Why Do You Need this New Edition?

If you're wondering why you should buy this new edition of *Racial and Ethnic Relations,* here are 4 good reasons!

1 All chapters have been thoroughly updated, most with numerous new research sources.

2 Chapter opening vignettes feature real-life experiences.

3 The authors examine (especially in Chapter 13) the implications of demographers' forecasts that by the mid-21st century the U.S. will be a country whose population majority is no longer European American, but instead composed of Latino, African, Asian, Middle Eastern, and Native Americans.

4 Most chapters focus on the economic, political, and demographic positions of major racial and ethnic groups, in the past and the present.

PEARSON

NINTH EDITION

Racial and Ethnic Relations

Joe R. Feagin
Texas A&M University

Clairece Booher Feagin

Prentice Hall

Boston ■ Columbus ■ Indianapolis ■ New York ■ San Francisco ■ Upper Saddle River ■ Amsterdam
Cape Town ■ Dubai ■ London ■ Madrid ■ Milan ■ Munich ■ Paris ■ Montreal ■ Toronto ■ Delhi
Mexico City ■ Sao Paulo ■ Sydney ■ Hong Kong ■ Seoul ■ Singapore ■ Taipei ■ Tokyo

Publisher: Karen Hanson
Editorial Assistant: Alyssa Levy
Associate Editor: Mayda Bosco
Executive Marketing Manager: Kelly May
Marketing Assistant: Janeli Bitor
Senior Production Project Manager: Roberta Sherman
Manufacturing Buyer: Debbie Rossi
Editorial Production and Composition Service: TexTech International
Photo Researcher: Martha Shethar
Cover Designer: Joel Gendron

Credits appear on page 493, which constitutes an extension of the copyright page.

Library of Congress Cataloging-in-Publication Data

Feagin, Joe R.
　Racial and ethnic relations / Joe R. Feagin. Clairece Booher Feagin. — 9th ed.
　　p. cm.
　ISBN-13: 978-0-205-79077-7
　ISBN-10: 0-205-79077-1
　1. Minorities—United States.　2. United States—Race relations.　3. United States—Ethnic relations.　I. Feagin, Clairece Booher.　II. Title.
　E184.A1F38 2011
　305.800973—dc22

　　　　　　　　　　　　　　　　　　　　2010027309

Prentice Hall
is an imprint of

www.pearsonhighered.com

10 9 8 7 6 5 4 3 2 1 EB 14 13 12 11 10

ISBN-10:　　0-205-79077-1
ISBN 13: 978-0-205-79077-7

Contents

Chapter 8   Mexican Americans   208

Chapter 10   Japanese Americans   283

Chapter 11   Chinese, Filipino, Korean, Vietnamese, and Asian-Indian Americans   307

Chapter 13   Ongoing Racial and Ethnic Issues in the United States: Some Final Considerations   367

PART III GLOBAL REALITIES   381

Chapter 14   Colonialism and Postcolonialism: The Global Expansion of Racism   384

Preface

Over the past few decades, numerous scholars, journalists, and politicians have argued that there is now a "postracial America." Some speak of a "declining significance of race" or an "end to racism" in the United States. They have written or spoken optimistically about a decrease in discrimination and about improving racial and ethnic relationships in the United States. Over the same period of time, however, the scholarly journals and mass media have been filled with accounts of hate crimes targeting people of color, accounts of the violent views and actions of white supremacist groups, college students and comedians doing openly racist skits and commentaries, talk-show hosts stereotyping people of color, public discussions of many lawsuits over racial discrimination in employment and public accommodations, studies showing widespread housing discrimination, descriptions of community rebellions against local police brutality incidents, and controversies over affirmative action and other antidiscrimination programs. In recent years, we have also seen intense debates about the character and impact of recent immigrants to the United States, many of whom are immigrants of color from Latin American and Asian countries.

As we move well into the twenty-first century, much scholarly and public discussion and argument still focus on continuing racial and ethnic discrimination, oppression, and conflict. Contrary to what some scholars and journalists assert about a postracial America, this discussion signals and reflects fundamental and foundational social, economic, and political realities in the United States. Today, many Americans are well aware, or are becoming aware, of the continuing significance of "race," racism, and ethnicity, not only in this country but also in other countries—from the Republic of South Africa to Northern Ireland, the former Yugoslavia, the former Soviet Union, France, Brazil, and the Middle East. Racial and ethnic oppression and conflict are extraordinarily important and persisting in the modern world, and they have the potential to tear apart any country, including highly industrialized countries that are said to be "advanced."

One result of the continuing interest in racial and ethnic issues in the United States is the creation of college and university courses that focus on racial and ethnic divisions, cultural diversity, immigration, and multicultural or multiracial issues. This ninth edition of *Racial and Ethnic Relations* continues to focus on U.S. racial and ethnic heritages, structures, developments, conflicts, and coalitions. This textbook is designed for sociology courses, other social science courses, and education courses variously titled "Racial and Ethnic Relations," "Race Relations," "Minority Groups," and "Minority Relations," as well as various other courses on cultural diversity, multiculturalism, and racial and ethnic groups offered in college, business, and governmental settings.

One purpose of this book is to provide readers with access to the important literature on racial and ethnic groups in the United States and, to a lesser extent, in certain other countries around the globe. We have drawn heavily on a broad array of important sources, including articles, books, and other data analyses by sociologists, political scientists, social psychologists, anthropologists, historians, economists, government demographers, investigative journalists, and legal scholars.

Limited space prevents us from dealing with all the important racial and ethnic groups in the United States. Instead, we focus on a modest number of major racial and ethnic groups, generally preferring to accent depth rather than breadth in the analyses. In recent decades, social science analyses have begun to dig deeper into the "what," "why," and "how" of racial and ethnic oppression, conflict, and resistance. We draw heavily on this ever-growing social science research.

The introduction to Part I briefly looks at the origins of the racial and ethnic mosaic that is the United States. It serves as an introduction to Chapters 1 and 2, which discuss major concepts and theories in the study of racial and ethnic relations.

The Part II introduction sketches the political and economic history of the United States in order to provide some context for understanding the adaptation and oppression of the various immigrant groups that have come, voluntarily or involuntarily, to U.S. shores. Only one major group, Native Americans, cannot be viewed as such immigrants; indeed, as the original inhabitants of North America, they were often the victims of actions by the early immigrants (colonists) from outside the continent. The situations and experiences of indigenous societies and the various groups that have immigrated to North America are considered in Chapters 3 through 13.

In Part III, Chapter 14 moves away from the United States to look at patterns of racial and ethnic adaptation, oppression, conflict, and resistance in several other countries around the world—mainly France, South Africa, and Brazil. In the latter two cases, we examine how patterns of racial oppression and conflict have often been developed or fostered by the outside European colonizers and their descendants during the colonial and decolonization periods in the histories of such countries.

In the ninth edition of *Racial and Ethnic Relations* we have made numerous changes and enhancements that make the text current and accessible to readers. We have kept the real-life vignettes in numerous chapters—real-life vignettes that capture for the readers some poignant aspects of the racial–ethnic issues raised throughout this textbook. Drawing on the last edition, we have continued to refine chapter organization with Big Picture Questions at the beginning of each chapter and with the positioning of important discussion questions throughout the chapters. In order to accent for readers many of the important racial and ethnic terms, we have also kept an important glossary of key terms at the end of the book, and have highlighted key terms in each chapter. To enhance the conceptual analysis, we have further developed and honed several relatively new social science concepts dealing with racial and ethnic matters.

We have significantly revised and updated each chapter, drawing on many recent research studies on racial and ethnic issues, including new social science research and population analyses published by the U.S. Census Bureau since our last edition. And we have incorporated significant material from media sources on current racial and ethnic issues of consequence in the United States and, particularly in the last chapter, in other countries. In addition, we have taken into consideration recent analyses of certain dramatic racial–ethnic events in U.S. society, such as intense debates and demonstrations over immigration issues and the nomination and election of Barack Obama, the first African American to serve as president of the United States.

To summarize our general perspective, the chapters of this textbook are designed to achieve the following educational goals:

1. To analyze fully the historical eras of migration that have diversified the United States and kept it demographically healthy while many other western industrialized countries have faced serious population difficulties or decline.

2. To develop a sense of the socioeconomic position of, and changes for, each major racial and ethnic group, both in the past and in the present.

3. To understand, for the past and the present, what each racial and ethnic group's members have experienced in dealing with racial-ethnic framing and other systemic racial-ethnic oppression in their everyday lives.

4. To assess the role and impact of U.S. economic and educational institutions in each racial and ethnic group's experiences in the United States.

5. To investigate the importance and character of family issues and religion in each racial and ethnic group's experiences in the United States.

6. To make sense of the difficulties each racial and ethnic group has encountered in dealing with the political systems and how its members have countered them.

7. To assess the character of resistance and countering actions that each racial and ethnic group has developed in reaction to the hostility, individual discrimination, and systemic oppression its members have faced in the past and in the present.

8. To consider and evaluate how major social science theories, especially assimilation theories and power-conflict theories, have been used, or might be used, to assess and interpret the oppressive, adaptive, and resistance experiences of each racial and ethnic group examined.

Throughout the chapters, and especially in Chapter 13, we examine the implications for the United States of the forecasts by demographers that by the middle of the twenty-first century the United States will become a country whose population majority is no longer European American but composed of Latino, African, Asian, Middle Eastern, and Native Americans. The United States has long been an interacting mosaic of many groups, and that mix is becoming ever more complex, interesting, and significant as the decades pass.

Supplements

Instructor's Manual with Tests (0-205-84212-7)

For each chapter in the text, this valuable resource provides a detailed outline and a list of objectives. In addition, test questions in multiple-choice, true/false, and essay formats are available for each chapter; the answers to all questions are page-referenced to the text.

MyTest (0-205-84213-5)

This computerized software allows instructors to create their own personalized exams, to edit any or all of the existing test questions, and to add new questions. Other special features of this program include random generation of test questions, creation of alternate versions of the same test, scrambling question sequence, and test preview before printing. The MyTest is available to adopters at www.pearsonhighered.com.

PowerPoint Slides (0-205-84214-3)

The Lecture PowerPoint slides follow the chapter outline and feature images from the textbook integrated with the text. They are available to adopters at www.pearsonhighered.com.

MySocKit (0-205-01482-8)

MySocKit is an online supplement that offers book-specific learning objectives, chapter summaries, flashcards, and graded practice tests, as well as video clips and activities to aid student learning and comprehension. Also included in MySocKit is MySearchLab, a valuable resource that includes tools for writing and conducting Internet research projects. It includes access to the EBSCO Content

Select Database, MySocLibrary, as well as Social Explorer, an interactive program for analyzing Census Data from 1790 to the present.

MySocKit is available with *Racial and Ethnic Relations, Ninth Edition,* when a MySocKit access code card is packaged with the text at no additional charge, or can be purchased separately.

Acknowledgments

In writing this and previous editions of this textbook, we have received useful comments and suggestions from numerous colleagues, students, teachers, correspondents, editors, and reviewers. We are indebted to those whose advice, suggestions, and insights have made this a better book.

Among these are Edward Múrgía, Jóse Cobas, Elizabeth Aranda, Susan Eichenberger, Louwanda Evans, Ruth Thompson-Miller, Leland Saito, Gary David, Amir Marvasti, Nijole Benokraitis, Nestor Rodríguez, Melvin Sikes, Hernán Vera, Jim Fenelon, Kristin Lavelle, Jennifer Mueller, Glenn Bracey, Ruth Thompson-Miller, Chris Chambers, Rosalind Chou, Joane Nagel, Howard Winant, Edna Bonacich, Karyn McKinney, Eileen O'Brien, Leslie Inniss, Richard Alba, Debra Van Ausdale, Robert Parker, Daniel Duarte, Teun Van Dijk, Harriett Romo, Alice Littlefield, Wendy Ng, John R. Sosa, Jaime Martinez, Bud Khleif, Howard Leslie, Larry Horn, Doris Wilkinson, Anthony Orum, James Button, Ward Churchill, S. Dale McLemore, Gideon Sjoberg, Gilberto Cardenas, Nikitah Imani, David Roth, Joseph Lopreato, John Butler, Eric Woodrum, Andrew Greeley, Graham Kinloch, Lester Hill, Chad Oliver, Marcia A. Herndon, Rogelio Nuñez, Tom Walls, Samuel Heilman, Phylis Cancilla Martinelli, José Limon, Devon

Peña, Diana Kendall, Robena Jackson, Mark Chesler, David O'Brien, Bradley Stewart, John Arthur, Barbara Mori, Robert Parker, William Smith, Leslie Houts Picca, Peter Chua, Lenard Wynn, Kenneth Stewart, Timothy Fong, Diane Wolf, Yanick St. Jean, Laurel Davis-Delano, Roberta Rosenberg Farber, Celestino Fernández, Tomás Jimenez, Akil Kokayi Khalfani, Deirdre Rouster, and Carol Ward. We are indebted to Natasha Ball, Louwanda Evans, and Shari Valentine for some library research assistance on this edition. We also thank Louwanda Evans for her help on proofreading and revising the test item guide and index for this edition. We are also indebted to many other colleagues and undergraduate and graduate students for their helpful comments on previous editions. We are especially indebted to Pinar Batur for revising Chapter 14.

We gratefully acknowledge the publisher's reviewers for this ninth edition:

Sharon Austin, University of Florida
Momodou Darboe, Shepherd University
Judi Kessler, Monmouth College
Sharon Kim, California State University, Fullerton
Frances Moulder, University of Connecticut
Xuefeng Zhang, Westmont College

We thank them for their timely and useful comments.

We hope that you find this ninth edition informative and intellectually stimulating. We welcome your comments. Please write to us at the Department of Sociology, Mailstop 4351, Texas A&M University, College Station, Texas 77843-4351.

Joe R. Feagin
Clairece Booher Feagin

Racial and Ethnic Relations

PART I

The Racial and Ethnic Mosaic

BIG PICTURE QUESTION

- *Why did the United States begin as a country that was substantially democratic but also rooted in racial oppression?*

More than two hundred years ago, the new United States severed its colonial ties with Europe. Born in revolution, this new nation was portrayed as centrally dedicated to freedom and equality. Over the next two centuries, a vigorous society would emerge, with great racial and ethnic diversity.

However, the new society had its seamy side. Racial and ethnic oppression and conflict were imbedded in the founding period and in the subsequent history of the new republic. The European immigrants often took the lands of indigenous societies by force. By the end of the seventeenth century, the enslavement of Africans and African Americans was fundamental to the economy of the North American colonies, and resistance and revolt by these enslaved Americans were recurring problems for white slaveholders. In succeeding centuries other non-European peoples, such as Mexican and Chinese Americans, would suffer serious yokes of racial oppression. However, non-Europeans were not the only ones to face oppressive conditions. Discrimination against European immigrant groups was also part of the sometimes forgotten history of both the pre- and post-revolutionary periods.

In the earliest period, the colonial population on the prospering Atlantic coast was predominantly English in its origins and basic social institutions. Because of England's huge appetite for raw materials and new markets, English authorities encouraged non-English immigration to the colonies. However, there was popular opposition, verbal and violent, to the long line of new European immigrants. "Foreigners" soon became a negative category for many colonists. "Despite the need for new settlers, English colonials had mixed feelings about foreign arrivals. Anglo-Saxon mobs attacked Huguenots in Frenchtown, Rhode Island, and destroyed a Scotch-Irish frontier settlement in Worcester, Massachusetts."[1] In the 1700s, colonies such as Virginia, Pennsylvania, and Rhode Island attempted to restrict non-British immigrants.[2]

The basic documents of the new republic reflected its patterns of racial subordination and privilege, and some of the republic's first laws were aimed at oppressing and hampering groups of non-English origin. A relatively radical Declaration of Independence, prepared mostly by the young Thomas Jefferson, originally contained language accusing King George III of pursuing slavery, of waging "cruel war against human nature itself, violating its most sacred rights of life and liberty in the persons of a distant people who never offended him, captivating them and carrying them into slavery in another hemisphere, or to incur miserable death in the transportation thither."[3] Jefferson further noted that the English king had not attempted to prohibit the slave trade and had encouraged enslaved Africans to "rise in arms" against white colonists. But because of pressure from white slaveholding interests in the South and slave-trading interests in New England, this strong critique of the slave trade was omitted from the final version of the Declaration.

Even in this revolutionary period, the grand new doctrines of freedom and equality could not be extended to the black population, for criticism of King George III on the issue of slavery was in fact criticism of much of the North American social and economic system. Jefferson himself was a major slaveholder, whose prosperity and wealth were closely tied to an extremely oppressive, slaveholding agricultural system.

The U.S. Constitution (1787) explicitly recognized racial subordination in several important places. First, as a result of a famous compromise between northern and southern representatives to the Constitutional Convention, Article I originally stipulated that three-fifths of a given state's enslaved population was to be counted in the total for apportioning the state's (white) legislative representation—that is, each enslaved American was officially viewed as three-fifths of a person. Significantly, at the Constitutional Convention white southern slaveowners, seeking to enhance their own representation in the new U.S. Congress, pressed for full inclusion of the enslaved African Americans in the population count, while northern interests were generally opposed.

In addition, a section was added to Article I permitting the slave trade to continue until 1808. The Constitution also incorporated a fugitive slave provision that required the return of runaways to their owners, a provision opposed by very few whites at the time.[4] Neither the statement in the Declaration of Independence that "all men are created equal" nor the Constitution's soon-to-be-added Bill of Rights was seen as applying to Americans of African descent. Slavery, ironically, would last much longer in the new "democratic" republic of the United States than in the older aristocratic Britain.[5]

African Americans and Native Americans were not the only groups to suffer from the new government's action. Numerous other non-English groups continued to find themselves much less than equal under the law. Anti-immigrant legislation in the late 1700s and early 1800s included the Alien, Sedition, and Naturalization Acts.[6] Irish, German, and French immigrants were growing in number by the late eighteenth century, and concern about the political sentiments of the new immigrants was great. The Naturalization Act stiffened residency requirements for citizenship from five to fourteen years; the Alien Act gave the president the power to expel foreigners. President John Adams was pressed to issue orders deporting immigrants under the Alien Act and did

so. Shiploads of European immigrants left the country because of fear of exclusion.

Inequality in life chances and wealth along racial and ethnic lines was a fundamental fact of the new country's institutions. At first, substantial liberty and justice were reserved for men of British descent. This situation did not go unchallenged. By the late eighteenth century, many Irish and German immigrants had come to the colonies. Indeed, a significant proportion of the 4 million persons enumerated in the first U.S. census in 1790 were of non-English origins.

Over the next two centuries, English domination was modified by the ascendance of other northern Europeans, such as the Irish. These groups in turn were later challenged by southern and eastern European and non-European groups trying to move up in the social, economic, and political systems. Gradually, the new society became an unprecedented mixing of diverse peoples.

Most in the non-British immigrant groups gradually came to adopt the English language and adjust to English-shaped economic, political, and legal institutions. All newly entering groups adapted, to some degree, to the dominant white Anglo-Saxon-Protestant culture and ways. European immigrant groups soon became viewed as "whites" and eventually gained substantial power and status in the process.

In contrast to white immigrants, the voluntary and involuntary immigrants from Africa, Asia, and Latin America, as well as Native Americans, have generally remained subordinate to white Americans in political, cultural, and economic terms. Racial and ethnic inequality and oppression were and continue to be part of the foundation of U.S. society. Nonetheless, racially oppressed Americans have long challenged their subordinate status, and they continue to do so. If current demographic trends continue, Americans of color will become the majority of the U.S. population by the middle of the twenty-first century. They already are the majority in several states and numerous large cities.

Today, as in the past, issues of oppression, immigration, adaptation, inequality, and ideology are at the heart of the sociological study of racial and ethnic relations in the United States. They will continue to be central issues for the foreseeable future. In the two chapters of Part I, we will define basic terms used by social scientists and examine these concepts from a critical perspective. Chapter 1 examines terms such as *race, racism, ethnic group,* and *prejudice.* Chapter 2 reviews major conceptual frameworks, including a variety of assimilation theories and power-conflict theories, for interpreting the complex structure and long-term development of racial and ethnic relations in the United States.

What are the problems with describing the United States as just a "nation of immigrants"?

Basic Concepts in the Study of Racial and Ethnic Relations

BIG PICTURE QUESTIONS

- *Why and how have human beings developed the powerful ideas of "race" and ethnicity?*

- *How does racial or ethnic discrimination become institutionalized?*

- *How do people respond to racial and ethnic oppression in the United States?*

I n the 1980s, Susie Guillory Phipps, a woman living in Louisiana, went to court to try to get the racial designation on her birth certificate at the Louisiana Bureau of Vital Records changed from "colored" to "white." A 1970 Louisiana "blood" law required that persons with one thirty-second (1/32) or more "Negro blood" (ancestry) were to be designated as "colored" on birth records; before 1970, "any traceable amount" of African ancestry had been used to define a person as colored. The light-skinned Phipps was the descendant of an eighteenth-century white plantation owner and an enslaved black American, and her small amount of African ancestry was enough to get her classified as "colored" on her official government birth certificate. Phipps lost her case.[1]

This significant controversy raises the question of how a person comes to be defined as *white* or *not white* in U.S. society. Only under traditional racist assumptions does having one black ancestor make one black, whereas having one white ancestor does not make one white. If one white ancestor made a person white under Louisiana law, many *black* residents there—those who have at least one white ancestor (often a white slaveholder)—could be classified as *white!* This revealing case illustrates that racial categories are constructed and defined socially and politically, not scientifically.

A logical place to start in making sense out of this U.S. system of racial and ethnic categorization is with basic terms and concepts. People have often used such terms as *racial groups* and *prejudice* without specifying their meaning. Because these are basic concepts in the study of intergroup relations, we will analyze them in detail.

Issues of Race and Racism

Racial Groups and Racialized Hierarchies

Both *racial group* and *race* have been used in a number of senses in social science and popular writings. *Human race, Jewish race, white race*—such terms in the literature suggest a range of meanings. In sixteenth- and early seventeenth-century Europe, the concept or word *race* was typically used for descendants of a common ancestor, emphasizing kinship linkages rather than physical characteristics such as skin color, hair type, or facial features. Only in the eighteenth century did **race** generally come to mean a

category of human beings with distinctive physical characteristics transmitted by descent, and set in a clearly racialized hierarchy.[2]

Soon, **racial hierarchy**, *a stratification of and substantial inequality among physically distinct groups,* came to be widely accepted, with white Europeans at the top. The often darker-skinned people from African and Native American societies were relegated by European observers to the bottom, in part because of their physical characteristics and allegedly "primitive" cultures, but also because they were subordinated by Europeans. Economic and political oppression resulted in a low position in the white classification system, or what can be termed *racial subordination.*[3]

Immanuel Kant's use of the German phrase for "races of mankind" in the 1770s was one of the early uses of the term *race* in the modern sense of biologically distinct, hierarchical categories of human beings. In 1795, Johann Blumenbach, a prominent German anatomist, established a racial classification system that became an influential typology. At the top of his racial hierarchy were the Caucasians (Europeans), followed in order by the Mongolians (Asians), the Ethiopians (Africans), the Americans (Native Americans), and the Malays (Polynesians). Blumenbach was the first to use the term *Caucasian;* he felt that the Europeans in the Caucasus Mountains of Russia were "the most beautiful race of men." Ever since, people of European descent have been called by a racist term that originally applied only to a small area of Europe.[4]

The concept of race as a biologically distinctive, hierarchical category was fully developed by northern Europeans who, for much of their histories, had been largely isolated from contact with people who differed from them physically or culturally. Before the development of large sailing ships in the late 1400s, Europeans had little contact with people from Asia, Africa, or the Americas. Soon, however, colonizing Europeans established slave systems in the Americas. Slave colonies were rationalized by colonizing Europeans, including the English, who classified enslaved Africans as a "lesser race." The idea of race was not developed from scientific observations of all human beings. Rather, it was a social "classification, a product of popular beliefs about human differences that evolved from the sixteenth through the nineteenth centuries."[5]

From the eighteenth century to well into the twentieth century, most white biologists, physical anthropologists, and other scientists accented this socially determined classification of what were seen as biologically distinctive groups. These scientists reflected their own racial prejudices and those of the white public. "The scientists themselves undertook efforts to document the existence of the differences that the European cultural worldview demanded and had already created."[6] Basic to this increasingly prevalent racist framing and worldview was the theory of a specific number of biologically distinct "races" with differing physical characteristics and the belief that these characteristics were hereditary and thus created a "natural" hierarchy of groups. By the late nineteenth century, numerous European and U.S. scientists and popular writers were systematically downgrading all peoples *not* of northern European origin, including southern and eastern Europeans (such as Polish and Jewish Europeans), as inferior "races."[7]

Thus, for four centuries of North American development, **racialization** has been *the process by which those in the dominant white group, especially its elites, have defined and constructed certain groups as being racially inferior or superior for the purposes of societal placement and of group enrichment, segregation, or oppression.* Racialization has historically operated in somewhat different ways for particular groups, but the process has generally been under the control of the dominant group, which, from the late 1600s forward, defined itself as "white." Since the seventeenth century, the dominant racial group has put into place a pervasive racial hierarchy, with a racial-status continuum that places white Americans at the top and African Americans and other Americans of color at or near the bottom. Over time, as we will see in later chapters, the white elite, assisted by rank-and-file whites, has determined where new immigrant groups, such as Irish or Chinese immigrants, are placed and where they are racialized within that already established racial hierarchy.

The singling out of people within the human species in terms of a strongly biologized "race" hierarchy seems to have been a distinctively European and Euro-American idea that has spread across all continents over recent centuries. In contrast, many indigenous peoples "have observed and appreciated cultural diversity as variations on cosmological themes. As a rule, the indigenous worldview encompasses all humanity."[8] In the

view of M. Annette Jaimes, many indigenous peoples across much of the globe have been more likely than Europeans to emphasize building alliances across various human groups. U.S. examples include the assistance in agricultural techniques given by indigenous Americans to early European colonists and later to Japanese Americans who were imprisoned during World War II (see Chapter 10) in U.S. concentration camps located near indigenous communities in the western United States.[9]

 How has the concept of "race" as a biologically distinctive category changed, or not changed, over several centuries?

Ideological Racism

The early development of ideological racism is rooted in the European global expansion that began in earnest in the late 1400s. We can define **ideological racism** specifically as *an ideology that considers a group's unchangeable physical characteristics to be linked in a direct, causal way to psychological or intellectual characteristics and that, on this basis, distinguishes between superior and inferior racial groups.*[10] The "scientific racism" of such European analysts as Blumenbach and Count Joseph Arthur de Gobineau, an influential French analyst in the nineteenth century, was used to justify the spread of European colonialism in Asia, Africa, and the Americas. A long line of racist theorists followed in Blumenbach's and Gobineau's footsteps, including the German Nazi leader Adolf Hitler. Sometimes they even applied the ideology of racial inferiority to culturally distinct European groups, such as Jewish Europeans. In a racist ideology, real or alleged physical characteristics are generally linked to *cultural* traits that the dominant group considers undesirable or inferior.

Significantly, the word *racism*, first used systematically in the 1930s by the German scholar Magnus Hirschfeld, is relatively new. Hirschfeld regularly used it for the ideology of biologically determined "races" accented by German Nazis and other Europeans to buttress their well-institutionalized system of racially oppressive practices. In its blatant and subtle forms, ideological racism has long been common in the United States. For example, in 1935, an influential white University of Virginia professor wrote this blatantly racist analysis:

> The size of the brain in the Black Race is below the medium both of the Whites and the Yellow-Browns, frequently with relatively more simple convolutions. The frontal lobes are often low and narrow. The parietal lobes voluminous, the occipital protruding. The psychic activities of the Black Race are a careless, jolly vivacity, emotions and passions of short duration, and a strong and somewhat irrational egoism. Idealism, ambition, and the cooperative faculties are weak. They love amusement and sport but have little initiative and adventurous spirit.[11]

This example of crude ideological racism clearly links physical and personality characteristics. Although this extreme, biologized, racist portrait passed for science before World War II—and in today's white supremacist organizations, it still does—it is *pseudoscience*. Modern biologists and anthropologists have demonstrated the wild-eyed irrationality of this racist mythology.

Found in many versions today, including some much more subdued, ideological racism accepts as true various stereotyped characteristics traditionally applied by whites to "outsider" groups of color. The assumption of this commonplace racist thinking is that physical differences such as skin color are intrinsically, even unalterably, tied to meaningful differentials in intelligence, culture, or "civilization." Yet, despite assertions of such a linkage by many people, including the pseudoscientists, no real scientific support for this assumed intrinsic linkage exists.

Indeed, there is *no* distinctive and enduring biological reality called "race" that can be determined by objective scientific procedures. Since at least the 1940s, the social, medical, and physical sciences have demonstrated this in numerous research studies. Nonetheless, in recent years a renewed insistence on the genetic reality of "races" has been triggered by a few dissenting white geneticists and social scientists. However, the older evidence and more recent research and analysis still strongly refute the notion of "races" being good categories for describing human genetic or biological diversity.[12] Given the constant blending and interbreeding of human groups over a great many centuries and into the present, it is impossible to sort human beings into unambiguously distinctive "races" on genetic grounds. There is far too much overlapping of genetic characteristics across various human populations. Two randomly selected individuals from the world's population would have in common, on average, about 99.8 percent of their genetic material. Even more important is the fact that most of the genetic variation with regard to human populations "occurs *within* populations, not *between* them."[13] There are genetic differences between geographically scattered human populations, but these differences are slight and exist because of different histories and geographical locations. The racial importance of the modest dissimilarities such as skin color variations is *socially*, not scientifically, determined.

Human populations singled out as "races" are simply groups with visible differences that certain people have collectively decided to emphasize as important in traditional social, economic, and political relationships. Such racial categorizing is neither objective nor scientific, but highly subjective. There are *many* different ways of classifying human populations in terms of physical and genetic characteristics: "One such procedure would group Italians and Greeks with most African blacks. It would classify Xhosa—the South African 'black' group to which [former South African] President Nelson Mandela belongs—with Swedes rather than Nigerians."[14] For example, antimalarial genes are not found among the light-skinned Swedes or the dark-skinned southern African groups such as the Xhosas, but they are commonly found in northern African groups and among Europeans such as Italians and Greeks. These antimalarial genes are likely *much* more important for human beings than those that determine skin color variations, yet they are *not* used by biological-race thinkers, the pseudoscientists, for their persisting racial classifications.[15]

In effect, there is only one human race (*Homo sapiens*), to which we all belong. Every human being is, in fact, distantly related to every other human being on earth. The indigenous peoples' view of human beings, previously noted, is now accepted by most scientists.[16] Nonetheless, the lack of scientific support has not lessened the popularity of blatantly racist ideologies of various types. Ashley Montagu, among many others, noted the extreme danger of ideological racism, a view shaped in part by the consequences of the German Nazi ideology, according to which there were physically distinct Aryan and Jewish "races."[17] That ideology lay behind Nazi-generated killings of millions of European Jews (and other Europeans) during the 1930s and 1940s.

In the case of North America, over several centuries now, variations on an old racist ideology have long been incorporated as part of a *white racial framing* of an ever more diverse society, a concept to which we will return later.

Racial Groups

Today, social scientists view "race" not as a given biological reality but as a socially constructed reality. Sociologist Oliver Cox, one of the first to underscore this social construction perspective, defined a *race* as "any people who are distinguished, or consider themselves distinguished, in social relations with other peoples, by their physical characteristics."[18] Similarly, a *racial group* has been defined by Pierre van den Berghe as a "human group that defines itself and or is defined by other groups as different from other groups by virtue of innate and immutable physical characteristics."[19]

Thus, a racial group is *not* something generated naturally as part of the self-evident order of societies. A person's race is typically determined by, and important to, certain outsiders, although a group's own self-definition can be important. Here we define a **racial group** as a *social group that persons inside or outside the group have decided is important to single out as inferior or superior, typically on the basis of real or alleged physical characteristics selected subjectively*. Racial group distinctions are rooted in ideological racism, which as noted previously links physical characteristics to "inferior" or "superior" cultural and intellectual characteristics.

In the United States, numerous groups fit this definition. Asian Americans, African Americans, Native Americans, and Mexican Americans have had their physical characteristics—such as skin color, facial features, and/or eye shape—singled out by the dominant white group as badges of social, cultural, and racial inferiority. In addition, this dominant group has generally viewed its own racially defined group as superior. Some groups once defined as racial groups, and as physically and mentally inferior groups, are no longer defined that way. In later chapters, we will see that Irish and Italian immigrants were for a time defined as inferior "races" by native-born white Anglo-Protestant Americans.

Later, the social definition of these European immigrants as distinctively inferior racial groups was replaced by a social construction of them as white and as *ethnic groups,* a term we examine later.

The examples of Irish and Italian Americans make clear that racial definitions are not necessarily fixed essences that last forever, but instead can be temporary social constructions shaped in sociopolitical struggles in particular times and places. Definitions of racial inferiority or superiority can and do change over time, albeit often slowly.

Why are some physical characteristics, such as skin color, selected as a basis for distinguishing racial groups, whereas certain other characteristics, such as eye color, seldom are? These questions cannot be answered in biological terms. They require historical and sociological analysis. Some have argued that such characteristics as skin color are "easily observed and ordered in the mind."[20] More important than ease of observation, however, is the way economic or political subordination creates a need to identify the powerless group in a certain way. In justifying economic or other exploitation, the dominant group often defines the real (or alleged) physical characteristics that are singled out to typify the exploited group as distinctive and inferior racial characteristics. For example, technological differences in weaponry and firepower between European and African peoples facilitated the enslavement of Africans in the American colonies. In turn, the generally darker skin of the Africans and their descendants came to be used by self-defined "white" groups as an indicator of subordinate racial and cultural status. Skin-color characteristics have no inherent meaning; in group interaction, they become important because they can be used to classify members of the dominant and subordinate groups.

In addition, knowledge of one's relatives often affects one's assignment to a racial group, particularly for those who lack the socially emphasized physical characteristics. At various times in many societies, people have been distinguished not only on the basis of their own physical characteristics but also on the basis of a socially determined "rule of descent."[21] For example, in Nazi Germany, Adolf Hitler's officials often identified Jewish Germans mainly on the basis of their having one or more Jewish relatives.

> **Q.** How is the concept of "race"
> understood presently by almost
> all social scientists?

Ancestry and Multiracial Realities

The socially applied rules of descent have varied greatly from society to society. For example, in some countries there are special categories or designations for mixed-ancestry groups, such as the "Coloureds" term once widely used for people with African and European ancestry in South Africa. Many Latin American countries recognize several mixed-ancestry categories. Mixed-ancestry distinctions have been rare in the United States, however. In the case of African Americans, interracial blending has, over time, caused dark skin color to become a less reliable characteristic for those determined to make racial distinctions, and the rule of descent has gained more importance as a mechanism of racial identification to perpetuate discrimination. Today, black Americans "evidence an unusually wide range of physical traits. Their skin color extends from ebony to a shade paler than many 'whites.'"[22] Indeed, relatively few black Americans are literally "black." Most have a skin color that is some shade of brown.

In many U.S. communities, the social aspect of the defining process becomes obvious when a light-skinned person, say, of one-eighth African ancestry but with none of the physical traits most whites associate with African Americans, is regarded as "black" because one of his or her ancestors or relatives is known to be of African ancestry. Sometimes termed the "one drop of blood" rule, this odd rule of descent is found mainly in the United States. Indeed, in Caribbean countries and many parts of Africa, a person who is one-eighth African in ancestry and seven-eighths European would ordinarily be considered "white."

Mixed racial ancestry does not fit neatly into traditional U.S. categorizing. Today, there are millions of children in interracial families, and growing numbers of interracial marriages take place annually. The existence and experiences of these Americans underscore the social construction of racial identities. Consider the case of Tiger Woods, a talented golfer who has won numerous major golf tournaments.[23] Woods has described his complex ancestry as one-eighth white, one-eighth Native American, one-fourth African American, one-fourth Thai, and

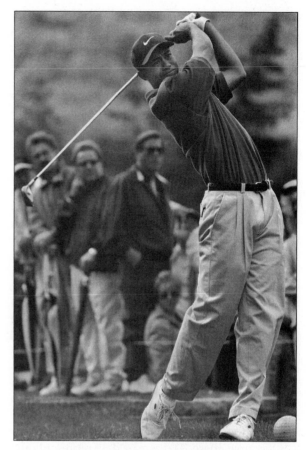

Golf star Tiger Woods hits a tee shot at a tournament.

one-fourth Chinese. However, the mass media have usually portrayed Woods as African American. Following his early golf victories, his father spoke of him as a black sports star, and Woods presented himself in early commercials as black. But later, Woods accented his mixed ancestry and seemed to some observers to play down his black ancestry and identity. After criticism by African Americans who were proud of his achievements and his African ancestry, Woods issued a statement that he was proud of his African American *and* other ancestry.[24]

Nonetheless, many people in the media and elsewhere have continued to view Woods mainly as a black sports star, and it seems likely that far more Americans see him as African American than as multiracial. After Woods won his first Masters Tournament, a white golfer, Fuzzy Zoeller, spoke about "that little boy" and joked that he hoped Woods would not choose collard greens and fried chicken for the Masters championship dinner.[25] Accenting foods that whites have long liked to associate with African Americans, Zoeller emphasized that Woods was indeed African American. He later apologized for his comments.[26]

In the late 1990s, Congress debated the addition of a "multiracial" category in the U.S. census for the year 2000, a change supported by many people of mixed racial ancestry and by organizations representing their views. However, some critics suggested that the presence of such a multiracial box for people to check on the census form might reduce the count in other categories, such as "black," which would hurt civil rights enforcement in some areas. Congress decided against the creation of a specific multiracial category for the 2000 census. Instead, individuals were allowed to mark multiple ancestry groups. This debate continued for the 2010 census, but again no specific multiracial category was added for that census. This debate clearly indicates that racial designations are socially constructed and maintained. Interestingly, in the 2000 census only 6.8 million Americans—out of a total of 281 million— indicated by checking multiple categories that they had multiracial ancestry. (At the time of this writing, such data for the 2010 census have not been published.)[27]

Of course, these 2000 census data represent only the tip of the iceberg; additional millions of Americans in fact have substantial multiracial backgrounds. Many Americans' ancestry is some mixture of European, African, Native American, Asian, Middle Eastern, or Latin American backgrounds, and today increasing numbers of people assert their multiracial (and/or multiethnic) identities. Attention to issues of multiracial ancestry, intermarriage, and interracial families will likely escalate as the United States becomes ever more diverse in future decades.

Ethnic Groups

What Is an Ethnic Group?

The term *ethnic group* has been used by social scientists in two different senses, one narrow and one broad. Some definitions of the term are broad enough to include socially defined racial groups. For example, in Milton Gordon's broad definition, an ethnic group is a social group distinguished

"by race, religion, or national origin."[28] Like the definition of *racial group*, this definition contains the notion of social set-apartness. However, here the distinctive characteristics can be physical or cultural, and language and religion are seen as critical markers or signs of ethnicity even when there is no physical distinctiveness. Today, a number of contemporary scholars, such as Werner Sollors, still view religious, national-origin, and racial groups as falling under the same umbrella term *ethnic group*.[29]

Other scholars prefer a narrower definition of ethnic group, one that omits groups defined substantially in terms of physical characteristics (those called racial groups) and that is limited to groups distinguished primarily on the basis of cultural or national-origin characteristics. *Cultural characteristics* include language; *national origin* refers to the country (and national culture) from which the person or her or his ancestors came.

The English word *ethnic* comes from the Greek word *ethnos*, originally meaning "nation." In its earliest English usage, in the fifteenth century, the word referred to culturally different "heathen" countries— that is, those not Christian or Jewish. The first usage of *ethnic group* to denote national origin developed in the period of heavy immigration from southern and eastern European countries to the United States in the early twentieth century. Since the 1930s, a number of prominent social scientists have suggested that the narrower definition of *ethnic group*, more in line with the original Greek meaning of "nationality," makes the term more useful.[30]

Social scientist W. Lloyd Warner, who was perhaps the first to use the term *ethnicity*, distinguished between ethnic groups—which he saw as characterized by cultural differences—and racial groups, characterized substantially by physical differences.[31] More recent scholars have also preferred the narrower usage. In van den Berghe's view, for example, ethnic groups are "socially defined but on the basis of cultural criteria."[32]

In this book, the usual meaning of **ethnic group** will be the narrower one—*a group socially distinguished or set apart, by others or by itself, primarily on the basis of cultural and/or national-origin characteristics*. Such set-apart groups, such as Irish Americans or German Americans, usually develop a sense of a common cultural heritage and ancestry. Some broad social categories, such as the religious category of "Baptists," have been considered by some to be ethnic groups, but in the sense we use the term here, they are not. Religious groups that are open to relatively easy conversion are not, strictly speaking, ethnic, because ethnicity says something about socially accepted lines of common descent or national origin as well as about current cultural characteristics.

Many social analysts who use the broader definition that includes racial groups argue that the historical experiences of people defined as "nonwhite" are essentially similar to experiences of white groups. Some have argued that in the United States the situations and experiences of non-European groups such as African or Asian Americans are in broad ways similar to those of immigrants from Europe, especially with regard to the process of gradual integration into the Anglo-Protestant core society. Some social scientists further assume that the experiences of both European and non-European groups are adequately explained by the same theoretical framework—typically some type of assimilation framework (see Chapter 2).[33]

In contrast, many analysts who prefer the narrower definition of *ethnic group* as a socially constructed category that differs in important ways from the term *racial group* view the historical and contemporary experiences of subordinated racial groups as distinctively different from those of white European ethnic groups.[34] Moreover, the public and scholarly use of the umbrella term *ethnic group* for all groups, including racial groups, in the past two decades has often had political and racial overtones: "Indeed, the substitution of 'ethnicity' for 'race' as a basis of categorization is accompanied by increasing unwillingness among the dominant group to accept responsibility for the problems of racism."[35] Although this criticism is accurate for much popular and scholarly writing that views such groups as African Americans and Mexican Americans as "just" ethnic groups that are no different in their societal experiences from groups such as Italian Americans and Irish Americans, it does not apply to those scholars who prefer the term *ethnic group* because they feel its use indicates that all groups have genuine and significant cultural histories.[36]

In addition, many scholars emphasize the point that all socially constructed racial groups include subgroups that can be seen as ethnic groups because they have distinctive cultural identities. Examples of this include Italian Americans within the white racial group and Jamaican Americans within the black racial group.

Definitions of *racial group* and *ethnic group* that emphasize their social meaning and social construction directly reject the biological determinism that views such groups as self-evident and possessing unchanging physical or intellectual characteristics. People themselves, both outside and inside racial and ethnic groups, determine when certain physical or cultural characteristics are important enough to single out a group for social purposes, whether for good or for ill.

Thus, a given social group may be viewed by different outsiders or at different times as a racial group or an ethnic group (in the narrow sense). During the 1930s, for example, Jewish Germans were identified as a "race" in Nazi Germany, in part because of physical characteristics that were alleged to be different from those of other Germans. However, the actual identification of Jewish Germans for persecution and killing by Nazi bureaucrats and soldiers was based more on certain ethnic characteristics—cultural characteristics such as religion or language—and genealogical ties to known Jewish ancestors than on physical characteristics.

In their first contacts with European societies, darker-skinned Africans were viewed in cultural-ethnic rather than biological-racial terms. St. Clair Drake's research on early African contacts with Europeans has shown that in the first centuries of historical contact—during the Egyptian, Greek, and Roman periods—European outsiders generally attached far greater significance to Africans' culture and nationality than to their physical characteristics. Before the sixteenth century, "neither White Racism nor *racial slavery* existed."[37] Similarly, Frank Snowden has demonstrated that the early encounters between African "blacks" and Mediterranean "whites" led to a generally favorable image of the Africans among Europeans and to substantial friendships and intermarriage—much different from the white–black relationships in modern race-conscious societies. Although some Europeans in these periods did express negative views of Africans' color, these views never developed into an acute color consciousness linked to a racially framed view of Africans as an inferior species with intellectual deficits. Virulent color prejudice in the form of ideological racism emerged only in the modern world, primarily in the imperial expansion into

Africa and the Americas by European nations seeking colonies between the 1400s and the 1800s.[38] Historical conditions have shaped whether and how skin color becomes a marker—usually in the social processes of group exploitation and oppression.

Ancestry is important to the concept of *ethnic group* whether it is defined in a narrow or a broad sense. Perception of a common ancestry, real or mythical, has been part of outsiders' definitions and of ethnic groups' self-definitions. Sociologist Max Weber saw ethnic groups broadly as "human groups that entertain a subjective belief in their common descent."[39] In addition to a sense of common ancestry, a consciousness of shared experiences and cultural patterns is typically important in shaping a group's identity.

A number of social scientists have focused on the ways in which people's constructions and conceptions of their own and others' ethnic identities change over time and from one situation to another. These social constructionists emphasize the importance of studying the "ways in which ethnic boundaries, identities, and cultures are negotiated, defined, and produced through social interaction inside and outside ethnic communities."[40] Drawing on field research, Mary Waters has shown the options white Americans have with regard to ethnic identity. A white person of English and Irish ancestry may choose either ethnic identity, both, or none, preferring in the latter case to identify only as "American."[41] Waters has documented how Afro-Caribbean immigrants sometimes view themselves as African Americans and sometimes as an ethnic group distinct from native-born people within the African American racial group.[42] Nonetheless, Afro-Caribbean Americans generally have no choice in how they are viewed—as black Americans—by most people in the dominant white group.

Yet other terms for socially distinguished groups are used by some researchers. Among these are *majority group* and *minority group*.[43] For example, Louis Wirth defined a **minority group** as "*a group of people who, because of their physical or cultural characteristics, are singled out from others in the society in which they live for differential and unequal treatment and who therefore regard themselves as objects of collective discrimination.*"[44] However, many scholars today consider it more accurate to use the term **dominant group** instead of *majority group* for *the racial or ethnic group with the greatest power and resources in a societal setting,* and the term **subordinate group** instead of *minority group* for *a group that is singled out because of physical and/or cultural characteristics for differential and unequal treatment and whose members become objects of substantial discrimination.* This usage is appropriate because a majority group can numerically be a minority, as was the case with white Europeans in numerous colonial societies. Indeed, if demographic trends continue, the white majority, in population terms, will likely become a statistical minority in the United States by 2050.

The United States is a racially and ethnically diverse society.

A Note on Cultures

Real cultural differences between groups are often at the heart of racial and ethnic conflict. Sociologists and anthropologists often define *culture* as the shared values, understandings, symbols, and practices of a group of people. The shared symbols are the means by which people "communicate, perpetuate, and develop their knowledge about and attitudes toward life."[45] There are cultural objects (the symbols and practices) as well as cultural creators and cultural receivers (the people who create and use the cultural objects).[46]

In Chapter 2, we will observe the importance of culture in the process by which one group adapts to another. We will examine the concept of *dominant culture*, the understandings and symbols created and controlled by a powerful group, as well as the concept of an *immigrant culture*, the understandings and symbols of an immigrant group entering the sphere of the dominant culture. Milton Gordon, an assimilation theorist, argued that immigrant groups coming into North America after the English gave up much of their own cultural heritage to conform to a dominant core culture:

> If there is anything in American life which can be described as an overall American culture which serves as a reference point for immigrants and their children, it can best be described, it seems to us, as the middle-class cultural patterns of, largely, white Protestant, Anglo-Saxon origins, leaving aside for the moment the question of minor reciprocal influences on this culture exercised by the cultures of later entry into the United States.[47]

In subsequent chapters, we will also see how subordinated racial and ethnic groups have drawn on their well-developed cultures to resist discrimination and slavish adaptation to a dominant white Anglo-Protestant culture. Some analysts describe these as *cultures of resistance*.[48] The cultural heritage and present cultural understandings of subordinated groups, such as African Americans or American Indians, not only foster a positive sense of identity and pride but also facilitate the group's survival and enhance its ability to resist oppression. Strong family and kinship values of Native American societies enabled them to survive the Euro-American invasions of their lands. Contrary to certain prevailing stereotypes, moreover, the strong family ties of African Americans have generally fostered a sense of pride and identity and have provided crucial support for coping with racial discrimination.

A Racial Framing of Society

Central to the persistence of racial hierarchies in countries such as the United States is the development of a comprehensive racial frame, primarily by the dominant racial group. This broad racial framing typically includes more than the ideological racism discussed previously. We can define a **racial frame** as an *organized set of racial ideas, narratives, stereotypes, images, emotions, and inclinations to discriminate.* Today, as in the past, a racial frame provides an all-encompassing interpretive scheme that shapes evaluations of everyday events and encounters with people from various racialized groups. A racial frame is very important socially because it interprets everyday worlds and generates discriminatory actions in line with the frame. A strong racial frame captures territory in minds and thus shapes how people act.[49]

In the case of North America, the European colonists and their descendants early developed a white racial framing of the new society to interpret and defend the increasingly institutionalized reality of white-on-black oppression and white-on-Indian oppression. This broad racial frame has been maintained, with some variation and periodic reworking, to the present day. Central to this frame is an interrelated set of emotionally charged understandings and narratives that whites (and others) have used to rationalize and legitimate racial oppression. Early political leaders, such as Thomas Jefferson, James Madison, and George Washington, participated actively, and often emotionally, in the development of this racial framing, including its ideological racism, in order to defend white power and privilege as natural for this society. Historically, variations on the white racial frame have regularly generated recurring discriminatory actions. Such racial framing of society has generated and rationalized anti-Indian genocide, African American slavery, Jim Crow segregation, and historical discrimination against Latinos and Asian Americans, as well as contemporary incarnations of racial discrimination targeting all these groups.

Historically and in the present, whites have combined racial stereotypes (the verbal-cognitive aspect), ideas and narratives (the deeper verbal-cognitive aspect), images (the visual aspect), emotions (feelings such as fear), and inclinations to take discriminatory action within a racial frame that is oriented to assessing and reacting to Americans of color in everyday situations. Learning racial framing typically begins at a young age. The language and framing of "race" that is picked up in social settings often becomes what psychologist Lev Vygotsky has called "inner speech"; that is, it is deeply internalized.[50] Racial words and terms that are learned as children usually carry complex understandings going well beyond their apparent denotative meanings. Particular racial words learned in childhood often embed and trigger an array of psychological linkages, emotions, and understandings. Our racialized language and broad racial framing thus shape and limit our thinking about this society.

Interestingly, there has been little research on the dominant white-generated framing, especially viewed as a whole. What evidence we do have suggests that there have been numerous variations on this white framing since the seventeenth century. Members of the dominant racial group in various regions of the country sometimes have accented different elements of the broad racial framing, although much of this old framing is shared across all subgroups and regions. From time to time in U.S. history, new immigrant groups, such as Asian and Latino Americans in the mid-nineteenth century, have been racialized and incorporated within the dominant framing. By constantly using the many elements of this old racial frame to rationalize and interpret this racialized society, by integrating new items into the frame periodically, and by applying learned stereotypes, images, and prejudicial interpretations in discriminatory actions, whites and others embed a racialized framing of the world deeply in their minds and, as well, the important societal institutions. Such deep embeddedness makes it difficult to alter or replace this centuries-old racial frame.

 How has the racial framing of this society been maintained and reworked from the seventeenth century to the present day?

Prejudices and Stereotypes

Typically, a racial or ethnic framing of society in the minds of members of dominant groups, and of others influenced by them, includes negative stereotypes and prejudices concerning those in subordinate groups, as well as assertively positive views of the dominant group and its major institutions. These elements are centrally about the ways various racial and ethnic groups are represented, named, and discussed in the dominant framing of them. Let us now examine some of these important elements.

One often discussed element is *prejudice*, which in popular discourse is associated mostly with negative attitudes about members of racial and ethnic groups, especially subordinate groups. Some understanding of how and why these negative attitudes develop can be achieved by considering the concept of *ethnocentrism,* which was long ago described as the "view of things in which one's own group is the center of everything, and all others are scaled and rated with reference to it."[51] Individuals who develop *positive ethnocentrism* are characterized by a loyalty to the values, beliefs, and members of their own group. Ethnocentrism often prompts negative views of out-groups through a constant evaluation of out-groups in terms of in-group values and ways. Such negative views are manifested in prejudices and stereotypes that influence the social, economic, and political interaction among groups.[52]

Prejudice has been defined by influential psychologist Gordon Allport as "thinking ill of others without sufficient warrant."[53] The term *prejudice* comes from the Latin word *praejudicium,* meaning "a judgment made prior to knowledge or experience." In English, the word evolved from meaning "hasty judgment" to the present connotation of unfavorable bias based on an unsupported judgment. Although prejudice can theoretically apply to favorable prejudgments, its current usage in both popular speech and social science analysis is usually negative. Thus, **prejudice** is, to closely paraphrase Allport, *an antipathy based on a faulty generalization. It may be felt or expressed. It may be directed toward a group as a whole, or toward an individual because she or he is a member of that group.*[54]

As used in this text, *prejudice* has both an emotional and a verbal-cognitive aspect; it involves a negative feeling or attitude toward the out-group as well as an inaccurate belief or image. An example might be "I, as a white person, hate black and Latino people because black and Latino people always smell worse than whites." The first part of the sentence expresses the negative emotion (the hatred); the last part makes an inaccurate generalization. This latter cognitive aspect has been termed a **stereotype**—that is, *an overgeneralization associated with a racial or ethnic category that goes beyond existing evidence.*

Why do many people stereotype other people? Why have Irish Americans been stereotyped as lazy drunkards, African Americans and Latinos as indolent, Italian Americans as criminals with "Mafia" ties, and Asian Americans as "treacherous Orientals"? Such questions encourage us to examine the role that prejudices and stereotypes play in the history and daily lives of individuals and groups and in the society in which they live.

Stereotypes involve social representations of various groups and take different forms. For example, anthropologist Jane Hill has researched the widespread use of "mock Spanish" as part of the negative representations and images of U.S. Latinos. Many non-Latinos sprinkle their language with mock-Spanish terms such as "no problemo," "el cheapo," and "hasty banana," and phrases such as "hasta la vista, baby." Mock-Spanish terms appear on billboards, in movies, in cartoons, on items in gift shops, and in elite boardrooms—often in association with racial caricatures of Mexican Americans or other Latino groups. This widespread mocking of the Spanish language and of Latinos typically signals racialized stereotyping.[55] Such ridicule of Mexican Americans' language or speech is racist because it has meaning mainly in relation to underlying racial stereotypes. Hill suggests that this mocking enables its (usually Anglo-white) perpetrators to support traditional hierarchies of racial privilege without seeming to be blatantly racist.

Recurring white attacks on certain distinctive language accents or on variants of English spoken by many Latinos, African Americans, Asian Americans, or other Americans of color are not just concerned with language, for they reveal a "general unwillingness to accept the speakers of that language and social choices they have made as viable and functional. . . . We are ashamed of them."[56] Language mocking and language subordination are not about standards for speaking as much as they are about determining that some people (usually people

of color) are not worth listening to and treating as equals. Thus, people who speak French-accented English rarely report such discrimination, whereas those who speak Spanish-accented English often do. Stereotyped language or accent mocking often becomes part of "hundreds of taken-for-granted commonplace utterances that function to 'racialize' their targets, constructing them as members of a human group represented as essentially inferior."[57]

Stereotyping operates at conscious and unconscious levels. For example, social psychologists have discovered that the overwhelming majority of whites who have taken a major test of unconscious stereotyping associate black Americans with negative words and traits, such as "evil character." In these research studies, whites have often had more difficulty linking black faces than white faces to pleasant words and positive traits. In addition, when shown photos of black faces, even for a few milliseconds, key areas of white subjects' brains that are designed to respond to perceived threats light up automatically when scanned. Such data suggest how deeply embedded in the brain traditional racial stereotypes can be. As a result, many whites do not approach new encounters with black Americans and other people of color with minds that are truly open to new information or interpretations.[58] In addition, social psychologists such as Patricia Devine have found that virtually all whites are aware of major racial stereotypes no matter what their personal inclinations to act on them may be. The reason: Automatic mental processing brings up such racial stereotypes for whites whenever an appropriate stimulus appears, such as a member of a racial outgroup. Moreover, the research shows that very prejudiced people are more inclined to act on the activated racial stereotypes, whereas less prejudiced people often engage in a type of mental processing that ignores or rejects the activated stereotype.[59]

Explanations of Stereotyping and Prejudice

Sociological analysts of stereotyping and prejudice tend to emphasize group pressures on individuals for conformity or rationalization, whereas psychological analysts tend to stress individual irrationality or personality defects. Much research has highlighted the expressive function of prejudice for the individual. Frustration–aggression theories, psychoanalytic theories, and authoritarian personality perspectives generally focus on the **externalization function of prejudice**—*the transfer of an individual's internal psychological problem onto an external object, such as a particular racial group, as a solution to that internal psychological problem.* Psychologically oriented interpretations sometimes attribute racial or ethnic prejudice to special emotional problems of "sick" or "abnormal" individuals, such as a deep hatred of their parents.[60]

In a classic study of prejudice and personality, *The Authoritarian Personality*, T. W. Adorno and his colleagues argued that people who hate such groups as Jewish Americans typically differ from tolerant people with regard to central personality traits—specifically, that they tend to exhibit "authoritarian personalities."[61] Those with **authoritarian personalities** *are characterized by a high degree of submission to authority, a strong tendency to stereotype, great concern for social status, a view of the world as threatening, and an intolerance of outgroups that occupy socially subordinate positions.*

Some scholars have raised questions about a too heavy stress on the expressive function of prejudice. They have suggested that social *conformity* may be a much more important factor for most prejudiced people. Most people accept their own social situations as given and hold the prejudices taught at home and school and by the mass media. The **conformity function of prejudice**—*holding prejudiced attitudes in order to conform to expectations of important social reference groups* such as relatives and friends—explains much individual prejudice. Many negative prejudices and stereotypes are formed from the informal lessons that people learn as children at home and in school and as adults as they absorb messages from the media and socialize with relatives, co-workers, and friends.[62] In this conformity view, most racial and ethnic prejudices are not the result of deep psychological pathologies; rather, they reflect shared social definitions of out-groups. In such cases, prejudice functions as a means of social adjustment. Most of us can think of situations in which we, or our acquaintances, have adjusted to new racial beliefs in moving from one region or setting to another. As Schermerhorn notes, "Prejudice is a product of *situations*," not "a little demon that emerges in people simply because they are depraved."[63]

An additional function of prejudice is to help rationalize a subordinate group's powerless position. Herbert Blumer suggested that prejudice is more than a matter of negative feelings possessed by members of one group for another; it is also "rooted in a sense of group position."[64] The dominant group comes to defend and rationalize its privileged position. Modern prejudice, Oliver Cox has argued, "is a divisive attitude seeking to alienate dominant group sympathy from an 'inferior' race, a whole people, for the purpose of facilitating its exploitation."[65] When people are racially subordinated, as in the cases of white enslavement of Africans in the North American colonies or of restrictive quotas for Jewish Americans in U.S. colleges in the 1920s, those in power—in both cases, Anglo-Protestant whites—develop prejudices and stereotypes as part of a framing that helps them to rationalize the oppression of others.

Some analysts have suggested that certain members of dominant racial groups who today discriminate against subordinate groups are motivated just by a desire for economic or political gain. Such people strive to maintain their undeserved privileges, whether or not they rationalize that striving in terms of racial prejudices and stereotypes.[66] Such striving takes place within a societal system of inequality in which the dominant racial group benefits economically, politically, and psychologically—and acts to maintain its ill-gotten benefits. In the everyday world of racial discrimination, however, it is likely that the desire to protect racialized privileges will almost always be accompanied by negatively stereotyped views of the subordinate group targeted for discrimination.

Are Racial Attitudes and Performances Changing?

Stereotyped images and other stereotypes of people of color held by whites today have many similarities with stereotypes of the past. Still, some changes have occurred, especially since the 1960s. Public opinion surveys of white attitudes toward Americans of color have shown a significant decline in the public expression of certain old-fashioned racist attitudes since the 1940s.

Researchers David Sears and John McConahay have identified what they term **symbolic** or **modern racism**—that is, *white beliefs that serious racial discrimination does not exist today and that black Americans in particular are making illegitimate demands for social changes.* Using survey-type measures, these social psychologists have suggested that, among whites, "old-fashioned racism" favoring rigid segregation and extreme stereotypes has largely been replaced by a modern racism whose white proponents accept modest racial desegregation but resist the large-scale changes necessary for full integration of U.S. society. Sociologist Lawrence Bobo has suggested that whites have an "ideology of bounded racial change"; that is, whites' support for changes in discrimination ends when such changes seriously endanger their standard of living.[67] Social psychologist Thomas Pettigrew has noted certain white reactions to black achievements in recent decades and suggested that an "ultimate attribution error" on the part of many whites includes not only blaming black victims for their failures but also discounting black successes by attributing the latter to luck or unfair advantages rather than intelligence and hard work.[68] Research on modern versions of whites' attitudinal racism has mostly examined attitudes toward black Americans, but these innovative concepts can likely be used to interpret whites' prejudices and stereotypes directed at other people of color.

Much social science research shows that many people today vary their presentations and performances of racial attitudes depending on the social setting. In a survey of white students on major college campuses, sociologists Eduardo Bonilla-Silva and Tyrone Forman discovered that racial attitudes expressed on short-answer survey items were frequently different from those expressed to questions requiring extended commentary. For example, on a brief survey item, 80 percent of 451 white students indicated that they *approved* of marriages between white and black Americans. However, when a smaller but similar group of white college students was interviewed in depth, this figure dropped to only 30 percent. Given more time to answer and explain their views in in-depth interviews, the majority expressed significant reservations about marriage across the color line. Other attitudinal views showed a similar pattern of racial expression varying by setting. Moreover, in her research social psychologist Maria Krysan increased the privacy of the settings in which her respondents could express their racial views. As the privacy of settings increased, white respondents expressed more negative attitudes toward black Americans. Other psychological research has found that whites who reject some

stereotypes, such as in settings where their expression is easy to control, nonetheless reveal these deeply held stereotypes in other situations where they are less able to control, or less concerned about controlling their expression. Social conformity and desirability concerns constantly are factors.[69]

Several social scientists have used qualitative research methods to explore the spatial and temporal variations in racist commentaries and performances. They too have demonstrated how whites vary commentaries and performances depending on whether they are in public or private social arenas. In research on interactions in an all-white country-and-western group, Nina Eliasoph found that overtly racist commentaries were critical for socially integrating whites when they were interacting with each other. Racist talk, or complacency about it, facilitated interaction. Whites were aware of when to engage in overtly racist discussions; they understood the setting was as important as the racist content. Researcher Karyn McKinney got college students to provide autobiographical journals about their private and public lives. One student pointed out that private settings were comfortable places for expressing attitudes: "I think that for people, other white people being around are a comfort zone to express any racist views. It is funny how some people assume that no white person will care about what they say or that they will even support their beliefs." Similarly, in an important and probing ethnographic study of "race talk," Kristen Myers and her associates recorded substantial comments made by ordinary people, both whites and people of color, in private places. Myers and her ethnographers found that many whites used blatantly racist slurs and categorizations—an often ritualistic degradation of people of color—in their everyday interactions.[70]

Particularly significant is the finding of contemporary social scientists that many whites still make blatantly racist commentaries and do racist performances, such as racist joking or frequent use of racist epithets, when they are in settings with white friends and relatives. This behavior is termed *backstage racism* by Leslie Houts Picca and Joe Feagin, who draw on the ideas of Erving Goffman. Making use of thousands of journal accounts from hundreds of college students across the country, Picca and Feagin found that whites often seem to behave differently depending on whether they are in a backstage setting with white friends and relatives or in a frontstage setting that includes people of color. They report this recent journal account from a white female college student about a night out with several other white students:

> Three of my friends (a white girl and two white boys) and I went back to my house to drink a little more before we ended the night. My one friend, Dylan started telling jokes. . . . Dylan said: "What's the most confusing day of the year in Harlem?" "Father's Day . . . Who's your Daddy?" Dylan also referred to black people as "Porch Monkeys." Everyone laughed a little, but it was obvious that we all felt a little less comfortable when he was telling jokes like that. My friend Dylan is not a racist person. He has more black friends than I do, that's why I was surprised he so freely said something like that. Dylan would never have said something like that around anyone who was a minority.[71]

Here, a white student told racist jokes, and others laughed along with him. Although they reportedly felt uncomfortable, the other whites did not openly object. The journal writer has rationalized her friend's racist actions, noting that he would not make such racist "jokes" in a frontstage setting with people of color around.

Although there clearly have been some important shifts in whites' racist attitudes in recent decades, many of the older racial stereotypes and prejudices, as well as much of the old racist framing of society, remain firmly embedded in many white minds and evident in many whites' everyday commentaries and performances.

 What are common methods of developing and rationalizing stereotypes and prejudices?

Discrimination

Distinguishing Dimensions

Public discussions of racial and ethnic discrimination and of government programs to eradicate it (for example, affirmative action) are often confusing because important dimensions of that discrimination are not fully distinguished. As a first step in sorting out the confusion, we suggest Figure 1.1. Key dimensions of discrimination include (a) motivation, (b) discriminatory actions, (c) effects, (d) the relation between motivation and actions, (e) the relation between actions and effects, (f) the immediate institutional context, and (g) the larger societal context.[72]

A given set of discriminatory acts—such as the exclusion of Jewish American applicants from Ivy League colleges in the 1920s or the exclusion of many children of color from numerous all-white

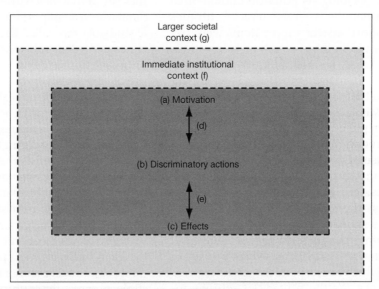

FIGURE 1.1 The Dimensions of Discrimination

Source: Adapted from Joe R. Feagin, "Affirmative Action in an Era of Reaction," *Consultations on the Affirmative Action Statement of the U.S. Commission on Civil Rights* (Washington, DC: U.S. Government Printing Office, 1982), pp. 44–48.

public schools until the mid-1960s—can be examined in terms of these important dimensions. One can ask what the motivation was for this discrimination. Was it prejudice, stereotyping, or another motive? One can also ask what form the exclusionary practices actually took. For example, in the case of segregated public schools in the South or West during earlier decades, white school administrators often refused, on overtly racist grounds, black, Latino, or Asian American children entrance into their buildings. Also of great importance are the many long-term effects of these discriminatory practices. For example, one effect was the much poorer school facilities that many black, Latino, and Asian American children encountered.

These historical practices were usually not just the actions of isolated white administrators. Rather, they were part of an institutionalized pattern of legally or customarily segregated education, the effects of which are still evident in society. Such patterns of official school segregation were part of a larger social context of the general subordination of black, Latino, and Asian Americans across various institutional areas. Indeed, today, as in the past, racial discrimination remains a multidimensional problem involving most institutional areas of U.S. society.

How do stereotypes and prejudices maintain racial or ethnic discrimination?

Research on Prejudice and Discrimination

Much social science research on discrimination has focused on one type of motivation—prejudice [(a) in Figure 1.1]. Many social scientists emphasize the relation between prejudice and discrimination [(d) in Figure 1.1], viewing racial and ethnic prejudice as the critical cause of discriminatory treatment of a singled-out group. Gordon Allport suggested that few prejudiced people keep their prejudices to themselves; they act out their feelings in discriminatory ways.[73] In his classic study, *An American Dilemma* (1944), Gunnar Myrdal saw racial prejudice as "the whole complex of valuations and beliefs which are behind discriminatory behavior on the part of white Americans." Later, sociologist Robert K. Merton wrote that for some people, discrimination is motivated not by their own prejudices, but by fear of the prejudices of others in their social group.[74]

Experimental studies by psychologists have focused on the relationship between prejudice and expressed discrimination. Numerous researchers have examined whether prejudiced people do, in fact, discriminate, and, if so, how that prejudice links to discrimination. Such studies have generally found only a weak positive correlation between expressed prejudice (for example, on questionnaires) and certain discriminatory behavior. Knowing how prejudiced a person is does not necessarily help predict the character of his or her actions.

Some experimenters have tried to develop nonobvious measures of discrimination. One such measure involved setting up an experimental situation in which whites encountered a person (an assistant of the researcher) who needed help with making a phone call at a public telephone. In this case, the researcher found that the racial identity of the person needing help often affected the type of white response. Whites were more likely to get assistance. One recent research project staged personal emergencies, one severe and one more moderate, and then assessed the quickness and quality of the helping actions that black and white victims got from black and white participants in the study. For the severe emergency setting, whites were slower on average in giving help and provided less help to black victims than to otherwise similar white victims. Whites who reacted this way were also found to interpret the black emergencies as less severe than identical white emergencies, as a way of dealing with their discriminatory responses in these situations. A related study found no such racial bias in helping behavior for black helpers, who treated black and white victims equally. As noted previously, public opinion surveys have shown a decline in public expression of blatantly racist attitudes among whites in recent decades. Thus, several experimental researchers have also asked whether whites responding to such surveys with relatively liberal racial answers are concealing many racial prejudices and stereotypes. Reviewing experimental studies that used less obvious measures of discrimination, such as the helping experiments, researchers have noted that experimental studies have found *much more* antiblack discrimination than they should have uncovered if the unprejudiced views that many whites express in surveys were their real views. As the backstage racism research cited previously also suggests, many whites do indeed hide their traditionally racist views in more public settings—including in public opinion surveys.[75]

Defining Institutional and Individual Discrimination

The emphasis on individual prejudice and bigoted individuals in traditional assessments of racial and ethnic discrimination has led some analysts to accent the institutionalization of discrimination. Stokely Carmichael (later, Kwame Ture) and Charles Hamilton distinguished between the concepts of individual racism and institutional racism. **Individual racism** involves *the racially hostile acts of an individual directed at members of another racial group* and is exemplified by the actions of a Klan-type terrorist bombing a black church. **Institutional racism** involves *the institutionalized practices that differentially and negatively affect members of a subordinate racial group,* such as the accumulating institutional practices that lead to large numbers of children of color suffering because of seriously inadequate health care facilities in most U.S. cities.[76] Carmichael and Hamilton moved beyond individual bigots. In their view, institutional racism often includes harmful actions in which many dominant group members have "no intention of subordinating others because of color, or are totally unaware of doing so."[77]

In his analysis of discrimination and mental health, Thomas Pettigrew has distinguished between *direct* and *indirect* racial discrimination. He has applied the latter term to restrictions in one institutional area (such as screening out job applicants because they do not have a college degree) that are shaped by racial discrimination in another area (such as the exclusion of Americans of color from adequate educational facilities, including colleges, in the past or present).[78]

Some conceptual work on discrimination emphasizes the close relationship between its individual ("micro") and institutional ("macro") dimensions, which should be seen as two aspects of the same phenomenon. Social psychologist Philomena Essed has underscored the "mutual interdependence of the macro and micro dimensions" of discrimination. From the macroperspective, racism is "a system of structural inequalities and a historical process." From a microperspective, racism involves individual discriminators whose specific actions are racist "only when they activate existing structural racial inequalities in the system."[79] In the U.S. case, the routine actions of discriminators are typically shaped and reinforced by an old hierarchical system of racial dominance and inequality.

The group context of discriminatory actions is very important. The working definition of the serious **discrimination** we emphasize in this book is as follows: *actions carried out by members of dominant groups, or their representatives, that have a differential and harmful effect on members of subordinate groups.* The dominant and subordinate groups we focus on are socially constructed racial and ethnic groups. From this perspective, the most extensive discrimination typically involves harmful practices taken by members of *powerful* racial and ethnic groups against those with much less power and fewer resources. (Those on the middle rungs of a racial–ethnic hierarchy can and do discriminate, especially against those below them in power.) Discrimination involves *actions* as well as one or more *discriminators* and one or more *victims*. A further distinction between *intentional* (motivated by prejudice or intent to harm) and *unintentional* (not motivated by prejudice or intent to harm) is useful for identifying different types of discrimination.[80]

Drawing on the two dimensions of scale and intention, we suggest four major types of discrimination. Type A, **isolate discrimination**, is *harmful action taken intentionally by a member of a dominant racial or ethnic group against members of a subordinate group, without the support of other members of the dominant group in the immediate social or community context.* An example is a white Anglo police officer who implements anti-Latino hostility by beating up Mexican American prisoners at every opportunity, even though the majority of Anglo officers and department regulations specifically oppose such actions. (If the majority of Anglo officers in that department behaved in this fashion, the beatings would fall under the heading of type C discrimination.) The term *isolate* should not be taken to mean that type A discrimination is rare, for it is indeed common.

Type B, **small-group discrimination**, is *harmful action taken intentionally by a small number of dominant-group individuals acting in concert against members of subordinate racial and ethnic groups, without the direct support of the norms and of most other dominant group members in the immediate social or community context.* The bombing of Irish Catholic churches in the 1800s by small groups of British Americans and the

A current member of the Ku Klux Klan, a terrorist group originally created in the nineteenth century.

burning of crosses at the homes of people of color in several cities in recent years by members of white supremacist groups are likely examples.

Type C, **direct institutionalized discrimination**, is *organizationally prescribed or community-prescribed action that by intention has a differential and negative effect on members of subordinate racial and ethnic groups.* Typically, these actions are not sporadic but are carried out routinely by a large number of dominant-group individuals guided by the legal or informal norms of the immediate organizational or community context. Historical examples include the intentional exclusion, by law, of African and Jewish Americans from traditionally white neighborhoods and jobs. Type C discrimination can be seen today in the actions of those white real estate agents and owners who regularly create barriers for people of color seeking homes in traditionally white residential areas. These

discriminating whites are today acting in accord with *informal* norms widely shared by many whites in their communities.[81]

Type D, **indirect institutionalized discrimination**, consists of *dominant-group practices that have a harmful effect on members of subordinate racial and ethnic groups even though the organizational or community-prescribed norms or regulations guiding those actions have been established with no intent to harm.* For example, intentional discrimination institutionalized in the inadequate school facilities provided for subordinate-group members such as black, Latino, and Native Americans—resulting in inadequate educations for many—has often handicapped their attempts to compete with dominant-group members in the employment sphere, where hiring and promotion standards usually include certain advanced educational credentials.

In addition, the effects of *past* discrimination linger on strongly in the *present:* Current generations of racial groups that were once severely and openly subordinated usually have less inherited wealth and fewer sociocultural (for example, educational or social networking) resources than current generations of the dominant racial group.

 What is the relevance of the four types of discrimination discussed to present-day racial relations in the United States?

The Sites and Range of Discrimination

Discrimination usually includes a spatial dimension. For instance, in a white-dominated society, a racially subordinated person's vulnerability to discrimination can vary significantly. If the latter is in a relatively protected site, such as with close friends at home, the probability of experiencing racial hostility or discrimination from dominant-group members is low. In contrast, if that same person—for example, a college professor—is in a moderately protected site, such as in a departmental setting within a once predominantly white university that has undergone significant desegregation, the probability of experiencing racial hostility and discrimination often increases, although the professional status of that professor will likely offer some protection there. The probability of overt racial hostility and discrimination often increases further as this person of color moves into historically white hotels, restaurants, and stores, or into city streets patrolled by white police officers. As we will see in later chapters, members of subordinate groups who venture the most into settings once reserved for members of dominant groups, in the past or present, have often been the most likely to face substantial racial hostility.[82]

In his classic book, *The Nature of Prejudice*, Gordon Allport notes that discrimination by members of a dominant group against those in a subordinate group ranges from antilocution (speaking against), to avoidance, to exclusion, to physical attack, and finally, to extermination.[83] For example, a dominant-group member, such as an English Protestant American, may still try to quietly exclude a Jewish American from his or her social club. Or a white American may hurl a racist epithet at a Chinese or Korean American walking nearby.

One can also distinguish subtle and covert categories of discrimination from the more blatant forms. **Subtle discrimination** can be defined as *unequal and harmful treatment of members of subordinate racial and ethnic groups that is obvious to the victim but not as overt as traditional, "door-slamming" varieties of discrimination.* In modern bureaucratic settings such as corporate workplaces, many white employers and managerial employees have internalized inclinations to subtle discriminatory behavior that they consider normal and acceptable. In such settings, subtle discrimination may not be noticed by nondiscriminating members of the dominant group, yet it is obvious to most people of color there.[84]

For instance, in research on African American managers who have secured entry-level positions in corporations, Ed Jones found a predisposition among whites, both co-workers and senior managers, to assume the best about persons of their own color and the worst about people different from themselves in evaluating job performance. Like Pettigrew's "ultimate attribution error," this critical predisposition, which can be conscious or subconscious, can result in discrimination in promotions and other areas that is more subtle than the blatant discrimination of exclusion. The black managers interviewed by Jones and other researchers report that their achievements often are given less attention than their failures, while the failures of comparable white managers are more likely to be excused in terms of situational factors or just overlooked. This negative feedback on a black worker's performance

makes it more difficult for her or him to perform successfully in the future.[85]

Covert discrimination, in contrast, is *harmful treatment of members of subordinate racial and ethnic groups that is hidden and difficult to document.* Covert discrimination includes acts of sabotage and tokenism. For example, in one research study, a black female mail carrier reported that white male co-workers were hiding some of her mail, so that when she returned from her route, there was still mail waiting to be delivered. Because of this sabotage, her white manager blamed her and gave her a less desirable route. Asian, African, and Latino Americans are hired sometimes as "tokens" or "window dressing": They are placed in certain conspicuous positions just to make an organization look good instead of being evaluated honestly in terms of their abilities for higher-level employment. Some employers hire a few for "front" positions to reduce pressures to expand the number of employees from racially or ethnically subordinated groups to more representative proportions. Tokenism can thereby become a serious barrier to individual and group advancement.[86]

Cumulative and Systemic Discrimination

Various combinations of blatant, covert, and subtle forms of discrimination usually coexist in a given organization or community. *Well-institutionalized patterns of discrimination that cut across major political, economic, and social organizations in a society* can be termed **systemic discrimination**. One National Council of Churches group portrayed systemic racial discrimination this way: "Both consciously and unconsciously, racism is enforced and maintained by the legal, cultural, religious, educational, economic, political, environmental and military institutions of societies. Racism is more than just a personal attitude; it is the institutionalized form of that attitude."[87]

Central to this systemic discrimination is the *cumulative* effect of much discrimination on its targets. Particular instances of racial or ethnic discrimination may seem minor to outside observers if considered in isolation. But when blatant actions, such as verbal harassment or physical attack, combine with subtle and covert slights, such as veiled sabotage, the cumulative effect of all this discrimination over months, years, and lifetimes is usually *far* greater than the sum of the individual instances.

Racial and ethnic oppression is typically both systemic and cumulative, and its targets usually pay a heavy price.

Responding to Discrimination

The responses of subordinate-group members to discrimination can range from deference or withdrawal to verbal and physical confrontation to legal action. Even when dominant-group members expect acquiescence in discrimination, some subordinate-group members may not oblige. The targets of discrimination often organize and fight back. Thus, a **civil rights movement** is a *collective movement to establish or improve the legal and political rights of a subordinate racial or ethnic group*. Such organized movements are exemplified by the black and Latino civil rights movements of the 1950s and 1960s. Sometimes however, the response is by individuals in everyday settings, especially if they are among those subordinate-group members with some monetary or legal resources. Discrimination that begins as one-way action may become two-way negotiation, often to the surprise of the discriminators.

Consider this example of a black woman manager in a U.S. corporation who describes a meeting with her white boss about her job performance:

> We had a five scale rating, starting with outstanding, then very good, then good, then fair, and then less than satisfactory. I had gone into my evaluation interview anticipating that he would give me a "VG" (very good), feeling that I deserved an "outstanding" and prepared to fight for my outstanding rating. Knowing, you know, my past experience with him, and more his way toward females. But even beyond female, I happened to be the only black in my position within my branch. So the racial issue would also come into play. And he and I had some very frank discussions about race specifically. About females, but more about race when he and I talked. So I certainly knew that he had a lot of prejudices in terms of blacks. And [he] had some very strong feelings based on his upbringing about the abilities of blacks. He said to me on numerous occasions that he considered me to be an exception, that I certainly was not what he felt the abilities of an average black person [were]. While I was of course appalled and made it perfectly clear to him. . . . But, when I went into the evaluation interview, he gave me glowing comments that cited numerous achievements and accomplishments for me during the year, and then concluded it with, "so

I've given you a G." You know, which of course just floored me. . . . [I] maintained my emotions and basically just said, as unemotionally as I possibly could, that I found that unacceptable, I thought it was inconsistent with his remarks in terms of my performance, and I would not accept it. I think I kind of shocked him, because he sort of said, "Well I don't know what that means," you know, when I said I wouldn't accept it. I said, I'm not signing the evaluation. And at that point, here again knowing that the best way to deal with most issues is with facts and specifics, I had already come in prepared. . . . I had my list of objectives for the year where I was able to show him that I had achieved every objective and I exceeded all of them. I also had . . . my sales performance: the dollar amount, the products . . . both in total dollar sales and also a product mix. I sold every product in the line that we offered to our customers. I had exceeded all of my sales objectives. You know, as far as I was concerned, it was an outstanding performance.

Then she noted the final result:

> So he basically said, "Well, we don't have to agree to agree," and that was the end of the session. I got up and left. Fifteen minutes later he called me back in and said, "I've thought about what you said, and you're right, you do have an O." So it's interesting how in fifteen minutes I went from a G to an O. But the interesting point is had I not fought it, had I just accepted it, I would have gotten a G rating for that year, which has many implications.[88]

This example of employment discrimination is a common one and illustrates a number of points made in this chapter. Because of certain physical characteristics, this woman was viewed by her white supervisor as a member of a racial group he stereotypes as generally incapable. He discriminated against her by downplaying her accomplishments with a low evaluation. The one-way action that probably was expected by the boss soon became two-way negotiation. This savvy woman made tactical use of her resources to win a concession and a changed evaluation.

Over the past few decades, there has been an increase in the number of middle-class people of color who have the resources to contest racial discrimination more directly and, sometimes, successfully. Microlevel discrimination may only be the first stage in a two-way encounter. The initial discrimination, the counter-framing and countering actions, and the discriminator's response, as well as the resources and perceptions of those involved, are important aspects of everyday racism.

Moreover, thinking broadly, we should recognize how important the individual and collective struggles against discrimination and for civil rights have been to the development of U.S. democracy. The United States has been an officially free country *only since the late 1960s*. Prior to the 1960s' civil rights acts (the last in 1968), this country had been substantially grounded either in slavery or in legal segregation since the 1600s. For more than three centuries, this country had a major portion of its population under such extreme oppression that describing the country generally as "free" was highly inaccurate. Over this period, moreover, the freedom struggles of African Americans and other Americans of color were central to creating the more democratic country that we live in today.

Conservative Reactions to Antidiscrimination Programs

Many conservative scholars and commentators have written about "reverse discrimination" and "reverse racism." They have intentionally tried to change the public discussion of traditional racial discrimination. Most argue that whites suffer seriously from the implementation of affirmative action and other remedial programs that attempt to redress the extensive discrimination historically faced by subordinated racial groups. (**Affirmative action programs** are *private and governmental programs that seek to improve the economic or educational opportunities for formerly excluded racial, ethnic, and gender groups*.) Conservatives and others often use the phrase *reverse discrimination* to deflect attention from the large-scale patterns of institutionalized discrimination still directed by whites against racially oppressed people.

Discrimination, as conceptualized by most social science scholars of racial and ethnic relations, emphasizes the dominant group–subordinate group context of discrimination. *Racial discrimination* usually refers to actions of members of dominant groups—for example, white Americans—that are made to harm members of subordinate groups, such as African, Latino, Asian, or Native Americans. Historically and today, systemic white discrimination is not just a matter of occasional white bigotry but involves the dominant group's power to enforce its

racial prejudices and stereotypes by means of discriminatory practices in most institutions.

On occasion, individual members of subordinated racial groups can be motivated by their prejudices and stereotypes to take action to harm those in the dominant white group. Yet, members of racially subordinate groups usually do not have the power or institutional position to express the prejudices they may hold about whites in the form of substantial and repeated everyday discrimination.

Think about the historical and contemporary patterns of discrimination directed by large numbers of whites against just one major group: African Americans. That mistreatment has meant, and still means, widespread blatant and subtle discrimination by whites against African Americans in most organizations in most institutions in society—in housing, employment, business, education, health services, and the legal system (see Chapter 7). For over four centuries, many millions of whites have participated directly in racial discrimination against many millions of African Americans. Judging from opinion polls and numerous research studies, a majority of whites currently hold some negative stereotypes of African Americans, and millions of these whites will discriminate under some circumstances. In addition, most whites still observe the antiblack discrimination that often takes place around them without working actively to stop it. This widespread and systemic discrimination has brought extraordinarily heavy social and economic losses for African Americans in many institutional sectors of society.[89]

What would the *reverse* of this centuries-old antiblack discrimination really look like? The reverse of the institutionalized discrimination by whites against African Americans would mean reversing the power and resource inequalities for several hundred years. In the past and today, most organizations in major institutional areas such as housing, education, and employment would be managed at the top and middle levels by a very disproportionate number of powerful black managers and officials. These powerful black officials would have aimed much racial discrimination at whites, including many years of slavery and legal segregation. As a result, millions of whites would have suffered—and would still suffer—trillions of dollars in economic losses such as lower wages, as well as high rates of unemployment and political disenfranchisement for long periods, widespread housing segregation, inferior school facilities, and violent lynchings. That societal condition would be something one could reasonably call a condition that "reversed the discrimination" against African Americans. It does not now exist, nor has it ever existed.

What is usually termed *reverse discrimination* is something much different from this fictional anti-white scenario. One usual reference is to private and public programs, such as affirmative action programs, that seek to remedy the past and present discrimination that has targeted Americans of color. These remedial programs, for a limited time and in certain places, have used racial screening criteria to overcome a small part of that past and present discrimination. Whatever modest costs a few years of these remedial programs have meant for whites, those costs do not add up to anything close to the total cost that inverting the historical and contemporary patterns of discrimination against people of color would involve.[90] A modest number of white men have occasionally paid some price for certain programs designed to remedy past and present discrimination. If such affirmative action is successful, it entails some cost to be paid by those who have benefited most from centuries of racial (and gender) discrimination. Yet, a white man who suffers as an individual from remedial programs such as affirmative action in employment or education suffers in just one area of his life (and often only once) and because he is an *exception* to his privileged racial group. A person of color who suffers from racial discrimination usually suffers *in many areas* of his or her life and primarily because the whole group has been and still is racially subordinated, not because he or she is an individual exception.[91] Moreover, in spite of continuing high levels of discrimination targeting Americans of color, many private organizations and public agencies have, in recent decades, cut back on their modest affirmative action and similar remedial programs because of white protests and judicial backtracking.

Summary

In this chapter, we have examined an extensive array of basic social science concepts that are essential for making sense out of racial–ethnic contacts and conflicts. These concepts loom large in contemporary discussions of racial–ethnic issues. More than a century of discussion of these concepts lies behind the voyage we have set out on here. We must carefully think through the meaning of such terms as *race* and *racial group,* because such concepts have historically been used in the shaping of racial contacts and racial oppression, as they still are today.

Ideas about "race" and racial groups have been particularly dangerous because they have played an active role in the triggering, or convenient rationalizing, of societal processes that have cost many millions of lives. Ideas do have a significant societal impact. The sharp cutting edge of "race," in the context of theorizing about "racial inferiority," can be seen in the enslavement by white Europeans of millions of Africans between the seventeenth and nineteenth centuries and in the genocidal German Nazi actions taken against European Jews, Gypsies, and others in the 1930s and 1940s. Sometimes it is easy to consider such concepts as harmless abstractions. However, some reflection on both recent and distant Western history exposes the error in this view. The concept may not be "mightier than the sword," to adapt an old cliché, but it can indeed be mighty.

Key Terms

race 5
racial hierarchy 5
racialization 6
ideological racism 6
racial group 8
ethnic group 10
minority group 12
dominant group 12
subordinate group 12
racial frame 13
prejudice 14
stereotype 15
externalization
   function of
   prejudice 16
authoritarian
   personalities 16
conformity function of
   prejudice 16
symbolic or modern
   racism 16
individual racism 20
institutional racism 20
discrimination 20
isolate
   discrimination 20
small-group
   discrimination 20
direct institutionalized
   discrimination 21
indirect
   institutionalized
   discrimination 21
subtle
   discrimination 22
covert
   discrimination 22
systemic
   discrimination 22
civil rights
   movement 23
affirmative action
   programs 24

CHAPTER 2

Adaptation and Conflict
Racial and Ethnic Relations in Theoretical Perspective

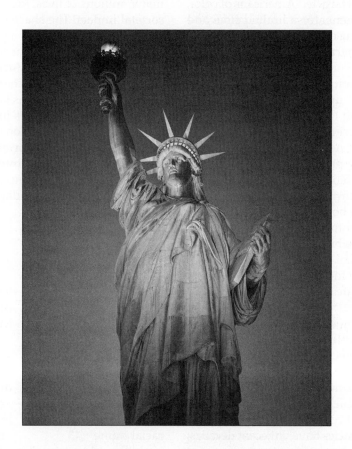

BIG PICTURE QUESTIONS

- *How do initial contacts contribute to the creation of dominant and subordinate racial and ethnic groups?*

- *Have long centuries of immigration made the United States a real melting pot?*

- *What is the role of systemic racism in the United States today?*

n 1790, the first U.S. Congress limited naturalized U.S. citizenship to "white persons" only. This discriminatory law remained in effect until 1952. Because of the law, numerous immigrants coming into the United States in this long era petitioned U.S. courts to be viewed as "white" so that they could officially become citizens. The first challenge to the law came from Ah Yup, a man who had immigrated from China and petitioned a California court to be admitted as a citizen of the United States. However, after some research on racial hierarchy, and citing Johann Blumenbach's racial typology, the white judge decreed that Ah Yup was not a "white person" under the law, but rather a person of the "Mongolian race."[1]

How do groups that are termed racial groups or ethnic groups develop? How do groups come into contact with one another in the first place? How do they adjust to one another beyond the initial contact? A number of important social science theories analyze how intergroup contact leads to initial patterns of racial and ethnic interaction and stratification. Various other theories explore the persistence of racial and ethnic patterns. Group domination and stratification, as well as intergroup conflict, are critical issues in these racial and ethnic theories.

Racial and Ethnic Hierarchies

Like numerous other societies, U.S. society is made up of a diversity of racial and ethnic groups. As in the 1790s, and so in the present, the number of racial and ethnic groups in North America remains impressive, although the mix of groups has varied over time. Racial and ethnic diversity is basic in the history of this society.

Yet, diversity, as the previously discussed terms *dominant group* and *subordinate group* suggest, has often been linked to a racial and ethnic *hierarchy*—to stratification, domination, and substantial inequality among groups. Human beings organize themselves for a number of different reasons—for example, for earning a living, for conducting religious rituals, and for governing. Among the important features of societal organization are social ranking systems. Such systems rank social categories of people, not just individuals.

In most societies, several social ranking systems coexist. Some classify people by their racial or ethnic group, whereas others rank people by their gender, age, disability, sexuality, or class position. Each ranking system has distinct social categories; rewards, privileges, and power vary with a group's position within the system. Some categories, such as English Americans in the racial and ethnic system, have generally had much greater power and resources than other categories, such as Native Americans, African Americans, or Latinos. Such power and resource inequality tends to persist from one generation to the next. In racial and ethnic ranking systems, certain ascribed (that is, attributed, not achieved) characteristics—such as one group's racial characteristics as perceived by another group—become the criteria for very unequal social positions, privileges, and rewards.[2]

The image of a ladder makes the concept of racial and ethnic stratification clearer. In Figure 2.1, the positions of five selected racial and ethnic groups at a specific time in U.S. history are diagrammed on a hierarchical ladder. Some groups are higher than others, indicating that they have greater privileges—social,

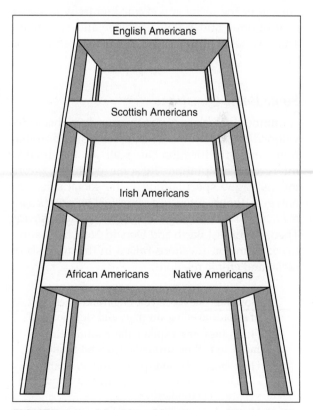

FIGURE 2.1   A Ladder of Dominance: The United States as of 1790

economic, and political—than the lower groups. A group substantially higher than another on an important dimension is viewed as a *dominant group;* one substantially lower than another is seen as a *subordinate group.* The more groups there are in a society, the more complex is the image, with middle groups possibly standing in a relation of dominance to some groups and in a relation of subordination to others.

Consider the United States in 1790, about the time of its founding. For that era one might roughly diagram the five groups in Figure 2.1 in terms of such factors as overall economic or political power, so that the top group would be English Americans, with Scottish Americans a little down the ladder. Farther down would be the early (usually Protestant) Irish immigrants, a group composed at the time mostly of poor farmers and indentured servants. At the bottom in terms of power and resources would be African Americans, most of who were in slavery in the South. Those Native American (Indian) groups and individuals within the boundaries of the new nation—most were still outside it—were also at the bottom of the racial and ethnic hierarchy in terms of economic and political power and resources. The new nation firmly embedded a racial and ethnic hierarchy from its beginning.[3]

Some Basic Questions

A number of social science theories have been developed to explain this societal diversity, domination, and stratification, as well as the related intergroup adaptation. In some contexts, *theory* means vague speculation; in the social sciences, however, **theory** refers to *a conceptual framework used to interpret or explain some aspect of everyday existence.* Theorists Ernest Barth and Donald Noel have summarized major questions raised in the analysis of racial and ethnic relations:

1. How does one explain the origin and emergence of racial and ethnic diversity and stratification?
2. How does one explain the continuation of racial and ethnic diversity and stratification?
3. How does one interpret internal adaptive changes within systems of racial and ethnic diversity and stratification?
4. How does one explain major changes in systems of racial and ethnic diversity and stratification?[4]

 What methods have been used to create the racial hierarchy in the United States?

Migration and Group Contact

Racial and ethnic relations and stratification systems originate with intergroup contact as different groups, often with no common ancestry, come into each other's spheres of influence. Contact can be between an established or indigenous people and a migrating people (group A → land of group B) or between two or more migrating groups moving into a previously uninhabited area (group A → new land ← group B). The movement of English colonists into the lands of Native Americans in the 1600s is an example of the first type of contact.

Migration has been viewed by Charles Tilly in terms of the following:

1. The actual migrating units (for example, individuals or families)
2. The situation at the point of origin (for example, the home country)
3. The situation at the destination (for example, a U.S. city)
4. The socioeconomic and political framework within which the migration occurs (for example, modern global capitalism)[5]

Certain precontact factors shape both the migration and the outcome of the contact that results from migration. *Push* factors include what is happening in the immigrants' home country—high unemployment or intergroup hostilities, for example. Depressed economies or painful religious or political conflicts in sending countries have generated major migrations to the United States. *Pull* factors also generate migration. Immigrants may be attracted by the portrayal, accurate or inaccurate, of better conditions—such as abundant jobs—at the destination. The outcome of the initial contact is influenced by the resources and characteristics of the migrating group (such as its economic resources or language) and of the receiving group (such as its receptiveness to newcomers). Technological assets, such as industrial skills or armaments (firepower), have proven an advantage to certain groups. Some argue, for example, that early European colonists were able to conquer (and often destroy) numerous

Native American societies in part because of the latter's less developed weaponry.[6]

Types of Migration

In a classic book, *Comparative Ethnic Relations*, R. A. Schermerhorn suggested four major types of migration that generate racial and ethnic relations. These constitute a continuum running from involuntary migration to completely voluntary migration:

1. Movements of forced labor
2. Contract-labor movement
3. Movement of displaced persons and refugees
4. Voluntary migration[7]

Movements of forced labor include *involuntary immigration, such as the forcible removal of Africans to North America.* **Contract-labor movement** includes the *migration of indentured Irish servants to the English colonies and of Chinese laborers to western North America.* **Political refugees** include the *streams of refugees produced by war,* such as Jewish immigrants from Europe in the 1930s and Vietnamese and Cuban refugees since the 1950s. **Voluntary migration** is *migration primarily by choice,* and includes the great migrations of southern and eastern European groups to the United States in the early twentieth century and of numerous Asian and Latin American groups since the 1960s.

The *voluntary migration of powerful colonizers,* sometimes termed **colonization migration**, often precedes the types just listed. Colonization migration can be seen in the English trading companies whose employees founded the first North American colonies, a development that soon led to the dispersal or brutal destruction of indigenous Indian societies already inhabiting the continent.[8]

Patterns of Racial and Ethnic Adaptation

The Initial Contact

What happens when different human groups come into contact as the result of migration? Outcomes vary. In the initial stage, outcomes include the following:

1. Exclusion or genocidal destruction
2. Egalitarian symbiosis
3. An exploitive hierarchy and stratification system

Genocide is *the deliberate and systematic attempt by one group to exterminate another group*—one outcome of contacts between European colonists and several Native American societies. **Egalitarian symbiosis** refers to *peaceful coexistence and a rough economic and political equality between two racial–ethnic groups.* Occasional examples of this outcome can be found in the history of world migrations, but they are rare, especially in North America. Some authors argue that by the early nineteenth century, Scottish Americans were approaching equality with English Americans in many areas. A more common result of migration and contact is **hierarchy,** *a significant socio-economic stratification.* Stanley Lieberson noted that **migrant superordination** occurs *when the migrating group imposes its will on indigenous groups, usually through more advanced weaponry and political or military organization.* The indigenous populations of the United States and Canada were subordinated in this fashion. **Indigenous superordination** occurs *when groups immigrating into a new society become subordinate to groups already there,* as was the case for Africans forcibly brought to North and South America by the established European colonists.[9]

Later Adaptation Patterns

Beyond the initial period of contact between two groups, the range of possible outcomes of intergroup contact includes the following:

1. Continuing genocide
2. Continuing egalitarian symbiosis
3. Replacement or modification of stratification by substantial inclusion along conformity lines
4. Replacement or modification of stratification by inclusion along cultural pluralism lines
5. Continuing subordination, ranging from moderate to extreme, of a racial or ethnic group

One type of outcome can be a continuing thrust by the dominant group to exterminate the subordinate group. Attempts by European Americans to kill off indigenous peoples continued until the early twentieth century. Alternatively, an egalitarian symbiosis can continue beyond initial peaceful interaction. The third outcome is for an initial hierarchy, characterized by a sharp inequality of power and resources, to be modified by extensive incorporation of the incoming group into the dominant culture and society. This can take two forms. In the first, inclusion of the new group occurs by means of substantial conformity to the dominant group's culture. By surrendering much of its cultural heritage and conforming to the dominant group, the incoming group gains increased acceptance and significant resource equality. Some have argued that many non-English European immigrant groups, such as Scots and Scandinavians, eventually gained rough equality with the English Americans in this way.

The fourth possibility is *cultural pluralism*—substantial economic and political assimilation and greater equality along with a significant persistence of subcultural (for example, religious) distinctiveness. In this outcome, the substantial adaptation of the immigrant group to the host group is primarily economic and political, with cultural distinctiveness continuing in certain major respects (such as religion). The interaction of certain white immigrant groups, such as Irish Catholic Americans, with the host-group English Americans offers a possible example of this outcome.

A fifth outcome of continuing intergroup contact is persisting and substantial racial or ethnic subordination and hierarchical stratification. The extent and inequality of this stratification can vary, but for many non-European groups, such as Native Americans and Mexican Americans, economic and political inequality has remained so great as to constitute what some term a condition of *internal colonialism*. Even in this case, however, partial acculturation usually occurs in terms of significant adaptation to the dominant group's culture (for instance, to the English language).

Types of Theories

In the United States, explanatory theories of racial and ethnic relations have been concerned with migration, adaptation, exploitation, oppression, stratification, and conflict. Most such theories can be roughly classified as either order theories or power-conflict theories, depending on their principal concerns and emphases. **Order theories** are *racial and ethnic theories that accent patterns of inclusion—the orderly integration and assimilation of particular racial and ethnic groups to a dominant culture and society,* as in the third and fourth outcomes just described. The central focus is on progressive adaptation to the dominant culture and on stability in intergroup relations. **Power-conflict theories** are *racial and ethnic theories that accent the persisting and great inequalities in the power and resource distributions associated with*

racial or ethnic subordination in a society, as in the first and fifth outcomes just described.

Assimilation and Other Order Perspectives

In the United States, much social theorizing has heavily emphasized **assimilation**, *the more or less orderly adaptation of a migrating group to the ways and institutions of an established host group.* Charles Hirschman has noted that "the assimilation perspective, broadly defined, continues to be the primary theoretical framework for sociological research on racial and ethnic inequality."[10] The English word *assimilate* comes from the Latin word *assimulare*, meaning "to make similar."

Robert E. Park

Robert E. Park, a major sociological analyst, argued that European out-migration was a major catalyst for societal reorganization around the globe. In his view, intergroup contacts regularly go through stages of a **race relations cycle**, in which *fundamental social forces, such as out-migration, lead to recurring cycles of contact and assimilation in intergroup history:* "The race relations cycle which takes the form, to state it abstractly, of *contacts, competition, accommodation* and *eventual assimilation,* is apparently progressive and irreversible."[11] In the contact stage, migration and exploration bring peoples together, which in turn leads to economic competition and thus to new social organization. Competition and conflict flow from the contacts between host peoples and the migrating groups. Accommodation, a critical condition in the race relations cycle, often takes place rapidly. It involves a migrating group's forced adjustment to a new social situation.

Park seems to view accommodation as involving a stabilization of relations, including the possibility of permanent caste systems. Sometimes he speaks of the race relations cycle as leading inevitably from contact to assimilation. At other times, however, he recognizes that the assimilation of a migrant group might involve major barriers and take a substantial period of time to complete.

Nonetheless, Park and most scholars working in this tradition have argued that there is a long-term trend toward large-scale assimilation even of subordinated racial and ethnic groups in modern societies. "Assimilation is a process of interpenetration and fusion in which persons and groups acquire the memories, sentiments, and attitudes of other persons or groups, and, by sharing their experience and history, are incorporated with them in a common cultural life."[12] Racially subordinate groups are expected eventually to fully assimilate into the "common culture" and major institutions of the society.[13]

Stages of Assimilation: Milton Gordon

Since Park's pioneering analysis in the 1920s, many U.S. racial and ethnic relations theorists and other analysts have adopted some version of the assimilationist perspective, although most have departed from Park's framework in important ways. Milton Gordon, author of the influential *Assimilation in American Life*, offers a multidimensional perspective. There is a variety of initial encounters between racial and ethnic groups and an array of assimilation outcomes. Gordon presents three competing images of assimilation—the melting pot, cultural pluralism, and Anglo-conformity—but he focuses on Anglo-conformity as having been the usual historical reality for the United States. In Gordon's view, immigrant groups entering the United States have over time given up much of their cultural heritage and conformed substantially to a white Anglo-Protestant core culture.[14] Cultural assimilation (also called *acculturation*)—the change of one group's cultural patterns to those of the host or dominant group—is a very important dimension of intergroup adaptation. Gordon's view emphasizes the way in which new groups must conform to the preexisting Anglo-Protestant culture that they face as they enter U.S. society.

Gordon notes that Anglo-conformity has been substantially achieved for numerous immigrant groups to North America, especially with regard to cultural assimilation. Most groups following the early English migration have adapted to the Anglo core culture. Gordon distinguishes seven dimensions of adaptation:

1. **Cultural assimilation:** *the change of one group's important cultural patterns to those of the core society*
2. **Structural assimilation:** *penetration of cliques and associations of the core society at the primary-group level*
3. **Marital assimilation:** *significant intermarriage*
4. **Identification assimilation:** *development of a sense of identity linked to the core society*
5. **Attitude-receptional assimilation:** *absence of prejudice and stereotyping*
6. **Behavior-receptional assimilation:** *absence of intentional discrimination*
7. **Civic assimilation:** *absence of value and power conflict*

A long line of European immigrants at Ellis Island (about 1900).

Whereas Park believed that structural assimilation, including new primary-group ties such as intergroup friendships, flowed from cultural assimilation, Gordon stresses that these are separate stages of assimilation and may take place at different rates.

For Gordon, structural assimilation generally relates to families and other primary-group relations. (*Primary groups* are small groups characterized by personal closeness, such as family groups and groups of close friends; *secondary groups* are specialized and impersonal groups, such as corporations.) In his view, the movement of a new immigrant group into the secondary groups of the host society—that is, into the employing organizations, such as corporations or government bureaucracies, and educational and political institutions—is *not* a distinctive type of structural assimilation that should be incorporated into an assimilation typology.

The omission of a thorough discussion of this secondary-structural assimilation is a major flaw in Gordon's typology. Looking at U.S. history, one sees that some admission into the society's important secondary groups, such as its economic institutions (workplaces), does not necessarily mean that one gets to enter the dominant group's friendship cliques or families. Also missing in Gordon's analysis is attention to residential integration and Anglo-conformity— to the movement of an incoming group away from segregated immigrant communities into the residential areas of the dominant group, a pattern that has received much attention in some demographic analyses. Moreover, the dimension Gordon calls *civic assimilation* is somewhat confusing because he includes in it "values," which are really part of cultural assimilation, and "power," which is a central aspect of structural assimilation at the secondary-group level.[15]

Still, this assimilation theory is useful and has influenced contemporary social scientists. For example, sociologist Silvia Pedraza has made significant use of Gordon's conceptual framework in her research on Cuban and Mexican immigration, and Richard Alba has contrasted his view of the loss of strong ethnic identities among white ethnic Americans with Gordon's idea of identificational assimilation. Alba and Victor Nee have also pointed out that Gordon's concept of the core culture needs to be modified to take account of the fact that the cultures of new immigrants have sometimes had an effect on that core, particularly in areas such as religion and music. They view the mainstream culture as now a composite of such diverse inputs. The cultural influence is not just one way. Moreover, in an assessment of Gordon's seven dimensions, J. Allen Williams and Suzanne Ortega examined interviews with a Midwestern sample and found that cultural assimilation was not necessarily the first type of adaptation to occur. Thus, in their data Mexican Americans were less culturally assimilated than African Americans, yet more assimilated structurally. Those of Swiss and Swedish backgrounds ranked about the same on the study's measure of cultural assimilation, but the Swedish Americans were less assimilated structurally. Williams and Ortega concluded that assimilation varies considerably from one group to another and that Gordon's seven types can be grouped into just three general categories of structural, cultural, and receptional assimilation.[16]

Focused on the millions of European immigrants and their societal adjustments, Gordon's model emphasizes *generational* changes within immigrant groups over time. For most European immigrant groups, substantial acculturation to the Anglo-Protestant culture has often been completed by the second or third generation. The partially acculturated first generation formed protective communities and associations, but the children of those immigrants were considerably more exposed to Anglo-conformity pressures from the media and in schools.[17] Gordon suggests that substantial assimilation along civic, behavior-receptional, and attitude-receptional dimensions has occurred for numerous European immigrant groups. Most have also made considerable progress toward equality at the secondary-structural levels of employment and politics, although the dimensions of this assimilation are not discussed in any detail by Gordon.

For many white, particularly non-Protestant, groups, substantial structural assimilation at the primary-group level is now accomplished yet still incomplete. Gordon suggests that substantially complete cultural assimilation (for example, full adoption of the English language) along with some structural (primary-group) separateness form a characteristic pattern of adaptation for many white ethnic groups. Even these relatively acculturated white ethnic groups today tend to have disproportionate numbers of informal friendships and marriage ties within their particular ethnic groups or within their general socioreligious community. Following Will Herberg, who argued that there are three great community "melting pots" in the United States—Jews, Protestants, and Catholics—Gordon and others have suggested that most primary-group ties beyond one's own group are typically developed within one's broad socioreligious community.[18] (According to the traditional **melting pot** view, *immigrants to the United States lose their racial and ethnic identities as they mix together in one new American blend.*)

Assimilation theorists like Gordon recognize that racial prejudice and discrimination have retarded structural assimilation, but they tend to view non-European Americans, including African Americans, particularly those in the middle class, as eventually being assimilated into the dominant culture and institutions. With regard to African Americans, Gordon argues, optimistically, that the United States has "moved decisively down the road toward implementing the implications of the American creed [of equality and justice] for race relations"—such as in employment and housing. The tremendous progress that he perceives African Americans to have made has created a government policy dilemma: Should it adopt a "corporate liberalism" that recognizes group rights along racial lines? Gordon includes under this corporate liberalism numerous government antidiscrimination programs, such as affirmative action, which he generally rejects.[19] The optimism of many assimilation analysts about the eventual implementation of the U.S. creed of equality for African Americans and many other non-European Americans is problematical, as we will see in later chapters.

In recent years, several assimilation analysts have argued that certain once-prominent ethnic identities, especially of European Americans, are fading. An advocate of the continuing usefulness of the concept of assimilation is sociologist Richard Alba. He has argued persuasively that, although ethnic identity is still of some consequence for many whites, a new ethnic group is being formed—"one based on a vague *ancestry* from anywhere on the European continent." Distinct ethnic identities as English American and Irish American are giving way to identification as "European American." Similarly, Herbert Gans has suggested that increasingly, especially for whites, ethnicity is only "symbolic" and weakening greatly in significance. Symbolic ethnicity involves little more than a desire to maintain some feeling for one's ethnic background without strong commitments to traditional ethnic behavior or social networks. Interestingly, research

on intermarriages linking white ethnic groups reveals that large proportions of the children of such marriages see themselves as having *multiple* ethnic identities, whereas others choose one of their heritages, or simply "American," as their identity.[20]

 Given the various assimilation theories, which one best describes the adaptation of present-day immigrants in the United States?

Ethnogenesis and Ethnic Pluralism

Some theorists working in the broad assimilation tradition also reject the argument that most European American groups have become or are becoming fully assimilated to a generic Anglo-Protestant or Euro-American identity and way of life. A few have explored models of adjustment that depart from Anglo-conformity in the direction of ethnic or cultural pluralism. It was a Jewish American of Polish and Latvian origin who early formulated a perspective called *cultural pluralism.* Horace Kallen (1882–1974) argued that membership in ethnic–cultural groups was not a membership one could readily abandon. Writing in *The Nation* magazine in 1915, he argued that ethnic groups necessarily adapted to the host society, but had a right to exist on their own terms; that is, democracy applied to ethnic groups. He argued against the ruthless Americanization advocated by many white Anglo-Protestant nativists at the time. By the 1920s, he had given the name **cultural pluralism** to *the view that each ethnic group has the democratic right to retain its own cultural heritage without being forced to assimilate to the dominant culture.*[21] Kallen's pioneering analysis set early precedents for the perspective now called *multiculturalism* (see Chapter 13).

Social scientists adopting a cultural pluralism perspective accept some Anglo-conformity adjustment as inevitable. For instance, in their classic *Beyond the Melting Pot,* Nathan Glazer and Daniel Moynihan recognize that the original customs and home-country ways of European immigrants were mostly lost by the third generation. This did not, however, bring an end to their ethnicity. The European immigrant groups usually remained distinct in terms of name, identity, and, for many, primary-group ties.[22]

Andrew Greeley developed the concept of *ethnogenesis* and applied it to white immigrant groups set off by nationality and religion. **Ethnogenesis** entails *the sociological theory that, over time, immigrant groups not only come to share cultural traits with the host group but also retain many of their own nationality characteristics.* The traditional assimilation perspective assumes "that the strain toward homogenization in a modern industrial society is so great as to be virtually irresistible."[23] The direction of this assimilation is assumed only to be toward the dominant Anglo-Protestant culture. However, from this ethnogenesis perspective, adaptation has meant much more than one-way conformity. The traditional Gordon assimilation model does not explain the persistence of ethnicity—the emphasis among immigrants on ethnicity as a way of becoming American and, in recent decades, self-conscious attempts to create ethnic identity and to manipulate ethnic symbols.

The complex ethnogenesis model of intergroup adaptation is portrayed in Figure 2.2. Greeley suggests, as is shown in the left-hand box (host/common/immigrant), that in many cases host and immigrant groups had a somewhat similar cultural inheritance. For example, some later European immigrant groups had a cultural background initially similar to that of earlier English colonists. As a result of the interaction of subsequent generations with each other and with descendants of earlier immigrants, such as in public schools and through the influence of the media (symbolized by long arrows in the figure), the number of cultural traits common to the host and immigrant groups often increased. Yet, as is illustrated in the right-hand boxes, late in the adaptive process certain aspects of the heritage of the home country have remained important to the character of the immigrant ethnic group. Ethnic groups share traits with the host group but also retain major characteristics of their nationalities. A modern ethnic group is one part home-country heritage and one part common culture, mixed together in a unique way because of a distinctive history of development within the North American crucible.[24]

As we noted in discussing Milton Gordon's ideas, some researchers argue that white ethnic cultures are blending and white ethnic identities are fading. Thus, they do not see a persistence of strong ethnic identities as Greeley does. Nonetheless, a number of research studies have documented the presence today of still-distinctive white ethnic groups, such as Italian Americans and Jewish Americans, in numerous cities, from New York to Chicago to San Francisco, New Orleans, and Tucson. Several researchers have also shown that ethnicity is often an *emergent phenomenon*—that its importance varies in cities and its character and strength depend on the specific historical conditions in which it grows.[25]

FIGURE 2.2   The Ethnogenesis Perspective

Source: Andrew M. Greeley, *Ethnicity in the United States* (New York: John Wiley, 1974), p. 309. Reprinted with permission.

Additional Problems with Assimilation Theories

Assimilation theorists such as Gordon have often taken as their primary examples of adaptation the European groups that migrated more or less voluntarily to countries such as the United States. But what about the adaptation and incorporation of the numerous non-European groups beyond the stage of initial contact? Most prominent assimilation analysts include non-Europeans in their theories, despite the problems that sometimes arise from such inclusion. They have argued that traditional assimilation, cultural and structural, is the necessary, if long-term, answer to the racial "problem" of the United States. One prominent analyst, Gunnar Myrdal, argued some decades back that as a practical matter it is "to the advantage of American Negroes as individuals and as a group to become assimilated into American culture, to acquire the traits held in esteem by the dominant white Americans."[26] In Myrdal's view there was an ethical contradiction between the democratic principles announced in the Declaration of Independence and the still-institutionalized discrimination against black Americans. For Myrdal this represented a "lag of public morals," a problem solved in principle but still being worked out in an ongoing, one-way assimilation process that may or may not be completed soon.

Optimistic assimilation analysts have emphasized *progressive inclusion,* which they believe will eventually provide racially subordinated groups with full citizenship—in fact as well as in principle. For that reason, they expect ethnic and racial conflict and tensions to disappear as various groups become fully assimilated into the dominant culture and society. Scholars such as Nathan Glazer, Milton Gordon, and Talcott Parsons have stressed what they see as the essential egalitarianism of U.S. institutions and what they view as the ongoing emancipation of non-European groups. They have often underscored what they see as a gradual assimilation of (middle-class) black Americans over several decades. Full membership for black Americans seems inevitable, notes Parsons, for "the only tolerable solution to the enormous [racial] tensions lies in constituting a single societal community with full membership for all."[27] The importance of racial, as well as ethnic, hierarchy and stratification is expected to decline as powerful, universalistic societal forces wipe out the

vestiges of earlier ethnocentric value systems. As these analysts see it, white European immigrants have desired substantial assimilation and have been absorbed. The same is expected to happen eventually for non-European groups.

Recently, sociologists Nee and Alba have accented a flexible theory of what they term "rational choice" assimilation, which allows for different patterns of adaptation for different racial–ethnic groups. They argue that the U.S. mainstream to which immigrants assimilate involves "a core set of interrelated institutional structures and organizations regulated by rules and practices that weaken, even undermine, the influence of ethnic origins. . . . A useful way of conceiving of the mainstream is that it is part of the society within which ethnic and racial origins have at most minor impacts on life chances."[28] Nee and Alba adopt a theory of assimilation that is more flexible than that of Gordon and are optimistic that descendants of immigrants of color will increasingly make their way fully into this societal mainstream without prohibitive discrimination. In their view, as the heavily white "baby boomer" generation in the United States continues to retire, many economic opportunities for Americans of color will open up. In this new era, skin color will likely not be the barrier to structural assimilation it once was. Perceptions of racial difference change, and in the future, immigrant groups of color may, like earlier white ethnic groups, be allowed by the dominant white group to integrate fully into core institutions. For example, Nee and Alba see signs of this in the favorable situation of many dark-skinned Asian-Indian Americans today (see Chapter 11).

However, other social scientists, such as Mia Tuan and Rosalind Chou and Joe Feagin, have been critical of such an optimistic assimilation perspective, at least for certain non-European groups. They have researched the situations of later-generation Chinese Americans, Japanese Americans, and other Asian Americans and found that, although they are substantially acculturated to the Anglo-dominant culture, most still have a strong sense of their racial identity because whites still regularly discriminate against them, overtly or subtly, and impose the identity of "Asian foreigner" on them. Many whites (and others) still view these groups in racialized terms—as somehow not "real Americans." Thus, it seems unlikely that most Asian Americans, to take just one important example of a non-European group, will soon be absorbed fully and equitably into white middle-class society.[29]

In addition, some assimilation arguments and theories have been criticized for having a serious nativist or "establishment" bias. For example, a number of Asian American scholars and leaders have reacted vigorously to the application of the concept of assimilability (and, thus, unassimilability) to Asian Americans, arguing that the modern version of this concept originated in a period (about 1870 to 1925) of intense attacks by white Americans on the then numerous Chinese and Japanese immigrants. The term *assimilation* was thus tainted from the beginning by its association with the notion that the only "good immigrant groups" were those that could assimilate rapidly and in Anglo-conformity fashion.

In recent years, several researchers have explored another assumption of traditional assimilationist thinking: the idea that new immigrants both should and do adapt to the core culture in a more or less linear, one-directional manner. One old and common view is that new immigrants must gradually "become American" in order to overcome the "inferiority" of their old languages, cultures, and societies. However, this perspective ignores the fact that the assimilation process can also have very significant negative effects. Some research indicates that in certain ways the physical or mental health of immigrant groups *declines* as they become better off economically and more assimilated into the core culture. For example, over time, most immigrants gradually adopt the relatively unhealthy diet of many native-born Americans (and many become overweight and obese) and/or experience family and social stresses (for example, teenagers become depressed) associated with adapting to mainstream U.S. customs. The shift from the culture of origin to the core culture is not necessarily a shift from an inferior to a superior culture, as many native-born Americans might assume.[30]

In addition, assimilation theorists often do not analyze sufficiently the historical development of a particular racial or ethnic group within the larger international context of modern capitalism. Numerous social scientists have developed a perspective called *transnationalism*, which assesses how migration across national boundaries takes place within a highly developed global capitalistic context in which the imperialistic actions of corporate and political actors in major industrial ("core") countries often have (intended or unintended) effects on international migration flows from countries in the "periphery." Like traditional assimilation analyses, transnationalism emphasizes the fact that individual migrants tend to migrate along family and friendship networks. However, as an analysis of Israeli immigrants to the United States puts it, transnationalism also involves "large scale economic, political, and legal structures within which immigrants develop their communities and lives." Transnationalism views immigration as an "on-going process through which ideas, resources, and people change locations and develop meanings in multiple settings."[31]

Thus, many immigrants and their children maintain a strong tie to the home country, with attachments to two "homes" at the same time. They seek opportunities in a new country but also maintain strong ties to the old country. Some immigrants, such as many Puerto Ricans, come to the U.S. mainland to escape pervasive poverty in their home areas, yet return home periodically because of racial discrimination and other factors that make their lives difficult in the United States. *Return* or *circular migration* is a term for this process. For many Israeli, Puerto Rican, and undocumented Mexican immigrants—and even some in the second generation—orientation and self-identity are very strongly linked to their place of origin.

Biosocial Perspectives

Some social theorists, including some assimilationists, offer a biosocial perspective on racial and ethnic relations. The old European and American notion that racial and ethnic groups are deeply rooted in human beings' biological makeup has received renewed attention from a few social scientists and biologists in the United States in recent decades. In *Human Nature, Class, and Ethnicity*, for example, Milton Gordon suggests that ethnic group ties are rooted in the "biological organism of man." Ethnicity is a fundamental part of the physiological as well as the psychological self. Ethnicity "cannot be shed by social mobility, as for instance social class background can, since society insists on its inalienable ascription from cradle to grave." Gordon seems to have in mind the rootedness of intergroup relations in the everyday realities of kinship and socially constructed group boundaries, not the old racist notion of the unchanging biological character of racial groups. He goes further, however, emphasizing that human beings tend to be "selfish, narcissistic and perpetually poised on the edge of aggression." In his view, these selfish tendencies lie behind contemporary racial and ethnic tensions.[32] Gordon is adopting a Hobbesian ("dog-eat-dog") view of human nature.

Critics of this biosocial view have suggested that it attributes to fundamental "human nature" what are in reality capitalism's highly individualistic values. That is, under modern capitalism, much selfishness and narcissism are *learned* rather than inherent in human biological makeup. Although decidedly different from earlier biological theories, the modern biosocial analysis remains problematical. The exact linkages between the deep genetic underpinnings of human nature and concrete racial or ethnic behavior are not spelled out beyond some vague analysis of kin selection and selfish behavior.

A major difficulty with any such biosocial approach is that in the everyday world, racial and ethnic relations are *immediately social* rather than biological. As numerous scholars have pointed out, many racial and ethnic groups have mixed biological ancestry. Jewish Americans, for example, have a very mixed ancestry—as a group, they share no distinctive biological characteristics. Biologically diverse Italian immigrants from different regions of Italy gained a sense of being Italian American (even Italian) in the United States. The bonds holding Jewish Americans and Italian Americans together were not genetically based or biologically primordial, but rather the result of real *historical* experiences as these social groups became firmly established in community settings in countries such as the United States. If ethnicity is primordial in a biological sense, it should always be a prominent force in human affairs. Sometimes historical ethnicity leads to ethnic conflicts, as in the case of Jews and Gentiles in the United States; in other cases, as with Scottish and English Americans, it mostly disappears in the mutual adaptation process. Sentiments based on common ancestry are important, but they are activated primarily in the concrete experiences and histories of specific migrating and host groups.[33]

Emphasizing Migration: Competition Theory

Competition theory is a contemporary example of the exploration of migration issues more or less in the tradition of Robert Park. **Competition theory** is *a view of ethnicity that emphasizes the relative stability of ethnic population boundaries over time and the intergroup*

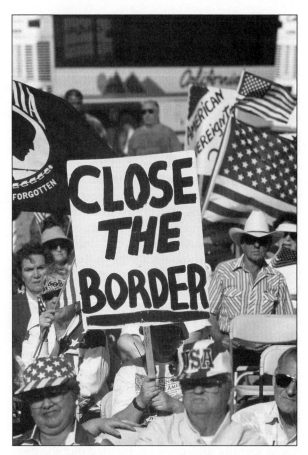

Protests against legal and undocumented immigration have increased in recent years.

competition over resources that result from shifts in these boundaries because of migration. Park emphasized that ethnic and racial relations stem from the migration of peoples, which in turn leads to competition for often scarce resources. Competition theorists have explored the contact and competition parts of the race relations cycle. Unlike some order-oriented theorists, they usually do address questions of protest and conflict, although they do not give much attention to racialized exploitation or wealth-inequality issues.[34]

Competition theorists view "ethnicity" in the broad sense as a social phenomenon distinguished by boundaries of language, skin color, and culture. They emphasize the general stability of many ethnic population boundaries, as well as the effects of shifts in these group boundaries; ethnic–group membership often coincides with the creation of a distinctive group niche within the larger labor force. Competition occurs when two or more ethnic groups attempt to secure the same socioeconomic resources, such as jobs or housing.[35]

According to group competition theorists, intergroup tensions and conflict are fostered by immigration across geographical borders and by the expansion of once-segregated ethnic groups into the same labor and housing markets to which other groups have access. Attacks on immigrant workers or native-born workers of color, for example, increase at the city level when a group moves out of traditionally segregated jobs and thus challenges other groups and not, as one might expect, in cities where ethnic groups are locked into segregation and poverty.

Sociologist Susan Olzak has examined empirical data on ethnic and racial violence in the nineteenth century to show that collective action, such as Anglo-Protestant crowds attacking the newer European immigrants entering the United States, increased when immigration expanded and when economic recessions occurred. The ethnic boundary of the native-born white Americans was mobilized against European immigrant (and black) workers "when ethnic competition was activated by a rising supply of low-wage labor and tight labor markets. In this case the ethnic groups that mobilized were not fully assimilated, but had retained aspects of their traditional identity and drew on that for mobilization against other groups."[36] Olzak distinguishes between (1) societal situations of economic decline, which can increase interethnic competition for jobs and other economic goals, and (2) situations of new ethnic mixing and integration, in which the breakup of once-segregated societies brings ethnic groups into new job competition and other economic competition.

Most recently, using data on ethnic groups in 100 countries, Olzak set these ethnic group competition issues within a broader international context. Examining various conflicts between ethnic groups in numerous countries, and between ethnic groups and their governments, she shows that local ethnic mobilizations are significantly influenced by the larger international setting of politics and world organizations. The more integrated a country is with international human rights organizations and similar world organizations, the more salient ethnic identities become within local country settings and the more likely that local inequalities and limits on human rights will generate ethnic-based group mobilization.[37]

Competition theorists have also emphasized that economic struggles often accompany political competition, which includes competition among ethnic groups for government positions and tax dollars. Joane Nagel has shown how contenders for political power often organize along ethnic lines and argued that "ethnicity is a convenient basis for political organizers due to the commonality of language and culture and the availability of ethnic organizations with ready-made leadership and membership."[38]

A power-conflict theorist might criticize these competition theorists for studying U.S. markets and urban interethnic competition over the last century without a developed analysis of the systemic racism that has long been foundational to the United States. Missing from competition theory is a substantial concern with issues of structural racial inequality, racial exploitation, and racial discrimination accented by numerous power-conflict theories discussed below.

Power-Conflict Theories

The past few decades have witnessed an increased development of major *power-conflict* frameworks that explain racial and ethnic relations in this and other countries. These perspectives place much greater emphasis on economic stratification, racial–ethnic hierarchy, and power issues than one finds in most assimilation and competition theories. Within this broad category of power-conflict theories are a number of subcategories, including the caste perspective, the internal colonialism viewpoint, and a variety of class-based and neo-Marxist theories.

The Caste School

One early exception to the assimilation perspective was the *caste school of racial relations*, which developed in the 1940s mostly under W. Lloyd Warner and Allison Davis and their associates.[39] Focusing on white-on-black oppression in the South, these researchers viewed the position of black Americans as distinctively different from that of other U.S. racial and ethnic groups. After the Civil War, a new societal system, a "caste" system, replaced the southern slavery system. The white and black castes were socially separated by a total prohibition of intermarriage as well as by great economic and social inequalities. These social scientists were critical of the emphasis in most social science analysis on prejudiced attitudes and feelings. Instead, these advocates of the **caste school of racial relations** accented *well-institutionalized racial discrimination as the foundation of a castelike system of U.S. segregation and apartheid.*[40]

Early Class Theories of Racial Relations

W. E. B. Du Bois, one of the first sociological analysts in the United States, was a black scholar and civil rights activist who had experienced the brutality of white racism firsthand. Drawing on Marxist class analysis in his later writings, Du Bois was perhaps the first major social science theorist to emphasize that racial oppression and social class oppression are closely linked. In his view, the linking together of racial oppression and modern capitalism explained why there has never been true democracy and freedom for all Americans. In a 1948 article titled "Is Man Free?," Du Bois argued that both black workers and white workers were prevented from exercising their full democratic rights because of the control of a small capitalist class (for example, the owners of major workplaces) over the U.S. economy and politics. He argued with evidence that a truly democratic society must include not only social and political equality for Americans of color but also substantial decision-making control of workplaces by workers. Du Bois's sociological ideas are still fresh and provocative, but to this point in time only a modest number of social scientists have used them to analyze the structure of U.S. society.[41]

An early power-conflict analyst who drew on Du Bois and social class analysis was Oliver C. Cox, a scholar whose work has been neglected. Cox also emphasized the role of the capitalist class in U.S. racism. He analyzed the economic dimensions of the forced slave migration from Africa and the great oppressiveness of later conditions for enslaved African Americans. In his view, the slave trade was "a way of recruiting labor for the purpose of exploiting the great natural resources of America." The color of Africans was not important; they were chosen "simply because they were the best workers to be found for the heavy labor in the mines and plantations across the Atlantic."[42] A search for cheap labor by a profit-oriented capitalist class of whites led to a system of racial subordination in the United States. Racial prejudice developed only later, as part of a white-generated ideology rationalizing this economic subordination.

Internal Colonialism

An emphasis on power and resource inequalities across racial lines is at the heart of the internal colonialism theory and its recent descendant, "coloniality" theory. The conceptual framework of internal colonialism is built in part on the work of analysts of external colonialism—the worldwide imperialism of certain capitalist nations, including the United States and European nations, over several centuries.[43] Balandier has noted that Europe's capitalistic expansion has affected non-European peoples across the globe since the fifteenth century: "Until very recently the greater part of the world's population . . . knew only a status of dependency on one or another of the European colonial powers."[44] **External colonialism** *involves the running of a country's economy and politics by an outside colonial power.* Over time, many European colonies in places like Africa became independent of their outside colonizers, such as Great Britain or France, but have continued to have their economies directed substantially by the capitalists and corporations of the former colonial powers.

In contrast, the European colonies in the Americas that experienced a large in-migration of whites have had a different pattern. In such cases, external colonialism has often become **internal colonialism**, in which *the control and exploitation of non-European groups in the colonized country passes from whites in the home country overseas to white immigrant groups within the newly independent country.*[45] Non-European groups in the United States have been viewed in terms of such internal colonialism. The origin and initial stabilization of this internal colonialism predate the Revolutionary War in the United States. The systematic subordination of non-Europeans began with "genocidal attempts by colonizing settlers to uproot native populations and force them into other regions."[46] A great many indigenous Americans were killed or driven off desirable lands. Enslaved Africans became a source of labor for white farmers before and after the Revolution. Later, Asian and Pacific peoples were imported as contract workers or annexed in the expansionist nineteenth-century period of U.S. development. Robert Blauner, an internal colonialism theorist, has noted that agriculture in the U.S. South depended on black labor; in the Southwest, Mexican agricultural development was forcibly taken over by European migrants there after the 1840s Mexican-American War.[47] From the internal colonialism perspective, contemporary racial–ethnic inequalities are grounded in the long-term economic interests of white employers in low-wage labor—the underpinning of capitalistic economic exploitation.

In recent years, colonialism theory has been reinvigorated by social science research showing how the global colonialism of the past created social structures of oppression that persist today. The scholars Ramón Grosfoguel and Chloe Georas have shown that the current situation for key racial–ethnic groups in the United States is still often one of "coloniality"—a situation of cultural, political, and economic oppression for subordinated racial–ethnic groups without the existence of an overt colonial administration and without legal segregation. Official decolonization does not mean an end to coloniality, for the colonial hierarchies of racial–ethnic oppression often remain more or less intact. Indeed, seen from this coloniality perspective, most mainstream analyses of racial relations underestimate the major continuities between the overtly colonial past and the racial and ethnic hierarchies of the present.[48]

Grosfoguel and Georas cite the examples of Puerto Ricans and African Americans. Both were early colonial-racial subjects of a global U.S. empire, and their situations today show many aspects of that old U.S. colonialism. Today, European Americans remain at the top of, and in control of, the racial hierarchy, and African Americans and Puerto Ricans remain racially subordinated groups at the bottom.

Cultural Resistance and Oppositional Cultures

Internal colonialism theorists accent the role of the cultural stereotyping and racist ideologies of dominant groups seeking to subordinate people of color. A racist ideology, itself part of a broader racist framing, dominates an internal colonialist society, intellectually dehumanizing the colonized. Stereotyping and prejudice, seen in many traditional social science theories as more or less *temporary* problems, are viewed by colonialism analysts as a way of rationalizing exploitation over a very long period. Attempts are made by the dominant group to envelop subordinate groups in dominant cultural values, traditions, and language—in the case of people of color, to "whiten" their cultures. In a system of internal colonialism, cultural as well as physical markers are used to set off subordinate groups such as Native Americans, Latinos, Asian Americans, and African Americans from the European American group.[49]

Thus, a number of power-conflict scholars have honed the idea of **oppositional culture**—*the culture of resistance often found among subordinate groups*—as a basis for understanding the resistance of non-European groups to the dominant Euro-American culture. Bonnie Mitchell and Joe Feagin have argued that the oppositional cultures of Americans of color are "distinct from the dominant Euro-American culture, while also reflecting or reacting to elements of the larger society. . . . In the colonies and later the United States the pressures on non-Europeans for conformity to the Euro-American culture forced minority Americans to become bicultural, to know both the dominant Euro-American culture and their own oppositional culture as well."[50]

The nation of the United States, created in the 1700s, encompassed African enslavement and genocidal attacks on the indigenous societies. Faced with oppression, these and other targets of colonialism have long drawn on their own cultural resources, as well as distinctive knowledge of Euro-American culture and society, to resist oppression. The cultures of those oppressed by European Americans have not only provided a source of individual, family, and community resistance to racial oppression but also infused a few new elements into the evolving cultural mix that now constitutes the U.S. culture. The cultures of racially colonized groups such as African, Latino, and Native Americans have also helped preserve key aspects of certain U.S. ideals, including the important tradition of civil rights, freedom, and social justice.[51]

Looking back over U.S. history, several social scientists have researched cultural strategies developed by subordinate racial and ethnic groups to resist oppression. For example, James Scott has shown that intentional deception is central to much interaction between the powerless and the powerful.[52] Most groups of color, including Asian, African, Latino, and Native Americans, have used a variety of techniques to hide their critical views of the U.S. system of racial oppression. The concealed discourse of oppressed groups includes critiques that cannot be discussed publicly. For example, early

Afro-Christianity often involved the enslaved African Americans resisting the "ideological hegemony" (attempts to brainwash) of their white slavemasters. In public religious services, enslaved African Americans usually pretended to accept Christian teachings about complete obedience. However, when and where no whites were present, Afro-Christianity might emphasize "themes of deliverance and redemption, Moses and the Promised Land, the Egyptian captivity, and emancipation."[53] For many of those enslaved the "Promised Land" meant the North and freedom, and the afterlife was often viewed as a place where white oppressors would be punished.[54] Surviving elements of African culture and religion were also major sources of this recurring inclination to resistance and rebellion.

 What are the major strengths and weaknesses of the order and power-conflict theories we have explained in this chapter?

Anticolonial Nationalism

Ideological resistance takes different forms. For example, anticolonial *nationalism* has developed as part of the cultural resistance to European colonialism and its racist ideology. Pan-Africanism and cultural nationalism are two examples of this resistance to both internal colonialism and liberal solutions for that colonialism.

From the early 1900s to the 1960s, for example, W. E. B. Du Bois was a major advocate of cultural nationalism. He saw pan-African nationalism as a partial solution for the colonized conditions in which people of African descent around the world found themselves.[55] Despite objections from the U.S. State Department, Du Bois succeeded in putting together the first Pan-African Congress in 1919, which was attended by delegates from fifteen countries. The Congress did not ask for immediate decolonization of Africans around the globe, but for more democratic treatment. The Congress called for abolition of slavery and curtailment of colonial exploitation. The Pan-African Congress was an important step toward uniting people of African descent and was perceived as radical by white European and American leaders.[56]

Many racially oppressed peoples have historically drawn on cultural nationalism as a means of resisting Euro-American cultural pressures and discrimination. For example, in Chapter 6 we will examine the cultural and other resistance of numerous Native American societies to the threat of both white violence and cultural imposition. In Chapter 8 we will examine protests by Mexican Americans in New Mexico. The Alianza Federal de Mercedes in the 1960s sought to recover lands in New Mexico taken by the Anglo-American invaders and to establish a stronger Mexican American identity with links to the Mexican heritage. A militant Chicano movement, which emphasized Mexican culture and national pride, emerged among Mexican Americans in a dramatic way in the 1960s and 1970s.

In recent decades, African American scholars and activists have developed a comprehensive Afrocentric perspective that includes a strong critique of the cultural imperialism of European Americans. Sociologist Molefi Kete Asante, among others, has spurred the development of this perspective, arguing for the concept and term *Afrocentricity*. Asante and his colleagues analyze the Eurocentric bias in the dominant culture, particularly the elements of that culture that have been absorbed by African Americans. Indeed, these analysts are critical of the language of much "ethnic" analysis: "The use of the terms *ethnicity, disadvantaged, minority,* and *ghetto* are antithetical to our political consciousness which is indivisible from the international political struggle against racism."[57]

Similarly, anthropologist Marimba Ani writes: "European cultural imperialism is the attempt to proselytize, encourage, and project European ideology. . . . European nationalism implies European expansion, that, in turn, mandates European imperialism."[58] Beginning in the 1400s, European imperialism was supported by a well-developed theory of European supremacy, a worldview that attempted to destroy the cultures of African and African American peoples. From this perspective, the Euro-American worldview includes the myth of European cultural and national superiority, a celebration of materialism over cooperative and spiritual values, and a belief in the superiority of the Judeo-Christian religious tradition over other religious traditions. Because of the profound effect this Euro-American framing of the world has had on the subordinated peoples, Afrocentric theorists argue that African Americans must direct their "energies toward the recreation of cultural alternatives informed by ancestral visions of a future

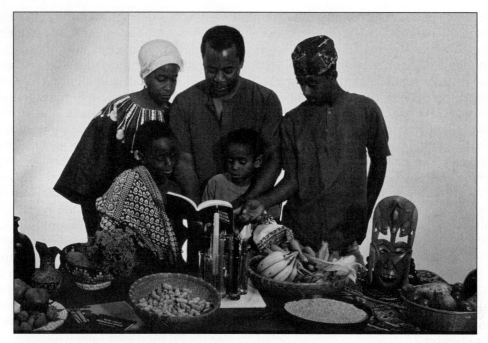

An African American family in African clothing celebrates Kwanzaa.

that celebrates . . . Africaness."[59] Numerous other Americans of color have engaged in similar struggles against what they view as a Eurocentric dominant culture.

A Neo-Marxist Emphasis on Class

Analysts of racial oppression have sometimes combined an internal colonialism perspective with an emphasis on class stratification, drawing on the Marxist research pioneered by such analysts as Du Bois and Cox. For example, Mario Barrera suggests that the heart of internal colonialism is an interactive structure of class and racial stratification that divides U.S. society. Social class, in the economic-exploitation sense of that term, is central in this perspective. Basic to current internal colonialism are four classes that have developed in U.S. capitalism:

1. *Capitalists:* a small group of people who control capital investments and the means of production and who buy the labor of many others
2. *Managers:* a modest-sized group of people who work as administrators for the capitalists and have been granted control over the work of others
3. *Petit bourgeoisie:* a group of small-scale merchants who control their own businesses and do most of their work themselves, buying little labor power from others
4. *Working class:* a very large group of blue-collar and white-collar workers who sell their labor to employers in return for wages and salaries

The dominant class in the U.S. political-economic system is the capitalist class, which routinely subordinates workers from various racial–ethnic groups for its own corporate profit and investment needs. It is the capitalists who usually decide whether and where to create jobs.

As shown in Figure 2.3, each class is crosscut by a line of racial segmentation that separates those who suffer from institutionalized discrimination—such as African, Latino, Asian, and Native American

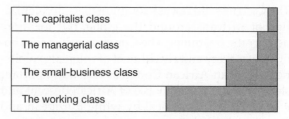

Note: Shaded area represents people of color.

FIGURE 2.3   The Class and Racial Structure of Internal Colonialism

workers—from those whites who do not. Take the example of the working class. Although these workers of color may share the same class position with white workers in that they are struggling against capitalists for better wages and working conditions, they are also in a subordinate position because of structural discrimination along racial lines within that working class. The dimensions of this discrimination often include lower wages for many subordinate-group workers, as well as their concentration in lower-status jobs.[60]

The Split Labor-Market View

Racial and ethnic analysts who emphasize class are sometimes unclear about whether all social classes of whites benefit substantially from the colonization of people of color, or just the dominant class of capitalist employers. A power-conflict perspective that helps in assessing this question is the **split labor-market view**, which *treats class in the sense of people's position in the economic "means of production" and argues that the white employer class and whites in the working class both discriminate against those in the working class who are not white.* Sociologist Edna Bonacich argued that in U.S. society, dominant-group (white) workers generally do not share the economic interests of the top social class, the capitalists, yet both the white employer class and the white part of the working class play key roles in discriminating against the racially subordinated part of the U.S. working class.[61]

Developing a neo-Marxist class analysis of racial subordination, Oliver Cox argued that the U.S. capitalist class, motivated by a desire for profit and cheap labor, sought African labor for the slave system in the United States. Ever since, this employer class has played the major role in keeping African Americans in a subordinate economic position in U.S. society. Similarly, Al Szymanski argued that because U.S. employers have not created enough jobs for all those who wish to work, white workers and workers of color are often pitted against each other for too few jobs, often to the broad advantage of capitalists as a class.[62]

However, Bonacich emphasizes that aggressive discrimination against black workers by white workers seeking to protect their own racial privileges is also very important in U.S. society. Historically, white workers have often resisted the full racial desegregation of their workplaces because they fear job displacement or lower wages. For example, until rather recently in U.S. history white workers' unions often openly restricted the access of workers of color to many job ladders, thus splitting the labor market and significantly reducing those workers' and their families' incomes. For example, from the 1880s to the 1960s, in states such as Alabama, the industrial unions controlled by white workers "helped forge a labor framework" that created and perpetuated rigidly segregated white and black jobs.[63] Informal job restrictions and other informal discrimination targeting workers of color are still maintained by white workers in some U.S. workplaces to the present day. White workers both gain and lose from this discrimination. They gain because there is less competition for better-paying job categories from workers of color who are restricted or marginalized. Historically, however, white workers have frequently lost in the long run because employers can use a cordoned-off sector of lower-wage workers of color to undercut white workers if they try to protest or to strike for better working conditions.[64]

In the 1930s, W. E. B. Du Bois explained how both of these class perspectives might be brought together. Du Bois examined the "public and psychological wage" that white workers have received in the U.S. system of racial oppression.[65] Most working-class whites—those with far fewer resources than whites in the higher classes—have come to accept less in the way of economic and political resources and power substantially because of their access to the racial privileges of whiteness. And it is the white elite that has historically convinced and actively pressured white workers to accept an ideology that celebrates "whiteness." When white working people, viewing themselves as racially superior, have refused to organize effectively with workers of color against white employers in order to secure better wages, they have often received fewer economic resources than might have been the case had they effectively organized *with* workers of color.

Ordinary whites suffer in the class-stratified society that is the United States, and the dominant racial frame—with its racist stereotypes of Americans of color—makes it harder for most of these whites to understand not only the situation of the racialized "others" but also their own oppressed economic situation in society. Most whites do not feel powerful or privileged, especially relative to the white elite, but many are unable to see clearly the real sources of class and racial inequality in this society. Indeed, many unfairly target Americans of color as bearing substantial responsibility for their, or the country's, serious economic difficulties. Some even join white supremacist groups, which engage in threats of overt violence against Americans of color.

Middleman Minorities, Ethnic Enclaves, and Segmented Assimilation

Social scientists have explored the in-between position, in terms of power and resources, that certain racial and ethnic groups have occupied in highly stratified societies. These groups periodically find an economic niche as small-business people positioned between more powerful producers and less powerful consumers (often consumers of color). Some ethnic and racial groups become small-scale traders and merchants doing jobs that dominant groups are not eager to do. For example, many first-generation Jewish and Japanese Americans, excluded from mainstream employment by white Protestant Americans, became small-scale merchants, tailors, and restaurant operators. Such groups have held "a distinctive class position that is of special use to the ruling class." That is, they often "act as a go-between to this society's more subordinate groups."[66]

Edna Bonacich and John Modell found that Japanese Americans fit what has been termed the *middleman minority model*. A **middleman minority** is *a racial or ethnic group that occupies an in-between position in terms of societal power and resources.* Before World War II, for example, Japanese Americans resided in highly organized communities, primarily on the West Coast. Their local economies were based on self-employment, including gardening and truck farming, and on other nonindustrial family businesses. The social solidarity of the first generation of Japanese Americans helped them establish successful small businesses. However, they faced hostility from whites. In fact, Japanese Americans were often driven into the businesses they developed because they were denied many other employment opportunities by white discrimination.[67]

Some middleman groups, such as Korean or Cuban American merchants in certain central cities today, have frequently become targets of hostility from groups that are less well off, such as low-income Mexican or African Americans. Strong in-group bonds can make the middleman group an effective competitor, and even white merchants and other entrepreneurs may sometimes become hostile toward an immigrant group of color that competes too effectively in the economy. Historically and in the present day, Korean or Jewish business people have periodically been viewed negatively by better-off, white Protestant merchants who have the power to discriminate against them, as well as by the poor renters and customers of color with whom they deal as landlords and merchants. Some scholars have criticized a broad application of "middleman minority" theory to certain Asian American groups, arguing that groups such as Chinese or Japanese Americans, even when substantially involved in trade, have rarely been a *middle* group of modest entrepreneurs situated between a poor racial–ethnic group and a richer racial–ethnic group. More generally, this middleman perspective also does not deal adequately with the movement, over time, of large numbers of small entrepreneurs in a particular middleman group into a yet more powerful business group, as has happened for many Jewish Americans over the last century.

A similar perspective, *enclave theory*, examines secondary-structural incorporation of a group into the U.S. economy, especially the ways in which certain non-European immigrant groups have created **ethnic enclaves**—that is, *distinctive social and economic niches in U.S. cities.* Both the middleman and the enclave perspectives give more emphasis to economic inequality and racial or ethnic discrimination than do the traditional assimilation perspectives such as Milton Gordon's. Enclave theorists stress the incorporation of certain groups—such as the Cubans, Chinese, and Koreans—into the United States through the means of small businesses and specialized "ethnic economies." The major differences between the two theories here seem to stem from the examples emphasized. Groups studied by enclave theorists, such as Cuban Americans, have generally created enclaves that are more than merchant or trading economies; they often include manufacturing enterprises, for example. These substantial economic enclaves may compete directly with established white-Anglo business elites. In contrast, the "middleman" groups have developed trading economies and have more often than not just filled an economic niche that has mostly complemented that of established white businesses.

Alejandro Portes and Robert Manning examined the communities of Cubans in Miami and Koreans in Los Angeles—groups that have developed many small businesses that cater to customers inside and outside their own communities. Enclave economies require an immigrant group with entrepreneurial talents, business experience, some capital, and a pool of low-wage labor. These characteristics enabled Cuban Americans in Miami to build a strong enclave economy. These enclaves, unlike the "colonies" of internal colonialism, typically do not relegate newcomers to a more or less permanent position of inferiority. Enclave scholars sometimes criticize the internal colonialism and split labor-market viewpoints for trying to encompass all subordinated groups, although they agree that the situations of African Americans, Mexican Americans, and Native Americans can perhaps be better explained as variations on internal colonialism. Yet, enclave analysts have so far paid insufficient attention to the economic exploitation that takes place in enclave economies, such as exploitation of low-wage immigrant workers by immigrant (for example, Cuban American) employers. They also tend to neglect the effects of the surrounding political and economic system—in the Cuban and Korean cases, multinational capitalism—that shapes the initial migration of these groups as well as the character of their specific enclave economies. In some ways enclave theorists straddle the fence between the order and power-conflict theories.[68]

Some researchers concerned with structural barriers that prevent immigrants of color from assimilating as might be predicted from a traditional assimilation perspective have suggested the concept of *segmented* assimilation. Rubén Rumbaut has underscored the diversity of the adaptation experiences of various immigrant groups, calling on immigration researchers to spell out what is "being 'assimilated,' by whom, under what circumstances, and in reference to what sector of American society." Alejandro Portes and Min Zhou have argued that over time the outcomes of adaptation by immigrants to U.S. society vary greatly, with some confined to the lower economic rungs of the societal ladder and others experiencing rapid economic development while maintaining much of their traditional culture. An example of segmented assimilation is the situation of many second-generation Mexican Americans today. Unlike the children and grandchildren of earlier white immigrants from Europe, who over these generations moved into better economic circumstances and living conditions, many second-generation and third-generation Mexican Americans continue to face difficult economic circumstances, with lower-paying jobs and inadequate housing (see Chapter 8). Moreover, in contrast, one 2008 New York City study, titled *Inheriting the City,* examined the situations of selected immigrants of color—for example, Dominicans, South Americans, and Chinese—and found that the second-generation children of these immigrants were so far mostly upwardly mobile and assimilating relatively well to certain "American ways," compared to their parents and to children in much older groups of color such as African Americans. Of course, one reason for the upward mobility of many recent legal immigrants of color (and their children) is the fact that many come into the United States with some socioeconomic resources, especially many who have come since 1990. In recent decades, much of the legal immigration to the United States has involved people from the middle and upper classes of the sending countries.[69]

Over the generations, then, the experiences of immigrants and their children can involve upward or downward mobility, and reflect a variable and segmented assimilation in key areas such as the economy. The arguments about segmented assimilation parallel to some degree the ideas of the ethnogenesis theory. The main difference lies in the greater attention given by segmentation theorists to major structural barriers such as the discrimination and entrenched segregation that have faced many people of color.

A Note on Market-Dominant Minorities

We should consider briefly who it is that has gained the top economic position in market-driven economies around the globe. In a provocative analysis of contemporary capitalism, Amy Chua has developed the concept of *market-dominant minorities*. She shows that in many areas, certain racial or ethnic minorities have come to economically dominate the population majorities in their countries. These market-dominant groups include, in her analysis, white South Africans in contemporary South Africa, people mainly of European descent (considered "whites") in many Latin American countries, Jewish Russians in contemporary Russia, Chinese Indonesians in contemporary Indonesia, Croatians in the former Yugoslavia, and Lebanese in several West African countries.

Historically, the European colonizers were market-dominant minorities in the areas on every continent where they came to dominate—almost always at the expense of impoverished indigenous peoples of color. Huge wealth increases came out of this process of greatly exploiting the labor, land, and natural resources of other peoples. In addition to these white Europeans becoming market-dominant minorities, the divide-and-conquer process of colonialism over time also favored certain other groups, "exacerbating ethnic wealth imbalances and fomenting group tensions. . . . most starkly in southern Africa but also in Latin America."[70]

Central to Chua's argument, as well as that of other recent U.S. analysts, is a concern that in many countries today the operation of capitalistic markets comes into serious conflict with the operation of expanding political democracies. Markets tend to favor small groups of people, often people who have accented their own racial or ethnic superiority. Yet, the opening up of democratic political institutions means that impoverished, often racially oppressed, majorities can gain political power and begin to counter the smaller, economically privileged racial or ethnic groups.

Women and Gendered Racism

Most theories of racial and ethnic relations have neglected gender stratification. In recent decades, numerous social scientists have researched the situations of women within various U.S. racial and ethnic groups. Their analyses often assess the ways in which male supremacy, or a **patriarchal system**—*a social hierarchy in which men as a group dominate women as a group, especially in terms of socioeconomic power and resources*—interacts with and operates within a system of racial and ethnic stratification. Discussing racial and ethnic cultures around the globe, Adrienne Rich has explained a patriarchal system in more detail as "a familial-social, ideological, political system in which men—by force, direct pressure, or through ritual, tradition, law and language, customs, etiquette, education, and the division of labor—determine what part women shall or shall not play, and in which the female is everywhere subsumed under the male."[71]

Asking whether racism or patriarchy has been the primary source of oppression, Philomena Essed examined the situations of black women in the Netherlands and United States. She found racism and sexism interacting. Thus, *societal oppression of women of color* is often a **gendered racism**.[72] For example, under slavery, African American women were exploited not only for labor but also often as sex objects for white men, including slaveholders. After slavery ended, under Jim Crow segregation these women were excluded from most job categories available to white men and women; major employment changes came only with the civil rights movement of the 1960s (see Chapter 7). Today, racism still has gendered forms. In the media, including on the Internet, the white woman is usually the standard for female beauty. Women of color are often stereotyped as exotic sex objects, matriarchs in female-headed families, or "welfare queens." In the economy they are often found disproportionately in lower-paid "female jobs," such as nurses' aides, fast-food restaurant workers, and clerical workers. Some women of color, such as Mexican American and African American women in the South and Southwest, are closely bound in their social relations with those who oppress them in such areas as domestic employment (as "maids").

Sociologist Patricia Hill Collins has argued that a solid black feminist theoretical framework analyzes critically the negative stereotypes of black women—the white-generated, historical, and contemporary stereotypes such as docile mammy, domineering matriarch, promiscuous prostitute, and irresponsible welfare mother. These severely negative images, which are also sometimes applied to Mexican American and Puerto Rican women, are central to the old white racial framing of these groups and persist because they are fostered by the media and undergird whites' discrimination against women of color.[73]

Scholars assessing the situations of women of color—including Native, Asian, Latino, and African American women—have emphasized the cumulative and interactive character of racial and gender oppression and the necessity of liberating these women from racial stereotypes and discrimination. Denise Segura has examined labor force data on Mexican American women and developed the concept of *triple oppression*—the mutually reinforcing and interactive set of racial, class, *and* gender forces whose cumulative effects "place women of color in a subordinate social and economic position relative to men of color and the white population."[74] Numerous social scientists have called for more research to explore the character, interaction, and consequences of these triple oppressions of race, class, and gender.

Men in some racial or ethnic groups also face a type of gendered racism. For example, gender-specific stereotypes are often directed at men of color. Whereas black women are frequently stereotyped by whites and others as matriarchs or "welfare queens," black men are often stereotyped as oversexed criminals. In addition, Asian American and Mexican American women are sometimes stereotyped as exotic sex objects, and Asian American men are sometimes stereotyped as impotent or unmasculine. Gendered racism takes many forms.

 How does gendered racism shape an individual's position in U.S. racial and gender hierarchies?

The State and Racial Formations

Looking at the important role of governments in creating racial and ethnic designations and institutionalizing discrimination, creative social theorists Michael Omi and Howard Winant have developed an innovative theory of *racial formation*. Racial tensions and oppression, in their view, cannot be explained solely in terms of social class or nationalism. In **racial formation theory**, *racial relations are substantially defined by government actions that range from the passing of racist legislation, such as restrictive immigration laws, to the racially motivated imprisonment of groups defined as a threat* (for example, Japanese American imprisonment during World War II, discussed in Chapter 10).

The U.S. government has greatly shaped the contours and stereotypes of racial and ethnic relations in this country: The U.S. Constitution and a lengthy series of laws have long defined racial groups and interracial relationships (for example, slavery) in openly racist terms. The U.S. Constitution, for example, counted each enslaved African American as only three-fifths of a person (for the purpose of white political representation), and the Naturalization Law of 1790 explicitly declared that only "white" immigrants could qualify to become naturalized U.S. citizens. Non-European immigrants,

such as Asians, were thereby prevented from becoming citizens. Japanese and other Asian immigrants, for example, were banned by racist laws from becoming U.S. citizens *until the 1950s*. In 1854, the California Supreme Court even ruled that Chinese immigrants should be classified as "Indians," thereby denying them political rights available to white Americans.[75]

For centuries, as we will see in later chapters, the U.S. government officially favored northern European immigrant groups over southern Europeans, such as Italians, and over people of color from other continents. For example, the Immigration Act of 1924 was used to exclude Asian immigrants and many immigrants from southern and eastern Europe—those whom the Anglo-Protestant political leaders in Congress and the White House saw as inferior and a threat to their control of society. Northern European Americans working through the government thereby greatly shaped the subsequent racial, ethnic, and religious mix of the United States. For example, today there are far fewer Catholic, Jewish, and Buddhist Americans than there would have been if the U.S. government had not enforced discriminatory immigration laws for many decades.

Toward a Theory of Systemic Racism

The social scientists and other scholars who were reviewed in the power-conflict theory section of this text are grappling with important dimensions of racial oppression as it has developed in countries like the United States. Drawing on the research and ideas of these authors—particularly Du Bois, Cox, Blauner, and Ture and Hamilton—and using much recent research work by Joe Feagin and his colleagues, we can trace out briefly the contours of a more comprehensive power-conflict theory, one we can call a *theory of systemic racism*. **Systemic racism** encompasses *the white prejudices, stereotypes, emotions, framing, discriminatory practices, and institutions that are integral to the long-term domination of Americans of color.* We suggest here key themes in the development and continuing maintenance of systemic racism in the United States:

1. *Initiation of oppression:* At an early point in time, European colonists established hierarchical group relations with the people of color they oppressed and exploited for their land (for example, Native Americans) and labor (for

example, African Americans). Later, descendants of these self-named "white" colonists would add many other Americans of color (for example, Latino and Asian American groups) to the system of racial exploitation and oppression.

2. *Mechanisms of oppression:* In the past and in the present, these substantial racial hierarchies have involved material oppression that is supported by a strong racial framing with its range of stereotyped ideas, narratives, and emotions. Racial hierarchies are perpetuated centrally by the exploitative and other oppressive (discriminatory) practices carried out by members of the dominant racial group (in this case, white Americans) against those in numerous subordinate racial groups.

3. *Privileges and costs of oppression:* Substantial material and symbolic privileges come to those in the dominant racial group. Much misery and serious social and economic burdens come to those in subordinate racial groups. Critical to the maintenance of hierarchical group relations is the ongoing societal reproduction of this unjust enrichment for white Americans and unjust impoverishment for many Americans of color, now over many generations.

4. *Elite maintenance of oppression:* Many actions of the white economic and political elites have created and maintained the societal institutions, interpretive frames, and ideologies that reflect the elites' interests in racial (and class and gender) hierarchies. Most non-elite whites have more or less accepted the society's racial hierarchy, along with fewer socioeconomic resources than the elites, because of their access to privileges and advantages associated historically with "whiteness."

5. *Rationalization of oppression:* Once the system of racial oppression and social privilege was firmly put into place in the 1600s and 1700s, it was increasingly defended and rationalized by a broad racist framing with its supporting racist ideology. Since at least the late 1600s, a broad racist frame accenting superior and inferior racial groups has been created and circulated by elite whites in power. For centuries now, that racist frame has been accepted and further circulated by most rank-and-file whites.

6. *Resistance to oppression:* Opposition to systemic racism is a constant in North American history. Native Americans, African Americans, and other Americans of color have a long history of individual and group counterframing and protest against the reality and burdens of racial oppression by white Americans. Some anti-racist whites have periodically joined in this centuries-old struggle against systemic racism.

To varying degrees, these dimensions of historical and contemporary racial oppression are relevant to understanding the oppressed situations of most non-European Americans, including Native Americans, African Americans, Latino Americans, Asian Americans, and Middle Eastern Americans. We will examine these dimensions in detail in later chapters, but let us illustrate them briefly here, with particular reference to white oppression of African Americans over nearly four centuries.

A previous history of oppression often explains many contemporary societal realities. For example, the pioneering W. E. B. Du Bois, in his book *The World and Africa* (1946), showed how the great misery and poverty evident in Europe's many African colonies were linked directly to the "wealth and luxury in Europe. The results of this poverty were disease, ignorance, and crime. Yet these had to be represented as natural characteristics of backward peoples."[76] Du Bois argued that a serious history of African colonization has been omitted from most mainstream histories of European development, wealth, and affluence. He further demonstrated that a complete understanding of European wealth and prominence must *center* on the history of African colonialism, for the material and labor resources of many Africans were exploited and taken to create much of that European wealth and prominence.

Similarly, a first step in developing a comprehensive theory of systemic racism in the United States is to put the four-centuries-long white exploitation and domination of people of color at the center of the social science analysis. From the beginning, European colonialism in North America involved racialized exploitation and oppression: European colonists built up much wealth by unjustly taking for themselves the material and labor resources of Native Americans and Africans. Today, a major educational task is to analyze critically the mythologized and falsified past history often taught in U.S. school books and to learn more about our actual racial and ethnic history.

Together with Du Bois, Oliver Cox was one of the first to examine the colonial origins of systemic racism in North America. He showed how capitalism, which was involved in the movement of Europeans overseas, created a situation that was "favorable for the development of white race prejudice."[77] Modern racial prejudice, ideology, and framing developed as these colonizers moved from viewing the early colonized populations of indigenous Americans and African Americans (and soon, Mexican and Chinese Americans) as "uncivilized savages" or "heathens" to seeing them as racially inferior and well below whites on the hierarchy of "races." This colonialism, with its substantial theft of land and labor, created our modern racial relations. The racial oppression of recent centuries did not arise out of some "abstract, natural, immemorial feeling of mutual antipathy between groups" but rather grew out of "a practical exploitative relationship" that was soon combined with a justifying racial framing with its racist ideology.[78]

Examining the origins of *racial hierarchies* in the colonialism and exploitation of particular historical periods, rather than in innate intergroup hostilities, is a second major theme for a comprehensive theory of systemic racism. "Race" is not an inborn human trait but rather a *way of relating* between individuals and groups. A comprehensive theory should begin with the real world of everyday exploitative and oppressive experiences and thus the historical relationships between large groups of human beings.

This systemic racism framework recognizes the centrality of the history of material and economic exploitation in North America, which began with the seizure by whites of Native American lands (see Chapter 6) and the enslavement of Africans (see Chapter 7) by violent means. Land and labor obtained unjustly, by theft and chicanery, formed much of the economic and social foundation of what became the United States. Most Native Americans were killed or driven out of major white-controlled areas, while enslaved Africans were forced to become a central part of the economies of the white colonial communities. The often genocidal action against many indigenous societies and the importation, subordination, and exploitation of enslaved Africans set in place the strong societal foundation for nearly 400 years of group oppression in North America.

By the mid-1600s, the liberty and lives of Americans of African heritage were controlled by a system of racial oppression put into place by European Americans. For most, this meant legalized slavery.

Transplanted and enslaved Africans became a major point of reference for European colonists in their construction of the colonial economy, polity, legal system, and values, and even their "white" selves. African American subjugation then became the common model for their treatment of other Americans of color in later periods. The white male elite among the colonizers reinforced this economy of oppression by legalizing it in the laws and political institutions of the new republic. Enslavement of African Americans was upheld in numerous provisions of the U.S. Constitution. Wealthy slaveholders—including George Washington, Thomas Jefferson, and James Madison—led in the creation of the legal and political arrangements of the new nation: Americans of color of that day, mainly Indian and African Americans, had *no* representation whatsoever in this nation-creating process. From the beginning, white-controlled local, state, and federal governments created and enforced an extensive system of racial exploitation and other oppression that would soon expand in the mid-nineteenth century to encompass yet other groups, such as Mexican and Chinese Americans.

A third theme in this comprehensive overview is the importance of the power and privilege of whites and the related burdens of the racial "others." Oppression operates from a socially framed set of ideas and practices that deny Americans of color the privileges, power, opportunities, and rewards that this society offers whites as a group. The racial hierarchy offers generally different resources and life chances for the racially dominant and racially subordinate groups.[79] Thus, white Americans and Americans of color have different group interests because they have historically had unequal access to "life, liberty, and the pursuit of happiness" and to the material and other resources that shape everyday life.

For systemic racism to persist across generations, it must reproduce the necessary socioeconomic conditions. These conditions include a greatly disproportionate control by whites of major economic resources and of the political, police, and ideological power to control subordinate racial groups. This *social reproduction process* is often hard to see because it is so much a part of everyday existence. Every new generation of whites has inherited an array of social, economic, and political privileges that are associated with being white. For more than three centuries of this country's existence, racial oppression was firmly enforced and reinforced by legal and political institutions. Once legal slavery and official segregation were finally eliminated—the latter only in the late 1960s—this action did not eliminate the *racial hierarchy* that put privileged whites generally toward the top and disadvantaged people of color on lower rungs of the hierarchical ladder. Over centuries now, the majority of whites have inherited some economic resources—often in the form of a farm, some house equity, or family savings—or other valuable social resources, such as job training or the ability to get a good education, from their white ancestors. These ancestors usually benefitted significantly from legal slavery, legal segregation, or other legalized discrimination.

For example, under just one major federal program (set up by a Homestead Act) from the 1860s to the 1930s, the U.S. government provided, for little or no money, some 246 million acres of land for some 1.5 million homesteads. Because of official discrimination and Klan-type violence, almost all of these homesteading families were white. Research by Trina Williams estimates that perhaps some 46 million (mostly white) people *today* are the descendants and heirs of those who received just this one major "affirmative action" benefit from the U.S. government.[80] The ancestors of contemporary African Americans were mostly excluded from this land and from many other economic resources by blatant, often violent, discrimination. (Note too that the land provided here had often been stolen, often by violence, from Native American societies.)

In addition, as we document in later chapters, many whites discriminate today against Americans of color in order to protect their group interests and privileges. For example, frequent discriminatory actions by whites still restrict the access of many Americans of color to better-paying jobs, higher political positions, and some residential areas. This persisting discrimination generally outweighs the expressed commitments of many whites now to the values of racial fairness and equality.[81] Note the continuing hierarchical structure of employment. Today, the majority of low-wage service and unskilled menial jobs in numerous employment sectors are held by workers of color; employees in these jobs often service better-off whites, such as employers, managers, and skilled workers. As a result, "these jobs entail a transfer of energies whereby the servers enhance the status of those served."[82]

The other side of white privilege is the set of material and psychological burdens that bear down on African Americans and other Americans of color. In its everyday operation, systemic racism *dehumanizes* those in a racially subordinated group. The most precious asset a person can have—substantial control over personal life and liberty—is often that which is most taken away. Institutionalized discrimination and inequality constitute the social structure of systemic racism, and part of its psychological dynamic is individual dehumanization. Our conceptual framework recognizes some degree of variation in these discriminatory burdens depending on the social position and gender of the oppressed individual. For example, middle-class Americans of color usually have more socioeconomic or political resources to counter some of the racial discrimination they face. In addition, women of color often face gendered racism—the double burden of suffering discrimination because they are not white and because they are female. Historically and in the present, institutionalized racial oppression has prevented most Americans of color, in all social classes, from developing to their full human potential.

A fourth aspect of this theory of systemic racism recognizes the differential role of different class and gender groups among white Americans. The actions of the white elite—originally centrally composed of slaveholding planters, other major farmers, merchants, and bankers, but later of industrialists and other major entrepreneurs—are critical in the creation and maintenance of the racist system at the foundation of U.S. society. As the scholars Du Bois and Cox made clear, in the process of protecting its top position, the overwhelmingly white (mostly male) elite has worked to create organizations, institutions, and ideologies that substantially incorporate its group interests. This elite group has long held disproportionate power and wealth. When its interests have conflicted with those of other groups, the elite has worked hard to deflect challenges to its dominance. The exploitative and discriminatory treatment of racially subordinated groups has varied, but in every case it is the dominant white group—and within it the ruling elite—that has set the basic terms for this treatment and, thus, for group development and mobility in society.[83]

In the economic arena, the white elite has been substantially interested in the exploitation of the land and labor of Americans of color, whereas the white working and middle classes have been more concerned about job, educational, and housing competition with Americans of color. Ordinary whites are important in enforcing discrimination in everyday life, because they constitute the majority of whites. Middle-class and working-class whites are responsible for much of the everyday discrimination against people of color, as contemporary studies of employment and housing discrimination show (see Chapters 6–12).

A fifth theme in our theory is that once racial oppression is in place, it is vigorously defended and rationalized. The taking of land and labor of Americans of color is rooted in this country's laws and founding documents. It is also rooted in a strong racial framing accenting the alleged cultural, intellectual, or biological inferiority of those on lower rungs of the racial ladder. This framing has been structured by certain white intellectuals and other white leaders and communicated to the general public in overt and subtle forms, often through schools, churches, and the media.

Since the seventeenth century, white intellectuals and other leaders have frequently tried to hide the actual sources of racial and class inequalities. The dominant group has regularly generated images of itself as racially superior and explained inequality in racist terms. A comprehensive theory of oppression must include this rationalization process. From the seventeenth century onward, religious, economic, political, intellectual, and media elites have perpetuated negative images of racialized outgroups to legitimate racial oppression. The often unseen power of the white elite still works through the white racial frame's strong stereotyped beliefs and images (for example, the woman or man of color as lazy or dangerous) perpetuated in the media, schools, workplaces, and churches.

A sixth aspect of a complete theory of systemic racism emphasizes the many resistance strategies developed by members of racially oppressed groups, individually and collectively. Protest against oppression includes overt confrontation with the dominant group and development of an alternative perspective on the everyday world, a counterframing of society generated over a long period of time by those fighting racial discrimination and domination. Americans of color are theorists of their own experience, as they have frequently made clear in the long history of antidiscrimination protest

and civil rights movements. Out of their everyday experiences with the white-generated system of racism, Americans of color have created counterframes and countercultures of resistance that are the basis for individual and group strategies to challenge or destroy oppression.

Evidence of a counterculture of resistance, for example, can be seen in the black, Native American, and Mexican American protest movements that were so powerful in the 1950s and 1960s. Organized protests against discrimination during this period included economic and bus boycotts, sit-ins, and demonstrations. African American resistance to segregation spurred the creation of civil rights organizations. Many civil rights demonstrations included large-scale participation by Americans from all class and racial backgrounds. This organized activism was often rooted in a strong local base of churches, clubs, and other organizations. These groups provided money and mobilized people to enable civil rights organizations to achieve success in fighting entrenched patterns of legal segregation.[84]

In summary, then, a racially oppressive society can best be comprehended in its totality. These several dimensions are important to a fully developed framework for understanding systemic racism in the United States.

 How has the U.S. racial hierarchy changed from the 1790s to the present?

A Note on the "Black–White Paradigm"

In recent decades, some academic researchers and other commentators have criticized what they see as a "binary black–white paradigm," which is said to dominate too much analysis of U.S. racial and ethnic relations.[85] These analysts feel that government, social science, and the media give (1) too much attention to white–black issues and (2) too little attention to the situations of other groups of color such as Asian, Latino, and Middle Eastern Americans. As we will see in later chapters, the view that these other non-European groups have not received adequate public attention and research is generally quite accurate.

However, the critical power-conflict analysts discussed previously have shown that a thorough understanding of the current and historical oppression of all non-European groups requires a recognition that the economic and social *foundation* of the North American colonies, and later of the United States, was created and concretized with the destruction of Native American societies and enslavement of Africans and African Americans. Once indigenous peoples were killed off or driven away and white-on-black oppression became an institutionalized foundation of the European-American–dominated society, that system was enshrined in legal institutions and rationalized in a racist framing and ideology that has endured to the present day.[86]

From this power-conflict perspective, U.S. society is not an array of disconnected racisms affecting peoples of color. Rather, this society has a racialized foundation and core that asserts and maintains substantial white superiority over all groups of color—a comprehensive system of racial domination that whites first developed for African Americans, and to some extent Native Americans, *within* the new society and extended later to other non-European groups. Since the mid-nineteenth century, other groups of non-European workers—for example, Japanese, Chinese, Filipino, Puerto Rican, and Mexican Americans—have been brought into the racialized system to be exploited for their labor. The generally more powerful white group exploited, evaluated, and imaged later non-European immigrants and their descendants from within the already well-institutionalized system of racial oppression and its rationalizing white racial frame.

The dominant white group has typically placed new non-European groups somewhere on a white-to-black continuum of status and privilege—with white Americans at the highly privileged end, black Americans at the bottom, and various other racial and ethnic groups placed somewhere in between, generally at the discretion of powerful elite whites. For nearly four centuries in North America, white minds and practices have constructed and maintained this hierarchical continuum of racial status, power, and privilege. As we demonstrate in later chapters, at certain points in U.S. history white Americans have come to view certain groups among Americans of color as more socially acceptable than African Americans or than the darker-skinned, or less acculturated, members of those particular groups of color. For example, whites have periodically granted some non-European groups, such as Japanese and Cuban Americans, an intermediate-group status

between the white and black ends of the white-generated racial ladder and continuum. The "model minority" stereotype that white commentators have often applied to Japanese, Chinese, and other Asian American groups (see Chapters 10 and 11) provides evidence of this strategy. These latter groups did not create this "model minority" perspective; elite white commentators did.

Indeed, at earlier points in U.S. history, Chinese and Japanese immigrants' character, values, and societal position were very negatively framed and stereotyped by whites—even as "black" or "near-black" on the socioracial continuum. However, in recent years, many whites have constructed certain groups, such as Japanese or other Asian Americans, as "model minorities" and as "nearer to white" on the socioracial continuum (see Chapter 10). They then criticize groups such as African or Mexican Americans for not possessing the work ethic, and for not achieving the economic successes, of such "model minorities." As Gary Okihiro has expressed it, whites have historically

> upheld Asians as "near-whites" or "whiter than whites" in the model minority stereotype, and yet Asians have experienced and continue to face white racism "like blacks" in educational and occupational barriers and ceilings and in anti-Asian abuse and physical violence. . . . This marginalization of Asians, in fact, within a black and white racial formation, "disciplines" both Africans and Asians and constitutes the essential site of Asian American oppression.[87]

By placing certain groups of color in an intermediate status on the socioracial ladder and continuum, white Americans as a group can effectively maintain and perpetuate the age-old racial hierarchy that began in this country with white oppression of Native Americans and African Americans.

 When new immigrants arrive in the United States, what criteria are used to place them in the persisting racial hierarchy?

Summary

In this chapter, we have reviewed major theories of migration and subsequent patterns of intergroup adaptation. Migration—varying from the movement of conquerors to slave importation to voluntary immigration—creates intergroup contact and thus racial and ethnic relationships and conflicts. Adaptation can have different outcomes in the period of initial contact, ranging from genocide to peaceful symbiosis to some type of societal hierarchy and large-scale inequality. Further adaptation may lead to further genocide, to egalitarian symbiosis, to full adaptation to the dominant culture and institutions, to some type of cultural pluralism, or to continuing large-scale inequality and a persisting socioracial hierarchy.

Most theories discussed in this chapter fall more or less under the two broad categories of order theories and power-conflict theories. Both types of theories offer useful insights into the character and development of certain racial or ethnic relationships. Assimilation theories tend to focus on voluntary immigrant groups and emphasize inclusion along conformity lines or pluralism outcomes. Assimilation analysts have pointed out the different dimensions of intergroup adaptation, such as acculturation and marital assimilation, and have often accented the role of value consensus in holding a racial and ethnic system together.

In contrast, power-conflict theories typically focus on involuntary immigration or colonial-type oppression and thus examine the substantial inequality and hierarchy in society. Power-conflict theories have certain recurring themes:

1. A central concern for major racial and ethnic inequalities in economic position, power, and resources
2. An emphasis on the interrelationship of racial oppression, the economic institutions of Western capitalism, and the subordination of women under patriarchal systems
3. An emphasis on the role of the government in legalizing and maintaining exploitation and segregation and in defining racial and ethnic relations
4. An emphasis on resistance to racial or ethnic domination by those who are oppressed

In analyzing U.S. history, power-conflict analysts have emphasized the forced character of much cultural and economic adaptation, particularly for non-European groups, and the role of coercion, segregation, exploitation, colonization, and institutionalized discrimination in keeping groups such as African, Latino, Asian, and Native Americans on or near the bottom rungs of the societal racial and ethnic ladder. Power-conflict theorists have also emphasized the importance of examining racial and ethnic relations in the context of the historical and global development of capitalism and patriarchy. In the introduction to Part II, we will explore the utility of such an approach in evaluating the broad contours of racial and ethnic relations over nearly four centuries of North American and world history.

Key Terms

theory 28
movements of forced
  labor 29
contract-labor
  movement 29
political refugees 29
voluntary
  migration 29
colonization
  migration 29
genocide 29
egalitarian
  symbiosis 29
hierarchy 29
migrant super-
  ordination 29
indigenous
  superordination 29
order theories 30
power-conflict
  theories 30
assimilation 30
race relations
  cycle 30
cultural
  assimilation 31
structural
  assimilation 31
marital
  assimilation 31

identification
  assimilation 31
attitude-receptional
  assimilation 31
behavior-receptional
  assimilation 31
civic assimilation 31
melting pot 33
cultural pluralism 33
ethnogenesis 34
competition
  theory 37
caste school of racial
  relations 39
external
  colonialism 39
internal
  colonialism 39
oppositional
  culture 40
split labor-market
  view 43
middleman
  minority 44
ethnic enclaves 44
patriarchal system 46
gendered racism 46
racial formation
  theory 47
systemic racism 47

PART II

A Nation of Immigrants
An Overview of the Economic and Political Conditions of Selected Racial and Ethnic Groups

BIG PICTURE QUESTIONS

- *How did the changing capitalistic economy influence major racial and ethnic groups immigrating to the United States?*

- *Why have so many people come to the United States?*

- *What push and pull factors have shaped large-scale migrations?*

I n the chapters that follow, we examine a number of important racial and ethnic groups in U.S. society. For each group, we look at its history and analyze its current situation in terms of theories of racial and ethnic relations reviewed in Chapter 2. Before examining groups in detail, we will here set some major groups in the historical context of four centuries of North American economic and political development. We accent two important dimensions in our overview: the ever changing capitalistic economy and the expanding political institutions. Within these frameworks, each racial or ethnic group has worked out its own cultural and social patterns in an increasingly complex United States.

Immigration, the Economy, and Government

Since the 1600s North American economic development under the control of Europeans and their descendants has seen several stages: mercantilism and early commercial capitalism coupled to a plantation/slave economy, competitive industrial capitalism, and advanced multinational capitalism. Economic institutions and developments and related government actions have shaped the character of all periods of immigration and immigrant incorporation and adjustment.

Significantly, indigenous peoples were the original inhabitants of the lands to which the European colonists and subsequent immigrants migrated. Many in the indigenous societies lost their lives and lands as a result of the often brutal European invasion and conquests. We will examine the past and present impacts of these immigrant invasions on Native Americans in some detail in Chapter 6.

The table on the following pages briefly lists many of the immigrant groups discussed in this book. Each group entered North America under particular historical circumstances. Many started in slavery, low-wage jobs, small-scale farming, or small businesses. Political and economic conditions at the time of entry were very important. Some groups entered when

Selected Immigrant Groups: An Overview

Immigrant Group	Time of Entry	Economic Conditions in North America	Government Conditions and Actions
Phase One: Commercial Capitalism and the Slave Society: Early 1600s–1860s			
1. English	1600s–1800s	Mercantilism; land taken from Native Americans; English entrepreneurs and yeoman farmers; commercial capitalism emerges.	English state creates land companies; colonial governments define individualized property and protect property.
2. Africans	1600s–1800s	Enslaved as property; became major source of labor for plantation capitalism.	Colonial governments establish slave codes; U.S. Constitution legitimates slave trade; U.S. government substantially controlled by slaveholding oligarchy.
3. Irish Catholics	1830s–1860s	Driven out of Ireland by English oppression and by famine; labor recruited for low-wage jobs in transport, construction.	U.S. government opens up western lands; Irish take over urban political machines from English Americans.
Phase Two: Industrial Capitalism: 1860s–1910s			
4. Chinese	1850s–1870s	Contract labor and low-wage work in mining, railroads, construction; menial service work for whites.	Local governments recruit Chinese labor; anti-Chinese laws passed in California; 1882 Exclusion Act.
5. Italians	1880s–1910s	Moved as European peasants into U.S. industrial capitalism; overseas recruitment for low-wage industrial and construction jobs in the cities.	Government backing for labor recruitment; U.S. treaties with Europe; intervention in European affairs (World War I); incoming numbers reduced by 1924 Immigration Act.
6. Eastern European Jews	1880s–1910s	Industrial capitalism utilized their skilled and unskilled labor; small entrepreneurs established themselves; much anti-Semitism.	Government backing for labor recruitment; U.S. treaties with Europe; incoming numbers reduced by 1924 Immigration Act.
7. Japanese	1880s–1900s	Recruited as agricultural laborers for Hawaii; later migrated to West Coast as laborers; served in domestic work; created small farms and businesses.	Government backing for labor recruiting; U.S. imperialism in Asia; conquest of Philippines and Hawaii; government actions soon exclude the Chinese and Japanese.
Phase Three: Advanced Industrial (Multinational) Capitalism: 1910s–2010s			
8. Mexicans	1910s–2010s	With Asian/European labor cut off, Mexicans recruited for low-wage jobs on farms and in industry; substantial immigration, especially during war periods.	U.S. government provides labor recruitment programs, fosters U.S. agribusiness in Mexico, stimulating out-migration; growing U.S. Border Patrol monitors immigration; new laws restrict immigration.

Selected Immigrant Groups: An Overview *(Continued)*			
Immigrant Group	**Time of Entry**	**Economic Conditions in North America**	**Government Conditions and Actions**
9. Puerto Ricans	1940s–2010s	Early farm labor migration; U.S. corporations recruit labor; blue-collar work in service economy; recurring and circular migration.	Conquest of Puerto Rico in 1898; U.S. government-supported agribusiness takes over economy, creates surplus labor, stimulates migration to mainland.
10. Recent Asian, Caribbean, Latin American, and Middle Eastern Groups	1960s–2010s	Many political and economic refugees; create economic niches, small businesses; important workers in the expanding service economy; face nativist racism.	U.S. involvement; in South Korea, Vietnam, Taiwan, Philippines stimulates out-migration; Cubans, Haitians, Middle Easterners flee political repression or wars.

low-wage jobs were plentiful on farms or in cities; others entered when fewer jobs were available. The extent of racial and ethnic discrimination and oppression varied considerably. Also important were the economic and other resources brought by or available to particular immigrant groups. Those immigrants who came voluntarily and with a little economic capital, some education, or entrepreneurial experience frequently had access to better jobs or developed small businesses—opportunities not available to immigrants with much less in the way of economic or cultural resources.

Commercial Capitalism and the Slave Society: 1600s–1860s

Colonial Society and Slave Labor

The colonial society that grew up on the east coast of North America during the 1600s was tied closely to England and the expansionist policies of the English political and economic elites. The early economic system in these colonies was a combination of government enterprises under the English king and enterprises developed by independent entrepreneurs, including, by the eighteenth century, the slave plantation owners in the South and merchants in the North. As was the case with other European colonial powers, the objective of English colonization was to secure raw materials and markets for English goods. The first joint-stock companies were formed

by merchants under the auspices of King James I of England. Employees of the Southern Company settled Jamestown; this was the English colony that secured the first enslaved Africans from a ship flying a Dutch flag in 1619.

Early capitalists, the English merchants and entrepreneurs, invested capital in the extraction of raw materials for home industries. The colonies served the empire as a source of raw materials and agricultural products and as a dumping ground for surplus workers and peasants displaced by the expansion of aggressive capitalism and other economic changes in Europe. Capitalistic production for profit was not the only important economic dimension, for the colonies also became home to many poorer English and other northern European immigrants—people displaced from the land in Europe and typically seeking to become small farmers or traders. In the colonies there were two major modes of production: the subsistence household (small-farm) mode and the profit-oriented capitalist (slave/plantation and merchant) mode.[1] The North American colonies had so much available land (often taken from indigenous Americans) that it was difficult for English and English American entrepreneurs to secure enough cheap European labor, particularly for large-scale agriculture. They tried using white indentured servants, but these immigrants generally worked off their terms of servitude and often went into farming.

From the late 1600s to the mid-1800s, people of African descent were a major source of (slave) labor for the white merchant and agricultural capitalists in the North American colonies. In the late eighteenth century, the emergence of cotton and sugar as international commodities created an even stronger demand for workers on slave plantations. The number of enslaved African Americans increased from 59,000 in 1714 to 3.9 million in 1860. This forced labor generated great wealth for many whites; it built up profits (capital) not only for further investments in expanding plantations and related business enterprises, but also for depositing in banks, where it could be used or borrowed by the white merchants, shippers, and industrialists of the North and South.

Civil War: The Southern Plantation Oligarchy versus Northern Entrepreneurs

The South was generally the most prosperous and powerful region in the country from the late 1700s to about the 1850s. White southerners owned much of the productive land, much of the agricultural produce for export, many processing mills and other valuable equipment, and millions of enslaved African American laborers. These African American laborers generated much wealth for white farmers and trading businesses, including capital later invested in manufacturing enterprises. White southerners dominated U.S. politics, and most presidents between George Washington and Abraham Lincoln were slaveholders or sympathetic to slavery. Until the 1860s, few major decisions made by the federal legislative and judicial branches went against the critical interests of the slaveholding oligarchy and associated merchants. The Civil War was to a substantial degree a struggle for economic and political power between northern industrialists and small farmers, on the one hand, and the southern plantation oligarchy, on the other. The victory of the North in that bloody war marked the arrival of northern industrialists as a dominant force in the U.S. economy and national government.[2]

Immigrant Laborers in the North

During the 1800s in the northern states, the growing industrial working class and the class of small farmers were increasingly populated by immigrants from Ireland, Germany, and Scandinavia. Immigrant labor often became the labor for the growing number of industrial enterprises—the textile mills, railroad

shops, and foundries. The pull factors motivating millions of Irish Catholic immigrants to cross the Atlantic after 1820 were the same as those that have attracted immigrants for centuries to a country portrayed by industrial labor recruiters and others as the land of opportunity. There were major push factors as well. In Ireland, a potato disease created severe food shortages; this crisis, plus the continuing political and economic oppression of Ireland by England, generated the migration of 1.6 million Irish to the United States over several decades. Many small farmers and artisans from Ireland sold their labor to U.S. employers; they became domestic servants, railroad laborers, miners, and industrial workers in cities.

The arrival of large numbers of white immigrants from northern Europe laid the foundation for new patterns of racial conflict. African Americans became a smaller percentage of urbanites in the North. Free black workers were used by white entrepreneurs in the North mostly as low-wage labor, sometimes as strikebreakers. Using them against white strikers increased the hostility of these workers toward black Americans. By the 1840s, free black workers in the North were being forcibly displaced from jobs by white immigrants, including Irish American workers. Although the Irish immigrants arrived from a country where the English oppressed and stereotyped them as an "inferior race," within a generation or so in the United States the majority of the Irish had come to see themselves as part of a "superior white race."

Western and Global Expansion

In the early decades of the nineteenth century, the new U.S. nation began to expand its empire well beyond that envisioned by its former British overlords. Since that time, the U.S. empire has gradually and continually expanded—first into Mexican and other lands to its west, later into Latin America, and eventually around the globe.

Fostered by U.S. governmental decrees and military protection, the great westward expansion across North America in the nineteenth century brought not only Native Americans but also a new group—Mexicans—into the orbit of exploitation and oppression by white entrepreneurs, soldiers, and farmers. The racist framing accenting the "white man's civilizing responsibility" for non-European groups guided white expansionists and justified for them the taking of Mexican and Native American lands in the West. Expansionists believed the "Mexican race" and the "Indian race" should become subordinate to the "Anglo-Saxon race." The first Mexican citizens, who had long been residents of the Southwest, did not migrate; they and their land were brought into the United States by force as the result of the Mexican-American War in the 1840s.

In 1822, President James Monroe announced, in what came to be called the Monroe Doctrine, that the Americas were now the U.S. sphere of influence and that no more European colonization would be tolerated. Soon, the United States replaced the European colonial powers as the dominant colonial power in the Americas. Since the middle of the nineteenth century, the U.S. government and businesses have expanded their involvement to western North America, Latin America, and all other continents. Since that time, U.S. economic and political ties have gradually become more extensive and complex than those of any other modern empire. They have included a myriad of business linkages and economic exploitations, as well as numerous military operations, government aid of many kinds, and far-reaching media and other cultural linkages.

Over the past century and a half, U.S. involvement in most other countries has had far-reaching consequences, not only for these countries but for the United States itself. As we will see, the character and history of immigration to the United States often parallels the development of economic involvement and political or military actions in other countries. Some have called this large-scale and continuing immigration "the harvest of the U.S. empire."

Industrial Capitalism: 1860s–1910s

Industrial Capitalism and Government Expansion Overseas

The Civil War was followed by westward expansion and an industrial boom. **Competitive capitalism**, *an economy dominated by small and medium-sized for-profit businesses,* gradually became one dominated by large enterprises. The growth of these businesses was dramatic, and the United States soon surpassed Great Britain in important industrial production categories. The proportion of workers engaged in agriculture declined between the 1860s and the 1920s, while the proportion in manufacturing doubled.

By the last decades of the nineteenth century, many corporations were growing dramatically through mergers and acquisitions.

Leading industrialists expanded corporate investments and activities in numerous countries overseas, often backed by a U.S. government growing in military power. The movement of U.S. Navy ships, as well as merchants and missionaries, into countries such as China, Japan, and the Philippines disrupted their economies and other social institutions, thereby increasing the surplus of farm workers and shaping out-migration. U.S. military and economic power pressured Asian countries to submit to U.S. influence. Given the often difficult economic conditions in these countries, U.S. labor recruiters enticed many Asian workers to Hawaii and the western United States. More than 200,000 Chinese laborers came to the United States between 1848 and 1882 to do hard work in West Coast mining, railroad, and service businesses. After the Chinese were excluded by a racist immigration law, Japanese immigrants were recruited for the low-wage jobs. Japan sent many thousands of emigrants to Hawaii and the United States, a migration triggered by U.S. political influence and labor recruiting by U.S. employers.[3]

The U.S. victory in the Spanish-American War of the 1890s resulted in the annexation of Puerto Rico and the Philippines by the expansionist U.S. government and the effective domination of Cuba. When the United States took over Puerto Rico, much of that island was owned by small local farmers, but soon large U.S. companies were controlling much of the production. Puerto Rico, the Philippines, and Cuba would later send large numbers of immigrants to the U.S. mainland.[4]

African Americans: Exclusion from Western Lands

The second half of the nineteenth century was a period of major governmental growth and bureaucratization. U.S. government action had a major influence on racial and ethnic relations. One of the first actions of President Abraham Lincoln and Republican legislators in the early 1860s was to pass a major Homestead Act, a wealth-building program for immigrant families seeking land, including Germans, Scandinavians, and Irish families. European American families who wished to farm were often provided 160 to 320 acres of land if they would develop it. After the Civil War, the U.S. Land Office ruled that most black Americans were ineligible for these land grants because they were not citizens when the act was passed. For the most part, black families did not have the opportunity that many white families had to build up landed wealth through farming, wealth passed down to millions of their descendants.[5]

In the late 1800s and early 1900s, southern black workers were one possible source of labor for northern industries. But the white oligarchy in the South, after a brief postwar Reconstruction period, took back control of the South's economy and state governments—to a substantial degree using terroristic Klan-type violence—and made certain that most newly freed black Americans remained in the South as low-wage laborers, tenant farmers, or sharecroppers. There was little distribution of plantation land to the black men and women who had made that land so fruitful for whites. They did not receive the "forty acres and a mule" that some government officials had promised them.

Southern and Eastern European Immigrants

Unable to use southern black labor, northern industrialists turned to Europe. The majority of the 20.7 million immigrants to the United States between 1881 and 1920 were from southern and eastern Europe. A 1910 survey of twenty major manufacturing and mining industries found that six of every ten workers were foreign born. Without this immigrant labor, the great industrial expansion of the United States would not have been possible.[6] In some cases these new workers displaced native-born white workers. Anti-immigrant hostility (nativism) among the workers in older European American groups increased as a result.[7]

European Immigrants and Black Americans

Writer Irving Kristol once argued that "The Negro Today Is Like the Immigrant of Yesterday." In this view the experience of black Americans moving to U.S. industrial cities has not been significantly different from that of white immigrant groups: African Americans should eventually move up economically and socially just as those immigrants did.[8] However, this argument overlooks important differences between the experiences of white and black immigrants to the industrial cities. Group mobility was possible for these new European immigrants because of the following:

1. Most arrived at a time when urban jobs were generally available, U.S. industrial capitalism was expanding, and opportunities were relatively abundant.

2. Many had some technical or other skills or a little capital—resources available to few African Americans at the time.

3. Most faced far less severe employment and housing discrimination than black workers in the cities.

4. Most found housing, however inadequate, reasonably near their workplaces.

5. In key cities, the political system was changing from Anglo-Protestant business dominance to shared power between these business elites and political machines oriented to new white immigrant voters.[9]

In the critical periods of large-scale European immigration, cities such as New York, Philadelphia, Boston, and Chicago were expanding centers of manufacturing. Blue-collar jobs were frequently available, if not plentiful. In the mid-nineteenth century, Irish and German immigrants were attracted to rural areas and to cities, where most found industrial, service, or government jobs. From 1890 to 1930, southern and eastern Europeans came in large numbers to cities. One study notes that "the Italian concentration in construction and the Polish in steel were related to the expansion of these industries as the groups arrived."[10] Many migrated as a result of labor recruiting by U.S. employers in Europe.

Among the European immigrants who arrived in the period between 1880 and 1920 were large numbers of Jewish immigrants fleeing European oppression. Although they were often poverty-stricken, many were part of an urban industrial proletariat and came with experience in skilled trades. One study found that two-thirds of Jewish immigrants were skilled workers, whereas other southern and eastern European immigrants were primarily peasant farmers or farm workers. When Jewish immigrants entered in large numbers around 1900, the clothing industry was moving to mass production and offered jobs for tailors and seamstresses, as well as unskilled jobs, and there were also chances for small-scale entrepreneurs in a number of cities.

The situation for the African Americans who began to move to the northern cities from the South after 1910 was quite different. Black workers who migrated from the South had little access to good government jobs and were regularly displaced by the white immigrant groups who forced them out of job after job, such as construction and transport jobs, and into marginal, low-paying jobs or unemployment. Stanley Lieberson has explored why southern and eastern European immigrants have done well in northern cities, compared with black Americans. Among his conclusions are that (1) black migrants were the victims of more severe discrimination over a longer period than were white immigrant groups and (2) economic competition between whites and the growing group of black workers in the urban North led to extensive hostility and institutionalized discrimination by whites.[11]

What factors contributed to the growing racial conflicts of the late 1800s and early 1900s?

Advanced Industrial (Multinational) Capitalism: 1910s–2010s

Mexican Immigrants

With the increased industrialization accompanying World War I came a sharp decline in the number of laborers available for agricultural work. The need was filled in part by Mexican labor, recruited with substantial governmental help. Mexican laborer and family migrations increased significantly in the 1920s. Agencies in cities such as Los Angeles and San Antonio recruited Mexican workers for agriculture and for low-skilled jobs in the steel, auto, and other urban industries. Internal colonialism theorist Robert Blauner has captured the contrast between the non-European and the European immigrants of this period and later: "America has used African, Asian, Mexican, and, to a lesser degree, Indian workers for the cheapest labor, concentrating people of color in the most unskilled jobs, the least advanced sectors of the economy, and the most industrially backward regions of the nation."[12]

Large Corporations and the U.S. Business Cycle

Since 1900, large corporations, many with an international orientation, have come to dominate the U.S. economy and politics. *The economic system that is dominated by large-scale, for-profit corporations that operate in many different countries, thereby creating an international market system*, is called **multinational capitalism**. By the 1920s, a large number of Americans, including immigrant workers, were working in the auto industry or in related industries such as steel. Aggressive competition among auto firms in the 1920s resulted in the production of more cars than were needed. This overproduction, a chronic problem in a capitalist economy, resulted in major cutbacks in employment in auto-related industries, thus helping trigger the Great Depression of the 1930s, which hit especially hard among African American and Mexican American migrants to industrial cities. Unemployed whites, including recent immigrants, took over many lower-paying jobs previously held by workers of color. The latter had very high unemployment rates. The federal government grew as U.S. political leaders tried to develop ("New Deal") government programs to save the foundering capitalist system. Nonetheless, racial discrimination was perpetuated in these New Deal social welfare programs of the 1930s. Typically, in these government-sponsored programs workers of color received lower wages than whites, were employed mainly as unskilled laborers, and were often employed only after whites.[13]

The Postwar Era: The United States and the World

For several decades after World War II, the U.S. government, the U.S. military, and U.S. multinational corporations substantially dominated world politics and the world economy, in large part because major industrial societies elsewhere, such as Germany and Japan, had been destroyed by that war. Since World War II, U.S. multinational corporations have more easily moved capital investments from the central city to suburbs, from northern to southern cities, and from U.S. cities to cities overseas. Capital flight and job exports have resulted in many economically abandoned central cities. The federal government has facilitated outward expansion of investment and jobs by funding large home mortgage programs and highway systems. Often these highway systems have been built in accord with the needs of large firms developing new workplaces and the needs of middle-class (disproportionately white) workers seeking to live outside central cities. As a result, since World War II, many white Americans—often the children and grandchildren of European immigrants—have followed new employment opportunities to the out-lying suburbs.

Into central cities have come yet other groups of workers and their families—African Americans, Puerto Ricans, Mexicans and Mexican Americans, Native Americans, Asian Americans, and Middle Eastern Americans. Since World War II, these immigrants to northern and western cities have inhabited central city areas increasingly abandoned by older industries and earlier European immigrants. For example, among these immigrants to central cities have been Puerto Ricans, many of whom have been recruited for low-wage city jobs. U.S. industrial and agribusiness development in Puerto Rico has helped to stimulate a large out-migration.

Government Involvement Overseas and Asian Immigration

Until the mid-1960s, U.S. immigration legislation was so restrictive that most people from Asian countries desiring to emigrate could not enter the United States. By the late 1960s, these discriminatory quotas had been lifted, and since then there has been a significant increase in immigrants, including Chinese, Korean, Filipino, Asian Indian, and Vietnamese immigrants. U.S. support for South Korea during and after its war with North Korea built strong ties between the United States and South Korea. A succession of dictators in South Korea drove out some dissenters, who migrated to the United States; other Koreans came for economic or educational reasons. The immigration of the Chinese, the Filipinos, and the Vietnamese is also generally related to the involvement of the U.S. government and corporations overseas. The U.S. arming and political support of the Philippine government and of the Nationalist Chinese government on Taiwan, and U.S. participation in the wars in Korea and South Vietnam, have played an important role in creating large groups of Filipinos, Koreans, Chinese, and Vietnamese oriented to the United States. More

recently, increasing corporate and political ties between the United States and mainland China have encouraged the immigration of Chinese here. As with earlier immigrants, Asian immigrants have migrated to the United States seeking economic opportunities and/or political freedom.

Latin American Immigration

Caribbean immigrants to the United States since the 1960s have included Cubans and Haitians, who have often moved to Florida. The U.S. government long supported a right-wing dictatorship in Cuba, which was overthrown by a guerrilla movement led by Fidel Castro. Many Cuban businesspeople and professionals fled in the first period of emigration after Castro took power. These Cubans, many of whom had some economic or educational resources, established a major economic enclave and gained political influence in Florida. After 1980, a significant number of working-class Cubans also migrated, some of them having been expelled as alleged "undesir-ables" by the authoritarian Castro government. Most Cuban immigrants have been welcomed by the U.S. government as political refugees, and many millions of dollars in federal subsidies have been provided to facilitate their adjustment. In contrast, Haitians, who have also fled politically repressive governments, have for the most part not been welcomed by the U.S. government. Many have been forced to return, and most of those allowed to stay have not been provided the type of government support provided to Cuban immigrants. A major reason is that the Communist government in Cuba is seen as a political opponent, whereas repressive governments in Haiti have mostly been viewed as political allies of the U.S. government.

In recent decades, much investment capital and federal aid for development have shifted from northern to Sunbelt cities. The growing economy of the Sunbelt has created a demand for low-wage workers in construction, manufacturing, and agriculture. Many have migrated there from Mexico and Central America for economic reasons. Others, like earlier European groups, have come fleeing political oppression in Central America. Mexican immigrants still make up a major portion of undocumented immigrants. They are constantly attracted by the possibility of jobs, and many are pushed by poor economic conditions in their country. Large U.S. corporations operating in Mexico have played a continuing role in generating Mexican out-migration. U.S. agribusiness firms have greatly stimulated the development of export-oriented agriculture in Mexico, in the process taking over large amounts of land and driving off many small Mexican farmers who had farmed the land to feed their families. Many small farmers and their families have become migrants to Mexican cities and the United States. Nativistic attacks on these immigrants by U.S. citizens ignore the U.S.-generated, economic push factors that frequently drive poor Mexicans to migrate to the United States.

Middle Eastern Immigration

Immigrants from the Middle East have been coming to the United States for more than a century. Arab immigrants from more than twenty countries comprise the largest group among these. Immigration from Arab areas has occurred in two major segments—the first from about 1880 to 1945, and the second, much larger immigration from 1946 to the present day. Between 1880 and World War II, Arab immigrants came in modest numbers. They were working-class and middle-class people who came mostly seeking economic opportunity. They were usually from what was then Greater Syria, an area that included what would later be known as Lebanon, Syria, and Palestine/Israel. By the mid-1920s, Arab Americans numbered 200,000; most were Christians. These early immigrants and their descendants make up a substantial proportion of Arab Americans today. The discriminatory 1924 Immigration Act sharply reduced immigration from the Middle East.

With the abolition of this discriminatory immigration law in the 1960s, immigration to the United States was opened to people of all countries, and the number of Arab immigrants increased. The 1970s Lebanese civil war and the 1980s Israeli invasion of Lebanon generated numerous immigrants; others have fled other Middle East wars. Large numbers have come from Lebanon, Syria, Egypt, and Palestine. Whether Muslim or Christian, most have a strong sense of their Arab origins and have settled in metropolitan areas. Although those who came during the earliest period of immigration were relatively poor, many who have immigrated since the 1960s have been educated professionals or businesspeople.

Early Arab immigrants were frequently cataloged with southern and eastern European immigrants as "inferior races" by native-born whites. In recent decades many people from the Middle East and Mediterranean areas, both Arab and non-Arab peoples, have continued to face widespread stereotyping. The U.S. media (including movies) have often portrayed Arabs, Arab Americans, and other Middle Eastern Americans in very negative and racially stereotyped terms.

Immigration Restrictions

European immigrants made up more than half of all those coming to the United States during the decade of the 1950s. Their proportion dropped to one-third by the 1960s and to less than one-fifth in recent years. The change is substantially the result of the abolition of the discriminatory national-origin quotas in the 1965 Immigration Act. Since the 1960s, many Asian, Latino, and Middle Eastern immigrants have been viewed as a "problem." Congress has passed additional immigration legislation with provisions to restrict the recent, mostly non-European, immigration to the United States. Many native-born workers and politicians are concerned that the country cannot absorb so many immigrants, even though the ratio of immigrants to the native-born population was *higher* in the early twentieth century than it is now. Implicit in many European American discussions of the new immigrants is a concern that most are from Asia and Latin America—that is, they are not white and not European.[14]

Significantly, new immigrants from Asia and Latin America, and their children and grandchildren, are part of a growing population of Americans of color. In many areas, including half the country's hundred largest cities and the states of Hawaii, New Mexico, Texas, and California, Americans of color are now a majority of the population. They soon will be the majority in other states. As their numbers increase, Americans of color will likely press harder for more equitable treatment in U.S. social, economic, and political institutions.

 When and how did changing immigration laws bar certain racial or ethnic groups from entry into the United States?

Summary

In this overview, we have briefly surveyed the economic and governmental contexts within which particular groups have immigrated and adjusted to life in the United States. The time of entry for particular groups and the resources they have brought have affected their relative economic and political success. A complete understanding of the character of U.S. immigration requires an analysis of the significant economic and political contexts of immigrants' entry and adaptation. Capitalist development and expansion, as well as U.S. political involvement overseas and domestic governmental action, have shaped the context and character of U.S. immigration and the patterns of racial and ethnic relations in North America for centuries. They also have provided crucibles within which the family patterns, distinctive cultures, and political resistance to discrimination of specific immigrant groups have constantly developed.

Key Terms

competitive
  capitalism   59

multinational
  capitalism   61

English Americans and the Anglo-Protestant Culture

BIG PICTURE QUESTIONS

- *Who were the English colonists who began the North American experiment?*

- *What influence did the English Americans have on major U.S. institutions?*

- *How was the dominant Eurocentric culture established, and how has it been maintained?*

Cleveland Amory tells a story about prominent English American families in Massachusetts. A Chicago banking firm wrote a Boston investment company for a letter of recommendation for a young Bostonian. Eloquently praising the young man's virtues, the company's letter pointed out that his mother was a member of the Lowell family, his father a member of the Cabot family, and his other relatives were members of other prominent New England families. The bank wrote back, thanking the company but noting that this was not the type of letter of recommendation they had in mind: "We were not contemplating using Mr. _____ for breeding purposes."[1] Apocryphal or not, this story illustrates the elite status of certain Boston families and suggests their prominence in New England's history.

The story indicates too the importance of inbreeding, descent, and interlocking family ties over the generations. Ethnicity involves cultural or nationality characteristics that are distinguished by the group itself or by important out-groups, but lines of descent are major channels for passing along these ethnic characteristics to later generations.

English Americans—that is, *Americans of English ancestry*—are the third largest white ethnic group in the United States, after German and Irish Americans. Approximately 27.5 million Americans are estimated to have substantial English ancestry according to a 2008 census report.[2] The term *English Americans* itself may sound a bit strange. Other terms are often used. Most common are the somewhat inaccurate terms *Anglo-Saxon* and *white Anglo-Saxon Protestant*. **Anglo-Saxon** *originally referred to Germanic tribes, the Angles and the Saxons, who came to the area now called England in the fifth and sixth centuries C.E. It was later applied to the inhabitants of England and to those English who came to North America.* **Anglo-Protestant Americans** is *a more accurate term for those often referred to as Anglo-Saxons* or as **white Anglo-Saxon Protestant Americans**. Although in-depth analyses of this ethnic group are rare, numerous authors have commented on its central importance: "Our American culture, our speech, our laws are basically Anglo-Saxon in origin."[3]

Milton Gordon's view of the shaping effect this first large group of European immigrants had on the dominant culture was noted in a previous chapter: "If there is anything in American life which can be described as an overall American culture which serves as a reference point for immigrants and their children, it can best be described . . . as the middle-class cultural patterns of, largely, white Protestant, Anglo-Saxon origins."[4] This comment suggests the importance of this dominant culture in the adaptation process faced by later immigrant groups.

As we noted previously, the term *Anglo-Saxon* derives from the names for Germanic tribes, the Angles and the Saxons, that came to the area now called England in the fifth and sixth centuries C.E.[5] However, in writing about the United States, some authors have used the term *Anglo-Saxon* and related terms in a loose way to include British groups other than the English, such as the Scots and the Welsh. Other northern European groups that have substantially adapted to the Anglo core culture—particularly Scandinavian and German Protestants—are sometimes included by scholars in the terms *Anglo-Saxon* and *Anglo-Protestant*. In any event, when the terms *Anglo-Saxon*, *Anglo-Protestant*, and *British American* are used by scholars, English Americans and the still-dominant culture they generated are usually at the heart of the discussion.

Early on, Americans of northern European descent expressed a sense of their superiority and prominence in the new nation. In the late 1780s, John Jay, the first chief justice of the U.S. Supreme Court, wrote in *The Federalist*, "Providence has been pleased to give this one connected country to one united people—a people descended from the same ancestors, speaking the same language, professing the same religion, attached to the same principles of government, very similar in their manners and customs."[6] This highly ethnocentric perspective—inaccurate at the time—has been a central problem for groups not from northern Europe ever since.

The English Migrations

Some Basic Data

Although the English were not the first Europeans to come to North America (the Spanish came earlier, for example), they were the first Europeans to colonize it in large numbers. By the early eighteenth century there were approximately 350,000 English and Welsh colonists in North America. At the time of the American Revolution, this number was approaching 2 million.[7]

Migration to the North American colonies was heavily English until the early 1700s. Then the

English migration generally receded to modest levels, until well into the nineteenth century.[8] Nearly 3 million English again migrated to the U.S. between 1820 and 1950, most heavily between 1880 and 1900. The English migration to the colonies, and later to the United States in the nineteenth century, was one of the largest population flows in this period. The English were the first sizable European group in what was to become the United States and continued to be an important segment of the European migration until World War I.[9]

The First Colonial Settlements

The English colonists' seventeenth-century migration, together with their pattern of settlement, was distinctive. This movement can be viewed as *colonization migration,* a concept explored in Chapter 2. Unlike other types of migration, colonization migration involves the subordination of indigenous societies. As we show in Chapter 6, the first victims of English and other European colonialism on this continent were indigenous societies. English colonists participated actively in killing Native Americans or otherwise driving them off their lands.[10]

Why did the English Crown become interested in establishing North American colonies? English advocates in the colonial period put forth various explanations. The need for trading posts and for new sources of raw materials, as well as for new markets for English goods, was cited as a rationale by advocates of North American colonization.[11] Yet other colonial advocates emphasized Protestant missionary objectives, the search for a passage to Asia, the need to stop Spanish or French expansion, and the need for a place for England's surplus population. As one researcher puts it, "What England primarily looked for in colonies was neither expansion of territory *per se* nor overseas aggregations of Englishmen, but goods and markets."[12]

The English colonization was a case of migrant superordination (see Chapter 2) with dire consequences for preexisting Native American societies. Geographical expansion proceeded rapidly. At first, some Native American groups were treated in a friendly fashion, if mainly because the colonists depended on Native American food and advice. As colonists gained numerical superiority over indigenous populations, they forced the latter back into frontier areas or slaughtered them outright.[13] Few

English colonists aboard The Mayflower *sign the Mayflower Compact.*

European colonists seemed concerned over the geno-cidal consequences of their aggressive colonialism.

The English established large settlements in North America, often using royal companies of various kinds. Recall from the introduction to Part I that some were early manifestations of European capitalism. The first joint-stock companies were formed by merchants under the auspices of James I of England in the 1600s. Employees of the Southern Company settled Jamestown, a colony where the primary goal was economic. Initially planning to develop the colony with poor laborers from Europe, the leaders soon perceived a labor shortage and secured enslaved Africans from a Dutch-flagged ship in 1619, laying the foundation for slavery in North America. The northern colony of Plymouth was settled in 1620 under the auspices of another royal company. Many New England colonists—later called "Pilgrims"—were Puritans who had broken with the Anglican church.[14] Both settlements nearly expired in their early years because of disease and starvation. The Plymouth colony managed to sur-vive only with the aid of Indian communities.[15]

According to historian David Fischer, several dis-tinctive English-speaking groups were among the first to immigrate. First came Puritans from England's eastern counties, who entered the Massachusetts area primarily between 1629 and 1640. They brought to New England "nucleated settlements, congregational churches, town meetings, and a tradition of ordered liberty."[16] A second group of immigrants came to the Virginia area between 1642 and 1675. This group con-sisted of a small number of Royalists from southern England and numerous indentured servants. Their culture was characterized by "extreme hierarchies of rank, strong oligarchies, Anglican churches, a highly developed sense of honor, and an idea of hegemonic liberty."[17] A third group—Quakers from the North Midlands of England and Wales, who came to the Delaware Valley between 1675 and 1725—established a "pluralistic system of reciprocal liberty" based on spiritual and social equality, austerity, and an intense work ethic.[18]

A fourth group of immigrants came to the Appalachian backcountry from the borderlands (for example, Scotland) of northern Great Britain and Ireland between 1718 and 1775. This group represented various ethnic ancestries (English, Scottish, and "Scotch-Irish") and had extreme socioeconomic inequalities, but its members

TABLE 3.1	
Surnames	White Population (%)
English	60.1
Scottish, "Scotch-Irish"	14.0
German	8.6
Irish (Free State)	3.6
Dutch	3.1
French, Swedish	3.0
Other	7.6
Total	100.0

shared the ideal of natural liberty.[19] Each of these four groups had a somewhat distinctive type of culture—distinctive speech patterns, architecture, family and child-rearing customs, dress and food ways, religious orientations, and conceptions of liberty and the organization of public life. Over time, their cultural patterns interacted and fused together to create the dominant Anglo-Protestant culture of the colonies and, later, the United States.

The American Historical Association has devel-oped rough estimates of the "national stocks" of the white population in 1790 based on surname analy-sis (see Table 3.1).[20] These estimates give the English the primary position among whites, with other British groups accounting for significant proportions then. In addition, African Americans, then mostly enslaved, made up about *one-fifth* of the total popu-lation in 1790.[21]

 Why did the English become interested in establishing North American colonies?

Later Migration

A modest number of British and other European immigrants entered the United States between the Revolution and 1820, but the century following 1820 saw the greatest Atlantic migration in history. English immigrants moved in large numbers from manufac-turing and mining industries in England to compa-rable positions in U.S. industry; their skills helped spur dramatic industrialization.[22] When English American workers were eventually displaced by machines or later immigrant groups, they or their children often moved up into managerial, professional, and technical positions. With their help, and substantial investments by English capitalists, U.S. industrial productivity soon surpassed that of Great Britain.[23]

The ease with which English immigrants moved into industrial workplaces suggests the swiftness of their incorporation at the level of U.S. secondary organizations. Their skills and backgrounds kept most from the poverty that other immigrants faced. Larger numbers moved into clerical and professional jobs than was the case with many later white immigrant groups. Acculturation was relatively easy. They were more readily hired where the ability to speak English was important. They avoided most anti-immigrant agitation. Indeed, new English immigrants often shared the ethnocentric or racist views held by previous English colonists, including the stereotyping of Jews, the hostility toward black Americans, and the dislike of southern Europeans. Structural assimilation in the *primary-relations sphere*, to use the concept of Milton Gordon, was usually rapid for them. English immigrants never faced enforced residential segregation, and marriage with other English Americans was commonplace.[24]

Relatively small numbers of English immigrants have come to the U.S. since 1910. In the 1930s, more people returned to England than came in as immigrants. The modest English migration since 1910, coupled with dramatic increases in immigration from other areas, has had a significant demographic effect. Since 1910, British Americans as a group have declined significantly as a proportion of the total population.[25]

Other Protestant Immigrants

The terms *Anglo-Saxon* and *Anglo-Protestant* have sometimes been used by researchers to include not only the English but also the Scots, the Welsh, and even the Scandinavians and the Germans. The Welsh entered the colonies in relatively small numbers, beginning in the early 1600s. Many found employment in industrial jobs or farming. The first generations retained their customs, language, and distinctive communities, but most were soon substantially assimilated to the white Anglo-Protestant mainstream.[26]

In terms of political and economic power, the Scots were the closest to the dominant English group

from the 1700s onward, although they too were subject to Anglo-conformity pressures. By the late eighteenth century there were perhaps 250,000 Scots in the United States, a number supplemented over the next century by three-fourths of a million migrants. In the colonial period, some were prosperous merchants, clerks, soldiers, and middle-income farmers, although the majority were probably servants, laborers, and poor farmers. Scots experienced hostility from some English Americans in the early period. Adaptation to the English core culture gradually accompanied inclusion in the economic system; by the early 1800s, many if not most had achieved parity with their English American neighbors. They, too, were becoming an important segment of the white Anglo-Protestant mainstream.

German immigrants made up the largest non-British group during the eighteenth century. Germans constituted nearly one-tenth of the colonists, and in the century after 1820, several million more came to the United States. Some were Catholics and Jews, but the largest proportion was Protestant. Many became farmers, merchants, and, later, industrial workers. Over several generations, much, but by no means all, of the German culture was reshaped or displaced by the well-established Anglo-American patterns. Cultural assimilation, together with substantial mobility in the economic and political spheres, came in a few generations for German Protestants. For years, however, some distinctiveness persisted in the form of certain German customs, festivals, and residential concentrations. Jewish Germans (see Chapter 5), who immigrated in the middle decades of the nineteenth century, remained somewhat distinctive, in part because of the often vicious anti-Semitism directed against them and later Jewish immigrants by many other Americans.

Scandinavian immigrants, such as Swedes and Norwegians, did not enter in large numbers until the 1870s and 1880s. In all, perhaps 2 million came. Many immigrants entered as farmers and laborers, but the second and third generations moved into skilled blue-collar and white-collar positions. Here, too, substantial adaptation to the British American core culture came in just a few generations. Still, some distinctiveness in family customs and residential location, especially in midwestern areas, persists today.

These white Protestant groups from northern Europe adapted relatively rapidly in the cultural, economic, and political spheres, although this process was not always peaceful. In the period of early contact, some northern European groups suffered physical attacks and extreme cultural conformity pressures from English Americans. However, within a generation English Americans were intermarrying with Scottish, Welsh, and "Scotch-Irish" Americans, and sometimes with Scandinavians and Germans. By the early twentieth century, the designations *white Anglo-Saxon Protestant* and *white Anglo-Protestant* increasingly came to blur the distinction between the English and the later northern European immigrant groups.

The Invention of the "White Race"

The eighteenth and nineteenth centuries saw the emergence of the "white race" as a deliberately constructed social group for the first time in North American or, for that matter, world history. From the beginning, English colonists and their descendants saw themselves as quite different from the indigenous Americans and black Americans, whom they initially stereotyped as "uncivilized" and "savages." English Americans saw themselves as "republicans" of great virtue; they were concerned with protecting the new nation and reserving it, as some stated in the 1790s, for the "worthy part of mankind."[27] By the late 1700s, the growing importance of southern plantations for the economy as a whole (northern entrepreneurs and bankers were often linked to the southern economy) increased demand for Indian lands and enslaved African American workers. At the same time, slavery was being abolished, sometimes rather slowly, in most northern states.

As a result, a white Anglo-Protestant elite circulated the idea of an advantaged "white race" and of inferior Indian and African "races." Famous U.S. founders, men of English or Welsh descent, played a central role in making this racial framing of society central to the thinking of most white Americans. These included three presidents: Thomas Jefferson, James Madison, and George Washington. Jefferson, the main writer of the Declaration of Independence, wrote extensively in the first major book by a U.S. intellectual that African Americans were greatly inferior to white Americans with regard to skin color, physical form, reason, familial love, forethought, and even the ability to feel pain and grief.[28] In an 1814 letter to a neighbor, Edward Coles, the aging Jefferson explained why he still thought that black Americans

should not be freed; black Americans are "brought from their infancy without necessity for thought or forecast, are by their habits rendered as incapable as children of taking care of themselves, and are extinguished promptly wherever industry is necessary for raising young."[29] Jefferson reiterated explicitly racist notions in his earlier writings as to the lack of forethought among black Americans and his view of their childlike dependency. In this letter to Coles, Jefferson described freed blacks thus: "In the mean time they are pests in society by their idleness, and the depredations to which this leads them." Many slaveholders like Jefferson, Madison, and Washington viewed those enslaved as a childlike and thus inferior "race."

These views were not confined to powerful whites. White elites of the founding era and later decades sought to provide some racial privileges for property-less European immigrants and their children, and thus to prevent the latter from bonding with other Americans of color. As sociologist W. E. B. Du Bois suggested, white workers often accepted a lesser economic position and lower wages in return for the "public and psychological wage" that went with being members of a "white race." In return for acceptance of their subordinate class position, white workers, including new immigrant workers, were allowed by the white elite to be part of a racial hierarchy in which all whites enforced deference from black Americans and other Americans of color.[30]

Historical research shows that many nineteenth-century European immigrants, who did *not* define themselves initially as "white" but rather as Irish, German, or Italian, gradually came to construct themselves as "white" as they moved up economically and politically in society. The development of a racist frame and its white-supremacist ideology was accelerated during Andrew Jackson's presidency (1829–1837). (Jackson himself was infamous as a slaveholder and for involvement in destroying Native American societies.) By the late nineteenth century or early twentieth century, not only the later English immigrants but also immigrants from Scotland, Scandinavia, Ireland, and Germany had come to accept a place in the "white race." Their racial privileges included the right to substantial personal liberty, to travel and immigrate, and (only for men initially) to vote. Similarly, the white elite's response to eighteenth- and nineteenth-century farmer protests and union organization among white immigrants included efforts to convince these farmers and workers to embrace racial solidarity within the socially invented "white race."[31]

 What structural and cultural factors led to the social construction of the "white race"?

Nativist Reactions to Later European Immigrants

In the 1700s and 1800s, some native-born white Americans, themselves descendants of earlier immigrants, expressed their hostility toward new European immigrants. **Nativism**, *an anti-immigrant ideology that advocates the protection of the native-born inhabitants of a country from immigrants who are seen as threatening or dangerous*, goes far back in North American history, but the term appears to have been first used in the 1840s. Nativists were nationalists who saw themselves as the *only* true Americans.[32]

Before the American Revolution, nativists focused on the religious and moral undesirability of new immigrants. Certain religious groups (especially Catholics), "paupers," and convicts were discouraged by English Americans from entering the colonies. Antiforeign sentiment was directed primarily at non-English immigrant groups, of whom French Huguenot refugees were one example. At least one Huguenot community was violently attacked by nativists. "In the early years Englishmen treated the increasingly numerous immigrants from other European countries . . . with much condescension and frequently with exploitative brutality." In Virginia and Maryland, discriminatory duties were placed on non-English servants coming into colonies. Catholics among the Irish were "doubly damned as foreign and Papist."[33]

Established colonists felt ambivalence about immigrants. On the one hand, immigrants provided needed labor for employers, ship captains profited from immigration, and new immigrants were encouraged to settle in frontier areas to increase colonial security. On the other hand, immigrants were sometimes seen as a threat, and English American mobs occasionally tried to prevent their landing.[34]

More Fear of Immigrants

Antiforeign sentiment took legal form in the late 1700s after the Federalist Party became concerned about political radicalism among new immigrants and about non-English immigrants' growing support for Jeffersonian Republicans. The 1798 Alien Act empowered the English American president (John Adams) to deport immigrants considered a threat. The period of residence required to be eligible for citizenship was raised from two to five years in 1795 and to fourteen years in 1798. Attempts were made to set an exorbitant fee for naturalization. These strategies were designed to limit the political power of non-English immigrants. Numerous attempts were made to reduce the influence of immigrants by vigorously pressuring them to assimilate to English-dominated institutions.[35]

A nativistic concern about non-English immigrants who did not know the English language and customs led Benjamin Franklin to establish a school in Pennsylvania in the 1740s.[36] Even the liberty-loving Franklin held strong ethnic prejudices about German immigrants and feared they would "shortly be so numerous as to Germanize us instead of us Anglifying them."[37]

Anti-Catholic sentiment fueled much nativist agitation. Irish and German immigrants entering during the 1840s and 1850s were targeted by bursts of nativist agitation; a variety of secret societies, sometimes termed the "Know-Nothing" movement, fought immigration and Catholicism. (When questioned, members of these societies are reported to have said, "I don't know nothing.") During the 1850s, ethnocentric Know-Nothings were elected to state legislatures, Congress, and state executive offices. They periodically precipitated violent attacks against both new immigrants and native-born Roman Catholics.[38]

Nativism was coupled with racist ideologies in the nineteenth century; other northern Europeans joined English Americans in this perspective. U.S. socioeconomic development was celebrated as the perfect example of what could be accomplished by the "Anglo-Saxon race." This racialized Anglo-Saxonism was picked up by white expansionists who lusted after Mexican lands in California and Texas. European Americans legitimated their vigorous military thrust into those areas by a perceived mandate to colonize "inferior races" there. One European American expansionist commented that "the Mexican race now see in the fate of the aborigines of the North, their own inevitable destiny. They must amalgamate or be lost in the superior vigor of the Anglo-Saxon race, or they must utterly perish."[39] This Anglo-Saxonism was to play an important role in racist thought for decades. It provided the rationalization for U.S. imperialist military and business expansion overseas, in places such as the Philippines, in the late nineteenth and early twentieth centuries.

After the Civil War, some U.S. intellectuals came under the influence of **social Darwinism**, *a perspective that extended Charles Darwin's evolutionary thinking into the societal realm and thus argued for a culture that embraces the "survival of the fittest."* This perspective developed in England and the United States and contained notions of Anglo-Saxon racial superiority linked to a theory of the social "survival of the fittest." One advocate, John Fiske, celebrated the superiority of English civilization and claimed it was the destiny of the English people to populate *all the world's* empty spaces.[40] Even more influential were popular U.S. writers such as Josiah Strong, a Congregationalist minister whose book, *Our Country* (1885), sold thousands of copies. Strong was a vigorous advocate of Anglo-Saxon superiority, which he and others combined with the view that native-born Catholics and non-British immigrants were highly undesirable. The English peoples were multiplying, he argued, and the U.S. was destined to be the seat of an "Anglo-Saxon race" whose numbers would approach (by the 1980s, he inaccurately predicted) a billion strong.[41]

Nativism and Racism Since 1890

Increased immigration from southern and eastern Europe and Asia around the turn of the twentieth century focused anti-immigration sentiment on these groups. Henry Cabot Lodge, an English American aristocrat from New England and a powerful political figure, was determined to defend the United States against immigrant "threats" in the 1890s and early 1900s. English Americans formed the Immigration League to halt southern and eastern European immigration. The League worked diligently for a literacy test, which passed Congress, and associated itself with the eugenics movement started by a prominent English Darwinist. Early U.S. eugenicists feared that allowing so-called "unfit" southern and eastern European (especially Catholic and Jewish) immigrants to enter would destroy the "superior race" of north Europeans. In their view,

the unfit should be sterilized, excluded, or even eliminated.[42]

Perhaps the most prominent American to contribute to racial nativism was Madison Grant, an American of English extraction who fused various racist ideas in his influential book, *The Passing of the Great Race* (1916). Worried about newer groups from southern and eastern Europe, Grant claimed that interbreeding with inferior European "races" would lead to mongrelization. Northern Europeans—the "Nordic race"—were the superior "race."[43] By the 1920s, this racist perspective (sometimes called "scientific racism") helped fuel pressures for immigration legislation that discriminated against non-British white groups. National-origin quotas were set to restrict the then-substantial immigration from southern and eastern Europe.

The 1920s and 1930s saw an outpouring of racial nativism. Nativist organizations such as the revived Ku Klux Klan, an old U.S. terrorist group, provided a social outlet for those who wished to subordinate African, Catholic, and Jewish Americans and preserve the "Anglo-Saxon race." Opposition to foreign immigration resurfaced again during and after World War II, when various members of Congress and (northern) European American organizations opposed legislation that would permit large numbers of political refugees, such as European Jews and Catholics, to migrate to the United States.

In more recent decades anti-immigrant and anti-Catholic nativism has continued to take the form of ethnic or racial stereotyping and harassment of Americans not of northern European ancestry. For example, Democratic Party presidential and vice-presidential candidates have sometimes been targeted because of their Catholic or southern European ancestry. In the 1984 national election, attacks were leveled at the Italian immigrant ancestry of Democratic vice-presidential candidate Geraldine Ferraro. Among other things, some Republicans (often of northern European ancestry) alleged that she and her Italian American husband had connections to organized crime. Since the 1990s, a number of Americans of Italian ancestry who are involved in politics, such as former Governor Mario Cuomo of New York, have suffered similar "Mafia" stereotyping.[44]

Another recent form of nativism can be seen in the various anti-immigration organizations that have flourished in the past two decades. Like their predecessors in the early twentieth century, these

At a demonstration in Denver, right-wing skinheads give the Nazi salute.

organizations have opposed and stereotyped recent immigrants, particularly those coming from Asia and Latin America since the late 1960s. Immigrants' languages and cultures have been the focus of nativist opposition. White-supremacy groups have held rallies, published racist literature, and established websites that attack non-European immigrant groups (sometimes viciously called, together with black Americans, the "mud people") as a threat to "American jobs" and to the Anglo-Protestant culture. Contemporary nativist groups include not only significant representations of northern European Americans but also, ironically, many whites with southern and eastern European ancestries—those whose parents or grandparents were targets of earlier nativist organizations.

The Dominant Culture and Major U.S. Institutions

Most analysts of the U.S. racial and ethnic scene have assumed that the dominant culture and institutions of the United States are substantially Anglo-Protestant in character. During the first century and a half of colonial settlement, an English heritage integrated most East Coast colonies. As historian

Sheldon Hanft has put it: "Since all but two of the original colonies were founded by Englishmen, were administered by English officials, were protected by England's army and navy, and were led by English-trained clergy, lawyers, and educators, they adapted English models in their laws, constitutions, educational system, social structure, and cultural pursuits." He adds that many wealthier colonists sent their sons to English universities, and "English styles in literature, poetry, music, architecture, industry, and clothing were the models to emulate until the twentieth century."[45]

The dominant U.S. political, legal, and economic institutions have generally been based on English models, but they have not been identical to those in England. For example, the early dominance of the Anglican church in several colonies soon gave way to significant religious diversity, and the availability of (Indian) land for (white) immigrants—the basis of much North American wealth—often fostered more democratic institutions here than in Europe at the time.[46]

Language

Although contemporary nativists have tried to bring it about, the United States as yet has no official language. Nonetheless, the *de facto* dominance of the English language signals the huge impact of early English colonists and their descendants. When the English came, perhaps a thousand indigenous languages were spoken. Today, only a few hundred are still spoken, and the number of Native Americans speaking indigenous languages is far smaller than those speaking the languages of the European conquerors.

The principal U.S. language over the past two centuries has not been a thorough blend of Native American and early immigrant languages, but an English language that has incorporated words from European and North American sources. Some scholars have argued that "our customary way of life is most like the English, and our language is but one of the several English dialects." Historically, assimilation pressures on non–English-speaking immigrants have first taken the form of language pressure. As early as the 1740s, native-born Americans of British background attacked new immigrants (such as Germans) for their alleged threats to the persistence of the English language and Anglo-American culture. From then to the present, the dominance of the English language has been a major concern of nativists.[47]

Today, as in the past, millions of Americans live in homes in which a language other than English is often spoken. In recent decades this group of non–English speakers has been attacked as un-American by organized nativists, who worry that many newcomers, especially Latin American and Asian immigrants, will not accept English as their primary language. They are especially concerned that Spanish, spoken by only about 12 percent of Americans at home, is challenging the dominance of English. (Yet, census surveys indicate that the majority of these home Spanish speakers speak English as well.) One result of lobbying by nativist organizations has been introduction of legislation to make English the official U.S. language. In 1986, California passed a ballot proposition that declared English to be the official language of this most populous state. Numerous other states have passed nativist legislation. Since 1981, an English Language Amendment to the U.S. Constitution has periodically been introduced in Congress, but has not yet been passed.[48]

In the 1990s, a group called National English Campaign announced that its goals were to (1) replace ethnic group identification and "hyphenated ethnicity" with an "American identity" based on individual citizenship and (2) establish English as the official language of government, schools, and elections. Most recently in the twenty-first century, numerous similar groups like U.S. English, Inc., have worked aggressively to get states and the federal government to make English the official language. Some thirty U.S. states now have some type of official English laws. Such efforts also suggest fear of a pluralism of U.S. racial and ethnic groups and cultures and an emphasis on an English-oriented U.S. identity.[49]

Contemporary organizations with nativist undertones, such as the California English Campaign and the National English Campaign, have fought bilingual programs across the country. In the late 1990s California passed a ballot initiative to limit instruction of immigrant children to only one year in their native language before they moved into classes taught in English.[50] The English-only groups argue that they are not trying to discriminate but wish immigrants to quickly become part of the mainstream by adopting English as their primary language. However, some like U.S. English, Inc., have also been part of a project of a conservative nonprofit organization supporting major immigration restrictions.[51]

Civil rights leaders have pointed out the discriminatory nature of actions advocated by pro-English groups, in particular the prohibition of Spanish usage by government agencies, elimination of bilingual programs, and elimination of bilingual ballots in states with numerous Latino voters. A number of research studies have shown that children who are "denied the right to view the world through their language and culture are made to feel inferior" and sometimes react in such negative ways as dropping out of school or engaging in drug use—outcomes that cost not only themselves but the greater society dearly.[52]

Nativist campaigns that promote use of the English language underscore the traditional dominance of that language—and the uneasiness that, ironically, some descendants of *earlier immigrants* still feel in the presence of languages and cultures brought by relative newcomers to this "nation of immigrants."[53] As one legal scholar notes, their "first myth is that our national unity somehow depends solely on the English language, ergo we must protect the language through constitutional amendment or legislation. A corollary is that the only language of true American identity is the English language."[54]

What is ironic about the aggressive English-only movements is that most of the immigrants being attacked not only recognize that English is the language of much political, social, and economic discourse, but also strive hard to learn it. In recent years tens of thousands of immigrants have been turned away or placed on waiting lists for adult English classes in several cities. Significantly, according to the Pew Hispanic Center's recent report, nearly 90 percent of Latino immigrants speak English well. The percentage is even higher for later generations.[55] Thus, English-only nativism is wrongheaded on the facts and mainly serves to further segregate English-only supporters from the rest of the world. In addition, lack of knowledge of languages other than English cripples many Americans who conduct business abroad or deal politically with people in other countries across the globe. A person who knows more than one language well, as many do in Europe, typically has greater knowledge and is therefore more intelligent in this regard than a person who knows but one.

Religion and Basic Values

English religious influence on this country has been great since colonial days. The various English (and British) denominations represented a variety of beliefs. Anglicans in Virginia were characterized by a hierarchy of priests and liturgical worship. This group favored a state church supported by compulsory church taxes. Presbyterian churches in the Appalachian backcountry favored a national church governed by strong ministers. Congregationalists in New England favored moderate separation of church and state and more democratic church governance. Baptists (Rhode Island) and Quakers (New Jersey and Pennsylvania) advocated strict separation between church and state. The communally organized Baptists favored a fellowship-centered form of worship. The spirit-centered worship of Quakers followed from a belief in an Inner Light that dwells in all people.[56] These latter groups established the principle of separation of church and state at the heart of the U.S. political system.

For the first 200 years, English religious denominations, or variations thereof, dominated the North American scene. The Anglican church received early government support but lost its privileged position during the American Revolution. Anglican and Congregational churches were in the majority at that time, although Baptist and Presbyterian churches and Quaker groups were becoming numerous. In the century after 1776, English dominance of the country's religious institutions decreased as Catholic, Jewish, and other religious groups grew with new immigration.[57]

The Catholic, Jewish, and Muslim faiths, as well as non-British Protestantism, have been greatly shaped by the "American way of life," a phrase the scholar Will Herberg applied to the dominant Anglo-Protestant culture.[58] One important study of Judaism has shown the substantial impact of Protestant institutions on eastern European Judaism. Immigrant synagogues made major changes over time in response to the dominant Anglo-Protestant culture. For example, Jewish religious schools adapted to Protestant American scheduling and Sunday school formats. Reform Jews adopted English as the language of worship and introduced Friday night services.[59] Yet, the Anglo-Protestant culture's effects on the non-Protestant religions of later immigrants have been uneven and incomplete. Although new immigrants have been expected to adapt in many areas, some religious heritages from the home countries have been preserved. Contemporary U.S. religious patterns can be accurately described as a type of cultural pluralism.

Certain Anglo-Protestant values have had significant effects on non-Anglo immigrants. The importance of the ascetic (austere and self-denying) Protestantism that early English immigrants brought to the colonies should not be underestimated. "American condemnation of British sexual and political impurities focused on the King. Idleness, wealth, and power had corrupted him."[60] Puritanism helped to establish the **Protestant work ethic**—*the idea of hard work as a duty of every individual, originally of an individual who seeks to please God*—at the center of the U.S. value system. This work ethic was linked by many to the persistent pursuit of personal profit. The expanding U.S. capitalistic system in the 1700s and the 1800s was pervaded by the "pursuit of profit, and forever *renewed* profit, by means of continuous, rational, capitalistic enterprise."[61]

The influence of English religious traditions on music and the arts in the first centuries is also evidence of the extensive effects of the English on early American culture. The first book published in New

England was the *Bay Psalm Book* (1640), which drew heavily on English music. "Yankee Doodle" was probably an English tune whose original lyrics satirized colonial soldiers. Only when the Revolution began did American soldiers take it over from the British. Before, during, and after the Revolution, English melodies were the basis of most popular songs.[62] Even the new national anthem, "The Star-Spangled Banner," took its melody from an English drinking song!

Interestingly, over the next two centuries English influence on popular music receded dramatically before the pervasive influence of African American music (jazz and rock and roll, for example), "Scotch-Irish" country music, and the Mexican American music of the Southwest. Today, popular music is one major area of U.S. culture from which the direct English influence has substantially disappeared.

Education

English and other British Americans took advantage of what few educational opportunities were available in the colonial period; more affluent parents sent their children to private schools established before 1800. With the public school movement, which began in earnest in the first decades of the nineteenth century, British American dominance of public schools became a fact of life. British Americans saw public schools as a means of socializing non-British immigrants into Anglo-Protestant values. In the nineteenth century, most school systems were established and fostered by British American industrialists and educators who shaped curricula and supervised schools. Although some—for example, John Dewey—believed education should bring mobility opportunities for poor immigrants, many elite educators emphasized social-control aspects of schools. The Americanization pressures on immigrant children were intense. Whether children were Irish, Jewish, or Italian, Anglicization was designed to ferret out non-Anglo-Protestant ways and assimilate the children to Anglo-Protestant manners, work habits, and values.[63]

Public schools' social-control function and the Anglo-American influence on their operation remain evident today. More recent immigrants, such as Asians and Latinos, have faced Anglo-conformity pressures similar to those experienced by earlier Irish and Italian immigrants. Indeed, the public schools are still a major battleground for those concerned with making English the official language of the United States.

Political and Legal Institutions

The political and legal institutions that affect all Americans have been shaped fundamentally, and are still being shaped greatly, by the English heritage in at least two ways: the laws and traditions more or less inherited from the English, and their concrete application today by English immigrants' descendants. Given the early majority of English immigrants in colonial society, English legal institutions became dominant. The Mayflower Compact (1620), a political framework that theoretically provided for equality under law, was part of this English political tradition. New England, with its Puritan institutions, often provided the model for later political and legal developments.[64]

The North American colonies developed distinctive political institutions—in some significant ways those characteristic of seventeenth-century England. The basic political ideas in England and the soon-to-be United States included unity of government and society, subordination of government to law, a balance of power between the legislature and the executive, and heavy reliance on local governments.[65] U.S. political and legal institutions, growing out of the U.S. Constitution, have generally reflected these ideas ever since. Nonetheless, some contrasts can be seen. Governmental authority and power were being centralized in England in the late 1700s, but in the new United States of 1789, governmental power was separated into three branches—executive, judicial, and legislative. The position of the U.S. president is unusual: The United States, unlike most modern political systems, does not distinguish between head of the government and chief of state. Indeed, numerous recent presidents have demonstrated how powerful the U.S. executive branch is relative to the Congress, whereas in most European countries parliaments are more powerful versus heads of governments. The United States is a relatively new society, but it is an "old" political state.

Representative government in the colonies and, later, in the United States is another example of English influence. Using Parliament as its model, the British Crown established representative colonial assemblies almost from the start.[66] Gradually, these assemblies grew in power vis-à-vis the London government. Indeed, Crown infringements on them helped to generate the Revolution.

The U.S. legal framework reflects great English influence. Before the Revolution, English common law was asserted to be "the measure of rights of Americans."[67] Tension between the new nation and England generated U.S. objections to the continuation of English-based laws. Some Americans wanted a new U.S. legal code, but for the most part, U.S. officials and lawyers only "sought to reshape or add to the existing stock of authoritative legal materials."[68] Although there was variation in how English statutes were brought into the U.S. legal system, their implementation was thoroughgoing: "The use of English statutes was provided for at an early stage in twenty-six of the twenty-eight jurisdictions organized between 1776 and 1836."[69] Although the U.S. legal system has been patched many times, the basic cloth today is still English common law.[70]

Officeholding

In addition to their fundamental impact on the establishment and structure of U.S. political institutions, English Americans have had a major impact on their operation. The first U.S. president, George Washington, was of English ancestry, as were many presidents who followed him. Americans with significant English ancestry have filled a disproportionate number of major offices at various political levels throughout U.S. history.

The colonial assemblies were "almost exclusively English in makeup."[71] The Declaration of Independence was signed by fifty-six European American men, thirty-eight of whom were English by background or birth; nine were Scottish or "Scotch-Irish," three Irish, five Welsh, and one Swedish.[72] A majority of the fifty-five members of the U.S. Constitutional Convention were also English; the Constitution was framed around their concerns not only for (partially) democratic institutions reminiscent of English institutions but also for the protection of their property and wealth. Most people of property and wealth in the new nation—merchants, slaveholders, financiers, shippers, wealthy farmers, and their allies—supported the new U.S. Constitution, substantially out of economic self-interest. Note too that enslaved Americans, indentured servants, poor farmers, laborers, and women had no say in the making of the U.S. Constitution.[73]

Studies of U.S. presidents, Supreme Court justices, and members of Congress have revealed a distinctive pattern persisting to the present. Of the U.S. presidents from George Washington to Barack Obama, about two-thirds had significant English ancestry and *all* but one of the others had other major northern European backgrounds.[74] No southern Europeans, Jewish Americans, Latino Americans, Asian Americans, or Middle Eastern Americans have ever been president. Just one American of color—President Barack Obama elected in 2008—has served, and his maternal ancestry is partially English. (His father was African.) A study of the origins of Supreme Court justices from 1789 to 1957 found that more than half were of English or Welsh extraction. Northern Europeans of Protestant backgrounds generally dominated the country's highest court from the 1790s to the early 1990s—that is, until the appointment of several black (Clarence Thomas), Jewish (Ruth Bader Ginsburg and Stephen Breyer), Italian (Samuel Alito), and Puerto Rican (Sonia Sotomayor) justices since the early 1990s.[75] Moreover, an analysis of 162 prominent political leaders (including presidents, representatives, senators, and Supreme Court justices) of the critical historical period between 1901 and 1910 found that more than half were of English or Welsh origin. These data show just how powerful elite members of the English or British American groups have been over most of the history of this country, even as their group's percentage of the population has long been less than 10 percent.[76]

Even when new immigrant groups periodically managed to break into U.S. politics in major ways, as in the case of Irish and Italian Americans in larger cities in the late nineteenth and early twentieth centuries, they often remained subservient to Anglo-Protestant leaders who continued to hold the highest political offices. Newer immigrants and their children finally gained significant electoral and political power in the first decades of the twentieth century in major cities like Chicago, but not as top elected officials at the national level. For example, as of 2010, only one Catholic American had *ever* been president: Irish American John F. Kennedy (1961–1963). His brief presidency marked only a temporary shift from a substantially north European Protestant political establishment at the very top, for Kennedy was followed by more white men of northern European Protestant stock as presidents, until the 2008 election of President Barack Obama.[77]

Although the disproportionate influence of northern European Americans at the very top of national politics and corporate decision making persists today, significant challenges to this dominance can be seen. For example, in the 2000s, the cabinets of presidents George W. Bush and Barack Obama have included a number of Americans whose ancestral backgrounds are not northern European. These cabinets have included numerous officials of Asian, Latino, and African American backgrounds, signaling the growing racial and ethnic diversity in national politics.

What about the English American impact on local governments? A study of New Haven, Connecticut, up to 1960 illustrates English political dominance in New England. For many decades an Anglo American patrician elite there "completely dominated the political system. They were of one common stock and one religion, cohesive in their uniformly conservative outlook on all matters, substantially unchallenged in their authority, successful in pushing through their own policies, and in full control of such critical institutions as the established religion, the educational system (including not only all the schools but Yale as well), and even business enterprise."[78] A study of the mayors of Cleveland, Ohio, in the period between 1836 and 1901 found that most were part of the Anglo-Protestant elite with strong ties to New England. Although midwestern, their political framework was substantially guided by what was termed the "New England creed," one proposition of which was "The good society is white and Protestant."[79]

In more recent decades Americans of British ancestry have had to compete with non-British immigrants and their descendants for power in local and state politics, and today the racial and ethnic mix in local and state political institutions varies considerably across the country. Irish, Italian, and, most recently, African, Latino, Middle Eastern, and Asian Americans have risen to political power in some large cities of the Midwest, East, South, and West. Still, English and other British Americans continue to exercise disproportionate political influence in many areas, especially in suburban politics, although they and their ethnicity still receive relatively little media attention.

Economic Institutions

Recall from previous sections that the English heritage is substantially reflected in U.S. economic institutions—in the norms and values that shape these capitalistic institutions and in the disproportionate dominance of individuals with English American backgrounds. Just as the U.S. legal system incorporated portions of the English legal system, the forms of capitalism that dominated much of northern Europe during colonial times also shaped the colonies' emerging economic system. The British Crown wished to increase raw materials and markets available to the home country. To this end, the first English colonies were often capitalistic, especially those established by state-chartered trading companies or English investors.

Mercantile capitalism, which still existed in the colonies at the time of the Revolution, was a state-directed capitalism linked to English nationalism. The American Revolution was in part a clash between English commercial interests and English American commercial interests, a clash that unified the colonies and brought a political break between two similar economic systems.[80]

Industrial capitalism developed in the United States after 1830, again with intimate connections to the English system. Much investment and many technologies used for U.S. industrial development came from England; increased numbers of English capitalists and skilled workers provided much of the know-how for U.S. economic development. After the Revolution, as before, Britain and the United States formed a single north Atlantic economy.[81]

Direct Participation in the Economy

English and other British Americans have regularly influenced the operation of the U.S. economy through direct control of critical business and political positions. In the beginning, they established most of the colonies and controlled much land and wealth. Control of the colonies lay substantially in the hands of English and other British American landowners and merchants.[82] In the late prerevolutionary period, farmers with their own farms small and medium-sized did come to have more influence.[83] In addition, English Americans with significant land and wealth often needed labor. Thus, the North American colonies imported labor from Europe and Africa. By the 1730s, a substantial Irish migration had begun, and a large proportion of these immigrants were indentured servants. A brutal African slave trade eventually supplanted this trade in indentured servants.[84]

As we move into the nineteenth and twentieth centuries, we find few studies on the English or British American dominance of the economy. A study of the wealth of men in 1860 concluded only that the wealth of "native-born males," doubtless mostly British Americans, was about twice that of "foreign-born males."[85] U.S. industrialization in the nineteenth century was often fueled by English and Dutch capital. U.S. business elites had long been dominated by Americans of British or other northern European descent. In the nineteenth century, the most famous of these were industrialists and financiers, many of whom have been regarded as exploitative "robber barons." They included John D. Rockefeller, Leland Stanford, and J. P. Morgan, men of great wealth and power. Their heritages were typically English, with a few other northern European heritages mixed in. Many of their associates or family members became U.S. senators, representatives, and governors.[86]

A study of top executives and entrepreneurs in the late-nineteenth-century iron and steel industry found that few came from recent immigrant families; most were native born and had fathers with capitalist or professional backgrounds. Thus, most did *not* fit the image of a poor immigrant "making good," as did the steel magnate Andrew Carnegie, who came to the U.S. as a poor boy. More than half were of English or Welsh ancestry; most of the rest were Scottish or Irish.[87] A survey of 200 major executives at the largest companies from 1901 to 1910 found that 53 percent were of English or Welsh origin, 7 percent were Scottish, 14 percent were Irish, and 8 percent were Canadian or British (unspecified).[88]

A few studies have also made clear the extent of British American dominance in local economies. For instance, in the 1930s, Burlington, Vermont, was dominated by "Old Americans"—those who had been in the U.S. for four generations, probably heavily English and English Canadian. They controlled banking and manufacturing, and also constituted a disproportionate number of professionals and political officials.[89] Only a few studies of the economically influential that examine ethnicity have been done since the 1930s. The 1940s "proper Philadelphians" about whom sociologist E. Digby Baltzell has written typically had English or British backgrounds. This is suggested by the dominance of Episcopalians and Presbyterians in the Philadelphia *Social Register* for the year 1940.[90] In an analysis of the 1950s and 1960s, Baltzell also underscored the continuing dominance of British Americans at the national level in these important decades.[91]

 What factors ensure the centrality of the Eurocentric culture and institutions?

Contemporary Elites

Thomas Dye's important 1970s study of major U.S. decision makers identified only 4000 people in top positions in corporations, government, and other sectors: "Great power in America is concentrated in a tiny handful of men. A few thousand individuals out of 200 million Americans decide about war and peace, wages and prices, consumption and investment, employment and production, law and justice, taxes and benefits, education and learning, health and welfare, advertising and communication, life and leisure."[92] Certainly, decisions of importance are reached at the middle and lower levels of society, but the few thousand in top positions make many of the most critical decisions—those affecting the lives of many millions in all racial–ethnic groups. Dye's research revealed that the social origins of the top 4000 were not representative of the population as a whole. Most were affluent, white, Anglo-Protestant men. There were very few African Americans and virtually no Mexican Americans, Native Americans, or Asian Americans. These elites were "at least 90 percent Anglo-Protestant," and Dye noted that "there were very few recognizable Irish, Italian, or Jewish names" in the group.[93]

In the last decade or two, popular U.S. magazines have proclaimed that those in the media, politics, and the universities who most influence American life are now a much more representative group. Elites "today represent a real break with their predecessors."[94] However, this view is inaccurate. One must be careful to distinguish social and economic realities from rags-to-riches myths. Today, the upper reaches of U.S. economic and other major institutions have broadened to include not only British Americans but also those with other northern European ancestry, particularly German, Irish, and Scandinavian Americans, and a handful of Catholic and Jewish Americans are now in the elite bastions of economic power. Yet, in the twenty-first century, Catholic and Jewish Americans are still *not* proportionately represented

TABLE 3.2   People with English Ancestry: Selected Population Characteristics (2008)

	People with English Ancestry	Total U.S. Population
Number	27,516,394	304,059,728
Median age (years)	46.9	36.9
High school degree or greater (25 years and over)	93.2%	85%
College degree or greater (25 years and over)	37.4%	27.7%
Foreign born	1.8%	12.5%
Female	52.2%	50.7%
Median family income	$75,954	$63,366
Percent individuals below poverty line	6.8%	13.2%

Source: U.S. Bureau of the Census, "2008 American Community Survey." All figures are estimates based on a national survey and have modest margins of error.

at the top of the corporate pyramid. And few non-Europeans can be found at the very top. Indeed, recent research on Fortune 500 companies shows that fewer than 4 percent of these corporations have people of color as their CEOs.[95]

English Americans as a Group: Economic and Other Demographic Data

Demographic analysts using the American Community Survey (Census Bureau) data estimate that 27.5 million Americans now claim English as their ancestry, about 9 percent of the population in 2008. According to Table 3.2, a very small percentage of those indicating substantial English ancestry were born abroad. The proportions of women and men in this English ancestry population are similar to those of the total population, but the English ancestry population is substantially older than the population as a whole.[96]

In the 2008 census survey data (see Table 3.2) we also see that the educational attainment of these Americans as a group was higher than that of the total population, for the category of high school diploma or greater (93.2 percent versus 85 percent) and the category of at least a college degree (37.4 percent versus 27.7 percent). The occupational distribution data (not in Table 3.2) also indicate that those of English ancestry are much more likely to hold managerial, professional, and other white-collar jobs than the total population of workers.

Taken as a group, these English American families were economically better off than those in the total population—with a substantially higher median family income of $75,954, as shown in Table 3.2. The poverty rate for individuals of English ancestry was also a little more than half that of all Americans.

English Americans Today

Although they constitute the group whose culture and institutions have usually been the standard against which other groups' degree of assimilation is measured, English Americans are rarely researched. A recent analysis by the first author using a major Internet search engine—and using many phrases with "English American" or "Anglo-Saxon American" in them—revealed *no* major research articles or books dealing centrally with this group today. On billions of websites there is no indication of a major recent research study of contemporary English Americans and their everyday lives. This extensive neglect of such a powerful group suggests just how much the English Americans have blended into the sociocultural background of U.S. society.

Some 27.5 million Americans today claim significant or total English ancestry. Those of English descent appear to have some tendency to marry others with similar backgrounds. One older analysis found that just over half the women with English ancestry had mates who were at least of partial English ancestry.[97]

Residential dispersal has been characteristic of English Americans and other northern European Americans. One study of the New York region found that, by the 1980s, respondents with English ancestry had dispersed throughout the region. Their ancestors had immigrated to the area in the seventeenth and eighteenth centuries, and later descendants had much time to move around. In this study, 95 percent of those with English or Dutch ancestry reported mixed ethnic backgrounds; many had ancestors from several countries. Moreover, some 40 to 50 percent of those with British backgrounds said that their ethnic identity had *no importance* to them. Sociologist Richard Alba cautions that this latter response may mean that many have come to see their English or British American identity as synonymous with a "truly American" identity. They may have so completely integrated their English or British identity with their definition of what is American that they see no need to identify assertively with their country of origin. In contrast, more recent immigrant groups (for example, southern Europeans) were much more likely to identify strongly with their national heritage.[98]

As we noted, very little contemporary research looks at the daily lives of English Americans today. However, one brief research commentary by Joan Marsh Schlesinger has addressed English Americans' mourning practices and the values associated with such practices. She suggests that English Americans tend to approach difficult family situations like funerals with a pragmatic and stoic attitude, one that plays down emotionality and accents planned process. They tend to prefer institutionalized care for loved ones who are near death, rather than the home care often preferred by other groups, and personal and family grief tends to be kept private. In Schlesinger's view, English Americans today, not unlike many other Americans, accent a private and often less emotional or intellectualized approach to dealing with difficult life and death issues.[99]

Although English Americans can be viewed for many purposes as one ethnic group, regional variations in broader elements of English American culture are evident, both in the past and in the present. For example, the concepts of liberty brought by the major groups of English immigrants in the 1600s and 1700s evolved in different ways in the colonies.

In New England, the English Puritans' concept of ordered freedom, codified in written laws, "became an instrument of savage persecution." Ordered freedom involved the liberty to impose individual restraints on Puritans themselves without interference by outsiders, to grant exemptions from these restraints to particular individuals, and to practice the "true" religion and persecute dissenters. In Virginia, the idea of hegemonic freedom—the belief that liberty was the birthright of the free-born English and gave those with high status the right to rule people of lower ranks—"permitted and even required the growth of race slavery for its support." In the Delaware Valley, the English Quakers' belief in reciprocal freedom, which recognized each individual's right to dissent, caused them to withdraw from the world. In contrast, the Appalachian "backcountry belief in natural freedom, which favored minimal government and the supremacy of private interests, sometimes dissolved into cultural anarchy."[100] The backcountry group included not only English immigrants but also immigrants from Scotland and Ireland. Thus, all those of English or other British descent emphasized the importance of individual freedom as they saw it. All these interpretations can still be found today as different regional variations on the theme of freedom.

Historian David Fischer has analyzed the relationship between regional diversity *today* in the United States and the distinctive colonial cultures of these four broad groups of English and British immigrants. Regional differences in homicide rates provide an interesting example. Homicide rates today are low in the areas of New England in which the early Puritans established a tradition of order and nonviolence, and high in the southern areas that were first settled by immigrants from Great Britain's northern borderlands of Scotland and Ireland, whose culture was somewhat violence prone before emigration. Other social indicators examined by Fischer include education, attitudes toward gender equality, and patterns of local government and public life. Those areas with high rates of high school and college graduation today are generally the ones whose colonial culture valued education highly. Those states that failed to ratify the Woman's Suffrage Amendment (1918–1921) and the Equal Rights Amendment (1972–1978) were those in whose colonial culture women had a comparatively low status. Many New England communities today continue the colonial practice of democratic governance by town meetings, and current regional differences in the levels of taxation and public spending are broadly similar to what they were in the colonial period. Significantly, "each of the four cultural regions of British America . . . [has] kept its own customs of enculturation for many generations."[101]

One distinctive region is the South, which was settled substantially by English and other immigrants from Britain's borderlands. The largest white ethnic group in the South today is still Americans of English descent. Sociologist Lewis Killian noted that another important part of the southern white population has descended from early Irish immigrants, those often called the "Scotch-Irish" Protestants (see Chapter 4). There are also large proportions of French, Spanish, or German descent in the South. Killian has argued that English and other British Americans have become mostly submerged in a larger, ethnically diverse white population that has emphasized whiteness above all else: "For a southerner, the salient fact was and is whether he was white or black; all else was secondary."[102]

The theoretical frameworks of assimilation analysts often take the English (or British) Americans and their culture and institutions as the starting point for the analysis of individual and group assimilation in the United States. Gordon's important seven-stage framework (Chapter 2) generally assumes Anglo-conformity as the general trend of adaptation by subsequent immigrant groups in the North American colonies and, later, in the United States.

Looking at the history of English Americans, however, power-conflict theorists would emphasize the ways in which the English colonization process initiated and maintained racial and ethnic stratification in the United States. The initial violent subordination or extermination of Native Americans by English colonists is a clear example of *migrant superordination*, which takes place when a migrating group imposes its will on an indigenous group. The entry of later groups of immigrants and their relegation to a subordinate position in the North American stratification system by that time fully dominated by English Americans, as was the case for enslaved Africans, is an example of *indigenous superordination*. Such concepts acknowledge the social hierarchy, with its unequal power and resources, that has developed and persisted over the long course of U.S. racial and ethnic history.

What are the major consequences of maintaining a Eurocentric culture and institutions?

Summary

This chapter examines one of the most neglected of U.S. ethnic groups: English Americans. The degree to which they now blend into the background of U.S. culture and society makes it difficult to assess the power, location, and achievements of these early immigrants and their many millions of descendants. Americans of English ancestry still make up a substantial proportion of the U.S. population, and they still tend to share certain values and customs and, in numerous areas, to marry others of northern European ancestry.

The English established major colonies in the area that became the eastern United States. *Dominance* is the appropriate term for English influence on North American religious, economic, and political institutions. The colonization migration of the English created a dominant culture and hierarchical social structure to which subsequent immigrant groups were required to adapt. The study of European group assimilation in North America begins with the English. For centuries, English migrants and millions of descendants have been disproportionately represented in key social, economic, and political positions in society.

Between the mid-1800s and today, English Americans have been joined in their dominant position by certain other European American groups. The result is a more diverse Anglo-Protestant group, but one that still holds disproportionately great power.

The tremendous impact of Anglo-Protestant Americans on North American culture and social institutions does not mean that substantial segments have not remained working class or poor. In addition, there have long been significant regional and denominational differences within the English and British American groups.

Since World War II, the English and British Protestant dominance has been challenged by Catholic and Jewish Americans with European ancestry as well as by non-European groups. Some analysts argue Anglo-Protestant influence is waning. Schrag, for instance, argued some time back that "Anglo-Saxon Protestants" were on the road to cultural decline and offered as evidence the increasing non–Anglo-Saxon dominance of music, literature, and art. However, even Schrag presented a different conclusion for the economic sphere: The Anglo-Protestant "elite still controls its own corporate offices, its board rooms, its banks and foundations."[103] Analyses declaring the elimination of Americans of English and British ancestry as a powerful force in many U.S. institutions are, as the preceding data suggest, still premature.

Key Terms

English Americans   66
Anglo-Saxon   66
Anglo-Protestant
  Americans   66
white Anglo-Saxon
  Protestant
  Americans   66

nativism   71
social Darwinism   72
Protestant work
  ethic   75

Irish Americans and Italian Americans

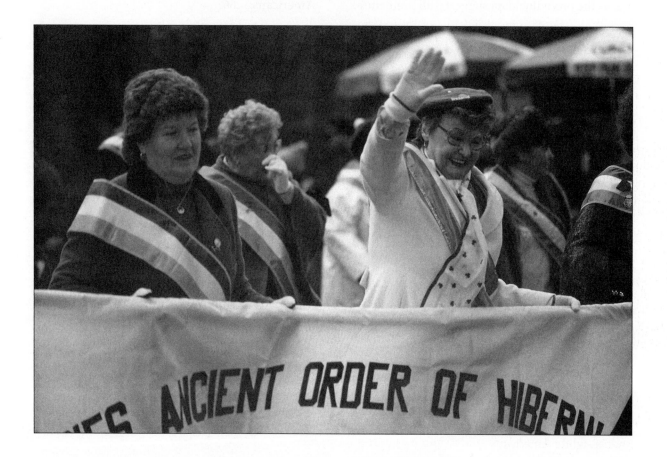

BIG PICTURE QUESTIONS

- *Why are the neglected experiences of white ethnic immigrants in the United States important?*

- *What factors have contributed to the incorporation of European immigrant groups into mainstream institutions?*

- *How have discrimination and related barriers been faced by Irish and Italian Americans?*

The Menace, a Missouri newspaper that reached 1 million in circulation by 1914, was created by editor Wilbur Franklin Phelps. Phelps used the weekly to circulate extreme anti-Catholic ideas, including the contention that the Vatican was pushing politically radical Italian Catholics to immigrate to the United States instead of the allegedly more docile, Americanizing Irish Catholics. Phelps's publication accused the Knights of Columbus of seeking the extermination and mutilation of religious heretics. Fierce anti-Catholicism characterized much popular writing in the media of the nineteenth and early twentieth centuries. Nativists sought to stop the flow of Catholic immigrants to the U.S., with Irish and Italian immigrants and their children often being the center of their attention.[1]

Numerous discussions of ethnicity have focused on "white ethnics," a term sometimes used for groups like white Catholic and Jewish Americans. White Anglo-Protestant Americans have, on occasion, blamed these groups for societal problems such as urban political machines or urban racism. They have spoken of white ethnic "hardhats" as uneducated people with a corrupt or authoritarian inclination. Not surprisingly, white ethnics have resisted, arguing that hypocritical Anglo-Protestants have little awareness of the historical experiences of Catholic and Jewish Americans with poverty and Anglo-Protestant-generated discrimination.

IRISH AMERICANS

The purpose of this chapter on Irish and Italian Americans, and the next chapter on Jewish Americans, is to analyze the neglected experiences of non-English white Americans who helped to build the United States. Irish Americans are one major group that comes to mind when white ethnic groups are mentioned.

Irish Immigration: An Overview

Placed on the migration continuum from slave importation to voluntary immigration, the Irish migration to North America falls toward the voluntary end. Even so, this movement was less voluntary than the migrations of other European groups, for economic and political pressures to leave Ireland were often great. More than 200,000 Irish left for the American

colonies before 1787; between 1787 and the 1820s, approximately 100,000 migrated.[2] The period of heaviest immigration was between 1841 and 1860, when 1.6 million Irish entered the United States. Migration peaked again in the 1880s and 1890s, then dropped sharply in subsequent decades.[3] For example, in the long period from 1961 to 1992, only about 107,000 Irish immigrants entered the United States.[4] In the 2008 American Community Survey, more than 36.2 million Americans listed Irish as their ancestry. Almost all were born in the United States. They now make up about 12 percent of the U.S. population.[5]

The Eighteenth-Century Migration

The first Irish came to the United States in the 1650s, when Captain John Vernon supplied 550 people from Ireland as workers for English colonists in New England. Large numbers did not begin to arrive on North American shores until the 1700s. Both push and pull factors influenced immigration. The image of North America as a land of opportunity was a pull factor, but domestic pressures were also important. Traditional scholars have held that virtually all Irish immigrants before 1800 were "Scotch-Irish" Protestants from northern Ireland.[6] **"Scotch-Irish" immigrants** is a term for certain *immigrants from northern Ireland, some of whose ancestors are said to have immigrated to Ireland from Scotland.* However, Michael O'Brien has cited "unquestionable proof that every part of Ireland contributed to the enormous emigration of its people, and while there are no official statistics now available—for none were kept—to indicate the numerical strength of those Irish immigrants, abundant proof of this assertion is found in authentic records."[7] Many southern Irish immigrants gave up traditional Catholicism because of the scarcity of Catholic churches in the American colonies and because hostile Protestant environments in many areas of Ireland and the colonies made open practice of Catholicism difficult.

Because the northern Irish in the first streams of immigration regarded themselves as Irish rather than "Scotch-Irish," the term *Scotch-Irish* was seldom used in the first centuries of Irish presence in North America. Migrants gave Irish names to their settlements and joined organizations such as the Friendly Sons of Saint Patrick, not Scottish societies. *Scotch-Irish* came into heavy use only after 1850, when older Irish Protestant immigrants (and English

Americans) sought to distinguish themselves from recent Irish Catholic immigrants, who were the focus of hostile English American discrimination.[8] By the late nineteenth century, Anglo-American politicians engaged in overt stereotyping when they praised the members of the "Scotch-Irish race" as exemplary pioneers and democrats while damning the "Catholic Irish race as inferior and lazy."[9]

Early Life

In North America, perhaps half of early immigrants became indentured servants; others became subsistence farmers or farm workers, often in frontier areas. English Americans often treated their Irish Protestant and Catholic servants and other workers as lowly subordinates, to the point of brutality. Faced with anti-Catholic hostility, significant numbers of Irish immigrants gave up Catholicism. Not all converted to Protestantism, however. Pressing for religious tolerance, prominent Irish Catholics wrote President George Washington in the late 1700s asking that the full religious rights of Catholics be protected.[10]

The pull factors motivating millions of Irish Catholics to cross the Atlantic after 1830 were the same as those that have attracted European immigrants for centuries to North America, which was portrayed, in exaggerated terms, as the land of golden opportunity. Push factors loomed larger. The Irish famine of the 1840s spurred emigration. A potato blight caused a massive failure of that crop, and many people died of starvation or hunger-related diseases. Ireland produced more than twice enough food to feed its population, but English landlords saw to it that most foodstuffs were exported or consumed by those in Ireland who had money. English leaders advocated emigration to the United States as a solution for the poor Irish.[11]

The Atlantic crossing was often dangerous. Few ships arrived that had not lost a number of their poorly accommodated passengers to starvation or disease. Survivors usually chose urban destinations. New York became a major center, eventually housing more Irish than the Irish city of Dublin. Early immigrants clustered in small, dispersed settlements within cities, unlike the huge segregated communities often characteristic of later groups. Irish settlements were reinforced by a second large group of immigrants from Ireland between 1870 and 1900 and by significant but declining numbers from 1900 to 1925.[12]

From the beginning, Irish American women have been very important in their communities. One distinctive aspect of Irish immigration was the large number of young single women. Because they had no hope of inheritance and little hope of marriage in poverty-stricken Ireland, they saw the United States as a land of opportunity. Once here, they usually did not subscribe to the cult of womanhood that emphasized that the woman's place was only in the home. Most did not live lives of sheltered domesticity but became self-sufficient individuals with work histories outside the home. They made important socioeconomic contributions to the upward mobility of the Irish into the middle class.

For decades, young unmarried women immigrated to avoid the terrible life that usually awaited them in Ireland. In contrast to male Irish immigrants and female immigrants from many other countries, these women were often willing to postpone or forego marriage and work as domestic servants. Many supported families in the "old country." Their daughters often became white-collar workers. The decisions they made were an expression of life-choice values that persist among Irish Americans today.[13]

Stereotypes

Both Protestant and Catholic Irish Americans suffered from nativistic English American concerns over their presence and political persuasions. Yet, it was the nineteenth-century Irish Catholics who were attacked the most frequently. From the 1820s onward, the Anglo-American stereotype of the Catholic Irish emphasized alleged character faults. With the increase in Irish migration in the 1840s, words such as *temperamental, dangerous, quarrelsome, idle,* and *reckless*—characteristics emphasizing conduct and character—came into use to stereotype the Irish. Anglo-American images hardened and became less tolerant as the number of immigrants grew.[14]

The Ape Image

Irish Catholics were stereotyped in media cartoons that used outrageous and hostile symbols—an ape-like face, a fighting stance, a jug of whisky, a shillelagh (a wooden club). The influential caricaturist Thomas Nast published cartoons of this type in *Harper's Weekly.* One caricature showed a stereotyped southern black man and an apelike Irishman,

Caricatures of Roman Catholic bishops as crocodiles supposedly threaten Protestant children on American shores.

both portrayed as ignorant voters and a threat to orderly politics. The apelike image of the Irish was imported from England. With the rise of debates over human evolution in England, the Irish poor had been viewed by many in England and the United States as the "missing link" between the gorilla and the human race. With the constant threat of Irish rebellions on the one hand and the press of evolutionary Darwinism on the other, "it was comforting for some Englishmen to believe—on the basis of the best scientific authority in the Anthropological Society of London—that their own facial angles and orthognathous features were as far removed from those of apes, Irishmen, and Negroes as was humanly possible."[15] In their rationalizing of the exploitation of the Irish and Africans, white-racist commentators on both sides of the Atlantic developed dehumanizing animal-like stereotypes.

Sociologist Andrew Greeley has underscored the parallels in the blatant stereotyping of early Irish Americans and African Americans:

> Their family life was inferior, they had no ambition, they did not keep up their homes, they drank too much, they were not responsible, they had no morals, it was not safe to walk through their neighborhoods

at night, they voted the way crooked politicians told them to vote, they were not willing to pull themselves up by their bootstraps, they were not capable of education, they could not think for themselves, and they would always remain social problems for the rest of the country.[16]

Changing Attitudes

In the early twentieth century, harsh attitudes toward Irish Americans gradually gave way to acceptance, as nativists' hostilities were transferred to newer groups. However, not all negative attitudes disappeared. As late as the 1930s, white students at Princeton were given a list of character traits and asked to identify those they associated with certain groups, including Irish Americans. Five of the ten traits most frequently assigned to Irish Americans—"pugnacious," "quick-tempered," "quarrelsome," "aggressive," and "stubborn"—make up much of the traditional stereotype of Irish aggressiveness. Significantly, fifty years later, a similar questionnaire given to a predominantly white sample of Arizona State University students found a significant decrease in negative imagery. Only "quick-tempered" and "stubborn" remained among the top ten traits assigned to the Irish.[17]

In a 1980s nationwide opinion poll that asked respondents whether various immigrant groups had, on balance, been good or bad for this country, Irish Americans received the second-highest percentage of *positive* answers, a little less than English Americans. The reduction in stereotyping of Irish Americans that appears to have taken place since the 1930s indicates substantial *attitude-receptional assimilation,* to use Gordon's conceptual term. Yet, even today, stereotypes of Irish Americans persist. In a study of white ethnic groups in New York, about one-fifth of those with Irish ancestry reported encountering various stereotypes of Irish as politicians and police officers, heavy drinkers, or poets.[18]

Protest and Conflict

From their first decades, Irish Americans suffered not only verbal abuse and stereotyping but also significant intentional discrimination and violence from Anglo-Protestants. On occasion, Irish Americans retaliated, sometimes to the point of counterviolence. Irish Americans have also been responsible for starting racial or ethnic conflict. As noted in Chapter 2, intergroup conflict often involves a struggle over resources and can be generated by substantial racial or ethnic group inequality.

Traditional assimilation theorists tend to neglect the substantial conflict characterizing interethnic and interracial relations. Indeed, some social science and popular views of U.S. history embody a myth of peaceful progress. According to this assimilationist view, the members of each white ethnic group have ascended the U.S. socioeconomic ladder mainly by pulling themselves up by their own bootstraps—by hard work, not by protest and collective violence. This image is incorrect. To secure their "place in the sun," Irish Americans have struggled vigorously against many groups, from established Anglo-Protestants (over political-economic issues) to Native Americans (over land). They have been involved in conflict with groups above and below them in the U.S. social hierarchy of power and position.

Early Conflict

Irish immigrants' first major conflict was with established groups that controlled major institutions in the North American colonies at the time of Irish immigration. A few eighteenth-century Irish settlements were damaged or destroyed by Anglo-Protestant attacks. British Americans attacked and destroyed an Irish community in Worcester, Massachusetts, in the eighteenth century. Catholic and Protestant Irish migrants faced widespread opposition from already-established white groups.[19]

In the colonial period, English Americans considered backcountry Irish Americans to be crude frontier people. Settling in frontier areas, these Irish Americans sometimes defied laws made by English American officials and engaged in aggressive protest against them, as in the Whisky Rebellion and the Regulation movement, to relieve domination and expand their political power. The Irish were encouraged to settle in frontier areas to shield the dominant Anglo-Protestant interests from indigenous Americans. Actually, the bloody practice of scalping was institutionalized by English and Irish settlers determined to exterminate these indigenous Americans. Placing bounties on the scalps of Native Americans became common in numerous colonies.[20]

By 1850, most large cities had seen anti-Catholic demonstrations and riots carried out by Anglo-Protestants. Philadelphia became a center for anti-Irish violence. There, in 1844, major riots "resulted in the burning of two Catholic churches. . . . the destruction of dozens of Catholic homes; and sixteen deaths."[21] In the 1850s, Anglo-Protestant nativist groups such as the Know-Nothings played a major role in open and violent attacks on Irish Americans.

Conflict with Other Groups

Conflict in mining areas was a major feature of the Irish experience in the nineteenth century. For example, a major coal strike in 1875, the Long Strike, forced many Irish American miners to the brink of starvation. British American owners broke the strike and crushed attempts at unionizing. In response, secret Irish organizations linked to the Ancient Order of the Hibernians (AOH) sometimes resorted to assassination or sabotage. Owners reacted with violence against AOH groups. The Anglo-Protestant establishment engineered the shooting deaths of numerous Irish workers, and the miners replied with armed defense and guerrilla warfare.[22]

In addition, Irish Americans found themselves contending with other groups for land and other economic resources. Irish American Protestant farmers seized Indian lands on the frontier. By the 1840s, Irish competition and discrimination against black workers in northern cities engendered substantial hostility between the two groups. Between the 1840s and the 1860s, Irish workers attacked black workers in several cities. During the Civil War, Irish hostility toward African Americans increased; the two groups competed for many low-wage jobs in northern cities. Irish opposition to free black workers was partially economic; they feared job competition from black Americans moving north. Excluded from discriminatory all-white unions, black workers sometimes were used by employers as strikebreakers. The use of black strikebreakers on the waterfront, combined with Irish opposition to the Civil War military draft, helped spur the 1863 Irish riot in New York City, usually termed the "Draft Riot"—the most serious riot in U.S. history. An estimated 400 white rioters were killed in the streets, together with some black residents and some white police officers and soldiers. Irish American rioters attacked "Yankees," the police, and black men, women, and children.[23]

Within a generation or two, Irish Americans—once attacked by other Europeans and English Americans as an "inferior race"—had come to see themselves (and be seen) as members of the "white race." As we discussed in Chapter 3, one response of the English American ruling class (political and business leaders) to unrest among these white immigrant farmers and laborers in the nineteenth century was to emphasize racial solidarity with them in what was termed the "superior white race."[24]

Between 1850 and 1890, most Irish Americans came to see themselves as white and, as a rule, began to develop the antiblack prejudices and framing shared by other whites. Historical analyses have shown that, among Irish Americans, the movement from sympathy for the oppression of African Americans to their own version of the white-racist framing of society was intentionally fostered by the Anglo-American press, some Anglo-Protestant and Roman Catholic religious and community leaders, and Democratic Party organizations.[25]

English Americans grudgingly accepted this change in the racial status of Irish Americans, in part because the Irish had growing political power in cities. "The emphasis on a common whiteness smoothed over divisions in the Democratic ranks within mainly northern cities by emphasizing that immigrants from Europe, and particularly from Ireland, were white and thus unequivocally entitled to equal rights."[26] Some Irish Americans aggressively opposed the racist thinking directed at black Americans, but were not able to stem the tide. Indeed, in the mid-nineteenth century a few Irish Americans bridged the racial gap by marriage. The famous boxer Muhammad Ali, for example, is known to have had an Irish great-grandfather, Abe Grady, who in the 1860s emigrated from Ireland and married an African American woman in Kentucky.

Irish–black conflict has now persisted for more than a century and a half, especially in large cities. In recent decades, Irish American and other white ethnic groups' concern over modest black gains from government antidiscrimination (e.g., affirmative action) programs has been a recurring issue. Many have felt that African Americans have received a disproportionate share of government attention and political-economic benefits, compared with what white ethnics have received. However, the evidence in this and later chapters shows that this common stereotyped notion is quite inaccurate.

 What were some important factors that contributed to conflicts between new immigrant groups and existing racial–ethnic groups?

Politics and Political Institutions

When the Irish began arriving in the seventeenth century, much of the political framework of the colonies had already been fashioned by the English. However, the Irish immigrants who came in the eighteenth century did play a role in shaping the new nation's institutions. Eight of the fifty-six signers of the Declaration of Independence were Irish immigrants. Seven Irish Americans were members of the Constitutional Convention, and at least four were members of the first U.S. Congress.[27]

Political Organization in the Cities

Most Irish who immigrated after the Revolutionary War settled in eastern cities, where they frequently became involved in urban politics. Discussions of politics have often focused on Irish Catholics and their "political bosses and machines." Many analyses have characterized these Irish Americans as being more corrupt in their political activities than other groups. In fact, Irish immigrants entered an urban political system that already included serious corruption. Anglo-Protestant political machines— by which those in power secured jobs, housing, and food for their poor constituents—already ruled in numerous cities before there were sizable Irish communities.

Urban politics was one means to upward socio-economic mobility for Irish Americans, a way to achieve economic and political power in the face of Anglo-Protestant opposition. In the nineteenth and early twentieth centuries, the dominant perspective on government tended toward a conservative hands-off view. Against this do-nothing background, desperate urban Irish residents, plagued by unemployment, low incomes, and poor housing, joined political organizations. Taking control of local party organizations, immigrant leaders often shaped government programs to benefit their poor. Providing jobs was one of the political machines' critical functions.[28]

One of the first political machines was New York City's Tammany Society. In 1817, a group of Irish Americans, incensed at discrimination by this Anglo-Protestant machine, broke into one of its meetings and demanded the nomination of an Irish American for Congress. Although they were driven away that time, a few decades later Irish Americans were able to take over two New York political organizations, including Tammany Hall. One Tammany Hall figure, William M. ("Boss") Tweed, has been singled out by critics who have claimed he was *uniquely* corrupt. In reality, Tweed was an urban political leader similar to many other urban political leaders, yet he represented the underdog, including Irish and Jewish Americans, in nineteenth-century New York. He was tolerant of various religious beliefs, family oriented, and ambitious. He identified with New York's poor immigrants and worked to build schools and hospitals.[29]

With the election of New York City's first Irish Catholic mayor in the 1880s, William Grace, Irish Americans began to play a major role in city politics. They held many elective posts and gained heavy representation in appointed positions. In vigorous competition with English and other British Americans, the Irish gradually won a place in the political sun in numerous east coast cities. By the 1960s, these Irish political organizations were mostly gone, except in Chicago, where the paramount Irish "boss," Mayor

Richard J. Daley, maintained enormous power into the 1970s. By the 1980s, Daley was dead, and Chicago's Irish-dominated political machine was weakening. However, in 1989, Richard M. Daley, son of the former mayor, was elected mayor and was still in office as of 2010. Today, Irish Catholic Americans hold many important local and state political offices.[30]

Pragmatism in Politics

In local politics, Irish Americans have often developed a pragmatic political style based on concern for individuals and loyalty to leaders. Indeed, pragmatic politics, with its themes of coalition and compromise, is a major Irish contribution to U.S. politics. In this framework, an urban political organization functions as a broker to balance the interests of a city's mosaic of racial and ethnic groups so that a coalition can hang together. Irish political leaders have pressed periodically for racially and ethnically balanced tickets, which have contributed to urban coalition building. Irish American political organizations have also made major contributions to the bricks-and-mortar development of cities. Irish contractors associated with city political machines helped to meet the then-pressing needs for public buildings, streets, and subways in many expanding cities.[31]

With suburbanization and intermarriage, this Irish political style has begun to fade, but it has by no means disappeared. One study of fifty-one cities found that those with large Irish populations were more likely than other cities to have a government (often Irish dominated) that provided a high level of public services for residents. Moreover, some analysts have attempted to link the upward mobility of Irish Americans to a growing "conservatism," noting that in the 1960s and 1970s Irish American electorates in areas such as New York and Connecticut preferred more conservative political candidates in mayoral, gubernatorial, and senatorial races. Research on recent national elections indicates that the majority of Irish Catholics are still inclined toward the Democratic Party, but have often split their votes roughly equally for Democratic and Republican presidential candidates. Nonetheless, in many areas Irish Americans have continued to vote for liberal and moderate Democrats, especially in local and state races. Indeed, the majority of Irish Catholics in the U.S. Congress in recent years have been Democrats.[32]

National and International Politics

One study of the period from 1901 to 1910 found that 13 percent of 162 prominent political leaders, including presidents, senators, representatives, and Supreme Court justices, were Irish American (mostly Protestant), compared with 56 percent who were of English or Welsh descent.[33] (Irish Catholic influence at the national level was weak in the nineteenth and early twentieth centuries.) Andrew Jackson, a slaveholder from Tennessee who served as president from 1829 to 1837, was the first Irish American (Protestant) president and the only one whose parents were both immigrants. Woodrow Wilson, a "Scotch-Irish" Protestant, was president from 1913 to 1921. Wilson was not sympathetic to Irish Catholic causes and did not support the Irish struggle against English domination. More recently, at a precedent-setting 1994 Saint Patrick's Day White House dinner, attended by prominent Irish American industrialists and politicians, Ireland's prime minister presented President Bill Clinton with a genealogy of Clinton's Irish ancestors. Clinton had shown much concern with political conflict in Northern Ireland.[34]

In recent decades the issue of an independent, united Ireland has generated substantial financial and political support among Irish Americans. In the 1980s, Irish Republican Army (IRA) member Joe Doherty became a rallying point for Irish American opposition to British rule of Northern Ireland. From a U.S. prison, Doherty wrote a popular column in the New York newspaper *Irish People* supporting the IRA's cause. In addition, he received visits from members of Congress, as well as from New York's Catholic Cardinal, in support of his request for political asylum.[35]

Irish American support for the Catholic Irish cause in Northern Ireland has created political tensions. Some non-Irish politicians have criticized Irish American support of the Catholic struggle in Northern Ireland and U.S. government efforts to broker peace between the British government and Sinn Féin, the political arm of the IRA. Several times in the 1990s, Gerry Adams, the head of Sinn Féin, was granted a visa to visit the United States—first to participate in a conference on Northern Ireland, then to meet with U.S. government officials following his announcement of an IRA cease-fire in Northern Ireland, and later to meet with President Clinton.[36]

Many observers feel that Irish American political leaders' peace negotiation efforts and President Clinton's decision to lift a twenty-year ban on official contacts with Sinn Féin played a significant and positive role in encouraging the peace agreements in Northern Ireland. By 2010, the republican and nationalist Sinn Féin had elected numerous members to the Northern Ireland Assembly, the second largest party in that political body. Sinn Féin had agreed with the Democratic Unionist Party (Irish Protestant) to share political power in Northern Ireland, holding several important ministerial posts, including deputy First Minister, in the Northern Ireland Executive. Irish Americans have continued to be oriented to the politics of Northern Ireland. Note too that the ongoing controversy over Northern Ireland's future independence from Britain not only illustrates an intergroup struggle between Catholics and Protestants in Ireland that continues today, but also demonstrates how events in the country of origin of one U.S. population group can long affect ethnic relations in the United States. This theme will reappear regularly in this book. World politics remains an important larger context influencing interethnic and interracial relations within the United States.

The Only Irish Catholic President to Date

Alfred E. Smith, the Democratic candidate for president in 1928, was the first Irish Catholic to carve out an important role in presidential politics. Yet, his Catholic religion counted heavily against him in this first Irish Catholic presidential campaign.[37] Not until 1960, more than 300 years after the first few Irish Catholics had come to the United States and more than a century after sizable Irish Catholic communities had been established, was the first and only Irish Catholic (also the only Catholic) president elected. Six of the presidents from Washington to Nixon had Irish American backgrounds, but except for John Kennedy all of these were Protestant Irish, as were the more recent presidents, Ronald Reagan and Bill Clinton.

In the 1960 presidential election, Irish Catholic votes in New England, New York, and Pennsylvania helped to create John Kennedy's narrow victory. As president, Kennedy acted not only on behalf of Irish Americans but also, to some extent, on behalf of America's other emergent urban political groups. Thus, Kennedy appointed the first Italian American

The only Catholic (Irish) president in U.S. history, John F. Kennedy, takes the oath of office.

and the first Polish American to a presidential cabinet and the first African American to head an independent government agency.[38]

The Irish in the Economy

One type of structural adaptation involves large-scale movement by members of an immigrant group into the secondary-organizational levels of society, such as into positions in government agencies and economic organizations, including farms and factories. Most immigrants started out at the bottom of the economic pyramid, filling the hard, often dirty, low-wage jobs in rural areas and cities. Irish immigrants found jobs through preexisting ethnic networks. "The process was cloaked in favoritism and operated quite independently of qualifications. The result can be called 'ethnic mobility, collective style.'"[39]

Irish labor was critical to industrial and commercial development. Irish immigrants after 1830 typically became urban workers, miners, or transportation workers. They migrated looking for work. Irish men found it in unskilled jobs, on the docks and in the factories of large cities; Irish women found it as servants, often in Anglo-Protestant homes. Many Irish immigrants were single females unattached to family groups. Impoverished, these women frequently moved into live-in domestic work. In contrast, Jewish and Italian women immigrants generally came with families. Irish women who came alone did so not by choice but because of adverse economic conditions in Ireland.[40]

Male immigrants became farm laborers, railroad laborers, miners, and textile workers. Many died helping to build transportation systems, as the old saying, "There's an Irishman buried under every railroad tie," indicates. Irish Catholics encountered some institutionalized discrimination in employment. Often stereotyped as dumb, unskilled, or rowdy, Irish American men and women were periodically denied well-paid jobs by employers.[41]

Upward Mobility

Significant numbers of Irish Catholics became upwardly mobile by the turn of the twentieth century. They entered the urban economy when expanding industries needed large numbers of low-wage workers. Major cities developed as Anglo-American capitalists centered new types of manufacturing in the industrial heartland, from Pittsburgh to Chicago to Detroit. Urban political machines facilitated mobility by providing jobs and other resources for the upward trek. Urban machines channeled money into building projects, facilitating the emergence of a business class. Irish Americans were important in East Coast labor organizations by the 1850s. By the early 1900s unions, had become important for Irish dockworkers, construction workers, and miners. To the present day, Irish Americans have been prominent in labor organizations, including the AFL-CIO.[42]

Mobility among Irish Americans since 1900 suggests increasing economic security for a growing segment. The mostly Protestant descendants of the pre-1830 immigrants were still disproportionately concentrated in farming areas, towns, and southern and border states in 1900. In the late nineteenth century and over the century since, a significant proportion have become relatively prosperous farmers, owners of small businesses, and skilled blue-collar workers, as well as part of many white-collar categories. Acceptance by the dominant white Anglo-Protestant group came slowly in many areas. Even by the 1930s, a great many Irish Catholics had not yet moved fully into the Anglo-Protestant-controlled economic mainstream. For example, a study of Newburyport, Massachusetts, found Irish Americans moving closer to the native-born Anglo-Protestant residents in socioeconomic status, yet no Irish Americans could be found at the top. In addition, the Depression of the 1930s postponed for a decade a major economic breakthrough, which finally came during and after World War II.[43]

Recent Successes

In recent decades, many Irish Catholics have been employed in government jobs, such as in police, fire, and public works departments; in the courts; and in schools and colleges. In seeking government jobs, like other groups after them (for example, African Americans), they often faced less discrimination in government than in the business sector. By the 1970s, two-thirds of younger Irish Catholic men held white-collar positions, compared with 38 percent of their fathers. Both generations were more likely to be found in better-paid, white-collar jobs than their counterparts in most other ethnic Catholic groups. The occupational distribution for Irish Americans now roughly parallels that of the total white population, and is a bit more oriented toward managerial, professional, and other white-collar positions than the one for the total U.S. population. Moreover, as Table 4.1 shows, the median income of Irish American families ($73,207) is now well above that of the total population and is only a little lower than that of English Americans (see Chapter 3). The percent poor in the Irish American population is higher than for English Americans, at 8.8 percent, but substantially lower than that for the U.S. population. (Note that these data include people who report sole or substantial Irish ancestry.)[44]

Today, Irish Americans hold positions of leadership in all areas of U.S. life. Media symbols of Irish

TABLE 4.1 People with Irish Ancestry: Selected Population Characteristics (2008 ACS)

	People with Irish Ancestry	Total U.S. Population
Number	36,278,332	304,059,728
Median age (years)	38.1	36.9
Foreign born	0.7%	12.5%
Percent female	52.2%	50.7%
High school degree or greater (25 years old and over)	92.2%	85%
Having at least a college degree (25 years old and over)	32.2%	27.7%
Median family income	$73,207	$63,366
Percent of individuals below poverty line	8.8%	13.2%

Source: U.S. Bureau of the Census, "2008 American Community Survey." All figures are estimates based on a large national survey and have modest margins of error. See endnotes for further explanation of ancestry choices.

American success have typically been athletes, entertainers, politicians, or, less often, entrepreneurs such as Joseph Kennedy, John Kennedy's influential father. Another group of Irish American heroes has received little notice—the growing group of Ph.D.s and academics. Catholics now make up a significant percentage of faculty members in top state colleges and universities, and a large percentage of these are Irish. In addition, many graduate-trained Irish Catholics continue to move into local, state, and federal governments as lawyers, administrators, researchers, and elected officials.[45]

Education

Organized education on a significant scale for Irish American ("Scotch-Irish") Protestants began after the Civil War. In the southern states, public schools spread during the often progressive Reconstruction period after slavery, and by the early twentieth century, many of the Protestant Irish there had taken advantage of them. The Catholic Irish relied on parochial and public schools in urban areas of the North for organized education. In part, because of the often severe anti-Catholicism, parochial schools did not become numerous until the period between 1820 and 1840. By the late 1800s and early 1900s, a parish and parochial school system had become the center of the Irish Catholic community in numerous cities.[46]

By the 1960s, the nearly 13,000 elementary and secondary Catholic schools in the United States had an enrollment of 5 million. Irish Americans were at the center of this immense network. Gradually too, these parochial schools have come to receive significant government aid—aid that, like that for other religious groups, has periodically raised the issue of the separation of church and state. By 1910, Irish Catholics were enrolled in college in large numbers, above the national average for all whites. Significant numbers of Catholic colleges were established, and college attendance continued to increase.[47]

Today, Irish Americans continue to place significant emphasis on education. As the 2008 census survey data in Table 4.1 show, the educational attainment of Irish Americans as a group is well above that of the U.S. population as a whole. Some 92.2 percent of those 25 years old or older have at least a high school diploma, and nearly one-third have at least a college degree. Older data also indicate that educational attainments of both Irish American Catholics and Protestants are increasing relative to the general white population.[48]

In the past decade, Irish American leaders have pressed for more coverage of Irish and Irish American history in U.S. schools and colleges. One California state senator of Irish heritage proposed a bill that would reshape the educational curriculum so that children in the diverse state of California could learn about the horrendous potato famines and the immigration discussed earlier. Similar efforts to enhance the educational curriculum to include more Irish history have been made in other states.[49]

Religion

In the religious sphere, the earliest Irish immigrants, whether Catholic or Presbyterian, mostly blended into various Protestant denominations, generally in southern and mid-Atlantic colonies. However, later groups of Irish Catholic immigrants played a major role in establishing what may be the most influential non-Protestant institution in the United States—the Roman Catholic Church. Although the Roman Catholic Church has had to adapt to the preexisting Protestant religious system, its growing strength has served to reinforce the right of all Americans to choose any faith. Indeed, the large migrations of Irish, other European, and Latin American Catholics to the United States have helped to make this country one of the most religiously diverse.

Initially, Irish Catholics had to fight intense anti-Catholic prejudice and sometimes violent discrimination designed to prevent the Roman Catholic Church from taking root in Anglo-Protestant soil. Still, new churches sprang up wherever Catholic workers lived. The U.S. Catholic Church's hierarchy has long been disproportionately composed of Irish Americans. One analysis of Catholic bishops from 1789 to 1935 revealed that 58 percent were of Irish extraction. In the 2000s, Irish Americans still account for a disproportionate number of Catholic priests, although this is now changing significantly.[50]

In northern cities, many Irish neighborhoods were built around a parish church, and local politics was often blended with church and school. However, over recent decades, many central city churches have been closed or merged, as Irish Americans have moved to suburbs. Today, the Irish

Catholic parish survives in the suburbs of many cities. Loyalty to the Church remains strong; one 1990s survey found that more than half of Irish Catholics go to services every week, a higher proportion than for other whites.[51]

Irish American priests have shaped the U.S. Catholic Church in a number of distinctive ways. Irish American archbishops and cardinals have often been politically and socially conservative, while many local Catholic priests have helped to lead progressive struggles, such as the struggle for expanded civil rights since the 1960s. For example, the former president of Notre Dame University and Congressional Gold Medal winner, Father Theodore M. Hesburgh, symbolizes the liberalism in Irish Catholicism. For many years, including those spent on the U.S. Commission on Civil Rights, Hesburgh has been outspoken in his support for civil rights laws, antisegregation action, and affirmative action to benefit African Americans and other Americans of color.[52]

Assimilation Theories and the Irish

There are now about 32.2 million Americans with Irish ancestry, more than one-tenth of the U.S. population. Irish Americans are one of the largest ethnic groups in the United States. As can be seen in Table 4.1, they are roughly similar as a group in median age and percent female to the U.S. population as a whole, but they are much less likely to be foreign born.

Let us now examine how the theories and concepts in Chapter 2 help to illuminate the experiences of Irish Americans. Some power-conflict analysts specifically omit immigrant groups such as "white ethnics" like the Irish Americans from their analyses, preferring to focus on racially subordinated groups because these have generally endured much greater violence and repression and for much longer. Assimilation theories in the tradition of theorists like Milton Gordon and Andrew Greeley have been the most used in analyses of groups such as Irish Americans. However, we should keep in mind something many assimilation analysts tend to neglect—the substantial conflict and discrimination that have characterized the experiences of these ethnic Americans.

Each generation of Irish Americans has become ever more incorporated into the core Anglocentric institutions than previous generations. Cultural

assimilation (acculturation) came relatively rapidly for early Irish immigrants and their descendants. Yet the eighteenth-century Irish, typically Protestants, moved up the socioeconomic ladder slowly. Substantial socioeconomic assimilation came by the late nineteenth century for many of their descendants. By the early 1900s, the successful assimilation of these mostly Protestant Irish was considered a standard for subsequent immigrant groups to follow. Sometime in the past century, many Protestant Irish became a difficult-to-distinguish part of the white-Protestant mainstream.[53]

Assimilation came more slowly for Irish Catholics who immigrated after 1830. Some adaptation to the dominant Anglo-Protestant culture, particularly learning English and the Anglo-Protestant culture's basic views and values, has been necessary to successful socioeconomic achievements within mainstream institutions. Significantly, Ireland's customs and U.S. customs had similarities to begin with. The English language was familiar to many immigrants. Although assimilation at other levels took several generations, significant acculturation took place in the first decade or so.[54]

Religion was an exception. Most Irish Catholic immigrants did not become Protestants. Conflict with the Anglo-Protestant nativists especially intensified Irish commitment to the Catholic Church. Still, Catholic churches made adjustments to the English-dominated environment in such areas as language and restructured church organizations. Such adaptations made the U.S. Catholic Church and school system an important medium within which Catholic immigrants began their acculturation and some structural assimilation (for example, priests helped immigrants secure jobs).[55]

Has commitment to the Catholic religion declined significantly in later generations of Irish American Catholics? Some analysts have claimed this. One Catholic scholar did a modest survey of Irish Americans and found that a substantial majority felt that their Irish heritage was more significant to them than their Catholic religion. Indeed, certain persisting Irish religious customs, such as large wakes and funerals in commemoration of those who have died, are probably rooted in Celtic Irish roots as much as in the Catholicism that came to Ireland later in its history. Still, social science studies over the last few decades have not found a significant decline in Catholic religious commitment. As a group, Irish

Americans have been among the most likely to attend mass of all Catholic groups.[56]

Since the mid-nineteenth century, the Catholic Irish have experienced substantial changes in the dimensions of societal incorporation that Gordon calls behavior-receptional assimilation and attitude-receptional assimilation—in effect, discrimination and prejudice. Stereotyping has declined substantially since the days when the apelike image was commonplace, although negative feelings directed against Irish Catholicism have persisted among some Protestant Americans. Anti-Catholic discrimination has also declined significantly, although it still can sometimes be seen at the very highest levels of the U.S. economy and government.

Patterns of Structural Assimilation

At the structural-assimilation (secondary-group) level, Irish Americans made slow but significant movement, over several generations, into Anglo-Protestant organizations and institutions. We have seen the steady movement of the Irish from unskilled work into white-collar occupations—and the relatively high occupational levels of Irish American Catholics in recent decades. Residential dispersal, often to suburban areas, has paralleled these developments, although some residential self-segregation persists in cities in the East and Midwest. Moreover, after a century of political struggle, Irish Catholics are now substantially integrated at the local and state government levels. In the past few decades, they have moved significantly into the judicial, legislative, and executive branches of the federal government, although they have sometimes had to struggle against anti-Catholic sentiments.

Some have argued that the higher status that accompanies economic assimilation is causing many Irish Americans to move away from the Democratic Party. However, urban politicians, particularly Democrats, have long given much attention to the Irish American community, and numerous Democratic Party leaders are still Irish. One research analysis found that 61 percent of Irish Catholics and 54 percent of Irish Protestants identified themselves as Democrats. These percentages question the accuracy of one assimilation theory of ethnic politics—that economic mobility destroys traditional ethnic voting patterns. As of today, absorption into a Republican Party dominated by white Protestants has not

happened for the majority of Irish American Catholics.[57]

As for structural incorporation at the level of primary-group ties, data on informal groups and voluntary associations point to some interesting trends. Since World War II, ethnic clubs and organizations have declined in importance for Irish Catholics. This probably indicates increasing integration into the voluntary associations of the larger white society. Irish American attendance at Catholic parochial schools has also declined.[58]

Intermarriage—*marriage between members of different racial or ethnic groups*—can be a major indicator of substantial assimilation at the primary-group level. One national survey in the 1960s reported substantial **endogamy**—*marriage within one's racial or ethnic group*—for Irish Catholics; 65 percent of respondents who had Irish fathers also had Irish mothers, and 43 percent of Irish married men had a wife with an Irish father. However, more than half the respondents to that national survey had a non-Irish spouse. One more recent survey of a large metropolitan area in New York found that 82 percent of Irish Americans were of mixed ethnic ancestry. And in the late 1990s, one commentator estimated that at least two-thirds of Irish Americans were then marrying outside the group.[59]

Is There an Irish American Identity Today?

The intermarriage rate poses challenges to continuing Irish American identity. Among the final stages of assimilation is what Milton Gordon and Andrew Greeley have seen as "identificational" adaptation. Ultimately, this type of assimilation would mean a significant loss of a sense of "Irishness" and the development of a sense of "peoplehood" solely American or Anglo-Protestant American. One's sense of identity would no longer be Irish. This may have happened for many Irish Americans with Protestant backgrounds, but the majority of Irish Catholics still have some sense of Irishness, however vague.

Some analysts argue that Irish Americans are losing their ethnic identity because of the sharp decline in immigration from Ireland in recent decades. Marjorie Fallows has argued that the American Irish are now fully acculturated to the Anglo-Protestant culture; distinctive ethnic traits that are culturally significant are rare today. Reginald Byron goes even further to argue from his 1990s data that most Irish Americans now operate with a symbolic or "virtual" ethnicity that has little to do with Ireland or the past history of Irish Americans, but is often a set of artificial views developed in response to the accent on multiculturalism in U.S. society. Moreover, even though there are still a few ethnically distinct Irish Catholic communities in certain large cities—especially Boston, Philadelphia, New York City, Chicago, and San Francisco—most Irish Catholics do not live there. From this viewpoint, cultural and structural (primary-group) assimilation are all but complete for those Irish Catholics who live outside traditional ethnic neighborhoods.[60]

Richard Alba interviewed respondents in eight white ethnic groups in a metropolitan area in upper New York State. He found a decline in the significance of ethnic identity among Irish Americans, especially in the fourth and later generations. However, those with pure Irish ancestry had a stronger sense of their ethnic identity than most of the other groups examined. Those with mixed Irish ancestry were also loyal to their Irish heritage. They were three times as likely to identify solely as Irish as they were to choose another ethnicity from their mixed background.[61]

Certainly, the Irish Catholic group has changed over generations of contact with the public school system and the mass media, but it has retained enough distinctiveness to persist as an ethnic group into the twenty-first century. The theory of ethnogenesis discussed in Chapter 2 seems appropriate to Irish Catholic Americans. Over several generations, the large numbers of Irish who came after 1830 and their descendants forged a distinctive U.S. ethnic group. Ethnicity was an important way for the Irish Catholics to assert their own identity in a buzzing confusion of diverse nationality groups. Because of nativistic discrimination, ethnic identity was less voluntary for Irish Catholics in the first few decades than later. Irish immigrants' cultural heritage was distinctly different from that of the Anglo American host culture. Over several generations of sometimes hostile interaction with Anglo-Protestants, the Irish immigrants and their descendants adapted substantially to the host society. This process created a distinctive Irish American ethnic group that reflects elements of its nationality background and also much of the dominant Anglo-Protestant culture.

In an analysis of opinion-poll data, Greeley examined survey questions that tap what he views as

traditional Irish Catholic sociocultural traits: gregariousness, gathering in a public house, religious intensity, and activity in religious organizations. Greeley concluded that Irish Catholic distinctiveness persists, particularly in certain large cities.[62] One obvious sign of this is the way in which Irish Americans celebrate the religious Saint Patrick's Day with very large parades, especially in cities with substantial Irish American populations such as Boston and New York. Some media reports have also indicated a resurgence of interest in things Irish among Irish Americans, a trend that some residents of Ireland describe as "plastic" Irish. One U.S. survey reported a growing interest in studying the Irish language (Gaelic), Irish dance, and Irish music among Irish Americans, including young people. Note too the pressures being placed on public schools to include more Irish history. Numerous colleges and universities have developed some type of research and teaching program in Irish studies, usually as part of humanities departments. Today, the impact of the Irish background on Irish American thought and behavior remains significant.[63]

 How would you apply assimilation theory to the experiences of Irish Americans?

ITALIAN AMERICANS

For many decades Italian Americans have been targets of hostility from other racial and ethnic groups, especially Anglo-Protestants. This mostly Catholic group has been attacked for being unsophisticated, super-patriotic "hardhats" with connections to the "Mafia." Since the 1960s, however, a major counterattack has developed. Many white ethnic leaders, including Italian Americans, have come to view Anglo-Protestant leaders critically and spoken out against such ethnic stereotyping.

The strong defense of things Italian and the achievements of Italian Americans had, by the twenty-first century, brought this group much greater acceptance among other Americans. The rising prominence of Italian Americans in the United States can be seen in the selection of Geraldine Ferraro, an Italian American member of Congress, as the Democratic Party's first female vice-presidential candidate (in 1984); in the elevation of Representative Nancy

Pelosi to be the first female Speaker of the U.S. House of Representatives in 2007; and in the appointment of judges Antonin Scalia and Samuel Alito to be associate justices on the U.S. Supreme Court since the 1980s. Today there are about 17.7 million Americans who claim Italian ancestry, with the largest concentrations in New England states and other northern states such as New York and Pennsylvania.

Italian Immigration

Italian explorers, including Cristoforo Colombo (Christopher Columbus), played a major role in opening the Americas to European colonization and exploitation. An Italian navigator, Amerigo Vespucci, made a number of voyages to the Americas shortly after Colombo's voyages. Because of his early maps, the continents came to be named the "Americas" after him.[64]

Many Immigrants

Since 1820, more than 5 million Italians have migrated to the United States. Between 1880 and 1920, Italian immigration was heavy, with more than 4 million recorded immigrants. After 1880, very large numbers, mostly poor farmers and laborers, immigrated from southern Italy. Most Italian Americans today are descendants of this southern migration.[65]

As we saw in Chapter 2, certain factors are relevant to such migration: the point of origin, the destination, the migrating units, and the larger context. As with the Irish, land and agricultural problems triggered much of Italian out-migration. Low income, poor soil, a feudal land system, unreasonable taxes, and government corruption were important push factors at the point of origin. The often exaggerated image of the United States as a place of expanding opportunity was a major pull factor. Some came to stay, but many early immigrants saw the United States as a temporary workplace.[66]

Migration along kinship networks, typical for poor and working-class migrants from European countries, lessened the pain of resettlement. Italians often came in groups from the same villages. Industrialized East Coast cities were popular destinations. In the larger cities, many immigrants settled in **ethnic enclaves**—*residential, social, and economic niches where fellow visitors already resided*—often called

"Little Italies." Remigration for Italians was well above that of other groups. In some years in the early 1900s, returnees to Italy equaled 60 percent or more of the new immigrants.[67]

Between 1924 and 1965, nativist-motivated immigration quotas sharply curtailed Italian immigration. The Immigration Act of 1924, passed by a disproportionately Anglo-Protestant Congress, established only a small discriminatory quota for Italians. By 1929, the annual quota for Italians was only 5802, compared with 65,721 for British immigrants. The quota system was based on nativists' belief that those countries that had furnished the most "good American citizens"—that is, northern European immigrants prior to 1890—should receive the largest quotas. The British, Germans, Irish, and Scandinavians were thus given three-fourths of the total, although the demand from those countries had slackened considerably by the time of this legislation.[68]

Pressure on Italy's small quota produced a backlog of 250,000 applicants by the time the 1965 Immigration Act replaced the discriminatory national-origin quota system. By the late 1970s, that backlog was exhausted, and since that time the annual number of Italian immigrants has dropped sharply. Counting both the first and second major ancestries listed by respondents, the Census Bureau has estimated that there were 15.7 million Italian Americans in 2000 and some 17.7 million in 2008, making them one of the largest European ancestry groups in the United States.[69]

Life for the Immigrants

What was life like for the large numbers of Italians who immigrated in the peak period? Most worked as unskilled laborers, often on transportation systems such as canals and railroads and on water and sewer systems. Pay was low, and individuals as well as families were usually poor. They were often segregated in "Little Italy" areas within cities. Italian Americans often replaced earlier immigrant groups in inner-city areas of large cities, as part of a residential invasion-succession process. Yet other new immigrant groups would follow on their heels.[70]

Some analysts have viewed working-class communities in cities as disorganized "slum" areas with little positive social life. This was not true for Italian Americans. As with the Irish, Italians developed extensive friendship and kinship circles, numerous political clubs, important avenues for upward mobility, and commonplace community celebrations. Festivals and indigenous organizations, including mutual-benefit societies, were central to Italian American communities.[71]

Stereotypes

By the end of the nineteenth century, nativist stereotypes of the "apelike" Irish were giving way to negative stereotypes of southern and eastern European immigrants, especially those who were Catholics or Jews. Italian immigrants were regularly seen as an "inferior race" and scorned by white nativists as "dangerous, contemptible, inferior, and disloyal"—the "off-scourings of the world." The dominant racial frame was extended to cover them, often classifying them with black Americans. For example, in 1890s New Orleans, one historian notes, "Native (non-Italian) whites generally classed (Italians) with Negroes, because they did what the natives looked upon as Negroes' work."[72]

Popular writers, scholars, and members of Congress warned of the peril of allowing these "inferior" racial–ethnic stocks from Europe into the United States. For example, Kenneth Roberts, a prominent journalist, expressed a common fear that the newer immigrants would make Americans a *mongrel* race: "The American nation was founded and developed by the Nordic race, but if a few more million members of the Alpine, Mediterranean and Semitic races are poured among us, the result must inevitably be a hybrid race of people as worthless and futile as the good-for-nothing mongrels of Central America and southeastern Europe."[73] Nativist writers of northern European origin included Italians and European Jews when they spoke of "Alpine, Mediterranean, and Semitic races."

Yet, in spite of these vicious attacks, Italian Americans were slowly and eventually treated by various government agencies at all levels as "white." Unlike most African Americans, and once they were citizens, they could vote, serve on juries, and intermarry with other European Americans. They had a paradoxical societal status and were pressured to become ever more acculturated to the northern European core culture.[74]

Stereotypes of Inferiority in Intelligence

In the first three decades of the twentieth century, Anglo-Protestant stereotypes of southern and eastern European immigrants' intellectual inferiority were based in part on misreadings of the results of new psychological tests inaccurately labeled intelligence quotient or **IQ tests**, *which are paper-and-pencil or object/symbol manipulation tests that advocates incorrectly claim can measure a global human intelligence.* The term *intelligence quotient (IQ) test* is inaccurate because the tests measure only selected, learned verbal and quantitative skills, not a basic or general intelligence. In 1912, the U.S. analyst Henry Goddard gave the European researcher Alfred Binet's diagnostic test and related tests to immigrants from southern and eastern Europe. His data supposedly showed that 83 percent of Jewish and 79 percent of Italian immigrants were "feeble-minded," a category naively defined in terms of low scores on the English-language tests. During World War I, prominent psychologists developed verbal and performance tests for large-scale testing of wartime draftees. Detailed analyses, published in the 1920s, gained public attention because of the racial-inferiority interpretation many northern European American psychologists placed on test scores of the southern and eastern European immigrants among the draftees.[75]

In 1923, Carl Brigham, a Princeton psychologist who later played a major role in developing college entrance tests, argued for the intellectual inferiority of these (white) immigrant groups, including Italian Americans, drawing on data from the Army tests. Average scores for foreign-born draftees ranged from highs of 14.87 for English draftees and 14.34 for Scottish draftees, to an average of 13.77 for all white draftees, to lows of 10.74 for Polish and 11.01 for Italian draftees. The relatively low test scores for groups such as Italian Americans were explained in aggressively *racial* terms; those low-scoring groups were considered not only unintelligent but "inferior racial stocks."[76]

The political implications of these tests were proclaimed: Immigration limits were necessary, and political means (immigration barriers and even government-ordered, forced sterilization) should be developed to prevent the continued propagation of these "defective strains" in the population.[77] Here was pseudoscientific support for such government action as the passage of the racist 1924 Immigration Act, which would soon severely restrict southern European immigration.

The U.S. government itself played an important role in the stereotyping of Italian immigrants, a point that Omi and Winant underscore in their racial formation theory (see Chapter 2). Psychologists working with government agencies helped to generate the official view of these immigrants as undesirable racial–ethnic groups, and Congress used their research to support racist arguments against continuing southern and eastern European immigration.

The "intelligence" differences measured by the usually brief psychological tests were assumed to reflect the inferior or superior genetic background of the European "racial" stocks. In the early decades of the twentieth century, few analysts and political leaders seriously considered the possibility that the linguistic (English), cultural (northern European American), and educational bias in the tests and in the psychologists' interpretive procedures could account for the "racial" differences.[78]

Immigrant leaders developed aggressive strategies for dealing with concern over "racial" lineage. One prominent Italian American leader, Fiorello La Guardia, suffered personal attacks that incorporated stereotypes. For his criticism of officials such as President Herbert Hoover he received letters such as the following: "You should go back where you belong and advise Mussolini how to make good honest citizens in Italy. The Italians are preponderantly our murderers and boot-leggers."[79] It is striking that even today, as one scholar has put it, "In TV shows, advertisements, children's cartoons, and even some university programs emphasizing cultural diversity, that bias [stereotypes of ignorance or criminality] persists despite the Italian-American intellectual foundation on the grandeur of Dante, the stateliness of Virgil, the experimentation of Pirandello, and the metaphysical complexity of Petrarch and the Troubadours," not to mention the art of Michelangelo and Da Vinci.[80]

Verbal slurs that have often been hurled at Italian Americans—*dago, wop,* and *guinea*—reveal the intensity of anti-Italian hostility. *Dago,* a corruption of the Spanish name Diego, was originally used for Spaniards or Mexicans. After 1880, it was applied by northern European Americans to Italian immigrants. The term *guinea* was an early term for African Americans, whose ancestors had come from the Guinea coast of Africa. After 1880, northern European Americans used *guinea* to classify Italians as "no better than blacks."[81] The way in which these old epithets from the dominant white racial frame were transferred to later racial and ethnic groups reveals not only the fear that established groups often have of newcomers but also the way in which certain European newcomers have come to be classified, as in the case of the Italian immigrants for a time, as somehow *not* white.

The Mafia Myth

The most persistent Italian American stereotype has been the **"Mafia" myth**—*the stereotyped image of Italian Americans as being substantially involved in organized crime*. As early as the 1870s, Italians were depicted as lawless, knife-wielding thugs. Even a report of the influential U.S. Immigration Commission, issued in the early 1900s, argued that criminality was "inherent in the Italian race." However, the validity of the criminality stereotype was early contradicted by government data. In 1910, the imprisonment rate for Italian immigrants was *much lower* than public stereotypes would suggest: 527 prisoners per 100,000 for the Italian born, compared with 727 for the allegedly "superior" English and Welsh foreign born.[82]

Small-scale crime, fostered by poverty and discrimination, was a problem in central city communities, but usually did not involve criminal conspiracy. In the 1930s Prohibition catapulted some Italian Americans into organized crime, at the time controlled mostly by Irish and Jewish Americans. By 1940, a few Italian American "crime families" were operating in cities. For many immigrant groups, such crime has been one of the only avenues for economic mobility. Unfortunately, the Sicilian word *Mafia* has been used to describe organized crime, although many of these gangsters have been neither Sicilian nor Italian. Significantly, Italian Americans had *low* crime rates in the 1920s and 1930s.[83]

The image of Italian criminality has taken on a mythological character. Well into the twenty-first century now, Italian names for criminals in various TV programs and movies have often implied ties to a "Mafia." Without exception, every non-Italian respondent in one study of white ethnics in California and Pennsylvania used the Mafia and gangsters to characterize Italian Americans; most said their ideas were based on media images. A mid-1990s national survey found that most of those surveyed still believed that the majority of Italian Americans were linked to organized crime. In addition, a recent survey of teenagers reported in *Parade* magazine revealed that most still associated Italian Americans "with blue collar jobs or the mob."[84]

In 1997, CBS aired a miniseries, *Bella Mafia,* about Italian American wives linked to organized crime. Some Italian Americans, including the National Italian American News Bureau, protested the gangster stereotypes and encouraged viewers to protest by not watching the program. This program was soon followed by a more popular television program, *The Sopranos,* and by stereotypical movies such as *Analyze This,* which presented Italian Americans as disturbed gangsters. *The Sopranos* show was praised by prominent media commentators as one of the great television shows. The Italic Institute of America did a survey of some 1200 Hollywood movies made between the late 1920s and the 2000s and found that some *70 percent* put Italian characters in negative roles. Today, the Institute regularly documents many negative stereotypes of Italians and Italian Americans still in various Hollywood, television, and other media presentations, including cartoons for children. Not only is there the problem with the obvious stereotyping in such media products but, as Alba and Abdel-Hady have noted, "On a deeper level, contemporary stereotypes present Italian Americans as individuals who have advanced materially in American society but have not absorbed the values and mores of its middle class; in their outlooks and their lack of appreciation for intellectual matters, they are depicted as little different from their immigrant peasant forebears."[85]

Over the last few decades, Italian Americans have fought these stereotypes. In the early 2000s, for example, the American Italian Defamation Association filed a lawsuit against Time Warner for televising *The Sopranos* series, thereby challenging its criminality stereotyping. Italian American groups have also fought against stereotyping on labels and trademarks. One lawyer working with the Commission for Social Justice of the Order of the Sons of Italy in America—a group with half a million members—successfully stopped the government from issuing label trademarks insulting to Italian Americans, including product labels with terms such as "Mafia Mob" or "Cosa Nostra." Moreover, school children

and their parents in New York protested the movie *Shark Tale* because its animated shark characters were depicted with the names, accents, and images of stereotypical "Mafia" types.[86]

Significantly, by the 1990s, FBI statistics showed that only a very small percentage of the 500,000 Americans involved in organized crime were Italian Americans. Except in a few New York City and Chicago neighborhoods, the power of Italian American "crime families" had declined significantly. As has often been the case, recent immigrant groups, including some from Asia and Latin America, have taken over much of organized crime in cities from previous immigrant groups.[87]

Stereotypes and Discrimination

One study of the portrayal of Italian Americans on prime-time television that examined a sample of 263 programs for one 1980s season found that negative images of Italian Americans outnumbered positive images by two to one. Most of the ninety-six Italian characters in the shows studied were men with low-status jobs, which was quite out of touch with the actual societal reality.[88]

One Italian American in California described his experience with ethnic slurs: "When I joined the office in the new location I became a member of the Rotary Club, and of course there were very few Italian members. So the minute I came on board, they started referring to me as the Godfather of the country." He went on to say that he found this humor degrading; he had to explain that he had no ties to a so-called Mafia. Numerous Italian Americans have reported similar experiences, including barbed Mafia jokes and discrimination in corporate workplaces.[89]

The Mafia myth has also caused serious problems for those in the public sphere. It was used by some Republicans in the 1984 presidential election, when a smear campaign aimed at Democratic vice-presidential candidate Geraldine Ferraro, an Italian American, insinuated that *she* had important "mob connections" because her husband inherited a business founded by his father and the brother of a New York crime figure. Recalling the first time her son had been called a "wop," when he was young, Ferraro indicated that her family's encounters with anti-Italian attitudes were common. One 1990s national survey by the Joint Civic Committee found that three-fourths of Americans still viewed Italians as somehow linked to crime. Not surprisingly, research has shown that this common stereotype has hurt Italian American political candidates in numerous elections in recent decades.[90]

Among all European ancestry groups in Alba's study of white ethnics in a metropolitan area in New York, Italian American respondents reported encountering the most ethnic stereotypes. Stereotyped images referred to physical appearance, mannerisms, family life, as well as Mafia connections. Non-Italian white respondents in a California and Pennsylvania study held both negative and positive stereotypes of Italian Americans. Some described Italians as dirty, loud, temperamental, selfish, unambitious, combative, and not bright; others listed characteristics such as having excellent food, doing well in business, being affectionate, and being family oriented.[91]

 How have the stereotypes used in portrayals of Irish Americans, Italian Americans, and African Americans been similar and different?

Conflict

The old myth of peaceful group progress is dispelled by the history of Italian Americans' struggles with Anglo-Protestant nativists, Irish Catholics, and African Americans. Irish and Italian Americans fought on the streets of Boston by the 1860s, and Italian parents sometimes accompanied their children to school for protection. By the 1880s, Anglo-Protestant nativist attempts to control immigrants from southern Italy took the form of vigilante action. In the 1880s, in Buffalo, New York, more than 300 Italians—most of the local Italian population—were detained by police after an incident in which one Italian killed another; only two were found to be holding weapons. Replying to the governor of New York, the police chief explained, stereotypically, that he thought Italian Americans as a rule carried concealed weapons and threatened local social order.[92]

Legalized Killings

In the South during this early period, dozens of Italian immigrants were killed by mobs motivated by economic competition and a desire to maintain racial–ethnic lines. Italian immigrants were viewed as a threat to white solidarity because they were more likely than other whites at that time to support civil rights for African Americans. They often worked as laborers alongside black Americans or sold to them as shopkeepers. In one town, five Italian American shopkeepers were lynched for this reason. Another well-publicized attack occurred in New Orleans after the 1891 murder of a police superintendent who was investigating crime among Italian immigrants. Numerous immigrants were jailed for the murder; the police refused to intervene when a large group led by prominent citizens stormed the jail and lynched eleven of them. Anglo-American newspapers and major political figures praised the deed, advancing the stereotype of Italian criminality. The Italian government insisted that lynchers be punished and reparations be paid to families. President Benjamin Harrison weakly apologized, but the Italian minister to Washington was brought home, thereby creating major tensions between the U.S. and Italian governments.[93]

One of the most famous U.S. murder trials was that of Nicola Sacco and Bartolomeo Vanzetti, Italian-born workers tried for robbery and murder in Massachusetts. Numerous witnesses testified that the defendants were elsewhere at the time of the crime, but the judge ignored the testimony of Italian-born witnesses. Anti-Italian prejudice was very evident at the trial, and the men did not receive a fair trial. As suspected "radicals," they were executed in 1927 in the midst of public hysteria over left-wing, "un-American" activities.[94]

Conflict and Cooperation with African Americans

Since the 1930s, conflict has arisen between Italian Americans and groups positioned lower on the U.S. socioeconomic ladder. "Law and order," school desegregation, and busing have been major issues in various metropolitan areas. During the 1960s and 1970s, some Italian American leaders complained that black Americans were the "darlings" of white liberals and received disproportionate government aid. Italian Americans in some areas of cities such as Newark and Philadelphia found themselves surrounded by large numbers of black immigrants from other regions, who were often poor. Realistic fears about urban crime were coupled with exaggerated views of the black role in crime, much as

Anglo-Protestant fears earlier had exaggerated the Italian role in urban crime.[95]

In 1990, a group of Italian American youth killed a black youth, Yusuf Hawkins, in predominantly Italian Bensonhurst in New York City. The attackers believed the victim was dating an Italian American woman. Actually, Hawkins had gone there to inquire about buying a car. Members of the Federation of Italian American Organizations actively sought to calm racial tensions, calling Italian residents' attention to their history of being discriminated against. [96]

Opinion surveys of Italian Americans in the 1960s and 1970s revealed significant antiblack prejudice and strong opposition to neighborhood desegregation. Nonetheless, a number of Italian Americans played a very important role in assisting the black civil rights movement of the 1960s. Included were singer Tony Bennett, Father Geno Baroni, and Father James Groppi, sometimes called the most important white activist in the movement. Grassroots activist Viola Liuzzo was killed by white supremacists for her involvement in the black civil rights movement. Moreover, by the 1990s, Italian American attitudes expressed in opinion surveys, like those of many other whites, had liberalized on some racial matters, at least in public opinion surveys. Sixty percent of Italian Americans, compared with 55 percent of all whites, said they would work for improved racial relations, and 85 percent of Italian Americans, compared with 79 percent of all whites, said they would vote for a black presidential candidate.[97]

Yet, today among Italian Americans, as among other white Americans, a sizable proportion remain openly racist in certain attitudes toward black Americans, a situation that has on occasion fueled antiblack discrimination and violence, such as the Bensonhurst attack. Many Italian Americans have abandoned much of the left-wing politics of their first generation for more conservative politics, including their viewpoints on racial issues. The scholar David Richards has shown the process by which Italian Americans came to "buy into" the racist system, thereby accepting a place in the "white race" and an orientation that weakened their earlier strong commitments to multiracial democracy. Another scholarly book, *Are Italians White?*, summarizes social science research, including some on New York communities, that shows how central-city location and struggles against northern European discrimination eventually led many Italian Americans "to assert a white identity in order to effectively distance themselves from their Brown and Black neighbors, and receive the ample rewards that come with being white."[98]

Politics

The first major Italian influence on U.S. politics was that of Filippo Mazzei, a friend of Thomas Jefferson who came to the colonies to help with agricultural development. Mazzei helped Jefferson bring legal reforms to Virginia. Mazzei's writings speak vigorously of freedom and include phrases similar to those Jefferson later used in the Declaration of Independence—such as Mazzei's phrase, "All men are by nature created free and independent."[99]

City Politics

During and after the great migration of 1880–1920, Irish political leaders recruited Italian Americans into the Democratic Party. In Chicago, Italian Americans benefited from political patronage, and many were employed by the city. By 1892, they elected a Chicago alderman, and soon had a few representatives in the Illinois legislature. Italians had won significant elective offices in New York City by the 1920s.[100] By the 1930s, Italian Americans were mayors of large cities such as New York, San Francisco, and New Orleans, and of a few smaller cities. Prominent Italian American mayors in recent decades have included Anthony Celebrezze (Cleveland), Joseph Alioto (San Francisco), George Moscone (San Francisco), Frank Rizzo (Philadelphia), and Rudolph Giuliani (New York City), the latter also a recent contender for the Republican presidential nomination.

State and National Politics

Prior to 1950, New York had sent only six Italian American representatives to Congress. The most famous was Fiorello La Guardia. In Congress he vigorously supported Italian immigration and attacked the anti-Italian immigrant quota system. He was the first Italian American to rise through ethnic politics in New York City, where he was elected mayor in 1934. In his political efforts, La Guardia demonstrated that Italian Americans often supported movements to reform urban machines and promote honest government.[101]

Members of the Order of the Sons (and Daughters) of Italy cheer at a recent New York parade.

International politics has affected Italian American political activities. During the economically oppressive Great Depression of the 1930s, Italian fascist and dictator Benito Mussolini became a hero for many Italian (as well as non-Italian) Americans, although antifascist activity was also a significant force in Italian American communities.

During World War II, Italian American spying and subversion were widely alleged, but not proven, and the use of the Italian language on the radio was prohibited in New York and Boston. Several hundred Italian Americans—legal residents—were imprisoned at a Montana concentration camp where Japanese Americans were interned. More than half a million were officially seen as "enemy aliens" and had to carry identity cards. The property of some was confiscated; restrictions were placed on travel; nighttime curfews were imposed; and some in coastal areas were forced to move. The justification for ignoring the civil rights of many Italian Americans was similar to the rationalizations for the internment of Japanese Americans (see Chapter 10). They were alleged without evidence to represent a security threat. Indeed, in the late 1990s, legislation was introduced in Congress to require the government to acknowledge these civil rights violations. Nonetheless, during World War II federal action against Italian Americans was far less severe than that against Japanese Americans—perhaps because Italian Americans were by that time considered to be "white" by most government officials.[102]

World War II contributed to Italian American mobility. The solidarity with other (especially white) Americans that was generated by the war effort against Germany and Japan helped Italian immigrants and their children assimilate more rapidly to the Anglo-Protestant culture and institutions. Italian Americans enlisted in the armed forces in significant numbers and served in ethnically integrated units. (In contrast, African and Japanese Americans served in segregated units.) The war helped create a vision of the United States that encompassed these ethnic Americans as fully white in terms of citizenship and privilege. In addition, numerous white ethnics, including Italian and Irish Americans, benefited greatly from a huge array of "welfare state" programs after World War II, such as federal home loan and veterans' programs, college aid programs, and Social Security programs. These and other whites had privileged access to these "affirmative action" programs, because white government officials regularly discriminated against Americans of color. In the postwar era, indeed, these ethnic Americans aggressively insisted on white privileges, to the point of violently resisting school and neighborhood racial desegregation and/or engaging in white flight to the suburbs. Over the last several decades, in contrast, small but significant numbers have joined groups—such as civil rights groups in the 1960s and, more recently, the Italian Americans for a Multicultural United States—attacking racism and supporting democratic diversity, even as the majority of these ethnic Americans have continued to accent their white privileges.[103]

Between the 1970s and today, the number of Italian American cabinet members, governors, and state legislators has grown. This signals substantial political advances. Mario Cuomo was a contender for the Democratic Party's presidential nomination in the 1990s, whereas Geraldine Ferraro was the first woman nominated for vice-president. In the late 1990s, New York City's mayor and one of the state's U.S. senators were of Italian ancestry. And since the early 2000s, New York's former longtime mayor, Rudolph Giuliani has been celebrated for his role in providing support for families of victims of the 9/11 World Trade Center attacks. As a result of his popularity, he ran for the Republican presidential nomination in 2008. In addition, in recent years each Congress has had more than two dozen Italian Americans serving as members of the U.S. House of Representatives and the U.S. Senate.

In the 1960s, Republican political strategists began efforts to win white ethnic votes, including the Italian American voters, away from the Democratic Party. Fears of the civil rights demands of Americans of color were manipulated for this purpose. By 1990, poll data indicated that 49 percent of Italian Americans called themselves Republicans, compared with 39 percent who called themselves Democrats. Since then, in national elections, Italian American voters have split their votes, but with a majority usually favoring Republican candidates at the national level. Analysis of national opinion data also indicates that over recent decades Italian Americans as a group have become more conservative on major issues such as capital punishment and immigration restrictions. Still, the data also indicate continuing political liberalism on such matters as

increased government spending to help the poor and troubled central cities.[104]

Italian Americans, like other U.S. ethnic groups, have lobbied politically on behalf of their home country. In the late 1990s, the United Nations was considering a U.S. proposal to add Germany and Japan, but not Italy, as permanent members of the Security Council. Italian American groups organized protests against this "blatant insult" and argued that Italy should be on the Security Council because of its great historical importance in UN activities.[105]

The Economy

Structural adaptation by immigrant groups includes their movement into secondary-organization levels of the host society—into economic as well as political and educational organizations. Economic mobility means attaining higher levels of employment and the attendant economic benefits. Italian Americans started near the bottom of the ladder. The southern Italian immigrants, who came after 1880, were often economically exploited by Anglo-Protestant employers. They had responded to the U.S. demand for unskilled labor in the late nineteenth century.[106]

Early Poverty and Discrimination

Urban poverty, coupled with often low-wage and/or dangerous working conditions, was the lot of most immigrants, as one report put it:

> The Italian immigrant may be maimed and killed in his industrial occupation without a cry and without indemnity. He may die from the 'bends' working in the caissons under the river, without protest; he can be slowly asphyxiated in crowded tenements, smothered in dangerous trades and occupations (which only the ignorant immigrant pursues, not the native American); he can contract tuberculosis in unsanitary factories and sweatshops.[107]

Some among the first generation of the post-1880 Italian immigrants were skilled workers, but most were unskilled. Women were often employed in low-paying trade occupations.

Isolate, small-group, and institutionalized discrimination (see Chapter 1) held Italian Americans back. From the first years, new Italian residents were "abused in public and isolated in private, cuffed in the works and pelted on the streets, fined and

Immigrant workers in a U.S. factory at the turn of the twentieth century.

imprisoned on the smallest pretext, cheated of their wages, and crowded by the score into converted barns and tumble-down shanties that served as boarding houses."[108] Discrimination was blatant. An early ad for laborers to build a New York City reservoir listed daily wages as $1.30 to $1.50 for "whites" and $1.15 to $1.25 for "Italians."[109] Then, as now, informal networks were a major means of circulating job information. In most job networks, Anglo-Protestant and Irish American sponsors functioned to protect their own workers and discriminated against Italian American workers.

Upward Mobility

Economic progress came slowly but steadily. The proportion of Italian American workers who were laborers dropped from 50 percent in 1916 to 31 percent fifteen years later. Small-business and skilled blue-collar positions were more common by 1931. The Great Depression slowed advancement but did not stop it. By 1939, Italian Americans had begun to supplant Jewish Americans as the major group in a number of important unions of skilled workers. Indeed, first- and second-generation Italian Americans were very important in the development of industrial unions, participating in numerous major strikes from the 1910s to the 1920s, as well as important leftist (for example, socialist) movements of the period. Socialist political movements in Italian communities were mostly ended by the execution of Sacco and Vanzetti, the repressive Red Scare by the federal government in the 1920s, and the repressive McCarthyism later during the 1950s. One result of this political repression was to pressure Italian Americans to become more conservative. Today, Italian Americans are more politically conservative as a group than are Italians in Italy, as well as than their own immigrant ancestors.[110]

By the 1920s, organized crime was providing some better-paying jobs for Italian Americans in cities. Significantly, the "good citizens" of the cities, often Anglo-Protestants and other non-Italian residents, were those who actively patronized the bootlegging, prostitution, and gambling operations of these Italian Americans. Later, money from organized crime would flow to legitimate enterprises, as with earlier groups. Children of those who were successful in organized crime often moved out of illegitimate enterprises. This trend supports "the thesis that for Italian Americans, as for other ethnic groups, organized crime has been a way station on the road to ultimately respectable roles in American society."[111] Of course, only a small percentage of Italian Americans ever achieved upward mobility in this way. Most did it by means of legitimate work efforts.

Numerous Italian Americans have become nationally prominent as entrepreneurs, professionals, authors, and scientists. Amadeo Giannini, founder of the Bank of America, made his fortune in California by financing businesses and ranches. Italian Americans such as Joseph Di Giorgio and the Gallo brothers began to play major roles in restaurant, agricultural, wine, and contracting businesses. Scientists Enrico Fermi and Salvador Luria won Nobel Prizes. Also, in recent decades the growth of the Italian American Writers Association has signaled the significant number of important Italian American writers, such as Gay Talese and Pietro DiDonato. Moreover, as with groups before and after them, Italian Americans have found upward mobility in sports. Notable examples include boxer Rocky Marciano and baseball Hall-of-Famers Joe DiMaggio, Ernie Lombardi, Yogi Berra, and Tommy Lasorda.[112]

 What key factors have contributed to the socioeconomic mobility of Irish Americans and Italian Americans?

Recent Decades

By the 1950s, Italian Americans had advanced economically, yet at least one study suggested that second-generation Italian Catholics had yet to equal white Protestants in the proportion holding higher-level white-collar jobs. Several decades later, the 1990 census showed more economic mobility. By then, compared with the total white population, Italian Americans had a greater proportion in professional, managerial, technical, and other white-collar jobs—and a smaller proportion in blue-collar jobs.[113]

Socioeconomic progress continues. As can be seen in Table 4.2, the 2008 census survey revealed that median family income for Italian Americans ($80,111) was substantially higher than that of the general population, while the poverty rate for Italian Americans was well below that of the general population, though higher than that for English Americans (see Chapter 3).[114]

Some Persisting Problems

Over the past few decades, ethnic discrimination targeting Italian Americans has sometimes been a problem at higher-level occupational levels. For example, the failure to hire Italian Americans at the City University of New York (CUNY) was documented in a 1970s study: "In decision-making positions of Dean,

TABLE 4.2   People with Italian Ancestry: Selected Population Characteristics (2008 Census)

	People with Italian Ancestry	Total U.S. Population
Number	17,748,513	304,059,728
Median age (years)	35.4	36.9
Foreign born	3.2%	12.5%
Percent female	50.3%	50.7%
High school degree or greater (25 years old and over)	91.8%	85%
Having at least a college degree (25 years old and over)	33.3%	27.7%
Median family income	$80,111	$63,366
Percent of individuals below poverty line	7.9%	13.2%

Source: U.S. Bureau of the Census, "2008 American Community Survey." All figures are estimates based on a large national survey and have modest margins of error. See endnotes for further explanation.

Director and Chairman of the system's 18 colleges, there are only 20 Italian Americans out of a total of 504 positions."[115] In addition, only a small percentage of the faculty members were Italian. In 1975, an affirmative action program for Italian American faculty was put into place, but over the years since then, the percentage of Italian American full-time faculty has not increased significantly (from 4.8 percent in 1978 to 5.9 percent in 2006). Today, Italian Americans still constitute less than 6 percent of CUNY's faculty, while the student body is estimated to be close to one-fifth Italian American.[116]

In the 1990s, thus, CUNY professors protested discrimination in the hiring of Italian Americans in a class-action suit against the university. Eventually, CUNY settled a lawsuit brought by the director of the university's Italian-American Institute; CUNY's administration agreed to make the Institute a permanent part of Queens College and to hire a distinguished senior professor in Italian American studies.[117]

In addition, one study by the American Academy of Arts and Sciences found a significant underrepresentation of Italian Americans among its 3700 distinguished U.S. members, drawn from numerous scientific and artistic fields. Although the percentage of the group that is Italian American has been growing, it still shows underrepresentation (1.3 percent of all members) when the percentage of Italian Americans on U.S. college and university faculties (4.6 percent) is used as a rough standard. By various mechanisms, probably including some anti-Italian stereotyping, Italian Americans are still excluded by the elite that chooses members of this prestigious organization.[118]

Over the past decade, some private clubs have continued to bar Italian Americans, and Italian Americans are still underrepresented in the top management of major corporations. Still, the overall picture of recent occupational and income mobility for Italian Americans, a white ethnic group discriminated against on a large scale only a few decades ago, is impressive. Some, such as Lee Iacocca, have been touted as presidential candidates; one (Rudolph Giuliani) was in the running for the nomination. Two (Antonin Scalia and Samuel Alito) are members of the U.S. Supreme Court. Italian American men are prominent among movie directors. Women of Italian American ancestry have moved into important positions in politics—notably the first woman Speaker of

the U.S. House (2007), Nancy Pelosi—and in the mass media, including major commentators such as Anna Quindlen. The majority of Italian Americans have made strides up the socioeconomic ladder, and on numerous socioeconomic indexes they have now surpassed Anglo-Protestant Americans.

Education

Many immigrants came from areas in Italy where the poor received little schooling. Numerous immigrant families made sacrifices to put their first child through elementary school and then expected this child to get a job to put later children through school. Anglo-Protestant educators were often concerned over the alleged inferiority of Italian Americans. Schools became "pressure cookers" of Americanization in which these educators sought aggressively to teach Italian immigrants' children Anglo-Protestant norms about dress, work, and language. Ethnic discrimination was often a fact of school life.[119]

Despite such obstacles, Italian Americans made dramatic progress. By 1970, Italian Americans' median level of educational attainment was higher than that of the total U.S. population and only slightly lower than that of the total white population. Table 4.2 shows that by 2008, Italian Americans 25 years old and older had achieved educational attainments—91.8 percent with at least a high school diploma and 33.3 percent with at least a college degree—well above those for the U.S. population as a whole.[120]

Religion

The Roman Catholic Church has been very important in the lives of most Italian Americans. Preexisting Irish Catholic churches were often overwhelmed by the numbers of Italian immigrants. For many Italians, Irish Catholicism was too orthodox. Religion was often not an intimate part of political identity for the Italian immigrant, as it generally was for the Irish immigrant, whose religious expression was tied to a nationalist heritage of anti-English agitation. Saints have been important to Italian Catholics, as have the religious festivals that have played an important role in socially cementing Italian communities.[121]

Irish American priests often held negative views of Italian parishioners. When some ethnic parishes for

Italian Americans were developed, the latter were warned away, on occasion forcefully, from Irish parishes. Many first-generation Italian Americans preferred to send their children to public schools rather than to Irish-dominated parochial schools. Gradually, Italian Catholicism, with its own festivals and ceremonies, took its place alongside Irish Catholicism.[122]

By the 1960s, one study of New York's Italian and Irish Catholics suggested that third-generation Italians were becoming more "Irishized" in their religious practices. In national surveys between 1988 and 1991, only 70 percent of Italian Americans classified themselves as Catholics, and many of those were nonpracticing. Today, Catholicism generally seems less central for Italian Americans than for Irish Americans. Some have joined Protestant denominations or become nonreligious. Still, today, numerous Italian American communities, such as that on New York's Long Island, have important parades, feasts, and church bazaars honoring traditional saints or the Virgin Mary.[123]

Assimilation or Ethnogenesis?

Today, Italian Americans make up nearly 6 percent of the U.S. population, at about 17.7 million Americans. As Table 4.2 shows, their median age is slightly lower than that of the U.S. median, as is their percentage female. The percentage of the group that is foreign born, at 3.2 percent, is significantly lower than that for the U.S. population as a whole, although higher than for English and Irish Americans.

Significantly, the pressures for acculturation to a British American culture came early for southern and eastern European immigrants. Often concentrated in "Little Italies," Italian immigrants learned Italian dialects other than their own, although most picked up some English. In addition to language and community factors, cultural adaptation was slowed by poverty, the intention of many to return home, and anti-immigrant discrimination.[124] The first-generation family was in transition, cross-pressured between the old Italian and new U.S. ways. Families often became less patriarchal, and kin solidarity often weakened somewhat, as did ties to a conservative Catholic religion. Children were more on their own. Speaking Italian at home was a point of intergenerational conflict, because younger members felt school pressures to speak only English.[125]

Marriage was a point of intergenerational conflict. First-generation parents saw it as a family matter, whereas children tended to see it as an individual matter. Given this tension, second-generation families adapted in different ways. One type substantially abandoned old ways, changing the Italian name and moving out of an Italian area. This was rare. A second type rejected the old ways in part, sometimes by moving out of a concentrated Italian community but maintaining close ties to the first generation. This was the largest group. A third type stayed in the old community and retained many of the old ways.[126] Today, although they have spread to states such as Florida and Illinois in significant numbers, Italian Americans are still concentrated in the North. They are no longer a predominantly central-city group but are about as likely to reside in suburbs as the average white American.

Structural Assimilation

Structural assimilation involves the movement of a group into the secondary organizations—the businesses and bureaucracies—of the larger society, as well as into its primary social networks: social clubs, neighborhoods, and friendship circles. Structural movement into workplaces and other areas by Italian Americans over the first several decades came with considerable resistance from earlier European groups. Positioning at the lower economic levels was a fact of life for a time. However, in recent decades Italian Americans have made impressive gains in employment, income, and education and significant advances in politics. This upward educational and occupational mobility has contributed to incorporation in other areas. Increasing equal-status contact with members of other white groups in the workplace, the suburbs, and colleges has in turn created cross-ethnic friendship networks and marriages.[127]

The economic success of Italian Americans and other white ethnic groups is sometimes compared with the relative lack of success of other groups, such as African Americans. Why were Italian Americans so successful in assimilating over time to Anglo-Protestant institutions and organizations? The answer to this lies not only in the hard work and sacrifice of several generations of Italian Americans, for those factors are also characteristic of African Americans. It lies also in the timing of Italian immigrants' entry into the United States. Jobs and housing near jobs were available to many Italians who arrived in the late nineteenth and early twentieth centuries. Second and third generations emerged with enough economic support from parents to obtain the education needed for better-paying jobs, which opened up for white ethnics during and after World War II.[128] Expansion of jobs on the middle rungs of the occupational ladder made upward mobility possible. Of even greater importance is the fact that the poverty and discrimination that Italian immigrants faced, although serious, were never as thoroughgoing as the extreme poverty and severe discrimination faced by African Americans and other non-European Americans.

During the World War II period, wartime solidarity hastened the assimilation of white ethnics, including Italian Americans, into Anglo-Protestant institutions, including regular units of the armed forces. In contrast, African and Japanese Americans were kept in segregated units. After the war, Italian Americans took advantage of new federal housing and veterans' programs, "affirmative action" oriented primarily to whites, in order to buy homes and get a college education.

Residential patterns have contributed to a continuing strong ethnic identity. One 1980s study in a large New York metropolitan area found that Italian Americans there were still one of the most residentially concentrated white ethnic groups. They were more likely than other groups to name a relative as a close friend, and they had one of the highest rates of intraethnic friendships.[129] Although kinship and primary-group ties often remain strong, suburbanization has shrunk their formerly large ethnic enclaves. In 1980 and 1990, most of the nearly 3 million Italian Americans in the Greater New York area already lived outside of concentrated Italian American neighborhoods. In the twenty-first century now New York's Italian Americans are much less concentrated in primarily Italian neighborhoods than in previous decades.[130]

Early studies of marriages in New Haven (1870) and Chicago (1920) found high rates of in-marriage for early Italians: 94 to 98 percent of all marriages were endogamous. In-marriage decreased significantly in subsequent decades. Although 84 percent of the respondents in a 1970s study reported that both of their parents were of Italian ancestry, only 44 percent were themselves married to Italian Americans. Still, the rate of religious endogamy was high: Most marriages with non-Italians were with Catholics. Exogamous marriages were more likely for those with higher-status educational and occupational achievements. More recently, one analysis estimated that 73 percent of Italian Americans in their 30s were marrying outside their ethnic group.[131]

Some social scientists, such as Richard Alba, have argued that, although ethnicity is still important for earlier Italian American generations, a transition is underway, with a strong sense of ethnicity receding for later generations. Italian Americans are becoming ever more structurally integrated into the white mainstream: Just over half of Italian American respondents in Alba's New York State study reported ethnically unmixed ancestry. For those born after 1940, the proportion dropped to one-third. National data today suggest high levels of mixed ancestry. A much more structurally assimilated Italian American group is likely emerging as younger generations replace earlier ones.[132]

An Italian Identity?

Identificational assimilation involves giving up one's ethnic identity for that of the dominant Anglo-Protestant culture. For many Italian Americans this seems to be happening, but rather slowly. Ethnic ties and accents are still found in older generations and among all generations in or near old ethnic community enclaves. In numerous substantially Italian American neighborhoods, especially in northern cities, older Italian Americans and new Italian immigrants of recent decades seem to be helping to keep some distinctive Italian cultural characteristics alive. One 1980s study of Belmont, a community in the Bronx with a substantial Italian American flavor, found some persisting ethnic neighborhoods and traditions.[133] And a 1980s study of Italian Americans in Scottsdale, Arizona, found that, rather than losing their cultural identity, these respondents had preserved some Italian American culture. In the New York State study cited earlier, Italian Americans were the most likely of the white ethnic groups to feel a sense of ethnic identity and to consider ethnic identity very important.[134]

Historian Marcus Lee Hansen once argued that there is often an increase in ethnic awareness in the third generation of an immigrant group; this substantially assimilated generation vigorously searches out its ethnic roots. One can extend this perhaps to even later generations. Younger Italian Americans have faced significantly less discrimination and stereotyping than older generations. This has enabled them to express their ethnicity more openly. Interestingly, in her 1990s New Jersey study, Tardi found a strong pride in ethnic identity among Italian Americans of the first, second, *and* third generations. Today, the structural factors associated with greater freedom to express ethnic pride, such as diminishing overt discrimination and increasing numbers of visible Italian Americans in public life, have doubtless affected all generations.[135]

One study of Italian Americans in California found a relationship between the strength of ethnic networks and identity and the work an individual does. Most working-class Italian Americans no longer worked with large numbers of other Italian Americans and therefore expressed their ethnic identity differently from shopkeepers and independent professionals, who were better able to express their Italian American ethnicity in their workplaces, such as by serving a partially ethnic clientele. Participation in the economy may not work to destroy ethnic identity, depending on the character of one's participation and where one works.[136]

Andrew Greeley's *ethnogenesis* model seems to fit the Italian experience. Italians came to the United States with significant differences from the dominant British American group, but they shared some historical background (in Europe) and a Christian religious tradition with that dominant group. Over time, interaction in schools and media influences served to narrow the gap. Italian Americans assimilated in major ways to the Anglo-Protestant host culture, but in other ways retained distinctiveness. Because of their strong national heritage, residential segregation, and strong community and kinship networks, a distinctive U.S. ethnic group developed over time. Today, Italian Americans are no longer dominated by their national heritage, but most have not yet become just like British Protestant Americans. For the most part, they remain Italian *and* American. As a group, Italian Americans have experienced very substantial adaptation and incorporation in the society, but without complete assimilation as yet, especially at the level of identity.

Some scholars see structural forces such as increasing intermarriage, increasing education, loss of the Italian language, and residential mixing in suburbs as further diminishing, if not eventually eradicating, this sense of ethnic identity among most Italian Americans. Membership in numerous Italian American organizations is declining. And the remaining sense of Italian American identity has not retarded the increasing rates of intermarriage.

Still, the continuing presence of important Italian American organizations such as the National Italian American Foundation, as well as significant numbers of foreign-born Italian Americans, continues to foster important connections to the old ethnic identity. Among Italian Americans, and in the larger society, there seems to be an increased interest in things Italian, such as opera, and in the Italian language, which has experienced a major increase in people interested in learning it and writing in it (for example, poetry) in recent years. Several colleges and universities, including Brooklyn College, Queens College, other parts of The City University of New York, and Stony Brook University have offered courses or programs in Italian American studies. And in cities where there are still large Italian American populations, there is still much evidence of Italian American culture—with its accent on certain types of food and sports, and on an array of Italian American religious-holiday feasts. These annual religious celebrations number in the hundreds and typically accent Catholic saints and religious devotion. Among the many feast celebrations is the Feast of San Gennaro in New York City, and St. Joseph's feast day is celebrated in several cities. These religious-holiday celebrations are helping to maintain a distinctive Italian American identity and to connect Italian American communities to each other and to Italy.[137]

Recently a leading Italian American social scientist, Michael Parenti, has argued there is continuing evidence of a strong ethnic heritage and identity for Italian Americans:

> At the present time ethnic awareness still retains a significant saliency even among those who attain high levels of education and professional training— as demonstrated by the rich offering of scholarly papers presented at the yearly meetings of the American Italian Historical Association. . . . Ethnic identity is not only reactive but proactive, not only a defense against derogatory stereotypes, not only a compensatory assurance of group worth, but a positive enjoyment, a celebration of our history and culture in this country and in Italy. It is a way of

connecting with others in what too often is a friend-less and ruthless market society, a nurturing identity that is larger than the self yet smaller than the nation.[138]

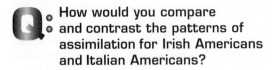

How would you compare and contrast the patterns of assimilation for Irish Americans and Italian Americans?

A Note on Ethnic Diversity among White Americans

There are numerous European ethnic groups other than the Italian, Irish, and English American groups that we have considered at some length. For reasons of space, we cannot assess in detail the many other groups that make up the white population. We will pause briefly to note how diverse this population is. A 2008 American Community Survey by the Census Bureau interviewed respondents across the country. The Census survey asked about ancestry of respondents and recorded the first and second ancestries given. Survey reports estimate the numbers for certain national-origin populations. Table 4.3 lists national-origin groups with more than 300,000 people giving first and second ancestry responses (combined).[139]

Those Americans in the largest ethnic groups mostly have ancestries linked to northern and central Europe. The largest groups listed are German, Irish (and Scotch-Irish), English, Italian, French, and Polish ancestries, in that order. Russia and the Netherlands, as well as Sweden and Norway, also have many representatives in the U.S. population. The second list refers to numerous countries or areas that have generally supplied fewer immigrants than the first list, but that still constitute major places of origin for many ancestors of these contemporary (mostly white) Americans. Distinctive in the second list of ancestral origins are numerous countries or areas in central, southern, and eastern Europe, with a few northern European countries or areas sprinkled in. Leading this list are those with Welsh, Czech, Hungarian, Danish, Portuguese, and Greek as their first or second ancestries. One country in the Americas, Canada, is represented—a country with a large population that also have English, Irish, Scottish, or French ancestries.

TABLE 4.3 Ancestry Groups (2008 American Community Survey)	
Estimated to Be Larger Than 2,000,000	
Dutch	4,928,607
English	27,516,394
French	9,446,760
German	50,271,790
Irish	36,278,332
Italian	17,748,513
Norwegian	4,643,339
Polish	9,887,099
Russian	3,129,738
Scotch-Irish	3,538,444
Scottish	5,827,046
Swedish	4,390,058
Estimated to Be in the 300,000–2,000,000 Range	
Austrian	771,531
Belgian	394,987
Canadian	716,075
Croatian	427,217
Czech	1,593,535
Danish	1,458,787
Finnish	687,682
Greek	1,350,600
Hungarian	1,538,824
Lithuanian	712,165
Portuguese	1,419,428
Romanian	468,804
Slovak	808,191
Swiss	997,233
Ukrainian	998,246
Welsh	1,980,323

Source: U.S. Bureau of the Census, "2008 American Community Survey." All figures are estimates based on a large national survey and have modest margins of error.

Although these data do not include vague choices and are general estimates from one major sample survey, they do provide insight into how diverse the white population is in the twenty-first century. The data also suggest how the early and large European immigrations were limited to a relatively few countries, for the English, Irish, and German ancestries are by far the largest categories.

Summary

Irish immigration to North America began with the arrival of indentured servants and farmers in the 1700s. This early immigration included more southern Irish than often exaggerated accounts of the northern "Scotch-Irish" have suggested. Most descendants of early migrants were, or became, Protestants and settled disproportionately in the South and frontier areas. Over several generations, many descendants of these early colonists became part of the white-Protestant mainstream. However, a significant proportion remained poor.

After the 1830s, large numbers of Irish Catholic immigrants settled in northern cities, where many suffered discrimination and violence at the hands of Catholic-hating nativists. Movement toward economic equality with older groups was slow for the poverty-stricken Irish Catholics. Conflict, sometimes violent, marked their climb. Frequently seen as political innovators, Irish Catholics shaped urban politics to facilitate their integration into the dominant political and economic institutions. They diversified U.S. religious institutions by bringing in a strong Catholic church-and-school complex.

Economic mobility was so dramatic that by the 1990s, Irish Americans ranked at or above the national average for all whites on important socioeconomic indicators, including educational level, occupational distribution, and income. Today, in the twenty-first century, Irish Americans are a major segment of Middle America.

Today, some descendants of Italian immigrants are still clustered in certain northern cities and states. However, large and increasing numbers are now scattered across suburban areas, mostly with other white groups. The majority remain Catholic, although many are inactive. Italian Americans have played an important role in the U.S. culture, politics, and economy.

Poverty and difficult working conditions greeted the hard-working Italian immigrants. They too were unprepared for intense nativist attacks from Anglo-Protestants, who stereotyped Italian Americans as an inferior, immoral, and criminal people and sought to prove Italian American "racial inferiority." To this day, Italian Americans have been stigmatized by a widespread "Mafia" mythology and have endured substantial discrimination from other white Americans.

Political avenues were closed for a time to Italian immigrants; the economy often consigned Italian Americans to low-paid jobs; and public schools sought to transform them into carbon-copy Anglo-Protestants. Despite these problems, however, immigrants and their descendants persevered. Particularly after World War II, they began to succeed ever more conspicuously in politics, the economy, and education. Economic and political mobility has made them another major U.S. success story, although a considerable cultural-conformity price was often exacted for that success.

Today, Italian Americans are one of the major groups in the U.S. drama of ethnic blending and pluralism. As a group they have retained ethnic distinctiveness that seems likely to persist for some time into the future. Some researchers predict that societal forces such as suburbanization and intermarriage may soon diminish the Italian ethnic identity and accelerate identification with a "European American" or "white American" identity. Other analysts disagree. In any case, they too are now an important segment of Middle America.

Key Terms

"Scotch-Irish"
  immigrants   85
intermarriage   96
endogamy   96

ethnic enclaves 98
IQ tests   99
"Mafia" myth   100

Jewish Americans

BIG PICTURE QUESTIONS

- *What factors have generated numerous Jewish migrations to the United States?*

- *What political and economic changes have Jewish Americans brought to the United States?*

- *What social factors have shaped Jewish Americans as a distinctive U.S. ethnic group?*

In 1913, Leo Frank, a Jewish American and hard-working president of the Atlanta B'nai B'rith, was accused of the murder of a non-Jewish teenager who worked in his factory. Later examination of the contradictory evidence indicated that he could not have committed the crime, but at the time the police were under heavy pressure to find the murderer of the young woman. Targeted by anti-Semitism, Frank was arrested, convicted, and sentenced to hang. Efforts by Jewish leaders to get his case appealed to higher courts failed, and many non-Jewish Georgians cited that legal effort as accelerating their anti-Semitic views. Rabid political demagogues such as Georgia's governor Tom Watson spoke of Jewish Americans as the "scum and dregs of the Parasite Race." Many people were angry when Watson commuted Frank's sentence to life imprisonment and began boycotts of Jewish merchants. Soon, a vigilante group of Georgia's "best citizens" took Frank from a prison farm and hanged him from a tree. For decades afterward, many non-Jewish Georgians strongly insisted that their anti-Semitism and the lynching were justified.[1]

Jewish groups have been scapegoats for the hatreds of the dominant peoples in various countries for thousands of years. From the Egyptian and Roman persecutions in ancient times to massacres in Spain in the 1400s to brutal pogroms in Russia in the 1880s to German Nazi massacres, Jews might be regarded as the most widely oppressed racial or ethnic group in world history. One reason we devote a chapter to Jewish Americans is because of this long and violent history, one that makes clear how oppressive societies can become in regard to modest cultural or physical differences between groups.

Today, a majority of adult Americans know little about this violent past. A survey in seven countries—the United States, Germany, Great Britain, Sweden, Austria, Poland, and France—found that the U.S. respondents were the *least* likely to know that Auschwitz, Dachau, and Treblinka were the names of German Nazi concentration and death camps. Majorities in all countries except the United States had heard of these extermination camps. Ironically, most U.S. respondents did agree that it is important to teach about the **Holocaust** (or **Shoah**), *the German Nazi extermination of millions of European Jews.*[2]

In spite of large-scale and long-term oppression, however, Jews across the globe have forged strong cultural traditions. Intellectual pillars of Western cultures—Karl Marx, Sigmund Freud, and Albert Einstein—were Jews. Jewish Americans have made enormous contributions to the United States—as pioneers in commerce, industrial workers, professionals, scholars, government officials, and entertainers. They have benefited from a political structure separating church and state that prohibits religious qualifications for public office. Jewish immigrants have often come from countries in which they were always outsiders struggling just to survive physically. Unlike the situation in other countries, for the most part U.S. law never became their enemy. Still, more than any other white ethnic group, Jews have been treated as outsiders even in the United States.

By tradition, Jewish ethnicity has been based on matrilineal ancestry: A Jew is one whose mother is Jewish. In the contemporary United States, many Jewish writers define Jews simply as those who identify themselves as Jews.[3] Some Jewish Americans focus their identity primarily on their religion; others define their Jewishness primarily in terms of group membership.*

Migration

From 1500 to World War II

Most early Jewish immigrants came to Atlantic coast colonies in the 1600s seeking economic opportunities denied in Europe. The first community dates from the arrival in 1654 of twenty-three Jews who fled the Catholic Inquisition in Brazil. Most were Sephardic Jews, whose background was the Jewish subculture of Spain.[4] Over the next one hundred years, small numbers of the descendants of those called **Marranos** (originally a derogatory term)—*Jews who were forced to convert publicly to Christianity during the*

---

*In this chapter we will often use the term *Jewish American* as shorthand for Jewish Americans of European descent. However, the reader should keep in mind that there are relatively small Jewish communities with national origins in Iran, Syria, North Africa, and the non-European areas of Russia. There are also small groups of African Americans who adhere to Judaism, as well as small groups of Latino and Asian Jews.

Spanish Inquisition under threat of death, but who privately maintained allegiance to Judaism—came to North American colonies. The immigration of Ashkenazi Jews from England, Germany, and Poland began in the 1700s, and this group soon outnumbered Sephardic Jews. Many were attracted by reports of American prosperity.[5]

After 1820, central European Jews arrived in the U.S. in dramatically increased numbers because of declining economic conditions and increasing anti-Semitism in Europe, as well as in response to U.S. economic expansion. These have often been called "German Jews," although they came from Bohemia and Moravia as well as Germany. By 1860, Jewish American communities and synagogues had been established in many cities.[6]

Eastern European Jews, the largest group of Jewish immigrants, began to arrive in the 1870s. Most came from Russian-controlled areas where anti-Semitism and lack of economic opportunities were push factors. In Russia during the late nineteenth and early twentieth centuries, a series of **pogroms**—*organized, often officially encouraged attacks on Jews*—contributed to significant out-migration.[7] Jewish immigration to the U.S. from 1881 to the 1920s totaled 2.5 million. By the mid-1920s, Jewish Americans composed 3.5 percent of the population. Eastern European Jews constituted a large proportion. These immigrants brought with them a distinctive language and culture, a strong sense of identity, and Orthodox religious observances.[8]

After the 1924 Immigration Act, an overtly racist law aimed at limiting eastern and southern European immigration, went into effect, the number of Jewish newcomers declined. Between 1921 and 1936, fewer than 400,000 entered the U.S. President Franklin Roosevelt's administration did permit a modest increase in refugees from Germany because of the Nazi persecution during World War II. Yet Roosevelt, and his State Department, soon adopted the policy of requiring affidavits of financial solvency and good character and used visa regulations to slow the flow of Jewish refugees. In 1940, the State Department put an end to most such immigration. More than 400,000 slots within U.S. immigration quotas for refugees from countries under German control were left unused between 1933 and 1943. Some unfilled slots likely represent lives lost to Nazi extermination because of the openly anti-Semitic U.S. immigration policy.[9]

From World War II to the Present

After the arrival of thousands of postwar refugees in the late 1940s, Jewish migration tapered off to an estimated 8,000 annually. By the 1970s, however, a new group—Israeli Jewish immigrants—were coming in significant numbers. Many were undocumented immigrants. By the 2000s, there were at least 200,000 in the United States.[10]

Between the late 1960s and today, a new group of Jews from areas in the Soviet Union (today Russia) have come to the United States. This immigration has so far totaled half a million. Many emigrated because of anti-Semitism or societal crises in Russia. Significantly, since the end of the Soviet Communist regimes, "old ethnic and religious hatreds have reentered political discourse, appearing now as a resurgent nationalism" in some eastern European countries.[11]

Estimates based on the National Jewish Population Survey (NJPS) put the current Jewish American population at about 5.2 million. Some analysts argue that, if a broader definition of who is Jewish is used, the figure is higher. An American Jewish Committee estimate based on figures from hundreds of local Jewish American communities puts the figure at nearly 6.5 million—a large proportion of the world's Jewish population. Most Jewish Americans were born in the United States, but about 14 percent are foreign born, a figure higher than for other white ethnic groups. Most live in large metropolitan areas, especially New York–northern New Jersey, Los Angeles–Riverside–Orange counties, and Miami–Ft. Lauderdale. Since the 1930s, Jewish Americans have declined as a percentage of the U.S. population, to about 2 percent of the population today.[12]

Prejudice and Stereotypes

Jewish Americans have frequently been socially defined by non-Jewish outsiders on the basis of physical and/or cultural characteristics. From the 1800s onward, numerous non-Jews in many countries have considered Jews to be a biologically inferior "race."[13] No group in history has suffered a broader range of negative stereotypes for a longer period than have the Jews. For centuries, they have been targets of hostility—that is, **anti-Semitism**, which includes *stereotyping or prejudice toward, or discrimination against, the Jews.* For many centuries some theological writings of Christendom have been rife with anti-Semitism. Jews have been cursed as "Christ killers," as those mainly responsible for Jesus's death—a view Christian immigrants brought to North America. This erroneous view is still articulated by some Christian writers and ministers, as well as in some movies. However, the earliest Christian biblical account, the Gospel of Mark, shows clearly that the Roman authorities were responsible for the crucifixion of Jesus, who was likely seen as a political threat, and only they had such killing power. The Roman authorities crucified thousands of Jews and others they considered as dissidents. If the Jewish authorities had been primarily responsible—and some did collude with the Romans—Jesus would have been stoned to death.[14]

Unlike African, Native, and Latino Americans, who are often stereotyped as unintelligent, Jewish Americans have often been seen as too intelligent and devious. This "devious" stereotype likely developed to explain Jewish Americans' success as "middleman" merchants in U.S. society.[15]

In the late 1800s, a stereotype of Jewish Americans as social climbers was circulated in the media, including then-popular vaudeville shows. Clumsy Jewish figures speaking oddly inflected English were depicted as being out of place in high-society positions. By the 1880s, newspaper and magazine cartoons were caricaturing Jewish Americans as long-nosed, garishly dressed merchants speaking broken English. During this period, Jewish Americans were excluded from many Anglo-Protestant organizations and institutions. For example, in 1877, a prominent banker was denied accommodation in a major New York hotel. The following year a Jewish American was excluded from the New York City Bar Association, and New York's City College banned Jewish Americans from fraternities.[16]

One particularly vicious attack on Jews was the fictional book called *The Protocols of the Elders of Zion*. This highly stereotypical tract was created by the Russian secret police and attempted to show that Jews, as anti-Christian agents, were taking covert control of the world and destroying Western civilization. Automobile pioneer Henry Ford worked to spread vicious anti-Semitic stereotypes. In May 1920, a summary of *The Protocols* appeared in Ford's newspaper in Michigan, boosting the circulation. By the 1920s, this book was widely circulated. Ford's newspaper and *The Protocols* played an important role in a burst of malicious

anti-Semitic stereotypes and discriminatory agitation.[17] Today, numerous hate groups and websites still circulate the vicious *Protocols*.

In subsequent decades, numerous media cartoons and reports stereotyped Jewish Americans as "Communist" sympathizers and alleged that "Jews were taking over the U.S. government." Right after World War II, a *Fortune* magazine poll found that three-fourths of those who felt some U.S. groups had more power than was good for the country cited Jewish Americans.[18]

Various forms of anti-Semitism persist today in the United States and Europe. For example, one recent opinion survey found that one-quarter of U.S. respondents blamed "the Jews" a moderate amount or a great amount for the recent (2009) financial crisis. Also, in the fall of 2009, two leading South Carolina Republican Party officials wrote an opinion piece for a major newspaper characterizing well-off Jewish Americans as penny-pinchers. Not only these officials, but also the newspapers' editors saw such traditional stereotyping as inoffensive. (After protests, the officials apologized.) In addition, the president of a major Baptist organization stated publicly that God does *not* hear the prayers of Jews, and the leader of one conservative group asserted that Jews had a "supernatural" talent for moneymaking. Recently, numerous conservative Christian ministers have written about Jews "being spiritually blind" and in need of Christianizing. Actor Mel Gibson's film *The Passion of the Christ* was assailed by Christian–Jewish dialogue groups and Jewish organizations for portrayals of Jewish leaders (or Jews) as primarily and collectively responsible for the death of Jesus—a fictional notion heard for centuries in some Christian rituals and Passion Plays around the globe.[19]

In a 2009 Annual Survey of American Jewish Opinion (ASAJO), 56 percent of Jewish Americans said that anti-Semitism *worldwide* was still a very serious problem; most of the rest agreed it was somewhat of a problem. Looking to the next few years, 45 percent also felt that anti-Semitism was likely to increase worldwide. Today, many Jewish Americans single out the "religious right" in the United States and other Western countries as the most anti-Semitic group.[20] Significantly, recent surveys have found that many non-Jewish Americans seriously overestimate the Jewish American presence, often placing that group at *about 25 percent* of the population (instead of 2 percent). For some this high estimate may indicate the negative view that Jews are too influential or dominant. Indeed, a recent national survey found that one-third of respondents believed Jews were more loyal to Israel than to the United States, and 15 percent thought that Jews did have too much power. Overall, one-seventh of the population was estimated to be very anti-Semitic in their beliefs. Nonetheless, substantial majorities in the survey felt that there should be tougher sentences for hate crimes and that the history of the European Holocaust should be taught to U.S. schoolchildren.[21]

Numerous researchers have examined stereotyped Jewish images. One study noted the stereotypical Jewish characters and other problems in television programs and other media: "The prevalence of interdating and intermarriage plots (to a point where they have become the paradigm for any romance involving a Jewish character); the virtual disappearance of Jewish families; the artificial limits on the number of Jewish characters on a single show, which might stigmatize it as 'too Jewish'; and finally, the often tasteless representation of religious themes and characters are related issues."[22]

Joyce Antler has documented the critical roles that Jewish women have played in their communities. Through contributions to literature, cinema, radio, and television, Jewish women have "helped to shape the main currents of modern and postmodern life." However, U.S. popular culture continues to perpetuate some negative stereotypes of Jewish women—images of the "Yiddish Mama," the too-assertive "Jewish Mother," and the "Jewish American Princess" (JAP). Negative images of women are still commonplace in public and private jokes and on greeting cards. Numerous scholars and media personalities have worked to reduce these negative images of Jewish women, as well as of Jews in general. In major films, Barbra Streisand, an influential Jewish American singer, has portrayed "feisty Jews and feisty women," creating positive images with staying power. Jewish filmmakers, as we will see later, have in recent decades worked to counter numerous negative images of Jewish Americans.[23]

Oppression and Conflict

During the 1880s, Jewish American merchants in the U.S. South suffered violent attacks from non-Jewish farmers who blamed them for economic crises; in the 1890s, farms and homes of Jewish merchants were burned in Mississippi. In the early 1900s, riots erupted against Jewish factory workers in New Jersey. Just before World War I, Leo Frank, a Jewish American in Georgia (mentioned at the beginning of the chapter), was convicted of killing an employee and then lynched by an angry mob. About this time the Ku Klux Klan was revived, and these white terrorists waged violence against black, Jewish, and Catholic Americans. During the 1920s and 1930s, crosses were burned on Jewish properties, and synagogues were vandalized. On occasion, Jewish victims fought back. In the 1920s, Jewish and Catholic immigrants openly protested parades and gatherings of the Klan in Ohio and New Jersey.[24]

Organized Anti-Semitism and Hate Crimes

Between 1932 and 1941, openly anti-Semitic organizations grew to more than 100. Two dozen were large-scale operations that held numerous anti-Semitic rallies, some drawing thousands of people. Millions of anti-Semitic leaflets and newspapers were distributed. Father Charles Coughlin's racist organizations—the National Union and the Christian Front—were active in anti-Jewish agitation in the 1930s. In 1940, the FBI arrested more than a dozen members of a Christian Front terrorist group that reportedly intended to kill "Jews and Communists, 'to knock off about a dozen Congressmen,' and to seize post offices, the Customs House, and armories in New York. In the homes of the group were found 18 cans of cordite, 18 rifles, and 5,000 rounds of ammunition."[25]

Increased anti-Semitism in Germany was an important factor in the rising number of Nazi attacks against Jewish Americans. The Nazi Holocaust began with restrictions on Jewish communities, which were followed by deportation to forced-labor camps and extermination. An estimated 6 million European Jews (as well as millions of others, such as Gypsies and homosexuals) were killed by the Nazis and their allies. In the United States, the sense of oppression among Jewish Americans was reinforced not only by newspaper reports of European refugees but also by the growing knowledge that the U.S. government was aiding Nazi actions in Germany—at first by continuing economic and diplomatic relations (until 1941) and later by turning its back on thousands of Jewish refugees.[26]

Anti-Semitic vandalism remains common in many areas of the United States.

Violent attacks on Jewish Americans, their property, and their synagogues were common after World War II. Over the last few decades these attacks have decreased, but still are a significant problem. Generally, only blatant instances of anti-Semitism are reported to the Anti-Defamation League (ADL). The League's first survey (1979) counted 129 reported cases of anti-Semitic vandalism, including arson and the painting of swastikas (the Nazi "twisted cross") on synagogues. Between 1979 and 1984, some 3694 anti-Jewish incidents were reported, and today annual figures still remain significant. Reported incidents include physical and verbal attacks on individuals, acts of vandalism against property, assaults, and harassment. For example, in 1996, a bomb was set off at a Jewish Center in New York. Members of one neo-Nazi group, The Order, which was formed to conduct war against the "Zionist Occupation Government," machine-gunned a Jewish talk-show

host in Denver, committed robberies, counterfeited money, set fire to a synagogue, and killed police officers. The number of hate crimes by racist skinheads (white neo-Nazis who shave their heads) has also grown in recent years.[27]

In 1990, Congress passed the Hate Crime Statistics Act, requiring the U.S. Justice Department to collect hate crime data from police departments. **Hate crimes** are defined as *crimes against people and property generated by prejudice against racial, ethnic, religious, disability, or sexual orientation groups.* In recent years there have been numerous violent attacks related to anti-Semitism and/or anti-Semitic groups. The most recent (2007) FBI hate crimes report counted thousands of hate crimes; about 12.7 percent (969) were anti-Semitic incidents. In addition, a 2009 report by the ADL covered more states than the FBI and recorded some 1460 incidents for that same year (2007), with just over half targeting Jewish individuals and the rest targeting Jewish organizations. Hundreds of the reported anti-Semitic attacks involved the use of the Nazi swastika, such as the football-field–sized swastika carved into a New Jersey cornfield. We should note too that most hate crimes are not reported to police and other agencies. According to the Southern Poverty Law Center, the actual annual figure is likely to be at least 50,000. In addition, activists (mostly white) have developed thousands of anti-Semitic and white supremacist hate sites on the Internet in recent years and have made much use of networking sites, such as MySpace and Facebook, and of video sites such as YouTube, in their organizing and propaganda efforts.[28]

In 2009, an anti-Semite and white supremacist attacked the Washington, DC, Holocaust Museum and killed an African American guard. During that year there were numerous other violent attacks by men linked directly or loosely to various anti-Semitic or white supremacist groups. These included assaults and shooting deaths of Jews and people of color in Brockton, Massachusetts; the killing of three police officers by an anti-Semitic, white supremacist in Pittsburgh; and a plot by an anti-Jewish extremist group to bomb synagogues in New York. Anti-Semitic incidents are also reported regularly in France, Germany, Italy, Russia, and Canada. The ADL has noted increases in anti-Semitic groups participating in organized networks working across the globe.[29]

In recent years more than forty state legislatures have passed hate crime laws, and numerous state legislatures have increased penalties for crimes involving racial–ethnic hatred. A more comprehensive federal approach to dealing with anti-Jewish and other hate crimes, such as the Hate Crimes Prevention Act (introduced in 1999), has long been supported by Jewish and other civil rights organizations. This Hate Crimes Prevention Act, after a decade of being blocked by white conservative legislators, finally passed the U.S. House and Senate in the fall of 2009 and was signed into law by President Barack Obama.[30]

Religious Discrimination and Conflict

Federal court cases have periodically dealt with religious discrimination. During the 1950s and 1960s, Jewish businesspeople contested local "blue laws" that required businesses to close on Sunday, the Christian holy day; they argued that such laws violated their First Amendment right not to be penalized for their (Friday–Saturday) religious practices. The Supreme Court, however, upheld the blue laws. Christian religious observances, such as reciting the Lord's Prayer, were once standard in public schools. The imposition of Christian religious practices on Jewish children was contested in state courts, and in the 1960s, the Supreme Court ruled against officially sanctioned religious practices in public schools. Although since the 1980s a more conservative Supreme Court has upheld the practice of prayers in legislatures and the government practice of putting Christian nativity scenes on public property, that Court has also reaffirmed the principle of the separation of church and state.[31]

In 1986, the Supreme Court ruled that the U.S. Air Force could require an Orthodox rabbi serving as a chaplain to remove his religious head covering—called a yarmulke—when working indoors. For Orthodox Jews, religious law requires adult men to wear head coverings at all times. The impact of such cases has been to give court sanction to government decisions that decide which religious expressions are permissible in the government sphere and which are not.

Over the last two decades Jewish civil rights organizations, such as the Anti-Defamation League, have worked with other civil rights organizations in a series of federal court cases to maintain the separation of church and state asserted in the First Amendment to the U.S. Constitution. These cases have involved such issues as religious charter schools funded by government aid, placement of a large monument in the form of a Christian cross on federal land, monuments and plaques in government facilities reproducing the King James (Protestant) Bible's version of the Ten Commandments, and government funding going to faith-based social aid programs. In the past and the present, Jewish Americans have played a critical role in preserving the First Amendment's requirement of the separation of church and state.[32]

 What has been the basis for much of the prejudice and discrimination targeting Jewish Americans?

Jewish Americans Fight Back

Fear of crime and anti-Semitism has periodically led to the formation of aggressive self-protective associations. In 1968, Rabbi Meir Kahane, an ultraconservative Jewish nationalist, organized the Jewish Defense League (JDL) in New York, in part to deal with threats against Jewish communities. The JDL's goals included reinvigoration of ethnic pride and use of armed patrols to protect communities from crime. During the 1980s, JDL members protesting the treatment of Jews in the old Soviet Union disrupted Soviet diplomatic activities and tried to assassinate diplomats.[33] Kahane himself was assassinated in 1990, but the organization has continued aggressive efforts to defend Jewish issues and communities, especially against neo-Nazi groups. In recent years the JDL has asserted that it is against all terrorism and has criticized the violent actions of earlier JDL activists. Today, the JDL is small, but it remains a vigorous supporter of self-defense and a critic of what JDL activists term the "Jewish establishment" and of secular trends among Jewish Americans. Today, most Jewish Americans condemn such groups as extremist.[34]

Jewish–Black Relations

African Americans and Jewish Americans share a long history of mutual assistance. This history has been important for both groups, as recent books on black–Jewish relations make clear. For example,

Cheryl Greenberg's book *Troubling the Waters* shows how, from the 1930s to the 1960s, the black–Jewish alliance helped build a strong civil rights movement in spite of conflicts. Actually, this important relationship goes back many years. In the 1850s, three Jewish immigrants participated in abolitionist John Brown's well-known armed struggle against slavery. In 1917, a Jewish newspaper condemned antiblack violence in the white-led East St. Louis riot. Joel Spingarn, a Jewish American, was chairperson of the civil rights organization, the National Association for the Advancement of Colored People (NAACP), between 1914 and 1939. Moreover, at the end of World War II, an all-black unit in the racially segregated U.S. armed forces was photographed as among the first units to liberate Jews in Nazi concentration camps. Although denied equality at home, black troops risked their lives for the U.S. cause and helped free Jewish victims of Nazism. Later, during the 1960s civil rights movement, Jewish Americans comprised more than half of the white students who went to the South to register black voters and of the white lawyers who defended imprisoned civil rights protesters. Some were murdered by white segregationists for this effort.[35]

Conflict has, however, erupted periodically between Jewish Americans and African Americans. In the 1960s urban rebellions—and in more recent rebellions—African American rioters have sometimes attacked local Jewish (and other) businesses considered to be exploiting black communities. These developments have generated a backlash among Jewish Americans. Controversies between Jewish and African Americans in New York City have more recently gained media attention. In the 1990s, tension escalated between Hasidic Jewish residents and black residents in Brooklyn after crime patrols, set up by the Hasidic community, harassed and beat black and Latino residents from nearby areas who ventured into the Jewish community. In nearby Crown Heights, a Hasidic driver accidentally ran over a black child, setting off anti-Jewish rioting by black residents in which a rabbinical student was killed. These events greatly increased tensions between black and Jewish residents.[36]

In recent decades some black anti-Semitism and certain black leaders' criticism of Israeli treatment of Palestinians have alienated numerous Jewish Americans from participation in intergroup coalitions. A few black leaders have aimed anti-Semitic remarks at Jewish merchants and landlords they believed were exploiting black communities.[37] Some black leaders have been unwilling to disavow the comments of Louis Farrakhan, a leader of the Nation of Islam whose anti-Semitic utterances included a reference to Judaism as a "gutter religion."[38] Into the 2000s, negative statements about Jews and Judaism by a few black leaders have helped to perpetuate major tensions between Jewish and black communities. In surveys, moreover, antiblack sentiments have also been found among some Jewish Americans.

Letty Pogrebin has suggested that "differences between blacks and Jews are rarely more obvious than when each group speaks about its own 'survival,' a word that both use frequently but with quite dissimilar meanings. . . . Blacks worry about their actual conditions and fear for the present; Jews worry about their history and fear for the future." Members of each group fear the other, but for different reasons: Some Jewish Americans fear the urban black Americans and leaders who make anti-Semitic remarks. Some African Americans, in contrast, fear Jewish Americans primarily because they are part of the dominant white group. Indeed, numerous social science analyses show that since World War II, Jewish Americans have clearly become part of "white" America. Thus, the many educational, veterans, and housing programs after World War II benefited Jewish Americans greatly, helping them move firmly into the (white) middle class, even as these programs often excluded or marginalized African Americans.[39]

Still, tensions between Jewish and African Americans have not substantially affected Jewish commitments to civil rights. Among white groups, Jewish Americans remain the most liberal on racial issues. In recent decades, opinion polls have found that Jewish views on racial matters are closer to those of black respondents than to those of white Protestants and Catholics. A major nationwide survey found that Jewish Americans were more likely than other whites to believe that black Americans do *not* receive equal treatment in the economic, educational, or judicial arenas.[40]

Today, many Jewish individuals and organizations strongly support black civil rights causes and communities. For example, although some Jewish businesses were burned by rioters during a 1990s Los Angeles riot, thirty synagogues and Hillel centers (campus organizations) provided substantial clothing and food for relief of black families in Los Angeles riot areas.[41] The pattern of mutual support has been evident in the national political arena for decades. One study by the American Jewish Congress of the votes of black and Jewish members of Congress found that much of the time the groups voted *alike* on matters of interest to both communities, including issues of separation of church and state and important public social services.[42] Moreover, in recent decades black and Jewish citizens in numerous community dialogue groups have sought ways to ease tensions between these traditional allies. For instance, in several cities black and Jewish teenagers join in celebrating Martin Luther King Jr.'s birthday. Operation Understanding, a cooperative group created by a black member of Congress and a Jewish executive, is sponsored by the Urban League and the American Jewish Committee. Each year the group has brought together significant groups of Jewish and black students in several major cities to build interracial bridges, such as by visiting sites of cultural importance to each group—Ellis Island, New York, where large numbers of eastern European Jews entered the United States, or the Mississippi site of the murder of black and Jewish civil rights workers.[43]

 Considering the decades since World War II, what has been the relationship between Jewish Americans and African Americans?

Politics

From their first arrival in the colonies, Jewish immigrants were treated as outsiders. Members of the first Jewish community, in Dutch New Amsterdam, were barred from holding public office; and, in general, voting and officeholding in the English and Dutch colonies were limited to Christians. Nonetheless, later on, Jewish Americans made substantial contributions to the American Revolution, and the government to which the Revolution gave birth brought benefits to Jewish citizens by establishing the (unique for the time) separation of church and state. The U.S. Constitution's prohibition of religious qualifications for public office and the Bill of Rights' protection of speech and religious choice granted political freedom at the federal level. Political enfranchisement

was slower to come at the state level. Indeed, by 1790, only five states had removed voting and officeholding restrictions; six others carried Christians-only provisions for political participation as late as 1876.[44]

In the first years of the U.S. republic, anti-Jewish practices by Federalist party officials, combined with their support for the new anti-immigrant Alien and Sedition Laws, guaranteed that most Jewish Americans would support the more liberal Jeffersonian political party, later to become the Democratic Party. Although Jewish Americans supported Democrats for decades, some gravitated to the antislavery Republican Party in the 1850s and 1860s.[45]

The voting power of Jewish Americans increased as they became concentrated in northern cities at the beginning of the twentieth century. Socialist Party candidates received strong support, but many Jewish Americans remained Republicans or supported the Irish-dominated Democratic machines, which provided jobs and shelter to growing numbers of poor European immigrants. Whereas Irish Americans used ethnic politics to advance immediate economic and family interests—for example, to create jobs—Jewish Americans, although concerned with bread-and-butter matters, were typically more political-issue oriented, particularly with regard to expanding civil rights.[46]

Jewish Americans and Political Parties

By 1910, few Jewish Americans had won electoral office. An occasional city council member, one or two state legislators, a judge—this was the extent of political success. Political representation at the national level was modest. The appearance of an internationalist Democratic candidate, Woodrow Wilson, again brought a majority of Jewish voters back to the Democrats. Wilson appointed a few Jewish Americans to important positions.[47] Franklin Roosevelt brought Jewish Americans firmly into the Democratic fold in 1932. Roosevelt's anti-Nazi rhetoric, support of social programs such as Social Security, and support of labor unions won over many Jewish voters. For the first time, Roosevelt brought numerous Jewish Americans into the federal government.[48]

Yet, Roosevelt did *not* take dynamic action on behalf of refugees from Nazi-dominated Europe. One reason was his fear of the intense U.S. anti-Semitism prevailing during the 1930s and 1940s, especially among the gentile (non-Jewish) members of

Congress. Anti-Jewish discrimination was common in politics, social affairs, education, employment, jury selection, and real estate decisions.[49]

Since the Roosevelt era, a substantial proportion of the Jewish vote has usually gone to Democratic presidential candidates. For example, in the 2009 Annual Survey of American Jewish Opinion (ASAJO), 53 percent of Jewish respondents identified with the Democratic Party, and only 16 percent with the Republican Party, probably the lowest for any white ethnic group. Other recent surveys indicate that 44 percent view themselves as liberal, 29 percent as middle-of-the-road, and only 26 percent as conservative. In the 2008 presidential election some 78 percent voted for Barack Obama, the first American of color to be elected president. Jewish Americans reveal a strong commitment to liberal sociopolitical issues, especially social justice, a view honed by centuries of anti-Semitic oppression.[50]

Historically, Jewish Americans have been underrepresented among elected and appointed officials. Not until 1974 did a Jewish American became mayor of New York City—a city with a large Jewish population. In the 1970s, Dianne Feinstein became the first Jewish woman to be elected mayor of a major city, San Francisco. Gradually increasing numbers of Jewish Americans have ever held the office of state governor, U.S. senator, or member of the U.S. House. The only Jewish American nominated for president by a major party was Republican Barry Goldwater (a convert to the Episcopal religion), who was defeated in 1964. So far, only a half-dozen Jewish Americans have served on the U.S. Supreme Court, even though Jewish Americans have been substantially represented among U.S. lawyers for some decades now. In 1993, President Bill Clinton appointed the first Jewish American woman (the second woman ever) to the Supreme Court—Ruth Bader Ginsburg. By the early 2000s, there were two Jewish Americans on that Court. As of 2008, Jewish Americans held numerous important positions in the U.S. House (30 members) and Senate (13 members), a proportion substantially higher than the Jewish percentage of the U.S. population—though likely one in line with the Jewish percentage of those Americans who are most active in U.S. politics. In 2000, the Democratic Party, for the first time in major party history, chose a Jewish American (who practiced Judaism), Senator Joseph Lieberman of Connecticut, as its vice-presidential candidate.[51]

Senator Joseph Lieberman (D–Conn.), here campaigning in 2000 with his wife Hadassah, was the first Jewish American to be nominated for vice-president by a major political party.

Subtle and covert discrimination still plays a role in limiting the number of Jewish Americans who occupy political offices in some states and cities. In these areas the proportion of Jewish Americans in elected office is low, especially given their high proportions among political activists and contributors.[52]

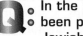 **In the political arena, what have been primary concerns for many Jewish American voters?**

Unions and Community Organizations

Eastern European immigrants protested oppressive working conditions in the 1890s, organizing to fight long hours, low pay, and unsafe conditions. Later, New York City data for the 1930s show large numbers in food, entertainment, clothing, and jewelry unions. Jewish union leaders often went beyond the problems of wages and working conditions to grapple with broader issues, such as developing health, pension, and educational programs that would be imitated by other unions. Jewish Americans also played an important role in the growth of the American Socialist Party and subsequent labor–liberal parties.[53]

By the 1930s, important civic and civil rights organizations were established: the Anti-Defamation League, the American Jewish Congress, the American Jewish Committee, and the United Jewish Appeal. Since 1906, the American Jewish Committee has vigorously fought anti-Semitic discrimination. The American Jewish Congress has long fought for civil rights. The Anti-Defamation League has carried out a long campaign to root out anti-Semitism. The United Jewish Appeal, established in 1939, has been a successful fund-raising organization that has aided numerous causes, including those of political refugees and the state of Israel. Voluntary organizations are critical to the preservation of Jewish identity and provide coordination for local Jewish community activities across the country.[54]

The survival of Israel has been a major concern. During the 1950s, political pressure for U.S. government support for Israel was unheeded, but by the 1960s, such support had sharply increased. Since then, Jewish American political pressure has been mobilized for numerous other causes, such as opposition to political candidates who support Middle Eastern policies viewed as hostile to Israel. Older organizations like the American Israel Public Affairs Committee (AIPAC) and the Conference of Presidents of Major American Jewish Organizations have helped Jewish Americans to influence U.S. policy on Israel. In recent years new liberal organizations have developed, revealing the diversity of views on the Middle East, Israel, and the rights of Palestinians among Jewish Americans. The New Israel Fund— a partnership involving Americans, Canadians, Israelis, and Europeans—provides funding for social justice efforts designed to benefit Arab and Jewish residents in Israel. The Jewish Peace Lobby and Jewish Voice for Peace attempt to provide constructive criticism of U.S. and Israeli policies and take a progressive approach to issues involving Israeli Jews and Palestinian Arabs.[55]

In addition to combating anti-Semitism, some Jewish organizations have worked to eliminate all racial prejudice and discrimination and to ensure separation of church and state. For example, early in his first term as president (2001), George W. Bush proposed a "faith-based initiative" to involve religious organizations in providing social services with federal aid. At a meeting between a Bush representative and the Jewish Council for Public Affairs, a coalition of Jewish organizations working on public policy and social service issues, concerns about separation of church and state were articulated. Jewish leaders feared that government support might go for specifically religious activities, thereby violating the U.S. principle of government neutrality.[56]

In recent years some Jewish Americans have accused well-off board members of the American Jewish Committee, the American Jewish Congress, the United Jewish Appeal, and the Anti-Defamation League of being more sympathetic to needs of employers than to traditional concerns for workers, the poor, and discrimination. This criticism highlights a dilemma faced by Jewish Americans. As one of the most affluent of white ethnic groups, Jewish Americans might be expected to develop the conservative orientation of other high-income white groups. Yet, given their past experiences with racial–ethnic discrimination and continuing anti-Semitism, Jewish Americans generally remain more liberal, both politically and economically, than non-Jewish white groups.[57]

The Economy

Jewish immigrants have contributed to the prosperity of North America. One immigrant from Poland, Haym Salomon, played a critical role in financing the American Revolution with a loan to the revolutionary government. The opening of commerce in the Americas presented opportunities for European Jews, especially those with centuries of experience as a "middleman" trading minority in Europe. However, success in certain commercial pursuits in Europe had made them a scapegoat for the non-Jewish poor, who often saw them as exploiters, and for the non-Jewish rich, who viewed them as an economic threat. In North America the often marginal nature of their businesses, as well as overt discrimination, fostered the growth of an ethnic economy in which Jews relied on economic aid from one another to maintain businesses and communities.[58]

Establishing an Economic Niche: A "Middleman Minority"?

The rate of penetration of a new immigrant group into the dominant economy depends on its economic background as well as conditions at the point of destination. Most German and other central European Jews were poor when they came to the U.S. However, they arrived when frontier development and industrial growth were expanding, and often found that their experience as merchants was in demand. Many eventually became prosperous shopkeepers.[59] By the 1890s, a majority of the German and other central European Jews were moving up the economic ladder.

The next large group of immigrants, from eastern Europe, also entered the expanding industrial economy at an opportune time. Most were poor, but their experience in coping with oppression in Europe provided them a heritage replete with strategies for finding economic niches in which to survive. Men, women, and children engaged in low-wage work. The long hours and poor working conditions of industrial capitalism's factories led to participation in union movements by these immigrants. In the early 1900s, more than one-third of eastern European Jewish immigrants were employed in the garment industry, one-fourth were in building trades, and one-fifth were in retail trade. The second generation was strongly encouraged by parents to seek white-collar jobs, and many went into law, medicine, and other white-collar professions.[60]

Jewish women contributed significantly to family incomes. A Philadelphia study in this period found that one in three Jewish households had a woman working outside the home. Because of the low wages of male and female workers, families needed the wages that women earned working outside the home or by taking in sewing or laundry at home. Wives often joined their husbands in small retail shops that supplied many neighborhoods. Many working-class women were left to raise children alone when their husbands died or deserted the family.[61]

From the Depression to the 1950s

The solidarity of the Jewish American community and heavy involvement in small and medium-sized businesses were sources of survival during the 1930s Great Depression. Whenever possible, Jewish businesses dealt with one another. Organized crime provided a way out of poverty for a small proportion, but participation in organized crime declined significantly as large numbers moved into the middle class and suburban areas following World War II.[62]

The Jewish ethnic economy provided a fallback position for those who faced discrimination. One goal of anti-Semitic organizations was to reduce the number of Jewish Americans in private and public employment. Non-Jewish whites in the teaching, banking, medical, legal, and engineering professions often sought to prohibit Jewish Americans from employment. The Great Depression increased this problem. Signs proclaiming "No Jews need apply" were commonplace. From 1900 to the 1950s, discrimination was widespread in housing, from Philadelphia to Boston and Chicago, as well as in smaller cities.[63]

One obsession of anti-Semites, to the present day, has been the alleged Jewish "dominance of banking." This fear increased in the Depression. Nonetheless, a 1936 *Fortune* magazine survey found very few Jewish Americans in banking and finance. Another survey found that *only 600* (far less than 1 percent) of the 93,000 U.S. banking officials were Jewish. Jewish Americans were also rare in heavy industries, public utilities, the press, and radio. The only sectors in which Jewish Americans were overrepresented were clothing, textiles, and the movies. The author of the 1936 *Fortune* article seemed puzzled by the clusters of Jews found in certain business areas and explained the situation in the stereotypical terms of Jewish clannishness. Such clustering patterns were not mysterious, for they reflected the extent to which Jewish workers and entrepreneurs were forced to work outside mainstream businesses because of blatant anti-Semitism. They were channeled by gentile discrimination into higher-risk economic spheres that were then often marginal to the mainstream economy.[64]

After World War II, extensive discrimination continued. Job advertisements included anti-Jewish restrictions, and employment agencies discriminated against Jewish workers. Even so, many Jewish Americans were able to share in postwar prosperity, particularly in new industries such as television and plastics. Jewish workers still were concentrated primarily in trade, clothing, and jewelry manufacturing, as well as in commerce and merchandising, light industries, mass communications, and certain other white-collar professions. In 1957, the Census Bureau found that three-fourths of Jewish men were employed in white-collar jobs, compared with 38 percent of white Protestants. Yet, in 1950, no more than 3 percent of corporate executives, presidents, and board chairpersons were Jews. Given the preponderance of Jewish Americans in commercial and business employment, this proportion was much lower than it would have been without discrimination.[65]

Individual and Family Success

The most recent (2000–2001) National Jewish Population Survey (NJPS) estimated median annual income for Jewish households (including both families and single individuals) to be $54,000. The median income for all U.S. households was then significantly less. Both figures have grown substantially since then. One 2008 Pew Research Center report on religion estimated from national survey data that 46 percent of Jewish American families had incomes above $100,000 a year, substantially more than the median income for all U.S. families.[66]

Continuing occupational mobility has characterized Jewish Americans over recent decades. In the 1960s, occupational data for major East Coast cities showed that 20 to 32 percent of Jewish American males were in various professional positions, with another 28 to 54 percent in various managerial positions. More than half of Jewish workers in all the cities fell into these two major categories, while most of the rest held clerical or sales positions. In comparison, the majority of workers in the total employed population in these cities held blue-collar positions. More recent data confirm this trend toward white-collar employment among Jewish Americans.[67]

In recent decades, as in earlier decades, Jewish executives have not come close to controlling banking. Excluding one New York bank (31 percent of whose top managers were Jewish), in 1976 only 2.5 percent of the executives of commercial banks nationwide were Jewish. A decade later, another analysis found that 3.4 percent of the executives at ten of the largest banks were Jewish.[68] A 1980s study of Jewish Americans then in the corporate elite found that most were in Jewish-founded corporations or occupied lower managerial positions in other corporations.[69]

A 1988 study of the distribution of Jewish executives in corporate America found that they constituted less than 5 percent of senior executives in many of the largest corporations. Interviews with

consultants and managers documented the "outsider" status of Jewish managers. These interviewees agreed that, to succeed in the corporate hierarchy, Jewish employees must divest themselves of *all visible Jewish identity*. This more or less forced one-way assimilation to the dominant white-Protestant norms and arrangements is still an oppressive aspect of U.S. society. Some Jewish respondents in this study cited specific anti-Jewish actions that had blocked career advancement.[70]

Until the past two decades, higher-level government positions have rarely been open to Jews. One Jewish American noted that when he began his career in the 1960s, "the State Department (and the CIA and FBI) was virtually closed to Jews."[71] Interestingly, in the late 1990s, the media made much of the fact that a dozen top people in the State Department were then Jewish, including then Secretary of State Madeleine Albright.

Perhaps because the academic sphere may offer greater freedom than other employment spheres, many of the country's college professors have been Jewish, although only in recent decades. Jewish Americans now make up about 10 percent of university faculties, and much higher proportions at numerous elite public and private universities. A number have served as presidents and other high-level administrators at major universities. Jewish Americans have been very well represented among U.S. Nobel Laureates (about 37 percent) and among top literary figures. They have included Nobel Laureate novelist Saul Bellow and prominent intellectuals such as linguist Noam Chomsky, biologist Stephen Jay Gould, writer and editor Irving Howe, and sociologist Seymour Martin Lipset.

 How did Jewish Americans come to play a role as a "middleman minority"?

Persisting Discrimination

Recall that in the 2009 Annual Survey of American Jewish Opinion, most Jewish Americans felt that anti-Semitism in the U.S. and overseas was still very serious; nearly half felt it would increase in the future.[72] One reason for this pessimism is continuing experience with anti-Jewish discrimination in public and private organizations. For example, one employee at a rental car company reported he was told by supervisors that Hasidic Jews were "the worst people to rent to." Two employees reported that supervisors rejected business accounts from Jewish applicants. Although the company denied it, the complaints suggested the likelihood of continuing discrimination against Jewish Americans. In another business setting, a Jewish barber was fired by a New York hair salon because he would not remove his yarmulke while he was cutting hair. And in late 2008, at Ft. Benning military base in Georgia, a Jewish trainee was verbally harassed by sergeants who forced him to remove his yarmulke while dining; he was physically assaulted by another military trainee. With help from the Anti-Defamation League, the Jewish soldier was successful in getting the military to punish his attackers and to move him to a safer area. In yet another area of discrimination, a federal lawsuit has alleged that a New York village has tried to keep out Orthodox Jews by prohibiting Jewish boarding schools.[73]

The effects of anti-Semitism keep many Jewish Americans from the full social recognition and political power that economic success brings to other whites. Only in 1985, for example, did New York City finally pass a law banning anti-Jewish and other discrimination in private clubs. In 1992, a bill banning such discrimination in private country clubs made its way through the New York State senate after being blocked for years by white Protestant opponents. In that year a similar bill banning discrimination in private clubs passed the Florida legislature. As of today, Florida is one of relatively few states with strong laws prohibiting racial or gender discrimination in private clubs. Recently, the governor of Maryland was criticized for attending a fundraising gathering at an all-white country club. Like numerous states, Maryland laws generally allow private clubs to exclude Jews, blacks, and women.[74] Some experts estimate that the majority of private country clubs have no black members, and many have no female or Jewish members. Others have very small numbers. Much discrimination has been hidden by secrecy at this high socioeconomic level of society. Often this discrimination is defended as private, yet many such "private" organizations benefit greatly from public laws and actions, such as tax exemptions and liquor licenses.

Education

Education was not as high a priority for the earliest groups of Jewish immigrants as it was for later groups; earlier arrivals focused on small-business success rather than on entering a profession or preserving their European tradition of religious scholarship. Significant participation in public schools came with the surge of eastern European immigrants, for whom secular education was a means of becoming "American." Parents pushed children to succeed in school so that they could prosper economically and be accepted socially. These immigrants established numerous schools that taught Jewish religious practices to ensure that U.S.-born children would retain their ethnic and religious identity. Educational mobility for second- and third-generation Jewish Americans often came swiftly. Large numbers graduated from high school; many pursued college educations.[75]

Discriminatory Quotas for Jewish Students

Jewish progress in higher education was countered to a degree by discrimination on the part of Anglo-Protestant whites. Restrictive quotas for Jewish students were imposed at numerous colleges and universities from the 1920s to the 1950s. In 1922, Harvard president A. L. Lowell called for discriminatory quotas. Covert methods to limit Jewish admissions, such as "character" tests and requirements for "geographic balance," were employed by many colleges.[76] Jewish Americans were often excluded from college and other teaching positions. Between the 1920s and the 1940s, Jewish Ph.D.s found it difficult to secure appointments at white-Protestant–dominated universities. However, the sudden growth in college enrollments following World War II created increased demand for college teachers. By 1970, the proportion of Jewish teachers on faculties in U.S. institutions of higher education had risen significantly, to 9 percent, well above the Jewish percentage of the population.[77]

Affirmative Action Programs

Since the 1960s, affirmative action programs, which seek to improve educational opportunities and job chances for black Americans and other groups of color, have become a political issue for some Jewish

Americans. Because of quota restrictions that once denied them access to education and jobs, Jewish Americans have long been among the vigorous supporters of the principle of individual merit. Thus, some have opposed contemporary affirmative action programs, such as in college admissions, because of their heavy commitment to higher education—a commitment that reflects past exclusion from many sectors of the academic world. College admissions preferences for non-Jewish groups, it has been argued by some, disproportionately affect Jewish access to college degrees and perpetuate the effects of past anti-Semitic discrimination.[78]

However, voicing support for affirmative action, Alan Dershowitz, a prominent Jewish American law professor, has noted that that people must make a major distinction "between the institutional impact and intensity of the hurt suffered as part of an invidious pattern of racial *subordination* and as part of a benevolent pattern of racial *equalization*." He points out the intentional and unfair bias in numerous college admission programs, including those at Ivy League universities, that often hold fairly constant the number of students admitted from white-Protestant pools (who are descendants and relatives of alumni and those admitted to achieve

"geographic balance"), yet at the same time make room for certain affirmative action applicants (Latinos and blacks) by reducing the numbers of yet other groups (Jewish and Asian Americans) who are admitted. Dershowitz argues that it would be much more equitable for those white-Protestant groups that have long benefited from the exclusion of many racial and ethnic groups to bear a heavier share of the costs of equalization through affirmative action than groups like Jewish Americans.[79] This analytical perspective takes history and societal background into serious consideration, suggesting how past white privileges should be taken into account in considering contemporary remedies for continuing racial–ethnic inequalities.

Continuing Achievements in Education

Severe anti-Jewish discrimination declined after World War II, and since that time the educational attainment of Jewish Americans has reached ever higher levels. One 2000 survey of 1010 Jewish adults found that an extraordinary 86 percent had secured some college education, with 60 percent reporting at least a college degree. The 2008 Pew Research Center report on religion estimated that more than

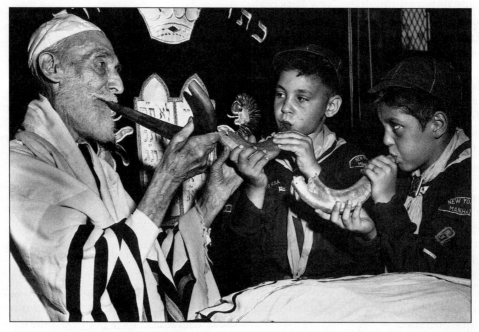

A Jewish elder shows youngsters how to blow a shofar, *the ram's horn used in religious observances.*

one-third of Jewish Americans today now have some postgraduate education beyond college. These attainment figures are much higher than for the U.S. population as a whole.[80]

Schooling in Jewish religion and culture also persists. Surveys of Jewish Americans in recent decades have found strong support among parents for some Jewish education for their children, and large percentages of adults and children have reported receiving such education. The most recent NJPS report on "more engaged" Jewish Americans estimated that much more than half of these adults and children had received some Jewish education. The emphasis on formal learning of one's heritage and religion in lower grades has carried over to colleges, for some 41 percent of current Jewish college and graduate students (the "more engaged" in the survey) reported having taken a Jewish studies class.[81]

Religion and Zionism

The degree of freedom allowed for people of various religious organizations varied across the early American colonies, but most restricted Jewish participation in colonial life. Such anti-Jewish bias generated and sustained a vigorous oppositional culture among Jewish Americans that has formed the base for protest of religious and other oppression to the present day. Although the new country remained substantially Christian after 1790, religious freedom gradually became law in each new state. As the numbers of central European (especially German) Jews increased in the nineteenth century, they founded numerous synagogues. Most Americanized their religious practices, in part to achieve greater respectability from non-Jews. The American Reform movement became organized in the Union of American Hebrew Congregations in the 1870s. Reform temples developed shorter services, organ music, and English prayers.[82]

The role of *Judaism* (the Jewish religion) in Jewish identity was a point of conflict between established German Jews and later eastern European immigrants. German Jews saw themselves as Americans whose religion happened to be Judaism. They generally endeavored to be inconspicuous. In contrast, new immigrants from eastern Europe generally had a strong desire to maintain their old ethnic identity. Most were Orthodox, observing the Sabbath and

kosher laws if they could. Theirs was a grassroots adaptation of Orthodoxy that focused on family and stressed charitable acts and observance of rituals.[83]

Conservative Judaism, which began in the 1880s as a modified traditionalism in reaction to Reform groups, appealed to later generations. Conservative synagogues observed many Orthodox traditions but discontinued dress codes and separation of men and women at services. By 1935, Orthodox synagogues had about 1 million members, Conservative synagogues about 300,000, and Reform temples about 200,000. The authority of the rabbi, as well as traditional ritual, became less important as one moved from Orthodox to Conservative to Reform congregations. Many synagogues built in middle-class neighborhoods after the 1920s were designed as community centers as well as religious centers. The Jewish atmosphere in concentrated neighborhoods provided a strong sense of group solidarity. However, secularism, socialism, labor radicalism, and Zionism became the new "religions" of many younger Jewish Americans during and after the 1930s Depression.[84]

Trends in Religious Practice and Identity

Expanding suburbanization for Jewish families after World War II brought an increase in suburban congregations. As a small minority in suburbs, Jewish families sought a way to ensure the Jewishness of their children. Synagogue membership and ritual observances saw marked increases.[85]

Jewish American religion currently reflects a substantial interest in the traditional heritage, maintenance of the synagogue as a community center, and home religious practices. However, at least four in ten Jewish Americans do not belong to a synagogue or temple. In the 2009 ASAJO, there was great diversity: 9 percent identified as Orthodox, 24 percent as Conservative, 27 percent as Reform, and 2 percent as Reconstructionist; 36 percent stated that they were "just Jewish." Clearly, today many Jewish Americans do not see themselves as traditionally religious.[86]

Judaism has become one of the major U.S. religious traditions. Some call much of contemporary Judaism a "cardiac" religion, emphasizing the "heart" (ethics) rather than traditional ritual and doctrine. There are still different denominations within U.S. Judaism, as within U.S. Protestantism. Orthodox Judaism, which bases Jewish identity on descent from a Jewish mother, still involves ritual observance with fewer adaptations to the secular world. In contrast, more liberal Reform Judaism accepts Jewish heredity through either a Jewish father or mother and emphasizes humanitarian Jewish principles rather than traditional ritual. Conservative Judaism represents a middle path between Orthodoxy's strong traditionalism and Reform's strong humanitarianism.[87]

Israel and Zionism

Concern for the survival of Israel occupies a place near the center of modern Jewish consciousness. Religiously active or not, many Jewish Americans share a commitment to **Zionism**—*a worldwide movement for the establishment in Palestine of a national homeland (Israel) for the world's Jewish communities.* This commitment to Israel has affected Jewish voting patterns, as well as Jewish philanthropy. In the 2009 ASAJO, nearly 70 percent of respondents said they felt close to Israel.[88]

Since 1990, there have been oscillating negotiations between the Israeli government and Palestinian officials over the future of the Palestinian population.[89] In the 2009 ASAJO survey, 49 percent of Jewish Americans supported the establishment of a Palestinian state, while 41 percent were opposed. However, 58 percent were opposed to Israel compromising on the status of Jerusalem as a united city under Israeli jurisdiction in order to secure any peace. In addition, 75 percent agreed with the pessimistic view that the "goal of the Arabs is not the return of occupied territories but rather the destruction of Israel." Sadly, just over half felt there would never be a time when "Israel and its Arab neighbors will be able to settle their differences and live in peace."[90]

One 2009 research study using focus groups with Jewish Americans found much ambivalence because of what researchers called a "new realism" about the conflict. Most respondents wanted Israel to make an agreement with the Palestinians and felt that the U.S. government might assist in this effort. "Most, however, remain skeptical that such a deal is possible, or that it would be honored by the other side. Caught between a realist's desire for security and an idealistic commitment to peace, they would like to see the United States engaged in mediating the conflict, but would also like the United States to be supportive of Israel against her enemies."[91]

Moreover, in recent years Jewish Americans have had to deal with right-wing Christian Zionists who are very supportive of a conservative Israeli approach to Palestinian issues. Some Jewish leaders have embraced these Christian Zionists as allies, but others have strongly opposed any alliances because these Christian Zionists seek Israel's dominance in the Middle East as a temporary condition that facilitates the second coming of Christ—with an apocalyptic destruction of all non-Christians, including Jews.[92]

Assimilation or Pluralism?

At least two different theoretical perspectives have been used to explain the experiences of Jewish Americans—Anglo-conformity perspectives and cultural pluralism approaches. Most scholarly analyses have reflected some type of assimilation viewpoint. The dominant perspective among Jewish Americans themselves has also been at least partially assimilationist: The view that substantial adaptation to the surrounding Anglo-Protestant culture is critical to achieving economic success and avoiding anti-Semitic discrimination. However, since the 1800s, certain Jewish leaders have favored cultural pluralism as an alternative to Anglo-conformity assimilation. Horace Kallen, a Jewish scholar, best formulated this perspective (see Chapter 2). He indicated that ethnic–cultural group membership is not easily abandoned by most people, and that ethnic groups have a right to exist on their own terms—that is, democracy should be fully applied to U.S. ethnic–religious groups. Kallen argued against the ruthless Americanization advocated for European immigrants by Anglo-Protestant Americans. He gave the name *cultural pluralism* to his view. However, more recent scholars have argued that Kallen's cultural pluralism is not a useful perspective for understanding the actual adaptive history of Jewish Americans, because massive acculturation and substantial adaptation in other areas have been facts of life for most Jewish Americans.[93]

Patterns of Assimilation

Partial cultural assimilation came relatively quickly for each major group of Jewish immigrants and their children. Most Sephardic and German Jews rapidly adapted, picking up English and certain dominant folkways but maintaining a commitment to Judaism.

Then, large numbers of eastern Europeans arrived. German Jews pressed these immigrants to Americanize, yet most new arrivals were committed to retaining their distinctiveness and sense of Jewish peoplehood. Their European Yiddish culture, which in the U.S. became in part an oppositional culture, played a crucial role in perpetuating their Jewish heritage. These immigrants had no illusions that they would cease to be outsiders in a predominantly non-Jewish society, yet they aggressively embraced opportunities for jobs, citizenship, and education.[94]

Second-generation (and later) eastern Europeans were more affected by assimilation pressures and rapidly picked up the language and Anglo-Protestant values pressed on them. Like young Italian Americans (see Chapter 4), they were caught between the culture of parents and the Anglo-Protestant culture—a situation guaranteed to create family tensions. Their Judaism was Americanized. Many of the third generation moved out of predominantly Jewish neighborhoods. Still, they too were often eager to accent their Jewishness in their religious and secular practices.[95]

Riv-Ellen Prell has researched the great pressures faced by Jewish women in the second and third generations. Many second-generation women were pressured to reject their mothers' strong-woman reality and adopt servile "lady-like" virtues of the Anglo-Protestant culture, which included devotion solely to home and family. Then, in their turn, later-generation women often struggled against their more conservative mothers for a more liberated woman's life less constrained by gender expectations and limitations.[96]

Central and eastern Europeans advanced relatively quickly in the sphere of structural assimilation at the secondary level of the economy and, sometimes, politics. A large portion achieved substantial economic success in the first generation. As a group, eastern Europeans moved occupationally from a blue-collar concentration to a white-collar concentration in three generations. Hard work and mastery of the educational system generally facilitated upward socioeconomic mobility. However, even today, Jewish Americans' occupational distribution underscores the point that many of the prosperous and well-educated among them are not yet fully integrated into upper reaches of the economy and society. The significant underrepresentation of Jewish Americans at the very top in numerous

spheres of U.S. economy and society is indicative of continuing, if often covert or subtle, anti-Jewish discrimination.

Why were Jewish Americans generally able to move up the economic ladder so successfully? Some have explained this in terms of values and religious traditions. According to Nathan Glazer, "Judaism emphasizes the traits that businessmen and intellectuals require, and has done so at least 1,500 years before Calvinism. . . . The strong emphasis on learning and study can be traced that far back, too. The Jewish habits of foresight, care, [and] moderation probably arose early."[97]

Others have argued that this relative success has had less to do with religion than with historical and structural conditions. Although eastern Europeans were among the poorest, least-educated European Jews, most were not illiterate. Those who came between 1880 and 1920 were generally from urban areas of Europe, where they had worked in urban occupations such as manufacturing, craftwork, and small-scale commerce. Their literacy was relatively high compared with that of most other immigrants of their day. European Jews migrated at a time of expanding manufacturing and trade in the United States. Thus, Jewish immigrants did not need to rely only on their religious values; they came in with "occupational skills that gave them a decisive advantage over other immigrants."[98] The fit between Jewish skills and economic circumstances at this critical time was better than it would be for later migrants (such as African Americans and Puerto Ricans) to the big northern cities.

In addition, Hertzberg attributes these immigrants' success to their "'Jewish head' . . . the heritage of siege mentality, of centuries of being an embattled bastion in a hostile 'exile,' and of having only one tool for survival, the use of one's wits." This interpretation suggests a type of oppositional culture that facilitates survival under anti-Semitic oppression.[99]

In recent decades the decreasing residential concentration of Jewish Americans has not eliminated their social cohesion and strong organizations. For example, the large Jewish community in Los Angeles has an active online journal and is substantially interconnected in terms of Jewish organizations, activities, and family ties—despite a dispersed housing pattern. Nationally, too, the pattern of having Jewish friends and related community connections still seems strong. In the most recent NJPS, over half of the more engaged Jewish respondents reported that at least half their close friends were Jewish.[100]

Some time ago, assimilation theorist Milton Gordon argued that, although Jewish Americans have experienced partial assimilation at the behavior-receptional level (that is, discrimination has declined), less assimilation has occurred at the attitude-receptional level because of the persistence of anti-Semitism.[101] Today, anti-Semitic prejudice—and indeed discrimination—can still be found in communities across the United States. Indeed, the development of white supremacist websites on the Internet in recent years has kept anti-Jewish images and organizations very much alive.

Intermarriage

Opposed by some on the grounds that it threatens the survival of the Jewish community, intermarriage with non-Jews has generally increased with each successive generation, probably reflecting in part a decline in negative images of Jews. The American Jewish Committee has recently concluded that the traditional taboo on such interfaith marriages has mostly disappeared. One 2000s study found intermarriage to be more common among young adults, those in the West, those with little Jewish religious education, those with less education generally, and children of those who had intermarried. Since the 1960s, the proportion of interfaith marriages has risen to 47 percent of those who married between 1996 and the early 2000s. In one national survey, 85 percent of the Jewish respondents (all ages) who were married had a Jewish spouse, but 64 percent reported that one or more of their children had a non-Jewish spouse.[102] According to another survey, more than half (56 percent) of the respondents disagreed with the assertion that "It would pain me if my child married a gentile." On another question, 40 percent said they were "neutral," while 16 percent viewed such marriages as a "positive good."[103]

Some analysts have speculated on whether Jewish Americans as a group will eventually disappear, given this significant intermarriage rate. Yet, some intermarried couples, along with their children, have strongly embraced Judaism and identify as Jewish. One study found that perhaps one-third of intermarried couples had taken this step.[104] Thus, Goldscheider has argued against the view that intermarriage

can be regarded as an unambiguous measure of assimilation because "strong communal bonds and networks link the intermarried to the community. . . . There is evidence as well that an increasing proportion of American Jews are accepting the intermarried within the community."[105]

Is the Jewish American community concerned that intermarriage is destroying Jewish identity and solidarity? Groups such as the American Jewish Committee have recently encouraged intense debates about such challenges to Jewish identity and community, with some arguing that intermarriage or lack of marriage and/or having few children were now more serious threats than anti-Semitism. Younger people are indeed marrying at much lower rates than older generations and are more likely to consider relationships with non-Jews. Still, a mid-2000s ASAJO survey suggests that a majority may not be so concerned. Asked whether anti-Semitism or intermarriage was the greater threat to the continuing Jewish presence in the United States, 62 percent of respondents picked anti-Semitism, 33 percent cited intermarriage, and 3 percent cited both. This survey found much more concern over external threats than over internal threats of intermarriage.[106]

Demographic trends—the declining birth rate and the related aging of the Jewish population—may be the most significant challenges. Jewish women in all age groups have had fewer children than all other women in those groups. The Jewish population's median age today is significantly higher than for the total population. Though there are some younger immigrants coming in, this likely means a declining Jewish population for the foreseeable future.[107]

 How well have Jewish Americans been assimilated into the dominant Anglo-Protestant culture and society?

Recent Immigrants: Strong Jewish Identity

The social and economic adjustment of recent Jewish immigrants raises interesting issues concerning assimilation and U.S. culture. Close ties between Israel and the U.S. make this trek westward easy for Israeli immigrants, who generally are more economically successful than most other immigrants. Many come with professional or managerial experience.[108]

In her research Annelise Orleck has shown a significant diversity in adaptive patterns for Jewish immigrants from the former Soviet Union. Immigrants from eastern regions of the Soviet Union were less assimilated to western European ways (and thus were more patriarchal and religious) than the immigrants from European-influenced areas of the Soviet Union (such as Moscow). Those who immigrated before the 1991 collapse of the Soviet Union were more likely to be anticommunist and more inclined to support the U.S. Republican Party, whereas those who immigrated after the collapse were more positive about the old Soviet Union, especially its social services. Many immigrants have reported difficulty adapting to U.S. culture. Although most émigrés in one survey rated their lives as Jews, as well as housing, income, and standard of living, as better here than in the former Soviet Union, most reported having trouble with English and finding a job. They considered their cultural environment worse here, and large percentages felt their friendships, social status, and workplace atmospheres were worse here. They liked the freedom, but disliked the "low" cultural tastes here. This mostly well-educated group appears to be adapting satisfactorily to the U.S. economy but is having trouble with certain social and cultural adjustments.[109]

Steven Gold examined adaptation among a diverse group of refugees from the former Soviet Union in Los Angeles and San Francisco. There, the Jewish population has been geographically concentrated; residents of the full-faceted Los Angeles community can lead active lives without much knowledge of English. Some, particularly younger, well-educated émigrés, found desirable jobs and moved into the middle class. But many middle-aged émigrés who had no transferable job skills or who were unwilling to take a lower-prestige job had difficulty adapting and often remained isolated from fellow émigrés. The strong sense of Jewish identity of these immigrants is another factor reinforcing Jewish American identity in the U.S. today.[110]

Although many immigrants from former Communist countries have aligned themselves with the Republican Party, most have been concerned over Republican attempts to limit immigration and government services. Interestingly, in one survey of all Jewish American groups, one-fifth supported increased immigration from countries overseas, and another 46 percent were satisfied with the current level of immigration.[111]

Contemporary Jewish Identity and the Future of the Community

What does it mean to be Jewish American today? Many scholars stress that U.S. Jews are "Jews by choice."[112] Although exaggerated, this view does indicate the degree of change that has occurred since the intense anti-Semitism of the early to mid-twentieth century. In that era, many gentiles targeted Jews for persecution. Today, most Jewish Americans can make identity choices in an atmosphere of much less discrimination.

Asked to specify the basis of Jewish identity, 90 percent of the respondents to one survey cited cultural or ethnic group membership. Fewer than 5 percent defined Jewishness only as religious. Still, the most recent NJPS found that most children of Jewish parents had some Jewish schooling, and that there had been an increase in children attending Jewish schools. Such schooling sustains identity. Significantly, Israel has been a major focus of Jewish American consciousness—which also reduces the possibility of Jewish identificational assimilation shifting to "just American."[113]

The *ethnogenesis* perspective (Chapter 2) recognizes the reality of persisting cultural differences among contemporary ethnic groups and helps in interpreting the Jewish experience. Jewish Americans are a composite group made up mostly of Sephardic, central European, eastern European, and Israeli origin. Jewish immigrants and their descendants have forged a *distinctive ethnic group*, shaped partially by their Jewish and (mostly) European cultural heritage and partially by the long history of adaptation to the white-Protestant culture. Despite substantial adaptation, ethnic distinctiveness remains. Some persisting anti-Semitism, respect for an ancient heritage, commitment to Israel, and parents' desire to socialize children in the Jewish heritage continue to shape the behavior and beliefs of most Americans of Jewish ancestry.

Sylvia Barack Fishman has described Jewish Americans' pattern of adaptation to the core culture as *coalescence*. The liberal American social and political values held by most American Jews have come to be seen simply as "Jewish" values. Through adaptive coalescence, Jewish Americans have merged their ideas with certain older American ideals, incorporating "American liberal values such as free choice, universalism, individualism, and pluralism into their understanding of Jewish identity." Ironically, Jewish Americans have often taken these historical values much more seriously than many other white Americans.[114]

How strong is Jewish identity today? Is it, as Herbert Gans argues, only a "symbolic ethnicity" without lasting significance? In this view, ethnicity for many white ethnic Americans is today little more than a desire to maintain some feeling for ethnic background without a strong commitment to traditional ethnic-religious behavior or to traditional social ties. Some Jewish scholars and agency officials in the United States and Israel have argued that weakening of religious ties and intermarriages among Jewish Americans indicate Jewish ethnicity is in significant decline. In 2009, an advertising effort cosponsored by the Israeli government criticized Jews abroad for their assimilation, weakened identity, and movement away from religious traditions. "It included newspapers ads and TV clips showing mock missing persons fliers emblazoned with Jewish-sounding names and the word 'Lost.'" After protests from Jews abroad the campaign was abruptly ended.[115]

One Jewish history professor, Robert Wolfe, has pointed out other identity dangers from Anglo-conformity assimilation, which is in reality "assimilation to Christian culture." In his view, "There is no such thing in the United States as a strictly secular organization. You cannot treat Sunday as a day of rest or hold a Christmas party and claim to be strictly secular . . . the choice is not between Jewishness and secularism. It is between a Jewish model of secularism and a Christian model. And given the inherent anti-Semitic bias of the Christian religion, it is suicidal . . . to choose the Christian model. It means placing yourself in a situation where you are always at a disadvantage, where you always have to prove yourself."[116] Thus, Jewish Americans have become *too* conforming and Christianized as they have adapted to the white-Protestant culture; and, if they are to survive as a specifically *Jewish* people, they must work hard to overcome the effects of substantial white-Protestant-Christian assimilation.

In recent years, Jewish American leaders have expressed concern over loss of traditional Jewish languages (Hebrew and Yiddish) and over changes at the voluntary organization level. Membership in some synagogues is declining, and some are having financial problems. Numerous philanthropic and service agencies have faced a decline in private or government support. Leaders are worried that too-assimilated Jewish Americans with a weaker sense of identity may not support traditional Jewish organizations as parents and grandparents did. However, the emergence of newer Jewish organizations, such as the Jewish Voice for Peace and the New Israel Fund, has involved many American Jews. Diverse cultural organizations and media have arisen, such as those for younger Jews and for gay-lesbian groups. Such newer organizations, as well as increases in Jewish day schools and festivals and the continuing importance of Jewish community centers, suggest that such worries are at least premature. Jewish community centers have long provided an array of important local programs, from health services to childcare to camping experiences, that sustain Jewish American communities.[117]

Recent surveys of Jewish Americans have found that most still seek, and have, substantial connections to Jewish subculture and communities. This subculture, including Jewish art, literature, and scholarship, is viewed as essential to the continuation of Jewish community and identity. One report concludes that "most Jews participate in selected holidays and forms of cultural involvement, maintain strong social connections to other Jews, and regard being Jewish as very important." But the report further noted that "smaller proportions of Jews—ranging from a quarter to a half—are variously engaged in other aspects of Jewish life as well, such as synagogue affiliation, charitable giving, volunteering, and many ritual observances." In effect, the majority are still connected to Jewish culture and community, and a substantial minority are very active in more organized Jewish American life.[118] Certain distinguishing features of Jewish culture and history—in particular, extensive social networks and the long tradition of survival as a minority in non-Jewish societies—support the long-term survival of ethnic identity. This seems to be true for younger generations as well, even though there are significant differences with older generations. One recent report on Jewish Americans under age 40 put it this way: "Young Jewish people are comfortable sharing Jewish events and space with non-Jews. Younger Jews, in fact, are likely to be much more comfortable with non-Jews and much less likely to have mostly Jewish friends than are Jews over 40." Nonetheless, only one-fifth of those surveyed had intermarried (many were still single), and six in ten said that being Jewish was "very important" to them.[119]

Significantly, there is greater acceptance of Jewish Americans in our largely non-Jewish society today, compared to some decades back. One distinctive change since the 1940s and 1950s has been an increase in Jewish Americans in movies made by Jewish and non-Jewish moviemakers. In recent decades many of these images have been relatively positive, and since the 1990s, a number of movies have been sympathetic to the problems faced by the nation of Israel (for example, *Munich* in 2005) or have probed issues of the Holocaust (for example, *Schindler's List* in 1993). Positive depictions of Jewish American families and individuals have also been central in movies like *Meet the Fockers* (2004) and *Knocked Up* (2007)—images that would have been unthinkable just a few years earlier. Jewish American moviemakers have played a central role in these changes. "Unlike the generation that preceded them, the Jewish moviemakers of the last quarter of a century have been forthright about their Jewishness. The Jewish characters they have developed on-screen are comfortable as Jews, not having to convert, assimilate, or hide their Judaism."[120] These movies have often done well at the box office. In addition, there is the related issue of the impact of Jewish Americans on the larger society. One recent review of research has assessed ways in which some Jewish characteristics, such as certain family styles and food habits, have penetrated popular culture (for example, television sitcoms).[121]

Interestingly, the increased acceptance of Jewish Americans among non-Jews seems to make Jewish Americans less likely to abandon their Jewishness, for their identity has ceased to be the focal point of massive discrimination and has instead become a badge of pride linked to a worldwide Jewish struggle such as that of Israel. Given these various factors, a sense of Jewishness is likely to remain strong for the majority of Jewish Americans for the foreseeable future. Thus, in the 2009 ASAJO, 51 percent ranked "being Jewish" as "very important" in

their lives; another one-third ranked it as "fairly important." Few ranked it as unimportant.[122]

Accepting and Challenging White Privilege

Jewish Americans remain significantly differentiated in identity, history, and experience from other white Americans, yet for the most part they are now accepted as "white." As recently as the 1920s, most white Anglo-Protestants regarded Jewish Americans as an "inferior race" that was not fully part of the "white race." After World War II, in part because of Nazism and its anti-Semitic oppression, as well as because of Jewish American soldiers serving in disproportionate numbers in the U.S. military, the dominant white gentile group gradually granted Jewish Americans numerous white privileges, especially greater occupational and residential mobility.

In addition, as Jewish social scientist Karen Brodkin has shown, many American Jews worked hard to become accepted as "white." Many moved to suburban areas, changed their names, or underwent cosmetic surgery in order to assimilate better to the omnipresent image of successful Euro-American whiteness. After World War II, many prominent Jewish Americans, such as writers and entertainers, publicly embraced white gentile values and institutions and actively accented images of Jewish Americans as a "high-achieving minority." Brodkin documents how many ordinary Jewish Americans came to accept a range of white-Protestant values and views as part of becoming white. Similarly, in his recent book, *The Price of Whiteness*, Eric Goldstein has shown how Jewish Americans sought acceptance and privileges as whites by conforming strongly to preexisting white-Protestant values, even as this meant giving up some of their distinctive Jewish group heritage or identity. Still, a heavy psychological price was paid for the pressured one-way assimilation and conformity.[123]

Both Brodkin and Goldstein have also shown that many American Jews have been uncomfortable with the group move to embracing white privilege, given their long history of fighting racial and ethnic oppression. Looking to the future, Brodkin suggests that "the challenge for American Jews today is to confront that whiteness as part of developing an American Jewishness that helps build an explicitly multiracial democracy in the United States."[124]

In what ways have many Jewish Americans challenged the "white" privilege that they have gained?

Summary

Jewish Americans, most of whom are descendants of central and eastern Europeans, are substantially assimilated in the dominant cultural arena. A prosperous ethnic group that has made dramatic progress up the socioeconomic mobility ladder, Jewish Americans have constantly struggled against widespread prejudice and discrimination. Theirs is substantially a success story, but they have paid a significant price. Anti-Semitism still persists today and often limits movement to the very top in the economy and in presidential politics. Coupled with substantial vertical progress over the decades has been horizontal mobility in the form of suburbanization.

Central to an adequate understanding of Jewish Americans today is an understanding of their ties to Israel. The creation of Israel and the periodic Arab–Israeli conflicts have generated a strong commitment to Israel, philosophically and financially. Jewish Americans continue to see Israel as an essential place of refuge for a people who survived the Roman persecution, the Spanish Inquisition, the Russian pogroms, and the Nazi Holocaust. This commitment has motivated thousands of Jewish Americans to visit Israel. Yet, in recent decades a significant number of Israeli immigrants have come to the United States seeking to escape the stress and violence of the Middle East. And many Russian Jews have come seeking better economic and political opportunities. These immigrants provide a contemporary reminder of the sojourner nature of much of the historical Jewish experience.

We have demonstrated here how diverse the United States still is—a diversity that fosters vitality and creativity. Jewish participation in U.S. institutions means that this country is *not* by official definition a Christian country. It is a country of many religious groups, including a diverse array of Protestants, Catholics, Jews, Muslims, Hindus, and others. One contribution of Jewish Americans has been their stand for the Jewish religious and cultural heritage— and thereby for the expansion of liberty for all U.S. residents.

Jewish Americans have contributed substantially to the national emphasis on education, to high achievement in arts and sciences, and to values of social justice and tolerance. Jewish Americans have not been passive victims of anti-Semitic discrimination; they and their organizations have often occupied the forefront of the fight against the prejudice and discrimination that still plague U.S. society.

Key Terms

Holocaust or
  Shoah   115
Marranos   115
pogroms   116

anti-Semitism   116
hate crimes   119
Zionism   130

Native Americans

BIG PICTURE QUESTIONS

- *What have been the consequences of colonization migration for indigenous American societies?*

- *What impact have Native Americans had on the dominant U.S. culture and society?*

- *How do conceptions of assimilation and resistance relate to the experiences of Native Americans?*

Not long ago, an Italian American leader in Denver, Colorado, tried to bring back the Columbus Day Parade, which was viewed as a celebration of the heritage of Italian Americans. This proposal was opposed by local Native Americans on the grounds that Columbus was a brutal conqueror who, along with his men, slaughtered indigenous peoples. The U.S. Justice Department worked out a modification whereby the march would be renamed The March for Italian Pride. Still, Native American, African American, and Latino American protesters objected to the celebration of Columbus under any name and sat down in the street to block the parade. This event is but one in a long series of protests by Native Americans against the genocidal conquests of indigenous peoples by European colonizers in the Americas.[1]

In the 1990s, Native American groups across the nation held protests against the celebration of the 500th anniversary of Columbus's 1492 voyage to the Americas. In Washington, DC, protesters spray-painted "500 years of genocide" on a statue of Columbus and read a list of human rights violations.[2] Suzan Shown Harjo has explained the prevalent Native American position regarding the Columbus Quincentenary: "As Native American peoples . . . we have no reason to celebrate an invasion that caused the demise of so many of our people and is still causing destruction today. The Europeans stole our land and killed our people."[3]

With this chapter we begin to consider in some detail the non-European groups that were racially subordinated during European colonial expansion. The term *white* as a racial self-designation for Europeans developed in the context of this contact with the usually darker-skinned peoples of Africa and the Americas, whom Europeans generally came to call *black* and *red*, respectively.[4] Many groups were subordinated economically, politically, and culturally. In this and subsequent chapters, we observe major differences in the past and present experiences of European and non-European Americans. We also examine the relevance of assimilation and power-conflict theories for interpreting the experiences of these important, often racially subordinated groups.

The first victims of European colonization on this continent were indigenous peoples—hundreds of Native American groups that were present at the time. Called collectively and erroneously "Indians" by their conquerors, indigenous peoples have long suffered at the hands of the European intruders and their descendants. Reflect for a moment on the odd notion of Europeans "discovering" America. In fact, the fifteenth-century European explorers were *latecomers,* for the continent they happened upon was already populated by millions of people. Ancestors of contemporary Native Americans had discovered the continent at least 20,000 years earlier—when, many scholars believe, they migrated across a land bridge from Asia to Alaska.

Conquest by Europeans and European Americans

Human migration varies from voluntary movement to forced slave importation. Migration often involves the incorporation of a new immigrant group into a societal framework by a dominant racial or ethnic group already established within certain geographical boundaries. In the case of Native Americans, however, the dominant group itself migrated: Europeans moved into the territories of indigenous groups. This process can be termed *colonization migration.* Unlike other migration, **colonization migration** involves the *conquest and domination of a preexisting geographical group by outsiders.* Such migration illustrates *external colonialism.*

How many Native Americans were there when the Europeans arrived in North America? Early on, some analysts estimated the indigenous population in the year 1500 at about 1 million. In recent years, this estimate has been revised upward. One considered estimate puts the number at 15 million at the time of conquest, with tens of millions in Central and South America as well. Other careful assessments support an even larger figure. Note too that low figures frequently have been used to legitimate the European conquest of an allegedly unoccupied land.[5]

By 1890, the combined effects of European diseases and violence had sharply reduced the number of indigenous people to approximately 250,000. This population remained below 400,000 until the 1950s, when it began to grow. Thus, in the 2000 census, 2,475,956 people identified themselves as American Indians (including indigenous Alaskans). Another 1,082,683 people identified themselves as white *and* Indian, and 182,494 identified themselves as black and Indian. (As of this writing, the 2010 census has not been completed and published.) The total of these groups and other (e.g., Indian-black) groups is more than 4.1 million—a substantial increase in the self-designated Indian population since 1990. The Census Bureau has estimated from the 2006–2008 American Community Surveys that there are now about 2,419,895 Native Americans, counting those who identified only as Indian. This represents a small decrease since the 2000 census count.[6]

Today, most of the more than 560 federally recognized Indian tribes have fewer than 10,000 members. According to 2000 census data, only five have populations of more than 100,000. In order of numbers, they are the Cherokee, Navajo, Choctaw, Sioux, and Chippewa tribes. Only 36 percent of Native Americans live on reservations, on trust lands, or in other Indian areas, most of which are rural. Most now live in towns and cities. There are about 350 Indian areas, which include 310 reservations covering about 72 million acres.[7]

In recent decades, the number of Americans claiming Indian ancestry has increased dramatically.[8] Drawing on interview data, sociologist Joane Nagel suggests that one reason for the increase is identity switching—the change in self-identification from non-Indian to Indian in response to activism promoting Indian pride. The tendency for Americans with partial Indian ancestry to openly assert this is increasing, likely because the stigma of being "part Indian" has declined. Some have also suggested that tribal benefits available to members of some Indian groups may have accelerated the willingness of non-Indians to falsely claim Indian ancestry.[9]

The term *Indian* and most government names for major Native American groups were created by whites. In most history books, not one major Native American group is regularly recorded under its own original name. For example, the so-called Navajo call themselves *Diné,* meaning "The People."[10] Renaming by outsiders is a result of Indians' subordination and suggests one major difference between colonized groups and European immigrants: Colonized peoples often have had little or no control over the group-naming process.

Although many non-Indians today think of Indians as a single category, the latter have for centuries been a diverse array of nations, with major differences in population, economies, polities, language, and customs. Native American groups have ranged from small bands to complex, hierarchically organized nations with large territories. The diversity is important to keep in mind, as the image of the typical Indian in the non-Indian mind is often of a Plains Indian living in a tipi, hunting bison, and wearing a feathered headdress.

Most Native Americans have never fit this image. As one researcher has noted, "Lumping Indians together into one group presumed to have the same cultural and physiological characteristics is the same as assuming that all Europeans are alike, that they speak the same language, have the same heritage, and share the same values. Historic tribes differed substantially in regard to religious beliefs and practices, language, dress, hairstyles, physiology, political organization, social structures, gender roles, world view and living conditions in response to the environment, which varied from forests, deserts, mountains, plains and coasts to subarctic and arctic areas."[11]

Early Cultural Borrowing

The cultures of the Native American societies encountered by European colonizers in the Western Hemisphere were often more highly developed than those of European societies. Some indigenous nations built great cities and roads, developed advanced agricultural systems, and created calendars and numerical systems superior to those of Europeans. In what came to be called "the Americas," most indigenous societies had complex and "sophisticated systems of government, community organizations, economy, means of communication, gender roles, arts, and elaborate clothing and hairstyles. Indians were and are extremely religious."[12] European invaders borrowed heavily. Thus, an estimated 60 percent of foods (for example, potatoes, corn, and many grains) eaten by people around the globe today were *first* developed by indigenous peoples in the Western Hemisphere. Many medicinal plants and their derivatives (for example, quinine) were borrowed from Native Americans.[13]

In the first decade of English settlement, numerous colonists deserted to Indian communities in search of better living conditions. In the winter of 1609–1610, one in seven of Jamestown (Virginia) colonists deserted to Algonquian communities. Better nourished than whites, the Algonquians hunted, fished, gathered food, and cultivated beans and maize. Their matrilineal society had no social classes, no state, and little economic specialization. The chiefs, who were not called by their titles, worked alongside other members. English workers were leaving a colony where the authorities had established severe punishments to prevent desertion. The reality of societies without property holding, kings, classes, and states provoked much worry among European American elites.[14]

Geographical Location and Relocation

Hundreds of indigenous societies were thriving at the time of European invasions. (In this chapter, we will sometimes speak of these many groups as though they were one Native American group; at other times, we will speak of one specific group within the larger category.) Initially, many were forced to move westward as whites advanced. *Forced migration* at gunpoint was the lot of some groups after their defeat by whites. Groups in the West, such as the Navajo, were rounded up after military engagements and forced to migrate to barren reservations. Perhaps the best known forced march was the "Trail of Tears," in which thousands of Cherokees, Creeks, Chickasaws, Choctaws, and Seminoles were relocated from their eastern lands to the so-called Indian Territory in present-day Oklahoma.

Internal migration over the past century has involved relocation from reservations and other rural areas to cities. During the 1950s and 1960s, as part of a tribal termination policy, an urban relocation program was expanded by the federal government to cover many Indian groups and numerous cities; a Bureau of Indian Affairs (BIA) branch was set up to oversee relocation services.[15] The scale of internal migration can be seen in the more than 200,000 Native Americans who moved to the cities between the 1950s and the 1980s. As of today, substantially more than half now reside in cities.[16]

The Colonial Period

Some white historians and others have asserted that the early white "settlers" encountered roving bands of Indians with whom they often came into conflict. In reality, it was often the indigenous Americans who were the settlers—they were the ones who had long settled the land, used it, and developed it. European colonists developed various strategies for dealing with those whose land they coveted. These ranged from honest treaty making with equals to deceptive treaty making, to attempts at extermination, to enslavement like that

of Africans, to confinement in often barren, prison-like areas called reservations.[17]

European colonists slowly gained dominance over Indian groups, usually forcing them into frontier areas or killing them off. Few whites seemed concerned about the genocidal consequences of this expansion. Some colonists relied on friendly Native Americans to survive the first devastating years, yet the colonists soon turned on their neighbors. In New England, a war with the Pequots in 1637 ended when whites massacred several hundred in a Pequot village and sent survivors into slavery.[18]

Treaties, Reservations, and Genocide

With the founding of the United States in 1787, indigenous peoples found themselves in a difficult position. They were viciously stereotyped and attacked in the Declaration of Independence, where Jefferson accused the British king of working "to bring on the [white] inhabitants of our frontiers, the merciless Indian Savages, whose known rule of warfare is an undistinguished destruction of all ages, sexes and conditions." Later, the U.S. Constitution only briefly mentioned Indians, giving Congress the power to regulate commerce with them.

By action or inaction, federal officials supported theft of Indian lands. A French observer of the 1830s noted the hypocrisy of official treaties: "This virtuous and high-minded policy [of treaty making] has not been followed. The rapacity of the settlers is usually backed by the tyranny of the government."[19] The procedure was often not one of immediate expropriation of land but rather of constant encroachment by whites, a gradual land-taking process sanctioned after the fact by the government treaties.

The violent subordination of Native Americans was encouraged by Andrew Jackson, a slave-holding president who was critical of much treaty making. Jackson encouraged states to defy Supreme Court rulings that favored Indians. Gradual displacement gave way to brutally oppressive marches over hundreds of miles at gunpoint, a near-genocidal policy designed to rid regions of those stereotyped by whites like Jackson as "savages." Congress passed the Indian Removal Act in 1830, and within a decade, many groups in the East had migrated "voluntarily" or at gunpoint to lands west of the Mississippi. Atlantic and Gulf Coast tribes, as well as midwestern tribes, were forcibly moved to the Indian Territory along the infamous "Trail of Tears." Large numbers died, and the relocated peoples faced serious survival problems in the new lands.[20]

In the nineteenth century westward-moving whites regularly precipitated struggles with Plains societies, many of which had, by that time, abandoned farming for a nomadic lifestyle. The nomadic, horse-oriented Plains peoples came to symbolize "the Indian" in most white imaginations, to the present day. Media presentations have severely distorted the reality of the Plains wars, which, unlike Hollywood's version, usually did *not* involve warriors in war bonnets on stallions facing a brave collection of U.S. Army officers backed by heroic soldiers on a sun-swept plain.[21]

 What are the consequences of being made a colonized people?

Myths about Conflict

Movies and television have portrayed the years between 1840 and 1880 as an era of large-scale and constant conflict between white overlanders and Indians. These media have created unforgettable, often racist images of the West—wagon trains moving across the West, wagons in a circle, whooping Indians on ponies, thousands of dead whites and Indians, and treacherous "red savages." However, research studies by John Unruh and others have made clear that these prevailing images are often mythical. Between 1840 and 1860, approximately 250,000 whites made the journey across the plains to the West Coast; fewer than two in every thousand died at the hands of the resident Native Americans. Between 1840 and 1860, a total of *only 362 whites* and *426 Native Americans* died in *all* the recorded battles between the two groups along wagon train routes. Indeed, there is only *one* documented attack by Indians on a wagon train in which there were as many as two dozen casualties for the white settler-invaders. Most white accounts of massacres by Indians are fictions or exaggerations of minor encounters.[22] In reality, Native Americans often provided food, horses, or guidance for weary white travelers.

A recurring pattern emerged in the conflict between whites and indigenous inhabitants. White farmers would move onto Indian lands. The U.S. government, by means of a treaty resulting from threat or coercion, would provide land for resettlement of the Indians affected. More white farmers, prospectors, or hunters would intrude on these new

An etching of a meeting between U.S. Army generals and Sioux and other Native American leaders at North Platte, Nebraska.

Native American lands. This theft of new land would later be legitimized by another weak or worthless government treaty, and the process would begin again. There were times when a U.S. government treaty promise of supplies to those Indians living in a restricted area would be broken, and some would leave the area, seeking food or revenge. The U.S. Army would take repressive action, sometimes intentionally punishing an innocent group and precipitating more uprisings.

Many treaties, still part of U.S. law, were masterpieces of fraud; consent was acquired by deception or threat. More than 300 treaties with Indian groups were made between 1790 and the Civil War. Very few were honored in full by the U.S. government. As time passed, treaties established regulations governing Indian behavior and provided for restricted areas whites called "reservations." This treaty process was finally abandoned by the U.S. government in 1871. Still, hundreds of ratified treaties between the United States and many Native American groups remain in effect.[23]

White Massacres of Native Americans

Serious treaty violations by whites often led to conflict. In an 1862 uprising in Minnesota, the eastern Sioux killed some white farmers after losing much of their land to invading whites and suffering at the hands of government agents. Delays in supplies promised by the government resulted in the Sioux burning and killing throughout the Minnesota Valley, and massive white retaliation followed. About the same time, conflict occurred in Colorado between indigenous groups and a state militia left in charge when the U.S. Army was withdrawn. Indian guerrilla warfare often was met with savage white retaliation. In 1864, Colonel John Chivington, a Christian minister, and his Colorado volunteers massacred nearly 200 Cheyennes in a peace-seeking band at Sand Creek. The massacre was one of the most savage: "Children carrying white flags were slaughtered and pregnant women were cut open. The slaughter and mutilation continued into the late afternoon over many miles of the bleak prairie."[24]

After the Civil War, with government support, railroad corporations gobbled up millions of acres in the West. White farmers, miners, and soldiers repeatedly violated treaties. One example was the Dakota Territory of the Sioux. Conflict over illegal white invasion escalated; U.S. troops were ordered to force Sioux bands onto a smaller reservation, even though the Sioux were already on what the government regarded as "unceded Indian territory." In this military force was Colonel George A. Custer. The most widely known battle of the Plains struggle occurred at the Little Big Horn in 1876, when a miscalculating Custer and his soldiers were wiped out by a Sioux-led group of Indians who had refused to settle on the reservation.

One of the last engagements took place at Wounded Knee Creek fourteen years later. Attempting to round up the last Sioux bands, the Army intercepted one and forced the Sioux to camp. A colonel ordered a disarming, which was carried out ruthlessly. One Sioux shot into a line of soldiers; the troops replied by shooting at close range with rifles and machine guns. Approximately 300 unarmed Indians, many of them old men, women, and children, were killed on the spot or while running from the camp.[25]

In the Southwest, indigenous resistance was, on occasion, substantial. Military expeditions against the scattered Navajo and Apache communities there attempted to destroy them or hem them in. Colonel Kit Carson convinced the Mescalero Apaches to agree to a reservation. Establishing headquarters in Navajo territory, Carson began a scorched-earth program, destroying Navajo fields and herds. He then herded his captives 300 miles to a reservation—the infamous "Long Walk" central to the Navajo collective memory of white oppression. By 1890, most remnants of the Indian groups had been forced onto reservations.[26] Still, even on the reservations, most attempted to maintain their historic cultures, including language and religion, and drew on their cultures to resist pressures of acculturation to white folkways.

 What are some long-term effects of the forced migrations of indigenous peoples?

Racist Images and Stereotypes

Soon after the arrival of European colonists in the Americas, stereotypes of Native Americans as lazy and wild and of Europeans as virtuous and hardworking, along with group classification by physical characteristics, served to distinguish colonizers from colonized. One early European myth about the Native American—that of the "child of nature" or the "noble savage"—was a mixture of patronizing appreciation and negative stereotyping. By the late 1600s, an array of anti-Indian stereotypes and ideologies became an early part of a comprehensive white racial framing of the new colonial society that was developing—a framing that included negative views of black Americans enslaved to work land taken from Indians. To the present day, elements of this old racist framing of Indians are maintained by many in the dominant white group.[27]

European colonists were initially shocked at the strength of Indian societies and their unwillingness to submit to the "civilizing" pressures of white missionaries and farmers. Violent resistance by these societies reinforced the white stereotype of the "Indian savage." By the mid-1600s, Europeans were writing that the Indians were only "wild beasts" who should be hunted.[28]

The era of westward expansion imprinted on the white mind, in popular novels and later in films and TV programs, the image of "cruel" Indian "warriors" attacking "helpless" white families. The media have seldom focused on the more significant savagery of attacks on Indian families, farms, and communities by white soldiers, hunters, and farmers. Ironically, a staggering number of fictional Indians have been killed in the media, especially in pulp fiction: "The Indian, who had been all but eliminated with real bullets, now had to be resurrected to be killed off again with printer's ink."[29] Cowboy-and-Indian movies added to false images of Indian "savagery." Numerous distorted or stereotyped images of Indians are still found in many books used in U.S. schools.

One erroneous image is that of the "primitive hunter" who made little use of land. Most indigenous groups that were killed off or forced off their lands were composed *not* of nomadic hunters but of part-time or full-time farmers. Groups such as the Cherokee had, by the time of their forced removal in the 1830s, developed significant agricultural enterprises.[30]

Paradoxical stereotypes have long been applied to Indian women, based mostly on the women's relationship with white men: a "Princess" who may save a white man from her own people, and a "Squaw" (another derogatory epithet) who becomes the white man's sexual partner. The image of the esteemed Princess—portrayed as only slightly darker-skinned than Europeans and often with distinctly European features in books and other media (such as in later Disney movies)—early became a symbol of the New World in Europe, a many-faceted "Mother figure—exotic, powerful, dangerous, and beautiful."[31] In contrast, the "Squaw" was often portrayed negatively by racist thinkers as darker, fatter, and cruder than the "Princess." She frequently shared the stereotyped traits of drunkenness, stupidity, and thievery attributed by whites to Indian men.

Research on elementary, high school, and college textbooks has found numerous racial stereotypes. Most history textbooks now deal at least briefly with indigenous peoples, but often only in the past. Some children's books today portray Indians as Pocahontas-type "princesses," "squaws," or "warriors." In an analysis of a social science textbook series for kindergarten through eighth grade, Communities United, a group that seeks to remove old racial stereotypes from textbooks, found "justifications and trivializations of some of the most vicious social practices in our history."[32] James Loewen's study of high school textbooks found significant improvements in recent years, with more attention to the diversity of early Indian societies and some recognition of their important cultures. Still, the textbooks are often riddled with erroneous assumptions about Indians and whites.[33]

Studies of the mainstream media, including popular films, have revealed numerous stereotypes, including the continuing use of "Indian warrior" and "Indian princess" images. Scholars have criticized the tendency of white observers to define Native Americans and their ancient traditions in terms of nineteenth-century white-racist images. This old imagery has influenced U.S. art, literature, media, and the mainstream view in general and has contributed to the invisibility of contemporary Indians.[34] The Academy Award–winning film *Dances with Wolves* (1990) is an example of the focus on the past. Although that now-classic film presents a more sensitive treatment of white–Indian history than its predecessors, it views the historical Indian experience as proceeding to an inevitable and negative conclusion. The film diverts attention from the *present* reality of Native Americans.[35]

Note, too, that *Dances with Wolves, Last of the Mohicans* (1993), and more recent Hollywood films often feature *white* actors playing Indians to attract white audiences. Even the still much-viewed Disney film *Pocahontas* (1995) continues to perpetuate backward stereotypes, often to child viewers. What appears as a movie about a real-life character is actually pseudo-history. One researcher notes that the Disney producer said he dramatized the "essence" of the real Pocahontas story. However, "the logic of that reasoning may be difficult to follow, but evidently to depict her 'essence' they needed to change her age and her body, and give her a motive for her actions that boils down to falling desperately in love with the first white man she sees."[36] The historical Pocahontas was actually a 10- to 12-year-old child when she was involved with John Smith, not the much older Barbie look-alike of the Disney movie. She was an Indian living when European colonizers were invading Indian lands—and soon would decimate her society and others by violence and disease. Her actual life included kidnapping and rape by whites, a trip to England, a marriage to a white planter, and early death from disease. This is *not* the story most non-Indians like to hear, and not the one told in the mainstream media.

These media are substantially responsible for communicating an array of negative and distorted images. One recent study asked a group of Americans to provide the name of an important Native American leader or personality. Participants listed "Tonto," the highly stereotyped fictional character on the old *Lone Ranger* radio and television shows. Another media center study examined television shows and found that only one-half of 1 percent of the speaking parts involved a Native American character. In addition, the television shows touching on Native Americans accented just a narrow range of unrepresentative or stereotyped themes. These included the Navajo code talkers of World War II, Indians as savages or primitive spiritual people in touch with nature, and Indians as a conquered but proud people (noble savage imagery).[37] The mainstream film industry has yet to make a fully honest film about the oppression of indigenous societies— one told substantially from the perspective of Native Americans and filled with Native American actors.

There are also remarkably few social science studies of white attitudes toward Native Americans for the contemporary era. In a 1920s research study, white college students were asked how close to themselves, on a scale from 1 ("would marry") to 7

("would not allow them in nation"), they would allow a given racial or ethnic group. White students rejected all close contact (such as friendships) with Native Americans. Using the same scale, a 1970s study found that white respondents still rejected Indians in primary-group relations, such as marriage and club membership. White views of Native Americans then mixed romantic stereotypes with traditional negative stereotypes, as they still do today. There is also a strong tendency today to see the negative socioeconomic conditions faced by many Indians as more or less self-imposed. For example, consider one 2008 study of white college students at a western university in a state with a substantial number of Native Americans. Researchers found that these students were more likely to accent individualistic explanations for white–Indian inequality than for white–black inequality, placing more emphasis on an innate lack of ability and on lack of Indian motivation as factors in explaining white–Indian inequality.[38]

Today, negative stereotypes remain commonplace in the mass media and elsewhere and thus have serious consequences. Stereotyped views in the minds of numerous white officials likely lead to discrimination in policing, arrests, and sentencing. Reports on prisons and juvenile facilities have shown that Indians are overrepresented and tend to receive harsher sentences compared with comparable white arrestees. One review of Montana prisons suggests that "socially sanctioned racism can and does seep into every level of the criminal justice system from the numbers of police arrests, severity of charges, sentencing, treatment by correction officers, and parole board decisions."[39] One reason is that many whites, including police officers, view Indians as outsiders and hold images of them as lazy, drunken troublemakers. The "drunken Indian" image is one of the most extreme stereotypes. Although indigenous societies have had problems with some members' alcohol abuse, relatively few Native Americans today have such problems. In one recent survey, only 5.8 percent of Native Americans, as compared to 5.1 percent of whites, had seriously abused alcohol over a recent year. Contrary to popular images, the vast majority were not and are not serious abusers of alcohol—despite facing the cultural destruction and intensive racial oppression that few other groups in society have encountered. In addition, numerous communities facing alcoholism problems have taken aggressive action against alcoholism, including the use of both traditional healing approaches and Western medical treatment programs. We might note too that there are now new national stereotypes of Native Americans as "well off" because of the gaming casinos developed by some Indian nations. As we will show later, this is yet another false stereotype that helps to downplay or rationalize, especially for white Americans, the persisting poverty and other inequalities still faced by many Native Americans, in both rural and urban areas.[40]

We should note too that in recent years white hate groups have carried out crimes against Indians and have developed Internet websites circulating negative, often vicious stereotypes of Indians. Suzan Shown Harjo, founding trustee of the National Museum of the American Indian, has noted, "There is no such thing as a good stereotype. . . . It reduces people or a person to a consumable, easily digestible, prejudged image or word. It sets up a system or prejudice either for or against a person or a people and, in that way, denies the humanity of that person or people . . . or it wrongly characterizes people."[41] In the 1990s, the Cable News Network (CNN) aired *Native Americans: The Invisible People,* a rare series that presented the historical circumstances surrounding contemporary Indian issues, including land-use treaty violations, federal recognition of Native American nations, and protection of sacred sites.[42] It is interesting that CNN was the first major television network to detail such historical and contemporary realities. CNN's founder, Ted Turner, also owned the Atlanta Braves baseball team, whose supporters have long helped perpetuate Indian stereotypes through continuing use of the team's name on sports gear and insistence on the famous "tomahawk chop." The team's name and fans' behavior have generated protests by Native American organizations, which largely have been ignored by both non-Indian fans and team owners.

The CNN program and some changes in the accuracy of school textbooks may signal a slow trend toward more honesty in dealing with U.S. history with regard to Native Americans. Interestingly, 57 percent of the respondents in a nationwide poll of registered voters reported that they believed public schools do not teach enough about Native American history, and three-fourths thought that colleges should provide more courses on Native Americans.[43]

In recent decades, numerous Native American writers, novelists, and moviemakers have fought traditional racist images and portrayed more realistic and nuanced images of Native Americans. For example, in his writings, such as the novels *Reservation Blues* (1995) and *The Absolutely True Diary of a Part-Time Indian* (2007), and the movie *Smoke Signals* (1998), Sherman Alexie generally portrays Native Americans in their own terms, constantly questioning stereotypes and accenting his studied representations of how Native Americans act and think. James Cox notes that Alexie's fictional characters constantly "struggle for self-definition and self-representation against the oppressive technological narratives that define Native Americans as a conquered people, as decontextualized, romanticized, subservient Tontos, and Native America as a conquered landscape." Similarly, Laguna poet and novelist Leslie Marmon Silko has dealt deeply with real Indian life, sense of place, spirituality, and struggle with the white world in her poetry and novels, such as *Ceremony* (1977), *Almanac of the Dead* (1991), and *Gardens in the Dunes* (2000). Native American writers have contributed much important and critical analysis to the public discussion of the commonplace stereotyped images and ideas of indigenous peoples and cultures.[44]

 How has a white racial frame persisted in the maintaining and reworking of stereotypes targeting Native Americans?

Politics

Native American Cultures and Societies: Before European Influence

European Americans have often viewed Native Americans as not having had "civilization" until it was brought to them by European colonists. Yet, at initial contact, most indigenous societies were at least as old as European societies and had civilizations that were at least as developed. Many indigenous societies were actually more egalitarian than European societies. Generally, in these societies both men and women had societal respect and significant status. Women often played as important a social or political role as men. Some groups, such as the Cherokees and the Iroquois, were matrilineal; the "husband-father role was to sire children, who belonged to their mother's clan, lived in their mother's family's home and inherited her property. Chiefs were from the women's side of the family."[45] Among the Iroquois, women elders chose the tribal leadership. Women had significant political input in other societies as well. Democratic political institutions were commonplace in Indian societies. Benjamin Franklin, Thomas Jefferson, and other colonial leaders admired and were influenced by the democratic institutions of certain indigenous nations such as the Iroquois. Even the symbol of the United States, an eagle clutching arrows, was copied from Iroquois symbols.[46]

The fact that much written Native American history was compiled by whites is perhaps one reason why the important roles of Indian women have usually been ignored or downplayed. Contact with Europeans frequently forced Indian groups to alter their gender roles; white leaders usually refused to deal with Indian women as leaders. Efforts of white officials and Christian missionaries to convince Indian groups about the inferiority of women and the superiority of men resulted in some decline in social power for women in numerous Indian communities.[47]

The Politics of the European Invasion

At first, European colonizers dealt with Native Americans as independent *nations*. As European communities gained strength, they began to treat these nations as groups to be exterminated or as dependent wards. Many eastern groups were destroyed or decimated. Those remaining in the East were militarily weak enough by the 1830s for the government to force them westward. During the 1830s, Supreme Court decisions made it clear that indigenous societies were only "domestic dependent nations" to be supervised by the U.S. government. The powerful agency Bureau of Indian Affairs (BIA) was established to coordinate federal relations with Indians; its work ranged from authoritarian supervision of reservations to provision of supplies. Until the 1880s, the BIA's role of attempting to protect Native Americans put it in conflict with a U.S. military policy that often promoted genocidal extermination.

Under BIA domination, traditional Indian leaders were often replaced by white-controlled Indian leaders. Indigenous religions were suppressed, and large numbers of Christian missionaries were imported. With the end of treaty making between the U.S. government and Indian nations in 1871 and the removal of many nations to reservations by the 1890s, Indians entered into a unique "trust relationship" with white America: They are the only subordinated racial or ethnic group whose life has been routinely administered over a long period of time by a bureaucratic arm of the U.S. government. The action of the BIA is a clear example of *government* defining and controlling U.S. racial and ethnic groups, a point underscored by the theory of racial formation (see Chapter 2). Later, we will see how the federal government has mismanaged Native American lands and trust funds that were supposed to be protected under this distinctive "trust relationship."[48]

From the Dawes Act to the New Deal

A major federal policy shift regarding land took place in the late nineteenth century. Indians, whites often argued, should be taught new rules of land ownership. Congress's 1887 Dawes Act stated that reservation lands should be divided among individual families—even though the European tradition of private ownership and development of land was an alien value system for most indigenous peoples. White advocates hoped that individual land allotments would convert Indian societies into collections of individualistic owners. Unallotted lands would be sold to land-hungry outsiders. This policy resulted in large-scale land sales to whites. Through fair means and foul, the remaining 140 million acres of Indian lands were further reduced to 50 million acres by the 1930s.[49]

In 1884, an Indian named John Elk moved to Omaha, Nebraska, where he adopted white ways and attempted to vote. Denied this right, Elk took his case to court, where he argued that the Fourteenth Amendment made him a citizen and the Fifteenth Amendment guaranteed his right to vote.[50] The all-white court ruled that Elk was *not* a U.S. citizen—that he was a citizen of a *foreign* nation and not entitled to vote. However, under the 1887 Dawes Act, Indian "wards" of the government could become citizens if they showed themselves competent in managing individual land allotments. Belatedly, in 1924, Congress passed the Indian Citizenship Act, granting citizenship to all Native Americans.

Later, in 1934, the Indian Reorganization Act (IRA) established yet another federal policy for indigenous peoples. Designed by Commissioner of Indian Affairs John Collier, the law was intended to establish Indian civil and cultural rights, allow for semi-autonomous tribal governments, and foster better economic development on reservations. The IRA would end land allotment, require BIA supervision of the land sales, and provide for preferential hiring of Indians at the BIA. Indian groups were supposed to vote on whether they wanted to come under this act.[51]

However, this supposedly progressive law ignored fundamental economic problems and maintained the subordinate relationship of Native Americans to the federal government. The law gave the Secretary of the Interior what Indians saw as excessive power. The Secretary, called the "dictator of the Indians," had the power to make rules for elections, veto constitutions, supervise expenditures, and regulate land management on reservations.[52] One analyst noted that "the expressed purpose of this law was finally and completely to usurp the traditional mechanisms of American Indian governance (e.g., the traditional chiefs, council of elders, etc.), replacing them with a system of federally approved and regulated 'tribal councils' . . . structured more along the lines of corporate boards than of government entities."[53]

Many Native Americans saw the IRA as a violation of the sovereignty guaranteed them by treaties, and the law was ratified locally often by manipulation of the voting process. After four years, 189 Native American nations were reorganized, many with central councils and constitutions reflecting the values of the surrounding white culture. The seventy-seven groups that voted down participation operated under more traditional cultures. Numerous groups began some self-government, managing their property and governing their affairs but with substantial federal supervision.[54]

The Termination Policy

In 1946, after World War II, with a growing number of claims being made with regard to U.S. government violations of older treaties made with various Native American communities, the federal government set up an Indian Claims Commission. This Commission received numerous claims for compensation for lands

taken, although in the first decade most of the Indian claims were denied.

In the 1950s, federal Indian policy again changed dramatically. House Concurrent Resolution 108 called for the *termination* of federal supervision of Indian groups. The intent was to reject the Indian Reorganization Act and return to the policy of forced conformity to white values with regard to land ownership. Termination was supported by land-hungry whites and their political supporters seeking to cut government costs, as well as by some acculturated Indians living off reservations. Thus, between 1954 and 1960, federal guardianship of several dozen Indian groups was "terminated." Because of its negative effects, including problems with unfriendly white officials and land entrepreneurs, this termination policy soon became a major failure. Termination was costly for many Indian groups that were still unprepared to deal with the land greed of the outside world.[55]

In the 1960s, federal policy toward Indians shifted once again. President Richard Nixon called on Congress to maintain Indians' close ties to the federal government and to prohibit termination without consent. Congress passed legislation that made credit available for business purposes and established a self-determination procedure whereby Indian nations would assume self-administration of certain federal programs. Thus, since the 1970s, numerous Native American groups have been able to run their own schools and social service programs. Even so, their budgets and many regulations are still controlled by the BIA. Interestingly, in 2009, President Barack Obama lived up to a campaign pledge and called the first White House Tribal Nations Conference. Obama also ordered each Cabinet agency to work to put into effect Executive Order 13175, titled "Consultation and Coordination with Indian Tribal Governments."[56]

The Controversial Role of the BIA

The powers of the Bureau of Indian Affairs have long been far-reaching. That agency defines who is an "Indian" by determining which tribal groups are officially acknowledged by the government. It keeps records of fractions of "blood" lines to identify who is eligible for tribal membership. Official status usually brings a number of benefits to a group, including development, health, education, and housing benefits. To obtain federal recognition, a tribal group must document a continuous history and prove that its members are Indians. Several groups have been denied recognition—an action that amounts to administrative death.[57] The government-controlled process of defining who is an Indian and what is a tribe is one that is emphasized by racial formation theorists.

Today, the BIA continues to supervise Indian governments, banking, utilities, and highways, as well as millions in Indian trust funds. The BIA supervises the sale of land, and, until relatively recently, all control of social services was in the hands of federal agencies. Some Native Americans regard the BIA as the lesser of two evils, noting that in recent decades it has protected them, to some extent, against predatory exploitation by white outsiders and has periodically expanded tribal self-determination. From this perspective, to terminate the BIA would be to end what protection the federal government does provide.[58]

Growing numbers of Indians have called for an end to BIA control and have worked for recognition of their groups as sovereign nations. The Indian Self-Determination and Education Assistance Act was amended to enable nations to plan for autonomous governance. Federal support for self-government expanded when a U.S. Senate investigation revealed extensive BIA mismanagement. One Indian leader pointed out that federal actions "still retain the legally groundless presumption that Indian nations are somehow inherently subordinate to the United States."[59]

In 1996, several Indian leaders filed a lawsuit on behalf of the half-million Indians who sought a financial accounting and reform of the government's trust account system, which had been mismanaged for a century. The U.S. government fought the lawsuit. Soon after the lawsuit was filed, a federal judge ordered the Departments of Interior and Treasury to produce records for the trust accounts for the named plaintiffs. These trust accounts stem from land allotments made to individual Indians in the nineteenth century. Profits from the land—such as leasing fees and royalties for oil, logging, and other land uses—should have been held in trust by the government. A federal district court decision referred to this as "fiscal and government irresponsibility," and an appellate court decision accented the critical point that the federal government must

still account for the trust funds. In 2006, an Indian Trust Reform Act was introduced in Congress, but it did not pass. If it had passed, this legislation would have provided $8 billion as a settlement (plaintiffs have requested $47 billion) to individual trust account holders and given some Indian groups control over trust assets on reservations. Moreover, as of mid-2010, the U.S. Justice Department has agreed to settle the lawsuit, conditional on congressional approval, with the Native American plaintiffs for a $1.41 billion settlement, far less than what these patient plaintiffs have sought.[60]

What are the strengths and weaknesses of government policies designed to assist Native Americans?

Growing Pressures for Political Participation

For Native Americans on reservations, political participation has often included participation in reservation elections and service in tribal governments. Indian governments have often combined legislative and executive functions into one elected council, and voter turnout for elections has frequently been substantial. Internal conflict has occurred periodically between leaders who prefer to work closely with the BIA and those who support greater tribal sovereignty.[61]

Native Americans did not have the right to vote in all states (outside reservations) until the 1924 Indian Citizenship Act. Even then, states such as Utah, Arizona, and New Mexico barred reservation Indians from voting until the 1940s; as late as 1970, some states made voting and jury participation difficult. State literacy tests and gerrymandered voting district lines have also reduced Indian voting power in several states. The number of potential voters has risen to substantial proportions in certain nonreservation areas; in some urban areas, Indian voting strength is great enough to function as a **swing vote** (*a bloc that can affect close elections*).

The number of Indians running for political office has gradually increased over the last few decades. Until recently, only a handful had ever served in state and federal legislatures. For example, the New Mexico legislature had its first Indian representatives only in 1964. By 2007, however, the number had grown significantly in the western states, including Alaska and Hawaii, to about seventy-three members of state legislatures. Few have ever served in Congress—perhaps a half-dozen representatives and two senators. The most famous, Charles Curtis, was born on the Kaw reservation in 1860. Said to be one-fourth Indian, Curtis was a representative for fourteen years, a senator for twenty, and vice-president under Herbert Hoover.[62]

Since 1935, only a handful of Native Americans have served in the U.S. Congress; rarely has there been more than one at any time. Ben Reifel, a Sioux, was a representative (R–S.D.) from 1961 to 1971. In 1992, Congress's only Native American member at the time, Representative Ben Nighthorse Campbell (R–Colo.), was elected a senator from that state. In 2000, Campbell was joined by Brad Carson, who was elected in Oklahoma with the help of an organized campaign to get out Indian voters. Carson was elected in the congressional district with the largest Indian population and was at the time the only Native American (Cherokee) in the House. In 2008, only one Native American from the continental United States, Thomas Cole (Chickasaw), a House member (R–Okla.), served in either branch of Congress. Senator Daniel Akaka (D–Hawaii) has Polynesian heritage, which links him to indigenous peoples of the Pacific. In the 2008 general election many Native Americans ran in various states; at least 23 were on the ballots in Montana, Oklahoma, New Mexico, and South Dakota. In this election, Native Americans ran in two major statewide elections— for governor in Washington (Dino Rossi lost) and for State Superintendent of Public Instruction in Montana (Denise Juneau won). The number of Indian voters has grown significantly over the past few decades, primarily because of numerous voter registration campaigns. As a result, Indian voters have been very important in some state races in the West, such as in helping Democratic candidates for the U.S. Senate win in a few states since 2004.[63]

The modest-to-slight Indian representation in state legislatures and Congress is paralleled in town and city governments. Even in metropolitan areas with substantial Indian populations, only a few have been elected to city councils, school boards, or county governments. Police harassment of Indians in towns near reservations is sometimes a problem, often revealing racial discrimination by local authorities. Periodically, complaints by Indian leaders have focused on the lack of efforts in various towns and cities with significant Native American populations to recruit Native Americans as police, parole officers, and government attorneys.[64]

The recent economic gains that have come from industrial and gaming operations, which we will examine later, have enabled a few Indian groups to contribute significant amounts of money to political campaigns and to fund lobbying in Washington, DC, thereby expanding their political influence. This political influence has already helped to stop the passage of legislation detrimental to Indian interests. In recent years, a few of the (white) lobbyists working for Indian interests, as well as for non-Indian interests, have been accused or convicted of corruption and illegal practices. In addition, we should note that the large majority of Native American groups have not yet been able to prosper economically and politically in the United States.[65]

Over the last decade or so, a conservative U.S. Supreme Court has handed down a series of major decisions that limit the political and judicial power of reservation governments. During the same era that tribal governments have asserted their rights and powers under treaties (including over whites on reservations), the U.S. Supreme Court has, as a National Congress of American Indians (NCAI) report puts it, "significantly limited the civil and criminal jurisdiction of tribal governments over events that occur within their territorial boundaries. The most recent Supreme Court cases make it clear that tribal governments are in an increasingly defensive posture in the federal courts. . . . In the long term, this erosion of jurisdiction threatens to make tribal governments ineffective in protecting the cultural identities of their communities."[66] Interestingly, one Indian response to continuing federal limitations on tribal governments has been an effort to raise $20 million to buy a prominent Embassy Row facility in Washington, DC—and thus to signal the historic importance and desired independence of the tribal nations and to coordinate their growing power to affect political decision making in the U.S. capital.

Protest and Conflict

Organized Native American protest against subordination has been the most sustained and lengthy of any group in the history of North America.

Armed resistance to European and European American oppression between the 1500s and the 1890s produced great protest leaders and movements; the end of armed conflict after the 1890s did not end the protests. By the late nineteenth century, new protest organizations had sprung up. One was the Indian Rights Association, founded by whites concerned with protecting and "civilizing" Native Americans. By exposing the corruption and discrimination on reservations, such progressive groups did lay the basis for reforms in federal policies. The Society of American Indians was one of the first formed by Native Americans. The goals of this self-help-oriented organization included developing a national Indian leadership and improving educational and job opportunities.[67]

In the 1920s, John Collier organized the American Indian Defense Association to fight attempts by government officials to establish "executive order reservations" not covered by treaty and thus more accessible to exploitation by whites who wished to extract minerals. The NCAI, the largest advocacy group today, was formed in the 1940s and has pressed for education, legal aid, and progressive legislation, among other important issues. The NCAI vigorously opposed the termination policy of the 1950s and campaigned for tribal self-determination. It has campaigned against anti-Indian stereotyping, including sports teams' use of caricatured Indian symbols. The National Indian Youth Council, created in 1961, has fought vigorously for civil rights, sometimes organizing civil disobedience protests. The Youth Council has been active in education and in protection of Native American lands.[68]

Significantly, over the last few decades many Native American groups have organized and pressed hard to relieve continuing discrimination and other contemporary effects of historical anti-Indian oppression. Many have reasserted their sovereignty over lands and reservations that have long been controlled by federal and local governments.

Confrontation with the Federal Government

The term *Red Power* appeared during a period of expanded Native American activism in the 1960s. Protest actions during the 1960s continued a long tradition of pressuring white-controlled institutions into fair concessions. Civil disobedience involved such activities as delaying dam construction, occupying government facilities, and picketing. Numerous protest actions have brought significant changes benefiting Native Americans.[69]

In 1968, the American Indian Movement (AIM) was organized to address problems ranging from police brutality to discrimination in housing and employment. In 1973, AIM organized a large-scale occupation of Wounded Knee, South Dakota, a hamlet on the Pine Ridge Reservation. Several hundred members participated in armed protest against the U.S. Justice Department's decision to send federal agents to Pine Ridge to support a Sioux leader who was being challenged by activists who wanted to replace him with a traditional council of elders. During the ten-week siege, two people were killed, and more than a thousand were arrested.[70]

In its attempts to convict AIM protesters, the government behaved like a police state and used illegal wiretaps, altered evidence, and paid witnesses, which led a federal judge to dismiss the case. Afterward, U.S. government agents participated in a campaign to destroy the AIM and were thought by knowledgeable observers to have been involved in suspicious accidents and murders involving AIM members. Two hundred AIM members were harassed and arrested, but few were ever convicted. This political struggle was a major example of an open confrontation between militant Native Americans and a Native American establishment supported by federal government officials.[71]

Leonard Peltier: A U.S. Political Prisoner

In recent years, numerous Native American protest efforts have sought to free Leonard Peltier, a Lakota Sioux. Seen by many, including the international civil rights group Amnesty International, as a political prisoner, Peltier has been in a federal penal institution for decades. He is accused of shooting two FBI agents in the confrontation between Indians and government agents at the Pine Ridge Reservation in the 1970s. Initially, several men were accused, but only Peltier was tried. Federal officials have admitted it is unclear who shot the agents, and numerous members of Congress have supported a new trial for Peltier. Revelations that the FBI withheld documents (including a critical ballistics test) from Peltier's defense attorneys have added support to international calls to free him. Millions around the globe have signed petitions or joined groups protesting Peltier's confinement as a U.S. political prisoner, and legal efforts to free him have continued to the present day. In 2009, he was once again denied parole, even after serving some 35 years in prison.[72]

Anti-Indian Racism and Sports Mascots

In recent decades, the AIM and other Indian organizations have protested the use of Indian names, sacred symbols, and "tomahawk chop" gestures by many sports teams. Before one Super Bowl, the AIM sponsored a conference on racism in sports. Nationally televised sports events have brought degrading caricatures into homes of Indians who otherwise have little contact with such imagery. "We couldn't ignore it anymore," one protester stated. "People started coming up to me at work and going, 'chop-chop' and 'woo-woo.'" Prominent team names such as *Redskins* are racially derogatory and vicious, yet many sports fans refuse to acknowledge this fact. Most names such as *Redskins, Chiefs,* and *Braves,* together with the associated caricatures used by many teams, involve age-old and offensive anti-Indian images and stereotypes. Parodies of sacred chants, face paint, headdresses, and drums for entertainment purposes are taken by many Indians as assaults on their cultures, in part because most of these have spiritual significance. Such imagery and actions often lump highly diverse Native Americans into one undifferentiated group whose stereotyped portrayal is mostly a fictional invention of the white imagination.[73]

For years now, people associated with the National Coalition on Racism in Sports and the Media have joined protesters challenging the Cleveland baseball team's use of the highly caricatured "Chief Wahoo" symbol. Called the *Indians,* Cleveland's team has come under intensive criticism for an image that is seen by many Native Americans and other Americans as extremely negative and racist. Images and mascots such as Chief Wahoo are "invented Indians," as the book *Team Spirits* (2001) puts it. They are not real but "perpetuate inappropriate, inaccurate, and harmful understandings of living people, their cultures, and their histories. . . . Through fragments thought to be Indian—a headdress, tomahawk, war paint, or buckskin—Native American mascots reduce them to a series of well-worn clichés, sideshow props, and racist stereotypes."[74]

Today, many colleges and universities still use such Indian logos, often in connection with sports. Debates similar to those in Cleveland have taken place around Chief Illiniwek, the dancing Indian present at sports events, who was long a symbol for the University of Illinois. In 2001, most of that university's trustees expressed support for this racist symbol. Finally, in March 2007, facing much protest, the university board of trustees belatedly retired the Chief Illiniwek image, name, and regalia. Researcher David Prochaska argues that Indian mascots catch on because of "imperialist nostalgia," a mutated celebrating by whites of those whom their ancestors killed or forced onto reservations. The fictional Chief Illiniwek, thus, was *not* dressed like the Woodlands Illiniwek after whom he was named. Instead, whites "playing Indian" at sports events dressed up in a pseudo-Sioux costume with a war bonnet like a Plains Indian. Such actions were *not* attempts to celebrate authentically the country's indigenous inhabitants.[75]

Such mascots and related fan actions are often based on stereotypes of Native Americans as wild "savages" or blood-thirsty warriors and ignore the historical reality of savage European takeovers of Native American lands and the often genocidal policies directed at indigenous peoples.[76] The symbolism chosen by colleges and sports teams also stereotypes Indians as historical peoples rather than as contemporary peoples. Indians are portrayed as a generic "Indian" group rather than as diverse nations and are thus robbed of control even over their public images. Vigorous opposition among some non-Indian men to the elimination of Indian sports symbolism may even suggest that the protest movement threatens a particular version of male identity rooted in the mythology of the American West. Note the following statement made by a prominent professional football player: "The reason there's so much violence in football is we can't kill Indians anymore."[77]

Significantly, the U.S. Census Bureau has decided not to include pictures of sports teams that use these stereotyped Indian symbols in the Bureau's promotional materials. In 2001, the U.S. Commission on Civil Rights issued a statement condemning the use of stereotyped Indian images as sports symbols, and in 2005, the National Collegiate Athletic Association (NCAA) decided that college sports teams that use Indian names will not be allowed to use that imagery in NCAA-related postseason games.

Nonetheless, some powerful universities have successfully pressured the NCAA to allow them to keep their racist Indian imagery, including Florida State University (Seminoles) and the University of Utah (Utes). Well into the twenty-first century, there are *at least 900* kindergartens, elementary schools, middle schools, high schools, and colleges in the United States that have these fictional Indian mascots.[78]

Recent Gains and Continuing Protests

The Indian rights movement has achieved some gains in raising public consciousness. Films portraying Native Americans as savages and white people as heroes have become less common. Films such as *Powwow Highway* and *Dances with Wolves* have portrayed Native Americans in a more sympathetic, if sometimes paternalistic, light. Since the 1970s, some colleges and universities, such as Dartmouth and Stanford, have dropped the name *Indians* for their teams. In 1992, in response to AIM protests, the *Oregonian* became the first newspaper to discontinue using names that stereotype Indians.[79]

In the 1990s, a coalition of petitioners sued to force the Washington Redskins football team to change its name. In 1999, a federal agency voided the trademark rights of the team because its logo was racially derogatory and violated the law. However, in 2005, a U.S. appellate court decision reversed the agency's decision, again allowing the very racist trademark. Over the last two decades, several colleges and universities have given up Indian logos, and numerous local governments, especially school boards, also have had to face the issue. Many public and private schools have changed team names and dropped offensive mascots. The Minnesota Board of Education and the Los Angeles and Dallas school districts have forced local schools to give up stereotyped Indian mascots.[80]

Other recent protests have focused on a variety of issues. Protests in Oklahoma led the legislature to pass a resolution that requires local governments to delete the derogatory word "squaw" from names of geographic places. In the early 2000s, in Austin, Texas, several hundred Native Americans and supporters rallied at the state capitol to press for a repatriation and grave-protection law. This legislation would protect unmarked Indian graves and their contents on both public and private lands in Texas. However, the Texas state government continued its anti-Indian reputation by opposing this reasonable law.[81]

Honoring Treaties: Fishing Rights and Land Claims

Fishing rights and land claims have provoked conflict between Indians and whites in several states. For more than a century, indigenous nations have struggled with whites over fishing rights in the Pacific Northwest and the Great Lakes regions. Shootings and court battles have occurred in Washington state over Indian rights to catch fish, particularly salmon and trout—rights guaranteed by official treaties between the Indian nations and the U.S. government. White anglers and commercial companies object because fishing opportunities are reduced when Native Americans exercise treaty rights. A court decision, *U.S.* v. *State of Washington* (1974), ruled that indigenous rights reserved by the treaties are different from those allowed to whites and ordered the state to protect Indian anglers.[82]

White anglers defied the decision. Indian fishers were harassed and assaulted, and white protests were directed at the judge. The federal government spent millions to increase fish availability and to compensate whites. In 1979, the Supreme Court upheld the lower-court ruling, and government enforcement gradually reduced illegal fishing by whites. This decision helped to revitalize reservation economies in Washington state.[83]

Historically, Native American lands were taken by force or secured by fraud and/or without adequate compensation. The underlying cause of one East Coast land-claims conflict was thus stated by the U.S. Commission on Civil Rights: "The basic Eastern Indian land claim is that Indian land in the East was invalidly transferred from Indians to non-Indians in the 18th and 19th centuries because the federal government, *although required to do so*, did not supervise or approve the transactions."[84] In recent decades, many groups, such as the Oneida and Mohawks in New York and the Passamaquoddy in Maine, have pressed land claims in court. The Mohawks successfully pressed a claim for the return of many acres of land in New York. After a court battle, the U.S. Supreme Court awarded the Lakota Sioux $122.5 million for more than 7 million acres taken illegally in the 1870s. Although the land had been guaranteed to the Sioux by an 1868 treaty made by the U.S. government, the land was later stolen by whites when gold was discovered on the reservation. Following a war between the Sioux and the U.S. Army, the Lakota and others lost control of a large area. In 1987, a U.S. senator introduced a bill to return substantial land and to offer money damages for some stolen land. The bill gained considerable support from the Lakotas before it was withdrawn. From 1981 to 1987, Native Americans staged an occupation of Camp Yellow Thunder in the Black Hills to protest the government's failure to live up to its treaty.[85]

More recently, Alex White Plume, president of the Oglala Lakota Nation, wrote a letter to then President George W. Bush, asking that the U.S. government "fulfill its obligation to respect and protect the human rights of Indian peoples in this country." He discussed sacred Indian sites endangered by white development, calling on the U.S. government to honor its legal obligation to protect these sites. He added: "We are also calling on the United States to fulfill its legal and moral obligations to Indian peoples by voting to approve the Declaration on the Rights of Indigenous Peoples at the upcoming September session of the U.N. General Assembly. The United States cannot meet its existing legal and moral obligations under international law, nor its fiduciary obligations under federal Indian law, by voting against (or abstaining from voting on) the declaration."[86] Sioux leaders were part of the U.N. committee that wrote this important Declaration on the Rights of Indigenous Peoples, which provides for the "restitution of the lands, territories and resources" and the "enforcement of treaties." Indigenous organizations representing more than 300 million indigenous people around the world pressed the U.N. General Assembly to pass this Declaration, which was approved overwhelmingly by the United Nations in 2007. However, strong "no" votes came from the United States, Australia, New Zealand, and Canada—all countries with large indigenous populations.[87]

White backlash against Native American land claims, fishing claims, and other protests led to the creation of a national organization called the Interstate Congress for Equal Rights and Responsibilities and other antitreaty organizations. A few white members of Congress introduced bills to break treaties, overturn court decisions, and extinguish Indian land claims, arguing that the demands by Indians had soured "friendly relations." Native

American groups responded that they were seeking what was *legally* theirs under official agreements with the U.S. government. Many whites had become hostile because of the expense of living up to U.S. law and, as one Indian leader noted, "because of the lack of educational systems to teach anything about Indians, about treaties."[88]

The Native American Rights Fund (NARF), a nonprofit national legal defense firm, has represented various tribes in lawsuits and negotiations for treaty-guaranteed land and natural resource rights and for restoration of the status of tribes as sovereign nations. The NARF has won hundreds of victories. Over recent decades, the organization has secured the return of land to the Passamaquoddy and Penobscot nations in Maine, and worked for increased Native American control over local taxation, local courts, and educational programs. As a 2009 NARF overview statement notes, the NARF has also succeeded in "Protecting and establishing the inherent sovereignty of tribes; Obtaining official tribal recognition for numerous Indian tribes; Helping tribes continue their ancient traditions, by protecting their rights to hunt, fish and use the water on their lands; Helping to uphold Native American religious freedom; Assuring the return of remains and burial goods from museums and historical societies for proper and dignified re-burial; [and] Protecting voting rights of Native Americans."[89]

Human rights groups have also worked to document and reduce the substantial racial harassment and violence targeting Native Americans. Many hate crimes have occurred in the rural, mostly white communities that border numerous reservations, and Indians in urban areas also have been targeted. Hate crime incidents seldom receive media coverage. One prominent author, Rodney Barker, has reported that numerous Native Americans have told him of hate crimes that they or their families experienced, but the local "newspaper was refusing to carry those reports." Recent FBI reports on hate crimes list about seventy-five a year targeting Native Americans, but the actual number is likely much higher. In a book on such crimes, Barbara Perry reports interviews with several hundred Native Americans, who noted the often substantial attacks they face at the hands of white police officers and other whites. Perry provides examples: "A student came to my office—a young Navajo woman whom I knew to be struggling financially and culturally to remain at

Northern Arizona University. . . . For the past three or four afternoons on her way home from campus, she had been taunted and harassed by a group of young white men—presumably also university students—hanging out on their front porch. Their taunts were filled with the standard racialized epithets—'Go home, squaw'; 'How many beers today?' The harassment was bad enough, but my young friend also feared that, with time, the harassment would escalate and they would, ultimately, physically attack her."[90]

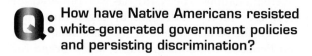 **How have Native Americans resisted white-generated government policies and persisting discrimination?**

Fighting for Fairness: Suing the Department of Agriculture

Native Americans are the oldest farmers in North America, yet most have had to struggle to maintain a living at this important occupation. The U.S. government has an uneven record regarding fairness to farmers who are not white. In 2000, more than 890 Native American families joined a class-action suit against the U.S. Department of Agriculture (USDA), charging that government agency with discrimination.[91]

The lawsuit, which as of mid-2010 was still pending, cites several types of discrimination. First, Indian farmers have often been discouraged from applying for USDA disaster assistance or farm support loans, whereas this has not been the case for most comparable white applicants. Second, Indian applicants have frequently been asked to fill out more complicated forms or to fill out forms with less assistance from USDA employees than has been offered to comparable whites. Third, USDA guidelines have been interpreted more advantageously for white than for Indian farmers. The latter have tended to receive smaller amounts when they do manage to secure loans. In addition, the USDA's locations have favored white farmers and made it difficult for many Indian farmers to get to the offices. The USDA has denied the lawsuit's charges of systemic discrimination. However, the history of U.S. government treatment of Native American (and African American) farmers suggests that extensive investigations of USDA policies are in order.[92]

Activism and Self-Determination

Since the 1970s, many Indian groups have renewed pressure on the U.S. government to accept the terms of long-neglected treaties with Indian nations. Protests of various kinds, including lawsuits, have led to restoration of lands and other resources and have been important to passage of congressional laws increasing Indian self-determination. Tribal control of lands and resources has increased because of such laws as the 1975 Indian Self-Determination and Education Assistance Act, the 1979 Archaeological Resources Protection Act, the 1983 Land Consolidation Act, and the 1988 Indian Gaming Regulatory Act. Numerous other acts are linked to this trend, including the 1978 American Indian Religious Freedom Act and the 1990 Native American Languages Act. This legislation indicates that earlier termination of tribal groups has ended. Coupled with these legislative changes are changes on reservations, where "communities are developing tribal court systems, establishing tribal education systems including tribal colleges, extending tribal sovereignty and control over resources and taxation, enforcing tribal hunting, fishing, and water rights, and building economic development programs."[93]

The resurgence of Indian self-determination has been accompanied by renewed emphasis on Indian cultures and spirituality. The National Museum of the American Indian Act authorized construction of a museum on the mall in Washington, DC, to bring together the Smithsonian's dispersed collection of Indian sacred objects. This museum is mostly under Native American control. The act requires that extensive government holdings of Indian funerary objects and burial remains be returned. The Native American Graves Protection and Repatriation Act requires museums to notify Indian groups of government holdings of Indian objects and to facilitate their return.[94]

Increased Native American activism is bearing fruit in a strong resurgence of Native American cultures and societies and a strong insistence on indigenous and civil rights. In communities near reservations, protests against racial discrimination periodically have been organized. In the fall of 2006, in Farmington, New Mexico, for example, a substantial number of Indians participated in a march down a major highway to protest recent hate crimes, police brutality, and other local discrimination that had taken place in urban areas bordering the Navajo nation.[95]

The Economy

Before being forced onto reservations, most indigenous groups—which ranged from the Pueblo agriculturalists of the Southwest to hunting societies on the Plains to mixed agricultural-hunting societies elsewhere across the continent—had self-sufficient, land-based economies.

The loss of land to whites substantially destroyed traditional economies. Melissa Fawcett Sayet, a Mohegan elder, has explained how she cried when her high school teacher taught the concept of **manifest destiny**, which stated that *the United States had a right to expand from the Atlantic Ocean to the Pacific and would inevitably do so.* By the 1880s, Native American nations had lost millions of acres as whites proceeded westward; millions more were lost with the breakup of remaining lands under the 1887 Dawes Act. In general, Native American lands were reduced to areas considered at the time to be the least valuable to white farmers and entrepreneurs. Today, Native Americans control only 3 percent of the land in the continental United States, although indigenous peoples still have legal claims to ten times that amount.[96]

Economic exploitation accompanied the growth of industrial capitalism and urbanization in the nineteenth century. Encroachment on Indian lands by white lumbering, ranching, and railroad interests redirected resources from rural Indian lands to fuel growth in cities. Bison and other game were killed for skins to be sold in eastern cities, and whites took lands for cattle raising and agriculture, hastening the impoverishment of Native Americans. Rural poverty increased as corporations reached out from metropolitan areas to develop more and more land; this in turn pressured many Native Americans to migrate to the cities. Joseph Jorgensen has shown that the poverty of rural Native Americans is "not due to rural isolation [or] a tenacious hold on aboriginal ways, but results from the way in which U.S. urban centers of finance, political influence, and power have grown at the expense of rural areas."[97] Over centuries, much Indian wealth and many resources have been unjustly transferred to the white population.

Poverty and Land Theft

On many reservations, poverty is rooted in the destruction of local economies and the mismanagement by BIA officials. Testifying before a congressional committee on the food situation in 1883, a member of the Assiniboine nation pointed out that its members were healthy until the buffalo were destroyed, and that substitute BIA rations were very inadequate:

> They gave us rations once a week, just enough to last one day, and the Indians they started to eat their pet dogs. After they ate all their dogs up they started to eat their ponies. All this time the Indian Bureau had a warehouse full of grub. . . . Early [the next] spring, in 1884, I saw the dead bodies of the Indians wrapped in blankets and piled up like cordwood in the village of Wolf Point, and the other Indians were so weak they could not bury their dead; what were left were nothing but skeletons.[98]

Government agents were responsible for supplies, instruction in farming, and supervision of lands. Unfortunately, many agents were corrupt or incompetent.

The 1930s reorganization policy, which provided for some self-government, put a partial brake on corruption, but federal policy later fluctuated between tribal self-determination and the forced individualism of the "termination" policy. Some Indian lands were sold to pay taxes, and many groups fell deeper into severe economic deprivation as land resources were depleted. For many years, Indian lands were taken for dams, national parks, and highways. Today, sale of lands to white lumbering and mineral businesses continues. In addition, much of the substantial money made from agriculture or ranching operations on Indian reservations has actually flowed to whites. Facing local and USDA discrimination and often having limited schooling, technical assistance, and capital to buy seeds, livestock, or machinery, many Indian farmers have faced a low agricultural yield or having to lease to white outsiders.[99]

Land, Minerals, and Industrial Development

Indian lands hold about 30 percent of coal reserves, 40 percent of uranium reserves, and 4 percent of oil and gas reserves. Hundreds of thousands of acres of Indian country have been developed to secure such mineral resources. Historically, whites have benefited the most from extracting such resources. White corporate executives have eagerly eyed these resources, and some have called for abolition of reservations and the Bureau of Indian Affairs so these resources can be better exploited. Historically, when desirable mineral resources have been found on Indian land, the land has often been taken over by white-run corporations. An example is the 1952 mineral agreement between the Navajo Tribal Council and Kerr-McGee Corporation. Over eighteen years, Kerr-McGee profited greatly, employing 150 Navajo men to mine uranium on Navajo land and paying them two-thirds of prevailing off-reservation wages. After the easy-to-reach deposits were mined, the company closed the facility, leaving radioactive debris that threatened water supplies. Many Indian miners have contracted terminal cancers related to their mining of uranium.[100]

One group of tribes made national headlines in the 1970s when they announced the creation of the Council of Energy Resources Tribes (CERT) and hired a former Iranian oil minister to help them get better contracts with white-owned companies. Many whites worried that CERT would seek to be completely independent in making contracts with energy corporations. Today, CERT's membership has expanded to nearly sixty U.S. and Canadian tribal groups. By providing technical and financial assistance to help member groups control their energy resources, the organization has brought new jobs and increased income to numerous communities. As a recent policy summary puts it, "Under the direction of the elected leadership of the 54 federally recognized U.S. Tribes and four First Nation Treaty Tribes of Canada, CERT dramatically restructured the federal–Indian relationship with respect to minerals, mining, taxation, and Tribal jurisdiction over environmental regulation on Indian lands."[101]

Persisting Economic Problems

Before 1940, most Indian men were poor farmers or unskilled workers. With urban migration, the proportion in farm occupations has dropped dramatically—from 68 percent in 1940 to about 1.6 percent today. Urban workers have usually been concentrated in the **secondary labor market**—*that sector characterized by job instability, low wages, and little mobility*, and disproportionately composed of workers who are not white. The **primary labor market**—*the sector characterized by skilled jobs, higher wages, and greater mobility*—is composed predominantly of white workers.

Recent census survey figures for workers aged 16 years and older (Table 6.1) compare the recent occupational distribution of workers who reported (only) Indian ancestry with that of all U.S. workers.[102] Today, Native Americans are less likely than U.S. workers as a group to hold managerial or professional positions (24.9 percent versus 34.5 percent). Native American men tend to be concentrated in blue-collar and service-sector jobs, while Native American women tend to hold clerical, sales, or service-sector jobs. Moreover, Native American civilian employees in the executive branch of the federal government are most heavily represented in clerical, technical, and blue-collar job categories.[103]

Through the years, unemployment rates for Indian workers have been far higher than for most other groups. In 1940, one-third of all Indian men were unemployed, compared with fewer than one-tenth of white men. By 1960, the rate had risen to 38 percent, compared with 5 percent for all men. This increase reflected, in part, the move from agriculture to the less certain work opportunities in urban areas. By 1990, the unemployment rate had dropped but was still high. For Native American men, the 15 percent rate was also three times that of white men, and the 13.1 percent rate for Native American women was almost three times that of white women. The unemployment rate for Native American workers, estimated for the 2006–2008 period in the American Community Survey, was 12 percent, then about twice the national unemployment rate of 6.4 percent. Between that time and 2010, both rates increased substantially. Note too that these U.S. government unemployment rates do *not* include the large proportion of workers who have given up looking for work or who find only part-time work.[104]

One racially stereotyped view of poor people of color is that they are unemployed because they are lazy or do not have necessary skills because of their "culture of poverty." However, research has made it clear that the *main* reason for their unemployment is the unwillingness or inability of employers in rural and urban areas to provide enough decent-paying jobs. Research by scholars such as Kathleen Pickering has shown that poverty-stricken Native

TABLE 6.1 Occupational Distributions: Native American Workers (Including Native Alaskans) and All Workers (2006–2008)

	Native American Workers	All Workers
Managerial and professional	24.9%	34.5
Sales and office	23.3	25.6
Service	22.6	16.8
Farming, forestry, and fishing	1.6	0.7
Construction, extraction, and maintenance	13.2	9.6
Production, transportation, and material moving	14.4	12.7
Total	100.0%	99.9%

Source: U.S. Bureau of the Census, "2006–2008 American Community Surveys." All figures are estimates based on large national surveys and have modest margins of error.

American communities, such as the Lakota Pine Ridge Reservation (South Dakota), involve local residents in much work activity. Many not only hold regular jobs in urban areas, often off and on, but also engage in much work in their home reservation areas—making traditional Lakota goods, making clothes, catering, repairing cars, and doing other personal services. Native Americans do a great deal of sharing goods and income across extended families. Like Native Americans in other communities, Lakota lives frequently involve movement back and forth between a reservation, where conventional paid work is scarce, and towns or cities where they work until (usually white) employers lay them off. In this way, the local community economy involves both subsistence work on the reservation and work beyond its borders—with supporting family networks being the central motivation for this extended economic effort across space and time. The vacillating economic conditions are imposed primarily by the larger white-controlled economy.[105]

For decades, Native Americans often had the lowest median family income and per-capita income of any major racial or ethnic umbrella group. The income of Native Americans on reservations has been lower than that of those living in nonreservation areas. In 1939, the median income of men on reservations was less than one-fourth of the median income for all U.S. men. Significant improvement has occurred in the decades leading up to the present, but the most recent government data (2006–2008 census surveys) show the median family income for Native American (including Alaskan) families to be

$42,428, which is still much less than the median family income for the total population of $63,211. The median income of households on rural reservations was even lower. Today, some 25.3 percent of Native Americans (including Alaskans) live below the official federal poverty line—much more than the 13.2 percent figure for the total population.[106]

Part of Native Americans' apparent economic improvement in recent decades may be an effect of the increase of people who now identify themselves as Native American. That is, people of mixed ancestry now reclaiming their heritage are frequently more affluent than others. Still, in this twenty-first century, many Native Americans remain among the poorest of all Americans. Note that poverty and unemployment are accompanied by inadequate living conditions. Generally speaking, Native Americans face the worst housing conditions of any U.S. group. Today, Native Americans are much more likely than white Americans to have inadequate nutrition, to die of tuberculosis or diabetes, to live in small apartments or houses, and to have inadequate water or lack of full plumbing facilities. Recent data on mortality rates for Indian adults and children show that they are much higher than for the white population as a whole. For example, mortality rates for children aged 1 to 4 are 59.2 deaths per 100,000 children for Native Americans, but only 27.0 deaths per 100,000 for whites.[107] For adults, the tuberculosis death rate is also much higher for Indians than for the U.S. population as a whole. Native Americans have the highest prevalence of type 2 (adult-onset) diabetes of any group. Although life expectancy for

Native Americans has increased in recent years, it too is still well below the national average. Many white officials tend to blame Native Americans for these problems, citing their lifestyles or diets. However, inadequate jobs, incomes, and medical facilities, as well as the stress of years of racial discrimination, are a major part of the problem. Today, numerous Indian nations are working hard to improve these health conditions as part of increased self-determination efforts allowed by the federal government in recent decades.[108]

Recent Economic Developments

With the growing self-determination movement and recognition of tribal sovereignty in federal courts, many Indian nations have developed new economic enterprises and improved local economies. Today, there are several hundred Indian gaming operations operated by some 233 tribal groups in twenty-eight states. Annual gross revenues for the year 2008 totaled about $25.9 billion. Of this, $10.6 billion were paid in taxes to local, state, and federal governments. While this tribal-generated development is significant, Indian gaming still constitutes a small percentage of the total U.S. gaming industry. Some 284,000 jobs were created in these and related enterprises.[109]

Media reports have greatly exaggerated the economic return from these operations, to the point that many non-Indian Americans hold to the myth that Indians are now mostly well off because of casinos (or oil wells). However, the majority of Native Americans have *not* benefited significantly from casino gaming revenues. The majority of the 500-plus federally recognized Indian groups have *no* gaming operations. Indeed, just a few dozen of the Indian operations receive most of the gaming revenues.[110]

Profits from gaming enterprises have constituted the first regular income for some Indian groups. Federal law requires that gaming profits be used for such things as education, economic development, courts and policing, and physical infrastructure. Where gaming revenues are significant, they have paid for educational and health care facilities, water treatment plants, job training, roads, and housing, and have reduced unemployment for some Indians. Gaming revenues have also helped create new nongaming businesses. For example, profits from the Choctaw Nation's bingo hall in Durant, Oklahoma, helped create truck stops, a motel, and a restaurant. These enterprises employ numerous Indians.[111]

Over recent decades, the Mississippi Band of the Choctaw Nation has been successful in developing

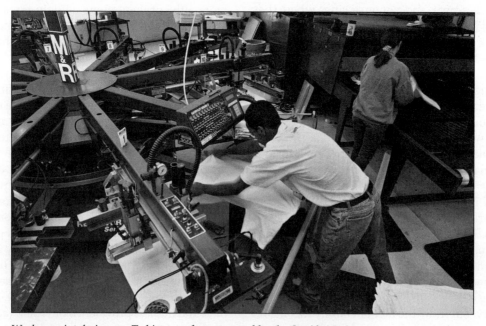

Workers print designs on T-shirts at a factory owned by the Oneida Nation.

industrial parks and other areas that have attracted Fortune 500 companies, thereby increasing local employment. They have also developed a forestry management company, a nursing home facility, and some golfing resort developments. They have become one of the ten largest private employers in the state of Mississippi, with an annual payroll of about $100 million. Similarly, in recent years Oregon's Confederated Tribes of Warm Springs have developed substantial tourism facilities, a casino, a hydroelectric enterprise, and a joint enterprise to develop diatomaceous earth products. In Oklahoma, the Cherokee Nation Industries has used gaming profits to build plants that manufacture cable boxes and cables, some of which have been used on the International Space Station. Thus, numerous Indian groups are investing gaming profits in more diversified businesses.[112]

Certain economic opportunities have been rejected by today's Native Americans. For example, in recent years numerous reservation leaders have been approached to provide landfill space for outside garbage or nuclear waste. Reservations are attractive to waste management companies because of their low population density and because they are not generally subject to state environmental regulations or taxes. Enforcement of federal pollution regulations has often been lax on reservations. Most tribes have rejected the offers, although some have become badly divided between tribal members seeking economic development and those trying to protect their lands.[113] The widespread problem of *government and private dumping in communities populated by Americans of color* is documented by a growing body of research. Such dumping is often a type of **environmental racism**.

Traditionally, indigenous nations' reservations have been government controlled, and federal government outsiders have had much to say about economic development on those reservations. As we have seen, this control has shifted to more self-determination by Native Americans over recent decades. A Harvard Project on American Indian Economic Development research summary by Stephen Cornell and Joseph Kalt notes that this "nation-building approach puts genuine, decision-making power in indigenous hands; it backs up that power with capable institutions of self-governance; it matches those institutions to indigenous political culture; it has a strategic orientation toward long-term

outcomes; and it is guided by public-spirited leadership. Over the last twenty-five years, this approach has begun to produce significant improvements in reservation socioeconomic conditions." However, a recent report by Kalt has also pointed out that "economic growth in Indian Country is fragile, particularly because it is founded on powers of self-determination that are under constant attack from certain state and federal quarters."[114]

Education

The first extended experiences of subordinated Native Americans with white-dominated education came early in the reservation period. Influential whites supported education as the channel of forced acculturation to white norms and values. In white-controlled schools, "wild Indians"—as whites stereotyped them—could be "civilized." By 1887, some 14,300 children were enrolled in 227 schools, most operated by the BIA or white religious groups.[115]

Still, by 1900, only a modest percentage of Native American children were receiving schooling in white-oriented schools. In the Southwest, perhaps one-fourth of school-age children in the four decades after 1890 had experience with BIA and other boarding schools; a small percentage of the rest attended public schools. The BIA and mission schools usually were run with an Anglo-conformity assimilationist approach. Intensive efforts were made to destroy Indian ways. By the 1930s, some boarding schools were being replaced by day schools closer to home, and a bilingual policy was being discussed by white government officials. Yet, even by 1945, large proportions of Native American children were still not enrolled in schools of any type.[116]

Enforced acculturation has been a recurring issue in BIA and local public schools, where white administrators and teachers have frequently blamed educational problems on cultural differences and thus emphasized the contrast between the often collective values of Indians and the intense individualism of most white Americans. Many white teachers have attempted to make their pupils "less Indian." To this day, many public and private school textbooks provide little to help Native American children identify with their own ancient and distinguished cultures.[117]

Partly because of organized protests since the 1960s, government aid for primary, adult, and vocational education has expanded substantially. Government attention has refocused on local public and BIA schools, and many federal schools have developed Native American advisory boards, added Native Americans to their staffs, and added classes in Indian art, dance, and language. However, in the words of one AIM member, the central "curriculum taught in Indian schools [has] remained exactly the same . . . indoctrinating children with exactly the same values as when the schools were staffed entirely by white people."[118]

The movement of many Native Americans to the cities has resulted in a decline in the proportion of children in BIA schools. Most now attend local public schools. One U.S. Department of Education task force concluded that local and federal educational systems have failed to meet the needs of Indian students. This report cited the absence of an Indian perspective in the curricula, the loss of Indian languages, the shift away from Indian values, and the racist views of many white teachers. The report called for implementation of multicultural curricula that embody respect for Indian history and culture. In addition, another recent report found that a large national sample of Native American fourth- and eighth-grade students had lower average reading and math test scores than did non-Indian students.[119]

Today, Native American educational attainment levels remain below those of the general population. Educational gains have been made since the 1960s, and recent American Community Surveys have found 76 percent of Native Americans over the age of 24 to be high-school graduates—a figure still lower than the 84.5 percent for all Americans. Some groups, such as the Navajos, have significantly lower high school attainment.[120] In addition, Indian students in predominantly white public school systems have often been disproportionately placed in "special education" classes and been disproportionately disciplined, often because of stereotypes in many teachers' minds. In several midwestern schools with significant numbers of Indian students, organizations such as the American Civil Liberties Union (ACLU) have documented discriminatory treatment of Indian students by white personnel, as well as recurring harassment by white students who throw rocks or hurl epithets such as "dirty Indian" or "greasy Indian" at the Indian students. Not surprisingly, then, U.S. Department of Education reports and other sources put the proportion of Indian students who drop out of many high schools at a figure of at least 60 percent, which is the highest for any racial or ethnic group and much higher than for whites.[121]

Over the last few decades, nonetheless, Indian youth have attended and graduated from two- and four-year colleges in increasing numbers. (Some 12.8 percent of Native Americans are now at least college graduates, compared to 27.4 percent of the total population.) Today, more than 170,000 Native American students are enrolled as undergraduate or graduate students in various types of colleges nationwide. Although most of these youth attend historically white colleges, some 27,000 students from 250 Indian nations attend the thirty-seven Indian-controlled colleges and universities, where significant efforts are made to integrate Indian history and cultures into courses. The American Indian Higher Education Consortium (AIHEC), created in 1972 by Indian

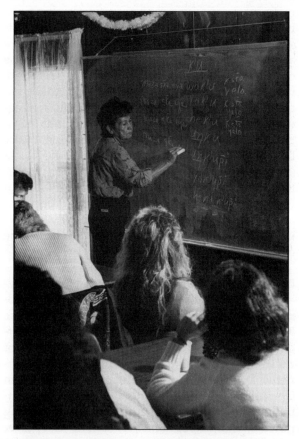

Lakota language teacher Doris Leader Charge writing words in the Lakota language for students at Sinte Gleska College.

educators, has worked aggressively to expand these colleges and their programs. Since the 1960s, moreover, more than one hundred U.S. colleges and universities have provided facilities for the study of Indian issues, such as by establishing American Indian Studies centers.[122]

Religion

Native American groups have periodically pressured museums and other facilities to return religious and art objects. They have protested the display of Indian skeletal remains in museums and have called for their return for proper burial ceremonies. Following enactment of the Indian Arts and Crafts Act (1988) and the Native American Graves Protection and Repatriation Act (1990), the U.S. government has required white-controlled museums to consult with Indian groups about returning these often illegal holdings. For example, in 1989, the Omaha tribe in Nebraska celebrated the return of their 400-year-old sacred pole, which had been in the possession of a Boston museum. The tribe has raised funds for a museum to house the sacred pole, which they regard as a living person, as *Umon'hon'ti*.[123]

Pressures on Native Americans to adapt to European American culture have long been very clear in the case of religion. Early white conquerors often attempted to convert those stereotyped as "heathen Indians" to Christianity. With the reservation period came a jockeying among Christian denominations for control; reservations often were divided among these denominations. For several reasons, including fear of whites, many Indians became loosely affiliated with a Christian denomination.[124] Today, however, only a minority identify exclusively with a Christian denomination.

Revitalization Movements as Protest

Colonized peoples have sometimes reacted to European oppressors by joining **millenarian movements** *oriented to a "golden age" in which supernatural events will change their oppressive conditions.* Among Native American millenarian movements were the Ghost Dance groups that emerged on the Great Plains. In the 1870s, a prophet called Wodziwob told of a vision in which ancestors of indigenous peoples would come on a train to Earth with explosive force, after which the Earth would swallow up the oppressive whites. Several Indian groups joined in the movement in hope of salvation from oppression. The movement declined when the cataclysm failed to occur, but it experienced a resurgence in the 1880s when a new prophet, Wovoka, told of a vision that ordered him to found another Ghost Dance religion. Religious fervor spread through the Plains tribes. The cooperation among indigenous peoples increased solidarity, but the movement was suppressed by white officials disturbed by the millenarianism. Indeed, most such Native American ceremonies were officially illegal until the 1970s, when the American Indian Religious Freedom Act was finally passed.[125]

Long used by Indian practitioners to treat sickness, peyote rituals became part of a new religion that spread through the Plains between 1880 and 1900. This new religion reflected an ambivalence toward Christianity. Rituals involved singing and praying but were distinctive in the visionary experiences induced by eating peyote (a hallucinogenic plant). Attacks on the religious movement by Christian missionaries and government officials welded believers together, and in 1918, the Native American Church was incorporated as an association of distinctive Christian groups using the traditional sacrament of Peyote. White legislators in several states passed anti-peyote laws, yet in the 1930s, the commissioner of Indian affairs came to the defense of indigenous religions and allowed their resurgence. By the 1960s, about 40 percent of Native Americans on some reservations were Native American Church members. Today, the Native American Churches' rituals are protected by federal religious freedom legislation, although some states still attempt to regulate the use of peyote by Native American Churches. The Church is estimated to have at least 200,000 members in numerous states, and many other adherents in other countries.[126]

In contrast to Christianity, most traditional religious beliefs and practices of Native Americans are not exclusive; a person can be both a Christian and a traditional believer. Because of this, a great variety of traditional and Christian religious practices have coexisted among Indian groups. Historically, numerous Native Americans have criticized Christianity as a crude religion stressing blood, crucifixion, and bureaucratized charity rather than practicing true sharing and love for others. Native American religious and political leaders often stress that Europeans are newcomers who sharply accelerated conflict in North America and mostly betrayed the Indians who aided them in becoming established.[127]

Indigenous Americans Overseas

Although most residents of the continental United States are unaware of it, the United States has significant colonies overseas. Because of imperial U.S. conquests in the 1800s and 1900s, numerous indigenous groups on Caribbean and Pacific islands came under U.S. political and economic control. Controlled by the Department of the Interior, these areas officially belong to the U.S. empire, and they do not have voting representation in Congress. These colonies include Puerto Rico (a commonwealth) and the Virgin Islands (an unincorporated U.S. Territory) in the Caribbean, and six colonial jurisdictions in the Pacific: the Northern Mariana Islands (a commonwealth); Guam and American Samoa (unincorporated U.S. Territories); and the Federated States of Micronesia, Republic of the Marshall Islands, and Republic of Palau ("sovereign nations"). The total indigenous population of these Pacific islands is nearly half a million. In addition, the official census designation, "U.S. Pacific Islanders," includes indigenous peoples of Hawaii—the largest single group. The latter have political rights in Hawaii, far from the continental U.S. In addition to indigenous residents, some islands (especially Hawaii and Guam) contain large populations of more recent immigrants of various backgrounds and their descendants. Pacific Islanders who live within the fifty U.S. states mostly reside in Hawaii and California.[128]

As a group, colonized Americans of Hawaiian, Polynesian, Micronesian, and Melanesian ancestry have a high poverty level and a median income much lower than that of the continental United States. They have worse disease and mortality rates than the U.S. population as a whole. Like other indigenous peoples, those in island communities have organized to deal with unjust impoverishment. They have aggressively raised the issue of European Americans taking lands and destroying their environments. Indigenous Hawaiians, for example, argue that the natural environment has been polluted seriously by the testing of weapons by the Department of Defense, as well as by tourism. Sacred sites have been desecrated by large developments for mainland U.S. immigrants. Leaders of the indigenous Hawaiian Nation have pressed for sovereignty, return of stolen lands, and a land trust for indigenous Hawaiians. In addition, U.S.-controlled Pacific islands have been sites of nuclear bomb and other military tests that polluted land and water with very dangerous chemicals.[129]

Our search of social science databases has found no serious articles on the political-economic conditions faced by these colonized Americans. Current research articles are almost entirely concerned with individual health issues or with substance abuse. Very little research examines the contemporary economic and political exploitation of these colonized peoples by Americans from the mainland.

Assimilation and Colonialism

The classical external colonialism model applies to early Native American encounters with Europeans, making this group distinct among North American racial–ethnic groups. In the earliest period, indigenous societies on the Atlantic coast had lands seized and members driven off or killed by European outsiders. The primary strategy was to remove indigenous peoples. This process prevailed as whites moved westward from the Atlantic over several centuries. A policy of genocide often preceded, or coexisted with, a segregation ("reservation") policy.

Assimilation Perspectives

Numerous U.S. analysts have argued that the opportunity to assimilate to the Anglo-American core culture has been more open for Native Americans than for other people of color. Since the 1920s, even a few Indian professionals have argued that Indians should voluntarily follow the lead of European immigrants and blend quietly into the dominant culture.[130]

Applying an assimilation model to Indians, some social science and other analysts tend to focus on the extent to which traditional cultures have undergone Europeanization. White-run schools and missions did bring changes in religion, language, and dress styles to indigenous groups. Other changes, such as land-ownership orientation, have likewise been substantial. Assimilation-oriented analysts cite the cultural adaptations to the dominant culture as evidence of Indians' movement toward gradual inclusion in the white-dominated society, yet also argue that Indian cultural traditions remain barriers to further incorporation.[131]

Living patterns and the sense of Native American identity today do vary widely. For example, people in the Sioux and Navajo societies generally have a strong identity, whereas certain other Native American groups have lost their old ways and strong identities. Some reservation groups, such as the Pueblos, Navajo, and Sioux, often confine substantial social contacts to their groups. Yet others, such as a significant segment of the Blackfeet, have intermarried with whites and substantially acculturated to European American ways.[132]

The intensive, often forced acculturation has failed to destroy many of the indigenous cultures. Cultural survival despite extremely unfavorable conditions is evident in the persistence of Indian languages. About 130 indigenous languages are spoken today, although most are slowly dying out. In 1990, the U.S. Congress passed the Native American Languages Act, which commits the government to working to "ensure the survival of these unique cultures and languages." Some Indian communities (for example, the Ojibwe and Blackfeet) have developed immersion language programs so that younger members can learn their indigenous languages.[133]

Structural integration at other than low-paid job levels in the economy has come slowly for Native Americans. Movement into the economic mainstream did not begin until the urban migration of the past few decades. Today, urban integration has often involved less-well-paid blue-collar positions and inadequate housing conditions, though great effort on the part of many Native Americans has gradually led to better educations and jobs. Some political advancement has taken place in towns and cities, though much political discrimination remains.

Social integration (at Milton Gordon's primary-group level) with white families has come slowly, especially for those on reservations. One 1960s Spokane, Washington, study found little social integration of Native Americans into white voluntary associations. In recent decades, intermarriage with other groups has been on the rise. Estimates suggest that at least half of Indian marriages now involve non-Indian spouses.[134]

A Native American dancer at a recent Pow Wow.

Assimilation-oriented analysts suggest that adaptation has occurred on Milton Gordon's other dimensions of assimilation (attitude-receptional, behavior-receptional, and identificational assimilation). Some movement can be glimpsed in the area of white attitudes; overt and public stereotyping of Native Americans by whites appears to have declined somewhat. However, the stereotypical use of Indian mascots by sports teams persists, often with racist defenses of such practices being made. Blatant discrimination against Native Americans may have decreased in certain sectors, but data on the economy, education, and politics indicate that many types of direct and indirect discrimination continue to restrict Native Americans today.

Attachment to ancestral identity is often strong among those who have predominantly Native American ancestry. Some have emphasized a broader umbrella identity. Several organizations, including the National Congress of American Indians and the National Indian Education Association, have tried to build a pan-Indian identity and promote unity across many groups. Since the 1980s, regular pan-Indian conferences and Pow Wows have been held in all regions. Still, local group membership remains very important for many, and most on reservation lands identify in local group terms rather than in pan-Indian terms.[135]

Research using the comprehensive 2000 census (the most recent available) shows that over the last few decades, Native Americans in major metropolitan areas have experienced a degree of spatial assimilation, at least as measured by residential dispersion within predominantly white neighborhoods. On standard measures of residential segregation from the white population, metropolitan Native Americans are the least segregated non-European group. That is, they are more likely than black, Asian, or Latino Americans to live among whites. Still, many urban Native Americans remain scattered among low-income neighborhoods populated by poor whites and other poor people of color. And a large proportion of Native Americans remain residentially separate in rural areas.[136]

Historically, when Indians have moved from reservations to cities, their ties to traditional tribal cultures have weakened in the urbanization process. However, in the last few decades, increased self-determination on numerous reservations has sparked some "retraditionalization." Many city dwellers regularly return to home reservations to participate in traditional ceremonies, thereby countering urban pressures for assimilation to the dominant culture.[137]

 How do assimilation concepts pertain to the experiences of Native Americans?

Power-Conflict Perspectives

Because of the colonialism history of Native Americans, numerous social science analysts have argued that power-conflict models are particularly relevant. They often discuss Native Americans as an "externally colonized minority."[138]

Power-conflict analysis accents the deception, genocide, and land theft that have been part of the long subordination process. Much assimilation rhetoric—"civilizing the Indians"—has been a cover for exploitation of indigenous peoples by often land-hungry whites. Treaties and certain other laws allowed individual Native Americans to become U.S. "citizens," usually after meeting such criteria as accepting individualized land allotments. Thus, becoming a citizen generally involved pressure, even coercion, to adapt in a one-way fashion to white customs and laws. Unlike most assimilation analysts, power-conflict analysts stress the reality of U.S. acculturation and incorporation processes often having *force* behind them. Government force is evident, for example, in the statement by the commissioner of Indian affairs in 1879:

> Indians are essentially conservative, and cling tenaciously to old customs and hate all changes: Therefore the government should force them to scatter out on farms; break up their tribal organizations, dances, ceremonies, and tomfoolery; take from them their hundreds of useless ponies, which afford the means of indulging in their wandering, nomadic habits, and give them cattle in exchange; and compel them to labor or to *accept the alternative of starvation*.[139]

On reservations, forced acculturation to the English language and white folkways was often the rule in Christian missions and public and private boarding schools.

From the 1970s to the 1990s, many Indian children were removed from their homes to white foster homes or institutions. In some areas, 25 to 35 percent were being removed, mostly to non-Indian families. White social workers sometimes argued that the homes of poor Native Americans were not "fit" places for these children. One Mormon child-placement program aggressively sought the removal of children. A Mormon church official stated: "When you go down on the reservations and see these hundreds of thousands of Indians living in the dirt and without culture or refinement of any kind, you can hardly believe it. Then you see these boys and girls [placed in Mormon homes] playing the flute, the piano. All these things bring about a normal culture."[140] White culture is held up as the "normal culture" against which poor Native Americans are judged, yet their poverty is substantially the result of whites' destruction of indigenous peoples' resources, theft of land, and continuing racial discrimination. In recent years, protests by Indian organizations such as the American Indian Movement (AIM) and implementation of the Indian Child Welfare Act (1978) have gradually achieved a major reduction in the number of children removed from parents.

Power-conflict analysts frequently accent the one-way character of social adaptation pressures. One older study of Indian students at the University of Oklahoma found that those students with a strong Native American identity were more likely than more "assimilated" Native Americans to drop out, regardless of academic ability. The conventional white-oriented college context is often problematic for students of color.[141] At all educational levels, Native American children typically face great and one-way acculturation pressures; most capitulate to some degree, with many thinking and behaving constantly in white-preferred ways. This adaptive behavior can damage the inner self and create great stress, and therefore bring about health problems. Caught between commitment to indigenous cultures and white pressures to conform, some children, as well as adults, have committed suicide or turned to drugs or alcohol. The suicide rate for Indians aged 10 to 24 is 20 per 100,000 for males and 6 per 100,000 for females, much higher than for other major groups.[142]

A colonialism analyst would stress that many Native Americans remain isolated politically and geographically—on the reservations, in rural areas, or in segregated urban areas. Many remain, in effect, colonized on their own lands. This is reminiscent of the external colonialism of imperialistic countries.

Today, whites, including policymakers, are often ignorant of Indian conditions. For example, in states such as Oklahoma, many whites hold the misconception that reservation groups such as Cherokees are dying out. The Cherokee nation, however, is one of the largest groups and is aggressively trying to hold on to many traditional values.[143] By denying the existence of enduring communities, many whites can ignore Native American neighbors and persisting problems of discrimination and inequality.

The continuing relevance of a colonialism model is seen in data on Indian income, employment, housing, education, and political participation. Although there have been important gains, many Native Americans remain on the lower rungs of the economic ladder. Many in rural areas and cities live in or near poverty and face high unemployment rates. To a disproportionate degree, Native Americans in urban areas have had to face a lack of economic resources, low-wage jobs, absentee landlords, and racial discrimination.

Still, many Native Americans are fighting back against white oppression, such as by organizing to protest the racist symbols used by sports teams and waste dumping on their lands by outsiders. A renaissance of Indian cultures can be seen in the numerous protest movements and Pow Wows of recent decades. We see a resurgence in strong self-determination efforts of many Indian nations and in numerous economic development projects. Growing numbers of Native Americans are reclaiming their Native American identities publicly and returning to reservations for recurring community celebrations.

Power-conflict analysts are likely to emphasize the importance of the struggle against white pressures and continuing racial oppression. Resistance and resurgence are often rooted in the historical Native American cultures, which frequently emphasize harmony with the natural world and dangers of self-indulgent individualism. Traditional cultures, then, provide a valuable source of the humanitarian, earth-centered values that many people now see as weak in U.S. society. A very critical source for Native American resistance to white discrimination and white values has been the home-culture framing of societal realities. Thus, one 2009 study involving interviews with Potawatomi Indians found that they often challenge the current realities of U.S. racism by accenting traditional values, their "cultural toolkit," which enables them not only to celebrate their group heritage but also to assess what is seriously weak or missing in the dominant culture.[144]

Richard Williams, current president of the American Indian College Fund and an Oglala Sioux, has noted that in recent decades North American Indians have "made their return from near annihilation to revival and renaissance in one of the greatest survival stories in all of human history." Since the 1960s, organized efforts by Native Americans have forced the federal government to uphold parts of some treaties and respect some Indian rights, and thus have assisted in a dramatic revival of Native Americans as a powerful national group. "For the first time," Williams notes, the government is "being held accountable to its own laws and treaties with Indian nations under its own legal system."[145] As a result, some recent federal government actions have indeed facilitated self-determination for Indian communities and improved education, health, and other social programs on and off reservations.

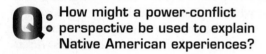 **How might a power-conflict perspective be used to explain Native American experiences?**

Summary

One recent Friends Committee report noted the barbed joking among some Native Americans. One leader of an Indian business association spoke softly the word *illegals*, then added loudly: "Illegals, illegals, illegals. . . . Everyone is always talking about illegal immigrants. Well, the only people in the country who aren't illegals are Native Americans." The report notes too that Sherman Alexie, the famous Indian novelist, once told a journalist that he "was walking in downtown Seattle when this pick-up truck pulls up in front of me. Guy leans out the window and yells, 'Go back to your own country,' and I was laughing so hard because it wasn't so much a hate crime as a crime of irony."[146] Indeed, Native Americans are descendants of the only groups that did *not* immigrate to North America within the past 600 years. They were brought into the European American sphere over a long period, during which many fought battles against the violent invaders. Genocide, the destruction of all Native Americans

in an area, was often the goal of these invaders. The era of battles with whites was followed by the present reservation era, with its long line of white bureaucrats and private actors, such as missionaries and entrepreneurs, seeking to dominate Native Americans.

Native Americans remain diverse, with many different rural and urban groups. Today, many are discriminated against by whites who have greater economic, political, and bureaucratic (for example, BIA) power. Often stereotyped as culturally or intellectually inferior, American Indians have long suffered and still face individual and institutionalized discrimination in the economic, political, religious, and educational spheres. In the economic realm, they have had lands taken and have been forced by job circumstances to relocate to racially inhospitable cities, and their socioeconomic mobility has been limited by continuing racial discrimination. Although significant economic gains have occurred in recent decades, for many on and off reservations this progress has been slow and has yet to be matched by substantial political influence. One 2008 research report has pointed out that economic progress in Native American areas is "fragile, particularly because it is founded on powers of self-determination that are under constant attack from certain state and federal quarters."[147] In addition, the BIA remains an intrusive bureaucracy, although it has gradually become more progressive and now employs many more Native American officials than in earlier years. Recently, the U.S. government was investigated for very serious mismanagement of its large Indian trust accounts, an issue that has yet to be fully resolved.

For centuries, protest movements have underscored the strengths and discontent of Native Americans. In recent years, activists have emphasized the cultural uniqueness of Indian respect for the larger human community and the natural environment. Many groups have organized to regain treaty rights and lands long ago stolen by whites. Calls for maintaining cultural distinctiveness and recognizing the virtues of indigenous cultures have been heard. Opposing celebrations of Columbus's "discovery of America," Native Americans have called attention to the reality of past and continuing oppression. Native Americans inhabited North America prior to European settlement and have a unique position with regard to citizenship. Indeed, some argue that they are *not* citizens of a United States. Because they *predate* the European invasions, they are citizens of their own long-established nations, which should regain their original sovereignty.

The desire for full recognition of sovereignty is strong for many Native American nations. Although the U.S. government has made moderate progress in returning land and control of various aspects of everyday life to many groups, most still have a neo-colonial relationship to the government. In recent years, many Native American nations have thus pressed for a direct government-to-government relationship that would replace this still mostly neo-colonial relationship with the U.S. government.[148]

Key Terms

colonization
  migration   138
swing vote   148
manifest destiny   155
secondary labor
  market   156

primary labor
  market   156
environmental
  racism   159
millenarian
  movements   161

CHAPTER 7

African Americans

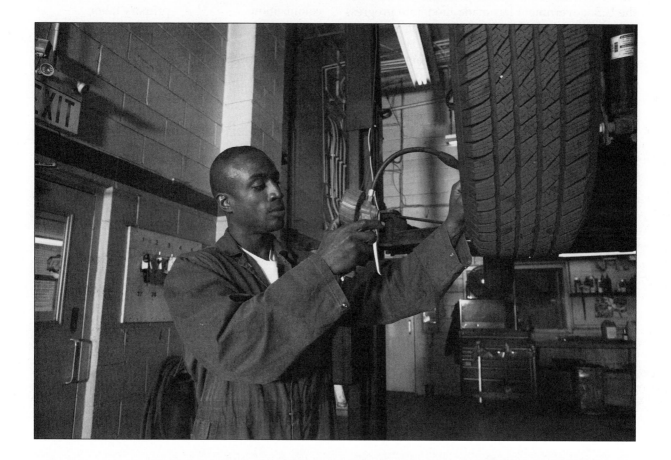

BIG PICTURE QUESTIONS

- *What role have African Americans played in building up this country's wealth and institutions?*

- *What are the long-term consequences of interracial contacts between European Americans and African Americans?*

- *What methods have African Americans used to resist systemic racism?*

One of the country's most talented journalists, Leanita McClain, committed suicide in 1984. Just 32 years old, she had won major journalism awards and was the first black person to serve on the *Chicago Tribune*'s editorial board. Why did such a talented person commit suicide? The answer is doubtless complex, but one factor looms large: the problem of coping with a discriminatory white world. Reviewing her life, one friend noted the conformity to white ways faced by black women in historically white workplaces: "Black women consciously choose their speech, their laughter, their walk, their mode of dress and car. They trim and straighten their hair. . . . They learn to wear a mask."[1] Black Americans in corporate workplaces not only face subtle and blatant racial discrimination but also suffer from intense pressures to adapt to the values and ways of that historically white world.

Interestingly, many African Americans have family trees in this country dating back to the 1600s or 1700s, before the American Revolution. They were among the first immigrants, and as a group they have been here far longer than many white immigrant groups. That a people who have been here almost as long as the first European colonists should still find themselves so discriminated against, so unwelcome in many historically white institutions, is a problematic dilemma for them and for the present and future of this country.

Forced Migration and Slavery

The black experience in North America is an example of the slave-importation end of the migration continuum discussed in Chapter 2. Formally, **slavery** involves *the legal ownership and exploitation of one human being by another*. Unlike white immigrants, who mostly came to this country voluntarily, most Africans had no choice until recently; for centuries they came enslaved and in chains. Their destinations were determined by European or European American slave traders and slaveholders. Many whites saw such enslavement as a solution to the demand for cheap labor on farms and plantations throughout the Americas.

The European Trade in Human Beings

Dutch and French companies early dominated the forcible importation of Africans; England entered the trade in the 1600s. Some were enslaved directly by Europeans, who raided local African societies and took people by force. In other cases, African coastal rulers, motivated by greed or fear of European firepower, succumbed to European slave-trade pressures and became go-betweens serving European slave traders. Nonetheless, this bloody Atlantic slave trade was invented and dominated by Europeans and, later, participated in extensively by European Americans.[2]

Once captured, enslaved Africans were often chained in corrals called *barracoons,* where they were branded and held for transportation. The Atlantic Ocean voyage was usually a living hell. Enslaved Africans were chained together with little room. The horror was summed up by one African:

> I was soon put down under the decks, and there I received such a salutation in my nostrils as I had never experienced in my life: so that with the loathsomeness of the stench, and crying together, I became so sick and low that I was not able to eat, nor had I the least desire to taste any thing. . . . On my refusing to eat, one of them held me fast by the hands, and laid me across, I think the windlass, and tied my feet, while the other flogged me severely.[3]

Suicides were common among enslaved Africans, and uprisings brought death to Africans and white sailors alike. The myth that Africans passively endured their fate is contradicted by the 155 recorded shipboard uprisings by Africans between 1699 and 1845; many other violent attacks on the white slavers doubtless went unrecorded.[4]

In 1619, twenty Africans were brought to the new European colony at Jamestown (Virginia) by a Dutch-flagged ship, and by the mid-1600s, the slave status of Africans had been fully institutionalized in colonial laws. From the mid-1600s to the 1850s, virtually all Africans were imported for the purpose of involuntary servitude. Estimates range from 10 to 15 million for the Western Hemisphere. Most were brought to the West Indies and South America; only 5 percent were brought directly to North America. From the 1600s to the Civil War, an estimated half-million Africans were brought into the colonies and, later, the United States.[5] In addition to those who arrived alive, millions of Africans died in the brutal process of transportation across the Atlantic.

Many European Americans in the early period were wealthy because they *owned* other human beings. These included the famous founders George Washington, James Madison, and Thomas Jefferson. In an early draft of the Declaration of Independence, the slaveholder Jefferson actually attacked the slave trade, but he was careful to blame it on England's King George III. Yet, because of other slave owners' opposition, this antislavery language was not included in the final version of the Declaration. One of the great democratic manifestos in world history was severely compromised by the unwillingness of slaveholding whites to include African Americans within its powerful framework.[6]

Slaveholding interests forced the recognition and support of slavery in several sections of the U.S. Constitution. These included a provision that each slave be counted as three-fifths of a person for the calculation of congressional representation (for whites); a fugitive-slave provision; and the postponement of prohibition of slave importation to 1808. Moreover, although the slave trade was officially abolished as of 1808, that ban was not seriously enforced. Thousands of Africans were still forcibly imported into a "democratic" United States.[7]

Most white families did not own enslaved African Americans. In 1860, only one-fourth of the 1.6 million white families in the South owned 3.8 million African Americans. A majority of those enslaved were held on larger farms and plantations, where they performed much of the labor and produced agricultural products to be marketed for the profit of slaveholders and their descendants. Most plantation owners were agricultural capitalists attuned to trade for profit. The wealth and power of the slaveholding gentry rose dramatically as a result of this slave-based agriculture. This plantation gentry dominated much of the economy and the federal government from the late 1700s to the 1850s.[8] Power-conflict theorists emphasize the government's role in creation of such oppressive arrangements (see Chapter 2). For many years, the U.S. government and southern and border (and some northern) state governments passed laws to benefit the powerful slaveholding gentry and to reinforce the racialized definition of and oppression of black Americans.

The Lives of Africans under Slavery

There has long been a magnolias-and-mint-julep mystique about the slave system, which lingers on, particularly in highly racist Hollywood movies such as the still-popular *Gone with the Wind*. According to this fictional imagery, residing in a big plantation house with multiple columns surrounded by magnolia trees, a paternalistic white master "cared kindly" for the "contented, happy slaves."

However, slave autobiographies describe the extreme brutality and oppressiveness of actual living conditions. Most rose before dawn and worked in the house or fields until dark or later. Food, clothing, and housing were typically crude and inadequate. The whip and chains, and other forms of torture, were mechanisms of control. White masters were frequently brutal and violent, such as the owner of one African American who told about moving from Georgia: "Then he chains all the slaves round the necks and fastens the chains to the hosses and makes them walk all the way to Texas. My mother and my sister had to walk. Emma was my sister. Somewhere on the road it went to snowing, and Massa wouldn't let us wrap anything round our feet. We had to sleep on the ground, too, in all that snow."[9] African Americans could not legally protest such brutality, for slaveholders controlled state militias and courts.

Although many analyses of slavery provide little discussion of enslaved women and children, one should recognize that the slave system included many of them. Most women, as one woman put it, "worked in the fields every day from 'fore daylight to almost plumb dark."[10] The brutality of many slaveholders was not tempered for women: "Beat women! Why sure he [master] beat women. Beat women just like men. Beat women naked and wash them down in brine."[11] African American women were victims of much coercion and violence, including frequent rape by white overseers and slaveholders, a major source over the slavery centuries of so-called racial mixing.

Whites, including many social scientists, have long been preoccupied with black families; contemporary problems of poverty and so-called broken families have often been traced back to the conditions of slavery. Until the 1970s, supportive family life was viewed as weak for the majority of enslaved African Americans. However, there is historical evidence that paternalistic slave owners often fostered enslaved families—if usually in their own self-interest—and, most significantly, that enslaved African Americans worked hard to preserve their families to the extent possible under extreme slavery conditions. Typical families may have been fragmented and frequently disrupted, but they attempted to be protective, supportive environments that helped enslaved African Americans survive. In his analysis of enslaved families, especially on large plantations, Herbert Gutman found that enslaved women were expected to have children by one man; that the names of fathers were given to sons; that adoption was used to ease disruption caused by death or breakup of families; and that many families managed to persist over generations. Of course, the threat to these enslaved families was typically great, a point that recent scholars like Wilma Dunaway (who studied smaller farms in the mountains of the South) have underscored. Marriages were very likely to be seriously disrupted at some point, by death or sale of a spouse by the slaveholder. Many families had spouses who were forced to be apart much of the time because of work assignments. Black wives and other black women were under constant threat of rape by white men. An accurate picture must include strong African American attempts to maintain family stability *and* the frequent disruption of families by callous white slaveholders seeking profits.[12]

Faced with physical torture and white attempts to eradicate their cultures, many peoples of Africa among those enslaved—the Yorubas, Akans, Ibos, Angolans, and dozens of other groups—became a single African American people and forged a distinctive African American culture.[13] Drawing on African roots, these new Americans shaped their religion, art and music, and philosophical and political thinking about oppression, liberation, and social justice. In the colonies and, later, the United States, pressures on African Americans to conform to the Eurocentric culture forced them to become *bicultural,* to know the dominant culture as well as their own. Since the first two centuries of slavery, African Americans have struggled to maintain what Bonnie Mitchell and Joe Feagin, among others, have termed an *oppositional culture*—a culture that is part African and part an African American adaptation to a history of white oppression.[14] It is this culture that has provided the foundation for active black resistance to oppression for centuries.

Active Resistance

Enslaved African Americans often had to be submissive, but this was only one response to domination.

A more assertive reaction, frequently grounded in African American culture, was common. Many observed the servile etiquette when necessary, but rebelled in dozens of small and large ways when they could.

Antislavery action included passive and violent resistance, flight to the North, and psychological withdrawal. The most famous route to freedom was the **Underground Railroad,** a *network of formerly enslaved and other antislavery Americans, black and white, who passed along tens of thousands to the North between the 1830s and the Civil War*. One famous "conductor" on this freedom trail was Harriet Tubman, one of the greatest of U.S. heroes. Formerly enslaved, she went back to the South nineteen times, risking her life to bring more than 300 enslaved people to freedom. Southerners committed to the "happy Sambo" view of enslaved workers sometimes went to absurd lengths to explain African American runaways. White physician Samuel Cartwright, incredibly, attributed the problem to a strange disease, "drapetomania," by which he meant the unhealthy tendency to flee one's owner![15]

Nonviolent resistance often took the form of a slow working pace, feigned illness, or strikes. Violent resistance was directed at property and slave owners or overseers. Tools, livestock, fields, and farmhouses were periodically destroyed; slavemasters and overseers were killed. In addition to mutinies aboard slave ships, there is evidence of at least 250 slave revolts or conspiracies to rebel during the long years of legal slavery.[16]

In 1800, a group of enslaved black Americans led by Gabriel Prosser gathered weapons and planned to march on Richmond. The governor of Virginia took action to protect the state capital from the rebels. One thousand armed African Americans rendezvoused, but a heavy rain cut them off from the city and they disbanded. Betrayed, the leaders were arrested; at least thirty-five were put to death.[17]

In 1831, Nat Turner, a very religious man, led a rebellion in Southampton County, Virginia. Seventy enslaved people recruited by Turner attacked, and dozens of whites were killed. The freedom fighters were eventually defeated by hundreds of white soldiers. Turner escaped but was captured and executed. Leaders of slave revolts took seriously the U.S. principle of "liberty and justice for all" and could be included among U.S. revolutionary heroes. African culture and religion were one important source of the black revolutionaries' resistance-oriented philosophy and inclination to rebellion.[18]

These revolts contradicted the white apologists' notion of "happy slaves"; given the opportunity, those enslaved did resist. Slavery destroyed lives and wasted energies of millions and denied most any opportunity to create wealth for their descendants. Slavery also brought major, though less recognized, costs for whites and their descendants. Especially in southern and border states, whites involved with slavery lost much of their own humanity, as well as much of their own freedom of speech and press, because of the repressive legal controls and requirements of a more or less totalitarian slave system.

Many free African Americans joined abolitionist organizations to work for the liberation of their brothers and sisters. Frederick Douglass, formerly enslaved himself, was an important leader among the abolitionists. In a July 4, 1852, speech in Rochester, New York, Douglass spoke eloquently: "What, to the American slave, is your Fourth of July? I answer: A day that reveals to him, more than all other days of the year, the gross injustices and cruelty to which he is the constant victim. To him your celebration is a sham."[19] Another influential black abolitionist was Isabella Van Wagener, better known as Sojourner Truth, who had been enslaved in New York; in the mid-1800s, she became an influential antislavery lecturer and an early advocate of women's rights. Clearly, black women and men played key roles in U.S. antislavery movements.

Outside the Rural South

Between the 1600s and the early 1800s, many *northern* whites either enslaved African Americans or considered the slavery system legitimate. Significant numbers of people were enslaved in northern areas. The wealth of many northern whites was built up directly or indirectly with forced black labor, as well as the labor of European immigrants. Benjamin Ringer notes that "despite the early emancipation of slaves in the North, [racialized colonialism] remained there, not merely as fossilized remains but as a deeply ingrained coding for the future."[20] Consider Massachusetts, where slavery was legalized in 1641, right after Africans were brought in. Massachusetts merchants played a central role in the slave trade. Not until the 1780s did public opinion and

court cases come together to abolish slavery in New England. Even then, it was not recognition of the rights of African Americans that ended slavery, but pressure from white working people who objected to competition from enslaved labor. In New York, those enslaved made up 7 percent of the population by 1786. A statute of emancipation was not passed there until 1799, and even then the law only provided for gradual emancipation. A realization that slavery was long entrenched in the North's economic and legal system is essential for an understanding of the discrimination that black Americans face today in the North.[21]

Before the Civil War, **"Jim Crow" laws** in the North already enforced *the racial segregation of ostensibly "free" African Americans in public transportation, hospitals, schools, churches, and cemeteries*. Racially segregated railroad cars were established first in Massachusetts. In northern cities, whites enforced severe housing discrimination and segregated housing areas. White residents in numerous northern areas tried to drive out any black immigrants who tried to settle there.

 What early methods of resistance were used by African Americans, and what were the consequences?

Racist Ideologies and Associated Stereotypes

Over time, the dominant group in a racial hierarchy, such as whites in the United States, develops strong beliefs to rationalize an unjustly gained economic, social, and political position. For nearly four centuries—in pamphlets, books, and articles—white intellectuals, theologians, politicians, and others have devised racist stereotypes and theories of the biological, mental, and moral inferiority of black Americans to rationalize the latter's exploitation. These racist stereotypes, theories, and ideologies are part of a comprehensive, deep racial framing of society—one created and maintained by the dominant racial group yet often accepted to some degree by members of other groups.

Negative views of African peoples existed in Europe before 1600, but until the 1700s, these did not develop into a systematic racist ideology and racist framing of society. Recall from Chapter 1 that eighteenth-century notions of a racist hierarchy included a social construction of an "African race" as inferior to "Caucasians." Thomas Jefferson took up these European notions and developed a racist ideology that personified the moral dilemmas of American whites in the eighteenth century: He wrote an indictment of slavery in the original draft of the Declaration of Independence, and yet he was the legal owner of 200 human beings. Jefferson wrote of his strong opposition to interracial sex, yet he enslaved a black teenager, Sally Hemings, who, according to DNA evidence, probably bore him at least one child, whom he also enslaved.[22] Jefferson wrote of the inferiority of black Americans and held many in slavery, but he occasionally foresaw that they would ultimately have to be freed if the country was to progress. Still, he freed few of those he enslaved, even at his death. And he, as an advocate of black colonization overseas, thought that those who were eventually freed should be pressed to leave the United States. Jefferson could not envisage the United States as a multiracial democracy.[23]

Seeing African Americans as Inferior: White Stereotypes

The white racial framing of society has long included a large array of antiblack stereotypes. For example, by the 1600s and 1700s, whites considered the dark color of enslaved African Americans to be problematical or ugly. By the mid-1800s, white defenders of slavery were even portraying African Americans as "apelike" creatures somehow not fully human. Significantly, this was the same vicious and stereotyped image that Anglo-Protestants had applied earlier to Irish immigrants.[24] Many antiblack stereotypes have become widespread since the first century of slavery. As Jefferson, among many other whites, asserted, black men and women were alleged to have an offensive odor. Black women have long been stereotyped as immoral or exotic; black men, as oversexed and potential rapists. Extreme white images of black sexuality may reflect white psychological problems with the idea and reality of "racial mixing." Indeed, much white anxiety, guilt, or anger over "racial mixing" may ultimately be linked to the historical fact that much interracial contact before and after 1865 involved the rape of black women by white men, such as white slave owners.

Patricia Williams, a distinguished law professor, has illustrated this reality by relating the story of Austin Miller, her great-great-grandfather. Miller, a 35-year-old white lawyer, bought Williams's 11-year-old black great-great-grandmother Sophie and her parents. Soon Miller forced the youngster Sophie to become the mother of Williams's great-grandmother Mary. Like many African Americans, Williams has had to deal with the reality that her influential white ancestor was not only a prominent lawyer but also a rapist and a child molester.[25]

The Pseudoscience of "Intelligence" Testing

The theme of intellectual inferiority along racial lines has received much attention since World War II. Earlier in the twentieth century, this theme was applied to immigrants from southern and eastern Europe who were considered to be inferior in intelligence to native-born Americans of northern European descent. Today, however, and in the past few decades, the focus has been on Americans of color.

For example, Arthur Jensen and Richard Herrnstein, along with a small handful of other white social scientists, have alleged that racial group differences in "intelligence test" (IQ test) scores are not determined primarily by environmental factors such as education, socialization, racial discrimination, and socioeconomic circumstances. Rather, say these authors, IQ scores reflect genetic differences between black and white groups. They argue that differences in intelligence can be reliably measured by relatively brief paper-and-pencil and object (or symbol) manipulation tests that are inaccurately labeled "IQ tests." Groups with low social status or income are argued to be, on the average, intellectually and genetically inferior to groups with greater status and income levels simply because the former average lower scores on these relatively brief white-created tests. Richard Herrnstein and Charles Murray's book, *The Bell Curve,* first published in 1994 and periodically reprinted, argued for the discredited theory that there are significant genetically determined differences in intelligence between black and white Americans.[26]

This view persists. James Watson, co-discoverer of the structure of DNA and a Nobel Prize winner, recently made the same argument that conventional IQ test data show black people are less intelligent than white people: "All our social policies are based on the fact that their intelligence is the same as ours—whereas all the testing says not really."[27]

Although the reactionary views of Watson, Jensen, Herrnstein, and Murray have been successfully refuted by many social scientists—especially their denial of environmental effects on test results—their notions about intelligence have spread to various other analysts and politicians around the globe. For example, Patrick Buchanan, an adviser to President Richard Nixon and who later became a Republican presidential candidate, picked up on Herrnstein's arguments. In a memo to Nixon, Buchanan alleged that "every study" showed black groups had lower IQs than white groups and that Herrnstein's views about race and IQ provided "an intellectual basis" for cuts in certain government support programs.[28]

In the 1930s, some social psychologists began seriously questioning whether IQ test results could be used as evidence of genetically determined group differentials. They showed how white–black differences in IQ test scores reflected major differences in education, income, and other living conditions. Numerous studies showed that test scores of black children improve with better economic and educational environments. Results from large-scale IQ testing revealed that black children and adults in some northern states scored *higher* than whites in some southern states.[29] Based on the logic of Watson, Herrnstein, and Murray, one would be forced to conclude that white southerners were mentally and "racially" inferior to black northerners. Most such white analysts would doubtless avoid this interpretation; obviously they, as defenders of a theory of black inferiority, do not wish to argue that data on IQ might actually show black intellectual superiority. Rather, they would accept an *environmental* explanation for uncomplimentary regional IQ-score differentials for whites. Not surprisingly, then, these testing differentials favoring whites are also most reasonably interpreted as reflecting significant environmental differences in such factors as family income and quality of schooling, not genetic factors.

Some analysts have focused on the cultural bias—specifically, the white middle-class bias—inherent in traditional achievement and other psychometric tests (including IQ, SAT, and GRE tests). These tests measure only certain types of learned skills and certain acquired knowledge—skills and knowledge that are *not* equally available to all racial–ethnic

groups because of centuries of discrimination and, thus, of low family incomes and lesser-quality educational facilities. For several decades now, social scientists have found that advanced skills in achievement-test taking are skills that white middle-class children are more likely to possess because they and their parents usually have access to more substantial learning resources (including expensive tutoring programs) and are typically more experienced with such paper-and-pencil testing.[30]

The most fundamental problem for those insisting on racial differences is the equation of these relatively brief tests' results with general intelligence. From the beginning, the so-called intelligence (IQ) tests have been intentionally misnamed. These tests measure only *selected* verbal, mathematical, or manipulative skills. Clearly, they do not measure (or measure well) many aspects of human abilities, such as musical, artistic, farming, fishing, and many other skills that reflect human intelligence. They penalize those who do not spend their lives enmeshed in the culture of the test makers. Intelligence is much broader than what relatively short paper-and-pencil or symbol-manipulation tests can measure. *Intelligence* is more accurately defined as a complex ability to deal creatively with one's environment, whatever that environment may be. At best, a very small portion of intellectual ability can be revealed on any conventional test. Given this problem of what social scientists call the *validity* of a measure, brief "intelligence" tests by no means reveal what the defenders of racial inequality claim they do.[31]

 Why was it important for whites to establish a racist ideology with negative stereotypes?

Contemporary Antiblack Prejudices and Related Views

To what extent does the white public still accept negative stereotypes of African Americans? Surveys of whites since 2000 continue to show that a majority still think in stereotypical terms about African Americans. One survey of whites by Harvard researchers found that a majority agreed that one or more of these stereotyped traits characterized African Americans: lazy, aggressive or violent, prefer to live on welfare, or complaining. One-third agreed with two or more of these negative traits. Similarly, a recent survey asked white college students to rate how other whites viewed African Americans. Views of African Americans as hostile, lazy, impolite, doing drugs, criminal, and unintelligent got the greatest emphasis.[32]

Negative images of black Americans seem to be deeply embedded in many whites' consciousnesses. Some psychological studies mentioned in Chapter 1 demonstrated that, when given a test of unconscious stereotyping such as the implicit association test, an overwhelming majority of white subjects quickly associate black faces (photos) with negative traits such as evil character or failure. The tests routinely reveal an antiblack, prowhite bias. In research where whites are showed photos of black faces for a few milliseconds, key brain areas designed to respond to threats light up automatically. Whites' underlying emotional states and deep racial framing, including fear of the racial "other," can apparently trigger such brain reactions and, probably, discriminatory actions.[33]

Negative stereotypes by whites are harmful for African Americans across the spectrum of life experiences. Take the example of healthcare. Surveying practicing psychiatrists some time back, Doris Wilkinson found that "cultural conditioning to racial beliefs and attitudes . . . pervades therapeutic contexts in which minority women are clients."[34] Recent research confirms this conclusion for various healthcare practitioners.

One study used actors to portray patients with symptoms of coronary disease. Several hundred physicians were asked to view recorded interviews and patient data to assess the probability of coronary artery disease and to suggest treatment. Black patients were less likely to be recommended for cardiac catheterization than white patients with similar dress, occupations, and medical histories. Another study of lung cancer patients found black patients were less likely than white patients to receive the best surgical treatment. Yet another recent study using implicit association tests taken by 2500 physicians found that 70 percent showed they implicitly preferred whites to blacks. The implications of this implicit bias are shown in a recent Harvard study in which the racial biases of 287 Boston and Atlanta physicians affected their thrombolysis recommendations for black and white patients. Although these mostly white doctors did not reveal much racial

prejudice on explicit racial questions asked of them, they did show a prowhite, antiblack bias on the implicit association tests given to them. As their prowhite implicit bias increased, so did their likelihood of discriminating in recommended medical procedures with regard to black patients. Clearly, white doctors' stereotyped images of black patients—for example, that blacks are not intelligent patients—may affect medical treatment. Yet other studies have found racial discrimination or inequality in cancer drugs carried by pharmacies, nursing home care, avoidable hospitalizations, and provision of medical care to communities of color. Building black trust in the medical care system is difficult in face of this widespread racial stereotyping and discrimination.[35]

Examining contemporary white racial views, John McConahay and colleagues have described what they call **modern racism**: *the white view that black Americans have illegitimately challenged cherished white values and are making illegitimate demands for changes in racial relations.* This hostility is reflected in negative views of certain black actions and achievements. Examining survey data, McConahay and associates have argued that extreme antiblack stereotypes and white opposition to all desegregation have, to some extent, been replaced by new racial prejudices and stereotypes. Unlike 1950s segregationists, most whites today publicly state support for equality of opportunity. Supporting this research perspective, Lincoln Quillian's recent review of social science literature found that in opinion surveys, whites mostly give public support to abstract ideals such as equality of opportunity and treatment, but the majority do not believe there is still widespread and major racial discrimination. As a result, the majority also oppose aggressive government intervention to secure racial equality. However, Quillian also concludes that "even among persons who hold a sincere belief in race blindness, images and depictions of members of racial groups learned beginning in childhood are influential in their thinking." That is, this modern racism is still undergirded by some old racist stereotypes and framing of subordinate racial groups.[36]

Many whites believe that African Americans today have opportunities equal to those of white Americans. One *Washington Post* poll found that on a general question about opportunities in life, 71 percent of white respondents thought African

Americans had opportunities in life equal to or better than those of whites. On specific issues, a majority viewed the average black person as having healthcare access equal to or better than that of the average white person. About half felt that blacks had a level of education similar to or better than that of whites. Half felt that, on average, blacks were about as well off as whites in jobs they hold, and 42 percent thought that the average black worker earned at least as much as the average white worker. Significantly, however, social science data on these questions show that *in no case* is there actually racial equality. Considering these four areas together, a large majority held one or more erroneous beliefs about white–black inequalities today.[37]

Today, racial discrimination remains a very serious problem in the United States, yet black and white Americans still often reveal dramatically different views about the reality of this discrimination. A recent Pew survey found that two-thirds of black respondents reported that black Americans always or often face job and housing discrimination, and one-half said the same for shopping and restaurants. In contrast, the majority of whites denied this black view of significant racial discrimination. Another survey by CNN found that most (87 percent) black respondents agreed that discrimination was still a national problem. In contrast, a 2008 *Newsweek* survey found that less than one-fifth of white respondents thought that discrimination was the main reason black Americans cannot get ahead. Instead, most said that black Americans themselves were mainly responsible for their current socioeconomic conditions.[38]

Do racial prejudices and stereotypes generate discrimination? One 1990s review of numerous studies found that whites who express prejudice tend to be more likely to discriminate than those who do not. Experimental research suggests that the apparently significant decrease in whites' racist attitudes on polls since the 1960s likely represents conformity to a more liberal social climate rather than a basic change in racist attitudes. One recent experimental study recruited 120 college-educated whites. These student subjects entered an experimental set-up that, without their knowledge, had actors playing out a scene where a black actor gently bumped a white actor on leaving the experimental room. The white actor did one of three things: (1) nothing; (2) blurted

out, "I hate when black people do that"; or (3) said "nigger." Soon afterward, the researcher entered and began the "study." Each white student was asked to select the white actor or black actor as a partner for the study. Researchers found that the white person's racist comments did not upset most white students or deter most from picking the white actor as a partner instead of the black actor.[39] Although there was no direct measure of prejudice, it seems likely that both unconscious racial biases and/or conscious racial thinking might have affected some white students' discriminatory choices in favor of white partners. At a minimum, the racialized comments of the white actor did not deter most students' choices.

Today, many whites continue to conceal antiblack views in order to appear socially acceptable. For example, research on white university students has found that racial attitudes expressed on short-answer survey items are often different from those expressed in reply to questions requiring detailed commentary. Recall that in one study cited in Chapter 1, 80 percent of 451 white students said that they approved of intermarriages between blacks and whites when the issue was presented as a brief survey item. However, when a similar but smaller group was interviewed in depth, the proportion that unequivocally approved of intermarriage dropped to 30 percent. Given time to explain, the majority expressed some reservations about intermarriages.[40]

Another research project had 626 white students at numerous colleges keep journals about racial events for part of a semester. In their brief journals these students recorded thousands of racial events, most involving negative and racist performances by whites, often college students. Many accounts of racist performances, such as the commonplace telling of "N-word" jokes at a party, described actions in "backstage" settings—that is, social settings composed only of white friends and relatives. After recounting racist performances by whites in these private spaces, the journal writers would often go on to say something like, "But these guys are really nice, and they would not say or do racist stuff in public." From the perspective of recent research, the apparent decrease in antiblack prejudices among whites seen in public opinion surveys over recent decades likely reflects, for a great many whites, increased concern for social acceptability (especially in more diverse "frontstage" settings) rather than an abandonment of the white racial framing and its old racist stereotypes.[41]

 How is the negative white racial framing of African Americans harmful across the spectrum of their life experiences?

Interracial Conflict

Antiblack Violence

Lynching is one of the most brutal forms of **ethnoviolence**—*violence directed at an individual or group because of that individual's or group's ethnic or racial identity*—in which human beings engage. **Lynching** is *a group killing carried out by vigilantes seeking revenge for an actual or imagined law violation by the victim.* Before the Civil War, most U.S. lynchings were carried out by white mobs targeting other whites. After the Civil War, lynching gradually became mostly a means of keeping African Americans subordinated under Jim Crow segregation. Table 7.1 shows the racialized pattern of recorded lynchings from the 1880s to the 1950s.[42]

Whites have also engaged in lynchings more recently. In 1981, in Mobile, Alabama, Ku Klux Klan members hanged a black man, and in 1998, white supremacists dragged James Byrd Jr. to death near Jasper, Texas. Experts estimate that, from the end of the Civil War to the present, at least half of all lynchings have gone unrecorded. Some estimate the number to be at least *six thousand* for the decades since the Civil War. African Americans have faced this extreme violence for more than a century; in many periods there was an "inclination to abandon such relatively mild and decent ways of dispatching the mob's victim as hanging and shooting in favor of burning, often roasting over slow fires, after preliminary mutilations and tortures . . . a disposition to revel in the infliction of the most devilish and prolonged agonies."[43]

White lynchers have usually expected that brutal lynchings would discourage black challenges of discriminatory practices such as legal segregation. Until the 1970s, white lynchers were rarely punished; many lynchings once took place with the acquiescence or active participation of white police officers. Many black civil rights advocates—and some white civil rights workers—were killed by whites, often in secret attacks, between the 1940s and the 1960s.[44]

Beginning in the World War I period, many black southerners moved to northern cities to escape oppressive conditions, but in the North they often met more violence. In a riot of whites in 1900 in New York City, for example, a substantially Irish American police force encouraged working-class whites to attack black residents. One of the most serious white-dominated race riots occurred in 1917 in East St. Louis. White workers, who saw new black workers as a job threat, attacked a black community. Thirty-nine black residents and nine of the white attackers were killed. This riot was followed in 1919 by a string of white-generated riots against black citizens from Chicago to Charleston.[45]

White supremacy groups have long been in the forefront of those who blame black, Latino, Asian, and Jewish Americans for U.S. social problems rooted elsewhere. The Ku Klux Klan, a leading supremacy group for more than a century, began as a terrorist group right after the Civil War, then went into decline after its victories in restoring the old white oligarchy's rule in the South. It regained strength in the 1920s, and again during the 1960s civil rights era. Other supremacist groups, such as the White Aryan Resistance (WAR), have emerged in recent decades. A recent count by the Southern Poverty Law Center found at least 900 Klan, neo-Nazi, racist-skinhead, Christian Identity, neo-Confederate, and other white

TABLE 7.1 Recorded Lynchings, 1882–1956		
Years	**White Victims**	**Black Victims**
1882–1891	751	732
1892–1901	381	1,124
1902–1911	76	707
1912–1921	53	533
1922–1931	23	201
1932–1941	10	95
1942–1951	2	25
1952–1956	0	3

Source: U.S. Census Bureau, *Historical Statistics of the United States.*

"hate groups," involving thousands of members, were still active in most states. Some groups now make extensive use of the hundreds of white supremacist websites, thereby increasing the readers of their literature. One Council of Europe estimate counted 4000 hate-based websites across the globe, including about 2500 U.S. websites.[46]

In recent years people associated with these groups, or reading their type of hate literature, have been involved in numerous hate-motivated crimes, including vandalism, assaults, and murders—many against African Americans. In a previously mentioned 1998 example, James Byrd Jr. was killed by white men whose racial views indicated ties to white-supremacist groups. They dragged him along a road until his body was dismembered. After this lynching-type killing, a Klan group held a rally nearby for the supremacist cause, and the murder triggered copycat crimes in other cities. Moreover, in Brooklyn's Flatlands area in the summer of 2005, ten white teenagers attacked a small group of black men, one of whom was unable to escape. He was chased in cars and on foot by the white group, some of whom yelled racist slurs. Once caught, he was beaten and ended up in the hospital. This incident was not isolated, for a few weeks before in the Queens area of New York City some white men had similarly attacked three black men and beaten one of them with a bat.[47]

Hate crimes come in many variations. After the 2008 presidential election there were at least 200 incidents of racialized vandalism and many threats of violence against President-Elect Barack Obama. In addition, the most recent (2008) FBI report on hate-based crimes reported nearly 5000 racialized crimes in the previous year, with some 70 percent of these apparently involving a racial bias against black Americans. (Note too that the FBI's report seriously underestimates the actual number of hate crimes because most U.S. police agencies do not report their hate crimes.)[48]

Some conservative political groups, such as Focus on the Family and the Traditional Values Coalition, have actually worked against tougher hate crimes legislation. In contrast, many civil rights groups have long called for increased legal penalties for U.S. hate crimes. In October 2009, the U.S. Congress—after years of conservative legislators blocking such legislation—passed the Hate Crimes Prevention Act, and President Barack Obama signed it.[49]

Black Protest against Oppression

Since the 1930s, black urbanites have, on occasion, rebelled violently against oppressive racial and socioeconomic conditions in their cities. Historically, large-scale white violence to enforce racial oppression preceded most black attacks on that continuing racial oppression.

A few urban revolts involving pitched battles between black residents and white police officers, often sparked by police brutality or other police malpractice, occurred during the 1930s and 1940s, especially in New York City. The underlying causes involved extensive job discrimination and discriminatory restrictions on political participation by whites—issues that have periodically prompted black Americans to lash out in nonviolent resistance movements as well as in violent revolts. During the 1960s and 1970s, many cities experienced black uprisings against local symbols of racial oppression, especially discriminatory white police officers, businesses, and landlords. Large-scale black rebellions occurred in Los Angeles in 1965, in Detroit and Newark in 1967, and in Washington, DC, in 1968. An angry generation of black Americans showed their willingness to engage in aggressive protests against discrimination and related economic problems.[50]

Rebellions against oppressive conditions have continued in recent decades. In the spring of 1980, black anger over local discrimination erupted in Miami. Black residents lashed out at discriminatory white and Cuban American police officers and at other racial discrimination. Those riots cost sixteen lives, caused 400 injuries, and resulted in $100 million in property damage.[51] More uprisings occurred in Miami between 1982 and 1991, all triggered by incidents involving police officers shooting an African American or being acquitted for such actions. In Los Angeles in the spring of 1992, the acquittal of officers videotaped beating an unarmed black man named Rodney King triggered the most costly uprising in U.S. history. During days of rioting in central Los Angeles, more than 10,000 blacks and Latinos were arrested, and more than fifty people were killed. Property damage exceeded $1 billion. At one point, 20,000 police officers and soldiers patrolled the area.[52] Protests also broke out in other cities. As in the 1960s riots, the underlying conditions fueling the uprisings included present-day discrimination and the poverty, unemployment, and poor housing that have resulted from long years of racial discrimination and racial inequality.

In 2001, the killing of a black man by white officers in Cincinnati sparked a large-scale rebellion by residents there. Local and national civil rights organizations had warned that police practices, as well as underlying employment and housing problems, could trigger rioting in major cities, including Cincinnati, 43 percent of whose population is African American. Numerous suspicious killings of black citizens by police officers had occurred in that city, and no officer had ever been convicted for such a killing. Days of rioting resulted in 800 arrests, dozens of injuries, and extensive property damage. In March 2001, the American Civil Liberties Union (ACLU) and local citizens filed a lawsuit against the city for **racial profiling**, *a practice used by some police departments that unfairly singles out citizens of color as potential criminals and often results in extensive harassment of innocent people.*[53]

In Cincinnati in June 2001, African Americans engage in a nonviolent protest against the killing of a young unarmed black man by the police.

The role of discriminatory white officials and police in generating or accelerating nonviolent protests and urban revolts by black Americans, while overlooked by many whites, has been significant. Police malpractice targeting Americans of color remains a major problem. In spite of improvements in U.S. policing since the 1970s, police violence and mistreatment have continued to oppress black Americans and their communities. In one important Gallup poll, *one-fifth* of the black respondents recently reported they had faced discrimination by police officers, a proportion that had increased over a previous poll. In yet another survey, more than eight in ten black respondents indicated that they had experienced some racial profiling by police or other authorities over the last year.[54] Moreover, in a search of major newspaper articles from a several-year period in the 1990s, one researcher found reports of 130 incidents of serious police brutality. White officers were involved in more than nine of every ten of these cases; black or Latino citizens were the victims in 97 percent of the incidents.[55]

For decades many police agencies have screened and stopped motorists because of their racial characteristics—what many black Americans refer to as the "crime" of "driving while black (DWB)." In one 2006 agreement, the Arizona Department of Public Safety (DPS), which protesting organizations and a lawsuit charged with racial profiling of black and Latino motorists, agreed to make data on traffic stops by state police officers public and take actions to reduce the likelihood of officers engaging in racial profiling. The Arizona DPS records revealed black and Latino motorists were indeed searched much more often than white motorists on suspicion of possessing contraband, yet were less likely than whites to have been found with that contraband. In another recent case, the ACLU and plaintiffs of color settled a lawsuit on profiling by Maryland State Police officers. Research data revealed that for some years, motorists of color were disproportionately stopped and searched without good reason. Thus, in numerous states police officers have been documented stopping motorists of color on vague notions that they might possibly have drugs. As a result, judges in various states—for example, California, Rhode Island, New Jersey, and Minnesota—have issued orders against such racial profiling.[56]

The Economy

According to traditional assimilation perspectives, most members of an immigrant group coming into U.S. society will gradually experience assimilation into the mainstream economy (see Chapter 2). Over several generations, most are expected to move into ever better levels of employment and living conditions. However, this assimilation view of economic mobility does not apply very well to African Americans. Although they have been in North America since at least 1619, they have still not been incorporated in representative numbers in many of the country's better-paying job categories, and they still face much racial discrimination in areas such as housing and healthcare.

White Enrichment, Black Losses

Over the course of North American history, whites at all class levels have benefited from white-on-black oppression. *White privilege* typically means an array of material benefits and other advantages inherited by most in each generation of whites. White privilege began in the monetary and status gains from the economic exploitation of 246 years of black slavery, persisted as a result of extensive discrimination under legal (Jim Crow) segregation, and continues as a result of contemporary discrimination and government failure to redress current effects of past discrimination.

For centuries, African Americans have been critical to the growth of U.S. prosperity. From the 1600s to the present, they have provided much of the hard labor necessary for economic growth and affluence. From the 1600s until the 1860s, the labor of most African Americans was stolen as they toiled for white slaveholders on farms and in cities. Much of the economic capital (wealth) and success of the country's white families and communities came directly, or indirectly by means of economic multiplier effects, from the African slave trade and the slave plantations. The slave trade and plantations generated many jobs for ordinary whites (such as overseers and government officials), much commercial trade, numerous banking enterprises, and many other enterprises throughout southern and northern regions. Much British, French, and North American industry, shipping, and banking depended on enslaved labor or the capital-generating effects of that labor. From the 1600s

to the 1800s, the majority of major agricultural exports in the Atlantic trade were produced by enslaved Africans. Without enslaved labor, it seems unlikely that successful British and U.S. textile industries would have developed when they did. Without that first major industry (textiles), it is unclear how or when Britain and the United States would have become major industrial powers.[57]

Since the 1600s, the exploitation of black Americans has directly or indirectly redistributed material rewards and wealth earned by black labor to many generations of whites, leaving the former relatively impoverished as a group and the latter relatively privileged as a group. Consider the value of the African American labor that was stolen. One researcher has calculated that the value (in 1983 dollars) of the slave labor expropriated by whites from 1620 to 1865 was somewhere between $1 and $97 trillion, depending on the rate of (lost) interest chosen. Even more labor was stolen under Jim Crow segregation in the form of discriminatory job placement and wages. Another study estimated the cost of this discrimination for just 1929–1969 (in 1983 dollars) at $1.6 trillion.[58] Calculating the cost of the massive antiblack discrimination from the end of slavery (1865) to the end of legal segregation (1969), and putting that calculation into current dollars, would likely increase the wage-loss estimate under segregation to several trillion dollars. Since the end of official segregation, which took place only about 1969, black Americans have suffered additional economic losses from continuing discrimination in employment and numerous other areas. The sum total for the current value of all black labor stolen through slavery, segregation, and contemporary discrimination is likely trillions of dollars.

Many whites have benefited from numerous federal programs providing critical resources that could be used to accumulate wealth over generations. Thus, in the late 1800s and early 1900s, the federal government distributed land, mineral rights, airline routes, radio/television frequencies, and other important resources. Throughout this period, black Americans, even though they were present in large numbers, were generally excluded from such benefits because of Jim Crow segregation and other discrimination. Under the 1860s Homestead Act, from that time to the 1930s, the government provided about 246 million acres at minimal cost to 1.5 million homesteads. The scholar Trina Williams estimates that roughly 46 million Americans today are likely beneficiaries, to varying degrees, of this huge wealth-generating, land-providing program.[59] Almost all these beneficiaries are white, for black families were largely excluded from this land give-away. (Note too that much of this land had been stolen from Indians.) Stephen DeCanio's research suggests that much of the long-term white–black gap in income and wealth is a direct result of this gap in access to arable homestead land.[60]

After the Civil War, some Republican Party proposals sought to give those formerly enslaved some arable land taken from slaveholders who rebelled—the famous "40 acres and a mule." Yet, this did not happen. With no major land distribution to accompany emancipation, most formerly enslaved workers were forced to sell their labor to whites because they continued to control the agricultural system in southern and border states. With much less money and legal protection than whites and faced with discrimination in land and consumer-product transactions, most freed blacks in the South were unable to become independent, land-owning farmers who could build up wealth to pass to later generations. Those who migrated to cities were mostly confined to service-sector jobs; unemployment was common. Few manufacturing jobs were open to black women or men.[61] The effect of racism-generated poverty was severe. For example, at the time, one black physician said, "Why should we be surprised at the great number of still-births among our women? . . . They do heavy washing, make beds, turn heavy mattresses, and climb the stairs several times during the day, while their more favored white sister is seated in her big armchair, and not allowed to move, even if she wanted to."[62]

What are some political and economic consequences of established white power and privilege?

The Migration North

In 1900, most black Americans lived in southern states. Soon, the bustling economy in northern and border cities, the declining significance of "King Cotton" in the South, and the violent cruelty of southern segregation stimulated increasing numbers to move north.[63] By the mid-twentieth century, millions had migrated to what many saw as an economic "promised land." They went to cities in the Northeast, Midwest, and West. Generally, they were forced to settle in low-income areas already occupied by black families. Some assimilation theorists argue that this migration brought great opportunities for mobility to black Americans, whom they see as just another immigrant group (such as the Irish or Italians) seeking to improve their lives in the cities. If we accept this view, we would expect that black economic gains between 1900 and today would have gradually closed the white–black economic gap. The reality, however, has been quite different.[64]

The racial division of labor in cities was enforced by discriminatory laws, violence, or informal discrimination. The urban economy has often been viewed as having primary and secondary employment sectors—the split labor market described in Chapter 2. The primary labor market, composed disproportionately of privileged white workers, is characterized by skilled jobs, high wages, and job ladders offering significant upward mobility. The secondary labor market, composed disproportionately of workers of color, is characterized by more job instability, lower wages, and less upward mobility.[65] The dramatic rise of corporate capitalism after 1900, which created new employment opportunities for many U.S. workers, resulted in unions organizing to expand workers' rights. However, to counter white workers' increasing demands, white employers often offered noneconomic concessions, including separating white workers from less privileged workers of color inside and outside the workplace. White workers got what W. E. B. Du Bois called a **psychological wage** (that is, *the white workers' sense of white superiority and privilege*) in return for accepting lower monetary wages than they probably would have gotten by organizing in unions with black workers.[66]

Increasing numbers of black men and women moving out of farm occupations found themselves channeled into unskilled jobs in urban industrial and service sectors. Principal occupations for black men became truck driver, porter, janitor, and cook. Black women served as maids, restaurant workers, and dressmakers, as white women began to move into clerical and professional jobs.[67] Census figures for 1930 revealed the continuing dominance of agricultural and domestic service jobs. Of every 1000 black workers, 648 were in agricultural or domestic service jobs, compared with 280 of every 1000 whites.

Most of the remainder held other unskilled blue-collar positions. Most of the few black professionals were teachers, ministers, and physicians serving the black community; likewise, black businesspeople usually served a black clientele. As a result of extensive discrimination, black incomes and savings were sharply lower than those of whites, which resulted in little in the way of resources to pass to future generations.[68]

Most labor unions were racially segregated. By the late 1930s, black pressure and federal legislation had forced many American Federation of Labor (AFL) unions to begin to reduce discrimination in recruiting black workers. The new Congress of Industrial Organizations (CIO) began with an official nondiscriminatory policy to attract black workers in the automobile, steel, and packing industries. However, in 1930, at least twenty-six major unions *officially* barred black workers from membership; by 1943, the number had dropped to fourteen. Nonetheless, official discrimination was usually replaced by informal exclusion or restriction of black workers on a large scale in the historically white unions. Some discriminatory practices have persisted in more subtle and covert forms in some historically white unions to the present day.[69]

Economic Changes Since the 1940s

During World War II, industries with labor needs were forced to make concessions to black demands for antidiscrimination laws and better opportunities. Under pressure from civil rights leaders, President Franklin Roosevelt issued executive orders that reduced job discrimination somewhat in war-related industries. At the end of the war this progress came to an end: Layoffs hit black workers much harder than whites, and discrimination increased again in most areas.[70]

During the civil rights era and the economic expansion that took place between 1955 and 1972, the proportion of black workers in professional, managerial, sales, clerical, crafts, and operatives jobs increased. By the 1980s, however, growth in the proportion of black employees in better-paid job categories slowed. Today, black workers are still significantly less likely than white workers to be in better-paid managerial, professional, technical, sales, and crafts job categories. For 2008, American Community Survey data showed that 27.5 percent of

black workers held managerial and professional jobs, compared with 38.7 percent of white workers. In contrast, black workers were more likely than white workers to hold jobs in the service workers category (24.5 percent versus 14.4 percent). (Note: Most comparative socioeconomic data in this chapter exclude from the white category "Hispanics" as defined by the U.S. Census Bureau.) Moreover, even within white-collar categories black workers tend to be in subcategories with lower pay and lesser job status. For example, within the professional category, black employees today are most commonly found in social work, kindergarten teaching, vocational counseling, dietetics, and healthcare. They are less often found among lawyers and judges, dentists, artists, engineers, and professors at historically white universities.[71]

Persisting Discrimination: A Business Example

Recall that 71 percent of white respondents in one national survey thought black Americans had at least the same opportunities as whites. Today, many whites refuse to accept the experienced testimony of the majority of African Americans that they still face serious discrimination in the workplace and other areas. Numerous research studies confirm that discrimination continues to confront black employees working for wages and those trying to succeed in businesses. In several studies, the first author has conducted or supervised interviews with hundreds of working-class and middle-class African Americans in numerous cities. Many have related concrete stories of discrimination in employment or business settings that document the types of discrimination discussed in Chapter 1. Recall that *isolate discrimination* involves actions of an individual acting alone, such as a white manager expressing antiblack views by discriminating against black employees without the support of fellow workers or a discriminatory company policy. Following is a description of the actual experience of the successful owner of a consulting firm:

> I have a contract right now with a southwestern city government. . . . I wanted the contract because I know I could do the work, and I have the background and the track record to do it. However, in negotiating the contract, they wanted to give it

to all these other people who never had any experience . . . simply because they're a big eight accounting firm, or they're some big-time institution. So, I had to compete against those people. But it was good because it proved that I could be competitive.

She then explained that a professional panel evaluating the bids gave her the highest rating because of her track record. But a barrier was thrown up, because

> the director of their department made a very racial statement, that "they were very sick and tired of these niggers and these other minorities because what they think is that they can come in here and run a business. None of them are qualified to run a business, especially the niggers." (Now, a white person, female, heard this statement, and because they had some confrontational problems—I think the only reason she really told me was because of that.) He was going to use that, not overtly, but in his mind that was going to be his reason for rejection. . . . Even though they [the panel] all recommended me (I got all five consensus votes), he was going to throw it out.[72]

This incident involved one white man's attempt to restrict a talented black person's business advancement, apparently without the help of other whites. Although this event happened about two decades ago, current research indicates that such everyday discrimination persists. Examples of such isolate discrimination motivated by racial prejudice and stereotyping are still common in the lives of African Americans.

Much well-institutionalized discrimination remains in the area of small business as well. One recent National Bureau of Economic Research study looked at the receipt of public contracts in the construction industry and found a major decrease for black contractors and other contractors of color. The causes include discrimination in the construction industry, as well as lawsuits by white contractors forcing a reduction of government antidiscrimination (for example, set-aside) programs. As the director of the Lawyers' Committee for Civil Rights has put it, "Self-employment rates of minorities, black contractors in particular, collapse when these programs are replaced or weakened through court challenges."[73] In another recent study, Adia Harvey Wingfield examined experiences of black

entrepreneurs starting beauty salons. She found that, "because of lenders' discriminatory practices, owners' limited social networks, and white patrons' unwillingness to patronize some of these establishments, black entrepreneurs find themselves limited in the types of business ventures they are able to develop."[74]

Discrimination in Corporations, Sports, and the Military

Recall from Chapter 1 that direct institutionalized discrimination involves organizationally prescribed actions carried out routinely by whites in various types of workplaces. Examples include outright exclusion, the relegation of black employees to special jobs or sections, or restricting the mobility of black employees beyond entry level. Several recent audit studies of employer responses to in-person applications and mail applications have shown that white applicants are much more likely to get callbacks about jobs than black applicants with similar resumes. In addition, a Massachusetts Institute of Technology study sent applications to job ads of Chicago and Boston employers. Using made-up names that sound like typically white or typically black first names, especially to whites, they found that job applicants with white-sounding names were much more likely to be contacted by employers than those with black-sounding names. When they increased the job credentials of the tester-applicants, this was far more likely to get white applicants a callback than black applicants.[75] Moreover, in 2005 some 417 lawsuits were filed by the federal Equal Employment Opportunity Commission (EEOC), and tens of millions in damages were won for employees. In that year, the federal Office of Federal Contract Compliance also won $45.2 million for nearly 15,000 workers who were targets of discrimination. This pattern has been true for other recent years as well. Numerous lawsuits and other agency actions demonstrate the reality of well-institutionalized and continuing discrimination in hiring, working conditions, and pay raises in a great array of workplaces.[76]

Having abandoned some overt racial barriers of earlier decades, numerous white employers have periodically retreated to a second line of discrimination: hiring black workers for nontraditional jobs and putting them in selective or marginalized positions. For decades now, research on the corporate world has shown that African Americans moving into professional and management jobs frequently find themselves tracked into "job ghettos," such as members or heads of departments of affirmative action, "community affairs," or "special markets."[77] Moreover, in one recent survey more than half of the 132 black and Latino professionals working in the field of public relations reported facing subtle and/or overt discrimination by current or past employers. Most felt that they had to be better qualified than a white person for the job they held. Some 60 percent felt that they were placed into slow-moving job career tracks, and more than half felt that they were often given menial jobs to do. The respondents also underscored the failure of top management in the industry to seek out more employees of color.[78] A survey of partners involved in hiring in eighty-three large law firms found that racial biases color the "way minority law students' achievements and aspirations are evaluated, that minority candidates are penalized for the high attrition rate of minority practitioners from law firms, and that there are still a significant number of inappropriate comments being made about minority candidates in the evaluation process." In the survey, one partner noted that senior (mostly white) lawyers in firms often set the stage for well-qualified lawyers of color to fail: They greatly exaggerate youthful mistakes and put them under the microscope, increasing their likelihood of failure.[79]

An example of racial problems in major corporations came to public attention in the late 1990s when the *New York Times* quoted from the taped transcript of a meeting of top executives at Texaco, then the country's fourteenth largest corporation, to discuss a lawsuit filed by black employees. According to the transcript, these top corporate officials discussed destroying documents requested by the plaintiffs. Black employees were called "black jelly beans" who "seem to be glued to the bottom of the bag." The EEOC found that Texaco had discriminated against black employees with regard to promotions.[80] Moreover, research on various U.S. industries, such as the finance industry, has found black employees underrepresented in key sectors (4.4 percent of professionals in the securities sector, for example). And in a 2008 analysis there were just five black CEOS at the head of *Fortune 500* companies, and just ten of these

companies had ever had a black CEO. In addition, there are fewer than one hundred black executives in the senior executive ranks of the country's top 1000 publicly traded companies. Even finding data on progress in desegregating corporate ranks is difficult. Many publicly traded companies have ignored federal government requests to report full data on the racial, ethnic, and gender characteristics of their employees.[81]

In numerous sports programs, one finds institutional discrimination at the coaching and front office levels. For example, even though black players have made up nearly half (46 percent in 2008) of Division 1 college football players for many years, data on 120 football head coaches at Football Bowl Subdivision (formerly Division 1A) universities indicated only six African Americans in 2008, some 5 percent of the total head coaches. Among the many Division 1 men's sports programs in 2008, moreover, some 89.2 percent of head coaches were white men. In the three NCAA divisions black head coaches constituted only 7.2 percent of Division 1, 5.3 percent of Division 2, and 4.0 percent of Division 3 head coaches in 2008. All 30 Division 1 conference commissioners were also white. In 2009, in the National Football League African Americans made up a more substantial number of the head coaches (6 of 32, some 19 percent), even as two-thirds of all NFL players were African Americans. In addition, all majority owners were white, as they always have been in the NFL.[82]

Considering the ordinary working-class and middle-class jobs in cities, the racial mismatch of jobs is often the result of corporate executives' intentional movement away from black populations in those cities. One research report on workers of color in Atlanta, Boston, Detroit, and Los Angeles found that, in general, the movement of jobs away from central cities to suburban areas by employers has severely limited employment opportunities. Apparently, some employers have intentionally selected workplace locations inaccessible to black workers. In Boston and Los Angeles, surveys found that employers were more likely to express a desire to move away from neighborhoods with increasing numbers of black families than from other city neighborhoods. In this large-scale study, numerous employers admitted that their hiring decisions involved a white racial framing, with its racist stereotypes about the personality traits, attitudes, and behaviors of workers of color. White employers held stereotyped images that white workers work better than black workers and rejected skilled black workers even before checking on their abilities. In addition, another study of California temporary employment agencies found white job applicants were significantly preferred over black applicants for jobs that often become a gateway to better jobs. Using similar white and black testers in sixty-four undercover tests, researchers found that "temporary agencies preferred white applicants 4–1 over African Americans in Los Angeles and more than 2–1 in San Francisco."[83]

A major survey of 40,000 U.S. military personnel, enlisted and officers, found that one-fifth of the black personnel had faced career-related racial discrimination in the previous year. Three-fourths had faced negative racial encounters; 52 percent had been told offensive racist stories; 49 percent had suffered unwelcome attempts to draw them into offensive discussions of race; 37 percent had encountered hostile racial stares; and 28 percent had endured racist comments or epithets.[84]

Government Action and Inaction on Discrimination

Freedom from centuries of slavery and Jim Crow segregation did not come for black Americans until the 1960s—that is, only in the last 10 percent of our history. The 1964 Civil Rights Act and its amendments prohibit discrimination in employment. The Equal Employment Opportunity Commission (EEOC) was created to enforce the act, primarily by investigating complaints, seeking conciliation, and filing suits to end discrimination by labor unions, private employers, state governments, and educational institutions. Until the 1980s, federal courts and the EEOC made significant progress in reducing racial barriers in traditionally white employment arenas.

However, under the Ronald Reagan and George H. W. Bush administrations in the 1980s and 1990s, aggressive EEOC efforts to halt discrimination declined substantially. The EEOC reduced field investigations of class-action complaints of discrimination as well as other broad, institutionally focused investigations of discrimination. The Reagan administration eliminated or weakened numerous civil

rights enforcement agencies, and, for the most part, President George H. W. Bush continued this approach. Presidents Reagan and Bush appointed justices to the Supreme Court who subsequently handed down backtracking decisions on civil rights enforcement and antidiscrimination issues.

During the 1990s, the Bill Clinton administration enforced the civil rights laws more vigorously, but this progress was significantly weakened under the administration of George W. Bush, beginning in 2001. Indeed, during his second term the EEOC had to deal with major budget cuts and the loss of many staff members. The EEOC is a very important U.S. antidiscrimination agency. Although the administration of Barack H. Obama has been much more committed to enforcing the civil rights laws and supporting the expansion of EEOC staff and discrimination reviews than the Bush administration, the agency continues to have a large backlog of discrimination complaints of all types. As a result, it often has had a slow resolution process for these complaints. In fiscal 2009, some 93,277 job discrimination complaints were filed that involved the private sector. The backlog was expected to still be very large at the end of fiscal year 2010.[85]

Our civil rights laws, then, do not guarantee real equality of opportunity in everyday settings. Relatively few of the millions of cases of discrimination perpetrated by white Americans each year against Americans of color are countered by effective antidiscrimination remedies. Generally, federal and state government agencies have neither the resources nor staff to vigorously enforce major antidiscrimination laws. Over the past few decades, many victims of discrimination have given up on the government's ability or willingness to deal with discrimination.[86]

Unemployment, Income, and Poverty

For decades the black unemployment rate has been more than twice the white rate (see Table 7.2).[87] In 1989, the black–white unemployment ratio reached a record high of 2.53. Since then it has fluctuated, but has remained high—at two times the white rate well into the twenty-first century. During economic recessions black workers tend to lose jobs at a higher rate than white workers and to be recalled at a slower rate. The movement of investment capital

TABLE 7.2   Unemployment Rates (Civilian Labor Force)

Year	Black (or Nonwhite)	White	Ratio
1949	8.9%	5.6%	1.6
1959	10.7	4.8	2.2
1969	6.4	3.1	2.1
1979	12.3	5.1	2.4
1989	11.4	4.5	2.5
1999	8.0	3.7	2.2
2008	10.1	5.2	1.9

Source: U.S. Bureau of Labor Statistics. U.S. Census Bureau.

and jobs to mostly white suburbs is a contributing factor to this unemployment difference.

Even higher than the unemployment rate is the **underemployment rate**, which includes *those with no jobs, those working part time, and those making poverty-level wages.* Surveys have found that large numbers of black workers have part-time work even though they want full-time work, receive very low wages, or are workers who have given up looking. Government reports indicate that one-quarter or more of black workers fall into subemployment categories, while the proportion for whites is usually much lower.[88]

For key years since 1950, black family income has not risen above 62 percent of white family income (see Table 7.3).[89] In the most recent (2008) American

Community Survey, the black median family income ($41,874) was less than 60 percent of the non-Hispanic white figure ($70,835).[90] Note too that families headed by single, separated, or divorced mothers tend to be poorer than those in which two parents are present. From 1970 until the present, the poverty rate for black female-headed families with children under age 18 has remained above 40 percent, and was at 41 percent in the most recent survey. In contrast, 21.9 percent of white female-headed families were below the poverty level in that survey.[91] One scholar has noted: "Families headed by black women are primarily poor, not because they do not have husbands, but *because they do not have jobs.*"[92] Like black men, black women face major

TABLE 7.3   Black (or Nonwhite) Median Family Income as a Percentage of White and Non-Hispanic White Family Income

Year	Percent of White Family Income	Percent of Non-Hispanic White Family Income
1950	54%	
1960	55	
1970	61	
1980	58	57%
1990	58	56
2008	62	59

Source: U.S. Census Bureau.
Note: Black family income figure for 2008 is also non-Hispanic.

employment problems in part because of intentional discrimination by white employers in the present and in part because of the continuing effects of past discrimination in contemporary workplaces and inadequate schooling facilities.

Whatever the type of family, black Americans have on average significantly fewer dollars than whites. In 2008, black families were three times as likely as white families to live in poverty (20.7 percent versus 6.1 percent). About one-fourth of all black Americans, and one-third of all black children, fell below the poverty line in "the world's richest country."[93]

Over several centuries, most African Americans have had little opportunity to build up multigenerational wealth because of slavery, Jim Crow segregation, and contemporary discrimination. Today, black households as a group have a much lower net worth than white households. Thus, one recent survey of U.S. families' finances placed the white families' median net worth at about $170,400. For black families the net worth figure was only $17,800. At the median point the wealth of white families was nearly ten times that of black families. Much of this inequality stems from such things as the home equities and savings accumulated by whites over generations of discrimination that seriously limited black access to housing and other economic resources.[94]

Wealth data show the long-term effect of centuries of racial oppression. Some data indicate that white families with modest incomes have *greater* net worth than black families with much higher incomes. The likely reason is that modest-income white families are more likely than the higher-income black families to have built up some significant equity in a house—which has often been made possible because white families have inherited a house or money from parents, or because they have not faced discrimination in finding a good job or decent housing in the past. Many middle-class African Americans are first-generation middle-class, and although their incomes may be good for the present, they have not inherited the wealth that enables them to build up much future wealth. Note too that recent research indicates that the proportion of African Americans in the middle class, as measured by income, has stayed roughly the same (about a quarter) and has not grown significantly since the early 1980s.[95]

 How do racial framing and discrimination relate to the unemployment and income inequality of African Americans?

Is There a Distinctive African American "Culture of Poverty"?

For decades, numerous commentators have contended that the black community is divided between an affluent middle class and the poor. Sometimes these analysts even argue that discrimination has mostly been eradicated for middle-class black Americans. Often the plight of the black poor is discussed as though their economic conditions were not the main problem; their values are said to be the main source of problems. From this perspective, poor black Americans (sometimes called "the underclass") are locked into a lower-class "culture" or "culture of poverty," with its "broken" families, delinquency, and lack of work emphasis. These stereotyped arguments about poor Americans are recent versions of the largely discredited culture-of-poverty views that have been argued since at least the 1960s.[96]

Perhaps the greatest weakness of arguments that focus on the alleged cultural inferiority of poor African Americans (and other poor Americans) is the serious neglect of centuries of structural discrimination and related socioeconomic factors. For example, many economic problems faced by poor Americans are created by white corporate executives who move good jobs overseas or from central cities to suburbs.

Overt, subtle, and covert discrimination also remains commonplace in workplaces and in housing, as we noted previously. Moreover, if the common notion that racial discrimination is irrelevant were true, poor black Americans should face roughly the same economic, political, and housing conditions as comparably poor white Americans. This is not generally the case. Because of continuing discrimination, overt and covert, poor black families mostly do *not* live in integrated neighborhoods with comparable white families. African Americans, including low-income workers, are *more* likely to be laid off in recessions than white Americans. Poor blacks are *less* likely than comparably poor whites to get unemployment compensation when they are laid off. They tend to hold lower-paying and less secure jobs than poor whites, and they face far more discrimination at the hands of white police officers and other whites than do poor whites. The "class" situation of poor black Americans does not account for the differences in treatment between them and poor white Americans. The cumulative effects of past and present racial discrimination on socioeconomic problems faced by poor black Americans must be recognized. As many research studies show, past official segregation and centuries of exploitative discrimination, coupled with blatant, subtle, and covert discrimination today, are likely reasons for much black poverty, unemployment, and underemployment.[97]

Discrimination in Housing

The 1968 Civil Rights Act, with later amendments, officially banned most housing discrimination. However, antidiscrimination laws have often been weakly enforced. A 2008 report of the National Commission on Fair Housing found that federal and state laws banning discrimination in rental and sales housing are weakly enforced or unenforced in most areas, even as housing discrimination is regularly documented. One 2000 study conducted across several cities, using numerous white and black housing testers, found that the white testers were favored over black testers 20 to 30 percent of the time with regard to such issues as housing availability, inspections, and cost. More recent studies of housing decisions have shown even higher rates of rental or sales discrimination. One recent study used black and white testers applying for housing in several southern cities. A National Fair Housing Alliance official summed up the results: We "measured what the apartment seekers were told about unit availability, . . . security deposit, rental rates, discounts for evacuees, and other terms and conditions of apartment leasing. In 66 percent of the tests—43 of 65 instances—White callers were favored over African-American callers."[98] This widespread discrimination can be blatant, subtle, or covert. Examples include a white landlord falsely telling a black renter that an apartment has been rented or a white real estate salesperson steering home buyers to informally segregated housing areas or providing less accurate housing information to people of color who are seeking housing.

Insurance companies also create discriminatory barriers. One investigation had black, Latino, and white testers pose as homeowners seeking insurance. They contacted major insurance companies in nine cities. Overall, 53 percent of the black and Latino testers—ranging from 32 percent in Memphis to 83 percent in Chicago—experienced discrimination in offers of insurance coverage and price. Whites were often offered more insurance options and lower rates. In both rental and sales housing sectors, as well as in the insurance sector, the omnipresent housing discrimination is generally met by weak government enforcement of state and federal antidiscrimination laws. In most residential areas, white landlords and real estate salespeople can discriminate more or less with impunity.[99]

Residential segregation is still a dominant U.S. reality. The white population of central cities has decreased, and a majority of suburbs are predominantly white. Today, most whites live in suburbs or nonmetropolitan areas, while the majority of people of color live in cities. Ironically, many whites now have some racial fears stemming from the residential segregation that they or their ancestors have created by centuries of racially exclusionary practices. Residential segregation has serious societal consequences, including little or no interracial contacts for many white Americans. Thus, one 1990s study by several journalists examined adjacent but largely segregated working-class residential areas of Chicago, one white and one black. The study found that the black residents were "fearful because much of their contact with white people was negative," whereas "whites were fearful because they had little or no contact."[100]

Politics and Protest

Before 1865, African Americans, whether enslaved in the South or theoretically free in the North, were not allowed to participate as equals with whites in the political system. Some petitioned white legislatures and officials for redress of their grievances, but most petitions were ignored. The Civil War brought an end to slavery and increased black participation in electoral politics. The Thirteenth Amendment to the Constitution abolished slavery, the Fourteenth Amendment asserted that civil rights of black Americans could not be denied by the states, and the

Fifteenth Amendment guaranteed black men (but not women) the right to vote.

From Reconstruction to the 1920s

Following the Civil War, the Reconstruction period came to the South as a breath of fresh air. **Reconstruction** was *the brief period in U.S. history following the Civil War during which an attempt was made by the federal government to disenfranchise the former slaveholding oligarchy and to improve the economic, educational, political, and human rights conditions of poor whites and blacks in the South.* Federally enforced Reconstruction policies were precipitated by southern white elites' unwillingness to make major changes in the highly discriminatory treatment of freed blacks or to prevent unrepentant leaders of the rebelling Confederacy from resuming political power. A brief period of limited federal military occupation resulted. Reconstruction brought political progress to black southerners. Black men gained the right to vote. New state constitutional conventions included black delegates, although in most states the majority of delegates were white. Between 1869 and 1901, twenty black men served in the U.S. House and two in the U.S. Senate. Hiram R. Revels and Blanche K. Bruce, from Mississippi, were the first ever to serve in the Senate.[101] Indeed, the fact that *only four* African Americans—Edward Brooke (R–Mass.), Carol Moseley Braun (D–Ill.), Barack Obama (D–Ill.), and Roland Burris (D–Ill.)—have served in the Senate since Revels and Bruce testifies to the continued pervasiveness of institutional discrimination in U.S. politics.

During Reconstruction, the new state governments were mostly controlled by whites who had not been wealthy supporters of the Confederacy, including farmers of modest means. But reactionary forces in the South brought an end to Reconstruction by the late 1870s and 1880s. Few Americans today know that a major reason for the end of this relatively progressive Reconstruction era was *white terrorism.* Many people in the South's white elite, helped by the neglect or collusion of U.S. presidents and many northern whites, conducted an extensive terrorist campaign against Reconstruction governments and newly freed black southerners. A former Confederate general, Nathan Bedford Forrest, was the first "Grand Dragon" of the newly created Ku Klux Klan, and no less a figure than General Robert E. Lee pledged his support to the Klan. The terrorist actions of Klan-type white supremacist groups helped to destroy the often progressive Reconstruction governments, and thousands of men, women, and children were severely beaten, raped, or killed by members of these violent groups. The Confederacy had lost the four-year war, but fought on for "twelve more years—using every weapon at its disposal, including the ultimate one of mass terrorism—until the nation finally acceded to most of the Confederacy's modified war aims."[102]

Although considerable racial segregation existed during Reconstruction, that segregation was not as all-encompassing as it would later become. By the early 1900s, enforced racial segregation became the rule in southern and border states. A U.S. Supreme Court decision, *Plessy* v. *Ferguson* (1896), upheld this racist segregation in railroad cars, asserting the legality of "separate but equal" facilities. The all-white Court reasoned openly that whites' racist attitudes were natural and that "legislation is powerless to eradicate racial instincts or to abolish distinctions based upon physical differences, and the attempt to do so can only result in accentuating the difficulties of the present situation."[103]

In 1915, the Supreme Court began a slow swing back to the protection of some black civil rights by declaring unconstitutional southern laws' "grandfather clauses" (stipulating that a person could vote only if eligible in a previous year when black southerners could not vote). Black voter registration increased slowly. By the 1920s, migration to cities had brought a few black leaders to the political forefront in the North. Independent political organizations were established, but the only major success was that of Adam Clayton Powell Jr. in New York City. In 1945, Powell, a black Democrat, became a member of Congress. In the North, most black voters supported the Republican Party, but by the 1930s (and the election of President Franklin Roosevelt), they had begun to shift to the Democratic Party.[104]

The Limits of Black Progress: Political Discrimination

Southern voter registration increased between the 1940s and the 1970s, raising the number of black voters from 250,000 to 4 million. A big jump in registration occurred after the belated passage of the federal Voting Rights Act of 1965. Since their reenfranchisement, black southerners have developed numerous effective political organizations and campaigns. In 1965, there were approximately seventy black elected officials in the South. Today, there are more than 9000 in all states. Nonetheless, black officials remain at less than 2 percent of all elected officials, and their percentage of elected officials has not grown over the last decade. They also are concentrated in the South—and substantially in Mississippi, Alabama, Illinois, Louisiana, and Georgia. Significantly, the increase in elected officials beginning in the 1960s was linked to the 1965 Voting Rights Act, "perhaps the single most successful civil rights bill ever passed."[105]

Over the past few decades, black voters have continued to face attempts to reduce the efficacy of their political participation. Researchers such as Chandler Davidson and a recent report by the Center for Voting Rights & Protection have demonstrated that serious discrimination persists in the twenty-first century in such forms as vote dilution, purges of voter registration rolls, unannounced changes in polling places, intentionally difficult registration procedures, changing elective offices into appointive ones, majority runoff requirements, annexing of white residential areas, unnecessary revisions in qualifications for office, and ballot security harassment. In recent elections a commonplace problem for voters of color has been the effort, mainly of local Republican operatives, to impose "ballot security" programs. One recent report notes how such security programs focus heavily on *minority* voting precincts, usually with little or no evidence of fraud being offered. In recent elections these programs have involved "Republican poll watchers or challengers who may slow down voting lines and embarrass potential voters by asking them humiliating questions," "people in official-looking uniforms with badges and side arms who question voters about their citizenship or their registration," and radio ads "targeted to minority listeners containing dire threats of prison terms for people who are not properly registered—messages that seem designed to put minority voters on the defensive."[106]

Responding to conservative white supporters in the 1980s, the Ronald Reagan administration tried to weaken the Voting Rights Act. In 1982, after a long battle, civil rights forces persuaded Congress to pass a 25-year extension. Between 1982 and 2006, the number of Department of Justice objections to local or state electoral changes, the frequent withdrawal of requests for changes, and the imposition of thousands of federal observers of local elections all indicated the continuing reality of discrimination in voting practices. In 2006, the nonpermanent features of the Voting Rights Act were again extended for 25 years.[107]

Since the early 1980s, voting rights issues have been at the center of debates about democracy in the United States. A number of legal scholars have pointed out that, although the enforcement of the Voting Rights Act has helped to increase the number of black-majority voting districts and elected officials, it has not reshaped local and state legislative bodies to give black officials a proportionate influence on their everyday operations.[108]

Thus, legal scholar Lani Guinier has suggested remedies that might increase black influence on government bodies, one of which is *cumulative voting,* a procedure in which each voter is given a number of votes equal to the number of positions to be filled in a legislative body. If ten members of a commission are to be elected, each voter has ten votes and may use them to vote for one candidate for each of the positions or may cast all ten votes for one candidate. Cumulative voting is currently used in selecting corporate directors. This strategy would increase the probability that a black candidate would be elected in an area in which the majority of voters are white. Some cities, such as Alamogordo, New Mexico, and Peoria, Illinois, have already experimented with this.[109]

Some analysts argue that increased black votes and more elected officials accomplish much for black voters, while others feel that black citizens are unlikely to gain much through an electoral process mostly controlled by whites. Certainly, in most jurisdictions black elected officials have been unable to dramatically reorder local priorities in employment, housing, or education. However, they have sometimes been able to bring some expansion of capital-based services to local black residential areas. In Florida, though, one study found black elected officials were often more effective in changing employment opportunities for constituents than in improving capital-based services. Many black officials have also had a positive influence on black voter turnout.[110]

Over the last few decades, African Americans have won mayoral elections in several major cities with substantial black populations—including

Philadelphia, Detroit, New York City, Atlanta, and Los Angeles—and also in a few predominantly white cities, such as Seattle, Asheville, Columbus, and Kansas City. In 1990, the state of Virginia elected L. Douglas Wilder as the first black governor of any state. By 2007, some 43 African Americans held statewide elected or appointive offices. In addition to one black senator (Illinois), these included two lieutenant governors (Maryland and New York), an attorney general (Georgia), a secretary of state (Illinois), and another governor (the second ever, in Massachusetts).[111]

The Federal Government

The New Deal era (1933–1940) was the first period since Reconstruction in which the federal government gave serious attention to the needs of its black citizens. President Franklin Roosevelt appointed more than one hundred African Americans to important positions. New Deal programs helped black Americans survive the Great Depression, even though most economic recovery agencies discriminated substantially in favor of white citizens.[112]

Between 1901 and 1929, Congress had *no* black members, and from 1929 until 1945, only one. In 1945, Adam Clayton Powell Jr. (New York) joined William Dawson (Illinois) in the House, and ten years later, Charles Diggs was elected from Michigan. By 1992, in part thanks to the registration of new black voters after the 1960s civil rights revolution, there were twenty-six black House members, including four women. By the late 1990s, there were thirty-nine black representatives, including eleven women, in the U.S. House and one black woman (the first ever), Carol Moseley Braun of Illinois, in the Senate. In 2009, there were still only thirty-nine black (mostly male) voting members of the U.S. House, and there was just one black senator (a temporary appointment) in the U.S. Senate.[113]

The first black person ever to serve in a U.S. presidential cabinet was Robert Weaver, appointed Secretary of Housing and Urban Development by President Lyndon Johnson in 1967. Johnson also appointed Thurgood Marshall as the first black Supreme Court justice. In 2008, the first black president, Barack Obama, was elected, and he appointed the first black attorney general (Eric Holder) in U.S. history. Nonetheless, African Americans

continue to be significantly underrepresented in the important federal legislative, executive, and judicial positions.[114]

The black vote has sometimes been very important in federal elections. Black voters played a role in Franklin Roosevelt's unprecedented fourth election in 1944 and were important to Harry Truman's close election in 1948. The black vote in a few key states reportedly decided the 1960 presidential election for the Irish Catholic John Kennedy. Black voters played a role in electing Lyndon Johnson in 1964 and Jimmy Carter in 1976. They voted overwhelmingly for Al Gore in 2000 and helped provide him with a popular vote (but not the electoral college) majority. They gave similarly huge majorities to candidates John Kerry (2004) and Barack Obama (2008). During recent elections, African American voters have continued to help elect numerous white and black members of Congress who strongly support civil rights issues. African American voters have long been centrally important in pressing the United States in the direction of its stated political ideal of "liberty and justice for all."[115]

 What are the societal implications of political segregation along racial lines?

The Republican Appeal to White Voters: A Shift from the Past

Black voters have often voted for losing presidential candidates since the late 1960s, who lost in part because of the barely disguised prowhite strategy of many leaders in the Republican Party. This strategy, used by Richard Nixon in winning the 1968 presidential election, was celebrated in Kevin Phillips's book, *The Emerging Republican Majority.* Phillips suggested that Republicans did not need "urban Negroes" to win elections. In recent decades, the Republican Party has moved from the party of Abraham Lincoln, which advocated expanded civil rights, to a party opposed to most aggressive government action (including affirmative action) to eliminate discrimination against Americans of color in employment and other institutional areas. Some version of this prowhite strategy was used successfully in the Ronald Reagan and George H. W. Bush campaigns of the 1980s and in the two George H. Bush campaigns in the 2000s.[116]

Not surprisingly, then, the overwhelming majority of black voters have generally supported Democratic candidates at local, state, and national levels. Between 1992 and 2008, the Republican Party got only 4 to 12 percent of the black vote in national elections. Recent Republican conventions have had a relatively small percentage of black delegates, and the Republican National Committee has had tiny numbers of black members. Consider the important 2008 Republican national convention, at which only 7 percent of delegates were people of color. (Just 1.5 percent were black.) In contrast, fully one-third of the delegates at the parallel 2008 Democratic Party convention were delegates of color. Moreover, most black Americans who are in official positions in state Republican organizations work in minority outreach, in contrast to the far more numerous black members of state Democratic Party organizations, who are active mostly outside such outreach programs. In 2008, *all* black members of Congress, and almost all black officeholders at various government levels, were members of the Democratic Party. This highly segregated pattern of political party interests and participation has characterized U.S. politics since the 1960s.[117]

Still, even with this inclination to the Democratic Party, black allegiance has not always been enthusiastic—in part because some white Democratic candidates have also used barely disguised antiblack tactics to court white voters and/or have ignored the educational or economic needs of their black supporters.

African American Organization and Protest

Certain basic commitments to liberty-and-justice values on the part of most African Americans have long provided a source of strength to resist discrimination, as well as a source of constant pressure for the United States to live up to its greatest ideals. Over the centuries, black resistance to white-generated discrimination and oppression has ranged from legal strategies and the ballot, to nonviolent civil disobedience, to violent attacks on the racist system.

The goals of protest movements over the past century and more have included desegregation of public accommodations and schools and the opening up to all Americans of housing and employment long reserved for whites. In 1905, in reaction to the prowhite accommodationist position of black leaders such as Booker T. Washington, the path-breaking sociologist W. E. B. Du Bois, together with other black and white leaders, formed the Niagara movement to press for legal rights as well as for economic changes. Soon, some of these leaders helped create the still-influential National Association for the Advancement of Colored People (NAACP).

From the 1900s to the 1950s, the influential Du Bois also played an important role in the development of pan-African nationalism, which was seen as a partial solution for oppression faced by people of African descent across the globe. In 1919, working with other black leaders, Du Bois put together the first pan-African Congress, to which delegates from fifteen countries came. About the same time, cultural nationalism was also strong in the 1920s Harlem Renaissance, which involved a dramatic flowering of literature and arts that celebrated black perspectives, traditions, and history.

Black organizations directed at self-help and philanthropic activity, such as the Urban League, were created in the early 1900s. These provided aid for the poor and worked to end Jim Crow segregation. Lawsuits were a major strategy. One early NAACP victory was a 1917 Supreme Court decision, *Buchanan v. Warley,* which knocked down a Louisville, Kentucky, law requiring residential segregation—one of the first steps in reversing the segregationist position the Supreme Court's white justices had aggressively taken since the late 1800s. Nonetheless, most Supreme Court decisions before the 1930s only reinforced racial segregation in schools, transportation, and the jury system.[118]

Against fierce white resistance, the NAACP began a large-scale attack on legal segregation in schools, voting, transportation, and jury selection. Beginning in the 1930s, NAACP and other civil rights lawyers won a series of cases that, over the next several decades, expanded legal rights of defendants, eliminated all-white political primaries, protected black voting rights, reduced union discrimination, voided discriminatory housing covenants, and desegregated schools and public accommodations. The Supreme Court's separate-but-equal doctrine in *Plessy* v. *Ferguson* increasingly came under attack. Dramatically reversing its 1896 position, the Supreme Court in *Brown* v. *Board of*

Education (1954) finally and unanimously ruled that "in the field of public education the doctrine of 'separate but equal' has no place."[119]

By the 1940s and 1950s, black communities were generating more antidiscrimination protests. During World War II, a threatened march by black Americans on Washington, DC, helped in getting President Roosevelt to issue an order desegregating wartime employment. After World War II, black leaders organized against the peacetime draft on the basis that black citizens should not have to serve in a racially segregated army. President Truman eventually set up an agency to rid federal employment of official discrimination and a committee to oversee the desegregation of the armed forces. The U.S. military became, and probably still is, the most racially desegregated of major U.S. institutions that were once highly segregated.[120]

The 1950s and 1960s brought another increase in protests. One strategy was the *boycott*, such as that of racially segregated buses in Montgomery, Alabama, in the 1950s, which began when NAACP member Rosa Parks refused a white driver's order to give up her seat on a racially segregated bus to a white person. Her arrest triggered a successful boycott by the black community that brought the young leader, Dr. Martin Luther King Jr., into national prominence. King became the head of the new Southern Christian Leadership Conference (SCLC). In 1960, a sit-in by students at a whites-only lunch counter in Greensboro, North Carolina, touched off a long series of sit-ins by thousands of black southerners and their white allies.

In 1963, Dr. King, other black leaders, and many black citizens launched demonstrations against discrimination in Birmingham, Alabama. Fire hoses and police dogs were used aggressively against peaceful demonstrators, many of whom were children. The police reaction to the Birmingham protests generated much national and international publicity for the civil rights movement. An agreement that desegregated businesses and employment ended these protests, but another round of demonstrations was touched off when a black home and motel were bombed. Then came the massive 1963 March on Washington, at which Dr. King dramatized rising aspirations for freedom in his famous "I Have a Dream" speech before thousands of black and nonblack supporters.[121]

Direct action against informal racial segregation in the North began in earnest in the 1960s with

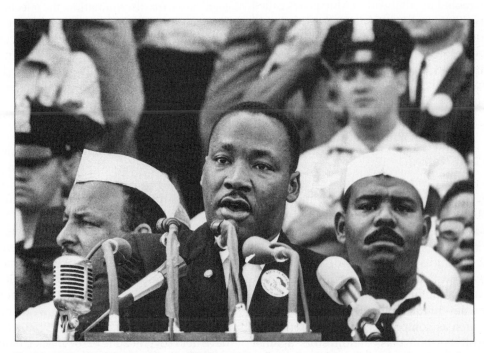

Dr. Martin Luther King Jr. gives his "I Have a Dream" speech at a large civil rights demonstration in Washington, DC, in 1963.

boycotts in Harlem, sit-ins in Chicago, school protests in New Jersey, and demonstrations in Cairo, Illinois. The Congress of Racial Equality (CORE) accelerated protests against discrimination in housing and employment. Led by Stokely Carmichael (Kwame Ture), the Student Nonviolent Coordinating Committee (SNCC) helped to germinate a national movement for racial desegregation, real "black power," and representative participation in all societal institutions. The growing number of organizations oriented toward black nationalism and self-help included the Black Panthers, a group of young men and women who started breakfast programs for children and engaged in surveillance of white police officers to try to reduce police brutality against black urbanites. The Nation of Islam was also expanding in membership and established black-controlled social programs and businesses.[122]

Some white commentators on the nonviolent civil rights era have suggested that Dr. King's strong image was largely a media creation and that the civil rights movement was primarily middle class. Yet, most local demonstrations included large-scale participation by black Americans from *all* backgrounds. Research on black movements has demonstrated that most were grounded in organized activism, which was rooted in what Aldon Morris has called "a well-developed indigenous base."[123] This broad base included community churches, clubs, and other voluntary organizations that provided money and mobilized people, thus enabling the more visible activists in organizations such as the SCLC and SNCC to successfully fight discrimination across the country.

Progress and Retreat

The 1960s civil rights movement played an important role in pressuring Congress to pass major legislation prohibiting discrimination in employment, voting, and housing—the Voting Rights Act of 1965 and the Civil Rights Acts of 1964 and 1968. However, many advances have been undercut since the 1980s by conservative presidential administrations. From 1981 to 1993, for example, government civil rights agencies reduced important enforcement activities, such as compliance reviews of government contractors and class-action suits against discriminatory employers. The 1980s Reagan administration even tried to cut back the Voting Rights

Act.[124] The George H. W. Bush administration (1989–1993) mostly continued the negative approach to African Americans, who responded by pressing their fight to improve civil rights enforcement. The Bill Clinton administration in the 1990s brought some improvements in enforcement. More black Americans were appointed to important positions, including judgeships, and the Clinton administration put greater emphasis on civil rights enforcement. There were some class-action suits brought on behalf of black individuals who reported discrimination. For example, discrimination complaints about service at Denny's restaurants were resolved by a consent decree in which the company agreed to pay millions in damages. This more aggressive Department of Justice involvement in antidiscrimination lawsuits was a clear break from the policies of previous administrations.[125]

The national elections in 2000 and 2004 brought another conservative president, George W. Bush, to power. His conservative appointments again brought backtracking on civil rights enforcement. A draft report by U.S. Commission on Civil Rights staff summarized Bush's first years in office: "While judicial and legislative achievements of the 1960s and 1970s largely broke down the system of segregation and legal bases for discrimination, the effects persist and hamper equal opportunity in education, employment, housing, public accommodations, and the ability to vote. President Bush has implemented policies that have retreated from long-established civil rights promises in each of these areas." Later reports by civil rights groups concluded that the Bush administration's antidiscrimination efforts were consistently weak or backtracking, with especially weak enforcement in areas such as employment, housing, and voting rights. As we noted previously in regard to the EEOC, the arrival of the Barack Obama administration in 2009 brought aggressive new enforcement of the civil rights laws.[126]

Over the last few decades numerous civil rights groups have continued to protest on behalf of expanded opportunities for African Americans and other Americans of color. Washington, DC, and other cities have witnessed important demonstrations against discrimination and the weakening of civil rights enforcement. Since the 1980s, black leaders have held several State of the Black Union overview conferences. In 2006, a document, "The Covenant with Black America," was presented to nearly 8000 attendees at the seventh conference in Houston, a book-length statement of strong recommendations to policymakers that would improve the lives of African Americans. In addition to suggesting action options for African Americans with regard to issues such as renewal of voting rights legislation and boycotting discriminatory companies, these conferences have generated renewed interest in political campaigns that accent issues of concern to black communities. Subsequent black conferences have confirmed these covenant goals, and the book version of "The Covenant" became a *New York Times* bestseller. The covenant organization has an active website working to meet its stated goals.[127]

From time to time, especially during conservative national presidential administrations, the NAACP Legal Defense Fund, the Leadership Conference on Civil Rights, and other black civil rights organizations have mounted enough pressure to stop top white government officials from achieving troubling political goals. These problematical goals include weakening civil rights laws and enforcement, and appointing people who are unsupportive of civil rights progress as federal judges. Moreover, even with its ups and downs, the black-led civil rights movement has contributed greatly to the expansion of civil rights for all Americans, especially since the 1960s. For example, civil rights organizations played an important role in getting the aforementioned Hate Crimes Prevention Act passed in Congress. We should note too that both black men and black women have been central to the centuries-old black movement for liberty and justice in the United States. Researchers such as Patricia Hill Collins and Bernice McNair Barnett have demonstrated that black women were an integral part of the civil rights movement of the 1950s and 1960s, even though leadership roles were generally reserved for men. In recent decades black women have gradually moved into numerous important positions in civil rights and political groups and have pressed for increased attention to the joint effect of sexism and racism on women of color.[128]

Education

During the Reconstruction period after the Civil War, black southerners gained their first access to schools, both those sponsored by the federal

African American author and professor Toni Morrison is a Nobel Prize winner.

government and by private organizations. However, by 1900, public schools in southern and border states were legally segregated under "separate but equal" laws, and educational facilities for black students were grossly inferior. In 1900, some southern counties spent *ten times* as much per capita for the education of white children as for black children.[129]

Despite relentless discrimination and segregation by whites, blacks pressed on toward their dream of a good education for all. By the early 1900s, 1.5 million black children were enrolled in schools. The South had thirty-four predominantly black colleges. Influenced by Booker T. Washington, who advocated vocational education, black college curricula typically focused on skills suitable for an agricultural economy, which at that time was declining. Other leaders, such as W. E. B. Du Bois, felt that Washington was too deferential to white views, and advocated instead a full range of educational opportunities for black youth.[130]

African Americans have long taken advantage of educational opportunities wherever these become available. In 1940, more than half of black adults over the age of 24 had less than a sixth-grade education. Fewer than 8 percent were high school graduates (versus 26 percent of whites). Forty years later, the proportion of black adults aged 25 and older with high school diplomas had risen above 50 percent. By 2008, according to the American Community Survey, 80.8 percent of black adults (age 25 and older) were high school graduates, and 17.5 percent had completed four years of college or more. These figures can be compared with 90.1 percent and 30.7 percent, respectively, of the adult white population in that year. Although educational opportunities and attainments for blacks today are still not equal, the educational attainment gap has narrowed much more than the large economic gap between white and black Americans.[131]

The Struggle for Desegregation

Movement toward school desegregation began in earnest in the 1930s with a long-term NAACP legal strategy. Lawsuits attacking discrimination in graduate schools were the first to expose the "separate-but-equal" doctrine for a sham. In the 1930s and 1940s, federal court decisions thus forced the racial desegregation of law schools and other graduate programs at major universities. Then, in 1954, brave black parents won the famous school decision, *Brown* v. *Board of Education of Topeka*. This decision forced the racial desegregation of schools in Topeka, Kansas, and a few other school systems, and set in motion government action to officially desegregate all public school systems. This government action met massive resistance. White judges, often fearing violent reactions by some whites, generally allowed school desegregation to proceed at a snail's pace during the decade after *Brown*. Most white-dominated school systems circumvented *Brown* as long as they could, and most black children remained overt targets of racial discrimination. Increasingly, whites set up private schools and/or resorted to open defiance and violence. In 1956, a reluctant President Dwight Eisenhower was forced by violent attacks on black children to federalize the Arkansas National Guard to protect the children braving violent white mobs to desegregate a high school in Little Rock.[132]

The 1960s and early 1970s finally brought widespread desegregation throughout the South and some court orders to desegregate certain northern school systems. In *Swann* v. *Charlotte-Mecklenburg Board of Education* (1971), one of a series of court cases following *Brown* that expanded the attack on racially segregated schooling, the Supreme Court upheld the use of busing as a means of disestablishing a dual school system. However, by 1974, a more conservative Court began to back off from comprehensive desegregation in a ruling that rejected inclusion of suburban districts in central-city desegregation plans. In *Milliken* v. *Bradley* (1974) the Court overturned a lower-court order requiring the integration of the substantially black Detroit school system with surrounding predominantly white suburban school systems. In one incremental step after another, between *Milliken* and the present, the Supreme Court and numerous other federal courts have retreated. In the major 1990s' cases of *Board of Education of Oklahoma* v. *Dowell* (1991) and *Freeman* v. *Pitts* (1992), the U.S. Supreme Court permitted informal resegregation of schools where there was no longer official segregation. Although many Americans of color have deplored and worked against this resegregation of public schools, relatively few white Americans have yet shown much concern about this backtracking trend.[133]

The Current Situation in Public Schools

Since the 1960s, the racial desegregation of public schools, when done reasonably well, has had positive effects on the academic achievement of African American children and other children of color who attend majority-white schools, when compared with achievement in schools that have a majority of children of color. A Charlotte, North Carolina, area study of 1800 children found that black *and* white children did better in terms of test scores and track placements in substantially desegregated schools than in more segregated schools. One reason for the better black performance lies in the better resources that are usually available in predominantly or substantially white schools. In this still discriminatory society, predominantly white schools generally get more than other schools in the way of economic and human resources, such as good media and Internet centers, newer and more computers, newer buildings, and more classes for advanced students. When formerly segregated black schools are racially desegregated, white officials tend to spend more money on them. When public schools resegregate, as many are doing, the opposite often happens. In addition, children of color from well-resourced desegregated schools usually have much better access to good job and information networks. Research shows too that they are more likely than similar students from segregated schools to attend desegregated colleges, work in desegregated settings, and acquire friends from other racial groups.[134]

Most black children who remain in schools composed predominantly of children of color do not have access today to first-rate educational opportunities and resources. Indeed, they have never had the level of socioeconomic resources invested in their educations that typical white children have received. In spite of the 1954 *Brown* decision, the promise of substantial school integration has never been delivered. Judge Robert Carter, an NAACP lawyer in *Brown,* has condemned the country's dismal record on educational equality: "Thus far, for most black children the constitutional guarantee of equal education opportunity which *Brown* held was secured to them has been an arid abstraction, having no effect whatsoever on the bleak offerings black children are given in the deteriorating schools they attend."[135]

Polls show that the overwhelming majority of Americans support equal educational opportunities, at least in the abstract. Opinion polls also show that the overwhelming majority of whites believe black Americans have at least the same chance to get a good education as whites—even though less than half of black Americans agree. And yet, as noted above, since the 1990s, school resegregation has taken place in many areas. Recent research drawing on government data indicates that segregation of black from white children in urban public schools remains very high. This segregation has increased even as urban residential segregation has decreased a little in recent years.[136] In the most recent school year, most black students attended predominantly segregated schools where more than half the children were children of color. Moreover, four in ten black and Latino children were in extremely segregated schools (schools where 90 to 100 percent of the children are of color). Such highly segregated schools tend to have fewer educational and economic resources, including relatively fewer dollars spent per pupil and less experienced teachers. Millions of children of color, as well as poor white children, remain "locked into 'dropout factory' high schools, where huge percentages do not graduate, have little future in the American economy, and almost none are well prepared for college."[137]

School resegregation is in part the result of the policies of presidential administrations that have opposed mandatory desegregation and supported voluntary desegregation or segregated neighborhood schools. Recent administrations have cut back efforts to desegregate schools and instead supported charter schools or tax deductions for private-school tuition. Local authorities, especially white officials, have mostly supported these resegregation policies. In some districts, school-choice policies have had an overwhelmingly negative effect on racial diversity. For example, a middle school in Winston-Salem, North Carolina, went from two-thirds white to 97 percent black over one summer after school choice was offered to parents. Indeed, today the U.S. educational system offers considerable choice for parents in the form of magnet schools, charter schools, home schooling, and private schools, yet such "choice" has not reduced racial segregation and inequality in the United States.[138]

School desegregation often increases housing desegregation. Historically, cities with metropolitan-area school desegregation plans have experienced more rapid housing desegregation than cities without such plans. Research has shown that the extent of housing desegregation in cities of similar size and racial mix is related directly to the scope of their school desegregation programs. Cities with school desegregation plans that cover only the central cities have had less housing desegregation than cities with desegregated schools in both central cities and suburbs. However, the ending of many school desegregation plans in recent years likely ends these positive effects on housing desegregation.[139]

Various forms of institutionalized discrimination persist in public school systems. One community organization report on New York City schools found widespread discrimination in the treatment of parents and children. Trained testers, posing as parents, were sent to twenty-eight elementary schools in half the city's community school districts. White parent-testers were able to speak with an educator, such as the principal, much more often than were black and Latino parent-testers. Whites were two-and-one-half times more likely to get a school tour and, on average, whites were given much more school information.[140]

Racial tracking is often a problem in desegregated schools. Black students are often placed in school tracks lower than their measured abilities indicate.

Students in higher tracks typically get more attention and better resources. Those put in privileged tracks in early grades tend to perform better in later schooling, and thus, over time, "racially stratified tracks create a discriminatory cycle of restricted educational opportunities." Eliminating or reducing ability tracking has had beneficial effects, as Roslyn Michelson has summarized: "When schools consistently employ practices to enhance equality of opportunity (including the elimination of tracking and ability grouping), desegregation brings clear, though modest academic benefits to black students and does no harm to whites."[141] In her Charlotte-Mecklenburg study, Mickelson found that breaking down tracking often benefits white students, for heterogeneous schooling helps to counter commonplace racial stereotyping.

Into the late 2000s, St. Louis was one of the few major cities with a long-standing school desegregation plan bringing together inner-city children of color with children in mostly white suburbs. By the voluntary interdistrict desegregation plan's eleventh year, black students made up at least 15 percent of the student population in most suburban school districts. Drawing on interviews with 300 educators, parents, students, and lawyers, an evaluation study of the impact of desegregation reported that many black students had achieved academic, and sometimes social, success in integrated suburban schools. Recently, white students and school boards in the suburban schools have strongly supported a continuation of their voluntary school desegregation programs.[142]

However, the majority of children of color in the St. Louis city school district have not benefited from this voluntary interdistrict program, which has been losing state funding and, as a result, its ability to serve as many students as in the past. "For the 2007–08 year, 3,662 black students from the city applied for only 1,163 available spaces in suburban schools. In other words, only 31% of the urban-to-suburban transfer applicants were placed in suburban schools."[143] Today, the St. Louis (central city) school system, composed mostly of black students, with small percentages of white students and other students of color, regularly faces financial crises, as it tries to serve a very large percentage of children from economically disadvantaged families. This central-city school system, like many others, is struggling to meet the needs of these poor children and continues to have a high dropout rate and low

high school graduation rate. Government remedial programs, such as those generated by the George W. Bush administration's No Child Left Behind Act, have documented continuing racial inequality in resources between predominantly white schools and those with mostly children of color, but have yet to provide the large-scale funding necessary to bring weakly performing schools up to the level of providing equal educational opportunities.[144]

As in the past, black parents today often face a major dilemma. What significantly desegregated school settings do still exist, while holding out promise of better educational resources, often remain hostile or unsupportive places for black children. White hostility in desegregated schools can have significant negative effects on children. Thus, since about 1980, many local black leaders have shifted their emphasis away from comprehensive school desegregation plans to other educational objectives. Many have become more concerned with the survival of black children, especially black males, than with desegregation, which is in any case declining.

Thus, educators in some cities with substantially black school enrollments, such as Atlanta and Washington, have developed a curriculum with more emphasis on the cultural heritage of African American children. In numerous cities, black educators have also created special schools, or programs within public schools, for poor black males. This survival strategy attempts to support black children and black community institutions in the face of continuing antiblack discrimination and little government action against that discrimination. However, this understandable strategy has significant limits, especially with regard to the majority of black children who still must attend regular public schools. Separate-but-equal policies for schools do not generally work because, for the most part, those children and parents with poor school opportunities are in communities with little political clout over the politicians who control the government money necessary for creating equal school opportunities. Black American children do not need white children in order to thrive educationally, but in this still-racist society they will ordinarily get the full array of educational resources they need only if they are in school with children whose parents have this substantial economic and political clout.[145]

Growing research indicates that whites also pay a significant price for continuing school and housing segregation. Gary Orfield, a leading school researcher, notes that most whites who grow up in relatively segregated suburban enclaves have "no skills in relating to or communicating with minorities."[146] As the country becomes more diverse, this lack of skills will become even more of a disadvantage in social and political interaction, and in getting jobs with globally focused companies and government agencies. Such white isolation will be a major handicap as the country becomes more involved in international trade and diplomacy in a world in which non-European nations are ever more powerful.

College Attendance and College Experiences

In one opinion survey, almost all (96 percent) of the black youth aged 11 to 17 stated that their biggest hope for their future was to go to college. Yet, in 2008, a substantially lower percentage (35.9 percent) of black students aged 18 and 19 years old were in college, as compared with 50.9 percent of their white counterparts. In recent years the proportion of African Americans between the ages of 25 and 29 who are college graduates has been about half that of whites in this age group.[147]

Until the 1960s, black college students in southern and border states were generally restricted by law to all-black colleges. The 1960s desegregation movements and laws opened many historically white colleges and universities for black students, including many in the North that had been informally segregated. By the 1970s, three-fourths of black college students nationwide were in predominantly white schools. Most black students attend predominantly white colleges today, but many continue to attend historically black colleges, where the campus culture is generally more hospitable to black students than that of traditionally white schools and where they may be more likely to graduate.[148]

In recent years, black students have continued to face serious problems of discrimination at predominantly white colleges and universities. One 1990s report put it this way: "Frequently black students find white universities to be hostile places where they are seen as 'special admits' and beneficiaries of affirmative action. Moreover, adjustment requires adherence to white cultural norms, thereby necessitating the abandonment of black cultural roots." And problems with hostile campus climates persist

today. For example, one recent report by Duke University's Campus Life project found that 44 percent of recent black graduates reported facing racial discrimination in dorms, classrooms, or other campus places during their first two years at Duke. One in seven reported discrimination by professors. In addition, in a recent survey at Eastern Kentucky University 23 percent of the faculty members and 18 percent of the students surveyed had seen incidents of racial discrimination on that campus. Moreover, research conducted by the first author at a major historically white university found many racial barriers. A questionnaire given to three dozen black juniors and seniors asked them to assess this statement: "Today [my university] is a college campus where black students are generally welcomed and nurtured." Most (89 percent) disagreed with this statement.[149]

Recently, in another social science study, Leslie Houts Picca and Joe Feagin asked students of color at more than two dozen historically white colleges and universities to keep journals of their everyday experiences with racial events. They received a great many accounts of racist incidents in and around these campuses from the 308 students of color in their sample. For example, one black student recorded this in his journal:

> This is one of those sad and angry nights for me. Tonight marks the third time since the beginning of the school year that I've been called a nigger by a bunch of white students on a . . . weekend. . . . At first I used to wonder where they actually take the time in their heads to separate me from everyone else by the color of my skin. I used to just blame alcohol consumption for their obvious ignorance and racist attitudes, but I have since stopped trying to make excuses for them. I have to admit that at times like this . . . I don't understand how such a system of hate could exist. . . . Sometimes it seems that if I am around all white people, then I become nothing more than a token black "exhibit" for their amusement. I guess that even I have to be careful not to judge all based on a few bad examples, which more often then not is the fate of many in the black community today. The saddest thing however, is that these people, these college students are supposed to be the supposed crème de la crème, the future business and political leaders.[150]

This student reports recurring incidents and feelings that are commonplace for many black students at historically white institutions like this one on the West Coast. Significant too is his final comment that the perpetrators of the discrimination seem to be the future white "business and political leaders." A tragic aspect of the barriers at predominantly white colleges is that African American students often identify these historically white colleges and universities not primarily with educational experiences to be savored but rather with an "agonizing struggle" with campus racism just to get a college degree.

Moreover, getting a college education does not necessarily lead to good jobs. One researcher studied the experiences of black and white students who graduated from a technical college. The black graduates, on average, generally worked harder and were better trained, yet they had substantially more difficulty in getting jobs than did white graduates. One major reason was that the preexisting social networks of the white students often provided them with much better job opportunities. Education alone cannot deal with this structural problem of lack of access to important, historically white, job information and employment networks in a still-segregated society.[151]

Religion and Culture

One of the first major stereotypes in the white framing of Africans and indigenous peoples in the Americas involved what Europeans saw as "savagery." The irony of slave-trading, warring Europeans seeing Africans as "savage" was lost on Europeans at the time and has been lost on most of their descendants. The enslaved Africans had brought sophisticated African religions and music to North America. At first, slave owners feared that "Christianizing" these African Americans would give them ideas of freedom. Oddly enough, Protestant missionaries were specifically instructed to tell their converts that conversion to Christianity did not bring freedom. Later on, however, white slave owners actively encouraged white missionaries, such as Baptists and Methodists, to convert enslaved African Americans so that they could be better controlled.[152]

Over time, much African American religion has mixed various African and European elements, and African perspectives have often been influential. Afro-Christianity developed a strong element of protest. The view of God that many of those

enslaved held—for example, the emphasis on God's having led the Israelites out of slavery—was not what slaveholders had hoped for. Hidden in Christian symbolism, the text of slave spirituals sometimes embodied a strong yearning to be free of slavery. Regular religious meetings periodically provided opportunities to plan open slave revolts. Enslaved men were frequently permitted to preach, and some preachers became important resistance leaders. Researchers have shown that the freedom discourse that African Americans developed in private was different from the discourse used in the presence of oppressive slave masters.[153]

Because African Americans, enslaved or free, were excluded from full participation in white churches, they developed their own churches. In Philadelphia, Absalom Jones and Richard Allen, after being mistreated at a white Methodist church, established the Free African Society in 1787. Later, Jones established the first Negro Episcopal church, and Allen played a role in the emergence of the influential African Methodist Episcopal church. Black churches became especially important after the Civil War as mutual-aid societies, which ministered to those facing sickness and death. They functioned as centers for pooling economic and other resources. Many schools established after the Civil War were under religious auspices. Later, with migration to cities after World War I, many African Americans shifted to a less otherworldly style in their numerous religious organizations. Urban social programs and civil rights activity, for example, increasingly became part of much church life. Urban churches became both religious and political forces. One important urban religious group that developed in the twentieth century is the Nation of Islam, a group that has broken with the black Christian heritage. Nation of Islam leaders have pressed for a religious approach suffused with black pride and a strong self-help philosophy. Afrocentric leaders have arisen from this movement, including the influential Malcolm X.[154]

Today, African Americans still mostly attend Protestant churches. They belong to a diversity of groups, from older Methodist and Baptist denominations to newer evangelical groups. Whatever its form, however, the black church is often, as one minister has explained, "the hub of existence in the black community," a "holistic ministry," and a "social center."[155]

Organizations protesting oppressive conditions have long been rooted in African American religion.

Religious gatherings and leaders have played a significant role in spreading protests against oppression, now for centuries. Since the 1800s, black ministers have often been political and protest leaders. The nonviolent civil disobedience movement that took place from the 1950s to the 1970s had significant religious underpinnings. The prominent minister Dr. Martin Luther King Jr., raised in a religious family known for support of civil rights, came naturally to his religious view of the legitimacy of nonviolent protest as a way to win concessions while at the same time healing the wounds of oppressed and oppressor. King led black and white citizens in effective civil rights protests, for which he earned a Nobel Peace Prize, and he died a hero whose example today inspires Americans of all backgrounds.[156]

The effectiveness of churches in providing leadership, and in mobilizing millions of formerly disenfranchised people in the civil rights movement, is rooted deeply in African American culture. The call-and-response format of many religious services, which allows the congregation to give the minister feedback on the sermon, has long provided, and continues to provide, a supportive context for response to calls to register to vote and participate in other political activities by black religious and political leaders. Today, as in the past, black political and protest leaders (for example, Jesse Jackson and Al Sharpton) often have religious connections and continue to harness the religious sentiments of African Americans to mobilize action against racial discrimination. In addition, we should note that African American music and singing have frequently reflected a strong element of protest against prejudice and discrimination—from the days of the spirituals to the more recent blues, jazz, gospel, and hip-hop traditions.[157]

Recent Immigrants from Africa and the Caribbean

In the mid-1990s and again in the 2000s, Colin Powell, a retired U.S. Army general and son of Jamaican immigrants, was frequently mentioned as a possible Republican vice-presidential or presidential candidate. For a time, General Powell, formerly head of the U.S. Joint Chiefs of Staff, was called by some "the most respected figure in American political life."[158]

In 2001, he became the first African American ever to serve as U.S. secretary of state. Powell is a representative of one of several distinctive ethnic groups that today make up the broad group called African Americans.

According to the 2008 American Community Survey, the black (non-Hispanic) foreign-born population is estimated to be 2.8 million. Today, about 7.7 percent of the black population is made up of such immigrants, who are mostly from Africa, the Caribbean, and Latin America. The substantial majority have arrived since the 1980s.[159]

The recent census survey estimates there are about one million (sub-Saharan) African-born individuals among black Americans, with most having arrived since 1990. Many have fled political problems in their home countries and are seeking greater economic opportunities. Large concentrations live

President Barack H. Obama addresses a town hall meeting in Los Angeles.

in Washington, DC, and New York. Most have at least a high school education, and they have a somewhat lower unemployment rate and poverty rate than native-born African Americans. Nonetheless, despite substantial achievements, they are still less well off economically than whites.[160]

The 2000 decennial census found about 1.5 million black Americans of Caribbean ancestry, a figure that had increased to more than 2.5 million according to the 2008 American Community estimate. Many have immigrated to the U.S. since the 1980s, and a majority live in New York or Florida. Caribbean Americans include numerous national-origin groups, including Martinicans, Guadeloupeans, Dominicans, Haitians, Trinidadians, and Jamaicans. The members of each usually do not identify as "Caribbean Americans," but rather expect their national-origin identities to be respected. They sometimes view themselves as African Americans and sometimes as an ethnic group distinctive from others in the general black group. (Some identify as Hispanic.) Nonetheless, Afro-Caribbean Americans have no choice about the negative "black" designation assigned to them by members of the dominant white group, most of whom see mainly their "blackness." This negative and imposed identity is linked to the racial discrimination they often face at the hands of whites.[161]

In recent decades, Haitian immigrants have received more public attention than other Caribbean newcomers. Since the 1970s, thousands have sought political refuge in the United States. Those fleeing a brutal dictatorship were permitted to enter the United States until 1981. In contrast to Cuban refugees who fled political persecution, and who have generally qualified for permanent residence and been provided with much support from the U.S. government, Haitians have received no significant financial support from the U.S. government and have generally been left to cope on their own. Indeed, between 1981 and mid-1994, most Haitians were refused entry; the U.S. Coast Guard intercepted immigrants and returned them to Haiti, where they often faced persecution. This U.S. policy drew criticism from human rights organizations. Amnesty International described Haitian prisons as death traps. Beginning in 1981, those reaching the United States were held at U.S. detention centers.[162]

The ouster in 1991 of Haiti's democratically elected president by military leaders created another flight of Haitians. To stop attempts to immigrate, the U.S. government repatriated 500 immigrants in 1991. In 1994, then President Bill Clinton announced that the U.S. government would no longer send Haitian refugees home without a hearing.[163]

Following the UN- and U.S.-supported overthrow of Haiti's military government in 1994, large numbers of the Haitian refugees opted to return home. Soon, however, the new government itself was overthrown, and Haitians again tried to immigrate to other countries, including the United States, where they still faced detention and deportation in the late 2000s. However, because the U.S. Coast Guard has been effective in intercepting Haitian boats and returning refugees to the island, relatively few have tried to come to the United States since the mid-2000s. One of the ironic aspects of the troubled situation of Haiti today is that it is the only country in the modern era whose enslaved African-origin population rose up and overthrew their colonial (French) slave masters. In the late eighteenth century, Haitians set up a new country led by their talented military leader, Toussaint L'Ouverture, an independent country that frightened U.S. slaveholders, including Thomas Jefferson.[164]

Economics and Education

Americans of Caribbean descent, substantially composed of immigrants and their children, are better off economically than some other groups among African Americans, although their situation is not as favorable as that of white Americans. For example, in the 2008 American Community Survey, the median family income of Americans of (non-Hispanic) Caribbean (West Indian) descent was $54,365. This can be compared with $41,874 for African Americans as a group and with $70,835 for white Americans as a group. In addition, poverty rates for individuals were 14.3 percent for these Americans of Caribbean (West Indian) descent, as compared to 24.1 percent for all African Americans and 9.3 percent for whites as a group. Some 81.5 percent of these Caribbean (West Indian) Americans had at least a high school education, with 22.4 percent having at least a college degree. These figures are a bit higher than the figures for African Americans as a group (80.8 percent and 17.5 percent), but substantially lower than the comparable figures for white Americans as a group (89.7 percent and 32.1 percent).

These Caribbean (West Indian) Americans are also a bit more likely to hold managerial and professional jobs than are African Americans as a group. For a few decades now, the U.S. laws governing regular legal immigration have encouraged a selective immigration of people from the world's middle and upper classes, and this has been true for Caribbean immigrants.[165]

Racial History and Racial Discrimination

Immigrants are often willing to take worse working conditions and/or to work with little protest against poor working conditions than are native-born Americans. This often benefits the image of black immigrants among white employers. Thus, one study of native-born and immigrant black workers at a New York City worksite found that white managers preferred immigrants over native-born black workers for certain food-service jobs because the former were thought to be "more flexible" and "loyal." In areas such as New York, white employers have often singled out West Indian immigrants as a type of "model minority," as "better" than native-born African Americans who are negatively stereotyped as lazy and criminal. This sometimes results in West Indian immigrants getting somewhat less discriminatory treatment from whites. Still, West Indians, particularly second and later generations, do indeed face substantial racial discrimination.[166]

We should note that relatively recent Caribbean and African immigrants have had a different racial history than those African Americans whose ancestors came to North America generations back, and usually in chains. In most cases neither these immigrants nor their children have experienced legal segregation in the United States. Most come from countries in which black people are the majority and in recent decades have had a significant role in running their major institutions, including politics, education, and the economy. In numerous Caribbean nations, for example, the majority of police officers, government officials, and white-collar workers are of African ancestry. Most immigrants have not grown up under recent white domination but only experience it when they immigrate to the United States.

Because they have lived in a society that is not controlled by whites, Caribbean Americans often question the U.S. system of racial categorization.

Thus, a common Haitian perspective is illustrated by a humorous story about one Haitian official's reply to a journalist who asked him what percentage of the Haitian population was white:

> "Ninety-eight percent." The startled American journalist was sure he had either misheard or been misunderstood, and put his question again. Duvalier assured him that he had heard and understood the question perfectly well, and had given the correct answer. Struggling to make sense of this incredible piece of information, the American finally asked Duvalier: "How do you define white?" Duvalier answered the question with a question: "How do you define black in your country?" Receiving the explanation that in the United States anyone with any black blood was considered black, Duvalier nodded and said, "Well, that's the way we define white in my country."[167]

African Americans who have grown up in the United States are constantly dealing with discrimination at the hands of whites and are routinely reminded of the significance of their African origin. In contrast, in the Caribbean immigrants' home countries, racial identity typically has much less significance in everyday life. When most of the population is black, it is common for a person not to be constantly conscious of racial identity.[168]

Haitian American sociologist Yanick St. Jean has noted that many Caribbean immigrants continue to see themselves as culturally different, as "foreigners" in the United States regardless of their length of residence. For that reason many feel that white Americans are more likely to accept them than they are to accept other African Americans and that racial discrimination is directed mainly at other blacks and only indirectly at them. Indeed, Mary Waters's interviews with Caribbean American workers revealed that many shared some white stereotypes of African Americans—that is, some of the old white racist framing.[169]

Although they have a strong black or African identity, Caribbean and African immigrants sometimes try to distance their self-identities from those of native-born African Americans. One reason is that there has been friction between these immigrants and native-born African Americans, many of whom expect immigrants to reject their island identities and traditions and to speak without a foreign accent. St. Jean has noted that for many Caribbean and African immigrants, the level of resistance to assimilation into African American groups is extremely high. As one social scientist correctly said: 'They want to be black; they are proud of being black; they just don't want to be black in the United States.' . . . The notion of blackness in this country is so different from their own. In the Caribbean, blackness is strength. In the United States it is not. Assimilating means moving from a positive image to a less than positive one.[170]

Initially, many Caribbean immigrants think that native-born African Americans exaggerate the discrimination they face at the hands of whites. However, after they have lived for a substantial time in the United States, they usually change this view because they too experience racial exclusion and other forms of antiblack discrimination. When asked in an interview by the first author, "How do you personally feel being black in a mostly white society?" one experienced Caribbean American professional (Mark R., a pseudonym) stated the following about life in the United States:

> I usually interact with American whites from a distance. Most are acquaintances, not friends. Co-workers do not know who I am, what I really want. I am not invited to their informal gatherings. Occasional exchanges in hallways are only superficial. I feel I am expected to live in an intellectual ghetto, a very special and preset place which I call "colonization of thinking." From all appearances, I am expected to fail. I am denied even the basic respect due to me as a human being. . . . Some things I would never admit to. They are just too demeaning.
>
> I feel my differences are neither acknowledged nor respected. I am a Haitian American. I cannot and will not discard my Haitian origins. But in this society everyone must move in the same direction. It simplifies. It unifies. And to the extent that it also inferiorizes, the denial is a perfect tool to keep "others," and blacks in particular, within the boundaries of American cultural definitions. If and when my differences are acknowledged, AIDS, poverty, and religion are quick to surface as if these were synonymous with Haitian.

Why do many U.S. whites associate AIDS and so-called "voodoo" religion with Haitian immigrants? Many Americans erroneously believe that AIDS originated in Haiti or that Haitians have extremely high rates of AIDS. In 1990, acceptance of this stereotype led officials in the U.S. Food and Drug Administration to ban blood donations by Haitians—an action

that provoked civil rights protests. The evidence contradicted the notion that Haitians then had a uniquely high AIDS rate. San Francisco's rate of new AIDS cases was then about *ten times* that of Haiti, and other U.S. cities also had rates significantly higher than Haiti's. Yet, people in these cities were not banned as a group from donating blood. Stereotypes of and discrimination against Haitian Americans are often rooted in racial images of "savage and exotic" African peoples. Many whites also devalue the cultures of other Caribbean Americans and hold racial stereotypes against people with any African background. Note, for example, the common white (and thus media) negative images of African-origin "voodoo" religion. White images of this religion (and other traditional African religions) are replete with racist stereotypes. Even the term *voodoo* is a white creation, for the more accurate term is *vodou* or *vodoun*, which means "spirit." A religion of distinctive rituals and imagery, vodoun is important in Haiti and in Haitian communities in other countries such as the United States. Its syncretic roots lie in the cultures of Africans uprooted long ago in the slave trade, as well as in cultures of the indigenous peoples of the Caribbean and in the Catholic religion learned under European influence.[171]

 What historical and societal pressures have led to the recent migration of people from Africa and the Caribbean?

Assimilation for African Americans?

Assimilation Theories

Assimilation theorists such as Milton Gordon and Nathan Glazer have long argued that the mainstream social science theory of assimilation is applicable to all ethnic and racial groups. Gordon applied his scheme to black Americans, whom he viewed as substantially assimilated at the cultural level (for example, to English and Protestant religion), with some cultural differences remaining because of a so-called lower-class subculture. Beyond acculturation, however, Gordon (writing in the 1960s) noted little integration of black Americans into what he viewed as the "core" (white Anglo-Protestant) society—that is, little intermarriage, modest erosion of discrimination, and no demise of racial group identity.[172] Nonetheless, Gordon wrote optimistically about what he saw as the eventual full assimilation of African Americans into a white-dominated society.[173]

In recent decades, numerous social scientists and popular analysts have argued that there has been a major collapse of antiblack discrimination in a "post-racial America" and that the full integration of black Americans into the core economy and society is well under way. These assimilationist scholars cite what they view as dramatic progress for the black middle class as proof. They often suggest that the major remaining problem is a black "underclass," whose difficulties are in their view not mainly related to current discrimination. While recognizing some discrimination remains, many assimilationist scholars have in effect blamed black Americans for their slower economic and social mobility. In a famous 1960s report, Daniel P. Moynihan viewed black families headed by women as a serious retardant to black progress. These family-blaming arguments have been regularly resurrected from the 1970s to the present. Some analysts have pointed to a so-called poverty subculture among low-income black Americans as a continuing barrier. The theme of certain white analysts boils down to "Why can't black people be like us?" This notion is an old part of the dominant white racial framing of black Americans and suggests that black individuals, like those in white immigrant groups, should be able to move up through the various levels of the white-dominated economy, society, and polity if they would only work harder and address their internal family and cultural problems.[174]

Power-Conflict Perspectives: The Continuing Significance of Racism

Power-conflict analysts reject the optimistic assimilationist view of African American mobility and incorporation into society. From this perspective, the traditional assimilationist perspective is viewed as denying the persistence of major discrimination and its large effects. The contemporary situation of African Americans is much more resistant to change than that ever faced by white immigrant groups. Once racial oppression became systemic in the 1600s, those whites initially in the top racial-hierarchy position, and their descendants, continued to monopolize the lion's share of the economic, political, and educational resources. Only since the late 1960s, when the last major civil rights law went into effect and ended Jim Crow segregation, has the United States been an officially "free" country. Even then, legal segregation in employment, education, and housing—which lasted nearly a century—has been replaced by informal, but still extensive, discrimination targeting Americans of color.

Articulating a theory of "internal colonialism," Robert Blauner has argued that major differences exist in the levels of social and economic oppression that black Americans and white immigrant (ethnic) groups have faced over long periods of time.[175] Africans were enslaved and brought in chains. Incorporated into the economy against their will, they and their descendants provided hard labor to build up the wealth of many whites in this society—first as enslaved laborers, later as exploited tenant farmers, then as exploited urban workers. Even with the great northward migration after World War I, their lesser economic position relative to whites was little altered. They faced extensive discrimination even as the U.S. economic system was industrializing. Historically, the initial incorporation of white immigrants occurred voluntarily, most often at the lower economic levels, but those levels offered some chances of upward mobility. This was not the case for most Africans and their descendants. Enslaved Africans suffered white attempts to destroy their African cultures and were forced to give up many traditional ways as part of their incorporation into slavery. Protestant religion and the English language were forced on them. They were generally forced to give up control of their own bodies, which became the property of whites. Over time, thousands of biracial children resulted from the rape of black women by white slaveholders or overseers—and, later on, by some white segregationists. In contrast with the assimilation view, power-conflict theorists emphasize the *forced* acculturation and *forced* secondary-structural incorporation of African Americans into a white-controlled society.

Power-conflict perspectives take a different view of the lack of full societal assimilation and incorporation of black Americans. They view the so-called subculture of poverty as actually a description of a structural condition historically created by whites' racial hostility, stereotyping, and discrimination, both individual and institutionalized. When European immigrants such as the Irish began arriving in U.S. cities, they did not gain socioeconomic mobility solely by hard work and fair competition. Coming to see themselves as "white" in the U.S. racial hierarchy, they often displaced and discriminated against free black urbanites who were thus relegated to the lowest-paid jobs or unemployment.[176]

After the Civil War, most black Americans in the South had to remain there, usually becoming poor tenant farmers or sharecroppers again exploited by whites. The new industrial economies of growing cities mostly drew workers from Europe, not the South. Widespread discrimination prevented black structural incorporation into the growing industrial economy on an equal-status basis with European immigrants. After World War I, with the large-scale trek northward, black southerners moved into low-paid jobs in northern industries; not until World War II did a significant proportion of black workers find some better-paid jobs in industry. Soon, however, increased racial discrimination against skilled black workers after World War II generated, once again, a major black unemployment and underemployment problem, which persists today. Southern migrants found that the economic opportunities in northern cities were much paler than the promised-land image that had drawn them. For many decades now, to the present day, racial discrimination in all U.S. regions has seriously limited black opportunities in jobs, education, housing, and other institutional areas.[177]

In Chapter 2 we noted the resurgence of an Afrocentric perspective emphasizing the long-term role of European imperialism in enslaving and dispersing Africans around the globe and in seriously damaging once-advanced societies in Africa. This approach examines the continuing Eurocentric bias in U.S. culture: Euro-American perspectives include a myth of white superiority over many other cultures. From this Afrocentric viewpoint, because of the Euro-American superiority myths' negative effects on African Americans, the latter should direct their efforts to re-create cultural alternatives more fully informed by their African heritage. They should develop a reinvigorated African diaspora culture.[178]

Power-conflict analysts often underscore the reality of oppression today: White racist framing and discrimination significantly handicap African Americans in numerous major institutional arenas, from public accommodations to employment, business, education, and housing. Power-conflict theorists are usually pessimistic about the full incorporation of African Americans into these critical institutional arenas without substantial and large-scale changes in the dominant racist framing and extensive discriminatory actions of the white majority.

Summary

Social, economic, and political progress by African Americans in this society has been severely restricted by the lasting effects of centuries of slavery and legal segregation, which existed for nearly 85 percent of our history. Even during the last great migrations of European immigrants in the early 1900s, African Americans—many of whom were already multigeneration Americans—were still extremely segregated and often violently oppressed. This was in great contrast to the upward mobility open to most European immigrants. Long decades of Jim Crow segregation greatly hampered the lives, including the economic mobility, of black Americans freed from slavery and several generations of their descendants. Later, the northward trek of black Americans reflected protest against southern oppression, protest in this case "by the feet." Other types of protest against racial subordination, nonviolent and violent, have regularly punctuated the long course of U.S. racism. The legal Jim Crow segregation period was followed by a long epoch, still in process today, of widespread and informal racial discrimination.

Today, most African Americans live in cities, North and South. In recent years, the migration pattern of African Americans has changed; more are now moving to the South than are leaving the South. Wherever they live, African Americans continue to face much racial discrimination and much educational, economic, and housing inequality. The Civil Rights Acts of 1964, 1965, and 1968 and later amendments have made many acts of racial discrimination illegal, but still have not ended the millions of cases of blatant, subtle, and covert discrimination in business, jobs, housing, education, and public accommodations each year. Government antidiscrimination programs have been too modest to remedy this widespread antiblack discrimination.

In spite of some much-publicized societal changes, such as the election of an African American to the

U.S. presidency in 2008, the twenty-first century specter of "slavery still unwilling to die" can be seen today everywhere: Major racial barriers to black voting continue in various states; most black children still attend racially segregated schools; the majority of black families still live in mostly segregated residential areas; most black Americans at all income levels face informal discrimination by banks, real estate agents, and landlords; many black defendants are tried by juries in which black citizens are underrepresented or absent; and most black workers at all class levels face some blatant or subtle discrimination in the workplace on a recurring basis.

The effects of this racial discrimination remain painful, stifling, and cumulative. Reflecting on the costs of racism and on strategies of resistance to racism, a successful black entrepreneur has commented on what it is like to be black today in a predominantly white society:

One step from suicide! What I'm saying is—the psychological warfare games that we have to play everyday just to survive. We have to be one way in our communities and one way in the [white] workplace or in the business sector. We can never be ourselves all around.[179]

Key Terms

slavery   169
Underground
  Railroad   171
"Jim Crow" laws   172
modern racism   175
ethnoviolence   177
lynching   177

racial profiling   179
psychological
  wage   181
underemployment
  rate   186
Reconstruction   189

CHAPTER 8

Mexican Americans

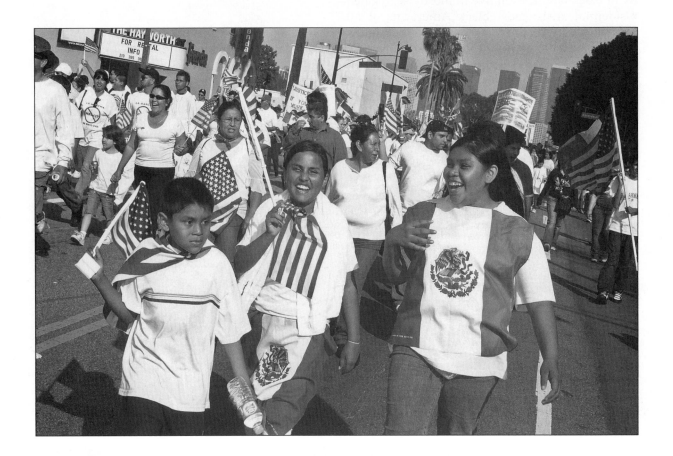

BIG PICTURE QUESTIONS

- *How does corporate globalization contribute to Latin American immigration to the United States?*

- *What role have Mexican Americans played in building up this country's wealth and institutions?*

- *What are the societal consequences of discrimination by European Americans against Mexican Americans?*

Not long ago, three men were drinking beer in suburban San Diego. After a while, these Anglo whites* decided to "shoot some aliens" at the U.S.–Mexico border. Using a rifle, one man killed a Mexican youngster who was crossing the border. The killer was sentenced to only two years in jail. The life of the immigrant was not considered valuable by his killer or, indeed, by the judge. In recent years, hostility toward Latin American immigrants has reached intense levels—with new white-dominated citizen groups, such as the "Minutemen," patrolling the Mexican border. One anti-immigration group burned a Mexican flag in front of a Mexican consulate in Arizona. In 2006, Congress passed expensive legislation to create hundreds of miles of security fencing and other barriers between the United States and Mexico; so far, billions of dollars have been spent. In 2010, conservative legislators in Arizona passed a controversial law allowing local police officers to arrest any person they had a "reasonable suspicion" was an undocumented immigrant—a law predicted to increase racial profiling. Much anti-immigrant hostility has been fed by stereotyped assertions about Mexican immigrants by poorly informed politicians and media. These assertions have helped to spur on white nativists, who have even made death threats against Latino leaders because of their speaking out on behalf of undocumented Mexican immigrants.[1]

Many Americans have historically held stereotypical views of the people in Mexico as sleepy farmers with big sombreros, "wetbacks," mustachioed banditos, or ignorant people involved with magical religious views. Popular images are supplemented by negative treatments of Mexicans and Mexican Americans in schoolbooks that distort the history of the Southwest, as in the historical myths that glorify heroic Texans in the 1830s confronting a backward

Mexican government and army. In addition, popular and scholarly accounts of U.S. history by European Americans frequently omit significant references to Mexican American contributions to the past and present development of the United States.

The 2000 census counted just over 35 million **Latinos (Hispanics),** *persons whose national origins (or whose ancestors' national origins) are in the countries of Latin America—that is, Mexico and much of the Caribbean, and Central and South America.* This figure was estimated to have grown by the late-2000s to some 46.9 million, about 30.7 million of whom were Mexican Americans.[2] U.S. Latinos are now one of the two largest groups of Americans of color, along with African Americans. The umbrella term *Hispanic,* coined by the U.S. government relatively recently, is widely used to designate persons of Mexican, Puerto Rican, Cuban, Dominican, and Central or South American heritage. And yet, *Hispanic* is an English word derived from *Hispania,* the Roman name for Spain. This term emphasizes Spanish heritage while ignoring other (for example, Indian and African) backgrounds. *Latino,* an alternative collective designation, recognizes the complex Latin American origins of these groups. It is a Spanish-language word preferred by many Spanish-speaking scholars, activists, and others. Although each term has critics, both are widely used not only by members of this group but also by outsiders.[3]

However, combining the various national-origin groups into one Latino or Hispanic category masks their significant diversity. Most people are likely to name their own group first and foremost in terms of its national origin, such as Mexican, Cuban, or Puerto Rican. Latino groups differ economically, politically, historically, and culturally—for example, in regard to food, religious practices, music, and political inclinations. Although the Latino population is increasingly dispersed, geographic distinctiveness remains. A substantial majority live in southwestern states or in Florida, Illinois, New York, and New Jersey. Mexican Americans are disproportionately concentrated in the Southwest; Puerto Ricans and most other Caribbean Latinos, in the Northeast; and Cuban Americans, in the Southeast.

In this and the following chapter, we examine three large Latino groups: Mexican Americans, mainland Puerto Ricans, and Cuban Americans—all of whom have diverse histories and heritages as well as different experiences in U.S. society. Today,

---

*The terms *whites* and *Anglos* are generally used in this and other chapters as shorthand for "European Americans," or what the U.S. Census Bureau calls "non-Hispanic whites." One survey of 2900 Latinos indicates that a significant majority, and more than 80 percent of Mexican Americans, do not prefer the term *white* for their group when given a wide range of choices. The largest percentage prefer *Hispanic/ Latino.* Cases where they opt for a "white" identity will be discussed later.

about two-thirds of Latinos are Mexican Americans, the group we focus on in this chapter.[4]

The Conquest Period, 1500–1853

Beginning in the 1500s, Spaniards conquered the indigenous populations in what is now Mexico and the southwestern United States and concentrated this exploited population in agricultural and mining communities. Because small numbers of Spanish women migrated, sexual liaisons, often forced, between Spanish men and indigenous women were common. The offspring, sometimes called *mestizos* ("mixed peoples"), soon outnumbered Spanish colonizers, and usually occupied a middle social position in the colonial societies' racial hierarchies—below the Spanish immigrants but above Indians, persons of mixed Indian and African heritage, and enslaved Africans.[5]

After centuries of exploitation, Mexico won independence from Spain in 1821. Before the invasion of the Anglo-American immigrants in the 1830s, Mexicans had already established numerous communities in what is now the southwestern United States. Several thousand, with a Mexican way of life and a self-sufficient economy, lived on land grants in what would eventually become the U.S. state of Texas. Thousands of immigrants from the United States moved into the area, and in a few years the new migrants outnumbered the preexisting Mexican population.[6]

The Texas Revolt: Myths and Reality

Mexican government actions, including freeing enslaved people and placing restrictions on U.S. immigration to northern Mexico, angered many U.S. immigrants to the area. The causes of the 1836 Texas revolt included the growing number of white immigrants coming illegally from what was the United States, the racist attitudes of these immigrants toward native-born Mexicans, and the resentment of immigrant slaveholders toward Mexican antislavery laws. Until recently, relatively few U.S. analysts have been inclined to see the Texas revolt as territorial aggression by U.S. citizens against another sovereign nation, which indeed it was. Many analysts have excused the behavior of the Texans and blamed the Mexican government.[7]

Myths about the revolt that praise white Texans' heroism persist. The most widely known is the legend of the Alamo, which portrays 180 or so principled, native-born, white Texans courageously fighting thousands of Mexican troops. Actually, most of the men at the Alamo mission, located in what is now San Antonio, were newcomers, not native-born Texans. Many, such as James Bowie and Davy Crockett, were also adventurers, not men of principle defending their homes. In addition, the Alamo was one of the best fortified sites in the West; its defenders had twice as many cannons, much better rifles, and better training in riflery than the poorly equipped Mexican recruits.[8]

The Texas rebellion was actually a case of U.S. colonizers going beyond an existing U.S. boundary and intentionally trying to incorporate new lands. The 1845 annexation of the Texas area by the U.S. precipitated a war. Intentionally provocative U.S. troop actions in a disputed Texas–Mexico boundary area generated a Mexican attack, which was followed by a U.S. declaration of war and victory. Mexico fell victim to what was in effect a U.S. conspiracy to seize its territory by force. In 1848, the Mexican government was forced to cede a huge area (now the U.S. Southwest and West) for just $15 million. Mexican residents there had the choice of remaining or moving to Mexico; most stayed, assured on paper of legal rights by the Treaty of Guadalupe Hidalgo.[9] However, white immigrants gradually used legal and illegal means to take much of the land still owned by the existing Mexican occupants.

California and New Mexico

In the early 1800s, the 7500 non-Indian residents of California lived mostly on Mexican-run ranches. After gold was discovered in 1849, however, U.S. whites poured into California, again taking lands from Mexicans.[10] At the time of U.S. acquisition in 1848, some 50,000 Mexicans in what became the New Mexico territory had long maintained their own cultural traditions. Established villages—Santa Fe dates from 1598—provided the organization to withstand some effects of the U.S. invasion. Initially, because there were few whites there, Mexican American landholders in these western areas continued to play an important role in commerce and politics.[11]

Soon, though, many lost their lands to the invading whites. By the mid-nineteenth century, the U.S. system of private land ownership was replacing a Mexican system that included significant communal lands. Despite U.S. treaty promises, old land grants were ignored, and communal land was treated as U.S. government land. Mexican landholders everywhere lost much land. The invasion of the Southwest was not a heroic period in which U.S. "settlers" appropriated unused land, but rather a period of imperialistic domination of Mexicans who had long been residents in the area.[12]

Past and Present Immigration

Estimates of Mexicans within the expanding United States range up to 118,000 for the 1850s. In the decades that followed, millions entered the United States, pushed by political upheavals and economic conditions in Mexico and pulled by expanding economic opportunities in U.S. fields and factories. Peak immigration periods have been 1910 to 1930, 1942 to 1954, and 1965 to the present. Immigrants have included (1) those with official visas; (2) **undocumented immigrants** (*immigrants without legal immigration papers)*; (3) **braceros** (*seasonal farm workers on contract)*; (4) commuters (those with official visas who live in Mexico but work in the United States); and (5) "border crossers" (those with short-term permits, many of whom become domestic workers).[13] Exclusion of Asian immigrants by federal action during the era from the 1880s to 1911 (see Chapter 11) and the pull of World War I–era industrialization sharply decreased the number of Asian immigrants and U.S.-born laborers available for agricultural work in the Southwest. Mexican workers were therefore drawn to the area. Under pressure from U.S. employers, federal government officials waived immigration restrictions, allowing thousands of Mexican workers to enter legally during World War I.[14]

This was an important indication of the globalizing character of U.S. capitalism. Recruitment of overseas labor by U.S. employers has for a century been a major source of racial and ethnic diversity. Several hundred thousand Mexican workers and family members entered the U.S. in the 1920s. Improved canning and shipping technologies opened markets for agricultural produce. The 1924 Immigration Act, which barred most southern and eastern European immigrants, did *not* exclude Mexicans, for Mexico had become a major source of low-wage labor for employers. Still, white nativists objected strongly to this growing Mexican population, which they feared would create a "problem" greater than, as they put it in their racist framing, "the negro [sic] problem of the South" and thus would threaten white racial "purity" in the United States.[15]

The Border Patrol of the U.S. Customs and Border Protection agency (part of the U.S. Department of Homeland Security) was created in the 1920s and has played a major role in the lives of immigrants. In 1929, legislation made illegal entry a felony. Although given the authority to keep out undocumented workers, until recently the Border Patrol has tried to regulate the number, allowing enough to come in to meet the labor needs of U.S. employers. In times of economic recession, the Border Patrol would conduct exclusion or deportation campaigns. Then, in better times, more Mexican immigrant workers would be allowed in, and enforcement of immigration restrictions would be less rigorous.[16] During the 1930s Great Depression, federal enforcement of literacy tests and local white hostility greatly reduced the number of immigrants. Considerable pressure was put on Mexicans already here, whether citizens or not, to leave. Many were forcibly deported in massive campaigns; thousands, *including numerous U.S. citizens,* were expelled in organized caravans by U.S. agencies eager to reduce government expenditures for relief during the Great Depression.[17]

Braceros *and Undocumented Workers: Encouraging Immigration*

In the World War II era, a 1942 Emergency Farm Labor (*bracero*) agreement between the United States and Mexico again provided Mexican workers for U.S. agriculture. Over two decades, nearly 5 million *braceros* were brought in at the request of employers, who were again going beyond U.S. borders for labor. This government program eventually stimulated the migration of yet more undocumented workers. Mexico, with the largest Spanish-speaking population of any country, has been the major supplier of immigrant workers for U.S. employers for many decades.[18]

Mexican workers' entry has periodically met intense opposition. Union officials have called for restrictions to protect the jobs of native-born Americans. Growing concern among nativist groups led to the inclusion of significant restrictions on legal Mexican immigration in the 1965 Immigration Act, which set an annual limit of only 20,000 per year for Mexican immigrants, thereby making it more difficult for Mexican immigrants to join relatives in the U.S. legally. Subsequent U.S. legislation has attempted to limit undocumented immigration.[19]

The U.S. economy, however, depends heavily on immigrants from Latin America. Undocumented workers are, as one report put it, the "backbone of Dole, Green Giant, McDonald's, Stouffers, Burger King, the Octopus car wash chain, Del Monte, Chicken of the Sea, Heinz, Hunt's, Rosarito, Campbell's *m-m-m good*, Wendy's, Taco Bell, Lean Cuisine, Dinty Moore, Hormel, midnight shifts, front lawn raking, pool scrubbing, gas station back rooms, blue-jean stitching, TV assembly, [and] athletic-shoe sole gluing."[20]

Migration and U.S. Involvement in Latin America

U.S. involvement in Latin America has long involved the U.S. government and major corporations, and the goals have frequently been political and economic colonization. The U.S. military has intervened many times in Latin America to protect U.S. political-economic interests. In addition, the growing U.S. economy has regularly created much demand for low-wage workers in sectors such as construction, agriculture, and food services.[21]

Many immigrants are attracted by these U.S. jobs, and many are also pushed by serious political or economic problems in their home countries. For example, the U.S. government and U.S. corporations are sometimes implicated in Mexico's recurring economic problems. For decades, U.S. corporations operating in Mexico have helped to generate out-migration. Some U.S. firms have built large farming operations in Mexico to grow food for export, thereby taking over large amounts of land and driving off small farmers who traditionally farmed the land to feed their families. U.S. corporations' expropriation of agricultural land and other resources in Mexico has forced many Mexicans to move from rural areas to large cities in Mexico, where jobs are often scarce. These urban workers frequently seek work in the United States to support their families. Indeed, a large proportion of Mexico's total revenues comes from money sent home to Mexico by immigrant workers in the United States.[22]

Since the 1960s, U.S. manufacturing and industrial corporations have built many factories in Mexico. Many companies have built **maquiladoras**, *manufacturing operations in northern Mexico near the U.S. border*, where they can take advantage of low-wage labor and weak environmental standards while avoiding certain tariffs and duties. International trade agreements such as NAFTA (North American Free Trade Agreement) have accelerated U.S. investment and manufacturing in Mexico. One consequence of border plants is that workers who migrate from southern Mexico to these border areas learn that working conditions are better across the border, and some then leave for the United States. The era of "free trade," which was supposed to bring economic benefits to most Mexican workers, has actually benefited, at most, a modest number of affluent Mexicans and U.S. capitalists.[23] The Mexican government has made little effort to stop cross-border migration, which relieves poverty pressures in Mexico. This Mexican perspective and increased U.S. hostility toward undocumented immigrants have created major tensions between the U.S. and Mexican governments.

The number of Mexican workers entering illegally for permanent residence is less than many U.S. media accounts and anti-immigrant groups suggest. Although some seek to settle permanently in the U.S., many border crossers apprehended by U.S. border agents annually "are temporary labor migrants who are caught more than once by the INS and who do not intend to live in the U.S. in any case. . . . A large reverse flow into Mexico goes virtually unnoticed and unreported."[24]

Many go back and forth across the border on a seasonal basis. The best estimate for the total number of undocumented immigrants from all countries for the late 2000s was about 11.9 million, with about 59 percent having come from Mexico. Up until the mid-2000s, an estimated 500,000 to 600,000 undocumented immigrants entered annually, but those numbers dropped off significantly because of the economic recession in the latter part of that decade. Indeed, in the case of Mexican immigrants, more than 430,000 were estimated to be *leaving* the United States in the years 2008 and 2009. One study of the undocumented workers found that most had friends or relatives in the U.S. through whom they found employment. The low-paid, often impermanent jobs available to most undocumented immigrants offer limited economic opportunities.[25]

Most undocumented workers—who make up about 5.4 percent of the current U.S. workforce—pay considerably more in income and other taxes than they get back in terms of government benefits such as Social Security and food stamps. Research studies indicate that undocumented immigrant workers work mainly in low-wage jobs that most U.S. workers consider undesirable, and thus they have little effect on, or in some cases even increase, the employment rate of native-born workers as a whole. The major exception is in urban areas where there are many unemployed workers of color. Native-born workers of color in the lowest-wage job categories in these areas are sometimes displaced by undocumented Latin American workers.[26]

 How has U.S. capitalism shaped Mexican migration and employment patterns?

The 1986 Immigration Act, the 2006 Secure Fence Act, and Undocumented Immigrants

Growing concern over the presence of undocumented immigrants led to passage of the 1986 Immigration Reform and Control Act (IRCA). It authorized (1) the legalization of undocumented immigrants resident continuously in the United States since 1982, (2) sanctions for employers who hire undocumented aliens, (3) reimbursement of governments for added costs of legalization, (4) screening of welfare applicants for migration status, and (5) programs to bring in agricultural laborers.[27] Just over 3 million undocumented immigrants applied for legalization by the deadline; 1.7 million applications were accepted for adjustment to legal residence. Mexican immigrants made up three-fourths of those who became legalized.[28]

After the law was passed, a federal study found that numerous firms discriminated against U.S. citizens to ensure they were not hiring undocumented workers. Other researchers found a similar response by many employers and "an IRCA-induced decline in job opportunities" for "unauthorized-looking natives."[29] A 1990 Immigration Act was passed to correct some of these problems, but employer discrimination against "immigrant-looking" native-born workers continues to be reported. This latter law reiterated family reunification as a major criterion for immigrant entry, but added more employment-related criteria for entry.

Debates over regulatory legislation have periodically revived anti-immigration arguments. Many native-born whites have long been concerned that the country could not absorb so many immigrants, even though the ratio of immigrants to the native-born population was higher in the early twentieth century, when southern and eastern Europeans were immigrating to the United States. In 1910, the foreign-born represented 14.6 percent of the population. In 2007, the figure was only about 12.6 percent, giving the United States a smaller percentage of foreign-born than some other contemporary nations.[30] Given its long history of successful absorption of immigrants, it is unlikely that the United States will soon be overwhelmed by these immigrants. Implicit in many public discussions of these new immigrants is a racialized concern that most are from Latin America and Asia—that is, that they are not whites of European origin.

Anti-immigrant stereotypes and political actions have been commonplace in recent decades. One white legislator in California distributed a racist poem titled "Ode to the New California" to state legislators that mocked Mexican immigrants with lines such as "I come for visit, get treated regal. So I stay, who care illegal. . . . We think America damn good place. Too damn good for white man's race."[31] Many newspaper and Web commentators have claimed that these immigrants cause employment problems for many Americans, significantly increase crime, and seriously overburden government services. Some white politicians and citizen groups forced the anti-immigrant Proposition 187 onto the California ballot, and it passed with a substantial majority in 1994. Proposition 187 sought to restrict undocumented immigrants' access to public services and required public employees to report undocumented immigrants. After legal challenges, it was overturned in 1999. In 2004, Arizona voters passed a similar measure, which has also faced legal challenges.

In 1996, the U.S. Congress passed yet another act: the Illegal Immigration Reform and Immigrant Responsibility Act (IIRIRA). This law established regulations restricting legal immigration as well as undocumented immigration. The IIRIRA increased the number of border control agents and imposed a substantial income requirement for families sponsoring immigrant relatives. These requirements

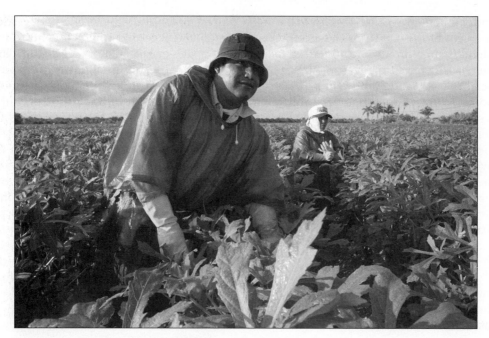

Farmworkers harvest crops in Florida.

discriminate against prospective Latino sponsors because their incomes are, on average, significantly lower than those of whites.[32]

In 2006, after months of debates, Congress passed another piece of punitive immigration legislation, the Secure Fence Act, which was estimated to cost taxpayers $35 billion. The law again increased the number of border enforcement personnel, as well as surveillance technology on the border. It required construction of physical barriers to Latin American immigrants, including a border fence. The 670-mile fence was only half completed by the 2008 deadline. (Other immigration reforms, such as amnesty for hard-working undocumented immigrants who had resided in the U.S. for a long time, were postponed.) From 1996 to the late-2000s, punitive actions such as those in the IIRIRA law have contributed to the deaths of an estimated 5100 undocumented men, women, and children trying to cross the dangerous U.S. border. And yet, political pressures from conservative elements and congressional elections have periodically resulted in a rush to pass more restrictive legislation especially targeting Mexican immigrants.[33]

The punitive immigrant legislation of recent decades has been motivated in part by a concern that immigrants come not to work but to get on government welfare programs. However, much research on Mexican and other Latino immigrants contradicts these stereotyped notions. The idea that Latino immigrants come just to get on welfare is contradicted by their high labor force participation rate (those employed or actively seeking work). Generally, even in severe economic recessions like the 2008–2010 period, Latinos, including immigrants, have higher labor force participation rates than non-Latinos. In 2008, the overall Latino labor participation rate was 68.5 percent, compared to 65.6 percent for non-Latinos. In addition, research shows that for the most part Latino immigrants use government social welfare programs much less often than native-born groups. Indeed, undocumented immigrants are legally prohibited from most government benefit programs, including federal housing programs, food stamps, Medicaid, and the Temporary Assistance for Needy Families program. In general, undocumented immigrants have less access to healthcare of any kind and must endure substandard living conditions.[34]

In the twenty-first century, Latin American immigration has become a major issue hotly debated in the media and by politicians. Undocumented immigrants have been constructed as a threat, as numerous conservative politicians and media commentators aggressively accent arguments about "homeland security" and an "unprotected border." Yet, the often harsh language about immigrants and security is very rarely extended to the even longer border that the United States has with Canada or the large number of undocumented immigrants from Canada and Europe. This is a sign that racialized thinking about the skin color and culture of those immigrating may be central to much opposition to unauthorized Latino immigrants. In addition, the increasing barricading of the U.S.–Mexican border since the 1980s has led to unintended consequences—such as increasing the number of undocumented workers living in the U.S. because the large number interested in working only for part of the year cannot easily return to Mexico.

 Have recent immigration laws contributed to discrimination against Mexican Americans?

Population and Location

The umbrella group referred to as *Latinos* is currently the fastest-growing major racial–ethnic segment of the U.S. population, now more than one-seventh of the total population. A substantial majority are Mexican Americans. Although immigrants make up a substantial portion, the majority have been born and raised in the United States. The Latino, mostly Mexican American, population of just one metropolitan area, Los Angeles, is now larger than the total population of numerous states. Latinos (again, mostly Mexican Americans) are more than one-third of the residents of California, the largest state, and growth in Latino communities has been substantial in other states in recent decades. Primarily because of recent growth in Latino and Asian populations, California and Texas now have population *majorities* that are not European American. In addition, U.S. Census Bureau and other data for the last decade reveal that the Mexican American population is increasingly becoming dispersed, for large numbers are now neighbors of other Americans in every region. Indeed, southern states from Arkansas to Georgia and South Carolina have seen particularly rapid growth in Latino populations, especially of foreign-born male workers filling low-wage jobs in these areas.[35]

Stereotypes and Related Images

Early Images

In the 1830s and 1840s, U.S. whites migrating to the Southwest generally did not react favorably to the people already there. Most of those people coming from the eastern and southern states applied the white racial framing and its stereotypes, developed previously for African Americans, to the resident peoples of the Southwest, including Mexicans and Indians. They attributed laziness and backwardness to what they saw as a distinctive "Mexican race." Most Mexicans in what would soon become the U.S. Southwest were of mixed ancestry, the descendants of Indians and Spaniards, and many also had some African ancestry. European American immigrants brought with them a well-developed racist framing that already rationalized the subordination of African Americans and that made it easy for them to stigmatize darker-skinned Mexican Americans as racially inferior.

Apparently, few white colonizers saw Mexicans as "white," but compared them to black or Indian groups. They placed Mexicans at the bottom of the old white-racist continuum. In the words of one land agent, Mexicans were "swarthy looking people resembling our mulattos, some of them nearly black." Sam Houston, a leader of white immigrants coming to Texas, called them inferior "half-Indians." The widespread white view that Mexicans had a "filthy, greasy appearance," as one traveler wrote, probably led to the derogatory epithet "greaser" for Mexicans. In the 1850s, John Monroe reported to Washington that the people in the New Mexico area "are thoroughly debased and totally incapable of self-government, and there is no latent quality about them that can ever make them respectable."[36] Ironically, these Mexicans' knowledge of ranching and mining laid the foundation for successful economic development by later white immigrants.

Later on, increased Mexican immigration after 1900 triggered more attacks. White-supremacist groups raided labor camps and beat workers. A "brown scare" hysteria developed in California between 1913 and 1918 amid fears that the Mexican Revolution would spread to the United States. Whites characterized Mexican immigrants as a menace to communities' health, and pressure for deportation mounted.[37] In the 1920s, a white member of

Congress stereotyped Mexicans as a mongrelized mixture of Spanish and "low-grade Indians" plus some African slave "blood." In 1928, an "expert" witness testified to the House Immigration Committee and branded the "Mexican race" a threat to the "white race."[38] Nativist writers expressed fear of "race mongrelization." A Princeton professor spoke fearfully of the future elimination of Anglo-Saxons through interbreeding in "favor of the progeny of Mexican peons who will continue to afflict us with an embarrassing race problem."[39] Interestingly, an explicit category of "Mexican race" was used in the 1930 census, the only census ever to include such.

Much public commentary since the 1920s has stereotyped the Mexican American male as crime oriented. For example, a report by a white lieutenant in the Los Angeles Sheriff's Department after the 1943 "zoot suit" riots (discussed later) alleged that the Mexicans' desire to spill blood was an "inborn characteristic," a view endorsed by his superior. Then, as now, stereotypes linked assumed social or cultural traits to alleged *biological* inferiority: "The Mexican was 'lawless' and 'violent' because he had Indian blood; he was 'shiftless' and 'improvident' because that was his nature."[40]

Since the 1920s, the results of so-called IQ testing have often been used to argue for the intellectual and group inferiority of Mexican Americans and other Latinos, as well as of black Americans. Indeed, a version of this highly stereotyped view of Latinos was expressed in a best-selling 1990s book called *The Bell Curve* (see Chapter 7).[41]

Contemporary Stereotypes and Prejudices

Negative stereotypes and prejudices can be found at all class levels. George Murphy, former senator from California, once argued that Mexicans were "ideal for 'stoop' labor—after all, they are built close to the ground."[42] In 1965, a leading U.S. historian, Walter Prescott Webb, wrote that "there is a cruel streak in the Mexican nature. . . . It may and doubtless should be attributed partly to the Indian blood."[43]

In recent decades, overtly racist stereotyping by whites, especially those in elites (discussed later), has often changed for the better, but there are still many who assert and act on negative anti-Mexican images. For example, speaking at a meeting on border issues and Mexican immigration in the 1990s,

a California state senator argued that public education should not be provided to the children of undocumented immigrants: "It seems rather strange that we go out of our way to take care of the rights of these individuals who are perhaps on the lower scale of our humanity." Latinos who criticized the senator's comments were themselves attacked in the media. Recently, moreover, U.S. Forest Service enforcement officers held a media briefing where they warned hunters and others that campers in Colorado national forests who "eat tortillas, drink Tecate beer and play Spanish music" could well be "armed marijuana growers." After protests from Latino organizations, which pointed out the lack of cultural awareness and need for multicultural training, Forest Service officials apologized for their "regrettable references."[44]

For many decades, numerous public commentators and scholars stereotyped Mexicans or Mexican Americans as passive or fatalistic. Some social science studies have reinforced the view that Mexican culture is one of fatalism, "machismo," and a too-extreme family orientation. Oscar Lewis and William Madsen portrayed what they thought was a folk culture of fatalism and familism in Mexican villages, a view later extended to Mexican American communities.[45] Numerous social scientists have pointed out the errors in such stereotyped assumptions. Many analysts have overlooked the substantial diversity in Mexican American culture and communities from Texas to California—and, more recently, in midwestern and southern states. A characteristic such as the assumed male domination in Mexican families varies significantly with the class and educational background of Mexican Americans, just as it does among other racial–ethnic groups.[46]

Drawing still-negative images from the media, political speeches, and other sources, many people often stereotype Mexican Americans and other Latinos. Thus, in one 1990s survey, white college students expressed the belief that Hispanics were more likely than whites to be physically violent, dirty or smelly, uneducated, poor, and criminally inclined. These respondents felt that, compared with whites, Hispanics placed less value on learning, mature love, physical fitness, and economic prosperity.[47] The majority of white respondents in a National Conference survey regarding interethnic attitudes believed that Latinos "tend to have bigger families than they are able to support." One-fifth of whites felt that Latinos lacked "ambition and the drive to succeed."[48] In contrast, an examination of data from twenty-one surveys of Mexican Americans and European Americans found that Mexican American workers were *not* less work oriented than European Americans; the former had a strong work ethic and were productive in their workplaces.[49]

In recent years, the "criminally inclined" stereotype in the white framing of Mexican Americans and other Latinos has often taken the form of aggressive "gangbangers" stereotyping—which we often see in movies and on television. In a recent study, Robert Durán examined the use of gangbanger imagery and gang-suppression models among law enforcement officials in two southwestern cities, Denver, Colorado, and Ogden, Utah. He concluded that the commonplace stereotyping of Mexican American neighborhoods as "gang infested" and the routine viewing of "gangs as synonymous with crime" lead to discriminatory police practices, which do not accent "criminal acts, but rather perpetual criminal people." With this stereotyped imagery in mind, gang-suppression approaches of numerous police departments become "over-inclusive and embedded with practices that create opportunities for abuse of authority." That is, most of the gang enforcement police stops were just racial profiling that involved no reasonable suspicion of criminal activity and that often included nongang members.[50]

 What are important commonalities in stereotypes targeting Native Americans, African Americans, and Mexican Americans?

Views of Immigration and Immigrants

In spite of increasing anti-immigrant discussions across the country, recent surveys have found that a substantial majority of Americans still think immigration is good for the country, although during major economic downturns many would like to see the level reduced. Several 2009 polls found that three-quarters of respondents want the government to do more to control immigration and U.S. borders, and two-thirds want employers who hire undocumented immigrants to be punished. At the same time in a 2009 ABC/*Washington Post* survey, 60 percent indicated their support for allowing undocumented immigrants to remain if they "pay a fine and meet other requirements." Other polls show a similar majority supporting legalization or other incorporation for those who have worked in the country for some time. There is only minority support for harsh measures. In a 2009 *New York Times* survey, only 24 percent agreed that the "borders should be completely closed." In addition, there is significant variation among Americans in negative views of recent immigrants. For example, a recent PEW poll found that Americans over age 65 are much more likely than those under age 30 to believe that "newcomers from other countries threaten traditional American customs and values." Not surprisingly, too, recent surveys of Latinos have found they are much more supportive of the current level of immigration than the non-Latino population.[51]

In numerous local areas, especially in Arizona, Nevada, Indiana, and North Carolina cities that have experienced substantial Mexican immigration, anti-immigrant sentiment is often stronger. Two-thirds of the respondents in a survey in North Carolina, where the Latino population has increased significantly in recent years, felt their neighbors would not accept Hispanics into the neighborhood.[52]

Moreover, in the mid- to late-2000s, numerous demonstrations against Latin American immigrants were held by white-supremacist groups, including Ku Klux Klan, neo-Nazi, and neo-Confederate groups, Today, on numerous websites as well as in videos and books, openly racist groups often describe Mexican and other Latino immigrants as a "cultural cancer," a "wildfire," or a "gang of illegals" making the country "less beautiful." Since the early 2000s, some whites have created violent video games with which one can play at killing undocumented immigrants coming across the U.S.–Mexico border.[53]

Using less flamboyant language, Harvard Professor Samuel Huntington has argued that Latin American immigrants are a serious danger to Anglo-American culture. In his ethnocentric view, certain immigrant groups are dividing the country because they and their allies "deny the existence of a common culture in the United States . . . and promote the primacy of racial, ethnic, and other subnational cultural identities and groupings." He is explicitly concerned here that the problematical immigrants are people of color, "overwhelmingly from Latin America and Asia." Yet, as we will show later, most of these immigrants either desire to return home after working for a while in the United States or aggressively seek to adapt to this dominant U.S. "common culture."[54]

Negative Images in the Mass Media

As a result of protests from Mexican Americans, extreme stereotypical depictions of Mexican Americans in advertising and the media have decreased in recent years. Organized protests and the recognition of the growing importance of Latino viewers have led U.S. media elites to present more positive images in the movies and on television, in part by featuring more Latino actors, such as Jennifer López, Eva Longoria, Edward James Olmos, and Javier Barem.

However, serious problems remain. One 1990s study of the portrayal of Mexican Americans and other Latinos in television programming found that most shows ignored Latinos or presented them disproportionately as criminals. Although the percentage of Latinos among actors on television shows has increased since then, one early 2000s study found that they were still only 2 percent of regular television characters and were still often portrayed as criminals or, more recently, in law enforcement occupations. Another study of local television news shows also found a bias, with Latinos being much less likely to be shown as defenders of the law than whites.[55]

Numerous Hollywood films remain problematical as well. One media scholar has commented: "The way we are treated in movies represents a way that we are marginalized in the larger society. In that way it is a very accurate portrayal."[56] For decades, Hollywood films, such as *Dirty Harry* (1971), *Falling Down* (1993), and *Gran Torino* (2008), as well as numerous theater and television crime movies, have portrayed Latinos disproportionately as "gangbangers," criminals, drug users, or welfare mothers. Moreover, the absence of Latinos in Hollywood and other U.S. movies has been significant. A study of films produced between 1990 and the mid-2000s, many of which are still widely viewed on DVDs in homes, found that 1.9 percent of the speaking characters were Latino, far less than the Latino proportion in the population over this period. Whites were substantially overrepresented. In newer media such as video games one also finds whites, especially men, overrepresented, and Latinos significantly underrepresented. One recent study examined 150 best-selling

video games and found not one Latino protagonist. Only 3 percent of the supporting characters were Latino. Yet Latinos now make up about 15 percent of the population. The researchers suggested that the lack of Latino protagonists and other characters signaled to people, young and old, that Latinos are not important in U.S. society. These findings signal too that game makers are mostly whites who are likely thinking out of a white racial framing of society.[57]

Media stereotyping, prejudice, and discrimination are often subtle, as in the absence or infrequency of positive pictures and images of Latinos in many magazines, newspapers, and other media, including those outside the entertainment industry. Marco Portales, a Mexican American scholar, has noted: "Since the 1950s, when I grew up, I have periodically observed that pictures of Hispanic people are not selected for the covers and inside pages of national and regional mainstream magazines, advertisements, and promotional brochures in the United States."[58]

Newspapers and magazines communicate negative images in the routine pictures, language, and metaphors they choose. One study by communications researchers examined recent and major U.S. women's magazines and found that white women were significantly overrepresented compared to women of color, and as judged against U.S. population proportions. In addition, analyzing everyday language used in a major U.S. newspaper, linguistics scholar Otto Santa Ana has shown that editors and reporters often write racialized reports on Latino immigrants. His examination of articles written around the time of the anti-immigrant California Proposition 187 (discussed earlier) documented the frequent use of negative language that portrayed Mexican and other Latino immigrants as animals, invaders, and disreputable persons. Numerous articles characterized public programs as "a lure to immigrants" and spoke of the electorate's appetite for "red meat of deportation," INS agents catching "a third of their quarry," Proposition 187 supporters who "devour the weak and helpless," and the need to "ferret out illegal immigrants." The articles' use of strong metaphorical language—words such as *burden, dirt, disease, invasion,* or *waves flooding the country*—conveyed an image of Latino immigration as very threatening or dangerous.[59]

Such metaphorical language, which non-Latinos often use without thinking, bolsters a negative view of, and plays down the humanity of, immigrants who are only seeking to make better lives for themselves.

Mocking Spanish

Anthropologist Jane Hill has examined the widespread use of a mocking type of Spanish by otherwise monolingual (in English) whites. *Mock Spanish* includes made-up terms such as "no problemo," "el cheapo," "watcho your backo," and "hasty banana," as well as phrases such as "numero uno" and "no way, José." On the surface, these terms often seem light-hearted, but they subtly incorporate "a highly negative image of the Spanish language, its speakers, and the culture and institutions associated with them." Mock Spanish—common in gift shops, in board rooms, at country club gatherings, and in the media—is mostly created by well-educated whites. They also create greeting card texts, coffee cup slogans, video games, and other cartoons that mock Spanish speakers. Characters in movies such as *Terminator 2* use "adiós," "hasta la vista, baby," and similar Spanish terms in an insulting way not common among native Spanish speakers. In a society in which openly racist talk is often frowned on, mock Spanish is used to perpetuate negative images of Mexicans and Mexican Americans: "Through this process, such people are endowed with gross sexual appetites, political corruption, laziness, disorders of language, and mental incapacity."[60]

Recently, an assistant director of the Texas Election Division made joking comments to the effect that local election officials should "speak slowly and loudly, in broken English" to Latino voters in need of language assistance, which is required under U.S. and Texas law. Such language mocking, like that mocking African American vernacular English, is often linked intimately to racialization and institutionalized discrimination. Certain accents in English are used as markers for this racialization. Whereas native speakers of languages such as French or Gaelic-Irish do not generally face serious discrimination because of their accents when they speak English, many speakers of Spanish-accented English do face such discrimination, especially at the hands of white native-English speakers. As one scholar has noted, "It is crucial to remember that it is not all foreign accents, but only accent linked to skin that isn't white, or which signals a third-world homeland, that

evokes such negative reactions."[61] Certain language accents are indeed closely linked to the stigmatization of groups such as Mexican Americans, Puerto Ricans, and Cuban Americans.

A Racialized Identity: The Contemporary Situation

Historically, Mexicans and Mexican Americans have been socially constructed by most Anglo whites as a distinctive, inferior racial group. Regardless of how they saw, or see, themselves, they have typically been racialized by the dominant group as inferior and not white. As David López and Ricardo Stanton-Salazar explain, "However ambiguous on the individual level for Mexican Americans, on the group level Mexicans have a history of stigmatization, economic exploitation and racial exclusion in California and the Southwest."[62] In recent decades, Mexican Americans, including recent immigrants from Mexico, have inherited this historical burden of being racialized in negative terms by a majority of whites.

Today, the terms *Mexican* and *Mexican American*, as used by those outside the group so designated (especially by those in the dominant white group), usually involve a view of Mexican Americans as being distinctive in racial and ethnic terms. Recall that a racial group is one that is socially constructed centrally on the basis of physical characteristics considered important by the dominant group, and an ethnic group is one that is socially constructed mainly on the basis of cultural or national-origin characteristics. Today, research evidence indicates that a substantial majority of whites view Latino groups as racially distinctive and as not white. We recently gave a questionnaire to 151 white college students asking them to place a list of major U.S. racial and ethnic groups into "white," "not white," and "other" categories. Overwhelming majorities did not classify any of the Latino groups listed—including Mexican Americans, Cuban Americans, and Puerto Ricans—as unambiguously white. The majority of these well-educated whites are operating with a white framing and racial-status continuum in mind when they place various U.S. groups into racial categories. For a majority of whites, all major groups of color seem to be viewed as closer to the black (or nonwhite) end of the old racial-status continuum than to the white end; no group among the many groups of color is, as yet, significantly "whitened." In addition, television and radio news discussions of Latino immigrants in recent years have revealed that leading white news commentators think of Latinos in racialized terms, such as by periodically alluding to them as a "race."[63]

Today, non-Latinos may use language, accent, or surname as well as physical characteristics to identify a person as Mexican American or Hispanic/Latino. This typically means that most of the latter who are lighter-skinned will usually be identified by Anglo whites as Hispanic/Latino—and therefore as *not* European American or white.

A subordinate group's reactions to being socially constructed by the dominant group adds yet more layers to the social reality. Typically, a subordinate group comes to see itself in certain racial or ethnic terms, yet this view is often not the same as that constructed for them by the dominant white group. Subordinated racial groups, including Mexican Americans and other Latinos, often resist the racialization imposed by whites in various ways. Some may insist that they are "white"—just like European Americans. This strategy is often painful and may involve alienation from relatives and other members of the group, but it does make some psychological and social sense, because "white" status carries with it privileges, power, and no racial subordination. A small percentage of Mexican Americans recognize the significant African ancestry of many people born in Mexico and assert their kinship with African Americans, while many others assert a distinctive Mexican American identity of their own that does not recognize this African ancestry. The latter often view themselves as part of a proud *la Raza Unida* (united people) and/or identify with a broader Hispanic/Latino community. Indeed, the Chicano movement since the 1960s (discussed later) has accented *la Raza* and thus accelerated the willingness of many to identify themselves as part of a multiracial group, which is not white and has some Indian ancestry. Today, surveys suggest the diversity of Mexican American (and other Latino) responses to their societal situation. One 1990s Houston-area survey found that the majority of Hispanic respondents, including nearly two-thirds of those born in the U.S., did not consider Hispanics to be part of the "white race." Similarly, an early-2000s national survey of 2900 Latinos by the Pew Hispanic Center found that a substantial majority of Latinos and Mexican Americans preferred to classify themselves

as something other than "white" or "black," with only 17 percent of Mexican Americans consistently preferring "white."[64]

Interestingly, when forced by the 2000 census (the most recent published census) to categorize themselves only in terms of a very limited racial-group listing—white, black, Indian, Asian, or other race—about half of those who self-identified as Hispanic or Latino on another census question chose for this question a racial category other than white. However, 48 percent of the self-identified Hispanics/Latinos did designate themselves on this limited census continuum as "white." This choice may indicate the strength of social pressures to appear and orient as white, as well as the complexity of racial identities today. Research by Sonya Tafoya has also shown that this identification as white increases over the generations of Latinos, as they become more distant from the immigration generation. Native-born children of Latino immigrants were more likely to check off the "white" box in the 2000 census than those in the immigrant generation. The centuries-old, white-imposed system of racial categorization, running from white to black, is often difficult to navigate for Americans of Latin American descent. As a result, some make a significant effort to identify with the white end of that continuum.[65]

 What methods of resistance are linked to the racialization of Mexican American identity?

Conflict and Protest

Oppression and Resistance

Anglo white coercion was a fundamental factor in Anglo white domination in the Southwest in the nineteenth and early twentieth centuries. Mexican land and agricultural development were taken over by theft and force. Not only were African Americans lynched to maintain white control, but an estimated 597 Mexicans and Mexican Americans were also lynched from the late 1840s to the 1920s. Many Mexicans and Mexican Americans resisted this violence. Folk ballads along the border have long praised the Mexican "bandits," who were often rebel Mexican leaders unwilling to bear quietly the burdens imposed on their people. Their resistance actions were regarded as "crimes" by whites, but often *not* by those subordinated. Mexican rebels (for example, Pancho Villa) were protected by people of Mexican origin on both sides of the U.S.–Mexico border. Moreover, white law-enforcement officers, including the Texas Rangers, periodically terrorized Mexicans and Mexican Americans.[66]

Since the 1920s, Mexican Americans and other Latinos have continued to suffer white violence. For example, in Los Angeles in the summer of 1943, violent attacks by white sailors on Mexican American youth, particularly those dressed in baggy attire whites called "zoot suits," marked the beginning of white-generated "zoot suit" riots. White mobs roamed Los Angeles, beating up Mexican Americans, and the latter sometimes organized retaliatory attacks. The media exaggerated Mexican American crime, and police harassment of Mexican Americans was common. The years leading up to the riots had seen a sharp increase in the *Los Angeles Times*'s use of "zoot suit" and other derogatory terms to refer to Mexican Americans, and such labeling fostered white hostility toward Mexican American residents.[67]

Over more recent decades, to the present, some whites have continued to use violence against Mexican Americans and other Latinos. We cite elsewhere the continuing attacks by whites on undocumented immigrants crossing the U.S.–Mexico border, as well as the numerous websites with violent anti-immigrant video games or intensely racist commentaries on immigrants and Spanish speakers. Hate crimes against Mexican Americans and recent Mexican immigrants are on the increase. The most recent FBI report counted some 830 Latinos as being victims of racialized crimes, a significant underestimate given that most law-enforcement agencies do not make a serious effort to report such crimes to the FBI. For example, in the San Diego area, a restaurant owned by a Mexican American family was firebombed, and racist graffiti were sprayed on its wall. Also, in Houston, a Latino teenager was attacked and raped by two white youth shouting racist comments.[68]

Protests Since the 1960s

During the 1960s and 1970s, dozens of protests against discrimination took place in southwestern cities. Young Mexican Americans, including groups such as the Brown Berets, took to the streets to fight back against police harassment and other discrimination.

Los Angeles protests were among the most significant. In August 1970, police attacked demonstrators at the end of a National Chicano Moratorium on the Vietnam War march, in which 20,000 Mexican Americans took part. (Activists in the 1960s and 1970s preferred the term *Chicano* to *Mexican American*. Today, the term *Chicano* is still used occasionally, mainly by activists and academics.) Other Mexican American protests during a Mexican Independence Day parade resulted in one hundred injuries and 68 arrests.[69]

Local governments have sometimes used their police forces, which historically have included few Mexican Americans, to counter legal protests by Mexican Americans. From the 1960s to the present, the common practice of preventive police patrolling in Mexican American communities, with its "stop and frisk" and "arrest on suspicion" tactics, has led periodically to unfavorable police contacts for Mexican Americans. Two-thirds of Latinos in one 1990s Los Angeles poll reported that incidents of police brutality were common. At public hearings, an independent citizens' commission investigating the Los Angeles Police Department heard testimony from Mexican Americans that the department "acted like an army of occupation," treating them as the "enemy."[70] This pattern has persisted to the present. In a more recent *Los Angeles Times* poll, 31 percent of Latinos were strongly critical of the local police department. In addition, recent national surveys by the Pew Center have found that less than half the Hispanics interviewed said they had confidence that local police would not use excessive force in dealing with the public, a proportion much lower than for white respondents in the same poll. Less than a majority of these Hispanics also felt that police officers and the courts treat Hispanics fairly.[71]

Widespread anti-immigrant sentiment and the introduction of anti-immigrant ballot measures have stimulated Mexican Americans to organize. In some communities Mexican Americans have responded to anti-immigrant nativism with school walkouts and protests. A large Los Angeles demonstration against one proposition (Proposition 187) illustrated broad-based community support for Mexican American political concerns. In the fall of 1996, about 30,000 Latino demonstrators in Washington, DC, denounced restrictions on immigrants and called for an increased minimum wage, better educational programs, and an end to discrimination.[72]

Over the first decade of the twenty-first century, anti-immigrant attitudes and legislation have generated numerous large-scale pro-immigrant marches, demonstrations, and strikes by hundreds of thousands of Mexican Americans and their allies from Washington and New York to Miami, to Chicago and Denver, to San Francisco and Los Angeles. Thus, in the spring of 2006, hundreds of thousands of demonstrators from numerous Latino and other groups participated in the largest public demonstrations in Chicago and Los Angeles history. In recent surveys some 24 percent of Latino respondents reported having participated in demonstrations for immigrants' rights.[73] Participants have demanded social justice, fair treatment, and legalization for undocumented immigrant workers and their families. Speaking at one demonstration, the mayor of Los Angeles and the son of Mexican immigrants, Antonio Villaraigosa, asserted, "We cannot criminalize people who are working, people who are contributing to our economy and contributing to the nation." On May 1, 2006, International Worker's Day, many millions of workers and activists in some 200 cities boycotted routine school, work, and shopping activities as part of a national protest against the treatment of immigrants. Not surprisingly, recent surveys of Latinos have found that more than 60 percent think the pro-immigrant protests signal a social movement "that will go on for a long time" and that over half say that they would participate in future protests. Numerous analysts have viewed these very large-scale movements as a sign of something new—protests clearly linked to transnationalism, border crossings, and the globalization of modern capitalism.[74]

The Economy

Mexicans were initially incorporated into the U.S. economy by often violent conquests of Mexican lands. Two million acres of private lands and 1.7 million acres of communal lands were lost to Anglo whites between 1854 and 1930 just in what is now New Mexico. Across the Southwest, those who lost land often became landless laborers. In the 1850s, one-third of Mexican Americans in the rural south Texas labor force were ranchers and farm owners, one-third were skilled laborers or professionals, and one-third were manual laborers. By 1900, the proportion of ranchers and farm owners had dropped sharply to 16 percent, while the proportion of laborers—many working on white-owned ranches or farms—had climbed to two-thirds.[75]

Mexican Americans were the original *vaqueros* (Spanish for "cowboys") on ranches across the Southwest, and large numbers became agricultural workers there. From the late 1800s to the early 1900s, working conditions in agriculture were often severe and the pay so low that few whites competed for these jobs. Women were concentrated in agriculture, domestic service, and manufacturing, particularly in the garment industry and canneries. Mexican American workers generally earned less than whites and were usually assigned the more physically demanding tasks.[76]

Stratification and Discrimination in the Workplace

Mexican Americans have long faced individual and institutional discrimination. Beginning in the early 1900s, many white-run agricultural firms, mining companies, and other firms openly paid differential rates for "whites" and "nonwhites"; the latter category included Mexican Americans. The availability of undocumented workers allowed white employers to keep wages low. White-controlled unions also discriminated against Mexican Americans. Attempts to create farm labor unions for low-income workers date back decades, but were unsuccessful until the 1960s. Moreover, by the 1940s, there was some improvement in employment conditions, but discrimination kept most Mexican Americans in low-wage positions. In 1943, President Franklin Roosevelt's antidiscrimination order and the tight labor supply temporarily opened some jobs at decent wages to Mexican Americans, but virtually none moved up into skilled positions. Poorly paid jobs and housing discrimination relegated most to segregated urban areas sometimes called *barrios*. Restrictive covenants were used by whites to exclude Mexican Americans from better housing areas. Since World War II, many Mexican American workers have occupied secondary-labor-market positions as farm workers, laborers, domestic-service workers, or other service workers, and earned wages far below those of whites.[77]

Beginning in the 1960s, U.S. firms began building the labor-intensive manufacturing plants (maquiladoras) noted earlier—mostly in the north-ern border region of Mexico to take advantage of low-wage labor. Today, there are an estimated 3000 maquiladoras, with about one million workers. Their number has declined in recent years. Wages in these maquiladoras have been far lower than in similar U.S. plants. Large numbers of workers in border cities live in shacks without water, electricity, or sanitation facilities. Many migrate to border areas to work in the maquiladoras just long enough to earn money to migrate to the United States.[78]

Many employers in southwestern, southern, and midwestern states have long sought Mexican work-ers who are undocumented because they will work, today as in the past, for low wages and can often be exploited more easily than U.S.-born workers. For example, if undocumented workers protest oppres-sive working conditions, an employer can report them to immigration authorities. Agricultural and service-sector employers frequently rely heavily on undocumented workers and circumvent laws that prohibit hiring them.[79]

In addition, large numbers of domestic workers, housekeepers, and nannies from Mexico, Central America, and the Caribbean work in affluent U.S. households. The "maids and servants" category of workers in the United States has long been racial-ized. In recent years this occupational racialization has developed a global dimension as affluent U.S. families purchase household and other services from workers who are from poor countries, especially Latin American countries. These workers tend to work long hours for less than a minimum wage. Interviewing 153 Latina domestic workers, Pierrette Hondagneu-Sotelo found that these women pay a high price for their employment: "the loss of dig-nity, respect, and self-esteem; the inability to even live with their [own] children; and the daily hard-ships of raising families on poverty-level wages." These immigrant workers are among the most eco-nomically and politically oppressed members of this society.[80] More generally, Latina workers, including immigrants and the native born, are more likely than U.S. women workers as a group to hold blue-collar jobs such as janitorial and maintenance jobs, per-sonal service positions, food preparation and simi-lar jobs, and various kinds of manufacturing jobs.[81]

In recent interview research, Mexican American and other Latino workers—immigrants and the native born, low income and middle class, and in southern and northern communities—have cited incidents of employment, housing, policing, and other discrimination by whites. Employment testing projects have documented discrimination against Mexican Americans and other Latinos, as well as for black Americans. Researcher Marc Bendick Jr. has examined sixteen studies of racial and national-origin discrimination. He found that researchers using white testers and testers of color have discov-ered whites are favored over applicants of color (Latinos and African Americans) about 20 percent of the time. Note too that the Latino and black work-ers typically face such discrimination not just once, but repeatedly over years and decades of work, and in many areas of employment.[82] Indeed, in one study, results showed that white job applicants with felony drug convictions are about as likely to be called back or given job offers as Latino applicants without a criminal record. In addition, many employers in cities such as Atlanta, Los Angeles, Detroit, and Boston have admitted their racial stereo-types about Latino and black workers. Many believe that workers of color are suitable primarily for lower-paying jobs regardless of their skills and sel-dom consider such workers for skilled positions. Even before they have specific knowledge, many employers stereotype Latino and black applicants as less likely than whites to possess skills of inter-personal communication. These applicants are less likely to be hired.[83]

Research by Millard and Chapa in several mid-western areas found significantly less job, housing, and school integration of Latinos and Anglos than they expected. "The two groups are quite separate in all sectors of the workplace, including factories, commerce, and services. . . . Anglos generally pay little attention to the newcomers, who are often left to the practices and prejudices of an Anglo minority that exploits them and another, larger group of Ang-los that rebuffs them." Discrimination by a minority of Anglos took place regularly in the context of majority Anglo indifference.[84]

Surveys also reveal problems with everyday dis-crimination. In one San Diego survey, two-thirds of Mexican American youth reported that they had personally faced discrimination. One young woman reported that as a high school senior, despite a good job interview over the phone, she failed to get the job. She noted, "I guess they heard me over the phone, and I guess I sounded kind of white. Once

I got to the store, I saw there were only white girls working there. Well, they never called me back." In addition, a survey of Latino workers in Los Angeles found that 31 percent reported discrimination in the workplace recently. This included racial slurs and being denied a job or promotion because of their racial background. National surveys of Mexican Americans and other Latinos have found that 38 percent view discrimination as a major problem in the workplace, with an additional 37 percent saying it is a minor but still present problem.[85]

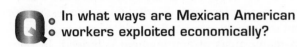

In what ways are Mexican American workers exploited economically?

Continuing Language Discrimination

Language discrimination in the workplace involves treating people unfairly because they speak a language that is not English, or because they speak a dialect of English that is not in favor. The Equal Employment Opportunity Commission (EEOC) has reported increases in complaints against employers who bar Spanish-speaking employees from speaking Spanish in job-related or private conversations at work. Many legal analysts, including those at the EEOC, interpret such employer practices as national-origin discrimination banned by the 1964 Civil Rights Act. EEOC regulations state that an English-only rule is discriminatory unless the employer can show a strong business necessity for it.[86]

Even though courts generally accept agency regulations implementing laws they enforce, federal court decisions have varied in whether they accept the EEOC regulations. In *García* v. *Gloor* (1981) the U.S. Supreme Court upheld an employer's right to fire an employee for speaking Spanish. A Mexican American employee of a lumber company was fired for answering a fellow employee's question in Spanish. The Court reasoned that Title VII of the 1964 Civil Rights Act did not equate national origin with primary language and that language discrimination was in this case permissible.[87] In a 1988 case, the Court of Appeals for the Ninth Circuit came to the opposite conclusion after evaluating an English-only rule: "The cultural identity of certain minority groups is tied to the use of their primary tongue." Referring to EEOC regulations, the court stated that "English-only rules . . . can 'create an atmosphere of

inferiority, isolation, and intimidation' [and] can readily mask an intent to discriminate on the basis of national origin."[88] In 1991, another federal district judge in California ruled that an English-only requirement for employees in a meat-packing plant was discriminatory. Fluency in English had not been a requirement when the employees were hired.[89]

The federal law on language discrimination is still developing. Bars to Spanish speaking are still viewed as illegal under EEOC guidelines and several court decisions. A few courts have knocked down English-only laws aimed at restricting Spanish speech in government settings, on First Amendment grounds. In 2000, the Court of Appeals for the Eleventh Circuit decided *Sandoval* v. *Hagan* and knocked down Alabama's English-only driver's license examinations as a violation of the 1964 Civil Rights Act. However, in 2001, the U.S. Supreme Court overturned the decision on grounds that applicable law did not allow a "private right of action," but the Court did not rule on whether language discrimination was national-origin discrimination prohibited under civil rights law. Moreover, a Catholic university in Texas reached a $2.4 million settlement in an EEOC lawsuit brought by cleaning personnel. Latino housekeepers charged that they were called "dumb Mexicans" and told by their supervisor to speak only English on breaks. And in a 2006 case, *Maldonado* v. *City of Altus,* the Tenth Circuit Court reviewed a district court case that examined Altus's English-only policy for all work-related interactions and overturned the district court ruling that had supported the town's policy, thereby signaling that the EEOC guidelines on language discrimination had shaped its decision in favor of Latino employees. However, in spite of these scattered cases the majority of federal court decisions dealing with employers' English-only requirements in workplaces have upheld such discriminatory requirements.[90]

Language discrimination has periodically generated organized protest from Latinos. For example, in a demonstration of intragroup solidarity in La Puente, a Los Angeles suburb, local Mexican American women organized with Mexican immigrants to stop school board attempts to replace their district's bilingual program with an English-only policy. In addition, the increasing multilingual diversity in a few states and associated political pressures have

TABLE 8.1   Employment Distribution (2008)

	European American	Mexican American
Managerial and professional specialty	38.7%	15.5%
Sales and office occupations	26.2	20.9
Natural resources, construction, maintenance	9.6	20.3
Production, transportation, materials moving	11.1	18.8
Service occupations	14.4	24.6
Total	100.0%	100.1%

Source: U.S. Bureau of the Census. "2008 American Community Survey." (European American is non-Hispanic white.)

recently led their legislatures to pass laws providing limited protections for non-native English speakers.[91]

Unemployment, Poverty, and Income

Unemployment rates for Mexican Americans have been relatively high for decades. In the 2008 American Community Survey, the unemployment rate for Mexican Americans (7.4 percent) was reported as significantly higher than that of non-Latino whites (5.2 percent). In Table 8.1, we see that Mexican American workers are more highly concentrated in lower-wage job categories than are Anglo workers. (Census data list a "non-Hispanic white" category. "European American" data here represent that category.) Although there is a significant proportion of Mexican American workers in the white-collar categories, Mexican American workers are heavily concentrated in the production, transportation, construction, natural resources, and service-worker categories, whereas European Americans are more heavily concentrated in white-collar positions. Indeed, Mexican American workers make up a significant percentage of the workers in numerous blue-collar and service categories in the U.S. economy.[92]

Mexican American incomes have been consistently low compared with those of white Americans. Table 8.2 compares family income levels and poverty rates as determined by the Census Bureau in its recent American Community Survey for Latinos of Mexican, Puerto Rican, and Cuban ancestry with figures for the European ancestry population. On family income measures, Mexican Americans as a group ranked as the poorest, followed by (mainland) Puerto Ricans. The median income for Mexican American families was less than 60 percent that of European American families. Mexican American families were more than three times as likely as European American families to be poor. In addition, the fact that many Mexican American workers hold relatively

TABLE 8.2   Family Income Levels and Poverty Rates (2008)

	Puerto Rican American	Mexican American	Cuban American	European American
Median family income (past 12 months)	$43,944	$41,538	$51,290	$70,835
Percentage of:				
Families below poverty line	21.1	20.7	11.0	6.1
Children less than 18 years old below poverty line	30.3	29.8	14.0	10.9

Source: U.S. Bureau of the Census. "2008 American Community Survey."

low-wage or temporary jobs has meant that economic slowdowns bring an actual decline in wages for workers in these families. Many of the poorest families include workers who immigrated from Mexico in recent decades with little in the way of educational or economic capital.[93] To make matters worse for these and other Mexican American families, there are dramatic differences in the reported wealth of Latinos (Mexican Americans and other groups) and European Americans. According to the most recent (2002) available data analyzed by the Pew Center, median net worth of Latino households, at just $7932, was less than 10 percent of the median net worth for white households in that survey.[94]

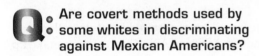

Q: Are covert methods used by some whites in discriminating against Mexican Americans?

Problems of Economic Adaptation

Some assimilation analysts have suggested that the process of adaptation for later immigrants, such as Mexican immigrants, are, or should be, similar to those for early-twentieth-century groups, such as Italian immigrants. However, the first large groups of Mexican immigrants and their children—those who came between World War I and the 1950s—did not achieve the same socioeconomic mobility as southern and eastern European immigrants because of discrimination, economic exploitation, and segregation. Later groups of Mexican immigrants, those who have come since the 1960s, have also faced different circumstances. The white southern and eastern European immigrants did not experience the high levels of job, residential, and school segregation and the racist stereotyping that have long been experienced by Mexican and other Latino immigrants. Most Europeans came during a period of rapid industrialization and had access to blue-collar jobs that required little education. These conditions generally enabled white immigrant workers and their children to advance economically.

In contrast, today the U.S. has a predominantly service-work–dominated economy with increasingly few manufacturing jobs. Most well-paid jobs today require more than a high school education. Unlike European immigrants in the early 1900s, many recent Mexican and other Latino immigrants, especially those with little formal education, have been

able to find only low-paid jobs with little chance of mobility. Segmented assimilation describes the experience of many Mexican American workers and their children. The children of these immigrants, second-generation Mexican Americans, today often do not move up the socioeconomic ladder as the second generation of earlier white immigrant groups did. This is substantially the result of the U.S. economy no longer providing enough decent-paying manufacturing and other blue-collar jobs, as it did for much of the twentieth century for white immigrants and their children.

Social science research shows two divergent patterns of mobility over the first generations of Mexican American adaptation. Zulema Valdéz has shown from census data that "earnings of low-skilled, foreign-born Mexicans *decrease* as immigrants reside in the United States longer. . . . In contrast, the earnings of high-skilled, foreign-born Mexicans *increase* as immigrants reside in the United States longer." Immigrant status, level of education, and continuing discrimination all make a difference. Elsewhere, Valdéz suggests that data indicating a large economic gap between Mexican Americans and whites and a persisting "intergenerational, low-wage, low-skilled Mexican laboring class" are not surprising for a country that has "a racialized and gendered labor market, growing wage inequality, tougher immigration policy, and an upsurge in anti-Mexican-immigrant sentiment."[95]

Moreover, as we saw in Chapter 7, the concept of a troubled "underclass"—one characterized by multigenerational poverty, high violent-crime rates, a school dropout problem, teenage pregnancy, and long-term drug use—has been accepted by some social scientists and media analysts as a way of explaining the impoverished conditions of certain racial and ethnic groups, including African Americans and Mexican Americans. Assessing working-class Mexican American and other Latino communities in cities from the West Coast to the East Coast, numerous social scientists have examined these communities' cultures and strengths, as well as their problems. They have found that even in the face of substantial poverty and political and economic discrimination, these communities usually maintain strong family and community support structures, community organizations, enclave economies, some significant mobility, and an accent on education. One recent example can be seen in the major California study by Edward Telles and Vilma Ortiz, *Generations of Exclusion*.[96] Even harsh conditions do not destroy communities. One older 1990s analysis of social and economic conditions in Laredo, Texas, found that the city's border location facilitates illegal drug trafficking, yet the area's strong Latino extended families and residential stability have created "a strong sense of community structure and identification."[97] In several such cities, small local businesses and off-the-books enterprises such as street vending have promoted the economic vitality of numerous Latino communities.

The movement of large numbers of immigrants into many Latino communities has also buttressed local economies and maintained a demand for businesses that provide Latino goods and services. The concentration of the poor that under-class theorists emphasize as negative can be positive. Thus, residential concentration of relatively low-income immigrants in cities such as Houston has stimulated development of an enclave economy, reinforced job and housing networks, and provided a supportive cultural setting. Recent research continues to confirm the strengths of families, religion, and organization in most Mexican American communities, with their still large populations of working poor.[98]

Contrary to conventional under-class notions, researchers do not find just one pattern of responses to poverty conditions. The character of poverty varies from community to community, but each has used its oppositional culture and social, economic, and religious resources for survival. Extended family and other networks, as well as strong cultural frameworks, remain at the core of these communities; these are reinforced by religious organizations and, frequently, additional community organizations.

Immigrant Workers: Targeted for Discrimination

Mexicans and Mexican Americans are now the neighbors of other Americans in all U.S. regions. For the most part, Mexican and other Latin American immigrants work hard under difficult conditions and often for modest pay. They perform much hard labor shunned by many other Americans: harvesting crops, building and cleaning houses, cutting lawns, and washing dishes in restaurants.

Nonetheless, many other Americans treat them as unwanted outsiders. They are often targets

of discrimination. Southern Poverty Law Center (SPLC) researchers recently interviewed about 500 Latino adults, mostly immigrants, in several southern states. These workers described much current discrimination, generally at the hands of whites:

> In Tennessee, a young mother is arrested and jailed when she asks to be paid for her work in a cheese factory. In Alabama, a migrant bean picker sees his life savings confiscated by police during a traffic stop. . . . [Latinos] are routinely cheated out of their earnings and denied basic health and safety protections. They are regularly subjected to racial profiling and harassment by law enforcement. . . . This treatment—which many Latinos liken to the oppressive climate of racial subordination that blacks endured during the Jim Crow era—is encouraged by politicians and media figures.[99]

Latino immigrant workers have faced discrimination in the North and West as well. Not long ago in New York, for example, Farmingville's legislative body vetoed a proposal to fund a new immigrant laborer hiring site and community center. The beating of two immigrant laborers, apparently by white supremacists, was not enough to secure action for improved hiring conditions for immigrant workers desired by local employers. Other northern communities have seen similar hostility toward immigrant workers.[100]

Growing numbers of immigrants report housing and related discrimination by white neighbors. Local officials periodically enforce housing codes so as to discriminate against Latino workers. A lawsuit by landlords on Long Island accused town officials of using rental permits and regulations to drive out immigrant workers. An organization representing Mexican American and other Latino farmworkers in Riverside County, California, reached a settlement with county officials resolving complaints of discrimination in code enforcement. A U.S. Department of Housing and Urban Development (HUD) investigation confirmed that county officials used discriminatory code enforcement to exclude Latino residents from mobile home parks.[101] HUD also cited officials in Elgin, Illinois, for violating an agreement to end discrimination in code enforcement. One recent SPLC report shows that at least thirty U.S. towns have considered, and some have passed, legislation aimed at discriminating against immigrant workers. In addition to housing discrimination, various new or proposed laws attempt to deny business permits to employers who hire undocumented workers or require the language of business or government to be English only.[102]

In many cities, housing discrimination by landlords plagues Latino families, both immigrant families and those whose members have been citizens for generations. Audit studies using Latino and white testers have found substantial rates of housing discrimination. Occasionally lawsuits also reveal such racial discrimination. For example, a large apartment management firm in Orange County, California, had to pay $226,000 in damages and penalties to settle a case brought by the county's Fair Housing Council that charged the company with discrimination against Latino and black renters in eight apartment complexes.[103]

Not surprisingly, given these patterns of intentional discrimination in housing, coupled with the desire to live with fellow Latinos who have similar experiences and backgrounds (including knowledge of how to cope with discrimination), more than 40 percent of Latinos now live in Latino-majority neighborhoods. Their segregation from whites is high, although somewhat less than that for African Americans, and has increased between 1990 and the present.[104]

Politics and Protest

Before 1910, only a few Mexican Americans, usually hand-picked by whites, held office in territorial and state legislatures in the Southwest. White ranchers and those who controlled railroads, mining interests, land companies, and other large enterprises dominated local and state politics.[105] By means of a restrictive "poll tax," an all-white political primary off-limits to voters of color, and numerous threats of violence, these white interests kept Mexican American voting strength low. Between 1910 and the 1940s, few Mexican Americans voted. Over subsequent decades, voting strength in the Southwest was expanded by the Twenty-Fourth Amendment, which banned discriminatory poll taxes, and by a California court case that knocked down English-only literacy requirements for voting.

In more recent decades, Mexican American voters have faced a variety of strategies designed to reduce their political strength. This has included the gerrymandering of voting districts to dilute Mexican American voting strength and prevent election of Mexican American candidates. Lawsuits—for example, *Garza* v. *County of Los Angeles* (1990) and *Williams* v. *City of Dallas* (1990)—have been necessary to challenge intentional discrimination by whites directed against the Latino voting population, such as the discriminatory use of at-large city council elections.[106] These lawsuits have forced some white-controlled governments to create single-member districts that allow for the possibility of elected Mexican American and other Latino political candidates.

Voter registration and voter turnout among Mexican Americans and other Latinos have risen substantially over the past three decades. As one recent report put it, "Between 2004 and 2008, the number of Latino eligible voters rose from 16.1 million in 2004 to 19.5 million in 2008, or 21.4%. In comparison, among the general population, the total number of eligible voters increased by just 4.6%."[107] The percentage of Latino voters among all eligible voters also increased, from 8.2 percent in 2004 to 9.5 in 2008. (Still, the percentage of eligible Latino voters actually registered to vote is lower than the figures for whites and blacks.) These increases in voters and in voter turnout played an important role in the 2008 election (discussed later).[108] However, we should also note that fewer than 40 percent of Latinos are U.S. citizens at least 18 years old and thus eligible to vote, as compared with more than three-quarters of whites who are eligible. Large numbers of potential Latino voters are, as of now, too young to vote or have not yet become citizens.

Growing Political Representation

Los Angeles, with the largest Mexican American population of any U.S. city, only elected its first Mexican American city council member in 1949. Even so, the city had no Mexican Americans on its council between the early 1960s and the early 1970s. Only in 1991 did Gloria Molina, the daughter of an immigrant laborer, became the first Mexican American, and the first woman, elected to the Los Angeles County Board of Supervisors.[109]

The National Association of Latino Elected and Appointed Officials (NALEO) has become one of the important organizations seeking to empower Latinos. The organization's thousands of members come from all government levels; the organization has played a major role in increasing Latino voter registration and turnout. One study of all 435 congressional districts found that a growing and significant number have a Latino population percentage of at least 12 percent, large enough to be politically significant. In recent years, many of these districts have had Republican members of Congress. Given that a majority of Latino voters—with the exception of Cuban Americans—still vote substantially Democratic most the time, the future translation of now-young Latino Americans into voters may bode well for future Democratic Party candidates.[110]

Since World War II, the total number of Mexican Americans serving as officials at all political levels has increased slowly but significantly, to more than 6000 today. Gradually, the growing numbers of registered Latino voters have brought the group greater political power. Mexican Americans and other Latinos currently constitute the largest voting bloc in cities such as Miami, San Antonio, Los Angeles, and New York.[111] Several cities, small and large, have had Mexican American mayors. In 1981, Henry Cisneros, later Secretary of Housing and Urban Development in the Clinton administration, was elected mayor of San Antonio, the first Mexican American mayor of a large city. His victory was the culmination of years

of organization. Cisneros was elected by means of a political alignment between the white business elite and the city's new Latino middle class. In 2001, a young city councilmember, Ed Garza, was elected as San Antonio's mayor with a similar coalition. Such coalitions of Anglo business elites and the Latino middle class have been successful in several southwestern cities. The most successful Latino politicians since the 1980s have tended to be business- or professional-oriented rather than community activists or labor leaders. In the first decade of the twenty-first century, several major cities have had Mexican American mayors (San José and Santa Ana, California; El Paso and San Antonio, Texas; and Albuquerque, New Mexico); four of these mayors have had a business or professional background. In 2005, Antonio Villaraigosa, the son of Mexican immigrants, was elected mayor of Los Angeles, the country's second largest city.[112]

Between the 1960s and today, the number of Latinos in state legislatures has increased significantly, with the largest numbers in Texas, California, and New Mexico. (Texas has about 2000 Latino elected officials in all offices, the largest number of any state.) The November 2008 election increased the number of Latinos in all state senates from 61 to 66, but the number in state lower houses actually

In a 2001 election, former California Assembly speaker Antonio Villaraigosa came close to being elected the first Latino mayor of Los Angeles. In a 2005 election, he was elected mayor.

decreased from 190 to 177, in part because some Latino state representatives were campaigning for higher offices.[113]

Today, the number of Mexican American and other Latino elected and appointed officials at the state and national levels still remains low relative to the Latino population percentage. Only a handful have ever served in top state executive positions, such as governors. In 1988, President Ronald Reagan appointed Lauro Cavazos as Secretary of Education, the first Mexican American (and Latino) ever appointed to a presidential cabinet. President Bill Clinton appointed two Mexican Americans to cabinet posts, and in 2001, President George W. Bush appointed one Latino, a Cuban American, to his cabinet. In addition, as of late 2009, there were twenty-four Latino members of the U.S. House of Representatives, mostly Democrats. This representation marks a significant increase over recent decades, but the Latino percentage (less than 6 percent) of House members is well below the Latino percentage of the U.S. population. By late 2009, there were also just two Latinos in the U.S. Senate (from New Jersey and Florida) and one Latino governor (in New Mexico).[114]

These growing numbers are politically significant. The international concerns of many Mexican Americans have helped to expand the involvement of U.S. political leaders in the Latin American arena, including the U.S. government placing a greater emphasis on relations between the U.S. and Mexico. Moreover, where Mexican Americans and other Latinos have been elected to office and increased their numbers in state and local bureaucracies, including as officials and teachers in school systems, significant educational and other socioeconomic advancements (such as rates of high school graduation) for Latino residents have been demonstrated.[115]

Support for the Democratic Party

In national elections since 1990, a majority of Latino voters nationwide have supported Democratic Party candidates. In the 1996 election, Latino voters, the majority of whom were Mexican American, for the first time voted at a rate greater than the national rate. This Latino turnout had an important impact not only on the presidential election but also on local and state elections from New York to California. Most voted for Democratic candidates. In the 2000 presidential election, an estimated 63 percent of Latinos voted for the Democratic candidate. Significantly, both the Democratic candidate, Al Gore, and the Republican victor, George W. Bush, spoke Spanish during the campaign and actively sought Latino voters, a first for presidential elections. In his first year in office, Bush became the *first* president to give a White House address in Spanish. Moreover, in the 2004 presidential election, exit polls suggested that 44 percent of Latino voters had given their votes to President Bush for reelection, an increase since 2000. However, in the 2006 elections for the U.S. Congress, the Latino vote increased for Democratic candidates across the country, as Latino voters apparently showed their negative reaction to the moves of the Republican-majority Congress to support anti-immigrant legislation.[116]

The 2008 presidential election saw Latino voters giving the African American presidential candidate, Barack Obama, two-thirds of their votes nationally, with Latino majorities for him in all states with substantial Latino populations. He won all major demographic subgroups—male, female, and younger voters. One legislative consultant, Andres Ramirez, noted that the Latino vote for Obama was greater than his winning margin in Florida and New Mexico: "In this election, the center-left coalition . . . dramatically increased turnout in the southwestern states, and saw a historic shift of the enormous Florida Hispanic vote from Republican to Democrat. Similar investments in future years in states like Arizona and Texas could very well make these states—home to George W. Bush and John McCain—as blue as New Mexico and Colorado are today."[117] Clearly, Latino voters are increasingly having a very significant influence on U.S. politics.

The Courts and the Police

Mexican Americans have long been significantly underrepresented in the U.S. judicial system, as jurors, judges, and prosecutors. In *Hernández* v. *Texas* (1954), the U.S. Supreme Court upheld an appeal of an all-white jury's conviction of a Mexican American defendant on the grounds that Mexican Americans were excluded from juries. The judge noted that the lack of Mexican American representation on any jury over a period of twenty-five years in a county that was 14 percent Mexican American was evidence of discrimination.[118]

Not until the 1960s was the first Mexican American federal judge appointed. Since the 1970s, the number has slowly increased, but is still relatively low today. No Mexican American has ever served on the U.S. Supreme Court. Mexican Americans are also underrepresented in most historically white police departments. Over recent decades, numerous Mexican American applicants have been denied police positions by the indirect discrimination of height requirements and by English-language requirements, as well as by too-low scores on conventional English-language examinations. One recent survey found that all Latinos taken together make up about 11 percent of police officers. They also make up only 3.5 percent of lawyers and 6 percent of various judicial workers. In addition, very few have ever served at the higher levels of federal justice-system agencies, although from 2005 to 2007, Mexican American Alberto Gonzáles served as the U.S. Attorney General. The same underrepresentation is to be found in state justice systems. One recent study of the Texas appellate court system found that, although black and Latino attorneys made up 16 percent of Texas attorneys, they held a very small percentage of important court-system positions. Thus, Latinos held just 8 of the 201 staff attorney positions for the sixteen Texas appellate courts, and 3 of the 55 law clerk positions. (The comparable numbers for black Texans were a minuscule 3 and 0.) Similarly small numbers were found for the higher Texas courts.[119]

Arizona, California, and Colorado have required jurors to be able to speak English, screening out many citizens. In these and other states, the pool of jurors was until recently selected by whatever method has suited (usually white) jury commissioners. Research in major Texas cities has shown that Latinos make up less than 10 to 13 percent of those called for jury duty in cities whose populations are at least 30 percent Latino. Many juries have included no Latinos. Thus, Mexican Americans and other Latinos charged with crimes have frequently been judged by juries containing few if any of their peers. Courtrooms in which no one understands Spanish present a problem for some defendants. Besides facing an absence of Spanish interpreters, defendants have been subjected to excessive bail, poor legal counsel, and stereotyped views of white judges. In some cases, white prosecutors have successfully excluded Latinos from juries on the basis of language. One 1990s Supreme Court decision upheld a prosecutor's exclusion of bilingual Latino jurors who had hesitated before agreeing to accept the official English translation of the Spanish-language testimony in a trial. In contrast, a judge in San Diego County, California, dismissed indictments by a grand jury because the pool from which jurors were selected did not represent a fair cross-section of the county.[120]

One survey of Latinos found that only 35 percent felt that Latinos usually or always "receive fair outcomes when they deal with the courts" in their communities, which compared to 57 percent of white respondents. Latino respondents also had substantially less favorable views of the police in their communities than did whites. In addition, some data for San Diego police officers stopping motorists have shown that Latino and black motorists were overrepresented in comparison to the driving-age population and were more likely to be searched when stopped. The same pattern of racial profiling characterizes other major cities. A recent national survey of local residents' views of police behavior found that 45 percent of Latino respondents felt that their local police officers were stopping people without good reason and were engaging in racial profiling.[121]

Some federal court data suggest a disproportionate focus on certain Latino lawbreakers, as compared to other groups of lawbreakers. For example, in recent years the federal law-enforcement system has focused much more heavily on undocumented immigrants to the U.S., and almost entirely on those crossing the U.S.–Mexico border. In the late 2000s, thus, about 24 percent of all federal court convictions were for immigration offenses, up from 7 percent in 1991. Some 80 percent of these involved Latino offenders; most were convicted for entering into or residing in the U.S. without authorization. This intensive federal government focus on Latino undocumented immigrants, while ignoring other undocumented immigrants, might be considered another type of discriminatory racial profiling.[122]

The Chicano Political Movement

Disenchantment with the accommodationist perspectives of some middle-class Mexican American leaders led to the emergence of the 1960s **Chicano political movement**, *a social movement that sought greater political power and less discrimination for Mexican*

Americans. During the 1960s and 1970s, many Mexican Americans, including college students, began to accent aggressively their historical culture and pride in their Mexican ancestry, and pressed for political and social equality in U.S. society. Since that time, the terms *Chicano* and *Chicanismo* have been associated with collective movements for change.

For example, lacking influence in mainstream political parties in the Southwest, many Mexican Americans joined the La Raza Unida Party (LRUP). The LRUP's goals included significant representation in local governments and pressing the latter to better serve the Latino community. The LRUP's major electoral and political successes occurred in Crystal City, a Texas city populated mostly by Mexican Americans. During the 1960s, the LRUP became a leading political force, and by 1970, Mexican Americans had won control of the school board and city council. However, white officials cut off state and federal funding, and then blamed the Mexican American leadership for government difficulties. By the 1980s, Mexican Americans were no longer identified with the LRUP but rather with the state Democratic Party. Yet, the LRUP had brought democratization to some southwestern communities and a substantial increase in Mexican American political participation.[123]

Women held important leadership roles within the LRUP. Most Mexican Americans elected in the Crystal City area were women. This type of feminism came "easily for Chicanas because of the woman's traditional role and strength as center or heart of the family. . . . The tradition of activism inherited from women's participation in armed rebellions in Mexico and in the political life of Mexico has also strengthened the Chicanas' position."[124] Mexican American feminists have faced major barriers. Indeed, for decades many issues of concern to them, including poverty and discrimination, have not been central to the mainstream (white) women's movement.

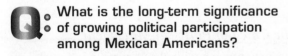 **What is the long-term significance of growing political participation among Mexican Americans?**

Other Organizations and Protests

Union organization has a long history among Mexican Americans. The first permanent organization was the Confederación de Uniones Obreras Mexicanas (CUOM), organized in California in 1927 with 3000 members. One CUOM strike was stopped by whites who used deportation of workers to Mexico and numerous arrests. Mexican American women participated in early strikes as members of the International Ladies Garment Workers Union. In addition, mutual-benefit associations developed early. These included worker alliances that pooled resources and provided individual and group support. The League of United Latin American Citizens (LULAC) was organized in southern Texas in the 1920s. Oriented toward civic activities, LULAC also pressed for an end to discrimination.[125]

After a Texas cemetery refused to allow the burial of a Mexican American World War II veteran, the American GI Forum was established to organize Mexican American veterans and work for expanded civil rights. In Los Angeles the Community Service Organization (CSO) worked to organize Mexican American voters. Two groups that formed about 1960—the Mexican American Political Association in California and the Political Association of Spanish-Speaking Organizations in Texas—focused mostly on political goals. Protests intensified in the 1960s. Youth organizations, including the Mexican American Youth Organization and the Brown Berets, worked for better education, employment, and housing conditions. A *Chicanismo* perspective, espousing a philosophy of self-esteem and antiracism, was linked to the actions of many in these organizations.[126]

Since the 1980s, the Southwest Voter Registration Education Project and similar groups have participated in many voter-registration campaigns and joined in filing lawsuits to dismantle discriminatory election systems. These groups played a major role in political victories by the Democratic Party in the late 2000s, and have pressed Democrats hard for reforms in the areas of healthcare and immigration. Another active force for change, the Mexican American Legal Defense and Education Fund (MALDEF), was founded in 1968 to address problems of jury discrimination, police brutality, and school segregation. Now the leading Latino legal rights organization, MALDEF has filed numerous lawsuits targeting discrimination and has worked to increase political representation. With the growth in Mexican American and other Latino populations in states outside the Southwest, MALDEF has expanded its civil rights efforts to the East Coast, opening an Atlanta office in 2002, where another Latino organization, the National Council of La Raza, has also set up a regional office. Widespread discrimination targeting Mexican Americans and other Latinos in most regions, which we noted previously, has influenced the expansion of antidiscrimination efforts by these important civil rights groups.[127]

Today, Mexican American women remain active in grassroots organizing and civil rights efforts. For example, Mothers of East Los Angeles (MELA) is an effective grassroots organization that works to defend its community's quality of life against environmental racism and local corporate pollution. At one neighborhood meeting, MELA members confronted an oil company representative seeking to build a pipeline through a Latino community in Los Angeles:

> "Is it going through Cielito Lindo [former President Ronald Reagan's ranch]?" The oil representative answered, "No." Another woman stood up and asked, "Why not place it along the coastline?" Without thinking of the implications, the representative responded, "Oh, no! If it burst, it would endanger the marine life." The woman retorted, "You value the marine life more than human beings?"[128]

Today, MELA members actively work, often with other local organizations, to protect the environment in which the residents of Los Angeles live, especially residential areas of concern to Latinos there.

Unions for Low-Wage Workers

In the 1960s, Jessie López, Dolores Huerta, and César Chávez created the Agricultural Workers Organizing Committee (AWOC) and the National Farm Workers Association (NFWA). In 1965, AWOC workers struck against Delano, California, growers. The NFWA met in Delano and voted to join the strike, demanding better wages. White growers refused to talk; picket lines went up; and guns were fired at workers. The NFWA remained nonviolent in the face of provocation by growers and police. A national grape boycott was organized and spread. Picket lines often formed where grapes were sold, and a massive march on Sacramento was organized. In 1966, AWOC and NFWA merged into the United Farm Workers Organizing Committee.[129]

In 1973, the largest California winery, Gallo Brothers, chose not to renew its contract with the United Farm Workers (UFW). As other wineries followed suit, many observers argued that the union was dying. But the workers' struggle continued. Governor Jerry Brown of California worked for legislation to protect farm workers, and in 1975, he signed the Agricultural Labor Relations Act, which provided for protection of union activities.[130] The UFW has been the most successful farm workers' union in U.S. history and has altered the structure of power in rural California by using the power of organized numbers of Latino and other farm workers to pressure for economic and political change. Among other issues, the UFW has addressed the issue of pesticide spraying of farm products in a nationwide campaign to force farmers to "stop poisoning workers and consumers."[131]

In spring 1994, one year after the death of César Chávez, more than eighty current and former farm

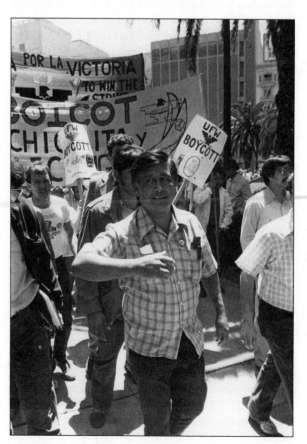

César Chávez marches at the head of United Farm Workers during a 1979 protest.

workers, some of whom had made the first such pilgrimage 28 years earlier, walked the 340 miles from Delano to Sacramento, California, signing up thousands of new UFW members along the way. From then to the present, the UFW has continued to organize and strike on behalf of farm workers. Recent reports from the UFW website summarize the results of organizing drives, including a campaign for a new contract with Gallo. In 2005, the union "mounted a major organizing drive among Central Valley table grape workers resulting in a summer election at Giumarra vineyards, America's largest table grape producer. Labor observers say it is one of the largest private sector union election campaigns in the nation." Most recently, the UFW signed a three-year contract with Beef Northwest Feeders, a major feedlot company; the contract provides medical and pension coverage and various workers' rights. Important contracts have also been signed on behalf of strawberry workers at Dole Berry locations and on behalf of thousands of agricultural workers at numerous other major agricultural firms, including D'Arrigo Bros, Monterey Mushrooms, and the Charles Krug-Mondavi winery. In recent years, thousands of UFW members and their supporters have also marched in numerous demonstrations in the West and Southwest in support of immigration reform.[132]

Today, nonetheless, many Mexican American and other farm workers across the country still get low wages and few benefits. They often live in crowded conditions; many who favor unions are harassed by employers. The majority of farm worker families still remain below the federal poverty line. In 2006, the UFW left the AFL-CIO and joined a more aggressive union coalition that included the Service Employees International Union, the Teamsters, and the United Food and Commercial Workers. Today, more farm workers are undocumented than in the past, and these workers are often afraid to organize. Still, in some areas union membership has been growing slowly.[133]

In recent decades, a significant number of Mexican Americans have become members of mainstream unions that represent auto workers, miners, teamsters, dockworkers, and railroad, cannery, garment, steel, and construction workers.[134] Unionizing efforts have also been successful among undocumented urban service workers. For example, in Los Angeles a local union of the Hotel Employees and Restaurant Employees International Union called for an international boycott of the New Otani Hotel because of its poor treatment of Latino and Asian service workers. Workers began large-scale picketing. Latinas, in particular, were critical to the union protests. Women activists proved wrong the traditional notions that women would be "unorganizable because of their family responsibilities, marginal commitment to the labor market, and submission to patriarchy." In August 2000, as the boycott and strike continued, a protest against working conditions at the hotel by 400 union workers was met by police officers in riot gear. Forty workers were arrested for blocking the intersection with clothes symbolizing the "dirty laundry" the hotel was unwilling to face.[135]

In the last decade or so, a few other unions, including the Service Employees International Union (SEIU), have aggressively organized Latino workers. Recently, an SEIU branch in Houston, called Justice for Janitors, has organized hundreds of janitors who clean a great deal of Houston office space. Most are Mexican American women and other Latinas. The union has drawn on a significant multiracial coalition of Houston community organizations, religious groups, and other labor unions. As sociologist Glenn Bracey describes it,

> Catholic churches and majority Latino organizations, such as CRECEN and LULAC, united with majority African American organizations, such as ACORN and NAACP, to push for improved living conditions for Houston's working poor. In many ways, Justice for Janitors' Houston campaign provides a model for interracial coalitions and exemplifies the power multiracial coalitions can have, even in traditionally hostile political environments.[136]

In Houston most such janitors have earned only a minimum wage and have often been limited to just four hours a day of work, with no health insurance benefits. In late 2006, the Houston union went on a successful strike against Houston cleaning companies that refused to sign a reasonable contract, one that eventually added important health and other benefits for these hard-working janitors. SEIU has had a number of similarly successful organizing efforts on behalf of Latino and other maintenance workers, including immigrant workers, in several other U.S. cities. Indeed, many of the more than 200,000 janitors organized by SEIU in numerous cities are Latino. Today, union efforts to improve

Latinos' working conditions persist across the United States.

Other Recent Challenges: Latinos and African Americans

The growing Mexican American and other Latino populations in urban areas have brought Latinos into situations of political conflict and cooperation with long-time African American residents. Together, the two groups now make up a majority or near-majority of the population in numerous U.S. cities. Capitalistic globalization is drawing many Mexican and other immigrant workers to the U.S., and the shift from an industrial to a service economy is reducing the number of higher-wage, unionized, blue-collar jobs available for both groups. U.S. capitalism sometimes pits new immigrants against established citizens who rely substantially on lower-wage blue-collar and service jobs.

Debates in the policy and scholarly literatures periodically focus on whether Latin American and Asian immigration in recent decades has affected the economic situations of native-born Americans. According to available data, employment problems have increased for many African Americans since the 1970s. National Research Council (NRC) and similar reports indicate that immigration has had a generally positive effect on the U.S. economy as a whole, but with some negative employment effects for other recent immigrants and some native-born Americans. Most undocumented workers labor in just two dozen or so low-wage occupations and earn wages near the minimum wage, if not below, and thus most native-born workers are not affected in a negative way. In recent decades, undocumented immigration has brought significant benefits to employers and better-off native-born workers, because they are the most likely to use the low-cost labor or services (for example, household work) of immigrants. The negative impact is greatest for high school dropouts and less skilled workers, including other Latinos and African Americans working in low-paid jobs.[137]

Corporate-generated competition between immigrants and less skilled native-born workers has the potential to generate recurring conflict, but so does general political competition between larger groups of Latinos and African Americans. In Dallas, for example, a struggle between the two groups over who should become school superintendent was resolved by the appointment of a black Puerto Rican candidate. Substantial conflicts between Latino and black groups related to elections in Miami and Houston, public housing in Chicago, and school and hospital hiring in Los Angeles have occurred. Some of the local political issues involve a growing Latino population that has not achieved full representation in public jobs and elected positions, which are often held by black urbanites. Several recent books have focused centrally on these issues, such as Nicolas Vaca's provocatively titled *The Presumed Alliance: The Unspoken Conflict Between Latinos and Blacks and What It Means for America*.[138]

The mass media tend to focus on conflict and neglect cooperation. For example, in recent years the media have accented tensions between Latino and black communities in California, tensions that became a topic of much discussion in the 2008 election year. In some areas of Los Angeles, Latino gang members attacked and/or killed black youth, and this got much media attention. Yet, what did not get similar media attention were the joint marches and organizing against gang violence in that area by Latino and black residents working together. In their turn, black residents of Los Angeles protested when a police SWAT team accidentally killed a Latino immigrant's child. Moreover, in the late 1990s, the head of the Los Angeles Human Rights Commission reported that at the neighborhood level, Latinos and blacks were generally finding ways to coexist and cooperate. Some black elected officials are working hard to better serve their new Latino constituents, many of whom have moved into formerly black residential areas.[139] Over recent decades, black and Latino communities in Texas have also often shown respect for one another. For example, black leaders and union members marched with Latinos in San Antonio to demonstrate against California's anti-immigrant Proposition 187, and in a late-1990s Houston election, Latino voters helped elect a black mayor against white opposition. In surveys, a majority of Houston's black and Latino leaders report that they interact frequently with leaders of other groups. In the late 2000s, black leaders and organizations in Houston worked closely with Latinos to create a strong service-workers union, the Justice for Janitors group mentioned previously.[140]

Moreover, Latino and black leaders and campaign volunteers, as well as Latino and black voters, worked together in a very sustained and effective way during the 2008 presidential campaign as they helped to elect the first U.S. president of color.

Education

In the early twentieth century, little official attention was given to the public education of Mexican Americans. Whites who controlled the economy of the Southwest pressed for low-wage labor without the expense of public education. Available public schooling was typically minimal. Before World War II, Mexican American schoolchildren from Texas to California were often racially segregated. However, as a rule, Mexican Americans were segregated by local laws or by informally gerrymandered school district lines rather than state law. Extensive white-generated discrimination in housing reinforced this omnipresent school segregation.[141]

Recurring Education Problems

After World War II, many communities began to demand changes. A major conference in 1946 called for an end to imposed segregation, the adoption of a Mexican-oriented curriculum, better teacher training, and improved school facilities. In *Méndez* v. *Westminster* (1946), a federal judge ruled that segregation of children in "Mexican schools" in California violated the Fourteenth Amendment because these children were separated on the basis of surnames. The educational theory expressed in the *Méndez* case anticipated the Supreme Court's ruling in *Brown* v. *Board of Education* almost a decade later. After *Méndez*, California laws allowing public segregation were repealed.[142]

For decades, some public schools with high percentages of Mexican American students prohibited all manifestations of Mexican American subculture. Teachers' classroom behavior, which has a strong relationship to student achievement, often downgraded the children's Latino heritage. Teachers frequently anglicized children's names (e.g., Roberto became Bobby). One 1960s study found that the average teacher praised white children more often than Mexican American children, questioned them more often, and used their ideas more often. Mexican American children were overrepresented in classes for the mentally retarded. Most in these classes were only "six-hour retarded" children—capable of functioning well in the outside world yet mislabeled largely as a result of in-school discrimination and

poor testing. Tests of Mexican American children's abilities and skills were (and often still are) usually conducted in English.[143]

Current Education Issues: Segregation and Bilingual Programs

Although certain discriminatory practices, such as disproportionate placement in classes for the "mentally retarded," had been eliminated from most schools by the 1980s, some discrimination has remained, even today. In the twenty-first century, public schools still place too many Mexican American children in classes for children with learning disabilities, school textbooks still neglect Mexican American history, and much *de facto* segregation persists. Research by the Civil Rights Project found that intense segregation for Latino students is greater today than at the beginning of the civil rights revolution more than 40 years ago. In 1968, some 23 percent of Latino students attended intensely segregated schools (minority enrollment of 90 percent or more); recent data indicate that about 40 percent of Latino (and black) students attend such highly segregated schools. In addition, year after year these Civil Rights Project studies report most segregated schools have high concentrations of children from low-income families.[144] The costs of such schools are high for communities of color, and for society as a whole. Year after year, millions of children of color, as well as many low-income white children, stay "locked into 'dropout factory' high schools, where huge percentages do not graduate, have little future in the American economy, and almost none are well prepared for college."[145]

Significantly, from its colonial beginning, the United States has been a land of many languages. In the eighteenth century the Articles of Confederation were officially published *in three languages*—English, German, and French. California's first constitution (1849), published in both Spanish and English, provided that "all laws, decrees, regulations, and provisions" be printed in both languages. New Mexico's laws were published in Spanish and English when it became a U.S. territory and through the first 40 years of statehood—until, under nativist pressure, languages other than English were labeled "foreign."[146]

When placed in English-only classrooms, Spanish-speaking children with limited English proficiency frequently become discouraged, develop low self-confidence, and fail to keep pace with native-English-speaking peers. For this reason, effective bilingual programs remain important. Although the Elementary and Secondary Education Act (1968) established a way for the federal government to fund bilingual programs in schools to meet the needs of language-minority children, by 1973 no southwestern state had taken more than a few token steps. The Supreme Court decision in *Lau* v. *Nichols* (1974), which established a child's ability to understand classroom instruction as a civil right, made it illegal for school systems to ignore English-language problems of language-minority groups. For a time, federal programs provided substantial funding for school district programs to increase English proficiency of children whose primary language is not English. Yet, apart from scattered, often stellar programs in schools with sensitive principals, the overall picture is now one of decline, backtracking, and organized opposition. A majority of voters in California, Massachusetts, and Arizona have voted in recent years to eliminate bilingual education, while one state's voters (Colorado) voted against ending programs. Forced "immersion" into English, regardless of the effects on children, is the view of a non-Latino majority in many areas. Interestingly, recent research indicates that a preexisting conservative political perspective is more important in fostering anti-immigrant voting (such as against bilingual education programs) by state legislators, and probably by voters, than increases in the actual number of Spanish-speaking immigrants in an area. Thus, researchers have concluded that "ideological framing is the most consistently important factor determining legislative responses to newcomers. . . . [Latino] immigrants have become part of a larger political dynamic and positioning based on racialized fears and misperceptions about the impact of immigration."[147]

One researcher has summed up the bleak trends in regard to bilingual education in the U.S. this way:

Bilingual educators find themselves increasingly isolated and hard-pressed to resist attacks. [Limited-English-proficient] students have fewer options, as many school districts limit access to native-language instruction and others convert to English-only models altogether. The nation's 30-year experiment with bilingual education, despite its success in many schools and its benefits to many children, is branded a failure in the public mind.[148]

One stubborn myth about bilingual instruction, often propagated by nativist organizations, is that there is no research evidence that bilingual programs are effective. Yet, numerous research studies show that well-crafted and adequately funded bilingual programs are successful. Effective bilingual programs do not create or foster social enclaves. Today, indeed, Latino immigrants and their children, including those in various kinds of quality bilingual programs, are generally learning English *faster* than did European immigrants in the first decades of the twentieth century. In addition, numerous researchers have shown the general advantages for all monolingual language speakers, whatever their age, in learning one or more additional languages.[149]

Educational Achievement and Continuing Problems

In 1950, more than half of Mexican American adults had less than a sixth-grade education, and less than 8 percent were high school graduates. Yet, in the 2008 American Community Survey, more than half reported being high school graduates and 9 percent had at least a college degree. However, Mexican Americans currently have the lowest levels of high school and college education of any major U.S. group. Table 8.3 compares educational attainment of Mexican American, mainland Puerto Rican,

TABLE 8.3   Educational Attainment, 2008 (Percentages at Selected Levels by Racial–Ethnic Group)

	Mexican American	Puerto Rican American	Cuban American	European American
Less than high school	45.2%	27.1%	24.4%	9.9%
High school graduate or more	54.8	72.9	75.6	90.1
Bachelor's degree or more	9.0	15.8	25.4	30.7

Source: U.S. Bureau of the Census. "2008 American Community Survey."

Cuban American, and European American adults over 24 years of age.[150]

Mexican Americans' educational attainment is the lowest of the three Latino groups and is lower than that of European Americans. This is in part because of the relatively recent large-scale infusion of poorly educated Mexican immigrants. In addition, in the United States, economic and other pressures often generate a significant school dropout rate for immigrants or their children. Thus, the educational levels of the Mexican American population today not only show evidence of decades of limited economic and educational opportunities, often because of discrimination, but also indicate the impact of this large-scale immigration of less educated immigrants.[151] Limited education in turn contributes to the wide income gap between Mexican American and white workers. "It's a vicious circle. This wage differential makes it so everyone in the family has to work, which is one of the biggest reasons for the [school] dropout rate."[152]

The school dropout rate—some critics call it the pushout rate—for Mexican American students remains quite high but is slowly declining. The U.S. Department of Education defines a "status dropout rate" as the percent of "16- through 24-year-olds who are not enrolled in school and have not earned a high school credential." The Hispanic status dropout rate for 2000 was 27.8 percent, but was down to 21.4 in the most recent year (2007) for which data are available. (Comparable figures for whites were 6.9 percent and 5.3 percent.) Thus, the estimate for all Hispanic groups combined is about four times that of whites. Poverty and the need to earn money to help support their families are major obstacles. Nonetheless, some public school systems have increased graduation rates significantly by providing programs to address such student concerns as jobs, substance abuse, and teen parenthood.[153]

In the late 1980s, researchers Harriet Romo and Toni Falbo began tracking a group of one hundred Mexican American high school sophomores at high risk of dropping out. Within two years, 40 percent had dropped out. Many who graduated did so with the help of special programs, and their skills were often scarcely better than those of the students who dropped out. Interviews with the students revealed that their school experience had often been demeaning and demoralizing. Some expressed the feeling that someone was "always on my back." Many students felt they were better off after they left school.[154]

Nonetheless, education was *highly* valued by the students and their families. Parents often felt angry or upset if a child dropped out of school. In most families, mothers were primarily responsible for children's education. The mothers derived much of their sense of self from the successes of children and tended to blame themselves, or felt that school personnel blamed them, for children's failures. These mothers' strategies for helping their children stay in school involved giving encouragement and pointing to individual models of success. They reported experiencing frustration over the school's unwillingness or inability to provide help and sometimes encountered hostility from teachers, counselors, or administrators.[155]

Mexican American parents and children generally understand the value of education. One 2009 Pew Hispanic Center survey of Latinos, including Mexican Americans, found that 89 percent of those aged 16 to 25 thought a college degree to be important "for success in life." However, only half of these young adults indicated they would seek a college degree. The report explains the discrepancy thus: "Nearly three-quarters (74%) of all 16- to 25-year-old survey respondents who cut their education short during or right after high school say they did so because they had to support their family. Other reasons include poor English skills (cited by about half of respondents who cut short their education), a dislike of school and a feeling that they don't need more education for the careers they want."[156] Moreover, in another (Zogby) survey of all Latino adults, some 90 percent indicated that it is important for children to get a college education. Three-quarters thought the government was spending too little on education and that an equal amount of money should be spent on schoolchildren no matter how affluent their school districts were. Field research has also shown that poor immigrant families are very interested in education for children, although, unlike middle-class parents, they frequently have little knowledge about how to become more involved in their children's schooling. This latter research also shows that public school administrators typically make little effort to help or involve immigrant parents with their children's education in a meaningful way.[157]

In a critique of typical explanations offered for poor school performance by students of color, researcher Catherine Walsh argues that mainly attributing school problems to individual or cultural inadequacies is blaming the victim. Blaming incompatibilities between Latino students and the usually white-dominated educational system on the victims is to overlook the historical and ongoing sociological significance of these differences. That all culturally different students do not perform equally poorly in school points to the relevance of additional factors. To locate the root of school problems, one must mainly look to the character of the largely Eurocentric school system, not to the student. The mainstream curriculum is typically built on European American culture and the centrality of English, and usually equates success with adoption of that dominant culture and language. Mexican American history, culture, language, and life experiences are typically ignored. The dominant group also generally controls the structure of public schools and often views Latino cultures as negative environments from which students need to escape. Walsh thus suggests that poor school performance is often a response to alienating and oppressive conditions that have robbed students of identity, dignity, and voice.

Other research has shown that Mexican American and other Latino high school students are far more likely than white students to attend very large public high schools, to be in classrooms with a high student–teacher ratio, and to be in schools with large numbers of students from low-income families. These very large public schools tend to have much less in the way of teaching and learning resources than those attended by whites in suburban areas.[158]

Thus, including the Spanish language and Mexican American culture in the classroom, involving the students' parents in the learning process, and increasing meaningful interaction between students and teachers are likely to improve education for these students. From the Walsh perspective, the severe imbalance of power and authority in school systems must also be corrected in order for Mexican American and other Latino students to be accorded full respect and to increase the possibility of establishing a positive identity in schools.

Once in college settings, moreover, Mexican Americans and other Latinos still face much subtle and blatant discrimination and threats to self-esteem and positive identity. Research involving interviews with middle-class Mexican Americans reveals this subtle and blatant discrimination in education and other institutional settings. For example, note this account from a recent interview study by José Cobas and Joe Feagin, given by a professional woman who reports that a white professor

> in college refused to believe that I had written an essay . . . because she assumed that Mexicans don't write very well and so therefore I couldn't have written this paper. . . . And so she asked that I write it over again. . . . I rewrote the assignment and she still didn't believe that it was my own. . . . She still refused to believe that it was my handwriting or my writing because she still felt that Mexicans could not express themselves well in English.[159]

Here, a well-educated white instructor, apparently with a head filled with Mexican stereotypes, used her power to discriminate twice against a talented Mexican American college student. Such occurrences are often reported by Latino and black students in colleges across the country, and can have a negative effect on self-esteem and thus on learning for success in society.

Religion

Historically, most Mexican Americans have been Roman Catholics, yet many formal doctrines of the Catholic Church are not now major factors in their lives. "Popular Catholicism," a blend of formal Catholicism and popular beliefs and rituals, has played a more important role. Indeed, a current concern among Latino theologians and their allies is that the Catholic Church does not take seriously these popular religious practices and does not "endorse their inclusion into the official and often traditional teachings of the Church." A key feature of the popular religion has been an emphasis on miracles and on the family aspects of Christianity, including an accent on the Virgin Mary and Our Lady of Guadalupe.[160]

Before 1940, the U.S. Catholic Church provided little sustenance to a Mexican American population troubled by poverty and discrimination. However, by the 1950s, some non-Mexican priests began to take an active role in community protests and union activities to benefit Mexican Americans. In the 1960s, War on Poverty programs were operated in connection with church projects, and a number of groups were formed to protest poverty. Initially, high-level Catholic officials prohibited priests from participating, although later on a few high Catholic officials supported Mexican American protests and unionization. In addition, relatively few Mexican Americans achieved positions of responsibility in the Church before the 1970s. The first Mexican American bishop was designated, in San Antonio, only in 1970. Today, only about 10 percent of the 281 active U.S. bishops are Latino, even though Latinos currently make up about 39 percent of U.S. Catholics.[161]

In recent decades, the Catholic Church's influence on secular views appears to be waning in Mexican American communities; rejection of the Church position on abortion and birth control has been widespread. Other changes are also evident. Many dioceses now require priests to study Spanish, and there is a growing Mexican American and other Latino lay leadership. Celebrations of the feast day of Our Lady of Guadalupe are popular. In response to rapidly growing numbers of Spanish-speaking parishioners, many older Catholic parishes in major cities have reoriented some services to needs of Mexican American and other Latino members. Numerous new churches have been established where Mexican immigration has been substantial. In cities such as Chicago, with its substantial Latino population, many Latinos (Mexican American, Puerto Rican, and other groups) have moved from central city areas to inner suburbs, a process that has resulted in a significant expansion of Catholic services, and construction of buildings, in these suburban areas.[162]

Recent surveys of Mexican American urban populations generally demonstrate a significant decline in identification with the Catholic Church. Whereas 81 percent of first-generation Mexican American respondents in San Antonio and Los Angeles identified themselves as Catholic, only 57 percent of the fourth-generation Mexican American respondents did likewise.[163]

One recent large-scale study of Mexican Americans and other Latinos by the Pew Hispanic Center found that a majority now identify as charismatic Catholics or Protestants, often evangelical Protestants. (Two-thirds reported going to churches with Latino clergy and services held in Spanish.) Many respondents indicated they were dissatisfied with the boring character of typical Catholic services. Indeed, many Mexican Americans and other Latinos have converted to Protestant denominations that increasingly welcome Mexican Americans and make them feel like "part of a family." Some scholars argue that Protestant evangelical churches often help Mexican Americans to move away from a hierarchical Catholic Church and way of thinking to a religious perspective that better fits in with the competitive individualism of U.S. society. Yet, there may be a reciprocal influence on U.S. society as well. The Pew Hispanic Center report suggests the "roles Latinos play in U.S. politics and public affairs are deeply influenced by the distinctive characteristics of their religious faith. Most Latinos see religion as a moral compass to guide their own political thinking, and they expect the same of their political leaders. In addition, across all major religious traditions, most Latinos view the pulpit as an appropriate place to address social and political issues."[164]

Assimilation or Internal Colonialism?

An assimilation perspective is implicit or explicit in much research on Mexican Americans. Numerous assimilation-oriented analyses argue optimistically that Mexican Americans are moving up the mobility ladder like earlier European ethnic groups, and are proceeding slowly but surely into the U.S. mainstream at all assimilation levels described by Milton Gordon. Reviewing the situation of Mexican Americans and other Latinos today, one article in *The Economist* concluded that "most of the evidence suggests that the latest immigrants are bedding in at least as quickly as their predecessors" and cites Latino rates of home ownership, intermarriage, and gaining citizenship as evidence.[165]

An assimilation theorist might emphasize that most Mexicans have arrived in the United States as voluntary immigrants and have generally been able to improve their economic circumstances relative to people in Mexico. Aspects of traditional culture have begun to disappear as acculturation has proceeded. Cultural assimilation for the first generation, the immigrants, primarily involves adjustment to English and conventional U.S. norms in public settings. Religious and other home-country values are less affected. Later generations, however, have experienced increased cultural adaptation as well as significant structural assimilation into the U.S. economy. Urbanization and increased incomes have

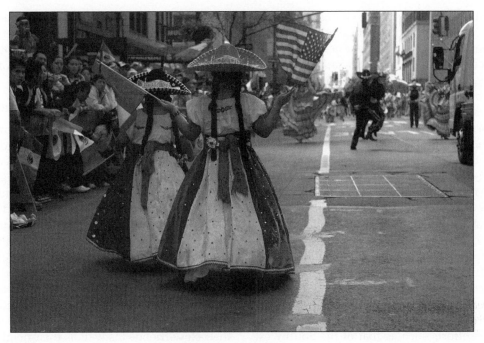

Mexican Americans celebrate Mexican Independence Day.

made possible separate residences for nuclear families, and the number of traditional large and extended families in urban areas has declined. Seen from this conventional assimilation perspective, Mexican American fertility and family values, as well as sociopolitical views, are now often similar to those professed by a majority of whites.[166]

A substantial degree of Mexican cultural heritage persists, however. Most Mexican Americans and other Latinos see no problem in adopting many aspects of the dominant culture, yet seek to preserve key elements of their own cultural background as well. Spanish remains part of a pattern of **bilingualism**, *the ability to speak two languages,* for many families into at least the second generation. Surveys have found that most Mexican Americans wish their children to retain some ties to Mexican culture, particularly to language, customs, and religion.[167] Still, most immigrant parents and their children recognize the clear social and economic advantages of learning English. Research reports indicate that *97 percent* of Latinos surveyed think that the ability to speak English is essential to success, and 84 percent think that government programs to teach English to immigrants should be expanded. Recent research also indicates that most Mexican Americans use English every day after they

have lived in the U.S. for a decade or so, and that by the third generation, English is the dominant or only language used by most Mexican Americans (and most in other Latino groups). By the fourth generation, Spanish is *not* spoken by 95 percent of Mexican Americans to their children.[168]

Research by the National Association of Latino Elected and Appointed Officials (NALEO) examined many organizations providing English-language training in sixteen states. More than half had waiting lists, some involving years of waiting. Numerous programs had a "decreased quality of instruction, from overwhelmed teachers, inadequate facilities and materials, to the inability to publicize services."[169]

Widespread use of English among immigrants and their children underscores how wrong-headed xenophobic calls for English-only laws and school policies are. In general, Mexican American and other Latino immigrants are learning English *somewhat faster* than their European immigrant predecessors. A review of the literature on several generations of Mexican Americans concluded that the fears of nativistic commentators about the unassimilability of Mexican immigrants is much too pessimistic: "Based on information about what happens to individual immigrants after entry and about what happens to their children, we find in the data examined here that many are undergoing changes that knit them more closely into the political and economic fabric of the country."[170] They make active efforts to become acculturated and move toward citizenship. Even undocumented immigrants often try to secure legal permanent-resident status and press hard for education for their children. Yet, half the Latino foreign-born population is undocumented; their ability to move up the socioeconomic ladder is limited unless they can convert to legal status, which is difficult to secure under U.S. law. Given that reality, Mexican American mobility will unlikely be the same as for earlier white ethnic immigrants.

Structural assimilation, especially upward mobility, at the economic level has come slowly even for many in the second and third generations. Discrimination and the concentration of many workers at lower wage levels persist. Mexican Americans' limited participation in political institutions has also been problematical, although recent progress can be seen. Registration efforts such as that of the Southwest Voter Registration Project and the success of court cases stipulating the use of more democratic single-member districts have increased Mexican American voter strength and representation in some areas.

Behavior-receptional assimilation and attitude-receptional assimilation, to use Milton Gordon's old terms, have varied considerably within the Mexican American group and over time. Widespread prejudice and discrimination faced the Mexicans who were conquered during the nineteenth-century U.S. expansion, as well as later immigrants. Over time, however, many Mexican Americans, especially those who were lighter-skinned and living in larger cities, often faced somewhat less prejudice and discrimination. In contrast, darker-skinned Mexican Americans, like African Americans, have often been treated in discriminatory ways by whites. Today, considerable prejudice and discrimination are still directed against Mexican Americans in many parts of the United States. Many whites still view Mexican Americans as an "inferior race" based primarily on certain physical features seen as typical of the group. And most still assert that Mexican Americans are definitely not white.[171] Moreover, as we showed previously, numerous research studies, such as those involving employment, have revealed continuing and substantial discrimination for Mexican Americans today. In our own field research involving

substantial interviews with middle-class Mexican Americans, we have also received numerous reports of racial discrimination in employment and other institutional areas still facing Mexican Americans.[172]

The Limits and Pacing of Assimilation

Neither structural assimilation at the primary-group level nor marital assimilation, to use Gordon's terms, for Mexican Americans has over recent decades reached the high level of white ethnic groups, but from a traditional assimilation viewpoint change in these and other areas seems to be proceeding rapidly.

Studies in the 1970s reported some increases in intergroup friendship contacts, particularly for Mexican American children in desegregated environments, although most still had predominantly Mexican American friends. Later on, in a 1990s survey, the vast majority of Latinos in predominantly Mexican American areas of the country reported that their close friends (as well as their neighborhoods) were Latino. The majority of marriages today are still within the Mexican American group. In the early 1900s, fewer than 10 percent of Spanish-surname individuals married outside the group. By the mid-1990s about 10 percent of first-generation Latinos were intermarried, compared with second- and third-generation percentages being at least double that percentage.[173] The current rate of out-marriage is growing and is higher for younger generations. One recent large-scale study of Mexican Americans in Los Angeles and San Antonio found that 9 percent of the first generation had out-married, but that percentage increased gradually to 29 percent for the fourth generation—a figure below that for white ethnic groups such as Italian Americans. Some recent studies have estimated intermarriage rates for Latinos as a group at even higher levels. Note too that most out-marriages are with whites.[174]

Significant numbers of Mexican Americans demonstrate movement toward what Gordon terms "identificational assimilation." Today, the diversity of self-identification labels used by persons with ancestral ties to Mexico—designations such as *Latino, Hispanic, Chicano,* and *Mexican American*—indicates a diversity of opinion about such naming and/or identity within an ever more multicultural and multiracial United States. One study of second-generation Mexican Americans found that those who were

Mexican born preferred the term *Mexican;* the U.S. born preferred *Mexican American, Latino,* or *Hispanic.*[175] In one 2000s survey, moreover, some 69 percent of Hispanic adult respondents reported that they were more Hispanic than American, 26 percent said they were equally Hispanic and American, and 5 percent said they were more American than Hispanic. Interestingly, when asked what of Hispanic culture and tradition was most important to preserve, 56 percent stressed strong family values. The importance of the Spanish language was stressed by 54 percent, and respect for parents and elders was emphasized by 47 percent. Two of these three top preservation concerns fit well with traditional family values emphasized in the dominant Anglo culture.[176]

Racial–ethnic identification varies with class, age, and experience, and with whether it is self-defined or imposed from the outside. For example, research in the 1990s at the University of California found that numerous Mexican American undergraduates had been sheltered by parents who encouraged them to view themselves as more or less "white" and to assimilate fully to Anglo-American ways. As a result, these students often experienced shock upon arrival at a campus where they were considered by many others to be "Mexican American" and/or as part of a distinctive racial group. Then, as now, historically white campus experiences often bring certain Latino (and black) college students out of rather sheltered families (as well as other families not so sheltered) and into a highly racialized society in which whites still mostly determine how racial or ethnic identities are imposed.[177]

Structural incorporation in numerous economic and social areas has its limits as well. Ease of movement and incorporation into white-controlled institutions often varies with perceived class and skin color. Middle-class professionals often face fewer overt racial barriers from whites than do members of the working class, although they face much subtle and covert racial discrimination. Several social science researchers have argued that Anglo whites today often allow lighter-skinned, middle-class Mexican Americans to fit in to some degree in historically white institutions.[178]

Today, as long as there are major immigration streams from Mexico into Mexican American communities, traditional assimilation processes will probably be slowed on some important dimensions. The movement of significant numbers of immigrants into established communities perpetuates certain aspects of traditional Mexican culture, supports much in-group marriage, and encourages respect for, and maintenance of, the Spanish language. Immigrants mean new customers and workers for Mexican American businesses. Immigrants from Mexico, as well as from Central and South America, have furnished the means and the reason for the growth of various enterprises, such as authentic Mexican-cuisine restaurants, healing centers, and Spanish-language media.

Many Mexican Americans and other Latinos are interested in developing or viewing their own mass media, including magazines, radio, and television. So far, Latinos are the country's fastest-growing television audience in the twenty-first century, and much of this audience is watching Spanish-language networks—Univision Television Network and Telemundo Network Group—both of which have been acquired by Anglo-controlled firms. In numerous cities, television stations affiliated with these networks have more viewers than major English-language stations. One recent analysis noted that among young adults in the cities of New York, Los Angeles, and Chicago, the leading nightly news watched was from Univision, and not from CBS, NBC, ABC, FOX, or CNN. These Spanish-language networks show programs from numerous Latin American countries and provide much more coverage of Latin America and U.S. Latinos than English-language stations.[179]

Is the white-oriented core culture itself responding to this growing Latino population? Some of the larger society's adaptations to the growing Latino population are modest, such as the use of Mexican food outlets and listening to Latino music. Other societal adaptations, such as bilingual education and Spanish-language ballots and Internal Revenue Service forms, represent a recognition of the reality of a different culture. In the twenty-first century, the mainstream media are also paying much more attention to Latino consumers, by selective advertising to Latinos and by featuring more Latino actors in movies and on television. Recognition of the changing character of the consumer market has prompted major corporations to recruit bilingual employees. Some observers have even spoken, usually in exaggerated ways, of these modest changes as the "Hispanicizing of America."[180]

Applying a Power-Conflict Perspective

Power-conflict analysts focus on the extent to which many Mexican Americans have *not* moved toward speedy incorporation into the dominant society and its institutions because of external discrimination and other persisting racial barriers. For example, significant economic assimilation and political incorporation into the higher socioeconomic levels of this society are not yet part of the societal reality for most Mexican Americans.

Internal colonialism analysts note that Mexican American history began with whites' ruthless conquest of northern Mexico between 1836 and 1853. This conquest created a colonial situation for early Mexicans, whose land and labor were brought into the United States by force. Parallels can be seen between their experience and that of externally colonized populations: Land is taken by military force, the indigenous population is subjugated, the indigenous culture is suppressed, and the colonizing power favors a small local elite to help maintain its economic and political domination.[181]

One problem in applying a traditional colonialism perspective to Mexican Americans is that over the last century most Mexicans have entered the U.S. as voluntary immigrants. Thus, internal colonialism analysts have focused on important differences between these Mexican immigrants and their European-immigrant predecessors. Mexican migrants have not come into a totally new environment; people of their background have long been in what is now the southwestern United States. Socially and culturally, they have to some extent moved within one geographical area, all of which was once Mexico. Relatively little time is usually required to move back and forth across the border (though this is becoming more difficult because of border patrolling and security barriers)—in sharp contrast with the travel time historically required of most earlier European immigrants.[182]

The most significant difference between the Mexican and earlier European immigrant experience lies in the intensive discrimination and great cultural subordination that later Mexican immigrants encountered. "The colonial pattern of Euro-American domination over the Mexican people was set by 1848 and carried over to those Mexicans who came later to the Southwest."[183] From the beginning to the present, the Mexican American experience has been different from that of European immigrant groups, whose level of residential and school segregation has generally declined sharply with length of residence in the United States. Mexican Americans have been racially subordinated and intentionally segregated to a far greater extent, and over a longer period, than European immigrant groups.

Mexican immigrants, for many decades now, have entered a societal environment in which their progress and mobility have generally been limited by low wages, inferior schools, and various types of discrimination. Intense societal pressure has historically been used to acculturate Mexican American schoolchildren and adults to the Anglo-American core culture. Some scholars have suggested that the rejection of public education by some Mexican American youth is a reaction to their enforced and colonized status.[184] Racial stereotyping, especially of darker-skinned Mexican Americans, has helped preserve the U.S. racial hierarchy and its supportive white racial framing. Land theft and exploitation of Mexican American labor have long been justified by theories of biological and/or cultural inferiority. Mexican immigrants have been forcefully subordinated by means of Border Patrol searches and the deportation of those immigrants (and sometimes citizens) whom authorities deemed unworthy. Residential segregation has long often reflected significant white discrimination. Indeed, much blatant, subtle, and covert discrimination against Mexican Americans persists today.

As discussed in Chapter 2, Mario Barrera analyzes the Mexican American experience using an internal colonialism model emphasizing institutionalized racism and exploitative capitalism in the shaping of past and present racial inequalities. In this view, each of the major classes of capitalism, the capitalist class and the working class, contains segments defined by racial characteristics. Each class is divided by a racial line that separates those who suffer institutionalized discrimination, such as Mexican Americans, from those Anglo whites who do not. Although Mexican American workers generally share a similar class position with ordinary white workers, in that both are struggling against employers for better working conditions, the former are also in a subordinate economic position *within* the working class because of structural discrimination along racial lines. The dimensions of this discrimination include lower wages for similar work and concentration in lower-wage occupations.[185]

Internal colonialism analysts argue that white employers have often created a split labor market from which they have received enormous profits; they have fostered distrust within the working class by focusing the attention of many white workers on Latino and other racially oppressed workers as a threat to white jobs. Given this dual-market segmentation of the labor force by employers, many white workers have periodically tried to solidify their positions and work in various ways to restrict or bar workers of color from better jobs.

Power-conflict analysts emphasize the continuing reality that the majority of whites still see Mexican Americans as not white and as usually an inferior racial group distinguishable by both physical characteristics and culture. Given this racialized reality, Mexican Americans would not be fully assimilated into the dominant institutions even if they were to abandon entirely their cultural heritage and Spanish surnames. Even most of those who are light enough to pass visually as "white" are not likely to abandon their families or give up their cultural heritage, whereas the latter heritage often enables whites to distinguish them for some continuing discrimination.[186]

Some assimilation analysts have questioned the extent of Mexican American support for certain protest movements. Sociologist Nathan Glazer, for example, has characterized the 1960s Chicano movement as having only "extreme views espoused by a minority."[187] However, in the 1960s and later, a majority of younger Mexican Americans supported much of the assertive Chicano perspective, and many in older generations were quietly supportive of Chicano movement goals to accent the Mexican heritage and end discrimination.

Indeed, since the 1960s, the perspectives and actions of political and union activists, such as those involved in recent Justice for Janitors organizing in cities, have reflected themes rooted in the Mexican historical heritage and garnered the support of many Mexican Americans. One important aspect of resistance, noted in Chapter 2, is that of counterframing against the dominant white framing of one's group. In the case of Mexican

Americans, research has shown that a strong antiracist counterframe has developed in some Mexican American civil rights movements, such as in the La Raza Unida Party and other organizations associated with the Chicano political movement in Texas and other states. Veteran activists in these groups have developed a sustained critical analysis of how a white-racist society oppresses Latinos. They have honed a perspective on how to resist anti-Latino racism. This antiracist counterframing is overtly political, as it often is in African American communities.[188]

Such contemporary antiracist framing often draws from the traditional Mexican American home-culture and its collective values. One recent research study has accented the ways in which this home-culture of Mexican Americans is used for self-support and resistance to the realities of contemporary institutionalized racism: "Emphasizing roots, values, and cultural toolkit through the rhetoric of tradition serves as both a valorization and a critique. Privileging particular traditions celebrates the practices of racial group members while simultaneously critiquing what is perceived as lacking in mainstream culture."[189] In particular, many Mexican Americans who do not have a fully developed Chicano antiracist framing of society still make use of a strong home-culture frame in a quiet type of everyday resistance. They frequently choose Mexican American cultural values and preferences over those accented by the dominant white-oriented culture. For example, these home-culture preferences shape daily choices in regard to language, food, music, and religion.

Nonetheless, there are numerous Mexican Americans, especially in the middle and upper class, who conform substantially, even aggressively, to problematical white norms and who have accepted important aspects of the white racial framing, even some negative framing of Latinos. Like some other Americans of color, many Latinos have used this whiteness strategy in trying to avoid being viewed by whites as black or near-black and in the bottom rungs of U.S. racial hierarchy. As historian Rodolfo Acuña has noted, Mexican Americans and other Latinos feel great pressure to see whiteness, and things white, as best. In the past, Mexican American organizations, such as the League of Latin American Citizens (LULAC) in its pressing lawsuits against segregation in the 1930s, argued that the U.S. census takers should classify Mexican Americans as "white." By insisting they are "white," in the past and in the present, some Mexican Americans have tried to overcome extensive discrimination by whites. Today, many Mexican American adults will comment unfavorably on the dark skin of a newborn child or play down their Indian and African backgrounds. In an effort to position their group closer to whites, they may also articulate anti-immigrant or antiblack attitudes. As Acuña notes, "the acceptance and internalization of the dominant society's racism by Mexicans and Latinos is irrational and produces a false consciousness. For instance, it is not uncommon for first-year Chicano university students to talk about reverse racism toward whites or express anti-immigrant sentiments."[190]

Indeed, many Latino immigrants come to the United States with some aspects of the white racist framing of Americans of color already in their heads, such as racially stereotyped attitudes directed against African Americans, even though they have met no (or few) African Americans. Based on interviews with Latino immigrants, one Mexican American scholar has explained that such negative views of black Americans are often created by the U.S. media: "I have traveled to Guatemala and have seen theaters showing the same violent, racist movies we show here. When I asked one migrant in Houston why some migrants have antiblack attitudes, he responded that they first learn about blacks from U.S. movies."[191] Similarly, a research study of foreign-born and U.S.-born Latinos in Houston found that the former had *more* negative attitudes toward black Americans than did the latter. New immigrants from all parts of the globe often arrive with negative views of African Americans and other Americans of color gleaned from white-controlled U.S. mass media productions, which now have a global circulation.

To make matters more complicated, some U.S.-born Mexican Americans believe that recent Mexican immigrants jeopardize the societal status of established Mexican Americans because whites still regularly link them to these new immigrants. One study of these tensions put it this way, "Realizing that members of the dominant society may not differentiate among the heterogeneous Mexican-origin community . . . [some] distance themselves spatially, socially, and culturally from immigrants."[192]

A Pan-Latino Identity

Continuing anti-Latino discrimination across the society has led many Mexican Americans and others to adopt a broader Hispanic or Latino identity in efforts to be "authentic Americans with dignity. They are beginning to embrace the new and less precise categories of Hispanic or Latino so that they can be part of a larger and more influential group."[193] Power-conflict analysts see the possibility of decreasing oppression and of an improved economic, political, and cultural situation in pan-Latino organizations and their periodic protests against discrimination.

The collective Latino/Hispanic consciousness has developed since the 1960s and unites people with such diverse national-origin identities as Mexican American, Cuban American, Puerto Rican, Salvadoran, Nicaraguan, and Dominican. Since that era, for example, many Mexican Americans and Puerto Ricans have to a significant degree transcended old identities and adopted the collective identity of Latino/Hispanic, while in some important ways still asserting their national-origin identities. The discrimination, imposed inequalities, and political opposition that Latinos have faced at the hands of whites have contributed to the formation of this new collective consciousness.[194]

On a national level, and in numerous cities where Hispanic/Latino populations contain more than one national-origin group, the Hispanic/Latino consciousness contributes to a broader sense of community and solidarity and helps subgroups achieve the collective strength to address local problems of education, bilingualism, jobs, and discrimination. A "dual identity" based on both national origin and a collective identity forged in the context of broader Hispanic/Latino concerns is clearly emerging.[195]

 What are some factors generating the significant differences in poverty and family income between European Americans and Mexican Americans?

Summary

Mexican Americans have an ancient and proud ancestry, substantially Indian with significant Spanish and African infusions. Their cultural background is partly Native American but heavily Spanish in language and Catholic in religion. After the European American conquest of what is now the U.S. Southwest, Mexican Americans became part of the complex U.S. mosaic of racial and ethnic groups. They have suffered racialized stereotyping similar to others with mostly non-European ancestry, and discrimination in the economy, education, and politics has been part of their lot from the beginning.

The literature on racial and ethnic relations has often compared the situations of Mexican Americans and African Americans, now the largest subordinated groups in the United States. Both face substantial racial prejudice and discrimination by whites even as we continue to move well into the twenty-first century, especially with regard to jobs, education, and housing. Today, across the country, we find both competition and cooperation between these two groups as they try to make a better place for themselves in a historically racist society.

A distinctive aspect of Mexican American communities is the constant infusion of documented and undocumented workers. This immigration often renews ties to Mexico, thereby undergirding Mexican American communities and identity. The Spanish language has a longer history in the U.S. than the languages of most white ethnic immigrants, and bilingualism is a facet of numerous Mexican American communities. A significant aspect of continuing Latino immigration is that many who come to the United States regularly return, if they are not prevented by major border barriers, to their home countries. A substantial majority of undocumented immigrants will, if not prevented, return to Mexico after a few years working in the U.S.; indeed, most Mexicans who have ever immigrated to the United States are *now* living in Mexico.[196]

Close ties to the culture of the home country Mexico—probably the closest for any U.S. immigrant group—slow certain aspects of the incorporation process by providing an external and supportive foundation for the home culture and social networks. Today, the dominant Eurocentric culture of the United States is under increasing pressure to change significantly as ever larger numbers of non-Europeans insist on the importance and validity of their own cultures and experiences.

Mexican Americans have helped to generate the pan-Latino consciousness that ties them to other Latinos and contributes to a stronger sense of social solidarity. A "dual identity" based on national origin and on a collective identity forged in the context of broader Latino American issues has indeed emerged for many across the United States.

Key Terms

Latinos (Hispanics) 209	maquiladoras 212
undocumented immigrants 211	Chicano political movement 231
braceros 211	bilingualism 241

Puerto Rican and Cuban Americans

BIG PICTURE QUESTIONS

- *What roles have Puerto Rican and Cuban Americans played in building this country's wealth and institutions?*

- *What are the persisting barriers to social and economic mobility of Puerto Rican and Cuban Americans?*

- *How would assimilation and power-conflict theorists explain current Puerto Rican and Cuban American socioeconomic realities?*

uerto Rico and Cuba, Spanish-speaking islands in the Antilles, are points of origin for large numbers of the 46.9 million Latinos on the U.S. mainland. For more than a century, the island of Puerto Rico has been a subordinated part of the U.S. empire. All Puerto Ricans are officially U.S. citizens, yet Puerto Rico is not a state and Puerto Ricans cannot vote in federal elections. Today, the island's future is debated by groups that support independence, statehood, or a continuation of commonwealth status. Unlike the Cuban case, these on-island political debates have been less important to migration, which is greatly influenced by the pull of the mainland U.S. economy, government-encouraged migration, and ease of migration for these U.S. citizens. Island Puerto Ricans are in fact only "quasi-citizens of the United States. They can give their lives fighting for the country in U.S. forces, but they cannot vote in national elections. They have only observer status in the U.S. Congress, but they can migrate to the mainland freely."[1] In the late-2000s, about 4.2 million Puerto Ricans resided on the mainland, while the population on the island was about 4 million. Including both groups, Puerto Ricans make up about 2.6 percent of the U.S. population.[2]

The island of Cuba has "oscillated between a corrupt democracy and dictatorships of both right and left, accompanied by a humiliating dependence on a superpower."[3] This oscillation has generated large out-migrations that have increased the populations of U.S. Latino communities, particularly on the East Coast. During several periods of migration, many Cubans came as refugees fleeing the Communist government on their island. Most settled in eastern cities, particularly in Florida, and today they and their descendants number about 1.6 million. Cuba has a long history of struggle for independence, replete with heroes such as Jose Martí, a nineteenth-century leader whose maxim was "A nation . . . but no master." The struggle for independence continues to be an important theme in the contemporary politics of Cuban Americans.[4]

Cuban Americans and mainland Puerto Ricans have been important to the expansion of the U.S. Latino population and culture in an increasingly multicultural United States. (*Mainland* refers to the U.S. mainland, as distinct from the territory of Puerto Rico.) Most in both groups express a strong identification with their homelands and traditions,

and both are committed to carving out a permanent place in the United States.

Puerto Ricans

Borinquén, the original name for Puerto Rico, had an indigenous population of 50,000 in 1493 when Spanish imperialism reached the island. Spain used indigenous residents as forced labor in mines and fields. Forced labor, disease, brutal killings, and violent suppression of rebellions caused a genocidal decline in population, and enslaved Africans were imported. Later, during the nineteenth century, immigrants from numerous countries, European and Latin American, made their way to Puerto Rico. A census in 1827 found the proportions of whites and people of color in Puerto Rico were almost equal. By 1900, the island's population was comprised of thirty-four nationalities. The inhabitants of Puerto Rico today are the product of several racial and ethnic heritages.[5]

From Spanish to U.S. Rule

In 1897, Puerto Ricans pressured the Spanish into granting them autonomy. The following year, during the Spanish-American War, U.S. troops occupied the island. In the 1899 treaty ending that war, Spain gave Puerto Rico to the U.S., whose leaders made it into a naval station and profitable agricultural enclave.[6] For some time Puerto Rico had an appointed governor: "The criterion used by the President of the United States to choose the colonial governor and his cabinet was, with very few exceptions, one of compensation for political favors received. Many of these men came to Puerto Rico without knowing the language or, at times, even the location of the island."[7] Acts of the local legislature were also subject to veto by the U.S. Congress, the president, or the appointed governor. English became mandatory in schools. In 1917, the Jones Act awarded U.S. citizenship to all Puerto Ricans.[8]

In 1948, Puerto Ricans were finally permitted to elect their governor, and in 1952, the Commonwealth of Puerto Rico was created with a constitution approved by the U.S. Congress. Considerable home rule was granted, including the right to elect officials, make legal codes, and run schools. But these changes came with the permission of the U.S.

government, the colonizing power that still oversees Puerto Rico. Today, those living in Puerto Rico still have no vote in national U.S. elections and have no voting members of the U.S. Congress.

When the U.S. government took over Puerto Rico, much land was owned by small farmers who raised coffee, sugar, and other foodstuffs. Puerto Ricans owned most farms. Under U.S. control, heavy taxes and restrictions on credit forced many to sell their land to U.S. companies. Independent farmers were also driven out by U.S.-forced devaluation of the Puerto Rican peso and the closing of European markets. By 1930, absentee-owned companies controlled most sugar production and monopolized tobacco production and shipping lines. The island had moved from a locally controlled, diversified economy to one dominated by external U.S. companies. Many small farmers and their families were thus forced to seek jobs with absentee-owned companies or leave for the mainland.[9]

In the 1940s, Operation Bootstrap, a program designed by the Puerto Rican governor to stimulate economic development by attracting U.S. corporations, was implemented. Lured by low wages and exemption from taxation, 1700 factories were located there by 1975. Per-capita income increased. However, tax exemptions for new industries left the burden of financing public infrastructure on the local population, resulting in a high income tax. Operation Bootstrap's emphasis on industry and neglect of agriculture also tilted the economy farther away from its heritage of locally owned farms. Today, little of the island's economy is agricultural.

Since the 1970s, high unemployment rates have hurt island workers, encouraging migration to the mainland. Recurring recessions have brought cutbacks in industrial plants, increasing unemployment.[10] In the 1990s, the Puerto Rican government privatized communications, shipping, and other public services and undertook major infrastructure projects in an attempt to attract more outside investors. But jobs did not increase rapidly, and the government has periodically faced major debt, employee layoffs, and major financial crises, including recently in 2009. In October 2009, thousands of workers took to the streets to protest government employee cutbacks, which had brought the unemployment rate to at least 15 percent. Moreover, the U.S. Congress recently ended the tax incentive encouraging U.S. corporations to locate in Puerto

Rico. As a result, even as some new local investments have been made, many factories have been moved to cheaper labor and taxation areas around the globe, continuing the economic crisis and stimulating yet more outmigration. [11]

Migration to the Mainland

Migration Patterns

Significant immigration to the U.S. mainland began only in the 1920s; by 1940, mainland Puerto Ricans numbered almost 70,000. Over the next two decades, the number increased more than tenfold, to 887,000, largely because of Operation Bootstrap, which resulted in a net loss of local jobs and encouraged emigration. Between 1945 and 1970, one person in three left the island. Major Puerto Rican communities were established in New Jersey, Connecticut, and Chicago, although the majority of immigrants settled in New York.[12]

Puerto Rican writer Jack Agüeros has described the impact of the new immigration: "Into an ancient neighborhood came pouring four to five times more people than it had been designed to hold. Men who came running at the promise of jobs were jobless as [World War II] ended. . . . The sudden surge in numbers caused new resentments, and prejudice was intensified. Some were forced to live in cellars."[13] Puerto Rican workers brought to New Jersey farms in the 1940s were "flown up here to a strange land, in the dark of the night, and by morning some are in the farmers' fields ready to work. There is no time for any sort of adjustment."[14] Workers also came to textile sweatshops in New York; steel mills in Pennsylvania, Ohio, and Indiana; foundries in Wisconsin and Illinois; and electronics industries in Illinois.[15]

The decades since 1970 have often involved the return or circular migration discussed in Chapter 2. Under conditions of globalizing capitalism, many Puerto Ricans fleeing the island's economic crises have come to U.S. cities, which also have problems of unemployment and poverty, as well as the problem of racial discrimination. Economic recessions along with deteriorating neighborhoods and discriminatory conditions on the mainland, and combined with family ties and a desire to nurture children in island culture, have prompted some number to return to Puerto Rico. Yet, as Gina Pérez has argued, one must be careful not to overemphasize this return migration, for it involves a modest minority of Puerto Ricans, with the rest settling down well into mainland communities. In addition, the circular migration has long been encouraged by the government and involves attempts to overcome built-in structural poverty in *both* places. It is not mainly the result of idiosyncratic personal factors. Often, those who return to Puerto Rico come back to the mainland after a time because of poor economic conditions on the island. Manufacturing wages on the island have been less than on the mainland, and Puerto Rico's per-capita income has been less than that of the poorest U.S. state. In recent years, the number of well-educated Puerto Rican workers coming to the mainland has increased, in part because of an absence of appropriate jobs in Puerto Rico. One recent study of these middle-class workers found that they too face economic difficulties on the island, and some make several cycles of mainland migration and return to the island. They develop, as Elizabeth Aranda puts it, "emotional bridges that connect island and mainland social spaces," a key reality that is an aspect of contemporary transnationalism. Facing discrimination on the mainland, and isolation from extended families, they periodically go back to recharge personal energies. They are caught between two emotional and social worlds.[16]

In the late 2000s, more than half of all Puerto Ricans resided in mainland communities, where they made up about 9 percent of all Latinos. Increasingly, many have settled in areas other than New York, where about 30 percent still reside. In recent years, secondary migrations from the Northeast to other areas have increased, especially to southeastern areas such as Miami, Tampa, and Orlando, where there are more Latino residents and often less overt discrimination.[17]

 Q: What are the strengths and weaknesses of the reciprocal social and economic relationship between the United States and Puerto Rico?

Joined by Other Latinos: Diversity in the New York Area

The U.S. census data show that New York City's population is currently about 8.4 million. During the 1980s and 1990s, the city's Anglo white population decreased significantly. Today, the American Community Survey estimates the non-Hispanic white percentage to be about 35 percent, with Hispanics at 27.4 percent and non-Hispanic black Americans at 23.7 percent. Most new growth has come from Latino and Asian immigrants. In the late 2000s, Puerto Ricans accounted for a little more than one-third of the city's Latinos. Like immigrant groups before them, many have gradually moved to suburban areas near New York City. In addition, in recent decades increasing numbers of Mexicans, Dominicans, Salvadorans, and other Latin Americans have moved to the bustling metropolitan area, including Long Island.[18]

By the early 2000s, Long Island's Latino population had increased to 282,693, more than 10 percent of the total population. This Latino population includes significant percentages of Puerto Ricans, Mexican Americans, Cuban Americans, and Latinos of other Caribbean, Central, or South American origin. Since the 1980s, large numbers of people from the Caribbean and Central and South America have joined Long Island's substantial Puerto Rican community.[19]

Increasingly, those who work in Long Island's restaurants and homes and on construction sites are Salvadorans, Colombians, and Dominicans. Many of the estimated 1.6 million Salvadorans in the U.S. today are refugees from civil wars in El Salvador. (One-third of people born there now live outside it.) Long Island is one of the major areas of Salvadoran settlement, the others being Los Angeles, San Francisco, Washington, DC, and Houston. Latino diversity in areas such as Long Island has encouraged a pan-Latino (pan-Hispanic) consciousness. For example, the town of Brentwood on Long Island renamed its Puerto Rican Day Parade the Hispanic Day Parade.[20]

Prejudices and Stereotypes

Puerto Ricans have long suffered racial stereotypes similar to those targeting Mexican Americans and African Americans. The first important stereotypes were developed by Anglo military officers and colonial administrators. (*White* and *Anglo* again refer to those identified by the U.S. census as non-Hispanic whites.) In the 1890s, one U.S. officer noted that "the people seem willing to work, even at starvation wages, and they seem to be docile and grateful for anything done for them. They are emotional."[21] Other U.S. officials saw colonized Puerto Ricans as "lazy natives."

Images of lazy, submissive, emotional Puerto Ricans have persisted to the present day. Even some white U.S. professionals who have Puerto Rican clients carry such stereotypes. Consider, for example, that some white teachers hold images of Puerto Ricans as lazy or immoral. Alfredo López reported attending a college meeting in New York at which an experienced teacher from a poor school spoke about instilling middle-class values of thrift, morality, and motivation in the children. López confronted the white teacher about her image of Puerto Rican children: "It was when I asked what morality was and where it was practiced among middle-class people or what motivation was lacking in our people and how she discovered this, or finally, how the hell a person could be thrifty on eighty-four dollars a week that she began to do some thinking." Although this is a report from the 1970s, this stereotyped framing of Puerto Ricans is still shown in social science research to be common today.[22]

Criminalizing Puerto Ricans

Often referred to by the derogatory term *spic*, Puerto Ricans have been viewed by many whites—like Italian, African, and Mexican Americans before them— as a criminal lot. An Aspen Institute conference report noted that the English-language media exaggerate certain aspects of Puerto Rican and Mexican American life—poverty, gang violence, and illegal immigration. Moreover, J. Edgar Hoover, one-time director of the FBI, famously promulgated the following racist stereotype: "We cooperate with the Secret Service on presidential trips abroad. You *never* have to bother about a President being shot by Puerto Ricans or Mexicans. They don't shoot very straight. But if they come at you with a knife, beware." Moreover, one of the more influential stereotyped portrayals of young Puerto Ricans as criminal and gang oriented is still seen in the many productions of the treasured American musical, *West Side Story*. One Puerto Rican critic, Frances Negrón-Muntaner, has recently offered a detailed critique of the overt and subtle racist imagery in this musical and the 1961 movie made from it: "The unanimous regard for the film's quality, which simultaneously

shames Puerto Ricans through its racist emplotment and valorizes us by the attachment of us to an appreciated [movie] commodity, continues to seduce audiences." Regularly performed today, *West Side Story* still communicates negatively stereotyped views of Puerto Ricans as gang members.[23]

Stereotypes of Puerto Ricans as criminals influence police actions in numerous Puerto Rican communities, which are often more closely patrolled than poor or affluent white areas. In the words of one Puerto Rican rights activist, "There is this idea that young Hispanics are all drug abusers who come here to terrorize people." Yet, a recent anonymous survey found that only small percentages (ranging from 1 to 15 percent) of Latino high school students had *ever* used hard drugs such as cocaine or heroin, percentages only a little higher than for white students.[24] However, such empirical data have not yet corrected the racial bias in drug-use stereotypes often circulated by government agencies and the media.

In Chapter 8, we cited data indicating Latino characters are rare in family movies and that Latino actors are often underrepresented on television programs, especially as primary recurring characters. When Puerto Rican and other Latino actors are used, they are often lighter-skinned (such as actor Jennifer López) or more likely than whites to be portrayed as criminals. In the early 2000s, Puerto Rican actor Esaí Morales was given a major part as a police lieutenant on then-popular television program *NYPD Blue*. This marked some modest change, even though Puerto Rican actors still were mostly getting roles as law enforcement officers, drug dealers, other criminals, drug or alcohol abusers, or, in the case of women, stereotyped sex objects. Morales is also a civil rights activist and co-founder of Washington's National Hispanic Foundation for the Arts. This organization has been very critical of the stereotyped roles that are frequently offered to Latino actors.[25]

Other Negative Images

In the 1970s, *New York Magazine* ran an article including the following negative metaphorical description of Puerto Ricans: "They came in swarms like ants turning the sidewalks brown, and they settled in, multiplied, whole sections of the city fallen to their shiny black raincoats and chewing-gum speech."[26]

Such negative metaphors of flooding have often been used by anti-immigrant analysts and nativist groups. In addition, negative imaging of Puerto Ricans has been circulated by some social scientists. In *Beyond the Melting Pot,* Nathan Glazer and Daniel Moynihan argued that Puerto Rican society was "sadly defective" in its culture and family system.[27] Anthropologist Oscar Lewis accented the concept of a **culture of poverty**—*the stereotyped idea that poor people usually develop a defective and deviant subculture.* He applied the concept to the poor on the island of Puerto Rico and in the United States, arguing that the culture of the poor is "a way of life which is passed down from generation to generation along family lines."[28] To the present day, popular and scholarly views of poor communities have been significantly influenced by Lewis's culture-of-poverty generalizations. However, culture-of-poverty and similar analyses usually do not recognize clearly the role that widespread structural unemployment and underemployment play in the creation of poverty and related problems for many Americans of color.

Another recent report on the local economy in New Britain, Connecticut, revealed some stereotypes similar to the traditional culture-of-poverty notion. The report, issued by the business elite, alleged that Puerto Ricans' "poor" language skills, family values, and work ethic contributed to the city's economic problems and suggested that Puerto Ricans should be encouraged to leave. Puerto Rican residents organized the Puerto Rican Organization for Unity and Dignity to counter anti-Latino stereotyping and discrimination and to increase their political clout. In such civil rights reports, one frequently finds local whites emphasizing the accents or Spanish language spoken by Puerto Ricans and other Latinos as problematical, yet they do not do the same for those who speak English with other types of accents (such as French-accented English). Social science research has shown that currently only a few selected accents in English, such as those of native Spanish speakers, are regularly used as markers for significant negative stigmatization and discrimination.[29]

In one 2000s radio interview, Republican Jim Hansen, a member of House Armed Services Committee, expressed concern about protests by Puerto Ricans against the U.S. Navy's target practice with bombs near the main island of Puerto Rico: "I don't see where Puerto Rico should get any favorite treatment over the rest of these people. Now what have they done to get it? They sit down there on welfare and very few of them are paying taxes, got a sweetheart deal." This image of lazy Puerto Ricans on welfare is still found at high levels of government. Some whites couple their negative images of Puerto Ricans and other Latinos with very fearful views of immigrants of color. In various urban areas, whites (including some in white supremacist groups) have acted to drive out Puerto Rican and other Latino immigrants. Thus, homeowners in one mostly white New York town received letters warning of a threat to their area by Latino immigrants, who were described as "forces of evil" and "low-income trash" seeking to convert the area to a Latino outpost.[30]

Color Coding and Anglo White Prejudices

People on the island of Puerto Rico, like those in other Latin American societies, generally recognize a spectrum of racial–ethnic categories based on multiple physical and cultural characteristics, not just skin color. One family's members may represent a variety of socially distinguished skin colors. Today, Puerto Rican society is more racially integrated than U.S. mainland society. An individual's treatment in the areas of housing, political rights, government policy, and education is less likely to be as racially differentiated, at least overtly, as on the mainland. Still, dark-skinned individuals sometimes face significant discrimination, particularly in socializing and marital arrangements, and there is often an attempt to disguise a particular family's African ancestry. Several researchers have recently shown how African ancestry is systematically played down by Puerto Ricans. For example, in the 2000 census many Puerto Ricans on the island chose "white" as their racial category, as compared to 8 percent choosing "black." Nonetheless, in the Caribbean and Latin American countries, as Marta Cruz-Janzen has underscored, there is indeed much African influence: "Africa is alive in all Latinos; the African [influence] . . . clamors in the Spanish flamenco, resonates in the Mexican corrida, palpitates in Mexico's *La Bamba,* and laments in the Argentinean tango. It is alive in Diego Rivera's painting. It calls to us in today's popular salsa sounds from the Caribbean. Just as earth is mother to us all, Africa is Latinos' other mother."[31]

The prevailing racial categorization system varies significantly by country, so that in Puerto Rico, as in much of the Caribbean and Latin America, there is a "European blood" rule, under which some known European ancestry usually makes one "white." Yet, on the U.S. mainland, the dominant racial rule is that some known African ancestry usually makes one "black." On the mainland, thus, European Americans have generally viewed Puerto Ricans as "not white," frequently grouping them with African Americans or Mexican Americans. One reason for this **color coding**—*social stratification or discrimination based on skin color*—is the long colonial relationship that Puerto Ricans have had with the U.S. government.[32] Whatever their color, Puerto Ricans have also been associated in most European American minds with colonized people. Until they come to the mainland, most Puerto Ricans, especially those whose complexion is medium brown in tone, have seldom dealt with blatant racial discrimination, especially on a large scale. Recalling an experience in high school when a girl whom he had asked to dance turned him down, Piri Thomas, a Puerto Rican who grew up in New York City and became well known as the author of the autobiographical *Down These Mean Streets*, wrote about his anger at whites' denial of his Puerto Rican identity:

"Who?" someone asked.
  "That new colored boy."
  I couldn't see them, but I had that for-sure feeling that it was me they had in their mouths. . . .
  "Christ, first that Jerry bastard and now him. We're getting invaded by niggers."[33]

The use of racist epithets in connection with an imposition of the white framing of Puerto Ricans as more or less black, when the home culture sees racial and ethnic diversity as a more complex matter, has often created confusion. Statements such as "You don't look Puerto Rican" or "Are you 100 percent Puerto Rican?" commonly confront Puerto Ricans on the mainland. Research has revealed a substantial difference in the self-perception of mainland Puerto Ricans and how they think others perceive them. In one survey, most Puerto Rican respondents indicated that they felt other Americans saw them as white (58 percent) or black (42 percent). However, this is not an accurate perception, at least for non-Hispanic whites in the twenty-first century. In a recent survey of a large number of non-Hispanic white college students in the southeastern United States, only 6.9 percent said unambiguously that they considered Puerto Rican

Americans to be a white group. Most saw Puerto Ricans as definitely not white.[34]

The 1980 U.S. census was the first to ask individuals if they were "Hispanic," with a separate question asking about racial categories. Just 4 percent of Puerto Ricans in New York City stated that their "race" was black; 44 percent classified themselves as white. Just under half wrote something like "Spanish" in the space of "Other—Specify." More recently, however, one twenty-first century Pew Center survey found that only 19 percent of Puerto Rican respondents chose "white" as their racial category, while a bit over half preferred "Hispanic" or "Latino." This shifting reaction over time probably indicates the impact of pressures generated by the mainland racial structure, which contrasts greatly in its operation with the island's racial categorizing system.[35]

Self-identity choices often remain in regular conflict with imposed identities from the larger society. Recurring tensions over skin color and other racial identifiers, such as hair texture, are revealed in several recent studies of Puerto Rican students and former students in New York and Newark public high schools. In one New York study Puerto Rican students had a strong sense of who they were, but still prized their somewhat lighter skin and straighter hair, which they contrasted with that of Dominican and African American students. According to the researchers,

> Patterns of resistance and accommodation in identity development are a reflection of the larger political and social context of the United States in which light skin is valued over dark skin, native-born Americans are valued over immigrants, and assertiveness is valued over shyness. It is also the context of New York City, where Puerto Ricans have little political or economic clout but they do have forms of celebrations (for example, the Puerto Rican Parade) that the city is willing to support each year and which reinforces both Puerto Rican pride.[36]

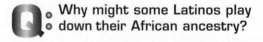 **Why might some Latinos play down their African ancestry?**

Economic and Related Conditions: The Mainland

Writing as an early immigrant, Jesús Colon explained that Puerto Ricans did hard labor for mainland society and that poverty was often their lot. He and his brother worked different hours and shared clothes: "We only had one pair of working pants between the two of us."[37] Discrimination was common for Puerto Rican immigrants; those with darker skin suffered the most. In *Down These Mean Streets,* Thomas recounted a 1945 interview for a job as a door-to-door salesperson. He was not hired; a lighter-skinned friend was. Dark-skinned Puerto Ricans, he discovered by asking other applicants, were discriminated against by white employers.[38]

Occupation and Unemployment

For decades Puerto Rican immigrants have brought with them a great diversity of skills. Some are artists and musicians; others are skilled in crafts. Some operated a business on the island; others held positions of responsibility in the educational, medical, legal, or political systems. On the mainland, however, immigrants' skills have often gone unused. Regardless of background, many have faced a limited range of jobs. They have often done the "dirty work" for European American firms, such as low-paying factory or restaurant jobs. They have cleaned up as busboys and janitors and worked in garment-industry sweatshops.[39]

Table 9.1 shows the occupational distribution for employed Puerto Ricans on the mainland in the late-2000s.[40] Although some progress has been made in recent decades, male workers are disproportionately in lower-paid blue-collar and service jobs. Once mostly less skilled blue-collar workers, Puerto Rican women are now concentrated in service, sales, and clerical jobs. Today, Puerto Rican men are significantly less likely to hold managerial or professional positions than European American men and are nearly twice as likely to be employed in service jobs. We should note too that those in the white-collar jobs tend to occupy lower-paid positions there, such as teacher or librarian, rather than doctor or lawyer.[41]

Unemployment at all points has been much higher for mainland Puerto Ricans than for European American workers. Unemployment and subemployment rates have been among the highest of any racial or ethnic group in eastern cities. In the recent American Community Survey, 6.3 percent of Puerto Ricans reported being unemployed, compared with 5.2 percent of non-Hispanic whites.[42] However, to ascertain the total percentage of job-troubled Puerto Ricans, we must add to this the large numbers who are discouraged from looking for work because of long-term unemployment, those who are working part time but desire full-time work, and those with very low wages. This would probably be a percentage double that of the unemployment rate.[43]

Employment Discrimination

Institutionalized discrimination against Puerto Ricans has long been rooted in color coding and

TABLE 9.1 Occupational Distribution (2008)				
	Men		**Women**	
	European American	**Puerto Rican American**	**European American**	**Puerto Rican American**
Managerial and professional specialties	36.1	22.8	41.7	31.2
Sales and office occupations	18.3	20.2	35.0	38.5
Production, transportation, and material moving occupations	16.8	20.5	4.7	6.7
Construction, extraction, and maintenance occupations	16.6	15.5	0.6	0.6
Service occupations	11.5	20.7	17.7	22.8
Farming, forestry, and fishing	0.7	0.4	0.2	0.2
Total	100.0%	100.1%	99.9%	100.0%

Source: U.S. Bureau of the Census. "2008 American Community Survey." (European American is non-Hispanic white.)

linguistic prejudice. This discrimination restricts access to many jobs, contributing to the disproportionate concentration of Puerto Ricans in lower-level employment and to a higher unemployment rate.

In recent decades, in places such as New York City, Puerto Ricans have been underrepresented, relative to their large population percentage, in government jobs. Thus, one study of nonprofit hospitals by the Institute for Puerto Rican Policy found relatively few Puerto Ricans and other Latinos "in policy-making positions at New York's private nonprofit hospitals . . . [and] concludes that Latinos face barriers in receiving care in these hospitals, including a lack of interpreters."[44] This absence of Latinos occurs in part because they are not well integrated into the important (white-dominated) job information networks. In addition, job tests that are often, and unnecessarily, given only in English screen out Puerto Ricans from some good jobs. This procedure is discriminatory when Puerto Rican applicants are capable of doing the jobs and screening tests are not job-related. Even trash collection jobs have sometimes required screening tests on which those who speak English score better.

Institutionalized discrimination can also be seen in height and weight requirements that use white men as the standard. Such requirements have sometimes disqualified Puerto Rican applicants, who are often smaller than Anglo white applicants, for police and fire department jobs. Even Puerto Ricans' status as U.S. citizens has been a source of discrimination. In some cases, mainland officials have asked Puerto Ricans to *prove* their U.S. citizenship. For other jobs, their citizenship status has proved to be a handicap. In a Civil Rights Commission interview, a Puerto Rican woman in California reported that employers there often prefer "Mexicans (particularly illegals) because they know that unions don't represent them, so they can be exploited easier. At least Puerto Ricans have citizenship and can get into unions."[45]

Employment opportunities are often significantly shaped by blatant or subtle discrimination. Numerous white employers classify Puerto Ricans as "black" or "nonwhite" and discriminate against them. Historically, many unions, especially those representing skilled workers, have excluded or restricted Puerto Ricans. Government officials have sometimes winked at these discriminatory practices. Recall the recent employment testing research we noted in Chapter 8. In one recent study, white job applicants with felony drug convictions were about as likely to be called back or given job offers as Latino (substantially Puerto Rican) applicants without criminal records. Research also shows that middle-class professional and managerial workers still face racial discrimination. Thus, one recent study of such Puerto Rican workers found that many go back to Puerto Rico periodically, to rest from the stress of discrimination as well as for family reasons. In spite of significant educational and other human capital, they had significant encounters with racial prejudice and discrimination in the United States.[46]

Industrial Restructuring

A variety of changing structural factors in the economy has contributed to high unemployment. Early Puerto Rican immigrants came to mainland cities to fill manufacturing jobs. By the time of the later migration of 1946 to 1964, however, the large central cities had mostly entered a period of gradual manufacturing decline. As New York City moved from an industrial to a service-oriented economy, production jobs once open to Puerto Ricans began to disappear. Between 1960 and 1980, New York City lost many manufacturing jobs, and this decline has generally continued to the present. Then, as well as in subsequent decades, the availability of low-paying service jobs has not kept pace with the decline in production jobs. Technological innovations have eroded the number of less-skilled production jobs. Many city plants have moved to the suburbs, the South, or overseas, taking jobs out of the geographical reach of city workers who do not qualify for white-collar jobs being newly created in cities.[47]

The presence of employed workers is crucial for any community's survival. Thus, in one area of Brooklyn, New York, numerous unemployed Puerto Ricans have lived in dire straights, yet have resided next to regularly employed blue-collar workers who help them and maintain the community's social institutions. A community can usually handle unemployment as long as this does not become the dominant economic reality.[48]

Income and Poverty

Mainland Puerto Ricans are relatively poor compared to other U.S. groups. As we saw in Table 8.2, in the late 2000s, median family income for mainland

Puerto Ricans ($43,944) was only 62 percent of that of Anglo whites ($70,835).[49] In areas such as New York City, where many Puerto Ricans reside and which has seen significant increases in its Latino population, their per-capita income is substantially less than half that of the Anglo population. In the late 2000s, the Census Bureau reported that 21.1 percent (and a larger proportion of children and individuals) of mainland Puerto Rican families fell below the federal poverty line, compared with just 6.1 percent of non-Hispanic white families.[50]

The desperate nature of some Puerto Ricans' economic situations is evident in their substantial use of public assistance, which is especially significant given the reluctance most have in taking such aid. "I'd rather starve than go on welfare" is an often-stated sentiment among Puerto Ricans.[51]

 What is the relationship of systemic racism to the unemployment, underemployment, and poverty facing Puerto Ricans?

Housing Problems

For decades, housing discrimination has been a significant problem for Americans of Puerto Rican descent. At one U.S. Civil Rights Commission hearing, a Rutgers University professor testified that Puerto Ricans had been excluded from most good housing markets and got only "housing scraps" no one else wanted. Today, when compared with other major groups, Puerto Ricans use a larger percentage of their income for housing and are more likely to live in rental and dilapidated housing. In the 2008 American Community Survey, just 40.2 percent of the Puerto Rican respondents lived in owner-occupied dwellings, compared to 73.4 percent of white households. As low-income renters, many Puerto Ricans are vulnerable to the effects of urban decay or gentrification. Overcrowding and deteriorating housing are characteristic of numerous neighborhoods. The South Bronx, home to a large Puerto Rican community, is a grim example. Once composed of stable communities, this area has been gutted by highway construction, redlined by bankers, and abandoned by employers. Since the 1970s, the area has lost much population. In addition to psychic stress and severed community ties, neighborhood decay has had negative effects on school

quality and increased distances to shopping and workplaces.[52]

In recent years, Puerto Rican neighborhoods in major cities such as Chicago and New York City—even including New York's famous East Harlem ("*El Barrio*")—have experienced significant gentrification because some affluent whites now seek central city housing and entrepreneurial opportunities. In the process of whites returning to the central city and generating housing gentrification, those with more money drive out those with less. Researcher Arlene Dávila shows how relatively poor East Harlem neighborhoods have faced increasing gentrification to the benefit of new white middle-class residents and businesses. One irony of such gentrification is how some officials have used the language of "Latin culture" (for example, on development signs) to get Puerto Ricans and other Latinos to acquiesce in urban development projects that result in white and other middle-class people displacing working-class Puerto Ricans and other Latinos.[53]

Over the last decade, Puerto Rican and other Latino leaders have pressed New York's attorney general for action against housing discrimination experienced by Latino workers in several New York communities. For example, numerous Puerto Rican, Dominican, and other Latino residents in Freeport have reported illegal searches and harassment by building inspectors. In other New York communities, Puerto Ricans, Dominicans, Salvadorans, and others have also reported that their homes are inspected for housing-code violations far more frequently than those of whites. They also report racial profiling and police harassment. Many local whites seem to prefer a community that segregates whites and Latinos in separate residential areas.[54]

Discrimination by local officials persists despite federal measures to stop it. Under a consent decree with the federal government, officials in Mount Kisco, in New York's Westchester County, agreed to stop using building codes and other regulations to discriminate against laborers, many from Central America. This consent decree had to be extended because of continuing complaints that a housing ordinance was being used to unfairly target Latino residents. Similarly, in 2005, a Puerto Rican legal defense organization won an injunction against the town of Brookhaven (Long Island) for evicting Latino renters, mostly laborers working there for white employers, without notice and due process.

Some workers even had to live in nearby woods as a result.[55]

Recent research using the latest tabulated national census shows that Puerto Ricans are generally quite segregated from whites, but that segregation has declined a little since 1990. In contrast, Mexican Americans are almost as segregated from whites as Puerto Ricans, but their segregation from whites has increased a little since 1990. A few studies show that certain Latino groups are *more* segregated from African Americans than they are from whites, but research also shows that Puerto Ricans and Dominican Americans are *less* segregated from African Americans than from whites. One likely reason is the substantial African ancestry of many Puerto Ricans and Dominican Americans. Dominican immigrants, yet another group under the Latino umbrella category, are more recent and somewhat more skilled and educated on average than Puerto Rican immigrants, and they have often settled in Puerto Rican communities. Grosfoguel and Georas have noted that despite their "higher-class background," whites usually place Dominican Americans in the same racially subordinate category in the "coloniality of power" (e.g., racial hierarchy) as they place Puerto Ricans.[56]

Surveys indicate that more than 80 percent of Puerto Ricans view racial discrimination to be a problem in general. More specifically, in one survey they cite discrimination against Latinos in workplaces (72 percent) and in schools (83 percent). Some 36 percent report that they or people close to them have been discriminated against in recent years. For Latinos, this proportion reporting significant discrimination increases with level of education, with 42 percent of the college educated reporting such discrimination. For Puerto Ricans, as for other Latinos, racial discrimination remains a serious problem.[57]

Education

According to recent American Community Survey estimates (see Table 8.3, Chapter 8), nearly 73 percent of Puerto Ricans more than 24 years old had completed high school, compared with about 90 percent of European Americans. Some 15.8 percent had completed college, about half the figure for whites.[58]

High school dropout rates, which are often pushout rates, today remain a nationwide problem for Puerto Rican and other Latino students. In many areas, nearly half of all Latino high school students do not graduate. These rates tend to be highest in central-city school districts, such as those of Chicago and New York City. Despite its high position among the states in per-pupil expenditures, New York City ranks near the bottom in dropout rates and student retention. The overall graduation figure for New York City schools has been near 50 percent. Some have characterized the poor educational opportunities of Puerto Rican youth as "premarket discrimination"—that is, discrimination that inhibits future success in the labor market.[59]

The low college graduation rate for mainland Puerto Ricans restricts socioeconomic mobility, with long-terms costs for individuals (and society) in terms of much lower lifetime earning power, poorer health, and sometimes more inclination to criminal activity. In addition, as with African and Mexican Americans, historically white college settings are often alien or difficult environments for Puerto Rican students. Morales-Nadal has noted the determination and struggles of Puerto Rican women to get educations in order to secure good jobs: "It is not uncommon for some mothers to take their children with them to class in some public colleges." Within the context of higher education, curricula and intergroup exchanges that respect the culture and identity of Puerto Ricans seem vital to the economic empowerment of more Puerto Rican youth.[60]

Recent research shows clearly that the main reasons for major Puerto Rican and other Latino educational problems do not lie in the conventional "causes" often cited by mainstream white analysts, such as language differences or Latinos placing little value on education. The main causes lie in the actions of (mostly white) decision makers at local and federal levels—for decades now—that have significantly weakened government educational and related programs that enhance socioeconomic opportunities for working-class families, especially working-class families of color. For many years, Puerto Rican parents have struggled against an underfunded and discriminatory educational system that has often failed their children. Puerto Rican community organizations have been formed to work for change, such as truancy prevention programs. When school boards have ignored the findings of their critical school evaluation reports, Puerto Rican leaders and community organizations have sometimes had to turn to the courts. Yet, deficient urban school systems have proved highly resistant to court-mandated change; white school administrators' attention to the needs of culturally different students has too often been resistive or half-hearted.[61]

Barriers to Social and Economic Mobility

Relatively few Puerto Rican Americans have moved into influential positions in education, and Puerto Rican communities usually have little control over educational decisions affecting their children. White authorities frequently are insensitive to Puerto Rican history and concerns; the standard curriculum is often based on the assumption that Puerto Ricans are culturally or linguistically deficient. Neglect of Puerto Rican history and culture undoubtedly contributes to a lack of self-esteem among students. The public schools attended by most students are *de facto* segregated, with a high concentration of students of color. One major study of northeastern public schools found that over three-quarters of Latino (many of them Puerto Rican) children were in schools in which over half the students were students of color. More than four in ten were in schools that were 90 to 100 percent children of color. In addition, the number of Puerto Rican teachers and administrators, especially compared to the number of Puerto Rican students, remains low.[62] As in the cases of African American and Mexican American students, racially segregated schooling often has negative impacts: low retention rates, many students who are reading below grade level, high student–teacher ratios, less qualified teachers, and low teacher expectations. In particular, researchers have found a strong relationship between teachers' low expectations and students' low academic achievement. Students, in any group, whose teachers respect them and expect them to achieve are more likely to succeed in life.

Language

Few schools today are structured appropriately to deal with non–English-speaking students. Prior to the American Revolution, bilingual education (in German, for example) was commonplace and continued to be available to many European immigrants and their children in private and public schools in the eighteenth, nineteenth, and early twentieth centuries. Only in recent decades has such bilingual education become "un-American."

In the current atmosphere of hostility to bilingual education, limited English proficiency creates barriers for Puerto Rican and other Latino students. Without well-crafted bilingual programs, children who are unable to understand English instruction fall behind native–English-speaking classmates. Puerto Rican students are often inaccurately assigned to low-ability groups, "language-disabled" classes, or lower grades. On average, Puerto Rican students do less well than white students on conventional achievement (skills) tests, most of which are given in English. One psychologist has underscored the inaccuracy of certain test scores: "In my clinic, the average underestimation of IQ for a Puerto Rican kid is 20 points. . . . When we test in Spanish, there is a 20 point leap immediately—20 higher than when he's tested in English."[63]

Puerto Rican educator Hermán La Fontaine once noted that a viable "definition of cultural pluralism must include the concept that our language and our culture will be given equal status to that of the majority population."[64] Many Puerto Rican educators have argued that children should be taught to read well in Spanish first, taught subjects in that language, and then taught English as a second language. Civil rights and community groups have pressed for substantial and well-designed bilingual programs for Latino children. In struggles against the current New York City and Chicago school systems, Puerto Rican parents and organizations have regularly sought comprehensive educational programs that recognize the significance of Puerto Rican history and culture and of the Spanish language. Interestingly, some researchers report that students in effective bilingual programs have higher attendance and completion rates and that those programs contribute to more positive self-concepts for students. Nonetheless, as we noted in Chapter 8, well-crafted, well-funded bilingual programs, which have been proven to work well for new English learners, have not become part of the public school curriculum for most Latino children. Numerous English-only groups have worked to end many of the effective bilingual programs.[65]

Official English Policies and Spanish Speakers

Support for English as the official U.S. language has grown dramatically in recent years. Much of this movement is nativist; Anglo-white leaders have mainly targeted Spanish and Spanish speakers, from Florida to California. An amendment to the Arizona Constitution went so far as to make English the language "of all government functions and actions," but a federal judge ruled that it violated the U.S. Constitution. In 2006 and 2007, attempts were made by some U.S. senators to add to an immigration bill a statement that English is the country's "common and unifying language," but the bills did not pass. Moreover, in 2007, voters in Nashville voted down a nativistic referendum proposal to make their city the largest one where government agencies were required to use only English.[66]

Xenophobic Americans often praise English-only government policies as a means to unify diverse groups and promote "traditional" (that is, European American) cultural values. Educator Catherine Walsh reports that, instead, "such efforts toward linguistic cohesion resonate with a kind of colonial domination, a hegemony that threatens to silence the less powerful . . . [and attempts] to render invisible the complex, abstract, socio-ideological nature of language."[67] Far more than just neutral symbols, language reflects and imbeds a group's history and culture and thus is inseparable from group and personal identity. Walsh has documented the struggle faced by language-minority students over whose language and therefore whose knowledge, perspectives, and experiences are recognized and whose are omitted. One young bilingual student put it this way: "Sometimes I two-times think. I think like in my family and in my house. And then I think like in school and other places. Then I talk. They aren't the same, you know." Realizing that the language context of home was not only different but less acceptable than that of the school, this child often told her teacher, "It makes me feel funny, all alone . . . different."[68]

Politics

Among mainland Puerto Ricans, voting rates have often been relatively low. As is the case with other subordinated racial communities, the weak electoral support of Puerto Rican candidates by white voters, the lack of campaign funds, the lack of representation in political party leadership, and a common feeling of hopelessness regarding change contribute to this relatively low political participation. In one older survey of mainland Puerto Ricans who were not registered to vote, the most frequently cited reasons were "not interested in politics" and "voting makes no difference."[69] However, voter registration and turnout have generally increased for mainland Puerto Ricans since 1990, especially in areas where governments are responsive to community needs. In several recent elections Puerto Rican voters have played an important role in deciding the results. Gradually, researchers have begun to examine the political views of Puerto Ricans. For example, in one 2000s national survey, half the Puerto Rican respondents indicated that they would be willing to pay higher taxes if government provided more services, a figure significantly higher than that for whites in similar surveys. Some 38 percent felt that one could trust government officials most or all the time, while 49 percent felt that one could trust them only some of the time. This trust response was similar to that of the white respondents.[70]

Election to major political offices has come slowly. Since the 1930s, Puerto Ricans have participated in Democratic Party politics in New York and New Jersey, but until recent years that participation has usually been very limited. The first Puerto Rican American was elected to the New York state assembly in 1937, but it would be 15 years before another was elected. In 1965, Hermán Badillo became the first Puerto Rican elected president of a New York City borough; six years later he became the first voting member of Puerto Rican background in the U.S. House. His seat was later filled by José Serrano. However, by the late 2000s, there were still just three Puerto Ricans in the U.S. House (two from New York City and one from Chicago), and none in the U.S. Senate. Interestingly, in 2009, Sonya Sotomayor, an appellate judge, became the first Puerto Rican and first Latina, as well as only the third woman, appointed to the U.S. Supreme Court. The U.S.-born daughter of a Puerto Rican immigrant, she grew up in the poverty-stricken South Bronx. Her nomination generated much conservative opposition, especially when her past comments at professional meetings were found to indicate she might draw on her experience as a woman of color in understanding court cases coming before her. Indeed, some of the media commentary even described Judge Sotomayor as presiding over a "hot judicial bench"—that is, as having a too-emotional and "ethnic" approach to the law. Such imagery is

CHAPTER 9   Puerto Rican and Cuban Americans   **261**

common today, as in the past, for Latinas. Numerous Hollywood and television movies have stereotyped Latinas (including actresses) as hot-headed or hot-blooded "spitfires."[71]

Local and State Governments

In recent decades, Puerto Ricans have served on numerous city councils and as mayors of small towns and a few cities. Miami had a Puerto Rican mayor from 1973 until 1985. They have also served as mayors of Hartford, Connecticut, and Camden, New Jersey. By the mid-2000s, more than 140 Puerto Ricans had been elected to municipal and state government positions—including nearly two dozen in New York state, where they were serving as Bronx Borough President, on the city council, and as state senators and assembly members. Over the last few decades, Puerto Ricans have won nearly two dozen elected positions in New York City. Moreover, in 1989, the National Hispanic Caucus of State Legislators was founded. As of the late 2000s, its members included several hundred Hispanic state legislators (including numerous Puerto Rican legislators) in the U.S., Puerto Rico, and the Virgin Islands. The organization's first legislative summit was in 2001, and in meetings since then its goals have included improving socioeconomic conditions and government services for Latinos across the United States and its territories.[72]

The long-term effects of institutional discrimination can be seen in state and city government employment, in which Puerto Ricans are still significantly underrepresented. Partly as a result of this modest representation, many Puerto Ricans report poor treatment by government and private agencies. Most government officials who serve them cannot speak Spanish. Government services have historically been less accessible to Puerto Ricans, and job training and employment services have often been slow in coming to Puerto Rican communities.[73]

In the 1980s, the governor of Puerto Rico announced a campaign to register mainland Puerto Rican voters and thus expand their political power. Local leaders welcomed this intervention, which demonstrated the close alliances between mainland and island communities. The project registered many new voters in areas such as New York City, and Puerto Rican voter turnout increased, resulting in more Puerto Ricans in government. In the 2000s, the Puerto Rico Federal Affairs Administration, an organization working for the Commonwealth of Puerto Rico in the United States, has continued to work aggressively to register many Puerto Rican and other Latino voters.[74]

Politics and Recent Intergroup Conflict

In Chapter 8, we noted the success of political coalitions between black and Latino communities in some cities. We can add to that discussion here. Latino voters have helped elect black mayors in Chicago (Harold Washington), Denver (Federico Peña), and Dallas (Ron Kirk). In New York City, where Latino and African Americans make up about half the population, there has been a long history of successful coalitions, as well as periodic tensions. Latino voters were critical to the elections of the city's first black mayor, David Dinkins, in 1989. Later, in the 2000s, a key New York black leader, Rev. Al Sharpton, went to jail with Puerto Ricans protesting the U.S. Navy's test bombing operations on a Puerto Rican island. A Puerto Rican mayoral candidate, Fernando Ferrer, was also supported that year by black officials, as was the case for Puerto Rican assembly candidates from New York City, Puerto Ricans running for elections in Boston, and a Mexican American running for mayor in Los Angeles. However, other cities have been characterized mostly by political competition. For example, consider the case of Providence, Rhode Island. The population is one-fourth Latino, half from the Dominican Republic and the rest from Puerto Rico, Mexico, and South America. African Americans make up 15 percent of the population; whites are a bare majority. In recent years, Latino political organizations have grown in strength. In 2000, two Latino candidates tried to unseat progressive black elected officials. The primary and general elections saw a large turnout of Latino voters, and one Latino successfully displaced a black official; a second came close to ousting another. Local observers suggested that the white elite had backed the Latino attempt to unseat black officials; others argued that the conflict was primarily the result of growing numbers of Latino voters. Local activists expressed much concern about the lack of a strong progressive coalition of voters of color.[75]

Sensitivity to these intergroup issues is great in the Latino and black communities. For example, the mainstream media paid little attention when, after the Census Bureau announced in 2002 that Latinos were now the largest U.S. minority group, numerous Latino writers, scholars, and activists signed an "Open Letter to African-Americans from Latinos." These Latino leaders made clear that they would "combat the competitiveness" of those who might try to stir up conflicts between Latinos and African Americans and displace the latter from their central position in the struggle for expanded civil rights.[76]

Protest

In Puerto Rico, protests against colonial status have periodically punctuated U.S. rule. Contrary to the stereotype of docility, Puerto Ricans have fought hard to retain their culture and end the island's status as the "last major U.S. colony." In the 1930s, large numbers of Puerto Ricans attacked colonial government buildings in periodic protests. On the mainland, Puerto Rican nationalists seeking independence conducted an armed attack on the residence of President Harry Truman and on members of the U.S. House while it was in session.[77]

Pro-statehood sentiment on the island has increased over the decades. In the late 1990s, the U.S. House passed a bill permitting a Puerto Rican plebiscite on the island's future, but the bill did not pass the Senate. Significantly, the bill admitted that the U.S. government had never permitted Puerto Ricans to have self-determination and recognized that commonwealth status was a temporary status on the way to statehood or "separate sovereignty." Today, island Puerto Ricans are divided between the options of commonwealth status and statehood. Supporters of statehood argue that commonwealth status is a second-class status. Opponents fear the economic changes and loss of Puerto Rican culture that statehood might bring. Rubén Berríos Martínez, president of the Puerto Rican Independence Party, has noted that "as a state, Puerto Rico is bound to pay the heaviest of prices: cultural assimilation. In the American system the only way out of an ethnic ghetto is through cultural assimilation into the Anglo-American mainstream, which would subordinate the island's Spanish language and distinct culture. . . . In any case, assimilation is unacceptable to Puerto Ricans, including statehooders."[78] One sign of this threat of forced assimilation is the view

of many mainland whites that Puerto Rico should not become a state unless it fully adopts English as its official language. In a significant show of support for independence, more than 200 delegates from nearly two dozen countries recently met in Panama as part of the Latin American and Caribbean Congress for Puerto Rico's Independence. Numerous Latin American leaders noted that Puerto Rico was the *only* Latin American country remaining under traditional colonial control.[79]

Tensions between island leaders and U.S. politicians increased significantly in the early 2000s. Numerous protest demonstrations targeted the U.S. Navy's bombing range on the small island of Vieques just off the main island of Puerto Rico. Island and mainland demonstrators regularly protested the negative impact of bombing on island inhabitants. Bronx Democratic Party chair Roberto Ramírez, assembly member José Rivera, and borough presidential candidate Adolfo Carrión Jr. were arrested in protests on the island. The Navy bombing was abandoned in 2003. Since that time, pro-independence activists have continued to struggle against U.S. domination of the island, on the island and the mainland. In recent years, the federal government has periodically sought to prosecute these Puerto Rican activists.[80]

On the Mainland

Arriving for the most part poor and/or stigmatized as inferior, Puerto Ricans have developed significant organizations to cope with discrimination and other barriers. Some major organizations are the Latino-Justice PRLDEF (formerly the Puerto Rican Legal Defense and Education Fund) and the National Puerto Rican Coalition (NPRC). Puerto Rican teachers associations have long worked to increase representation of Puerto Ricans among teachers and to expand bilingual programs. Puerto Ricans have also been active in union organizations on the mainland since the 1800s.[81]

In the spring of 1969, the Young Lords, a militant Puerto Rican youth group, occupied the administration building of Chicago's McCormick Theological Seminary to publicize urban poverty there. They opened a community day-care center and school, protested the use of urban-renewal land for a tennis club, and set up a people's park on urban-renewal land.[82]

New York City council member Margarita Lopez denounces U.S. bombing on the Puerto Rican island of Vieques.

In New York City, another Young Lords group occupied the First Spanish Methodist Church and organized a day-care center, set up breakfast and clothing programs, created a newspaper, and led a demonstration to protest squalid conditions at a hospital. The Young Lords articulated a thirteen-point program for a democratic-socialist society. Asserting their Puerto Rican identity, they called for "liberation and power in the hands of the people, not Puerto Rican exploiters." At the peak of their influence, Young Lords had chapters in twenty cities. The Young Lords, like other militant groups of color in that era, were subject to police repression, including secret infiltration by government agents. Leaders were prosecuted, sometimes in rigged trials, or co-opted into government antipoverty programs. By the 1970s, the Young Lords had disbanded. Still, many former members later became influential professionals and leaders in community organizations.[83]

In recent decades, numerous Puerto Rican organizations have worked for a better quality of life and increased participation in the political process. In cities with a significant number of Puerto Ricans, social and cultural clubs preserve elements of traditional Puerto Rican culture. Grassroots activists have created a number of organizations in New York and New Jersey, seeking to improve day-care, bilingual education, and social services. The LatinoJustice PRLDEF organization, which has expanded to include all Latinos, has since 1972 engaged in litigation in support of civil rights. They recently filed a federal lawsuit on behalf of five Puerto Rican voters, to force some Florida counties to provide ballots and election assistance in Spanish. The lawsuit was brought under a provision of the Voting Rights Act. And in December 2008, they also filed a petition with the Inter-American Commission on Human Rights of the Organization of American States, in which they argued that the U.S. government was violating international human rights agreements— including the American Declaration of the Rights and Duties of Man agreed to by many countries of the Americas in 1948—by not protecting U.S. Latinos from local violence and other racial discrimination.[84]

In addition, the organization Aspira has worked hard to improve education for Latino youth; and the National Puerto Rican Forum has focused on employment and job training. The National Puerto Rican Coalition, representing many local organizations, has served as a liaison between Puerto Rican communities and government officials and lobbied for educational, health, economic, voting rights, and other civil rights programs. Under the pressure of organizations such as these, as well as activism by Puerto Rican students and professors, several New York and New Jersey universities have developed important Puerto Rican studies and research programs. This effort has encouraged new research on Puerto Ricans and the creation of the Puerto Rican Studies Association, as well as a new generation of Puerto Rican researchers, artists, and writers. Puerto Ricans have also led in struggles to keep low-cost "open admissions" for public New York City universities.[85]

More Community Protest

Puerto Rican communities have long protested racial discrimination by local whites. The previously cited research on the gentrification of East Harlem neighborhoods also describes how local Puerto Rican organizations have fought against that discrimination by getting involved in politics, including lobbying school boards and planning boards. Puerto Rican groups there have made use of the idea of *Latinidad* (Latino cultural unity) in struggles against gentrifying development projects. Chicago community organizations have similarly protested gentrification by affluent whites moving back into the city, as well as housing discrimination and police brutality directed at Puerto Ricans and other Latinos. Substantial reports of police injustice, including unwarranted searches and use of excessive force, are common in cities with significant Latino populations. Indeed, in the 1990s, a major Miami riot involving hundreds of Puerto Ricans occurred after six police officers were acquitted in the fatal police beating of a Puerto Rican drug dealer. Residents of the impoverished neighborhood reported the violent uprisings were related directly to the powerlessness that many there felt.[86]

Problems with police have persisted. In 2001, after a National Puerto Rican Day parade in New York, a milling crowd protested and rioted when police began arguing with, and then pepper-spraying, people in the crowd. Some community residents were injured. Police authorities defended their violent actions as appropriate, but some in the community questioned what they saw as a pattern of police malpractice in the area. Recent research in Chicago has found similar community reports of police discrimination against Puerto Ricans and other Latinos on the streets, as well as poor police responses to citizen reports of crimes. In the last few years, Puerto Rican and other Latino civil rights groups have filed lawsuits against local law-enforcement personnel for arbitrarily singling out Latinos because of the way they "look" and various other types of racial profiling, some of which is aimed at finding immigration violations. One recent lawsuit involves a complaint against a Frederick County, Maryland, sheriff for arresting a Latina who was not engaged in criminal activity, but simply eating her sandwich at a work break.[87]

In some areas community protest movements have brought significant changes. For example, pressures from community activists led to the founding of a community college in the South Bronx and helped create supportive programs for Latino students at the City University of New York. City and state governments have provided more funds for community services and hired more Puerto Ricans. Public schools have added Puerto Rican studies and bilingual programs and hired more Puerto Rican teachers, and colleges have set up Puerto Rican studies programs.[88]

Coalitions of grassroots organizations and older established groups, including the National Congress for Puerto Rican Rights, have been created to improve economic conditions. Since the 1990s, leaders and members of state branches of the National Congress have pressed local governments for fairer treatment in the justice system and for better schools; they have participated in protest demonstrations against government indifference to poverty, discrimination, and police brutality. The National Congress and other Puerto Rican organizations have pressed the mass media for better reporting on Latino communities and more Puerto Rican and Latino journalists and editors.

Numerous media outlets have belatedly responded to community pressures for better coverage and representation. By the late 1990s, some Puerto Ricans, such as David González, the first Latino to write the *New York Times* column "About New York," were articulating a Latino perspective in mainstream media. Also the *Times*'s Caribbean and Central America bureau chief, González noted that he "took the column's title at face value. I wanted to make sure the groups I knew, my people, were reflected not just in terms of the usual issues—the social issues, which are important—but also the cultural issues in these neighborhoods whose residents exist in New York."[89] Integrating local media outlets not only voices historically excluded communities but also increases the knowledge available to all citizens and policymakers in an increasingly diverse society. The deepest understandings of this society's distinctive racial–ethnic communities often come from those who are native to those areas' cultures and languages.

Annual Puerto Rican Day parades, celebrating Puerto Rican culture and heritage, have been held since the 1950s in several cities, especially in New York and New Jersey. One late 1990s parade in New York City drew 200,000 people, including elected officials, and celebrated the strong sense of Puerto Rican identity and concern over discrimination. Significantly, a few days before this parade, a white businessperson urged businesses to protect their premises during the event, and a white columnist writing in a prominent magazine called Puerto Ricans "fat," "dusky," and "semi-savages." These comments, which triggered protests, reveal continuing stereotypes of Puerto Ricans in certain white business and media elites. Significantly, in recent years these annual New York parades have been quite friendly and family oriented—with as many as 80,000 participants, many thousands also participating in associated events, and a great many more watching from the sidelines.[90]

Religion

Catholicism has long been the main religion among Puerto Ricans and Cuban Americans. Yet, both groups have developed some distinctive branching religions. For example, some Puerto Ricans have adopted aspects of the syncretic Santería religion that blends traditional practices of once enslaved Africans (mainly Yoruba) with those of Catholicism. (We discuss Santería and Cuban Americans later in the chapter.)

On the mainland, Puerto Rican Catholics have generally been led by non–Puerto Rican clergy. One exception to the dependence on non–Puerto Rican clergy is the bishop of Puerto Rico, who periodically visits mainland parishes. Sociologist Joseph Fitzpatrick has argued that Puerto Rican Catholicism is more a religion of the community than of the parish. Community celebrations and processions are important, as is reverence for the Virgin Mary and certain saints. Formal church worship has often been less important than communal celebrations and home ceremonies. Still, many remain devoutly religious whether or not they attend mass regularly. On the mainland, Puerto Ricans have often shared parishes with other Latino parishioners. Research by Susan Eichenberger suggests that the pan-Latino diversity of some parishes leaves some Puerto Rican parishioners feeling alienated because of the diverse approaches to religion among the Latino groups. Increasingly, Latino caucuses have developed within the Catholic Church to press for Spanish-language services and for more priests of Latino background.[91] Gradually, the U.S. Catholic Church has moved to integrate Puerto Ricans and other Latinos into parishes and leadership positions.

As is the case for other Latinos, many Puerto Ricans have left the Catholic Church for evangelical Protestant churches, which they feel offer a warmer reception and a community feeling. Protestant evangelical groups have made significant inroads into Puerto Rican communities, and many communities now have numerous evangelical churches. Moving out of Catholicism has been seen by some Puerto Ricans as assisting social mobility in a predominantly Protestant society. Interestingly, one recent Pew Hispanic Center report on Latino religions draws these comparative conclusions: "Some differences in religious traditions are apparent among Latinos . . . based on country of origin. Mexicans, for example, are more likely to be Catholic than are Puerto Ricans, who in turn are more likely to be evangelical than are Latinos from any other country. Larger shares of Cubans than Latinos as a whole are seculars [non-religious]."[92]

Assimilation or Colonialism?

Assimilation Perspectives

In an influential 1971 book, Joseph Fitzpatrick uses an assimilation model to interpret Puerto Rican experiences. At that time he reported significant overall assimilation, including major cultural assimilation, particularly for mainland-born Puerto Ricans who identified with the dominant society and adopted the English language.[93] Other scholars, such as Catherine Walsh, have argued that this cultural adaptation is more variable and limited and generally gives a "false hope" of full sociocultural inclusion in a white-dominated society. There is a significant cost to conformity to that dominant culture. Thus, in *Up from Puerto Rico* (1958), Elena Padilla argued that second-generation Puerto Ricans generally have a different reference group than first-generation immigrants—the mainland society rather than island society—and as a result many hide their Spanish-language facility in an attempt to assimilate culturally in a Eurocentric environment.[94]

Manuel Maldonado-Denis suggests that the "American ethic is a messianic one, and all ethnic groups are required to assimilate culturally as a condition for achieving a share in the material and spiritual goods of American society."[95] Cultural assimilation pressures begin in Puerto Rico, where for decades the colonial governments pressured islanders to assimilate to a Eurocentric U.S. culture, such as by requiring English in schools. More recently, in a 1990s survey, Strategy Research Corporation ranked the cultural assimilation level of Latinos. The majority of mainland Puerto Rican heads of household were classified as partially assimilated, with only 10 percent fully assimilated. English language use was one measure they used for cultural assimilation. Many were bilingual or only Spanish speakers. Since the 1990s, however, an ever-growing percentage of mainland Puerto Ricans have come to speak mainly or only English. Indeed, recent research shows that the ability to speak any significant Spanish dies out in three generations or less for Puerto Ricans and other Latinos.[96]

Over the decades, many Puerto Ricans have resisted complete acculturation. The quest for a Puerto Rican identity in the U.S. has sometimes taken the "form of a strong assertion of the significance of Puerto Rican culture, including language, and also the definition of Puerto Rican interests around militant types of political and community action."[97] Puerto Rican studies programs in some public schools and colleges have buttressed the sense of a distinctive Puerto Rican identity. However, some Puerto Rican leaders argue that they must assimilate more thoroughly with key aspects the Eurocentric culture to secure better jobs and socioeconomic positions. They argue this can be done with a minimum of "selling out"—that is, with a strong persistence of Puerto Rican culture. Others worry about the heavy cost of thoroughgoing cultural assimilation to Puerto Rican identity; they fear that assimilation pressures will lead to rootlessness. In addition, one should distinguish those Puerto Ricans who have made a permanent home on the mainland and cut many ties with the island and those who maintain very strong ties to families and communities on the island—and often return there periodically. One recent study of middle-class Puerto Ricans who return periodically suggests that they engage in selective acculturation—that is, they "embrace U.S. patterns of living" and certain U.S. measures of success, but maintain strong cultural and family ties to the island of Puerto Rico. They are part of an increasing global migration, and caught between two sociocultural worlds. With this large group among mainland Puerto Ricans, it is unlikely that Puerto Ricans will ever fully adapt to the dominant white-oriented culture and society as did earlier European immigrants.[98]

One further barrier to full incorporation is the continuing racialization of Puerto Ricans. For example, some research shows that many white school teachers are engaged in an ongoing cultural struggle with their Puerto Rican and other Latino students. Researchers have found that favorable treatment of Latino students in school increases as their "difference" from whites, as perceived by non-Latino teachers, decreases. For earlier white immigrants, acculturation frequently led to significant denial of their ethnicity. For Americans of color, however, full cultural assimilation and loss of racial identity are generally impossible; the differences usually are too visible and important in contemporary whites' racial judgments. Rather than becoming de-racialized or de-ethnicized "Americans," Puerto Ricans typically remain distinctive and substantially subordinated.[99]

Today, overt job discrimination against Puerto Ricans appears to be declining, although substantial covert and subtle discrimination remains. Blatant, covert, and subtle forms of mistreatment continue in other areas such as housing rentals and sales. For the most part, the level of behavior-receptional assimilation, to use Gordon's term, is relatively low. Secondary-structural incorporation at the level of higher-paying white-collar jobs has been slow; Puerto Ricans are still disproportionately concentrated in blue-collar, service, and lower-wage white-collar jobs, as well as among the unemployed. The level of Puerto Rican participation in mainland political institutions also remains relatively low, although it has grown significantly in the last decade.

Structural assimilation of Puerto Ricans at the primary-group level and marital assimilation have not reached levels comparable to those of most European immigrants. Several studies have found regular and significant interaction between immigrant parents and their U.S.-born married children. Despite the wrenching experiences of migration and several decades on the mainland, the older immigrant generation remains substantially linked socially to children and grandchildren. The better jobs and educations of many in the second and later generations have not ended this family networking for most. However, out-marriage appears more significant for second and later generations and may be slowly breaking down intergenerational ties. One 1990s study of New York City marriage records showed that some 87 percent of first-generation

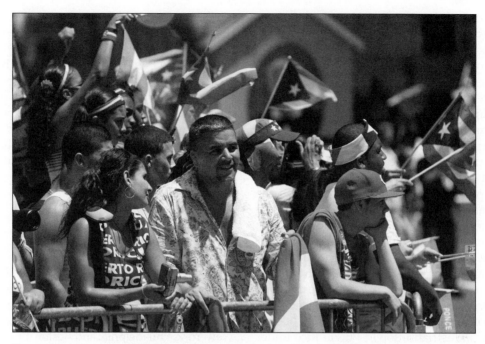

Puerto Ricans wave the flag of Puerto Rico while viewing a New York City parade.

Puerto Rican brides married within their group or married other Latinos. The percentage was still about three-quarters for second-generation brides. In addition, 2000 census data showed that, taking the country as a whole, Puerto Ricans were more likely to be married to non-Latinos (at 21 percent) than Cuban Americans and many other Latinos.[100]

As in other immigrant communities, generational conflict has sometimes been a problem. Children who grow up in the mainland U.S. culture pick up values that can conflict with certain traditional Puerto Rican values. Moreover, identificational assimilation, in Gordon's terms, has come slowly for young and old. Most, whether island-born or mainland-born, still see themselves as Puerto Rican.[101]

Power-Conflict Perspectives

Power-conflict analysts agree that Anglo-conformity pressure on Puerto Ricans has been heavy, but they also stress how colonized Puerto Rican Americans as a group remain. Their assimilation into historically white economic and political institutions has been relatively slow. This suggests that they, like many other non-European migrants, are not being progressively incorporated into U.S. society just like the European immigrants earlier in the twentieth century. This latter optimistic view has been common among mainstream assimilation theorists.

Issues of a multiracial Puerto Rican identity and history surfaced in a late-1990s debate among some Puerto Ricans about a new Puerto Rican "Barbie" doll issued by Mattel Corporation in its "Dolls of the World" series. Puerto Rican critics argued that the doll's appearance (skin and hair) was too white-European and did not reflect Puerto Ricans' strong Indian and African ancestries. Some noted that the description of the island on the doll's box neglected this ancestry, as well as the long U.S. colonial oppression of the island. Today, many scholars and other analysts are paying much more attention to the substantial African ancestry and cultural background, as well as colonial history, of Puerto Ricans.[102]

Power-conflict analysts of the U.S. treatment of Puerto Ricans are generally concerned more than most assimilation analysts about the continuing negative effects of racial discrimination, unemployment, and deteriorating housing on the lives and futures of Puerto Ricans of all ages. Much of the research is not encouraging. For example, one recent study of Puerto Rican adolescents found that they had generally good mental health, but that "those with greater experience with discrimination in their lives had lower scores in some of the mental health indicators than did their peers." Nearly half these adolescents reported significant discrimination in their young lives, and their perception of, and level of anxiety over, discrimination was clearly related to stress, depression, and negative self-esteem.[103]

Moreover, Puerto Ricans are one U.S. racial–ethnic group that still endures *external* colonialism. Unemployment in the U.S. "possession" of Puerto Rico is one major reason for out-migration from the island; the prosperity of the mainland economy is a major pull factor. However, unemployment and mainland prosperity would not have created the great migrations without the long colonial relationship. The economic history of Puerto Ricans is grounded in the history of the colonial relationship between the U.S. and the island of Puerto Rico. After the war with Spain, the U.S. government took the island by force as an external colony. Since that time the inhabitants have been subject to constant U.S. economic and political intervention.

After the industrialization of Puerto Rico under the auspices of U.S. corporations, many Puerto Rican workers became part of a surplus labor population that made its way to mainland cities. These immigrants from an external colony often became part of the *internal* colonialism of U.S. central cities, where Puerto Ricans have usually been racialized by whites as "not white" and lived mostly in significantly segregated communities. Colonialism theorists argue that today a co-opted (by whites) Puerto Rican middle- and upper-class elite frequently exerts social control over Puerto Rican communities to keep the populations from openly rebelling against oppressive conditions.[104]

Internal colonialism may also be seen in the "urban enterprise zones" and other urban development projects created in numerous central cities' communities of color since the 1980s. Typically these are urban poverty areas, some substantially Puerto Rican, that offer significantly reduced taxes and regulations to corporations that open plants or other developments there. Some power-conflict analysts view such urban enterprise programs as involving significant economic exploitation of Latino and black communities, because participating corporations have often paid low wages even as they have received major government tax benefits.[105]

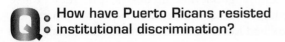 **How have Puerto Ricans resisted institutional discrimination?**

Cuban Americans

Cuban Americans are one of the largest U.S. Latino groups. Like Puerto Ricans, this group has its roots in an important Caribbean island, Cuba, one with more than a century of close ties to the United States. Even through the decades of dramatic political conflict between the U.S. and recent Cuban governments, the U.S. government has maintained a major symbol of past colonialism there—the large military base at Guantánamo Bay, Cuba.

Patterns of Immigration

Early Immigration: 1868–1959

Most migrations from Cuba to the United States have stemmed from political upheaval or economic distress on the island. Nineteenth-century wars of independence brought the first immigrants. Some went to New York, Philadelphia, and Boston, but most settled in Florida because of its proximity to Cuba. After 1885, Ybor City and Tampa in south Florida became home to many Cubans when cigar factories located there. These Cuban Americans were committed to independence of their homeland from Spain and contributed soldiers and financial assistance to the U.S. war with Spain. When Cuba won its independence, many returned. Yet, tens of thousands stayed in the United States where they had homes and jobs. These early Cuban Americans made major contributions to their adopted homeland; they organized Florida's first labor union and established Key West's first fire department and bilingual school.[106]

In 1898, Spain was driven out of Cuba by the U.S. military, and in 1902, Cuba became a U.S. protectorate. Cuba was in effect a U.S. colony from 1898 until the Cuban revolution in the 1950s. During this long period, U.S. financial domination was no less extensive than its political domination. By the late 1950s, U.S. businesses controlled 90 percent of Cuba's mines, 80 percent of its utilities, one-half of its railways, 40 percent of its sugar production, and one-fourth of its bank deposits. Cuba was indeed an economic and political U.S. colony.[107]

The political turbulence accompanying a succession of repressive dictators in Cuba during the first half of the twentieth century periodically brought political refugees to the United States. For example, during the corrupt dictatorship of Fulgencio Batista in the 1950s, between 10,000 and 15,000 refugees per year entered the United States.[108]

Recent Immigration: 1959 to the Present

Large numbers of Cubans migrated to the United States after Cuba's 1959 revolution, when Fidel Castro, a U.S.-educated leader of the grassroots insurrection that overthrew Batista, came into power. To the majority of Cubans, Castro's victory brought hope for economic and political reforms. Land grants to tenant farmers, guaranteed compensation for small growers, and nationalization of utility companies were among Castro's stated goals. However, these reforms were not welcomed by Cuba's business, industrial, and political elites, or by U.S. investors. Exaggerated views of the Cuban revolution's threat to U.S. business and political interests, suspicions that Castro was a Communist, and Castro's declarations that he would not tolerate outside manipulation of Cuba led to open U.S. government and business hostility, a break in diplomatic relations, and a U.S. government policy that welcomed refugees from Cuba's "Communist oppression."[109] This U.S. opposition helped tilt Cuba even more toward supportive Communist regimes in Europe.

The first major immigration after the revolution began with Cuba's monied elite—former government officials, bankers, and industrialists who had done well under the Batista dictatorship. During a second wave of immigration, which began in 1961, large numbers of middle-income and upper-income Cubans chose exile from their native island rather than life under Fidel Castro's increasingly authoritarian government. This group was predominantly composed of professionals, managers, merchants, and landlords, and included more than half of Cuba's teachers and doctors. Many cited loss of jobs, possessions, or sources of income as reasons for departure. Others reported political persecution. Early groups of immigrants were composed primarily of lighter-skinned Cubans. By 1962, almost 200,000 Cubans had entered the United States. Smaller numbers continued to arrive by boat or by way of other countries after air travel between Cuba and the United States was suspended in 1962.[110]

As with earlier Cuban immigrants, Florida, only 90 miles from Cuba, was the usual destination. Both the immigrants and the U.S. government initially viewed Cubans as refugees forced into temporary exile. Guillermo Grenier has accented this distinctiveness. Among all U.S. Latinos, only the Cuban immigrant majority defined itself not as an immigrant community, but socially and politically as an "exile community," one seeking to overthrow the Castro government and return to the island. Moreover, to provide for the needs of refugees, the U.S. government created the Cuban Refugee Emergency Center in Miami and allocated major federal funds. The John Kennedy presidential administration expanded aid by establishing a Cuban Refugee Program that assisted refugees with resettlement, helped locate employment, and provided for health services, education and training programs, and food distribution. Unlike many other Latino and Caribbean immigrants, Cubans were well treated and welcomed as allies in the U.S. political struggle against globalizing Communism.[111]

A third group of immigrants, totaling more than 250,000, arrived between 1965 and the 1970s. Hope for a better standard of living in the United States as well as political disagreement with Cuba's regime were major push factors for this largely lighter-skinned working-class and small-business group. These refugees also settled primarily in Florida, although by the 1970s, some were spread among Cuban communities in other states. More than three-fourths of new immigrant families had relatives already in the United States.[112]

By the late 1960s, increasing numbers had begun to think of themselves as permanent residents of the United States, more interested in improving their lives in the United States and less aggressively involved in efforts to bring about the demise of Castro's government. Many were developing businesses, had bought homes, and had become integrated into the social, economic, and political institutions of their communities. Many became naturalized citizens.

The Mariel Immigrants

A fourth infusion of immigrants, *the entry of about 125,000 Cubans who came from Cuba to the United States in 1980,* often called the **Mariel boatlift** (after a Cuban port), gave rise to stereotypes of these refugees as "undesirables"—poorer and less educated than earlier immigrants and containing a large percentage of criminals and the mentally ill. Some left Cuba voluntarily and some, considered undesirable by the Cuban government, were forced to leave. However, of the entire group, only a few hundred were mentally ill and required institutionalization, and fewer than one in five had been in prison. Among this latter group, almost one-fourth had been political prisoners, and the offenses of an additional 70 percent consisted of acts that were not crimes in the United States. (Fewer than 2 percent were subsequently imprisoned in a U.S. penitentiary.) Their education level was actually similar to that of the 1970s immigrants. More than 11 percent were professionals; 71 percent were blue-collar workers. However, unlike earlier immigrants, about 40 percent of the Mariel group were darker-skinned Cubans, with substantial African ancestry. More than half came to waiting families or sponsors, and two-thirds of the rest were easily placed in communities across the country.[113]

Most Mariel immigrants were working class and came with often different political experiences from earlier immigrants. They had lived under a Communist government for long periods. Yet, they were ineligible for the U.S. financial support available to earlier political refugees. They were allowed to stay by the creation of a special category, which included eligibility for emergency assistance, medical services, and supplemental income. Some were held in processing centers for an extended time while the U.S. government attempted to identify those who were supposedly "dangerous." Many became angry at the contrast between their new socioeconomic conditions and exaggerated reports they had heard in Cuba about life in the United States. Most were eventually integrated into Cuban American communities, but as a group they have not done as well as earlier immigrants. The racialized and other stereotypes and related discrimination have had a negative impact. Although many have managed to do relatively well in U.S. society, Gastón Fernández argues, "for many others the costs of the stigmatization remain very high and adaptation elusive in the face of unusually high levels of depression, incarceration, and economic hardship. Levels of unemployment and reported discrimination by others, including other Cuban-Americans, are high."[114]

In 1994, the Cuban government again lifted its ban on emigration, and 35,000 Cubans left for Florida, mostly on rafts and small boats. Reversing earlier policy, the U.S. government stopped admitting immigrants, sending them instead to camps at the Guantánamo Bay naval base in Cuba. The U.S. and Cuban governments negotiated an agreement whereby the United States would increase visas for Cubans to at least 20,000 annually, to facilitate legal immigration,

Some of the Cuban refugees not allowed into the United States were held at the Guantánamo Bay naval base in Cuba.

and Cuba would halt the exodus. The U.S. government agreed to send back Cubans who had not departed legally and were intercepted by the Coast Guard. Since the mid-1990s, the number of immigrants has often not reached the allowed quota because of fees and other barriers imposed by the Cuban government. The sometimes heated discussions over immigration and travel issues have continued between the two governments to the present. Attempts to reach the United States illegally have persisted. Under U.S. law, migrants who reach the U.S. shoreline are permitted to stay (at least temporarily). In addition, the Nicaraguan Adjustment and Central American Relief Act, in effect since the late 1990s, has given legal resident status to many Cubans and Central Americans who came illegally.[115]

Today, about 1.6 million Cuban Americans live in the United States, mostly in major urban areas on the East Coast, but with increasing numbers in smaller towns and cities in states such as Pennsylvania and North Carolina. In a recent American Community Survey, the median age for Cuban Americans was just over 41 years, significantly higher than for the U.S. population as a whole (36.9 years) and for other Latino groups. About 60 percent were born in Cuba.[116]

 What pressures and attractions have led to Cuban migrations?

Intergroup Conflict

One major result of these numerous Cuban migrations is the significant change in the population mix of Florida. By the 1980s, Latinos had become a majority in the city of Miami; over the next two decades they became a majority in the larger metropolitan area. The Cuban migrations after 1980 swelled public-assistance rolls, increased school overcrowding, and created major expenses for local governments. The millions paid to care for new Cuban immigrants angered many non-Latinos, many of whom unfairly blamed immigrants for local social problems.

Tensions between Cuban Americans and African Americans

Tensions accelerated between Cuban immigrants and Miami's black residents, many of whom felt Cubans were getting too much government assistance and were taking jobs away from native-born African Americans. Today, the larger and generally more affluent Cuban American community in south Florida controls numerous businesses, many of which prefer to hire Cuban Americans. This creates friction with the black population, which often faces high unemployment. In one 1980s mayoral election, most black voters voted against the Cuban candidate. Since 1980, several racial riots have occurred in the Miami area. Miami's 1980 Liberty City riot and 1982 Overtown riot by working-class African Americans were precipitated in part by police involvement in killing black men. The Overtown uprising began after a Cuban American police officer shot and killed a black man playing a video game. More rioting took place in 1984 when this officer was acquitted. After the riots some Anglo landlords and businesses that had been damaged were replaced by Latino landlords and businesses in black communities. One black school official claimed that "after a generation of being Southern slaves, blacks now face a future as Latin slaves." The 1989 shooting of an unarmed black motorist by a Latino officer precipitated yet another black uprising in Miami. After the incident, the U.S. attorney began an inquiry into complaints of police brutality by Anglo and Latino officers.[117]

More recently, Cuban American leaders have been critical of the friendliness of some black leaders, inside and outside the United States, to the Cuban Communist government. In turn, some Cuban American officials angered the black community in south Florida when they ignored visiting black officials, including then South African President Nelson Mandela, who had maintained relations with the Cuban government. In addition, black groups have sued Cuban-controlled local governments in Florida for what they see as discriminatory obstruction of fair political representation for black residents. Recent research has also shown that, among major Latino groups, Cuban Americans are the most likely to move away from communities with large African American populations.[118]

Political tensions between African Americans and Cuban Americans have surfaced periodically in presidential elections since 2000. In the 2000, 2004, and 2008 elections, black voters in Florida overwhelmingly supported Democratic candidates, whereas Cuban Americans voted in large numbers for the Republican candidate. In these elections, black leaders have charged that local officials, including some Cuban Americans, have played a role in creating discriminatory barriers for black voters. Today, intergroup rivalry and competition remain strong in Florida, where a very old involuntary immigrant group (African Americans) often loses in a political power struggle with a relatively new immigrant group substantially composed of political refugees and their children (Cuban Americans).

Inconsistent U.S. government treatment of the often lighter-skinned Cuban refugees and the usually darker-skinned Haitian refugees, discussed in Chapter 7, has been another source of intergroup tension. Thousands of Haitians, as well as hundreds of thousands of Salvadorans and Guatemalans, have been refused political refugee status in the U.S. since the 1970s; many have been deported to face persecution at the hands of governments often more oppressive than the Cuban government. In a clearly biased maneuver, Cuban immigrants were for years defined as "political refugees" eligible for U.S. citizenship by U.S. officials, and yet most Haitian and Central American immigrants were classified by U.S. officials as "economic refugees" ineligible even for entry. (Beginning in 1994, the federal government did place more restrictions on Cuban immigrants.) Not surprisingly, this differential treatment of immigrants has fueled significant tensions between Miami's Cuban and Haitian communities.[119]

Racial Divisions among Cuban Americans

The Cuban American population is diverse in terms of the racial gradient that is central to U.S. society. In Cuba, before the revolution, the society was substantially segregated; lighter-skinned Cubans generally had more residential and economic privileges than darker-skinned Cubans with more African ancestry. After the revolution, Castro's government decreed that darker-skinned Cubans should be treated equally with lighter-skinned Cubans, and the former generally gained greater access to better jobs and housing. Racial status became less important, though it by no means disappeared. In the U.S., Cuban immigrants faced a world in which the dominant Anglo Americans have long classified people

on a continuum running from preferred "white" to denigrated "black" and in which major societal privileges are linked to the top of that racial classification. For example, one *New York Times* report described the experiences of two men who had been close friends in Cuba, but who had grown apart when they recently moved to the Miami area.[120] The light-skinned one integrated easily into the predominantly light-skinned Cuban population already in Miami, while the darker-skinned man was viewed as black by local Anglo Americans and forced to reside in a black community. Although they lived a few miles apart, the friends inhabited separate racialized worlds. The reporter who interviewed them recounted the experiences of the darker-skinned man (Mr. Ruiz):

> He had seen barrios in Havana with more blacks than others, but he had never lived in a place where everybody was black. Far from feeling comfortable, he yearned for the mixing he had known in Cuba. . . . [H]e had been taught to see skin color . . . as not much more important than, say, the color of his eyes. But this was not Cuba. This was Miami, and in Miami, skin color easily trumps nationality.[121]

In the United States, Ruiz felt constantly under surveillance from Anglo whites. Many of the latter, as well as many lighter-skinned Cubans, stereotype black Americans as dangerous, lazy, or criminal. Soon after arrival, Ruiz faced police harassment from a light-skinned Cuban American officer, just because he was black. The rigid U.S. racial divisions force Latin American immigrants into a new racialized world that is often hard for them to navigate.

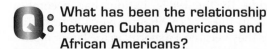 **What has been the relationship between Cuban Americans and African Americans?**

Stereotypes and Discrimination

Cuban Americans are sometimes stereotyped as mostly being anti-Castro militants or extremists and have been described in some media reports, including newspaper editorials, as "crazies" for their aggressive protests over such incidents as the one involving the Cuban boy Elián González (discussed later) in the year 2000. Certainly, some media accounts of this case suggested stereotypes of Cubans as overly emotional and foreign. Myriam

Márquez, a Cuban American journalist, noted that many other Americans hold a stereotyped view: "We are circling our wagons, hunkering down for battle and waving a foreign flag on American soil. You are sure we will riot because there's no question in your mind that Miami long ago turned into a Banana Republic with a Wild West flair."[122]

Some analysts have stereotyped Cuban Americans, especially early immigrants, as a predominantly successful group that does not face discrimination. However, as Susan Eckstein has noted, "Cuban separateness resulted partly from Anglo rebuff. The Anglo upper class and the Anglo professional and business community *excluded* Cuban immigrants from their informal social circles and from their economic interest groups."[123] Cuban Americans as a group are generally more prosperous than other Latino groups, but this relative affluence should not be exaggerated, for a large proportion live in modest circumstances or poverty.

Cuban Americans also do not escape some of the criminal stereotyping other Latinos face. For example, in the still-popular cult movie *Scarface* (1983) the central character is a hyper-violent Cuban (Mariel) immigrant who takes over a Miami drug empire. The movie was made just after the inflow of Mariel immigrants, and its preface greatly exaggerated the number of criminals in the Mariel exodus from Cuba. The movie, and numerous Anglo white movie critics, bought into and perpetuated the media stereotyping of Mariel immigrants as violent criminals. As we noted previously, very few actually were such criminals.[124]

Many non-Latinos regularly express distaste for Spanish and other aspects of Latino cultures. In the 1980s, for example, Florida voters overwhelmingly approved an "official English" ballot initiative that many Latinos understandably considered hostile. This initiative mandated that government business be conducted only in English. One Cuban American leader noted that such legislation "opens the way for bigotry and discrimination."[125] (The legislation was later reversed in another election.) The desire of some private clubs in Florida to provide a place in which Anglo members do not have to hear Spanish spoken has led them to establish policies that exclude Latinos. Federal judge Kenneth Ryskamp's connection to a Miami club with such a policy was one action that apparently led the Senate Judiciary Committee to reject his nomination to a Court of Appeals seat. Judge Ryskamp echoed sentiments of many Florida Anglos when he explained that his wife was annoyed because many store clerks spoke mostly Spanish and many stores stocked merchandise preferred by Spanish-speaking customers.[126]

Like other Latinos, Cuban Americans have experienced an array of discrimination at the hands of Anglo whites. In the 1960s, signs outside some apartment buildings proclaimed, "No Dogs, No Kids, No Cubans." For several decades, Cuban Americans have faced employment barriers. One Cuban American FBI agent, Fernando Mata, helped bring a successful class-action lawsuit against the FBI. The court ordered the agency to eradicate discrimination against its Latino employees. However, after the lawsuit, Mata, a decorated counterintelligence specialist, lost his security clearance and was suspended because of allegations that he was spying for Cuba. However, civil rights activists outside the agency saw no proof of spying activity and argued that Mata was being harassed because of the lawsuit. Mata's attempt to sue the FBI for retaliation was rejected by a federal court for "national security" reasons.[127]

Cuban Americans have reported discrimination in yet other government agencies. In the early 2000s, a Drug Enforcement Administration (DEA) senior agent, Sandalio González, sent materials to Congress indicating that he was being transferred out of the Miami office for what appeared to be discriminatory reasons. The highest-placed Cuban American in the agency, González had protested anti-Latino discrimination in the office. He filed a lawsuit seeking to stop the transfer. In addition, in the early 2000s, several immigration agents working for the old Immigration and Naturalization Service (INS, now part of the Department of Homeland Security) reported significant anti-Cuban stereotyping and discrimination in the Miami INS office. There were reports of "jokes about shooting Elián, and several derogatory comments from INS Miami officials against the Cuban American community. One poster in the INS Miami office called Cubans 'lazy, loud-mouthed criminals.' Banners were hung with the City of Miami seal and a headline reading 'banana republic' and cup-holders were produced showing the image of a Cuban flag with a line slashed through it." With the help of the organization Judicial Watch, one Latino agent filed a lawsuit against the INS alleging discrimination against Cuban Americans and other

Latinos there. The case was settled in the fall of 2002, after which the judge underscored the "hostile work environment for employees of Cuban-American and Hispanic national origin" there.[128] In addition, we should also note that some research has shown that racially hostile workplaces are more likely for darker-skinned Cuban Americans than for those who have lighter skin.

Significantly, one recent national survey found that 45 percent of Cuban American respondents thought that national debates over immigration made anti-Latino discrimination worse, albeit a figure somewhat lower than that for Puerto Ricans (59 percent) and Mexican Americans (58 percent).[129]

The Economic Situation

Many Cuban immigrants experienced a dramatic decline in occupational status when they entered the U.S. economy. A 1966 survey of Cubans in the Miami metropolitan area found that the percentage of immigrants who were employed as professionals, proprietors, technicians, and managers dropped from about 48 percent to about 13 percent, whereas the percentage of those employed as unskilled laborers doubled. Even though many were willing to take jobs far below their previous occupational level, unemployment was also widespread.[130]

The increased Cuban presence in Florida has elevated Florida's importance as a center for Latin American and other international commerce. The area's growth has expanded international trade and the number of corporations with headquarters for Latin America. In the eyes of many, Miami has become the "capital of Latin America" because of its dominant position in Latin American trade and banking, as well as in the underground economy of the drug trade.[131]

Compared with other Latino groups, Cuban Americans have generally enjoyed a greater degree of economic success. The relatively high-level educational and occupational characteristics of many immigrants, especially earlier arrivals, have helped many attain significant success. In addition, the large numbers of immigrants in one metropolitan area (Miami) make possible the development of an "ethnic enclave" (a concentrated community) with strong support networks facilitating social and economic adjustment. Examining Miami's Cuban

enclave, some researchers have suggested that Cubans have done relatively well economically because they migrated not as poor individuals in isolated circumstances over long periods of time but rather as a group that had substantial resources, access to important social networks, and major support from federal government programs. Researchers such as like Silvia Pedraza have underscored this government role. Motivated greatly by government concern to "fight Communism," large-scale federal programs played a major role in advancing the structural assimilation of these immigrants by reinforcing their initial social-class advantage and creating a cumulative advantage for them in the U.S. economy.[132]

The first federally funded bilingual programs were started for Cubans in the 1960s, and the Cuban Refugee Program lasted until 1974. Over time the federal government provided $1.2 billion in aid to Cuban refugees, an average of about $63,000 per family (in 2000 dollars). About three-fourths received government assistance. Specific programs to support businesses, such as loans from the Small Business Administration, were targeted to Cuban Americans. However, as Grosfoguel and Georas found in their data analysis, "in Miami, as well as in Union City, New Jersey, and in New York City, metropolitan areas where large numbers of Cubans settled, the Small Business Administration (SBA) practiced institutionally racist policies against Puerto Ricans and African-Americans while favoring disproportionately the Cubans in the provision of loan programs."[133] Numerous local government programs were also established to benefit refugees. Cuban immigrants are the only large group of Latin American immigrants who have ever been granted such extensive government aid, which has been critical in helping Cuban refugees and their descendants to adapt to the mainstream economy and institutions.

In addition, the wide range of occupations among the Cuban immigrants has facilitated the development of a large and interdependent local economy capable of providing jobs and incomes for many in Florida's Latino communities, including immigrants from Central and South America. The enclave economy has also given Cuban American entrepreneurs access to less skilled workers arriving later from Cuba. Appeals to group solidarity have even helped some businesspeople exploit their compatriots economically, as low-wage workers.[134]

Although these individual and group factors are important in Cuban Americans' economic adjustment, they do not fully account for this group's mobility. Another factor is the family. The Cuban American family has generally been "organized around realizing aspirations of economic achievement." Although relatively few women participated in the paid labor force prior to the Cuban revolution, gainful employment became an economic necessity for upward mobility in the United States. Cuban American women, including those married with husband present and those with children, have over the decades been more likely than other Latinas to do paid labor. In addition, three-generation families under one roof are common among Cuban Americans, and provide a major source of child care and additional wage earners.[135]

Among Latino groups, Cuban Americans have relatively high levels of economic status. In the 2008 American Community Survey (see Table 9.2), some 29.5 percent of men and 34.5 percent of women reported being in managerial and professional occupations, with 18.5 percent of men and 38.5 of women being in sales and office positions. The rest were in blue-collar and service positions, with nearly the same male and female percentages in these categories as for European Americans.

Our comparison of income, poverty rates, and educational attainment for Mexican Americans, Puerto Ricans, and Cuban Americans in Chapter 8 shows that Cuban Americans are nearer the non-Latino white population on several socioeconomic measures than are Mexican Americans and Puerto Ricans. As we saw in Table 8.3, the proportion of Cuban Americans with at least a high school diploma is the highest of the three large Latino groups (at 75.6 percent), but significantly less than the 90.1 percent for Anglo whites. The rate of college completion for Cuban Americans is also substantially higher than for Puerto Ricans and Mexican Americans. As we saw in Table 8.2, the median family income ($51,290) for Cuban Americans is about 72 percent of that ($70,835) of Anglo whites. In contrast, median family income for mainland Puerto Ricans and Mexican Americans was substantially less. Cuban Americans also have a high rate of home ownership. The relatively higher economic status of Cuban Americans compared with other Latino groups does not mean that they face no racial–ethnic discrimination. Given this group's relatively high level of education, their median income figure is lower than it is for comparably educated Anglos. Employment discrimination by some Anglo employers has long been a problem for Cuban Americans, as we noted previously.[136]

The prosperity of Cuban Americans compared with other Latino groups does not mean that all Cuban Americans are affluent. In the late 2000s, as we saw in Table 8.2, the poverty rate for Cuban American families (11.0 percent) was nearly double

---

TABLE 9.2   Occupational Distribution (2008)

	Men		Women	
	European American	Cuban American	European American	Cuban American
Managerial and professional specialties	36.1	29.5	41.7	34.5
Sales and office occupations	18.3	18.5	35.0	38.5
Production, transportation, and material moving occupations	16.8	19.9	4.7	6.6
Construction, extraction, and maintenance occupations	16.6	17.2	0.6	0.5
Service occupations	11.5	14.5	17.7	19.9
Farming, forestry, and fishing	0.7	0.4	0.2	0.0
Total	100.0%	100.0%	99.9%	100.0%

Source: U.S. Bureau of the Census. "2008 American Community Survey." (European American is non-Hispanic white.)

that of Anglo whites (6.1 percent). In addition, about 14 percent of Cuban Americans under age 18 lived below the official poverty line.[137]

Politics

The expectation that the Fidel Castro regime would be short-lived led most post-1959 Cuban immigrants to remain politically inactive for some years, but the 1970s saw an increase in naturalized citizens, voter registration, and political participation. Political views were often shaped by continuing concern with Cuba's government. In the 1980s, for example, the Cuban American marketing director of the *Miami News* stated, Cuban Americans are "definitely super-conservative. Communism for us is the enemy. On domestic issues, we will be more toward the center . . . but the Cuban business community is still more in favor of Reaganomics than Mexicans or Puerto Ricans."[138] Thus, many today identify with the Republican Party, which is considered to be more anti-Castro. Recently, one survey found that a substantial majority of Cuban American adults surveyed were registered Republicans, with those immigrating before 1980 being the most likely to be Republicans.[139]

Since the 1980s, Cuban Americans have become very politically active. Two-thirds of adults are citizens, and they register and vote in large numbers. They hold many elective and appointive offices in Florida, including powerful positions in the Florida legislature. In recent years, the mayor of Miami, the mayor of Miami-Dade County, the superintendent of the Miami-Dade County public schools, the county police chief, the presidents of major local colleges, and numerous state legislators from the area have been Cuban Americans. In 1993, Ileana Ros-Lehtinen, a Cuban American from Miami, became the first Latina ever to serve in the U.S. House of Representatives. In the early 2000s, President George W. Bush appointed the first Cuban American, Mel Martínez, to a cabinet position, as Secretary of Housing and Urban Development. Martínez was later elected to the U.S. Senate (Florida). In the mid-2000s, Robert Menendez, a Democrat, became the first Cuban American to serve in the U.S. Senate from New Jersey. In 2010, there were only four Latinos serving as Republican members of the U.S. Congress; all were Cuban Americans from Florida.[140]

Many Cuban Americans remain involved in the politics of Cuba. One major example is the 2000 case of Elián González, a Cuban boy whose mother drowned while trying to bring him to the United States. Elián's U.S. relatives waged a custody battle with his father, who sought to return with Elián to Cuba. In April 2000, U.S. immigration agents seized the boy from U.S. relatives and let him return. Both actions upset many Cuban Americans. This is yet another example of how many U.S. racial–ethnic groups remain actively concerned with the politics of home countries. Some conservative political analysts, such as the late Samuel Huntington, have worried that U.S. foreign policy is no longer unified but has become a "balkanized" collection of the overseas interests of diverse U.S. nationality groups. In his view Cuban Americans and other Latinos have intentionally created a separate America and are therefore seriously threatening the dominant Anglocentric culture. However, he offered no substantial data to support such notions.[141]

One influential political group has been the Cuban American National Foundation (CANF), established in 1981 and eventually involving thousands of members and offices in Miami, Washington, and other cities. It has been active in lobbying Congress on legislation dealing with Cuba. In a 2001 speech, for example, the chair of CANF indicated that his organization still supported the extensive U.S. embargo on trade with Cuba, which was under increasing attack from humanitarian groups. However, by late 2006, with the serious illness of Fidel Castro and the rise of his brother Raúl Castro to prominence, the CANF and other Cuban American organizations were shifting their hard-line approach to working for more contacts and interaction with the Cuban people and government. Still, a 2006 survey of Cuban Americans in south Florida found that 49 percent supported (with 45 percent opposed) tough new George W. Bush administration restrictions on family travel and remittances to Cuba. The restrictions were added because of the lobbying efforts of a new far-right organization called the Cuba Liberty Council.[142]

However, in the fall of 2008 and again in the spring of 2009, CANF again called publicly for a shift away from the Bush administration's emphasis on harsh restrictions and on changing the Cuban government to a major focus on helping the Cuban

U.S. Senator Robert Menendez (D–N.J.) speaks during a campaign rally in October 2006.

people. Playing down the importance of the embargo, in a long 2009 statement, CANF called for new actions directing more resources to Cuba, for setting up regular discussions with the Cuban government on renewing migration from Cuba, and for improving other diplomatic relationships. Significantly, in the spring of 2009, President Barack Obama announced modest changes in the U.S. policy toward Cuba. He lifted the harsh Bush restrictions on family travel and family remittances to Cuba, allowed improved telecommunications with Cuba, and permitted more humanitarian items to be exported to Cuba.[143]

Clearly, today there are important political divisions within the Cuban American community over U.S. government policy toward Cuba, with those who immigrated in the post-1980 era being more supportive of liberalized relationships than those who immigrated earlier. Those who came in the pre-1980 period have tended to be politically conservative, and have had more political influence in Florida and the country, than those who have come later. The latter have often been working-class and have not moved up economically and politically as rapidly. The latter are also more likely to reject trade and travel restrictions to Cuba. One reason this internal division is not widely recognized is that post-1980 immigrants have been slower to become

citizens and voters, and thus they have much less political impact.[144]

In the past, some Cuban exiles have engaged in paramilitary training and terrorist acts directed against the Fidel Castro government. Exiles recruited by the CIA were involved in the unsuccessful Bay of Pigs invasion in 1961. Members of at least one anti-Castro group practiced mock invasions well into the 1990s. In addition, Cuban Americans have been active in the operation of Radio Martí, a federally funded station, and its affiliate, TV Martí, which transmit news and public affairs programming from Washington to Cuba via Florida. Recently, some critical analysts have suggested that the programming is often of propagandistic quality and that 99 percent of Cubans have never heard of these expensive efforts (a half billion dollars over the years). These broadcasts are also considered violations of international law by the International Telecommunications Union (ITU).[145]

The collapse of the Soviet Union in 1991 brought severe economic hardships to Cuba's people; the two countries had been linked by billions of dollars in trade for decades. In 2001, a group of prominent Cuban Americans met to hear a presentation from Ramón Saul Sánchez regarding nonviolent actions to help the Cuban people with humanitarian supplies and undermine the Cuban government.

Sanchez has headed up the Democracy Movement, a Cuban-exile group that has demonstrated on behalf of Cubans trying to sail from Cuba. Over the 1990s and 2000s, the group has brought a flotilla of boats to Cuba numerous times on anti-Castro and pro-democracy missions, and the U.S. Coast Guard has tried to stop the efforts.[146]

The recurring involvement of Cuban Americans in the politics of Cuba is yet another example of the ways in which the development and situations of U.S. racial and ethnic groups interact with and are dependent on the world context. U.S. racial and ethnic relations are often intrinsically international.

How did migration to the United States change the economic situation of many Cuban Americans?

Religion

Like many Puerto Ricans, many Cuban immigrants to the U.S. brought with them *a type of syncretic religion that included aspects of both Catholicism and older African religions*—religious practices referred to as Cuban **Santería**. Over centuries, Santería practitioners have dressed up African nature deities (orishas) in the religious symbolism of Catholic saints, combining aspects of Catholic ideas and ritual with folk religious practices rooted in religions of Africans once enslaved in Cuba. Today, Santería practices and ideas are important for many Cubans. They provide therapeutic support for many people, and also shape the ways in which people practice Catholicism in the U.S. and Cuba.[147]

Interestingly, surveys from the late 2000s have found that Cuban Americans are less likely than those in other Latino groups to say that religion is the most important thing in their lives. Just 39 percent reported being regular (at least weekly) attenders of church services—a figure lower than that for other major Latino groups. (In addition, Cuban Americans report that they are significantly less opposed to abortion, but significantly more opposed to gay marriage, than are Puerto Ricans or Mexican Americans.) Those who are actively involved in Catholic parishes, especially in Florida, may find an increasingly diverse Latino Church. Numerous formerly white Catholic parishes have become mostly Latino, with a significant number

ministering to a diversity of Latino populations—Cuban Americans, Puerto Ricans, Mexican Americans, Dominican Americans, and South and Central Americans. As with Puerto Ricans, this pan-Latino diversity leaves some Cuban parishioners feeling somewhat alienated from Catholicism because of the different approaches to the Catholic religion even among Latinos.[148]

Assimilation or Colonialism?

Assimilation Issues

Cuban Americans are a relatively recent addition to the bubbling cauldron that is the United States. Like other Latinos, they have faced major prejudice and discrimination, including language discrimination and restriction or exclusion in Anglo-dominated organizations and institutions.

Efforts to maintain the Cuban culture and social order, as well as to bypass country club discrimination by European Americans, led to the creation in the 1960s of the Big Five Club, an elite, mostly Latino, Miami social club. Over the decades, the club's membership has included many of the Cuban American community's most distinguished families. (Affluent Anglos have their own, mostly Anglo clubs.) Over the last decade or so, however, the younger, U.S.-born generation has seemed less interested in joining elite Cuban social clubs, and so the Big Five Club has encompassed an ever more socially diverse membership. In addition, many Cuban Americans in various generations have joined an array of mostly or entirely Latino business and professional associations and are sending their children to predominantly Latino parochial schools. Significantly, private-school segregation can be seen in south Florida. Affluent Anglos often place their children in elite private schools where few Latino children are enrolled.[149]

Identificational assimilation, in Gordon's sense of that term, has come slowly. Some, especially those who are older and Cuban born, still consider themselves exiles rather than immigrants, and may speak of having a "fractured identity." Others—especially those who left Cuba as children and U.S.-born generations (the latter about 40 percent of the Cuban American population)—say they have a double identity. Additionally, one recent survey found only 13 percent of Cuban Americans expressing an inclination to return to Cuba permanently if the Castro government comes to an end. Over half have also indicated that the U.S. government should be in overt dialogue with the Cuban government. In addition, more than 70 percent of Cuban Americans surveyed recently favored negotiations between the U.S. government and a new Cuban government if it showed a willingness to improve relations with the U.S. and the Cuban exile community.[150]

One psychological study compared national identifications of Cuban American and African American women. The African American women generally felt they were indeed "American," but that they were not seen as such by Anglo whites; and they felt that they still were economically and socially excluded by whites. In contrast, Cuban American women generally did not feel they were American and did not think Anglo whites saw them as American. However, for the latter feelings of societal inclusion increased with length of residence. The longer they had been in the U.S., the more economically and socially included they felt.[151]

The preservation of Cuban culture and identity in the enclave communities in Florida provides a crucial foundation for Cuban Americans' economic and political integration into U.S. society. The community solidarity originally created by the first groups of immigrants was rooted in kinship and friendship ties and formed the social and economic context into which later immigrants entered. In the 1970s, researchers interviewed 590 male immigrant heads of household at the time of their arrival in Miami and again several years later. In the initial interview, 99 percent expressed an intention to remain in the Miami area; at the time of the final interview, 97 percent still resided there. The Miami area's strong enclave community has provided a context in which immigrants and their children adapt to the dominant Anglo culture yet continue to carry out routine activities within a Cuban American setting. Six years after these respondents entered the United States, more than one in five were self-employed in the Cuban American community, and almost half worked for a Cuban American business. At the economic level, a significant majority of these immigrants did not assimilate directly to the dominant economic institutions but rather to the local Cuban enclave economy.[152]

Over time, Cuban immigrants and their children have made significant economic achievements. One

reason is that the Cuban migration to the U.S. has been different from that of other Latinos, in that it has included a substantial percentage of professionals and businesspeople. David Hayes-Bautista and Robert Stein note that "Latino entrepreneurship has turned Miami into a bustling center of international trade, self-declared gateway to the economies of Latin America and self-appointed music center of Latino USA. Latino politicians run the city and county; Latinos are involved in the fine arts, academia, journalism and broadcasting."[153] Although this summary neglects continuing problems with discrimination and stereotyping that Cuban Americans face, it underscores the important point that, of all major Latino groups, they are probably the most integrated into Anglo-dominated economic and political institutions.

Many Cuban immigrants did not have to wait their turn in the urban economic queue, as did Italian, Polish, and other immigrant groups. Instead, many in the first three immigrant groups advanced into an economic niche as small-business owners or professionals, often laying a basis for their children's movement into even better business and professional jobs. As a result, many of their children and grandchildren are relatively advantaged. For example, children's first communions (receiving the Roman Catholic sacrament) for many families have become costly celebrations. Daniel Álvarez noted, "We are a very tight community, and we want to do whatever we can to hold on and keep our kids in touch with their Cuban Catholic heritage."[154] The presence of a large cohesive group of immigrants in an enclave community provides much support for later generations. However, the enclave community has brought significantly less socioeconomic mobility for more recent (Mariel and later) immigrants. One recent review has reported that the "benefits of enclave entrepreneurship accrued primarily to its original builders and, secondarily, to their offspring. . . . Later Cuban arrivals also followed the entrepreneurial route, but they were hampered in their efforts by the rupture of networks (and hence the opportunities and resources that they provided) with the older exile community."[155]

Cultural assimilation pressures on Cuban immigrants have created cross-generational problems similar to those of earlier European immigrants. Language assimilation is significant for the younger generation. One survey of Miami's Cubans revealed that by the 1980s, many youth preferred English-language programs on radio and TV, whereas parents switched between English and Spanish programs. Like other immigrant grandparents, Cuban grandparents preferred to speak Spanish. Parents and grandparents worried about the excessive freedom of U.S. teenagers. Parents and grandparents tended to emphasize Cuban traditions, while grandchildren preferred things American. Older generations were generally committed to overthrowing Cuba's Communist government and returning home. Less politically active youth saw the U.S. as their permanent home. Family and community ties were strong, and the youth were proud of their Cuban identity.[156]

In the 1990s, Strategy Research Corporation (SRC) ranked the Cuban Americans as the least *culturally* assimilated of major Latino groups, based on language use and behavioral and attitudinal measures. The high density of Cuban Americans in a few Florida cities and the group's older average age were likely factors. Less than one-third reported then that they spoke or wrote English well. However, the SRC survey presented a different picture for younger Latinos in the Southeast. Less than half of the youth classified themselves as "very Hispanic," and only 40 percent felt they would be "very Hispanic" in the future. Three-fourths spoke English at school and felt more comfortable speaking English than Spanish. More recently, a mid-2000s Miami survey found that nearly half of Cuban Americans spoke English outside their homes and most worked with non-Cubans. And another recent survey by the U.S. Census Bureau found that the overwhelming majority of Cuban Americans under age 18 spoke English well. As with most other Latinos, the Spanish language seems to be slowly decreasing in importance as the Cuban generations pass.[157]

Cuban Americans have adapted selectively to their new country. They have developed a vigorous enclave economy and substantial group resources, with increasing and major links to the outside, Anglo-dominated economic and political institutions. Yet, many have tried to preserve the Spanish language and Cuban traditions. Nonetheless, the younger generations are assimilating more rapidly than the Cuban-born to the dominant Anglo culture. Interestingly, one recent survey found that Cuban Americans were the *only* major Latino group in which a majority said that they preferred to identify as "white" over other common identifications such

as Latino, Hispanic, and black. The survey also found that for Latinos as a group, and probably for Cuban Americans, the tendency to identify as "white" was much higher for those over age 55 than for those who were younger.[158]

The dominant Euro-American culture does regularly make some modest adjustments to new groups entering the society. For example, as the U.S. Latino population has grown, Cuban, Mexican, and other Latino music and foods have become popular. Many restaurants now feature Cuban and Mexican foods, and major grocery chains, especially in areas with substantial Latino populations, carry foods of interest to Latinos. In southern Florida cities, grocery chains carry such things as plantains, guava paste, and corn husks. Although smaller Latino-operated stores (*bodegas*) have more goods for Latinos, chain retailers have discovered this group's buying power and are striving to discover what products they seek. In this process, non-Latino customers are also exposed to Latino tastes in food and other products.[159]

A Power-Conflict Perspective?

To our knowledge, no one has applied a sustained power-conflict perspective to the case of Cuban Americans. Some might argue that the internal colonialism and other power-conflict perspectives are not useful for interpreting the development of the predominantly light-skinned Cuban American group. This group has not been so strongly racialized and victimized by long-term economic and political discrimination as other Latino groups. Many of the relatively well-off Cubans who migrated to the United States before 1980 had been, to some degree, the beneficiaries of U.S. economic and political control over Cuba prior to the 1959 revolution. Instead of becoming low-wage laborers for non-Latino agribusiness and other capitalists, as was (and often still is) the case for many Mexican Americans and Puerto Ricans, many Cuban Americans have become part of a southern Florida niche economy and enclave society that have helped speed their economic and social adaptation and mobility.

The opportunities and accomplishments of the U.S.-born generations of Cuban Americans (at least of the lighter-skinned majority), which include growing numbers of businesspeople, professionals, and managerial workers, seem in some ways more similar to those of older white ethnic groups (for example, Italian Americans) at a comparable time than to those of other U.S. Latinos. Indeed, the adaptive development of lighter-skinned Cuban Americans might best be interpreted as a variation on the ethnogenesis model. This group has experienced substantial cultural adaptation as well as some economic and political integration into certain Anglo-controlled institutions. Still, the process of ethnogenesis means that *major* aspects of home-country heritage remain *very* important to the immigrant-ethnic group identity for a long period of time. Relatively new groups like (lighter-skinned) Cuban Americans are, to a substantial degree, increasingly being integrated politically and economically with the dominant European American group, yet retain major characteristics of their home culture and nationality as well. From the ethnogenesis perspective, a new ethnic group is one part home-country heritage and one part common culture mixed together in a distinctive way because of a unique history of social development within the U.S. crucible.

Clearly, substantially greater political and civic integration with the dominant Anglo group can occur only if later generations of Cuban Americans disperse residentially from what is now a relatively concentrated and cohesive community in southern Florida. Residential dispersion will likely accelerate this societal incorporation.

There are also major language-related obstacles to the full cultural and structural assimilation of Cuban Americans to the Anglo culture and institutions. Powerful English-speaking Anglos have periodically organized to impose English as the dominant language. Such nativism marks a cultural colonialism that rejects pluralism if it threatens the core culture. As a group, Cuban Americans will not be fully accepted by the dominant Anglo group until they generally reject Spanish and other important aspects of their Cuban heritage. Perhaps more important, most Anglo whites still seem to classify Cuban Americans, even those who are lighter skinned, as *not white*. In particular, the many Cuban Americans whose ancestry is perceptibly African (especially as seen from an Anglo viewpoint) will likely not be admitted into European American social groups and institutions on the same terms as Anglos. Indeed, given persisting problems of anti-Latino discrimination and Anglo cultural domination (including the "English only" movements), one

could well construct a developed power-conflict perspective in regard to understanding the troubled societal reality that exists today for the majority of Cuban Americans.

 How do you explain the economic and educational differences among Cuban Americans, Puerto Ricans, and Mexican Americans?

Summary

The United States has the fourth largest Spanish-speaking population among all countries, and in the near future the Latino population will reach 50 million people. In Chapter 8, we examined Mexican Americans, the largest Latino group. In this chapter, we have examined two other large Latino groups.

Puerto Ricans on the mainland are second in population size to Mexican Americans. Puerto Ricans are an important American group with an ancient heritage. Like Mexican Americans, they represent a fusion of Native American, Spanish, and African heritages. Today, Puerto Ricans as a group are a people with one foot on the mainland and one foot on a Caribbean island. The more or less external-colony situation of the island population complicates its future political-economic development.

The island of Puerto Rico is self-contained, with a variety of social classes, including a local capitalist class and working class, as well as a small elite of U.S.-based multinational capitalists. Some argue that social-class problems on the island are different from those on the mainland, where most Puerto Ricans are working class; there are few mainland Puerto Rican capitalists. Other commentators downplay class and stress that there is only one Puerto Rican people. As one Puerto Rican social scientist once stated, "No matter how we see ourselves internally, the Yanqui always sees us and deals with us as one class and one people with the same problems. Therefore we should band together and not divide ourselves to fight for our nation against the colonizer."[160]

Concentrated in the Northeast, mainland Puerto Ricans have been important to the social and economic vitality of the New York City area, especially now that many whites are leaving the area. Many

Puerto Rican workers face hard lives doing difficult, low-wage jobs. Levels of poverty and unemployment remain relatively high.

Like Puerto Ricans, Cuban Americans are rooted in a Caribbean island. One of the largest Latino groups, they are relatively better off as a group than most other Latino groups, with higher levels of education and income. (But they are still less well off than white Anglos.) Today, they are an urban population significantly concentrated in the southeastern United States. Cuban Americans' relative prosperity stems substantially from the fact that many early Cuban immigrants migrated with some important personal and group resources, including access to major federal assistance. Smaller families and a relatively high level of participation of women in the paid labor force have contributed to their upward socioeconomic mobility. Cuban Americans' achievements affirm the advantages of migrating under the auspices of strong family networks and of receiving significant federal government support.

Cuban Americans have developed a powerful community centered in the Miami metropolitan area. Their population size and socioeconomic resources have allowed them to develop a strong economic and political niche and to maintain their Spanish language as well as other important Cuban cultural practices. However, as is the case with numerous other immigrant groups, members of the younger generation have moved rapidly toward the dominant culture in many areas, including language, often to the disappointment of older generations.

The pride that most Latinos feel in their heritages can be seen in their desire to maintain the Spanish language as well as other cultural patterns. The growing numbers of U.S. Latinos provide support for Spanish-language media, Latino organizations, and the marketing of Latino-oriented products. Puerto Ricans and Cuban Americans have helped generate a new pan-Latino consciousness. They generally share with Mexican Americans and other Latinos a common language, a common religious background, and similar home cultures. The pan-Latino consciousness contributes to a sense of solidarity that is reflected in efforts to address common problems of education, jobs, and discrimination.

In recent years, the now substantial Latino population has had an increasing impact on the larger society. Latin American immigration is a major source of the country's population and economic growth, and U.S. Latinos are the Americans most likely to see this immigration in a positive light.[161] Increasingly in some areas, major U.S. corporations are actively recruiting Puerto Rican, Cuban American, and other Latino American workers—especially the better educated. Big corporations, as varied as Chevron, PepsiCo, Bank of America, American Airlines, General Motors, and Miller Brewing Company, have operated recruitment programs at high schools and colleges with large Latino populations, hired Spanish interpreters, and provided mentoring for Spanish-speaking employees. Executives in these and other major companies are also acutely aware of the substantial increase in Spanish-speaking consumers (now a trillion-dollar market), as well as growing international trade with Spanish-speaking countries. In addition, growing numbers of Latinos are citizens and voters, and thus are having an increasingly major impact on U.S. politics, as was seen in the 2008 presidential election.[162]

Key Terms

culture of
  poverty   253
color coding   254

Mariel boatlift   269
Santería   278

CHAPTER 10

Japanese Americans

BIG PICTURE QUESTIONS

- *What role have Japanese Americans played in building up this country's wealth and institutions?*

- *How has a white racial framing shaped negative perceptions of Japanese Americans?*

- *Does the "middleman minority" theoretical perspective fit the experiences of Japanese Americans?*

Mitsuye Yamada, a Japanese American professor, has described white students in an Ethnic American Literature class who read a book in which Asian American writers wrote critically of discrimination they faced. One white student "blurted out that she was offended by its militant tone and that as a white person she was tired of always being blamed for the oppression of all the minorities." Other students were nodding in agreement. Professor Yamada pointed out to the students that they had read other critics of society who were black, Native American, and Latino, but that the students had not been as offended by these analyses. Significantly, white students indicated that they had expected the anger of these others, but not anger about discrimination from Asian American writers. One white student summarized the feelings of numerous students: "It made me angry. *Their* anger made *me* angry, because I didn't even know the Asian Americans felt oppressed. I didn't expect their anger."[1]

Introduction: Asian Americans

Changes in U.S. immigration laws since 1965, especially elimination of discriminatory quotas, have allowed a substantial increase in immigration from Asia and the Pacific Islands. Asian-Pacific Islander Americans constitute the fastest-growing U.S. racial group. More than a dozen groups of Americans have roots in Asia or the Pacific Islands. Since their earliest days of immigration, Asian-Pacific groups have sought to maintain their distinctive cultures and identities even as they adapted to the dominant U.S. culture and institutions.

Diverse groups are included under the relatively new terms **Asian American** and **Asian-Pacific American**, *umbrella terms for Americans with ancestral roots in Asia or the Pacific Islands*. In 1940, these Americans were less than one-half of 1 percent of the population. By 2000, they numbered more than 10 million. Today, their numbers are still growing, now at about 13.4 million people who claim only Asian ancestry and about 15.3 million if you add those with partial Asian ancestry in the most recent census survey. The latter figure constitutes about 5 percent of the U.S. population. Table 10.1 shows the numbers for various groups at three points in time (1980, 1990, and 2008). In the 2008 American Community Survey estimates, the largest of the Asian-Pacific groups was Chinese American. Including those

of partial Chinese ancestry (the U.S. Census Bureau tabulates certain groups for sole reported ancestry as well as those with partial ancestry), they totaled more than 3.6 million. In numbers, Filipino Americans were not far behind, at nearly 3.1 million. Japanese, Asian-Indian, Korean, and Vietnamese Americans constitute the other large Asian American groups.[2]

In this chapter, we examine the critical case of Japanese Americans; then we turn to other groups in Chapter 11.

Japanese Americans

Americans with substantial Japanese ancestry now number nearly 1.3 million. They represent one of the oldest Asian American groups and hold a distinctive place in U.S. history because of their unique experiences during World War II. They are the *only* group of Americans to have been forcibly placed in U.S. concentration camps on a large scale in the past 80 years. Japanese Americans are still paying a significant price for this violation of their human rights by the U.S. government and California state government. Today, they are considered by many to be the most successful and assimilated of Asian Americans, and since the 1960s, they have been central to the white-constructed **model minority stereotype**— *which characterizes certain Asian American groups as exemplary in socioeconomic and moral characteristics, often as compared to other people of color*. For these reasons, we devote an extended discussion to their experiences.

Although large proportions of Asian groups live in western states, Japanese Americans are among the most heavily concentrated in the West. Japanese Americans have by far the highest percentage (a substantial majority) who are U.S. born, an indication of the group's early entry and small number of recent immigrants.[3] For many non-Asian Americans, Japanese Americans still conjure up stereotypes of "crafty Orientals," images of militaristic Japanese expansionism in the 1930s, or resentment of "unfair" Japanese economic competition today. Even in recent years, as we demonstrate later, movies, political speeches, and vandals' graffiti have sometimes included such phrases as "fat Japs" and "little Nips," and Japanese and other Asian Americans have been targets of significant vandalism and violence. Periodically, Japanese American community facilities are vandalized, and Japanese firms are considered

TABLE 10.1   Asian-Pacific American Groups (1980 to 2008)

	1980 Census	1990 Census	2008 Census Survey (Group Alone)*	2008 Census Survey (Group Alone Plus Combinations)**
Japanese	716,331	866,160	710,063	1,298,890
Chinese	812,178	1,648,696	3,077,783	3,622,496
Filipino	781,894	1,419,711	2,425,697	3,088,000
Korean	357,393	797,304	1,344,267	1,609,980
Vietnamese	245,025	593,213	1,431,980	1,728,532
Asian Indian	387,223	786,694	2,495,998	2,725,594
Hawaiian	172,346	205,501	147,201	437,590
Cambodian	16,044	149,047	186,068	240,142
Laotian	47,683	147,375	159,347	217,175
Hmong	5,204	94,439	171,316	221,948
Thai	45,279	91,360	139,208	219,943
Samoan	39,520	57,679	71,831	126,194

*This category includes census estimates from a survey for people who reported only one specific Asian group.

**This category includes census estimate from a survey for people who reported one detailed Asian group plus people reporting two or more Asian groups and people who reported some Asian and some non-Asian ancestry.

dangerous if they purchase U.S. properties or companies.[4] Periodic verbal and physical attacks seem to be motivated by fear of Japanese product imports and corporations or resentment of Japanese competition in world trade.

Migration: An Overview

Serial and Chain Migration

Asian and Pacific Americans include many immigrant groups: the Chinese, Japanese, Koreans, Filipinos, Vietnamese, and Asian Indians, as well as smaller groups such as Cambodians, Laotians, Hmong, Thai, Samoans, and Micronesians. Historians have often neglected Asian immigrants in the epic story of U.S. migration.[5]

Historically, immigration of early Asian groups proceeded serially. This was largely the result of actions of white employers seeking new laborers, and also of white workers on the West Coast motivated by racist framing and acting to stop immigration by Asian worker groups. As we discuss in Chapter 11, the first substantial group of Asian immigrants was Chinese. From the 1860s to the 1880s, many Chinese workers migrated to the West Coast of the U.S. to do low-wage work in construction and other industries. After racist agitation and exclusionary legislation stopped Chinese immigration in the 1880s, Japanese workers were recruited to fill the demand for labor on white-owned farms and in construction and mining projects. Similarly, the termination of Japanese immigration in 1908 in turn spurred white employers to recruit Filipinos to fill their labor needs on the mainland and in Hawaii.[6]

Early Immigration

Japan's initial contact with the United States involved **gunboat imperialism** (*imperialism backed by the use or threat of military force*). In 1853, U.S. Commodore Matthew Perry sailed warships into Tokyo Bay and coerced a treaty granting the U.S. trading rights with Japan. Later, the U.S. colony of Hawaii became the first destination for Japanese immigrants entering the U.S. sphere. At least 231,000 migrated there between 1868 and 1929. After 1884, thousands of Japanese laborers were brought to Hawaiian plantations under contract labor agreements. There were relatively few white laborers on the islands, and Japanese immigrants became part of a racial hierarchy headed by white planters. When contracts expired, most stayed, laying the basis for Hawaii's present-day Japanese American population. In 1898, Hawaii came under firm U.S. government control.[7]

Japanese workers were numerous. Dependent on plantations owned by big corporations, they learned that they could not "advance themselves through individualism and small business," as on the mainland. Rather, as laborers, they adopted a strategy of "unionization, politics, and collective action."[8]

Mainland Migration

Between the 1880s and the so-called Gentlemen's Agreement in 1908 (see below), more than 150,000 Japanese came to the mainland. Those who immigrated to the mainland settled into a greater range of diverse economic positions, from farm labor and mining to shopkeeping and truck farming, than did those who immigrated to Hawaii. Some came under contract to employers, some under the auspices of relatives, and others on their own. The pre-1908 *Issei* (literally, "first generation") had a harder time than those who came afterward, since later immigrants were able to move directly into Japanese American communities.[9] (*Issei, Nisei, Sansei,* and *Yonsei* are Japanese terms for the first four generations of Japanese Americans. *Issei* were born in Japan.)

White employers generally favored labor immigration; white workers and unions generally opposed it. About 1900, one San Francisco mayor campaigned against the Japanese, arguing that they were "unassimilable" and a competitive threat. In 1905, white-run California newspapers began a racist campaign against what they called the "yellow peril"—in other words, "threatening" Asian immigrants. The all-white California legislature passed a resolution calling for exclusion of the Japanese because, given their racial differences, they supposedly would not "assimilate." Racist agitation and related factors led President Theodore Roosevelt to negotiate a prohibition of such immigrants. In 1907–1908, Roosevelt persuaded the Japanese government to agree to an infamous Gentlemen's Agreement whereby no passports would be given by Japan to Japanese workers except those already in the U.S. and their close relatives.[10]

Unlike earlier Chinese immigrants, Japanese immigrants were able for a time to bring in families. Before 1920, thousands of "picture brides" arrived, after proxy wedding ceremonies conducted in Japan, to husbands they had never met. The large proportion of women and children among Japanese immigrants between 1910 and 1920 led white supremacy groups to allege that a "disloyal alien race" would soon overpopulate California.[11]

More Racist Agitation and Restrictions

White writers and politicians who proclaimed a political and economic threat posed by southern and eastern European immigrants to "Anglo-Saxon superiority" also expressed fear of Asian immigrants. The American Legion and the California Farm Bureau Association pressed for their exclusion. By the 1920s, Congress succumbed to agitation by passing the 1924 Immigration Act, which established racist quotas giving preference to "Nordic" countries and excluding the Japanese by prohibiting all "aliens ineligible for citizenship" coming into the United States. (In *Ozawa* v. *United States* [1922], the U.S. Supreme Court ruled that only white or African immigrants could become U.S. citizens.) One feature of the new immigration restrictions was that Japanese and other Asian immigrants in the United States, unlike their European counterparts, were prohibited from bringing in their wives. The Cable Act (1922) also stipulated that *any* U.S. woman, white or Asian, who married an alien ineligible for citizenship (that is, an Asian) would lose *her own* citizenship. These restrictions served to block many avenues of incorporation into the larger society for Asian immigrants.[12]

Government action against Asians, often spurred by white unions and hate groups, persisted. Not until 1952 did the U.S. government provide a small quota for the Japanese and permit first-generation Japanese Americans to become naturalized citizens. Anti-Asian restrictions were not fully removed from U.S. immigration law until 1965.[13]

As late as 1965, Asian Americans numbered about 1 million, and Japanese Americans were the largest group. The reform-oriented 1965 Immigration Act finally permitted significant numbers of new immigrants from Asia, and since the 1970s, Asian and Pacific peoples have been a major component of U.S. immigration.[14] After the end of openly racist immigration quotas in 1965, Japanese immigrants have been allowed, but relatively few have taken the opportunity. Japanese numbers have been lower than those of other Asian groups, in part because of the advanced character of the Japanese economy. However, immigration of a modest number of students and of professionals and executives in U.S. branches of Japanese corporations and their families has contributed to the revitalization of some Japanese American communities.

 How did U.S. government action shape Japanese migration to the United States?

Stereotypes

White and other non-Asian Americans have long held strong stereotypes about Asian Americans, which take a variety of forms. For example, in recent decades Japanese and other Asian Americans have often been called "model minorities"—that is, viewed as especially successful in moving up the socioeconomic ladder because of supposedly different cultural values. In contrast, movies about World War II and the Vietnam War have often portrayed Asians as devious, corrupt, or evil "gooks" (a racist epithet). In recent years, moreover, anti-Asian graffiti such as "Japs," "Chink," "Go back to your country," and "Look out for the Asian invasion" have often been scrawled on buildings, college dorm walls, and highway overpasses.[15]

Robert Lee has listed the racist images applied to those whom non-Asians view as "Orientals" (an offensive term): "Six images—the pollutant, the coolie, the deviant, the yellow peril, the model minority, and the gook—portray the Oriental as an alien body and a threat to the American national family."[16] White Americans, in particular, have applied stereotypes developed for early Chinese and Japanese immigrants to later Asian immigrants. All Asian groups have suffered from similar stereotypes, such as the "dangerous or wily Oriental" image. For example, in the nineteenth century and later, Chinese immigrants were stereotyped as "docile," "crafty," or "dirty." Initially, white Americans considered the new Japanese immigrants around 1900 less threatening and more family oriented than the Chinese. Soon, however, white images came to include negative notions that the Japanese too were docile, servile, and devious.

Immigrants heard cries of "Jap go home."[17] Since those early decades, and especially since World War II, the word *Jap* has become a shorthand term used by non-Asian Americans for Japanese Americans or the Japanese, usually by those with hostile intent or those who do not clearly understand its derogatory meaning.

Within a short period, early Japanese laborers gained land to farm by contract or lease. However, hostile white farmers and workers often exaggerated the extent of this Japanese American land use, which never involved more than a small percentage of western farmland. Another widespread myth was that Japanese Americans were incapable of assimilation because of their culture. Like other whites, V. S. McClatchy, a Sacramento editor, argued that the Japanese workers were "for various reasons unassimilable, and a dangerous element."[18] The irony in this was clear to anyone who understood that by state or federal law Japanese immigrants were not even allowed to become U.S. citizens, own land directly, or marry whites. They were legally prohibited from assimilating along these dimensions.

From U.S. presidents and senators to ordinary whites, many exaggerated the differences between themselves and these immigrants. For example, in the 1910s, James Phelan, U.S. senator from California, argued that Japanese Americans were a threat to the "future of the white race, American institutions, and Western civilization."[19] Again we see how a common and influential framing of whiteness is based on biased views of the meaning of "civilization," as well as on negative views of disliked outgroups.

The U.S. movie industry has played an important role in circulation of stereotypes of Asian Americans. In the early twentieth century, for example, Chinese and Japanese characters were often pictured as outsiders and dangerous villains. They and other Asian Americans were stereotyped as "inscrutable" and poor at speaking English.[20] Between 1900 and 1930, vicious images of forward, buck-toothed "Japs" exploded across the U.S. media. In widely circulated "Letters of a Japanese Schoolboy," journalist Wallace Irwin articulated and stimulated various anti-Japanese stereotypes, including a mode of speech mocked with phrases such as "so sorry, please" (with *l* often replacing *r*, and vice versa). White leaders often spoke of the alleged immorality of Japanese Americans, sometimes using the ape-like imagery applied earlier to Irish or African Americans.[21]

War Propaganda

From the 1890s to the 1930s, anti-Japan sentiment grew. The Japanese were considered an "inferior race" with the brashness to challenge U.S. interests in the Pacific. Well before the Japanese attack on Pearl Harbor, white politicians and labor leaders were portraying Japanese Americans as disloyal. This image expanded after the bombing of Pearl Harbor, and white-generated rumors of spying circulated, including unsubstantiated stories of Japanese American farmers planting flowers in a pattern to guide attacking airplanes.[22]

California's attorney general (later U.S. chief justice), Earl Warren, depicted Japanese Americans as dangerous. In 1943, the West Coast General John DeWitt argued, "A Jap's a Jap. . . . The Japanese race is an enemy race, and while many second- and third-generation Japanese born on U.S. soil, possessed of U.S. citizenship, have become 'Americanized,' the racial strains are undiluted."[23] With no evidence, the national press argued there were many enemy agents in this "large alien population." Ironically, the main reason for this "alien" population was the racist law that prohibited Japanese immigrants from becoming U.S. citizens. Significantly, and contrary to recent books again trying to justify this World War II discrimination, *no* Japanese American was *ever* proven to have collaborated with the enemy during World War II—a reality that contrasts with that of German Americans, who included a few supporters of Hitler's regime but who (as whites) were never put into concentration camps on a large scale (discussed later).

After the war, some stereotypes slowly began to change. By the 1960s, new ones developed. Magazines and newspapers periodically praised Japanese Americans for being very acculturated and successful. However, as Dennis Ogawa noted, the "highly Americanized" and "successful citizens" stereotypes are not really positive, for they usually suggest that one must act "very white" to be a good U.S. citizen. The "model minority" stereotyping was, and continues to be, used to defend the overall U.S. record on racial matters (discussed later). It implies that because Japanese Americans have been English-speaking,

work-ethic models of virtue, they can now be accepted by whites as "better" than certain other non-European groups.[24]

Recent Distortions, Stereotypes, and Omissions

One study of Japanese American images in 1970s school textbooks found numerous distortions of Japanese American history along with the model minority stereotype. Most omitted the fact that U.S. employers in Hawaii and California brutally exploited Japanese laborers. In addition, few textbooks dealt with the Japanese American experience in U.S. concentration camps until the U.S. government apologized in the late 1980s. Today, analyses of textbooks have shown that many have finally included a mention of the wartime camps but still do not assess critically this illegal internment. Like recent best-selling popular books, many school textbooks—termed "whitewashed" by one *AsianWeek* commentator—view the wartime oppression of Japanese Americans as just part of the "hysteria of war," argue it was legitimate, and/or do not discuss the long history of anti-Japanese discrimination leading up to the imprisonment. One result is that many people are so uninformed about the concentration camp events that they now defend them, as did leading U.S. House member Howard Coble in 2003. On a talk show, the ill-informed Coble argued that the U.S. government did the right thing to protect national security, an assertion that provoked protests from civil rights groups. Similar ignorance of decades of research is revealed in recent books by conservative commentators, such as Michelle Malkin's book *In Defense of Internment*. These books downplay the oppressiveness of the concentration-camp experiences of Japanese Americans, thereby justifying past and present racial profiling (such as of Middle Eastern Americans) by the government. Such revisionist history has been strongly protested by civil rights organizations such as the Japanese American Citizens League and has been thoroughly refuted with much data by leading researchers. However, it is a sign of the inequality in communications in this society that such revisionist books have usually gotten far more attention in the public media than have the refutations of their arguments by experienced researchers and civil rights groups.[25]

Misperceptions remain commonplace. In the 1980s, Senator Spark Matsunaga of Hawaii, a Japanese American at a White House reception for visiting Japanese officials, was mistaken for the latter by U.S. Secretary of State Alexander Haig, who wished him a nice visit! In addition, Senator Daniel Inouye, a Japanese American who lost an arm fighting for the U.S. in World War II, has periodically received hate mail telling him he should "go home to Japan where he belongs." Japanese American and other Asian American officials have reported that whites frequently congratulate them on how well they speak English, as though they were foreign born. Many non-Asian Americans seem unaware that the United States has numerous Japanese American elected officials, that their birthplace is the United States, and that their native language is English.[26]

As we have seen in previous chapters, racist framing and actions often include mocking the language and cultures of Americans of color. On a radio show, U.S. Senator Alfonse D'Amato (R–N.Y.) once spoke in a mock Asian accent as he criticized a Japanese American judge who had *no* such accent and who, like D'Amato, was a third-generation American. Recently, a Chicago Cubs baseball player, Kosuke Fukudome, was mocked by offensive T-shirts that read "Horry Kow" (mocking language for "Holy Cow") on the front and his number on the back with a bear drawn with slanted eyes and oversized glasses. Apparently, many whites consider such mocking to be harmless and "humorous," yet Fukudome himself was offended by the shirt, and the Cubs management also condemned the shirt once the story broke in the newspapers.[27]

Previously we noted that several sports teams have discontinued use of stereotyped racial symbols of groups such as Native Americans. Similarly, Seattle's Shoreline Community College finally abandoned its Japanese Samurai Warrior mascot, a Japanese caricature. Still, racist caricatures of Japanese people periodically surface today in the media, in novels, in advertising, and on Internet websites. For example, a recent issue of *Nation's Restaurant News* had a restaurant ad with text urging people to "Come Face to Face with a New Oriental Tradition." Not only did it use the offensive term *Oriental* but it also portrayed a Japanese sumo wrestler about to face a heavyset white man in sumo garb. Numerous media ads and commentaries have presented images of sumo wrestlers in ignorant, caricatured, or mocking

ways. Such presentations of a very ancient, respected, and religion-linked (to Shinto religion) athletic profession constitute major insults to the Japanese people and culture.[28]

U.S. movies have often perpetuated racial stereotypes. Michael Crichton's famous novel, *Rising Sun*, and the 1990s movie made from it, developed old and racialized caricatures. Japanese characters in this mystery are portrayed as "inscrutable, technologically proficient, predatory aliens who . . . subsist through unpalatable foods, manipulate *everything* and *everyone*, and enjoy kinky, violent sex with white women." The Media Action Network, an organization formed to combat Asian stereotyping, initiated talks about the film's racist content with the movie company and organized demonstrations against the film.[29] Debates about negative Asian images in movies emerged again in the 2000s with the release of the Disney movie *Pearl Harbor*. The film's use of the derogatory epithet "Japs" and its one-sided portrayal of Japanese military actions in World War II resulted in an increase in anti-Japanese sentiment in some areas of the United States. Japanese Americans reported numerous derogatory comments from non-Asians because of the movie—responses that indicated that old racist stereotyping and prejudices are still alive. One California news report quoted Japanese American students who stated that others blamed them for starting World War II and called them derogatory epithets such as "Nips," "Japs," or "Chino."[30]

Moreover, late in 2009, Japanese American civil rights officials met with the head of Paramount Pictures about the racial stereotyping in the Paramount film *The Goods: Live Hard, Sell Hard*. In that movie a white car-dealership executive makes derogatory references to "Japs" and cites the Pearl Harbor attack as he manages to incite coworkers' violence against an Asian American employee. This mocking and derogatory use of "Japs" or "Jap" for the Japanese or for Japanese Americans is commonplace today. Thus, the Japanese American Citizens League has recently and strongly criticized the use of the word "*Jap*" as an abbreviation for Japan (correct is "Jpn") in televised Olympic swimming trials programs, a major newspaper's crossword puzzle, an episode of the NBC television program *Heroes*, toy doll packaging, motorcycle magazines, and tourist travel guides, as well as on a California nursery sign and on language-translation machines.[31]

Language mocking is commonplace. In the mid-1990s, a white disk jockey for a San Francisco radio station was suspended for anti-Asian comments and allowing callers to make anti-Asian remarks. He reportedly spoke of "stinking Japanese," told a Japanese American caller he would hate the Japanese forever, and predicted war with Japan. The station received vigorous complaints from Asian American groups. More recently, in 2006, a disc jockey at a Toledo radio station called Japanese and other Asian restaurants numerous times making offensive mock-Asian commentaries, such as "ching, chong, chung" and "me speakee no English," to those who answered. That same year, a talk-show host on the CBS radio network mocked an Asian Excellence Awards ceremony by playing a fake excerpt with "Asian men" saying things such as "ching chong, ching chong, ching chong." In addition, comedian Rosie O'Donnell used a repeated "ching chong" to mock Chinese speech on an ABC talk show. In the mid-2000s, the Adidas company was also criticized by civil rights groups for making shoes that had a negative caricature of a buck-toothed, slant-eyed Asian as a logo, an image like that used in earlier decades against Japanese and Chinese groups. Such aggressive stereotypes are integral parts of the old white racial framing of society and are therefore long-lasting.[32]

Repression and Violent Attacks

For more than a century Japanese Americans have suffered not only hostile racial framing but also economic discrimination and physical attacks. The first acts of violence came within a decade of their arrival. After the 1906 San Francisco earthquake, mob violence directed at Japanese Americans increased. Scientists sent by Japan to help with earthquake relief were attacked by white men, and major newspapers condoned such violent actions. Japanese businesses were boycotted, and shopkeepers were attacked. Anti-Japanese exclusion movements also sometimes turned to violence, as in California in 1921, when large numbers of Japanese farm workers were driven out of some areas by white farmers. Violent attacks again escalated at the beginning of World War II. In 1942, whites carried out dozens of violent attacks on Japanese Americans and their property, all along the West Coast.[33]

The Ugly Specter of U.S. Concentration Camps

Japanese military victories in the Pacific in the 1930s and 1940s, including the attack on Pearl Harbor, increased fear of a Japanese invasion of the U.S. mainland. Members of Congress and the media frequently parroted anti-Japanese stereotypes and thereby escalated fear of Japanese Americans across the country. By 1942, the "evacuation" and "relocation," to use the government's euphemistic terms, of Americans of Japanese ancestry was suggested by many whites. Some were motivated by economic self-interest; for example, the Western Growers Protective Association and similar white groups seemed committed to destroying Japanese American business competition.[34]

In the first major phase of federal action against Americans whose ancestry was linked to countries at war with the United States, a small number of Japanese, German, and Italian aliens were moved from sensitive areas and their travel was restricted. The second stage began with Executive Order 9066, issued on February 19, 1942, by President Franklin Roosevelt and validated by Congress, which instructed the secretary of war to establish areas from which any person could be excluded. The West Coast military commander established western California, Washington, and Oregon, and southern Arizona, as areas where no Japanese, Italian, or German aliens could reside. However, *only* those of Japanese ancestry—citizens and noncitizens alike—were detained in large numbers in assembly centers and transported under guard to barbed-wire concentration camps in the West.[35]

Japanese American businesses usually had to be sold at a loss. By the fall of 1942, inland areas in the West housed about 120,000 Japanese Americans, more than two-thirds native-born U.S. citizens whose only "crime" was to be perceived by whites as racially different.[36] Racial oppression took many forms. The administration at California's Tule Lake Camp arranged for inmates to be hired out as domestics at the very low wage of $30 per month. The camp administration spent some of these earnings on facilities for white personnel. Barracks were typically bare-board with few furnishings. Families were forced to live in small rooms or partitioned-off areas. Men, women, and children faced severe discrimination and the consequent psychological and physical stress.[37]

Japanese Americans forced out of their homes in San Francisco await transportation to U.S. concentration camps.

Japanese Americans protested their discriminatory treatment in numerous demonstrations; 6000 renounced their citizenship. Gradually, several thousand college students and workers on agricultural assignments were released, and others were allowed to join the Army, where many served in Europe with extraordinary valor in racially segregated units.[38] In 1944, the order to evacuate was rescinded. Most returned to the West Coast region and found their farms and businesses in white hands or in ruin, household goods destroyed, and whites hostile if not violent. The U.S. government spent about $250 million on the process of imprisonment; Japanese American losses are estimated to have been at least $400 million. The other human losses were incalculable.[39]

Why the Camps Were Created

The U.S. Supreme Court upheld the military decision—even though two-thirds of those imprisoned were U.S. citizens. This imprisonment was a clear violation of civil rights guaranteed by the U.S. Constitution. President Franklin Roosevelt believed that people of Japanese descent were racially inferior,

and he and other leaders saw the struggle in the Pacific as a *racial* war. Racist attitudes made it easier for top officials to intern U.S. citizens of Asian descent (but not large numbers of citizens of German descent) in barbed-wire concentration camps.[40]

Japanese Americans fought this oppression unsuccessfully in courts and with demonstrations. When evacuees confronted oppressive authorities at a California assembly center, some rioted. The freedom-oriented revolt was suppressed by armed police. In the fall of 1942, internees called a strike at the Poston camp to protest imprisonment.[41] In December 1942, at the Manzanar camp in California, an assault on a Japanese American who collaborated with whites and the imprisonment of the attacker led to a meeting attended by 4000 and demands for an investigation of camp conditions. The director, escorted by police armed with machine guns, met the crowd. A crowd again formed at night and was fired upon; two Japanese Americans were killed.[42] Ironically, this authoritarian, racialized oppression of U.S. citizens occurred at a time when the U.S. government was fighting a racist German Nazi regime and proclaiming the values of "freedom" and "democracy" to a war-torn world.

Later Impact

After World War II, Japanese Americans on the West Coast continued to face economic discrimination and violent attacks. The epithet "Jap" became commonplace in white comments and anti-Japanese graffiti. Hate crimes—including murders, assaults, threats, and other harassment—targeting Japanese and other Asian Americans in their homes, businesses, and places of employment and on the streets have persisted now well into the twenty-first century. Indeed, the fastest-growing category of hate crimes in recent decades has been that involving Asian Americans as targets.[43]

One can also see the effects of the concentration-camp experience in many areas of the lives of Japanese Americans today (discussed more later). Here, consider one individual example: the recent court martial of Lieutenant Ehren Watada, a U.S. Army officer of Japanese and Chinese descent. A fine student and Eagle Scout, he joined the Army in the early 2000s for patriotic reasons. When ordered to go to Iraq, and after careful study of the Iraq invasion rationale, he decided the war violated U.S. law and became the first commissioned officer to refuse to be sent to the war zone. The Army decided to court-martial him, rejecting his arguments. The charges included his public comments critical of the war. His parents, veterans for peace groups, and civil liberties groups supported his decision, often strongly, but the Japanese American community was divided, with Representative Michael Honda speaking on behalf of his conscientious stand, while several Japanese American veterans groups condemned his actions. Interestingly, in one interview Watada directly connected his conscientious stand with that of Japanese Americans during the World War II concentration camp era who had stood up to that political oppression. His first court-martial in 2007 ended in a mistrial, and a second court-martial was blocked by a federal judge, a decision the U.S. Army appealed. However, in 2009, President Barack Obama's Justice Department sought a dismissal of the case, which was finally granted in May 2009.[44]

 What have been some long-term socioeconomic consequences of Japanese American internment in U.S. concentration camps?

The Political Arena

Because of racist U.S. naturalization laws, the Issei and other first-generation Asian Americans were not allowed to become citizens until the 1950s. Thus, they could not be active politically. However, political organizations were gradually created in the 1930s, when some Nisei (second generation) formed political clubs in West Coast cities. Formed in 1929, the Japanese American Citizens League (JACL), under Nisei leadership, initially advocated accommodation strategies of self-help and pressed moderately for civil rights and voter registration. The oldest Asian American civil rights organization, the JACL soon began to press more aggressively for the expansion and enforcement of civil rights laws and regulations.[45]

Compensation Pressures and Political Progress

Since World War II, the JACL, working with other Japanese American organizations, has won important political and legal victories. By 1946, the JACL and some newer organizations were pressing for compensation for the imprisonment losses, citizenship for the first generation, and changes in discriminatory laws. Meager compensation for business and property losses came with the 1948 Japanese American Evacuation Act; Japanese American recipients were paid less than 10 percent of actual losses.[46]

These organizations continued to press the government for adequate repayment for losses. As advocates for the country's "liberty and justice" tradition, they helped secure public admission of racial discrimination. In 1987, after years of foot-dragging by congressional leaders and initial opposition from the White House, Congress passed a bill, which President Ronald Reagan signed into law, that provided $1.2 billion in reparations. The law contained an admission that the "basic civil liberties" of Japanese Americans were violated because of "racial prejudice" and included a formal apology.[47] Finally, by 1994, all reparations checks were mailed. Each internee, or his or her heirs, received a modest $20,000. President George H. W. Bush wrote each a letter of apology. Some, such as U.S. Representative Robert Matsui of California, refused the check but accepted the apology.[48] Not all Americans were willing to see Japanese Americans receive justice. In Oxnard, California, for example, non-Asians unable to distinguish between Japanese Americans, who are U.S. citizens, and the Japanese government, circulated anti-Japanese leaflets that claimed that no apology to Japanese Americans for unconstitutional imprisonment was necessary because the Japanese government had detained U.S. soldiers in World War II.[49]

In 2001, a memorial to Japanese Americans who were incarcerated and to Japanese American soldiers who served in the U.S. military was dedicated in Washington, DC.[50] Since then, several "never again" monuments have been established in West Coast areas, such as on Bainbridge Island, Washington (where the first detainment took place), to memorialize the experiences of Japanese Americans. Congress has also recently approved funding to preserve some of the internment camps as historical monuments. In addition, pressure from Japanese American civil rights organizations in the 1970s helped win repeal of Title II of the 1950 Internal Security Act, which permitted government imprisonment of U.S. citizens deemed potential collaborators with an enemy in time of crisis, and the rescinding of Executive Order 9066, which ordered wartime imprisonment of Japanese Americans.[51] These were actions of significance for the civil rights of all U.S. citizens.

Government Officials

In 1930, the first Japanese Americans were elected to the territorial legislature of Hawaii. Later on, World War II veterans, intent on expanding participation, became active in Democratic attempts to replace the Republican domination of those islands, and several were elected to the legislature. Their efforts facilitated Congress's conferral of statehood on Hawaii in the 1950s. Statehood had been opposed for the racially diverse islands by some white politicians, such as rabidly racist Senator Strom Thurmond (R–S.C.).[52]

War hero Daniel Inouye was elected the first U.S. representative from the new state and the first Japanese American to ever serve in Congress. In 1962, Spark Matsunaga became the second to serve in the House, when Inouye was elected to the U.S. Senate. In 1964, a second House seat was won by Patsy Takemoto Mink, the first Japanese American woman, and first woman of color, to serve in Congress.[53] In 2010, Inouye and Daniel Akaka, the

latter of native Hawaiian and Chinese American ancestry, were Hawaii's U.S. senators.

Political victories on the mainland have been difficult because of the dilution of Japanese American votes in predominantly non-Asian populations. Few have been elected until recent decades. In the 1960s, several were elected to city offices in Los Angeles County, Oakland, and San Jose, California. In 1972, Carl Ooka was elected county commissioner in Washington state, the first Japanese American elected to office in that state. Since the 1970s, only a handful of mainland Japanese Americans have held elected positions at higher levels. In the 1970s, Samuel Hayakawa was elected U.S. senator from California, the first on the mainland, and Norman Mineta of California became the first mainland representative of Japanese descent to the U.S. House. Robert Matsui was elected in 1978 and remained alone until 2001 when he was joined by fellow Californian Michael Honda, also Japanese American. In 2006, Mazie Hirono was elected to the U.S. House from Hawaii, the first Japan-born person elected there. As of 2010, Hirono, Honda, and Matsui's wife Doris (elected in 2005 to replace Matsui after his

Norman Mineta, a leading Japanese American official, has served in the cabinets of Democratic and Republican presidents.

death), together with Senator Inouye, were the Japanese American members of Congress.

Only two Japanese Americans have ever held a presidential cabinet post. Norman Mineta was appointed Secretary of Commerce by Bill Clinton in 2000. In 2001, he became Secretary of Transportation in the George W. Bush administration. In 2009, Eric Shinseki, the first Japanese American (and Asian American) to become a top general and Army chief of staff, became Barack Obama's Secretary of Veterans Affairs. In spite of these advancements, the Japanese American population and the Asian-Pacific American population generally remain seriously underrepresented in federal elective and appointed positions, including the federal court system. Just 1 percent of federal judges (8 of 850) are currently from this group, although Asian-Pacific Americans make up 5 percent of the U.S. population. In 2009, President Barack Obama did appoint three new Asian-Pacific American judges in California.[54]

Historically, many Asian Americans, including Japanese Americans, have been reluctant to participate actively in politics out of fear of intensifying discrimination against their group. Even in the past decade or so, Japanese and other Asian Americans have been less likely than whites to register or vote. Researchers have speculated that many Asian Americans tend to view politicians as disreputable or to vote for white politicians rather than run their own candidates because they feel whites have "more political clout."[55]

Japanese and other Asian Americans who venture into the political arena sometimes encounter overtly racist reactions. For example, in 1992, a Democratic Party leader at a Spokane, Washington, party meeting referred to owners of a local hotel as "chinks." Later, at a meeting to examine the incident, the party's white vice-chair bowed and clasped her hands in front of her in response to a Japanese American participant who would not shake her hand. This mocking gesture combined with the racial slur led the JACL to sue the state party for discrimination.[56]

Politics, Stereotyping, and Competition with Japan

Acts of vandalism and other violence by whites against Japanese Americans have often been motivated by fear of economic competition from Japan. For example, an exhibit at a 1980s Flint, Michigan,

auto show portrayed a car with a Japanese face falling like a bomb on Detroit.[57] In recent decades, Japan's economic development has surpassed that of the United States in some areas. In response, "Buy American" cartoons featuring caricatures of "wily Japs" and "crafty Orientals" have periodically appeared in U.S. media. Old racist stereotypes have reappeared on the Internet, in public conversations among whites, and in newspaper articles. Increasing unemployment in local and national recessions of the 1980s–2000s era have periodically fueled a tendency among some non-Asians to blame the Japanese, Chinese, and other Asians for U.S. troubles. This scapegoating is sometimes reflected in political action. Anti-Japanese and other anti-Asian protectionist bills have periodically been introduced in Congress. Yet, congressional and other critics have often ignored Japanese and other Asian investments in the U.S. that create thousands of jobs. U.S. recessions are not the result of Japan's investments or its competitive economy; the real causes lie elsewhere—often in poor U.S. corporate management and in capital flight.[58]

In 1992, a Japanese businessperson was killed in the Los Angeles area. Not long before, he had been threatened by a man who blamed him for a U.S. economic recession. And in Beaumont, Texas, a Japanese American resident who tried to get a road sign reading "Jap Road" changed received hate mail and death threats. Clearly, anti-Japanese hostility among non-Asians can still turn to threats or violence today.[59]

Protest Organizations and Group Pride

Voluntary associations were formed in the early 1900s to combat anti-Japanese discrimination. Japanese workers in Hawaii participated in work stoppages to protest poor conditions, and substantial labor organizing took place on the mainland, with strikes for better wages and work conditions from the 1890s onward. Japanese American workers were involved in agricultural and mining strikes in California, Utah, Colorado, and Washington. However, white labor leaders often blocked admission of Japanese Americans into white-run unions with the old racist argument that the latter were racially unassimilable.[60]

Japanese Americans protested incarceration in World War II concentration camps; thousands renounced their citizenship and returned to Japan after the war. Later, during the 1960s, new pan-Asian organizations and publications appeared, often established by younger generations. *Amerasia Journal* and similar journals urged collective attention and action in regard to major problems of Japanese and other Asian Americans, including discrimination.[61] Helping to stimulate new scholarship on Asian Americans questioning traditional white stereotyped views and providing a more honest appraisal of U.S. history, numerous colleges and universities have developed Asian American studies programs, including campuses of the University of California and the California State University, the University of Washington, and the University of Hawaii.[62]

In recent years, hate crimes directed against Japanese and other Asian Americans have persisted on and off college campuses. For example, in the late 1990s, a naturalized U.S. citizen from El Salvador, writing under the alias "Asian hater," and upset by successful Japanese and other Asian American students at the University of California, was sentenced to a year in prison for emailing death threats to Asian students.[63] Serious racist incidents on college and high school campuses have been protested numerous times by civil rights organizations since that time. For example, in 2009, the Midwest office of the JACL sent a strong protest letter to the police department in Lancaster, Pennsylvania, asking for a major investigation of a racial attack on three Asian students at Franklin and Marshall College in that city. A group of young people (apparently white students) hurled racist insults at them and assaulted them. Because of such hostility, which often increases as the number of Asian American students on historically white campuses grows, many Japanese American and other Asian American students have become more interested in development of strong Asian American organizations and academic programs on these campuses.[64]

In addition, other recent off-campus hate crimes reported and condemned by the JACL involved a southern California white man who was proud of being a tough "whitey" drug dealer. He was sent to prison for life for killing three Asian Americans, including an Asian American waitress, at a bar in a Japanese American community in San Francisco.[65]

The Economy

Most Japanese immigrants started out at the bottom of the U.S. economic pyramid, filling hard farming,

mining, and construction jobs. One California study in 1909 found 65 percent of Japanese American workers in agriculture, 15 percent in domestic service, 15 percent in small businesses, and 5 percent in other work. In many areas Japanese workers did much of the difficult "dirty work" and generally were paid less than whites.[66]

Finding an Economic Niche

Gradually, many first-generation immigrants (Issei) found land to farm on their own. Although the amount of land was not large, their economic role was important. In some areas they grew most of certain important food crops. Some created small businesses in urban areas in which institutionalized discrimination barred them from manufacturing and white-collar employment. The Issei came to play a "middleman minority" role in some western states (see Chapter 2). Operated on a small scale, some of their enterprises catered primarily to a Japanese American clientele, but many eventually served non-Asians. Issei solidarity created a niche economy, and this small-business economy in turn reinforced group solidarity. Sociologists Bonacich and Modell conclude that "the Japanese minority filled a particular and specialized niche in the western economy and was important to it, providing key products and services."[67]

Most early immigrants came from just eleven Japanese prefectures, and each was represented by an association in the United States. These prefectural clubs became mutual-aid associations for immigrants caught in a racially hostile environment. They aided immigrants' movement into the economy by providing training for workers and directing clients to small businesses. Businesses succeeded because they could draw on prefectural networks for workers and loans. Informal money-pooling organizations called *tanomoshi* provided modest capital for entrepreneurs who could not secure funds from white-owned banks.[68]

Opposition to Japanese immigrant workers and entrepreneurs came swiftly. In urban areas, white-controlled labor movements often led the opposition, using boycotts and anti-Japanese advertising. One such action by the Anti-Jap Laundry League attempted to drive Japanese Americans out of the laundry business.[69] A 1913 California Alien Land Law, passed under pressure from white farmers, stipulated that "aliens" could not buy land or lease it for more than three years. (Recall that all Issei were forced to remain "aliens" because of naturalization laws.)[70] This California law interfered with agricultural activity, but some found ways to circumvent it, such as by registering land ownership under children's names. Discriminatory laws significantly reduced the number of Japanese American farms. These laws were passed in other states and remained on the books of Florida, New Mexico, Kansas, and Wyoming into the twenty-first century.[71]

Those forced out of farming or otherwise attracted to cities often became gardeners or nursery operators. The 1930 California census showed that half of male Japanese workers were in agriculture or gardening, one-fourth were in trade or business, 2 percent were in the professions, and most of the rest were in other urban occupations.[72] By the beginning of World War II, some were moving into white-collar positions. Half the Japanese American men in Los Angeles County in 1940 held white-collar positions; most of the rest had blue-collar jobs.[73] Then their economy collapsed. Median economic losses per family in Los Angeles from the wartime imprisonment were estimated at about $10,000 (in 1940 dollars) in goods, property, income, and expenses. Losses were similar elsewhere.

Researching the labor of women before World War II, Evelyn Nakano Glenn found that "from the moment they arrived, Japanese American women labored alongside the men to secure their own and their families' livelihood."[74] Much hard work done by Issei women was unpaid family labor, but some worked as domestic servants for whites. Before World War II, discrimination kept Japanese American women out of the white-collar work available to European immigrant women. Domestic workers often resisted their oppression in covert ways, such as by evading work pressed on them by exploitative employers. Resistance gave them a sense of self-reliance, which was critical for their personal and political development and that of their children. They sometimes struggled against husbands as well; subordination to white women in domestic employment was often reinforced by subordination to husbands at home. Yet, these Japanese American women struggled to maintain dignity, and "despite the menial nature of employment, the Issei achieved a sense of their own strength, and in some cases, superiority to employer and husband within their own area of competence."[75]

 What methods have been used by Japanese Americans to resist racial discrimination?

The Postwar Economy

As the need for labor grew in the booming postwar economy, white employers finally began to hire Japanese Americans. Racial discrimination persisted, however, keeping the second generation (Nisei) out of numerous occupations. University of California education departments discouraged Japanese American students from considering the teaching profession because of difficulties in placement. Self-employment continued to be important. By 1960, there were 7000 Japanese-owned businesses in Los Angeles. The "middleman" model seems to fit the Issei well, but second and later generations have gradually moved away from the small business niche economy to professional and other white-collar jobs. In 1960, half the Nisei were involved in niche businesses, but many others had used educations funded by parents to move into good white-collar jobs.[76]

Occupational Mobility, Income, and Persisting Employment Barriers

Numerous popular and scholarly books and articles have related the postwar Japanese American experience as a story of great achievement. The usual socioeconomic indicators in census data show that the Japanese Americans' progress since the 1950s has indeed been dramatic. For those reporting only Japanese ancestry, in 2008, both men and women were more likely to hold managerial or professional jobs than were their white counterparts (53.7 percent versus 36.1 percent for men; 50.8 percent versus 41.7 percent for women). These occupational percentages are only a little lower when those with partial Japanese ancestry are added in. In the late 2000s, moreover, Japanese Americans' unemployment rate was less than that of whites (3.0 percent versus 5.2 percent). If those with partial Japanese ancestry were added in, the unemployment rate climbed to 4.5 percent.[77]

Income data reveal economic success. According to the 2008 census survey of those reporting only Japanese ancestry, the median income for families was substantially more than that for white families ($83,762 versus $70,835). Income for families with partial Japanese ancestry was only a little less ($81,779). In addition, only a small percentage of Japanese American families (4.7 percent) fell below the federal poverty line—a figure lower than for whites (6.1 percent). Note, however, that Japanese American workers are significantly concentrated in a few states, especially Hawaii and California, with both high wages *and* a high cost of living.[78]

Although Japanese Americans have achieved significant socioeconomic success, they still face exclusion from certain positions in many business, entertainment, political, and civil service areas, regardless of their abilities. Examinations of television and Hollywood filmmaking in recent decades have found relatively few Japanese and other Asian American actors, except in stereotypical positions such as gardener, geisha, tourist, martial arts expert, or gangster. One recent examination of television programs on major networks found continuing underrepresentation—with slight improvements recently in the number of Asian American actors in key roles but a *decline* in the number of Asian American writers and producers.[79]

A similar problem persists in Hollywood. In numerous movies, past and present, Hollywood executives have portrayed Asian characters using white actors, reducing opportunities for Asian American actors. Moreover, movies like *Orange County* (2002), a county with a large Asian American population, have no Asian American characters or actors. Even the film *21* (2008), based on a true story of an Asian American MIT professor and his mostly Asian American students outfoxing casinos, had white actors in lead roles. Another recent example is Paramount Pictures' *The Last Airbender* (2010). Although based on an animated television series set in an Asian world, where lead characters are all Asian and Inuit/Yupik, white actors were chosen for all four leading movie roles. This discriminatory reality generated large-scale protests by civil rights groups, including the Media Action Network for Asian Americans (MANAA), and thousands of fans in a letter-writing campaign. Apparently, Hollywood producers often feel white audiences cannot relate to movies with several Asian American actors in lead roles. The MANAA organization has put out a memo to Hollywood that lays out the numerous ways Hollywood executives create in some films negative portrayals of Japanese Americans, other Asian Americans, and Asians generally—such as by using racist epithets, showing Asians only in certain clichéd occupations, accenting Asian racial features and accents, and having the few Asian actors that are in the films act in stereotyped comic or criminal ways. In this way, Hollywood executives communicate a stereotyped Asian image in movie theaters across the globe.[80]

Note also that the direct discrimination motivated by anti-Asian stereotypes and the indirect discrimination in the form of white-normed height and weight requirements have played a restrictive role for Asian American entry into, and promotion in, occupations such as firefighters, police officers, and flight attendants. Most protective service agencies, such as the New Haven Fire Department, which was made famous in the *Ricci* (2009) Supreme Court firefighters' case, have very few or no Asian American employees, often because the latter are stereotyped as "foreign" or "weak."[81]

Moreover, while Japanese Americans and other Asian Americans (and Pacific Islanders) are about 5 percent of the population, currently their percentage on boards of *Fortune 100* companies is only 2.2 percent. And only two of these current board members are Japanese Americans. Most corporate boards have no Asian American representation. The same problem exists for top corporate executive positions. Only four Asian Americans (all Asian-Indian) are currently chairs or CEOs of a *Fortune 500* company. Even in the San Francisco area, where Asian Americans are one-fourth of the population, and probably even more of the professional workforce, a recent study found that in the largest 25 corporations headquartered in the area Asian Americans hold only 5.5 percent of corporate board positions and 9.3 percent of corporate executive-officer positions.[82]

Japanese and other Asian American employees often face a "glass ceiling" in corporations or exclusion from business networks. (A **glass ceiling** is *an unwritten policy in some organizations that limits* *advancement of certain people based on their racial group or gender.*) Top corporate executives, typically white men, have argued that Asian Americans are best as technical workers and not as executives who need excellent "people skills." Asian Americans may be hired as engineers, computer experts, or technicians, but they are frequently not considered for the higher administrative, managerial, and professional levels in numerous corporations and agencies. Moreover, knowing about that type of stereotyping, many younger Asian Americans have pursued scientific and technical educations and rejected the humanities, social sciences, and business disciplines. The "promotion ceiling" also exists in higher education. One recent study estimated that the ratio of Asian American college administrators to Asian American college faculty and professionals is a little more than one-third that for other major racial groups. In addition, Japanese Americans and other Asian Americans remain significantly underrepresented in the upper administrative positions in many federal government agencies.[83]

Blatant discrimination still occurs in numerous major institutions. For example, a third-generation Japanese American, Bruce Yamashita, entered a Marine Corps' Officer Candidate School. A talented man with a law degree, Yamashita faced overt discrimination from the first day, when a sergeant told him to "go back to your own country." A fellow candidate asked why he had not joined the Japanese army. No officers intervened to stop the harassment, and Yamashita was terminated for "leadership failure." In 1994, after a legal battle during which Yamashita, with the assistance of the JACL, uncovered a pattern of military discrimination against non-European American officer candidates, the Secretary of the Navy finally commissioned Yamashita a captain in the Marine Corps.[84]

Similarly hostile racial climates have been found in other workplace settings. For example, in the spring of 2009, one JACL office pressed the Missouri Commission on Human Relations to take action to end the workplace discrimination faced by a Japanese American truck driver at the hands of a fellow employee who repeatedly used racist slurs against him. And at a Veteran's Administration hospital in Indianapolis an employee requested that an old framed newspaper article headlined "Japs Surrender" be removed, but the removal was resisted by retired white Marines. A JACL official had to explain to these white veterans the offensiveness of the racialized term.[85]

Education

Racism and Early Segregation

The Issei had a strong commitment to education, and most viewed education as a way to escape arduous farm and nursery jobs and secure better-paying positions. Parents enrolled children in school more often than most other immigrant parents, and many pursued formal education themselves. However, they faced much opposition. In 1906, the white mayor of San Francisco, in a move supported by newspapers, secured a resolution from the board of education establishing a segregated public school for Asian American children. Reflecting white fears of "racial mixing," one legislator spoke aggressively of the danger to "pure maids of California" posed by older Japanese students in primary grades. The Japanese government protested, and the U.S. government took action to force the San Francisco board to give Japanese American children the equal rights promised by a U.S.–Japan treaty. White Californians were so angered by this rare federal show of support for Japanese Americans that they talked of *state secession*. President Theodore Roosevelt and local officials worked out a compromise allowing most Japanese American children into integrated schools. In exchange, Roosevelt executed the infamous Gentlemen's Agreement, which terminated most Japanese immigration.[86]

Japanese Americans also developed their own schools to educate children in the Japanese language and culture. By 1928, there were more than 4000 pupils in 118 schools. White supremacists vigorously attacked language schools as centers of emperor worship and Buddhism that they alleged made children "disloyal" to the United States.[87]

Educational Progress

By the 1930s, Japanese Americans were making great strides, from primary grades to college, despite widespread discrimination. Data on University of California branches indicated that the ratio of Japanese American college students there to the Japanese American population was a little higher than the comparable student figure for the total population.

A 1930 survey showed that Japanese Americans' educational attainments were equal to those of whites in California.[88]

Wartime imprisonment interrupted these educational pursuits. Many second- and third-generation Japanese Americans received some schooling behind barbed wire. After the war, the educational gains resumed. In recent decades the median educational level for adult Japanese Americans has been substantially higher than that for all adult Americans. Recent American Community Survey data for those reporting only Japanese ancestry, who were twenty-five and older, showed that most (93.5 percent) had a high school education or higher, and 46.3 percent had a bachelor's degree or higher, compared with 90.1 percent and 30.7 percent of whites, respectively. These figures change only slightly when those with partial Japanese ancestry are added in.[89]

However, racial discrimination persists. Japanese Americans and other Asian Americans in elementary and secondary schools, as well as colleges, are often targets of hostile racialized actions. Recall the hate crimes at colleges mentioned previously: The "Asian hater" who emailed death threats to Asian American students at the University of California, and the (apparently white student) group that attacked Asian students on the Franklin and Marshall College campus. Moreover, in January 2009 the JACL publicly condemned yet another attack on two Japanese American high school students who were targeted and taunted by other students with racial slurs such as "Jap," "flat face," and "Asian bitch"—and told to "Go back to where you came from." One newspaper report detailed how the students had been racially harassed, physically threatened, and mocked *for many years* by other students and mistreated by some school personnel in their predominantly white schools in northern California. In a letter to the school superintendent the JACL noted that these Japanese American children "are Americans—Asian Americans—and those who either don't accept or understand that fact require a lesson in American history and tolerance."[90] In this last case the school officials had been slow to develop substantial diversity training. Such inaction is unsurprising, given that Asian Americans remain seriously underrepresented in higher administrative positions in many public education settings, often because of continuing stereotypes about their personalities, foreignness, or technical abilities.[91]

Religion

Japanese immigrants brought Buddhism and Shintoism—still the main religions in Japan—and these religious traditions became important in the United States. Once immigrants arrived, white missionaries tried to convert many to Christian beliefs. Protestant missions were crucibles of acculturation in which many young Japanese Americans began to absorb the language and values of the dominant culture.[92]

By the 1920s, there were many Buddhist temples, which often adopted Protestant-Christian-style Sunday schools and church organizations. White exclusionists, ignorant of the fact that Buddhism does *not* involve emperor worship, claimed the temples were hotbeds of emperor worship and antipatriotic teaching.[93] Jingoistic agitation branded Buddhism (and Shintoism) as un-American, and for decades some temples have been vandalized. After World War II, the number increased as Buddhism regained its important position in local communities. Japanese Americans founded the Buddhist Churches of America, the oldest U.S. Buddhist group, one involving Jodo Shinshu Buddhism. Today, there are many Buddhist temples across the country, including yet other types of Buddhist groups brought by other Asian immigrants.[94]

Many Japanese Americans are members of Protestant churches today. A San Francisco study found that churches of various kinds were second in importance only to family in cementing the community together; a majority of respondents were at least occasional participants in church activities. One trend that has emerged in recent decades is an emphasis on pan-ethnic Protestant churches, which include members from several Asian groups. Moreover, the percentage of Buddhists has declined in recent years. Buddhist groups tend to attract older members; younger Japanese Americans tend to prefer Protestant churches, or no religion at all.[95]

Yet, there has been some resurgence of interest in Buddhism in recent decades among many Americans, Asian and non-Asian. Buddhist festivals have been celebrated in Japanese and other Asian communities. Colonel Ellison Onizuka, the first Asian

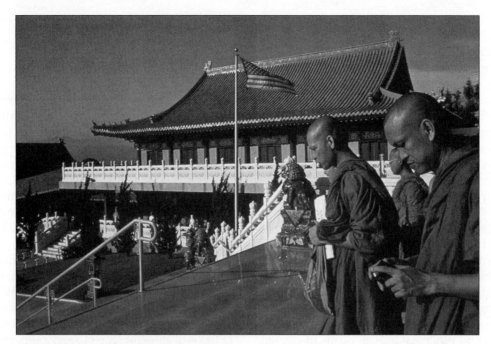

A Buddhist temple in Los Angeles.

American in space (who died in the 1986 *Challenger* explosion), was a member of the Buddhist Churches of America. His Buddhist funeral made many people aware of the significance of U.S. Buddhists. We might also note that a recent (2008) survey of Asian Americans found that one-fifth indicated their religious affiliation was with an Asian religion such as Buddhism, whereas 27 percent said they had no affiliation and 38 percent said they were affiliated with some Christian denomination. This marks a significant shift from the religious affiliations of majorities of the populations in the Asian countries such as Japan from which they or their ancestors came.[96]

Assimilation Perspectives

Japanese Americans have received much attention in social science and popular theorizing about their group adaptation. Early on, many whites considered Japanese Americans to be "unassimilable." In recent decades, however, many white (and other) social scientists and popular analysts have adopted a strong assimilation perspective and heralded Japanese Americans as probably the most assimilated to the Euro-American core culture of all Americans of color.

Because relatively few Japanese immigrants have come to the U.S. in recent decades, Japanese

Americans' ties to the home country are often not as strong as for other Asian American groups. Most were born in the U.S. and have grown up under the pressures of the dominant culture and white-controlled institutions.

An assimilation theorist might argue that some cultural assimilation came at an early point for most Issei. Some sought to acculturate rapidly, at least in those areas where acculturation was permitted, while maintaining strong ties to relatives and friends. Yet, many sought to survive racial discrimination by socially isolating and immersing themselves in things Japanese. Historically, Issei influence in the Japanese community was wide-ranging, but their ability to cope with the dominant culture was restricted by massive discrimination. Cultural assimilation, especially with regard to language, religion, and orientation to white-collar employment, has come rapidly for later generations. Second-generation Nisei became bicultural and operated successfully in their communities and in Euro-American institutions. Studies of third-generation Sansei and fourth-generation Yonsei underscore the significant closing of the gap with certain important aspects of the dominant culture. In one study, Nisei and Sansei respondents showed substantial acculturation in that they spoke mostly English and seldom read Japanese literature.

By the late 1980s, about half of Japanese Americans in Los Angeles spoke English only, the highest proportion for any Asian American group.[97]

A 1990s study of Japanese and Chinese Americans in California found that later generations were highly oriented to the norms of white middle-class culture and retained few Japanese and Chinese traditions. They chose to keep only the parts of ancestral cultures fitting their current way of life. One analyst asserted, "What they have retained of cultural traditions is largely symbolic and a novelty."[98] However, a deeper assessment of their worldview would likely have shown strong continuity with some basic values of parents and grandparents, particularly with regard to family, community, and education.

By the 1990s and 2000s, some important community institutions were in decline. Several civic organizations have disappeared; major Japanese American newspapers have ceased publication. In the 2000s, *Rafu Shimpo,* a Japanese American newspaper in publication since 1903, has been changing, such as by adding an Internet website; today, it reports only 45,000 daily readers. This is the largest remaining Japanese American paper (and largest bilingual newspaper in the U.S.) and now covers issues relating to all Asian Americans. Current readers are often younger-generation Japanese Americans, as well as more recent Asian immigrants and their children.[99]

Structural assimilation at secondary-group levels has been significant for Japanese Americans, particularly in the economy. Typically, second- and later-generation families have achieved relatively high levels of education, income, and occupational position. Explanations for this success tend to focus on work, family values, and community or economic organization. Sociologist Ivan Light, for example, has opted for a traditional-culture explanation for the Japanese American small-business economy—a niche economy that in his view sets them apart from African and Mexican Americans. Light emphasizes the role of a "culturally preferred style of economic organization," by which he means rotating-credit associations and similar organizations established by Japanese immigrants and their children.[100]

What Milton Gordon refers to as behavior-receptional assimilation and attitude-receptional assimilation showed little change for Japanese Americans until after World War II. Blatant discrimination and prejudice severely marred the

lives of Issei and Nisei for the first sixty years. Since World War II, overt racial discrimination and prejudice have decreased. In the early 1900s, Japanese Americans were seen by whites as the "lowest of the low." But, according to analysts such as Paul Spickard, by the 1980s, whites did "not see them as very different from themselves, and that fact is remarkable."[101] However, Spickard mainly judges white attitudes indirectly from such factors as relatively high rates of Japanese American intermarriage with whites.

Analysts such as Spickard, however, are too optimistic in equating intermarriage rates with consistently positive white views. In recent decades, as the studies cited previously show, white stereotyping and discrimination have periodically been directed at Japanese and other Asian Americans. Thus, in one 1980s survey, one-fifth of those surveyed reported experiencing considerable discrimination as adults; another 65 percent reported a little discrimination. Three-fourths felt that Japanese Americans as a group did experience discrimination. Moreover, numerous in-depth interviews with Japanese and other Asian Americans in the 2000s by Rosalind Chou have shown that the majority still experience *substantial* levels of subtle, blatant, and/or covert discrimination, although such discrimination rarely gets the attention of social scientists or the media.[102]

Assimilation analysts often accent assimilation at the level of primary social ties and voluntary associations. Integration in these areas did not occur to any significant degree until after World War II. During the post-1950s decades, researchers found that primary-group integration with outsiders was relatively limited for the Nisei, but more extensive for younger generations. By the 1960s and 1970s, a majority of Japanese Americans were living in neighborhoods where at least half their neighbors were white. Much research suggests a trend toward significant primary-group assimilation since the 1960s, especially for those who moved away from urban areas that had a critical mass of Japanese Americans.[103]

Until the late 1940s, laws in western states made Asian–white marriages officially illegal. Los Angeles data show an out-marriage rate of just 2 percent in the years between 1924 and 1933 and a rate of 11 to 20 percent for the 1950s.[104] Some decades later, 1990 census data on intermarriage indicated that for Japanese Americans in California the out-marriage rates to whites was relatively high—13 percent for men and 28 percent for women. Moreover, an examination of the most recent (2006) census data for Japanese Americans found that 63.9 percent of husbands and 47.4 percent of wives had Japanese spouses, while 9.9 percent of husbands and 6.4 percent of wives were married to other Asian Americans. Some 19.7 percent of husbands had white wives, with 38.2 percent of wives having white husbands—significant increases since 1990. (The others who were intermarried had black or "other" spouses.) Nonetheless, a majority were married within the Asian American umbrella group.[105]

Viewed from Gordon's concept of identificational assimilation, few Japanese Americans have rejected their Japanese cultural heritage or identity. They hold this identity for positive reasons, yet it is also imposed by non-Asians who view them as "foreigners." In recent interviews with many third- and later-generation Japanese and Chinese Americans, Mia Tuan found that, although they were significantly assimilated along important dimensions, a substantial majority had a strong sense of a racialized identity because whites imposed the identity of "foreigner" on them. As a result, they felt themselves caught between worlds, as "forever foreigners." In their daily lives most must be bicultural, with a foot in two cultural worlds. One 1980s study asked Japanese Americans whether they saw differences in Japanese American and white American orientations toward social affairs, church life, and family relations. Large percentages saw significant differences. In addition, most did not consider that they were assimilating rapidly to the dominant culture in regard to family and religious orientations.[106]

Younger Japanese Americans are retaining some distinctive organizations and traditions. Where possible, many younger Japanese and other Asian American college students have joined Asian American fraternities and sororities (today, about 65 with 420 branches) rather than white-dominated organizations, which often have a history of racial discrimination. The Sansei and Yonsei have maintained numerous Japanese American rituals, parades, and festivals. Although the number of geographical concentrations ("Japantowns") has declined, significant family and community connections and networks remain, even for many who have intermarried. One entrepreneur has noted, "The community's alive and well and thriving. What's declining are these historical and geographic icons like Japantowns."[107]

Surveys of Japanese American college students reveal that, although the students show signs of significant acculturation to the core culture and support interracial marriage, most hold important values close to those of their parents—with regard to family, community, hard work, and education. Many of the students report being most comfortable with people of Asian descent.[108]

Kitano and Daniels suggest that Japanese and other Asian Americans can be grouped into major categories based on (1) degree of overall assimilation to the dominant Eurocentric culture and institutions and (2) the strength of what they term "ethnic identity." Among Japanese (and other Asian) Americans, many in third and later generations are in a "high assimilation, low ethnic identity" category. They have made many adaptations to the dominant Anglo American culture in language and lifestyle and retain weak ties to the traditional culture. They have strong social ties to whites or are married to whites. In contrast, another large group belongs to a "high assimilation, high ethnic identity" category. They move easily in Japanese American culture and the dominant culture. In contrast with the first group, they are more knowledgeable about Japanese American history and culture and have a stronger racial–ethnic identity. A third, much smaller group includes those who immigrated in recent decades and those who have spent most of their lives within Japanese American communities; they belong to a "low assimilation, high ethnic identity" category. Marriages are only within the Japanese American group; Japanese identity is very strong. Still, assimilation is incomplete even for the first two subgroups because many whites still regard Japanese Americans as racially and ethnically distinct, and this visibility forces "the retention of ethnic identity, no matter how slight."[109]

One might view Japanese Americans as an example of Greeley's concept of ethnogenesis—partly in but partly outside the dominant European American culture and society. To our knowledge, no analyst has yet developed this perspective for Japanese Americans, although Petersen argued that this group has become a U.S. "subnation," achieving integration in the economy and making some cultural adaptation, but often maintaining family-centered communities and networks.[110]

Younger generations of Japanese Americans are among the most integrated of all non-European groups into European American culture and communities. How this will develop in the future is unclear. The level of intermarriage to whites and to other Asian Americans has significantly increased in recent years, the latter as Asian American populations have grown. For many Asian Americans today, integration with whites may not be quite as important, at least in the primary-social sphere, as integration with other Asian Americans. In addition, some Japanese Americans view the children of mixed marriages as Japanese American and are working to integrate them well into Japanese American traditions. Those of *mixed ancestry* called **Hapa** (Hawaiian for "half") are seen as the leading edge of change. Greg Mayeda has suggested that eventually the typical Japanese American will be a *Hapa*: "Community leaders must recognize this and encourage *Hapas* and their multicultural families to participate in Japanese-American organizations and customs. If given the opportunity, *Hapas* can unify and reinvigorate the Japanese-American community."[111]

A Power-Conflict View

Few analysts have interpreted the Japanese American experience from a developed power-conflict perspective. Robert Blauner has suggested that Japanese Americans could be viewed as partially colonized in the first half-century of their U.S. experience. Many early immigrants worked in a position of debt servitude or migrated under significant economic or political pressure.

Over centuries an important economic relationship has existed between the labor needs of U.S. capitalism and the infusions of immigrant workers. Asian labor has often filled the needs of U.S. capitalism, as on the West Coast in the nineteenth century. Chinese and Japanese laborers were seen as "colored" labor, with few rights. Because the U.S. was an imperial power in the Pacific, labor agents had easy entry into Asian countries and could dictate agreements benefiting U.S. employers. The latter recruited Asian laborers because they could be made to work for low wages. The U.S. employers had the backing of the U.S. government in securing low-wage labor from Japan and China. Neither country possessed the power European nations had to protect their immigrant workers.[112]

In the beginning, Japanese Americans, like Mexican Americans, were forced by white-generated discrimination to mostly become low-wage laborers. Alien-labor laws that barred land ownership, the race-based exclusion of Japanese immigrants in 1924, and the massive imprisonment in World War II constituted semi-colonial treatment. Japanese Americans' experiences were different from experiences of most European immigrants on which conventional assimilation models are based.

Pressures to acculturate were largely coercive for the first generations. Early commitment to cultural assimilation in Japanese communities was substantially a reaction to severe racial discrimination. By 1910, Japanese American leaders were exhorting constituents to be exemplary in their hard work and to defer to whites in order to gain some acceptance. In early decades, Japanese Americans' experiences with systemic racism were similar to those of African, Mexican, and Native Americans.

Note that the early "assimilation" theorizing of early social scientists emerged during an era of white agitation *against* Japanese immigration and reflected white scholars' often racist views of the Japanese. Indeed, applying the assimilationist perspective to Japanese and other Asian Americans prior to the 1950s is inappropriate in one fundamental respect: Asians were often *prevented* from trying to assimilate in important areas. Unlike European immigrants, Asian immigrants were denied the right to become naturalized citizens.

U.S. government agencies have long played a central role in defining racial groups, a point underscored in racial formation theory (see Chapter 2). For example, in the 1922 *Ozawa* case, the Supreme Court ruled that Asian immigrants were *not white* and could not become citizens. In a similar case the following year, *U.S.* v. *Bhagat Singh Thind*, racist reasoning was applied to an Asian Indian who sought to become naturalized. The Court declared that, in contrast to children of Asian parentage, "the children of English, French, German, Italian, Scandinavian, and other European parentage quickly merge in to the mass of our population and lose the distinctive hallmarks of their European origin."[113] This racist reasoning misses the point that at the time— and indeed into the 1950s—Asian immigrants were legally barred from political and civic assimilation.

Returning to the present situation, some intermarriages might be viewed differently from a power-conflict perspective. Numerous Asian Americans now marry within the Asian American umbrella group, rather than with whites. The interethnic marriage rate has grown because of the increasing size of the Asian American population, the consequent expansion of networks, the similarity in economic achievements, and a shared Asian American identity. Another factor is "a growing racial consciousness in American society, which is perceived by many Asian Americans as increasingly racially polarized and stratified. . . . Race, more so than ethnicity, [now] shapes the experiences and the development of identity among Asian Americans."[114]

How is the "model minority" stereotype harmful to Japanese and other Asian Americans?

Criticizing the "Model Minority" Stereotype

Paramount among the weaknesses in many assimilation analyses in social science and popular media is reliance on a "model minority" stereotype. In recent decades, newsmagazines and television commentators have carried glowing reports on the achievements of Asian Americans in various occupations and education. The success of Japanese and other Asian Americans, frequently viewed as rooted in distinctive cultural values and family styles, is cited in the white-dominated mainstream media and by other whites as a reflection of the great opportunities in the United States and a model for what other people of color, particularly African Americans and Latinos, could achieve if they would follow the Asian example. However, stereotypes of Japanese Americans as paragons of hard work and docility often carry a negative undercurrent. The model imagery was created not by Asian Americans but by white scholars and media analysts, for their own ideological reasons. When African Americans aggressively protested during the 1960s, these whites intentionally created the *model minority* term to suggest that African Americans could achieve the American dream by working harder rather than by protesting discrimination.[115]

However, one must recognize the historical realities. Pre–World War II educational opportunities (greater than those available to African Americans) in states such as California helped prepare many Japanese Americans for white-collar jobs that gradually opened up after that war. Asian American values alone did not bring success, but better access to education and certain white-collar jobs. Critics of the model minority notion have documented other factors in the success of Japanese Americans: the Japanese government's early support of their immigrants and the availability of an important small-business niche in West Coast areas. At an early point, Japanese Americans created many successful businesses through which they served one another and the needs of the economy of the West. Out of economic necessity, Japanese American employers and employees, many with strong kinship ties, worked together against hostile white competitors.

Success often came at the price of being marginalized in the small-business economy and, later, in certain white-collar jobs. As with Jewish Americans, Japanese Americans have, to a substantial degree, succeeded economically by carving distinctive occupational and geographical niches—a process of adaptation not in line with more idealistic assimilation models. The long-term effects of discrimination are still reflected in the disproportionate concentration of Japanese and other Asian Americans in certain professional and technical occupations. In addition, movement into white-collar jobs did not end whites' discrimination. One 1980s study of Japanese American workers in San Francisco found that those in white-collar jobs were clustered in certain occupations such as computer programming, clerical work, architecture, engineering, dentistry, and pharmacy. The highest-level white-collar personnel, such as managers, financial officers, and management analysts, still tended to be white men, which is still true today. Indeed, the model minority stereotype operates in many white minds to downplay Japanese Americans' and other Asian Americans' concerns and protests about continuing racial discrimination in the twenty-first century, especially at higher managerial, business, and professional levels.[116] Note too that Japanese Americans still often receive smaller economic benefits from their generally high level of education than do comparably educated whites.

An important bias in the traditional cultural-background explanation of Japanese American success is the idea that racial or ethnic groups whose values are closest to those of the dominant white group are the ones who should be and will be successful. Societal success is thus evaluated in terms of values prized by the dominant group. Although Japanese Americans have acculturated in numerous ways, the price paid in hyper-conformity, lost creativity, and lost contributions to this society has often been great.[117]

In important documentary work, media analyst Janice Tanaka examined negative impacts of the great pressures for assimilation on third-generation Sansei. Interviews with Sansei found that most of their parents were interned in the wartime camps. These Nisei were greatly affected by that incarceration, and during and after World War II they placed great pressure on themselves and their children to conform aggressively to white perspectives and customs. Fearful of a recurrence of extreme white oppression, they responded to white racism with the orientation that would later get them stereotyped, in an ironic twist, as "model minorities." However, the effects of aggressive conformity often have been negative, to the present day. According to Tanaka and other recent researchers, many Nisei and Sansei have encountered, and continue to endure, great personal distress, painful self-blame, mental and physical illnesses, or alcoholism and drug abuse. Some have committed suicide because of the intense pressures to conform.[118]

Not surprisingly, the negative reactions of the Sansei have in turn affected their own children, the Yonsei. The costs of white-imposed racism persist over generations. Tuan has concluded from her interviews with third-generation Japanese and Chinese Americans that some "have embraced the model minority label" and that especially the youth "were convinced that with hard work, patience, and a little help from the model minority stereotype, they would someday gain the full approval of white Americans." Like Tuan, the research of Chou and Feagin also shows the substantial mental and physical energy that Asian Americans today must expend in dealing with whites' racial hostility and discrimination, which also affects their often cautious interactions with whites.[119]

Over recent decades, Japanese Americans have reported that no amount of cultural assimilation protects them from whites who insist on stereotyping Japanese and other Asian Americans as outsiders—and on discriminating against them. Ronald Takaki, a University of California professor, once visited an East Coast city where a taxicab driver congratulated him on his good English and inquired how long he had been in the country. Ironically, Takaki's family had been here for *three* generations—since 1886. Despite the fact that many Japanese Americans have grown up in mostly white neighborhoods and gone to mostly white schools, they and other Asian Americans often report such "foreigner" reactions and discrimination and do not feel they are fully accepted by many whites.[120]

From the beginning, Japanese immigration and integration into the dominant society have been shaped by U.S. corporations' intervention in the world economy. The action of the U.S. government in forcing Japan into the world economy in the nineteenth century was followed by the recruitment of Japanese laborers for business enterprises. Today, as the Japanese economy vies with the U.S. economy for Pacific and world dominance, the world economy still forms the backdrop. New economic alliances on the Pacific Rim, such as the Association of Southeast Asian Nations, are bypassing the United States. Japan is powerful in these alliances, and that success is one reason there has been relatively little recent migration from Japan to the United States.

Some non-Asian Americans, angry over domestic economic troubles, confuse Japanese Americans and other Asian Americans with the Japanese and blame them unfairly for economic troubles caused by U.S. employers investing overseas or by the federal government. As a Japanese American Citizens' League commentary has stated,

> When the U.S. economy declines, attention often shifts to the role that other countries play in providing "unfair" competition. Asian-Pacific Americans are often perceived to be "foreigners" who take jobs away from "real" Americans. . . . [For a time] Japan was perceived as "taking over" the U.S. by buying companies and real estate. Little attention was given to the fact that Great Britain was then the largest foreign investor in the U.S., while Canada held the largest percentage of foreign-owned real estate.[121]

Such periodic negative imaging and attacks are yet another constant indication to Japanese Americans that somehow they have not been accepted as "true Americans" by many non-Asian Americans.

 How would you use assimilation or power-conflict perspectives to explain key aspects of the Japanese American experience?

Summary

Japanese Americans are a very important group in U.S. history. In the beginning they were severely exploited and treated as a greatly "inferior race." Many entered the United States as laborers, facing violence and intense discrimination. They later endured complete exclusion as a result of overtly racist immigration legislation. During World War II, they suffered the only large-scale imprisonment of U.S. citizens in U.S. concentration camps. Against terrible odds they worked very hard and prospered. Yet, in spite of substantial cultural and other assimilation, Japanese Americans are still not fully integrated into the dominant European American institutions.

Students of racial and ethnic matters should realize that the success story of Japanese and other Asian Americans is partially mythological. Japanese Americans have suffered greatly from past and present racial discrimination. Fewer Japanese Americans than whites fully realize earnings levels that parallel their high educational levels. Few rise to top management in *Fortune 500* corporations, law firms, or government agencies. Although significant numbers of Asian Americans have lived in the U.S. for more than 150 years, not one has ever served as a Supreme Court justice, Speaker of the House, or U.S. president or vice-president. Relatively few have ever served in Congress.

Japanese Americans have often been racially stereotyped. Across the United States, white employers, government officials, and media figures have viewed Japanese and other Asian Americans as "slant-eyed" oddities or "foreigners," not "true Americans." Japanese Americans are considered by many other Americans to be a "model minority" with no need of government protection against discrimination. However, there is still anti-Japanese sentiment that results in overt and subtle discrimination. David Mura, author of *Turning Japanese: Memoirs of a Sansei,* has argued that, for real change to occur, whites must see that the "problem of race is one of giving up power" and begin "dismantling racism and redistributing power."[122]

Working harmoniously together, the seven-person crew of the ill-fated space shuttle *Challenger* included an African American born to sharecroppers (Ronald McNair), a Jewish American of the Orthodox faith (Judith Resnik), and a Japanese American of the Buddhist faith (Ellison Onizuka). Onizuka, grandson of laborers who immigrated to Hawaii in the 1890s, was born on a farm. He became an engineer and participated in space missions. As the first Asian American astronaut, Onizuka has symbolized for many the heroic character of the Asian American struggle for success.

Some decades back, Hawaii was (with New Mexico) one of the first two U.S. states in which no racial or ethnic group constituted a majority. Today Japanese Americans are (with Filipino Americans) one of the two largest nationality groups there. Compared with other U.S. areas, racial–ethnic relations have generally been more cooperative and less conflict-ridden. Although Hawaii has seen some serious interracial tensions between groups, and indigenous Hawaiians have suffered much discrimination and poverty, some knowledgeable observers have suggested that the highly multiracial, multiethnic state of Hawaii can provide valuable lessons on how diverse racial–ethnic groups on the mainland can work together to build a more viable, truly multiracial democracy.[123]

Key Terms

Asian American 284	gunboat imperialism 285
Asian-Pacific American 284	glass ceiling 297
model minority stereotype 284	*Hapa* 303

Chinese, Filipino, Korean, Vietnamese, and Asian-Indian Americans

BIG PICTURE QUESTIONS

- *What role have Asian American groups played in building up this country's wealth and institutions?*

- *How has systemic racism affected the Asian American experience?*

- *Why have numerous Asian groups recently migrated to the United States?*

Elaine H. Kim, a Korean American professor, has written insightfully about the major 1990s Los Angeles riot. She has noted how the mass media played up visual images of conflict between black and Latino rioters and Korean merchants, yet ignored important group histories. Korean Americans, African Americans, and Latino Americans have all been victims of much violence and other discrimination by white Americans. Recalling her experiences, Kim noted that "Korean-Americans have been and continue to be used for someone else's agenda and benefit, whether we are hated as foreigners who refuse to become 'good Americans,' stereotyped as diligent work machines or simply treated as if we do not exist."[1] Korean Americans are one of five major Asian American groups—each with a strong identity and rich history of adaptation and struggle—discussed in this chapter. The others are Chinese, Filipino, Vietnamese, and Asian-Indian Americans.

Asian Americans often find themselves pressured by the dominant Eurocentric culture to conform in a one-way direction to that culture. For example, in recent edited books titled *YELL-Oh Girls!* and *Asian American X*, several hundred young Asian Americans write about their lives and understandings. Many recount frequent experiences with intense, often coercive pressures to assimilate to white-dominated ways of dress, speech, goal attainment, thinking, and physical being. Most are torn between the culture of parents, which provides respect for their "Asian-ness," and the pressures of the white-dominated society. As one Korean American who grew up in a white community puts it, the historical dominance of whiteness helps explain the "thoughtless ways white Americans often inhabit a sense of entitlement and egocentric normality. But when that entitlement becomes married to an acute perception of moral authority and clarity borne of a patriarchal and Anglocentric notion of rectitude and religion, the outcome . . . is acidic and threatening to nuanced or complex thought."[2]

Migration: An Overview

Since the 1980s, Filipinos, Chinese, Koreans, Vietnamese, and Asian Indians have been among the fastest-growing U.S. immigrant groups. For key periods from 1820 to the present, Table 11.1 lists those immigrants gaining permanent legal resident status.[3] Relatively few Filipinos, Koreans, Vietnamese, or Asian Indians immigrated to the U.S. mainland before the 1960s. Thereafter, immigration increased dramatically. More than 4 million immigrants have come since 1980. The data reveal different patterns. Most Asian Indians have arrived in the U.S. since the 1960s. In contrast, Chinese immigration has involved two major periods. The first began about 1850 and lasted until 1882, the year of the Chinese Exclusion Act, which prohibited direct immigration from China. Large-scale immigration did not resume until the immigration reforms in 1965.

The discriminatory 1924 Immigration Act excluded Asians from immigrating. The 1952 Immigration and Nationality Act began to eliminate some anti-Asian discrimination and established principles for immigration policy: (1) reunification of families; (2) protection of the domestic labor force; and

TABLE 11.1	**People with Legal Permanent Resident Status, by Country of Last Residence, 1820–2009**						
	1820–1899	**1900–1919**	**1920–1939**	**1940–1959**	**1960–1979**	**1980–1999**	**2000–2009**
Chinese*	304,208	40,800	36,522	39,410	314,896	993,679	741,951
Filipino	**	**	391	21,344	408,386	1,036,394	545,463
Korean	**	**	**	4,928	268,240	502,478	209,758
Vietnamese	**	**	**	290	124,665	476,011	289,616
Asian-Indian	687	6,504	2,630	3,542	166,635	584,177	590,464

Figures include Hong Kong and Taiwan.
**Figures not available for this period.*

(3) immigration of persons with needed skills. The act permitted small-scale Asian immigration and for the first time made Asian immigrants eligible for citizenship. In 1965, Congress took a major step toward providing Asians the opportunity to immigrate on a scale similar to that of earlier European groups. The 1965 Immigration Act abolished racist national-origin quotas and established a significant annual quota for Asian countries. The proportion of Chinese, Filipinos, Koreans, Vietnamese, and Asian Indians among the total number of immigrants rose from 0.2 percent for the years 1901 to 1920 to 27 percent in the 1970s, and has remained substantial to the present.

Because the 1965 act and its amendments give preference to family members, many recent legal permanent residents are relatives of previous immigrants. The majority of immigrants have gone to areas where earlier immigrants settled. Today, the largest Asian-Pacific American populations are in major cities; Los Angeles, New York, Honolulu, and San Francisco lead the list. Because of past immigration barriers, most today are foreign-born immigrants or the children of foreign-born parents. Chinese and Japanese American populations have the largest third- and later-generation components.

Chinese Americans

Chinese immigration began in substantial numbers in the decade before the U.S. Civil War, with a quarter-million coming during three decades after 1860. Most were men and entered as low-wage workers, brought in to do the "dirty work" for white employers in the West. Many were recruited to remedy labor shortages in railroad work or to fill menial positions in such personal-service areas as laundry work. The few women who immigrated usually came alone, often brought by force to work as prostitutes. In 1875, Congress passed a law prohibiting the importation of women for prostitution—the first direct regulation of U.S. immigration. Significant numbers of Chinese women were not permitted to enter until the 1940s.[4]

As the 1870s began, the U.S. economy entered a depression. White labor leaders, newspaper editors, politicians, and the general public on the West Coast accused Chinese Americans of driving wages to substandard levels and taking white jobs. Anti-Chinese laws were passed at state and federal levels.[5] The

federal government's 1882 Chinese Exclusion Act officially prohibited direct immigration. Over the next decades, the act reduced the flow of immigrants, which had reached 123,201 in the years from 1871 to 1880. Because most were male, exclusion resulted in a 40 percent decline in the Chinese American population by 1920.[6] In 1905, President Theodore Roosevelt stated that Chinese laborers must be kept out of the U.S. "absolutely."[7] Significantly, this openly racist Exclusion Act was not repealed until 1943, when China became a wartime ally against Japan. Then, a tiny quota of 105 was set for new Chinese immigrants. (In July 2009, the California state legislature finally apologized for California's anti-Chinese laws in this era.)[8]

The second major period of immigration took place after the 1965 immigration reform. Between 1960 and 1979, more than 300,000 Chinese, mainly from Hong Kong and Taiwan, came to the United States. Large numbers have entered since 1980 (see Table 11.1). During recent decades, the proportion from Hong Kong and Taiwan has fallen and that from mainland China has grown. Between 1980 and 2008, the Chinese American population, the largest among Asian Americans, increased substantially—from 812,178 to more than 3.6 million, including those with partial Chinese ancestry. Chinese Americans constitute nearly one-fourth of Asian Americans.[9]

Filipino Americans

When the Philippine Islands were taken over by the U.S. after the Spanish-American War, the U.S. government ignored Filipino desires for independence. U.S. military forces killed many who fought for independence. A U.S. form of government was established. Because the Philippine Islands were a U.S. colony, Filipinos were exempt from anti-Asian provisions of the 1917 and 1924 Immigration Acts. This allowed them to immigrate freely, and U.S. employers recruited them to work on sugar plantations in Hawaii and in fields on the West Coast.[10] After passage of the 1924 Immigration Act, employers increased recruitment of Filipinos as laborers to replace Asian and other workers excluded by the act. As numbers increased, so did anti-Filipino sentiment among white workers. In 1934, Congress responded to this racist sentiment by granting independence to the Philippines and imposing an immigration quota of only fifty persons per year.[11]

Although Filipinos could enter without restriction until 1934, advantages ended there. Filipino Americans held an ambiguous legal position. Most states did not allow Filipinos to practice law, medicine, or other professions. Congress began moving toward U.S. citizenship for Filipino Americans during World War II, since it was hard to defend the idea of freedom for the Philippines from Japanese rule while denying such citizenship.

During World War II, 30,000 Filipinos were recruited to fight with U.S. forces battling the Japanese. President Franklin Roosevelt promised these fighters they could come to the U.S. and become U.S. citizens. The government backed out of the promise, leaving thousands stranded. These veterans were not granted the right to U.S. citizenship until passage of the Immigration Act of 1990.[12] Even then, most who had resided in the U.S. in recent decades were ineligible for many veterans' benefits until, in 2009, critical provisions of the Filipino Veterans Equity Act, first introduced in Congress in 1993, finally became law. A study of Filipino American veterans found that most have lived on low incomes, often with serious medical problems. In recent years, groups such as the Filipino-American Service Group have fought hard to secure justice for these veterans.[13]

Between the 1950s and the 1970s, the number of Filipinos residing in the United States almost doubled. Since the 1960s and 1970s, Filipino immigration has increased dramatically (as shown in Table 11.1). In 2008, the Census Bureau estimated from a national survey that nearly 3.1 million Americans had some Filipino ancestry, the second largest Asian-Pacific group. Today, a large majority are foreign born. Many live in the Los Angeles area, and they are also numerous in other large western and midwestern cities.[14]

Korean Americans

Immigration of a few Koreans began in the early 1900s. They too confronted discriminatory wages and other discrimination. They were racially segregated, refused housing in many areas, and denied public services. After learning of these conditions, Japan, which occupied Korea beginning in 1910, pressured the Korean government to ban emigration to the United States, thereby restricting immigrants for decades.[15] Nonetheless, a few—primarily "picture brides" and students—managed to come. Because most who arrived before the 1910 restrictions were single men, and because interracial marriage was banned by U.S. laws, numerous Korean men sent pictures to prospective brides in their homeland. Thus, *marriages were arranged on the basis of photographs, without the bride and groom having met*, leading to the term **picture brides**. From 1910 to 1924, more than 1000 brides came to the United States.[16]

Because of U.S. military intervention in the 1950s Korean War, many Koreans came to admire and be interested in migrating to the United States. Most who immigrated from 1950 to 1965 were brides of U.S. soldiers. Children and grandchildren stemming from these marriages are today part of a substantial U.S. multiracial population making its voice heard for greater respect for multiracial ancestry.

Changes in immigration laws in 1965 opened up new possibilities. Lack of economic or educational opportunities in Korea has prompted many to emigrate over several decades now. Some have been political dissidents who opposed the dictatorial regimes that dominated South Korea for decades. Others have been students who completed their education and stayed. Once established, immigrants have used the immigration law's family reunification clause to bring in family members. After 1965 the numbers increased significantly; within a decade the annual number exceeded 30,000. Over the last decade it has declined a bit but continues at a significant level of around 19,000 to 26,000 annually.[17]

A recent Census Bureau estimate is that there are 1.6 million Americans with Korean ancestry, nearly 10 percent of the Asian American population. A substantial proportion still reside on the West Coast, although in recent years many have moved to the larger midwestern and eastern cities.[18]

Vietnamese Americans

Most Vietnamese immigrants to the United States have come since 1975, when U.S. involvement in the Vietnam War ended. U.S. plans to evacuate some South Vietnamese included those employed by the U.S. government or U.S. businesses, and their families. Thousands fled their country.[19] The large number of immigrating Vietnamese were admitted outside the usual immigration process as political refugees. As Table 11.1 shows, very few immigrated before 1960, in part because of anti-Asian immigration laws. Following changes in immigration laws and the end of the U.S. military intervention in Vietnam, many entered the United States between 1975 and 1980.[20]

In the 1980–1990 period, the number of Americans with Vietnamese ancestry grew 142 percent, and between 1990 and 2000, this population again increased dramatically. The population continues to increase, with 20,000 to 30,000 immigrants annually, and numbers more than 1.7 million today. A large percentage of Vietnamese Americans are foreign born, and many live in western and southwestern states.[21]

Asian-Indian Americans

Of all the major Asian-Pacific groups, perhaps the least well known is the group the Census Bureau calls "Asian Indians"—those from India. The first Indian immigrants were Sikhs who worked on railroads or in agriculture on the West Coast in the 1800s, but their number remained very small until the 1960s. Asian Indians have immigrated in significant numbers only since the 1965 Immigration Act. The 1990 census reported almost 787,000 Asian-Indian Americans, but by 2008, this population had increased sharply to about 2.5 million.[22]

Three periods are evident in the Asian-Indian migrations. In the 1960s, many immigrants were male professionals and managers; wives were usually not well educated. A second group came in the 1970s; it included a more diverse occupational mixture, with more well-educated women. A larger and more diverse group has come since the 1980s and includes many well-educated immigrants like those in previous migrations. Also in this group are many relatives sponsored by earlier immigrants who are less well educated and likely to move into service work or family businesses.[23]

Most Asian-Indian Americans do not live on the West Coast of the United States. The majority live in the Northeast, and a large portion live in the Midwest and the South. In metropolitan areas many Asian-Indian Americans have had the economic resources to move directly into suburbs rather than settling first in central-city areas like other immigrant groups, past and present. As a result, there are no large central-city concentrations as there are for other Asian groups. Even so, wherever there is a substantial Asian-Indian population in a metropolitan area, there are usually numerous community organizations, such as Indian (for example, Hindu) houses of worship.[24]

Asian Women as Immigrants

Many discussions of Asian immigrants, and Asian Americans in general, stereotype the women in these groups as being rather withdrawn and docile. However, Asian immigrant families do include many women who are strong and successful figures in their own right. Min Zhou and James Gatewood write, "As immigrants, Asian American women are agents in their own destiny, often making painful decisions to come to America but, more often than not, having some control over their choices. They play an active role."[25] The immigration experience often reshapes traditional gender relationships so that these women immigrants take a more active role in providing economic and other support for their families than they typically did in the home country. This in turn can reshape their relationships with men in their families. As with women in earlier immigrant groups, such as the Irish, Asian women often become important decision makers in the immigration process and in their group's adaptation to the host society.[26]

 How have anti-Asian sentiments shaped U.S. immigration laws and decisions?

Stereotypes

Anti-Asian stereotyping and hostility have a long history. One common stereotype held by European Americans is that Asian Americans are all basically the same, physically and culturally. Japanese Americans are commonly mistaken by non-Asians for Chinese Americans, who in turn may be mistaken for other Asian American groups. Asian Americans are frequently viewed as "foreigners" rather than "Americans" because of their non-European appearance. Historically, U.S. films and television programs have portrayed Asians as criminal, dangerous, or fanatical. Stereotyped images, such as the "evil Jap" of World War II and the "gook" more recently, were created primarily by whites and have been recycled as U.S. foreign policy has changed. This *uninformed and stereotypical way of thinking of Asian peoples,* sometimes called **Orientalism,** shapes much anti-Asian discrimination and some U.S. government policies.[27]

Studies of Asian American students at colleges and other educational institutions have found they are regularly targets of stereotyping as "foreigners," "Chinks," or "nerdy Asian students."[28] Anti-Asian stereotypes have serious implications. For example, a white member of South Carolina's Board of Education commented at a board meeting, "Screw the Buddhists and kill the Muslims." Even with this outburst, he was able to keep his position. Moreover, a study of relatively recent Chinese immigrants who settled in Monterey Park, California, found that many long-term residents—both powerful white residents and even some older Japanese American and Latino residents—had developed a stereotyped view distinguishing between "good immigrants" for their own ancestors and "bad immigrants" for recent Chinese immigrants. Good immigrants were said to have blended in and been subservient, whereas bad immigrants were those like some Chinese who questioned the established social and economic order.[29]

As noted in Chapter 10, numerous Asian American groups have been stereotyped as "model minorities." According to this view, which many think is only positive, Asian Americans have moved ahead in society unhindered by racial prejudice and discrimination, mainly by dint of hard work. For example, in a major 2009 national survey, a majority of the respondents agreed with the statement that Asian Americans "often or always" had more success in society than other Americans, thereby generally associating hard work, intelligence, and family values with Asian Americans.[30] There are many exemplary individuals in Asian American communities, but the model minority stereotype overstates their economic situation and underplays the racist barriers they face.

Specific Images of Asian Americans

Coming to the West Coast, the first Chinese workers became subjects of white anger. They were called "coolies" and maligned as "heathen," "mice-eaters," or "Chinks." For decades, the white leaders and public openly portrayed Chinese Americans not as Americans, but as an alien "race." Chinese and other Asian Americans have long been negatively evaluated along the axes of superior/inferior and insider/foreigner.[31] For example, in 1896, even as he defended some rights for black Americans as the dissenter in the infamous *Plessy* v. *Ferguson* Jim Crow segregation decision, Supreme Court Justice John Marshall Harlan added this: "There is a race so different from our own that we do not permit those belonging to it to become citizens of the United States. Persons belonging to it are, with few exceptions, absolutely excluded from our country. I allude to the Chinese race."[32] "Alien race" images have persisted to the present.

Modest changes in white attitudes came after the United States declared war on Japan in 1941. China and the United States became allies against Japan. After the U.S. entry into World War II, *Time* magazine printed this racist explanation of differences between the Chinese "friends" and the "Jap" enemies:

> Virtually all Japanese are short. Japanese are likely to be stockier and broader-hipped than short Chinese. Japanese are seldom fat; they often dry up and grow lean as they age. Although both have the typical epicanthic fold on the upper eyelid, Japanese eyes are usually set closer together. The Chinese expression is likely to be more placid, kindly, open; the Japanese more positive, dogmatic, arrogant. Japanese are hesitant, nervous in conversation, laugh loudly at the wrong time. Japanese walk stiffly erect, hard heeled. Chinese, more relaxed, have an easy gait, sometimes shuffle.[33]

Ironically, the white editors who published this wildly stereotyped statement thought they were saying something positive about their "friends" the Chinese. Yet, this is an example of the crude racial stereotyping that has long been part of much white racial framing of Asian Americans.

Historically, racial stereotypes of Filipino immigrants have fluctuated according to their usefulness to white employers seeking their low-wage labor, such as for Hawaiian agricultural plantations. Employers recruiting Filipinos often characterized them as "unintelligent" and "docile." When no longer needed, they were also stereotyped as "lazy, shiftless, and unmanageable." Such anti-Asian stereotypes have often been drawn out of an old racist framing of society that whites developed earlier for other Americans of color.[34]

The Vietnamese arrived in the U.S. during the 1970s, when unemployment was relatively high, and many non-Asian Americans feared these refugees would take their jobs and/or seriously drain government resources. Anti-Vietnamese sentiment was reflected in one national poll in which 54 percent of respondents felt Vietnamese refugees should not be permitted to stay.[35] Some non-Asian Americans still view Vietnamese Americans as alien or the "enemy" because of the Vietnam war and/or still use the racist epithet, *gooks*. For example, Senator John McCain, a Republican presidential candidate, has used the racialized "gook" for the Vietnamese who fought U.S. intervention in Vietnam. Moreover, a Dallas-area police chief recently retired early after making a comment that he would not have "gooks" on his police force. Many non-Asians still regard Vietnamese Americans as strange, clannish, or hard to approach. One survey of Vietnamese residents of Orange County, California, found that six in ten believed that anti-Vietnamese prejudice was still a problem.[36]

Today, many non-Asian Americans harbor negative views of specific Asian American communities and also of Asian Americans as a group. One recent national survey found that one-quarter of respondents admitted holding negative attitudes about Chinese Americans. A similar proportion opposed the idea of intermarriage with an Asian American. In 2009, another large national survey found that a sizable majority of respondents believed Asian Americans were more than 8 percent of the U.S. population, when in fact they were just 5 percent. A significant proportion also held anti-Asian stereotypes, and those who reported little interaction with Asian Americans were more likely than others to hold anti-Asian prejudices. Also, those with a high level of prejudice were more likely than others to view China as a threat to the United States.[37]

The mass media, including the movie industry, have long perpetuated negatively stereotyped images of Asian adults. Especially in recent decades, Asian men have often been portrayed as weak, sexless, or effeminate. For example, the Hollywood film *The Hangover* (2009) had an array of stereotyped Asian and African American characters, including an effeminate Asian man. As Russell Leong noted, "Racist myths and assumptions about smaller stature—smaller eyes—and less sexual and erotic drive—have stymied the development and

acceptance of Asian American men as full erotic beings."[38]

One severe stereotype faced by Asian American women is that of the exotic sex object. Numerous Asian women have written of how some men, especially white men, seek them out with heads full of images of exotic relationships or submissive wives. Numerous websites are devoted to finding Asian sexual partners and wives for white men. Other gendered stereotyping can be seen in the mainstream U.S. standard of ideal female beauty—typically, white, fair-haired, and relatively busty and tall. Faced with this constant imaging, and like some other women of color, many Asian Americans feel themselves to be inferior—even to the point of having plastic surgery to "improve" facial or breast characteristics. One recent report showed a sharp increase in cosmetic surgery for Asian Americans, with the most common surgeries for Asian American women being eyelid surgery, nose reshaping, and breast augmentation. Much surgery is directed at making them look more like the white beauty ideal. Writing at age 19 about her reaction to pressures from relatives to have plastic surgery on her face, one Chinese American has commented thus: "Asian is beautiful. After all these years of wanting to open up my eyes with tape and glue and surgery, I have opened up my eyes to a different definition of beauty, one that embraces differences and includes every girl . . . because being *Asian is beautiful*."[39]

More Stereotyping in the Media and Popular Entertainment

Interestingly, the martial arts movies of Bruce Lee and his imitators have created certain positive images of strong and virtuous Asians, and have become popular. However, as sociologist C. N. Le has put it,

> The success of these martial arts movies . . . also demonstrates the fine line that the Asian American community must walk. On the one hand, most of us are proud of the success of these martial arts movies and Asian and Asian American stars. However, we must be wary . . . [as] it could be very easy to see all Asian Americans as martial arts experts and then associate that with being a "foreign thing" and that therefore, all Asian Americans are again foreigners.[40]

Much moviemaking imbeds racial stereotyping. For example, for two decades the popular musical *Miss Saigon,* often produced as a musical play and made into a movie, has been strongly criticized because its central character, a Vietnamese "bar girl" abandoned by a white GI, is a crude stereotype. Asian American leaders have called on theatergoers and actors to boycott the play. As we noted in Chapter 10, numerous Hollywood and other movies made since 2000 have used an array of these stereotyped and mocking images of Asian women and men, as well as of Asian cultures and religions.[41] One example is the *Mr. Wong* cartoon made by an animation company that used a caricature of a Chinese "hunchbacked, yellow-skinned, squinty-eyed character who spoke with a thick accent and starred in an interactive music video titled 'Saturday Night Yellow Fever.'"[42] There was significant national protest from Asian Americans over the cartoon, while many whites and a few Asian Americans defended it as "only humor." When the Asian Pacific American Media Coalition heard that a company was considering making it into a movie, they conducted a letter-writing campaign to convince advertisers to pull ads from the company's website. Also, the filmmakers of a puppet movie, *Team America: World Police,* had a Korean political leader speaking gibberish in a mock Asian accent. As one reviewer noted, "*Team America* was an hour and a half of racial mockery with an 'if you are offended, you obviously can't take a joke' tacked on at the end." Such reactions to these movie examples reveal how racist stereotypes are frequently passed off as harmless joking, when in fact "joking" reinforces the racist framing lying behind ongoing discrimination against Americans of color.[43]

Over several decades, the mostly white-controlled television and radio industries have also produced numerous programs with negative stereotyping and mocking of Asian groups. Television series such as *The Simpsons* have derided South Asian clerks, while *The Late Show with David Letterman* has made fun of Bangladeshi newsstand operators. Recently, numerous television and radio personalities have used mocking language and gestures when discussing Asians or Asian Americans. For example, Asian American organizations protested racial stereotyping engaged in by former police detective Bo Dietl on a 2009 radio show hosted by Don Imus. Dietl mocked broadcaster Katie Couric's physical appearance, commenting that,

"She's got her eyes pulled so far, she's starting to look Chinese herself . . . ten years ago, she looked American. Today she looks Oriental." He also engaged in the eye-pulling slant-eye gesture commonly used to mock Asians. In addition, two popular teen-age stars and one older country and western star have recently been photographed making similar eye-pulling, mocking gestures in various settings.[44] Such negative mocking has deep roots in the stereotyped mannerisms and language found among whites and other non-Asian Americans, beginning in childhood. Indeed, over recent decades, many Asian Americans, of all ages, have noted that they periodically encounter hostile words from whites and other non-Asians, including young people, such as these: "Ching chong Chinaman sitting on a rail, along came a white man and snipped off his tail"; "Ah so. No tickee, No washee. So sorry, so sollee"; and "Chinkee, Chink, Jap, Nip, zero, Dothead . . . Flip, Hindoo."[45]

In addition, various news media have often engaged in stereotyping Asians and Asian Americans. One 1990s study of images in news coverage found numerous portrayals of Asian Americans as manipulative, mysterious, and inscrutable, as well as widespread trivialization of Asian customs, ridicule of Asian American pronunciation, and use of inflammatory phrases such as "Asian invasion," all of which actions reinforce views of Asian Americans as undesirable foreigners. In recent decades, some Asian Americans have been targets of widespread stereotyping in news media investigations of alleged illegal contributions to political campaigns. For example, under pressure to raise money for the Democratic Party in the 1990s, John Huang, a Chinese American, and other Asian American fundraisers raised millions in contributions, some of which were alleged to have been illegally contributed by overseas donors. News media discussions included considerable stereotyping of Asian Americans as mysterious and underhanded. A graphic commentary on the fund-raising investigations appeared on the cover of *National Review* magazine, which had caricatures of Bill and Hillary Clinton as slant-eyed, buck-toothed Chinese in Mao suits and Chinese hats. White cartoonists have long portrayed Asian Americans in such terms to express fear of the "yellow peril." Later on, significantly, during the 2008 presidential primaries U.S. Chinese-language media reporters were turned away from a San Francisco fundraiser luncheon for the Hillary Clinton presidential campaign, apparently because the organizers did not want Clinton to be associated in the public mind with Asian "foreigners" and the earlier fund-raising scandal.[46]

Although investigation of illegal contributions is certainly legitimate, blatant stereotyping is another matter. In the Huang case, the news media did *not* so vigorously target for investigation other foreign contributions, such as those from overseas corporations, to Democratic and Republican Party activities. And the white-controlled media also did not single out the racial or ethnic characteristics of other questionable contributors.

These examples indicate that elite, media, and public stereotypes of Asian Americans still include notions of the latter as threatening, relatively unassimilated, culturally odd foreigners. Much of this negatively framed imagery is new for Asian immigrants who, research studies show, often do not see themselves in racialized terms until their arrival to the U.S. Sharmila Rudrappa has summarized this point from field research: "Upon arrival in the United States we postcolonial immigrants suddenly become racialized. . . . From being persons with no tangible race—we do not think of ourselves in racial terms in India—we become people of color in this society."[47]

Discrimination and Conflict

Hate Crimes and Other Racial Attacks

Asian immigrants and their children have faced much harassment and violence since the earliest days of Asian immigration. Until fairly recently, few local governments collected data on racial violence. Each year now, many anti-Asian hate crimes are reported to law-enforcement agencies. Since the late 1990s, at least fifteen Asian Americans have died in hate crime attacks. Hate crimes range from killings to vicious verbal slurs and hate messages painted on homes and businesses.[48]

Periodically, these anti-Asian hate crimes get some attention in the media. For example, in 1997, several Asian American students were denied service at a Syracuse restaurant. When they left, they were beaten by white patrons, and the restaurant's security personnel did not intervene. A lawsuit was filed against the restaurant, but the case was dismissed. More recently, in 2008, a former Asian American student at the University of Colorado was walking with friends near campus when he was challenged by white men. One man harassed him with racist epithets ("chinaman") and nativistic questions like "Do you think you are an American?" and then hit him several times, insisting that he say "I love America." Not long before, a student newspaper had published a column saying that, "If it's war the Asians want . . . it's war they'll get." Although the incidents may not have been connected, they suggest the intensity of anti-Asian feelings in and around some college communities.[49]

The U.S. Civil Rights Commission has noted that such hate crimes are underreported, especially for Asian Americans. Many of the latter are immigrants who distrust the police and have a limited understanding of their civil rights. Some have been mistreated or killed by police officers. One important county where many Asian Americans live, Orange County, California, has reported 150 to 170 hate crimes annually in recent years. Los Angeles has also reported hundreds of hate crimes each year. Although African American residents are usually the most frequent targets, Asian Americans have been singled out for a variety of hate crimes, ranging from racist graffiti painted on homes or circulated on the Internet to violent threats and attacks.[50]

The U.S. Civil Rights Commission and its advisory boards have found that adequate police protection is often not provided for Asian Americans. Community organizations in various cities have urged police officials to prosecute hate and other crimes more vigorously.[51] Some white-dominated police departments seem very insensitive to Asian American communities. When Asian Americans do have contact with white officers, their rights are sometimes jeopardized by language barriers, and few police departments have adequate interpretive services for non–English-speaking Americans. When Asian Americans report a crime, they frequently do not receive an adequate police response.[52] One controversial police strategy is photographing youth because they fit a "gang profile." Asian Americans—like African Americans, Latino Americans, and Arab Americans—are sometimes the targets of extensive racial profiling by white authorities. A spokesperson for one Asian American organization explained,

"Culturally, the Asian community does not speak out against such things as police harassment. By nature, our people do not complain or report abuse, so by having some speak out, we hope to encourage others to do the same."[53]

 Have hate crimes targeting Asian Americans been similar to or different from those involving other racial and ethnic groups?

Chinese Americans

During the nineteenth century, anti-Chinese sentiments and hostility were common in union policies and in political platforms, as well as in the media. Chinese immigrants were violently attacked by whites in western states. In more recent decades, Chinese Americans have continued to be the targets of racially motivated attacks. For example, in the 1990s, a Chinese woman in New York was pushed in front of a subway train by a man with a "phobia about Asians." And a teen-aged white supremacist in California was charged with numerous felony crimes, including the attempted murder of a Chinese American council member and the fire-bombing of NAACP and Japanese American Citizens League offices.[54]

In Detroit in 1982, the infamous murder of Vincent Chin, a Chinese American, brought racially motivated actions against Asian Americans to public attention. Two white auto workers, apparently believing Chin was Japanese and blaming him for auto industry problems, started an argument with Chin and then beat him to death. A Michigan judge sentenced each only to probation and a fine of $3780. Many people expressed outrage. The U.S. Commission on Civil Rights concluded that this extreme leniency was "suggestive of very little value being placed on an Asian American life."[55] The U.S. Department of Justice later brought federal charges against the assailants for civil rights violations. A U.S. District Court jury found one of the defendants guilty of violating Chin's civil rights, thereby acknowledging the racial motivation. The other was acquitted. The guilty defendant was sentenced to 25 years in prison, but his conviction was overturned by an appellate court for technical reasons. In a retrial he was acquitted.[56]

A similar incident took place in Raleigh, North Carolina, in 1989. This time the Chinese American victim, Ming Hai Loo, was killed by white brothers who thought he was Vietnamese and were angry about U.S. battle deaths in Vietnam. In 1990, the brother who struck the fatal blow was sentenced to 37 years in prison, but with the possibility of parole after 4½ years. The other assailant, who made racist remarks, received a six-month misdemeanor sentence. The following year he was found guilty in federal court of violating the victim's civil rights and received a 4-year sentence. Significantly, this case was the *first* successful federal prosecution of a civil rights case in which the target was Asian American. Yet, this violence, like more recent violence against Asian Americans, has received little national attention—a neglect that perpetuates non-Asian Americans' lack of awareness of anti-Asian violence.[57]

For example, in the summer of 2006 in Queens, New York, several Chinese American teenagers were attacked and beaten by whites whom a witness said were yelling racist slurs and saying, "Stay out of our neighborhood." Such attacks make the local news, but again there is no significant national discussion of these hate crimes. In July 2007, two Chinese Americans were attacked by two white men in New York's Chinatown area. The whites were yelling racist slurs ("Chink") and hostile phrases ("Go back to your country" and "This is for the Korean War"). And in 2009, two teenagers with a reputation for targeting Asian Americans were arrested for robbing and strangling a Chinese American businessperson in the New York City area.[58]

Anti-Asian attacks often illustrate not only racist violence but also the confusion of non-Asians about Asian Americans. Many non-Asians do not seem to be very aware that Asian-Pacific Americans include many nationality groups, and many non-Asians periodically mistake a person from one Asian American group for someone from another. This confusion may have been reflected in several incidents over recent decades in which Secret Service and other federal guards have treated Asian Americans entering various government buildings with suspicion, as though they were foreigners.[59]

In the late 1990s, the federal Los Alamos National Laboratory was investigated for security compromises, and Dr. Wen Ho Lee, a naturalized U.S. citizen from Taiwan, was fired for allegedly being a spy for the Chinese government. In the fall of 2000, after months of media speculation about Chinese intrigues and Lee's involvement, and after Lee had served months in confinement, he was freed on a plea bargain in which all but one minor charge (downloading files to an unsecured computer) were dropped. Numerous news stories portrayed him and Chinese Americans as mysterious or disloyal. Then President Bill Clinton, while critical of the incarceration, asserted that no anti-Asian animosity lay behind it. Nonetheless, many Asian Americans protested the stereotyping of Chinese Americans as disloyal, as well as the discrimination against Dr. Lee. In 2006, Dr. Lee finally won some degree of vindication when the federal government and several media companies agreed to pay him $1.6 million in damages, and a federal judge apologized for the role of government officials in the discrimination.[60]

Given the numerous examples of racial hostility we have just noted, and will note in following sections, it is not surprising that in a 2009 survey some seven in ten Chinese American respondents said that they faced "a lot or some prejudice" in their everyday lives.[61]

Filipino Americans

Among the earliest of Asian-Pacific immigrants, Filipino Americans have also suffered many violent attacks. In the period from the 1910s to the 1930s, white farm laborers often clashed with Filipino workers in California. Filipino wages were set considerably lower by white employers than wages of white workers, yet the latter still attacked Filipino workers. In October 1929, whites rioted against Filipino workers in the San Joaquin Valley. Bitter about white farmers' use of Filipinos, whites went to a labor camp, ordered Filipinos out, and burned the camp. The police chief refused to take action against the mob. A prolonged riot by whites occurred near Watsonville, California, in 1930—a riot reflecting a decade of tensions and exacerbated by newspaper commentaries blaming Filipino Americans for problems. Anti-Filipino demonstrations erupted; a vigilante mob of hundreds of whites marched on a Filipino dance hall. On January 22, 1930, the anti-Filipino attacks reached a peak when hundreds of vigilantes attacked the Northern Monterey Filipino Club. One person was killed, and many Filipino Americans were severely beaten.[62]

In more recent decades, whites have periodically directed some hostility toward Filipino Americans. In the 1990s, for example, white guests at a party at Chicago mayor Richard Daley's estate called several Filipino American youth racist names and threw them out.[63] Moreover, in 1999, Joseph Ileto, a Filipino American mail carrier, was killed in Los Angeles by a white supremacist who murdered him because of his skin color. In response, Ileto's family has become active in protests against such crimes, including pressing the U.S. Congress to pass new hate crimes legislation. And yet, such anti-Asian crimes persist. More recently, another white supremacist, a woman who had published a racist newsletter, went on a rampage in Santa Barbara, California, and killed fellow postal workers. She targeted six people—one Filipino, one Chinese, one Latino, and three black workers. In recent years, various levels of violence have been used against Filipino Americans. For example, a young Filipino American was recently beaten up on a New York bus because her numerous attackers thought she was Chinese.[64]

Filipino Americans have been targeted via racial profiling by government officials. In one incident, U.S. officials detained, treated roughly, and derided ten Filipino American airline mechanics on allegations that they were linked to "terrorist cells." After being detained for months without bail for routine immigration problems, seven were released with misdemeanor violations and three others, who were tried, were acquitted. None was convicted of any terrorist act. Other Filipinos picked up at the same time for similar offenses were quickly released, leading community leaders to suspect aggressive racial profiling.[65]

Korean Americans

Koreans are relatively recent U.S. immigrants, yet they too have been hit by anti-Asian harassment and violence. Like white ethnic merchants, Korean American merchants in some urban communities have faced hostility. Black residents have sometimes charged that some merchants treat black customers rudely and discriminate against black employees and customers. Korean American merchants, in turn, sometimes cite the crimes they periodically face at the hands of poor black and Latino criminals.

African American residents in New York and California cities have periodically demonstrated against

Korean American businesses. Each group has accused members of the other of racially motivated violence. In 1991, for example, a Korean American storekeeper in Los Angeles killed a young black teenager (Latasha Harlins), whom the storekeeper mistakenly thought was shoplifting. Black rage over this incident, which intensified after a judge imposed a lenient sentence on the shooter, played a role in a major 1992 Los Angeles riot. Historian Mike Davis described the looting of Korean-owned businesses during that riot as, in part, the product of "the black community's unassuaged grief over Harlins's murder."[66]

During the riot, Los Angeles's Korean Americans felt betrayed as they saw mostly white police officers protect large shopping centers owned by whites while smaller Korean-owned stores were destroyed by black and Latino rioters. This was a three-way conflict. Social scientist Elaine Kim has commented that "the so-called black–Korean problem masks a deeper racism in this country. . . . When the Los Angeles Police Department and the state government failed to respond to the initial outbreak of violence in South Central, I suspected that Korean Americans were being used as human shields to protect the real source of rage."[67]

One factor in continuing Korean–black tensions is that many Asian immigrants already have antiblack stereotypes when they arrive. They, like other recent immigrants, pick up negative stereotypes from U.S.-made movies and television programs seen by millions in countries around the globe. In one study, Asian respondents in rural Taiwan were interviewed about their views of black Americans. Although they had never been to the United States, and although some realized U.S. television programs, movies, and newspapers engaged in racial stereotyping, most still accepted negative stereotypes of African Americans learned from the now-global U.S. media.[68]

The negative stereotypes Korean and other immigrants bring with them can become a basis for negative interactions with African Americans. In their turn, African Americans sometimes develop negative views of Asian immigrants who stereotype them. Negative stereotyping of Asian Americans that African Americans pick up from the mainstream media often affect how black Americans feel about Asian American merchants in their communities. Negative attitudes of immigrants toward African Americans—and negative attitudes of African

Americans toward Asian immigrants—are typically part of a much larger, indeed global, system of mostly white-generated racial framing of numerous social groups.

Claire Jean Kim has shown that Korean–black conflict should be understood in the context of this systemic racism. Such conflict is not just about stereotyping and scapegoating by Korean and African Americans, but it reflects the larger white-racist framework and hierarchy. As noted previously, in this racial hierarchy, white Americans are at the top and black Americans are at the bottom; the other racially oppressed groups, such as those of Asian descent, are often positioned in between (see Chapter 2). This white-created hierarchy stimulates conflict among groups positioned differently in it. The hierarchy generates legitimate protests against a group's hierarchical placement and the racist barriers associated with that. "The differential positioning of Blacks and Asian Americans (including Korean immigrants) in the American racial order and their physical juxtaposition in the urban economy creates an immanent tendency for conflict between the two groups."[69] Collective black actions against Korean merchants in black communities are not just about black stereotyping of these merchants. They are also part of centuries of black resistance to outside economic control of their communities. Resistance arises no matter who (Irish, Jewish, or Korean) the outside merchants are.

Another source of bitterness on the part of some African Americans is the largely unfounded belief that the U.S. government helps Koreans start small businesses. In fact, Korean Americans usually pool family resources to purchase businesses.[70] Many immigrants have started small businesses in low-income black and Latino communities because such businesses require modest capital and can be very profitable. The gamble the Korean American entrepreneurs take in poor communities is "necessitated by the constraints they face—the near impossibility of a professional career or white-collar work, and the daunting difficulties in opening a store in an affluent neighborhood."[71] Contrary to the conventional "American dream," however, Korean immigrants are usually unable to start businesses in predominantly white areas because they face anti-Asian discrimination or do not have enough capital. Many have graduated from Korean colleges, yet are unable to find employment in line with their educations, in part because of white discrimination and in part because they do not yet have the necessary language skills. Like white ethnic merchants before them, Korean American merchants have sometimes become the latest "middleman minorities."[72]

In recent years, conflict has also erupted between Korean American entrepreneurs and Latinos in California. Some studies have found strong antagonism between the groups. For example, many rioters looting Korean businesses during the major 1992 Los Angeles riot were Latinos. In addition, Korean American garment industry subcontractors are often seen by their low-wage Latino employees as profit-seeking exploiters indifferent to workers' well-being. In their turn, these Korean American contractors report frequent verbal disputes in the workplace and acts of vandalism by Latino workers. The Korean American subcontractors are themselves in turn exploited by white manufacturers, who make use of a subcontracting system designed for flexible and profitable production of garments.[73]

In recent years, Korean Americans have also been targets for hate crimes in other regions, many of which are apparently perpetrated by whites who view them as generic Asian Americans or who cannot distinguish among Asian groups. For example, in one recent Georgia incident involving a Korean American church, much church property was vandalized and painted with swastikas and racist epithets, including "chink mobile" written on the church van.[74]

Vietnamese Americans

Many Vietnamese immigrants fished as a livelihood in their homeland, and some have moved to fishing communities on the U.S. coasts. In the 1970s, they were encouraged to move to the Gulf Coast because of its labor shortage. They generally took low-paying jobs, such as cleaning fish or working in restaurant kitchens, and in these positions were mostly accepted. But as they began to buy boats and offer competition to white fishers, white attitudes changed. Many whites have resented the Vietnamese Americans' success and have blamed them for economic problems on the Gulf Coast.

They have faced hostility and violence. A 1979 conflict between Vietnamese Americans and whites in Seadrift, Texas, culminated in the shooting death of a white fisher. Vietnamese refugees were arrested for the shooting, which followed an argument over placement of crab traps. Within hours of the death, Vietnamese boats were burned, a house was fire-bombed, and an attempt was made to bomb a packing plant where Vietnamese Americans worked. The attacks caused most Vietnamese Americans to flee. Those arrested were acquitted. In response, some whites turned to the Ku Klux Klan for "protection of their industrial interest."[75]

Vietnamese Americans have faced racialized violence elsewhere. For example, in the mid-1980s, the Boston police department reported that nearly one-fourth of Boston's racial violence was directed at Vietnamese and other Asian Americans. In 1989, one Vietnamese and four Cambodian children were gunned down in Stockton, California, by a white man who attacked children at his old school, which now had mostly Asian children. He had expressed much hostility toward Asians. Significantly, most media reports ignored his anti-Asian racism.[76]

Conflict similar to that between Korean American business owners and the black residents of the communities where they operate has also arisen between Vietnamese American owners and community residents. In summer 1996, open conflict arose in New Orleans, including a fight between the son of a Vietnamese American shopkeeper and a black resident. Black residents and their Committee for Justice boycotted the Vietnamese-owned grocery store, charging the owners with discrimination and other mistreatment. In their turn, the owners charged black residents with "untrustworthiness and years of tolerating obscene language and repeated taunts to 'go back to your own country.'"[77] The owners closed the store and filed a lawsuit against black organizations. Both sides engaged in intensive stereotyping of the other. Eventually, several hundred Vietnamese and African American church members met to try to better understand each others' perspectives and cultures.

In the last few years, Vietnamese Americans have been targets of numerous hate crimes. Recently in Santa Barbara, California, a Vietnamese American student and his friend were aggressively called racist slurs ("gook," "Chink," and "Chinaman") by white college students and were physically attacked near a University of California fraternity house. Moreover, a white man in Seattle was recently charged with verbally abusing and attacking a Vietnamese

American in a parking lot. After he was in police custody, the man continued to threaten to kill immigrants. And in Portland, Oregon, another Vietnamese American reported being attacked by men yelling racist slurs and hitting his car while he was stopped at a red light.[78]

Asian-Indian Americans

Asian-Indian Americans have faced significant racialized hostility and discrimination. In public schools, Asian-Indian children have been called numerous derogatory names (e.g., "dot heads" and "terrorists") and physically abused because of their ancestry. Religion-based hazing targeting South Asians has become common in schools and other settings. In recent years, white politicians have made hostile comments about South Asians. In his 2006 try for reelection, Senator George Allen (R–Va.) publicly called a South Asian campaign worker of his opponent a racist epithet ("macaca"). Politicians and others often view and call Asian-Indian Americans "foreigners." Especially since the 9/11 terrorist attacks, South Asian Americans have become confused in some ignorant non-Asian minds with Middle Easterners. For example, in a 2005 city council election in Orange City, Florida, a white candidate spoke of his Asian-Indian opponent as being linked to 9/11 ("these kind of people") and asserted that "I don't want an Indian in my government."[79]

Asian-Indian and other South Asian Americans have faced significant violence. In Queens, New York, Rishi Maharaj received multiple injuries when beaten with bats by white men shouting racist epithets and threats. Two days later, a Pakistani American gas attendant was killed with a baseball bat on Long Island. Asian-Indian American men who are religious Sikhs seem particularly likely to be attacked, often because of turbans they wear. In November 2007, a Seattle Sikh cab driver was called racist slurs and "an Iraqi terrorist," and viciously attacked by a drunken football fan. In addition, the Sikh Coalition in New York City reports that 40 percent of Sikhs there have been targeted with religious or racial harassment, and that a majority of Sikh students have suffered mocking, often because of the religious head covering (patka) they wear.[80]

In recent years, Asian-Indian Americans have also faced significant harassment by police officers and other community members. In Edison, New Jersey,

a community rally was held recently by Asian Indians to protest incidents they viewed as police brutality targeting people of Asian descent. When local authorities refused to address the problem, several dozen members of the South Asian communities held a protest demonstration, which was countered by whites with racist and anti-immigrant signs saying "You must've slid under the border to come here" and "You're all cockroaches! Go home!"[81]

 How does the dominant white racial frame shape relations between Asian Americans and other Americans?

Organizing and Activism in the Political Arena

The number of Asian American voters is increasing dramatically in numerous areas, especially in major coastal cities. Some call this vote a "sleeping giant" of U.S. politics. Indeed, Asian Americans' increased voting power was on display in the 2008 election, where they voted substantially (62 percent according to exit polls) for the Democratic Party presidential candidate, Barack Obama, thereby helping put the first American of color in the U.S. presidency. Nonetheless, except in Hawaii, Asian Americans still have limited political and judicial representation. Even in the last few years, as noted in Chapter 10, federal appointed offices, including judges, cabinet positions, and congressional staff positions, have been relatively hard to secure. Norman Mineta, a Japanese American, has held two presidential cabinet posts. In 2001, President George W. Bush appointed Elaine Chao as Secretary of Labor, making her the *first* Chinese American and Asian American woman to hold a Cabinet post. President Obama appointed two more Asian Americans to cabinet positions—Chinese Americans Gary Locke (Commerce Secretary) and Steven Chu (Energy Secretary).

In early 2010, there were also just eleven voting members in both houses of Congress with some Asian ancestry, three of whom were from Hawaii. Four were Japanese Americans (Matsui, Honda, Hirono, and Inouye) mentioned in the last chapter. Three others were Chinese Americans. Of Chinese and native Hawaiian ancestry, Daniel K. Akaka

Taiwan-born U.S. Congressman David Wu of Oregon (left) *is greeted by Taiwanese President Chen Shui-bian at the Presidential Palace in Taipei.*

(D–Hawaii) was elected U.S. senator in 1990. In 1999, David Wu (D–Ore.) became the first Chinese American ever to serve in the U.S. House; he remained in that office in 2010, joined there in 2009 by Judy Chu (D-Calif.). Another representative, Robert Scott (D–Va.), is of Filipino, black, and white ancestry and has served since 1993. Serving since the 2000 election, Senator John Ensign (R-Nev.) is one-eighth Filipino American. Elected in 2008, Representative Steve Austria (R-Ohio) is of more substantial Filipino heritage. In 2008, Representative Anh Cao (R-La.) became the only Vietnamese American to ever serve in Congress. In 2003, Bobby Jindal (R–La.) became only the second Asian-Indian American ever elected to Congress. He remained there one term, then became governor of Louisiana. Over the decades, only a few Asian Americans have served in the U.S. Congress.[82]

Advances at the state level have come slowly, although growing numbers of Asian Americans have run for office since the 1990s. In the mid-1990s, the state of Washington elected a Chinese American governor, Gary Locke, the first Asian American elected governor outside Hawaii. In 2010, however, in California, where Asian Americans made up more than 12.4 percent of its voting-age population, there were only three Asian American members of Congress and

three members in its state legislature. In early 2010, only sixty-seven Asian Americans were serving among the country's 7424 state legislators, less than 1 percent. (The figure is 0.2 percent if Hawaii is omitted from the count.) A substantial majority of Asian American elected officials at the state level serve in Hawaii's legislature or executive branch. A serious lack of representation in government also exists in most local areas with substantial Asian American populations. For example, until 2002, when Chinese American John Liu became a councilmember from Queens, no Asian American had ever served on New York City's council. Although Asian Americans have had little representation in big-city politics in the past, the number of Asian American candidates running for office has grown significantly in recent years.[83]

Nationally, a large proportion of Asian Americans have immigrated too recently to be eligible to vote, and the registration rate of those eligible has been relatively low, although this is now changing. Many have not registered or voted because they come from countries with undemocratic political systems and do not trust politicians. In addition, anti-Asian discrimination by mostly white government and party officials has played a role in reducing political involvement. U.S. Civil Rights Commission conferences have noted general barriers to political participation, including apportionment policies diluting the strength of Asian American voting blocs. Several field studies have found that Asian American voters periodically face discrimination at the polls, including faulty translations of candidates' names on ballots and racist remarks from poll workers. One study in nine states by the Asian American Legal Defense and Education Fund gathered 200 reports of voting barriers, including poll workers making excessive requests for identification, using erroneous voter lists, not allowing required provisional ballots, giving voters the runaround on poll-site addresses, restricting voters from required interpreters and voting materials, and otherwise failing to assist voters with limited English proficiency. Significant proportions of older Asian American voters in numerous cities have limited English proficiency and thus difficulty in voting. Asian American civil rights groups have filed lawsuits contending there is such discrimination in local voting procedures.[84]

Pan-Asian Organizations and Coalitions

Nineteenth-century and early twentieth-century Asian immigrants, divided by language and cultural differences and historical tensions between their countries of origin, held fast to distinctive cultural identities, resisting the tendency of non-Asian Americans to lump all Asians together. This has remained true for most first-generation immigrants in recent decades. However, among the large number of second- and later-generation Asian Americans, language and cultural barriers are not as significant, and a pan-Asian identity and solidarity have developed in many cities.

Beginning on college campuses in the 1960s and spreading to community activists and professional organizations by the 1970s, pan-Asian organizations and news media have helped to forge a group consciousness among many students, artists, professionals, and other Asian Americans. This movement to **panethnicity**—*the generalization of solidarity among ethnic subgroups*—is fostered by shared cultural backgrounds, but especially common experiences of racial and ethnic oppression in the United States and a common interest in fighting that oppression. All Asian American groups have experienced being considered unwanted "foreigners" by other Americans, especially white Americans. Indeed, one recent

research study found that most Asian American respondents from various nationality groups now have a strong group consciousness and identification with the umbrella concept of "Asian American." This group consciousness was enhanced for them when they were shown photos of prominent Asian Americans. In addition to pressures internal to Asian American communities, the researchers suggest that the use of classifications such as "Asian race" by the U.S. Census Bureau and other government agencies, and the general use by whites of terms and concepts such as "model minority" and "foreigners," have helped to foster Asian American as a general racial-group consciousness among the diversity of Asian American nationalities.[85]

The term *Asian American* is now generally preferred to the term *Oriental*, with its roots in European colonialism and imperialism. Asia is East (Oriental) only if the point of reference is Europe. The term *Oriental* has long been associated with white-generated stereotypes of Asian deviousness, passivity, and acquiescence. For many, *Asian American* now includes a significant sense of respect and empowerment.[86]

Not all Asian Americans were empowered by the pan-Asian organizations of the 1960s. Women reported that they were often restricted to subordinate roles in organizations, and those who challenged sexism in the movement were often ridiculed as "traitors" to Asian American unity. Feeling alienated from the mainstream (mostly white) women's movement, as have other racially oppressed women, Asian American women have formed their own groups within the context of the Asian American identity, often emphasizing their triple oppression based on gender, racial group, and class. Indeed, organizations of racially oppressed women have helped bring the issue of multiple forms of stratification—of race, gender, and class—into sharper focus in recent racial–ethnic scholarship.[87]

Not until the 1980s did a national pan-Asian *political* organization specifically address broad Asian American concerns. The first major political effort began in 1986 with the founding of the Asian-American Voters Coalition, which included organizations representing Japanese, Chinese, Asian-Indian, Filipino, Korean, Vietnamese, and Thai Americans. Since then, groups like this organization have sought to consolidate Asian Americans into an effective voting bloc that can influence elections from California to New

York; protect Asian Americans' civil rights; and fight anti-Asian legislation, distorted media images, hate crimes, and employment discrimination. From the 1980s to the present, the Asian Pacific American Legal Center of Southern California, the country's largest legal organization serving Asian-Pacific Americans, has often taken action to protect Asian immigrants' rights, such as the right to speak their languages in workplaces, and has addressed numerous other civil rights and community issues.[88]

In the 1990s, numerous (now twenty-one) Asian American organizations, including the Japanese American Citizens League and the Organization of Chinese Americans, joined to form the National Council of Asian Pacific Americans (NCAPA). Today, the NCAPA continues to be concerned with such problems as hate crimes, discrimination, immigration rights and restrictions, and the unfair singling out of Asian Americans during various government investigations.[89]

Coalitions with non-Asian groups have also been created. Latino, African, Vietnamese, Korean, Chinese, and other Asian American leaders in Los Angeles created the Multicultural Association for Voter Registration to encourage all Americans of color to register to vote and become more active politically. Numerous coalitions in major cities continue to reflect a growing awareness that cooperation generates greater political power.[90]

Chinese Americans

Chinese Americans have a long history of immigration and have been among the most politically active of groups in this chapter. After World War I, Chinese Americans became increasingly involved in worker and political organizations. Labor-oriented organizations were created, such as in New York's relatively large Chinese American communities. Between 1900 and 1930, the Chinese-language newspaper *Chung Sai Yat Po* was an advocate of civil rights for Chinese Americans, including rights of women. The paper's emphasis on political events in China, where the status of women was progressing toward equality, contributed to the social awakening of many Chinese American women.[91]

With the new immigration after 1965 came renewed political activity. Explaining the slowness

Unionized Asian American healthcare workers picket for better wages and working conditions in Los Angeles.

of change, Michael Woo, one of few to hold a major city government position, has argued that one challenge in getting out the vote is that Chinese and other Asian Americans "traditionally view all political activity as suspect."[92] Irving Chin, chair of the Chinatown Advisory Committee to the Borough President of Manhattan, told a U.S. Senate committee that Chinese American political activity was limited because of problems with English and a traditional reluctance to engage in political action. Professor Ling-chi Wang, then chair of Asian American studies at the University of California (Berkeley) and sometimes called the "Chinese Martin Luther King Jr.," spoke to this committee, urging social support programs. Influenced by Wang and others, immigrant parents pressed a lawsuit for bilingual education in public schools, an effort that resulted in a 1974 U.S. Supreme Court decision ordering such bilingual education. More recently, Chinese American and other Asian American activists have worked to get rid of discriminatory height requirements for police officers and fire fighters and to eliminate disproportionately tough admissions standards for Asian American students at elite U.S. universities.[93]

Concerned about various local and national issues, including nativistic attacks on immigrants, Chinese and other Asian Americans have become more politically active. For example, in 2006, Chinese and other Asian Americans organized a protest in New York City against a bill in the U.S. House that turned undocumented immigrants into felons. Action on various local issues is also increasing. One example is Monterey Park, California, a Los Angeles suburb whose population is predominantly Chinese Americans, other Asian Americans, and Latinos. When white council members passed a resolution saying that Monterey Park was not a sanctuary for "illegal aliens" and that English should be the official language, Asian American residents were outraged. Thousands signed petitions demanding the council rescind the resolution, which it did. The controversy indicated a serious rift between fearful whites, who contended that the Asians are "taking over," versus Asian Americans who are only seeking the traditional middle-class dream.[94] Moreover, in 2008, an estimated 10,000 Chinese and other Asian American demonstrators gathered outside CNN offices in Los Angeles to actively protest anti-Chinese comments of the CNN commentator, Jack

Cafferty, who had said about China: "We continue to import their junk with the lead paint on them and the poisoned pet food and export . . . [and send] jobs to places where you can pay workers a dollar a month to turn out the stuff that we're buying from Wal-Mart. . . . I think they're basically the same bunch of goons and thugs they've been for the last 50 years."[95]

Chinese Americans are growing in political influence, with a number of "firsts" in recent years. Recall that in the 1990s, Gary Locke, the son of immigrants, became the first Chinese American to serve as a mainland governor. In 1998, Oregon's David Wu was the first Taiwan-born American to serve in Congress. In the 2006 election, the first Asian American was elected to Connecticut's legislature, Chinese American William Tong. Several Chinese Americans have served on city councils in communities in the Los Angeles area and in San Francisco. California elected Leland Yee in 2006, the first Asian and Chinese American to serve in its Senate. However, getting political representation remains an uphill battle against stereotyping and discrimination. Thus, in the spring of 2001, David Wu and his legislative director, both Chinese Americans, were detained and questioned at a Department of Energy security check-in about their citizenship status and about whether their identification cards were legitimate. Apparently, they did not fit what congressional officials were supposed to look like.[96]

Chinese Americans have become increasingly active in national politics and have pressed major political parties to select Chinese candidates. Yet, as we have noted, few Chinese Americans have so far served in the U.S. Congress. One 2009 survey found that eight in ten Chinese Americans believed that Asian Americans have too little political power today in Washington, DC. Like other groups with numerous immigrants, Chinese Americans are very concerned about U.S. foreign policy. Since the 1980s, many have pressed for changes in U.S. policies toward China. The killing of protesting students in Beijing's Tiananmen Square in 1989 prompted the creation of an organization called the Committee of 100. Headed by influential Chinese Americans, the organization has regularly sought to increase cultural exchanges, improve discussions on outsourcing, and change U.S. government policy on China. Many Chinese Americans have pressured the U.S. government to take stronger action to persuade

China to improve human rights. Even though there is continuing concern about the Chinese government's authoritarian record, many Chinese Americans throughout the United States were pleased when Beijing hosted the 2008 Olympic Games, and many have suggested that bringing the world's media there has had liberalizing effects in China.[97]

Filipino Americans

The most successful farm workers' union, the United Farm Workers (see Chapter 8), was created by a merger between a Mexican American organizing drive and a Filipino labor organization, the Agricultural Workers' Organizing Committee (AWOC). These groups conducted a major strike against poor working conditions on California farms. Larry Itliong, head of the AWOC and a Filipino American activist, worked hard to organize laborers from Alaska to California to South America. Numerous other Filipino labor and political organizations have been created in recent decades.[98]

New resistance tactics have emerged in recent decades. The National Federation of Filipino American Associations (NaFFAA), which evolved from earlier groups, has chapters in most major cities with numerous Filipino American members; it serves as a nonpartisan umbrella group of hundreds of Filipino American organizations. This group actively monitors government policies and legislation of interest to Filipino Americans and works with similar groups on these issues, including enforcement of civil rights laws, fairer immigration laws, and building of global networks in the Filipino diaspora. Since the 1990s, Filipino Americans have held numerous conferences to generate political strategies to win elected and appointed offices in areas where they make up a significant percentage of the population. For example, at several conferences of Filipino organizations, one major issue was getting the provisions of the Filipino Veterans Equity Act passed. The 2009 economic stimulus legislation finally provided support for these Filipino veterans.[99]

Filipino immigrants have long had one of the highest naturalization rates of any immigrant group. Despite stereotyped images of "foreigners," Filipinos and members of other Asian immigrant groups have often been eager to become naturalized U.S. citizens.[100] Yet, even with this strong commitment to being citizens, Filipino Americans have

rarely been elected or appointed to major political offices, even in areas where their numbers are large. In 1990, David Valderrama was the first Filipino elected to a state legislature in a mainland state (Maryland). In 1994, Benjamin Cayetano became the first Filipino American elected to a top state office, as governor of Hawaii. And in recent years, a few have been elected as state senators and representatives, mayors, city council members, and school board members. By 2000, there were about ten Filipino Americans serving in state legislatures, and another dozen serving as elected officials in urban areas. By the late 2000s, numerous Filipino Americans were running for office, but none had yet made it into mainland gubernatorial positions. However, as of 2010, as noted earlier, three serve in the U.S. Congress. A substantial majority voted for Barack Obama for president in 2008.[101]

Numerous Filipino American organizations have responded to the Philippine government's call for investment in the islands to overcome economic crises. Again, we see global influences on U.S. racial groups. In addition, the overthrow of the Ferdinand Marcos dictatorship in the Philippines in the 1980s boosted Filipino American pride. Filipino identity was strengthened by the advent of political democracy, and that change reinforced the commitment of Filipino Americans to greater political participation in the United States. Significantly, in the late 1990s, Filipino American leaders in San Francisco protested the installation of a granite column celebrating Commodore George Dewey's victory over the Spanish in Manila Bay in 1898. Dewey was accurately criticized for bringing U.S. colonialism to the Philippines. Moreover, like other Asian American groups, organized Filipino Americans protest against the significant discrimination they face. Recently, a group of Filipino Americans and other Asian Americans actively protested the mistreatment of a Filipino American female shopper and Air Force veteran by a white male employee who taunted her with being a "mail-order bride" and mocked her with comments like "ching, ching, chang" at a major Chicago department store.[102]

Korean Americans

Only in recent years have Korean Americans gained some significant political power in the United States. Since the 1980s, Korean American Coalition chapters have been formed in several cities, and operate as social and advocacy organizations seeking to increase Korean American participation in political and civic affairs. Recent efforts have accented education, voter registration, citizenship drives, and community service programs. Although Korean Americans have been active in the Asian American political organizations, not one had held major political office in a western state until the early 1990s. In 1992, in California, Jay C. Kim became the first and only Korean American—and the first East Asian immigrant—ever elected to the U.S. House.[103]

After the 1992 Los Angeles riot, the local Korean American Coalition became active. Jerry Yu, a member of the coalition, noted that during the riot, "Korean Americans really saw with their own eyes the lack of political strength that we as a community have."[104] In the last several presidential elections, Korean and other Asian Americans have become very active in registering voters and in supporting candidates of their choice. During the Democratic Party's January 1997 inaugural celebrations, many Korean Americans attended the first-ever Asian American inaugural ball, an indication of growing political influence. Although there are more registered Republicans than Democrats among Korean Americans, a substantial majority voted for

Democrat Barack Obama in the 2008 presidential election.[105]

Periodically, Korean Americans have vigorously demonstrated against discrimination and other mistreatment. Not long after the 1992 Los Angeles riot, in which many Korean American businesses were targeted, more than 30,000 Korean Americans marched to protest these attacks, police brutality, injustice in the legal system, and media bias. It was the largest protest demonstration ever carried out by Asian Americans against injustice, yet it received little media attention. More recently, Asian Americans organized to support a major march in Los Angeles against growing anti-immigrant sentiment and legislation, and in other cities Asian American activists have organized forums on current immigration issues.[106]

Many Korean Americans maintain close ties to Korea. After the 1992 riot, officials from Korea visited riot areas of Los Angeles, arriving even before U.S. presidential candidates that election year. When North Korea faced food shortages, Korean Americans sent more than 1 million dollars for assistance. In recent years, many Korean Americans have signed petitions to the U.S. Secretary of State supporting U.S. negotiations with the North Korean government to unite Korean families divided by the

Korean Americans and others march for peace after a major 1992 Los Angeles riot.

Korean War. Since the late 2000s, many Korean Americans have become involved in U.S. policy debates over the securing of nuclear weapons by North Korea, fearing that their families might be among the first to suffer if such weapons were ever used.[107]

Vietnamese Americans

In recent years, the once icy political relationship between Vietnam and the United States has thawed. By the late 1980s, surveys found half of Vietnamese Americans favoring the establishment of diplomatic ties with Vietnam. Nonetheless, the issue of reestablishing ties to a Communist homeland has been a topic of heated debate within Vietnamese American communities. Indeed, in the late 1990s, many Vietnamese Americans protested outside a store in Westminster, California, when the owner put up a picture of the Vietnamese Communist leader Ho Chi Minh. Others have been successful in getting some city and state governments to replace the current flag of Communist Vietnam with the old South Vietnamese flag when there is need for a Vietnamese flag to be used in the United States. In recent years they have often protested actions of the Vietnamese government, and among Asian American groups they have been the most likely to vote Republican because of their view that the Republican Party is more anti-Communist.[108]

Like other Asian Americans, Vietnamese Americans are still stereotyped as "foreigners." In Orange County, California, a group of Vietnamese Americans seeking a permit for a parade to honor Vietnamese war dead was turned down by the council because whites did not consider that to be "American." Vietnamese stores were defaced by white vandals. A white council member remarked, "If they want to be South Vietnamese, go back to South Vietnam." After protests from the community, the council member apologized. For more than a decade, southern California has had an active Vietnamese American Political Action Committee working for expanded political influence for Vietnamese Americans. Texas has also seen increased Vietnamese American and other Asian American political organization.[109]

Vietnamese Americans have, in recent decades, created numerous important community organizations and institutions, including Buddhist temples

and Vietnamese radio stations. In the 1990s, the Vietnamese Community of Southern California was created to unify 300 local Vietnamese American organizations and to develop employment, immigrant, and youth programs. Similar organizations have been created in other areas. Because of these efforts, over the past two decades several Vietnamese Americans have been elected to local and state political offices in California and Texas, including to the Orange County Board of Supervisors and the city councils of Westminster, Garden Grove, and San Jose, California, as well as to the legislatures of California and Texas. Thus, in 1992, Tony Lam, a restaurant owner, was elected to the Westminster City Council in Orange County and became the first Vietnamese American elected to political office. In the mid-2000s, Van Tran and Hubert Vo were the first to be elected to the California and Texas legislatures. By 2010, more than two dozen Vietnamese Americans had run for political office, mainly in California. Still, only a few have served as elected officials anywhere in the United States.[110]

Vietnamese Americans have played an important role in developing national organizations working for southeast Asian concerns. One such group, the Southeast Asia Resource Action Center (SEARAC) in Washington, DC, engages in political action and educational efforts for the Asian American community and has worked on domestic social programs and U.S. foreign policy, as well as on immigrant rights and other civil rights issues. SEARAC provides leadership training and technical assistance for numerous Asian American organizations. In addition, some local communities, such as the large Vietnamese American community in New Orleans, have begun to flex their political muscles. After Hurricane Katrina (2005), the Vietnamese Americans there successfully stopped plans to put tons of debris from the flooding in a landfill near their community.[111]

Asian-Indian Americans

Because of their relatively recent arrival in large numbers, Asian Indians have relatively little political visibility. In the history of the U.S. Congress, only two Asian-Indian Americans have served, the first being Californian Dalip Singh Saund, elected in the 1950s. He was also the first Asian American member of Congress. By the 1990s, Asian-Indian Americans were forming organizations designed to increase political influence. Benefitting from this activity, Pitambar Somani was appointed Ohio's director of health in the mid-1990s, the first Asian Indian to serve in a governor's cabinet. Since then, the number of Asian-Indian Americans running for political office has slowly grown in New Jersey and other states with rapidly increasing Asian-Indian American populations. Recall that in 2003, Jindal (R–La.) became the second Asian-Indian American elected to Congress. In 2006, two South Asians were elected to the state legislature of Maryland, and a few others were elected to other state legislatures. Slowly, their representation is increasing. Moreover, in recent decades, Asian-Indian Americans have created organizations to fight discrimination. For example, a Hartford, Connecticut, group has pressed for changes in discriminatory licensing requirements for foreign-born physicians and has lobbied for government aid for India. This is yet another example of the influence of international contexts on the political orientations of U.S. immigrant groups.[112]

The New York Taxi Workers Alliance organized a large group of South Asian taxi drivers in the 1990s to protest poor working conditions and poor treatment by city officials. Representing many taxi drivers, the group included Asian Indians as well as taxi drivers from Pakistan and Bangladesh. Faced with twelve-hour shifts, low incomes, and no fringe benefits, the drivers staged a successful strike against officials' attempts to impose unfair regulations on taxis. The strike helped organize drivers from a diverse array of South Asian groups to work together for better working conditions.[113]

Broad South Asian coalitions such as the New York Taxi Workers Alliance have increased in number. Especially since 9/11, groups have organized to counter the numerous hate crimes committed against South Asians, often because ignorant non-Asians think South Asians are Middle Easterners. New Asian-Indian American organizations, such as the United States India Political Action Committee (USINPAC, created in 2002), have been established "to impact policy on issues of concern to the Indian American community in the United States. USINPAC provides bipartisan support to candidates for federal, state and local office who support the issues that are important to the Indian American community."[114] Currently, this organization has worked on immigration, hate-crime legislation,

civil rights, and equal opportunity issues, as well as on enhancing U.S.–India business and government relationships.

 How have pan-Asian organizations and coalitions helped in resisting stereotypes and discrimination?

The Economy

In recent decades, the U.S. Civil Rights Commission has documented the exploitation of Asian and other immigrants, who are often unaware of their rights, by employers who violate laws regarding fair working conditions, wages, and hours. As with other Americans of color, civil rights laws and Supreme Court decisions have often failed to protect Asian American workers from serious discrimination.

Even highly educated Asian immigrants with managerial or professional experience have faced significant barriers. Employers often discount immigrants' experience and credentials. They may be hired for research, engineering, and other technical positions, yet remain underrepresented at management levels in most large companies. A 1990s study found that U.S.-born Asian American men with good English proficiency were less likely to hold managerial positions than white men with comparable qualifications. Today, as then, Asian Americans are rare in top management and professional positions in major corporations. Those seeking to be directors, top managers, and senior professionals report a "glass ceiling." Recall from Chapter 10 that Asian Americans (and Pacific Islanders), about 5 percent of the population, currently hold only 2.2 percent of board positions at *Fortune 100* companies. Most boards have had no Asian American representation. In addition, only four Asian Americans are currently chairs or CEOs of a *Fortune 500* company. Asian Americans qualified to be directors and top executives face "good old boy networks" and stereotyping about their "lack of leadership abilities" and "nerdiness." One study of Asian American managers found that they were often seen as docile workers who could be hired and fired at will because they would not complain.[115]

Out of frustration, numerous Asian American professionals and lower-level managers have drawn on their entrepreneurial skills, left major corporations, and started companies. Even then, they face discrimination. For example, recent studies and court cases in Chicago have found major racial disparities and discrimination in construction contracting for businesspeople of color including Asian Americans. Asian Americans were found to have less than their share of government construction contracts, as compared with their percentage of construction-related firms. They have also suffered discrimination at the hands of banks and other lending organizations.[116]

One 1990s U.S. Civil Rights Commission study found discrimination to be even more severe for Asian American women. These workers are vulnerable not only to discrimination but also to sexual harassment and other gender discrimination on the job. They are frequently excluded from informal networks of white co-workers and enjoy fewer sources of support than white women when confronted with harassment. Recent studies have found continuing job problems. Asian American women professionals and other workers frequently report being channeled into jobs seen as appropriate for women, being limited in training they can get for promotion, and being excluded from critical "good old boy" networks that provide essential job information. Their experiences also include making significantly less than men, and especially white men.[117]

Discrimination based on physical appearance, language proficiency, or verbal accent is also commonplace for Asian American employees. Recently, for example, nine Asian American and Latino plaintiffs sued Abercrombie & Fitch Co. for hiring discrimination. They charged the company's policy of hiring "attractive" employees favored "a blond, blue-eyed staff" and discriminated "against people of color in hiring, job assignment, compensation, and termination." In addition, in a major decision, the Ninth Circuit Court of Appeals upheld an employer's right to consider an Asian applicant's verbal skills when these were relevant to job performance. As noted previously (see Chapter 8), many Asian and Latin American immigrants, and sometimes their children, are adversely affected by English-only rules in the workplace, many of which are inappropriate because they are not relevant to job requirements. In one recent example, the LPGA established a "good English only" rule for all its women golfers because numerous Korean American golfers had English skills and accents that were viewed by the white leadership as displeasing to

(presumably white) sponsors of U.S. women's golf tournaments. After significant protests, however, the LGPA backed off of its discriminatory rule.[118]

Chinese Americans

In the nineteenth century, Chinese immigrants were recruited to fill less-skilled jobs in the U.S. The first large-scale use of Chinese labor was in the construction of the transcontinental railroad, completed in 1869. Early workers converted swampland in California to farmland; their planting, cultivating, and harvesting skills were used extensively at white-owned vineyards, orchards, and ranches. Chinese factory workers were an important part of the California economy. Most of them labored for long hours in poor conditions for very low wages. Later, the demand for large numbers of factory workers in World War II defense plants opened better opportunities for Chinese Americans. Between 1940 and 1950, more than one-third of Chinese American men remained in service occupations, but percentages in craft, technical, and professional occupations more than doubled. War industries provided increasing numbers of women with clerical and technical jobs.[119]

In recent decades, many working-class Chinese immigrants' prospects have not been good because they have lacked money, skills, or the ability to speak English well. Most have settled in preexisting urban Chinese American communities, where men often find service jobs and women work in nonunion garment factories. Working conditions are frequently substandard, and pay is low. The better educated among these postwar immigrants—such as engineers, doctors, mathematicians, and scientists trained in China, Taiwan, or the United States—have usually found better jobs in U.S. industries and universities and generally have had an easier time adjusting to their new country than poorer immigrants.[120]

Globalization of the U.S. economy since the 1970s can be seen in the major growth in high-tech industries, including those on the West Coast. U.S. employers' desire for cheaper labor has led many high-tech employers to recruit skilled labor from overseas, especially from China, India, and the Philippines. Attracted by high-tech employment, many new U.S. engineers and medical personnel since the 1980s have been immigrants from abroad, often from Asia. Many have been educated in over-seas universities oriented to a Western curriculum or have been international students at Western universities.[121] Some have become entrepreneurs, creating high-tech U.S. firms.

By the early 2000s, white executives at some major companies doing business in Asia had discovered that hiring Chinese and other Asian American executives for overseas management positions was smarter than sending white executives. One business report notes that "when Starbucks was looking to hire someone to lead its Asia Pacific operation in the late 1990s, it chose Pedro Man, a Canadian Chinese. In 2002, David Wang, a Chinese American, was appointed president of Boeing-China. Many of these newly appointed executives were born in Asia and educated in the West." The article notes that such executives are familiar with Asian and U.S. cultures and can act as human bridges operating in different countries and cultures. Nonetheless, Asian American

managers and professionals are much less likely to be chosen to head up major corporate facilities within the United States.[122]

Table 11.2 shows the most recent data for occupational distributions of the groups in this chapter and of whites. (All chapter tables include data for those who reported only one group for ancestry.) Today, workers who listed only being of Chinese descent in the recent American Community Survey are heavily concentrated in white-collar and small-business jobs; some 53.2 percent hold professional and managerial positions, a category that includes some small entrepreneurs. The proportion of Chinese Americans exceeds that of whites in this category, but whites are more likely to be in higher-paying jobs in this broad category. Chinese Americans are a little more likely to be in the blue-collar service-sector jobs than whites. (The occupational distribution for people who listed both Chinese ancestry and non-Chinese ancestry is very similar.)

TABLE 11.2 Occupational Distribution by Group (2008)

	Chinese American	Filipino American	Korean American	Vietnamese American	Asian-Indian American	White American
Managerial and professional specialty	53.2%	42.2%	44.7%	30.0%	65.1%	38.7%
Sales and office occupations	20.1	24.7	27.1	17.9	18.9	26.2
Construction, extraction, maintenance, and repair occupations	2.8	3.9	4.1	6.1	1.6	9.1
Production, transportation, and material moving occupations	7.7	9.6	8.6	19.4	7.0	11.1
Service occupations	16.1	19.4	15.3	26.3	7.2	14.4
Farming, forestry, and fishing	0.1	0.2	0.1	0.3	0.1	0.5
Totals	100%	100%	99.9%	100%	99.9%	100%

Source: U.S. Bureau of the Census. "2008 American Community Survey."

In the late 2000s, Chinese Americans' unemployment rate was lower than that of the population as a whole (4.7 percent versus 6.4 percent).[123]

The Chinese American community is significantly represented at both ends of the economic spectrum. An Wang (1920–1990), head of his own firm, became a billionaire. I. M. Pei (1917–) is one of the country's leading modern architects. In recent decades, Chinese American novelists have written insightfully about their group's experiences. One of the first was Maxine Hong Kingston, whose 1970 novel, *The Woman Warrior,* won major book awards. Amy Tan is another well-known author. Her novel, *The Joy Luck Club,* which became a movie, has helped to stimulate much novel writing by Asian Americans. Kingston and Tan draw on important experiences in Chinese communities, especially mother–daughter relationships. Maya Lin, an innovative Chinese American architect, designed the National Vietnam Veterans Memorial on the Washington, DC, mall while in her twenties, as well as a memorial to civil rights workers in Montgomery, Alabama.[124]

At the other end of the economic continuum, however, nearly 9.2 percent of Chinese American families live below the poverty line. Table 11.3 presents the most recent data available on income and poverty for the Asian American groups (those reporting one ancestry). In the late 2000s, median family income for Chinese American families ($81,823) was significantly higher than that of white families.[125] In evaluating these higher incomes for Asian American groups, however, one should recognize that, generally speaking, average Asian American families have more workers per family and/or more family members than average white families. The typical Asian

American family is also more likely to be in an expensive metropolitan area on the West Coast or in the New York City area than the average white family. Note too that in the late 2000s, the proportion of Chinese American families living in poverty was significantly greater than that of white families. (These economic data change little when those reporting both Chinese and non-Chinese ancestry are added in.) In addition, U.S.-born Chinese Americans tend to be better educated, to hold managerial or professional jobs outside the small-business economy, and to live outside dense "Chinatowns" in large cities. In contrast, recent Chinese immigrants are more likely to have less education, be unemployed or hold low-wage jobs, and/or live in inner cities.[126]

One study of Manhattan's Chinese American community revealed that the area did not fit the common image, sometimes seen in movies or on television crime shows, of an exotic urban zone with dangerous and mysterious "Orientals" and "red light districts." Instead, it is mostly peopled by hard-working Chinese Americans who have created a booming local economy and a community "that is the center of economic and social life for the Chinese population throughout the New York City metropolitan area."[127] Yet, such communities periodically face urban redevelopment pressures, such as when non-Asian officials who view the areas in "exotic" terms propose redevelopment projects to "clean them up."

Current workplace and business discrimination faced by Chinese and other Asian Americans takes many forms. Nearly half of the general (mostly white) respondents in a 2009 survey thought that Asian Americans were generally promoted as fairly as whites, and half felt they were fairly represented on

---

TABLE 11.3   Income Level by Group (2008)

	Chinese American	Filipino American	Korean American	Vietnamese American	Asian-Indian American	White American
Median family income	$81,823	$87,069	$66,055	$60,566	$99,783	$70,835
Below poverty level (families)	9.2%	3.9%	10.9%	11.7%	4.9%	6.1%

Source: U.S. Bureau of the Census. "2008 American Community Survey."

corporate boards. However, a substantial majority of Chinese Americans in another survey felt that Asian Americans were *not* fairly treated in regard to such employment matters.[128] Also, a study by sociologist Leland Saito examined the redevelopment of a shopping center in Monterey Park, California, which is now a majority Asian American community. The white minority forced an important redevelopment project to be done *their* way. "Rather than reflecting the city's current and future position as a major node for Asian-themed businesses, the shopping center was remodeled [with a Mediterranean design] to provide a place where whites could shop and 'feel at home.'"[129]

Filipino Americans

Filipinos were first recruited as farm workers for Hawaiian sugar plantations and West Coast farms. Most were single men who endured grueling work and meager wages. In the 1930s, thousands, constituting 40 percent of California's Salinas Valley agricultural workforce, formed the Filipino Labor Union (FLU). An FLU-led strike of workers was met with violence from white growers supported by police. Strikers eventually won wages of $0.40 an hour and recognition of the union. This labor union involvement signaled a consciousness that economic mobility would have to involve much struggle against racial and class oppression in the United States. Military-related Filipino communities were created on the West Coast in the 1950s and 1960s, when U.S. armed forces began recruiting Filipinos into its civilian workforce. For decades, U.S. hospitals have recruited Filipino nurses. Many Filipino engineers and other professionals have emigrated because of political and economic crises at home.[130]

Table 11.2 shows a concentration of Americans reporting only Filipino ancestry in white-collar jobs. They are somewhat less heavily represented in professional and managerial positions and more heavily represented in technical, sales, and administrative support jobs than Chinese Americans. Filipino Americans are more likely to hold service-sector jobs and less likely to hold skilled blue-collar jobs than are whites. Significantly, the unemployment rate for Filipino Americans in the late 2000s was 4.8 percent, somewhat lower than that of the general population (6.4 percent).[131]

As we observe in Table 11.3, in the late 2000s, Filipino Americans reported a relatively high median family income, higher than that for whites ($87,069 versus $70,835). Again, these figures are somewhat misleading. On average, more family members work among Filipino Americans than in the white population, and thus families have a lower per capita income. Most Filipino Americans also live on the West Coast, where wages and living costs are higher than many other parts of the United States. Note too that Filipino Americans have the lowest family poverty rate of any group in Table 11.3.

For decades now, Filipino Americans have faced serious job discrimination, including language discrimination. A 1988 lawsuit filed with the Equal Employment Opportunity Commission charged that the San Francisco city government systematically discriminated against Filipino Americans. Statistical data indicated that Filipino Americans held only 1 percent of the city's administrative and supervisory positions although they made up 12 percent of the city's professional workers. Filipino American organizations charged that whites in government stereotyped Filipino American professionals as incapable of leadership and penalized them because of their accents. Then, in the 1990s, a federal judge upheld a Los Angeles hospital's ban on speaking Tagalog, the native language of many Filipinos. The hospital prohibited Filipino nurses from speaking Tagalog at any time, even on their breaks. In Hawaii, a Filipino American unsuccessfully sued officials who discriminated against him by turning him down for a white-collar job because of his Filipino-accented English. Over the 1990s and the 2000s, as we discussed in Chapter 8, numerous court cases have continued to target English-only workplace rules and discrimination by employers against employees who speak a certain type of accented English, especially that of Asian and Latino American employees. While bars to non–work-related speech other than English are illegal under EEOC guidelines, most federal judges dealing with English-only workplace requirements have upheld such discriminatory requirements.[132]

We should note too that the impact of discrimination today on Filipino American and other Asian American workers is often serious. In several recent studies Filipino American respondents have reported significant levels of everyday discrimination. One recent study of 1652 Filipino Americans asked about

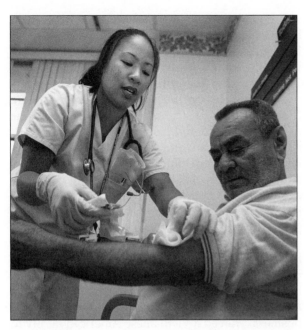

Filipino Americans constitute a large proportion of the nurses in New York area hospitals.
Source: The New York Times.

discrimination they faced at work and about a long list of negative health conditions ranging from asthma and diabetes to hypertension and heart problems. The researchers found that the extent of workplace discrimination was significant and "associated with an increased number of health conditions. . . . Racial discrimination in the workplace was positively associated with poor health among Filipino Americans after we controlled for . . . general concerns about one's job."[133]

Korean Americans

Language barriers and racial discrimination kept early Korean immigrants from obtaining employment in accordance with their abilities. The early–twentieth-century Korean immigrants typically engaged in hard labor for low wages. Many, including educated professionals, worked as agricultural laborers or as dishwashers, housekeepers, or janitors in urban areas. Koreans arriving in recent decades have included a great array of abilities and backgrounds, including scientists and other professionals. A significant percentage have become entrepreneurs, starting small stores, often in low-income

areas. With the largest self-employed percentage of any Asian (or white) group (24 percent in the most recent tabulated census), Korean Americans have filled an important small-business niche in New York, Philadelphia, Los Angeles, and other large cities. Surveys of Korean American small-business owners have found that few had been small-business owners in Korea. Indeed, most had held white-collar jobs in their homeland.[134]

Many Asian immigrants have moved into self-employment because of *exclusion* from professions for which they were trained. Limited English proficiency is one factor, but anti-Asian discrimination is also a reality. Like other Asian Americans, as we have noted previously, Korean Americans holding white-collar jobs are often passed over for promotions, especially to higher management ranks, regardless of education or language skills. Indeed, several news reports have indicated that some managers and professionals have actually moved back to Korea, where their skills allow them to move up the corporate ladders.[135]

Given discriminatory barriers, many Koreans prefer the freedom afforded by self-employment. Korean immigrants have arrived at a time when earlier immigrant groups are moving out of the inner-city small-business niche into white-collar jobs. Many, especially women, have little knowledge of English, and their main employment option is a family business. One of the dramatic changes brought by international immigration is the greatly increased participation of Korean women in the workforce, often in family businesses. This participation has had some effect on the strong patriarchal values that immigrants brought with them from Korea. These new roles for Korean American women have often "reduced their husbands' patriarchal authority, creating new sources of marital conflict and sometimes leading to separation and divorce." They have also influenced the preference among growing numbers of Korean women for white men as partners and husbands.[136]

Many Korean immigrants arrived with some capital, and often have the support of the larger Asian American community, including local banks. Korean American businesses tend to be smaller and more likely to serve members of their group or customers in low-income urban areas than businesses started by immigrant groups from some other countries (for example, Iran). In addition, one Los Angeles survey found that those Korean American merchants whose customers are primarily black or Latino actually earn more than those whose customers are primarily white. Many of these merchants take the profits earned in low-income communities and move out to middle-class areas. Black resentment over Korean merchants taking money out of the black community has contributed to the hostility that many black urbanites feel toward these entrepreneurs. Researchers have found a high degree of geographic mobility among Korean Americans in Los Angeles. Many live for only a short time in a heavily Korean inner-city area before moving out to a suburb.[137]

Table 11.2 reveals that today Americans who report only Korean ancestry are more likely to hold professional and managerial jobs, and sales and office jobs, than whites. Korean Americans are a little more likely to be in service occupations and less likely to hold skilled blue-collar jobs than whites. In the late 2000s, the unemployment rate for Korean Americans was below that of the general population (5.1 percent versus 6.4 percent). The median family income for Korean Americans ($66,055) was below the white median ($70,835). Korean Americans also have a relatively high poverty rate among groups in Table 11.3. In addition, one recent report on Korean immigrant workers found that many of them were low-wage service workers—often working in restaurants, groceries, nail salons, construction, and dry cleaning businesses. Some 30 percent of these were undocumented, and they were seriously exploited by employers. They were often made to work long hours and not given employee benefits—to which they were entitled. Probably because of the significant number of undocumented Korean immigrant workers in numerous Korean American communities, there is significant support among Korean Americans for the protests in some cities against nativistic groups and anti-immigrant legislation.[138]

Vietnamese Americans

Among the 1.7 million Vietnamese Americans, a majority have a relatively short history in the United States. Those who came right after the Vietnam War were often more affluent and better educated than those who came later. Some had been in business. After immigrating, many suffered downward mobility. One survey then found that more than six in ten immigrants with white-collar jobs in Vietnam held blue-collar jobs in the United States. The remainder held white-collar jobs, primarily clerical or sales work.[139]

Vietnamese Americans still face significant discrimination. In the 1990s, one convenience store chain settled a class-action lawsuit charging that one manager had ordered discrimination against Vietnamese American employees. Two supervisors reported they were told to fire Vietnamese workers and hire whites. In the settlement the company agreed to hire more Vietnamese managers. Soon, however, employees of the chain were back in court, protesting continuing discrimination in company stores. Vietnamese immigrants and their children have faced discrimination when they have tried to run a small business. In one recent account a white health inspector, who made openly racist comments like "You yellow people don't know how to run a business," forced a Vietnamese American family to close a business in a town in Oregon.[140]

One study in California found that Vietnamese male and female employees were paid less than comparable white workers. As we have seen in other studies of Asian American workers, Vietnamese men and women were found to be less likely to be promoted to management positions than white counterparts. Another recent study also found that Vietnamese Americans reported a significant level of discrimination, one that linked to personal stress and health problems.[141] Note too the data in Table 11.2. In 2008, Americans reporting only Vietnamese ancestry held lower (but still substantial) percentages of professional-managerial positions or sales-office positions than other Asian Americans or whites. Vietnamese Americans held the highest proportions of blue-collar jobs among Asian groups. More than half held various blue-collar (especially service) jobs. This occupational situation was reflected in median family income ($60,566), which was substantially below that of whites ($70,835) and other large Asian groups (Table 11.3). About one in nine Vietnamese families fell below the U.S. poverty line. In the late 2000s, moreover, their unemployment rate was lower (5.3 percent) than the total population figure (6.4 percent), but the highest of any major Asian American group. (Many later Vietnamese immigrants have faced low-wage jobs and poverty. They have not been as economically successful as first arrivals.) Consider too that, like other

Asian Americans, many Vietnamese live in the relatively high-cost state of California. Nonetheless, they are today upwardly mobile, with younger generations becoming better educated and moving into better-paying white-collar jobs.[142]

Asian-Indian Americans

Most of the country's more than 2.7 million Asian-Indian Americans have roots in relatively recent immigration. Most have not settled in preexisting communities on the West Coast, but have created new neighborhoods, mostly in East Coast cities. Many immigrants have brought significant monetary capital and cultural capital in the form of college educations and professional training. Today, the majority are white-collar workers or businesspeople. The rate of creation of Asian-Indian American businesses has been twice that for the country as a whole. By the 1990s, Asian-Indian Americans owned 93,000 U.S. businesses, most in retail trade or services. Today, they are estimated to own at least 30 percent of all motels and hotels and 60 percent of convenience stores in the United States.[143]

Since the 1980s, numerous skilled Asian-Indian immigrants have gone to California, especially to the high-tech Silicon Valley. Many prospered in the high-tech boom there, and one business journal estimates that 35 percent of start-up high-tech firms there are owned by Asian-Indians. However, those with limited work visas have often had to return to India; others have scrounged for low-wage jobs in order to remain in the United States.[144]

Americans reporting only Asian-Indian ancestry have *by far* the largest proportions of college graduates and professional and managerial employees among all Asian-Pacific American groups in Tables 11.2 and 11.4 (p. 338). The proportions are also much higher than for whites. According to one estimate, about 38 percent of U.S. doctors are now Asian-Indian, as well as 12 percent of all scientists, including 36 percent of NASA scientists. Reportedly, some 40 percent of New York diamond traders are Asian-Indian. Not surprisingly, by the late 2000s, Asian-Indian Americans had the highest median family income ($99,783) among Asian groups in Table 11.3—a figure much higher than for whites ($70,835).[145]

This success has not come without problems, some that may not be initially apparent to unreflective observers. For example, a recent article in the business magazine *Forbes* celebrates Asian-Indian American immigrants and their children as the "new model minority" for their employment success, other economic achievements, and educational success, yet only briefly notes that many such immigrants come from India's well-off classes. Instead, the author emphatically accents their culture, "obsession" with education, and IQ scores. He makes clear that, once again, the notion of a "model minority" is useful as a racial weapon, as he criticizes immigrants from Mexico for not becoming "wealthy and educated . . . after many years in the country" like Asian-Indian immigrants. Among other things, this conventional stereotyping ignores the significant discrimination that successful Asian-Indian Americans face from whites and others inside and outside their workplaces. One recent survey found some 60 percent reporting verbal hostility and harassment in various settings, with a smaller percentage reporting physical harassment because of their racial group. (Some 77 percent of all Asian American respondents in that survey reported verbal harassment, and 19 percent reported physical harassment.) In addition, exaggerated stereotypes of their success have contributed to interracial struggles in several states, including California. For example, non-Asians in San Francisco have vigorously opposed attempts to include Indians as Asians in programs designed to help small Asian American businesses.[146]

This *Forbes* perspective also ignores the reality that many Asian-Indian Americans work in lower-paying positions as taxi drivers and sales clerks, or are unemployed. Not all have achieved significant economic success. In the recent American Community Survey, some 4.9 percent of Asian-Indian American families were below the poverty level, and 5 percent were unemployed. Certainly, large numbers of less well-educated Asian-Indian immigrants in California and East Coast cities have had a much harder economic struggle in recent years than most of the Asian-Indian American professionals and managers who work in the same urban areas.[147]

 What effects have anti-Asian stereotypes and discrimination had on Asian American economic and educational achievements?

Education

In earlier decades, Chinese, Japanese, and other Asian American children were often segregated in separate schools. Thus, a 1927 decision by an all-white Supreme Court upheld Mississippi's racialized segregation of children of the "Mongolian race." This Jim Crow segregation began to break down only after World War II, but *de facto* school segregation persisted in many cities because discriminatory housing covenants kept Asian Americans out of white residential areas.[148] Still, this overt discrimination did not keep Asian Americans from pressing hard for better educational opportunities.

Substantial Achievements amid Persisting Problems

Most Asian American groups place great stress on educational success. Not surprisingly, then, Asian American students have often been overrepresented among those who do well in science competitions. However welcome these prizes are, they constitute a mixed blessing because winning competitions has reinforced stereotypes of Asian Americans as "naturally" gifted in science. Asian Americans have criticized such stereotypes, pointing out Asian Americans excelling in areas other than the sciences. Being stereotyped as high achievers puts a heavy burden not only on the achievers but also on the many Asian students not at the top of their classes. In addition, many Asian American children, especially poorer children, do not have well-funded educational environments, yet the "model minority" stereotype often reduces the likelihood of significant government action to meet their needs.

Some Asian Americans, particularly youth in predominantly white suburbs, come to accept these stereotypes themselves. Some view themselves or their group in terms of the white-crafted model minority imagery because it appears only positive. However, these young people often do not understand the ideological purpose for which this stereotyped imagery was created by whites, and that their acceptance of it may limit their own life choices, as well as their ability to work with other people of color in coalitions against continuing discrimination faced by all.[149]

Many younger immigrants, along with some U.S.-born children of immigrants, face problems of limited English proficiency and/or the shock of an unfamiliar Eurocentric culture in U.S. schools. Non-Asian teachers and administrators are often ignorant of Asian American cultures and insensitive to their needs. Some have been unwilling to protect Asian students from mistreatment by non-Asian students. And some administrators and teachers have shown other types of insensitivity or even racial hostility. For example, in 2008, a local Louisiana school board considered adopting a regulation requiring commencement addresses by students to be entirely in English. They took this strange step because two co-valedictorians of a local high school had spoken thanks to their limited-English-speaking parents with a few Vietnamese words. The director of the midwestern JACL spoke out against this discrimination: "It is deeply troubling that a school would think to censor students for their bilingual abilities. Their multicultural roots should be celebrated, not punished."[150]

Moreover, a 1990s U.S. Civil Rights Commission report noted that only a small proportion of limited-English-proficiency Asian American students had teachers who spoke their native languages. Many non-Asian school authorities have shown little concern for these children's language problems. Contrary to media stories, recent Asian immigrants who are not proficient in English frequently have low grades and high dropout rates. A study of San Diego high school students found that Vietnamese, Cambodian, and Pacific Islander students had higher dropout rates than white students. In addition, an important report from the late 1990s showed that only 1.2 percent of teachers in U.S. schools were Asian American, yet 3.2 percent of the children in these schools were Asian American. Studies today continue to show similar patterns of low Asian teacher–Asian student ratios, especially for Southeast Asians. There is also the problem of a Eurocentric bias in most school curricula. One 2009 survey of hundreds of Chinese Americans found that two-thirds felt there was not enough taught about the culture of China and the Chinese people in U.S. schools.[151]

In addition, many urban schools have been settings where Asian American students often face substantial hostility from non-Asian students. In one study, more than 60 percent of Asian American students reported other students were harassing them. Such harassment, both verbal and physical, was

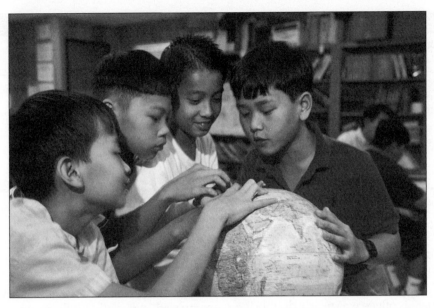

In Austin, Texas, Vietnamese American children work on their geography lesson.

given as a reason for disliking school. Similarly, another report found that a New York City high school had "repeatedly denied Asian immigrant students an adequate education by discharging them early, and also had not addressed repeated incidents of hate violence against Chinese and Pakistani immigrant students on school grounds."[152] Recent reports from various civil rights groups indicate they get many complaints from Asian and Pacific Islander students about verbal and physical violence from other students and from employees at their local schools.[153]

This discrimination does not disappear once the students move on to the college level. Research studies indicate numerous, often racialized, problems are commonly faced by Asian American college students, who may be viewed positively only with regard to their educational achievements. One recent summary of research notes that most stereotypes of Asian American students by non-Asians "are negative, such as non-Asians' perceptions that Asians 'don't speak English well,' 'have accents,' and are 'submissive,' 'sneaky,' 'stingy,' 'greedy,' etc."[154] Such stereotypes often create hostile campus climates and much everyday stress. In addition, there are periodic hate crimes, such as the aforementioned attacks on a Vietnamese American student and his friend near a University of California fraternity house and

on an Asian American graduate of the University of Colorado. Moreover, at the University of California (Davis), a group of whites, including students, beat up five Korean American students while spouting racist epithets. Even college presidents are not immune from anti-Asian attacks. In 2009, a racist commentary on the "Generic Good Morning Message," an email notice system at Dartmouth College, mocked the incoming president of Dartmouth College, Dr. Jim Yong Kim, for his Asian background. Initially, the stereotyped e-mail was downplayed just as poor humor by other top Dartmouth administrators.[155]

Educational Attainment

Many observers have noted the fact that Asian Americans have higher educational levels than the U.S. population as a whole. As an umbrella group, they are much more likely to have a college degree than the average American. This figure is misleading, however, because of wide variations among the Asian American groups as well as within each group. Using the latest available data for persons over 24 years of age, Table 11.4 compares the educational attainment of five groups with that of whites and the total population.[156] Vietnamese Americans ranked the lowest in educational attainment among

TABLE 11.4   Educational Attainment by Group (2008)

	Chinese American	Filipino American	Korean American	Vietnamese American	Asian-Indian American	White American	Total Population
High school graduate or more	80.2%	91.6%	89.7%	73.3%	90.6%	90.1%	85.0%
Bachelor's degree or more	52.1	48.0	49.8	27.8	70.1	30.7	27.7

Source: U.S. Bureau of the Census. "2008 American Community Survey."

the Asian and white groups. Although Chinese Americans fell a little below the national percentage for high school graduation, the rate at which this group had completed college was nearly double the national rate. In addition, Asian-Indian, Korean, Filipino, and Chinese Americans are much more likely to have graduated from college than whites or the general population.

Various theories have been offered to explain much of the success Asian Americans experience in education. Some argue that it is rooted in Asian cultures' traditional reverence for learning or in strong family support. However, most U.S. groups that are not Asian also have high educational expectations for their youth. There is more to these educational statistics than quick cultural interpretations suggest. One should keep in mind that the contemporary U.S. immigration system strongly *favors* immigrants with significant socioeconomic resources. (Some argue it "creams off" many people from the world's middle and upper middle classes.) Many Asian immigrants have entered the U.S. already with significant economic and educational resources that are important for their mobility, as well as that of their children. In addition, many aggressively pursue education as a weapon against extensive anti-Asian prejudice and discrimination in U.S. society; educational effort has thus become part of a resistance strategy in which education is viewed as a matter of group achievement and a counter to negative racial barriers. We should also remember the significant variation in educational access and achievement within Asian American groups, as well as the fact that continuing discrimination in job markets has kept many Asians from achieving the economic suc-

cess they should have gained based on their abilities and educational achievements.[157]

Asian American educational achievement is often compared, especially by those accenting the model minority stereotype, with black or Latino achievements. This comparison is problematical for reasons already mentioned, as well as for certain geographical reasons. As a group, Asian American students have had greater access to better-resourced educational institutions, such as those in California's suburbs, that have historically facilitated socioeconomic mobility better than many of the public schools attended by black and Latino students in less affluent states from the Carolinas to New Mexico. In addition, Asian American students in most metropolitan areas are not as likely as other students of color to be segregated residentially from white middle-class students whose schools usually have much better educational resources and facilities.

Controversy in Higher Education

In recent decades, some elite colleges and universities have reportedly discriminated against Asian American applicants, often in covert and subtle ways. For example, Ivy League universities began admitting a large percentage of Asian American applicants in the 1970s, but acceptance rates often dropped as the number of Asian American applications increased. Critics accused some universities of using such nonacademic pretexts as lack of alumni parents ("legacies") and the necessity for a regional distribution to exclude many Asian American students. Asian American leaders and applicants to leading colleges and universities have argued that

Asian Americans are often discriminated against because of stereotypes among the mostly non-Asian college admissions officers about them being "too studious" and uninvolved in "extracurricular activities" in high school and/or because of admissions policies favoring only one or two other groups of color.[158]

For example, the proportion of Asian Americans among the students admitted at Brown University rose from 2.6 percent for the class of 1979 to 14.8 percent for the class of 1993, although the proportion of Asian American applicants admitted fluctuated wildly, between 14 percent and 41 percent, during this period. Studying the sharp drop in the proportion of Asian applicants admitted there between the years 1982 and 1983, investigators found that the admissions staff had assigned comparatively low nonacademic ratings to Asian American applicants and had sought to hold steady the number of Asian American students admitted, even though their applicant pool had tripled.[159] Harvard, Yale, and Princeton have faced similar charges of covert discrimination against Asian American applicants. Recently one student, the child of Chinese immigrants with perfect SAT scores and near-perfect grades, filed a lawsuit against Princeton University for allegedly discriminating against him in admissions on nonmerit grounds.[160]

How does the "model minority" stereotype relate, if at all, to Asian American socioeconomic attainments?

Full Assimilation for Asian Americans?

Assimilation Views

Milton Gordon argued that his assimilation theory applied to a wide range of ethnic and racial groups. Although Gordon did not apply his scheme to Asian Americans, other assimilation-oriented analysts have argued that most Asian American groups are on their way to full integration into the Eurocentric core society—at least at the dominant-culture level and at the secondary-structural level in terms of job placement. Assimilation-oriented analysts tend to be optimistic about the eventual thoroughgoing

assimilation of Asian American groups, including full incorporation into the middle class.

Assimilation-oriented analysts have underscored Asian American progress in economic integration. Sociologist Talcott Parsons argued that racial–ethnic inclusion is a powerful ongoing process, and this includes Americans of color (see Chapter 2). Numerous scholarly analysts of Asian Americans argue that anti-Asian discrimination is collapsing and assimilation into dominant institutions is well underway. For example, some media analysts of Filipino Americans have argued that way. "With a command of English, light brown skin, and Spanish-sounding names, Filipinos have few problems assimilating into American society," asserted James Madore of the *Christian Science Monitor*.[161] Not surprisingly, many assimilation-oriented analysts view Filipino and other Asian Americans as indeed "model minorities." In their view, a non-European group has succeeded when its economic attainments, measured by quantitative indicators of occupation, education, and income, are at least comparable to those of the dominant white group.[162]

Interestingly, the National Asian Pacific American Bar Association (NAPABA) opposed U.S. Supreme Court nominee Clarence Thomas at his 1991 Senate confirmation hearings, in part by challenging Thomas's publicly asserted image of Asian Americans as "model minorities." Thomas argued that Asian Americans "transcended the ravages caused even by harsh legal and social discrimination" and should not be beneficiaries of government affirmative action because they are "overrepresented in key institutions." Then, as now, the NAPABA pointed out the racial hostility and discrimination still widely faced by Asian Americans. In the NAPABA's experienced view, affirmative action programs continue today to be critical for diversifying colleges and universities, as well as to Asian American workers' employment in historically white job categories.[163]

Recall Kitano and Daniels' assimilation model (Chapter 10) distinguishing types of group adaptation: (1) high assimilation, low ethnic identity; (2) high assimilation, high ethnic identity; and (3) low assimilation, high ethnic identity. In this view, Asian Americans who fall into the high assimilation/low ethnic identity category are more "core American" or "white-like" than Asian. Their language, lifestyle, and expectations are more like those of whites, and traditional culture is mostly forgotten. High rates of marriage to non-Asians occur in this group. Although a significant proportion of Japanese Americans are viewed by many as falling into this Kitano-Daniels category of advanced assimilation, the proportions for the Asian American groups in this chapter appear to be smaller.

From this perspective, those Asian Americans in the high assimilation/high ethnic identity category differ from those in the first category because they retain a strong group identity. They move easily in and out of both cultures, and their friendship patterns and interests reflect a bicultural perspective. They are usually comfortable with their identity and resist persisting anti-Asian discrimination. Numerous analysts have suggested that a significant proportion of Filipino and Asian-Indian Americans fall into this category. They remain substantially bicultural. One scholar has suggested that Asian-Indian children are constantly operating in two cultures. Most speak English well and are influenced by U.S. pop music and movies, yet also watch Indian movies and often "follow the ways of their elders when it comes to such traditions as marriage and child-rearing." Most Asian-Indian American young people still have a strong sense of their group identity.[164]

One study of Chinese and Japanese Americans found that those in the third and fourth generations were often highly oriented to white middle-class cultural styles. They were assimilated culturally and retained little traditional Asian culture. However, most of these culturally assimilated Asian Americans had a strong sense of group identity. Unlike white ethnics such as Italian or Polish Americans, Asian Americans do not have a choice, for their racial position as "Asian" or "Oriental" is constantly imposed on them by whites and other outsiders (especially those with power). The latter ask repeatedly, "What are you?" or "Where are you from?" Answers such as "American" or "New York City" often anger the questioners.[165]

Asian Americans listed in Kitano and Daniels's third major category, low assimilation/high group identity, are usually relatively recent immigrants or those who have spent all their lives in traditional urban enclaves. All have made some adaptations to the dominant culture but prefer their communities and form most friendship and marriage bonds there. Many if not most recent Korean and Vietnamese immigrants are often viewed as falling into this category. A significant proportion of recent Filipino and Chinese immigrants seem modestly assimilated at the cultural level but firmly rooted culturally and socially in their communities.[166] Moreover, tensions between recent immigrants and the native born are often seen. Immigrants in Chinese American communities sometimes call the native born "ABCs" (American-born Chinese). New immigrants criticize the ABCs as out of touch with traditional Chinese culture. In return, native-born Chinese and other Asian Americans sometimes call new Chinese and other Asian American immigrants "FOBs" (fresh off boats) and make fun of certain traditional ways that they accentuate.[167]

Recent surveys of the children of Asian immigrants indicate that 70 to 90 percent in each group can speak only English; only small minorities are fluent in their parents' language. They are highly assimilated in language terms. By the third generation there is little trace of fluency in their ancestral languages. Only the immigrant generation itself retains a substantial majority fluent in the ancestral language, and usually a majority of them can speak English adequately. Not surprisingly, then, the United States (and especially California) has been termed the "graveyard of immigrant languages."[168]

In numerous Asian American communities generational conflicts are still conspicuous. In recent years, for example, Vietnamese parents have complained that their children have given up the Vietnamese language, are uninterested in entering the family business, and move away from old neighborhoods. For their part, the youth today refer to the conflict in the hyphenated term "Vietnamese-American" as "riding the hyphen." Vietnamese American leaders in Garden Grove, California, have met to set up an institute of Vietnamese studies to offer courses in the Vietnamese language and history. One purpose is to combat a too-rapid assimilation of the younger generation. Today, California's numerous Vietnamese-language radio and television stations and programs help to keep Vietnamese culture and language alive.[169]

Many first-generation Korean immigrants are also committed to their home-country language and culture and to maintaining close ties to relatives, and they have built strong institutions within their communities. In "Koreatown," in Los Angeles, Korean Americans have created many important institutions, including newspapers, schools, an orchestra, and churches. Religion has often facilitated the adjustment of many Korean immigrants and their children. In California, as elsewhere, Korean immigrants and their children have established many churches, combining Western practices and Korean-language services. Churches provide much support and important networking and other social capital.[170]

A study by Karen Pyke examined the views that children of Korean and Vietnamese immigrants had of family life. Most accepted the dominant U.S. conception of the "normal" family as their framework. They often criticized parents as too strict or distant and thought the latter should more closely resemble those in the "normal" U.S. family. These children had assimilated the dominant view of family. However, when they discussed plans for taking care of parents in later life, they expressed strong traditional Korean and Vietnamese values, described parents' family practices positively, and retained important filial values. Other studies of Korean American and Chinese American young people have also shown significant assimilation to the dominant culture, especially with regard to popular culture. Many have become aggressively consumerist to "prove" they are really "American." The adaptation pattern for children and grandchildren of Asian immigrants blends aspects of the culture of origin with aspects of the dominant culture, as suggested by Greeley's ethnogenesis perspective. However, such adaptation can be very stressful, and some develop mental health problems. A recent study by Christine Yeh of Korean, Chinese, and Japanese American high school students found mental health problems for youth who experienced substantial "cultural stress, such as being caught between two cultures, feeling alienated from both cultures, and having interpersonal conflicts with whites." In addition, Rosalind Chou and Joe Feagin have recently documented this same stressful reality in interviews with Asian Americans of various ages.[171]

Many Asian-Indian Americans are well integrated into the dominant culture. Coming from a country that was once a British colony, they often know English well, and many reside in predominantly white neighborhoods. The majority are well-educated and work in predominantly white settings. Most have adopted key aspects of the Eurocentric core culture. One study of first-generation Asian-Indian Americans found most came from urban areas in India and were already exposed to many aspects of U.S. culture through the media. The group as a whole scored in the middle range on a cultural assimilation scale that included language use and music, food, and media preferences. Yet, most families maintain essential aspects of traditional culture. The majority still marry within the group (see below). Asian-Indian Americans have built numerous Hindu temples. For example, the Hindu temple in Silicon Valley opened in a warehouse in 1994 with 380 families, but with immigration had grown to 4800 families by the 2000s.[172] This community-building pattern can be seen in numerous cities. Asian-Indian Americans are generally highly acculturated on some dimensions of adaptation and highly Indian on others.

One sign of the somewhat slower overall assimilation of most Asian-Pacific groups in this chapter, compared with the assimilation rate for Japanese Americans, may be their lower out-marriage rates to non-Asians. For example, 1990 census data showed relatively high out-marriage rates to whites for California's younger-generation Japanese Americans. But rates of out-marriage to whites were generally lower for younger adults in the four other Asian American groups discussed in this chapter.[173] Significantly, an analysis of these census data found that interethnic marriages (within the Asian American umbrella group) were increasing.

More recent 2006 census data for all U.S. states reveal an interesting pattern. A recent examination by C. N. Le and J. J. Huang of data for Chinese, Korean, Filipino, Vietnamese, and Asian-Indian Americans found that 82.4 to 92.3 percent of husbands and 61.1 to 93.6 percent of wives had spouses from within their own group. Another 0.9 to 4.5 percent of husbands or wives were married to spouses from other Asian American groups. There was much variation in terms of intermarriages with whites, with about one-quarter of Korean and Filipino wives having white husbands, but much smaller percentages (4.3 to 13.9 percent) of Asian-Indian, Vietnamese, and Chinese wives having white husbands. (The percentages of white spouses for Asian American husbands were, with the exception of Asian-Indians, significantly lower than those for wives, in the 2.9 to 9.2 percent range.) In 2006, the overwhelming majority in all these Asian American groups were married within their own group. And all groups examined in this chapter were out-married to whites at substantially lower rates than were Japanese Americans (see Chapter 10). However, for both men and women in these Asian American groups, with one exception, white out-marriage percentages were significantly *higher* for those marriages that involved both partners who were raised in the United States. This suggests that in the future there may be much higher overall rates of out-marriage for each group. However, even then there may be a limit to out-marriages, as the one exception today is for the largest out-marrying group—that is, for U.S.-raised Japanese American women. They now seem to be out-marrying with whites somewhat less often than in the recent past.[174]

In some areas the rate of marriage within the Asian American umbrella group has grown in recent years, in part because of the now large and growing population of Asian Americans and because of a growing panethnic consciousness among Asian Americans, especially with regard to continuing discriminatory treatment at the hands of others because they are Asian.[175]

Significantly, one study of Asian–white interracial relationships in the Southwest found that "contrary to popular utopian celebration of mixed-race marriage as a sign of multiracialization, interracial intimacy is still regulated by racial, gender, class, and national hierarchies." That is, the Asian American women who were interviewed "saw white men as sources of power through which they might transform their [socioeconomic and gender] marginality" in their communities and the larger society.[176] Thus, Asian and Asian American women sometimes see white men as avenues of liberation and mobility from the patriarchal or modest-income realities of their own backgrounds, even as white men are sometimes attracted to them because of old stereotypes of Asian female docility or exotic sexuality. Clearly, interracial partnering and marriage involving such motivations do not necessarily signal a trend to a less racist society.

Researcher Nazli Kibria has used the ethnogenesis model to assess the adaptations of Asian groups to each other. Her research on second-generation, middle-class Chinese and Korean Americans revealed what she calls a "pan-Asian ethnogenesis." Members of each second-generation group are developing a sense of a shared Asian American identity in addition to their country-of-origin identities. The construction of this Asian American identity is a

"process that involves recognition of the shared personal experiences and orientations of Asian-origin persons, including that of being racially labeled as Asian by the dominant society, of growing up in an Asian home, and of adhering to the Asian values of an emphasis on family, education, hard work, and respect for elders."[177] However, particular nationality ties are strong and will likely continue to exist alongside a shared Asian American identity. In addition, a white frame–imposed identity of "foreign Asian" cannot be escaped. Being defined as racially different plays a significant role in shaping this broad Asian American identity. Racial consciousness is particularly strong where there has been a recent history of anti-immigrant campaigns, hate crimes, and white flight. To make full sense of this reality, one needs a sustained analysis of the systemic-racism context in which these immigrants and their children must adapt.[178]

Some Questions from a Power-Conflict Perspective

Power-conflict analysts of Asian Americans reject numerous aspects of optimistic assimilationist perspectives, including "model minorities" notions. Among other things, model minority stereotypes ignore the origins of many Asian immigrants who came with good educations and some money or social capital. It also downplays continuing problems many have with poverty and racial discrimination.[179]

The image of Asian immigrants is often one of poor immigrants working their way up to success by dint of hard work. Although they were certainly hard-working, the majority of the Asian immigrants who came between the 1960s and the mid-1970s were middle-class people with white-collar backgrounds. Their monetary capital or educational backgrounds often enabled them to establish themselves as middle-class Americans and provide advantages for their children. In contrast, immigrants who came after the mid-1970s included more working-class people, many of whom secured low-wage jobs in garment or assembly industries. Asian Americans, "particularly immigrant Asian workers, have a highly visible position in both ends" of the economy. "Despite the fact that a large number of Asian Americans are successful, a disproportionate number of [some Asian groups] are poor."[180]

Recall that, in response to black and Latino Americans protesting discrimination, some whites developed the model minority notion to argue all Americans of color could achieve the American dream just by working as hard as Asian Americans. This negative assessment of African Americans is illustrated in a 1960s *U.S. News & World Report* article that compared Chinese and African Americans. By praising the hard work and morality of Chinese Americans, the article implied that if black Americans possessed such virtues (which of course most do), it would not be necessary to spend "hundreds of billions to uplift" them. The article omitted any mention of the widespread racial discrimination facing African Americans.[181]

Power-conflict analysts have shown how, over centuries, powerful whites have positioned non-European groups in the established racial hierarchy. The earliest and most fundamental of the racial oppressions generated *within* the early colonies, and later *within* the United States, targeted enslaved African Americans brought in to do labor to build up white wealth. Later, white employers brought other non-European groups, including Mexican, Chinese, Japanese, and Filipino immigrants, into the economy as low-wage labor. Whites have evaluated these later non-European immigrants and their descendants from within the earlier, well-established framework of racial oppression, with its framing and ideology of white superiority. New immigrant groups are placed somewhere in the long-established white-to-black hierarchy of exploitation and status.[182]

At certain times in U.S. history, powerful whites have elevated some Asian Americans, as individuals or groups, from a lower rung to an intermediate rung in this white-to-black hierarchy of racial status. At least in their image of society, white leaders and the white public often position certain non-European groups in this intermediate racial status, which helps to maintain an intact but flexible hierarchical system. When white commentators and politicians write positive things about the success of Asian American groups, they usually single out those who are most white-oriented and acculturated.[183]

However, as some power-conflict analysts note, at earlier points in history most Asian Americans were placed on or near the bottom rung of the racial hierarchy for economic and other exploitation—and

were thus typed negatively as "black" or "near-black" in status. Frank Wu has noted how historically various racially oppressed people, such as Asian Americans, have often been seen by whites as "constructive blacks," at or near the black end of the racist hierarchy.[184]

Today, in contrast, certain Asian American groups are often publicly constructed as "nearer-to-white," but again usually to serve white purposes. Given this construction, these whites then frequently criticize African or Latino Americans for not being like the stereotyped Asian American model in efforts or achievements. As Gary Okihiro has noted, whites have periodically "upheld Asians as 'near-whites' or 'whiter than whites' in the model minority stereotype, and yet Asians experienced and continue to face white racism 'like blacks' in educational and occupational barriers and ceilings and in anti-Asian abuse and physical violence."[185]

The model minority perspective obscures the problems and needs of many Asian Americans who face continuing discrimination and stereotyping. As sociologist Nadia Kim has recently demonstrated, we must assess and accent "the specificity of Asian-American racialization" and thus "take seriously the denial of social citizenship to Asian groups on a racial basis and . . . how it is linked to anti-black subordination and the racial system writ large."[186]

In addition, we must understand that many East and Southeast Asian immigrants, especially those with less education, have experienced severe economic strain from the 1980s to the present. One recent large-scale study of Korean American families in a major Orange County community in California found much to contradict the image of a generally well-off Asian American community. Korean families had a higher poverty rate than for Orange County residents as a whole, more than a quarter were on government assistance, and a third had no health insurance. The study found serious health problems. The Korean community had a higher percentage of people with high cholesterol, asthma, and strokes than the county population as a whole. The study found a high level of psychological distress, four times the rate for the county as a whole, but a lower utilization rate of mental-health facilities. Alcohol and cigarette use were relatively high for Californians. This is not the Pollyanna portrait that the media typically like to report for Asian Americans.[187]

Instead of dealing with these difficult socio-economic realities, media commentators and politicians typically celebrate Asian individuals who have been successful. For example, Chang-Lin Tien, the distinguished former chancellor of the University of California (Berkeley), is portrayed as a poor immigrant who came without knowing English. What is seldom noted, however, is that he was from a wealthy Chinese family with close ties to the pre-Communist ruler of China, Chiang Kai-shek. Numerous other leading Asian Americans have come from overseas families with substantial economic or other resources. Indeed, given the significant variation in assimilation among Asian groups and subgroups, the segmented assimilation view of analysts such as Min Zhou seems appropriate. Those Asian immigrants with greater family and group resources generally have had a different experience adapting to U.S. society than those with fewer resources, such as the many working-class Asian immigrants.[188]

The secondary-structural integration of many Asian Americans into the economy is not as untroubled as numerous assimilation analysts suggest. Many suffer racial discrimination in employment and educational institutions. We have noted the informal quotas still used to reduce Asian American participation, such as those at some colleges and universities. Once in a historically white institution, moreover, many Asian Americans report that numerous racial barriers are thrown in their paths. In employment settings many find that the jobs available are not as good as what their educational and experience credentials should secure. Many excel in college, but often receive a lower rate of return on educational investments than whites. Although many are hired by major companies, many also find that promotions to higher management and upper professional levels are unlikely.[189]

Optimistic assimilation analysts generally pay insufficient attention to continuing racial violence and profiling that handicap Asian Americans and affect long-term adaptation probabilities. Many white Americans still view Asian Americans in racialized terms and as foreigners or even "mud people." We have seen recent violence on both coasts, such as the killing of Joseph Ileto in California, the killings in Santa Barbara, and the various attacks on Asian-Indian Americans in East Coast cities. In numerous areas, anti-Asian violence has persisted to the present.

The aforementioned study of third- and later-generation Chinese and Japanese Americans found that, although most are culturally assimilated, they have a strong group identity because many outsiders impose the identity of "foreigner" on them. Many whites and others view them as not "real Americans." A power-conflict analyst would suggest that for this reason most Asian Americans will not soon be fully absorbed into the white middle-class mainstream. While analyzing experiences of second-generation Filipinos, for example, Le Espiritu found that they encounter much pressure to assimilate fully and yet face racial hostility and discrimination that signals "they will never be accepted." They must adapt to the dominant culture, yet maintain aspects of the home culture, in part because they have never been fully accepted because of physical appearance. Indeed, one recent national survey found that a substantial minority of the respondents thought Asian Americans "should think in more American ways," thereby suggesting that in their view many or most Asian Americans are not yet well assimilated to the dominant culture.[190]

The pressure to conform to whiteness is intense, yet conforming does not bring acceptance because of the white racial framing of Asian Americans. Mia Tuan has noted that "generations of highly acculturated Asian ethnics who speak without an accent have lived in this country, and yet most white Americans have not heard of or ever really seen them. They are America's invisible citizenry." Interviewing many later generation Chinese and Japanese Americans, she found that, although they were well adapted to much of the dominant culture, most had a strong racial identity because whites imposed this "Asian foreigner" identity on them. Research on younger Vietnamese Americans by Hung Cam Thai and on Asian Americans of all ages by Chou and Feagin has shown that a great many try hard to "fit in" to U.S. society by behaving and operating in ways seen as pleasing to whites, especially those whites who are important in shaping their life circumstances.[191]

Nonetheless, Asian Americans have also long struggled to protect their civil rights and growing political power. In 1992, for example, the Asian American Legal Defense and Education Fund fought hard for an extension of the 1965 Voting Rights Act in order to protect the right of non-English speakers to bilingual election materials. Some white senators argued that Asian American voters needed no protection, even though the Senate then included not one Asian American from the mainland states. To the present day, such organizations continue to fight actively against anti-Asian hostility and discrimination in many institutional areas in the United States.[192]

 Using assimilation or power-conflict perspectives, how would you explain differences in economic mobility and political achievements among Asian American groups?

Summary

Many Korean, Filipino, Asian-Indian, and Vietnamese Americans—and the newest Chinese Americans—are among the most recent of the immigrant additions to the bubbling U.S. cauldron. Like immigrants before them, they have been targets of much racial framing, hostility, and violence. In general, their socioeconomic success has been so significant that several groups have been recently stereotyped as model minorities. Those who portray Asian Americans in this way often have the ulterior motive of criticizing non-Asian groups such as African and Latino Americans for alleged deficiencies. Assimilation-oriented social scientists and other commentators are inclined to focus on Asian American socioeconomic progress but downplay persisting problems of hate crimes, discrimination, and poverty.

From a power-conflict perspective, an Asian American group has not achieved complete success until it can participate fully in the mainstream economy, politics, and society without paying significantly higher social, material, and psychological costs than the dominant group.[193] No Asian American group has attained full and comfortable equality with the descendants of the oldest white immigrant groups. Physically distinguishable, Asian Americans have remained disadvantaged and have experienced political or economic problems, racist framing, recurrent discrimination, and only modest recent gains in political power.

Immigration has again taken "a central position on the American social agenda" and nativist talk and action have again focused on regaining "control of U.S. borders."[194] Much white opposition to immigration seems to go beyond the question of immigrants taking jobs to the issue of their racial characteristics, because most recent immigrants have been Asian and Latin American. Thus, Asian immigrants continue to be the victims of extensive anti-Asian stereotyping.

However, Asian and other recent immigrants contribute greatly to the success and progress of the United States. They are the ones who have supplied much of the energetic imagination and new labor necessary as the older immigrant groups and their descendents age. The hard work and abilities of these new immigrants have helped make the United States a vigorous country, yet one that is still very much in the making.

Key Terms

picture brides   310   panethnicity   322
Orientalism   312

CHAPTER 12

Arab Americans and Other Middle Eastern Americans

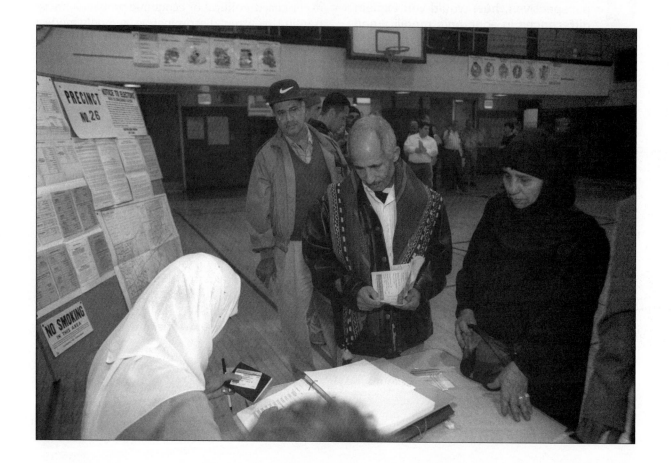

BIG PICTURE QUESTIONS

- *What role have Arab Americans played in building up this country's wealth and institutions?*

- *What effect has the ideology of Orientalism had on U.S. society?*

- *How have Arab Americans challenged U.S. religious and racial stereotypes?*

An Arab American correctional officer at a federal prison in Virginia has described experiences there after the attacks of September 11, 2001 (9/11). An immigrant from Lebanon, he was one of a few Arab Americans working there. Before 9/11 he had suffered discrimination because of his appearance in this area of Virginia, but after the attacks he suffered more. Fellow employees quit speaking to him and told him to "go back where you came from" or "go bomb something—your people are good at that." Called "camel jockey" and "sand nigger," he endured hate emails and a note that said "death to Muslims." Someone ransacked his office. His superiors would not let him transfer. "It was degrading. Suddenly I became a second-class citizen. I became a criminal, a target, a person with no rights for something I had nothing to do with."[1]

Middle Eastern Americans

Many people in the United States seem confused about three important categories of Americans: Middle Eastern Americans, Arab Americans, and Muslim Americans. These are *not* the same. One of the fastest-growing umbrella groups, **Middle Eastern Americans** (*a term for Americans whose ancestry lies in any of the Middle Eastern countries*) is a category in the process of formation and one much like umbrella groups such as Latino Americans and Asian Americans. **Arab Americans** is an umbrella term as well, covering *people from numerous Arab countries*. Arab Americans are but one major group within the category of Middle Eastern Americans. Within the latter are also non-Arabs, especially Iranian, Turkish, and Pakistani Americans. Both the Middle Eastern and Arab American umbrella categories include Muslim Americans, a religious group, but this designation of Muslim encompasses many people who are not Middle Eastern. Muslim Americans include many African Americans and South Asian Americans.

Especially since 9/11, this umbrella group of Middle Eastern Americans has become more conspicuous and important. They often face violence and other racial or religious discrimination no matter what their Middle Eastern ancestry is or whether they are Christian or Muslim, Arab or non-Arab. In recent years, government agencies, as well as private organizations and individuals, have frequently used "Arab," "Middle Eastern," and "Muslim"

interchangeably to name a new political "enemy" and target them with discrimination, including unfounded interrogations, arrests, detentions, wiretapping, property seizures, and deportations. These discriminators have had an effect: By targeting people from the Middle East, discriminators frequently force those targeted to see themselves as sharing significant experiences, backgrounds, and identities.[2] Indeed, census data and social science research reveal that a growing number prefer to identify themselves as "Arab American" or "Middle Eastern American" rather than by their specific countries of family origin.

Consider three eras of immigration. The first Muslim migration involved the involuntary immigration of enslaved people from Muslim societies in Africa. Brought to the Americas from the 1600s to the 1800s, they were the first Muslims in what later became the United States. The next period of immigration came much later, between the 1880s and World War II. These immigrants were mostly Arabs from the Middle East, including Christians and Muslims. In recent decades, a third era of immigration has encompassed more Arab immigrants and many non-Arab immigrants from countries such as Iran, Turkey, and Pakistan.

In this chapter we will touch on, but not consider in much detail, non-Arab Middle Eastern groups, yet they should be kept in mind as we explore the situations of Arab Americans. For example, Iranian Americans are a significant portion of recent Middle Eastern immigrants and a growing U.S. group, one with a very different background than Arab Americans. Indeed, their increased presence has helped to create the umbrella designation of Middle Eastern Americans.[3]

Arab Americans

Most Americans are not aware that European civilization was heavily influenced by advanced Arab cultures from the tenth to twelfth centuries. In that period, Arab scholars made breakthroughs in mathematics, such as the development of the place-value decimal system, well before European scholars. They made major contributions to the physical sciences and seafaring technologies, such as the compass. Much knowledge from Arab scientists and scholars was imported into European civilizations.[4]

The widespread use of Arabic indicates how far the Arab empire once spread. Today, Arabic is a first language spoken by more than 280 million people, and by millions more as a second language. It is spoken in the Middle East and North Africa, Malta, and Sicily, and was spoken in Spain for centuries prior to 1500. From the eighth century to the fifteenth century, Arab Islamic (Moorish) culture was influential in Spain and Spanish colonies. From this Moorish period and other avenues of Arabic influence, at least 2400 Arabic-origin words have come into English—such as *algebra, almanac, chemistry, cipher, coffee, cotton, jar, nadir, orange,* and *zero.* These reveal the substantial global influence of Arab cultures, including on sciences and commerce.[5]

Today, the Arab World ranges from Mauritania and Morocco in North Africa to Iraq and Saudi Arabia in what is now termed the *Middle East.* It includes countries in the League of Arab States, those with Arabic cultures. (Some countries in the Middle East, such as Turkey and Iran, are not Arab states but have large Muslim populations.) Although many Americans with origins in Arab countries consider themselves Arab Americans, others—some Lebanese Maronites, Coptic Americans, Armenians, and Chaldean Americans—often do not. They accent instead ethno-religious origins.[6]

Since the 1960s Arab–Israeli conflicts, a very strong pan-Arab identity has developed in the Middle East. In the United States a strong pan-ethnic Arab American identity has also emerged, in part as a reaction to the stereotyping of Arab Americans and in part as a reaction to what is seen as an anti-Arab tilt by the U.S. government in Middle Eastern conflicts. Even with the political, religious, and cultural differences in the Middle East and the U.S., this strong Arab pan-ethnic identity persists in both areas. Numerous pan-Arab organizations, including the National Association of Arab Americans, the Arab American Institute, and the Arab American University Graduates, have been created since the 1960s Middle East conflicts. These groups have spent much energy trying to influence U.S. foreign policy with regard to Middle Eastern political and economic issues.[7]

This chapter focuses on Arab Americans. According to the 2008 census estimate, there are more than 1.5 million Americans with substantial Arab ancestry (see Table 12.1).[8] They have roots in nearly two dozen different countries. The largest group is

TABLE 12.1	Estimated Population with Arab Ancestry by Detailed Group (2008)
Detailed Group	
Lebanese	501,907
Egyptian	179,592
Syrian	149,541
Palestinian	85,745
Jordanian	59,233
Moroccan	77,468
Iraqi	69,277
"Arab" or "Arabic"	260,427
Other Arab	190,340
Total	1,573,530

Source: U.S. Bureau of the Census. "2008 American Community Survey."

Lebanese, followed by the next largest groups, Egyptian and Syrian. These three groups make up over half the Arab American population. Some Arab American leaders consider the official census figure to be a serious undercount because of weaknesses in census techniques, significant out-marriage, and other factors. A current estimate by the Arab American Institute is that there are about 3.5 million Arab Americans.[9]

 How have Arab civilizations in the Middle East shaped the development of European and American societies?

Migration

The Early Period

Today, many Arab Americans are immigrants or children of immigrants. There have been two major periods of immigration from Arab areas to the U.S.—from 1880 to 1945, and from 1946 to the present. Between 1880 and World War II, immigrants entered in modest numbers. They were primarily Christians from villages and, like most immigrants, viewed the U.S. as a land of opportunity. *Many planned to make some money and return home,* a type of **sojourner immigration.** They were generally from "Greater Syria," an area that then included what would later be known as Lebanon, Syria, Jordan, and Palestine/Israel. By the 1920s, Arab Americans numbered about 200,000. Their descendants now make up a major proportion of Arab Americans.[10] Significantly, the openly discriminatory 1924 Immigration Act sharply reduced immigration from the Middle East, as well as from southern Europe and Asia.

Later Immigration

Most Arab immigrants have entered the United States since 1967. According to the 2008 American Community Survey of the foreign-born Arab American population, some 60 percent arrived between 1990 and 2008—about the same as for the total foreign-born U.S. population. Many immigrants have fled violent conflicts in the Middle East and Africa. Immigrants have come from at least twenty countries, ranging from Morocco in western Africa to the United Arab Emirates in the Middle East. The 1970s Lebanese civil war and the 1980s Israeli invasion of Lebanon generated numerous immigrants. Others fled wars between Iraq and Iran and between Iraq and Kuwait. Many are Palestinians. Most are now Muslims. Whether Muslim or Christian, immigrants have often entered with a strong Arab nationalism and greater inclination to criticize U.S. Middle Eastern policies than earlier immigrants. Most have settled in metropolitan areas, especially Washington, DC, New York, Chicago, Detroit, and Los Angeles.[11]

However, since 9/11, Arab immigrants, Muslim and non-Muslim, and other Muslim immigrants have faced much racial profiling by U.S. government officials. The latter have rejected more Arab visa applications, such as from tourists and businesspeople. Immigration regulations have been violated, or restrictions have been applied disproportionately to Arab and other Muslim immigrants. A year after the creation of the Department of Homeland Security in 2002, the new agency gained control of immigrants and conducted a special registration program for men who had entered legally from twenty-five countries, all but one predominantly Arab or Muslim. These men were required to be photographed and fingerprinted. Although much of this profiling program was soon ended, an array of other government actions have resulted in significant mistreatment of Arab immigrants—mistreatment the American-Arab Anti-Discrimination Committee (ADC) has viewed as racially discriminatory.[12]

In recent decades, immigrant groups have generally coalesced into an Arab American umbrella group, at least for key social and political goals. Most third-generation descendants of earlier Greater Syrian immigrants now see themselves as Arab Americans. One Detroit study surveyed leaders of Middle Eastern (including Arab) organizations to discern if there were cultural traits shared across diverse Middle Eastern groups. Most stressed the importance of kinship networks. One respondent commented, "The most important [thing] in our tradition is respect for the family. And closeness of family."[13] Middle Eastern leaders, and presumably immigrants they represent, worry that the dominant culture tends to break up families through divorce and too-lenient supervision of children.

Many of these Detroit respondents accented religion, which has been central to Arab cultures and to various other Middle Eastern cultures. Most Arab Americans come from backgrounds with a "common language, tradition, cultural traits, and values," even though they have diverse national identities.[14] Although there are differences within the Arab American community between Christians, Muslims, and Jews, prevailing anti-Arab stereotypes and hostility generate pressures that tend to unite Arab Americans. In addition to family and religion, other traits accented by this midwestern study's respondents included an emphasis on tracing ancestry to Arab or Middle Eastern lands, an orientation to Arabic and other Middle Eastern languages, and a strong commitment to entrepreneurship.[15] Americans from Arab areas and other Middle Eastern areas may have different physical features and religious backgrounds but often share certain cultural traits and political concerns. Still, only in a loose way can one speak of umbrella groups called "Arab Americans" and "Middle Eastern Americans."

 What are the consequences of racial profiling for Arab Americans and the larger U.S. society?

Stereotyping and Prejudice

Classified as an "Inferior Race"

In the first period of Arab immigration, U.S. officials sometimes classified these immigrants as "Turks" and sometimes as "Syrians." Between 1909 and 1944, at least eight court decisions by white judges legally assessed whether certain Arab Americans were "white." Four ruled that they were, and four ruled that by "common knowledge" or "legal precedent" they should *not* be considered white. Thus, in 1914, a South Carolina court ruled that while a Syrian immigrant "may be Caucasian," he or she was not what the 1790 Naturalization Act called a "free white person" and could not become a U.S. citizen. This decision was reversed in 1915 on the grounds that the relevant laws were those of 1873 and 1875, which allowed Syrians to be considered enough like Europeans to be officially "white." Later decisions would sometimes disagree, again asserting that Arab Americans were not white.[16]

The right of Arab immigrants to citizenship and to claim whiteness continued to be challenged in many institutional arenas, including courts, until the 1940s. White supremacist writers of the early twentieth century saw them as "parasites" and "Mongolian plasma" that would "contaminate the pure American stock."[17] Syrian immigrants were cataloged with southern and eastern Europeans as "inferior races" by European American intellectuals. Nativists termed Syrians the "most foreign" of immigrants. They suffered extreme stereotypes that many whites drew from the already entrenched white racist frame, including old derogatory terms such as "blackie," "camel jockey," and "sheeny."[18]

In addition to physical features such as skin color and facial features, many whites, in the early period and today, have used distinguishing markers that are cultural in character, such as clothing (*hijab* or turban), language accents, and religious customs. Thus, in the racial–ethnic framing of Arab Americans and Middle Eastern Americans, certain cultural markers are added to skin color marking to target them for discrimination. One scholar has noted the racialized categorizing associated with anti-Islam hostility: "As a result of this racialized process, Islamophobia affects Christians, Muslims and Sikhs from all backgrounds and, in particular, people who have ancestry in North Africa as well as in western and southern Asia. Islamophobia, in short, affects a racialized group of people."[19]

Recent Stereotyping and U.S. Politics

Strong negative images of Arab Americans and other Middle Eastern Americans have been circulating among other Americans for decades now. For example, a 1975 Columbia University undergraduate guide described an Arabic course with a comment that every other word in Arabic was about violence. And a 1981 national survey found 44 percent of respondents then considered Arabs to be "barbaric" or "cruel," while about half thought they were "treacherous" or "cunning."[20]

Moreover, a national *USA Today*/Gallup survey recently found that many Americans still hold negative stereotypes and favor discrimination against Muslim Americans, many of whom are Arab Americans. More than four in ten thought Muslims were extreme in religious beliefs; a majority felt they were not respectful of women. Some 31 percent admitted that they would be fearful of a Muslim man on a plane. One-fifth said they would oppose a Muslim as a neighbor, and 40 percent favored discriminatory security measures—such as requiring Muslims to carry special identification and searching Muslims more thoroughly at airports. For many Americans the term *terrorist* conjures up images of Middle Eastern or Muslim men, so much so that when major terrorist events happen, such as the bombing of the Murrah Federal Building in Oklahoma City by white men, police and others often at first search for dark-skinned Middle Easterners.[21]

Since the 1960s, U.S. government policies regarding the Middle East have helped spread negative stereotypes of Arabs and Arab Americans. Terrel Bell, Ronald Reagan's Secretary of Education, reported that in the 1980s, mid-level aides in the White House and government agencies made comments about Arab people as "sand niggers."[22] The common labeling of Arab people and other Middle Eastern people with old terms such as "camel jockeys" and "sand niggers" during the Gulf War of the 1990s and in recent Middle Eastern conflicts has helped to rationalize U.S. interventions overseas in the minds of many Americans. The influential Arab scholar, Edward Said, described these negatively stereotyped views of Middle Eastern peoples as part of a western ideology of *Orientalism*. Orientalism has negatively targeted Middle Eastern and Asian peoples for centuries in Western thought, pervading much scholarly work as well as popular thinking.[23]

Today, as in the past, political figures in the Middle East are sometimes characterized in biologically racist terms. Cartoons have long shown Arab leaders as evildoers with "sharply hooked noses" and a "mustachioed leer." Palestinian leader Yasser Arafat was often portrayed by U.S. newspapers as having "pendulous lips," and other Arab leaders have been portrayed in the media as having similar imagery, including "beak-like noses."[24] The mass media, including cartoonists, participate actively in creating a wide array of racist stereotypes. For example, one study of the animated cartoons *Family Guy* and *South Park* (2001–2007) found they too had images of Arab people and various other Middle Eastern people as barbaric, untrustworthy, and religious extremists.[25]

Recently, Middle Eastern Americans active in the movie and entertainment industries have also criticized the executives and producers there for regularly portraying Middle Easterners as terrorists, "lunatics," and veiled and subordinated women. Such stereotyping seems to be some of the last openly and aggressively racist stereotyping still allowed in Hollywood movies. John Tehranian summarizes the situation thus: "In a haunting recycling of the past, the racist tropes historically employed against blacks, Jews, and other persecuted minorities are now pointed against Arabs, culminating in a discourse that juxtaposes our Western values against their Oriental barbarism."[26]

The absurdity of much common stereotyping is underscored in Evelyn Shakir's comments on her family: "Terrorist, oil sheik, master of the seraglio— it was impossible for me to connect these terms with my uncle who baked blueberry muffins for his wife's breakfast and washed out her underthings by hand, or with my other uncle who belonged to the Rotary Club, voted Republican, and was a deacon in the Baptist church." Note the omission from much of the mainstream media of such positive images of Arab Americans and other Middle Eastern Americans. As Karyn McKinney Marvasti has put it, "So the only cultural resources 'average' Americans have to draw on in thinking about these groups are the negative, 'terrorist' images they've seen the most. This is particularly likely since relatively few non-Arab Americans have Arab American neighbors and friends."[27]

We should note that only a few U.S. political leaders outside Middle Eastern American communities have been willing to challenge these common images. In a speech to the 1984 Democratic Party national convention, Jesse Jackson, an African American leader, was perhaps the first political leader to speak publicly of Arab Americans in strongly positive terms and

as a people facing racial and religious stereotyping and discrimination. Since then, few U.S. political leaders outside Middle Eastern American communities have had similar courage to speak out.[28]

Stereotypes and Arab American Women

Arab and Arab American women, as well as women from other Middle Eastern countries, have faced many stereotypes. Whites and others have portrayed them as exotic, passive, or totally dominated by men, with the latter often stereotyped as hot-tempered. Islam and Arab culture are frequently viewed in the West as extremely oppressive of women.[29]

However, the reality of life for women in Arab countries and in the U.S. is varied and should be put in a comparative context. For example, several Arab and other Middle Eastern countries—such as Iraq, Pakistan, and Afghanistan—have had a greater percentage of women in their governing bodies than has the United States. Women in numerous Arab countries do face issues of an imposed *hijab* or *burka*—that is, covering clothing—though in many cases they choose such covering out of respect for traditions or to be liberated from a "sex object" status. The issues here are complex. As Kristine Ajrouch has noted, "Many veiled women report feeling full of dignity and self-esteem and enjoy that their physical, personal self does not enter into social interactions." In addition, indigenous feminist movements in Middle Eastern societies are currently pressing to reduce barriers and improve the lives of women. We should also note that U.S. women are not free of gender domination. They face being objectified in an often extreme form that accents a certain image of female beauty (e.g., white, thin, or sexually provocative), which frequently leads to pressure to diet in extreme ways or have cosmetic surgery to meet a socially constructed, usually male-oriented image. Historically, most women in Arab societies have lived under strong patriarchal conditions, yet this condition has also been characteristic of most non-Arab families in Western societies until recent decades. Indeed, today, many non-Arab U.S. families are still strongly patriarchal, especially those most firmly situated in conservative religious traditions. In addition, today, as in the past, when it comes to everyday household decisions, many wives and mothers in Arab families have substantial decision-making power.[30]

Generally speaking, traditional values in Arab countries have emphasized family honor and stipulated that women be modest and protected when around male strangers. For Arab American women, this gendered value system sometimes comes into conflict with prevailing U.S. values relating to such behaviors as dating or to adolescent independence. Some Arab American women "have engaged in outright rebellion against their parents' or husbands' authority. Others have been able to invoke traditional values to justify unconventional behavior; in the name of service to family and community, much has been permitted."[31] Over time, many Arab American women have gained greater autonomy, sometimes creating tensions in families. Moreover, women are particularly important to the persistence of Arab culture in the United States; some studies have found them to be the "anchor of the group's sense of identity." Research on Arab American and Muslim women shows that they are quite diverse in their perspectives and gender role adaptations in the United States.[32]

The centrality of certain body imagery in the U.S. media—such as that of the often thin, light-skinned, or blonde models in advertising—creates problems for Arab American women. As a result, "dark pigmentation and, especially, dark body hair, have been sources of shame to [Arab American] girls growing up in the United States." Some feminist groups have emerged among Arab American women, in part because of concern with this dominant image of ideal female beauty. Indeed, recent studies have shown that feminist views are now frequently espoused by Arab American and Muslim American women, especially those who are politically active.[33]

 How have U.S. government policies regarding the Middle East shaped the spread of racial and ethnic stereotypes?

Oppression, Discrimination, and Conflict

Past and Present Patterns of Discrimination

Early Arab immigrants and their children faced racialized discrimination, especially in southern areas. Considered "not white" by many self-defined whites, Arab Americans were turned away from voting places, restaurants, and restrooms. Across the United States they faced less discrimination than African Americans, but were nonetheless often seen as not being white.[34]

Although the Census Bureau today defines Arab immigrants and their descendants as "white," most non-Arab Americans still view them as "not white." One survey of white college students found that just 5 percent felt that the group listed as "Arab Americans" was unambiguously white, with only 7 percent indicating that the group listed as "Middle Eastern Americans" was white. For a majority of these well-educated (self-identified) white Americans, Arab Americans were not white. Thus, classification as "white, non-European" by the U.S. Census Bureau has not prevented continuing racial imaging, prejudice, and discrimination. Unlike older white ethnic groups, a majority of Arab Americans do not have the choice of escaping their racial and ethnic identities, even if they wished to do so. One recent survey of adolescents found that Arab American youth had a substantial awareness of their racial identity in U.S. society and reported facing significant discrimination because of it.[35]

For decades, to the present day, racial and religious discrimination has been a serious problem. The Council on American-Islamic Relations (CAIR) has dealt with many complaints of discrimination faced by Arab Americans and other Muslim Americans in recent years. The U.S. Equal Employment and Opportunity Commission reported that the number of employment discrimination complaints from Middle Eastern Muslim Americans and other Muslim Americans has increased dramatically, to a high of 907 in a recent annual report. In addition, these formal reports are likely the tip of the iceberg, according to knowledgeable Arab American officials. One study by the Discrimination Research Center sent 6000 fictitious job résumés from qualified applicants to various California employers. Those with an identifiably Middle Eastern name, Abdul-Aziz Mansour, got the *lowest* response rate from these employers.[36]

The array of contemporary discrimination is broad—from being forced to endure racist jokes, cartoons, and emails from fellow employees, to not being hired or promoted because of Islamic religious observance, to being taunted with racial slurs. Many cases of employer discrimination involve workplace prohibitions against religious practices, such as not allowing Muslim men to have beards, not permitting Muslim women to wear the *hijab,* or not permitting daily prayers. Much everyday discrimination comes from fellow workers or clients. For example, one study of Arab nurses in the Detroit area found that numerous respondents had faced some discrimination from colleagues and patients. Moreover, in recent years, Muslim Americans have filed at least 70 lawsuits against various discriminators, but not one has received significant redress from juries or judges. In one flagrant discrimination case, a Muslim Afghanistani American was harassed in his workplace with many racist comments, including racist epithets. He also suffered physical attacks such as being made to put pork in his mouth, got notes with Nazi symbols, and endured hostile commentary on his religion. At the trial the jury decided this was discrimination, but did not consider it to have caused enough suffering to be worth redressing with compensation. Not surprisingly, some lawyers have feared actually going to jury trials for Arab American clients because of negative depictions of Arab peoples in the mainstream media.[37]

International Politics and Discrimination

The commonplace "Orientalist" distortions of Arab people and other Middle Eastern people have serious implications for U.S. government policies regarding overseas matters. This is especially true for U.S. policies in the Middle East, a region where the U.S. government has long been heavily invested, in part because of concern for oil supplies. For decades many U.S. policymakers and Middle Eastern diplomats have not been well informed about the region's history or cultures. The scholar Edward Said's earlier assessment is still accurate: "The Middle East experts who advise policymakers are imbued with Orientalism. . . . If in the meantime the Arabs, the Muslims, or the Third and Fourth Worlds go unexpected ways after all, we will not be surprised to have an Orientalist tell us that this testifies to the incorrigibility of Orientals and therefore proves that they are not to be trusted."[38] Orientalist views have become conspicuous in recent U.S. interventions in the Middle East, such as in Iraq and Afghanistan. Such invasions and occupations of sovereign countries have often been conducted by

people with little accurate knowledge of these countries, limited ability to speak local languages, and/or a propensity to stereotype people there as backward.

In recent decades, various kinds of discrimination against Arab Americans, Muslim and non-Muslim, and other Muslim Americans have been linked to international issues and related racial or religious stereotypes. For example, influenced by his negative framing of Middle Easterners, President Richard Nixon responded to the 1972 killing of Israeli athletes in Germany by a few Palestinians by establishing a secret government operation targeting Americans of "Arab ancestry." Although the terrorist attacks on Israelis had nothing to do with the United States, the CIA and the FBI collected information on Arab Americans and harassed many of these U.S. citizens.[39]

In addition, the 1990s Anti-Terrorism and Effective Death Penalty Act and the Illegal Immigration Reform and Immigrant Responsibility Act have given federal authorities powers to detain and interrogate immigrants suspected of links to terrorist organizations without the usual constitutional and civil rights protection, such as the right to a fair legal hearing at which the evidence for detention is presented. (In addition, in the 1990s, the FBI and the Immigration and Naturalization Service also developed a plan to imprison Arab Americans in the event of a war between the United States and any Arab country.) These and more recent laws and regulations have been used in discriminatory ways against U.S. immigrants and citizens with Arab or Muslim backgrounds, or against Americans who look like they might be Arab or Muslim (but are not).[40] As noted in the chapters on Japanese and Italian Americans, in the past some U.S. citizens have been viewed by their government as guilty until proven innocent, in contradiction to U.S. law, and only because of their racial or ethnic backgrounds.

Since the 1970s, Arab American community and civil rights activists, especially those critical of government policies, have been special targets of harassment and violence. Some have received threatening phone calls or had property vandalized. In the mid-1980s, a regional director for one Arab American organization was killed by a bomb. Police authorities attributed the bombing to the extremist Jewish Defense League, which did express satisfaction at the bombing.[41]

The September 11, 2001, attacks by Middle Eastern terrorists—who were apparently angry about
U.S. policies in the Middle East—generated many
hate crimes against Arab Americans or those who
were thought to look like Arabs. Such crimes were
principally about hostile racial and religious framing, for they were committed even though no Arab
American was implicated in the attacks and seven-
teen of the nineteen men involved were from Saudi
Arabia and the United Arab Emirates, countries of
origin for few Arab Americans and, ironically, close
allies of the U.S. government. In just nine weeks after
September 11, there were at least 520 violent attacks
in the United States on people thought to be of
Middle Eastern ancestry. These attacks included
assaults, arson, and several murders. Some of those
assaulted or killed were not Middle Eastern but were
assumed to be so by ignorant attackers.[42]

In addition, the 2001 USA Patriot Act, passed
quickly after the 9/11 attacks, together with the
earlier laws mentioned previously, gave the federal
government broad authority to detain noncitizens
with little or no due process and to carry out
searches and surveillance with less judicial review.
Many Americans concerned about civil liberties
feared that laws said to be designed to reduce the
possibility of terrorism would be used to target
selected immigrants, particularly those who looked
like Middle Eastern Americans. As the American-
Arab Anti-Discrimination Committee put it, "These
serious civil liberties concerns should be alarming
to all Americans, but there can be little doubt that it
is the Arab American and Muslim communities who
are facing the gravest threats to their rights and that
these communities will bear the brunt of any major
diminution of civil liberties in the United States."[43]

This assessment has been accurate, to the present
day. Many Arab and other Middle Eastern Americans have been targeted by federal agents and private security personnel in recent years only because
of the way they look. They have been removed from
airliners. In one recent case, Muslim religious officials (imams) were taken off a plane just because they
were praying. This surveillance problem has become
so general that Arab Americans have a term for it—
FWA, for "flying while Arab." Over the last few
years, the intensive, often stereotypical media focus
on Middle Eastern people and terrorism has helped
to generate numerous incidents where people who
look like they are Middle Eastern have been banned

from airplanes by airline personnel only because of
their appearance. Little or no evidence is required
for such discrimination, as these corporate personnel operate out of a fearful framing of Middle Easterners. In addition, the FBI, among other police
agencies, has targeted Islamic mosques since 9/11,
but has apparently not done the same surveillance
of conservative Christian churches, a few of whose
members have been linked to various terrorist acts in
the United States. And near the end of the Bush
administration in late 2008, the FBI implemented
new regulations that allow agents to use subjective
racial and ethnic assumptions in deciding who is a
suspect for a crime. No evidence is necessary to begin
a criminal investigation "in the national interest."
Only "suspicious" racial or ethnic characteristics are
needed for such investigation. A major reason for
such regulations is to allow racial profiling of Middle
Eastern people by government agents.[44]

Today, such racial profiling is a serious problem,
one sometimes associated with violence. In a recent
incident in Miami, Florida, two vacationing Arab
American brothers were stopped by the police at
night, and one was shot and killed as he turned to
the police with his hands in the air. After the killing,
the police asked nearby witnesses if the unarmed
men had been speaking "Arabic," which apparently
had something to do with the police shooting.
Indeed, much recent research shows that Arab Americans and Muslim Americans constantly encounter
other Americans who view their home countries, cultures, and languages as enemies of the United States,
thereby forcing them to constantly defend their patri-
otism and right to be in the United States.[45]

The hostile framing of Arab and other Middle
Eastern Americans has also generated periodic out-
breaks of hate-crime violence against Arab Americans. Since the late 1980s, and increasingly since
2001, Islamic mosques have been bombed or set on
fire; others have been vandalized. Many physical
attacks on Americans of Middle Eastern descent
took place following the 1991 Gulf War. In the early
1990s, more than 150 anti-Arab hate crimes were
reported to police. Since then, Arab Americans have
been blamed for events such as the 1995 Oklahoma
City bombing by white terrorists. In the days after
that bombing, there were more than 200 attacks on
Arab Americans and Muslim Americans. More
recently, the attacks and other discrimination have
continued. A CAIR report indicates there were

116 hate crime incidents targeting Middle Eastern Americans nationally in 2008 alone, adding to more than 1000 that had already taken place since 2001. Nationwide, the total number of civil rights complaints processed that year by CAIR and its affiliates was 2728, up from the previous year.[46]

One recent hate crime targeted eight Muslim female students at the University of California in Berkeley. Three white men threw water bottles at them, sprayed them, and yelled racist slogans ("East Oakland nigger"), including mocking comments about their *hijabs*. Two students also reported they had previously suffered much verbal harassment. Sometimes other dark-skinned Americans are attacked because they are mistaken for Arab or other Middle Eastern Americans. For example, at a lake beach in Nevada an Asian-Indian man suffered major injuries when he was beaten by whites who called him and his relatives "terrorists," "relatives of Osama Bin Laden," and other slurs indicating the attackers thought their victims were from the Middle East. Even so, a judge dismissed the hate crime charges against these whites, who reportedly were charged with only misdemeanor crimes.[47]

In addition, one national poll found that since 2001, nearly three-quarters of Muslim respondents had experienced anti-Muslim harassment or physical attack, or knew someone who had experienced it. Another poll of Arab Americans found that nearly 30 percent had endured some discrimination, and also that one-third had not traveled by air since 2001 for fear of such discrimination. Indeed, many Arab and other Middle Eastern Americans have reacted to such recurring discrimination by changing the way they dress, the way they talk about social and political matters, and the way they practice their religion.[48]

 Is anti-Arab discrimination in the United States connected to international actions by the U.S. government?

Taking Action against Discrimination

Arab Americans have often taken action against racial and religious framing and discrimination. For example, lawsuits by civil rights groups such as the American Arab Anti-Discrimination Committee have sharply criticized the Homeland Security Department

for its racial profiling and targeting of Middle Eastern entrants into the United States. Civil rights protests have been aimed at the *Chicago Sun-Times* newspaper for racially stereotyping Arabs and neglecting reporting on Arab American communities. Arab American groups organized a boycott of the paper; protests called attention to editorials claiming Palestinian leader Yasser Arafat was primarily responsible for Middle Eastern violence. Antidiscrimination groups have also protested dozens of television and Hollywood movies such as *Rules of Engagement* (2000) and *The Siege* (1998), which show Arabs as terrorists and/or threats to the United States and constantly feed old anti-Arab images. *The Siege* directly links Islam to terrorism, showing Muslim rituals being conducted before acts of violence. Hala Maksoud, head of an antidiscrimination organization, described this film as "insidious, dangerous, and incendiary" and as inciting "hate which leads to harassment, intimidation, discrimination, and even hate crimes." Indeed, from the Rudolph Valentino movie *The Sheik* (1921), to the most recent movies, negative images of Arabs and Muslims have periodically been important in Hollywood movies. In one Detroit area survey, Arab and other Middle Eastern American leaders actively expressed concern about the frequency of these negative images of Arabs and Muslims, as well as the infrequency of positive commentaries in the mass media.[49]

Many Arab Americans have supported civil rights organizations such as CAIR that have taken action against anti-Arab and anti-Muslim discrimination. Various strategies are used. CAIR sometimes attempts mediation with employers to make them more sensitive to the religious needs of their Arab and other Muslim employees. If that fails, they may go to court. Numerous other civil rights organizations—such as the American-Arab Anti-Discrimination Committee, Arab American Institute, Islamic Society of North America, and the Muslim American Society—have worked aggressively to increase active political participation among Arab Americans and other Middle Eastern Americans, as well as to reduce discrimination and hate crimes.[50]

Local Conflict and Cooperation with Other Groups

In areas such as metropolitan Detroit, where Arab Americans have established many small businesses,

Amre Moussa, Secretary General of the Arab League, helps Arab Americans celebrate the opening of the Arab American National Museum in Dearborn, Michigan.

periodic conflicts with other racial and ethnic groups have occurred. Some black groups have reported that relatively new Arab American merchants sometimes treat black customers with disrespect or discrimination. Merchants have in turn complained that black customers sometimes steal from their stores. This conflict is reminiscent of similar conflicts between Korean (or, earlier, Jewish) merchants and black urbanites. Some local efforts—for example, at Detroit's Wayne State University and on Youth Day at Belle Isle in Detroit—have been directed at improving communication between the African American, Arab American, and other area communities.[51]

In recent years, some local Jewish American and Arab American groups have made substantial efforts to increase contacts and dialogue. For example, in Chicago, members of the Arab-American Bar Association and the Decalogue Society of Jewish lawyers have committed themselves to more positive intergroup contacts. In addition, groups of New York Muslims, Jews, and Arab Christians have met to work for increasing understanding between these groups and to reduce local interpersonal and intergroup violence.[52]

 What strategies of resistance have Arab Americans used to counter stereotyping and discrimination?

Politics and Political Emergence

Gradual Increase in Political Activity

By the 1930s, a few Syrian Americans held elected public office, but not until 1958 was the first Arab American elected to Congress. The first U.S. senator of Arab descent, South Dakota's James Abourezk, was not elected until 1980. By the 1980s, a few Arab Americans were named to major appointed positions in government, including White House chief of staff. Over the recent decades, however, a slowly increasing number of Arab Americans moved into positions of influence in the U.S. political system.

Recent Political Involvement

Arab Americans and Muslim Americans have increased their political activity significantly since 1990. Major voter registration drives have led to a substantial increase in Arab voter participation. Nearly

90 percent are registered to vote, and surveys suggest that these citizens pay more attention to politics than most other Americans. One recent study of Arab Americans found that both "women and men have high levels of political engagement, in part reflecting their relatively affluent socioeconomic positions."[53] The political campaigns of the 1990s and 2000s have seen many Muslim and Arab American political candidates. In the 2006 and 2008 elections, from California to Michigan to West Virginia, numerous Arab Americans ran for local, state, and federal positions. As of late 2009, Arab Americans were governors of Maine and Indiana and mayors of St. Louis and numerous smaller towns and cities. They were also on numerous city councils across the country. Seven served in state senates, and fourteen served in state assemblies. Many others served in other elective and appointive positions in many states. The presence of Arab American officials has effects, large and small. For example, some congressional aides have held Friday (Muslim) prayer services in the Capitol building, and more attention is being given to the Arab American view of ongoing Middle Eastern conflicts.[54]

For the first time, the 2000 Republican and Democratic national conventions had Muslim clergy giving prayers. In the November 2000, 2004, and 2008 elections there were many Arab American voters. In these presidential elections, states with significant numbers of Arab American and Muslim American voters received attention from presidential candidates. Candidate George W. Bush consulted with Islamic leaders in Michigan, where the Muslim community supported his 2000 presidential bid, but shifted away from Bush in his 2004 campaign and from John McCain in the 2008 election because of concerns over racial profiling and other discrimination by federal agencies. The 2008 Democratic presidential convention had more than forty Arab American delegates, and the Obama campaign had the first official webpage ever for Arab Americans on its campaign website. A substantial majority voted for Obama in 2008. Bush appointed Arab Americans Spencer Abraham (Energy Secretary) and Mitchell Daniels (Director of the Office of Management and Budget) to his cabinet. Donna Shalala had been the first Arab American to serve in a presidential cabinet in the 1990s. In the late 2000s, three Arab Americans served in Congress: Nick Joe Rahall II (D–W. Va.), Charles Boustany (R–La.), and Darrell Issa (R–Calif.) in the U.S. House. In 2008,

Spencer Abraham, a Lebanese American, has served as U.S. Secretary of Energy.

Obama appointed Ray LaHood as U.S. Secretary of Transportation. About a dozen others have served in the U.S. House and Senate since George Kasem was the first to be elected to Congress in 1958. Consumer advocate Ralph Nader, a Lebanese American, ran for president in several recent elections.[55]

Negative images of Arab Americans have interfered with their ability to participate fully in politics. In recent decades, several local and state political candidates have returned the monetary contributions of Muslim Americans, often with a public display, because the candidates were afraid to be seen as accepting Muslim contributions. During the 2008 presidential campaign, Barack Obama and John McCain avoided mosques and being photographed with Middle Eastern Americans, especially those in traditional dress. Conventional stereotyping of Arab Americans and Muslim Americans seems to be just below the surface of such discriminatory reactions. In addition, in the 2006 and 2008 elections numerous Arab American voters contacted Arab American and other civil rights organizations because they had been led to believe they were ineligible to vote if their English was poor, because they had heard that they had to take a citizenship oath, or because they had encountered other discriminatory barriers to voting.[56]

International Politics and Linkages

Social and political ties to countries of origin remain important to immigrants and their descendants generations after they have become fully established.

Today, for many Arab Americans, such as Lebanese, Iraqi, or Palestinian Americans, ties to home countries or lands are of much importance. They closely watch political events in the Middle East and the U.S. government's involvement there.

In recent years, many Arab Americans have been critical of U.S. foreign policy in the Middle East, faulting it for tilting too far in support of Israel (Israel is currently the largest recipient of U.S. foreign aid) and too much against the interests of the numerous Arab countries in the region. Arab Americans are often critical of Israel's treatment of Palestinians. Ibrahim Hooper, communications director of CAIR, has put it thus: "You're not going to find a Muslim who is not going to support the Palestinians' efforts to free themselves from occupation." Nonetheless, most Arab Americans and most Muslim Americans do *not* support terrorism anywhere. As Dr. Agha Saeed, chair of the American Muslim Alliance, an organization working for civic education, has noted: "We are critical of Israel but not supporters of terrorism."[57] Not surprisingly, then, Arab Americans in cities from Atlanta to Detroit to Riverside, California, have peacefully protested Israeli treatment of Palestinians and called for increased efforts to bring peace there.

The influence of Arab American organizations' efforts to bring their perspective into U.S. discussions of the Middle East may be seen in some recent opinion polls. The majority of U.S. respondents in national polls express a desire for the U.S. government to take an even-handed approach to the Israeli–Palestinian conflict. In addition, most Americans feel Palestinians should have equal rights with Israelis and support an independent Palestinian state under conditions of peace for Israel. Recent surveys also show that majorities of both Arab Americans and Jewish Americans favor an independent Palestinian state and the right of Israel to be secure and independent.[58]

Arab American political activists and organizations have also actively focused on critical domestic issues such as immigration reform and healthcare. Arab Americans and other Middle Eastern Americans have created a large array of important voluntary associations and organizations to provide support for their communities. Cities with large Middle Eastern communities have many voluntary associations, including Islamic and Christian religious groups, media groups, village societies,

professional groups, educational associations, human service groups, and political organizations such as the Arab American Political Action Committee.[59]

Many Middle Eastern community leaders are working to build greater community and political cooperation across various Arab American and other Middle Eastern organizations. One leader noted, "The one thing I wish is for a united community with one organization and leaders . . . who are most qualified and can accomplish things whether they're Palestinian, Lebanese, Yemeni, Shi'a, Sunni, Muslims, non-Muslims." To promote such cooperation, organizations such as the American Muslim Alliance have been formed to link Arab Americans and other Middle Eastern Americans politically across the country. Today, the Alliance has thousands of members in many states.[60]

The Economy

Like other immigrants, some early Arab immigrants were attracted by the relatively high wages paid by Henry Ford in his early 1900s automobile plants in Michigan. However, unlike many European immigrants, most early–twentieth-century Arab immigrants, those from Greater Syria, bypassed new industrial occupations expanding in the decades after 1890, and instead became small merchants. As a result, they often had somewhat higher incomes than new industrial workers. Most settled in just a few cities, where many established small grocery stores, fruit stands, and dry-goods stores. There they built residential and economic enclaves like other immigrant groups such as Italian Americans.[61]

Early immigrants were often working class, but many who immigrated more recently have become professionals and businesspeople. Indeed, Arab Americans today are disproportionately self-employed. Table 12.2 gives the current occupational distribution for those who gave their ancestry as Arab in the 2008 American Community Survey.[62]

Compared to all U.S. workers, Arab Americans are more likely to be white collar and in managerial, professional, sales, and office occupations (which include entrepreneurs). They are less likely than U.S. workers as a whole to be in blue-collar, service, and farming occupations. Numerous Arab Americans have achieved prominence in professional and managerial occupations. Some we have already mentioned. Others include Dr. Michael DeBakey

TABLE 12.2 Occupational Distribution (2008)

Occupation	Arab Americans	All Workers
Managerial, professional, and related	43.7%	34.9%
Sales and office	29.0	25.5
Construction, extraction, and maintenance	5.0	9.3
Production, transportation, and material moving	8.5	12.5
Service	13.7	17.1
Farming, fishing, and forestry	0.1	0.7
Total	100%	100%

Source: U.S. Bureau of the Census. "2008 American Community Survey."

(inventor of the heart pump), Gibran Khalil Gibran (poet), John Abizaid (top U.S. general), Steve Jobs (Apple computer co-founder), Helen Thomas (dean of the White House press corps in the 1990s and 2000s), and schoolteacher, Christa McAuliffe, who was among the astronauts who died in the space shuttle *Challenger* explosion.

Arab Americans are more prosperous economically than some other racial and ethnic groups. In Table 12.3 we observe that Americans with Arab ancestry had a median family income ($70,073) about 10 percent higher than that for the total population. Yet, there are some who are not doing well. At that time Arab Americans had a poverty rate for families significantly greater (at 12.7 percent) than that for the total population.[63]

Arab Americans are concentrated in a few major cities, with the largest number living in the Detroit metropolitan area. Although the Detroit metropolis is frequently viewed as a distinctively African American city, its population includes hundreds of thousands of Middle Eastern Americans. It has the largest Arab American population of any city and the largest Arab-origin population outside the Middle East and northern Africa. Areas of the city have significant Iraqi, Egyptian, Lebanese, Palestinian, and Syrian communities. Metropolitan Detroit is home to the national headquarters of the U.S. Chaldean church and an Islamic Institute. Arab and other Middle Eastern immigrants and their children have helped greatly to bring renewed development and prosperity to areas of Detroit and Michigan. Many Middle Eastern restaurants operate in the area, and Arabic-language signs advertise many Arab American shops and professional offices. Today, thousands of Arab American businesses are located in metropolitan Detroit. Dearborn, part of metropolitan Detroit, is called the center of Arab America because of its large Arab population. Once known principally for being the home of the automobile industry, this area has become a city of mosques and Middle Eastern restaurants and shops and, recently, home of the country's only museum about Arab Americans.[64]

Education

The average Arab American is better educated than the average American. The 1980, 1990, and 2000 censuses all reported that Arab Americans had higher average educational levels than the U.S. population averages. Table 12.4 shows two examples from the 2008 American Community Survey.[65]

TABLE 12.3 Median Family Income and Poverty Rates (2008)

	Arab Americans	Total Population
Median family income	$70,073	$63,366
Family poverty rate	12.7%	9.7%

Source: U.S. Bureau of the Census. "2008 American Community Survey."

TABLE 12.4   Educational Attainment: Percent of Population 25 Years and Older (2008)

	Arab Americans	Total Population
High school graduate or more	88.7%	85.0%
Bachelor's degree or more	45.5	27.7

Source: U.S. Bureau of the Census. "2008 American Community Survey."

For Americans of Arab ancestry, 88.7 percent had at least a high school diploma, and 45.5 percent had completed at least a bachelor's degree. Both figures are higher than those for the general population. One major survey of leaders of Middle Eastern organizations found a very strong emphasis among them on the importance of education, an emphasis uniting various Middle Eastern American subcommunities. These leaders stressed education in part because education and knowledge have long been important within Islamic and other Middle Eastern cultures and in part because of its importance in facilitating advancement in U.S. society.[66]

Some parents send their children to private Muslim schools, but most send them to public schools. As with earlier immigrants and their children, tensions have sometimes arisen between schoolteachers and administrators, on the one hand, and students or parents, on the other. One Arab educator has noted that non-Arab teachers often fail to realize that not all Arab Americans share the same cultural background. Conflicts arise when teachers are unaware that their Arab students come from diverse countries and cultures, when they make incorrect assumptions about the cultural backgrounds of students, or when they impose certain ill-considered school restrictions. For example, one teacher made the stereotyped and very inaccurate assumption that Lebanese women are not allowed to walk freely in the street. Other non-Arab teachers are unaware of the strong tradition of education and the extensive systems of schools in many Arab countries. Misunderstandings about appropriate roles and behaviors are another source of conflict. Muslim students have been suspended from schools, just for wearing the *hijab*. In addition, non-Arab teachers often see Arab American parents as too strict with children, while the Arab parents may view teachers as too lax with disruptive students.[67]

The peers of Arab American and other Middle Eastern American children are often problematical as well. One large recent study of Muslim students in public and private high schools in New York City found that they were very likely to be the victims of racialized teaching and taunting, including hostile comments calling them "terrorists." These problems of taunting and attacks extend, as we have seen previously, to college settings. In a recent study, Arab American and other Muslim American students at community colleges in California and Michigan reported significant levels of racialized harassment on and around their campuses, as well as some reluctance to talk about the extent of the discrimination they faced.[68]

Educator Wendy Schwartz notes that public schools have a responsibility to deal with racial and ethnic stereotyping faced by children: "Because prejudice against Arab Americans increases when political events involve Arabs, or are even speculated to involve them, educators need to be prepared to respond to possible harassment of Arab American students resulting from negative news reporting, and to invoke school policies against hate crimes and discrimination as appropriate."[69] Schwartz calls on educators to become sensitive to major cultural practices of Arab Americans, such as by respecting major Islamic holidays, and to become better informed about Middle Eastern history and contemporary issues in the Middle East.

Religion

Religion has long been central to Middle Eastern countries and cultures, and many Arab Americans take religion very seriously. Many are Christian, a few are Jewish, and many others are Muslim. Most early Arab immigrants were Christian. Generally, they immigrated from Maronite, Melkite, and Syrian

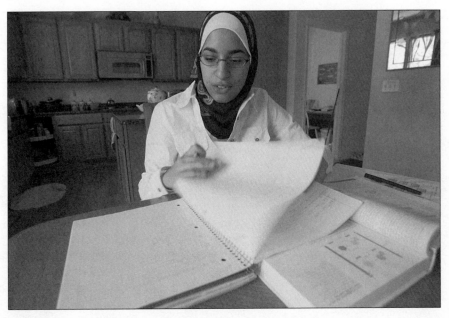

An Arab American student studies at her parents' home in Michigan.

Orthodox areas in what was then Greater Syria. As late as the 1960s, most Arab Americans were Christian. Since the 1960s, however, most immigrants have been Muslim. They and their descendants account for a significant proportion of the U.S. Muslim population, which is put at 2.4 million Americans by the U.S. Census Bureau. Estimates vary as to the percentage of Muslims among Arab Americans, but the Arab American Institute estimates the Muslim percentage at 24 percent, with 63 percent estimated to be various types of Christians. Other analysts estimate the Muslim percentage now to be much higher, at nearly half, because of the many recent Arab Muslim immigrants.[70]

In the early twentieth century, many Arab Americans were Maronite Catholics or Eastern Orthodox Christians, and many still are today. Numerous Maronite Catholic and Eastern Orthodox churches and orders exist in various U.S. cities, including New York City.[71]

Islam has been practiced in North America since the first century of European settlement (some enslaved Africans were Muslims) but did not become visible to most Americans until the 1940s or so. By the 1950s, when the Federation of Islamic Associations of the United States and Canada was created, there were fifty-two mosques in the U.S., not includ-

ing African American mosques. Note that many U.S. Muslims are South Asian Americans and African Americans, with many of the latter being associated with distinctive subgroups such as the Nation of Islam. Indeed, the first Muslim elected to the U.S. Congress, in 2006, was Keith Ellison, an African American who had converted to Islam. By 2010, there were more than 2000 mosques in the United States, representing a large increase over recent decades. According to some estimates, Muslims are now the second largest U.S. religious group.[72]

The arrival of Arab and other Middle Eastern Muslim immigrants since the 1960s has brought conflicts to some Islamic mosques and organizations. New arrivals have expressed surprise at deviations in U.S. mosques from what they regard as traditional Islamic practices. Like Christian churches and Jewish synagogues, mosques have been significantly shaped by the U.S. environment. For example, Sunday schools have been set up, and Sunday prayer services have become more popular than traditional Friday services. Conservative Islamic revivalists have worked to bring U.S. mosques back to more traditional practices, seeking elimination of such events as raffles and teenage dances, and greater segregation or reduction of participation of women in mosque affairs.[73]

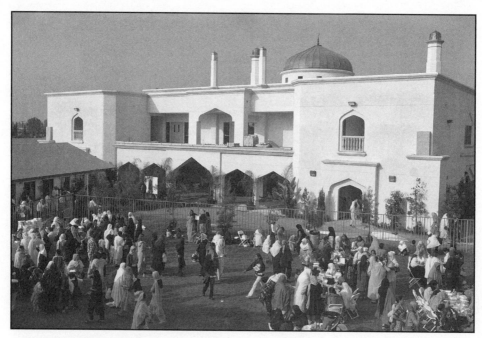

People gather outside a new mosque in Orange County, California.

In a recent Pew poll nearly three-quarters of Muslim Americans said religion was very important in their everyday lives, as compared with 60 percent of those Americans who indicated they were Christians. Some 40 percent of the Muslims went to mosque services at least once a week, as compared to 45 percent of Christian Americans who attended church at least once a week. They were less likely than Christian Americans to believe that their religious organizations should actively express political and social views. In addition, as of the late 2000s, less than 5 percent of children with Muslim backgrounds are receiving direct schooling in Islam outside the home.[74] In the 1990s, a training program for religious leaders was established in Herndon, Virginia, by the International Institute of Islamic Thought, which offers degrees in Imamate Studies and provides U.S. Islamic communities with religious imams educated in the United States. Until this now thriving Institute was established, most leaders came from overseas, and the inability of some overseas leaders to understand U.S. society created tensions with those served, especially with youth influenced by the dominant U.S. culture. Even so, one recent study of Muslim students in New York City high schools showed that they were three times as likely as non-Muslim students to view religion as very important in their everyday lives.[75]

Unlike the various denominations of Christianity that are strong among Arab Americans and other Middle Eastern Americans, Islam is not yet fully accepted in the United States. As we have seen, Arab and other Middle Eastern practitioners still suffer widespread prejudice and stereotyping. In this regard the practitioners of Islam suffer much as Jewish Americans once did for practicing Judaism. The U.S. media periodically connect mainstream Islam to extremists. The media often refer to overseas incidents as involving "Islamic terrorists"—as though the religion of Islam routinely generated this terrorism. Yet, these reporters and editors would never refer routinely to terrorists in Northern Ireland as "Christian terrorists," even though Christian sectarian ideologies (Catholic versus Protestant) have often been linked to terrorism on that island. In neither case is the broader religion responsible for extremist terrorism. Today, as Suad Joseph has noted, the portrayal of Islam is too often "achieved by misrepresenting and then essentializing and homogenizing *a highly complex and diverse religion* that has many different sects, legal systems, beliefs, and practices."[76]

The recurring linkage of the religion of Islam to extremist terrorism creates serious dilemmas for many Muslim Americans, including Arab Americans. Much religious intolerance still confronts them in their everyday lives. Continuing anti-Arab and anti–Middle Eastern stereotyping and discrimination can create serious problems of identity and self-esteem for Arab Americans and other Middle Eastern Americans. As a result, some have decided to deny or "de-emphasize their Arab or Islamic background." This reaction is the same as that of numerous other immigrants groups, past and present, for whom the U.S. sociocultural context has often been a painful Procrustean bed, one with great pressure for one-way conformity to the dominant culture.[77]

Adaptation and Assimilation Issues

Patterns of Assimilation

Partial cultural assimilation has come relatively quickly for most Arab immigrants and their children. Earlier Greater Syrian immigrants soon adapted to new cultural and social environments, picking up English and certain U.S. folkways, even as most maintained their distinctive religious traditions. Intentional discrimination by European Americans played a role in frustrating the rise of first-generation Arab Americans and their children. In response to discrimination, they often anglicized their names, gave up Arabic, and/or tried to appear as Anglo-American as they could, especially in public.[78]

In the sphere of structural assimilation at the secondary level of economy and politics, these early Arab Americans advanced and gradually achieved substantial success. In the early period whites saw their nationality as "Syrian," not "Arab." Indeed, most did not see themselves as Arabs at that point, although most had deep Arab cultural roots. Although many had come to make money and return home, in the entrepreneurial process they came to be proud of their U.S. contributions. Constant contacts with other Americans drew them into the individualistic values and language habits of the dominant culture. As they became more attached to their new homeland, attachment to Syria and Lebanon declined significantly.[79]

In contrast, Arab immigrants who have entered since the 1960s have generally assimilated more slowly at most levels, perhaps because their numbers have been much larger and because of the more intense anti-Arab and anti-Islamic sentiment in the U.S. in recent decades.

Contemporary Assimilation Issues and Patterns

One major survey of Middle Eastern Americans in Michigan found that the issues receiving the greatest emphasis were immigration, cultural preservation, citizenship, and assimilation. Preservation of traditional home cultures, especially language and religion, is of great concern to many in Arab American and other Middle Eastern American communities.[80]

Generally speaking, significant language and other cultural assimilation is taking place in Arab American communities today. Although the last tabulated census (2000) revealed that a majority of Arab Americans over the age of 4, and either foreign born or born of two Arab parents, speak a language besides English at home, speaking two languages is the norm. Today, surveys indicate that in many homes English is increasingly dominant. This is especially true for those who have intermarried with people from other racial or ethnic groups. Probably because of the growing Arab American population and continuing Middle East crises, interest in Arabic language and culture among native-born Arab Americans has increased in recent years. However, those in the second and third generations usually have to take Arabic classes to become fluent, for most do not develop Arabic fluency at home.[81]

Although some Arab Americans oppose marriage outside the group because it threatens group solidarity, intermarriage is increasing. Many second- and third-generation Arab Americans, as well as other Middle Eastern Americans, are moving out of enclave communities and intermarrying outside traditional nationality and religious groups. One study of Muslim Americans (mostly Arab Americans) and converts in Houston found two types of contemporary patterns. Twelve of the twenty-seven respondents, mostly of the first or second generation, had traditional arranged marriages that were also endogamous. However, fifteen of the twenty-seven had exogamous marriages outside their immediate nationality group, all of which were self-initiated. In addition, along with vertical economic progress for Arab Americans has come horizontal mobility, especially suburbanization. First-generation immigrants, like those in other immigrant groups, tend to live in older urban areas, but subsequent generations have been the most likely to move to suburbia. Indeed, many in all generations have moved to the suburbs.[82] This suburbanization, however, has often reduced attendance at mosques and weakened commitment to Islamic traditions.

Assimilation and Generational Conflicts

Today, Arab American and other Middle Eastern American groups are relatively young U.S. populations; many are under the age of 25. This pattern is characteristic of populations containing large numbers of recent immigrants. As with earlier Arab immigrants, strong assimilation pressures have led more recent Arab immigrants and their children to adopt the English language and some mainstream values constantly articulated in the media and public schools. As they become better educated, Arab Americans and other Middle Eastern Americans, especially the young, are being drawn away from cultures of origin to the dominant U.S. culture. Education is essential for advancement, but results in greater acculturation to the Eurocentric core culture. Some in U.S.-born generations even mock the first generation, especially newcomers, as "boaters" who speak English with a strong accent or are not in tune with the dominant culture. In turn, the first generation sometimes views later generations as far too assimilated and losing touch with their ancestral heritage.[83]

Like children of other immigrants, Arab children are caught between parents' home culture and the dominant U.S. culture; family conflicts often result. Parents and community leaders worry that young people are enticed away from traditional values and practices by certain negative aspects of U.S. culture, such as drugs and sexual promiscuity. As in other groups, many Arab American teenagers often prefer aspects of the more permissive core culture. U.S.-born teenagers may seek to fit in by adopting such practices as coloring their hair unusual colors, wearing tight jeans, and listening to rap music. Some arrange dates away from parents. While parents are disturbed at their children's lack of respect for the old ways, children frequently feel they are unfairly restricted.[84]

Some community leaders fear that anti-Arab prejudice and discrimination will cause the youth to desire to abandon their heritage or ancestry even more rapidly. Indeed, some youth do try to hide their identities. In one interview, an Arab American girl told of a friend who passed herself off as half-black and half-Puerto Rican to avoid anti-Arab racism. However, she herself said, "I could constantly find an excuse to deny my culture, but I'm not."[85] In addition, the targeting of Arab Americans, Muslim and non-Muslim, and other Muslim Americans by racist outsiders and discriminators has often had the effect of encouraging youth to accent these identities. Thus, one research study of second-generation Arab Americans on the West Coast found that many were accenting their Muslim identities (often in a Muslim first, then Arab pattern) in response to stereotyping and discrimination. This became one of the vehicles "for self-reinvention and public action, particularly among those who participated in Muslim student activism on college campuses."[86]

 How might assimilation or power-conflict theories be used to explain generational conflicts among Arab Americans?

Creating a Hybrid Culture

Recall Andrew Greeley's ethnogenesis perspective (Chapter 2), which recognizes the reality of cultural differences within contemporary racial and ethnic groups and seems to fit the Arab American experience in certain ways. Arab Americans constitute more than a single Middle Eastern group. Their origins lie in nearly two dozen different countries, including a few in northern Africa. Today they are becoming a composite group of diverse cultural origins. Within the U.S. context, immigrants from various Arab countries and their descendants have increasingly forged a distinctive Arab American umbrella group shaped by their Arab heritages and by adaptation to the European American culture. Despite substantial adaptive changes, significant Arab cultural distinctiveness remains.

One study found that Michigan's Arab American organizations have helped young people become assimilated to certain good features of U.S. culture and society while at the same time cautioning them about its bad features and emphasizing traditional Arab family and religious values. As one leader has put it, "We even actually encourage our kids to assimilate in American society."[87]

Gary David and Kenneth Ayouby have defined **mediated assimilation** as *the process whereby Arab American organizations act as cultural filters to screen out some undesirable features of U.S. culture.* The pattern of using strong community organizations for both assimilation to and resistance to the dominant culture has been typical of many immigrants. This view of the effects and role of community organizations differs from the view that these organizations are interested only in promoting and maintaining old cultural ways. In the mediated assimilation model, these organizations attempt to maintain some adherence to home country traditions, but also help create a new "Arab American" mixture. A hybrid culture appears to be developing, one that includes elements of home-country practices but that also adapts these elements to the assimilation patterns within a specific U.S. community. The hybrid Arab American culture is "specific to the community's experiences both in the new and old lands."[88] This hybrid particularly helps to blend together groups of people, young and old, whose ancestral roots are in different countries into an umbrella Arabic American culture.

Power-Conflict Issues: Identities in the Face of Hostility

A power-conflict perspective underscores certain distinctive aspects of the Arab American experience. The dominant European American majority has the major say in how Arab Americans are portrayed in the media and how they are viewed and treated in most U.S. institutions. In public discussions and settings, the European American view of Arab Americans customarily decides whether the latter as a group are placed toward the darker, more socially undesirable end of the prevailing racial–ethnic continuum or toward the lighter, more socially desirable ("white") end. Recall the numerous European American judges who, between 1909 and 1944, vacillated on whether certain Arab American groups could be considered "white." Indeed, one important dimension of daily interaction with European Americans for Arab Americans is that they are treated as, at worst, "sand niggers" and "terrorists," or, perhaps with less overt hostility, as "not yet white," even as they are officially listed as "white" by the U.S. Census Bureau.

Continuing societal stereotyping and discrimination, often at the hands of European Americans, have pressed some Arab Americans to deny or de-emphasize their Islamic or Arab ties. For example, recent research on Arab-origin people in the Detroit area has found significant variations in identification with "Arab American." Some subgroups among Arab Americans try to hold to both strong Arab American and "white identities, while others report a strong white identity, yet distance themselves from the pan-ethnic 'Arab American' label."[89] Although the majority continues to openly claim their nationality and religious backgrounds, they will often restrain their reactions to the anti-Arab prejudice and discrimination they regularly face, even as they may work quietly to eliminate this prejudice and discrimination.

Recently, an Arab American civil rights leader, Imad Hamad, has argued that being officially designated as white by the U.S. Census Bureau is actually "unfair because we are not treated as white in society."[90] Indeed, some Arab American leaders have sought to have Arab Americans officially classified as a distinctive non-European group, like the "Hispanic" category devised by the U.S. Census Bureau, but so far this has been rejected. Interestingly, many Arab Americans now publicly identify themselves as "people of color," and thus link themselves to the long struggle of movements against racial oppression in the United States.[91]

Clearly, the racial–ethnic identity of Arab Americans today is much more than a "symbolic identity" without lasting significance—the view some analysts hold of group identities in white ethnic groups such as Irish Americans. In this color-conscious society, Arab Americans' array of physical characteristics presents a continuing problem for their group and for European and other Americans who think in racial terms about them. Arab Americans vary from very dark-skinned to blue-eyed and blond, although most have brown eyes, dark hair, and olive or light brown skin. Some can and do pass as phenotypically white, but many others who might do so in fact reject this option and emphasize certain differences from European Americans.[92] Most European Americans, for their part, seem to view Arab Americans and other Middle Eastern Americans, taken as a group, as "not white." The persistence of anti-Arab stereotyping and hostility both encourages and discourages movement away from a strong Arab American identity.

Summary

Middle Eastern immigrants have been coming to the United States for more than a century. One of the largest groups among these immigrants consists of Arab immigrants from more than twenty countries. By the 1920s, there were about 200,000 Arab Americans, mostly Christians. They and their descendants make up a substantial proportion of today's Arab American population. The rest of this group encompasses many recent immigrants from Arab countries, most of whose religious background is Muslim. These immigrants and their descendants have helped make Islam the second largest U.S. religion. As has been the case for other immigrant groups, economic and political conditions in countries of origin are major reasons for recent migration. Many immigrants have fled wars in the Middle East. Most have a strong sense of Arab origins and an inclination to be critical of certain U.S. government policies in the Middle East.

Today, Arab Americans have established strong communities in a number of large cities. Many live in metropolitan Detroit. Many have become successful professionals or businesspeople, and some are beginning to move into important political offices. Arab Americans and other Middle Eastern Americans still face widespread stereotyping and significant and sometimes violent discrimination. Hate crimes have frequently targeted Islamic mosques, as well as Middle Eastern individuals and their families and homes. Negative images of Arabs and Arab Americans are common in some media; men are often portrayed as extremist or domineering and women as servile or repressed. Only a few U.S. leaders outside Arab American communities have, as yet, been willing to challenge these stereotyped images in a regular and sustained way.

Arab Americans are today in the forefront of those fighting racial and ethnic stereotyping and religious discrimination. Like other groups facing serious discrimination, they have created important community and civil rights organizations that have pressed for expanded civil rights not only for Arab Americans and other Middle Eastern Americans but also for all Americans.

Key Terms

Middle Eastern
  Americans   347
Arab
  Americans   347

sojourner
  immigration   348
mediated
  assimilation   365

CHAPTER 13

Ongoing Racial and Ethnic Issues in the United States
Some Final Considerations

BIG PICTURE QUESTIONS

- How is the commonplace rhetoric about current immigrants similar to that for past immigrants?

- How does the changing U.S. demographic situation challenge white Americans' traditional power and privilege?

- Is the United States truly a democracy?

In the 1990s, David Spritzler, a 12-year-old student at the distinguished Boston Latin School, refused to say the Pledge of Allegiance with other students. He explained that, because "liberty and justice for all" does not exist in the United States, he did not want to do something that violated his principles. Facing disciplinary action, the boy went to the Massachusetts Civil Liberties Union, which sent the headmaster a letter noting that federal court decisions supported the boy's understanding of free speech. Inside and outside the school, reaction to Spritzler's courageous assertion of his rights was positive and negative. One hostile letter that he received was accompanied by a copy of his newspaper photograph marked with a bullet-riddled Star of David and a swastika.[1]

The United States began as a land of great promise for colonists who came from Europe. Early poets, such as Philip Freneau in his 1788 poem "The Pictures of Columbus," spoke of the new land as "paradise anew." Thomas Jefferson and other founders used strong language about liberty, freedom, and democracy for the new nation created in the late 1700s.[2] Yet, as Latino scholar Ilan Stavans has noted, this celebrated image is not the reality of the past four centuries. Instead, North America has always been "the crossroads of hope and violence, democracy and intolerance. America the beautiful and America the ugly."[3] Today, the United States is still a country of hope with grand ideals of equality, freedom, and democracy, but it is also "America the ugly," where a great many "others" are still second-class citizens who face racial or ethnic discrimination or other oppression that is substantially under the control of still-dominant European Americans.

Currently, U.S. society is undergoing important changes in its racial and ethnic composition. Challenges and conflicts brought by these major demographic changes will likely continue for decades. Among these are challenges to traditional white domination, in terms of both the white population majority and white power and privilege. Significant challenges to traditional white social, political, and educational domination are already arising from large-scale population changes and new organizational developments those changes bring. Today, people of European descent are less than one-fifth of the world's population and still decreasing in proportion. They are also a decreasing proportion of the U.S. population.

Currently, white Americans are a statistical minority in the central-city areas of the major metropolises of New York City and Chicago and of the entire metropolitan areas of Los Angeles and Houston. They are a minority in many of the country's one hundred largest cities. Whites are also a minority of the population in California, Texas, New Mexico, and Hawaii. If future birth and immigration rates are at least roughly similar to those of the present, more than half the population will be Americans of color by about 2050. By that year, the U.S. Census Bureau estimates a majority of about 429 million Americans will be Americans of color—with the Latino population increasing rapidly to about 30 percent, the black population growing more slowly to about 15 percent, and the Asian American population growing rapidly to about 9 percent.[4]

This ongoing demographic shift is significant, for European Americans have not been a statistical minority of the U.S. population since the 1700s. Today, much discussion of these demographic changes, especially among European Americans, has a fearful tone. Many have a deep concern about non-European challenges to the dominant Euro-American culture. For example, Patrick Buchanan, former contender twice for the Republican presidential nomination and presidential candidate for the Reform Party, has expressed the concerns of many whites about a country that is no longer predominantly white. Buchanan has asserted, "Our Judeo-Christian values are going to be preserved and our Western heritage is going to be handed down to future generations and not dumped on some landfill called multiculturalism." In a recent best-selling book, *State of Emergency*, that got him on many television programs, Buchanan draws in part on white-nationalist and other extremist authors to argue that the United States is being submerged by "third world" immigrants who will take over the country socially in coming decades—that is, that current young people will live to see the "end" of the United States if something is not done to stop this migration.[5]

Writing in the influential policy journal *Foreign Affairs*, the late Harvard professor Samuel Huntington asserted a similar point: "If multiculturalism prevails and if the consensus on liberal democracy disintegrates, the United States could join the Soviet Union on the ash heap of history."[6] He, too, feared that domestic forces pushing toward heterogeneity, diversity, and multiculturalism were disintegrating the country.

Even otherwise liberal analysts have expressed variations on this strongly negative view of cultural pluralism and multiculturalism. Historian Arthur Schlesinger Jr. has written about multiculturalism as dominating all levels of education. In his view, this involves "an astonishing repudiation" of "a unifying American identity" and an "assault on the Western tradition" by multicultural "tribalism."[7] Many such fearful white analysts, therefore, see efforts to create a multiracial democracy whose core culture is no longer predominantly European as a disturbing challenge to European American values and interests and to "European civilization."

A Nation of Immigrants

Historically, the United States has *always* been a nation of immigrants. Recurring immigration is its uniqueness and generally one of its strengths. In numbers and diversity, the many millions who have come from all corners of the globe are unparalleled in the rest of the world. These millions have brought dozens of languages and cultures, a great diversity of resources, and an array of physical and cultural characteristics. This diversity can be seen in something as simple as the array of Asian, Mexican, African, European, Middle Eastern, Asian-Indian, and South American restaurants in cities, or in something as complex as recent racial–ethnic voting patterns in the 2008 presidential election and in ongoing debates over multicultural education in the schools.

European countries have supplied well over half of the 75 million immigrants who have entered the United States over the 189-year period shown in the next column.[8] Numerous European countries have supplied at least 700,000 immigrants to the growth of the United States; and Austria/Hungary, Germany, Ireland, Italy, Norway/Sweden, Russia, and the United Kingdom have each contributed more than 2 million immigrants. Canada, populated mostly by European immigrants and their descendants until relatively recently, has supplied more than 2 million. Only a few from the populous areas of Asia and the Middle East have so far contributed at least 700,000 immigrants to the U.S. mix. Only four countries in the Caribbean, Central America, South America, Africa, or Oceania have yet sent that

---

IMMIGRANTS TO THE UNITED STATES, 1820–2009

Persons Obtaining Legal Permanent Resident Status by Region and Country of Last Residence (1820–2009)**

Official government records show that between 1820 and 2009, about 75 million immigrants entered the United States. Only a small number of countries have sent more than 700,000 people. Listed below are the countries from which at least 700,000 immigrants have arrived during this long period. Single-asterisked countries are those from which at least 2 million immigrants have come during this period.

Europe (total = 39,621,305)
    Austria and Hungary*
    France
    Germany*
    Greece
    Ireland*
    Italy*
    Norway and Sweden*
    Poland
    Russia*
    United Kingdom*

North America (12,348,734)
    Canada and Newfoundland*
    Mexico*

Asia and Middle East (11,730, 420)
    China (including Hong Kong and Taiwan)*
    India
    Korea
    Philippines*
    Vietnam

The Caribbean (4,591,001)
    Cuba
    Dominican Republic
    Jamaica

Central America, South America, Africa, and Oceania (6,145,666)
    El Salvador

Source: Department of Homeland Security, *Yearbook of Immigration Statistics: 2010.*

**Data for years prior to 1906 refer to country of origin; data from 1906 to 2009 refer to country of last residence.

many. Moreover, Mexico, China (including Hong Kong and Taiwan), and the Philippines are the only countries outside of Europe and Canada that have so far contributed more than 2 million immigrants to the mix. These patterns reflect the discriminatory effects of U.S. immigration laws before 1965.

Some groups of immigrants do not appear in official statistics for various reasons. One group is Puerto Ricans, who are not counted because they are officially U.S. citizens. And from the 1600s to the 1850s, many Africans were forced to immigrate. For most, their point of origin on the African continent is unknown because of the brutal conditions of forced emigration. These involuntary immigrants numbered at least a half-million, but they are uncounted in government records. Undocumented immigrants in the contemporary era are also not included in these figures.

Why do people migrate? What affects migration? We have examined these issues throughout this book. Distinctive economic and political conditions in the United States and sending countries for particular historical periods have shaped which countries supply immigrants and how many come. For many decades between the late nineteenth century and the mid-1960s, the U.S. government imposed major barriers to immigrants from many areas. For those who were able to come more or less voluntarily, economic and political conditions in their homelands that were barriers to personal and family development pressed many to leave. During boom times, when many jobs are available, the U.S. economy has particularly attracted immigrants from many lands.

Old indigenous societies were already present in North America when strangers from distant shores arrived. Immigration from Europe brought genocide, forced migration to reservations, and many material and other losses for indigenous peoples.

Political actions by colonial and U.S. governments have long helped to determine the character of immigration patterns. For centuries now, the U.S. political-economic empire has expanded as the government and corporations have expanded activities globally. U.S. ties overseas, more extensive than those of previous empires, include corporate and military linkages, often generated by U.S. military interventions overseas; extensive government aid to countries; and far-reaching media linkages, including television and movies. Large-scale immigration often parallels the development of U.S. political and economic linkages internationally. We saw this in the first great migrations of European workers to

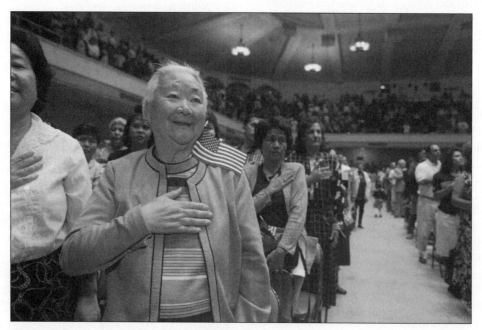

An elderly Chinese American woman recites the Pledge of Allegiance with a diverse group of 1700 other new U.S. citizens in San Jose, California.

North America, the migration of English and Irish laborers in the eighteenth and nineteenth centuries. We have also seen it in later migrations, such as the Chinese laborers who built infrastructure projects in western states, the Mexican laborers who have done much hard labor in agriculture since 1900, and the Korean and Asian-Indian immigrants who have established thousands of small businesses in cities.

Over the course of U.S. history, leading government officials, usually of north European ancestry, have often used restrictive laws to control migration according to their racial–ethnic framing and preferences. As an article in a 1914 magazine noted, "Immigrants who came earlier and their descendants have always tried to keep this country for those who were already here and for their kinfolk."[9] The racist Chinese Exclusion Act (1882) and the discriminatory national-origin quotas in the 1924 Immigration Act guaranteed that by the twenty-first century the U.S. population mix would include fewer Americans from Asia and from southern and eastern Europe than would otherwise have been the case. By intention, the 1924 law sharply reduced the number of Catholic immigrants from countries such as Italy and Poland and of Jewish immigrants from eastern Europe. As a result, just over half of adult Americans today are Protestant; a minority of the population is Catholic, Jewish, or Muslim. And Asian Americans still constitute only about 5 percent of the population.[10]

Beginning in 1965, openly exclusionary and racist quotas in U.S. immigration laws were replaced with general limits on the number of immigrants allowed to enter from any country. Still, the 1986 Immigration Reform and Control Act and later immigration acts have reflected dominant-group concerns about who was immigrating. For example, the 1986 act was intended to limit immigrants from south of the border, particularly from Mexico. Not surprisingly, the act's restrictive provisions have led to some racial profiling of, and other discrimination against, Latinos who are U.S. citizens.

The 1990 Immigration Act set an official annual limit of all legal immigrants at 675,000. This limit most affects immigrants from countries (such as Asian countries) from which many people seek to emigrate and contrasts with the generally unlimited immigration allowed before 1910, when most potential immigrants were European. The 1990 act established several visa categories, the largest of which is for family members of legal U.S. residents in order to facilitate family reunification. In addition, 140,000 employment-based visas are reserved primarily for highly skilled workers, and visas for unskilled workers are virtually unavailable. The act also designated a special category of visas to provide legalization for certain illegal immigrants from some (mostly European) countries and to set aside visas for wealthy immigrants willing to invest to create U.S. jobs.

A 1996 immigration act increased federal surveillance over undocumented immigrants, and other federal legislation excluded undocumented immigrants from most public welfare benefits. Other immigration acts (especially in 2005) further increased these restrictions, including limits on judicial appeals by immigrants. Statistical calculations including regular legal immigrants, refugees, and undocumented immigrants—and excluding temporary visitors, workers, and students and subtracting out-migrants—indicate that a net figure of about 1.2 to 1.5 million people have been added to the United States so far annually since 2000.[11]

In recent years, immigration and proposed immigration restrictions (including such things as a fence on the Mexican border) have been debated by Congress, by the public, and by media commentators. Many native-born business leaders and politicians question the character and values of the Latin Americans and Asians who constitute the majority of recent newcomers. These arguments are similar to those made by opponents of immigration in the late nineteenth century and early twentieth century against a great many immigrants from Europe.

Most respondents in recent opinion surveys indicate that they feel the diverse cultural composition of the United States is an important asset. However, when commenting on legal and undocumented immigration, the public shows mixed feelings. For example, a recent Pew Research Center national survey asked respondents to indicate the most important problem facing their communities. Crime, education, unemployment, drugs, traffic, taxes, and roads all ranked higher in the list than immigration issues. Still, when asked specifically, 52 percent agreed that immigrants were a burden in terms of jobs, housing, and healthcare. About 42 percent, however, accented an alternative view—that immigrants strengthen the country with hard work and talents. A majority felt the level of legal immigration should stay the same or be increased; about half thought today's immigrants were at least as willing to assimilate as European immigrants in the early 1900s. In addition, most negative opinion about immigrants was directed at the undocumented immigrants. A majority felt they should not have access to social services; about half thought that employers should be penalized for hiring them. Recall too the 2009 ABC/*Washington Post* survey cited in Chapter 8, in which 60 percent of the respondents agreed with allowing undocumented immigrants to remain if they "pay a fine and meet other requirements." A 2009 *New York Times* survey also found that only 24 percent of Americans wanted the "borders [to] be completely closed." However, in 2010, conservative white legislators in Arizona passed major legislation making it a serious crime for undocumented immigrants to be in that state and pressuring police officials to aggressively question those they suspected of being undocumented. A national Pew Center survey found that a bare majority of Americans supported this legislation, and more than two-thirds of the respondents approved of requiring Americans to show documents proving their legal-resident status to police officers and of allowing police to hold those without such documents on them. Nonetheless, the new law caused much controversy across the country, and many demonstrations were called to protest what many saw as "police state" legislation.[12]

Although many respondents in national polls believe immigrants are taking away many jobs, most research studies have shown that immigrants do not generally take away more jobs than they create. Immigrants' presence creates new demands for housing and other commodities. Drawing on several research studies, one Council of Economic Advisors report concluded that the low-wage jobs "taken by immigrants in years past have . . . increased employment and income for the population as a whole." An overview study by the National Academy of Sciences concluded that "the evidence points to the conclusion that there is only a small adverse impact of immigration on the wage and employment opportunities of competing native groups. This effect does not appear to be concentrated in the local areas where immigrants live, but instead is dispersed across the United States." Most recent studies have found little effect on job opportunities for most native-born Americans. The main exception to this is a finding in some studies of negative effects on those seeking

and holding working-class jobs—those jobs often held by working-class black and native-born Latino Americans. Even in this latter case there are contradictory findings, with one recent study showing no immigration effects for these latter workers.[13]

Over the past decade, growing misinformation about and stereotyping of immigrants, especially undocumented immigrants, have too seldom been countered by educators and officials willing to speak on the facts about immigration. Census Bureau data indicate that immigration from Asia and Latin America since the 1960s is not fueling a uniquely large population expansion. The 1980s saw a U.S. population increase of 9.8 percent, the second-lowest rate for any decade in U.S. immigration history. The 1990s saw a faster increase of 13 percent, but in the period from 2000 to 2010, the increase was significantly less—about 9.9 percent. All these increases are smaller than the increases for most decades over the past century and a half. Thus, in the decades from the 1850s to the 1920s, the percentage increases in population ranged from 15 percent over the 1910s to 36 percent over the 1850s.[14]

Between 1901 and 1910, some 8.8 million immigrants entered the U.S., mostly from Europe. This was the largest number for any decade prior to the 1990s, and it occurred when there was little government restriction on immigration. U.S. government immigration data for 1991 to 2000 show that total legal immigration was the largest to that point—about 10 million. For the period from 2001 to 2010, the figure is also estimated to be about 10 million. Note, however, that during the earlier 1901–1910 decade, the U.S. population was very much smaller—about 92 million, as compared with 281 million in 2000 and more than 309 million in mid-2010.[15] The ratio of legal immigrants to native-born Americans is thus *lower* today than that ratio was in the late nineteenth and early twentieth centuries. Adding in current undocumented immigrants to the total immigration figure is difficult because their numbers are, at best, rough estimates, and many also return home. Today, even adding in estimates for undocumented immigrants who stay permanently, the U.S. not only has a smaller percentage of foreign-born than it had in earlier decades but also has a smaller percentage of foreign-born than some other countries. Given its long history of successful absorption of immigrants and the size of its native-born population and geographical area, the

United States is unlikely to be overwhelmed by the current rate of immigration.

Some social analysts argue that immigrants make mostly positive contributions to this country: As a group, immigrants are "upwardly mobile, ambitious, saving; they have traditional values, care about their children, all that sort of stuff. They've done something very dramatic to upgrade themselves."[16] Immigrants are generally hard working and seek to make a good life for themselves and their families. If it were not for the many immigrants in recent decades, numerous cities would now have declining populations. The 2000 census showed that several major cities—including Chicago, Boston, and New York City—whose populations have declined over the past half-century are growing again. (Several of the states with the largest percentages of the foreign-born have also seen significant economic growth.) Other major cities, including Pittsburgh and Philadelphia, without as great an immigrant influx, have continued to decline. Judging from American Community Surveys since 2000, the official tabulations for the 2010 U.S. Census (not yet available) are likely to show a similar pattern. Thus, some city officials have sought to support their economies by aggressively encouraging immigration.[17]

Interestingly, over the next half-century, the U.S. will likely face a shortage of workers as large numbers of baby boomers retire, and the next generation of workers born in the U.S. from the mid-1960s to the mid-1980s is significantly smaller. A decreasing workforce, especially at the 30 to 60 age level, will be insufficient to meet many job demands, including heavy demands for the public and private services the aging population will require. Numerous analysts have shown that the future U.S. economy will probably be in serious trouble without a constant and substantial infusion of new immigrant workers from abroad.[18]

The Melting Pot: Early Images of Immigrant Incorporation

There has never been a consensus on how new immigrants are to be incorporated into U.S. society. Pressures for cultural assimilation are often matched by immigrants' desires to maintain their own cultures. For more than a century, one prominent idealized image for immigrant incorporation has

been the "melting pot." In the early 1900s, immigrant playwright Israel Zangwill made an influential statement of this in his play *The Melting Pot*, in which a Russian immigrant argues:

> America is God's Crucible, the great Melting-Pot where all races of Europe are melting and reforming! Here you stand, good folks, think I, when I see them at Ellis Island, here you stand in your fifty groups, with your fifty languages and histories, and your fifty blood hatreds and rivalries. But you won't be long like that, brothers, for these are the fires of God. . . . A fig for your feuds and vendettas! Germans and Frenchmen, Irishmen and Englishmen, Jews and Russians—into the Crucible with you all! God is making the American.[19]

Zangwill's optimistic image of a crucible that melts many different groups to form an "American blend" symbolizes a mutual adaptation process in which old and new groups blend together on a more or less equal basis. However, as we have seen throughout this book, actual intergroup adaptation has usually involved much more one-way assimilation and group conflict. Also, many Americans—including African, Asian, Latino, Middle Eastern, and Native Americans—seem to be absent from this early melting-pot imagery.

Assimilation theorists such as Milton Gordon argue that in practice the melting pot has diverged greatly from Zangwill's ideal. Immigrant adaptation has typically been in the direction of Anglo-conformity as those in each new group of immigrants have given up much of their cultural heritage for the dominant culture: "If there is anything in American life which can be described as an overall American culture which serves as a reference point for immigrants and their children, it can best be described, it seems to us, as the middle-class cultural patterns of, largely, white Protestant, Anglo-Saxon origins."[20]

 How have U.S. government immigration policies shaped past and present demographic trends?

Multicultural and Multiracial Democracy Issues

In recent years, melting-pot and pluralistic imagery have become common. As we have seen, some modern-day assimilationists have expressed great concern over full integration of groups from Asia and Latin America into the U.S. mix. Popular and scholarly debates over the meaning of the melting-pot idea occur in colleges, corporate boardrooms, Congress, and the White House. Indeed, in the late 1990s, President Bill Clinton even set up a White House advisory panel to hold hearings on how to deal with growing diversity and preserve "One America." Contemporary discussions are filled with terms such as **multiculturalism**—*the idea that modern societies should include and accept diverse racial and ethnic groups with equal social and political status*—and **cultural diversity**—*acceptance of a variety of cultures*—that stress the importance of respecting the many groups and subcultures contributing to U.S. development, especially the contributions of non-European groups. A variation of the cultural pluralism perspective (see Chapter 2), multiculturalism, emerged out of the racial and ethnic protest movements of the 1960s and has spread. Some multiculturalists seek modest changes in existing institutions, while others, often called "strong" multiculturalists, seek fundamental structural and cultural changes, especially in institutionalized racial and ethnic discrimination.

Numerous colleges and universities, as well as elementary and secondary schools, have developed a few multicultural programs to give greater voice to the racially oppressed people (and sometimes white women) who have done much of the hard work that has built this society. Since the 1980s, universities as different as Stanford University, the University of Michigan, the University of California at Irvine, Texas A&M University, and Tufts University have added courses on aspects of U.S. (and global) cultural and/or racial–ethnic diversity to B.A. or B.S. requirements. Today, over half of major U.S. colleges and universities report having some type of diversity requirement. Studies show that these courses are often effective in reducing some racial–ethnic and other stereotyping. Multicultural programs, usually modest in scope, have been implemented at many public schools. Teachers at one high school in Brooklyn's predominantly white Bensonhurst section, where a black man shopping for a used car was killed by a white mob, pioneered a successful multicultural class that was imitated in other high schools. Their goal was to shatter racial and ethnic stereotypes and provide students with an opportunity to discuss the causes of intergroup stereotyping and strife.[21]

Some publishers and voluntary organizations have made multicultural teaching materials more

Many U.S. colleges and universities, such as the University of California (Berkeley), have become more racially and ethnically diverse over the past few decades.

readily available to colleges and public schools. For example, the Southern Poverty Law Center in Montgomery, Alabama, has developed a substantial website and program for public schools that today include the high-quality magazine *Teaching Tolerance* and other curriculum materials for multicultural school programs.[22]

A "strong" version of multiculturalism has been enthusiastically embraced by numerous scholars and other Americans with roots in Africa, Asia, Latin America, and the Middle East, as well as in indigenous North America societies. They seek a sharp reduction in ideological racism and racial and ethnic discrimination, as well as a greater respect for their home countries and their cultures. Some white analysts view this stronger variant of multicultural thought as an attack on the dominant Euro-American culture. The late historian Arthur Schlesinger put it thus: "The contemporary ideal is not assimilation but ethnicity. We used to say *e pluribus unum*. Now we glorify *pluribus* and belittle *unum*. The melting pot yields to the Tower of Babel."[23]

Social scientists and popular writers who make such arguments generally reflect the "order theory" framework we have discussed. Critics of an assertive multiculturalism, fearful of losing the centripetal forces of Euro-American culture, argue that Anglo-conformity is still the best assimilation model for non-European groups. Their "melting pot" is not so much a mutual blending as a melting of newcomers (and some older groups) into the dominant Euro-American culture. Although they may recognize contributions of non-Europeans to the core culture, critics of a strong multiculturalism emphasize Anglo-conformity assimilation when they assert that the U.S. is founded on European individualism, not on a philosophy of racial–ethnic pluralism. Schlesinger argued, "It is not that the Western cultures are superior to other cultures as much as it is, for better or worse—our culture."[24] From this perspective, the Eurocentric bias generally found in the educational system, as well as other societal sectors, is not problematic but essential to the integration of diverse groups into "our" one societal whole.

The strong version of multicultural thought and practice suggests that the U.S. should be viewed not as a melting pot but as a grand mosaic, a country celebrating its real diversity with egalitarian and social justice language and conceptual framing. Traditional images of the melting pot assume that European culture and institutions should continue to be the foundation of U.S. society. No early melting-pot analysts paid serious attention to Americans of color, and even many pluralists have "presupposed a set of criteria for successful participation in American plural society: middle-class values, English-language dominance, and acceptance of Western political and cultural ideas."[25] In contrast, these strong mosaic theorists do not see the dominant Anglocentric culture as necessarily central to the American identity, but rather see an evolving and increasingly diverse, just, and egalitarian country. "Ironically, it is in minority communities that the idea of the 'gorgeous mosaic' has been embraced most enthusiastically: the least powerful are advancing the most encompassing and egalitarian notion of social relations."[26]

Strong multicultural analysts believe that vigorous multiculturalism and diversity programs provide a necessary corrective to the dominance of Euro-American culture. One reason is that relatively few Americans, of any age, know much detail about the country's variegated history. One survey, using multiple-choice questions, found that most respondents could *not* choose 1775 as the year the Revolutionary War started, nor could they pick Virginia as the area where that war ended. A government survey of high school seniors found that most lacked knowledge even of simple historical facts. And a 2000 survey of more than 500 seniors at dozens of our major colleges and universities found that most scored very low on a modest high school history test. More recent tests have shown a little improvement, but most students still score low.[27] Even those who think they know U.S. history often accept many misconceptions taught in school. Research shows that high school textbooks communicate much inaccurate, distorted, or elliptical information about U.S. history, particularly with regard to racial and ethnic matters. Typical high school and college textbooks put a pleasant face on an often bloody U.S. racial and ethnic history. Most leave out inconvenient historical information—such as the fact that New York's Wall Street was once a large colonial market where whites sold enslaved Africans, a savage business that lasted there until well after the Civil War started.[28]

Many multicultural analysts and projects "have encouraged us to look at traditionally excluded cultures and study them on their own terms rather than seeing them through the eyes of the dominant class." Contemporary multiculturalism is not separatist, but encourages "people to see in plural ways, so that they are not seeing through the lens of any single culture, but understanding the relationships of cultures to each other."[29] Analyses such as that of Schlesinger also miss the fact that strong multicultural education is in tune with the changing U.S. demographic reality.

Debates over multiculturalism and cultural diversity programs often become heated when they encompass issues of racial and ethnic inequality and white privilege and power. Some social science and other analysts view the function of multicultural courses as simply to expose students to various racial–ethnic groups and their cultures, but other analysts, such as "critical race" theorists, want such courses to analyze deeply the oppressive stratification that underlies U.S. racial–ethnic relations. The focus of this strong and anti-racist multiculturalism is power and resource inequality, and its goal is to eventually effect major societal changes through large-scale, authentically democratic, restructuring of this still-inegalitarian society.[30]

Power-conflict analysts often argue that multiculturalism in college curricula should acquaint all students well with the perspectives of nondominant racial and ethnic groups, and that college administrators and faculty should carefully scrutinize and change the curricula in all disciplines so that they "fairly represent the variegated nature of American culture."[31] From this perspective, a strong multiculturalism should also bring a real change in college hierarchies so people of color (and white women) are well and fairly represented at all levels of the faculty and administration and are an empowered presence in policy making on admission of students, hiring of administrators and faculty, drafting of curricula, and overseeing college investments. These analysts suggest that a strong commitment to meaningful multiculturalism and multiracial democracy should lead to a major alteration of the oppressive hierarchies of private and public organizations, including corporations and government agencies, so that people of color (and white women) are meaningfully represented at all levels of decision making.[32]

Equality and a Pluralistic Democracy

An Egalitarian Society?

The equality and social justice sought by all subordinated racial and ethnic groups has an ancient heritage. Indeed, the view that "all men are created equal" was articulated for and by the white male "founders" in the Declaration of Independence. Many other groups since that time have taken this ideal seriously. However, these words were initially meant to apply only to white, European, Protestant male immigrants and their male descendants—and generally only those with property. This very limited equality of access to political institutions was a dramatic step forward in an autocratic era, but it excluded the North American *majority*, which at the time included women, African Americans, and Native Americans. Even the few Jewish and Catholic Americans at the time usually had limited citizenship.

Over the centuries, the conception of who could claim this equality and justice has become more inclusive. The ideal of equality has been a major driving force in U.S. history as the social, economic, and political systems have gradually become more inclusive and egalitarian. The concept of equality has evolved to include equality of worth among individuals, equality of opportunity, equality before the law (including civil rights), and, for many, equality of results in the socioeconomic system. Over time, most subordinated racial and ethnic groups have achieved some advancement in at least some of these categories.

Between the early 1800s and the early 1900s, dramatic economic development brought opportunity and advancement to millions of European immigrants. Although they suffered initial discrimination, substantial majorities of these groups eventually achieved much socioeconomic and political success, often as a result of major government programs, such as the Homestead Act and the veterans' and housing assistance programs after World War II. Many contemporary assimilation analysts argue that the non-European groups are also moving, if more slowly, toward substantial social, economic, and political equality.

However, the rosy view of U.S. society as long committed to "liberty and justice for all" remains today, as always, very inaccurate. Substantial movement up the economic and political ladders did come for white immigrants from Europe. But an overly optimistic view ignores the great misery and discrimination that many white ethnics endured, for a generation at least, as poorly paid laborers, servants, or peddlers in an exploitative economic system. We have documented capitalistic and ethnic exploitation of early Italian, Irish, and Jewish Americans. Immigration for the allegedly "inferior races" from southern and eastern Europe was severely restricted by the discriminatory U.S. immigration law in effect until 1965. These white ethnic Americans faced serious stereotyping and some significant discrimination for several decades; for some, such as Jewish Americans, serious stereotyping and prejudice persists, sometimes resulting in very significant discrimination.

The optimistic picture of U.S. equality and freedom glosses over continuing large-scale discrimination faced by Americans with roots outside of Europe. Historically, Native, Asian, African, Latino, and Middle Eastern Americans have pressed hard for expanded equality and an end to discrimination and other oppression. Periodically, over U.S. history, significant improvements have occurred in legal rights and socioeconomic opportunities, such as those that led to the dismantling of Jim Crow segregation during and after the 1960s civil rights movement. Nonetheless, major problems of continuing racial and ethnic discrimination remain imbedded in the informal operation of U.S. economic, educational, political, and other social institutions, in which whites frequently discriminate against people of color. Today, major U.S. civil rights laws are often only weakly enforced.

How egalitarian is U.S. society today?

Racial Discrimination: The Present Day

The year 1992 marked the 500th anniversary of the landing of Christopher Columbus and his soldiers in the Americas. The Quincentenary celebrations generated protests from many Americans, especially Native Americans, who have worked hard to counter mythical images of beneficent European explorers "discovering" America. They have shown how arrogant and imperialistic it was for Europeans to claim to discover a land already occupied by millions of people for thousands of years. As we documented in Chapter 6, "liberty and justice for all" has often bypassed the original Americans, who still often remain forgotten Americans.

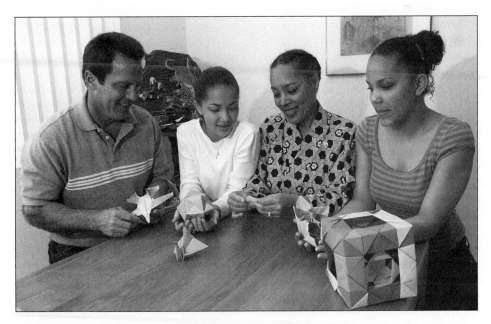

Family members, who are proud of their mixed racial and ethnic ancestries, explore the art of origami at their home in Arizona.

As we saw in Chapters 10 and 11, the broad category of Asian Americans includes many groups, including Chinese, Korean, Filipino, Vietnamese, Asian-Indian, and Japanese Americans. Today, they too struggle with much anti-Asian sentiment and discrimination from white and other non-Asian Americans concerned about immigration, job competition, and other economic issues. Anti-Asian sentiment continues to generate serious discrimination, including violence, against Asian-Pacific Americans across the country.

Latinos, including Puerto Ricans, Mexican Americans, and Cuban Americans, continue to face many problems in securing justice and equality. As we saw in Chapters 8 and 9, research studies provide much evidence of continuing anti-Latino framing and discrimination. Studies document discrimination by white employers against Latinos, as well as by white landlords. As a group, Latinos, from California to Texas to New York, continue to find progress toward equality and justice limited by racist framing and discrimination.

African Americans, as we have seen in Chapter 7, still face many obstacles in securing the equality and justice promised by the old American creed. The late 1860s and 1870s Reconstruction era, one of important economic and political progress for African Americans, was soon followed by a dramatic resurgence of extreme white-generated oppression, including legal Jim Crow segregation. A century later, in the late twentieth and early twenty-first centuries, just a few decades after public policy expanded opportunities for Americans of color in the 1960s and 1970s, U.S. society and most federal, state, and local governments again moved backward. From 1981 to 1992, and again from 2001 to 2008, conservative white political leaders, including Republican presidents, cut back or kept ineffective various equal opportunity, affirmative action, and other programs designed to redress persisting racial discrimination. In the 1990s, the Democratic (Clinton) presidential administration placed somewhat greater emphasis on enforcing civil rights laws, but the election of more conservative congresses in the 1990s brought renewed efforts to curtail affirmative action and other antidiscrimination programs. After the election of George W. Bush in 2000 (and 2004), the executive branch of the U.S. government moved even farther away from an aggressive commitment to reduce racial discrimination in its many forms.[33]

Decades after civil rights laws were passed, racial and ethnic discrimination remains very serious and widespread, and many federal and local government agencies and private institutions have backed away from effective programs to counter such persistent discrimination. No truly large-scale and lasting changes in racial composition and power have yet occurred at or near the top levels in most major, historically white institutions. Whites (frequently white men) still overwhelmingly dominate upper-level and often middle-level positions in most major organizations—from the executive branch of the U.S. government to *Fortune 1000* corporations, major universities, most state legislatures, major banks, and large chain stores.[34]

As we demonstrated in Chapter 7, many research studies show that discrimination against African Americans, mainly by white Americans, remains common in employment, housing, and education. Since the 1980s, the majority of white Americans have shifted their attention away from even reducing pervasive racial discrimination. Indeed, in recent years the majority of whites signal in many ways that they are in denial about the severity of continuing discrimination. However, the deep reality and pain of discrimination can be seen by any person who sincerely wishes to see it. For example, when asked what it is like being black in the United States, a retired education professor who has lived in several regions of the country replied,

> I feel angry. I feel betrayed. Sometimes I feel very cynical. Most of the time I feel that I live in a country where I'm still not respected as a person. I lived at a time when I was told that if I got a good education, did all the right things, that I could be anything I wanted to be. I got a good education. I did all the right things, but even today I run into situations where my opportunity structure is limited because I am black. So I found that all along, no matter what I did, no matter how hard I tried, limitations were placed on me strictly because of the color of my skin. So I feel betrayed by the Constitution that guaranteed me certain rights. I feel betrayed by the Pledge of Allegiance to the flag, which says "liberty and justice for all."[35]

This statement was originally made in the late 1980s but, when we recently asked him and other African Americans if they still feel this way, they have indicated that the racial barriers and reactions described here still persist. In the aftermath of civil rights protests in the 1960s, and numerous demonstrations more recently, many white Americans have asked why black Americans and other Americans of color still protest and rebel. Across the country, Americans of color have protested because of continuing frustration and anger over pervasive individual and institutional discrimination. The equality-and-justice agenda of this country remains substantially rhetorical and unfinished. Contrary to the views of many, periodic group protests by Americans of color about the serious flaws in U.S. society are usually realistic and at base about persisting institutional racism and about fully implementing that equality-and-justice agenda.

 How has the global expansion of the U.S. government and corporate operations shaped patterns of U.S. immigration?

Summary and Conclusion

We began this chapter with a discussion of demographic changes. In some ways the U.S. remains segregated geographically along racial and ethnic lines. Many new immigrants, primarily Asian and Latin American, have settled on the coasts—in Los Angeles, New York City, San Francisco, Miami, Baltimore, Houston, San Diego, Boston—and in certain midwestern cities such as Chicago and Detroit. In addition, the African American population has continued to grow somewhat, and since the 1990s, many African Americans, especially retirees and younger people, have moved back to the South. Yet, over these same decades, the white population has grown more slowly than the Latino, Asian, and African American populations. In recent years, the white population has declined in many of the largest metropolitan areas, including coastal cities like New York and Los Angeles. However, in other metropolitan areas in the southern and mountain states, the white population has grown, often significantly.[36]

Even though the U.S. population has grown substantially in recent decades, without immigration many major cities, such as New York and Los Angeles, from which many whites have departed, would have experienced serious population declines. Numerous high-immigration metropolitan areas are now heavily populated by Americans of color, while much of the center of the U.S. remains disproportionately white. Today, about half the white population lives in the Northeast or Midwest, but a much smaller proportion of all Americans of color live in those same areas. Americans of color are a majority in California, New Mexico, Hawaii, and Texas. The populations of eight additional states, including New York, New Jersey, and Florida, are projected to be more than 40 percent Americans of color relatively soon. In contrast, twelve states, including several in New England and in the Mountain and North Central areas, are projected to be overwhelmingly white.[37]

The ongoing population shift from a predominantly white country to one in which no racial or ethnic group has a population majority has significant economic, social, and political implications. In our view, much more thought and action needs to be devoted by all Americans, including social researchers and policymakers, to the likely effects of these changes and to ways to create a truly democratic multiracial country.

For example, consider the educational system. Many of the eighty-eight metropolitan areas with populations over a half-million already have populations under 15 years of age that are a majority of children of color. These include Los Angeles, San Francisco, Phoenix, Miami, Las Vegas, Tucson, and Washington, DC. School systems in these and many other cities already have majority populations that are not white. Indeed, no later than the late 2030s, the U.S. educational system as a whole will be composed predominantly of students of color. Such a change will increasingly pose major challenges to traditional white control of the structure, administration, and curriculum of public schools. Increasingly, parents, students, and teachers of color will likely press for much more input into how these schools are structured and run. Current discrimination against Americans of color in school systems, as well as in other historically white institutions, is less likely to be tolerated when these groups have increased organizational and political power. School officials and other officials will likely become much more concerned with issues of expanded multiculturalism, enhanced diversity, and imbedded institutional racism.[38]

In addition, by the late 2040s, if not before, demographic forecasts suggest that a majority of working

Americans will no longer be white, while a majority of the older retired population will be white. One can wonder how, to take just one important issue, workers of color will view paying taxes to support elderly whites on Social Security and other support programs when many of those whites are the ones who have created and/or maintained the patterns of discrimination that have oppressed workers of color and their parents over some decades.

Intergroup debates about and conflict over sociopolitical power, discrimination, diversity, and related public policy issues—such as serious affirmative action programs or laws to restrict immigrants—are likely to increase. Areas in which a majority of voters are people of color are not likely, depending on the area and groups involved, to elect whites who have a history of strong opposition to legal immigration, affirmative action, or other antidiscrimination programs. We already see this in states such as California and New York. As voting constituencies change to reflect ongoing demographic changes, the composition of political bodies, juries and justice systems, educational systems, and other government institutions at all levels is likely to change significantly—unless, as some analysts fear, reactionary white political and business leaders take aggressive action to stop these likely changes in the direction of expanded democracy.[39]

Is it possible to move in the direction of much greater racial and ethnic equality and justice? These ideals have long been part of an authentic American dream and framing of a better society. The roots of that dream lie in many Americans' aspirations for liberty, human rights, and social justice over four centuries. These ideals were articulated in the Declaration of Independence, a path-breaking document that more than two centuries ago reflected this country's movement toward greater liberty and democracy. However, the Declaration and the U.S. Constitution were very seriously marred by a capitulation to white supporters of the slavery system. After the nineteenth century abolitionist movement and the Civil War, the U.S. Constitution was amended to abolish slavery and expand the liberties of African Americans, although Supreme Court and other government decisions soon severely limited the benefits stemming from those constitutional changes. Later, in the mid- and late twentieth century, under pressure from the numerous civil rights and women's movements, Supreme Court decisions and new civil rights laws brought formal equality and greater opportunities for Americans of color and white women. Still, antidiscrimination laws and court decisions have often been weakly enforced. In addition, these civil rights laws do not protect against, and thus cannot eradicate, many informal types of serious racial and ethnic discrimination that persist now in the twenty-first century.

Whether equality and social justice for subordinated racial and ethnic groups can become the U.S. reality yet remains to be seen. In the recent and distant past, the expansion of human rights, equality, and justice has often resulted from the effective and large-scale organization of racially and ethnically oppressed people and their white allies against persisting racial and ethnic oppression. History suggests that the likelihood of a further expansion seems to be conditional on renewed and successful political action and organization by Americans of all backgrounds and creeds who are committed to the eradication of oppression and to the full implementation of the grand ideals of human rights, equality, and justice.

Key Terms

multiculturalism   374   cultural diversity   374

PART III

Global Realities

BIG PICTURE QUESTIONS

- *How has European imperialism affected racial and ethnic oppression and conflict in the colonized societies?*

- *How does neocolonialism continue the process of domination of former European colonies?*

Today, there is much racial and ethnic oppression and conflict in countries across the globe. In this third section, we go beyond the United States to look at some major racial and ethnic issues as they have arisen on other continents—South America, Europe, and Africa. Until European imperialism and colonialism began in earnest in the 1400s, most local intergroup oppressions and conflicts were shaped only by local histories and contexts. In the long period of European imperialism, numerous European countries sent explorers and colonists to seize the labor, lands, and other material resources that would expand the wealth of the home countries. Eventually, most of the globe was under some type of European domination. This colonialism involved the organized exploitation of the labor and land of many indigenous societies.

In his probing book, *The World and Africa*, the savvy sociologist W. E. B. Du Bois summarized the bloody effects of much colonialism:

> There was no Nazi atrocity—concentration camps, wholesale maiming and murder, defilement of women and ghastly blasphemy of childhood—that the Christian civilization of Europe had not long been practicing against coloured folk in all parts of the world in the name of and for the defense of a Superior Race born to rule the world.[1]

Indigenous societies were destroyed or greatly reshaped by the impact of the European colonizers and their military, political, economic, and religious organizations. Colonization was usually defended by an ideology of white European (usually Christian) superiority.

In addition, if there was already intergroup conflict in the colonized country, it was usually shaped or redirected by the European intervention. European imperialism had a rebound effect, later or at the same time, on racial and ethnic oppression and conflicts within the colonizing societies themselves. We see this in the major example of France in the next chapter, as we have already seen evidence of this effect in the case of U.S. involvement overseas, such as in South Korea and Vietnam.

After centuries of direct European colonialism, colonizers and colonized have often remained linked. In *The World and Africa*, Du Bois examined how the poverty and disease of Europe's many African colonies have been closely linked to the great wealth and continuing prosperity that have persisted over centuries now in numerous European countries. A full understanding of that European prosperity must incorporate how extensive European colonialism took by force the labor and mineral resources of many colonized countries, especially those African countries (indeed, most of them) that were European colonies.

Today, economic neocolonialism typically continues the process of resource exploitation of most former colonies. We see the effect of this colonialism and neocolonialism in the cases of South Africa and Brazil, which are examined in Chapter 14. In

381

major ways the stolen economic resources of land and labor created the basis for much wealth in contemporary European countries while leaving the former colonies with major, and lasting, social and economic problems often not of their own making. Thus, the histories and current societal realities of the three countries examined in the next chapter are closely connected to the European colonization of Africa and Latin America. These case studies show the major and continuing effects of Europe's overseas colonization on both the colonized and the colonizers.

Global Racism in Systemic Perspective

The global colonialism and imperialism examined earlier in this book and in the chapter that follows were typically rationalized in terms of a white racial framing. As we have shown, especially in Chapters 1 and 2, social theorists have examined the origins of racial and ethnic formation and differentiation, as well as reasons for the adaptation, perpetuation, and alteration of thereby-created racial and ethnic groups. Theorists are interested in group interaction over long periods, which interaction has varied from peaceful coexistence and cooperation to substantial exploitation to genocidal destruction. Theorists examine differences in political, economic, and cultural foundations of racial and ethnic patterns of behavior that link to group enslavement, marginalization, and assimilation, among other possibilities of group interaction. In order to answer the question of how and why racial and ethnic patterns change over time, theorists frequently explore key historical factors, such as the development of modern capitalism, that often generate social formations such as external and internal colonialism.

Considering this history, our concept of *systemic racism* provides a solid basis for understanding the origins, perpetuation, and maintenance of global racial oppression, as well as the large-scale resistance to it. Previously we have shown how this oppression has long been systemic and well-institutionalized, and how its modern forms have been generated and maintained, principally but not exclusively, by people of European descent—who by the 1400s were oppressing peoples around the globe and who saw themselves as civilizing the "uncivilized" peoples.

Understanding the institutionalized reality of this oppression, this systemic racism, provides us with a comprehensive theory with which to examine racial (and ethnic) relations shaped by centuries of white domination of people of color in areas of the globe where Europeans intruded. As Chapter 2 explains, Du Bois and Oliver Cromwell Cox were probably the first to evaluate this racialized oppression from a deep global perspective, from which they examined the distinctive historical route of the North American experience and how this experience paralleled the imposed changes of Eurocentric imperialism globally. As a result of this European performance, somewhat similar racialized patterns have emerged in the experiences of people of color in numerous countries. Thus, we have the pervasiveness of institutionalized racism on a global level.

In Chapter 14, we examine global racism further. We put the theory of systemic racism even more within a cross-cultural context to better understand its constituent elements. As previous chapters demonstrate, the study of racial and ethnic relations and oppressions, of racial–ethnic domination and resistance, requires a multifaceted inquiry. Studying the comparable cases of South Africa, Brazil, and France gives us an enhanced perspective on global racial oppression, including an increased understanding of our racialized United States.

Besides the crucial step of putting European and Euro-American domination of people of color at the center of historical and cross-cultural analysis, a theory of systemic racism encourages us to understand how deeply imbedded racial hierarchies of societies reflect centuries of institutionalized material and economic exploitation. For example, in North America, white colonizers seized Native American lands, just as white colonizers seized Bantu and Zulu lands in South Africa and the lands of indigenous peoples in Brazil. Enslaved African laborers were forced to work stolen lands. Once land and labor were stolen, through a centuries-old social reproduction process, systemic racial oppression persisted and expanded, destroying or limiting socioeconomic and other life possibilities for many groups over the generations. Just in regard to economic conditions, the racial hierarchy means racially fractured and segmented job markets. The worldwide reality is that the majority of low-wage jobs are now held by workers of color, and unemployment rates are typically much higher for those on the lowest rungs of the racial hierarchy in the United States, South Africa, Brazil, and France. In addition, racial segregation has long been part of the experience of domination for various racial groups in these countries. Moreover, in the U.S., beginning in the slavery era, individual and group resistance to racial oppression has been ongoing. This struggle is by no means unique. The battle for freedom has been fought, and is still being fought, in South Africa, Brazil, and France—in each case in terms demanding that allegedly democratic governments deliver on old promises of equality, justice, and progress for all.

Throughout this book we have seen how this system of racial oppression overlaps and interrelates with other systems of social domination, especially gender and class domination. Thus, white male elites in the United States, South Africa, Brazil, and France generally maintain great privilege and power over both white women and women and men of color.

Not only reproducing the system, but also legitimizing it and creating institutions for such ends have become important aspects of the perpetuating racial framing of systemic racism, so much so that not only the white oppressors but also people of color begin to believe that it is "normal" and it cannot be changed.

Nonetheless, as we have seen, societal change is very possible. The struggle against oppression is an integral part of the racial–ethnic history of the U.S.; and the overthrow of apartheid in South Africa, the civil rights groups' efforts to force the Brazilian government to fulfill its commitments to "racial democracy," and the protests by African Muslims in France all demonstrate the imperative and importance of confronting oppression, as well as the difficulties of overcoming deeply imbedded systems of oppression. By looking at important global manifestations of systemic racism in the next chapter, we begin to understand how societal structures exhibit the significance, depth, and adaptability not only of racist ideology and oppression but also of antiracist resistance and confrontation, often at the global scale.

 How does the concept of systemic racism help in understanding global racial oppression?

Colonialism and Postcolonialism
The Global Expansion of Racism

BIG PICTURE QUESTIONS

- *How has modern capitalism shaped global patterns of racial exploitation and inequality?*

- *What are the legacies of European colonialism in African and Latin American countries?*

- *Where can systemic racism be found outside the United States?*

This chapter was written by Pinar Batur of Vassar College.

In the spring of 1994, after the first elections in which black and white South Africans voted together, South Africa's new black president, Nelson Mandela, commented, "Today is a day like no other before it. Today marks the dawn of our freedom. . . . We are starting a new era of hope, reconciliation and nation-building."[1] That day, 30 million South Africans felt free of racial **apartheid**, *the rigidly institutionalized system of racial segregation and social, economic, and political inequality that had long invaded most aspects of daily life in South Africa*. The newly elected South African government outlawed apartheid and promised to move toward equality in rights and in black access to everything whites had in South Africa.

With this assurance, Nkosingthi Msesizwe, a black miner, believed he could now ride the same elevator with white miners in post-apartheid South Africa. But Msesizwe was beaten by white miners, who shouted that "this hoist is for whites. It is not for you."[2] Even though South Africa's new government assured South Africans that equality would be achieved through constitutional changes, the transition has been difficult. More than a decade and a half after the election that marked the end of apartheid, institutionalized racism, including overt discrimination, is the everyday reality in contemporary South African society. The proportion of households earning less than $90 a month rose from 20 percent of the population in 1995 to 28 percent in 2000. As a result, the poorest half of all South Africans, almost all black, earned just 9.7 percent of the national income in 2000, down from 11.4 percent in 1995. Now, in the twenty-first century, half the people of South Africa live below the poverty line, and 91 percent of those are black.[3] The pattern seems similar to the persistent pattern of U.S. racial inequality, as well as that of other countries. When we examine Brazil, considered a "racial democracy" by some, we see that it too has one of the world's most unequal distributions of income, one of the indicators of persistent racial inequality between white and black Brazilians. The data indicate that white Brazilians earn at least 50 percent more than black Brazilians with the same level of education.[4] Why does examination of these countries, on different continents, with different histories and cultures, reveal similar patterns?

In this chapter, we assess the cases of South Africa, Brazil, and France in order to examine how colonialism and the global reality of systemic racial discrimination and other elements of racism have been implemented and maintained by whites of European ancestry in countries other than the United States. The case of South Africa demonstrates the major life-determining and life-threatening consequences of European colonialism and the thoroughgoing institutionalization of overt antiblack racism, whereas Brazil exhibits how a racist culture overtly and covertly links to and maintains racist institutions. Turning to France, we explore the legacy and effects of racialized colonialism in one of the major European colonizing powers. In our view, students of contemporary racial and ethnic relations should know about more than intergroup relations and stratification in their own country. In order to understand global realities of the twenty-first century, students must know about the development of colonialism, imperialism, and racialized societies around the globe.

Colonialism and Racism

In F. Scott Fitzgerald's classic 1920s novel *The Great Gatsby*, one discussion among wealthy white characters focuses on a racist book that argued that, if not prevented, "the white race will be . . . utterly submerged. It's all scientific stuff; it's been proved. . . . It is up to us, who are the dominant race, to watch out or these other races will have control of things." One of the white characters then whispers, "We've got to beat them down."[5] As revealed in such novels as well as in government policy decisions, the white racial frame and its ideological racism have long validated for the white public imperialist expansion and colonialism around the world. Economic and political exploitation has long targeted people who are not of the dominant racial group, while the white-generated ideology of racism has rationalized this exploitation. This white-racist framing has long rationalized the subordination of people of color in many societies colonized by Europeans, including not only the United States but also South Africa and Brazil.

The expansion of Western capitalism around the globe since the 1400s has fostered the division of people according to racial group, including the assignment of superior and inferior characteristics to certain designated "races." As we noted in Chapter 2, the dynamics of Western capitalistic expansion, which created numerous colonies of subordinated peoples, made racial inequality a permanent part of global existence through its white racial framing and racist ideologies, and associated discriminatory practices. Western capitalistic expansion integrated white racist framing and action into global and local economic and political arrangements and cultural production. The international development of Western capitalism also fostered the advancement of ideological and "scientific" racism, integrating such perspectives into a global system of oppression with its distinctive racialized culture. The examination of racism as a global reality is important to the study of racial relations because white racism's institutions superimpose themselves on local institutions in societies that such racism invades, and those institutions shape the construction of identities and everyday experiences of both colonizers and colonized.[6] By the eighteenth century, global racism had become a process of defining and building communities and societies based on racial privileges and a continuing hierarchy of power with whites of European background at the top and racially oppressed people at or near the bottom.

The global expansion of European capitalism through colonialism gave white racist thinking and framing a global scope; indeed, by the early 1900s, a majority of the earth's peoples were more or less under the control of European colonizers. In W. E. B. Du Bois's famous words, these dynamics have led to establishment of a global demarcation: "The problem of the twentieth century is the problem of the color line," because "force and fear have hitherto marked the white attitude" and permeated every major aspect of many societies. "Regardless of color, we carry the color abhorrence in our hearts."[7]

The History and Legacy of Colonialism

Western colonialism began with the major overseas expansion of Spain and Portugal, where their rulers sought to enhance their treasuries with gold, silver, and other goods taken from the world's peoples. The legal and ideological rationale for this was provided by Roman Catholic popes in papal bulls, declarations echoing papal justifications for Christian crusades against Muslims in earlier centuries.[8] On May 3, 1493, Pope Alexander VI issued a bull of

demarcation, a document resolving Spanish and Portuguese disputes over colonization. As revised by the Treaty of Tordesillas in 1494, this bull put all the world's non-Christian ("pagan") peoples at the economic disposal of these growing colonial powers.[9] The Christian justification for expansion was for a time in tension with the profit-making desire of European entrepreneurs for land and slave labor. For a short period, some Catholic theologians and priests, most notably the Spanish priest Las Casas, opposed the ruthless enslavement of the indigenous populations. However, in a 1550 debate with Las Casas in Spain, theologian Gaines de Sepulveda carried the day with his argument that it was lawful to make war on and enslave the indigenous populations because of their heathen, sinful, and barbarous "natures," which obligated them to serve those (the Spanish) with the "superior" culture and virtues.[10]

After the 1500s, European expansion led by the Netherlands, England, and France (and later by Germany and Belgium) spurred the global expansion of capitalism, in the process fostering great economic and racial inequality between colonizers and colonized.[11] These countries generated scholars, theologians, and politicians who developed theories of the superiority of white Europeans and the animal-like inferiority of non-Europeans. Europeans distinguished themselves from so-called savages. Often, colonized peoples were demonized and considered to have the vices that the English and other Europeans feared in themselves: wildness, brutishness, cruelty, laziness, sexual promiscuity, and heathenism. "Far from English civilization, they had to remind themselves constantly what it meant to be civilized—Christian, rational, sexually controlled, and white."[12] By the 1700s and 1800s, well-developed theories of the cultural and racial inferiority of the overseas "savages" were pronounced by English and other European leaders, as we noted in Chapter 1. As one of the major racist ideologues of the nineteenth century, Joseph de Gobineau, put it:

> [White people] are gifted with reflective energy, or rather with an energetic intelligence. . . . They have a remarkable, even extreme love of liberty, and are openly hostile to the formalism under which the Chinese are glad to vegetate, as well as the strict despotism which is the only way of governing the Negro.[13]

At an early point in time, colonialism became a system of control based on a colonial political administration, an exploitative commercial trade, and a missionary zeal to convert indigenous populations to Christianity and "civilization." In Asian, Oceanic, African, and American societies, this threefold domination fostered colonial administrations' oppressive rule, unequal trade practices, and the imposition of Christianity and Western culture. Desire for raw materials motivated European colonial expansion, such as the desire to obtain black pepper and lumber from Brazil or tea and spices from India. Securing these resources frequently required use of military violence—violence that, after the initial conquest, was carried out by a colonial administration. Everyday life in the colonies was reshaped by the European oppressors who controlled colonized societies politically, economically, and culturally. Exploitation of colonized peoples and their many valuable natural resources was usually accompanied by systematic violence.[14]

Violence and exploitation were justified through an ideology of cultural and racial superiority that penetrated religious and political views and everyday language. White racial framing and its racist ideology not only were an integral aspect of the dominant group's racial identity, but often seeped into the subordinate group's racialized construction of its self-conception. Pervasive material and ideological racism fostered the view of the colonized as subordinate and powerless.[15] Albert Memmi, a North African author educated in French colonial schools, wrote about the penetrating effects of such colonial rule:

> I am ill at ease in my own land and I know of no other. My culture is borrowed and I speak my mother tongue haltingly. I have neither religious beliefs nor tradition and am ashamed of whatever particle of them has survived deep within me. . . . I am Tunisian, but of French culture.[16]

European colonialism altered the lives of the colonized; it also had major effects on the colonizers and their home countries. The flow of raw materials from highly exploited colonies demanded a docile working class in the colonized and colonizing societies. Thus, the French Empire subjugated African areas such as Algeria, and the system of economic subjugation and racist rationalization reached well back into French society, negatively shaping conditions for the white working class in France. The white working class's acceptance of colonialism and the ideology of white racism, as well as of their own class oppression, was fostered by their false sense of racial superiority and their uncritical acceptance of their own political and economic system. For example, French colonialism long oppressed Algerians in Africa, and in today's postcolonial France, whites' racist views and actions greatly influence the political and economic positions of first- and second-generation Algerians now residing in France. In the U.S. case, European colonial oppression included African slavery, the extermination of Native Americans, and the conquest of Puerto Rico and the Philippines. The scars of this colonial oppression continue to influence contemporary social and political events.

Drawing on old racist ideologies and verbally or physically attacking racially oppressed people in their midst, white neo-Nazi groups and racist political parties have reemerged in most of the former colonized societies of Europe and North America. The ongoing relationships between colonizing and colonized societies have firmly established the white framing and its ideology of racial superiority as a central mode in global thinking—a racial framing that shapes images of the (formerly or currently) colonized as well as the institutionalized practices of everyday oppression.[17] During the postcolonial era, the white framing and the practices of institutional racism are continuing global realities.

We now turn to an exploration of the effects and the legacy of colonialism in the colonized societies of South Africa and Brazil and in the colonizing society of France.

To Whom Does Southern Africa Belong?

In many areas, those who come to occupy the land often ask, "To whom does this land really belong?" According to racist constructions of colonial history, the land is "discovered" by "civilized" white people, who are the first to "use the land in a productive way." For white colonizers, the real history of a place begins with European or Euro-American colonization.

The Khoisan people resided in the area now called South Africa when ancestors of the current Bantu-speaking black majority arrived there around 300 C.E.[18] The first European expedition to the area came much later in the form of Portuguese explorers in

1487. The first significant European settlement in southern Africa dates to 1652, when Jan van Riebeeck established a station for the Dutch East India Company. As Dutch settlements spread, encounters with the Bantu peoples led to a series of confrontations, which Europeans called "kaffir wars."

In Arabic, *kaffir* originally meant "infidel." In South Africa, whites used it as a degrading racist term (such as "nigger" in the U.S.) for black Africans. Early European invaders and occupiers there saw their colonization as a religious and civilizing mission that justified the killing, subjugation, and enslavement of indigenous people. Drawing on the powerful white-racist framing, Europeans rated themselves as racially and religiously superior to indigenous Africans, whom they considered to be animal-like, and they often stereotyped them as heathens, "idolatrous and licentious, thieving and lying, lazy and dirty."[19] Europeans often rationalized what they saw as the inferiority of Africans through "scientific" racism, arguing that the tropical environment was responsible for producing immature, childish, and "beastlike" creatures who could be "civilized" only by the European work ethic and Christian discipline. European colonists thus legitimated their invasion, occupation, and enslavement of black Africans as a vehicle to lift the latter from their "barbarism."[20]

Although the white invaders agreed among themselves about the black "inferiority," they continued to fight each other for control. The Dutch colonial interest in southern Africa collided with British determination to control the sailing route to India around the tip of Africa. Britain's conquest of southern Africa's Cape Colony in 1806 and British colonial settlement beginning in 1820 fueled the out-migration of 15,000 **Boers**—*white South Africans of Dutch descent*—into the interior, a movement these whites called the "Great Trek." The British imperialists abolished slavery and changed the regulations on black labor. The Boers interpreted British actions as putting black people "on an equal footing with [white] Christians, contrary to the laws of God and the natural distinction of race."[21] These views were asserted by Dutch ministers and also reflected the goals of the Dutch East India Company, which had tried to create a racially divided society to maintain the slave trade and their theft of raw materials.[22]

Dutch leaders began to promote Dutch settlers as the true "white tribe of Africa" and called themselves **Afrikaners** (*white speakers of the Afrikaans language*).[23] According to the racist ideology, there were "no native blacks" prior to the arrival of Europeans. This erroneous view persists today: "Basically we came here more or less at the same time. We both belong to South Africa. There is no one black man who can say that this is his country more so than a white. We belong here as much as they do."[24] In addition, in defense of earlier slavery and current labor conditions, the Afrikaners have long argued that "we make the [black] people work for us in consideration of allowing them to live in our country."[25]

 Are there similarities in contacts between Dutch colonists and Bantu peoples and those of European colonists and Native Americans?

Formation of the State and Apartheid

European interest in southern Africa was further stimulated by the discovery of diamonds and gold in the late nineteenth century. Under growing colonial control and violence, the oppressive working conditions in mines as well as on agricultural plantations shaped the brutality of everyday life for black Africans. In 1910, the Union of South Africa was created, which united British areas with Boer areas and redefined South Africa in terms of the common heritage of European Christianity and a "civilizing" mission. The new white-controlled state imposed extensive racial segregation on the politically defined population of "blacks" and **coloureds**, the latter being *people of mixed white–black ancestry*. The 1913 Native Lands Act limited land ownership and settlement for black and coloured South Africans (but not for white South Africans) to restricted areas. Voting rights and political representation were reserved for whites. As gold and diamond mining and other industries expanded, the labor force was sharply divided between whites, who held skilled and supervisory positions with better wages and working conditions, and black workers, who were unskilled and worked under severe conditions with little pay.[26]

Black South Africans drew on their home cultures to resist the racialized oppression and inequality. Organized opposition to increasingly racist policies came from the African National Congress (ANC), founded in 1912 to demand voting rights, freedom of residence, and land ownership for black Africans.

White voters elected the National Party in 1948 on a platform of apartheid that mandated separate development and complete racial segregation. The supporters of apartheid drew on a virulent form of white-racist and fascist ideologies. Afrikaner whites, like the Nazis in Germany, constructed South Africa as a "special nation with a special mission: The Afrikaner believes that it is the will of God that there should be a diversity of races and nations and that obedience to the will of God therefore requires the acknowledgment and maintenance of that diversity."[27] Afrikaner nationalists argued that "the preservation of the pure race tradition of the [Boers] must be preserved at all costs. . . . Any movement, school, or individual who sins against this must be dealt with as a racial criminal by the effective authorities." Church-sanctioned racist thinking was a great buttress for racial oppression; the Dutch Reform Church of South Africa became a citadel for the National Party.[28]

Apartheid had several interconnected aspects. One was the racially hierarchical structure in which whites, about 18 percent of the population, ruled over the 82 percent who were "not white." This racialized hierarchy was fostered by a white-controlled nation-state that denied full citizenship to Africans of color. A critical aspect of apartheid was well-institutionalized discrimination, which included extensive racial segregation in everyday life.[29]

Apartheid was reinforced by many racist laws. For example, the 1950 Population Registration Act established legal registration by racial group; the Group Areas Act prohibited black South Africans from residing outside of racially zoned areas. In the 1950s, the government sought to control opposition to apartheid by passing security legislation against so-called Communist activities, and until the 1980s this law enabled the government to silence any black or white South Africans opposed to government racial policies through the use of aggressive intimidation, imprisonment, and state violence. To control the transfer of knowledge, in 1953, the white government took control of public education, creating a separate and inferior educational system for black South Africans.[30] In addition, the Bantu Self-Government Act forced much of the black population into territorially fragmented areas, called *homelands,* with very limited material resources. Recognized by white South Africans, and only by them, as "independent countries," these homelands were yet another form of racial apartheid.

Another example of the brutality of apartheid was the 1956 decision to order 100,000 non-Europeans to leave their homes in the city of Johannesburg within one year in order to make residential space available for whites. In 1964, new laws expanded apartheid by regulating black employment, giving the police power to hold suspects for months without trial, and prohibiting political organizations composed of racially diverse members.

Scholars have debated the role of South African capitalists in maintaining apartheid. Clearly, white capitalists benefited greatly from apartheid, yet some were opposed to its more extreme manifestations. A good example is Harry Oppenheimer, who in 1957 inherited the Anglo-American Corporation and DeBeers Consolidated Mines, which controls much of South Africa's and the world's gold, diamonds, and copper, as well as almost all coal production in South Africa. After 1959, Oppenheimer supported the Progressive Party, which advocated incorporation of black Africans into the political system. In 1976, he established the Urban Foundation for social support projects in black areas. However, Oppenheimer took advantage of the racist labor structure by holding down the wages of black workers. Even though some capitalists objected to apartheid because it was bad for the country's image, they mostly played a key role in supporting apartheid because it kept labor costs down.[31]

Opposition to Apartheid

As apartheid intensified, so did efforts of the ANC and another resistance group called the Pan-African Congress (PAC), both of which were banned by the government in 1960.[32] In 1964, after the Sharpeville massacre, in which police killed sixty-nine black demonstrators in an urban area, Nelson Mandela and other ANC and PAC leaders were sentenced to life in prison. These imprisonments were followed by the torture and deaths of some leaders in police custody. As the support for apartheid became more violent, the antiapartheid movement in South Africa became stronger. A growing number of demonstrations, including numerous student demonstrations, resulted in hundreds of deaths of black protesters at the hands of brutal police forces.[33]

By the late 1970s, open opposition to apartheid in black townships near larger cities forced the government to search for new ways to legitimize its

Black South Africans line up to use their new voting rights in democratic municipal elections in Cape Town.

control. White leaders tried co-optation. Beginning in 1978, restrictions on black labor unions and multiracial political parties were lifted. Meanwhile, the ANC enlarged its political base and changed its emphasis from armed struggle to mass political mobilization.[34]

For a time, the white government maintained control by exacerbating divisions in the black and coloured populations. Differences among black South Africans were used by white leaders to channel anger away from white oppression. Thus, the South African government funded the black Inkatha Zulu separatist movement and secretly provided it with military training in order to fuel Zulu (one black group) hostility toward the ANC and its primary supporters, especially the Xhosa people (a different black group).[35] Also, by providing for some limited political participation by Asian and coloured people in the 1984 constitution, the white-controlled government tried to divide the population further, provoking widespread opposition among black South Africans. Demonstrations in townships were met with brutality. Declaring a state of emergency, the government tried to prevent the press from reporting clashes and detained thousands; some 250,000 black mineworkers responded to these actions with a three-week strike.[36] For a few years, such divide-and-conquer strategies allowed the white government to continue its domination; but,

by accentuating racial and ethnic divisions, these actions produced lasting problems for the development of a democratic South Africa in the current era.

White resistance to the antiapartheid movement had its limits. Black protests, together with an international economic boycott, made life increasingly difficult for whites. The white elite, particularly the economic elite, was disturbed by the societal chaos and loss of profits. In 1989, after becoming head of the government, F. W. deKlerk began to dismantle the policies of apartheid under pressure from black and white opponents of the old racist regime. After 12,000 deaths in political clashes over four years, the South African government finally moved to hold the first free elections. In April 1994, two and one-half years after being freed from prison, Nelson Mandela, the head of the ANC, was elected to the presidency of South Africa. This marked a dramatic shift in political power, from oppressors to oppressed, something rare in human history without a large-scale revolution.

The Future of South Africa

Today, however, the racist past is still having an effect on South Africa. Racial oppression is well institutionalized in everyday life, from the city of Pretoria—which white Afrikaner separatists still see as their spiritual capital—to rural Zulu homelands, where many Zulus still consider the ANC and its leaders to be the continuation of white oppression.[37] In the most recent period, critical issues for South Africa have included (1) "black on black" violence, which often reflects group differences among black South Africans; (2) the political and economic problems that plague the segregated homelands; and (3) the perpetuation of racial inequality in housing, education, employment, and healthcare.

After his election as president in 1999, Thabo Mbeki tried to facilitate economic relief for many poor black South Africans, but his policies largely failed to reach the black rural population. According to government statistics, as the average black African household income fell 19 percent from 1995 to 2000, to about $3700 per year, white household income enjoyed a 15 percent increase, to about $22,600 per year. Unemployment for black workers worsened in the first ten years of the post-apartheid era.[38] Today, the new president, Jacob Zuma, elected in 2009, has been rattled by corruption charges by the white establishment and is questioned by the black middle class for his lax attitude about HIV/AIDS. At present, about one-fifth of South African adults are HIV positive. The infection of one in five adults not only increases the mortality rate but contributes to higher infant mortality and lower population growth among black South Africans. The previous Mbeki government had planned to extend antiretroviral therapy from 235,000 to 650,000 by 2011.[39] The Treatment Action Campaign general secretary at the time, Sipho Mthathi, had said, "Our task is to end 1000 new HIV infections daily and to reduce the AIDS death rate of more than 900 deaths every day," but critics argued these efforts were too late and too little.[40] As a result of relatively weak government policies, South Africa today faces the challenge of one of the world's highest HIV infection rates, with AIDS likely claiming the lives of one in three adults in the first half of the twenty-first century if the government does not take strong action.[41]

Today, many black South Africans are, slowly or quickly, dying from unemployment, poor healthcare, and disease. In the context of global racism, poor healthcare is emerging as a new articulation of racism, as it too is tied increasingly to skin color. Many black South African voters seem to be losing hope for real economic development and prosperity and are growing disinterested in politics. Turnout in elections has dropped precipitously in the twenty-first century.[42] Frantz Fanon once asked, "What is South Africa?" He answered, "A boiler into which thirteen million blacks are clubbed and penned in by two and a half million whites."[43] Today, South Africa is changing, but whites still have much economic control, and most black South Africans feel the country is not changing fast enough to provide them hope and real sustenance. South Africa shows how European colonialism has historically operated through a trilogy of domination—administration, trade, and religion—to establish a system of white control and violence and to extract, vampire-like, an area's great resources for (mostly) white use and wealth. After long centuries of intensive colonial exploitation for white profit, the lives of the black people of southern Africa have been changed fundamentally and irrevocably, mostly for the worse. These changes have made the struggle against systemic white racism integral to the past, present, and future of South Africa.

 How have black South Africans resisted segregation and other racial oppression?

Brazil: The Legacy of Slavery and the Illusion of Equality

The country of Brazil in South America has the largest African-origin population outside of Africa—reported to be just under half, about 80 million, of the country's 170 million people. Slavery was abolished in Brazil more than one hundred years ago, but systemic racism still has major effects on black Brazilians today. For example, in many restaurants black customers are harassed or excluded by being told that all empty tables are reserved. A major television soap opera that showed a white man and black woman kissing generated numerous angry protests. Black women complain that in apartment buildings they are presumed to be maids and shown the service elevator. Almost all of the many thousands of teenagers on whom the police reportedly have detailed files are not white. Many employers routinely choose white over black applicants for better-paying jobs.[44]

Even without the many decades of legal segregation the U.S. experienced, or a long era of racial apartheid as in South Africa, politically and economically, the differences between black and white Brazilians demonstrate the harsh realities of great inequality. For example, in a recent year only 15 of the 513 members of the Brazilian Congress, and 3 of 81 senators, were black. The judicial system is dominated by the 98.5 percent of judges who are white.[45] About 40 percent of the black population works in minimum-wage jobs.[46] Although they comprise nearly half the population, black Brazilians constitute just 2 percent of students enrolled in the universities, and only 17 percent of university graduates admit to mixed racial ancestry.[47] At the large University of São Paulo, for instance, few of the 5000 faculty members are black. Overall, black Brazilians have the highest rates of unemployment, underemployment, illiteracy, and substandard housing.[48] This reality of major social, economic, and political inequality along racial lines is the legacy of European colonization and slavery.

Brazil was colonized during the early period of the imperialistic expansion of Spain and Portugal, when European knowledge of the world beyond Europe was sketchy. The Portuguese sought to establish a commercial empire, and explorer Pedro Alvarez Cabral claimed this land for the Portuguese crown. The Portuguese elite named the land after a dye extracted from native trees. The emerging European textile industry consumed so much of the dye that, by the end of the 1500s, one hundred ships traveled regularly between Brazil and Portugal. The Portuguese established sugar cane plantations in numerous colonial settlements. Some indigenous inhabitants were enslaved, although most were slaughtered during wars between indigenous groups and the European colonizers or in wars between the Portuguese and other European powers coming into Brazil. Or, like indigenous peoples in the United States, these indigenous peoples died from European diseases because they had no immunity to them.[49]

By the nineteenth century, Brazil resembled the U.S. South. Large numbers of enslaved Afro-Brazilians worked on large plantations to produce sugar, coffee, and rubber for the ever-expanding, Europe-dominated, capitalist world market.[50] Brazil's enslaved population, mostly of African origin, numbered about 5 million—more than half its population—just before the abolition of slavery in 1888. Brazil became independent of Portugal in 1822, and in 1889, the local military overthrew the monarch and declared a republic. Since that time, Brazilian history has been marked by recurring military intervention in national politics and by continuous debates about the establishment of real democracy in a multiracial society.

Human rights marchers protest racism in Brasilia, Brazil.

Ever a Racial Democracy?

When Brazil's slave system ended, one stated national goal was to establish racial equality, but this did not develop. Indeed, black citizens continued to live under slavery-like conditions. Nonetheless, an official myth emerged that Brazil had "benign patterns" of racial relations and that Brazil was, and currently is, a unique *racial democracy*. Many Brazilians, especially whites, have loudly proclaimed their society to be a true racial democracy. This notion usually does not recognize the existence of significant and widespread racial prejudice and discrimination, much less the need for major policies of racial remediation and reparation. Instead, it claims that black Brazilians are equal in this multicultural society. The mainstream white ideology in Brazil argues that because of "Brazilian exceptionalism"—the allegedly equal treatment of the formerly enslaved population and the allegedly equal opportunities available to all—multicultural Brazil is not so starkly divided along racial lines as the United States and South Africa. However, this view ignores Brazil's continuing, large-scale patterns of institutional racism and associated white racist framing and ideology, all of which foster economic and political inequalities and cultural marginalization of black and indigenous Brazilians. Even in the city of Salvador area, once a major slave-importing port and a place where black Brazilians comprise 80 percent of the population, very few blacks hold government positions. Salvador has never elected a black mayor or representative.[51]

Since the late nineteenth century, one aspect of Brazil's racial framing has been an obsessive focus on racial mixing. Many whites, including intellectuals, have argued that people of mixed descent exhibit the worst characteristics of their parents' racial groups and that Brazilian society will degenerate with the increased "mixing of the races." This societal-degeneration view was imported from the racist framing of the United States and Europe. Based on nineteenth-century assumptions about the origins and hierarchy of "races" (see Chapter 1), this notion fits well with white stereotypes and fears about losing control to a growing Afro-Brazilian population. Opponents of racial mixing have often supported their argument with a "whitening thesis," which claims that "stronger and better white genes" are essential to "progressive" evolution of the population. Even though these racist notions assume the superiority of whites, they are contradictory. On the one hand, the fear of racial mixing seems to encourage racial segregation; on the other hand, the whitening notion seems to favor interracial marriages that would supposedly improve society's "gene pool."[52]

Emerging together in the nineteenth century, these racist assumptions remain part of Brazil's culture and still influence many white (and some black) Brazilians' thinking about the state of their country. Today, this perspective can be seen in immigration policies that favor white Europeans, in negative white attitudes to interracial marriages, and even in many black Brazilians' adherence to a color hierarchy that shows a decided preference for lighter skin tones.

Many light-skinned Brazilians believe that differences between racial groups are less important in their country than such differences in South Africa or the United States. However, Brazilians use many words for racial identification. The word for "black" does not have the same meaning in Brazil as in the United States or South Africa. In Brazil, *preto* (black) describes a person with mostly or all African ancestry. Yet, a racially mixed person who would likely be called "black" in the United States is identified in Brazil as *pardo* (brown) or *moreno*. Morenos are further divided into light (*morenos claros*) and dark (*morenos escuros*). The term *mulatto* is used to refer specifically to a person of mixed African and European backgrounds. In addition, because the term *Negro* includes *pretos* and *morenos*, it has provided a political term for black-power movements, as in Brazil's *Movimento Negro*.[53] As displayed by this diverse terminology, the country's racial hierarchy is supported by strong white stereotypes that view black people as "bad-smelling, dirty, unhygienic, ugly" and that view those termed mulattos as "pushy and envious of whites." According to one revealing Brazilian ditty, "The white man goes to heaven, the mulatto stays on earth, the caboclo (mestizo) goes to purgatory, the black goes to hell." Stereotypes are still prevalent, with one result being the absence of blacks from most advertisements. Note too that, in a recent survey by the Brazilian Advertising Association, 44 percent of the Brazilian respondents did acknowledge the existence of racial discrimination against blacks and also the negative character of much black imagery.[54]

Today, as in the past, whiteness is a symbol of superiority and the key to social and political power. Indeed, in national censuses the number of people who identify as "mulatto" has grown faster than is statistically possible. Many people who are not white seem to be choosing this term because they believe that "brownness" is an escape hatch that will allow them to achieve greater upward mobility by acquiring an intermediate, and whiter, racial status. Moreover, by downplaying real racial differences in much public discussion, Brazil's white elites and political leaders avoid addressing problems of racially based economic inequality, as well as racial inequalities in education and mortality rates. Brazil has periodic economic booms, but benefits have flowed heavily to the upper middle class and upper class, which have long been almost exclusively white.[55]

 Are the present consequences of European colonialization in Brazil similar to those for the United States?

A Century of Lies

The colonial histories of Brazil and the United States are different, but racial inequalities are similar. The inequality between Brazil's racial groups has sharpened between the 1960s and today, during the country's movement to economic modernization. Transnational corporations, many headquartered in the U.S., have sought low wages and new markets and invested heavily in Brazil. As black Brazilians have confronted elites and demanded equal-opportunity legislation to secure greater access to education and employment, they have developed important political movements resembling U.S. civil rights and black-power movements. Moreover, since the 1980s, as U.S. politicians and administrations have reduced federal commitments to expanded civil rights and to affirmative action and have curtailed government efforts to reduce inequality (see Chapter 7), Brazil's government has acted in a similar backtracking fashion. As in the United States, powerful whites have criticized affirmative action for Afro-Brazilians with the inaccurate and confused term "reverse racism."[56]

Although affirmative action policies are relatively new, the country has a history of significant racial policies, including some in its constitution and other major laws. In 1960, the government declared racism a punishable offense. The 1988 Constitution declared such racism a crime with no statute of limitations, included provisions to protect black cultural practices, and granted some economic reparations—such as land titles to surviving families of the "quilombos," the communities formed by runaway slaves prior to emancipation in 1888. The 1995 election of Fernando Henrique Cardoso, a progressive sociologist, led to comprehensive policy initiatives regarding the goal of racial equality. Substantial gains were made with the 1996 Human Rights Program, which officially recognized racial groups and the need for targeted remedial policies.

Following the 2001 World Conference on Racism—from which U.S. officials withdrew, in part to avoid discussing reparations for indigenous nations and black Americans—Brazil announced multilayered affirmative action policies. The Agrarian, Culture, Justice and Foreign Ministries announced affirmative action programs involving 30 percent quotas for black Brazilians. In 2001, Rio de Janeiro established a 40 percent quota for its universities. Cardoso argued for active confrontation of racial inequality and declared that the Brazilian image of a perfect racial democracy had never existed. Today, racial inequality continues to influence Brazilian society regardless of government policies. As Janaina des Virgens Santos of Salvador has said, "If you have 10 black people and one white [apply for a job], the white person would get preference."[57]

The aforementioned changes occurred as a result of pressures from black individuals and organizations. For example, on May 13, 1988, marking the centennial of slavery's abolition, the government organized a celebration, but Afro-Brazilian groups put together counterdemonstrations. Demonstrators protested persisting racial inequality and institutionalized discrimination. Labeling the celebration a "farce" and "100 years of lies," they called for a "march for the real liberation of the race." Afro-Brazilians demanded the elimination of inequality in jobs and political power; they addressed issues of racial categorization and the African influences on Brazilian culture. They advocated a strengthening of cultural and other ties between black Brazilians and others in the African Diaspora in order to challenge white-imposed racial oppression everywhere.[58] Another protest movement demanded significant land reform. Because 5 percent of the

Brazilian population, which is overwhelmingly white, controls 95 percent of the land, more than 50,000 rural poor marched in the late 1990s to protest the slow pace of change and to demand much-needed land reform.[59]

Another growing social movement is that of indigenous Brazilians. Although the last census indicates a rapid growth of the indigenous population—from 294,000 in 1991 to 386,000 in 2001—12 of the 216 indigenous groups in Brazil are still facing extinction. Indigenous groups make up an important part of the population, yet their voices have been undermined or ignored for centuries.[60]

In 1995, President Cardoso's administration began to include blacks in the government administration, and Brazil gained its first black government minister, second black general, and first black police commander. A new president, Luiz Inacio Lula da Silva, was elected in 2002 and reelected overwhelmingly in 2006, for a term to end late in 2010. Under Lula, the first working-class Brazilian president, social projects such as improving the socioeconomic conditions of the urban poor have begun to take center stage. Nonetheless, Jocalio Teles of the Federal University of Bahia has noted that "the quality of life of the black population is terrible . . . how will the future be for the black population in our city and our country?"[61] Not surprisingly, many black Brazilians have demanded much faster change. Interestingly, some rap groups are strengthening the black civil rights movement by using popular music to criticize racial prejudice and discrimination in Brazilian society.[62]

Helio Santos, a black university professor, has underscored the contradictions in his country today: "Brazilian society discriminates against blacks at every point, but it is hidden, disguised. . . . There is an illusion of social democracy in Brazil. . . . Blacks internalize discrimination so often they can't see it."[63] As in the United States, the illusion of equality serves elites' social and political purposes while racial discrimination remains integral to society. According to C. L. P. Oliveira, a researcher in Brazil, "People have an idea of the proper place for blacks in society. . . . They see blacks as soccer players, musicians, workers . . . but it's very hard for many people to recognize them as doctors or lawyers, and other highly qualified professionals."[64] These realities indicate the continuation of struggle for black Brazilians. Indeed, whites receive college degrees at

a rate much greater than that of black and indigenous Brazilians of the same age.[65] Only 17 percent of university graduates are of mixed racial ancestry, and only 2 percent are black. Some government affirmative action policies are now targeting these problems through setting up such things as remedial quotas for college student admission. The retention rate in college, however, has been influenced by black students' economic conditions, which often force them to leave school in favor of low-paying jobs to support themselves or their families. As a result, the large racial gap in advanced education has not changed significantly for over one hundred years in Brazil. The aforementioned Jocalio Teles observes that "a majority of people with access to higher education are white."[66]

The Brazilian case shows the effects of European colonialism not only on economic and political institutions but also on ideological racism's perpetuation in popular culture. Racial subordination of black Brazilians, although considered by whites to be eliminated, remains a central part of Brazil's present and promises to continue to influence the country's future through the dominance of the white racist framing and ideology in elite thinking, institutionalized practices, and the mass media.

 Does the systemic racism concept help explain racial conflict in Brazil?

Colonialism and Colonizer in France: The Violence of Inclusion and Exclusion

European colonialism legitimated using violence on subordinated peoples through a dichotomous construction of the colonial world in terms of "good" and "evil."[67] This symbolism of "good" colonizing Europeans and "evil" and unworthy colonized subjects was an integral aspect of racial subordination and conflict during the long colonial period and during the subsequent postcolonial period. This symbolism of good Europeans and evil "colonials" has deep religious roots and has long been part of the white racist framing of non-Europeans. Attempts at assimilation and integration in colonial areas have long been fundamentally challenged by these racist assumptions, and postcolonial societies are still confronted by them. Although there are many examples of this, contemporary France is a very important case that we will examine here.

The Character of French Colonialism

French colonialism differed from British and Portuguese colonialism in that it claimed the newly colonized peoples as "citizens of France." To realize this social fiction, colonial administrators propagated French culture and language in a vigorous attempt to assimilate colonized peoples into the French culture and empire. However, at no point in its history has France itself been unified or monocultural. Subordinated racial and ethnic groups in France, such as Jews, have long been targets of racial hostility and exclusion. In a famous case, Alfred Dreyfus, a Jewish captain in the French army, was falsely accused by his superiors and convicted in 1898 of selling military secrets to Germans. The trial became a major issue in French elections, and candidates adopted anti-Semitic platforms. Yet, Jews made up a tiny 0.2 percent of the population. In the first two months of 1898, French Jews were the targets of no fewer than sixty-nine anti-Semitic riots in which 4000 people participated; rioters destroyed Jewish businesses and synagogues and attacked many individuals.[68]

France's anti-Semitic orientation emerged again during World War II in the southern pro-Nazi Vichy area of France. While the French-run Vichy government opposed exportation of French Jews to German extermination camps, it did not resist deportation of foreign Jews.[69] When former French President Francois Mitterand's association with the pro-Nazi Vichy government was later revealed in the press, he responded that, at the time, "I did not think about the anti-Semitism of Vichy."[70] Official and popular obliviousness to racist framing and action, even among some "left" politicians, is integral to France's enduring system of racism.

 What role has anti-Semitism played in French patterns of racial thought and discrimination?

Muslim Immigrants and Racism

Since the period of overseas colonialism, debates surrounding immigration to France have often reflected overt and subtle racist thinking about government immigration policies. Today, it is estimated that one in every four French citizens has a non-French parent or grandparents.[71] Contemporary complexities surrounding the integration of immigrants stem substantially from the French government's relations with about 5 million immigrant Muslims from Africa, most of whom settled in France after the Algerian War of 1954–1962. About two-thirds of this relatively new population became French citizens.

Algeria, a country in northern Africa, became a French colony in the 1830s, although the Algerians vigorously resisted the invasion. French colonists confiscated land and stripped Algerians of political and economic rights. In response, some Algerians advocated complete assimilation into French social and cultural ways; others demanded independence from France through organized resistance. Interestingly, when France was controlled by the Germans during World War II, Algiers (in Algeria) became the capital of "Free France." During the war, Algerians even fought in the French army against Germans, largely in expectation of Algerian independence from France. However, this political liberation did not come. Following the war, a growing Algerian nationalist movement led by the National Liberation Front (FLN) met with violent suppression from the French government. The Algerian war of independence did not end until 1962, when Algeria finally gained political independence from France.

Since the 1960s, the migration of Algerians to France has made Islam the country's second major religion, after Roman Catholicism. The large number of darker-skinned Muslims in France has not only kept alive memories of the brutal colonial war but also brought a hostile and racialized reaction from many whites who fear the loss of the "essence" of French culture.[72] Many French whites have argued that the cultural differences between them and the African immigrants are more important than the racial division. Intellectual and popular debates among whites tend to focus on immigrants' assimilation into, or conflict with, existing French culture, and try to play down the importance of racial perceptions held by whites—a strategy that is also common in the United States.[73] For example, when French whites view the omnipresent racial segregation in housing as a result of immigrants' "individual choices," they intentionally dismiss the dynamics of the racial discrimination routinely directed against Afro-French groups in housing markets in France.

Indeed, the term *immigrant* in French (as, increasingly, in English) is popularly used to define only immigrants of non-European origin, especially Muslim Africans. According to one social worker, *immigrant* and *foreigner* are pejorative: "I am a foreigner. You and I are foreigners. We are not victims of racism. An immigrant is someone who is forced to leave his country, the poor bloke—Arabs and so on."[74] Officially, people in France are classified in terms of nationality as "foreigners" or "nationals." There is little white recognition that Muslim Africans who are naturalized are citizens of France. The proportion of immigrants in the population has not increased: Immigrants account for about the same proportion of the population today as in 1931. In addition, 80 percent of those popularly classified as

"immigrants" have lived in France for more than ten years, and one-fourth were actually born in France.[75]

Especially since 1980, the issue of African immigration has come to the forefront of political debate, pressed in particular by the reactionary Jean-Marie Le Pen and the French far right, which has received as much as 15 percent of the vote in elections. Le Pen's support is greatest from white French voters in urban areas with sizable numbers of Muslim Africans. Far-right groups advocate ending African immigration, providing job priority only for native-born French whites, forcing Africans to return to Africa, and reimposing the death penalty for criminals. The far-right particularly objects to the acquisition of French nationality by second-generation Africans, whose parents are often criticized for their attachment to certain African cultural values and for teaching these values to their French-born children.[76] Some rightist white politicians have made arguments that the increasing numbers of Muslims in Europe are a threat to the "Christian core" of Western civilization, thereby sounding like some political extremists in the United States. Such arguments have roots dating back to the early Christian Crusades.

This extremism can also be seen in a rise in anti-Semitism. Anti-Semitic incidents in Europe increased in 2009, especially in France, where there were 631 anti-Semitic incidents, including 113 that were violent. Moreover, in an effort to attract voters who support the racist right, the French government has pursued repressive policies against African immigrants and their supporters. For example, in summer 1996, when 300 African immigrants and non-African intellectuals staged a mass protest in a church, the government sent 1000 police officers to break down church gates to maintain "law and order."[77] Today, only 4 percent of the French population is black, but a new survey suggests that more than half of the black population believe that they have been victims of everyday discrimination. More than one-third feel the problem is getting worse, and one in five report they have been denied jobs because of the color of their skin. The Council of Black Associations, which conducted the survey, argues that the (white) French refusal to collect information on the basis of racial background compounds the problem of racism.[78] Attacks against blacks have been increasing among racist public commentators such as Pacal Sevran, who has said, "Africa is dying from all the children born there . . .

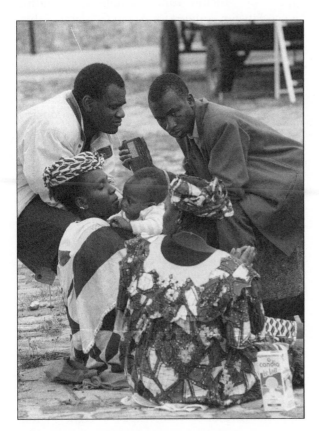

Sitting in a courtyard, these undocumented African immigrants await a court decision on whether they can stay in France.

we need to sterilize half the planet." Even supposed progressives are often anti-immigrant. One socialist party leader has commented, after finding out that nine of the eleven starting players on France's national soccer team were not white, "I'm ashamed of my country."[79]

Issues of racism have divided France in recent decades. An anti-racist association called SOS Racism, which includes native-born French and immigrants, has challenged xenophobia, anti-Semitism, and racism. SOS Racism advocates equality of rights and giving immigrants the right to vote. The organization had 350 local committees and 50,000 followers at its inception and attracted media attention in the 1980s when it organized an anti-racist demonstration attended by hundreds of thousands.[80]

Still, the attacks on African (especially Arab) immigrants continue. The most extreme form of discrimination is "Arabicide," a term some use for the more than 200 unsolved murders of Muslim Arab residents of France in recent decades. French law includes no category for hate crimes, and police do not classify such killings in a way that shows the pattern of violence against the Arab community. Murders are often dismissed by whites as the "settling of accounts" between Arab factions. This government attitude is similar to the French government's response to the 1961 Papon massacre during the Algerian War. In that case, a demonstration in Paris organized to protest the nightly curfew for Algerians in France was met with massive police violence. Protesters were clubbed, machine gunned, or driven into the Seine River by the police. At least 140 Algerians were killed, and 400 people were declared missing. According to the official government report, these were all "gangland killings" between the National Liberation Front and the Algerian National Movement. The police were thereby excused for their many killings.[81]

In addition to anti–African-Muslim violence, discrimination in housing, workplaces, and education is commonplace. Muslim communities also face attacks on their culture and traditions. One issue is the right of Muslim girls to wear traditional head scarves in French schools. In the Muslim community, depending on the circumstances, the wearing of these head scarves has different meanings. Some Muslim feminists have argued that the traditional head scarves of women represent the oppression of

patriarchy forced on women by men. However, other Muslim feminists have argued that the head scarves represent an assertion of women's rights if they are worn by women of their own free will. Thus, they can represent a political statement. The controversy in France began in 1989, when Arab students wearing head scarves were excluded from school classes. In 1994, the French government banned the wearing of head scarves in public schools, arguing that the practice violated the tradition of secular education. The Education Minister claimed, "We must respect the culture and faith of Muslims, but the history and will of our people was to build a united secular society specifically where schools were concerned."[82]

In this view, scarves divided Muslims from non-Muslims, therefore violating separation of church and state. The French government has interpreted the increasing number of students wearing head scarves in schools as an indication of the increasing appeal of Muslim fundamentalism, including French Muslim support for Algeria's Islamic Salvation Front, which is fighting to establish an Islamic state in Algeria. In fact, the Education Ministry's ban on head scarves coincided with police raids in which the residents of Arab neighborhoods in cities were arrested on suspicion of being Muslim militants.[83]

France's former President Jacques Chirac aroused the racist sentiments of whites by accusing Algerian immigrants of being "welfare cheats" who produce children just to benefit from the welfare system. President Nicholas Sarkozy, in contrast, during his visit to Algeria declared that French colonial rule was "profoundly unjust," and added that "there is nothing that more closely resembles anti-Semitism than Islamophobia. Both have the same face: that of stupidity and hate."[84]

France's movement into the European Union (EU) has brought the complexities of the "New Europe" into its own society. The European Union stresses workers' rights, the standardization of policies with regard to communities of color, and a stable immigration policy. However, EU politics have also fostered a resurgence of rightist, protectionist, racist, anti-immigration, and anti-community rights political platforms in several countries. Le Pen supporters in France would expel "foreigners" from the country. These pressures are fostering anti–European Union movements, sometimes known as "EuroNat."[85] Hate crimes against people of color have risen significantly. Indeed, racist music, such as the song "Beating Up Blacks," has had some popularity. A French television executive was fined for allowing this song to be performed on air, which includes lines such as "can't stand the foreigners, the darkies . . . flick on the lighters, we're going to set them on fire."[86]

In the summer of 2005, a French newspaper asked, "Suburbs: A Colonial Problem?"[87] Unlike in the United States, where the urban poor are in inner cities mostly separated from those in suburbs, in France the poor are often concentrated in suburbs. As a response to this article, a group called Indigénes de la République published a manifesto accenting "liberté, egalité, fraternité!" (liberty, equality, brotherhood)—the same cry of the peasants and workers during the 1789 French Revolution. The manifesto announced: "We the daughters and sons of colonized peoples and immigrants, are engaged in a struggle against oppression and discrimination by the post-colonial-republic." A few months later in many towns and cities, riots resulted in the burning of 10,000 cars and 200 public buildings, and in three deaths. Most who participated in the rebellions were young men living in the poverty-stricken suburbs and suffering from a 40 percent unemployment rate. Most in these predominantly Muslim and African areas had lost hope that the French government would address their severe economic problems. Some expressed the desire to live under an Islamic government, but most said that they wanted a French government that would assist them economically, and without discrimination.[88]

Significantly, Muslim voters' political patterns are similar to those of others in France who share their socioeconomic backgrounds. According to opinion polls, Muslim French voters opposed the European Union Constitution in about the same proportion as the country as a whole.[89] In a way, assimilationist government policies have succeeded on this political front. Even as a group of citizens who have been racially targeted, Muslims do not act as a distinct voting bloc. Perhaps that is one reason why in 2007, President Chirac, serving his last term, did not make any attempts to address the economic needs of many Muslim Arab citizens.

Colonialism brings oppression and violence not only to the land of the colonized but also to the land of the colonizer, especially if the colonized migrate to the colonizing country. In the postcolonial era,

both the racial framing of non-Europeans and the well-institutionalized discrimination that accompanies it persist vigorously in European countries such as France.

 What are some important consequences of recent African immigration to France?

The Future of Colonialism and Postcolonialism

Some General Considerations

During the era of European colonialism as well as during the postcolonial era, Europeans and European Americans have often believed that the seeds of "Westernization" and "modernization" would eventually bring "civilization" to colonial or formerly colonial areas. Expecting a slow evolution, modernization theorists have argued that European colonialism spread Western culture and ideology to the lands of the "uncivilized" and "inferior." Following Westernization, conflict between the colonizers and colonized was expected to disappear as the colonized peoples gradually assimilated into the "superior" European culture. Thus, the Westernization process demands that colonized peoples acquiesce in the continuation of global patterns of racial and ethnic inequality by accepting external European and U.S. cultural, economic, and political domination. This view is clearly racist in its assumptions, and is based on the oppressed willingly accepting their oppression.

Challenging such racist perspectives, power-conflict analysts generally reject the assimilationist Westernizing perspective. They argue that today, as in the past, white-generated racism is a global reality. From the power-conflict perspective, the awareness of global diversity should emphasize the creation of new terms of human coexistence and equality in order to establish real societal and international peace. Current world conditions often do not allow for the careful exploration of political and economic alternatives to external colonialism or its postindependence indirect colonialism. This is in part because warring factions in many postcolonial countries are rooted in divisions created by past colonialism and continue to practice group subordination backed by violence. In addition, in the United States, South Africa, Brazil, and France, systemic racism, with its many discriminatory mechanisms, continues to destroy the lives and communities of large numbers of oppressed people.

From a power-conflict perspective, colonialism is an exploitative system that has brought great racial and ethnic inequalities and misery to many countries. Racial subordination has integrated segregation and racial inequality into the everyday lives of people in North America, South Africa, Brazil, and France, as well as people in many other countries. In the postcolonial era, the painful realities of Euro-colonialism are evident in the continuing racial inequality in such areas as education, housing, business, employment, public accommodations, and healthcare. Around the globe, such inequalities influence the life chances of all people who were (and are) racially, ethnically, and religiously oppressed. Although the modes of inequality and segregation may be different, oppression and associated state violence have been perpetuated in the postcolonialist era in both colonizing and colonized societies.

The enslavement of human beings, whether of indigenous or imported populations, which was a common aspect of colonialism, had effects that have lasted to the present. As slavery destroyed human beings and their cultures, it and its ideology became integrated into social institutions that still dominate postcolonial societies. For example, South Africa is today confronting the lingering effects of slavery and its racist ideology under its now disintegrating apartheid system; African Americans and Afro-Brazilians are demanding abolition of the contemporary effects of slavery in their lives and communities. From a strong power-conflict perspective, a realistic assessment of the present and future of postcolonial societies requires a confrontation with entrenched inequality and segregation and a major struggle against the persisting practices and effects of systemic racism and its global realities. After World War II, the conditions of the Cold War era often defined the possibilities for colonial societies as they revolted against their colonial masters. The Cold War between the Soviet Union and the United States and its European allies shaped the economic dependency and cultural experiences of many postcolonial societies. **Neocolonialism**—*the continuation of the economic and cultural dominance of the former colonial states*—is an extension of the Cold War. When the Soviet Union

and its empire broke up after the late 1980s and the Cold War ended, many people in the former Soviet Union and in its satellites pressed toward full independence. They expected that colonialism and neocolonialism, including that of the former Soviet Union, would end.

However, this has not been the case. In most of these countries, Communism has been replaced by a form of capitalism that constitutes a new type of economic and political colonialism with close ties to Western banks and corporations. Former European colonies in Africa and Asia have faced a similar neocolonialism. As the capitalist system recreates itself in new neocolonial forms, it creates new modes of inequality and segregation that usually remain pervaded by the global system of racial and ethnic hostility and subordination.[90]

Colonialism, Capitalism, and Racism: A Note on Contemporary Genocide

The last century has often been marred by large-scale hate and massive killings, increasingly forcing the term *genocide* into widespread use. Genocide has come to be understood as "the coordinated plan of different actions aiming at the destruction of essential foundations of the life of national groups with the aim of annihilating the groups themselves."[91] As Israel Charny warned,

> There needs to be a growing consensus on the part of human beings and organized society that penetrates the very basis of human culture that mass killing is unacceptable to civilized peoples, otherwise the prevailing momentum of historical experience will continue for generation after generation that genocide is a phenomenon of nature, like other disasters, and this view of the inevitability of genocide as an almost natural event will continue to justify it in the sense of convincing people that nothing can be done.[92]

Genocide is an old human problem, as we saw in Chapter 6 when we assessed Euro-American tactics that attempted to exterminate indigenous Americans. In recent decades, numerous examples of genocide have remained terrifying and inhuman in the extreme. In the late twentieth and early twenty-first centuries, a common response of many white Europeans and Euro-Americans is to view genocide among peoples of color as natural and inevitable. Typically, they view such genocidal events through the old white frame, which inclines them to not notice, or to excuse, genocidal events. The global system of racial oppression, gradually expanded by Europeans from the fifteenth century onward until it circled the globe, not only involved early genocidal attacks on indigenous peoples but also developed the racist framing of "superior" peoples and "inferior" peoples that rationalized genocide and other forms of racial oppression.

Now that this racial framing of superior and inferior, of civilized and uncivilized, has been firmly in place for centuries—in some form in the minds of most in the world's ruling elites—a great many people have acted on, and continue to act on, its racialized stereotypes, images, emotions, and interpretations. Thus, not surprisingly, recent genocides in Africa and the former Soviet Union implicate the white racist framing and its contextual system of racial–ethnic hierarchy and oppression. Those perpetrating genocidal action are often acting out of racial and ethnic categories generated, in part or in whole, by the white racial frame, and/or in relation to territorial boundaries created by Euro-colonialism's administering officials. At least as important is the fact that the old white racist framing legitimates great indifference and inaction on the part of the world's powerful European and Euro-American elites and associated international organizations. Wherever they have occurred in recent decades, as in earlier centuries, genocidal thinking and actions have often been linked in one way or another to the long history of European colonialism and neocolonialism.

One recent example is that of the Darfur region of Sudan in Africa, where at least 100,000 people have died and millions have been displaced, are starving, and are in desperate need of emergency aid for food, shelter, and medical treatment. The Darfur conflict has been escalated by two groups of allies. The Sudan Liberation Army and the Justice & Equality Movement, allies seeking federation or independence and representing the non-Arab majority, are fighting against what they view as intense political oppression of the Sudanese government's army and affiliated militia units, allies representing the country's Arab minority. (We use here the terms *Arab* and *non-Arab*, although the groups in opposition sometimes overlap in ancestry and religious commitments.)

Events in Darfur are complex. The minority-controlled government is northern and Arabized, whereas rebels are southern and western and fighting

political and economic oppression. The current Sudanese government is the direct descendant of the British colonial government, which handed over power to the Sudanese Arab elite. Some of the numerous groups resisting this minority and repressive government are Islamic in religion, as are the government leaders, yet others in the resistance in the south are Christian or animist. There is also a division today between non-Arab farmers and nomadic Arab herders over control of fertile lands.[93]

The current divisions and fighting in Sudan link closely to the long direct and indirect (through Egyptian officials who the British government controlled) colonization of the area by the British, who withdrew in 1956 after decades of colonial control. During many years of control, British colonial administrators used the method of "divide and conquer." To establish full control and incorporation of the area into Euro-capitalism, which they legitimated in terms of a strong white-racist and colonialist framing, British oppressors manipulated existing group tensions between Arabized peoples mostly in northern Sudan and non-Arab (sometimes termed "black") Africans in southern and western areas. The British imposed their racialized thinking in ways that *inferiorized* the darker-skinned local population, a framing to some extent picked up, later on, by Sudan's Arab leaders and government officials who have sought the subordination and Arabization of Sudan's southern non-Arab areas.[94]

Much fighting has been linked to control of the oil extracted from southern Sudan and piped through a pipeline to the Red Sea. One of the southern non-Arab groups, the Nubas, are among the major victims of the Arab government in this complex conflict. The Nuba Mountains, bordering Sudan's oil pipeline, are on the front line of conflict. Although they are non-Arab Africans, the Nuba speak Arabic, the official language of the country. About half are Muslim, and half are Christian and/or animist. When the Nuba joined the Sudan Liberation Army, government forces pushed them up into the mountains, where they could no longer grow food. When the government banned humanitarian airlifts, many Nuba died of hunger, especially children.[95]

In spite of earlier colonial involvement and their significant shaping of political events in Sudan for many decades, Western (and other) leaders have so far delayed responding significantly to this ongoing violence, even debating whether events in Darfur represent "genocide." Westerners have debated how long killings on a large scale have been occurring, how to count nomadic peoples and villagers who have fallen victim, and how to calculate victims when some have fled to neighboring countries or perished from the side effects of violence such as related malnutrition and disease. Central to the debate on "genocide," which belatedly began in 2004, has been whether these horrific events are just internal, civil war skirmishes that do not warrant international intervention. Finally, in July 2004, the U.S. House of Representatives unanimously passed a resolution labeling the violent events as "genocide." The resolution called on the George W. Bush administration to act according to the international Genocide Convention. Secretary of State Colin Powell then insisted that naming the Darfur events "genocide" would not change favorable U.S. policy toward Sudan's government even as he commissioned an in-depth study on whether the events merited the term. The U.S. government was not alone in being slow to call the events genocide, for Canadian, British, and EU officials, along with the UN secretary general, continued to call Darfur "a massive violation of human rights," not genocide.[96] Groups such as Human Rights Watch called the Darfur situation "ethnic cleansing" and argued that it involved the "forced removal of an ethnic group," not its annihilation. Belatedly too, U.N. Secretary General Kofi Annan finally appointed a U.N. commission to determine whether genocide had occurred there. Debates came to a halt when Colin Powell finally did assert that genocide, not just civil war, was taking place in the Sudan.[97]

A peace accord was signed in May 2005 between the Arab-led government and the non-Arab opposition forces, but it did not end the killings. The African Union sent 7000 peacekeepers to monitor the refugee camps, but this small force and the vastness of the county seriously hampered their effectiveness. The African Union withdrew in late 2006.[98] In the summer of 2007, the Sudanese government, under international political pressure, agreed to the deployment of a new peacekeeping force. Even though United Nations and African Union soldiers have tried to keep order, direct and indirect killing has continued to the present. Violent deaths are on the rise, as are deaths from diseases. The Center for Epidemiology in Brussels declared that their data show more than 80 percent of deaths were from disease, the result of unsanitary conditions in refugee camps and makeshift settlements, rather than directly from violence. The International Criminal Court issued an arrest warrant for the Sudanese president al-Bashir for war crimes, but he has rejected both the court's authority and the charge of genocide. In fact, even the court has said it fails to find sufficient evidence of al-Bashir's specific intent to "destroy, in whole or in part, a national, ethnic, racial or religious group," which is crucial in determining whether genocide is being committed.[99]

The racial and ethnic differences among the people that were fostered and accentuated during British colonial rule have survived today under neocolonialism. Western leaders seem relatively unconcerned with violence in Sudan (as earlier in the case of Rwanda), yet seem very concerned about who gets oil flowing out of southern Sudan. The past actions of, and current collective indifference of, leaders in Western countries exhibit the ways in which white political-economic control, directly or indirectly, but always in terms of the pervasive racial framing, still dominates the globe.

Summary

White racism became a global reality substantially as a result of European and Euro-American colonialism, which operated through bureaucratic administrations, exploitative trade, and a missionary type of Euro-Christian culture. European and later U.S. colonizers rationalized colonial expansion and violence by defining themselves as superior peoples whose duty it was to Westernize and modernize the "uncivilized." The construction of colonized peoples as racially inferior, within the age-old white racist framing, was fundamental to legitimizing colonial exploitation. Colonialism destroyed local economies and political arrangements, and shaped colonized peoples' conceptions of themselves and their future possibilities. Racist framing, culture, and social institutions were integral to European colonialism, and white racial oppression has persisted into the postcolonial era. Around the globe, systemic racism can be still seen in pervasive racial prejudices, emotions, practices, and institutions.

The colonization of black South Africans by European states began in the seventeenth century. Over a 400-year period, a powerful white racist framing, ideology, and society evolved that has shaped most aspects of the existence of black and other South Africans, from housing to education to employment. The racist system of apartheid created separate racial communities. Since the free election of 1994, white, black, and other South Africans have attempted to reconcile deep differences and inequalities within a post-apartheid system. However, they still face major obstacles because of persistent racist thought and discriminatory action, as well as continuing neo-colonialism in the form of white control of the country's powerful economy.

In contrast to systemic racism in South Africa, Brazilian racism is often more subtle and wrapped in the myth of "racial democracy." Brazil was colonized in the sixteenth century. Even today, however, Brazilian politics, economy, and society reveal the effects of that colonization and the slavery system imposed by whites. Even though slavery was abolished more than one hundred years ago, systemic racism is evident in widespread racial discrimination, in many media and intellectual discussions, and in elements of popular culture. A white racist framing penetrates the images that Brazilians have of who they are and works to divide Brazilians, including those with African ancestry, according to shades of skin color. More than a century after the abolition of slavery, systemic racism persists in the discriminatory ways in which whites treat people of African ancestry and in the ways in which most Brazilians see themselves and their communities.

European colonialism left major scars on the colonized lands and also on the colonizing countries. The postcolonial lives of colonized and colonizers have been plagued by chronic racist framing, social disruption and oppression, and much group violence. For example, France, a colonizer, has experienced continuing racial violence in the post-colonial era. Racialized framing and practice still target French Muslims from Africa, who experience job discrimination, destruction of property, and attacks on their Muslim culture.

The European community, the United States, and even the United Nations have been hesitant to condemn many of the oppressive acts, including violence and genocide, that are shaped by global racism. They have often been reluctant to name and confront forms of institutionalized racism in societies around the world. Today, the world appears to be in the increasingly tight grip of a culture of racist thinking and hostility and a global structure of racial oppression long propagated by variations on European colonialism and neocolonialism. And this world of oppression is often accepted as an everyday reality.

Further confrontation of and resistance to white-generated racism will likely come from bridging various local understandings and from the everyday struggles of people in numerous societies with racial oppression. From this perspective, a greater understanding of white-generated racism in France or Brazil can contribute significantly to confronting and resisting similar racial oppression in the Americas or South Africa. Similarly, understanding racism better in the latter areas can contribute substantially to resistance to racial oppression in the former areas. Undoing contemporary systems of racism remains a major and enduring challenge for all concerned peoples in the twenty-first century.

Key Terms

apartheid 385	coloureds 388
Boers 388	neocolonialism 400
Afrikaners 388	

Glossary

affirmative action programs　Private and governmental programs that seek to improve the economic and educational opportunities for formerly excluded racial, ethnic, and gender groups.

Afrikaners　White South African speakers of the Afrikaans language.

Anglo-Protestant Americans　A more accurate term for those often referred to as Anglo-Saxon Protestant Americans.

Anglo-Saxon　A term that originally referred to Germanic tribes that came to the area now called England in the fifth and sixth centuries C.E.; it was later applied to white inhabitants of England and to those English who came to North America.

anti-Semitism　The stereotyping of, prejudice toward, or discrimination against Jews.

apartheid　The rigidly institutionalized system of racial segregation and social, economic, and political inequality that invaded virtually every aspect of daily life in South Africa from 1948 until the 1990s.

Arab Americans　An umbrella term for Americans whose ancestral roots are in Arab countries in the Middle East and northern Africa.

Asian Americans　An umbrella term for Americans whose ancestral roots are in Asia.

Asian-Pacific Americans　An umbrella term for Americans whose ancestral roots are in Asia or the Pacific Islands.

assimilation　An incoming group's adoption of the cultural traits (e.g., language) and/or identity of the host group and/or integration into the primary networks and secondary organizations of the host group.

attitude-receptional assimilation　Milton Gordon's term for the absence of prejudice and stereotyping.

authoritarian personalities　Personalities that are characterized by a high degree of submission to authority, a strong tendency to stereotype, great concern for status, a view of the world as threatening, and an intolerance of out-groups that occupy socially subordinate positions.

behavior-receptional assimilation　Milton Gordon's term for the absence of intentional discrimination.

bilingualism　The ability to speak two languages; relates to school programs for non–English-speaking children learning to speak English.

Boers　White South Africans of Dutch descent.

braceros　Farm workers on seasonal contracts (e.g., some Mexican farm workers).

caste school of racial relations　Power-conflict theory that emphasizes well-institutionalized discrimination as the foundation of a castelike system of U.S. segregation and apartheid.

Chicano political movement　A militant movement that began during the 1960s and has sought increased power and respect for Mexican Americans.

civic assimilation　Milton Gordon's term for the absence of value and power conflict between two racial or ethnic groups, mainly between a host group and a newer immigrant group.

civil rights movement   A collective movement to establish or improve the legal and political rights of a subordinate racial or ethnic group.

colonization migration   The conquest and domination of a preexisting geographical group by outsiders.

color coding   Social discrimination or stratification based on skin color.

coloureds   The South African term for people of mixed black–white ancestry.

competition theory   A view of ethnicity that emphasizes the relative stability of ethnic population boundaries over time and the intergroup competition over resources that results from shifts in boundaries because of migration.

competitive capitalism   An economic system dominated by competition between small and medium-sized for-profit businesses.

conformity function of prejudice   Prejudiced attitudes held in order to conform to the expectations of an important social reference group.

contract-labor movement   Migration under contract, such as that of indentured Irish servants to English colonies and Chinese laborers to western North America.

covert discrimination   Harmful treatment of members of subordinate racial and ethnic groups that is hidden and difficult to document.

cultural assimilation   The change of one group's important cultural patterns to those of the host or dominant group.

cultural diversity   The variety of cultures in a specific region, a nation, or the world; often relates to respect for diverse cultures.

cultural pluralism   The view that each racial or ethnic group has the democratic right to preserve and practice important elements of its own cultural heritage without being forced to assimilate to a dominant culture.

culture of poverty   A stereotyped concept asserting that poor people typically develop a defective and/or deviant subculture.

direct institutionalized discrimination   Organizationally prescribed or community-prescribed action that by intention has a differential and negative effect on members of subordinate racial and ethnic groups.

discrimination   Most often, the actions carried out by members of dominant groups, or their representatives, that have a differential and harmful effect on members of subordinate racial or ethnic groups.

dominant group   A racial or ethnic group with the greatest power and resources in a society; also called **majority group.**

egalitarian symbiosis   A peaceful coexistence and a rough economic and political equality between two racial or ethnic groups.

endogamy   Marriage within one's own racial or ethnic group.

English Americans   Americans of English ancestry.

environmental racism   Government and private waste dumping and other environmental discrimination in communities populated by Americans of color.

ethnic enclave   The economic (often market), social, and often residential niche that certain racial and ethnic groups have developed as a way of surviving or prospering in U.S. cities.

ethnic group   A group that is socially distinguished or set apart, by others or by itself, primarily on the basis of cultural and/or national-origin characteristics.

ethnogenesis   The sociological theory that, over time, immigrant groups not only come to share cultural traits with the host group but also retain many of their own nationality characteristics.

ethnoviolence   Violence directed at an individual or group because of the individual's or group's ethnic or racial identity.

external colonialism   The economic or political exploitation of a society by a powerful group, such as (imperialistic) aristocrats or capitalists, from another, geographically separate society.

externalization function of prejudice   The transfer of an individual's internal psychological problem to an external racial or ethnic group as a way of repressing or denying that problem.

gendered racism   The interaction of racial discrimination and gender discrimination, which especially affects women of color.

genocide   The deliberate and systematic extermination of a nationality or racial group.

glass ceiling   An unwritten and unofficial policy in organizations that limits the potential for advancement of certain persons, usually based on their racial, ethnic, or gender group.

gunboat imperialism   Nineteenth-century imperialism backed by the use or threat of military force.

Hapa   Persons of mixed Japanese-other ancestry (from a Hawaiian word meaning "half").

hate crimes   Crimes against people and property generated by prejudice against racial, ethnic, religious, disability, or sexual orientation groups.

hierarchy   A significant socioeconomic stratification.

Hispanics   Persons of Mexican, Puerto Rican, Cuban, Dominican, and Central or South American heritage; also called **Latinos**.

Holocaust   The planned extermination of the Jews by the government in Nazi Germany in the 1930s and 1940s, in which an estimated 6 million European Jews (and many others) were murdered.

identification assimilation   Milton Gordon's term for an incoming group's development of a sense of identity linked to that of the dominant host group.

ideological racism   An ideology that considers a group's unchangeable physical characteristics to be linked in a direct, causal way to psychological or intellectual characteristics, and that on this basis distinguishes between superior and inferior racial groups.

"illegals"   See **Undocumented immigrants.**

indigenous superordination   A societal condition in which incoming immigrant groups are placed in a subordinate position to a dominant host group.

indirect institutionalized discrimination   Dominant-group practices that have a harmful effect on members of subordinate racial and ethnic groups even though the organizational or community-prescribed norms (informal or legal rules) guiding the actions were established with no intent to harm.

individual racism   Racially hostile acts of an individual directed at one or more members of another racial group.

institutional racism   Institutionalized practices that differentially and negatively affect members of a subordinate racial group.

intermarriage   Marriage between members of different racial or ethnic groups.

internal colonialism   The colony-like control and exploitation of subordinate groups by a dominant group *within* a given society.

IQ tests   Paper-and-pencil or object/symbol manipulation tests that advocates inaccurately claim can measure a global human intelligence.

isolate discrimination   Harmful action taken intentionally by a member of a dominant racial or ethnic group against members of a subordinate group without direct and significant support from the immediate social or community context.

"Jim Crow" laws   State and local laws, in the North before the Civil War as well as in the South afterwards, that enforced racial segregation of "free" African Americans in public transportation, hospitals, schools, churches, and cemeteries.

Latinos   See **Hispanics**.

lynching   The illegal killing of a person by a mob, such as by hanging.

"Mafia" myth   A stereotype of Italian Americans as being substantially involved in organized crime.

majority group   See **dominant group**.

manifest destiny   A white-framed concept put forth in the nineteenth century that the United States had a right to expand from the Atlantic Ocean to the Pacific and would inevitably do so.

maquiladoras   Manufacturing operations of U.S. firms that are located in northern Mexico near the U.S. border, where U.S. firms can take advantage of low-wage labor and weak environmental standards while avoiding certain tariffs and duties.

Mariel boatlift   The immigration of 125,000 Cubans who departed from Cuba's Mariel Harbor for the United States in 1980.

marital assimilation   Significant intermarriage between one racial or ethnic group and another racial or ethnic group.

Marranos   Jews who were forced to convert publicly to Christianity during the Spanish Inquisition under threat of death but who privately maintained allegiance to Judaism.

mediated assimilation   David and Ayouby's term for the process whereby Arab American organizations act as cultural filters to screen out undesirable features of U.S. culture (applicable to other groups).

melting pot   The view that immigrants to the United States should or do lose their racial and ethnic identities as they mix together in one new American blend.

Middle Eastern Americans   An umbrella term for Americans whose ancestral roots lie in any of the Middle Eastern countries.

middleman minority   A racial or ethnic group that occupies an in-between position in terms of societal power and resources.

migrant superordination   A societal condition in which immigrants assume a dominant position over an indigenous population.

millenarian movements   Movements among indigenous groups, such as Native Americans, that have included the belief in a golden age in which supernatural events would change present oppressive conditions.

minority group   A group that is singled out because of physical and/or cultural characteristics for differential and unequal treatment and whose members become objects of discrimination; it typically has less power and resources than the dominant group; also called **subordinate group.**

model minority stereotype   The stereotype that views certain Asian American (and sometimes other) groups as exemplary in socioeconomic and moral characteristics, often as compared to other people of color.

modern racism   See **symbolic racism**.

movements of forced labor   Involuntary immigration, such as the forcible removal of Africans to North America.

multiculturalism   Cultural pluralism; the political or educational movement to respect the human rights of all Americans and recognize the diverse cultural ways of the many U.S. racial and ethnic groups, particularly those that have suffered widespread racial–ethnic discrimination.

multinational capitalism   An economic system dominated by large-scale, for-profit corporations that operate in many different countries, thereby creating an international market system.

nativism   An anti-immigrant perspective that advocates the protection of the native-born inhabitants of a country from recent immigrants who are seen as threatening or dangerous.

neocolonialism   The continuation of the economic and cultural dominance of former colonial states over former colonies.

oppositional culture   The culture of resistance often found among subordinate groups; somewhat or greatly distinct from the dominant culture, it reflects in part the struggle with that dominant culture.

order theories   Racial and ethnic theories that accent group adaptation patterns involving the orderly and progressive assimilation of particular racial and ethnic groups to a dominant culture and its related institutions.

Orientalism   A typically uninformed and stereotypical way of thinking of Asian and Middle Eastern peoples.

panethnicity   The generalization of solidarity among ethnic subgroups.

patriarchal system   A social system in which men generally predominate in power and status over women and in which men work to maintain or reinforce subordinate social roles for women.

picture brides   So called because their marriages were arranged on the basis of photographs, without the bride and groom having met.

pogroms   A Russian term, originally meaning "riot," that came to be applied to a series of organized, often officially encouraged attacks on Jews, especially during the late nineteenth and early twentieth centuries.

political refugees   Streams of refugees produced by war or political oppression.

power-conflict theories   Racial and ethnic theories that accent persistent and great inequalities in, and conflicts over, the power and resource distributions associated with racial or ethnic subordination in a society.

prejudice   An antipathy (negative feeling), felt or expressed, that is usually based on a faulty generalization and directed toward a group as a whole or toward individual members of a group.

primary labor market   The sector characterized by skilled jobs, higher wages, and greater mobility.

Protestant work ethic   A religiously based view of everyday life that promotes hard work and strong self-discipline.

psychological wage   W. E. B. Du Bois's term for white workers' sense of white superiority and privilege.

race   A term fully developed in the 1700s by European analysts to refer to what is also called a racial group. See **racial group**.

race relations cycle   Robert E. Park's view of a progressive sequence of intergroup events that usually results from one group's migration into a host society: contact, competition, accommodation, and eventual assimilation.

racial formation theory   The view that racial and ethnic relations and identities in a society are socially defined, especially by the historical actions of governments.

racial frame   An organized set of racial ideas, narratives, stereotypes, images, emotions, and inclinations to discriminate.

racial group   A social group that persons inside or outside the group have decided is important to single out as inferior or superior, typically on the basis of real or alleged physical characteristics that are selected subjectively.

racial hierarchy (racialized hierarchy)   Stratification of, and substantial inequality among, a society's racial groups.

racial profiling   A practice used by some police departments that unfairly singles out citizens of color as potential criminals and often results in extensive harassment of innocent people.

racialization   The process by which those in the dominant white group, especially its elites, have defined and constructed certain groups as being racially inferior or superior for the purposes of societal placement and of group enrichment, segregation, or oppression.

Reconstruction   The period in U.S. history following the Civil War during which an attempt was made by the federal government to disenfranchise the slaveholding oligarchy and improve the economic, educational, political, and human rights conditions of poor whites and blacks in the South.

Santería   A type of syncretic religion that includes aspects of both Catholic and older African religions.

"Scotch-Irish" immigrants   Immigrants from northern Ireland, some of whose ancestors are said to have immigrated to Ireland from Scotland.

secondary labor market   That sector characterized by job instability, low wages, and little mobility.

Shoah   See **Holocaust**.

slavery   The legal ownership and exploitation of one human being by another; the system that makes the trade in and ownership of human beings possible.

small-group discrimination   Harmful action taken intentionally by a small number of dominant-group individuals acting in concert against members of subordinate racial and ethnic groups without the support of the immediate organizational or community context.

social Darwinism   A perspective that extended Charles Darwin's evolutionary thinking into the social realm and that accents a perspective on society that embraces the notion of the "survival of the fittest."

sojourner immigration   Nonpermanent immigration for the purpose of making money and then returning to the country of origin.

split labor-market view   A power-conflict perspective that argues that the white employer class and the white part of the working class both discriminate, to a substantial degree independently, against the racially subordinated part of the working class.

stereotype   An overgeneralized image, usually negative, of a racial or ethnic outgroup that is false or that greatly distorts the real characteristics of the targeted group.

structural assimilation   Milton Gordon's term for an incoming group's penetration of the primary social networks of the host group; extended by other analysts to include penetration of secondary groups.

subordinate group   A group that is singled out because of physical and/or cultural characteristics for differential and unequal treatment and whose members become objects of discrimination; it typically has less power and fewer resources than the dominant group.

subtle discrimination   Unequal and harmful treatment of members of subordinate racial and ethnic groups that is obvious to the victim but not as overt as traditional "door-slamming" varieties of discrimination.

swing vote   A bloc that can affect close elections.

symbolic racism   Beliefs held by many whites that serious antiblack discrimination does not exist today and that African Americans and other people of color are making illegitimate demands for social and racial change.

systemic discrimination   Institutionalized patterns of discrimination that cut across major political, economic, and social organizations in a society.

systemic racism   The white prejudices, stereotypes, emotions, framing, discriminatory practices, and institutions that are integral to the long-term domination of Americans of color.

theory   In the social sciences, a conceptual framework used to interpret or explain some aspect of everyday existence.

underemployment rate   Includes not only those with no jobs, but also those who are working part time and those who are making poverty-level wages.

Underground Railroad   A network of formerly enslaved and other antislavery Americans, black and white, who passed along tens of thousands of enslaved people from the South to the North between the 1830s and the Civil War.

undocumented immigrants   Immigrants without legal immigration papers.

voluntary migration   Migration primarily by choice.

white Anglo-Saxon Protestant Americans   A label often applied to white Protestant Americans whose ancestry is English or British.

Zionism   A worldwide movement for the establishment in Palestine of a national homeland for the world's Jewish communities.

Notes

Part I

1. Leonard Dinnerstein and Frederic C. Jaher, "Introduction," in *The Aliens,* ed. Leonard Dinnerstein and Frederic C. Jaher (New York: Appleton-Century-Crofts, 1970), p. 4.
2. Leonard Dinnerstein and Frederic C. Jaher, "The Colonial Era," in *The Aliens,* ed. Dinnerstein and Jaher, p. 17.
3. Quoted in Peter M. Bergman, *The Chronological History of the Negro in America* (New York: Harper & Row, 1969), p. 52.
4. John Hope Franklin, *From Slavery to Freedom,* 2nd ed. (New York: Knopf, 1963), pp. 141–143.
5. Ibid., p. 143.
6. Samuel E. Morison, *The Oxford History of the American People* (New York: Oxford University Press, 1965), p. 353.

Chapter 1

1. Frances F. Marcus, "Louisiana Repeals Black Blood Law," *The New York Times,* July 6, 1983, p. A10.
2. Wilton M. Krogman, "The Concept of Race," in *The Science of Man in the World Crisis,* ed. Ralph Linton (New York: Columbia University Press, 1945), p. 38.
3. Winthrop D. Jordan, *White over Black* (Baltimore, MD: Penguin, 1969), p. 217.
4. Stephen J. Gould, "The Geometer of Race," *Discover,* November 1994, pp. 65–66.
5. Audrey Smedley, *Race in North America* (Boulder, CO: Westview, 1993), pp. 303–305.
6. Ibid, p. 26.
7. Peter I. Rose, *The Subject Is Race* (New York: Oxford University Press, 1968), pp. 32–33; Thomas F. Gossett, *Race* (New York: Schocken Books, 1965), p. 3.
8. M. Annette Jaimes, "Liberating Race," in *The State of Asian America: Activism and Resistance in the 1990s,* ed. Karin Aguilar-San Juan (Boston: South End Press, 1994), p. 369.
9. Ibid., p. 370.

10. See Pierre L. van den Berghe, *Race and Racism* (New York: Wiley, 1967), p. 11.
11. Robert Bennett Bean, *The Races of Man* (New York: University Society, 1935), pp. 94–96, quoted in *In Their Place: White America Defines Her Minorities, 1850–1950,* ed. Lewis H. Carlson and George A. Colburn (New York: Wiley, 1972), p. 106. See also Magnus Hirschfeld, *Racism* (Port Washington, NY: Kennikat Press, 1973 [1938]), pp. 35–99, 266–318.
12. Eugenia Shanklin, *Anthropology and Race* (Belmont, CA: Wadsworth, 1994); Josephy L. Graves, "What We Know and What We Don't Know: Human Genetic Variation and the Social Construction of Race," Social Science Research Council, http://raceandgenomics.ssrc.org/Graves (retrieved June 12, 2006); Alan Goodman, "Two Questions about Race," Social Science Research Council, http://race andgenomics.ssrc.org/Goodman (retrieved June 12, 2006).
13. James Shreeve, "Terms of Estrangement," *Discover,* November 1994, p. 60; see also Paul Hoffman, "The Science of Race," *Discover,* November 1994, p. 4.
14. Jared Diamond, "Race Without Color," *Discover,* November 1994, p. 84.
15. Michael Banton and Jonathan Harwood, *The Race Concept* (New York: Praeger, 1975), pp. 13–50.
16. See Nathan Rutstein, *Healing Racism in America* (Springfield, MA: Whitcomb, 1993), pp. 1–51, 121–129.
17. Ashley Montagu, *Race, Science and Humanity* (Princeton, NJ: D. Van Nostrand, 1963).
18. Oliver C. Cox, *Caste, Class, and Race* (Garden City, NY: Doubleday, 1948), p. 402.
19. Van den Berghe, *Race and Racism,* p. 9.
20. Michael Banton, *Race Relations* (New York: Basic Books, 1967), p. 57; see also p. 58.
21. Charles Wagley and Marvin Harris, *Minorities in the New World* (New York: Columbia University Press, 1958), p. 7.
22. Thomas F. Pettigrew, *A Profile of the Negro American* (Princeton, NJ: D. Van Nostrand, 1964), p. 69.

23. Bill Zimmerman and Bob Herzog, "Golf: From Sheep to Tiger," *Newsday,* August 13, 1997, p. A34.

24. Denene Millner, "In Creating a Word to Describe His Racial Makeup, Golfer Tiger Woods Has Also Stirred Up a Round of Controversy Among Blacks," *New York Daily News,* June 8, 1997, p. 2.

25. Wire reports, *Newsday,* May 20, 1997, p. A57.

26. Joe Drape, "Woods Meets Zoeller for Lunch," *The New York Times,* May 21, 1997, p. B13.

27. Barbara Vobejda, "Hill Reassured on Racial Checkoff Plan for Census," *The Washington Post,* July 26, 1997, p. A4; Art Shriberg and Carol Lloyd, "Interracial Marriages Still Taboo," *Tampa Tribune,* June 5, 1997, p. 1.

28. Milton M. Gordon, *Assimilation in American Life* (New York: Oxford University Press, 1964), p. 27.

29. Werner Sollors, *The Invention of Ethnicity* (New York: Oxford University Press, 1989).

30. William M. Newman, *American Pluralism* (New York: Harper & Row, 1973), p. 19.

31. W. Lloyd Warner and Leo Srole, *The Social Systems of American Ethnic Groups* (New Haven, CT: Yale University Press, 1945), pp. 284–286.

32. Van den Berghe, *Race and Racism,* p. 10.

33. See Nathan Glazer, "Blacks and Ethnic Groups: The Difference, and the Political Difference It Makes," *Social Problems* 18 (Spring 1971): 447.

34. D. John Grove, *The Race vs. Ethnic Debate: A Cross-National Analysis of Two Theoretical Approaches* (Denver, CO: Center on International Race Relations, University of Denver, 1974); Robert Blauner, *Racial Oppression in America* (New York: Harper & Row, 1972).

35. Philomena Essed, *Understanding Everyday Racism* (Newbury Park, CA: Sage, 1991), p. 28.

36. Letter to authors from Edna Bonacich, October 1994.

37. St. Clair Drake, *Black Folk Here and There* (Los Angeles: UCLA Center for Afro-American Studies, 1987), vol. 1: xxiii. See also vol. 2 of this work.

38. Frank Snowden, *Color Prejudice* (Cambridge, MA: Harvard University Press, 1983), pp. 3–4, 107–108.

39. Max Weber, "Ethnic Groups," in *Theories of Society,* ed. Talcott Parsons et al. (Glencoe, IL: The Free Press, 1961), vol. 1, p. 306.

40. Joane Nagel, "Constructing Ethnicity: Creating and Recreating Ethnic Identity and Culture," *Social Problems* 43 (February 1994): 152.

41. Mary Waters, *Ethnic Options: Choosing Identities in America* (Berkeley, CA: University of California Press, 1990).

42. Mary Waters, "The Intersection of Race and Ethnicity," paper presented at the Annual Meeting of the American Sociological Association, Cincinnati, OH, 1991.

43. This term was suggested by Donald M. Young in *American Minority Peoples* (New York: Harper, 1932), p. xviii.

44. Louis Wirth, "The Problem of Minority Groups," in *The Science of Man in the World Crisis,* ed. Linton, p. 347.

45. Clifford Geertz, *The Interpretation of Cultures* (New York: Basic Books, 1973), p. 89.

46. Wendy Griswold, *Cultures and Societies in a Changing World* (Thousand Oaks, CA: Pine Forge Press, 1994), p. xiv.

47. Milton M. Gordon, *Assimilation in American Life* (New York: Oxford University Press, 1964), pp. 72–73.

48. See Bonnie Mitchell and Joe Feagin, "America's Racial-Ethnic Cultures: Opposition Within a Mythical Melting Pot," in *Toward the Multicultural University,* ed. Benjamin Bowser, Gale Auletta, and Terry Jones (Westport, CT: Praeger, 1995), pp. 65–86; Patricia Hill Collins, *Black Feminist Thought: Knowledge, Consciousness, and the Politics of Empowerment* (Boston: Unwin Hyman, 1990).

49. I draw here on the framing ideas of George Lakoff, David Snow, and Rob Benford. See George Lakoff, *Don't Think of an Elephant: Know Your Values and Frame the Debate* (White River Junction, VT: Chelsea Green, 2004). Also, generally, in this section we draw heavily on Joe R. Feagin, *Systemic Racism: A Theory of Oppression* (New York: Routledge, 2006), especially pp. 25–27.

50. L. S. Vygotsky, *Mind in Society: The Development of Higher Psychological Processes,* eds. M. Cole, V. John-Steiner, S. Scribner, and E. Souberman (Cambridge, MA: Harvard University Press, 1978). We draw here on Debra Van Ausdale and Joe R. Feagin, *The First R: How Children Learn Race and Racism* (Lanham, MD: Rowman & Littlefield, 2001), Chap. 1.

51. William G. Sumner, *Folkways* (New York: Mentor Books, 1960), pp. 27–28.

52. Robin M. Williams Jr., *Strangers Next Door* (Englewood Cliffs, NJ: Prentice-Hall, 1964), pp. 22–25.

53. Gordon Allport, *The Nature of Prejudice,* abridged ed. (New York: Doubleday Anchor Books, 1958), p. 7 (italics omitted); see also pp. 6–7.

54. Ibid., p. 10 (italics added).

55. Jane H. Hill, *The Everyday Language of White Racism* (New York: Wiley-Blackwell, 2008), pp. 134–157; Joe R. Feagin, *Racist America: Roots, Current Realities, and Future Reparations* (New York: Routledge, 2000), p. 119.

56. Rosina Lippi-Green, *English with an Accent* (New York: Routledge, 1997), p. 201.

57. Jane H. Hill, "Mock Spanish: A Site for the Indexical Reproduction of Racism in American English," unpublished research paper, University of Arizona, 1995.

58. Nilanjana Dasgupta, Debbie E. McGhee, Anthony G. Greenwald, and Mahzarin R. Banaji, "Automatic Preference for White Americans: Eliminating the Familiarity Explanation," *Journal of Experimental Social Psychology* 36 (2000): 316–328; Andrew Scott Baron and Mahzarin R. Banaji, "The Development of Implicit Attitudes: Evidence of Race Evaluations from Ages 6 and 10 and Adulthood," *Psychological Science* 17 (2006): 52–53. See summaries in Shankar Vedantam, "Many Americans Believe They Are Not Prejudiced. Now a New Test Provides Powerful Evidence That a Majority of Us Really Are," *The Washington Post,* January 23, 2005, p. W12; Associated Press, "Racism Studies Find Rational Part of Brain Can Override Prejudice," www.beliefnet.com/

story/156/story_15664_1.html (retrieved November 28, 2004); Siri Carpenter, "Buried Prejudice: The Bigot in Your Brain" *Scientific American,* May 2008, http://www.sciam.com/article .cfm?id=buried-prejudice-the-bigot-in-your-brain (retrieved June 1, 2008).

59. Patricia G. Devine, "Stereotypes and Prejudice: Their Automatic and Controlled Components," *Journal of Personality and Social Psychology* 56 (1) (1989): 5–18; Patricia G. Devine and A. Elliot, "Are Racial Stereotypes Really Fading? The Princeton Trilogy Revisited," *Personality and Social Psychology Bulletin* 21 (1995): 1139–1150; R. H. Fazio, J. R. Jackson, B. C. Dunton, and C. J. Williams, "Variability in Automatic Activation as an Unobtrusive Measure of Racial Attitudes: A Bona Fide Pipeline?" *Journal of Personality and Social Psychology* 69 (1995): 1013–1027; Joe Feagin, *The White Racial Frame: Centuries of Racial Framing and Counter-Framing* (New York: Routledge, 2010).

60. See Thomas F. Pettigrew, *Racially Separate or Together?* (New York: McGraw-Hill, 1971), pp. 134–135.

61. T. W. Adorno et al., *The Authoritarian Personality* (New York: Harper, 1950), pp. 248–279.

62. See Williams, *Strangers Next Door,* pp. 110–113; Pettigrew, *Racially Separate or Together?*, p. 131; Charles R. Lawrence, "The Id, the Ego, and Equal Protection," *Stanford Law Review* 39 (January 1987): 317–323; Gerald D. Jaynes and Robin Williams Jr., eds., *A Common Destiny: Blacks and American Society* (Washington, DC: National Academy Press, 1989).

63. R. A. Schermerhorn, *Comparative Ethnic Relations* (New York: Random House, 1970), p. 6.

64. Herbert Blumer, "Race Prejudice as a Sense of Group Position," *The Pacific Sociological Review* 1 (Spring 1959): 3–7.

65. Cox, *Caste, Class, and Race,* p. 400.

66. David M. Wellman, *Portraits of White Racism* (Cambridge: Cambridge University Press, 1977).

67. David O. Sears, "Symbolic Racism," in *Eliminating Racism,* ed. Phyllis A. Katz and Dalmas A. Taylor (New York: Plenum, 1988), pp. 55–58; John B. McConahay, "Modern Racism," in *Prejudice, Discrimination and Racism,* ed. John F. Dovidio and Samuel L. Gaertner (Orlando, FL: Academic, 1986); and Lawrence Bobo, "Group Conflict, Prejudice, and the Paradox of Contemporary Racial Attitudes," in *Eliminating Racism,* ed. Katz and Taylor, pp. 99–101.

68. Marylee Taylor and Thomas Pettigrew, "Prejudice," in *Encyclopedia of Sociology,* ed. Edgar F. Borgatta and Marie L. Borgatta (New York: Macmillan, 1992), p. 1538.

69. Eduardo Bonilla-Silva and Tyrone A. Forman, "'I Am Not a Racist but . . .': Mapping White College Students' Racial Ideology in the U.S.A.," *Discourse and Society* 11 (2000): 51–86; Maria Krysan, "Privacy and the Expression of White Racial Attitudes: A Comparison across Three Contexts," *Public Opinion Quarterly* 62 (Winter 1998): 506–544.

70. Nina Eliasoph, "'Everyday Racism' in a Culture of Political Avoidance: Civil Society, Speech and Taboo,"

Social Problems 46 (November 1999): 479–495; Karyn McKinney, *Being White: Stories of Race and Racism* (New York: Routledge, 2005), p. 205; Kristen Myers, *Racetalk: Racism Hiding in Plain Sight* (Lanham, MD: Rowman & Littlefield, 2005).

71. Leslie Houts Picca and Joe R. Feagin, *Two-Faced Racism: Whites in the Backstage and the Frontstage* (New York: Routledge, 2007), pp. 17–18.

72. Figure 1.1 is adapted from Joe R. Feagin, "Affirmative Action in an Era of Reaction," in *Consultations on the Affirmative Action Statement of the U.S. Commission on Civil Rights* (Washington, DC: U.S. Government Printing Office, 1982), pp. 46–48.

73. Allport, *The Nature of Prejudice,* p. 14.

74. Gunnar Myrdal, *An American Dilemma* (New York: McGraw-Hill, 1964 [1944], vol. 1, p. 52; Robert K. Merton, "Discrimination and the American Creed," in *Discrimination and National Welfare,* ed. Robert MacIver (New York: Harper, 1949), p. 103.

75. Faye Crosby, Stephanie Bromley, and Leonard Saxe, "Recent Unobtrusive Studies of Black and White Discrimination and Prejudice," *Psychological Bulletin* 87 (1980): 546–563; Jonathan W. Kunstman and E. Ashby Plant, "Racing to Help: Racial Bias in High Emergency Helping Situations," *Journal of Personality and Social Psychology* 95 (2008): 1499–1510. See also Joe R. Feagin and Douglas L. Eckberg, "Discrimination: Motivation, Action, Effects, and Context," in *Annual Review of Sociology,* ed. Alex Inkeles, Neil J. Smelser, and Ralph H. Turner (Palo Alto, CA: Annual Reviews, 1980), pp. 3–4.

76. Charles Hamilton and Stokely Carmichael, *Black Power* (New York: Random House/Vintage Books, 1967), p. 4. See also *Institutional Racism in America,* ed. Louis L. Knowles and Kenneth Prewitt (Englewood Cliffs, NJ: Prentice-Hall, 1969), p. 5.

77. Anthony Downs, *Racism in America and How to Combat It* (Washington, DC: U.S. Commission on Civil Rights, 1970), pp. 5, 7.

78. Thomas F. Pettigrew, "Racism and the Mental Health of White Americans: A Social Psychological View," in *Racism and Mental Health,* ed. Charles V. Willie, Bernard M. Kramer, and Bertram S. Brown (Pittsburgh: University of Pittsburgh Press, 1973), p. 271.

79. Essed, *Understanding Everyday Racism,* p. 39.

80. Joe R. Feagin, "Indirect Institutionalized Discrimination," *American Politics Quarterly* 5 (April 1977): 177–200.

81. Diana M. Pearce, "Black, White, and Many Shades of Gray: Real Estate Brokers and Their Racial Practices" (Ph.D. dissertation, University of Michigan, Ann Arbor, MI, 1976); Diana Kendall, "Square Pegs in Round Holes: Nontraditional Students in Medical Schools" (Ph.D. dissertation, University of Texas, Austin, TX, 1980).

82. Joe R. Feagin, "The Continuing Significance of Race: Antiblack Discrimination in Public Places," *American Sociological Review* 56 (February 1991): 101–116.

83. Allport, *The Nature of Prejudice,* pp. 14–15.

84. Nijole V. Benokraitis and Joe R. Feagin, *Modern Sexism,* 2nd ed. (Englewood Cliffs, NJ: Prentice-Hall, 1995), pp. 39–43.

85. Ed Jones, "What It's Like to Be a Black Manager," *Harvard Business Review* 64 (May/June 1986): 84–93; Thomas Pettigrew and Joanne Martin, "Shaping the Organizational Context for Black American Inclusion," *Journal of Social Issues* 43 (Spring 1987): 41–78. See also Joe R. Feagin and Melvin Sikes, *Living with Racism: The Black Middle Class Experience* (Boston: Beacon Press, 1994). Examples in law-enforcement departments are documented in Ken Bolton and Joe Feagin, *Black in Blue: Black Police Officers in White Departments* (New York: Routledge, 2004).

86. Benokraitis and Feagin, *Modern Sexism,* p. 135.

87. Quoted in Itabari Njeri, "Words to Live or Die by," *The Los Angeles Times Magazine,* May 31, 1992, p. 23. See also Joe R. Feagin, *Systemic Racism: A Theory of Oppression* (New York: Routledge, 2006).

88. Feagin and Sikes, *Living with Racism,* pp. 145–147. Other recent examples can be seen in Feagin, *Systemic Racism,* and in Bolton and Feagin, *Black in Blue.*

89. See Joe R. Feagin and Hernán Vera, *White Racism: The Basics* (New York: Routledge, 1995), Chap. 8; Feagin and Sikes, *Living with Racism.*

90. See Joe R. Feagin and Aaron Porter, "Affirmative Action and African Americans: Rhetoric and Practice," *Humboldt Journal of Social Relations* 21 (1995): 81–104; Nijole Benokraitis and Joe R. Feagin, *Affirmative Action and Equal Opportunity: Action, Inaction, Reaction* (Boulder, CO: Westview Press, 1978).

91. We draw in part here on Feagin and Porter, "Affirmative Action and African Americans: Rhetoric and Practice."

Chapter 2

1. *In re. Ah Yup,* 1 F. Cas. 223 (C.C.D.Cal. 1878).

2. Tamotsu Shibutani and Kian M. Kwan, *Ethnic Stratification* (New York: Macmillan, 1965), pp. 28–33; Donald L. Noel, "A Theory of the Origin of Ethnic Stratification," in *Majority and Minority,* ed. Norman R. Yetman and C. Hoy Steele (Boston: Allyn & Bacon, 1971), p. 32.

3. William M. Newman, *American Pluralism* (New York: Harper & Row, 1973), pp. 30–38.

4. Ernest A. T. Barth and Donald L. Noel, "Conceptual Frameworks for the Analysis of Race Relations: An Evaluation," *Social Forces* 50 (March 1972): 336.

5. Charles Tilly, *Migration to an American City* (Wilmington, DE: University of Delaware Agricultural Experiment Station, 1965).

6. Barth and Noel, "Conceptual Frameworks," pp. 337–339.

7. R. A. Schermerhorn, *Comparative Ethnic Relations* (New York: Random House, 1970), p. 98.

8. Ibid., p. 99.

9. Stanley Lieberson, "A Societal Theory of Racial and Ethnic Relations," *American Sociological Review* 29 (December 1961): 902–910.

10. Charles Hirschman, "America's Melting Pot Reconsidered," *Annual Review of Sociology* 9 (1983): 397–423.

11. Robert E. Park, *Race and Culture* (Glencoe, IL: The Free Press, 1950), p. 150 (italics added).

12. Robert E. Park and Ernest W. Burgess, *Introduction to the Science of Society* (Chicago: University of Chicago Press, 1924), p. 735.

13. Janice R. Hullum, "Robert E. Park's Theory of Race Relations" (Master's thesis, University of Texas, Austin, TX, 1973), pp. 81–88; see Park and Burgess, *Introduction to the Science of Society,* p. 760.

14. Milton M. Gordon, *Assimilation in American Life* (New York: Oxford University Press, 1964), pp. 72–73. See also Milton M. Gordon, *Human Nature, Class, and Ethnicity* (New York: Oxford University Press, 1978), pp. 67–89.

15. On the levels, see ibid., p. 71. On residential assimilation, see Doug Massey and Nancy Denton, "Suburbanization and Segregation in U.S. Metropolitan Areas," *American Journal of Sociology* 94 (1988): 592–626.

16. Silvia Pedraza, *Political and Economic Migrants in America: Cubans and Mexicans* (Austin: University of Texas Press, 1985), pp. 5–7; Richard Alba, *Ethnic Identity: The Transformation of White America* (New Haven, CT: Yale University Press, 1990), p. 311; Richard Alba and Victor Nee, "Rethinking Assimilation Theory for a New Era of Immigration," *International Migration Review* (1997): 829–837; J. Allen Williams and Suzanne T. Ortega, "Dimensions of Assimilation," *Social Science Quarterly* 71 (1990): 697–709.

17. Gordon, *Assimilation in American Life,* pp. 78–108.

18. See Will Herberg, *Protestant–Catholic–Jew,* rev. ed. (Garden City, NY: Doubleday/Anchor Books, 1960).

19. Milton M. Gordon, "Models of Pluralism: The New American Dilemma," *Annals of the American Academy of Political and Social Science* 454 (1981): 178–188.

20. Alba, *Ethnic Identity,* p. 3; Herbert J. Gans, "Symbolic Ethnicity," *Ethnic and Racial Studies* 2 (1979): 1–20; Stanley Lieberson and Mary Waters, "Ethnic Mixtures in the United States," *Sociology and Social Research* 70 (1985): 43–53; Mary Waters, *Ethnic Options: Choosing Identities in America* (Berkeley, CA: University of California Press, 1990).

21. Milton R. Konvitz, "Horace Meyer Kallen (1882–1974)," in *American Jewish Yearbook, 1974–1975* (New York: American Jewish Committee, 1974), pp. 65–67; Milton Gordon, *Assimilation in American Life,* pp. 142–159.

22. Nathan Glazer and Daniel P. Moynihan, *Beyond the Melting Pot* (Cambridge, MA: M.I.T. Press and Harvard University Press, 1963).

23. Andrew M. Greeley, *Ethnicity in the United States* (New York: Wiley, 1974), p. 293.

24. Ibid., pp. 295–309.

25. William L. Yancey, D. P. Ericksen, and R. N. Juliani, "Emergent Ethnicity: A Review and Reformulation,"

American Sociological Review 41 (June 1976): 391–393. See also Greeley, *Ethnicity in the United States*, pp. 290–317.

26. Gunnar Myrdal, *An American Dilemma* (New York: McGraw-Hill, 1964), vol. 2, p. 929.

27. Talcott Parsons, "Full Citizenship for the Negro American? A Sociological Problem," in *The Negro American*, ed. Talcott Parsons and Kenneth B. Clark (Boston: Houghton Mifflin, 1965–1966), p. 740.

28. Victor Nee and Richard Alba, "Assimilation as Rational Action," *Handbook of Rational Choice Social Research*, ed. Rafael Wittek, Tom Snijders, and Victor Nee (New York: Russell Sage Foundation, 2006), p. 8. See also Richard Alba, *Blurring the Color Line: The New Chance for a More Integrated America* (Cambridge, MA: Harvard University Press, 2009).

29. Mia Tuan, *Forever Foreigners or Honorary Whites?: The Asian American Experience Today* (New Brunswick, NJ: Rutgers University Press, 1998); Rosalind Chou and Joe R. Feagin, *The Myth of the Model Minority* (Boulder, CO: Paradigm, 2009).

30. Rubén G. Rumbaut, "Paradoxes (and Orthodoxies) of Assimilation," *Sociological Perspectives* 40 (1997): 483.

31. Steven J. Gold, "Transnationalism and Vocabularies of Motive in International Migration: The Case of Israelis in the United States," *Sociological Perspectives* 40 (1997): 410–411. We draw here too on Gina M. Pérez, *The Near Northwest Side Story: Migration, Displacement, and Puerto Rican Families* (Berkeley: University of California Press, 2004), pp. 12–14.

32. Gordon, *Human Nature, Class, and Ethnicity*, pp. 73–78; see also Clifford Geertz, "The Integrative Revolution," in *Old Societies and New States*, ed. Clifford Geertz (New York: The Free Press, 1963), p. 109.

33. Edna Bonacich, "Class Approaches to Ethnicity and Race," *Insurgent Sociologist* 10 (Fall 1980): 11.

34. Frederik Barth, "Introduction," in *Ethnic Groups and Boundaries: The Social Organization of Culture Difference* (Oslo: Universitets Forlaget, 1969), pp. 10–17.

35. Susan Olzak, "A Competition Model of Collective Action in American Cities," in *Competitive Ethnic Relations*, ed. Susan Olzak and Joane Nagel (Orlando, FL: Academic, 1986), pp. 17–46.

36. Susan Olzak, "Have the Causes of Ethnic Collective Action Changed over a Hundred Years?" (technical report, Department of Sociology, Cornell University, Ithaca, NY, 1987), p. 18; Susan Olzak, *The Dynamics of Ethnic Competition and Conflict* (Stanford, CA: Stanford University Press, 1992).

37. Susan Olzak, *The Global Dynamics of Racial and Ethnic Mobilization* (Palo Alto: Stanford University Press, 2006).

38. Joane Nagel, "Resource Competition Theories," *American Behavioral Scientist* 38 (January 1995): 442.

39. W. Lloyd Warner, "Introduction," in Allison Davis et al., *Deep South* (Chicago: University of Chicago Press, 1941), pp. 4–6; W. Lloyd Warner and Leo Srole, *The Social Systems of American Ethnic Groups* (New Haven, CT: Yale University Press, 1945), pp. 295–296.

40. Compare Robert Blauner, *Racial Oppression in America* (New York: Harper & Row, 1972), p. 7.

41. William E. B. Du Bois, "Is Man Free?" *Scientific Monthly* 66 (May 1948): 432–434. See also Manning Marable, *How Capitalism Underdeveloped Black America* (Boston: South End Press, 1983), pp. 3–15.

42. Oliver C. Cox, *Caste, Class, and Race* (Garden City, NY: Doubleday, 1948), p. 332.

43. Ronald Bailey and Guillermo Flores, "Internal Colonialism and Racial Minorities in the U.S.: An Overview," in *Structures of Dependency*, ed. Frank Bonilla and Robert Girling (Stanford, CA: privately published by a Stanford faculty–student seminar, 1973), pp. 151–153.

44. G. Balandier, "The Colonial Situation: A Theoretical Approach," in *Social Change*, ed. Immanuel Wallerstein (New York: John Wiley, 1966), p. 35.

45. Pablo Gonzalez-Casanova, "Internal Colonialism and National Development," in *Latin American Radicalism*, ed. Irving L. Horowitz et al. (New York: Random House, 1969), p. 130; Bailey and Flores, "Internal Colonialism," p. 156.

46. Bailey and Flores, "Internal Colonialism," p. 156.

47. Blauner, *Racial Oppression in America*, p. 55. Our analysis draws here on Blauner's discussion.

48. Ramón Grosfoguel and Chloe S. Georas, "Coloniality of Power and Racial Dynamics: Notes toward a Reinterpretation of Latino Caribbeans in New York City," *Identities: Global Studies in Culture and Power* 7 (2000): 85–125.

49. Guillermo B. Flores, "Race and Culture in the Internal Colony: Keeping the Chicano in His Place," in *Structures of Dependency*, ed. Bonilla and Girling, p. 192.

50. Bonnie Mitchell and Joe Feagin, "America's Racial-Ethnic Cultures: Opposition Within a Mythical Melting Pot," in *Toward the Multicultural University*, ed. Benjamin Bowser, Gale Auletta, and Terry Jones (Westport, CT: Praeger, 1995), pp. 65–86. See also Michael Hechter, Debra Friedman, and Malka Appelbaum, "A Theory of Ethnic Collective Action," *International Migration Review* 16 (1982): 412–434.

51. Carol B. Stack, "Sex Roles and Survival Strategies in an Urban Black Community," in *Woman, Culture and Society*, ed. Michelle Zimbalist Rosaldo and Louise Lamphere (Stanford, CA: Stanford University Press, 1974), p. 128; Ronald Angel and Marta Tienda, "Determinants of Extended Household Structure: Cultural Pattern or Economic Need?" *American Journal of Sociology* 87 (1981–1982): 1360–1383.

52. James C. Scott, *Domination and the Arts of Resistance* (New Haven, CT: Yale University Press, 1990); John Gaventa, *Power and Powerlessness* (Urbana, IL: University of Illinois Press, 1980).

53. Scott, *Domination and the Arts of Resistance*, p. 116.

54. Sterling Stuckey, *Slave Culture* (New York: Oxford University Press, 1987), pp. 27, 42–46.

55. W. E. B. Du Bois, "The Future of Africa," *Advocate of Peace* 81 (January 1919): 12, as quoted in Manning

Marable, *W. E. B. Du Bois: Black Radical Democrat* (Boston: Twayne, 1986), p. 100.

56. Marable, *W. E. B. Du Bois*, p. 101.

57. Molefi Kete Asante, *The Afrocentric Idea* (Philadelphia: Temple University Press, 1987); Molefi Kete Asante, *Afrocentricity* (Trenton, NJ: Africa World Press, 1988).

58. Marimba Ani, *Yurugu: An African-Centered Critique of European Cultural Thought and Behavior* (Trenton, NJ: Africa World Press, 1994), p. 567.

59. Ani, *Yurugu*, p. 570.

60. Mario Barrera, *Race and Class in the Southwest* (Notre Dame, IN: University of Notre Dame Press, 1979), pp. 214–217.

61. Bonacich, "Class Approaches to Ethnicity and Race," p. 14.

62. Cox, *Caste, Class, and Race*; Al Szymanski, *Class Structure* (New York: Praeger, 1983), pp. 420–440; Al Szymanski, "Racial Discrimination and White Gain," *American Sociological Review* 41 (1976): 403–414.

63. Stanley B. Greenberg, *Race and State in Capitalist Development* (New Haven, CT: Yale University Press, 1980), p. 349.

64. Barrera, *Race and Class in the Southwest*, pp. 201–203; Bonacich, "Class Approaches to Ethnicity and Race," p. 14.

65. W. E. B. Du Bois, *Black Reconstruction in America 1860–1880* (New York: Atheneum, 1992 [1935]), p. 700; Joe R. Feagin, *Racist America: Roots, Current Realities and Future Reparations* (New York: Routledge, 2000), pp. 30–31, 178.

66. Bonacich, "Class Approaches to Ethnicity and Race," pp. 14–15.

67. Edna Bonacich and John Modell, *The Economic Basis of Ethnic Solidarity* (Berkeley, CA: University of California Press, 1980), pp. 1–37.

68. Alejandro Portes and Robert D. Manning, "The Immigrant Enclave: Theory and Empirical Examples," in *Competitive Ethnic Relations*, ed. Olzak and Nagel, pp. 47–68.

69. The quote is from Rumbaut, "Paradoxes (and Orthodoxies) of Assimilation," p. 483; Alejandro Portes, "Segmented Assimilation Among New Immigrant Youth: A Conceptual Framework," in *California's Immigrant Children*, ed. Rubén Rumbaut and Wayne Cornelius (La Jolla, CA: Center for Mexican American Studies, University of California, 1995), pp. 71–76; Min Zhou, "Growing Up American: The Challenge Confronting Immigrant Children and Children of Immigrants," *Annual Review of Sociology* 23 (1997): 63–95; Philip Kasinitz, John Mollenkopf, Mary C. Waters, and Jennifer Holdaway, *Inheriting the City: The Children of Immigrants Come of Age* (Cambridge, MA: Harvard University Press, 2008); Rubén G. Rumbaut, "Paradise Shift: Immigration, Mobility and Inequality in Southern California," *Commission for Migration and Integration Research*, Working Paper 14, Austrian Academy of Sciences, 2008.

70. Amy Chua, *World on Fire: How Exporting Free Market Democracy Breeds Ethnic Hatred and Global Instability* (New York: Doubleday, 2003), p. 121. See also pp. 22–30 and 120–123.

71. Quoted in Michael Albert et al., *Liberating Theory* (Boston: South End Press, 1986), p. 35.

72. Philomena Essed, *Understanding Everyday Racism* (Newbury Park, CA: Sage, 1991), pp. 30–32.

73. Patricia Hill Collins, *Black Feminist Thought: Knowledge, Consciousness, and the Politics of Empowerment* (Boston: Unwin Hyman, 1990), pp. 40–48.

74. Denise A. Segura, "Chicanas and Triple Oppression in the Labor Force," in *Chicana Voices: Intersections of Class, Race and Gender*, ed. Teresa Cordova et al. (Austin, TX: Center for Mexican American Studies, 1986), p. 48.

75. Omi and Winant, *Racial Formation in the United States*, pp. 75–76.

76. William E. B. Du Bois, *The World and Africa* (New York: International Publishers, 1965 [1946]), p. 37; for a more detailed development of these ideas, see Feagin, *Racist America*.

77. Cox, *Caste, Class, and Race*, p. 578.

78. Ibid., p. 332.

79. Andrew Hacker, *Two Nations: Black and White, Separate, Hostile, Unequal* (New York: Scribner's, 1992).

80. Trina Williams, "The Homestead Act—Our Earliest National Asset Policy," paper presented at the Center for Social Development's symposium, Inclusion in Asset Building, St. Louis, MO, September 21–23, 2000. See also Feagin, *Racist America*, Chapter 6.

81. Ian Craib, *Modern Social Theory: From Parsons to Habermas* (New York: St. Martin's, 1984), p. 53.

82. Iris Young, *Justice and the Politics of Difference* (Princeton, NJ: Princeton University Press, 1990), p. 52.

83. Tomas Almaguer, *Racial Fault Lines* (Berkeley, CA: University of California Press, 1994), p. 7.

84. Aldon Morris, *The Origins of the Civil Rights Movement* (New York: The Free Press, 1984).

85. See, for example, Juan F. Perea, "The Black/White Binary Paradigm of Race: The 'Normal Science' of American Racial Thought," *California Law Review* 85 (October 1997): 1219–1221.

86. See, for example, Lewis R. Gordon, *Her Majesty's Other Children: Sketches of Racism from a Neocolonial Age* (Lanham, MD: Rowman & Littlefield, 1997), pp. 5, 53. This section draws on Feagin, *Racist America*, Chapter 7.

87. Gary Y. Okihiro, "Is Yellow Black or White?" in *Asian Americans: Experiences and Perspectives*, ed. Timothy P. Fong and Larry H. Shinagawa (Upper Saddle River, NJ: Prentice-Hall, 2000), p. 75.

Part II

1. Edna Bonacich, "United States Capitalist Development: A Background to Asian Immigration," in *Labor Immigration Under Capitalism*, ed. Lucie Cheng and Edna

Bonacich (Berkeley, CA: University of California Press, 1984), p. 82.

2. Herbert Aptheker, lectures on American history, University of Minnesota, 1984.

3. Lucie Cheng and Edna Bonacich, "Imperialism, Distorted Development, and Asian Emigration to the United States," in *Labor Immigration Under Capitalism*, ed. Cheng and Bonacich, pp. 214–217.

4. Bonacich, "United States Capitalist Development," pp. 99–110.

5. Coretta Scott King, "It's a Bit Late to Protest Preferential Treatment," *Detroit Free Press*, December 13, 1985, p. 9A.

6. Stephen Steinberg, *The Ethnic Myth* (New York: Atheneum, 1981), p. 36.

7. Bonacich, "United States Capitalist Development," pp. 112–115.

8. Irving Kristol, "The Negro Today Is Like the Immigrant of Yesterday," *The New York Times Magazine*, September 11, 1966, pp. 50–51, 124–142.

9. Theodore Hershberg et al., "A Tale of Three Cities: Blacks, Immigrants, and Opportunity in Philadelphia: 1850–1880, 1930, 1970," in *Philadelphia*, ed. Theodore Hershberg (New York: Oxford University Press, 1981), pp. 462–464.

10. William Yancey, E. P. Ericksen, and R. N. Juliani, "Emergent Ethnicity," *American Sociological Review* 41 (June 1976): 393.

11. Stanley Lieberson, *A Piece of the Pie* (Berkeley, CA: University of California Press, 1980), pp. 377–383.

12. Robert Blauner, *Racial Oppression in America* (New York: Harper & Row, 1972), p. 62.

13. H. Sitkoff, *A New Deal for Blacks* (New York: Oxford University Press, 1978), pp. 37–38; C. G. Wye, "The New Deal and the Negro Community," *Journal of American History* 59 (December 1972): 634.

14. Charles B. Keeley, "Population and Immigration Policy: State and Federal Roles," in *Mexican American and Central American Population Issues and U.S. Policy*, ed. Frank D. Bean, Jurgen Schmandt, and Sidney Weintraub (Austin, TX: Center for Mexican American Studies, 1988).

Chapter 3

1. Cleveland Amory, *The Proper Bostonians* (New York: Dutton, 1947), p. 11.

2. See Table 3.2. See also U.S. Census Bureau, *Census 2000 Supplementary Survey*. Table PCT 024. Ancestry-First Reported, http://factfinder.census.gov/home; U.S. Census Bureau, *Census 2000 Supplementary Survey*. Table PCT 025. Ancestry-Second Reported, http://factfinder.census.gov/home (retrieved January 28, 2002); U.S. Bureau of the Census, *1990 Census of Population: Social and Economic Characteristics: United States*, CP-2-1 (Washington, DC: U.S. Government Printing Office, 1993), p. 166.

3. Carl Wittke, "Preface to the Revised Edition," in *We Who Built America*, rev. ed. (Cleveland, OH: Case Western Reserve University Press, 1967).

4. Milton M. Gordon, *Assimilation in American Life* (New York: Oxford University Press, 1964), p. 72.

5. Rowland T. Berthoff, *British Immigrants in Industrial America* (Chicago: University of Chicago Press, 1953), p. 1.

6. John Jay, Alexander Hamilton, and James Madison, *The Federalist* (London: Penguin Classics, 1987 [1788]), p. 91.

7. Wilbur S. Shepperson, *British Emigration to North America* (Oxford: Basil Blackwell, 1957), p. 3.

8. Conrad Taeuber and Irene B. Taeuber, "Immigration to the United States," in *Population and Society*, ed. Charles B. Nam (Boston: Houghton Mifflin, 1968), p. 316.

9. Immigration and Naturalization Service, *1975 Annual Report* (Washington, DC, 1975), pp. 62–64.

10. Alice Marriott and Carol K. Rachlin, *American Epic* (New York: Mentor, 1969), p. 105.

11. Samuel Eliot Morison, *The Oxford History of the American People* (New York: Oxford University Press, 1965), pp. 48–49.

12. Klaus E. Knorr, *British Colonial Theories, 1570–1850* (Toronto: University of Toronto Press, 1944), p. 126.

13. Marriott and Rachlin, *American Epic*, pp. 104–106; Winthrop D. Jordan, *White over Black* (Baltimore, MD: Penguin, 1969), p. 89.

14. This paragraph and the following paragraph draw on Morison, *Oxford History of the American People*, pp. 50–154, and Maldwyn A. Jones, *American Immigration* (Chicago: University of Chicago Press, 1960), pp. 10–38.

15. Morison, *Oxford History of the American People*, p. 74.

16. David Hackett Fischer, *Albion's Seed: Four British Folkways in America* (New York: Oxford University Press, 1989), pp. 6, 13–205, 785–786.

17. Ibid., pp. 207–418.

18. Ibid., pp. 419–603.

19. Ibid., pp. 605–782.

20. Proceedings of the American Historical Association, vol. 1 of *Annual Report of the American Historical Association* (Washington, DC: American Historical Association, 1932), p. 124.

21. Jones, *American Immigration*, pp. 34–35.

22. Berthoff, *British Immigrants in Industrial America*, pp. vii, 28–29; Charlotte Erickson, "English," in *Harvard Encyclopedia of American Ethnic Groups*, ed. Stephan Thernstrom (Cambridge, MA: Harvard University Press, 1980), pp. 324–332.

23. Shepperson, *British Emigration to North America*, pp. 27–32, 84; Berthoff, *British Immigrants in Industrial America*, pp. 46–87, 122; Charlotte Erickson, "Agrarian Myths of English Immigrants," in *In the Trek of the Immigrants*, ed. O. Fritiof Ander (Rock Island, IL: Augustana Library Publications, 1964), pp. 59–64.

24. Berthoff, *British Immigrants in Industrial America*, p. 125.

25. Stanley Lieberson and Mary C. Waters, *From Many Strands* (New York: Russell Sage, 1988), pp. 40–41.

26. In the next few paragraphs we summarize material from several sources, especially Charles H. Anderson, *White Protestant Americans* (Englewood Cliffs, NJ: Prentice-Hall, 1970), pp. 28–71, 79–87; Ian C. Graham, *Colonists from Scotland* (Ithaca, NY: Cornell University Press, 1956); Albert B. Faust, *The German Element in the United States* (New York: Steuben Society, 1927); Wittke, *We Who Built America*, passim.

27. Ronald Takaki, *Iron Cages* (New York: Oxford University Press, 1990), pp. 12–14.

28. Thomas Jefferson, *Notes on the State of Virginia,* ed. Frank Shuffelton (New York: Penguin, 1999 [1785]), pp. 144–166; We draw on Joe Feagin, *Systemic Racism: A Theory of Oppression* (New York: Routledge, 2006), especially Chapter 3.

29. "The Letters of Thomas Jefferson: 1743–1826; Emancipation and the Younger Generation," http://odur.let .rug.nl/~usa/P/tj3/writings/brf/jefl232.htm (retrieved May 10, 2004).

30. William E. B. Du Bois, *Black Reconstruction in America: An Essay toward a History of the Part Which Black Folk Played in the Attempt to Reconstruct Democracy in America, 1860–1880* (New York: Atheneum, [1935] 1992). We draw here on Joe R. Feagin and Aaron Porter, "White Racism: Bibliographic Essay," *Choice* 33 (February 1996): 903–914.

31. Theodore W. Allen, *The Invention of the White Race* (New York: Verso, 1994), pp. 21, 184; David Roediger, *Towards the Abolition of Whiteness: Essays on Race, Politics, and Working Class History* (New York: Verso, 1994).

32. John Higham, *Strangers in the Land* (New York: Atheneum, 1963), p. 4.

33. Quotes are from Jordan, *White over Black*, pp. 44, 86. See also Henry P. Fairchild, *Immigration* (New York: Macmillan, 1920), p. 47; Jones, *American Immigration*, p. 44.

34. Jones, *American Immigration*, pp. 41–46.

35. Fairchild, *Immigration*, pp. 57–58.

36. Michael Kammen, *People of Paradox* (New York: Knopf, 1972), p. 66.

37. Quoted in Nancy F. Conklin and Margaret A. Lourie, *A Host of Tongues* (New York: The Free Press, 1983), p. 69.

38. Higham, *Strangers in the Land*, p. 6; Marcus L. Hansen, *The Immigrant in American History* (New York: Harper Torchbooks, 1964), pp. 111–136; Wittke, *We Who Built America*, p. 505.

39. Quoted in Richard Hofstadter, *Social Darwinism in American Thought*, rev. ed. (Boston: Beacon Press, 1955), pp. 171–172.

40. Higham, *Strangers in the Land*, p. 33.

41. Hofstadter, *Social Darwinism in American Thought*, pp. 178–179; Lewis H. Carlson and George A. Colburn, *In Their Place* (New York: John Wiley, 1972), pp. 305–308. Carlson and Colburn provide excerpts from the writings of Strong.

42. Higham, *Strangers in the Land*, pp. 96–152.

43. E. Digby Baltzell, *The Protestant Establishment* (New York: Random House/Vintage Books, 1966), pp. 96–98; Higham, *Strangers in the Land*, pp. 148–157.

44. Richard Alba, *Ethnic Identity: The Transformation of White America* (New Haven, CT: Yale University Press, 1990), p. 365.

45. Sheldon Hanft, "English Americans," www.every culture.com/multi/Du-Ha/English-Americans.html (retrieved June 15, 2006).

46. Jones, *American Immigration,* pp. 36–38.

47. The quote is from W. Lloyd Warner and Leo Srole, *The Social Systems of American Ethnic Groups* (New Haven, CT: Yale University Press, 1945), p. 287; Juan F. Perea, "Demography and Distrust: An Essay on American Languages, Cultural Pluralism and Official English," *Minnesota Law Review* 77 (1992): 269.

48. Susanna McBee, "A War over Words," *U.S. News & World Report,* October 6, 1986, p. 64; U.S. Census Bureau, "Facts for Features," Press Release, July 16, 2007.

49. "National English Campaign Supports English as the Official Language of the United States," *Business Wire,* February 11, 1997; U.S. English, Inc., "Official English," http://www.us-english.org/view/8 (retrieved September 17, 2009).

50. "English for the Children—California English Campaign Endorses Initiative," *Business Wire,* August 28, 1997.

51. Clarence Petersen, "Tribune Books," *Chicago Tribune,* October 31, 1993, p. C8.

52. Bill Piatt, *Only English? Law and Language Policy in the United States* (Albuquerque: University of New Mexico Press, 1990), p. 159.

53. Amado Padilla et al., "The English-Only Movement," *American Psychologist* 46 (February 1991): 120–130; National Education Association, *Official English/English Only* (Washington, DC: National Education Association, 1988), pp. 5–7.

54. Perea, "Demography and Distrust."

55. Pew Hispanic Center, "English Usage among Hispanics in the United States," 2007, http://pewhispanic.org/ reports/report.php?ReportID=82 (retrieved September 17, 2009). See also Daniel Gonzalez, "Immigrants Jam English Classes," *The Arizona Republic,* July 26, 2005; Carl J. Veltman, *Language Shift in the United States* (Berlin: Mouton, 1983).

56. Fischer, *Albion's Seed*, pp. 795–797.

57. Edwin S. Gaustad, *Historical Atlas of Religion in America* (New York: Harper & Row, 1962), pp. 1–20.

58. Will Herberg, *Protestant–Catholic–Jew*, rev. ed. (Garden City, NY: Doubleday/Anchor, 1960), p. 82.

59. Marshall Sklare, *Conservative Judaism* (Glencoe, IL: The Free Press, 1955), pp. 31–117.

60. Takaki, *Iron Cages*, p. 7.

61. Max Weber, *The Protestant Ethic and the Spirit of Capitalism,* trans. Talcott Parsons (New York: Scribner's, 1958), p. 17; see also p. 50.

62. David Ewen, *History of Popular Music* (New York: Barnes & Noble, 1961), pp. 1–10.

63. See Samuel Bowles and Herbert Gintis, *Schooling in Capitalist America* (New York: Basic Books, 1976).

64. Morison, *Oxford History of the American People*, p. 55.

65. Samuel P. Huntington, "Political Modernization: America versus Europe," *World Politics* 18 (April 1966): 147–148.

66. Jack P. Greene, *The Quest for Power* (Chapel Hill: University of North Carolina Press, 1963), pp. 1ff.

67. Roscoe Pound, *The Formative Era of American Law* (Boston: Little, Brown, 1938), pp. 7–8.

68. Ibid., p. 12.

69. Elizabeth G. Brown and William W. Blume, *British Statutes in American Law, 1776–1836* (Ann Arbor: University of Michigan Law School, 1964), p. 44. See also Lawrence M. Friedman, *A History of American Law* (New York: Simon & Schuster, 1973), pp. 96–100.

70. Pound, *The Formative Era of American Law*, p. 81.

71. Maurice R. Davie, *World Immigration* (New York: Macmillan, 1939), p. 36.

72. Henry J. Ford, *The Scotch-Irish in America* (Princeton, NJ: Princeton University Press, 1915), p. 491.

73. Charles A. Beard, *An Economic Interpretation of the Constitution of the United States* (New York: Macmillan, 1947), p. 17.

74. See Joseph N. Kane, *Facts about the Presidents*, 3rd ed. (New York: Wilson, 1974).

75. John R. Schmidhauser, "The Justices of the Supreme Court: A Collective Portrait," *Midwest Journal of Political Science* 3 (February 1959): 1–57.

76. William Miller, "American Historians and the Business Elite," *Journal of Economic History* 9 (November 1949): 202–203.

77. On Protestant presidents before Kennedy, see ibid., p. 21.

78. Robert A. Dahl, *Who Governs?* (New Haven, CT: Yale University Press, 1961), pp. 15–16.

79. Matthew Holden, Jr., "Ethnic Accommodation in a Historical Case," *Comparative Studies in Society and History* 8 (January 1966): 172.

80. Rowland Berthoff, *An Unsettled People* (New York: Harper & Row, 1971), p. 13; Oliver C. Cox, *Caste, Class, and Race* (Garden City, NY: Doubleday, 1948), pp. 338–339; Barrington Moore Jr., *Social Origins of Dictatorship and Democracy* (Boston: Beacon Press, 1966), pp. 112–113.

81. Frank Thistlewaite, *The Anglo-American Connection in the Early Nineteenth Century* (Philadelphia: University of Pennsylvania Press, 1959), pp. 5–11.

82. Jesse Lemisch, "The American Revolution Seen from the Bottom Up," in *Toward a New Past*, ed. Barton J. Bernstein (New York: Random House, 1968), p. 8; J. O. Lindsay, ed., *The Old Regime*, vol. 7 of *The New Cambridge Modern History* (Cambridge: Cambridge University Press, 1957), pp. 509–511.

83. Morison, *Oxford History of the American People*, p. 89.

84. Abbot E. Smith, *Colonists in Bondage* (Chapel Hill: University of North Carolina Press, 1947), pp. 25, 336; Jordan, *White over Black*, p. 47; Howard Zinn, *The Politics of History* (Boston: Beacon Press, 1970), p. 68.

85. Lee Soltow, *Men and Wealth in the United States, 1850–1870* (New Haven, CT: Yale University Press, 1975), p. 149.

86. Matthew Josephson, *The Robber Barons* (New York: Harcourt, Brace & World, 1934), pp. 32–35, 315–452.

87. John N. Ingham, *The Iron Barons* (Westport, CT: Greenwood, 1978), pp. 14–16.

88. Miller, "American Historians and the Business Elite," p. 202.

89. Elin L. Anderson, *We Americans* (Cambridge, MA: Harvard University Press, 1937), p. 137; see also pp. 21–247.

90. E. Digby Baltzell, *An American Business Aristocracy* (New York: Collier, 1962), p. 267.

91. Baltzell, *The Protestant Establishment*, p. 321.

92. Thomas R. Dye, *Who's Running America?* (Englewood Cliffs, NJ: Prentice-Hall, 1976), pp. 3–8, 150–153. See also Thomas R. Dye, *Who's Running America? The Carter Years* (Englewood Cliffs, NJ: Prentice-Hall, 1979), pp. 171–177.

93. Thomas R. Dye, letter to author, April 11, 1977.

94. Julia Reed, "The New American Establishment," *U.S. News & World Report*, February 8, 1988, p. 38.

95. Richard D. Alba and Gwen Moore, "Ethnicity in the American Elite," *American Sociological Review* 47 (June 1982): 373–383; see also Dye, *Who's Running America?* pp. 170–173.

96. U.S. Census Bureau, "2008 American Community Survey," http://factfinder.census.gov/servlet/IPCharIterationServlet?_ts=273424629497 (retrieved October 16, 2009); see also U.S. Census Bureau, *Census 2000 Demographic Profile Highlights: Selected Population Group: English,* http://factfinder.census.gov (retrieved June 16, 2006); U.S. Bureau of the Census, *990 Census of Population: Ancestry of the Population of the United States*, CP-3-2 (Washington, DC: U.S. Government Printing Office, 1993), p. 33. According to the U.S. Census Bureau, the American Community Survey is a large survey by the Census Bureau that involves mailing questionnaires to a random "sample of addresses to obtain information about households—that is, about each person and the housing unit itself. The survey produces annual and multi-year estimates of population and housing characteristics." Ancestry is determined by survey respondents' replies to a question about their ancestral or ethnic background. The first two choices are coded, and most in tabulations are those who list English first. Thus, English Americans are those who indicate English ancestry as their first or second choice.

97. Lieberson and Waters, *From Many Strands*, p. 173.

98. Alba, *Ethnic Identity*, pp. 49–82.

99. Joan Marsh Schlesinger, "Mourning Families of English Heritage," in *Living Beyond Loss: Death in the Family*, ed. Froma Walsh and Monica McGoldrick (New York: W. W. Norton, 2004), pp. 122–124.

100. The quotes are from Fischer, *Albion's Seed*, pp. 199–205, 412, 597, 777–782, 897–898.

101. Ibid., pp. 887–897, quotation on p. 896.

102. Lewis M. Killian, *White Southerners* (New York: Random House, 1970), p. 16.

103. Peter Schrag, *The Decline of the WASP* (New York: Simon & Schuster, 1971), p. 164.

Chapter 4

1. John Higham, *Strangers in the Land: Patterns of American Nativism 1860–1925,* rev. ed. (New York: Atheneum, 1975), p. 180.

2. U.S. Department of Justice, Immigration and Naturalization Service, *Annual Report* (Washington, DC: U.S. Government Printing Office, 1973), pp. 53–55. The figures for the period between 1820 and 1867 represent "alien passengers arrived"; for later periods they represent immigrants arrived or admitted.

3. Cited in William Peterson, *Population,* 2nd ed. (New York: Macmillan, 1969), p. 260.

4. U.S. Bureau of the Census, *Statistical Abstract of the United States 1991* (Washington, DC: U.S. Government Printing Office, 1991), p. 10; U.S. Bureau of the Census, *Statistical Abstract of the United States 1994* (Washington, DC: U.S. Government Printing Office, 1994), p. 11.

5. See Table 4.1. See also U.S. Census Bureau, *Census 2000 Demographic Profile Highlights: Selected Population Group: Irish,* http://factfinder.census.gov (retrieved June 16, 2006); U.S. Bureau of the Census, *1990 Census of Population: Ancestry of the Population in the United States,* CP-3-2 (Washington, DC: U.S. Government Printing Office, 1993), pp. 50, 65; U.S. Bureau of the Census, *1990 Census of Population: Social and Economic Characteristics: United States,* CP-2-1 (Washington, DC: U.S. Government Printing Office, 1993), p. 166; U.S. Census Bureau, *Census 2000 Supplementary Survey.* Table PCT 024.

6. Philip H. Bagenal, *The American Irish* (London: Kegan Paul, Trench, 1882), pp. 4–5; Henry Jones Ford, *The Scotch-Irish in America* (Princeton, NJ: Princeton University Press, 1915), pp. 125–128, 183–186; James G. Leyburn, *The Scotch-Irish* (Chapel Hill: University of North Carolina Press, 1962), pp. 160ff.

7. Michael J. O'Brien, *A Hidden Phase of American History* (New York: Devin-Adair, 1919), p. 249; we also draw on pp. 267, 287–288.

8. Thomas D'Arcy McGee, *A History of Irish Settlers in North America* (Boston: Office of American Celt, 1851), pp. 25–34; Leyburn, *The Scotch-Irish,* pp. 331–332.

9. Quoted in Ford, *The Scotch-Irish in America,* pp. 520–521.

10. Winthrop D. Jordan, *White over Black* (Baltimore, MD: Penguin, 1969), pp. 86–88; McGee, *A History of Irish Settlers in North America,* p. 79.

11. Arnold Shrier, *Ireland and the American Emigration, 1850–1900* (Minneapolis: University of Minnesota Press, 1958), pp. 13–16; T. A. Jackson, *Ireland Her Own* (New York: International Publishers, 1970), pp. 243–245; Kerby A. Miller, *Emigrants and Exiles* (New York: Oxford University Press, 1985), p. 556.

12. Carl Wittke, *The Irish in America* (Baton Rouge: Louisiana State University Press, 1956), pp. 24–27; Theodore Hershberg et al., "A Tale of Three Cities," in *Majority and Minority,* 3rd ed., ed. Norman Y. Yetman and C. Hoy Steele (Boston: Allyn & Bacon, 1982), pp. 184–185; Bagenal, *The American Irish,* p. 72; Wittke, *The Irish in America,* p. 46.

13. Ronald Takaki, *A Different Mirror* (Boston: Little, Brown, 1993), pp. 154–160; Hasia R. Diner, *Erin's Daughters in America* (Baltimore, MD: Johns Hopkins University Press, 1983), pp. xiii–xv.

14. Dale T. Knobel, *Paddy and the Republic* (Middletown, CT: Wesleyan University Press, 1986), pp. 24–27; Bill Bryson, *The Mother Tongue: English and How It Got That Way* (New York: William Morrow, 1990).

15. Lewis P. Curtis Jr., *Apes and Angels: The Irish in Victorian Caricature* (Washington, DC: Smithsonian Institution Press, 1971), p. 103. See also p. 59.

16. Andrew M. Greeley, *That Most Distressful Nation* (Chicago: Quadrangle, 1972), pp. 119–120.

17. Leonard Gordon, "Racial and Ethnic Stereotypes of American College Students over a Half Century," paper presented at meetings of the Society for the Study of Social Problems, Washington, DC, August 1985, pp. 14–15.

18. American Institute of Public Opinion, Roper Center, 1982; Richard D. Alba, *Ethnic Identity: The Transformation of White America* (New Haven, CT: Yale University Press, 1990), p. 156.

19. Leonard Dinnerstein and Frederic C. Jaher, "Introduction," in *The Aliens,* ed. Leonard Dinnerstein and Frederic C. Jaher (New York: Appleton-Century-Crofts, 1970), p. 4.

20. Leyburn, *The Scotch-Irish,* pp. 234, 301–316; Ford, *The Scotch-Irish in America,* pp. 291–324; Leyburn, *The Scotch-Irish,* pp. 225–230.

21. Dennis Clark, *The Irish in Philadelphia* (Philadelphia: Temple University Press, 1973), p. 21; see also Wittke, *The Irish in America,* p. 120.

22. Wayne G. Broehl Jr., *The Molly Maguires* (Cambridge, MA: Harvard University Press, 1964), pp. 198–199; Anthony Bimba, *The Molly Maguires* (New York: International Publishers, 1932), pp. 70–73.

23. Takaki, *A Different Mirror,* pp. 150–152; Oscar Handlin, *Boston's Immigrants, 1790–1865* (Cambridge, MA: Harvard University Press, 1941), p. 137; James McCague, *The Second Rebellion* (New York: Dial Press, 1968).

24. Theodore W. Allen, *The Invention of the White Race* (London: Verso, 1994), p. 21; David Roediger, *Towards the Abolition of Whiteness* (London: Verso, 1994), p. 12.

25. Allen, *The Invention of the White Race,* pp. 21–50; Joe R. Feagin and Hernán Vera, *White Racism: The Basics* (New York: Routledge, 1995), pp. 1–18.

26. Quote is from Roediger, *Towards the Abolition of Whiteness,* p. 140. On Ali, see "Ali has Irish Ancestry," *BBB Sport,* February 9, 2002, http://news.bbc.co.uk/sport2/hi/boxing/1810535.stm (retrieved October 13, 2009).

27. Ford, *The Scotch-Irish in America*, pp. 246, 462, 491; McGee, *A History of Irish Settlers in North America*, p. 71; Shane Leslie, *The Irish Issue in Its American Aspect* (New York: Scribner's, 1919), p. 8.

28. Wittke, *The Irish in America*, p. 104; Edward M. Levine, *The Irish and Irish Politicians* (Notre Dame, IN: University of Notre Dame Press, 1966), pp. 6–9.

29. Leo Hershkowitz, *Tweed's New York* (New York: Doubleday/Anchor Books, 1987), pp. xiii–xx.

30. Nathan Glazer and Daniel P. Moynihan, *Beyond the Melting Pot* (Cambridge, MA: MIT Press and Harvard University Press, 1963), pp. 218–262; Robert A. Dahl, *Who Governs?* (New Haven, CT: Yale University Press, 1963), p. 41; Mike Royko, *Boss: Richard J. Daley of Chicago* (New York: Dutton, 1971); Sam Roberts, "In Search of Irish, or the Greening of the Suburbs," *The New York Times*, March 17, 1988, p. B1; Alba, *Ethnic Identity*, p. 156.

31. Greeley, *That Most Distressful Nation*, pp. 206–209; Dennis J. Clark, "The Philadelphia Irish," in *The Peoples of Philadelphia*, ed. Allen F. Davis and Mark H. Haller (Philadelphia: Temple University Press, 1973), p. 145.

32. Terry N. Clark, "The Irish Ethnic and the Spirit of Patronage," *Ethnicity* 2 (1975): 305–359; Mark R. Levy and Michael S. Kramer, *The Ethnic Factor* (New York: Simon & Schuster, 1972), pp. 130–135; Andrew M. Greeley, *The Irish Americans* (New York: Harper & Row, 1981), pp. 168–169; George J. Marlin, *The American Catholic Voter: Two-Hundred Years of Public Impact* (New York: St. Augustine's Press, 2004), pp. 300–340.

33. William Miller, "American Historians and the Business Elite," *Journal of Economic History* 9 (November 1949): 202–203.

34. John Aloysius Farrell, "Clinton Staff Alters Blair Brown's Status," *Boston Globe*, March 19, 1994, p. 3.

35. Linda Greenhouse, "Supreme Court Ruling Clears Way for Deportation of an I.R.A. Man," *The New York Times*, January 16, 1992, p. A1; "O'Connor Seeks Aid for I.R.A. Fugitive," *The New York Times*, February 1, 1992, sec. 1, p. 25; Cal McCrystal, "Notebook: A Tug-of-War for America's Irish Soul," *Independent*, February 2, 1992, p. 23.

36. Steve Fainaru, "Adams, in New York Limelight, Asks for U.S. Help on Peace," *Boston Globe*, February 2, 1994, p. 1; Gerald Renner, "Sinn Fein Leader Urges Peace Plan Support," *Hartford Courant*, September 26, 1994, p. A1; Kevin Cullen, "Loyalist Extremists Call Ulster Cease-Fire," *Boston Globe*, October 14, 1994, p. 1; "Northern Ireland Peace Talks," National Public Radio, "Weekend Edition," September 21, 1997.

37. William V. Shannon, *The American Irish* (New York: Macmillan, 1963), pp. 151–181.

38. Glazer and Moynihan, *Beyond the Melting Pot*, p. 287; Shannon, *The American Irish*, pp. 395–411; Levy and Kramer, *The Ethnic Factor*, pp. 126–127.

39. *Reporting for the Russell Sage Foundation*, no. 6 (May 1985): 6.

40. Stephen Steinberg, *The Ethnic Myth* (New York: Atheneum, 1981), pp. 160–164.

41. Handlin, *Boston's Immigrants*, p. 67.

42. Greeley, *That Most Distressful Nation*, p. 120; Clark, "The Philadelphia Irish," p. 143; Wittke, *The Irish in America*, pp. 217–227.

43. Lloyd Warner and Leo Srole, *The Social Systems of American Ethnic Groups* (New Haven, CT: Yale University Press, 1945), pp. 93–95.

44. Ronald P. Formisano, *Boston Against Busing: Race, Class, and Ethnicity in the 1960s and 1970s* (Chapel Hill: University of North Carolina Press, 1991), p. 15; Harold J. Abramson, *Ethnic Diversity in Catholic America* (New York: Wiley, 1973), pp. 41–44; Levy and Kramer, *The Ethnic Factor*, p. 125; see also U.S. Bureau of the Census, "2008 American Community Survey," http://factfinder.census.gov/servlet/ IPCharIterationServlet?_ts=273424629497 (retrieved October 16, 2009). See also *1990 Census of Population: Ancestry of the Population in the United States*, pp. 353, 371, 455, 473; U.S. Bureau of the Census, *1990 Census of Population: Social and Economic Characteristics: United States*, pp. 45, 48, 49.

45. Roberts, "In Search of Irish," p. B1; Tim Unsworthy, "The Irish: Faith Persuasive as Metamucil in an Old Priest's Diet," *National Catholic Reporter*, March 15, 1996, p. 16.

46. John T. Ellis, *American Catholicism* (Garden City, NY: Doubleday/Image Books, 1965), p. 62; Clark, *The Irish in Philadelphia*, p. 123.

47. David O. Moberg, *The Church as a Social Institution* (Englewood Cliffs, NJ: Prentice-Hall, 1962), p. 193; Andrew M. Greeley, *Ethnicity, Denomination and Inequality* (Beverly Hills, CA: Sage, 1976), pp. 45–53.

48. U.S. Census Bureau, *2008 American Community Survey*, http://factfinder.census.gov/servlet/IPCharIterationServlet?_ts=273424629497 (retrieved October 16, 2009).

49. "Bill to Require Teaching of Irish Famine," United Press International, March 17, 1997.

50. Wittke, *The Irish in America*, pp. 52–61, 205; Owen B. Corrigan, "Chronology of the Catholic Hierarchy of the United States," *Catholic Historical Review* 1 (January 1916): 267–389; Edwin S. Gaustad, *Historical Atlas of Religion in America* (New York: Harper & Row, 1962), p. 103; Ellis, *American Catholicism*, p. 56; Wittke, *The Irish in America*, p. 91; Greeley, *That Most Distressful Nation*, p. 93.

51. National Opinion Research Center, 1990 General Social Survey. Tabulations by authors.

52. Greeley, *The Irish Americans*, pp. 130–132.

53. *Saturday Evening Post*, December 12, 1901; *Saturday Evening Post*, August 28, 1902.

54. Clark, *The Philadelphia Irish*, p. 178.

55. Stephan Thernstrom, *Poverty and Progress* (Cambridge, MA: Harvard University Press, 1964), p. 179.

56. Bede Jagoe, "Celtic Cult to Celtic Culture," paper presented at O.P. International Conference on Constructions of Irishness: The Irish in Ireland, Britain and Beyond, March 23, 2002; Abramson, *Ethnic Diversity in*

Catholic America, p. 111; Greeley, *The Irish Americans,* pp. 149–151.

57. Andrew M. Greeley, "The Success and Assimilation of Irish Protestants and Irish Catholics in the United States," *Sociology and Social Research* 72, no. 4 (July 1988): 236; Raymond E. Wolfinger, "The Development and Persistence of Ethnic Voting," *American Political Science Review* 60 (1965): 907.

58. Joseph P. O'Grady, *How the Irish Became American* (New York: Twayne, 1973), p. 141; Marjorie R. Fallows, *Irish Americans: Identity and Assimilation* (Englewood Cliffs, NJ: Prentice-Hall, 1979), p. 147.

59. Abramson, *Ethnic Diversity in Catholic America,* p. 53; Alba, *Ethnic Identity,* p. 47. On the 1990s, see Nona Claren, "The Trouble with the Melting Pot," *Baltimore Sun,* June 24, 1997, p. 9A.

60. Fallows, *Irish Americans,* pp. 148–149; Reginald Byron, "Ethnicity and Generation," *Ethnologia Europaea* 28 (1998): 27–36. See also Richard D. Alba, "Social Assimilation among American Catholic National-Origin Groups," *American Sociological Review* 41 (December 1976): 1032.

61. Alba, *Ethnic Identity,* pp. 55, 61.

62. Greeley, *The Irish Americans,* p. 206; Andrew M. Greeley, *Ethnicity in the United States* (New York: Wiley, 1974), p. 311.

63. S. L. Berry, "In Step with the Irish Heritage; Irish-Americans Struggle to Learn Ancestral Language," *Indianapolis Star,* March 17, 1997, p. E1; Jagoe, "Celtic Cult to Celtic Culture."

64. Giovanni Schiavo, *The Italians in America Before the Civil War* (New York: Vigo Press, 1934), pp. 55–180.

65. U.S. Department of Justice, Immigration and Naturalization Service, Annual Report (Washington, DC: U.S. Government Printing Office, 1973), pp. 52–54; Schiavo, *The Italians in America,* p. 204; Carl Wittke, *We Who Built America,* rev. ed. (Cleveland, OH: Case Western Reserve University Press, 1964), p. 441; Humbert S. Nelli, *The Italians in Chicago, 1880–1930* (New York: Oxford University Press, 1970), p. 5; Grazia Dore, "Some Social and Historical Aspects of Italian Emigration to America," in *The Italians,* ed. Francesco Cordasco and Eugene Bucchioni (Clifton, NJ: Augustus M. Kelley, 1974), p. 7.

66. We are indebted to Phyllis Cancilla Martinelli for her useful suggestions in sections that follow. Joseph Lopreato, *Italian Americans* (New York: Random House, 1970), pp. 23–27; John S. MacDonald, "Agricultural Organization, Migration, and Labor Militancy in Rural Italy," *Economic History Review,* 2d ser., 16 (1963–1964): 61–75; Luciano J. Iorizzo and Salvatore Mondello, *The Italian-Americans* (New York: Twayne, 1971), pp. 57–59; Michael La Sorte, *La Merica* (Philadelphia: Temple University Press, 1985), pp. 1–13, 189–202.

67. Antonia Stella, *Some Aspects of Italian Immigration to the United States,* reprint ed. (San Francisco: R & E Associates, 1970), p. 33; Rudolph J. Vecoli, "Contadini in Chicago," in *Divided Society,* ed. Colin Greer (New York:

Basic Books, 1974), p. 220; William Petersen, *Population,* 2nd ed. (New York: Macmillan, 1969), p. 260; La Sorte, *La Merica,* pp. 189–202.

68. John Higham, *Strangers in the Land,* rev. ed. (New York: Atheneum, 1975), pp. 312–324.

69. U.S. Bureau of the Census, *Statistical Abstract of the United States 1994* (Washington, DC: U.S. Government Printing Office, 1994), p. 11; U.S. Bureau of the Census, *1990 Census of Population: Ancestry of the Population in the United States,* CP-3-2 (Washington, DC: U.S. Government Printing Office, 1993), p. 50; U.S. Census Bureau, "2008 American Community Survey," http://factfinder.census.gov/servlet/IPChar IterationServlet?_ts=273424629497 (retrieved October 16, 2009).

70. Stanley Lieberson, *Ethnic Patterns in American Cities* (Glencoe, IL: The Free Press, 1963), pp. 209–218; La Sorte, *La Merica,* pp. 61–158.

71. William F. Whyte, *Street Corner Society,* 2nd ed. (Chicago: University of Chicago Press, 1955), pp. 272–273; Walter Firey, *Land Use in Central Boston* (Cambridge, MA: Harvard University Press, 1947), pp. 187–188; Wittke, *We Who Built America,* p. 446.

72. The first brief quotes are from Rita J. Simon and Susan H. Alexander, *The Ambivalent Welcome: Print Media, Public Opinion, and Immigration* (Westport, CT: Praeger, 1993), pp. 84, 131; the longer quote is from George Cunningham, "The Italian, a Hindrance to White Solidarity in Louisiana, 1890–1898," *The Journal of Negro History* 50 (1965): 25. See also Eliot Lord, John J. D. Trenor, and Samuel J. Barrows, *The Italian in America,* reprint ed. (San Francisco: R & E Associates, 1970), pp. 17–18.

73. Kenneth L. Roberts, *Why Europe Leaves Home,* excerpted in "Kenneth L. Roberts and the Threat of Mongrelization in America, 1922," in *In Their Place,* ed. Lewis H. Carlson and George A. Colburn (New York: Wiley, 1972), p. 312.

74. Jennifer Guglielmo, "White Lies, Dark Truths," in *Are Italians White?: How Race Is Made in America,* ed. Jennifer Guglielmo and Salvatore Salerno (New York: Routledge, 2003), p. 11.

75. Leon J. Kamin, *The Science and Politics of I.Q.* (New York: Wiley, 1974), pp. 15–19.

76. Carl C. Brigham, *A Study of American Intelligence* (Princeton, NJ: Princeton University Press, 1923), especially pp. 124–125 and 177–210. Brigham later recanted.

77. See Roberts, *Why Europe Leaves Home,* for earlier views.

78. See Kamin, *The Science and Politics of I.Q.,* p. 30.

79. Quoted in E. Digby Baltzell, *The Protestant Establishment* (New York: Random House/Vintage Books, 1966), p. 30.

80. Fred Misurella, "Truth Behind the Fiction of Italian-Americans," *The Christian Science Monitor,* April 15, 2002, p. 9.

81. Irving L. Allen, *Unkind Words* (New York: Bergin and Garvey, 1990), pp. 32, 60.

82. Iorizzo and Mondello, *The Italian-Americans,* pp. 35–36; quotation in Nelli, *The Italians in Chicago,* p. 126; Stella, *Some Aspects of Italian Immigration,* pp. 60–61, 73.

83. Philip di Franco, *The Italian American Experience* (New York: Tom Doherty Associates, 1988), pp. 84–86; Richard Gambino, *Blood of My Blood* (Garden City, NY: Doubleday/Anchor Books, 1975), pp. 293–298; Lopreato, *Italian Americans*, p. 126; Nelli, *The Italians in Chicago*, pp. 154–155.

84. Mary C. Waters, *Ethnic Options: Choosing Identities in America* (Berkeley: University of California Press, 1990), pp. 142–143; the earlier survey is cited in Richard Alba and Dalia Abdel-Hady, "Galileo's Children: Italian Americans' Difficult Entry into the Intellectual Elite," *The Sociological Quarterly* 46 (2005): 7; a *Parade* survey is cited in Italic Institute, "Shark Tale—Overview, Argument, & Position Summary," http://italic.org/shark.htm (retrieved July 6, 2006).

85. Alba and Abdel-Hady, "Galileo's Children," p. 6. The movie report was issued by PR Newswire, as reported at Alfano Digest, http://groups.yahoo.com/group/italian americansunite/message/2834 (retrieved October 15, 2009). See also http://www.italic.org/anti_defamation/ExhibitA.php (retrieved October 15, 2009).

86. Peter Bondanella, *Hollywood Italians: Dagos, Palookas, Romeos, Wise Guys, and Sopranos* (New York: Continuum International Publishing Group, 2004); "Italian American Group Rips CBS for 'Mafia' Stereotypes," (New York) *Daily News*, November 18, 1997, p. 96; William F. Miller, "Lawyer Fights Italian American Stereotypes," *(Cleveland) Plain Dealer*, June 15, 1996, p. 7B; Italic Institute, "Shark Tale— Overview, Argument, & Position Summary."

87. Selwyn Raab, "The Mob in Decline," *The New York Times*, October 22, 1990, p. A1; Gambino, *Blood of My Blood*, pp. 300–301.

88. Robert Lichter and Linda Lichter, "Italian-American Characters in Television Entertainment," report prepared for the Commission for Social Justice, Order of Sons of Italy, May 1982.

89. Quotation cited in Micaela di Leonardo, *The Varieties of Ethnic Experience* (Ithaca, NY: Cornell University Press, 1984), pp. 160–161; see also Susanna Tardi, *Family and Society: The Case of the Italians in New Jersey* (Ann Arbor, MI: UMI Dissertation Service, 1991), p. 189.

90. S. Luconi, "Mafia-Related Prejudice and the Rise of Italian Americans in the United States," *Patterns of Prejudice* 33 (1999): 43–57; Donna Haupt, Jan Mason, and Penny W. Moser, "The Embattled Queen of Queens," *Time*, October 1, 1984, p. 34; Vivienne Walt, "Cuomo: Hurt by Prejudice Toward Italians," *Newsday*, July 23, 1991, p. 19.

91. Alba, *Ethnic Identity*, pp. 141–142; Waters, *Ethnic Options*, pp. 142–43; see also Ross Harano and Jeryl Levin, "Capone Image Hurts Italian-Americans," *Chicago Tribune*, August 3, 1993, p. N16.

92. William F. Whyte, "Race Conflicts in the North End of Boston," *New England Quarterly* 12 (December 1939): 626; Iorizzo and Mondello, *The Italian-Americans*, pp. 35, 66.

93. Luciano J. Iorizzo, "The Padrone and Immigrant Distribution," in *The Italian Experience in the United States*, ed. Silvano Tomasi and M. H. Engel (New York: Center for Migration Studies, 1970), pp. 49–51; Gambino, *Blood of My Blood*, pp. 118, 119, 280–281; Higham, *Strangers in the Land*, p. 169; di Franco, *The Italian American Experience*, p. 85; Cunningham, "The Italian, a Hindrance to White Solidarity in Louisiana, 1890–1898," p. 28.

94. William Young and David E. Kaiser, *Postmortem* (Amherst: University of Massachusetts Press, 1985); Gambino, *Blood of My Blood*, pp. 120–121.

95. See Erika Hayes James and Lynn Perry Wooten, *2004 Census of African Americans on Boards of Directors of Fortune 500 Companies* (Institute for Leadership Development and Research, 2004), pp. 5–9.

96. Curtis Rist, "Prosecutor: Race Riot in Bensonhurst," *Newsday*, April 17, 1990, p. 4.

97. Levy and Kramer, *The Ethnic Factor*, p. 174; National Opinion Research Center, General Social Surveys, 1989 and 1990.

98. Guglielmo, "White Lies, Dark Truths," p. 4; see also David A. J. Richards, *Italian American: The Racializing of an Ethnic Identity* (New York: New York University Press), 1999.

99. Schiavo, *The Italians in America Before the Civil War*, pp. 163–166.

100. Nelli, *The Italians in Chicago*, pp. 75–76; Wittke, *We Who Built America*, p. 447; Lopreato, *Italian Americans*, pp. 113–117; Giovanni Schiavo, *Italian American History* (New York: Vigo Press, 1947), pp. 499–504.

101. di Franco, *The Italian American Experience*, pp. 146–147. Salvatore J. LaGumina, "Case Studies of Ethnicity and Italo-American Politicians," in *The Italian Experience in the United States*, ed. Tomasi and Engel, p. 147; Richard Krickus, *Pursuing the American Dream* (Garden City, NY: Doubleday/Anchor Books, 1976), pp. 174–181, 280.

102. "World War II Italian American Internment," Bill Ritter, Charles Gibson, ABC Good Morning America, October 30, 1997; Stephen Fox, *The Unknown Internment: An Oral History of the Relocation of Italian Americans during World War II* (Boston: Twayne Publishers, 1990); Wittke, *We Who Built America*, p. 450; Iorizzo and Mondello, *The Italian-Americans*, pp. 200–205, 208; Gambino, *Blood of My Blood*, p. 316.

103. Richard Alba, *Italian Americans* (Englewood Cliffs, NJ: Prentice-Hall, 1985), pp. 78–81; Guglielmo, "White Lies, Dark Truths," pp. 11–12.

104. Alba, *Italian Americans*, p. 143; General Social Surveys, 1989 and 1990. See also Andrew M. Greeley, *Ethnicity in the United States* (New York: Wiley, 1974), pp. 94–101; "Italian Americans: Big Swing?" *Campaigns & Elections*, August 1996, p. 63.

105. John M. Goshko, "Italian Americans Lobbying UN for Their Motherland," *International Herald Tribune*, September 18, 1997, p. 10.

106. Iorizzo, "The Padrone and Immigrant Distribution," p. 43.

107. Stella, *Some Aspects of Italian Immigration*, p. 94. See also Gambino, *Blood of My Blood*, p. 85; Leonard Covello, "The Influence of Southern Italian Family Mores upon

the School Situation in America," in *The Italians,* ed. Cordasco and Bucchioni, p. 513; Lord, Trenor, and Barrows, *The Italian in America,* pp. 16–19; E. P. Hutchinson, *Immigrants and Their Children, 1850–1950* (New York: Wiley, 1956), pp. 137–138.

108. Higham, *Strangers in the Land,* p. 48.

109. Gambino, *Blood of My Blood,* p. 77; see also Stephan Thernstrom, *The Other Bostonians* (Cambridge, MA: Harvard University Press, 1973), p. 161.

110. John J. d'Alesandre, "Occupational Trends of Italians in New York City," *Italy-America Monthly* 2 (February 1935): 11–21; Marcella Bencivenni, "Lost and Found: The Italian-American Radical Experience," *Monthly Review* 57 (January 2006): 60; W. Lloyd Warner and Leo Srole, *The Social Systems of American Ethnic Groups* (New Haven, CT: Yale University Press, 1945), pp. 96–97; Gambino, *Blood of My Blood,* p. 101; Wittke, *We Who Built America,* p. 443.

111. Nelli, *The Italians in Chicago,* pp. 211–214; Smith, *The Mafia Mystique,* p. 322; Ianni, *A Family Business,* p. 193.

112. Andrew F. Rolle, *The American Italian* (Belmont, CA: Wadsworth, 1972), pp. 89–93; "Introduction," Italian American Writers' Association, http://www.iawa.net/database.htm#General (retrieved October 13, 2009).

113. Thernstrom, *The Other Bostonians,* p. 171; U.S. Bureau of the Census, *1990 Census of Population: Ancestry of the Population in the United States,* p. 356; U.S. Bureau of the Census, *1990 Census of Population: Social and Economic Characteristics: United States,* p. 45.

114. See Table 4.2. See also U.S. Bureau of the Census, *1990 Census of Population: Ancestry of the Population in the United States,* pp. 307, 356, 458.

115. *National Center for Urban Ethnic Affairs Newsletter* 1, no. 5 (1976): 8.

116. Robert Viscusi, "Giving the Boot to Italians," *Newsday,* May 30, 1991, p. 74; John D. Calandra Italian American Institute, The City University of New York: Affirmative Action Trends from 1978 to 2006 and the Average Annual Employment Rates since 1993 by Race and Ethnicity, University-Wide Summary, October 1, 2007.

117. "CUNY Settles Suit by Italian Institute," *The New York Times,* January 9, 1994, sec. 1, p. 22; Felipe Pimentel, "The Decline of the Puerto Rican Fulltime Faculty at the City University of New York (CUNY) from 1981–2002," Hunter College, www.centropr.org/downloads/Faculty Brief(R) .pdf (retrieved July 6, 2006).

118. Alba and Abdel-Hady, "Galileo's Children," pp. 3–18.

119. Lawrence A. Cremin, *The Transformation of the School* (New York: Alfred A. Knopf, 1961), pp. 67–68; Colin Greer, *The Great School Legend* (New York: Basic Books, 1972), pp. 3–6.

120. See Table 4.2. See also U.S. Bureau of the Census, *U.S. Census of Population, 1970: Subject Reports—National Origin and Language,* PC(2)-1A (Washington, DC: U.S. Government Printing Office, 1973), p. 165; U.S. Census Bureau, "2008 American Community Survey," http://factfinder.cen sus.gov/servlet/IPCharIterationServlet?_ts=273424629497 (retrieved October 16, 2009).

121. Rudolph J. Vecoli, "Contadini in Chicago: A Critique of the Uprooted," in *The Aliens,* ed. Leonard Dinnerstein and Frederic C. Jaher (New York: Appleton-Century-Crofts, 1970), p. 226; Harold J. Abramson, *Ethnic Diversity in Catholic America* (New York: Wiley, 1973), pp. 136–139.

122. Silvano M. Tomasi, "The Ethnic Church and the Integration of Italian Immigrants in the United States," in *The Italian Experience in the United States,* ed. Tomasi and Engel, pp. 167–188; Nelli, *The Italians in Chicago,* p. 195; di Franco, *The Italian American Experience,* pp. 269–270.

123. National Opinion Research Center, "A Profile of Italian Americans: 1972–1991," March 1992; Stuart Vincent, "Devotion to Saints a Part of Life; Festivals Have an Italian Flavor," *Newsday,* May 1, 1996, p. A6.

124. Covello, "The Influence of Southern Italian Family Mores," p. 515.

125. Paul J. Campisi, "Ethnic Family Patterns: The Italian Family in the United States," *American Journal of Sociology* 53 (May 1948): 443–449; Covello, "The Influence of Southern Italian Family Mores," pp. 525–530.

126. Irvin L. Child, *Italian or American?* (New Haven, CT: Yale University Press, 1943). (An important excerpt from this book can be found in *The Italians,* ed. Cordasco and Bucchioni, pp. 321–336); Alba, *Italian Americans,* p. 114.

127. Alba, *Italian Americans,* p. 166.

128. See ibid.

129. Alba, *Ethnic Identity,* pp. 47–48, 59–61, 70–71, 224–226.

130. Commentary from Richard Alba given to authors, May 1994 and June 1997; Anthony L. LaRuffa, *Monte Carmelo: An Italian-American Community in the Bronx* (New York: Gordon & Breach, 1988), pp. 135–139.

131. Francis X. Femminella and Jill S. Quadagno, "The Italian American Family," in *Ethnic Families in America,* ed. Charles H. Mindel and Robert W. Habenstein (New York: Elsevier, 1976), pp. 74–75; Ruby Jo Reeves Kennedy, "Single or Triple Melting Pot? Intermarriage in New Haven, 1870–1950," *American Journal of Sociology* 58 (July 1952): 56–59; Nelli, *The Italians in Chicago,* p. 196; James A. Crispino, *The Assimilation of Ethnic Groups: The Italian Case* (New York: Center for Migration Studies, 1980), p. 105; Alba, *Italian Americans,* pp. 146–147; Waters, *Ethnic Options,* p. 104; Nona Claren, "The Trouble with the Melting Pot," *Baltimore Sun,* June 24, 1997, p. 9a.

132. Alba, *Italian Americans,* pp. 159–162; Alba, *Ethnic Identity,* p. 47.

133. LaRuffa, *Monte Carmelo,* pp. 17–28.

134. Phyllis Cancilla Martinelli, *Ethnicity in the Sunbelt* (New York: AMS Press, 1989), pp. 234–258; Alba, *Ethnic Identity,* pp. 59–60, 70.

135. Marcus Lee Hansen, "The Third Generation," in *Children of the Uprooted,* ed. Oscar Handlin (New York: Harper & Row, 1966), pp. 255–271; P. J. Gallo, *Ethnic Alienation* (Rutherford, NJ: Fairleigh Dickinson University Press, 1974), p. 194; John M. Goering, "The

Emergence of Ethnic Interests," *Social Forces* 49 (March 1971): 381–382; Tardi, *Family and Society,* pp. 179–192.

136. di Leonardo, *The Varieties of Ethnic Experience,* p. 156.

137. Richard D. Alba, "Identity and Ethnicity Among Italians and Other Americans of European Ancestry," in *The Columbus People: Perspectives in Italian Immigration to the Americas and Australia,* ed. Lydio Tomasi, Piero Gautaldo, and Thomas Row (Staten Island, NY: Center for Migration Studies, 1994), pp. 21–41. On religious feast days, see "Italian American," Wikipedia, http://en.wikipedia.org/wiki/Italian_Americans#cite_ref-2 (retrieved October 13, 2009).

138. Michael Parenti, "Italian American Identity: To Be or Not To Be," http://hnn.us/roundup/entries/116023.html (retrieved October 15, 2009).

139. U.S. Census Bureau, "2008 American Community Survey," http://factfinder.census.gov/servlet/IPCharIterationServlet?_ts=273424629497 (retrieved October 16, 2009); see also "Census 2000 Supplementary Survey," Table PCT 024, Ancestry-First Reported; Table PCT 025, Ancestry-Second Reported.

Chapter 5

1. Leonard Dinnerstein, *Anti-Semitism in America* (New York: Oxford University Press, 1994), pp. 181–184; John Higham, *Strangers in the Land: Patterns of American Nativism 1860–1925,* rev. ed. (New York: Atheneum, 1975), p. 186.

2. American Jewish Committee, "Thinking about the Holocaust 60 Years Later: A Multinational Public-Opinion Survey," March–April 2005, www.ajc.org/site/apps/nl/content3.asp?c=ijITI2PHKoG&b=846741&ct=1025513 (retrieved July 12, 2006).

3. Arthur Hertzberg, *The Jews in America* (New York: Simon & Schuster, 1989), pp. 377–388; Bernard J. Wolfson, "African American Jews: Dispelling Myths, Bridging the Divide," in *Black Zion: African American Religious Encounters with Judaism,* ed. Yvonne Chireau and Nathaniel Deutsch (New York: Oxford University Press), pp. 34–38.

4. Hertzberg, *The Jews in America,* pp. 13–28.

5. Charles E. Silberman, *A Certain People* (New York: Summit Books, 1985), pp. 42–45; Chaim I. Waxman, *America's Jews in Transition* (Philadelphia: Temple University Press, 1983), pp. 6–8.

6. Silberman, *A Certain People,* pp. 42–49; Hertzberg, *The Jews in America,* pp. 102–104.

7. Hertzberg, *The Jews in America,* pp. 152–154, 185; Silberman, *A Certain People,* p. 49; Waxman, *America's Jews in Transition,* p. 43. See also Frank K. Flinn, "Who Killed Jesus? A Guide to Viewing Mel Gibson's Movie," Washington University, http://newsinfo.wustl.edu/news/page/normal/711.html (retrieved January 25, 2007).

8. Hertzberg, *The Jews in America,* pp. 160–176, 224; Silberman, *A Certain People,* pp. 49–51.

9. Milton Meltzer, *Never to Forget: The Jews of the Holocaust* (New York: Harper & Row, 1976), p. 45.

10. Douglass Stanglin, Kenneth Walsh, Edward Pound, Charles Fenyvesi, and Josh Chetwynd, "Quale's Newest Place in the Sun," *U.S. News & World Report,* August 26, 1996, pp. 16, 19.

11. Maurice J. Karpf, *Jewish Community Organization in the United States* (New York: Arno, 1971), p. 33. See also Sidney Goldstein, "American Jewry: A Demographic Analysis," in *The Future of the Jewish Community in America,* ed. David Sidorsky (New York: Basic Books, 1973), p. 71; Alvin Chenkin, "Jewish Population in the United States," in *American Jewish Yearbook, 1973* (New York: American Jewish Committee, 1973), pp. 307–309; Arthur A. Goren, "Jews," in *Harvard Encyclopedia of American Ethnic Groups* (Cambridge, MA: Harvard University Press, 1980), pp. 591–592; Rita J. Simon and Julian L. Simon, "Social and Economic Adjustment," in *New Lives,* ed. Rita J. Simon (Lexington, MA: Heath/Lexington Books, 1985), pp. 26–41; Stanglin et al., "Quale's Newest Place in the Sun," pp. 16, 19; Annelise Orleck, *The Soviet Jewish Americans* (Westport, CT: Greenwood, 1999), p. 7.

12. United Jewish Communities, "The National Jewish Population Survey 2000-01: Strength, Challenge and Diversity in the American Jewish Population," 2003–2004, www.ujc.org/content_display.html?ArticleID=60346 (retrieved July 7, 2006); "Religion in Brief," *Atlanta Journal and Constitution,* September 6, 1997, p. 6E; Ira M. Sheskin and Arnold Dashefsky, Jewish Population in the United States," in *American Jewish Year Book, 2008,* ed. D. Singer and L. Grossman (New York: American Jewish Committee, 2008), p. 118; Jerome A. Chanes, *A Primer on the American Jewish Community* (New York: American Jewish Committee, 2008), p. v.

13. David Sidorsky, "Introduction," in *The Future of the Jewish Community in America,* ed. Sidorsky, pp. xix–xxv; Stephen D. Isaacs, *Jews and American Politics* (Garden City, NY: Doubleday, 1974), pp. ix–x.

14. Charles Y. Glock and Rodney Stark, *Christian Beliefs and Anti-Semitism* (New York: Harper & Row, 1966), p. 64 and passim. On the centuries of obsession with and attacks on Jews, see Adam Garfinkle, *Jewcentricity: Why the Jews Are Praised, Blamed, and Used to Explain Just About Everything* (New York: Wiley, 2009).

15. Carey McWilliams, *A Mask for Privilege* (Boston: Little, Brown, 1948), pp. 164–165, 170–173; John Higham, "Social Discrimination Against Jews in America, 1830–1930," *Publication of the American Jewish Historical Society* 47 (September 1957): 5.

16. Silberman, *A Certain People,* p. 48; Hertzberg, *The Jews in America,* pp. 86–87, 188–189; Higham, "Social Discrimination Against Jews in America," p. 47.

17. Leonard Dinnerstein, *Antisemitism in America* (New York: Oxford University Press, 1994), pp. 80–82.

18. Gustavus Meyers, *History of Bigotry in the United States,* rev. ed. (New York: Capricorn Books, 1960), pp. 277–313; Isaacs, *Jews and American Politics,* pp. 51, 98.

19. Neil Malhotra and Yotam Margalit, "Anti-Semitism and the Economic Crisis," *Boston Review,* May/June 2009, http://bostonreview.net/BR34.3/malhotra_margalit.php (retrieved October 29, 2009); Anti-Defamation League, "ADL Condemns Anti-Semitic Characterization of Jews by South Carolina GOP Leaders," press release, October 20, 2009; Gary A. Tobin, *Jewish Perceptions of Anti-Semitism* (New York: Plenum, 1988), pp. 106–112; "Anti-Jewish Elements Intact in Gibson's 'Passion Recut,'" www.adl.org/PresRele/ASUS_12/4665_12.htm (July 10, 2006); "Resources on the Mel Gibson movie, The Passion of the Christ," Boston College Center for Christian-Jewish Learning, www.bc.edu/research/cjl/meta-elements/texts/cjrelations/resources/education/PASSION_resources.htm (retrieved July 10, 2006).

20. American Jewish Committee, "2009 Annual Survey of American Jewish Opinion," http://www.ajc.org/site/c.ijITI2PHKoG/b.5472819/k.D6D7/2009_Annual_Survey_of_American_Jewish_Opinion.htm (retrieved October 25, 2009).

21. "Anti-Semitism Concerns Surveyed," *San Diego Union-Tribune,* June 6, 1997, p. E5; Anti-Defamation League, "ADL Survey: Anti-Semitism Declines Slightly in America; 14 Percent of Americans Hold 'Strong' Anti-Semitic Beliefs," www.adl.org/PresRele/ASUS_12/4680_12.htm (retrieved July 11, 2006).

22. American Jewish Committee, "Introduction," *Television's Changing Image of American Jews,* www.ajc.org/pre/jour nal12-index.asp (retrieved March 13, 2001).

23. Joyce Antler, "Introduction," in *Talking Back: Images of Jewish Women in American Popular Culture,* ed. Joyce Antler (Hanover, NH: Brandeis University Press, 1998), pp. 1, 10.

24. Henry L. Feingold, *Zion in America* (New York: Twayne, 1974), pp. 143–144; C. Vann Woodward, *Tom Watson* (New York: Oxford University Press, 1963), pp. 435–445; Rufus Learski, *The Jews in America* (New York: KTAV Publishing House, 1972), pp. 290–291; John Higham, *Strangers in the Land* (New York: Atheneum, 1975), pp. 298–299.

25. Milton R. Konvitz, "Inter-Group Relations," in *The American Jew,* ed. O. I. Janowsky (Philadelphia: Jewish Publication Society of America, 1964), pp. 78–79; Donald S. Strong, *Organized Anti-Semitism in America* (Washington, DC: American Council on Public Affairs, 1941), pp. 14–20, quotation on p. 67.

26. Lucy S. Dawidowicz, *The War Against the Jews: 1933–1945* (New York: Holt, Rinehart & Winston), p. 148; see also pp. 164, 403.

27. Lewis H. Carlson and George A. Colburn, "The Jewish Refugee Problem," in *In Their Place,* ed. Lewis H. Carlson and George A. Colburn (New York: Wiley, 1972), pp. 290–291; Stephanie Chavez, "Anti-Semitic Incidents Reported Rising," *Los Angeles Times,* February 7, 1992, p. A3; Lenni Brenner, *Jews in America Today* (Secaucus, NJ: Lyle Stuart, 1986), pp. 205–206, 209.

28. Leadership Conference on Civil Rights Education Fund (LCCREF), *Confronting the New Faces of Hate: Hate Crimes in America, 2009* (Washington, DC: Leadership Conference, 2009), pp. 27–29; Anti-Defamation League, "Anti-Semitism—U.S.," www.adl.org/main_Anti_Semitism_ Domestic/default.htm (retrieved July 10, 2006).

29. Anti-Defamation League, "Shooting At U.S. Holocaust Museum Part Of A 'Wave Of Hate' Against Jews," http://www.adl.org/PresRele/Extremism_72/5547_72.htm (re-trieved October 27, 2009).

30. Greg Wilson, "Hate Crimes Law to Make Debut in Attack on Bronx Synagogue," (New York) *Daily News,* October 20, 2000, p. 30; see www.adl.org on hate crimes legislation.

31. Konvitz, "Inter-Group Relations," pp. 85–95; Alan Dershowitz, *Chutzpah* (Boston: Little, Brown, 1991), p. 326; Linda Greenhouse, "Justices Affirm Ban on Prayers in Public School," *The New York Times,* June 25, 1992, p. A1.

32. Robert F. Drinan, "The Supreme Court, Religious Freedom and the Yarmulke," *America,* June 12, 1986, pp. 9–11; Anti-Defamation League, "Separation of Church and State," http://www.adl.org/civil_rights/ab/Church State.asp (retrieved October 27, 2009).

33. Gerald S. Strober, *American Jews* (Garden City, NY: Doubleday, 1974), pp. 149–176.

34. Anti-Defamation League, *Extremism in the Name of Religion: The Violent Legacy of Meir Kahane* (Washington, DC: ADL, 1995); Jewish Defense League, "Ideology and Advocacy," http://www.jdl.org/index.php/ideology-advocacy (retrieved October 27, 2009).

35. Cheryl Lynn Greenberg, *Troubling the Waters: Black-Jewish Relations in the American Century* (Princeton, NJ: Princeton University Press, 2006); Ronald Takaki, *A Different Mirror: A History of Multicultural America* (Boston: Little, Brown, 1993), p. 406.

36. "Two Deaths Ignite Racial Clash in Tense Brooklyn Neighborhood," *The New York Times,* August 21, 1991, p. A1; Scott Minerbrook and Miriam Horn, "Side by Side, Apart," *U.S. News & World Report,* November 4, 1991, p. 44.

37. Silberman, *A Certain People,* pp. 41, 340.

38. Ibid., pp. 333, 339–343; Dershowitz, *Chutzpah,* pp. 241, 301–302.

39. The quotation is from Letty Cottin Pogrebin, *Deborah, Golda, and Me: Being Female and Jewish in America* (New York: Crown, 1991). We draw on Karen Brodkin, *How The Jews Became White Folks: And What That Says About Race in America* (New Brunswick, NJ: Rutgers University Press, 1998); Ira Katznelson, *When Affirmative Action Was White: An Untold History of Racial Inequality in Twentieth-Century America* (New York: W. W. Norton, 2005).

40. Joe R. Feagin and Leslie Inniss, "Racial Attitudes in Four Socio-religious Groups," research paper, University of Florida, Spring 1992; Anti-Defamation League, *Highlights from an Anti-Defamation League Survey on*

Racial Attitudes in America (New York: ADL, 1993), pp. 51, 55, 61, 80–86.

41. Tom Tugend, "L.A. Jews Step Up Aid to Riot-Hit Areas," *Jerusalem Post,* May 12, 1992, n.p.

42. Buddy Nevins, "Idea of Saving Bucks Doesn't Compute with School Officials," *Ft. Lauderdale Sun-Sentinel,* December 18, 1994, p. B4.

43. Gene Warner, "Black, Jewish Teens Team Up to Honor King Legacy," *Buffalo News,* January 21, 1997, p. 1B; Judith Reitman, "Black, Jewish Teens Look to Past to Find New Understanding," *(New Orleans) Times-Picayune,* March 9, 1997, p. A3; Jenna Portnoy, "Going Far to Get Close," Citypaper.net, http://citypaper.net/articles/2006-06-29/naked.shtml (retrieved October 2006).

44. Waxman, *America's Jews in Transition,* pp. 5–10, quotation from p. 10; Hertzberg, *The Jews in America,* pp. 62–69; Lawrence H. Fuchs, *The Political Behavior of American Jews* (Glencoe, IL: The Free Press, 1956), pp. 23–25; Silberman, *A Certain People,* p. 44.

45. Hertzberg, *The Jews in America,* pp. 108–109; Mark R. Levy and Michael S. Kramer, *The Ethnic Factor* (New York: Simon & Schuster, 1972), p. 101; William R. Heitzmann, *American Jewish Voting Behavior* (San Francisco: R & E Research Associates, 1975), pp. 27–28.

46. Irving Howe, *World of Our Fathers* (New York: Simon & Schuster, 1976), pp. 362–364; Emanuel Hertz, "Politics: New York," in *The Russian Jew in the United States,* ed. Charles S. Bernheimer (Philadelphia: John Winston, 1905), pp. 256–265; Edward M. Levine, *The Irish and Irish Politicians* (Notre Dame, IN: University of Notre Dame Press, 1966); Isaacs, *Jews and American Politics,* pp. 23–24; Feingold, *Zion in America,* p. 321.

47. Hertz, "Politics," pp. 265–267; Heitzmann, *American Jewish Voting Behavior,* p. 37; Fuchs, *The Political Behavior of American Jews,* pp. 57–58.

48. Hertzberg, *The Jews in America,* pp. 282–283.

49. Heitzmann, *American Jewish Voting Behavior,* p. 49; Fuchs, *The Political Behavior of American Jews,* pp. 99–100.

50. American Jewish Committee, "2009 Annual Survey of American Jewish Opinion"; see also American Jewish Committee, "2005 Annual Survey of American Jewish Opinion."

51. Chanes, *A Primer on the American Jewish Community;* Isaacs, *Jews and American Politics,* pp. 23, 201; Levy and Kramer, *The Ethnic Factor,* pp. 102–103; Howe, *World of Our Fathers,* p. 118; Milton Plesur, *Jewish Life in Twentieth Century America* (Chicago: Nelson Hall, 1982), pp. 143–145; Andrew Herrmann, "Buddhists See Cup as Half Full," *Chicago Sun-Times,* January 21, 1995, p. 13.

52. See Isaacs, *Jews and American Politics,* pp. 12, 118–119. For a recent conservative perspective on Jewish liberalism and activism, see Norman Podhoretz, *Why Are Jews Liberals?* (New York: Doubleday, 2009).

53. Nathan Reich, "Economic Status," in *The American Jew,* ed. Janowsky, pp. 70–71; Karpf, *Jewish Community Orga-*nization in the United States, pp. 11–12; Howe, *World of Our Fathers,* pp. 391–393; Feingold, *Zion in America,* pp. 235–236.

54. Karpf, *Jewish Community Organization in the United States,* pp. 62–65; Naomi Cohen, *Not Free to Desist* (Philadelphia: Jewish Publication Society of America, 1972), pp. 3–18, 37–80, 433–452; Podhoretz, *Why Are Jews Liberals?;* Jonathan S. Woocher, *Sacred Survival* (Bloomington: Indiana University Press, 1986), pp. vii–viii; Chanes, *A Primer on the American Jewish Community,* p. 14.

55. Arnold Foster and Benjamin R. Epstein, *The New Anti-Semitism* (New York: McGraw-Hill, 1974), pp. 155–284; Strober, *American Jews,* pp. 7–42; Chanes, *A Primer on the American Jewish Community.*

56. Leonard, Mary, "Many Jews Hit Faith Plan Funding," *Boston Globe,* February 28, 2001, p. A2.

57. Brenner, *Jews in America Today,* p. 10; Podhoretz, *Why Are Jews Liberals?*

58. Hertzberg, *The Jews in America,* pp. 17–28, 63; Feingold, *Zion in America,* p. 12; McWilliams, *Brothers Under the Skin,* pp. 305–306.

59. Wittke, *We Who Built America,* p. 325; George Cohen, The Jews in the Making of America (Boston: Stratford, 1924), pp. 120–122; Silberman, *A Certain People,* pp. 44–45; Waxman, *America's Jews in Transition,* pp. 22–24.

60. Nathan Goldberg, *Occupational Patterns of American Jewry* (New York: Jewish Teachers Seminary Press, 1947), pp. 15–17; Marshall Sklare, *America's Jews* (New York: Random House, 1971), p. 61; Isaac M. Rubinow, "Economic and Industrial Conditions: New York," in *The Russian Jew in the United States,* ed. Bernheimer, pp. 110–111; Jacob Lestschinsky, "Economic and Social Development of American Jewry," in *The Jewish People* (New York: Jewish Encyclopedic Handbooks, 1955), 4: 74–77; Rubinow, "Economic and Industrial Conditions," pp. 103–107; Waxman, *America's Jews in Transition,* p. 58; Hertzberg, *The Jews in America,* p. 198.

61. Charlotte Baum, Paula Hyman, and Sonya Michel, *The Jewish Woman in America* (New York: Dial Press, 1976), p. 98; Hertzberg, *The Jews in America,* pp. 198–201.

62. Karpf, *Jewish Community Organization in the United States,* pp. 9–14; Lestschinsky, "Economic and Social Development of American Jewry," pp. 91–92; W. Lloyd Warner and Leo Srole, *The Social Systems of American Ethnic Groups* (New Haven, CT: Yale University Press, 1945), p. 112; Silberman, *A Certain People,* pp. 127–130.

63. McWilliams, *A Mask for Privilege,* pp. 38, 40–41; Karpf, *Jewish Community Organization in the United States,* pp. 20–21; Higham, "Social Discrimination Against Jews in America," pp. 18–19.

64. For the February 1936 *Fortune* survey, see Karpf, *Jewish Community Organization in the United States,* pp. 9–11; McWilliams, *A Mask for Privilege,* pp. 143–150.

65. Lestschinsky, "Economic and Social Development of American Jewry," pp. 71, 87; McWilliams, *A Mask for*

Privilege, p. 159; Reich, "Economic Status," pp. 63–65; Dershowitz, *Chutzpah,* p. 74; Barry R. Chiswick, "The Labor Market Status of American Jews," in *American Jewish Handbook,* ed. M. Himmelfarb and D. Singer (New York: American Jewish Committee, 1984), p. 137; Mabel Newcomer, *The Big Business Executive* (New York: Columbia University Press, 1955), pp. 46–48.

66. United Jewish Communities, "The National Jewish Population Survey 2000-01," p. 6; Brian J. Grim and David Masci, "The Demographics of Faith," http://www.america.gov/st/diversity-english/2008/August/20080819121858cmretrop0.5310633.html#ixzz0VRKb866Z (retrieved October 30, 2009).

67. Goren, "Jews," p. 593; Sklare, *America's Jews,* pp. 61–62; Goldscheider and Goldstein, *The Jewish Community of Rhode Island,* pp. 11–12; Barry A. Kosmin et al., *Highlights of the CJF 1990 National Jewish Population Survey* (New York: Council of Jewish Federations, 1991), p. 12.

68. Abraham K. Korman, *The Outsiders: Jews and Corporate America* (Lexington, MA: Heath/Lexington Books, 1988), pp. 79–82.

69. Richard L. Zweigenhaft and G. William Domhoff, *Jews in the Protestant Establishment* (New York: Praeger, 1982), p. 46.

70. Korman, *The Outsiders,* pp. 35–41, 66–88.

71. Dov B. Levy, "Top Jobs," *Jerusalem Post,* March 30, 1997, p. 6. See also Chanes, *A Primer on the American Jewish Community,* p. v.

72. American Jewish Committee, "2009 Annual Survey of American Jewish Opinion."

73. Allen Myerson, "At Rental Counters, Are All Drivers Created Equal? Avis Finds Itself at the Center of Discrimination Complaints," *The New York Times,* March 18, 1997, p. D1; Ellen Neuborne, "Car Renters Outline Charges at State Hearing," *USA Today,* April 1, 1997, p. 1B; Anti-Defamation League, "Fort Benning Adds Support Services for Jewish Trainees After Consultation with ADL on Mistreatment Complaint," press release, August 6, 2009; "Jean Louis David Hair Salons Sued for Discrimination Against Jewish Barber," PR Newswire, January 18, 2001; *USA* v. *Village of Airmont,* http://www.justice.gov/crt/religdisc/airmont_order.pdf (retrieved October 30, 2009).

74. "Florida Legislature Passes Bill," PR Newswire, March 13, 1992; Sklare, *America's Jews,* p. 65; McWilliams, *Brothers Under the Skin,* pp. 310–311.

75. Hertzberg, *The Jews in America,* pp. 50, 273; Silberman, *A Certain People,* p. 51; Waxman, *America's Jews in Transition,* p. 53; J. K. Paulding, "Educational Influences: New York," in *The Russian Jew in the United States,* ed. Bernheimer, pp. 186–197; Cohen, *The Jews in the Making of America,* pp. 140–141; Karpf, *Jewish Community Organization in the United States,* p. 57; Waxman, *America's Jews in Transition,* p. 137.

76. Silberman, *A Certain People,* pp. 52–55; Hertzberg, *The Jews in America,* pp. 246–247; Higham, "Social Discrimination Against Jews in America," p. 22; Karpf, *Jewish*

Community Organization in the United States, p. 19; McWilliams, *A Mask for Privilege,* pp. 128–129.

77. Silberman, *A Certain People,* pp. 98–100; Hertzberg, *The Jews in America,* p. 309; Dershowitz, *Chutzpah,* pp. 73–74.

78. Strober, *American Jews,* pp. 120–130; Maurice R. Berube and Marilyn Gittell, "The Struggle for Community Control," in *Confrontation at Ocean Hill–Brownsville,* ed. Maurice R. Berube and Marilyn Gittell (New York: Praeger, 1969), pp. 3–12 et passim; Joe R. Feagin and Harlan Hahn, *Ghetto Revolts* (New York: Macmillan, 1973), pp. 327–328; Nathan Glazer, *Affirmative Discrimination* (New York: Basic Books, 1975), pp. 33–76, 196–221.

79. Dershowitz, *Chutzpah,* pp. 75–79, quotation from pp. 78–79.

80. Hertzberg, *The Jews in America,* p. 309; Kosmin et al., *Highlights of the CJF 1990 National Jewish Population Survey,* pp. 10–11; Holly J. Lebowitz, "High Holy Days Can Be Lonely for Students," *(Cleveland) Plain Dealer,* September 7, 1996, p. 6E; American Jewish Committee, "Responding to Intermarriage Survey, Analysis, Policy"; American Jewish Committee, "2000 Annual Survey of American Jewish Opinion"; Grim and Masci, "The Demographics of Faith."

81. United Jewish Communities, "The National Jewish Population Survey 2000-01," p. 15. Silberman, *A Certain People,* pp. 171–172; Robert Alter, "What Jewish Studies Can Do," *Commentary* 58 (October 1974): 71–74.

82. Waxman, *America's Jews in Transition,* p. 10; Hertzberg, *The Jews in America,* pp. 117–123, 146–147, 254–262, quotation from p. 120. See also Silberman, *A Certain People,* p. 46.

83. Hertzberg, *The Jews in America,* pp. 159–161, 167–168, 195, 214–236.

84. Ibid., pp. 277–279; Waxman, *America's Jews in Transition,* p. 17; Wolfe Kelman, "The Synagogue in America," in *The Future of the Jewish Community in America,* ed. Sidorsky, pp. 157–158; Louis Lipsky, "Religious Activity: New York," in *The Russian Jew in the United States,* ed. Bernheimer, pp. 152–154; Silberman, *A Certain People,* pp. 170–177; Hertzberg, *The Jews in America,* pp. 277–279.

85. Silberman, *A Certain People,* pp. 176–181.

86. American Jewish Committee, "2009 Annual Survey of American Jewish Opinion."

87. J. L. Blau, *Judaism in America* (Chicago: University of Chicago Press, 1976), as summarized in Samuel C. Heilman, "The Sociology of American Jewry," in *Annual Review of Sociology,* ed. Ralph Turner, vol. 8 (Palo Alto, CA: Annual Reviews, 1982), p. 147; Michael Greenstein, *The American Jew: A Contradiction in Terms* (New York: Gefen, 1990), pp. 1–5.

88. American Jewish Committee, "2009 Annual Survey of American Jewish Opinion"; see also American Jewish Committee, "2005 Annual Survey of American Jewish Opinion."

89. Monty Noam Penkower, *At the Crossroads: American Jewry and the State of Israel* (Haifa, Israel: University of

Haifa, 1990), p. 27; "U.S. Jews Favor Palestinian State: Poll," *Agence France Presse,* September 29, 1997; Stanley Reed, "Will Palestine's Peace Dividend Buy Peace?" *Business Week,* May 16, 1994, p. 53.

90. American Jewish Committee, "2009 Annual Survey of American Jewish Opinion."

91. Theodore Sasson, *The New Realism: American Jews' Views about Israel* (New York: Koppelman Institute, American Jewish Committee, 2009), p. 36.

92. Ethan Felson, "National Affairs," in *American Jewish Year Book, 2008,* p. 118.

93. Howe, *World of Our Fathers,* p. 645; Karpf, *Jewish Community Organization in the United States,* pp. 37–39, 49–50; Milton R. Konvitz, "Horace Meyer Kallen (1882–1974)," in *American Jewish Yearbook, 1974–1975* (New York: American Jewish Committee, 1974), pp. 65–67; Milton Gordon, *Assimilation in American Life* (New York: Oxford University Press, 1964), pp. 142–159.

94. Hertzberg, *The Jews in America,* pp. 102–130, 167–176, 195.

95. Sidney Goldstein and Calvin Goldscheider, *Jewish Americans* (Englewood Cliffs, NJ: Prentice-Hall, 1968), p. 226; Silberman, *A Certain People,* pp. 173–181.

96. Riv-Ellen Prell, *Fighting to Become Americans: Jews, Gender, and the Anxiety of Assimilation* (Boston: Beacon Press, 1999), p. 8. See also pp. 6–10.

97. Nathan Glazer, "The American Jew and the Attainment of Middle-Class Rank: Some Trends and Explanations," in *The Jews,* ed. M. Sklare (Glencoe, IL: The Free Press, 1958), p. 143, as quoted in Stephen Steinberg, *The Ethnic Myth* (New York: Atheneum, 1981), p. 93.

98. Steinberg, *The Ethnic Myth,* pp. 94–102.

99. Hertzberg, *The Jews in America,* pp. 167–171, 195, 254–255, quotation from p. 171; Waxman, *America's Jews in Transition,* pp. 55–58.

100. Calvin Goldscheider, *Jewish Continuity and Change* (Atlanta, GA: Scholars Press, 1986), pp. 17–18; Sidney Goldstein, "Jews in the United States: Perspectives from Demography," in *American Jewish Yearbook, 1981* (New York: American Jewish Committee, 1980–1981), p. 28; Kosmin et al., *Highlights of the CJF 1990 National Jewish Population Survey,* p. 35; United Jewish Communities, "The National Jewish Population Survey 2000-01," p. 7; "The Federation's Causes," http://www.jewishla.org/The Federations_Causes .cfm (retrieved October 30, 2009).

101. Gordon, *Assimilation in American Life,* pp. 76–77.

102. United Jewish Communities, "The National Jewish Population Survey 2000-01," p. ix; American Jewish Committee, "2000 Annual Survey of American Jewish Opinion."

103. American Jewish Committee, "Responding to Intermarriage Survey, Analysis, Policy."

104. United Jewish Communities, "The National Jewish Population Survey 2000-01," p. 130; see Alan Dershowitz, *The Vanishing American Jew: In Search of Jewish Identity for the Next Century* (New York: Little, Brown, 1997).

105. Goldscheider, *Jewish Continuity and Change,* pp. 15–19, quotation from p. 16.

106. Arianne R. Sanua, "AJC and Intermarriage: The Complexities of Jewish Continuity, 1960–2006," *American Jewish Yearbook, 2007* (New York: American Jewish Committee, 2007), pp. 4-32; American Jewish Committee, "2005 Annual Survey of American Jewish Opinion"; Jacob B. Ukeles, Ron Miller, and Pearl Beck, *Young Jewish Adults in the United States Today* (New York: American Jewish Committee 2006), pp. 6–8.

107. United Jewish Communities, "The National Jewish Population Survey 2000-01," p. 3.

108. Marilyn Henry, "Israeli Immigrants to the United States Moving Up the Ladder," *Jerusalem Post,* August 13, 1996, p. 12; Henry summarizes a report in the *1996 American Jewish Yearbook* by Steven Gold and Bruce Phillips.

109. Orleck, *The Soviet Jewish Americans,* p. 3, see also pp. 4–100; Steven J. Gold, "Review of The Soviet Jewish Americans," *Journal of American Ethnic History* 20 (Fall 2000): 107; Simon and Simon, "Social and Economic Adjustment," pp. 27–38.

110. Steven J. Gold, *Refugee Communities* (Newbury Park, CA: Sage, 1992), pp. 39–44, 67–89.

111. Orleck, *The Soviet Jewish Americans,* pp. 190–193; American Jewish Committee, "2000 Annual Survey of American Jewish Opinion."

112. David Biale, "The Melting Pot and Beyond," in *Insider/Outsider: American Jews and Multiculturalism,* ed. David Biale, Michael Galchinsky, and Susan Heschel (Berkeley: University of California Press, 1998), p. 31.

113. Kosmin et al., *Highlights of the CJF 1990 National Jewish Population Survey,* pp. 3–6, 14–17, 28; United Jewish Communities, "The National Jewish Population Survey 2000-01," p. 15.

114. Sylvia Barack Fishman, *Jewish Life and American Culture* (Albany, NY: SUNY Press, 2000), pp. 1–16.

115. Quote is from Amy Teibel, "Ads against Jewish Assimilation Pulled over Uproar," *The Boston Globe,* September 10, 2009, p. 4. See also Hertzberg, *The Jews in America,* p. 386; Herbert J. Gans, "Symbolic Ethnicity," *Ethnic and Racial Studies* 2 (1979): 1–20; Richard Alba, *Ethnic Identity: The Transformation of White America* (New Haven, CT: Yale University Press, 1990), p. 306.

116. Robert Wolfe, "Reviving the Jewish Left," http://pnews .org/art/5art/JEWISHleft.shtml (retrieved July 13, 2006).

117. Lawrence Grossman, "Jewish Communal Affairs," in *American Jewish Yearbook, 2008,* pp. 134–135; Ira Rifkin, "Jewish Social Agency Finds Support Eroding," *Sacramento Bee,* December 2, 1995, p. G5. Chanes, *A Primer on the American Jewish Community,* p. 27; Leon Wieseltier, "American Jewry at the Start of a Century: What Should We Worry About Next? At a Century's End," *At a Century's Beginning: Symposium On the Prospects for Judaism and the Jews* (New York: American Jewish Committee, 2007), pp. 17–18. We are indebted to Diane L. Wolf for suggestions here.

118. United Jewish Communities, "The National Jewish Population Survey 2000-01," p. viii; see also Chanes, *A Primer on the American Jewish Community*, p. 37.

119. Ukeles, Miller, and Beck, *Young Jewish Adults in the United States Today*, p. 3. See also Alba, *Ethnic Identity*, p. 310.

120. Eric A. Goldman, *The American Jewish Experience Through the Lens of Cinema* (New York: American Jewish Committee, 2008), p. 31.

121. Caroline Forman Litwack, "'You Don't Have to Be Jewish': The Representation of Jews on Television Sitcoms," M.A. thesis, Georgetown University, Washington, DC, 2006, p. 89.

122. American Jewish Committee, "2009 Annual Survey of American Jewish Opinion"; see also Silberman, *A Certain People*, pp. 25, 159–324.

123. Brodkin, *How the Jews Became White Folks*, pp. 139–178; Eric Goldstein, *The Price of Whiteness: Jews, Race, and American Identity* (Princeton, NJ: Princeton University Press, 2006).

124. Brodkin, *How the Jews Became White Folks*, p. 187.

Chapter 6

1. Peggy Lowe, "Columbus Day Case Dropped; Charges to Be Dismissed Against 139 Protesters Arrested at October March," *Rocky Mountain News*, March 7, 2001, p. 5A.

2. "Counter-Quincentenary Protesters Encounter Celebrators at Kickoff of Quincentenary Year," *Indigenous Thought* 1, nos. 4 and 5 (October 1991): 1–3.

3. "We Have No Reason to Celebrate an Invasion," *Rethinking Columbus* (Milwaukee, WI: Rethinking Schools, 1991), p. 4.

4. For a discussion of the development of the designations white and red, see David R. Roediger, *The Wages of Whiteness* (New York: Verso, 1991), pp. 21–23.

5. Henry F. Dobyns, "Estimating Aboriginal American Population," *Current Anthropology* 7 (October 1960): 395–416; Kirkpatrick Sale, *The Conquest of Paradise* (New York: Knopf, 1990); Lenore A. Stiffarm and Phil Lane, Jr., "The Demography of Native North America," in *The State of Native America*, ed. M. Annette Jaimes (Boston: South End Press, 1992), pp. 23–28; see also Russell Thornton, *American Indian Holocaust and Survival* (Norman: University of Oklahoma Press, 1987); C. Matthew Snipp, *American Indians: The First of This Land* (New York: Russell Sage Foundation, 1989).

6. U.S. Census Bureau, "Overview of Race and Hispanic Origin, Census 2000 Brief," March 2001, pp. 2–5; U.S. Census Bureau, "2006–2008 American Community Surveys," American Factfinder, http://factfinder.census.gov (retrieved November 3, 2009).

7. Public Information Office, U.S. Census Bureau, "Census Bureau Facts for Features," November 2000, CB00-FF.13, www.census.gov (retrieved June 7, 2001); U.S. Census Bureau, *The American Indian and Alaska Native Population: 2000* (Washington, DC: U.S. Government Printing Office, 2002), pp. 1–11.

8. Carol Morello, "Native American Roots, Once Hidden, Now Embraced," *The Washington Post*, April 7, 2001, p. A01.

9. Joane Nagel, *American Indian Ethnic Renewal: Red Power and the Resurgence of Indian Identity and Culture* (New York: Oxford University Press, 1996); Morello, "Native American Roots, Once Hidden, Now Embraced."

10. Edward H. Spicer, *Cycles of Conquest* (Tucson: University of Arizona Press, 1962), pp. 20–23; Clyde Kluckhohn and Dorothy Leighton, *The Navajo*, rev. ed. (Garden City, NY: Doubleday/Anchor Books, 1962), pp. 23–27 et passim.

11. Devon A. Mihesuah, *American Indians: Stereotypes and Realities* (Atlanta, GA: Clarity Press, 1996), p. 20.

12. Ibid., p. 43.

13. Jack Weatherford, *Indian Givers: How the Indians of the Americas Transformed the World* (New York: Ballantine, 1988), pp. 39–133.

14. Peter Linebaugh and Marcus Rediker, *The Many-Headed Hydra: Sailors, Slaves, Commoners, and the Hidden History of the Revolutionary Atlantic* (Boston: Beacon Press, 2000), pp. 32–34.

15. Howard M. Bahr, "An End to Invisibility," in *Native Americans Today*, ed. Howard M. Bahr, Bruce A. Chadwick, and Robert C. Day (New York: Harper & Row, 1972), pp. 407–409; James E. Officer, "The American Indian and Federal Policy," in *The American Indian in Urban Society*, ed. Jack O. Waddell and O. Michael Watson (Boston: Little, Brown, 1971), pp. 45–60.

16. U.S. Bureau of the Census, *1990 Census of Population: General Population Characteristics: Urbanized Areas*, CP-1-1C (Washington, DC: U.S. Government Printing Office, 1992), p. 48.

17. Spicer, *Cycles of Conquest*, pp. 5, 306–307; Murray L. Wax, *Indian Americans* (Englewood Cliffs, NJ: Prentice-Hall, 1971), pp. 6–7; Lynn R. Bailey, *Indian Slave Trade in the Southwest* (Los Angeles: Westernlore Press, 1966), pp. 73–140.

18. D'Arcy McNickle, *The Indian Tribes of the United States* (London: Oxford University Press, 1962), pp. 13–28; Alice Marriott and Carol K. Rachlin, *American Epic* (New York: Mentor Books, 1969), pp. 104–108; John Collier, *Indians of the Americas* (New York: Mentor Books, 1947), p. 115; William T. Hagan, *American Indians* (Chicago: University of Chicago Press, 1961), p. 14; Ruth M. Underhill, *Red Man's America* (Chicago: University of Chicago Press, 1953), pp. 321–322; Wax, *Indian Americans*, p. 13.

19. Alexis de Tocqueville, *Democracy in America* (New York: Random House/Vintage Books, 1945), 1:364.

20. Virgil J. Vogel, "The Indian in American History, 1968," in *This Country Was Ours*, ed. Virgil J. Vogel (New York: Harper & Row, 1972), pp. 284–287; McNickle, *The Indian Tribes of the United States*, pp. 40–41.

21. Ralph K. Andrist, *The Long Death* (London: Collier-Macmillan, 1964), p. 3.

22. John D. Unruh, *The Plains Across* (Urbana: University of Illinois Press, 1979), p. 185 et passim.

23. Vogel, "The Indian in American History, 1968," p. 285; Wendell H. Oswalt, *This Land Was Theirs* (New York: Wiley, 1966), pp. 501–502.

24. William Meyer, *Native Americans* (New York: International, 1971), p. 32; Andrist, *The Long Death*, pp. 31–68, 78–91; Thornton, *American Indian Holocaust and Survival*.

25. Andrist, *The Long Death*, pp. 240–250, 350–353; Alvin M. Josephy, *The Indian Heritage of America* (New York: Bantam, 1968), pp. 284–342; Theodora Kroeber and Robert F. Heizer, *Almost Ancestors* (San Francisco: Sierra Club, 1968), pp. 14–20.

26. Spicer, *Cycles of Conquest*, pp. 216–221, 247–270.

27. Robert F. Spencer, Jesse D. Jennings, et al., *The Native Americans* (New York: Harper & Row, 1965), pp. 495–496; David Miller, "The Fur Men and Explorers View the Indians," in *Red Men and Hat Wearers*, ed. Daniel Tyler (Fort Collins, CO: Pruett, 1976), pp. 26–28; Roediger, *The Wages of Whiteness*, pp. 21–23.

28. Peter Farb, *Man's Rise to Civilization as Shown by the Indians of North America from Primeval Times to the Coming of the Industrial State* (New York: Dutton, 1968), pp. 246–249; Tyler, ed., *Red Men and Hat Wearers*, passim.

29. Lewis H. Carlson and George A. Colburn, "Introduction," in *In Their Place*, ed. Lewis H. Carlson and George A. Colburn (New York: Wiley, 1972), p. 44.

30. Vogel, "The Indian in American History, 1968," pp. 288–289; de Tocqueville, *Democracy in America*, 1:355–357.

31. Rayna Green, "The Pocahontas Perplex: The Image of Indian Women in American Culture," in *Unequal Sisters*, ed. Ellen Carol DuBois and Vicki L. Ruiz (New York: Routledge, 1990), pp. 15–21, quotation from p. 17.

32. "Children's Secret Lessons," *Indigenous Thought* 1, nos. 4 and 5 (October 1991): 24.

33. James W. Loewen, *Lies My Teacher Told Me: Everything Your American History Textbook Got Wrong* (New York: The New Press, 1995), p. 91; James W. Loewen, *Teaching What Really Happened* (New York: Teachers College Press, 2010), pp. 141–154 and passim.

34. See Jacquelyn Kilpatrick, *Celluloid Indians: Native Americans and Film* (Lincoln: University of Nebraska Press, 1999; Snipp, *American Indians*, pp. 23–25; Jimmie Durham, "Cowboys and . . .," in *The State of Native America*, ed. Jaimes, pp. 423–425.

35. Ward Churchill, *Fantasies of the Master Race* (Monroe, ME: Common Courage Press, 1992), pp. 243–247, quotation from p. 246.

36. Kilpatrick, *Celluloid Indians: Native Americans and Film*, p. 152; see also pp. 151–153.

37. Patricia R. Powers. "Native Americans and the Public: A Human Values Perspective," *Research Report, Friends Committee on National Legislation* (Winter 2006–2007): 23; Robert Lichter, "Framing, Messaging, Content Analysis," as reported in Powers, "Native Americans and the Public," p. 83.

38. Howard M. Bahr, Bruce A. Chadwick, and Robert C. Day, "Introduction: Patterns of Prejudice and Discrimination," in *Native Americans Today*, ed. Bahr, Chadwick, and Day, pp. 44–45; Emory S. Bogardus, *Immigration and Race Attitudes* (Boston: Heath, 1928); Beverly Brandon Sweeney, "Native American: Stereotypes and Ideologies of an Adult Anglo Population in Texas," M.A. thesis, University of Texas at Austin, 1976, pp. 125–133. The 2000 study is Tamela McNulty and Matthew Steffens, "Religious Affiliation and Beliefs about Racial Inequality: White College Students' Attitudes about Black-White and Native American-White Inequality," *Social Science Journal* 46 (2009): 506–520.

39. Alexandra Witkin-New Holy, "American Indian Religious Rights: Inside Montana Prisons," Center for Native American Studies, Montana State University (Bozeman), http://tlc.wtp.net/american_indian_religious_rights.htm (retrieved June 7, 2001).

40. Bridget F. Grant, Deborah A. Dawson, Frederick S. Stinson, Patricia Chou, Mary C. Dufour, and Roger P. Pickering, "The 12-Month Prevalence and Trends in DSM–IV Alcohol Abuse and Dependence: United States, 1991–1992 and 2001–2002," *Alcohol Research & Health* 29 (2006): 84; Powers, "Native Americans and the Public: A Human Values Perspective."

41. Gayle Pollard Terry, "Los Angeles Times Interview with Suzan Shown Harjo: Fighting to Preserve the Legacy and Future of Native Americans," *The Los Angeles Times*, November 27, 1994, p. M3.

42. Jeff Cohen and Norman Solomon, "Using History, CNN Delivers Improved Coverage of Indians," *Star Tribune*, November 30, 1994, p. A17.

43. "Nationwide Poll Shows Support for Native Issues; Saginaw-Chippewa Commissions Zogby Research Firm to Reach Average Americans," Oklahoma Indian Times Online, www.okit.com/gaming/2001/feb/poll.htm (retrieved June 6, 2001).

44. James Cox , "Muting White Noise: The Subversion of Popular Culture Narratives of Conquest in Sherman Alexie's Fiction," *Studies in American Indian Literatures* 9 (Winter 1997): 57; Robert M. Nelson, "A Laguna Woman," in *Leslie Marmon Silko: A Collection of Critical Essays*, ed. Louise Barnett and James Thorson (Albuquerque: University of New Mexico Press, 1999), pp. 15–22.

45. Mihesuah, *American Indians: Stereotypes and Realities*, pp. 61–63.

46. Loewen, *Lies My Teacher Told Me*, p. 104.

47. Mihesuah, *American Indians: Stereotypes and Realities*, pp. 63–65.

48. U.S. Bureau of Indian Affairs, *Federal Indian Policies* (Washington, DC: U.S. Government Printing Office, 1975), p. 6.

49. Ibid., p. 7; Spicer, *Cycles of Conquest*, p. 348.

50. *Elk v. Wilkins*, 112 U.S. 94 (1884); see also Vine Deloria, Jr., *Of Utmost Good Faith* (New York: Bantam, 1972), pp. 130–132.

51. Spicer, *Cycles of Conquest*, pp. 351–353; McNickle, *The Indian Tribes of the United States*, p. 59; Alison R. Bernstein, *American Indians and World War II* (Norman: University of Oklahoma Press, 1991), pp. 4–10.

52. Virgil J. Vogel, "Introduction," in *This Country Was Ours*, ed. Vogel, pp. 196–197.

53. M. Annette Jaimes, "Federal Indian Identification Policy: A Usurpation of Indigenous Sovereignty in North America," in *The State of Native America*, ed. Jaimes, p. 124.

54. Ibid., pp. 95–98.

55. W. A. Brophy and S. D. Aberle, *The Indian* (Norman: University of Oklahoma Press, 1966), pp. 179–193; Rebecca L. Robbins, "Self-Determination and Subordination: The Past, Present, and Future of American Indian Governance," in *The State of Native America*, ed. Jaimes, pp. 98–100.

56. U.S. Bureau of Indian Affairs, *Federal Indian Policy*, p. 12.

57. Jaimes, "Federal Indian Identification Policy," pp. 123–137; Susan Campbell, "A Mohegan Family," *Hartford Courant*, March 1, 1992, p. 10; Anne Fullam, "Tribe Seeks U.S. Recognition," *Newsday*, February 11, 1992, p. 20.

58. Jack Forbes, *Native Americans of California and Nevada* (Berkeley, CA: Far West Laboratory for Educational Research and Development, 1968), pp. 80–82; Alan L. Sorkin, *American Indians and Federal Aid* (Washington, DC: Brookings Institution, 1971), pp. 48–65; Vogel, "Introduction," p. 205; James S. Olson and Raymond Wilson, *Native Americans in the Twentieth Century* (Provo, UT: Brigham Young University Press, 1984), p. 209; E. S. Cahn, *Our Brother's Keeper* (New York: World, 1969), pp. 157–158.

59. Robbins, "Self-Determination and Subordination," pp. 98–112, quotation from p. 109.

60. Elouise Cobell, "After Five Years of Delay, Will the Bush Administration Treat the Trust Accounts Lawsuit Any Differently?" Oklahoma Indian Times Online, www.okit .com/opinion/2001/janfeb/trust.htm (retrieved June 7, 2001); NCAI, "Senate Committee Schedule to Meet with Tribes to Discuss Indian Trust Reform Act of 2006 and Fractionation Problem," www.ncai.org/Home.9.0.html? &no_cache=1 (retrieved September 7, 2006); Ari Shapiro, "U.S. In $3B Settlement with American Indians," www .npr.org/templates/story/story.php?storyId=121216558 &sc=emaf (retrieved December 11, 2009).

61. Brophy and Aberle, *The Indian*, pp. 33–44; Olson and Wilson, *Native Americans in the Twentieth Century*, pp. 189, 191.

62. Virgil J. Vogel, "Famous Americans of Indian Descent," in *This Country Was Ours*, ed. Vogel, pp. 310–351.

63. U.S. Census Bureau, "Census Bureau Facts for Features," October 26, 2004, www.census.gov/Press-Release/www/releases/archives/facts_for_features_

special_editions/002957.html (retrieved September 5, 2006); "Election 2008: Impact in Indian Country," National Congress of American Indians, press release, November 6, 2008.

64. Olson and Wilson, *Native Americans in the Twentieth Century*, p. 186.

65. "Indians Flashing Casino Profits in D.C.: The Mashantucket Pequot Tribe, for Example, Employs a Full-Time Lobbyist in Washington," *Providence Journal-Bulletin*, July 13, 1997, p. 5A.

66. NCAI, "Tribal Sovereignty Protection Initiative," www .ncai.org/Sovereignty_Protection.91.0.html (retrieved September 7, 2006); NCAI, "San Manuel Band of Serrano Mission Indians Contributes $100,000 to NCAI's Embassy of Tribal Nations Capital Campaign," press release, October 23, 2008; see also Powers, "Native Americans and the Public: A Human Values Perspective," p. 52.

67. Hazel W. Hertzberg, *The Search for an American Indian Identity* (Syracuse, NY: Syracuse University Press, 1971), pp. 20–21, 42–76, 180–200.

68. Ibid., pp. 200–208, 291–293; Isabel Wilkerson, "Indignant Indians Seeking Changes," *The New York Times*, January 26, 1992, p. 14.

69. Robert C. Day, "The Emergence of Activism as a Social Movement," in *Native Americans Today*, ed. Bahr, Chadwick, and Day, pp. 516–517.

70. Robbins, "Self-Determination and Subordination," p. 103.

71. Meyer, *Native Americans*, p. 88; "Pine Ridge After Wounded Knee: The Terror Goes On," *Akwesasne Notes* 7 (Summer 1975): 8–10.

72. Greg Toppo, "Group Wants a Peltier Pardon," *Santa Fe New Mexican*, December 8, 1996, p. B1.

73. Richard Meryhew, "Be It Redskins, Chiefs, or Lions, Indians to Protest," *St. Paul Star Tribune*, January 3, 1992, p. 1B; Wilkerson, "Indignant Indians Seeking Changes," p. 14.

74. The quotation is from C. Richard King and Charles Fruehling Springwood, "Introduction," in *Team Spirits: The Native American Mascots Controversy*, ed. C. Richard King and Charles Fruehling Springwood (Lincoln: University of Nebraska Press, 2001), p. 7. We also draw on "Doby's Best Pitch Comes at Playground," *Austin American-Statesman*, July 9, 1997, p. C4.

75. Susan Dodge, "Illiniwek Not Going Anywhere," *Chicago Sun-Times*, March 08, 2001, p. 1; David Prochaska, "At Home in Illinois: Presence of Chief Illiniwek, Absence of Native Americans," in *Team Spirits*, ed. King and Springwood, pp. 165–169.

76. Laurel R. Davis, "Protest Against the Use of Native American Mascots: A Challenge to Traditional American Identity," *Journal of Sport and Social Issues* 17 (April 1993): 9–22; quotation on p. 13.

77. Ibid., p. 19.

78. Randi Hicks Rowe, "NCAA Decides; New Policy Prohibits Usage of Racially Abusive Names by College

Teams," *American Indian Report* 21 (2005): 8–9; Joseph J. Hemmer, Jr., "Exploitation of American Indian Symbols: A First Amendment Analysis," *American Indian Quarterly* 32 (Spring 2008): 121–140.

79. Quoted in "Newspaper Defends Dropping Native American Names from Teams," Reuters News Service, February 19, 1992.

80. Terry, "Los Angeles Times Interview with Suzane Shown Harjo"; "Indian Mascots Are Out, Says Vote in L.A.," *The Los Angeles Times,* September 10, 1997, p. A6; C. Richard King and Charles Fruehling Springwood, "Introduction," in *Team Spirits,* ed. King and Springwood, p. 5.

81. Zach Maxwell, "Rally for Repatriation," *Oklahoma Indian Times* Online, www.okit.com/news/2001/feb/rally.htm (retrieved June 7, 2001).

82. U.S. Commission on Civil Rights, *Indian Tribes: A Continuing Quest for Survival* (Washington, DC: U.S. Government Printing Office, 1981), pp. 61–99; Institute for Natural Progress, "In Usual and Accustomed Places," in *The State of Native America,* ed. Jaimes, pp. 223–226.

83. Institute for Natural Progress, "In Usual and Accustomed Places," pp. 224–226.

84. U.S. Commission on Civil Rights, *Indian Tribes,* p. 103. Italics added.

85. Olson and Wilson, *Native Americans in the Twentieth Century,* p. 195; Ward Churchill, "The Earth Is Our Mother," in *The State of Native America,* ed. Jaimes, pp. 151–169.

86. Alex White Plume, "An Open Letter to President George W. Bush, *Indian Country Today,* August 31, 2006, www.indiancountry.com/content.cfm?id=109 6413572 (September 12, 2006).

87. Haider Rizvi, "Indigenous Rights: Native Peoples Demand Self-Determination," Inter Press Service, August 9, 2006, n.p.; "United Nations Declaration On the Rights of Indigenous Peoples," http://www.un.org/esa/socdev/unpfii/en/declaration.html (retrieved November 2, 2009).

88. U.S. Commission on Civil Rights, *Indian Tribes,* pp. 1–2 (Hatfield quotation from p. 1; quotation from tribal leader from p. 2); Institute for Natural Progress, "In Usual and Accustomed Places," pp. 223, 231, 233–234.

89. The quotation is from "About NARF," http://www.narf.org/about/about_whatwedo.html (retrieved November 8, 2009). We draw here on "Shattering the Myth of the Vanishing American," *Ford Foundation Letter* 22, no. 3 (Winter 1991): 1–5.

90. "The Hidden Victims: Hate Crimes Against American Indians Under-Reported," *Southern Poverty Law Center Intelligence Report,* October 1994, pp. 1–4; Rodney Barker quotation is on p. 4. The student quotation is in Barbara Perry, *Silent Victims: Hate Crimes Against Native Americans* (Tucson: University of Arizona Press, 2008), as excerpted at www.uapress.arizona.edu.

91. Jeff Shaw, "Bitter Harvest; Indian Farmers Allege Years of Discrimination at the USDA," *In These Times,* October 2, 2000, p. 20.

92. Ibid.

93. Alvin M. Josephy, Jr., Joane Nagel, and Troy Johnson, "Introduction: 'You Are on Indian Land!'" in *Red Power: The American Indians' Fight for Freedom,* 2nd ed., Alvin M. Josephy, Jr., Joane Nagel, and Troy Johnson (Lincoln: University of Nebraska Press, 1999), p. 5. We also draw on pp. 3–6.

94. Alvin M. Josephy, Jr., Joane Nagel, and Troy Johnson, "The National Museum of the American Indian Act," in *Red Power,* ed. Josephy, Nagel, and Johnson, p. 228; Alvin M. Josephy, Jr., Joane Nagel, and Troy Johnson, "The Native Americans Graves Protection and Repatriation Act," in *Red Power,* ed. Josephy, Nagel, and Johnson, p. 233.

95. Associated Press, "Navajos March Against Discrimination, Violence," www.lakotaarchives.com/ictnews.html (retrieved September 8, 2006).

96. Ward Churchill and Winona LaDuke, "Native North America: The Political Economy of Radioactive Colonialism," in *The State of Native America,* ed. Jaimes, pp. 241–262; Campbell, "A Mohegan Family," p. 10. See also Sar A. Levitan, Garth L. Mangum, and Ray Marshall, *Human Resources and Labor Markets,* 2nd ed. (New York: Harper & Row, 1976), p. 441.

97. Joseph G. Jorgensen, "Indians and the Metropolis," in *The American Indian in Urban Society,* ed. Waddell and Watson, p. 85.

98. Quoted in Deloria, *Of Utmost Good Faith,* pp. 380–381; see also Hagan, *American Indians,* pp. 126–127; Spicer, *Cycles of Conquest,* pp. 349–356.

99. Cahn, *Our Brother's Keeper,* pp. 69–110; Rupert Costo, "Speaking Freely," *Wassaja* 4 (November–December 1976): 2; Sorkin, *American Indians and Federal Aid,* pp. 70–71; Jorgensen, "Indians and the Metropolis," pp. 96–99.

100. Olson and Wilson, *Native Americans in the Twentieth Century,* p. 181; Robert Bryce, "Indians Seek Control of Tribal-Land Resources," *The Christian Science Monitor,* September 14, 1994, p. 4.; Churchill and LaDuke, "Native North America," pp. 247–248; Harvard Project on American Indian Economic Development, *The State of the Native Nations: Conditions Under U.S. Policies of Self-Determination* (New York: Oxford University Press, 2008), pp. 161–163.

101. The quotation is from "About CERT," http://www.certred earth.com/aboutus-philosophyHistory.html (retrieved November 9, 2009). We also draw on Michael Parfit, "Keeping the Big Sky Pure," *Perspectives* 13 (Spring 1981): 44; Bryce, "Indians Seek Control of Tribal-Land Resources"; Michelle Dearmond, "Tribes, Officials Talking Energy," *Riverside Press Enterprise,* June 21, 2005, p. B01.

102. U.S. Bureau of the Census, "American Fact Finder: Selected Population Profiles in the United States," "American Indian and Alaska Native Alone," http://factfinder.census.gov (retrieved November 9, 2009). In Chapters 3–12, we use data from the American

Community Survey (ACS), a large national survey done to supplement the decennial census. It provides excellent survey estimates for key population statistics, but not full population counts.

103. "Annual Report to the Congress," http://www.opm.gov/About_OPM/Reports/FEORP/2006/feorp2006.pdf (retrieved November 9, 2009).

104. U.S. Bureau of the Census, *Sixteenth Census of the United States: The Labor Force, Part I: U.S. Summary* (Washington, DC: U.S. Government Printing Office, 1943), p. 39; U.S. Department of Health, Education and Welfare, *A Study of Selected Socio-Economic Characteristics of Ethnic Minorities Based on the 1970 Census, vol. 3, American Indians* (Washington, DC: U.S. Government Printing Office, 1974), p. 49; U.S. Bureau of the Census, *1990 Census of Population: Social and Economic Characteristics: United States*, p. 44; U.S. Bureau of the Census, *1990 Census of Population: Social and Economic Characteristics: American Indian and Alaska Native Areas*, CP-2-1A (Washington, DC: U.S. Government Printing Office, 1993), p. 56; U.S. Bureau of the Census, "American Fact Finder: Selected Population Profiles in the United States," "American Indian and Alaska Native Alone."

105. Kathleen Pickering, "Alternative Economic Strategies in Low-Income Rural Communities," *Rural Sociology* 65 (2000): 148–167.

106. U.S. Bureau of the Census, "American Fact Finder: Selected Population Profiles in the United States," "American Indian and Alaska Native Alone."

107. See Nagel, *American Indian Ethnic Renewal*; U.S. Department of Health and Human Services, *National Vital Statistics Reports* 56 (2005).

108. Charles W. Grim, "Statement before the Senate Committee on Indian Affairs on the Status of Indian Health," Department of Health And Human Services, April 13, 2005, www.senate.gov/~scia/2005hrgs/041305hrg/grim.pdf (September 11, 2006); Harvard Project, *The State of the Native Nations*, pp. 219–257.

109. Kavan Peterson, "Indian Casinos Boon to Tribes and States," Stateline.org, June 21, 2006, www.stateline.org/live/ViewPage.action?siteNodeId=136&languageId=1&contentId=121398 (September 11, 2006); National Indian Gaming Association, "The Economic Impact of Indian Gaming in 2008," http://www.indiangaming.org/info/pr/press-releases-2009/NIGA_08_Econ_Impact_Report.pdf (retrieved November 9, 2009).

110. Indian Gaming Association, "The Economic Impact of Indian Gaming in 2008"; National Indian Gaming Commission, "Helping Indian Nations Recover from Centuries of Economic and Social Neglect," Oklahoma Indian Times Online, www.okit.com/gaming/2001/feb/helping.htm (retrieved June 7, 2001).

111. Bob Doucette, "Tribes Compete and Contribute," *The Oklahoman*, June 6, 2001, www.oklahoman.com/cgi-bin/showarticle?ID=696797&TP (retrieved June 7, 2001); National Indian Gaming Commission, "Help-ing Indian Nations Recover from Centuries of Economic and Social Neglect."

112. Bob Doucette and Mark A. Hutchison, "Tribes Build Businesses from Gaming," *The Oklahoman*, June 4, 2001, www.oklahoman.com/cgi-bin/show_article?ID=696799&pic=none&TP=getarticle (retrieved June 7, 2001); Choctaw Nation, "Overview of Tribal Businesses," http://www.choctaw.org/MBCI%20Economic%20Development/Overview%20of%20Tribal%20Businesses/Overview%20of%20Tribal%20Businesses.html (retrieved November 9, 2009); "Recreation and Tourism," http://www.warmsprings.com (retrieved November 9, 2009).

113. Associated Press, "Goshute Reservation in Skull Valley, Utah—2006 Update, Nuclear Dump Glance," June 24, 2006; Bob von Sternberg, "Tribe Fights Storage of Reactor's Spent Fuel," *St. Paul Star Tribune*, November 27, 1991, p. 2B.

114. Stephen Cornell and Joseph P. Kalt, "Two Approaches to Economic Development on American Indian Reservations: One Works, the Other Doesn't," *Harvard Project on American Indian Economic Development and the Native Nations Institute for Leadership, Management, and Policy 2006*, as summarized at http://www.jopna.net/ (retrieved November 3, 2009); the last Kalt quote is from his book, as quoted at Rob Capriccioso, "A Complex Tale to be Told," *Indian Country News*, http://indiancountrynews.net/index.php?option=com_content&task=view&id=1615&Itemid=84 (retrieved November 9, 2009).

115. U.S. Bureau of Indian Affairs, *Federal Indian Policies*, p. 5; Jorge Noriega, "American Indian Education in the United States," in *The State of Native America*, ed. Jaimes, pp. 371–383.

116. U.S. Bureau of Indian Affairs, *Federal Indian Policies*, pp. 5–6; Spicer, *Cycles of Conquest*, p. 349; Noriega, "American Indian Education in the United States," pp. 381–383; U.S. Bureau of Indian Affairs, *Federal Indian Policies*, p. 9.

117. Noriega, "American Indian Education in the United States," pp. 384–385.

118. Phyllis Young, as quoted in ibid., p. 387.

119. *Indian Nations at Risk: An Educational Strategy for Change*, report of U.S. Department of Education Task Force (Washington, DC: U.S. Government Printing Office, 1991), cited in Kenneth Cooper, "Multicultural Focus Recommended for Education of Native Americans," *The Washington Post*, December 27, 1991, p. A19; National Center for Education Statistics, *National Indian Education Study, Part 1: The Performance of American Indian and Alaska Native Fourth- and Eighth-Grade Students on NAEP Reading and Mathematics Assessments* (Washington, DC: U.S. Government Printing Office, 2006), executive summary, n.p.

120. U.S. Bureau of the Census, "American Fact Finder: Selected Population Profiles in the United States," "American Indian and Alaska Native Alone"; see also U.S.

Bureau of the Census, *We the People: American Indians and Alaska Natives in the United States* (Washington, DC: U.S. Government Printing Office, 2006), p. 8.

121. David Melmer, "ACLU Intervenes at High School," *Indian Country Today,* July 4, 2005, www.indiancountry. com/content.cfm?id=1096411180 (September 12, 2006); Valerie J. Shirley, "On the Right Path," *Black Issues in Higher Education* 21 (2004): 88; Institute for Higher Education Policy, *The Path of Many Journeys: The Benefits of Higher Education for Native People and Communities* (Washington, DC: U.S. Government Printing Office, 2007).

122. Institute for Higher Education Policy, *The Path of Many Journeys,* pp. 1–51; National Center for Educational Statistics, "Digest of Education Statistics," 2005, http:// nces.ed.gov/programs/digest/d05/tables/dt05_205 .asp (September 14, 2006); Noriega, "American Indian Education in the United States," pp. 391–392; Office of Indian Education Programs, *Fingertip Facts: 1994* (Washington, DC: U.S. Bureau of Indian Affairs, 1994), p. 16.

123. Paul Hammel, "Tribes Offered Help in Preserving Relics, Treasured Artifact," *Omaha World-Herald,* February 26, 2001, p. 1.

124. Vine Deloria Jr., *Custer Died for Your Sins* (London: Collier-Macmillan, 1969), pp. 108–116.

125. Vittorio Lanternari, *The Religions of the Oppressed* (New York: Mentor Books, 1963), pp. 110–132; Spencer et al., *The Native Americans,* pp. 498–499; Wax, *Indian Americans,* p. 141.

126. Lanternari, *The Religions of the Oppressed,* pp. 99–100; Hertzberg, *The Search for an American Indian Identity,* pp. 239–240, 251, 280; Hertzberg, *The Search for an American Indian Identity,* pp. 246, 257, 271–274, 280–284; Elaine G. Eastman, "Does Uncle Sam Foster Paganism?" in *In Their Place,* ed. Carlson and Colburn, p. 29; Deloria, *Of Utmost Good Faith,* pp. 177–180; "About NAC," http://www.native americanchurch.net/Native_American_Church/NAC.html (retrieved November 10, 2009).

127. Olson and Wilson, *Native Americans in the Twentieth Century,* p. 219; Deloria, *Custer Died for Your Sins,* pp. 122–124.

128. National Asian Pacific American Families Against Substance Abuse, "Pacific Islander Substance Abuse Fact Sheet," Los Angeles, April 26, 2005.

129. Intercultural Cancer Council, "Native Hawaiians/ Pacific Islanders & Cancer," http://iccnetwork.org/cancerfacts/cfs5.htm (July 20, 2006); Anonymous, "Pacific Islanders Threatened," *Environmental Action* 25 (Winter 1994): 32.

130. For example, Lurie, as quoted in John A. Price, "Migration and Adaptation of American Indians to Los Angeles," *Human Organization* 27 (Summer 1968): 168–175.

131. See Snipp, *American Indians,* pp. 23–25.

132. Olson and Wilson, *Native Americans in the Twentieth Century,* p. 212; see also pp. 210–211.

133. Alvin M. Josephy, Jr., Joane Nagel, and Troy Johnson, "Native American Languages Act," in *Red Power,* ed.

Josephy, Nagel, and Johnson, p. 199; Michelle Nijhuis, "Tribal Immersion Schools Rescue Language and Culture," *The Christian Science Monitor,* June 11, 2002, www.csmonitor.com/2002/0611/p11s01-legn.html.

134. Prodipto Roy, "The Measurement of Assimilation: The Spokane Indians," *American Journal of Sociology* 67 (March 1962): 541–551; C. Matthew Snipp, *American Indian and Alaska Native Children in the 2000 Census* (New York: The Annie E. Casey Foundation and The Population Reference Bureau, April 2002).

135. Lynn C. White and Bruce A. Chadwick, "Urban Residence, Assimilation, and Identity of the Spokane Indian," in *Native Americans Today,* ed. Bahr, Chadwick, and Day, p. 243; Brophy and Aberle, *The Indian,* p. 10; Spicer, *Cycles of Conquest,* p. 577.

136. Joan Weibel-Orlando, *Indian Country, L.A.* (Urbana: University of Illinois Press, 1991), pp. 22–43; John Iceland, Daniel H. Weinberg, and Erika Steinmetz, "Racial and Ethnic Residential Segregation in the United States: 1980–2000," paper presented at the annual meeting, Population Association of America, Atlanta, GA, May 9–11, 2002.

137. Josephy, Nagel, and Johnson, "Introduction," in *Red Power,* pp. 7–8; Nijhuis, "Tribal Immersion Schools Rescue Language and Culture."

138. Robert Blauner, *Racial Oppression in America* (New York: Harper & Row, 1972), p. 54; Spicer, *Cycles of Conquest,* pp. 573–574.

139. Quoted in Francis McKinley, Stephen Bayne, and Glen Nimnicht, *Who Should Control Indian Education?* (Berkeley, CA: Far West Laboratory for Educational Research and Development, 1969), p. 13 (italics added).

140. Quoted in Shirley Hill Witt, "Pressure Points in Growing Up Indian," *Perspectives* 12 (Spring 1980): 31.

141. Wilbur J. Scott, "Attachment to Indian Culture," *Youth and Society* 17 (June 1986): 392–394; Ellen Herman, *Kinship by Design: A History of Adoption in the Modern United States* (Chicago: University of Chicago Press, 2008), p. 241.

142. Witt, "Pressure Points in Growing Up Indian," pp. 28–31; Robert W. Blum et al., "American Indian–Alaska Native Youth Health," *Journal of the American Medical Association* 267 (March 25, 1992): 1637–1644; U.S. Department of Health and Human Services, *Regional Differences in Indian Health* (Washington, DC, 1994), p. 56; Donald Warne, "Research and Educational Approaches to Reducing Health Disparities Among American Indians and Alaska Natives," *Journal of Transcultural Nursing* 17 (July 2006): 266–271; Jennifer Langhinrichsen-Rohling, John Friend, Ashley Powell, "Adolescent Suicide, Gender, and Culture: A Rate and Risk Factor Analysis," *Aggression and Violent Behavior* 14 (2009): 402–414.

143. Albert L. Wahrhaftig and Robert K. Thomas, "Renaissance and Repression: The Oklahoma Cherokee," in *Native Americans Today,* ed. Bahr, Chadwick, and Day, p. 81; "Cherokee Nation News," http://www.cherokee

.org/NewsRoom/Default.aspx (retrieved November 12, 2009).

144. Jessica M. Vasquez and Christopher Wetzel, "Tradition and the Invention of Racial Selves: Symbolic Boundaries, Collective Authenticity, and Contemporary Struggles for Racial Equality," *Ethnic and Racial Studies* 32 (2009): 1569.

145. Richard B. Williams, "The Indian Renaissance in America," *Denver Post,* June 6, 2001, p.B7.

146. Both are quoted in Powers, "Native Americans and the Public: A Human Values Perspective," p. 56.

147. Harvard Project, *The State of the Native Nations,* p. 121.

148. See Institute for Natural Progress, "In Usual and Accustomed Places," pp. 228–236.

Chapter 7

1. Bebe Moore Campbell, "To Be Black, Gifted, and Alone," *Savvy* 5 (December 1984): 69.

2. James H. Dorman and Robert R. Jones, *The Afro-American Experience* (New York: Wiley, 1974), pp. 72–74; Thomas R. Frazier, preface to chapter 1, in *Afro-American History: Primary Sources,* ed. Thomas R. Frazier (New York: Harcourt, Brace & World, 1970), pp. 3–5.

3. Olaudah Equiano, "The Interesting Narrative of the Life of Olaudah Equiano," in *Afro-American History,* ed. Frazier, pp. 18, 20.

4. Dorman and Jones, *The Afro-American Experience,* pp. 80–82.

5. Philip D. Curtin, *The Atlantic Slave Trade* (Madison: University of Wisconsin Press, 1969), pp. 87–93; U.S. Bureau of the Census, *Historical Statistics of the United States* (Washington, DC: U.S. Government Printing Office, 1960), p. 770.

6. Carl N. Degler, *Out of Our Past* (New York: Harper, 1959), pp. 161–163; John Hope Franklin, *From Slavery to Freedom,* 4th ed. (New York: Knopf, 1984), p. 88.

7. Franklin, *From Slavery to Freedom,* pp. 132–133.

8. U.S. Bureau of the Census, *Historical Statistics of the United States,* p. 11; Degler, *Out of Our Past,* pp. 163–164; Ulrich B. Phillips, *Life and Labor in the Old South* (Boston: Little, Brown, 1929), pp. 339ff; Kenneth M. Stampp, *The Peculiar Institution* (New York: Random House/Vintage Books, 1956), pp. 383–418.

9. Ben Simpson, "Ben Simpson: Georgia and Texas," in *Lay My Burden Down,* ed. B. A. Botkin (Chicago: University of Chicago Press, 1945), p. 75; see also John W. Blassingame, *The Slave Community* (New York: Oxford University Press, 1972), pp. 155–160.

10. Quoted in Jacqueline Jones, *Labor of Love, Labor of Sorrow: Black Women, Work, and the Family, from Slavery to the Present* (New York: Random House/Vintage Books, 1985), p. 16. We have amended the quotation slightly for clarity.

11. Quoted in ibid., p. 19.

12. Herbert Gutman, *The Black Family in Slavery and Freedom, 1750–1925* (New York: Pantheon, 1976); Stanley

Elkins, "The Slavery Debate," *Commentary 46* (December 1975): 46–47; Wilma A. Dunaway, *The African-American Family in Slavery and Emancipation* (Cambridge: Cambridge University Press, 2003).

13. Patricia Williams, "Alchemical Notes: Reconstructing Ideals from Deconstructed Rights," *Harvard Civil Rights and Civil Liberties Review* 22 (1987): 415.

14. Bonnie Mitchell and Joe Feagin, "America's Racial-Ethnic Cultures: Opposition Within a Mythical Melting Pot," in *Toward the Multicultural University,* ed. Benjamin Bowser, Gale Auletta, and Terry Jones (Westport, CT: Praeger, 1995), pp. 65–86; see also Patricia Hill Collins, *Black Feminist Thought: Knowledge, Consciousness, and the Politics of Empowerment* (Boston: Unwin Hyman, 1990), pp. 40–48.

15. Eugene G. Genovese, *Roll, Jordan, Roll* (New York: Random House, 1974), p. 650.

16. Herbert Aptheker, *American Negro Slave Revolts* (New York: International, 1943), pp. 12–18, 162.

17. Ibid., pp. 165, 220–225, 249–250, 267–273.

18. Herbert Aptheker, *Essays in the History of the American Negro* (New York: International, 1945), pp. 39, 49–51; Sterling Stuckey, *Slave Culture* (New York: Oxford University Press, 1987), pp. 42–46.

19. Quoted in *Bartlett's Familiar Quotations,* 15th ed., ed. Emily M. Beck (Boston: Little, Brown, 1980), p. 556.

20. Benjamin B. Ringer, *"We the People" and Others* (New York: Tavistock, 1983), p. 533.

21. A. L. Higginbotham, *In the Matter of Color* (New York: Oxford University Press, 1978), pp. 144–149.

22. Jerry Fresia, *Toward an American Revolution: Exposing the Constitution and Other Illusions* (Boston: South End Press, 1988), pp. 1–2; Dinitia Smith and Nicholas Wade, "DNA Evidence Links Thomas Jefferson to Slave's Offspring," *Gainesville (Fla.) Sun,* November 1, 1998, p. 4A.

23. Thomas F. Gossett, *Race* (New York: Schocken Books, 1965), pp. 42–43; see Thomas Jefferson, *Notes on the State of Virginia,* ed. Frank Shuffelton (New York: Penguin Books, 1999 [1785]).

24. See, for example, Samuel Cartwright's infamous 1850s article, "The Prognathous Species of Mankind," in *Slavery Defended,* ed. Eric L. McKitrick (Englewood Cliffs, NJ: Prentice-Hall, 1963).

25. Williams, "Alchemical Notes," pp. 401–434. See also Duncan J. MacLeod, *Slavery, Race, and the American Revolution* (London: Cambridge University Press, 1974), p. 158.

26. Richard J. Herrnstein, *IQ in the Meritocracy* (Boston: Little, Brown, 1973); Arthur R. Jensen, "How Much Can We Boost IQ and Scholastic Achievement?" *Harvard Education Review* 39 (1969): 1–123; Tom Wilkie, "The American Association for the Advancement of Science: Research Revives Dispute over IQ," *Independent,* February 19, 1991, p. 7; Richard J. Herrnstein and Charles Murray, *The Bell Curve: Intelligence and Class Structure in American Life* (New York: The Free Press, 1994), pp. 295–316.

27. "Nobel Winner in 'Racist' Claim Row," CNN.com, October 18, 2007, http://edition.cnn.com/2007/TECH/science/10/18/science.race/index.html?iref=mpstoryview (retrieved January 20, 2009).

28. "Buchanan Campaign Rhetoric," *Boston Globe,* January 12, 1992, p. 68; Samuel Francis, "Out of the Mouths of Japanese," *The Washington Times,* February 11, 1992, p. F1.

29. See data gathered by Otto Klineberg as cited in I. A. Newby, *Challenge to the Court* (Baton Rouge: Louisiana State University Press, 1967), p. 74. See also Thomas F. Pettigrew, *A Profile of the Negro American* (Princeton, NJ: D. Van Nostrand, 1964), pp. 123–126.

30. Leon J. Kamin, *The Science and Politics of IQ* (New York: Wiley, 1974), pp. 175–178.

31. N. J. Block and Gerald Dworkin, "IQ, Heritability, and Inequality," in *The IQ Controversy,* ed. N. J. Block and Gerald Dworkin (New York: Random House, 1976), pp. 410–540.

32. Lawrence Bobo, "Inequalities That Endure?: Racial Ideology, American Politics, and the Peculiar Role of the Social Sciences," paper presented at conference on "The Changing Terrain of Race and Ethnicity," University of Illinois, Chicago, October 26, 2001; Srividya Ramasubramanian, "Effects of Media Literacy Training on Explicit and Implicit Racial Stereotypes," Ph.D. dissertation, Penn State University, State College, PA, 2004, p. 16.

33. Nilanjana Dasgupta, Debbie E. McGhee, Anthony G. Greenwald, and Mahzarin R. Banaji, "Automatic Preference for White Americans: Eliminating the Familiarity Explanation," *Journal of Experimental Social Psychology* 36 (2000): 316–328; Associated Press, "Racism Studies Find Rational Part of Brain Can Override Prejudice," www.beliefnet.com/story/156/story_15664_1.html (retrieved November 28, 2004); Shankar Vedantam, "Many Americans Believe They Are Not Prejudiced. Now a New Test Provides Powerful Evidence that a Majority of Us Really Are," *Washington Post Magazine,* January 23, 2005, p. W12; Andrew Scott Baron and Mahzarin R. Banaji, "The Development of Implicit Attitudes: Evidence of Race Evaluations from Ages 6 and 10 and Adulthood," *Psychological Science* 17 (2006): 52–53.

34. Doris Wilkinson, "Minority Women: Social-Cultural Issues," in *Women and Psychotherapy,* ed. Annette M. Brodsky and Rachel T. Hare-Mustin (New York: Guilford, 1980), pp. 295–297. See also A. Thomas and S. Sillen, *Racism and Psychiatry* (New York: Bruner-Mazel, 1972), pp. 57–58.

35. Kevin A. Schulman et al., "The Effect of Race and Sex on Physicians' Recommendations for Cardiac Catheterization," *New England Journal of Medicine* (February 25, 1999): 618–626; Peter B. Bach et al., "Racial Differences in the Treatment of Early-Stage Lung Cancer," *New England Journal of Medicine* (October 14, 1999): 1198–1205; Robert W. Putsch and Linda Pololi, "Distributive Justice in American Healthcare," *American Journal of Managed Care* 10 (September 2004): SP48–SP49; Vanessa Housing, "Doctors in Study Prefer Whites to Blacks: UW Researchers Take a Look at Physician Biases," SeattlePI.com, October 29, 2008, http://seattlepi.nwsource.com/local/385343_doctorbias29.html?source=rss (retrieved April 6, 2009); and Alexander R. Green et al. "Implicit Bias among Physicians and Its Prediction of Thrombolysis Decisions for Black and White Patients," *Journal of General and Internal Medicine* 24 (January 2009): 137–140. We draw in this section on Chapter 4 of Joe R. Feagin, *Racist America: Roots, Current Realities, and Future Reparations,* 2nd ed. (New York: Routledge, 2010).

36. John B. McConahay and Joseph C. Hough, "Symbolic Racism," *Journal of Social Issues* 32 (1976): 38; Lincoln Quillian, "New Approaches to Understanding Racial Prejudice and Discrimination," *Annual Review of Sociology* 32 (2006): 299–328.

37. Richard Morin, "Misperceptions Cloud Whites' View of Blacks," *The Washington Post,* July 11, 2001, p. A01; for the actual data on these areas, see Joe R. Feagin and Karyn McKinney, *The Many Costs of Racism* (Lanham, MD: Rowman & Littlefield, 2003), pp. 10–17. We draw on this discussion here.

38. Pew Research Center, "Blacks See Growing Values Gap Between Poor and Middle Class: Optimism about Black Progress Declines," November 13, 2007, http://pewsocialtrends.org/pubs/700/blackpublic-opinion (retrieved May 5, 2008). All the other surveys are reported in "Race and Ethnicity," http://www.pollingreport.com/race.htm (retrieved February 27, 2009).

39. The lead researcher in the student study was Kerry Kawakami. We use summaries of the study in "Racism: What We Say Doesn't Match What We Do," http://www.msnbc.msn.com/id/28563183/ (retrieved June 29, 2009); and in "Study Finds Gap between What We Say, Do about Racism," http://www.freep.com/article/20090108/NEWS07/90108092/1118/RSS (retrieved March 13, 2009). On older studies, see John F. Dovidio, John C. Brigham, Blair T. Johnson, and Samuel L. Gaertner, "Stereotyping, Prejudice, and Discrimination: Another Look," in *Stereotypes and Stereotyping,* ed. C. Neil Macrae, Miles Hewstone, and Charles Stangor (New York: Guilford, 1995), pp. 276–319.

40. Eduardo Bonilla-Silva and Tyrone A. Forman, "'I Am Not a Racist but . . .': Mapping White College Students' Racial Ideology in the U.S.A.," *Discourse and Society* 11 (2000): 51–86; we draw here on Joe R. Feagin, *Racist America: Roots, Current Realities, and Future Reparations* (New York: Routledge, 2000).

41. Leslie Houts Picca and Joe R. Feagin, *Two Faced Racism: Whites in the Backstage and Frontstage* (New York: Routledge, 2007).

42. U.S. Bureau of the Census, *Historical Statistics of the United States,* p. 218.

43. W. J. Cash, *The Mind of the South* (New York: Random House/Vintage Books, 1960), p. 125.

44. See Gunnar Myrdal, *An America Dilemma* (New York: McGraw-Hill, 1964), 2: 1–198.

45. Gilbert Osofsky, *Harlem: The Making of a Ghetto* (New York: Harper & Row, 1963), pp. 45–51; Arthur I. Waskow, *From Race Riot to Sit-In, 1919 and the 1960s* (Garden City, NY: Doubleday, 1966), pp. 209–210 et passim; Elliot M. Rudwick, *Race Riot at East St. Louis* (Carbondale: Southern Illinois University Press, 1964), pp. 3–30.

46. Southern Poverty Law Center, "Hate Group Numbers Up By 54% Since 2000," http://www.splcenter.org/news/ item.jsp?aid=366 (retrieved June 19, 2009). See also "Going After the Klan," *Newsweek,* February 23, 1987, p. 29; Jessie Daniels, *Cyber Racism* (Lanham, MD: Rowman and Littlefield, 2009), pp. 5–6. We draw in this section on Feagin, *Racist America,* 2nd ed., Chapter 8.

47. Thomas Fields-Meyer, Bob Stewart, Michelle McCalope, and Michael Haederle, "One Deadly Night: Deep in the Woods of East Texas, James Byrd Died a Terrible Death, Leaving a Town and a Nation in Shock," *People,* June 29, 1998, p. 46; Howard Chua-Eoan and Hilary Hylton-Austin "Beneath the Surface; A 'New South' Town is Haunted by 'Deep South' Ghosts—And a Fresh, Ugly Murder," *Time,* June 22, 1998, p. 34; Andy Newman, "Plea Agreements Worked out in Brooklyn Hate-Crime Beating," *The New York Times,* March 9, 2006, http://gothamgazette.com/community/45/news// 184 (retrieved September 18, 2006); Robert D. McFadden, "Black Man Is Attacked by Whites in Brooklyn, Police Say," *The New York Times,* www.nytimes.com/ 2005/08/08/nyregion/ 08bias.html?ex=1281153600& en=8f7ecc53eb288e6a&ei=5090&partner=rssuserland& emc=rss (retrieved September 19, 2006).

48. Greg Mitchell, "Racial Incidents and Threats Against Obama Soar," November 15, 2008, www.huffingtonpost .com/greg-mitchell/racial-incidents-and-thre_b_144061.html (retrieved December 29, 2008); FBI, "Hate Crime Statistics," October 2008, http://www.fbi .gov/ucr/hc2007/victims.htm (retrieved May 17, 2009).

49. People for the American Way, "Right Wing Organizations," www.pfaw.org/pfaw/general/default.aspx?oid =7069& print=yes&units=all (retrieved September 19, 2006); "U.S. Supreme Court Upholds Stiffer Sentences for Hate Crimes," *Intelligence Report,* September 1993, pp. 4–5.

50. Joe R. Feagin and Harlan Hahn, *Ghetto Revolts* (New York: Macmillan, 1973), p. 134.

51. "The Mood of Ghetto America," *Newsweek,* June 2, 1980, pp. 32–34.

52. Lara Parker, "Violence After Police Shooting Exposes Miami Racial Tensions," *The Washington Post,* June 29, 1991, p. A2.

53. Associated Press, "Cincinnati City Manager Resigns," *The New York Times,* May 2, 2001, www.nytimes.com (retrieved May 3, 2001).

54. Gallup Organization, *A Downturn in Black Perceptions of Racial Harmony* (Princeton, NJ: Gallup Organization, 2007), http://www.gallup.com/poll/28072/Downturn-Black- Perceptions-Racial-Harmony.aspx (retrieved January 18, 2008); Gallup Organization, *Black-White Relations 2001 Update* (Princeton, NJ: Gallup Organization, 2001), pp. 1–4.

55. Kim Lersch, "Current Trends in Police Brutality: An Analysis of Recent Newspaper Accounts," Master's thesis, University of Florida, Gainesville, 1993.

56. Howard Fischer, "DPS to Track Stops for Profiling," *Arizona Daily Star,* July 29, 2006, www.azstarnet.com/ allheadlines/139930.php (retrieved September 19, 2006); ACLU, "Landmark Settlement Reached With Maryland State Police In 'Driving While Black' Case," http://www.aclu.org/racialjustice/racialprofiling/34753 prs20080402.html (retrieved May 15, 2009); ACLU, "Racial Profiling Alert," April 2006, http://www.aclu. org/racialjustice/racialprofiling/28283res20060401. html (retrieved May 15, 2009).

57. William M. Wiecek, "The Origins of the Law of Slavery in British North America," *Cardozo Law Review* 17 (1996): 1711–1792; Robert S. Browne, "Achieving Parity Through Reparations," in *The Wealth of Races: The Present Value of Benefits from Past Injustices,* ed. R. F. America (New York: Greenwood Press, 1990), pp. 199–206.

58. Cited in David H. Swinton, "Racial Inequality and Reparations," in *The Wealth of Races,* pp. 153–162.

59. Trina Williams, "The Homestead Act—Our Earliest National Asset Policy," paper presented at the Center for Social Development's symposium, Inclusion in Asset Building, St. Louis, MO, September 21–23, 2000.

60. Stephen J. DeCanio, "Accumulation and Discrimination in the Postbellum South," in *Market Institutions and Economic Progress in the New South 1865–1900,* ed. G. Walton and J. Shepherd (New York: Academic Press, 1981), pp. 103–125.

61. Doris Y. Wilkinson, "The Segmented Labor Market and African American Women from 1890 to 1960," in *Research in Race and Ethnic Relations,* vol. 6, ed. Rutledge M. Dennis (Greenwich, CT: JAI Press, 1991), p. 89. See also Ray Marshall, *The Negro Worker* (New York: Random House, 1967), pp. 7–12; MacLeod, *Slavery, Race, and the American Revolution,* pp. 151–153; Pete Daniel, *The Shadow of Slavery: Peonage in the South* (London: Oxford University Press, 1972); Myrdal, *An American Dilemma,* 1:228.

62. Quoted in Jones, *Labor of Love, Labor of Sorrow,* p. 123.

63. Karl E. Taeuber and Alma F. Taeuber, *Negroes in Cities* (Chicago: Aldine, 1965), pp. 12–13.

64. Charles Tilly, "Race and Migration to the American City," in *The Urban Scene,* ed. Joe R. Feagin (New York: Random House, 1973), p. 35; Taeuber and Taeuber, *Negroes in Cities,* pp. 144–147.

65. Edna Bonacich, "Class Approaches to Ethnicity and Race," *Insurgent Sociologist* 10 (Fall 1980): 11. See also Bennett Harrison, *Education, Training, and the Urban Ghetto* (Baltimore: Johns Hopkins, 1972).

66. W. E. B. Du Bois, *Black Reconstruction in America: An Essay Toward a History of the Part Which Black Folk Played in the Attempt to Reconstruct Democracy in America, 1860–1880* (New York: Atheneum, 1992 [1935]).

67. Wilkinson, "The Segmented Labor Market and African American Women from 1890 to 1960," pp. 90–94.

68. U.S. Bureau of the Census, *Negroes in the United States, 1920–1932* (Washington, DC, 1935), p. 289; Jones, *Labor of Love, Labor of Sorrow*, p. 179; Myrdal, *An American Dilemma*, 1:304–306.

69. Marshall, *The Negro Worker*, pp. 23–24, 56–57.

70. U.S. Bureau of the Census, *Population, vol. 3, The Labor Force* (Washington, DC: U.S. Government Printing Office, 1943); see also Sidney M. Wilhelm, *Who Needs the Negro?* (Cambridge, MA: Schenkman, 1970), p. 57.

71. U.S. Census Bureau, "Population Group: Black or African American Alone, Not Hispanic or Latino," "2008 American Community Survey," http://factfinder.census.gov (retrieved November 19, 2009); U.S. Census Bureau, "Population Group: White Alone, not Hispanic or Latino," "2008 American Community Survey," http://factfinder.census.gov (retrieved November 23, 2009). The data here are for non-Hispanic whites and blacks. See also U.S. Bureau of Labor Statistics, "Annual Average Tables from the January 2005 Issue of Employment and Earnings, Table 10: 'Employed Persons by Occupation, Race, Hispanic or Latino Ethnicity, and Sex,'" January 2005, www.bls.gov/cps/home.htm#annual (retrieved September 19, 2006).

72. Joe R. Feagin and Melvin P. Sikes, *Living with Racism: The Black Middle Class Experience* (Boston: Beacon Press, 1994), pp. 191–194; more recent studies can be found in Feagin, *Racist America*, 2nd edition, pp. 135–188.

73. "Statement of Barbara R. Arnwine Executive Director Lawyers' Committee for Civil Rights Under Law," U.S. Equal Employment Opportunity Commission, www.eeoc.gov/abouteeoc/meetings/4-19-06/foreman.html (retrieved September 19, 2006).

74. Adia Harvey Wingfield, personal communication. See Adia Harvey Wingfield, *Doing Business With Beauty: Black Women, Hair Salons, and the Racial Enclave Economy* (Lanham, MD: Rowman and Littlefield, 2008).

75. Lincoln Quillian, "New Approaches to Understanding Racial Prejudice and Discrimination," *Annual Review of Sociology* 32 (2006): 308; Devah Pager and Bruce Western "Discrimination in Low-Wage Labor Markets: Evidence from an Experimental Audit Study in New York City," research paper, Princeton University, http://72.14.209.104/search?q=cache:hltEuw40fgkJ: paa2005.princeton.edu/download.aspx%3FsubmissionId%3D50874+discrimination+job+Hispanic+testers+matched+cities+research&hl=en&gl=us&ct=clnk&cd=1H (retrieved October 24, 2006). The MIT study, by Marianne Bertrand and Sendhil Mullainathan, is summarized in David Wessel, "Racial Discrimination: Still at Work in the U.S.," *The Wall Street Journal Online*, at www.careerjournal.com/myc/diversity/20030916-wessel.html (retrieved May 26, 2005). We also draw in this section on Feagin, *Racist America*, 2nd ed., Chapter 5.

76. LRA Online, "Backtracking at the EEOC," June 13, 2006, www.laborresearch.org/story2.php/418 (retrieved September 19, 2006).

77. Sharon M. Collins, "The Making of the Black Middle Class," *Social Problems* 30 (April 1983): 369–381; Sharon Collins, "Blacks on the Bubble: The Vulnerability of Black Executives in White Corporations," *Sociological Quarterly* 34 (August 1993): 429–447.

78. Public Relations Society of America, New York Chapter, "National Survey of Multicultural Public Relations Practitioners Reveals Barriers to Diversity," Press Release, New York, June 9, 2005.

79. Arin N. Reeves, "Colored by Race: Bias in the Evaluation of Candidates of Color by Law Firm Hiring Committees," Minority Corporate Counsel Association, www.mcca.com/site/data/magazine/2006-09/colored_by_race.shtml (retrieved September 25, 2006).

80. Kurt Eichenwald, "Texaco Executives, on Tape, Discussed Impeding a Bias Suit," *The New York Times*, November 4, 1996, p. A1; Kurt Eichenwald, "The Two Faces of Texaco," *The New York Times*, November 10, 1996, sec. 3, p. 1.

81. U.S. Equal Employment Opportunity Commission, *Diversity in the Finance Industry* (Washington, DC: EEOC, 2006), executive summary; "Study: Networking Hinders Black Women Executives," Associated Press, January 7, 2009, http://www.foxnews.com/wires/2009Jan07/0,4670,BlackWomenExecutives,00.html (retrieved March 19, 2009); Walden Asset Management, "Report: Nearly Half of America's Largest Companies Responding to Survey Do Not Voluntarily Disclose Equal Employment Opportunity Data on Women, Minorities," Washington, DC: Walden Asset Management, December 7, 2005, p. 1. See also Feagin, *Racist America*, 2nd ed., Chapter 6.

82. The Institute for Diversity and Ethics in Sports, "The 2008 Racial and Gender Report Card: College Sport," University of Central Florida, February 19, 2009, pp. 1–6; The Institute for Diversity and Ethics in Sports, "The 2009 Racial and Gender Report Card: National Football League," University of Central Florida, September 24, 2009, pp. 1–18.

83. "The Multi-City Study of Urban Inequality," *Russell Sage Foundation Newsletter*, Fall 1999, pp. 1–3, and an attached supplement; Philip Moss and Chris Tilly, *Stories Employers Tell: Race, Skill, and Hiring in America* (New York: Russell Sage, 2001); the quote is from Jenny Bussey and John Trasviña, "The Treatment of White and African American Job Applicants by Temporary Employment Agencies in California," research report, Discrimination Research Center, December 2003, http://72.14.209.104/search? q=cache:9B6I8O0NUi0J:www.impactfund.org/DRC%2520December%25202003%2520Report.pdf+%22employment+testing%22+testers+matched+cities+research&hl=en&gl=us&ct=clnk&cd=2 (retrieved October 24, 2006).

84. Jacquelyn Scarville et al., *Armed Forces Equal Opportunity Survey* (Arlington, VA: Defense Manpower Data Center, 1999), pp. 46–85; Office of the Under Secretary of Defense Personnel and Readiness, *Career Progression of Minority and Women Officers* (Washington, DC: U.S. Department of Defense, 1999), pp. 83–85.

85. "Private Sector EEOC Complaints on the Rise, Requiring Compliant Postings as First Line of Legal Defense," http://www.posterguard.com (accessed May 10, 2010).

86. See, for example, *Wards Cove Packing Co.* v. *Atonio*, 109 S. Ct. 2115 (1989).

87. Bureau of Labor Statistics, *Characteristics of the Employed: 2008,* Table 5: "Employment Status of the Civilian Non-institutional Population by Sex, Age, and Race," http://www.bls.gov/cps/tables.htm#charemp (retrieved November 19, 2009). The black figure is higher in U.S. Census Bureau, "Population Group: Black or African American Alone, Not Hispanic or Latino," American Community Survey (2008). See also U.S. Bureau of the Census, *The Social and Economic Status of the Black Population in the United States, 1971* (Washington, DC: U.S. Government Printing Office, 1972), p. 52; U.S. Department of Labor, Bureau of Labor Statistics, "Annual Average Data, Table 24: Unemployed Persons by Marital Status, Race, Hispanic or Latino Ethnicity, Age, and Sex," ftp://ftp.bls.gov/pub/special requests/lf/aat24.txt (retrieved September 24, 2005).

88. See the figures for Laura Dresser and Joel Rogers, *The State of Working Wisconsin: Update 2003* (Madison: Center on Wisconsin Strategy), August 31, 2003, www.cows.org/pdf/jobs/soww/rp-soww-03.pdf (retrieved September 22, 2006).

89. U.S. Census Bureau, "Historical Income Tables—Families, Table F-5: Race and Hispanic Origin of Householder—Families by Median and Mean Income: 1947 to 2004," published December 20, 2005, www.census.gov/hhes/income/histinc/incfamdet.html. "Nonwhite" here consists mostly of black Americans.

90. The data here are again for non-Hispanic whites and blacks. U.S. Census Bureau, "Population Group: Black or African American Alone, Not Hispanic or Latino," "2008 American Community Survey"; U.S. Census Bureau, "Population Group: White Alone, not Hispanic or Latino," "2008 American Community Survey." See also U.S. Bureau of the Census, *Income, Poverty, and Health Insurance Coverage in the United States: 2005,* Table 1: Income and Earnings Summary Measures by Selected Characteristics: 2004–2005, published August 2006, www.census.gov/prod/2006pubs/ p60-231.pdf.

91. Joseph Dalaker and Bernadette D. Proctor, U.S. Census Bureau, Current Population Reports, Series P60-210, *Poverty in the United States, 1999* (Washington, DC: U.S. Government Printing Office, 2000), pp. B-15, B-17; U.S. Bureau of the Census, *Income, Poverty, and Health Insurance Coverage in the United States: 2005,* published August 29, 2006, www.census.gov/prod/2006pubs/p60-231.pdf; U.S. Census Bureau, "Population Group: Black or African American Alone," "2008 American Community Survey"; U.S. Census Bureau, "Population Group: White Alone, not Hispanic or Latino," "2008 American Community Survey."

92. Robert B. Hill, "The Economic Status of Black Americans," in *The State of Black America, 1981*, ed. J. D. Williams (New York: Urban League, 1981), pp. 5–6, 33. Italics added.

93. U.S. Census Bureau, "Population Group: Black or African American Alone, Not Hispanic or Latino," "2008 American Community Survey"; U.S. Census Bureau, "Population Group: White Alone, Not Hispanic or Latino," "2008 American Community Survey."

94. U.S. Bureau of the Census, *Asset Ownership of Households* (Washington, DC: U.S. Government Printing Office, 2005), Table 4, www.census.gov/hhes/www/wealth/ 1998_ 2000/wlth00-4.html (see also note 90); Brian K. Bucks, Arthur B. Kennickell, Traci L. Mach, and Kevin B. Moore, "Changes in U.S. Family Finances from 2004 to 2007: Evidence from the Survey of Consumer Finances," *Federal Reserve Bulletin* 95 (February 2009): A1–A55; Thomas M. Shapiro, *The Hidden Cost of Being African American: How Wealth Perpetuates Inequality* (New York: Oxford University Press, 2004), p. 31.

95. U.S. Census Bureau, "Asset Ownership of Households: 1995, Table 1: Median Value of Assets for Households, by Type of Asset Owned and Selected Characteristics: 1995," published April 9, 2001, www.census.gov/hhes/ www/wealth/1995/wealth95.html; U.S. Census Bureau, "Asset Ownership of Households: 1995, Table 2: Asset Ownership Rates for Households, by Selected Characteristics: 1995," published April 9, 2001, www.census.gov/hhes/www/wealth/1995/wealth95.html; U.S. Commission on Civil Rights, *The Economic Stagnation of the Black Middle Class* (Washington, DC, 2005), pp. 7–9.

96. See William J. Wilson, *The Declining Significance of Race* (Chicago: University of Chicago Press, 1978); Ken Auletta, *The Underclass* (New York: Random House, 1982); William J. Wilson, *The Truly Disadvantaged* (Chicago: University of Chicago Press, 1987); Joe R. Feagin, *Subordinating the Poor* (Englewood Cliffs, NJ: Prentice-Hall, 1975), p. 22.

97. For evidence see Feagin, *Racist America*, 2nd ed.; Joe R. Feagin, *Systemic Racism: A Theory of Oppression* (New York: Routledge, 2006); Joe R. Feagin, *The White Racial Frame: Centuries of Racial Framing and Counter-Framing* (New York: Routledge, 2010).

98. Quillian, "New Approaches to Understanding Racial Prejudice and Discrimination," p. 306; the quote is from Shanna L. Smith, National Fair Housing Alliance, "Testimony Before the House Financial Services Committee, Subcommittee on Housing and Community Opportunity," February 28, 2006, http://www.house.gov/financialservices/media/pdf/022806ss.pdf. (retrieved May 18, 2009). See also National Fair Housing Alliance, *Fair Housing Enforcement: Time for a Change*, May 1, 2009, Washington, DC.

99. Shanna L. Smith and Cathy Clous, "Documenting Discrimination by Homeowners Insurance Companies Through Testing," in *Insurance Redlining: Disinvestment, Reinvestment, and the Evolving Role of Financial Institutions,* ed. Gregory D. Squires (Washington, DC: Urban Institute, 1997), pp. 106–117; and "Housing Segregation Background Report: Brooklyn, New York," National Fair Housing Alliance, New York, NY, October 2006, pp. 2–3.

100. Isabel Wilkerson, "The Tallest Fence: Feelings on Race in a White Neighborhood," *The New York Times,* June 21, 1992, sec. 1, p. 18.

101. Franklin, *From Slavery to Freedom,* pp. 252–253; Chuck Stone, *Black Political Power in America,* rev. ed. (New York: Dell, 1970), pp. 30–31.

102. Stetson Kennedy, *After Appomattox: How the South Won the War* (Gainesville: University Press of Florida, 1995), p. 3; see also Cedric J. Robinson, *Black Movements in America* (New York: Routledge, 1997), pp. 86–88. We also draw here on Feagin, *Racist America,* 2nd ed., Chapter 2.

103. *Plessy* v. *Ferguson,* 163 U.S. 551–552.

104. Hanes Walton, Jr., *Black Politics* (Philadelphia: Lippincott, 1972), pp. 100, 119.

105. Earl Ofari Hutchinson, "Obama's Rise As Black Representation Slows," New America Media, *Commentary,* February 28, 2009, http://news.newamericamedia.org/news/view_article.html?article_id=c172110aedc8c978a6f63abe5153774d (retrieved November 20, 2009). We draw here on Chandler Davidson and Bernard Grofman, "The Voting Rights Act and the Second Reconstruction," in *The Quiet Revolution in the South* (Princeton, NJ: Princeton University Press, 1994), p. 386. Some data are from the Joint Center for Political and Economic Studies, at http:// nuance.dhs.org/ibotalk/0012/0083.html (retrieved May 3, 2001).

106. Chandler Davidson, Tanya Dunlap, Gale Kenny, and Benjamin Wise, *Republican Ballot Security Programs: Vote Protection or Minority Vote Suppression—Or Both?* Report to Center for Voting Rights & Protection, September 2004; Chandler Davidson, *Minority Vote Dilution: An Overview,* Reprint 85-1 (Houston, TX: Institute for Policy Analysis, Rice University, 1985), pp. 17–18.

107. Frank R. Parker, *Black Votes Count* (Chapel Hill: University of North Carolina Press, 1990); Davidson, *Minority Vote Dilution,* pp. 17–18.

108. Earl Ofari Hutchinson, "Bamboozled at the Voting Booth," *Mother Jones,* November 16, 2000, www.motherjones.com/reality_check/bamboozled.html (retrieved May 3, 2001).

109. William E. Forbath, "Civil Rights, Economic Justice, and the Meaning of the Guinier Affair," *Legal Times,* June 28, 1993, p. 21; Michael Isikoff, "Readings in Controversy: Guinier's Pivotal Articles," *The Washington Post,* June 4, 1993, p. A10; Lani Guinier, *The Tyranny of the Majority: Fundamental Fairness and Representation Democracy* (New York: The Free Press, 1994).

110. James W. Button, *Blacks and Social Change* (Princeton, NJ: Princeton University Press, 1989), pp. 226–227.

111. The data are from the Joint Center for Political and Economic Studies, http://www.jointcenter.org (retrieved November 20, 2009).

112. Myrdal, *An American Dilemma,* 1:503; Raymond Wolters, *Negroes and the Great Depression* (Westport, CT: Greenwood Press, 1970), p. xi and elsewhere.

113. Congressional Black Caucus, *Directory of the 104th Congress* (Washington, DC, 1995); http://www.jointcenter.org (retrieved November 20, 2009).

114. Stone, *Black Political Power in America,* pp. 68–72; Adia Harvey Wingfield and Joe R. Feagin, *Yes We Can? White Racial Framing and the 2008 Presidential Election* (New York: Routledge, 2010).

115. Stone, *Black Political Power in America,* p. 47. Cf. Henry L. Moon, *Balance of Power* (Garden City, NY: Doubleday, 1948); Wingfield and Feagin, *Yes We Can?*

116. Kevin Phillips, *The Emerging Republican Majority* (New Rochelle, NY: Arlington House, 1969); Joe R. Feagin, "White Elephant: Race and Electoral Politics in Texas," *Texas Observer,* August 23, 1991, pp. 15–16.

117. Feagin, *Racist America,* 2nd ed., Chapter 8; David A. Bositis, "Blacks and the 2004 Republican National Convention," Joint Center for Political and Economic Studies, Washington, DC, 2004, pp. 1–10; Paul Jenkins, "The GOP's White Supremacy," *Huffington Post,* December 28, 2008, http://www.huffingtonpost.com/paul-jenkins/ the-gops-white-supremacy_b_ 153823. html (retrieved December 29, 2008); James Wright, "Black Republicans Ponder Their Future," *Afro Newspapers* November 24, 2008, http://news.newamericamedia.org/news/view_article.html?article_id=(retrieved December 18, 2008).

118. Feagin and Hahn, *Ghetto Revolts,* pp. 81–85; Loren Miller, *The Petitioners* (New York: Random House, 1966), pp. 250–256; see also Mitchell and Feagin, "America's Racial–Ethnic Cultures," pp. 65–86.

119. Miller, *The Petitioners,* pp. 260–347.

120. Lerone Bennett Jr., *Confrontation: Black and White* (Baltimore, MD: Penguin, 1966), pp. 164–169.

121. Ibid., pp. 223–234; Bryan T. Downes and Stephen W. Burks, "The Historical Development of the Black Protest Movement," in *Blacks in the United States,* ed. Norval D. Glenn and Charles Bonjean (San Francisco: Chandler, 1969), pp. 322–344.

122. Feagin and Hahn, *Ghetto Revolts,* pp. 92–94; Bennett, *Confrontation,* pp. 234–237; Inge P. Bell, *CORE and the Strategy of Nonviolence* (New York: Random House, 1968), pp. 13–16.

123. Aldon Morris, *The Origins of the Civil Rights Movement* (New York: The Free Press, 1984).

124. U.S. Commission on Civil Rights, *The Federal Civil Rights Enforcement Effort: Fiscal Year 1983* (Washington, DC, 1982), pp. 5–7; Andrew Rosenthal, "Reagan Hints Rights Leaders Exaggerate Racism to Preserve Cause," *The New York Times,* January 14, 1989, p. 8.

125. Joe R. Feagin and Hernán Vera, *White Racism: The Basics* (New York: Routledge, 1995), pp. 52–57.

126. The quote is in Office of Civil Rights Evaluation, U.S. Commission on Civil Rights, *Redefining Rights in America: The Civil Rights Record of the George W. Bush Administration, 2001–2004,* www.thememoryhole.org/pol/usccr_redefining_rights.pdf (April 12, 2005). See also Law Librarian Blog, "One Step Closer to Book Burning," http://lawprofessors.typepad.com/law_librarian_blog/2005/02/one_step_closer.html (retrieved September 25, 2006); "Politicizing Civil Rights Enforcement," http://southernstudies.org/2007/04/politicizing-civil-rightsenforcement.html (retrieved November 23, 2009).

127. "Home Page," http://www.covenantwithblackamerica.com/background.htm (retrieved November 23, 2009); Michael H. Cottman, "7th State of the Black Union Gathers but HUD's Alphonso Jackson Misses It," February 27, 2006, www.blackamericaweb.com/site.aspx/bawnews/ stateofblackunion227 (retrieved November 2006).

128. "NAACP-Supported Hate Crimes Prevention Legislation Passes U.S. Senate," http://naacp.org/get-involved/activism/alerts/111thaa-2009-07-30-c/index.htm (retrieved November 23, 2009); Sheila D. Collins, *The Rainbow Challenge* (New York: Monthly Review Press, 1986), pp. 128–143; Collins, *Black Feminist Thought;* Bernice McNair Barnett, "Invisible Southern Black Women Leaders in the Civil Rights Movement: The Triple Constraints of Gender, Race, and Class," *Gender & Society* 7 (1993): 162–182.

129. Franklin, *From Slavery to Freedom,* pp. 280–281; Myrdal, *An American Dilemma,* 1:337–344; Henry A. Bullock, *A History of Negro Education in the South* (New York: Praeger, 1967), pp. 1–99.

130. Bullock, *A History of Negro Education in the South,* pp. 170–186; Franklin, *From Slavery to Freedom,* pp. 284–286.

131. U.S. Census Bureau, "Population Group: Black or African American Alone, Not Hispanic or Latino," "2008 American Community Survey"; U.S. Census Bureau, "Population Group: White Alone, not Hispanic or Latino," 2008 American Community Survey. See also U.S. Bureau of the Census, *We the People: Blacks in the United States* (Washington, DC: U.S. Government Printing Office, 2006), p. 10; U.S. Bureau of the Census, *Statistical Abstract of the United States 1993,* p. 152.

132. Bullock, *A History of Negro Education in the South,* pp. 211–212, 225–230; Miller, *The Petitioners,* pp. 347–358.

133. *Milliken* v. *Bradley,* 418 U.S. 717 (1974); *Swann* v. *Charlotte-Mecklenburg Board of Education* 402 U.S. 43 (1971); U.S. Commission on Civil Rights, *Twenty Years After Brown* (Washington, DC: U.S. Government Printing Office, 1975), pp. 11–41.

134. We draw here on Joe R. Feagin, "Heeding Black Voices: The Court, Brown, and Challenges in Building a Multiracial Democracy," *University of Pittsburgh Law Review* 66 (Fall 2004): 57–81; and R. A. Mickelson, "The Academic Consequences of Desegregation and Segregation," *North Carolina Law Review* 81 (2003): 1513–1546. See also Joe R. Feagin and Bernice M. Barnett, "Success and Failure: How Systemic Racism Trumped the *Brown* v. *Board of Education* Decision," *University of Illinois Law Review* 2004 (2004): 1099–1130; Gary Orfield, *Reviving the Goal of an Integrated Society: A 21st Century Challenge* (Los Angeles: UCLA Civil Rights Project, 2009); Gary Orfield and Susan Eaton, *Dismantling Desegregation: The Quiet Reversal of Brown v. Board of Education* (New York: The Free Press, 1996); Rethinking Schools Project, *The Return to Separate and Unequal* (Milwaukee: Rethinking Schools Project, 2001); J. H. Braddock and T. M. Eitle, "The Effects of School Desegregation," unpublished manuscript, University of Miami, n.d.

135. Quoted in William H. Freivogel, "Black, White, and Brown: Desegregation Ruling Established a Legal Landmark, Unkept Promises," *St. Louis Post-Dispatch,* May 15, 1994, p. 1B.

136. "Vital Statistics," *The Journal of Blacks in Higher Education,* Summer 2008, http://www.jbhe.com/vital/60_index.html (retrieved April 6, 2009); John R. Logan, *Choosing Segregation: Racial Imbalance in American Public Schools, 1990–2000,* unpublished research report, Lewis Mumford Center, University at Albany, Albany, NY, March 29, 2002, n.p.

137. Gary Orfield and Chugmei Lee, *Racial Transformation and the Changing Nature of Segregation* (Cambridge, MA: Harvard Civil Rights Project, 2006), pp. 6–12. The quote and current data are from Orfield, *Reviving the Goal of an Integrated Society,* pp. 3–6.

138. Gail Russell Chaddock, "U.S. Schools Slip Back toward Segregation," *The Christian Science Monitor,* July 18, 2001, www.csmonitor.com; Brett Lane, "Choice Matters: Policy Alternatives and Implications for Charter Schools," Northwest Regional Educational Laboratory, www.nwrel.org/charter/policy.html (retrieved October 3, 2006).

139. Orfield and Lee, *Racial Transformation and the Changing Nature of Segregation,* p. 32.

140. New York ACORN Schools Office, *Secret Apartheid: A Report on Racial Discrimination Against Black and Latino Parents and Children in the New York City Public Schools* (New York: ACORN, 1996), p. 2.

141. Roslyn A. Mickelson, "The Academic Consequences of Desegregation and Segregation: Evidence from the Charlotte-Mecklenburg Schools," *North Carolina Law Review* 81 (2003): 1513–1529.

142. Amy Stuart Wells, Robert L. Crain, and Susan Uchitelle, *Stepping over the Color Line: African American Students in White Suburban Schools* (New Haven, CT: Yale University Press, 1997).

143. Amy Stuart Wells et al., *Boundary Crossing for Diversity, Equity and Achievement: Inter-District School Desegregation and Educational Opportunity* (Cambridge, MA: Charles Hamilton Houston Institute For Race and Justice, 2009), p. 9.

144. We draw here on St. Louis City School District, "2004-05 School Accountability Report Card," http://dese.missouri.gov/planning/profile/arsd115115.html (retrieved October 3, 2006); and Orfield and Lee, *Racial Transformation and the Changing Nature of Segregation,* p. 38.

145. Feagin, "Heeding Black Voices," pp. 76–80; see also Juan Williams, "The Seduction of Segregation, and Why King's Dream Still Matters," *Washington Post,* January 16, 1994, p. C1.

146. Gary Orfield, as quoted in George J. Church, "The Boom Towns," *Time,* June 15, 1987, p. 17.

147. U.S. Bureau of the Census, "School Enrollment—Social and Economic Characteristics of Students: October 2008," http://www.census.gov/population/www/socdemo/school/cps2008.html (retrieved November 24, 2009); U.S. Department of Education, "Action Plan for Higher Education: Improving Accessibility, Affordability and Accountability," published September 2006, www.ed.gov/about/bdscomm/list/hiedfuture/actionplan-fact sheet.html (retrieved November 24, 2009).

148. Kim Clark, "The Challenge for Black Colleges: Like All Schools, Historically Black Colleges Have Their Strong Points and Their Drawbacks," http://www.usnews.com/articles/education/bestcolleges/2009/08/19/the-challenge-for-black-colleges.html?PageNr=2 (retrieved November 24, 2009); Mary Jordan, "Black College Enrollment Up," *The Washington Post,* January 20, 1992, p. A14; "Is the Dream Over?" *Newsweek on Campus,* February 1987, pp. 10–14.

149. The 1990s quote is from Komanduri S. Murty and Julian B. Roebuck, "The Case for Historically Black Colleges and Universities," *Journal of Social and Behavioral Sciences* 36 (1992): 177–178. The university data are from "Report Finds That Large Numbers of Black Students at Duke Face Discrimination in the Classroom and Also Elsewhere on Campus," *JBHE Weekly Report,* as cached at Google (retrieved November 24, 2009); "Race Relations on the Campus of Eastern Kentucky University," *JBHE Weekly Report,* http://www.jbhe.com/latest/index102209_ p.html (retrieved November 24, 2009).

150. The quote is from an ongoing field study: Leslie Houts Picca and Joe R. Feagin, "Experiences of Students of Color," University of Dayton, unpublished research, 2010. See also Joe R. Feagin, Hernán Vera, and Nikitah Imani, *The Agony of Education* (New York: Routledge, 1996).

151. Deirdre A. Royster, *Race and the Invisible Hand: How White Networks Exclude Black Men from Blue-Collar Jobs* (Los Angeles: University of California Press, 2003).

152. Stampp, *The Peculiar Institution,* pp. 156–162; Aptheker, *American Negro Slave Revolts,* pp. 56–60.

153. Stuckey, *Slave Culture,* p. 27; James Scott, *Domination and the Arts of Resistance* (New Haven, CT: Yale University Press, 1990).

154. Richard C. Wade, *Slavery in the Cities* (New York: Oxford University Press, 1964), pp. 161–163; Winthrop Jordan, *White over Black* (Baltimore: Penguin, 1969), pp. 422–425; E. Franklin Frazier, *The Negro Church in America* (New York: Schocken Books, 1964), pp. 35–39; Myrdal, *An American Dilemma,* 2:938–939; E. U. Essien-Udom, *Black Nationalism* (New York: Dell, 1964).

155. Quoted in Michael Hirsley, "Churches Are Sources of Power," *Chicago Tribune,* February 5, 1992, p. C6.

156. Frazier, *The Negro Church in America,* p. 44; Joseph R. Washington Jr., *Black Religion* (Boston: Beacon Press, 1964), pp. 2–29; David L. Lewis, *King* (Baltimore: Penguin, 1970), p. 390.

157. We draw here on research by Bonnie Mitchell for Mitchell and Feagin, "America's Non-European Cultures." See also Feagin, *Racist America,* 2nd ed., Chapter 8.

158. Joe Klein, "Can Colin Powell Save America?" *Newsweek,* October 10, 1994, p. 26.

159. U.S. Bureau of the Census, *We the People: Blacks in the United States,* p. 7; U.S. Census Bureau, "Population Group: Black or African American Alone, Not Hispanic or Latino."

160. John R. Logan and Glenn Deane, *Black Diversity in Metropolitan America* (Albany, NY: Lewis Mumford Center, 2003), pp. 4–6; U.S. Census Bureau, "Population Group: Black or African American Alone, Not Hispanic or Latino."

161. Logan and Glenn Deane, *Black Diversity in Metropolitan America,* pp. 3–6; personal communication from Yanick St. Jean, September 1994.

162. Felix Robert Masud-Piloto, *With Open Arms: Cuban Migration to the U.S.* (Totowa, NJ: Rowman & Littlefield, 1988), pp. 111–125; Paul Farmer, *The Uses of Haiti* (Monroe, ME: Common Courage Press, 1994); Amy Wilentz, *The Rainy Season: Haiti Since Duvalier* (New York: Simon & Schuster/Touchstone, 1989).

163. Gwen Ifill, "President Names Black Democrat Advisor on Haiti," *The New York Times,* May 9, 1994, p. A1; Eric Schmitt, "Tents for Haitians Rise Again at Guantánamo," *The New York Times,* July 2, 1994, p. 1.

164. Testimony of Steven David Forester, Esq., Senate Foreign Relations Committee Hearing on the "Success and Challenges of United States Policy to Haiti," July 15, 2003, http://foreign.senate.gov/testimony/2003/ForesterTestimony030715.pdf (retrieved October 3, 2006); "Haitian Refugees and Immigrants" (Indianapolis, IN: Refugee and Immigration Ministries, Disciples (of Christ) Home Missions, 2007); Yoku Shaw-Taylor, "The Intersection of Assimilation, Race, Presentation of Self, and Transnationalism in America," in *The Other African Americans: Contemporary African and Caribbean Immigrants in the United States,* ed. Yoku Shaw-Taylor and Steven A. Tuch (Lanham, MD: Rowman and Littlefield, 2007), p. 5.

165. U.S. Census Bureau, "Population Group: Black or African American Alone, Not Hispanic or Latino," 2008 American Community Survey; U.S. Census Bureau, "Population Group: White Alone, Not Hispanic or Latino," 2008

American Community Survey; U.S. Census Bureau, "Population Group: West Indians (excluding Hispanic origin groups)," www.factfinder.census.gov (retrieved November 25, 2009).

166. Ramón Grosfoguel and Chloe S. Georas, "'Coloniality of Power and Racial Dynamics: Notes toward a Reinterpretation of Latino Caribbeans in New York City," *Identities: Global Studies in Culture and Power* 7 (2000): 85–125; Mary C. Waters, "Ethnic and Racial Identities of Second Generation Black Immigrants in New York City," *International Migration Review* 28 (Winter 1994): 795–820; Shaw-Taylor, "The Intersection of Assimilation, Race, Presentation of Self, and Transnationalism in America," in *The Other African Americans*, pp. 4–5.

167. Barbara J. Fields, "Ideology and Race in American History," in *Region, Race, and Reconstruction: Essays in Honor of C. Vann Woodward*, ed. J. Morgan Kousser and James M. McPherson (New York: Oxford University Press, 1982), p. 146.

168. Lewis R. Gordon, "Thinking about Identities," in *The Other African Americans*, pp. 69–90; Waters, "Ethnic and Racial Identities of Second Generation Black Immigrants in New York City."

169. Personal communication between authors and Yanick St. Jean, September 1994; see also Waters, "Ethnic and Racial Identities of Second Generation Black Immigrants in New York City."

170. Shaw-Taylor, "The Intersection of Assimilation, Race, Presentation of Self, and Transnationalism in America," in *The Other African Americans*, pp. 4-5; Regine O. Jackson, "Beyond Social Distancing: Intermarriage and Ethnic Boundaries among Black Americans in Boston," in *The Other African Americans*, pp. 217–221. The final quote is from a discussion with sociologist Yanick St. Jean, September 1994.

171. Paul Farmer, *AIDS and Accusation* (Berkeley: University of California Press, 1992), pp. 215–226; Michaela Alfred-Kamara, *Recovered Histories: Reawakening the Narratives of Enslavement, Resistance and the Fight for Freedom* (Anti-Slavery International, October 2008), p. 84. See www.antislavery.org.

172. Milton Gordon, *Assimilation in American Life* (New York: Oxford University Press, 1964), p. 78.

173. See also Talcott Parsons, "Full Citizenship for the Negro American? A Sociological Problem," in *The Negro American*, ed. Talcott Parsons and Kenneth B. Clark (Boston: Houghton Mifflin, 1965), p. 740.

174. Nathan Glazer, *Affirmative Discrimination* (New York: Basic Books, 1975), pp. 40–76; Daniel P. Moynihan, *The Negro Family* (Washington, DC: U.S. Government Printing Office, 1965); Frazier, *The Negro Church in America*; Myrdal, *An American Dilemma*.

175. Robert Blauner, *Racial Oppression in America* (New York: Harper & Row, 1972), pp. 51–110.

176. Wade, *Slavery in the Cities*, pp. 273–275; Herman D. Bloch, *The Circle of Discrimination* (New York: New York University Press, 1969), pp. ix–xiii.

177. Wilhelm, *Who Needs the Negro?*; Robert L. Allen, *Black Awakening in Capitalist America* (Garden City, NY: Doubleday/Anchor Books, 1970), pp. 4–6; Report of the National Advisory Commission on Civil Disorders (New York: Bantam, 1968), pp. 278–279.

178. Marimba Ani, *Yurugu: An African-Centered Critique of European Cultural Thought and Behavior* (Trenton, NJ: Africa World Press, 1994), pp. 567–569.

179. Feagin and Sikes, *Living with Racism*, p. vii. On the contemporary health costs of racial discrimination, see Feagin and McKinney, *The Many Costs of Racism*, Chapters 2–5, and David R. Williams, Harold W. Neighbors, and James S. Jackson, "Racial/Ethnic Discrimination and Health: Findings from Community Studies," *American Journal of Public Health* 93 (February 2003): 200–208.

Chapter 8

1. Juan Gonzalez, *Harvest of Empire: A History of Latinos in America* (New York: Penguin, 2000), p. xii; Ruben Navarrette, "Calm Down, It's Not an Assault on America," Realclearpolitics Blog, May 03, 2006, www.realclearpolitics.com/articles/2006/05/calm_down_its_not_an_assault_o.html (retrieved October 26, 2006).

2. U.S. Census Bureau, "The Hispanic Population," *Census 2000 Brief*, May 2001, pp. 1–2, www.census.gov/prod/cen2000; U.S. Bureau of the Census, "Population Group: Mexican," "2008 American Community Survey," http:// factfinder.census.gov (retrieved November 27, 2009).

3. Edward Múrguía, "On Latino/Hispanic Ethnic Identity," *Latino Studies Journal* 2, no. 3 (September 1991): 8–18.

4. "Hispanics: A People in Motion," research report, Pew Hispanic Center, Washington, DC, January 2005, p. 3.

5. Teresa L. Amott and Julie A. Matthaei, *Race, Gender, and Work* (Boston: South End Press, 1991), pp. 64–67.

6. Américo Paredes, *With His Pistol in His Hand* (Austin: University of Texas Press, 1958), pp. 3–14; Rodolfo Acuña, *Occupied America* (San Francisco: Canfield Press, 1972), pp. 10–12.

7. Acuña, *Occupied America*, p. 15; S. Dale McLemore, "The Origin of Mexican American Subordination in Texas," *Social Science Quarterly* 53 (March 1973): 665–667; Rodolfo Alvarez, "The Psycho-Historical and Socioeconomic Development of the Chicano Community in the United States," *Social Science Quarterly* 53 (March 1973): 925; David Montejano, *Anglos and Mexicans in the Making of Texas, 1836–1986* (Austin: University of Texas Press, 1987).

8. William Lord, "Myths and Realities of the Alamo," *American West* 5 (May 1968): 20–25.

9. Carl N. Degler, *Out of Our Past* (New York: Harper, 1959), pp. 109–110; Acuña, *Occupied America*, pp. 23–29.

10. Joan Moore and Harry Pachon, *Hispanics in the United States* (Englewood Cliffs, NJ: Prentice Hall, 1985),

pp. 18, 22–23; Leo Grebler, Joan W. Moore, and Ralph G. Guzmán, *The Mexican-American People* (New York: The Free Press, 1970), pp. 43–44; Acuña, *Occupied America*, p. 105; Joan W. Moore, "Colonialism: The Case of the Mexican Americans," *Social Problems* 17 (Spring 1970): 468–469.

11. Moore and Pachon, *Hispanics in the United States,* p. 21; Ellwyn R. Stoddard, *Mexican Americans* (New York: Random House, 1973), pp. 9–13; Carey McWilliams, *North from Mexico* (New York: Greenwood, 1968), pp. 70–76; Acuña, *Occupied America,* pp. 60–62; Grebler, Moore, and Guzmán, *The Mexican American People,* pp. 43–44; Nancie L. Gonzales, *The Spanish-Americans of New Mexico* (Albuquerque: University of New Mexico Press, 1967), pp. 204–210.

12. Alvarez, "Psycho-Historical and Socioeconomic Development," p. 925.

13. Oscar J. Martinez, "On the Size of the Chicano Population: New Estimates: 1850–1900," *Aztlán* 6 (Spring 1975): 55–56; U.S. Department of Justice, *Immigration and Naturalization Service, Annual Report* (Washington, DC, 1975), pp. 62–64; Julian Samora, *Los Mojados: The Wetback Story* (Notre Dame, IN: University of Notre Dame Press, 1971), pp. 7–8.

14. Leo Grebler, *Mexican Immigration to the United States: The Record and Its Implications* (Los Angeles: UCLA Mexican-American Study Project, 1965), pp. 20–21.

15. Mark Reisler, *By the Sweat of Their Brow: Mexican Immigrant Labor in the United States, 1900–1940* (Westport, CT: Greenwood, 1976); Grebler, *Mexican Immigration to the United States,* pp. 23–24; Manuel Gamio, *Mexican Immigration to the United States* (New York: Dover, 1971), pp. 171–174; Ronald Takaki, *A Different Mirror* (Boston: Little, Brown, 1993), pp. 326–334.

16. Samora, *Los Mojados,* pp. 48–52.

17. Gilberto Cardenas, "United States Immigration Policy Toward Mexico," *Chicano Law Review* 2 (Summer 1975): 73–75; Grebler, *Mexican Immigration to the United States,* p. 26.

18. Samora, *Los Mojados,* pp. 18–19, 24–25, 44–46, 57; Joan Moore, *Mexican Americans,* 2nd ed. (Englewood Cliffs, NJ: Prentice-Hall, 1976), pp. 49–51; Strategy Research Corporation, *1991 U.S. Hispanic Market* (Miami: Strategy Research Corporation, 1991), pp. 39, 51.

19. Cardenas, "United States Immigration Policy toward Mexico," pp. 84–85; Cheryl Anderson, "Immigration Bill Under Attack on Several Fronts," *Austin American-Statesman,* December 12, 1982, p. C1.

20. Luis Alberto Urrea, *By the Lake of Sleeping Children: The Secret Life of the Mexican Border* (New York: Anchor Books), 1996, p. 18; see also Ann V. Millard and Jorge Chapa, *Apple Pie and Enchiladas: Latino Newcomers in the Rural Midwest* (Austin: University of Texas Press, 2004).

21. See Ilan Stavans, *The Hispanic Condition: Reflections on Culture and Identity in America* (New York: Harper Collins, 1995).

22. Ibid., p. 22.

23. See Gonzalez, *Harvest of Empire,* pp. 234–236. See also "Maquiladoras," http://en.wikipedia.org/wiki/Maquiladora#cite_ref-5 (retrieved November 27, 2009).

24. Michael Fix and Jeffrey S. Passel, *Immigration and Immigrants: Setting the Record Straight* (Washington, DC: Urban Institute, 1994), p. 24.

25. Jeffrey S. Passel and D'Vera Cohn, "Mexican Immigrants: How Many Come? How Many Leave?" research report, Pew Hispanic Center, Washington, DC, July 22, 2009; Jeffrey S. Passel and D'Vera Cohn, "A Portrait of Unauthorized Immigrants in the United States," Pew Hispanic Center, Washington, DC, April 14, 2009; Leo R. Chávez, *Shadowed Lives: Undocumented Immigrants in American Society* (Orlando, FL: Harcourt Brace Jovanovich, 1992), pp. 19–151.

26. Douglas S. Massey, "Five Myths about Immigration," *Immigration Policy in Focus* 4 (August 2005), p. 1; Fix and Passel, *Immigration and Immigrants,* pp. 24–25, 51, 60, 62, 71, 81.

27. Stephen Koepp, "Rotten Shame: Who Will Pick the Crops?" *Time,* June 22, 1987, p. 49.

28. Jacqueline Maria Hagan and Susan González Baker, "Implementing the U.S. Legalization Program," *International Migration Review* 27 (Fall 1993): 514; Susan González Baker and Frank Bean, "The Legalization Programs of the 1986 Immigration Reform and Control Act," in *In Defense of the Alien,* ed. Lydio F. Tomasi (New York: Center for Migration Studies, 1990), pp. 3–11; Susan González Baker, *The Cautious Welcome: The Legalization Programs of the Immigration Reform and Control Act* (Washington, DC: Urban Institute, 1990); some information here was provided by Demographics Statistics Branch, Immigration and Naturalization Service, January 1995.

29. Jose A. Pagan and Alberto Davila, "On-the-Job Training, Immigration Reform, and the True Wages of Native Male Workers," *Industrial Relations* 35 (January 1996): 45–58.

30. "Statistical Portrait of the Foreign-Born Population in the United States," Pew Hispanic Center, Washington, DC, March 5, 2007; Lisa Lollock, *The Foreign Born Population in the United States: March 2000, Current Population Reports,* P20-534, (Washington, DC: U.S. Census Bureau, 2001). See also Karen A. Woodrow and Jeffrey S. Passel, "Post-IRCA Undocumented Immigration to the United States," in *Undocumented Migration to the United States,* ed. Frank Bean, Barry Edmonston, and Jeffrey Passel (Santa Monica, CA: Rand Corporation, 1990), p. 42.

31. Quoted from *The Los Angeles Times* in Donaldo Macedo, "Foreword," in Enrique T. Trueba, *Latinos Unidos: From Cultural Diversity to the Politics of Solidarity* (Lanham, MD: Rowman & Littlefield, 1999), pp. xviii–xix. See also Otto Santa Ana, *Brown Tide Rising: Metaphors of Latinos in Contemporary American Public Discourse* (Austin: University of Texas Press, 2002).

32. Lynda Gorov, "Poor Immigrants Face New Hurdles," *Boston Globe,* November 30, 1997, p. A1.

33. "5,100 Crosses at Mexico Border Mark Migrant Deaths," Press Release, Associated Press, October 30, 2009; "Major Provisions of 'The Secure Fence Act of 2006,'" Justice for Immigrants, Press Release, www.justice-forimmigrants.org/HR6061.html (retrieved October 22, 2006); "Fencing in Immigration Reform," American Friends Service Committee, Press Release, www.afsc.org/news/2006/fencing-in-immigration-reform.htm (retrieved October 22, 2006).

34. Rakesh Kochhar, "Latino Labor Report," research report, Pew Hispanic Center, Washington, DC, September 27, 2006, p. 7; Rakesh Kochhar, "Latino Labor Report," research report, Pew Hispanic Center, Washington, DC, June 4, 2008; Francine J. Lipman, "The Taxation of Undocumented Immigrants: Separate, Unequal, and Without Representation," *Harvard Latino Law Review* 9 (Spring 2006): 1–7; Elizabeth Chesler, "Notes: Denying Undocumented Immigrants Access to Medicaid: A Denial of Their Equal Protection Rights?" *Public Interest Law Journal* 17 (June 2008): 255–258.

35. "Country of Origin Profiles of U.S. Hispanics," research report, Pew Hispanic Center, Washington, DC, October 15, 2009.

36. The first three quotations are from Arnoldo De León, "Initial Contacts: Niggers, Redskins, and Greasers," in *The Latino/a Condition: A Critical Reader,* ed. Richard Delgado and Jean Stefancic (New York: New York University Press, 1998), p. 161. Monroe is quoted in Philip D. Ortego, "The Chicano Renaissance," in *Introduction to Chicano Studies,* ed. Livie I. Duran and H. Russell Bernard (New York: Macmillan, 1973), p. 337.

37. Ricardo Romo, *East Lost Angeles: History of a Barrio* (Austin: University of Texas Press, 1983), pp. 89–111.

38. Cardenas, "United States Immigration Policy Toward Mexico," pp. 70–71.

39. Quoted in Ralph Guzmán, "The Function of Anglo-American Racism in the Political Development of Chicanos," in *La Causa Politica,* ed. F. Chris Garcia (South Bend, IN: University of Notre Dame Press, 1974), p. 22.

40. McWilliams, *North from Mexico,* p. 213.

41. William Sheldon, "Educational Research and Statistics: The Intelligence of Mexican-American Children," in *In Their Place,* ed. Lewis H. Carlson and George A. Colburn (New York: Wiley, 1972), pp. 149–151.

42. Quoted in Guillermo V. Flores, "Race and Culture in the Internal Colony: Keeping the Chicano in His Place," in *"Structures of Dependency,"* ed. Frank Bonilla and Robert Girling (Stanford, CA: privately published by a Stanford faculty–student seminar, 1973), p. 194.

43. Quoted in George A. Martinez, "Mexican Americans and Whiteness," in *The Latino/a Condition,* p. 178.

44. The senator is quoted in Otto Santa Ana, "'Like an Animal I Was Treated': Anti-Immigrant Metaphor in U.S. Public Discourse," *Discourse & Society* 10 (1994): 220. The Forest Service story is at "Forest Service apologizes to Hispanic campers," http://www.inform.com/article/Forest%20Service%20apologizes%20to%20Hispanic%20campers (retrieved December 15, 2009).

45. Octavio Ignacio Romano, "The Anthropology and Sociology of the Mexican-Americans," *El Grito* 2 (Fall 1968): 13–19; Oscar Lewis, *Five Families* (New York: Wiley, 1962); William Madsen, *Mexican Americans of South Texas* (New York: Holt, Rinehart and Winston, 1964).

46. G. Marin, "Stereotyping Hispanics," *International Journal of Intercultural Relations* 8 (1984): 17–27.

47. Linda A. Jackson, "Stereotypes, Emotions, Behavior, and Overall Attitudes toward Hispanics by Anglos," *Research Report* 10, Julian Samora Research Institute, Michigan State University, East Lansing, MI, January 1995, www .jsri.msu/RandS/research/irr/rr10.htm (retrieved June 9, 2001). On the issues here , see also the older research of Américo Paredes, *With His Pistol in His Hand;* Romano, "The Anthropology and Sociology of the Mexican Americans"; Stoddard, *Mexican Americans,* pp. 42–44; Lea Ybarra, "Empirical and Theoretical Developments in the Study of the Chicano Family," in *The State of Chicano Research on Family, Labor, and Migration,* ed. Armando Valdez, Albert Camarillo, and Tomás Almaguer (Stanford, CA: Stanford Center for Chicano Research, 1983), p. 96.

48. National Conference of Christians and Jews, *Taking America's Pulse: The National Conference Survey on Inter-Group Relations* (New York: National Conference, 1994).

49. Charles N. Weaver, "Work Attitudes of Mexican Americans," *Hispanic Journal of Behavioral Sciences* 22 (August 2000): 275–295.

50. Robert J. Durán, "Inner-City Mexican American Experiences with Police Gang Enforcement," *Journal of Contemporary Ethnography* 38 (2009): 143–168.

51. The 2009 surveys are reported in "Fact Sheet: Public Opinion on Immigration," ImmigrationWorksUSA.org, http://www.immigrationworksusa.org/uploaded/file/IW_polling_round-up.pdf (retrieved December 1, 2009); and in "America's Immigration Quandary: No Consensus on Immigration Problem or Proposed Fixes," research report, Pew Hispanic Center, Washington, DC, March 30, 2006, pp. 1–4.

52. James H. Johnson Jr., Karen D. Johnson-Webb, and Walter C. Farrell Jr., "A Profile of Hispanic Newcomers to North Carolina," *Popular Government* 65 (Fall 1999): 2–12. On Latino immigrant responses to living with black residents, see also Paula D. McClain et al., "Racial Distancing in a Southern City: Latino Immigrants' Views of Black Americans," *The Journal of Politics* 68 (August 2006): 581–582.

53. Southern Poverty Law Center, *Under Siege: Life for Low-Income Latinos in the South* (Montgomery, AL: SPLC, 2009); and "Blood on the Border," *Intelligence Report,* Southern Poverty Law Center, Spring 2001, pp. 8–11; Navarrette, "Calm Down, It's Not an Assault on America."

54. Samuel P. Huntington, "The Erosion of American National Interests," *Foreign Affairs* (September/October 1997): 28ff; see also Samuel P. Huntington, *Who Are We: The Challenges to America's National Identity* (New York: Simon & Schuster, 2005).

55. Joe Kelly and Stacy L. Smith, "Generally Movies Give Boys a D: Portraying Males as Dominant, Disconnected and Dangerous," research report, Duluth, Minnesota, Dadsanddaughters.org, 2006, p. 4; National Council of La Raza, "Distorted Reality: Hispanic Characters in TV Entertainment," September 1994. See also Gregory Freeman, *Crisis*, October 1994, p. 5; Travis L. Dixon and Daniel Linz, "Overrepresentation and Underrepresentation of African Americans and Latinos as Lawbreakers on Television News," *Journal of Communication* 50 (2000): 131–135; Children Now and National Hispanic Foundation for the Arts, "Latinos on Prime Time: 2001–02 Prime Time Television Season," 2002, http://72.14.209.104/search?q=cache:x880r4C_busJ:www.hispanicarts.org/Media/Latinoson Prime TimeIII .pdf+%22latinos+on+prime+time%22+2001-2002&hl= en& gl=us&ct=clnk&cd=1 (retrieved November 13, 2006).

56. Ansel Martinez, "Study Shows Television Shows Stereotype Hispanics," *All Things Considered* (Washington, DC: National Public Radio), September 10, 1994.

57. Marco Portales, *Crowding Out Latinos: Mexican Americans in the Public Consciousness* (Philadelphia: Temple University Press, 2000), p. 101; Dmitri Williams, Nicole Martins, Mia Consalvo, and James D. Ivory, "The Virtual Census: Representations of Gender, Race and Age in Video Games," *New Media & Society* 11 (2009): 815–834. See also Brendan Sinclair, "Study: Minorities Underrepresented in Games," http://www.gamespot.com/news/6229016.html (retrieved December 1, 2009).

58. Portales, *Crowding Out Latinos*, p. 31.

59. Santa Ana, "'Like an Animal I Was Treated,'" pp. 194–220; see also Santa Ana, *Brown Tide Rising*. The magazine research is reported in Juanita J. Covert and Travis L. Dixon, "Representation and Effects of the Portrayal of Women of Color in Mainstream Women's Magazines," *Communication Research* 35 (2008): 232–256.

60. Jane H. Hill, "Mock Spanish: A Site for the Indexical Reproduction of Racism in American English," unpublished research paper, University of Arizona, Tucson, 1995. For more recent data, see Jane H. Hill, *The Everyday Language of White Racism* (New York: Wiley-Blackwell, 2008).

61. Rosina Lippi-Green, *English with an Accent* (New York: Routledge, 1997), pp. 238–239. The quote on the Texas official is from "MALDEF Urges Texas Secretary of State to Re-Issue Language Assistance Guidance to County Election Officials in Light of Recent Comments," November 12, 2009, http://maldef.org/news/releases/TX_election_11122009 (retrieved December 8, 2009).

62. David E. López and Ricardo D. Stanton-Salazar, "Mexican Americans: A Second Generation at Risk," in *Ethnicities: Children of Immigrants in America*, ed. Rubén Rumbaut and Alejandro Portes (Berkeley: University of California Press, 2001), pp. 57–90.

63. Joe R. Feagin and Danielle Dirks, "'Who Is White?': College Students' Assessments of Key U.S. Racial and Ethnic Groups," unpublished research manuscript, Texas A&M University, College Station, TX, 2006; "Reaction to Lou Dobbs Town Hall on Broken Borders," www.mydd.com/story/2006/10/27/112734/61 (retrieved October 27, 2006).

64. Ariela J. Gross, "Texas Mexicans and the Politics of Whiteness," *Law and History Review* 21 (Spring 2003), www.historycooperative.org/journals/lhr/21.1/comment_gross.html (Retrieved October 30, 2006); the survey is in Tatcho Mindiola, Néstor Rodríguez, and Yolanda Flores Niemann, "Intergroup Relations between African Americans and Hispanics in Harris County," unpublished research report, Center for Mexican American Studies, University of Houston, 1996; Pew Hispanic Center/Kaiser Family Foundation, "2002 National Survey of Latinos," research report, Washington, DC, December 2002, pp. 32–33.

65. U.S. Census Bureau, "Overview of Race and Hispanic Origin," *Census 2000 Brief*, March 2001, pp. 2–5, www.census.gov/prod/cen2000; Sonya Tafoya, "Shades of Belonging," Pew Hispanic Center, research report, December 6, 2004.

66. E. J. Hobsbawm, *Primitive Rebels* (New York: W. W. Norton, 1959), pp. 15–16; Paredes, *With His Pistol in His Hand*, pp. 27–32; McWilliams, *North from Mexico*, p. 127; Moore, "Colonialism," p. 466; Stoddard, *Mexican Americans*, p. 181; William D. Carrigan, "The Lynching of Persons of Mexican Origin or Descent in the United States, 1848 to 1928, *Journal of Social History* 37 (Winter 2003): 411–438.

67. Ralph H. Turner and Lewis M. Killian, *Collective Behavior* (Englewood Cliffs, NJ: Prentice-Hall, 1957), pp. 125–128; McWilliams, *North from Mexico*, pp. 229–238.

68. Navarrette, "Calm Down, It's Not an Assault on America"; Southern Poverty Law Center, *Under Siege: Life for Low-Income Latinos in the South* (Montgomery, AL: SPLC, 2009), pp. 1–5; Mark Potok, "Diversity and Its Discontents," *Intelligence Report*, Spring 2009, http://www.splcenter.org/intel/intelreport/article.jsp?aid=1010 (retrieved May 17, 2009).

69. Armondo Morales, *Ando Sangrando* (Fair Lawn, NJ: R. E. Burdick, 1972), pp. 100–108.

70. U.S. Commission on Civil Rights, *Mexican Americans and the Administration of Justice in the Southwest* (Washington, DC, 1970), pp. 6–10; Robert Lee Maril, *Poorest of Americans* (South Bend, IN: University of Notre Dame Press, 1989), p. 52; Andrea Ford and Sheryl Stolberg, "Latinos Tell Panel of Anger at Police Conduct," *The Los Angeles Times*, May 21, 1991, p. A1.

71. Patrick J. McDonnell, "Latinos Recover Optimism Lost in '90s," *The Los Angeles Times*, March 11, 2001; Mark Hugo Lopez and Gretchen Livingston "Hispanics and

the Criminal Justice System," research report, Pew Hispanic Center, April 2009.

72. Antonio H. Rodríguez and Carlos A. Chávez, "Latinos Unite in Self-Defense on Proposition 187," *The Los Angeles Times,* October 21, 1994, p. B7; Beth Shuster and Chip Johnson, "Hundreds of Students Stage Walkouts to Protest Proposition 187," *The Los Angeles Times,* October 21, 1994, p. B3; Frank Trejo, "Thousands of Hispanics March in Washington; Texas Residents Join Call for End to Discrimination, Rights Abuses," *Dallas Morning News,* October 13, 1996, p. 1.

73. "Topline Survey Results," www.icrsurvey.com (retrieved December 3, 2009).

74. Andrew Gumbel, "A Million Turn out for Proimmigration March in Los Angeles," *The Independent,* March 27, 2006, www.findarticles.com/p/articles/mi_qn4158/is_200603 27/ai_n16175884 (retrieved October 17, 2006); Robert Suro and Gabriel Escobar, "2006 National Survey of Latinos: The Immigration Debate," research report, Pew Hispanic Center, Washington, DC, July 2006, pp. 8–9; William I. Robinson, "'Aqui estamos y no nos vamos!' Global Capital and Immigrant Rights," *Race & Class* 48 (2006): 77–91.

75. Abel G. Rubio, *Stolen Heritage* (Austin, TX: Eakin Press, 1986); Clark Knowlton, "Recommendations for the Solution of Land Tenure Problems Among the Spanish Americans," in *Chicano: The Evolution of a People,* ed. Renato Rosaldo, Robert A. Calvert, and Gustav L. Seligmann (San Francisco: Rinehart Press, 1973), pp. 334–335; George I. Sánchez, *Forgotten People* (Albuquerque: University of New Mexico Press, 1940), p. 61; Arnoldo Deleón, *The Tejano Community, 1836–1900* (Albuquerque: University of New Mexico Press, 1982), pp. 63–91.

76. Tomas Almaguer, "Historical Notes on Chicano Oppression: The Dialectics of Racial and Class Domination in North America," *Atzlán* 5 (Spring–Fall 1974): 38–39; Richard del Castillo, "Myth and Reality: Chicano Economic Mobility in Los Angeles, 1850–1880," *Atzlán* 6 (Summer 1975): 153–154; Charles Wollenberg, "Huelga, 1928 Style: The Imperial Valley Canteloupe Workers' Strike," in *Chicano,* ed. Rosaldo, Calvert, and Seligmann, pp. 185–188; Amott and Matthaei, *Race, Gender, and Work,* pp. 76–77.

77. Samora, *Los Mojados,* p. 130; Grebler, Moore, and Guzmán, *The Mexican-American People,* p. 91; Ruth H. Tuck, *Not with the Fist* (New York: Harcourt, Brace & World, 1946), pp. 173–183; Anne Brunton, "The Chicano Migrants," in *Introduction to Chicano Studies,* ed. Duran and Bernard, pp. 489–492; McWilliams, *North from Mexico,* pp. 217–218.

78. Roberto Suro, "Border Boom's Dirty Residue Imperils U.S.–Mexico Trade," *The New York Times,* March 31, 1991, p. 1; Patrick McDonnell, "Foreign-Owned Companies Add to Mexico's Pollution," *The Los Angeles Times,* November 18, 1991, p. A1; Richard W. Stevenson, "Economic Scene: The Hidden Costs of Mexico Plants," *The New York Times,* July 19, 1991, p. D2; Judy Pasternak, "Firms Find a Haven from U.S. Environmental Rules," *The Los Angeles Times,* November 19, 1991, p. A1; Patrick McDonnell, "Mexico: Progress and Promise," *The Los Angeles Times,* October 22, 1991, p. 11; "Maquiladoras," http://en.wikipedia.org/wiki/Maquiladora#cite_ref-5 (retrieved November 27, 2009).

79. Chávez, *Shadowed Lives,* pp. 19, 139–155.

80. Teresa Puente, "When Hope Turns into Slavery," *Chicago Tribune,* August 10, 1997, p. 1C; Pierrette Hondagneu-Sotelo, *Domestica: Immigrant Workers Cleaning and Caring in the Shadows of Affluence* (Berkeley: University of California Press, 2001), p. 210.

81. Felisa Gonzales, "Hispanic Women in the United States, 2007," research report, Pew Hispanic Center, May 8, 2008, p. 3.

82. On interview studies, see José Cobas and Joe R. Feagin, "Latinos/as and the White Racial Frame," *Sociological Inquiry* 78 (February 2008): 39–53. On testing, see Marc Bendick, Jr., "Situation Testing for Employment Discrimination in the United States of America," *Revue Horizons Stratégiques,* Centre D'analyse Stratégique, July 2007, pp. 6–18.

83. Devah Pager and Bruce Western, "Discrimination in Low-Wage Labor Markets: Evidence from an Experimental Audit Study in New York City," research paper, Princeton University, http://72.14.209.104/search?q=cache:hltEuw40fgkJ: paa2005.princeton.edu/download.aspx%3FsubmissionId% 3D50874+discrimination+ job+Hispanic+testers+matched+ cities+research&hl=en&gl=us&ct=clnk&cd=1H (retrieved October 24, 2006); Philip Moss and Chris Tilly, *Stories Employers Tell: Race, Skill, and Hiring in America* (New York: Russell Sage, 2001), pp. 130–150.

84. Millard and Chapa, *Apple Pie and Enchiladas,* p. 5; López and Stanton-Salazar, "Mexican Americans: A Second Generation at Risk," in *Ethnicities,* p. 76.

85. Lawrence D. Bobo and Susah A. Suh, "Surveying Racial Discrimination: Analyses from a Multiethnic Labor Market," in *Prismatic Metropolis: Inequality in Los Angeles,* ed. Lawrence D. Bobo, Melvin L. Oliver, James H. Johnson Jr., and Abel Valenzuela Jr. (New York: Russell Sage, 2000), p. 528; John Zogby, John Bruce, and Rebecca Wittman, "Hispanic Perspectives," Zogby International Report, June 2004, p. 16; "2006 National Survey of Latinos," pp. 4–5.

86. Jim Doyle, "Court Curbs 'English-Only' Company Rules," *San Francisco Chronicle,* October 5, 1991, p. A12; Juan Perea, "English-Only Rules and the Right to Speak One's Primary Language in the Workplace," *University of Michigan Journal of Law Reform* 23, no. 2 (Winter 1990): 265–318.

87. *Garcia* v. *Gloor* 618 F.2d 264 (5th Cir. 1980), cert. denied, 449 U.S. 1113 (1981).

88. *Gutierrez* v. *Municipal Court,* 838 F.2d at 1039, quotations from Perea, "English-Only Rules," pp. 271–272; *Gutierrez* v. *Municipal Court,* vacated as moot, 109 S. Ct. 1736 (1989).

89. *Garcia* v. *Spun Steak Co.,* DC NCalif, No. C91-1949 RHS, October 14, 1991; Doyle, "Court Curbs 'English-Only' Company Rules." On recent laws, see "An Act Opposing Unnecessary Language Restrictions in the Workplace (H. 1851)," www.massenglishplus.org/content/ Language_ Rights/Workplace_Rights/English_Only_ FAQ.pdf (retrieved December 4, 2009).

90. *Sandoval* v. *Hagan,* 197 F3d 484 (11thCir. 1999); *Alexander* v. *Sandoval,* Case No. 991908, decided April 24, 2001; Lawrence Siegel, "The Argument for a Constitutional Right to Communication and Language," *Journal of Deaf Studies and Deaf Education* 7 (2002): 258–266; and Associated Press, "School Settles Bias Suit; Texas University to Pay $2 Million," April 21, 2001; *Maldonado* v. *Altus,* 433 F.3d 1294 (10th Cir. 2006), abrogated on other grounds by *Burlington N. & Santa Fe Ry. Co.* v. *White,* 548 U.S. 53 (2006). We draw here on Andrew J. Robinson, "Language, National Origin, and Employment Discrimination: The Importance of the EEOC Guidelines," *University of Pennsylvania Law Review* 157 (2009): 1522–1524.

91. Gilda Laura Ochoa, "Mexican Americans' Attitudes toward and Interactions with Mexican Immigrants: A Qualitative Analysis of Conflict and Cooperation," *Social Science Quarterly* 81 (March 2000): 84–105.

92. See Table 8.1. For earlier data see U.S. Bureau of the Census, "2005 American Community Survey, American Fact Finder: Selected Population Profile in the United States," http://factfinder.census.gov (retrieved June 15, 2007); U.S. Department of Labor, Bureau of Labor Statistics, "Annual Average Data, Table 6: Employment Status of the Hispanic or Latino Population by Sex, Age, and Detailed Ethnic Group January 2006," ftp://ftp.bls.gov/pub/special.requests/lf/ aat6.txt (retrieved October 17, 2006); U.S. Bureau of the Census, "Historical Income Data—Families," Table F-5: Race and Hispanic Origin of Householder—Families by Median and Mean Income: 1947 to 2004, published December 20, 2005, www.census.gov/hhes/www/ income/histinc/f05.html.

93. See Table 8.2. For earlier data, see U.S. Bureau of the Census, "2005 American Community Survey, American Fact Finder: Selected Population Profile in the United States," http://factfinder.census.gov (retrieved June 15, 2007); U.S. Bureau of the Census, "The Hispanic Population in the United States: 2004," published December 14, 2005, www.census.gov/population/ www/socdemo/hispanic/cps2004 .html.

94. U.S. Bureau of the Census, "Asset Ownership of Households," Table 4: Characteristics: 2000, published January 28, 2005, www.census.gov/hhes/www/wealth/ 1998_2000/wlth00-4.html; Rakesh Kochhar, "The Wealth of Hispanic Households: 1996 to 2002," research report, Pew Hispanic Center, Washington, DC, October 18, 2004, p. 3.

95. The first quote is from Zulema Valdéz, "Segmented Assimilation among Mexicans in the Southwest,"

96. Edward E. Telles and Vilma Ortiz, *Generations of Exclusion: Mexican Americans, Assimilation, and Race* (New York: Russell Sage Foundation, 2008); see also Joan Moore and Raquel Pinderhughes, *In the Barrios: Latinos and the Underclass Debate* (New York: Russell Sage, 1993).

97. Avelardo Valdez, "Persistent Poverty, Crime, and Drugs: U.S.–Mexican Border Region," in *In the Barrios: Latinos and the Underclass Debate,* ed. Joan Moore and Raquel Pinderhughes (New York: Sage, 1993), pp. 184–194.

98. Nestor Rodríguez, "Economic Restructuring and Latino Growth in Houston," in *In the Barrios: Latinos and the Underclass Debate,* ed. Moore and Pinderhughes, pp. 101–126; and Edward Telles, "Mexican Americans and the American Nation: A Response to Professor Huntington," *Aztlán* 31 (Fall 2006): 7–23. See also Valdéz, "Segmented Assimilation among Mexicans in the Southwest."

99. Southern Poverty Law Center, *Under Siege: Life for Low-Income Latinos in the South* (Montgomery, AL: SPLC, 2009), p. 4.

100. "A Time for Courage," *Newsday,* April 6, 2001, p. A48; Southern Poverty Law Center, *Under Siege: Life for Low-Income Latinos in the South,* pp. 1ff.

101. National Fair Housing Advocate, "Farmworkers Represented by CRLA and the County of Riverside Settle Major Fair Housing Case," www.fairhousing.com/ news_ archive/releases/crla5-23-00.html (retrieved March 1, 2001).

102. Dan Rozek, "Elgin Denies Housing Bias against Hispanics," *Chicago Sun-Times,* October 3, 2000, p. 32; "Center Calls for the Rejection of Anti-Immigrant Ordinances," *Southern Poverty Law Center Report,* September 2006, p. 3.

103. Daryl Strickland, "O. C. Business Plus; Yoder-Shrader Settles Housing Bias Suit," *The Los Angeles Times,* August 1, 2000, p. C3.

104. "Hispanics: A People in Motion," p. 7; Michael E Martin, *Residential Segregation Patterns of Latinos in the United States, 1990–2000* (New York: Routledge, 2007); "Ethnic Diversity Grows, Neighborhood Integration Lags Behind," Unpublished research report, Lewis Mumford Center, University at Albany, April 3, 2001, n.p.

105. Moore, *Mexican Americans,* p. 33.

106. *Garza* v. *County of Los Angeles,* 918 F.2d 763; 1990 U.S. App.; *Williams* v. *City of Dallas,* 734 F. Supp. 1317; 1990 U.S. Dist.

107. Mark Hugo Lopez and Paul Taylor, "Dissecting the 2008 Electorate: Most Diverse in U.S. History," research report, Pew Research Center, April 2009. See also U.S. Hispanic Leadership Institute, "Latino Vote," www .ushli.org/about_us.html (retrieved October 26, 2006).

108. "Hispanics and the 2006 Election," research report, Pew Hispanic Center, Washington, DC, October 2006, pp. 1–3.

109. Zogby, Bruce, and Wittman, "Hispanic Perspectives," p. 7. Data on officials in these paragraphs are from Juan Gómez-Quiñones, *Chicano Politics: Reality and Promise, 1940–1990* (Albuquerque: University of New Mexico Press, 1990), pp. 167–169, 173; National Association of Latino Elected and Appointed Officials, *National Report* 11, no. 1 (Fourth Quarter 1991): 1, 3; personal communications with Rodolfo de la Garza and Robert Brischetto; Hector Tobar and Richard Simon, "Molina's First Goal Expand County Board," *The Los Angeles Times,* February 21, 1991, p. A1; and Carla Rivera, "Heated Meeting Marks Burke's Debut as Leader," *The Los Angeles Times,* December 8, 1993, p. B3.

110. The National Association of Latino Elected and Appointed Officials Educational Fund, press release, May 9, 2001; Lopez and Taylor, "Dissecting the 2008 Electorate: Most Diverse in U.S. History."

111. Juan Gonzalez, *Harvest of Empire,* p. 169.

112. NALEO Education Fund, "2008 General Election Profile: Latinos in Congress and State Legislatures after Election 2008: A State-by-State Summary," research report, Washington, DC, November 2008; Gregory Rodriguez, "Mayoral Election; A Novel Latino Strategy," *The Los Angeles Times,* June 3, 2001, p. M1.

113. NALEO Education Fund, "2008 General Election Profile: Latinos in Congress and State Legislatures after Election 2008: A State-by-State Summary." See also their website, www.naleo.org.

114. Ibid.; and from the U.S. House website.

115. Rodolfo O. de la Garza, Nestor Rodríguez, and Harry Pachon, "The Domestic and Foreign Policy Consequences of Mexican and Central American Immigration: Mexican-American Perspectives," in *Immigration and International Relations,* ed. Georges Vernes (Santa Monica, CA: Rand Corporation, 1990), pp. 135–147; Kenneth J. Meier and Laurence J. O'Toole, Jr., "Political Control Versus Bureaucratic Values: Reframing the Debate," *Public Administration Review* (March/April 2006): 177–188.

116. Ray Suarez, "Latinos Politics," National Public Radio, Talk of the Nation, August 5, 1997; Telles, "Mexican Americans and the American Nation," p. 17; Marjorie Connelly, "The 1994 Elections," *The New York Times,* November 13, 1994, p. 24; Bob Wing, "White Power in Election," *ColorLines,* Spring 2001, www.arc.org/ C_Lines/CLArchive (retrieved June 19, 2001); "How Did Latinos Really Vote in 2004?" National Council of La Raza, memorandum, January 15, 2005; "Hispanic Voters Reassessing Ties to Republicans," *Hispanic News,* October 24, 2006, www.hispanic.cc/hispanic_voters_ reassessing_ties_to_republicans.htm (retrieved October 27, 2006).

117. Andres Ramirez, "An Updated Analysis of the Hispanic Vote, 2008," NDNBlog.org, November 13, 2008, http:// ndnblog.org/node/3249 (retrieved December 17, 2008). We draw also on Jody Herman and Lorraine Minnite, "The Demographics of Voters in America's 2008 General Election: A Preliminary Assessment," Project Vote Research Memo, November 18, 2008; Mark Hugo Lopez, "The Hispanic Vote in the 2008 Election," Pew Hispanic Center, research report, November 2008. For extensive 2008 election analysis, see Adia Harvey Wingfield and Joe R. Feagin, *Yes We Can? White Racial Framing and the 2008 Presidential Election* (New York: Routledge, 2010).

118. *Hernandez* v. *Texas,* 347 U.S. 482 (1954). Cited in Ricardo Romo, "Mexican Americans in the New West," in *The Twentieth-Century West,* ed. Gerald D. Nash and Richard W. Etulian (Albuquerque: University of New Mexico Press, 1989), p. 135.

119. U.S. Commission on Civil Rights, *Mexican Americans and the Administration of Justice in the Southwest,* pp. 79–86; U.S. Bureau of Labor Statistics, *Current Population Survey,* Table 11: Household Data, www.bls.gov/cps/ cpsaat11.pdf (retrieved November 9, 2006); Mary Alice Robbins, "Few Minorities Hold Positions as Court Law Clerks, Staff Attorneys in Texas," *Texas Lawyer,* December 04, 2009,www.law.com/jsp/article.jsp?id= 1202436038028&Few_Minorities_Hold_Positions_as_ Court_Law_Clerks_Staff_ Attorneys_in_Texas (retrieved December 16, 2009).

120. Robert Walters and Mark Curriden, "A Jury of One's Peers? Investigating Underrepresentation in Jury Venires," *Judge's Journal* 43 (Fall 2004): 17–21. On court decisions, see *Hernandez* v. *New York,* 1991, 111 S. Ct. 1859, and Juan Perea, "*Hernandez* v. *New York:* Courts, Prosecutors, and the Fear of Spanish," *Hofstra Law Review* 21 (Fall 1992): 1–61.

121. The survey is in David B. Rotman and Randall M. Hansen, "How Recent Court Users View the State Courts: Perceptions of Whites, African-Americans, and Latinos," http:// 72.14.209.104/search?q=cache: reUHK336gmIJ:www.flcourts .org/gen_public/family/ diversity/bin/perceptions2.pdf+How+Recent+Court+ Users+View+the+State+Courts:&hl=en&gl=us&ct=cln k&cd=1 (retrieved October 27, 2006). The data on polic profiling is from Police Assessment Resource Center, "Racial Profiling," March 2002, research report, pp. 7–8; Police Assessment Resource Center and Vera Institute of Justice, "Assessing Police-Community Relations in Pasadena, California," Los Angeles, CA, research report, August 2006, p. 70.

122. Mark Hugo Lopez and Michael T. Light, "A Rising Share: Hispanics and Federal Crime," research report, Pew Hispanic Center, Washington, Washington, DC, February 2009.

123. Romo, "Mexican Americans in the New West," pp. 136–139; Michael V. Miller and James D. Preston, "Vertical Ties and the Redistribution of Power in Crystal City," *Social Science Quarterly* 53 (March 1973): 772–782; John S. Shockley, *Chicano Revolt in a Texas Town* (Notre

Dame, IN: University of Notre Dame Press, 1974), pp. 28–148, 162–177; Maril, *Poorest of Americans*, p. 52; Armando Gutiérrez and Herbert Hirsch, "The Militant Challenge to the American Ethos: 'Chicanos' and the 'Mexican Americans,'" *Social Science Quarterly* 53 (March 1973): 844–845; Carlos Muñoz, Jr., *Youth, Identity, Power: The Chicano Movement* (New York: Verso, 1989); Ignacio M. Garcia, *United We Win* (Tucson: University of Arizona Press, 1989), pp. 228–231.

124. Marta Cotera, "Feminism, the Chicana and Anglo Versions," in *Twice a Minority*, ed. Margarita B. Melville (St. Louis: C. V. Mosby, 1980), p. 231; see also Amott and Matthaei, *Race, Gender, and Work*, pp. 83–84; Cotera, *Feminism*, pp. 213–233.

125. McWilliams, *North from Mexico*, pp. 191–193; Grebler, Moore, and Guzlán, *The Mexican-American People*, pp. 91–92; Stoddard, *Mexican Americans*, p. 180; Gamio, *Mexican Immigration to the United States*, pp. 135–138.

126. Grebler, Moore, and Guzmán, *The Mexican-American People*, pp. 543–545; Stoddard, *Mexican Americans*, p. 188; Moore, *Mexican Americans*, p. 152; U.S. Commission on Civil Rights, *Mexican Americans and the Administration of Justice in the Southwest*, pp. 15–17; Rees Lloyd and Peter Montague, "Ford and La Raza: 'They Stole Our Land and Gave Us Powdered Milk,'" in *Introduction to Chicano Studies*, ed. Duran and Bernard, pp. 376–378; Frances L. Swadesh, "The Alianza Movement: Catalyst for Social Change in New Mexico," in *Chicano*, ed. Rosaldo, Calvert, and Seligmann, pp. 270–274.

127. Steve Taylor, "SVREP Leader Issues Warning to Democrats in D.C.," *Rio Grande Guardian*, September 1, 2009, http:// www.svrep.org/press_room/press_clippings/ 09/20090901_riograndeguardian.htm (retrieved December 8, 2009); Mark Bixler, "Latino Advocacy Groups Plan Offices Here for Anti-Bias Efforts," *Atlanta Journal and Constitution*, May 30, 2001, p. 3B; "MALDEF's 40th Anniversary," http://maldef.org/about/40th_anniversary (retrieved December 8, 2009).

128. Mary Pardo, "Mexican American Women Grassroots Community Activists: 'Mothers of East Los Angeles,'" *Frontiers* XI, no. 1 (1990): 4. See also Jane Braxton Little, "The Lake and the 'Hood,'" http://www.yesmagazine .org/issues/whose-water/the lake-and-the-hood (retrieved December 8, 2009).

129. Jacques E. Levy, *César Chávez* (New York: W. W. Norton, 1975), pp. 182–201; Peter Matthiessen, *Sal Si Puedes* (New York: Delta Books, 1969), pp. 59–216; John G. Dunne, *Delano* (New York: Farrar, Straus & Giroux, 1967), pp. 110–167.

130. Levy, *César Chávez*, pp. 495, 522–535.

131. J. Craig Jenkins, *The Politics of Insurgency* (New York: Columbia University Press, 1985), pp. x–xi; Robert Reinhold, "Environmental Agency Moves to End Most Uses of Deadly Agricultural Pesticide," *The New York Times*, September 6, 1991, p. A17; "Cubans in the United States," research report, Pew Hispanic Center, Washington, DC, August 2006, p. 6.

132. Ann Bancroft, "10,000 at Rally for Farm Workers," *San Francisco Chronicle*, April 25, 1994, p. A1. The quotation and history are from "UFW Chronology," www .ufw.org/_page.php?menu=research&inc=_page.php? menu=research&inc=history/01.html (retrieved October 17, 2006); and "Recent UFW Successes," http:// www.ufw.org/_board.php?b_code=about_suc (retrieved December 8, 2009).

133. Mark Arax, "UFW Pledges New Activism as March Ends," *The Los Angeles Times*, April 25, 1994, p. A3; Letisia Marquez, "Farm Workers Union Has Work Cut Out for It," *Ventura County Star*, March 29, 2001, http://web.insidevc.com/news/372065.shtml (retrieved July 2, 2001).

134. Zaragosa Vargas, *Labor Rights Are Civil Rights: Mexican American Workers in Twentieth-Century America* (Princeton, NJ: Princeton University Press, 2004); Hector L. Delgado, *New Immigrants, Old Unions: Undocumented Workers in Los Angeles* (Philadelphia: Temple University Press, 1993).

135. Margaret M. Zamudio, "Organizing Labor among Difference: The Impact of Race/Ethnicity, Citizenship, and Gender on Working-Class Solidarity," in *Places and Politics in the Age of Global Capitalism*, ed. Arif Dirlik (Lanham, MD: Rowman & Littlefield, 2001), p. 116; Antonio Olivo, "Hotel Workers, Riot Police Clash during Protest," *The Los Angeles Times*, August 4, 2000, p. B1.

136. Glenn Bracey II, "Black and Latino Coalitions and Interest Convergence Theory: A Case Study of the Justice for Janitors Campaign in Houston, Texas," master's thesis, Texas A&M University, College Station, TX, 2007. We also draw here for SEIU data on Peter Costantini, "A New Internationalism Rising," Inter Press Service International Association, January 9, 2006, www.ipsnews.net/news.asp? idnews=31695 (retrieved October 30, 2006).

137. Frank D. Bean and Stephanie Bell-Rose, "Immigration and Its Relation to Race and Ethnicity in the United States," in *Immigration and Opportunity: Race, Ethnicity, and Employment in the United States*, ed. Frank D. Bean and Stephanie Bell-Rose (New York: Russell Sage, 1999), pp. 13–14; Rakesh Kochhar, "Growth in the Foreign-Born Workforce and Employment of the Native Born," research report, Pew Hispanic Center, Washington, DC, August 2006, pp. 1–4; and Rakesh Kochhar, "Latino Workers in the Ongoing Recession: 2007 to 2008," research report, Pew Hispanic Center, Washington, DC, December 2008.

138. Martin Kasindorf and Maria Puente, "Hispanics, Blacks Find Futures Entangled," *USA Today*, September 10, 1999, p. 4; Bracey, "Black and Latino Coalitions and Interest Convergence Theory"; Nicolas C. Vaca, *The Presumed Alliance: The Unspoken Conflict Between Latinos and Blacks and What It Means for America* (New York: HarperCollins, 2004.)

139. "Coverage of 'Brown-Black' Divide Overlooks Nuance, Complexity," April 15, 2008, http://www.mije.org/reg

gieroyston/blackbrowndivide (retrieved December 17, 2009); Earl Ofari Hutchinson, *The Latino Challenge to Black America* (Los Angeles, CA: Middle Passage Press, 2007), especially chapter 1; Kasindorf and Puente, "Hispanics, Blacks Find Futures Entangled."

140. Chandler Davidson and Charles M. Gaitz, "Ethnic Attitudes as a Basis for Minority Cooperation in a Southwestern Metropolis," *Social Science Quarterly* 53 (March 1973): 747–748; Néstor Rodríguez, "U.S. Immigration and Intergroup Relations in the Late 20th Century: African Americans and Latinos," *Social Justice* 23 (1996): 111–124; Bracey, "Black and Latino Coalitions and Interest Convergence Theory."

141. Thomas P. Carter, *Mexican Americans in School* (New York: College Entrance Examination Board, 1970), pp. 204–205; George I. Sánchez, "History, Culture, and Education," in *La Raza,* ed. Julian Samora (Notre Dame, IN: University of Notre Dame Press, 1966), pp. 1–26; Paul Taylor, *An American-Mexican Frontier* (Chapel Hill: University of North Carolina Press, 1934), pp. 196–204; Guadalupe San Miguel Jr., *Let All of Them Take Heed: Mexican Americans and the Campaign for Educational Equality in Texas, 1910–1981* (Austin: University of Texas Press, 1987), pp. 1–58.

142. Charles Wollenberg, *All Deliberate Speed: Segregation and Exclusion in California Schools, 1855–1975* (Berkeley: University of California Press, 1976), pp. 125–135.

143. Carter, *Mexican Americans in School,* pp. 97–102; Thomas P. Carter, "The Negative Self-Concept of Mexican-American Students," *School and Society* 96 (March 30, 1968): 217–220; George I. Sánchez, "Bilingualism and Mental Measures, a Word of Caution," *Journal of Applied Psychology* (December 1934): 767–769. See also Wollenberg, *All Deliberate Speed,* pp. 118–119; Jane Mercer, *Labelling the Mentally Retarded* (Berkeley: University of California Press, 1973), pp. 96–189.

144. Gary Orfield and Chugmei Lee, *Racial Transformation and the Changing Nature of Segregation* (Cambridge, MA: Harvard Civil Rights Project, 2006), pp. 11–12; Gary Orfield, *Reviving the Goal of an Integrated Society: A 21st Century Challenge* (Los Angeles: UCLA Civil Rights Project, 2009), pp. 1–8.

145. Orfield, *Reviving the Goal of an Integrated Society,* pp. 3–6.

146. Juan F. Perea, "Demography and Distrust: An Essay on American Languages, Cultural Pluralism, and Official English," *Minnesota Law Review* 77 (1992): 269.

147. Kenji Hakuta and Eugene E. Garcia, "Bilingualism and Education," *American Psychologist* 44 (February 1989): 374–379; Dick Kirschten, "Speaking English," *National Review,* June 17, 1989, pp. 1556–1561; Manuel Ramirez and Alfredo Castaneda, *Cultural Democracy, Bicognitive Development, and Education* (New York: Academic Press, 1974); San Miguel Jr., *Let All of Them Take Heed.* The concluding quote is from Jorge M. Chavez and Doris Marie Provine, "Race and the Response of State Legislatures to Unauthorized Immigrants," *Annals of the American Association of Political and Social Science* 623 (May 2009): 79–92.

148. James Crawford, "Language Politics in the U.S.A.: The Paradox of Bilingual Education," *Social Justice* 25 (Fall 1998), http://ourworld.compuserve.com/homepages/JWCRAWFORD/paradox.htm (retrieved November 13, 2006).

149. Susan Baker and Kenji Hakuta, "Bilingual Education and Latino Civil Rights," www.law.harvard.edu/groups/civilrights/papers/bilingual/bilingual.html (retrieved July 2, 2001); W. Steven Barnett et al., "Two-Way and Monolingual English Immersion in Preschool Education: An Experimental Comparison," *Early Childhood Research Quarterly* 22 (2007): 277–406. See also Ofelia Garcia, *Bilingual Education in the 21st Century: A Global Perspective* (New York: Wiley-Blackwell, 2008).

150. See Table 8.3. For earlier data, see U.S. Bureau of the Census, 1950 Census of Population, P-E no. 3C, Table 3; U.S. Census Bureau, "Hispanic Population, Table 7.1: Educational Attainment of the Population 25 Years and Over by Sex, Hispanic Origin, and Race: March 2000," published March 6, 2001, www.census.gov/population/www/socdemo/hispanic.html; U.S. Bureau of the Census, "2005 American Community Survey, American Fact Finder: Selected Population Profile in the United States," http:// factfinder.census.gov (retrieved June 15, 2007).

151. "Educational System Fails Chicano Students at Every Level, Says Report," *Staff and News Wire Report,* March 24, 2006, www.diverseeducation.com/artman/publish/article_5664.shtml (retrieved October 17, 2006); U.S. Census Bureau, "The Foreign-Born Population, Table 4.1: Latin American Foreign-Born Population by Sex, Age, and Region of Birth: March 2000," published January 03, 2001, www.census.gov/population/www/socdemo/foreign.html.

152. Quote is in Beth Barrett, "College Disparity Costly: Mexican-Americans' Wage Gap Up, Study Says," *Daily News of Los Angeles,* May 27, 1997, p. N1.

153. National Center for Education Statistics, *The Condition of Education* (Washington, DC: U.S. Department of Education, 2009). We also draw on U.S. Census Bureau, *Current Population Survey,* October 1999, p. 4; Barbara Kantrowitz with Lourdes Rosado, "Falling Further Behind," *Newsweek,* August 19, 1991, p. 60.

154. See Harriett Romo and Toni Falbo, *Defying the Odds: Keeping Latino Youth in School* (Austin: University of Texas Press, 1995).

155. Ibid.

156. Mark Hugo Lopez, "Latinos and Education: Explaining the Attainment Gap," research report, Pew Hispanic Center, October 2009, p. 1.

157. Zogby, Bruce, and Wittman, "Hispanic Perspectives," pp. 11–12. See also Concha Delgado-Gaitan and Henry Trueba, *Crossing Cultural Borders: Education for Immigrant Families in America* (Philadelphia: The Falmer Press, 1991); Richard Fry, "The High Schools Hispanics Attend," research report, Pew Hispanic Center, Washington, DC, November 2005, pp. i–ii.

158. Catherine Walsh, *Pedagogy and the Struggle for Voice* (New York: Bergin and Garvey, 1991), pp. 95–113. See also Orfield, *Reviving the Goal of an Integrated Society.*

159. José A. Cobas and Joe R. Feagin, "Language Oppression and Resistance: Latinos in the United States," *Ethnic and Racial Studies* 31 (February 2008): 390–410.

160. The quote and source is Paul Vanderwood, "Religion: Official, Popular, and Otherwise," *Mexican Studies* 16 (Summer 2000): 418.

161. Moore, *Mexican Americans,* pp. 88–91; Stoddard, *Mexican Americans,* p. 93; Grebler, Moore, and Guzmán, *The Mexican-American People,* pp. 459–460; Gómez-Quiñones, *Chicano Politics,* p. 179; "Latinos Shift Loyalties," *Christian Century,* April 6, 1994, p. 344; "Cultural Diversity in the Church," U.S. Conference of Catholic Bishops, www.usccb.org/hispanicaffairs/rememberingpast.shtml (retrieved December 10, 2009).

162. David A. Badillo, "Mexicanos and Suburban Parish Communities," *Journal of Urban History* 31 (November 2004): 23–42; see also Grebler, Moore, and Guzmán, *The Mexican-American People,* pp. 436–439, 473–477.

163. Telles, "Mexican Americans and the American Nation," p. 16.

164. Pew Hispanic Center and Pew Forum on Religion & Public Life, "Changing Faiths: Latinos and the Transformation of American Religion," research report, Washington, DC, April 2007, pp. 1–3. The Pew quote is on p. 1. We also draw here on Jill Leovy, "More Hispanics Hear Call of Witnesses," *Seattle Times,* March 25, 1991, p. E1; Vanderwood, "Religion," pp. 476–477.

165. "The Mixture as Never Before," *The Economist,* March 11, 2000. See also Richard Alba, *Blurring the Color Line: The New Chance for a More Integrated America* (Cambridge, MA: Harvard University Press, 2009), pp. 16–183.

166. Telles and Vilma Ortiz, *Generations of Exclusion,* passim. On earlier decades, see Edward Múrguía, *Assimilation, Colonialism, and the Mexican American People* (Austin: University of Texas Press, 1975), pp. 4–5; Rodolfo Alvarez, "The Unique Psycho-Historical Experience of the Mexican-American People," *Social Science Quarterly* 52 (June 1971): 15–29; Stoddard, *Mexican Americans,* p. 103; Benjamin S. Bradshaw and Frank Bean, "Trends in the Fertility of Mexican Americans, 1950–1970," *Social Science Quarterly* 53 (March 1973): 696–697.

167. Strategy Research Corporation, *1991 U.S. Hispanic Market,* pp. 107–108. See also Telles and Vilma Ortiz, *Generations of Exclusion.*

168. Zogby, Bruce, and Wittman, "Hispanic Perspectives," p. 15; "Hispanic Attitudes toward Learning English," research report, Pew Hispanic Center, Washington, DC, June 2006, p. 1; Shirin Hakimzadeh and D'Vera Cohn, "English Usage Among Hispanics in the United States," research report, Pew Hispanic Center, Washington, DC, November 2007; Rubén Rumbaut, Douglas S. Massey, and Frank D. Bean, "Linguistic Life Expectancies," *Population and Development Review* (September 2006): 1–2; Telles, "Mexican Americans and the American Nation," p. 13; Telles and Vilma Ortiz, *Generations of Exclusion.*

169. "Newcomers Eager to Learn English Face Waiting Lines across the Nation," National Association of Latino Elected and Appointed Officials, October 6, 2006, www.naleo.org/pr100606.html (retrieved October 17, 2006).

170. Frank Bean, Susan Brown, and Rubén Rumbaut, "Mexican Immigrant Political and Economic Incorporation," *Perspectives on Politics* 4 (June 2006): 312. We also draw here on Robert Suro, "A Developing Identity: Hispanics in the United States," *Carnegie Reporter* (Spring 2006): 24–25.

171. Edward Múrguía and Edward E. Telles, "Phenotype and Schooling Among Mexican Americans," *Sociology of Education* 69 (October 1996): 276–289; Feagin and Dirks, "'Who Is White?': College Students' Assessments of Key U.S. Racial and Ethnic Groups."

172. Bendick, "Situation Testing for Employment Discrimination in the United States of America"; Cobas and Feagin, "Language Oppression and Resistance," pp. 390–410.

173. Strategy Research Corporation, *1991 U.S. Hispanic Market,* pp. 111–115; Edward Múrguía, *Chicano Intermarriage: A Theoretical and Empirical Study* (San Antonio, TX: Trinity University Press, 1982), pp. 45–51; Amitai Etzioni, "The Monochrome Society," *Heritage Foundation Policy Review,* February 2001, p. 53.

174. Telles, "Mexican Americans and the American Nation," pp. 15, 56; Marta I. Cruz-Janzen, "Lives on the Crossfire," *Race, Gender & Class* 9 (2002): 55–57. See also Telles and Vilma Ortiz, *Generations of Exclusion.*

175. Walter Connor, "Who Are the Mexican Americans? A Note on Comparability," in *Mexican-Americans in Comparative Perspective,* ed. Connor, pp. 4–28; López and Stanton-Salazar, "Mexican Americans: A Second Generation at Risk," in *Ethnicities,* pp. 57–90.

176. Cheskin Company, *Hispanic Trends* (Redwood Shores, CA: Cheskin, 2002), p. 5.

177. Peter Skerry, "Not Much Cooking," *Brookings Review,* June 22, 1993, p. 42. For discussion of students facing barriers, see Alberta M. Gloria, Jeanett Castellanos, Nicholas C. Scull, and Francisco J. Villegas, "Psychological Coping and Well-Being of Male Latino Undergraduates," *Hispanic Journal of Behavioral Sciences* 31 (2009): 317–339; Alberta M. Gloria, Jeanett Castellanos, Ambrocia G. Lopez, and Rocio Rosales, "An Examination of Academic Nonpersistence Decisions of Latino Undergraduates," *Hispanic Journal of Behavioral Sciences* 27 (May 2005): 202–223; Alberta M. Gloria and T. M. Segura-Herrera, "Ambrocia and Omar Go to College: A Psychosociocultural Examination of Chicanos and Chicanas in Higher Education," ed. R. J. Velasquez, B. McNeill, and L. Arellano, in *Handbook of Chicana and Chicano Psychology* (Mahwah, NJ: Erlbaum, 2004), pp. 401–425.

178. Montejano, *Anglos and Mexicans in the Making of Texas, 1836–1986*; Múrguía, *Assimilation, Colonialism, and the*

Mexican American People, p. 112; Edward Múrguía and Misael Obregon, "From Colorism to Presentation in the Case of Mexican Americans and African Americans," unpublished research paper, Texas A&M University, College Station, TX, 2006. See also Joe R. Feagin, *Racist America: Roots, Current Realities, and Future Reparations,* 2nd ed. (New York: Routledge, 2010), Chapter 7.

179. Roberto Suro, "Changing Channels and Crisscrossing Cultures: A Survey of Latinos on the News Media," research report, Pew Hispanic Center, Washington, DC, April 2004, pp. 1–3; Mireya Navarro, "Complaint to Spanish TV: Not Enough Americans; Few U.S. Plots for Growing U.S. Audience," *The New York Times,* August 21, 2000, p. B1; *Hispanic Trends,* p. 15; David Kaplan, "Spanish-Language Networks Become Titans," Hispanic American Center for Economic Research, http://www.hacer.org/current/Titans.php (retrieved December 10, 2009).

180. See Suro, "Changing Channels and Crisscrossing Cultures"; Kaplan, "Spanish-Language Networks Become Titans"; Achy Obejas, "A Changing Nation: Shades of Future Seen in Census Report on Hispanics," *Chicago Tribune,* March 31, 1996, p. 1; Cheskin Company, *Hispanic Trends,* p. 15.

181. Acuña, *Occupied America,* p. 3.

182. Alvarez, "Psycho-Historical and Socioeconomic Development," pp. 928–930.

183. Múrguía, *Assimilation, Colonialism, and the Mexican American People,* pp. 8–9.

184. John U. Ogbu, *Minority Education and Caste* (New York: Academic Press, 1987), pp. 236–237; John Obgu, "Variability in Minority Responses to Schooling: Non-immigrants vs. Immigrants," in *Interpretive Ethnography of Education,* ed. George Spindler and Louise Spinder (Hillsdale, NJ: Erlbaum, 1987), pp. 255–275.

185. Barrera, *Race and Class in the Southwest,* p. 213.

186. Geoffrey Fox, *Hispanic Nation: Culture, Politics, and the Constructing of Identity* (Tucson: University of Arizona Press, 1996), pp. 240–241; Joe R. Feagin and Danielle Dirks, "'Who Is White?': College Students' Assessments of Key U.S. Racial and Ethnic Groups," unpublished research manuscript, Texas A&M University, College Station, TX, 2006.

187. Nathan Glazer, "The Political Distinctiveness of the Mexican Americans," in *Mexican-Americans in Comparative Perspective,* ed. Walter Connor (Washington, DC: Urban Institute, 1985), pp. 212–216.

188. We also draw here on Chapter 7 of Joe R. Feagin, *Racist America: Roots, Current Realities, and Future Reparations,* 2nd ed. (New York: Routledge, 2010).

189. Jessica M. Vasquez and Christopher Wetzel, "Tradition and the Invention of Racial Selves: Symbolic Boundaries, Collective Authenticity, and Contemporary Struggles for Racial Equality," *Ethnic and Racial Studies* 32 (2009): 1569. We are indebted here to discussions with Hernán Vera, Nestor Rodriguez, and José Cobas. See also José Cobas and Joe R. Feagin, "Latinos/as and the

White Racial Frame," *Sociological Inquiry* 78 (February 2008): 39–53.

190. Rodolfo Acuña, *Anything but Mexican: Chicanos in Contemporary Los Angeles* (London: Verso, 1996), p. 8. The historical data are from Gross, "Texas Mexicans and the Politics of Whiteness." See also Cobas and Feagin, "Latinos/as and the White Racial Frame," pp. 39–53.

191. Nestor Rodriguez, personal communication, March 1996; the study cited is Yolanda Flores-Niemann, Tatcho Mindiola, and Nestor Rodriguez, "U.S.-Born and Foreign-Born Latinas' Perceptions of Black/Brown Relations: Implications for Future Inter-Group Relations," unpublished research paper, University of Houston, 1997, pp. 12–13. See also Tatcho Mindiola, Yolanda F. Niemann, and Nestor Rodriguez, *Black-Brown Relations and Stereotypes* (Austin: University of Texas Press, 2002).

192. Gilda L. Ochoa, *Becoming Neighbors in a Mexican American Community: Power, Conflict and Solidarity* (Austin: University of Texas Press, 2004), p. 128.

193. Fox, *Hispanic Nation,* p. 241.

194. Felix M. Padilla, *Latino Ethnic Consciousness: The Case of Mexican Americans and Puerto Ricans in Chicago* (Notre Dame, IN: University of Notre Dame Press, 1985), p. 7. See also pp. 138–139; and Andrés Torres, "Latinos in New England: An Introduction," in *Latinos in New England,* ed. Andrés Torres (Philadelphia: Temple University Press, 2006), p. 17.

195. Múrguía, "On Latino/Hispanic Ethnic Identity."

196. Massey, "Five Myths about Immigration," pp. 1–13.

Chapter 9

1. Daniel Adams, "Puerto Ricans Vote on Independence from U.S.," *The Independent,* December 9, 1991, p. 14.

2. U.S. Census Bureau, "Selected Population Profile in the United States: Puerto Rican," "2008 American Community Survey," http://factfinder.census.gov (retrieved May 26, 2010). For earlier data, see U.S. Census Bureau, "2005 American Community Survey," "General Demographic Characteristics: 2005," http://factfinder.census.gov (retrieved November 05, 2006).

3. Enrique Fernandez, "Puerto Rican Independence: Is It a Dream?" *Newsday,* February 27, 1992, p. 94.

4. See Eric Williams, *From Columbus to Castro: The History of the Caribbean 1492–1969* (London: André Deutsch: 1970), pp. 109, 291.

5. Manuel Maldonado-Denis, *Puerto Rico, A Socio-Historic Interpretation,* trans. Elena Vialo (New York: Random House/ Vintage Books, 1972), pp. 13–19; Luis Antonio Cardona, *A History of the Puerto Ricans in the U.S.A.* (Rockville, MD: Carreta Press, 1990), pp. 8–9; Williams, *From Columbus to Castro,* pp. 109, 291.

6. U.S. Commission on Civil Rights, *Puerto Ricans in the Continental United States: An Uncertain Future* (Washington, DC: U.S. Government Printing Office, 1976),

pp. 11–12; Jorge Heine, "A People Apart," *Wilson Quarterly* 4, no. 2 (Spring 1980): 119–123.

7. Maldonado-Denis, *Puerto Rico*, p. 77.

8. U.S. Commission on Civil Rights, *Puerto Ricans in the Continental United States*, p. 12.

9. Maldonado-Denis, *Puerto Rico*, pp. 305–306; Heine, "A People Apart," p. 123.

10. U.S. Bureau of the Census, *Statistical Abstract of the United States 1994*, Table 1342 (Washington, DC: U.S. Government Printing Office, 1994), p. 835.

11. Kristin S. Krause, "Post-incentive Puerto Rico; Island's Future as Manufacturing Center in Doubt as Congress Phases Out Income Tax Break," *Traffic World*, October 27, 1997, p. 20; César F. Rosado Marzán, "Facing Financial Crisis, Puerto Rican Government Lays Off 100,000," *Labor Notes*, http:// labornotes.org/node/232 (retrieved November 10, 2006); "Strike Protests Job Cuts in Puerto Rico," CNN, October 16, 2009, http://edition.cnn.com/ 2009/WORLD/americas/10/15/puerto.rico.strike (retrieved December 14, 2009).

12. Adalberto Lopez, "The Puerto Rican Diaspora: A Survey," in *Puerto Rico and Puerto Ricans: Studies in History and Society*, ed. Adalberto Lopez and James Petras (New York: Wiley, 1974), p. 318; Clara E. Rodríguez, *Puerto Ricans: Born in the U.S.A.* (Boston: Unwin Hyman, 1989), pp. 1–10.

13. Jack Agueros, "Halfway to Dick and Jane," in *The Immigrant Experience: The Anguish of Becoming American*, ed. Thomas C. Wheeler (New York: Dial Press, 1971), p. 93.

14. Cardona, *A History of the Puerto Ricans in the U.S.A.*, pp. 95–96.

15. U.S. Commission on Civil Rights, *Puerto Ricans in the Continental United States*, p. 25; Rodríguez, *Puerto Ricans*, pp. 4–13; Cardona, *A History of the Puerto Ricans in the U.S.A.*, pp. 95–112; Felix M. Padilla, *Puerto Rican Chicago* (Notre Dame, IN: University of Notre Dame Press, 1987), pp. 66–72.

16. Pedro A. Rivera, "Angel and Aurea," *Wilson Quarterly* 4, no. 2 (Spring 1980): 146–152; Rodríguez, *Puerto Ricans*, pp. 4–8, 28; Gina M. Pérez, *The Near Northwest Side Story: Migration, Displacement, and Puerto Rican Families* (Berkeley: University of California Press, 2004), pp. 196–198; the "emotional bridges" quote is from Elizabeth M. Aranda, *Emotional Bridges to Puerto Rico: Migration, Return Migration, and the Struggles of Incorporation* (Lanham, MD: Rowman & Littlefield, 2007), pp. 172–176.

17. U.S. Census Bureau, "Selected Population Profile in the United States: Puerto Rican," "2008 American Community Survey"; U.S. Census Bureau, "American Community Survey," "General Demographic Characteristics: 2005," http://factfinder.census.gov (retrieved November 5, 2006); Elizabeth Aranda, personal communication, November 15, 2006.

18. Candice Choi, "Fewer Puerto Ricans in NYC, but More Mexicans, Asian Indians," DiversityInc.com, www.diversityinc.com (retrieved July 8, 2001); "New York City,"

"American Community Survey" (2006–2008), http:// factfinder.census.gov (retrieved December 14, 2009).

19. Bart Jones, "Census 2000: Island's Little El Salvador," *Newsday*, May 23, 2001, p. A2.

20. Ibid.; Kern Resource Center, "Spanish for Health Care Workers," Bakersfield, CA, http://72.14.209.104/ search? q=cache:brQ2ex8Gy7sJ:www.health-careers.org/ resources/ Spanish%2520Handbook%2520Revised. pdf+%22million+ Salvadorans%22+%222000+census%22+2005&hl=en& gl=us&ct=clnk&cd=1 (retrieved November 13, 2006).

21. Quoted in Frank Bonilla, "Beyond Survival: Porque Sequiremos Siendo Puertoriquenos," in *Puerto Rico and Puerto Ricans*, ed. Lopez and Petras, p. 439.

22. Alfredo Lopez, *The Puerto Rican Papers* (Indianapolis, IN: Bobbs-Merrill, 1973), p. 120; see also Laura A. Szalacha et al., "Discrimination and Puerto Rican Children's and Adolescents' Mental Health," *Cultural Diversity and Ethnic Minority Psychology* 9 (2003): 141–155.

23. Hoover is quoted in Lopez, *The Puerto Rican Papers*, p. 211. Frances Negrón-Muntaner is quoted from his *Boricua Pop: Puerto Ricans and The Latinization of American Culture* (New York: NYU Press, 2004), p. 61.

24. Danice K. Eaton et al., "Youth Risk Behavior Surveillance—United States, 2005," *Morbidity and Mortality Weekly Report* 55(SS05) (June 9, 2006): 1–108.

25. Kristal Brent Zook, "Esai Morales, Good Cop; 'NYPD Blue' Casts New Recruit Against Type," *Washington Post*, May 21, 2001, p. C1.

26. Quoted in Juan Gonzalez, *Harvest of Empire: A History of Latinos in America* (New York: Penguin, 2000), p. 253.

27. Nathan Glazer and Daniel P. Moynihan, *Beyond the Melting Pot* (Cambridge: M.I.T. Press and Harvard University Press, 1963), pp. 88–90.

28. Oscar Lewis, *La Vida* (New York: Random House, 1965).

29. Mirta Ojito, "A Movement Is Born; New Britain Puerto Ricans React to Report Revealing Bias," *The New York Times*, June 28, 1997, p. 23.

30. The congressman's quote is from Associated Press, "Congressman Criticized for Vieques 'Welfare' Slam," June 20, 2001, http://salon.com/politics/wire/2001/ 06/20/welfare/index.html. Community examples are from Dexter Filkins, "Racial Slurs and Intrigue on City Island," *The New York Times*, February 16, 2001, p. B3.

31. Marta I. Cruz-Janzen, "Latinegras," *Frontiers* 22 (2001): 18; Rodríguez, *Puerto Ricans*, pp. 51–56. On race in Puerto Rico, see Jorge Duany, "The Rough Edges of Puerto Rican Identities: Race, Gender, and Transnationalism," *Latin American Research Review* 40 (October 2005): 179–185.

32. Ramón Grosfoguel and Chloe S. Georas, "'Coloniality of Power' and Racial Dynamics: Notes toward a Reinterpretation of Latino Caribbeans in New York City," *Identities: Global Studies in Culture and Power* 7 (2000): 85–125.

33. Piri Thomas, *Down These Mean Streets* (New York: Knopf, 1967), pp. 85–86.

34. Rodríguez, *Puerto Ricans,* pp. 56–59, Angel R. Martínez, "The Effects of Acculturation and Racial Identity on Self-Esteem and Psychological Well-Being among Young Puerto Ricans," Ph.D. thesis, City University of New York, 1988; Joe R. Feagin and Danielle Dirks, "Who Is White?": College Students' Assessments of Key US Racial and Ethnic Groups," unpublished manuscript, Texas A&M University, 2004.

35. Rodríguez, *Puerto Ricans,* pp. 61–68; Pew Hispanic Center/Kaiser Family Foundation, "2002 National Survey of Latinos," research report, Washington, DC, December 2002, pp. 32–33.

36. Constance Kim-Gervey, "To Be or Not to Be: An Exploration of Ethnic Identity Development in Context," in M. Azmitia, M. Syed, and K. Radmacher, eds., *The Intersections of Personal and Social Identities: New Directions for Child and Adolescent Development* 120 (2008): p. 77. See also pp. 61–79.

37. Jesús Colon, "The Early Days," in *The Puerto Ricans: A Documentary History,* ed. Kal Wagenheim (Garden City, NY: Doubleday/Anchor Books, 1973), p. 286.

38. Thomas, *Down These Mean Streets,* pp. 102–104.

39. Rodríguez, *Puerto Ricans,* p. 2; U.S. Commission on Civil Rights, *Puerto Ricans in the Continental United States,* p. 54; Frank Bonilla and Ricardo Campos, "A Wealth of Poor: Puerto Ricans in the New Economic Order," *Daedalus* 110 (Spring 1981): 158.

40. U.S. Census Bureau, "Selected Population Profile in the United States: Puerto Rican," "2008 American Community Survey." For earlier data, see U.S. Bureau of the Census, "The Hispanic Population in the United States: 2004, Detailed Tables, Table 10.2: Occupation of the Employed Civilian Population 16 Years and over by Sex and Hispanic Origin Type: 2004," published December 14, 2005, www.census.gov population/www/socdemo/hispanic/cps2004.html.

41. Juan Gonzalez, "Puerto Ricans on the Mainland," *Perspectives* 13 (Winter 1982): 16; U.S. Commission on Civil Rights, *Puerto Ricans in the Continental United States,* p. 52; Bonilla and Campos, "A Wealth of Poor," p. 160.

42. U.S. Census Bureau, "Selected Population Profile in the United States: Puerto Rican," "2008 American Community Survey."

43. See Gonzalez, *Harvest of Empire.*

44. "Latinos and Hospital," *Gotham Gazette,* www.gothamgazette .com/resource/housing/report/10 (retrieved November 14, 2006); see also U.S. Commission on Civil Rights, *Puerto Ricans in the Continental United States,* pp. 59–62.

45. Western Regional Office, U.S. Commission on Civil Rights, *Puerto Ricans in California* (Washington, DC: U.S. Government Printing Office, 1980), p. 17.

46. The first study is Devah Pager and Bruce Western "Discrimination in Low-Wage Labor Markets: Evidence from an Experimental Audit Study in New York City," research paper, Princeton University, http:// 72.14.209.104/search?q=cache:hltEuw40fgkJ:paa2005. princeton.edu/download.aspx%3FsubmissionId% 3D50874+discrimination+job+His panic+testers+ matched+cities+research&hl=en&gl=us&ct=clnk&cd= 1H (retrieved October 24, 2006). The last study is Aranda, *Emotional Bridges to Puerto Rico,* p. 174. See also Rodríguez, *Puerto Ricans,* pp. 92–93.

47. U.S. Commission on Civil Rights, *Puerto Ricans in the Continental United States,* p. 60; Vilma Ortiz, "Latinos and Industrial Change in New York and Los Angeles," unpublished research paper, 1990; Clara E. Rodríguez, "Economic Factors Affecting Puerto Ricans in New York," in *Labor Migration Under Capitalism: The Puerto Rican Experience,* ed. History Task Force (New York: Center for Puerto Rican Studies, 1979), pp. 208–210; Rodríguez, *Puerto Ricans,* pp. 85–91.

48. Mercer L. Sullivan, "Puerto Ricans in Sunset Park, Brooklyn: Poverty amidst Ethnic and Economic Diversity," in *In the Barrios,* ed. Joan Moore and Raquel Pinderhughes (New York: Russell Sage, 1993), pp. 1–25.

49. U.S. Census Bureau, "Selected Population Profile in the United States: Puerto Rican," "2008 American Community Survey."

50. See Table 8.2. U.S. Census Bureau, "Selected Population Profile in the United States: Puerto Rican." See also Marianne McCune, "Puerto Ricans in New York Struggling. . . Still," November 20, 2009, http://blogs.wnyc .org/news/2009/11/20/puerto-ricans-in-new-york-struggling-still/ (retrieved December 16, 2009).

51. Agueros, "Halfway to Dick and Jane," pp. 96–102; Rivera, "Angel and Aurea," p. 148.

52. Padilla, *Puerto Rican Chicago,* pp. 117–123; U.S. Bureau of the Census, The Hispanic Population in the United States: March 1993, *Current Population Reports* P20–475 (Washington, DC: U.S. Government Printing Office, 1994), pp. 16–17; Rodríguez, *Puerto Ricans,* pp. 106–116.

53. Jordan Green, "City Life; Gentrification Puts Whites on the Hook," *Newsday,* June 21, 2001, p. A45; Arlene Dávila, *Barrio Dreams: Puerto Ricans, Latinos, and the Neoliberal City* (Berkeley: University of California Press, 2004).

54. Joseph Mallia, "Matter of Rights in Freeport," *Newsday,* February 11, 2001, p. G17; Joseph Mallia, "Complaints against Inspectors," *Newsday,* January 25, 2001, p. A8.

55. Randal Archibold, "Mount Kisco Agrees to Extend Ban on Bias Against Hispanics," *The New York Times,* February 8, 2001, p. B7; "Federal Court Finds That Brookhaven Discriminated Against Latinos in Evicting Day Laborers and Day Laborers," Puerto Rican Legal Defense and Education Fund, press release, December 16, 2005.

56. William Vêlez, Michael E. Martin, and Edgar Méndez, "Segregation Patterns in Metro Areas: Latinos and African Americans in 2000," *Centro Journal* 21 (Spring 2009): 129; Lance Freeman, "A Note on the Influence of African Heritage on Segregation: The Case of Dominicans," *Urban Affairs Review* 35 (September 1999): 137–146;

Grosfoguel and Georas, "'Coloniality' of Power and Racial Dynamics," p. 110.

57. Pew Hispanic Center/Kaiser Family Foundation, "2002 National Survey of Latinos," research report, Washington, DC, December 2002, pp. 72–76; see also Clay F. Richards, "Jobs Top Latinos' List of Concerns," *Newsday*, October 13, 1991, p. 27.

58. U.S. Census Bureau, "Selected Population Profile in the United States: Puerto Rican."

59. Clive R. Belfield, *The Economic Consequences of Inadequate Education for the Puerto Rican Population in the United States* (New York: Centro de Estudios Puertorriqueños, Hunter College [CUNY], 2008), pp. 1–8; Rodríguez, *Puerto Ricans*, pp. 122–123, 127; George Borjas and Marta Tienda, eds. *Hispanics in the U.S. Economy* (New York: Academic Press, 1985); Lucy Hood, "High School Students at Risk: The Challenge of Dropouts and Pushouts," *Challenge Papers*, Carnegie Corporation, New York, 2004, pp. 1–16.

60. Milga Morales-Nadal, "Puerto Rican/Latino(a) Vistas on Culture and Education," unpublished research paper, 1991, n.p.; Belfield, *The Economic Consequences of Inadequate Education for the Puerto Rican Population in the United States*, pp. 3–10 and passim.

61. Patricia Gándara and Frances Contreras, *The Latino Education Crisis: The Consequences of Failed Social Policies* (Cambridge, MA: Harvard University Press, 2008); Rodríguez, *Puerto Ricans*, pp. 139–140; Louie F. Rodríguez and Gilberto Q. Conchas, "Preventing Truancy and Dropout Among Urban Middle School Youth," *Education and Urban Society* 41 (2009): 216–247.

62. Gary Orfield and Chugmei Lee, *Racial Transformation and the Changing Nature of Segregation* (Cambridge, MA: Harvard Civil Rights Project, 2006), p. 11. See also Gary Orfield, *Reviving the Goal of an Integrated Society: A 21st Century Challenge* (Los Angeles: UCLA Civil Rights Project, 2009). We also draw here on Rodríguez, *Puerto Ricans*, pp. 139–140; Hood, "High School Students at Risk."

63. Quoted in U.S. Commission on Civil Rights, *Puerto Ricans in the Continental United States*, p. 99; Rodríguez, *Puerto Ricans*, p. 126.

64. Quoted in U.S. Commission on Civil Rights, *Puerto Ricans in the Continental United States*, p. 103.

65. Pérez, *The Near Northwest Side Story*, pp. 157–191; Rodríguez, *Puerto Ricans*, pp. 139–148; Edna Acosta-Belén and Carlos Santiago, *Puerto Ricans in the United States: A Contemporary Portrait* (Boulder, CO: Lynne Rienner, 2006), p. 159; W. Steven Barnett et al., "Two-Way and Monolingual English Immersion in Preschool Education: An Experimental Comparison," *Early Childhood Research Quarterly* 22 (2007): 277–406. See also Ofelia Garcia, *Bilingual Education in the 21st Century: A Global Perspective* (New York: Wiley-Blackwell, 2008).

66. Catherine Walsh, *Pedagogy and the Struggle for Voice* (New York: Bergin and Garvey, 1991), pp. 101, 127; "U.S. Senate Roll Call Votes 110th Congress—1st Session,"

http://www.senate.gov/legislative/LIS/roll_call_lists/roll_call_vote_cfm.cfm?congress=110&session=1&vote=00197 (retrieved December 17, 2009); Isabel Cowles, "English-Only Measure Defeated in Nashville," http://www.findingdulcinea.com/news/Americas/2009/jan/English-Only-Measure-Defeated-in-Nashville.html#0 (retrieved December 17, 2009).

67. Walsh, *Pedagogy and the Struggle for Voice*, p. ix.

68. Ibid., pp. vii–xi, 1–27, 65–68, quotations from p. vii. See also Garcia, *Bilingual Education in the 21st Century*.

69. Migration Division, Department of Labor and Human Resources, Commonwealth of Puerto Rico, *Puerto Rican Voter Registration in New York City* (New York: Commonwealth of Puerto Rico, 1988), pp. 5–6.

70. General information was provided by the Midwest–Northeast Voter Registration Education Project; Pew Hispanic Center/Kaiser Family Foundation, "2002 National Survey of Latinos," pp. 64–65.

71. In these sections we draw on information provided by Maria Merrill-Ramirez and the Midwest–Northeast Voter Registration Education Project (now U.S. Hispanic Leadership Institute); and Peter Baker and Jeff Zeleny, "Obama Hails Judge as Inspiring," www.nytimes.com/2009/05/27/us/politics/27court.html (retrieved December 12, 2009). On images of "hot" Latinas, we draw on "Interview with Isabel Molina-Guzmán," http://illinois.edu/lb/article/72/27530/page=4/list=list (retrieved December 18, 2009).

72. Some information here provided by the Midwest–Northeast Voter Registration Education Project (now U.S. Hispanic Leadership Institute). We also draw on Jorge Duany, "The Puerto Rican Diaspora to the United States: A Postcolonial Migration?" http://www.centropr.org/docu ments/events/Jorge_Duany_Puerto_Rican_Diaspora.pdf (retrieved December 17, 2009); "About Us," http://ushli.org/about/ (retrieved December 17, 2009); and U.S. Hispanic Leadership Institute "About Us," http://www.nhcsl.org/aboutus.php (retrieved December 17, 2009).

73. Lopez, "The Puerto Rican Diaspora," p. 329; Western Regional Office, U.S. Commission on Civil Rights, *Puerto Ricans in California*, p. 16; Duany, "The Puerto Rican Diaspora to the United States."

74. David E. Pitt, "Puerto Rico Expands New York Voter Drive," *The New York Times*, October 14, 1987, p. A18; "Puerto Rico Governor to Announce Nation's Largest Nonpartisan Hispanic Voter Registration Campaign Succeeded in Registering over 300,000 Hispanic Voters," Hispanic Prwire, www.hispanicprwire.com/news.php?l=in&id=2865&cha=10 (retrieved November 22, 2006).

75. Shannah Kurland, "Brown Power vs. Black Power," *ColorLines*, Spring 2001, www.ard.org/C_Lines/CLArchive.htm; Lori Robinson, Paul Cuadros, Alysia Tate, and Raul Yzaguirre, "In the Pursuit of Opportunities and Justice, Should the Black and Latino Communities Join Forces or Go It Alone?" *The Crisis*, January/

February 2004, www.findarticles.com/p/articles/mi_qa4081/is_200401/ai_n9382156/ pg_1 (retrieved November 26, 2006); "Coverage of 'Brown-Black' Divide Overlooks Nuance, Complexity," April 15, 2008, http://www.mije.org/reggieroyston/blackbrowndivide (retrieved December 17, 2009).

76. Earl Ofari Hutchinson, *The Latino Challenge to Black America* (Los Angeles, CA: Middle Passage Press, 2007), chapter 1.

77. Lopez, *The Puerto Rican Papers*, pp. 55–58.

78. Bonilla and Campos, "A Wealth of Poor," pp. 166–167; Larry Rohter, "Puerto Rico Votes to Retain Status as Commonwealth," *The New York Times*, November 15, 1993, p. A1; Gonzalez, *Harvest of Empire*, pp. 263–266. The quote is from Rubén Berríos Martínez, "Puerto Rico's Decolonization," *Foreign Affairs* (November/December 1997): 100–114; "Puerto Rico Crosscurrents Likely to Wash over Florida," *Broward Daily Business Review*, March 21, 1997, p. A5.

79. Georgie Anne Geyer, "Puerto Rico Should Teach the Language That Binds," *Tulsa World*, September 5, 1997, p. A21; "Regional Congress Rejects Puerto Rico Colonial Regime," *Prensa Latina*, November 22, 2006, www.independencia.net/noticias/pl_ingl_congr_rejects_colol_status22n06.html (retrieved November 26, 2006).

80. Associated Press, "Congressman Criticized for Vieques 'Welfare' Slam," June 20, 2001, http://salon.com/politics/wire (retrieved July 3, 2001); Robert Barreto, "Puerto Rican Activists Facing Repression," http://socialistworker.org/2008/08/19/puertorican-activists (retrieved December 13, 2009).

81. Joseph Fitzpatrick, "Puerto Ricans," in *Harvard Encyclopedia of Ethnic Groups*, ed. Stephen Thernstrom (Cambridge, MA: Harvard University Press, 1981), p. 866; Padilla, *Puerto Rican Chicago*, pp. 54, 99–143; "About NPRC," http://www.bateylink.org/about (retrieved December 18, 2009).

82. John Adam Moreau, "My Parents, They Cry for Joy," in *The Puerto Ricans*, ed. Wagenheim, pp. 327–330.

83. Lopez, "The Puerto Rican Diaspora," pp. 331–332.

84. LatinoJustice PRLDEF, "Judge Refuses to Dismiss Voting Rights Case Brought by Puerto Ricans Against Volusia County," press release, August 25, 2009; Anne Barnard, "Rights Group Accuses U.S. of Failing to Protect Latinos," *New York Times*, December 18, 2008, http://www.nytimes.com/2008/12/19/nyregion/19latino.html?_r=1 (retrieved December 15, 2009); Acosta-Belén and Santiago, *Puerto Ricans in the United States*, pp. 157–165.

85. Acosta-Belén and Santiago, *Puerto Ricans in the United States*, pp. 157–165.

86. Pérez, *The Near Northwest Side Story*, pp. 152-154; Gonzalez, "Puerto Ricans on the Mainland," p. 17; Padilla, *Puerto Rican Chicago*, pp. 117–125; Steven A. Holmes, "Puerto Ricans' Alienation Is Cited in Miami Rampage," *The New York Times*, December 5, 1990, p. A24.

87. Jennifer Weil, Joe Williams, and Alice McQuillan, "Violence Follows Parade: 42 Arrested as Cops and Angry Crowd Clash in Bronx," *Daily News*, June 12, 2001, p. 7; Pérez, *The Near Northwest Side Story*, p. 169; CASA de Maryland, LatinoJustice PRLDEF, Nixon Peabody LLP, "Groups Sue Frederick County [Maryland] Sheriff for Racial Profiling," press release, November 9, 2009.

88. Lopez, "The Puerto Rican Diaspora," p. 332; Acosta-Belén and Santiago, *Puerto Ricans in the United States*, pp. 160–167. See also "About Us," http://www.ncprr.us/About_Us.html (retrieved December 18, 2009).

89. Quoted in Gigi Anders, "Talking the Talk," *American Journalism Review*, November 2000, p. 30.

90. Joseph Torres, "Racism Mars Puerto Rican Parade," New America News Service, September 10, 1997; "National Puerto Rican Day Parade 2005," www.nationalpuertoricandayparade.org/parade.html (retrieved November 26, 2006).

91. Fitzpatrick, "Puerto Ricans," p. 865; Susan E. Eichenberger, "Where Two or More Are Gathered: The Inclusion of Puerto Ricans in Multiethnic Latino Parishes in Southeastern United States," Ph.D. dissertation, University of Florida, Gainesville, 2004.

92. Andrew Greeley, "Defection among Hispanics (Updated)," *America* 177 (September 27, 1997): 12–13; Acosta-Belén and Santiago, *Puerto Ricans in the United States*, pp. 185. The Pew quote is from *Changing Faiths: Latinos and the Transformation of American Religion* (Washington, DC: Pew Forum on Religion in Public Life and the Pew Hispanic Center, 2007), p. 12.

93. Joseph P. Fitzpatrick, *Puerto Rican Americans: The Meaning of Migration to the Mainland* (Englewood Cliffs, NJ: Prentice-Hall, 1971), pp. 22–43.

94. Elena Padilla, *Up from Puerto Rico* (New York: Columbia University Press, 1958). See also Walsh, *Pedagogy and the Struggle for Voice*, pp. 101–102; Milton Gordon, *Assimilation in American Life* (New York: Oxford University Press, 1964), pp. 75–77.

95. Maldonado-Denis, *Puerto Rico*, p. 319.

96. Lloyd H. Rogler and Rosemary Santana Cooney, *Puerto Rican Families in New York City: Intergenerational Processes* (Maplewood, NJ: Waterfront Press, 1984), pp. 76–79; Strategy Research Corporation, *1991 U.S. Hispanic Market* (Miami: Strategy Research, 1991), p. 78; Rubén Rumbaut, Douglas S. Massey, and Frank D. Bean, "Linguistic Life Expectancies," *Population and Development Review* (September 2006): 1–2; Telles, "Mexican Americans and the American Nation," p. 11.

97. Fitzpatrick, *Puerto Rican Americans*, p. 43.

98. Aranda, *Emotional Bridges to Puerto Rico*, p. 175.

99. Dávila, *Barrio Dreams*, p. 18; see also Chapter 8.

100. Aranda, *Emotional Bridges to Puerto Rico*, pp. 60–120; Greta A. Gilbertson, Joseph P. Fitzpatrick, and Lijun Yang, "Hispanic Intermarriage in New York City," *International Migration Review* 30 (Summer 1996): 445–459; Sharon Lee and Barry Edmonston, "New Marriages, New Families: U.S. Racial and Hispanic Intermarriage," *Population Bulletin* (June 2005): 13–15.

101. Rogler and Cooney, *Puerto Rican Families in New York City*, pp. 76–79; Acosta-Belén and Santiago, *Puerto Ricans in the United States*, pp. 226–228.

102. Nancy Rivera Brooks, "Barbie's Online Critics See Guise in Dolls; Toys: Puerto Rican Incarnation Is at Center of Latest Mattel Brouhaha. First, the Hair . . .," *The Los Angeles Times*, November 21, 1997, p. D1; Acosta-Belén and Santiago, *Puerto Ricans in the United States*, pp. 15–17.

103. Gonzalez, *Harvest of Empire*, p. 95; the study cited is Laura A. Szalacha et al., "Discrimination and Puerto Rican Children's and Adolescents' Mental Health," *Cultural Diversity and Ethnic Minority Psychology* 9 (2003): 141–155.

104. Lopez, "The Puerto Rican Diaspora," p. 343; Duany, "The Puerto Rican Diaspora to the United States."

105. Bonilla and Campos, "A Wealth of Poor," p. 172; Don Hirasuna and Joel Michael, "Enterprise Zones: A Review of the Economic Theory and Empirical Evidence," research report, Minnesota House of Representatives, 2005.

106. Felix Robert Masud-Piloto, *With Open Arms: Cuban Migration to the U.S.* (Totowa, NJ: Rowman & Littlefield, 1988), pp. 7–11. We also draw in next few paragraphs on additional references in note 110.

107. Ibid., pp. 13–20.

108. Ibid., p. 11.

109. Ibid., pp. 20–35.

110. Ibid., pp. 1, 32–35, 39–41; "U.S. Hispanics: Who They Are, Whence They Came, and Why," in *The Hispanic Almanac* (Washington, DC: Hispanic Policy Development Project, 1984), pp. 17–18; Antonio Jorge and Raul Moncarz, *The Political Economy of Cubans in South Florida* (Miami: Institute of Interamerican Studies, 1987), pp. 4, 18; Hugh Thomas, *Cuba: The Pursuit of Freedom* (New York: Harper & Row, 1971), p. 117; Silvia Pedraza-Bailey, "Cuba's Exiles: Portrait of a Refugee Migration," *International Migration Review* 19, no. 1 (Spring 1985): 9–11, 23; Silvia Pedraza, "Cubans in Exile (1959–1989): The State of the Research," *Scholarship on the Cuban Experience: A Dialogue among Cubanists*, ed. Damian Fernandez (Gainesville: University of Florida, 1992).

111. Guillermo J. Grenier, "The Creation and Maintenance of the Cuban American 'Exile Ideology' in Miami," *Circunstancia* 10 (May 2006), pp. 1–2; Masud-Piloto, *With Open Arms*, pp. 1–5, 83–87. See also Eckstein "Cuban Émigrés and the American Dream."

112. Pedraza-Bailey, "Cuba's Exiles," pp. 15–17; Michael G. Wenk, "Adjustment and Assimilation: The Cuban Refugee Experience," *International Migration Review* 3, no. 1 (Fall 1968): 44, 48.

113. Pedraza-Bailey, "Cuba's Exiles," pp. 22–26; Masud-Piloto, *With Open Arms*, pp. 92–108.

114. Masud-Piloto, *With Open Arms*, pp. 83–87; Zulema E. Suarez, "Cuban Americans in Exile: Myths and Reality," in *Family Ethnicity: Strength in Diversity*, ed. Harriette P. McAdoo (Thousand Oaks, CA: Sage, 1999),

pp. 135–152. The quotation is from Gastón A. Fernández, "Race, Gender, and Class in the Persistence of the Mariel Stigma Twenty Years after the Exodus from Cuba," *International Migration Review* 41 (Fall 2007): 620–621.

115. Tim Golden, "U.S.-Cuban Accord Sets off a Surge of New Refugees," *The New York Times*, September 11, 1994, p. 1; "Prepared Statement of the Honorable Phylis E. Oakley, Assistant Secretary of State, Bureau of Population, Refugees and Migration, Before the Senate Committee on the Judiciary, Subcommittee on Immigration," Federal News Service, July 31, 1997; Andrew I. Schoenholtz and Thomas F. Muther, Jr., "Immigration and Nationality," *The International Lawyer* 33 (Summer 1999): 517.

116. U.S. Bureau of the Census, "Population Group: Cuban," "2008 American Community Survey," http://factfinder.census.gov (retrieved November 27, 2009); see also U.S. Census Bureau, *The Hispanic Population, Census 2000 Brief*, May 2001, pp. 1, 7, 8.

117. "Trouble in Paradise," *Time*, November 23, 1981, pp. 24–32; Max J. Castro and Guillermo J. Grenier, "Black–Latino Relations Under Conditions of Latino Empowerment: The Miami Case," unpublished research proposal, Miami, 1991, pp. 3–4; Jeffrey Schmalz, "Miami Tensions Simmering 3 Months After Violence," *The New York Times*, April 10, 1989, p. A8; Holmes, "Puerto Ricans' Alienation Is Cited in Miami Rampage," p. A24.

118. Mike Clary, "Black, Cuban Racial Chasm Splits Miami," *The Los Angeles Times*, March 23, 1997, p. A1; Jeremy F. Pais, Scott J. South, and Kyle Crowder, "White Flight Revisited: A Multiethnic Perspective on Neighborhood Out-Migration," *Population Research Policy Review* 28 (2009): 321–46.

119. "757 Haitians Cleared to Seek Refuge in U.S.," *The New York Times*, December 10, 1991, p. A8.

120. Mirta Ojito, "Best of Friends, Worlds Apart," *The New York Times*, June 5, 2000, p. 1A.

121. Ibid.

122. Myriam Marquez, "'Ugly Cuban-American' a Malicious Stereotype," *Houston Chronicle*, April 20, 2000, p. A29.

123. Susan Eckstein, "Cuban Émigrés and the American Dream," *Perspectives on Politics* 4 (June 2006): 305. (Italics added.) The census data here are from U.S. Bureau of the Census, "Population Group: Cuban," "2008 American Community Survey."

124. See Roger Ebert, "Scarface," http://rogerebert.suntimes.com/apps/pbcs.dll/article?AID=/19831209/REVIEWS/312090301/1023 (retrieved December 21, 2009).

125. Quoted in Matt Spetalnick, "Florida Declares English Official Language," Reuter Library Report, November 9, 1988, n.p.

126. Neil A. Lewis, "Committee Rejects Bush Nominee to Key Appellate Court in South," *The New York Times*, April 12, 1991, pp. A1, A11.

127. Philip Shenon, "FBI Suspends Veteran Agent," *The New York Times,* March 5, 1990, p. A1.

128. David Kidwell, "Miami Agent Lashes out at DEA," *Miami Herald,* February 22, 2001, p. 1B; the quotations are from the summary of events at "Whistleblower Protection—Ricardo Ramirez," http://www.judicialwatch.org/rramirez.shtml (retrieved December 22, 2009). See also Rodolfo Espino and Michael M. Franz, "Latino Phenotypic Discrimination Revisited: The Impact of Skin Color on Occupational Status," *Social Science Quarterly* 83 (2002): 612–624.

129. "Cubans in the United States," research report, Washington, DC, Pew Hispanic Center, 2006, pp. 6–7.

130. Jorge and Moncarz, *The Political Economy of Cubans in South Florida,* pp. 16–19.

131. Ibid., p. 9.

132. Lisandro Perez, "Immigrant Economic Adjustment and Family Organization: The Cuban Success Story Reexamined," *International Migration Review* 20, no. 1 (Spring 1986): pp. 4–7; Silvia Pedraza-Bailey, "Cubans and Mexicans in the United States: The Functions of Political and Economic Migration," *Cuban Studies* 11, no. 2/12, no. 1 (July 1981–January 1982); Alejandro Portes and Robert L. Bach, *Latin American Journey* (Berkeley: University of California Press, 1985), pp. 200–220.

133. Grosfoguel and Georas, "'Coloniality' of Power and Racial Dynamics," p. 113; other data here are from David E. Hayes-Bautista and Robert M. Stein, "Los Angeles; A Choice of Two Destinies: Will It Be Miami or San Antonio?" *The Los Angeles Times,* March 11, 2001, p. 1M.

134. Perez, "Immigrant Economic Adjustment and Family Organization," pp. 4–20.

135. Ibid., quotation on p. 18.

136. U.S. Census Bureau, "Selected Population Profile in the United States: Puerto Rican," "2008 American Community Survey." See older data at U.S. Census Bureau, "Hispanic Population, Table 1: Selected Summary Measures of Age and Income by Hispanic Origin and Race: March 2000," published March 6, 2001, www.census.gov/population/www/socdemo/hispanic.html.

137. U.S. Census Bureau, "Selected Population Profile in the United States: Puerto Rican," "2008 American Community Survey."

138. Quoted in "Widespread Political Efforts Open New Era for Hispanics," *Congressional Quarterly,* October 23, 1982, p. 2,709.

139. "Survey of Cuban and Cuban American Resident Adults in Miami-Dade and Broward," Bendixen & Associates, September 2006, www.miami.com/multimedia/miami/news/Cuban%20Exile%20Poll.pdf (retrieved December 7, 2006).

140. Some information was provided by the Midwest–Northeast Voter Registration Education Project. See also "Cubans in the United States," pp. 6–7.

141. Andrew Gumbel, "U.S. Presidential Election: Mayor Denies 'Betrayal' of Democrats," *The Independent* (London), December 4, 2000, p. 12. See also Samuel P. Huntington, "The Erosion of American National Interests," *Foreign Affairs,* September/October 1997, p. 28.

142. Jorge Mas Santos, "Make a Difference. Have a Purpose. Shine a Light," February 7, 2001, www.canfnet.org (retrieved July 12, 2001); Ana Menendez, "The 'Transition' Has Begun—In Cuba and U.S.," MiamiHerald.Com, December 6, 2006, www.miami.com/mld/miamiherald/16173093.htm (retrieved December 7, 2006).

143. Damien Cave, "Cuban American National Foundation Calls for New US Cuba Policy," *Miami Herald,* April 11, 2009, http://havanajournal.com/cuban_americans/entry/cuban-american-national-foundation-calls-for-new-us-cuba- policy (retrieved December 21, 2009).

144. Benjamin G. Bishin, Feryal M. Cherif, Andy S. Gomez, and Daniel P. Stevens, "What to Expect from the Cuban-American Electorate," http://www.brookings.edu/articles/2008/08_cuban_americans_gomez.aspx (retrieved December 21, 2009); Eckstein, "Cuban Émigrés and the American Dream," pp. 301–303.

145. Richard Boudreaus, "Cuba Strikes Democracy Movement," *The Los Angeles Times,* January 19, 1992, p. A1; Deborah Sharp, "Execution in Cuba," *USA Today,* January 22, 1992, p. 3A.; Peter Kornbluh and Jon Elliston, "Will Congress Kill TV Marti?" *The Nation,* August 22/29, 1994, pp. 194–196; "Radio and TV Marti," Council on Hemispheric Affairs, March 29, 2006, www.coha.org/2006/03/29/radio-and-tvmarti-washington-guns-after-castro-at-any-cost (retrieved December 7, 2006); David Adams, "Time to Scrap TV Marti, Critics Say," *St. Petersburg Times,* February 19, 2009, http://www.tampabay.com/news/world/article976246.ece (retrieved December 21, 2009).

146. Kirk Nielsen, "Sail Away and Stay and Stay," *Miami New Times* Online, May 10, 2001, www.miaminewtimes.com (retrieved July 12, 2001); "Bush Urges Cubans to Push Democracy," CNN.COM, www.cnn.com/2006/POLITICS/08/03/us.cuba/index.html (retrieved August 3, 2006).

147. Cathay Smith, "Santería: The Way of the Saints," http://home.wlu.edu/~lubint/Touchstone/Santeria-Smith.htm (retrieved November 19, 2006).

148. Robert Suro et al., *Changing Faiths: Latinos and the Transformation of American Religion* (Washington, DC: Pew Forum on Religion in Public Life and the Pew Hispanic Center, 2007); "Cubans in the United States," p. 7; Eichenberger, "Where Two or More Are Gathered."

149. "Big Five Club Keeps Cuban Traditions Alive," *Miami Herald,* February 2, 2008, http://www.latinamericanstudies.org/exile/big-five.htm (retrieved December 27, 2009); Jon Nordheimer, "Where Old Havana Plays," *The New York Times,* April 3, 1991, p. C1; Eckstein, "Cuban Émigrés and the American Dream," pp. 297–299.

150. Deborah Sontag, "The Lasting Exile of Cuban Spirits," *The New York Times,* September 11, 1994, sec. 4, p. 1. The

survey is cited in "Cubans in the United States," p. 7. See also "Survey of Cuban and Cuban American Resident Adults in Miami-Dade and Broward"; and "Hispanics of Cuban Origin in the United States, 2007," research fact sheet, Pew Hispanic Center, Washington, DC, 2007.

151. Kelly M. Barlow, Donald M. Taylor, and Wallace E. Lambert, "Ethnicity in America and Feeling 'American,'" *Journal of Psychology* 134 (November 2000): 581–600.

152. Portes and Bach, *Latin American Journey*, pp. 91–93, 193–199.

153. Hayes-Bautista and Stein, "Los Angeles: A Choice of Two Destinies," p. 1M.

154. Amie Parnes, "First Communions Turn Lavish in South Florida; Cuban-Americans among Big Spenders," *Boston Globe*, June 27, 2001, p. A2. See also Portes and Bach, *Latin American Journey*, pp. 246–247.

155. Alejandro Portes and Steven Shafer, "Revisiting the Enclave Hypothesis: Miami Twenty-five Years Later," in *The Sociology of Entrepreneurship* (Bingley, United Kingdom: Emerald Group Publishing Limited, 2007), p. 190.

156. "Trouble in Paradise," pp. 30–31.

157. Strategy Research Corporation, *1991 U.S. Hispanic Market*, pp. 78–130; Eckstein, "Cuban Émigrés and the American Dream," p. 299.

158. Strategy Research Corporation, *1991 U.S. Hispanic Market*, pp. 78–130; Matea Gold, "Cultural Celebration Sways to a Cuban Beat; Heritage: About 20,000 Attend L.A.'s Third Annual Cuban American Festival of Art, Music, and Food in Echo Park," *The Los Angeles Times*, May 19, 1997, p. B1; "2002 National Survey of Latinos," pp. 32–33.

159. Andrew Meadows, "Catering to Latin Tastes; Tapping the Hispanic Market," *Tampa Tribune* (Florida), April 20, 2001, p. 1, Business & Finance.

160. Private communication with Maria Merril-Ramirez, July 1982.

161. Robert Suro and Gabriel Escobar, "2006 National Survey of Latinos: The Immigration Debate," research report, Pew Hispanic Center, Washington, DC, July 2006, p. 16.

162. Stephanie Armour, "Welcome Mat Rolls Out for Hispanic Workers: Corporate America Cultivates Talent as Ethnic Population Booms," *USA Today*, April 12, 2001, p. 1B; Robert Crosslin, Jennifer Davis, Janet Marinaccio, Eric Olson, "Opportunities for Hispanic/Latino Workers," research report, Goodwill Industries International, Inc., April 2007; "Increasing Wealth in the Latino Community," research report, Los Angeles, Tomás Rivera Policy Institute, University of Southern California, 2007.

Chapter 10

1. Mitsuye Yamada, "Invisibility Is an Unnatural Disaster: Reflections of an Asian American Woman," in *Feminist Theory Reader: Local and Global Perspectives*, ed. Carole K. McCann and Seung-Kyung Kim (New York: Routledge, 2003), p. 174.

2. U.S. Bureau of the Census, *U.S. Census of Population, 1980: Asian and Pacific Islander Population in the United States*, PC80-2-1E (Washington, DC: U.S. Government Printing Office, 1988), p. 1; U.S. Bureau of the Census, *1990 Census of Population: Social and Economic Characteristics: United States*, CP-2-1 (Washington, DC: U.S. Government Printing Office, 1993), pp. 105–106; U.S. Bureau of the Census, "American Fact Finder: Census 2000 Demographic Profile Highlights: Selected Population Group," http://factfinder.census.gov; (retrieved December 1, 2006); U.S. Bureau of the Census, "2008 American Community Survey, American Fact Finder: Selected Population Profile in the United States," [Various Asian American groups], http://factfinder.census.gov (retrieved January 3, 2010).

3. U.S. Commission on Civil Rights, *Civil Rights Issues Facing Asian Americans in the 1990s* (Washington, DC: U.S. Government Printing Office, 1992), p. 15; Robert Daniels, *Coming to America* (New York: HarperCollins, 1990), p. 350; U.S. Bureau of the Census, "2008 American Community Survey, American Fact Finder: Selected Population Profile in the United States, Japanese Alone," http://factfinder.census.gov (retrieved January 3, 2010); U.S. Bureau of the Census, "2008 American Community Survey, American Fact Finder: Selected Population Profile in the United States, Japanese Alone or in Any Combination," http://factfinder.census.gov (retrieved January 3, 2010).

4. Kathryn Tolbert, "Pacific Grim," *Boston Globe Sunday Magazine*, March 29, 1992, p. 14.

5. Ronald Takaki, *Strangers from a Different Shore: A History of Asian Americans* (New York: Penguin, 1989), p. 7.

6. Alan T. Moriyama, *Imingaisha: Japanese Immigration Companies and Hawaii, 1894–1908* (Honolulu: University of Hawaii Press, 1985); Wayne Patterson, *The Korean Frontier in America: Immigration to Hawaii, 1896–1910* (Honolulu: University of Hawaii Press, 1988).

7. Roger Daniels, *The Politics of Prejudice* (New York: Atheneum, 1969), pp. 3–6; Hilary Conroy, *The Japanese Frontier in Hawaii, 1868–1898* (Berkeley: University of California Press, 1953), passim; Moriyama, *Imingaisha*, pp.xvi–xix.

8. Takaki, *Strangers from a Different Shore*, p. 179.

9. U.S. Immigration and Naturalization Service, *1975 Annual Report* (Washington, DC, 1975), pp. 62–66.

10. Arinori Mori, *The Japanese in America* (Japan Advertiser Press, 1926), pp. 19–21; Kaizo Naka, *Social and Economic Conditions among Japanese Farmers in California* (San Francisco: R & E Research Associates, 1974), p. 6; John Modell, "On Being an Issei: Orientations Toward America," Unpublished research paper presented to the American Anthropological Association, San Diego, November 1970, p. 4.

11. Sucheng Chan, *Asian Americans: An Interpretive History* (Boston: Twayne, 1991), pp. 103–117; Roger Daniels, *Asian America: Chinese and Japanese in the United States*

Since 1850 (Seattle: University of Washington Press, 1988), pp. 100–154.

12. Jacobus Tenbroek, Edward N. Barnhart, and Floyd W. Matson, *Prejudice, War, and the Constitution* (Berkeley: University of California Press, 1968), pp. 42–43; *Takao Ozawa v. United States*, 260 U.S. 178 (1922); Takaki, *Strangers from a Distant Shore*, pp. 14–15.

13. Hillary Conroy and T. Scott Miyakawa, "Foreword," in *East Across the Pacific*, ed. Hillary Conroy and T. Scott Miyakawa (Santa Barbara, CA: ABC-CLIO, 1972), pp. xiv–xv.

14. The statistics are from U.S. Census Bureau publications.

15. Takaki, *Strangers from a Different Shore*, pp. 479–481; Leadership Conference on Civil Rights Education Fund, *Confronting the New Faces of Hate: Hate Crimes in America* (Washington, DC: Leadership Conference, 2009).

16. Robert G. Lee, *Orientals: Asian Americans in Popular Culture* (Philadelphia: Temple University Press, 1999), p. 8.

17. E. Manchester-Boddy, *Japanese in America* (San Francisco: R & E Research Associates, 1970), pp. 25–30.

18. V. S. McClatchy, *Japanese Immigration and Colonization*, reprint ed. (San Francisco: R & E Research Associates, 1970), p. 42.

19. Quoted in Edward K. Strong Jr., *The Second-Generation Japanese Problem* (Stanford, CA: Stanford University Press, 1934), p. 133.

20. Tenbroek, Barnhart, and Matson, *Prejudice, War, and the Constitution*, p. 31.

21. Dennis M. Ogawa, *From Japs to Japanese* (Berkeley, CA: McCutchan, 1971), p. 12; Carey McWilliams, *Brothers under the Skin*, rev. ed. (Boston: Little, Brown, 1964), pp. 148–149; Stanley Sue and Harry H. L. Kitano, "Stereotypes as a Measure of Success," *Journal of Social Issues* 29 (1973): 83–98.

22. Tenbroek, Barnhart, and Matson, *Prejudice, War, and the Constitution*, pp. 66–70.

23. Quoted in Ogawa, *From Japs to Japanese*, p. 11.

24. U.S. Department of the Interior, War Relocation Authority, *Myths and Facts about the Japanese American* (Washington, DC, 1945), pp. 7–8; Ogawa, *From Japs to Japanese*, pp. 35–54. Survey data document attitude changes in the period 1942–1961. See also Roger Daniels, "Why It Happened Here," in *The Social Reality of Ethnic America*, ed. R. Gomez et al. (Lexington, MA: D. C. Heath, 1971), p. 236.

25. Council on Interracial Books for Children, *Stereotypes, Distortions and Omissions in U.S. History Textbooks* (New York: Racism and Sexism Resource Center for Educators, 1977), pp. 42–46; Funie Hsu, "Textbook Companies Dictating Whitewashed History," *AsianWeek*, September 2, 2005, http://news.asianweek.com/news (retrieved December 17, 2006); Sam Chu Lin, "Extended Life for 'Chinese Experience' Series," *AsianWeek*, February 20, 2004, http://news.asianweek.com/news (retrieved December 17, 2006); "Latest Headline News," Media Action Network for Asian Americans, http://www.manaa.org (retrieved December 18, 2006). See also

Michelle Malkin, *In Defense of Internment: The Case for Racial Profiling in World War II and the War on Terror* (New York: Regnery Publishing, 2004); for systematic refutation of her arguments by major scholars, see "Dangerous Revisionist History," http://www.densho.org/about/revisionism.asp (retrieved January 4, 2010).

26. Letta Tayler, "Dateline: Washington," *States News Service*, May 8, 1987, n.p.; Takaki, *Strangers from a Different Shore*, p. 6.

27. Mia Tuan, *Forever Foreigners or Honorary Whites?: The Asian American Experience Today* (New Brunswick, NJ: Rutgers University Press, 1998), p. 1. The baseball incident is in the Press Release on Fukudome T-Shirts, Japanese American Citizens League, April 2009, www.jacl.org (retrieved January 4, 2010).

28. Bill Stamets, "Asians Wary of Ad Stereotypes," *The Chicago Reporter*, http://www.chicagoreporter.com/index.php/c/Cover_Stories/d/Asians_Wary_of_Ad_Stereotypes (retrieved January 3, 2010).

29. The quote is from Karl Taro Greenfield, "Return of the Yellow Peril," *Nation* (May 11, 1992): 636. See also Michael Crichton, *Rising Sun* (New York: Knopf, 1991); Helen Zia, *Asian American Dreams: The Emergence of an American People* (New York: Farrar, Straus & Giroux, 2000), p. 134.

30. Erika Hayasaki, "'Pearl Harbor' Making Its Marks," *The Los Angeles Times*, May 29, 2001, p. 6–1.

31. "JACL Meets with Paramount Pictures Executives," Press Release, Japanese American Citizens League, November 12, 2009 (retrieved January 5, 2010). These listed examples are from press releases in 2008–2009 by the Japanese American Citizens League, at http://www.jacl.org/public_policy/response.htm (retrieved January 4, 2010).

32. Steven A. Chin, "KFRC Deejay Draws Suspension for On-Air Derogatory Remarks," *San Francisco Examiner*, December 6, 1994, p. A2; "Current Affairs," *JACL News*, www.jacl.org/index.php (retrieved December 19, 2006); Media Action Network for Asian Americans, "Latest Headline News," www.manaa.org (retrieved December 18, 2006).

33. Herbert B. Johnson, *Discrimination against the Japanese in California* (Berkeley, CA: Courier, 1907), pp. 73–74; Daniels, *The Politics of Prejudice*, pp. 33–34; Howard H. Sugimoto, "The Vancouver Riots of 1907: A Canadian Episode," in *East across the Pacific*, ed. Conroy and Miyakawa, pp. 92–110; Jean Pajus, *The Real Japanese California* (San Francisco: R & E Research Associates, 1971), pp. 164–166; Daniels, *The Politics of Prejudice*, p. 87; Tenbroek, Barnhart, and Matson, *Prejudice, War, and the Constitution*, p. 73.

34. Lemuel F. Ignacio, *Asian Americans and Pacific Islanders* (San Jose, CA: Pilipino Development Associates, 1976), pp. 95–96; Tenbroek, Barnhart, and Matson, *Prejudice, War, and the Constitution*, passim; Raymond Y. Okamura, "The American Concentration Camps: A Cover-up through Euphemistic Terminology," in *Understanding*

Prejudice and Discrimination, ed. Scott Plous (New York: McGraw-Hill, 2003), pp. 149–164.

35. Dorothy Swaine Thomas and Richard S. Nishimoto, *The Spoilage* (Berkeley: University of California Press, 1946), pp. 8–16; Tenbroek, Barnhart, and Matson, *Prejudice, War, and the Constitution,* pp. 118–120.

36. Tenbroek, Barnhart, and Matson, *Prejudice, War, and the Constitution,* pp. 120, 126–129, 130; Thomas and Nishimoto, *The Spoilage,* pp. 10–20; Edward H. Spicer et al., *Impounded People* (Tucson: University of Arizona Press, 1969), pp. 141–241.

37. Richard Drinnon, *Keeper of Concentration Camps* (Berkeley: University of California Press, 1987), pp. 47, 153; Valerie Matsumoto, "Japanese American Women During World War II," in *Unequal Sisters,* ed. Ellen C. DuBois and Vicki L. Ruiz (New York: Routledge, 1990), p. 373.

38. Thomas and Nishimoto, *The Spoilage,* pp. 54–71; Tenbroek, Barnhart, and Matson, *Prejudice, War, and the Constitution,* pp. 126–132, 149–155; Spicer et al., *Impounded People,* pp. 252–280.

39. Leonard Bloom and Ruth Riemer, *Removal and Return* (Berkeley: University of California Press, 1949), pp. 124–157, 198–204; Tenbroek, Barnhart, and Matson, *Prejudice, War, and the Constitution,* pp. 155–177, 180–181.

40. Bradford Smith, *Americans from Japan* (New York; Lippincott, 1948), pp. 10–12, 202–276; Carey McWilliams, *Prejudice* (Boston: Little, Brown, 1944), p. 4; Tenbroek, Barnhart, and Matson, *Prejudice, War, and the Constitution,* pp. 211–223; Harry H. L. Kitano, *Japanese Americans,* 2nd ed. (Englewood Cliffs, NJ: Prentice-Hall, 1976), pp. 82–88; S. Frank Miyamoto, "The Forced Evacuation of the Japanese Minority During World War II," *Journal of Social Issues* 29 (1973): 11–29; Drinnon, *Keeper of Concentration Camps,* pp. 255–256. See also Christopher Thorne, *Allies of a Kind* (New York: Oxford University Press, 1978).

41. Kitano, *Japanese Americans,* p. 73.

42. Gary Y. Okihiro, "Japanese Resistance in America's Concentration Camps: A Re-evaluation," *Amerasia Journal* 2 (Fall 1973): 20–34; Arthur A. Hansen and David A. Hacker, "The Manzanar Riot: An Ethnic Perspective," *Amerasia Journal* 3 (Fall 1974): 112–142. See also Roger Daniels, *Concentration Camps, U.S.A.* (New York: Holt, Rinehart & Winston, 1971).

43. Southern Poverty Law Center, *Intelligence Report,* March 1994, pp. 17–29; C. N. Le, "Anti-Asian Racism and Violence," *Asian-Nation,* www.asian-nation.org/racism.shtml (retrieved December 21, 2006).

44. Mike Honda, "Watada Chose to Stop Fighting," *San Francisco Chronicle,* January 30, 2007, www.thankyoult.org/content/view/107/23 (retrieved February 2, 2007); and "Ehren Watada," http://en.wikipedia.org/wiki/Ehren_Watada (retrieved February 2, 2007); Gene Johnson, "Justice Department Won't Pursue War Objector Case," Associated Press, May 6, 2009, http://

abcnews.go.com/US/wireStory? id=7521494 (retrieved January 5, 2010).

45. Ivan H. Light, *Ethnic Enterprise in America* (Berkeley: University of California Press, 1972), pp. 174–179; Bill Hosokawa, *The Nisei* (New York: Morrow, 1969), pp. 199–200; Kitano, *Japanese Americans,* pp. 55–58.

46. Hosokawa, *The Nisei,* pp. 439–446; Kitano, *Japanese Americans,* pp. 89–90.

47. Nathaniel C. Nash, "House Votes Payments to Japanese Americans," *The New York Times,* September 18, 1987, p. A15.

48. Ken Miller, "U.S. Pays Japanese Internees $20,000—and Apologies," Gannett News Service, October 9, 1990, n.p.

49. Santiago O'Donnell and Psyche Pascual, "Kato Slaying Raises Fears of Hate Crime," *The Los Angeles Times,* March 1, 1992, p. B1.

50. Benjamin Forgey, "Imagery Says It All at New Monument; Artistry, Apology Merge at Japanese American Memorial," *The Washington Post,* June 30, 2001, p. C1.

51. Rodolfo Acuña, *Occupied America* (San Francisco: Canfield Press, 1972), pp. 212–213; "JACL Announces Success In Camp Preservation Funding," Japanese American Citizens League, Press Release, November 3, 2009.

52. Harry H. L. Kitano and Roger Daniels, *Asian Americans: Emerging Minorities,* 3rd ed. (Englewood Cliffs, NJ: Prentice-Hall, 2001), p. 47.

53. Kitano, *Japanese Americans,* pp. 174–186; Daniel Inouye and Lawrence Elliot, *Journey to Washington* (Englewood Cliffs, NJ: Prentice-Hall, 1967), pp. 248–250; Hosokawa, *The Nisei,* pp. 460–469.

54. Hosokawa, *The Nisei,* pp. 486–487; Christine Munteanu, "In the U.S. Federal Courts, Asian Pacific Americans Are Left Off the Bench," *JACL Network Update,* Fall 2009, p. 1.

55. Stanley Karnow, "Apathetic Asian Americans?" *The Washington Post,* November 29, 1992, p. C1; Jeffrey Passel, "The Latino and Asian Vote," www.urban.org/publications/900723.html (retrieved December 19, 2006).

56. "Slur Stirs Party In-fighting," *Commercial Appeal,* May 4, 1994, p. 5A.

57. U.S. Commission on Civil Rights, *Recent Activities Against Citizens and Residents of Asian Descent* (Washington, DC: U.S. Government Printing Office, 1986), pp. 3–6.

58. Kenneth Walsh, Gloria Borger, Susan Dentzer, and Carla A. Robbins, "The 'America First' Fallacies," *U.S. News & World Report,* February 3, 1992, p. 22.

59. O'Donnell and Pascual, "Kato Slaying Raises Fears of Hate Crime," p. B1; Kitano and Daniels, *Asian Americans,* 3rd ed., p. 83.

60. Yuji Ichioka, "A Buried Past," *Amerasia Journal* 1 (July 1971): 1–25; Karl Yoneda, "100 Years of Japanese Labor History in the U.S.A.," in *Roots,* ed. Amy Tachiki et al. (Los Angeles: UCLA Asian American Studies Center, 1971), pp. 150–157; Takaki, *Strangers from a Different Shore,* p. 200.

61. See *Roots*, ed. Tachiki et al.

62. Russell Endo and William Wei, "On the Development of Asian American Studies Programs," in *Reflections on Shattered Windows*, ed. Gary Y. Okihiro et al. (Pullman: Washington State University Press, 1988), pp. 6–12.

63. Randal C. Archibold, "UC Irvine Expected to Offer Asian Studies Major; Education: On a Campus Where More Than Half the Students Are of Asian Background, Absence of Such a Program Has Been a Concern and a Topic of Protests," *The Los Angeles Times*, May 13, 1997, p. A3; Wired News Report, "E-mail Hate Scribe Sentenced," Wired News, www.wired.com/news/print/0,1294,12090,00.html (retrieved August 12, 2001).

64. Japanese American Citizens League, Press Release, April 2009, http://www.jacl.org/public_policy/response.htm (retrieved January 4, 2010). See also Leadership Conference on Civil Rights Education Fund, *Confronting the New Faces of Hate: Hate Crimes in America* (Washington, DC: Leadership Conference, 2009).

65. "News report," *JACL Network Update*, Fall 2009, p. 2. See also Leadership Conference on Civil Rights Education Fund, *Confronting the New Faces of Hate: Hate Crimes in America*.

66. Cited in Sidney L. Gulick, *The American Japanese Problem* (New York: Scribner's, 1914), p. 11; Japanese Association of the Pacific Northwest, *Japanese Immigration* (San Francisco: R & E Research Associates, 1972), pp. 22–25; Daniels, *The Politics of Prejudice*, pp. 7, 10–12.

67. Edna Bonacich and John Modell, *The Economic Basis of Ethnic Solidarity* (Berkeley: University of California Press, 1980), pp. 38–47.

68. Kitano, *Japanese Americans*, pp. 19–21; Light, *Ethnic Enterprise in America*, pp. 27–29; S. Frank Miyamoto, "An Immigrant Community in America," in *East across the Pacific*, ed. Conroy and Miyakawa, pp. 223–225.

69. Gulick, *The American Japanese Problem*, pp. 11, 32–33; Light, *Ethnic Enterprise in America*, p. 71.

70. See also Roger Daniels, "Japanese Immigrants on the Western Frontier: The Issei in California, 1890–1940," in *East across the Pacific*, ed. Conroy and Miyakawa, p. 85.

71. Pajus, *The Real Japanese California*, pp. 147–151; Light, *Ethnic Enterprise in America*, p. 76.

72. Bloom and Riemer, *Removal and Return*, pp. 115–117; Strong, *The Second-Generation Japanese Problem*, pp. 209–211.

73. Bloom and Riemer, *Removal and Return*, pp. 17–20.

74. Evelyn Nakano Glenn, "The Dialectics of Wage Work: Japanese American Women and Domestic Service, 1905–1940," in *Unequal Sisters*, ed. DuBois and Ruiz, p. 345.

75. Ibid., p. 369.

76. Bloom and Riemer, *Removal and Return*, pp. 44, 144; Bonacich and Modell, *The Economic Basis of Ethnic Solidarity*, pp. 256–259.

77. U.S. Bureau of the Census, "American Fact Finder: 2008 American Community Survey," http://factfinder.census.gov (retrieved January 7, 2010).

78. Ibid.

79. Kitano and Daniels, *Asian Americans*, 3rd ed., p. 81; "Asian Representation Increasing on TV, Slowly," Goldsea Intelligence, http://goldsea.com/Asiagate/612/08tv.html (retrieved December 13, 2006).

80. "Paramount Discriminates Against Asian American Actors for Movie Adaptation of Asian-Based TV Series," *MANAA* (April 29, 2009), http://www.manaa.org/paramountdiscriminates.html (retrieved January 8, 2010); "Restrictive Portrayals of Asians in the Media and How to Balance Them," MANAA, http://www.manaa.org/asian_stereotypes.html (retrieved January 8, 2010). We also draw from other news reports at www.manaa.org.

81. U.S. Commission on Civil Rights, *Success of Asian Americans: Fact or Fiction?* (Washington, DC: U.S. Government Printing Office, 1980), pp. 14–15; and research studies cited in "Brief of Amici Curiae, Asian American Justice Center, Asian American Institute, Asian Law Caucus, et al., In Support of Respondents," in *Ricci v. DeStefano*, 557 U.S. ___ (2009).

82. LEAP, *APA Representation on Fortune 100 Boards* (Los Angeles: Leadership Education for Asian-Pacifics, 2009), pp. 1–6; Gerrye Wong, "Where are the Asian CEOs?" *AsianWeek*, http://www.asianweek.com/2009/05/01/where-are-the-asian-ceos (retrieved January 10, 2010).

83. S. B. Woo, "How to Vote in 2004 to Win 'The Big Interests,'" 80-20Initiative, www.80-20initiative.net/empower.html (retrieved December 20, 2006); Winfred Yu, "Asian Americans Charge Prejudice Slows Climb to Management Ranks," *The Wall Street Journal*, September 11, 1985, n.p., quoted in Takaki, *Strangers from a Different Shore*, pp. 476–477; "Brief of Amici Curiae"; Roli Varma, "Asians in the U.S. Public Service: Diversity, Achievements and Glass Ceiling," United Nations Expert Group Meeting on Managing Diversity in the Civil Service, May 2001; Anne Fisher, "Piercing the 'Bamboo Ceiling'" *Fortune*, August 22, 2005, http://money.cnn.com/magazines/fortune/fortune_archive/2005/08/22/8270002/index.htm (retrieved January 10, 2010).

84. Art Pine, "Marines Pin Bars on Man They Dismissed," *The Los Angeles Times*, March 19, 1994, p. A4; Judy Tachibana, "Triumph over Racism in the Marines," *Sacramento Bee*, April 20, 1994, p. B3.

85. These accounts are from March 2009 press releases of the Japanese American Citizens League, at http://www.jacl.org/public_policy/response.htm (retrieved January 4, 2010).

86. K. K. Kawakami, *The Japanese Question* (New York: Macmillan, 1921), pp. 143–145; John Modell, "Tradition and Opportunity: The Japanese Immigrant in America," *Pacific Historical Review* 40 (May 1971): 163–182; Johnson, *Discrimination Against the Japanese in California*, pp. 3–20, 40–47; Franklin Hichborn, *The Story of the Session of the California Legislature of 1909* (San Francisco: James H. Barry Press, 1909), p. 207; Pajus, *The Real*

Japanese California, pp. 170–178; Kawakami, *The Japanese Question,* pp. 168–169.

87. William Petersen, *Japanese Americans* (New York: Random House, 1971), p. 183; Strong, *The Second-Generation Japanese Problem,* pp. 201–204; Kawakami, *The Japanese Question,* pp. 146–151; Pajus, *The Real Japanese California,* p. 181.

88. Pajus, *The Real Japanese California,* p. 183; Strong, *The Second-Generation Japanese Problem,* pp. 185–188.

89. U.S. Bureau of the Census, "American Fact Finder: 2008 American Community Survey."

90. JACL, Press Release, January 2009 (retrieved January 4, 2010); Sheila Sanchez, "Parents Hope to File Civil Rights Lawsuit against Fall River Joint Unified School District," NikkeiWest, n.d. (c. late 2008–early 2009).

91. Jacqueline Mac, *Myths and Mirrors: Real Challenges Facing Asian American Students* (San Francisco: Japanese American Citizens League, 2009); Varma, "Asians in the U.S. Public Service: Diversity, Achievements and Glass Ceiling." See also U.S. Commission on Civil Rights, *Social Indicators of Equality for Minorities and Women* (Washington, DC, 1978).

92. Manchester-Boddy, *Japanese in America,* p. 118.

93. Petersen, *Japanese Americans,* p. 177; Manchester-Boddy, *Japanese in America,* pp. 114–118.

94. Andrew W. Lind, *Hawaii's Japanese* (Princeton, NJ: Princeton University Press, 1946), pp. 212–257; Petersen, *Japanese Americans,* pp. 177–178, 185.

95. Hosokawa, *The Nisei,* p. 131; Kitano, *Japanese Americans,* p. 115; Christie Kiefer, *Changing Cultures, Changing Lives* (San Francisco: Jossey-Bass, 1974), pp. 34–38; Petersen, *Japanese Americans,* p. 187.

96. John Dart, "Military Opens Chaplain Ranks to Buddhists," *The Los Angeles Times,* October 27, 1987, p. 1; Barry A. Kosmin and Ariela Keysar, *American Religious Identification Survey (ARIS) 2008: Summary Report* (Hartford, CT: Trinity College Program on Public Values, 2008), p. 14.

97. John Modell, "The Japanese American Family: A Perspective for Future Investigations," *Pacific Historical Review* 37 (February 1968): 79; Joe R. Feagin and Nancy Fujitaki, "On the Assimilation of Japanese Americans," *Amerasia Journal* 1 (February 1972): 15–17.

98. Tuan, *Forever Foreigners,* p. 155.

99. Peter Y. Hong, "Japanese American Newspaper's Layoffs Anger Community," *The Los Angeles Times,* November 15, 1997, p. B1; "Welcome to The Rafu Shimpo Online Edition," http://www.rafushimpo.com/en/rafu/welcome.html (retrieved January 10, 2010).

100. Petersen, *Japanese Americans,* pp. 6–7; Light, *Ethnic Enterprise in America,* passim; William Caudill, "Japanese American Personality and Acculturation," *Genetic Psychology Monographs* 45 (1952): 3–102; Harry H. L. Kitano and Roger Daniels, *Asian Americans: Emerging Minorities* (Englewood Cliffs, NJ: Prentice-Hall, 1988), p. 179.

101. Paul Spickard, *Mixed Blood* (Madison: University of Wisconsin Press, 1988), p. 347.

102. David J. O'Brien and Stephen S. Fugita, "Generational Differences in Japanese Americans' Perceptions and Feelings about Social Relationships between Themselves and Caucasian Americans," in *Culture, Ethnicity, and Identity,* ed. William McCready (New York: Academic Press, 1983), pp. 235–236; Rosalind Chou and Joe R. Feagin, *The Myth of the Model Minority* (Boulder, CO: Paradigm Books, 2009).

103. Darrel Montero, *Japanese Americans: Changing Patterns of Ethnic Affiliation over Three Generations* (Boulder, CO: Westview Press, 1980), p. 80; Modell, "The Japanese American Family," pp. 76–79; Kitano, *Japanese Americans,* pp. 189, 196; George Kagiwada, "Assimilation of Nisei in Los Angeles," in *East Across the Pacific,* p. 273; Feagin and Fujitaki, "On the Assimilation of Japanese Americans," p. 23.

104. Akemi Kikumura and Harry H. L. Kitano, "Interracial Marriage: A Picture of Japanese Americans," *Journal of Social Issues* 29 (1973): 67–81; John N. Tinker, "Intermarriage and Ethnic Boundaries: The Japanese American Case," *Journal of Social Issues* 29 (1973): 55; John W. Connor, *Tradition and Change in Three Generations of Japanese Americans* (Chicago: Nelson-Hall, 1977), p. 308; Gene N. Levine and Colbert Rhodes, *The Japanese American Community* (New York: Praeger, 1981), p. 145.

105. C. N. Le and J. J. Huang, "Interracial Dating and Marriage," http://www.asian-nation.org/interracial.shtml (retrieved January 10, 2010). See also Larry H. Shinagawa and Gin Yong Pang, "Asian American Panethnicity and Intermarriage," in *Asian Americans: Experiences and Perspectives,* ed. Timothy P. Fong and Larry H. Shinagawa (Upper Saddle River, NJ: Prentice-Hall, 2000), pp. 334–343.

106. O'Brien and Fugita, "Generational Differences," pp. 231–235; Tuan, *Forever Foreigners or Honorary Whites?*

107. Kitano and Daniels, *Asian Americans,* p. 80; Annie Nakao, "Homing in on Japan," *San Franciso Chronicle,* September 10, 2000, www.sfgate.com/cgi-bin/article.cgi?file=/examiner/archive/2000/09/10/NEWS12211.dtl (retrieved December 21, 2006).

108. Kitano and Daniels, *Asian Americans,* p. 81.

109. Ibid., pp. 191–192.

110. Petersen, *Japanese Americans,* pp. 214–221.

111. Greg Mayeda, "Japanese Americans Don't Lose Identity," *The New York Times,* December 28, 1995, p. A20; Nakao, "Homing in on Japan."

112. Edna Bonacich, "United States Capitalist Development: A Background to Asian Immigration," in *Labor Immigration under Capitalism,* ed. Lucie Cheng and Edna Bonacich (Berkeley: University of California Press, 1984), p. 82.

113. *U.S. v. Bhagat Singh Thind,* 261 U.S. 215 (1923).

114. Shinagawa and Pang, "Asian American Panethnicity and Intermarriage," in Fong and Shinagawa, *Asian Americans,* pp. 343–344.

115. Takaki, *Strangers from a Different Shore,* p. 474; Robert Blauner, *Racial Oppression in America* (New York:

Harper & Row, 1972), pp. 54–55; Paul Takagi, "The Myth of 'Assimilation in American Life,'" *Amerasia Journal* 2 (Fall 1973): 149–158; Peter Uhlenberg, "Demographic Correlates of Group Achievement: Contrasting Patterns of Mexican-Americans and Japanese-Americans," *Demography* 9 (February 1972): 119–128; B. Suzuki, "Education and the Socialization of Asian Americans," in *Asian Americans: Social and Psychological Perspectives*, ed. R. Endo, S. Sue, and N. Wagner (Palo Alto, CA: Science & Behavior Books, 1980), pp. 155–178; William Petersen, "Success Story, Japanese-American Style," *The New York Times*, January 9, 1966, p. 21.

116. Amado Cabezas and Gary Kawaguchi, "Empirical Evidence for Continuing Asian American Inequality: The Human Capital Model and Labor Market Segmentation," in *Reflections on Shattered Windows*, pp. 144–164; Wong, "Where Are the Asian CEOs?"; Fisher, "Piercing the 'Bamboo Ceiling'"; Amado Cabezas, "Testimony to U.S. Commission on Civil Rights," in *Civil Rights Issues of Asian and Pacific Americans* (Washington, DC: U.S. Government Printing Office, 1980), pp. 389–393.

117. Takagi, "The Myth of 'Assimilation in American Life,'" pp. 149–158; Ogawa, *From Jap to Japanese*, pp. 43ff.

118. "When You're Smiling: The Deadly Legacy of Internment," a documentary produced and directed by Janice D. Tanaka, Visual Communications, 1999; see also C. Browne and A. Broderick, "Asian and Pacific Island Elders: Issues for Social Work Practice and Education," *Social Work* 39, 1994 (3): 252–259.

119. The quotation is from Tuan, *Forever Foreigners or Honorary Whites?*, pp. 8, 162; see also Chou and Feagin, *The Myth of the Model Minority*, pp. 140–216.

120. Brad Knickerbocker, "U.S. Japanese Retain Cultural Ties," *The Christian Science Monitor* (July 27, 1993): 11; Miranda Ewell, "Japanese American Still Trying to Find a Way to Belong in U.S.: Asians Have Achieved Measurable Success but Continue to Face a Complex Racial and Ethnic Landscape," *Orange County (CA) Register*, August 19, 1996, p. A10; Chou and Feagin, *The Myth of the Model Minority*, pp. 16–220.

121. JACL, "Causes of Anti-Asian Sentiment," www.jacl.org/antihate/index.html (retrieved December 21, 2006).

122. David Mura, "Whites: How to Face the Angry Racial Tribes," *Utne Reader* (July/August 1992): 80. See also David Mura, *Turning Japanese: Memoirs of a Sansei* (New York: Atlantic Monthly Press, 1991).

123. See Charles Burress, "Looking to Hawaii for Harmony: Japanese American Panel Wants a Model for the New California," *San Francisco Chronicle*, October 21, 1997, p. A17.

Chapter 11

1. Elaine H. Kim, "They Armed in Self-Defense," *Newsweek*, May 18, 1992, p. 10.

2. Vickie Nam, "Introduction," in *YELL-Oh Girls*, ed. Vickie Nam (New York: Quill, 2001), pp. 111–116; Michael Kim, "Out and About: Coming of Age in a Straight White World," in *Asian American X: An Intersection of 21st Century Asian American Voices*, eds. Arar Han and John Hsu (Ann Arbor, MI: University of Michigan Press, 2004), p. 141.

3. U.S. Department of Homeland Security, "Yearbook of Immigration Statistics: 2009, Table 2: Persons Obtaining Legal Permanent Resident Status by Region and Selected Country of Last Residence: Fiscal Years 1820 to 2009," May 4, 2010, http://www.dhs.gov/files/statistics/publications/LPR09.shtm (retrieved May 18, 2010).

4. Ronald Takaki, *A Different Mirror* (Boston: Little, Brown, 1993), pp. 211–214; Roger Daniels, *Asian America: Chinese and Japanese in the United States Since 1850* (Seattle: University of Washington Press, 1988), pp. 16–17, 44; Bill Ong Hing, *Making and Remaking Asian America through Immigration Policy: 1850–1990* (Stanford, CA: Stanford University Press, 1993), p. 23, 48–49, 80.

5. U.S. Commission on Civil Rights, *Recent Activities against Citizens and Residents of Asian Descent* (Washington, DC: U.S. Government Printing Office, 1986), p. 7.

6. Immigration and Naturalization Service, *1985 Statistical Yearbook*, pp. 2–5; Ronald Takaki, *Strangers from a Different Shore: A History of Asian Americans* (Boston: Little, Brown, 1989), pp. 111–112.

7. U.S. Commission on Civil Rights, *Recent Activities Against Citizens and Residents of Asian Descent*, p. 8.

8. U.S. Commission on Civil Rights, *The Tarnished Golden Door: Civil Rights Issues in Immigration* (Washington, DC: U.S. Government Printing Office, 1980), p. 10.

9. Immigration and Naturalization Service, *1985 Statistical Yearbook*, pp. 2–5; U.S. Census Bureau, "Table DP-1: Profile of General Demographic Characteristics for the United States: 2000," www.census.gov (retrieved August 29, 2001); U.S. Census Bureau, http://factfinder.census.gov/basicfacts.html (retrieved August 29, 2001); U.S. Bureau of the Census, "American Fact Finder: Census 2000 Demographic Profile Highlights: Selected Population Group," http:// factfinder.census.gov/home/saff/main.html?lang=en (retrieved December 16, 2006); U.S. Bureau of the Census, "2008 American Community Survey, American Fact Finder: Selected Population Profile in the United States," http://factfinder.census.gov (retrieved January 14, 2010).

10. Stephan Thernstrom, ed., *Harvard Encyclopedia of American Ethnic Groups* (Cambridge, MA: Harvard University Press, 1981), pp. 357–359.

11. U.S. Commission on Civil Rights, *Recent Activities against Citizens and Residents of Asian Descent*, p. 9.

12. Vanessa Ho, "Filipinos' American Dream Comes True," *Seattle Times*, April 29, 1992, p. B1.

13. David Pierson, "Plight of Filipino Vets Studied," *The Los Angeles Times*, August 1, 2001, Part 2, p. 8; see also the website http://www.fasgi.org (retrieved January 14, 2010).

14. U.S. Census Bureau, "Table DP-1: Profile of General Demographic Characteristics for the United States: 2000"; U.S. Census Bureau, http://factfinder.census .gov/basicfacts.html; U.S. Bureau of the Census, "American Fact Finder: Census 2000 Demographic Profile Highlights: Selected Population Group"; U.S. Bureau of the Census, "2008 American Community Survey, American Fact Finder: Selected Population Profile in the United States."

15. Wayne Patterson, The *Korean Frontier in America: Immigration to Hawaii, 1896–1910* (Honolulu: University of Hawaii Press, 1988), p. 177; Takaki, *Strangers from a Different Shore*, pp. 270–271; U.S. Commission on Civil Rights, *Recent Activities against Citizens and Residents of Asian Descent*, p. 9.

16. Warren Y. Kim, *Koreans in America* (Seoul: Po Chin Chai Printing Co., 1971), pp. 22–25.

17. David M. Reimers, *Still the Golden Door: The Third World Comes to America* (New York: Columbia University Press, 1985), pp. 110–111; U.S. Department of Homeland Security, "Yearbook of Immigration Statistics: 2009, Table 2: Persons Obtaining Legal Permanent Resident Status by Region and Selected Country of Last Residence: Fiscal Years 1820 to 2009."

18. U.S. Bureau of the Census, "2008 American Community Survey, American Fact Finder: Selected Population Profile in the United States." See also U.S. Census Bureau, "Table DP-1: Profile of General Demographic Characteristics for the United States: 2000"; U.S. Census Bureau, http:// factfinder. census.gov/basicfacts.html; U.S. Bureau of the Census, "American Fact Finder: Census 2000 Demographic Profile Highlights: Selected Population Group."

19. Darrel Montero, *Vietnamese Americans: Patterns of Resettlement and Socioeconomic Adaptation in the United States* (Boulder, CO: Westview Press, 1979), pp. 1–3.

20. Morrison G. Wong and Charles Hirschman, "The New Asian Immigrants," in *Culture, Ethnicity, and Identity,* ed. William C. McCready (New York: Academic Press, 1983), p. 381.

21. U.S. Bureau of the Census, *1990 Census of Population: United States Summary,* CP-2-1 (Washington, DC: U.S. Government Printing Office, 1993), p. 4; U.S. Census Bureau, "Table DP-1: Profile of General Demographic Characteristics for the United States: 2000"; U.S. Census Bureau, http://factfinder.census.gov/basicfacts.html.

22. U.S. Bureau of the Census, "2008 American Community Survey, American Fact Finder: Selected Population Profile in the United States."

23. This paragraph draws on research of Arun Jain, as cited in Marcia Mogelonsky, "Asian-Indian Americans," *American Demographics,* August 1995, p. 36.

24. U.S. Bureau of the Census, "American Fact Finder: Census 2000 Demographic Profile Highlights: Selected Population Group"; U.S. Bureau of the Census, "2005 American Community Survey, American Fact Finder: Selected Population Profile in the United States."

25. Min Zhou and James V. Gatewood, "Introduction: Revisiting Contemporary Asian America," in *Contemporary Asian America: A Multidisciplinary Reader,* ed. Min Zhou and James V. Gatewood (New York: New York University Press, 2000), p. 35.

26. Ibid., p. 10.

27. Harry H. L. Kitano and Roger Daniels, *Asian Americans: Emerging Minorities* (Englewood Cliffs, NJ: Prentice-Hall, 1988), p. 176.

28. "Hate Crime Attack at UCSB," April 20, 2009, http:// www.angryasianman.com/2009/03/hate-crime-attack-at-ucsb.html (retrieved January 7, 2010); K. Connie Kang, "Building Bridges to Equality," *The Los Angeles Times,* January 7, 1995, p. A1.

29. "Prepared Testimony of Karen Narasaki, Executive Director, National Asian Pacific American Legal Consortium Before the House Judiciary Committee, Subcommittee on the Constitution," Subcommittee Hearing on H.R. 1909: The Civil Rights Act of 1997, Federal News Service, June 26, 1997; Nazli Kibria, "College and Notions of 'Asian Americans,'" in *The Second Generation: Ethnic Identity among Asian Americans,* ed. Pyong Gap Min (Lanham, MD: Rowman & Littlefield, 2002), p. 204; Leland T. Saito, "The Politics of Adaptation and the 'Good Immigrant': Japanese Americans and the New Chinese Immigrants," in *Asian and Latino Immigrants in a Restructuring Economy: The Metamorphosis of Southern California,* eds. Marta Lopez-Garza and David R. Diaz (Palo Alto, CA: Stanford University Press, 2001), pp. 332–349.

30. Committee of 100, *Still The "Other?" Public Attitudes toward Chinese and Asian Americans* (New York: Committee of 100, 2009), pp. 14–21.

31. Claire Jean Kim, "The Racial Triangulation of Asian Americans," *Politics and Society* 27 (March 1999): 105–138.

32. *Plessy* v. *Ferguson* 163 U.S. 537, 561 (1896).

33. Quoted in Takaki, *Strangers from a Different Shore*, p. 370.

34. Miriam Sharma, "Labor Migration and Class Formation among the Filipinos in Hawaii, 1940–1946," in *Labor Immigration Under Capitalism,* ed. Lucie Cheng and Edna Bonacich (Berkeley: University of California Press, 1984), pp. 583, 593.

35. Montero, *Vietnamese Americans*, pp. 3–4.

36. Paul Sweeney, "Tolerance in a Texas Town," *Texas Observer,* September 17, 1982, pp. 7–9; K. Connie Kang, "U.S. Asians Seen as 'Alien,' Study Finds," *The Los Angeles Times,* March 2, 2000, p. A3; Steve Emmons and David Reyes, "Gangs, Crime Top Fears of Vietnamese in Orange County," *The Los Angeles Times,* February 5, 1989, p. 3; Anti-Defamation League, "American Attitudes towards Chinese Americans and Asian Americans," Press Release, April 25, 2001, www .adl.org/misc/american_attitudes_towards_chinese .asp (retrieved December 20, 2006).

37. Anti-Defamation League, "American Attitudes towards Chinese Americans and Asian Americans"; Committee

of 100, *Still The "Other?" Public Attitudes toward Chinese and Asian Americans*, pp. 14–21.

38. As quoted in C. N. Le, "Sex and the Asian Man," *Asian-Nation,* www.asian-nation.org/asian-man.shtml (retrieved December 28, 2006). The text was originally written by David Pierson for the *Los Angeles Times*. See also Rosalind Chou, "Asian American Sexual Politics: The Construction of Race, Gender, and Sexuality," Ph.D. dissertation, Texas A&M University, Spring 2010.

39. C. N. Le, "Cosmetic and Plastic Surgery," *Asian-Nation,* www.asian-nation.org/cosmetic-surgery.shtml (retrieved December 21, 2006); the quotation is in Olivia Chung, "Finding My Eye-Identity," in *YELL-Oh Girls*, p. 139. On white male sexism, see Meggy Wang, "For Those Who Love Yellow Girls," in *YELL-Oh Girls*, pp. 129–132.

40. C. N. Le, "Martial Arts Movies Kick @#!" *Asian-Nation,* www.asian-nation.org/martial-arts.shtml (retrieved December 28, 2006).

41. Sonni Efron, "'Saigon' Is Under Fire Once More," *The Los Angeles Times*, September 7, 1990, p. F1; Holly Hee Won Coughlin, "My Breakup with Miss Saigon," Minnesota Women's Press, July 7, 1999, www.modelminority.com (retrieved December 31, 2006); "Paramount Pictures & Asian Americans: Tarnished Legacy," http://www.racebending.com/v3/featured/paramount-pictures-and-asian-americans-a tarnished-legacy (retrieved January 3, 2010).

42. Doris Lin, "The Death of (http://Icebox.com's) Mr. Wong," USAsians.net, http://us_asians.tripod.com/articlesmrwong.html (retrieved December 14, 2006).

43. Jennifer Fang, "Team America: Racism, Idiocy, and Two Men's Pursuit to Piss Off as Many People as Possible," *Asian Media Watch,* October 28, 2004, www.asianmediawatch.net/teamamerica/review.html (retrieved December 17, 2006).

44. Helen Zia, *Asian American Dreams: The Emergence of an American People* (New York: Farrar, Straus, 2000), p. 199; "OCA Criticizes Bo Dietl for Offensive Behavior," Press Release, November 16, 2009, http://www.ocanational.org/index.php?option=com_content&task=view&id=586&Itemid=94n (retrieved January 3, 2010). The eye-pulling gestures are reported in press releases by the Japanese American Citizens League at http://www.jacl.org/public_policy/response.htm (retrieved January 4, 2010).

45. Zia, *Asian American Dreams*, p. 109; *YELL-Oh Girls*, pp. 111–200; *Asian American X*, passim.

46. Center for Integration and Improvement of Journalism, *News Watch: A Critical Look at Coverage of People of Color* (San Francisco: San Francisco State University, 1994), pp. 40–43; Ling-chi Wang, "Foreign Money Is No Friend of Ours," in *Asian Americans: Experiences and Perspectives,* ed. Timothy P. Fong and Larry H. Shinagawa (Upper Saddle River, NJ: Prentice-Hall, 2000), p. 402; Steven Rosenfeld and Liane Hansen, "Asian Americans," *NPR Weekend Sunday,* November 23, 1997; Andrea Stone and Robert Silvers, "Asian Americans See Rising Racism," *USA Today,* July 15, 1997, p. 8A; "Daphne Kwok, Organization of Chinese Americans, and John O'Sullivan, National Review, Discuss Recent Cover Story for That Magazine That Asian Americans Are Saying Is Offensive and Racist," NBC News Transcripts, March 21, 1997; Mae M. Cheng, "Magazine Cover Ripped; Coalition Calls National Review Illustration Racist," *Newsday,* April 11, 1997, p. A4; "Clinton Campaign Shuns Chinese American Media," http://www.asian-nation.org/headlines/2007/03/clinton-campaign-shuns-chinese-american-media (retrieved January 13, 2010).

47. Sharmila Rudrappa, "Disciplining Desire in Making the Home: Engendering Ethnicity in Indian Immigrant Families," in *The Second Generation*, p. 85.

48. U.S. Commission on Civil Rights, *Civil Rights Issues Facing Asian Americans in the 1990s* (Washington, DC: U.S. Government Printing Office, 1992), pp. 5–6; Jocelyn Y. Stewart, "Lest Hate Victim Be Forgotten," *The Los Angeles Times,* January 25, 2001, p. A1.

49. Lena H. Sun, "Anti-Asian American Incidents Rising, Civil Rights Group Says; Organization Executives to Meet with Reno Today," *Washington Post,* September 9, 1997, p. A2; "Prepared Testimony of Karen Narasaki," Federal News Service, June 26, 1997. For the 2008 incidents, we draw on Press Release, Japanese American Citizens League, November 2008, http://www.jacl.org/public_policy/response.htm (retrieved January 4, 2010); Howard Pankratz, "Asian Assault Victim in Boulder," *Denver Post,* October 31, 2008, http://www.asianam.org/hate.htm (retrieved January 2, 2010).

50. U.S. Commission on Civil Rights, *Civil Rights Issues Facing Asian Americans in the 1990s*, pp. 22–48; "Hate Crimes Rise in Orange County," *The Race Relations Reporter* (May 15, 1999): 1; Orange County Human Relations Commission, "Hate Crimes and Incidents in Orange County," http://64.233.161.104/search?q=cache:2B69Ym6YOgAJ:www.ochumanrelations.org/pdf/Hate_Crime_report.pdf+%22orange+county%22+reported+%22hate+crimes%22+2005&hl=en&gl=us&ct=clnk&cd=3 (retrieved January 1, 2007).

51. David Reyes, "Coalition Urges More Prosecutions of Hate Crimes," *The Los Angeles Times,* September 9, 1994, p. B1; Mara Rose Williams, "Asian Americans Say Police Are Biased," *Atlanta Journal and Constitution,* September 9, 1994, p. C5; Maryland Advisory Committee, U.S. Commission on Civil Rights, "City Services and the Justice System: Do Korean American Storeowners in Baltimore, Maryland Get Equal Treatment?" July 2004, http://64.233.161.104/ search?q=cache:3QEAKAn9wJ: www.usccr.gov/pubs/sac/md0704.pdf+%22adequate+police+protection%22+%22asian+americans%22&hl=en&gl=us&ct=clnk&cd=1 (retrieved January 1, 2007).

52. U.S. Commission on Civil Rights, *Civil Rights Issues Facing Asian Americans in the 1990s*, pp. 49–69.

53. Mimi Ko, "Forum to Examine Police Harassment," *The Los Angeles Times*, June 11, 1994, p. B2; see also Utah Task Force on Racial and Ethnic Fairness in the Legal System, "Perceptions of Racial and Ethnic Fairness in the Criminal Justice System: Listening to Utahns," Client Committee Report on Public Hearings, 1999, http://64.233.161.104/search? q=cache:2i_I1Gbt5K0J: www.utcourts.gov/specproj/retaskforce/clrpt24.pdf+ photographing+youths+%22gang%22+%22racial+ profiling%22+%22asian+american%22&hl=en&gl=us& ct=clnk&cd=4 (retrieved January 1, 2007).

54. U.S. Commission on Civil Rights, *Civil Rights Issues Facing Asian Americans in the 1990s*, pp. 5–6; U.S. Commission on Civil Rights, *Recent Activities Against Citizens and Residents of Asian Descent*, pp. 3–6; Ann Bancroft, "Jury Gets Racist Firebombings Case in Sacramento," *San Francisco Chronicle*, August 25, 1994, p. A20.

55. U.S. Commission on Civil Rights, *Recent Activities against Citizens and Residents of Asian Descent*, pp. 43–44; U.S. Commission on Civil Rights, *Civil Rights Issues Facing Asian Americans in the 1990s*, pp. 25–26; quotation from p. 28.

56. U.S. Commission on Civil Rights, *Civil Rights Issues Facing Asian Americans in the 1990s*, pp. 25–26.

57. Ibid., pp. 26–28.

58. "Hate Crime in Queens," *AsianWeek*, August 25, 2006, http://news.asianweek.com (retrieved December 18, 2006); "OCA-NY Commends NYPD for Arrest of Hate Crime Assailants; Urges District Attorneys Office to Vigorously Prosecute to the Fullest Extent of the Law," Asianam.org, July 6, 2007, http://www.asianam.org/ hate.htm (retrieved January 13, 2010); Kirsten Fleming, Philip Messing, and Andy Geller, "Two Teens Targeting Asians Arraigned for Murder," *New York Post*, June 10, 2009, http://www.asianam.org/hate.htm (retrieved January 2, 2010).

59. Julie Chao, "Berkeley Students Claim Bias in D.C.; Asian Americans Offended by Guards," *San Francisco Examiner*, September 30, 1997, p. A1.

60. Harry H. L. Kitano and Roger Daniels, *Asian Americans: Emerging Minorities*, 3rd ed. (Englewood Cliffs, NJ: Prentice-Hall, 2001), pp. 54–55. For an up-to-date summary, see "Wen Ho Lee," http://en.wikipedia.org/wiki/ Wen_Ho_Lee (retrieved January 18, 2010).

61. Committee of 100, *Still The "Other?" Public Attitudes toward Chinese and Asian Americans*, pp. 14–21.

62. Howard A. DeWitt, *Anti-Filipino Movements in California: A History, Bibliography and Study Guide* (San Francisco: R & E Research Associates, 1976), pp. 27–66.

63. Ibid.; David Ibata, "Asians Seek Spot in America's Melting Pot," *Chicago Tribune*, April 26, 1992, p. 1.

64. Stewart, "Lest Hate Victim Be Forgotten," p. A1; "Death Climbs to 8 in Postal Rampage," Asianweek.com, February 9, 2006, www.asianam.org/hate.htm (retrieved January 2, 2007); Caroline Aoyagi-Stom, "AA Community Rallies Around 17-Year-Old Teen Beaten on New York MTA Bus," April 6, 2007, http://www.asianam. org/hate.htm (retrieved January 13, 2010).

65. Gus Mercado, "Lessons Learned from the Texas 10 Trials," National Federation of Filipino American Associations, www.naffaa.org/2005naffaa/files/texas10lessons. pdf (retrieved January 3, 2007).

66. Andrea Ford, "Slain Girl Was Not Stealing Juice, Police Say," *The Los Angeles Times*, March 19, 1991, p. B1; Itabari Njeri, "Perspectives on Race Relations," *The Los Angeles Times*, November 29, 1991, p. B5; Mike Davis, "In L.A., Burning All Illusions," *Nation* 254, no. 21 (June 1, 1992): 743–746, quotation on p. 745.

67. Kim, "They Armed in Self-Defense," p. 10.

68. Hsia-Chuan Hsia, "Imported Racism and Indigenous Biases: The Impacts of the U.S. Media on Taiwanese Images of African Americans," research paper presented at the Annual Meeting of the American Sociological Association, Los Angeles, August 5–9, 1994; Joe R. Feagin, *Racist America: Roots, Current Realities, and Future Reparations*, 2nd ed. (New York: Routledge, 2010), pp. 252–255.

69. Claire Jean Kim, *Bitter Fruit: The Politics of Black–Korean Conflict in New York City* (New Haven, CT: Yale University Press, 2000), p. 11.

70. Moon H. Jo, "Korean Merchants in the Black Community: Prejudice among the Victims of Prejudice," *Ethnic and Racial Studies* 15 (1992): 395–411; Robert L. Bach, *Changing Relations: Newcomers and Established Residents in U.S. Communities* (New York: Ford Foundation, 1993).

71. Nancy Abelmann and John Lie, *Blue Dreams: Korean Americans and the Los Angeles Riots* (Cambridge, MA: Harvard University Press, 1995), pp. 140–141.

72. Njeri, "Perspectives on Race Relations," p. B5.

73. Ku-Sup Chin, "New Immigrants, Industrial Flexibility, and Ethnic Conflicts: Korean and Hispanic Immigrants in the Los Angeles Garment Industry," paper presented at the Annual Meeting of the American Sociological Association, Los Angeles, August 5–9, 1994.

74. Press Release, Japanese American Citizens League, June 2008, http://www.jacl.org/public_policy/response.htm (retrieved January 4, 2010).

75. U.S. Commission on Civil Rights, *Recent Activities against Citizens and Residents of Asian Descent*, pp. 50–52; Sweeney, "Tolerance in a Texas Town," pp. 7–10.

76. Michael McCabe, "U.S. Leaders Urged to Fight Hate Crimes," *San Francisco Chronicle*, February 29, 1992, p. A1; Zia, *Asian American Dreams*, p. 91.

77. Eric K. Yamamoto, "Healing Our Own," Boston College, www.bc.edu/bc_org/avp/law/lwsch/journals/bctwj/ 20_1/08_TXT.htm (retrieved January 2, 2007).

78. "Hate Crime Attack at UCSB," April 20, 2009, http:// www.angryasianman.com/2009/03/hate-crime-attack-at-ucsb.html (retrieved January 7, 2010); Press Release, JACL Network Update, Fall 2009, p. 3; Press Releases, JACL, http://www.jacl.org/public_policy/response .htm (retrieved January 4, 2010).

79. Jonathan Schuppe and Aditi Kinkhabwala, "Education a Family Affair; Asian Indians Work Hard for Success in Classroom," *Asbury Park Press* (Neptune, NJ), August 17, 1997, p. 27A; "Documented Incidents of Xenophobia and Intolerance in Political Discourse," South Asian Leaders of Tomorrow (SAALT), press release, August 30, 2006.

80. Zia, *Asian American Dreams,* pp. 219–221; Press Release, Japanese American Citizens League, February 2008, http://www.jacl.org/public_policy/response.htm (retrieved January 4, 2010); Press Release, Japanese American Citizens League, June 2008, http://www.jacl.org/public_policy/response.htm (retrieved January 4, 2010).

81. Asian American Legal Defense and Education Fund, "Public Statement from Concerned Organizations Regarding the Recent Incidents in Edison, NJ Involving the South Asian Community," www.aaldef.org/article.php?article_id=144 (retrieved December 13, 2006).

82. "Asian Americans Called the New 'Sleeping Giant' of California Politics," AsianConnections.com, September 7, 2006, http://asianconnections.com (retrieved December 18, 2006); Adia Harvey Wingfield and Joe R. Feagin, *Yes We Can? White Racial Framing and the 2008 Presidential Election* (New York: Routledge, 2010), pp. 174–176; U.S. House of Representatives, "Daily Press Gallery: Demographics," www.house.gov/daily/hpg.htm (retrieved January 19, 2010).

83. K. Connie Kang, "Group Seeks to Boost Profile of Asian American Voters," *The Los Angeles Times,* August 22, 2000, p. B1; "The Immigrant Vote in New York City Is Topic of Panel Discussion," *Barnard Campus News,* May 2, 2001, p. 1; Center for Voting and Democracy, "Asians in State Legislatures and Voting Age Population," http://archive.fairvote.org/vra/asianleg.htm (retrieved January 19, 2010).

84. Paul Ong and Don Nakanishi, "Becoming Citizens, Becoming Voters," in *Asian Americans,* ed. Fong and Shinagawa, pp. 380–383; "The Immigrant Vote in New York City Is Topic of Panel Discussion," *Barnard Campus News,* May 2, 2001; U.S. Commission on Civil Rights, *Civil Rights Issues Facing Asian Americans in the 1990s,* pp. 157–163; Asian American Legal Defense and Education Fund, "The Asian American Vote 2004: A Report on the Multilingual Exit Poll in the 2004 Presidential Election," *Outlook* (Fall 2006), www.aaldef.org/article.php?article_id=67 (retrieved December 13, 2006); "New Report: Asian American Voters Face Discrimination, Improper Voter ID Checks in 2006 Elections,"https://www.aaldef.org/article.php?article_id=354 (retrieved January 12, 2010).

85. Daniels, *Asian America,* p. 113; Zhou and Gatewood, "Introduction: Revisiting Contemporary Asian America," p. 27; Jane Junn and Natalie Masuoka, "Asian American Identity: Shared Racial Status and Political Context," *Perspectives on Politics* 6 (December 2008): 729–736.

86. Yen Le Espiritu, *Asian American Panethnicity* (Philadelphia: Temple University Press, 1992), pp. 19–49; see also Edward W. Said, *Orientalism* (New York: Vintage Books, 1979).

87. Lisa Lowe, "Heterogeneity, Hybridity, Multiplicity: Marking Asian American Differences," *Diaspora* 1 (1991): 31; Espiritu, *Asian American Panethnicity,* pp. 47–49.

88. Espiritu, *Asian American Panethnicity,* pp. 50–51; Paul Sweeney, "Asian Americans Gain Clout," *American Demographics* 8 (February 1986): 18–19; Kang, "Building Bridges to Equality." See also articles on the website http://www.apalc.org (retrieved January 19, 2010).

89. Frank Wu, "Asian Americans Finally Organize the NCAPA," New America News Service, November 27, 1997; "Civil Rights," http://ncapaonline.org/index.php?option=com_content&view=article&id=56&Itemid=64 (retrieved January 19, 2010).

90. For examples in the 1990s, see Carla Rivera, "Orange County Focus," *The Los Angeles Times,* April 28, 1992, p. B3.

91. Peter Kwong, *Chinatown, N.Y.: Labor and Politics, 1930–1950* (New York: Monthly Review Press, 1979), pp. 45–67; Judy Yung, "The Social Awakening of Chinese American Women," in *Unequal Sisters,* ed. Ellen Carol DuBois and Vicki L. Ruiz (New York: Routledge, 1990), p. 196.

92. Martin F. Nolan, "California Confronts the Politics of Growth," *Boston Globe,* October 23, 1991, p. 1.

93. Kitano and Daniels, *Asian Americans,* p. 49; K. Connie Kang, "Activist for a New Era of Civil Rights; Berkeley Professor Has Fought Many Battles for the Asian American Community in the Past Three Decades," *The Los Angeles Times,* July 6, 2001, part 2, p. 1.

94. Ronda Kaysen, "Waving Stars and Stripes, Chinatown Rallies against Immigration Bill," http://www.downtownexpress.com/de_153/wavingstarsandstripes.html, April 14–20, 2006 (retrieved January 25, 2010); Timothy Fong, *The First Suburban Chinatown: The Remarking of Monterey Park, California* (Philadelphia: Temple University Press, 1994), passim; Bert Eljera, "The Chinese Beverly Hills," http://asianweek.com/052496/LittleTaipei.html (retrieved January 25, 2010). On earlier issues, see Nicholas Lemann, "Growing Pains," *Atlantic Monthly* (January 1988): 57–62.

95. The demonstrations and Cafferty quotation are reported in David Pierson, "Protesters Gather at CNN: A China Commentary Draws an Angry Crowd to the L.A. Offices," *Los Angeles Times,* April 20, 2008, http://articles.latimes.com/2008/apr/20/local/me-cnn20 (retrieved January 19, 2010).

96. Pei-te Lien, M. Margaret Conway, and Janelle Wong, *The Politics of Asian Americans: Diversity and Community* (New York: Routledge, 2004), p. vii.

97. Committee of 100, *Still The "Other?" Public Attitudes toward Chinese and Asian Americans,* pp. 14–21; Frank Wu, "What Do Chinese Americans Think of China?" New America News Service, October 30, 1997; see

"Issues," Committee of 100, www.committee100.org/aboutus/aboutus_issues.htm (retrieved January 3, 2007); K. Connie Kang, "The 2008 Summer Games; Chinese Americans Feel Joy, Concern at Choice," *The Los Angeles Times,* July 14, 2001, p. A10.

98. John Gregory Dunne, *Delano: The Story of the California Grape Strike* (New York: Farrar, Straus & Giroux, 1967), p. 77; Lemuel F. Ignacio, *Asian Americans and Pacific Islanders* (San Jose, CA: Pilipino Development Associates, 1976), pp. 11–56; Kitano and Daniels, *Asian Americans,* p. 86.

99. "What is NAFFAA," http://www.naffaa.org/main/?p=3 (retrieved January 21, 2010); Michelle Mizal, "Filipino Americans Hope to Build Unity; Group Also Hopes to Build Political Clout at D.C. Event," *Virginian-Pilot* (Norfolk, VA), August 21, 1997, p. B1; Tony Perry and Richard Simon, "Now the Stimulus Bill Has Authorized $198 Million in Payments," *Los Angeles Times,* February 18, 2009, http://articles.latimes.com/2009/feb/18/local/mefilipino-veterans18 (retrieved January 21, 2010).

100. Kitano and Daniels, *Asian Americans,* 3rd ed., p. 117.

101. "D.C. Groups Congratulate David Wu and Stress the Importance of the APA Vote," Asian Pacific American Institute for Congressional Studies, press release, November 9, 1998; Gus Mercado, "Obama wins Filipino Vote at Last-Hour," *Philippine Daily Inquirer,* November 10, 2008, http:// globalnation.inquirer.net/mindfeeds/mindfeeds/view/20081110-171290/Obama-wins-Filipino-vote-at-last-hour (retrieved January 21, 2010).

102. James T. Madore, "Long-Quiet Asian Group Starts to Mobilize," *The Christian Science Monitor,* May 20, 1988, p. 7; "Filipino Americans Protest S.F. Memorial," United Press International, March 31, 1997; Mary Owen, "Protest at H&M Backs Claim of Harassment," October 7, 2007, http://archives.chicagotribune.com/2007/oct/07/business/chi-h&mstory_07oct07 (retrieved January 21, 2010).

103. Bong-youn Choy, *Koreans in America* (Chicago: Nelson-Hall, 1979), pp. 141–189; "About Us," *Korean American Coalition* (Los Angeles), http://www. kacla .org/?p=363 & language = enslaved (retrieved January 21, 2010).

104. Quoted in Greg La Motte, "Asian Americans: A Diverse Voting Block," Cable News Network, June 1, 1992, transcript no. 76-5.

105. Julie Ha, "Korean American Political Power," New America News Service, March 18, 1997; "Survey Report," http://www.naasurvey.com (retrieved January 21, 2010).

106. Zia, *Asian American Dreams,* p. 184; Wendy Koch, "Asians Are Becoming More Vocal in the Debate," *USA Today,* May 2, 2006, p. 7A.

107. "Korean Americans Send 100,000 Dollars in Aid to North Korea," Agence France Presse, April 3, 1997; Barbara Slavin, "Korean-Americans Want Families on Agenda," *USA Today,* May 9, 2001, p. 13A; "Korean Americans Fear Ramifications of Nuclear Test," The Online News Hour, October 31, 2006, http://64.233.161.104/search?q=cache: RURtiM2z30gJ: www.pbs.org/newshour/bb/politics/julydec06/koreanams_1031.html+%22korean+ americans%22+2006+family+%22north+korea%22+government+pol icy & hl = en & gl = us & ct = clnk & cd =1 (retrieved January 3, 2007).

108. Steve Emmons and David Reyes, "The Orange County Poll," *The Los Angeles Times,* February 5, 1989, p. 1; "Vietnamese Americans," Wikipedia, http://en.wikipedia.org/wiki/Vietnamese_American (retrieved January 21, 2010); Jane Junn, Taeku Lee, S. Karthick Ramakrishnan, and Janelle Wong, "National Asian American Survey: Asian Americans and the 2008 Election," http://www.naasurvey.com/assets/NAAS-National-report.pdf (retrieved January 21, 2010).

109. "Vietnamese Americans," Wikipedia (2010); and "Vietnamese Americans," Wikipedia, http://en.wikipedia.org/wiki/Vietnamese_American (retrieved January 3, 2007).

110. Quyen Do, "Little Saigon Readies for Community Balloting; Vietnamese Americans Will Elect Their Unofficial Leaders," *Orange County (CA) Register,* January 13, 1996, p. B1; Bert Eljera, "Big Plans for Little Saigon," www .asianweek.com/051796/LittleSaigon.html (retrieved August 15, 2001); Leland Saito, personal communication, April 18, 2001; My-Thuan Tran, "Vietnamese Americans Join Panels in Final Tally: Truong Diep and Andrew Do Win Westminster and Garden Grove City Council Seats," *Los Angeles Times,* December 2, 2008, http://articles.latimes.com/2008/dec/02/local/me-ocvote2 (retrieved January 21, 2010).

111. Carolyn Leung, "Redefining Advocacy for the Southeast Asian American Community," *Journal of Asian American Studies* 3 (2000): 237–241; "History and Mission," http://www.searac.org/mission.html (retrieved January 21, 2010); Leslie Eaton, "A New Landfill in New Orleans Sets Off a Battle May 8," 2006, http://www.nytimes.com/2006/ 05/08/us/08landfill. html?_r=1 (retrieved January 21, 2010); S. Leo Chiang, "New Orleans: A Village Called Versailles," August 28, 2008, http://www.pbs.org/frontlineworld/rough/2008/08/a_village_calle.html (retrieved January 21, 2010).

112. Kotkin, "Asian Indians in California Spotlight After Years in Shadows," p. H2; Newman, "Festival Reflects Indians' Growth," sec. 12NJ, p. 1; Vindu P. Goel, "The Rise of Asian Indians," *(Cleveland) Plain Dealer,* July 28, 1996, p. 8.

113. Zia, *Asian American Dreams,* pp. 198–202; Tianlong Yu, "Challenging the Politics of the 'Model Minority' Stereotype," *Equity & Excellence in Education* 39 (2006): 328; "The Continuing Impact of September 11th and the South Asian Community," South Asian American Leaders of Tomorrow, http://64.233.161.104/ search?q=cache:p_e8QXcjwUEJ:www.saalt.org/pdfs/Philly Impact9-11.pdf+%22south+asian+coalition%22+indian+-india+villages+servitude&hl=en&gl=us&ct=clnk&cd=2 (retrieved January 3, 2007).

114. "About USINPAC," http://www.usinpac.com/mission_objective.asp (retrieved January 21, 2010).

115. U.S. Commission on Civil Rights, *Civil Rights Issues Facing Asian Americans in the 1990s*, pp. 131–136, 145–148; LEAP, *APA Representation on Fortune 100 Boards* (Los Angeles: Leadership Education for Asian-Pacifics, 2009), pp. 1-6; Gerrye Wong, "Where are the Asian CEOs?" *AsianWeek*, http://www.asianweek.com/2009/05/01/where-are-the-asian-ceos (retrieved January 10, 2010); E. J. Park, "Asian Americans in Silicon Valley: Race and Ethnicity in the Postindustrial Economy," unpublished doctoral dissertation, University of California, Berkeley, Department of Ethnic Studies, 1992; Cliff Cheng, "Are Asian American Employees a Model Minority or Just a Minority?" *Journal of Applied Behavioral Science* 33, no. 3 (September 1997): 277–290.

116. Asian American Institute, *Asian Pacific Americans and Public Contracting: Equal Opportunity Laws and Policies* (Chicago Asian American Institute, 2008).

117. U.S. Commission on Civil Rights, *Civil Rights Issues Facing Asian Americans in the 1990s*, pp. 131–136, 153–156; Johanna Shih, "Circumventing Discrimination: Gender and Ethnic Strategies in Silicon Valley," *Gender & Society* 20 (April 2006): 177–206; National Asian Pacific American Women's Forum, Press Release, www.napawf.org/file/issues/issues-wage_gap.pdf (retrieved January 4, 2007). See also Rosalind Chou and Joe R. Feagin, *The Myth of the Model Minority* (Boulder, CO: Paradigm Books, 2009), passim.

118. "Got the Look? Abercrombie & Fitch's Hiring Policy: Hot or Not?" *Current Events* 103 (2003): 3; U.S. Commission on Civil Rights, *Civil Rights Issues Facing Asian Americans in the 1990s*, pp. 136–148; Mike Walker, "LPGA's English-Only Policy is Unsportsmanlike and Un-American," http://www.golf.com/golf/tours_news/article/0,28136,1836266,00.html (retrieved January 21, 2010).

119. *Harvard Encyclopedia of American Ethnic Groups*, ed. Thernstrom, pp. 218–220; Takaki, *Strangers from a Different Shore*, pp. 374–375.

120. Reimers, *Still the Golden Door*, p. 107. See also Chou and Feagin, *The Myth of the Model Minority*.

121. Zhou and Gatewood, "Introduction: Revisiting Contemporary Asian America," in *Contemporary Asian America: A Multidisciplinary Reader*, ed. Zhou and Gatewood, p. 10.

122. Bettina Boxall, "Asian Indians Remake Silicon Valley; Immigrants: As Their Numbers Surge, High-Tech Skills Ease the Transition for Many," *The Los Angeles Times*, July 6, 2001 p. A1; "Demand for Asian Exec a Sign of the Times," Nwasianweekly.com, July 30, 2005, www.nwasianweekly.com/20052431/editorial20052431.htm (retrieved December 20, 2006).

123. U.S. Bureau of the Census, "2008 American Community Survey, American Fact Finder: Selected Population Profile (Chinese Alone)," http://factfinder.census.gov (retrieved January 22, 2010).

124. Roger Daniels, *Coming to America* (New York: Harper-Collins, 1990), p. 355; C. N. Le, "Writers, Artists and Entertainers," *Asian-Nation*, www.asian-nation.org/artists.shtml (retrieved December 28, 2006).

125. U.S. Bureau of the Census, "2008 American Community Survey, American Fact Finder: Select Population Profile (Chinese Alone)."

126. Mylinh Uy, "Tax and Race: The Impact on Asian Americans," *Asian Law Journal* 11 (May 2004): 129–138.

127. Jan Lin, *Reconstructing Chinatown: Ethnic Enclave, Global Change* (Minneapolis: University of Minnesota Press, 1998), p. ix.

128. Committee of 100, *Still The "Other?" Public Attitudes toward Chinese and Asian Americans*, pp. 14–21.

129. Leland Saito, *Race and Politics: Asian Americans, Latinos, and Whites in a Los Angeles Suburb* (Urbana: University of Illinois Press, 1998), pp. 39–54; Leland Saito, *The Politics of Exclusion: The Failure of Race-Neutral Policies in Urban America* (Palo Alto, CA: Stanford University Press, 2009).

130. Takaki, *Strangers from a Different Shore*, pp. 322–323; Steve Lohr, "Filipinos Flocking to the U.S. as Manila's Troubles Grow," *The New York Times*, June 6, 1985, p. A14.

131. U.S. Bureau of the Census, "American Fact Finder, Selected Population Profile in the United States (Filipino Alone)," http://factfinder.census.gov (retrieved January 22, 2010).

132. United Press International, press release, March 30, 1988; Irene Chang, "Ruling on Foreign Language Ban Criticized," *The Los Angeles Times*, October 26, 1991, p. B3; Kari Gibson, "English Only Court Cases Involving the U.S. Workplace: The Myths of Language Use and the Homogenization of Bilingual Workers' Identities," *Second Language Studies* 22 (Spring 2004): 1–6; Andrew J. Robinson, "Language, National Origin, and Employment Discrimination: The Importance of the EEOC Guidelines," *University of Pennsylvania Law Review* 157 (2009): 1522–1524.

133. Gilbert C. Gee, Michael S. Spencer, Juan Chen, and David Takeuchi, "A Nationwide Study of Discrimination and Chronic Health Conditions Among Asian Americans," *American Journal of Public Health* 97 (July 2007): 1–6; Arnold B. de Castro, Gilbert C. Gee, and David T. Takeuchi, "Workplace Discrimination and Health Among Filipinos in the United States," *American Journal of Public Health* 98 (March 2008): 520–526.

134. Choy, *Koreans in America*, pp. 123–133; U.S. Bureau of the Census, *1990 Census of Population: Social and Economic Characteristics: United States Summary*, pp. 47, 113; U.S. Bureau of the Census, *1990 Census of the Population: Social and Economic Characteristics: Urbanized Areas*, CP-2-1C (Washington, DC, 1993), p. 4759; Takaki, *Strangers from a Different Shore*, pp. 441–444; Reimers, *Still the Golden Door*, pp. 111–112; Ivan Light, "Immigrant Entrepreneurs in America: Koreans in Los Angeles," in *Clamor at the Gates*, ed. Nathan Glazer (San

Francisco: ICS Press, 1985), p. 162; John Lunn and Todd Steen, "The Heterogeneity of Self-Employment: The Example of Asians in the United States," *Small Business Economics* 24 (March 2005): 143–158.

135. "Korean Americans Adjust to Life in Korea," *New America News Service,* February 3, 1997.

136. Pyong Gap Min, *Changes and Conflicts: Korean Immigrant Families in New York* (Boston: Allyn & Bacon, 1998), p. 120.

137. Pyong Gap Min and Mehdi Bozorgmehr, "Immigrant Entrepreneurship and Business Patterns: A Comparison of Koreans and Iranians in Los Angeles," *International Migration Review* 34 (Fall 2000): 707–738; Emily MacFarquhar, "Fighting over the Dream," *U.S. News & World Report,* May 18, 1991, p. 34; Ivan Light and Edna Bonacich, *Immigrant Entrepreneurs* (Berkeley: University of California Press, 1988); Keeley Webster, "Brokers, Investors Banking on Koreatown's Growing Attraction," California Real Estate Journal, June 12, 2006, http://209.85.165.104/search?q=cache: FVGTS8TQWqUJ:themercuryla.com/the-extras/banking-on-koreatown.php+ %22moving+back+to+koreatown%22+ %22los+angeles%22&hl=en&gl=us&ct=clnk&cd=1 (retrieved January 5, 2007); Lunn and Todd Steen, "The Heterogeneity of Self-Employment: The Example of Asians in the United States," pp. 145–156.

138. U.S. Bureau of the Census, "2008 American Community Survey, American Fact Finder: Selected Population Profile (Korean Alone)," http://factfinder.census.gov (retrieved January 22, 2010); Asian American Legal Defense and Education Fund, "AALDEF Releases Groundbreaking Report on Low-Wage Korean Workers," *Outlook* (Fall 2006), www.aaldef.org/article.php?article_id=206 (retrieved December 13, 2006); Aruna Lee, "Korean Americans: Crackdown Could Hurt Linked Communities," New America Media, March 30, 2006, http://news.newamerica media.org/news/view_article.html?article_id=c43694580a1dbba141a6e50e37d93577.

139. Montero, *Vietnamese Americans,* p. 39.

140. "Prepared Testimony of Karen Narasaki," Federal News Service, June 26, 1997; Linh Ngo, "The Lawsuit," in *YELL-Oh Girls,* pp. 150–153.

141. Linus Yamane, "The Labor Market Status of Foreign Born Vietnamese Americans," Claremont Colleges, Working Papers in Economics, 2001; Gilbert C. Gee, Michael S. Spencer, Juan Chen, and David Takeuchi, "A Nationwide Study of Discrimination and Chronic Health Conditions Among Asian Americans," *American Journal of Public Health* 97 (July 2007): 1–6.

142. U.S. Bureau of the Census, "American Fact Finder, Selected Population Profile in the United States (Vietnamese Alone)," http://factfinder.census.gov (retrieved January 22, 2010). See also Dennis McLellan, "Writer Urges the U.S. to See 'A Hidden Treasure of Talents,'" *The Los Angeles Times,* February 7, 1992, p. E3; Sonni Efron, "Few Viet Exiles Find U.S. Riches," *The Los Angeles Times,* April 29, 1990, p. A1.

143. "Asian, Indian Firms Growing," *Omaha World Herald,* August 5, 1996, p. 13; Arturs Kalnins and Wilbur Chung, "Ethnic Links, Location Choice and Performance: A Test of the Rural Motel Industry," University of Southern California, 2000, http://www.rhsmith.umd.edu/faculty/wchung/pdfs/Patel Hotels.pdf (retrieved January 25, 2010).

144. Boxall, "Asian Indians Remake Silicon Valley"; "The Market: Potential and Opportunity," http://mediakit.indusbusinessjournal.com/03_ibj_mediakit07_market_potential.pdf (retrieved January 5, 2007).

145. U.S. Bureau of the Census, "2008 American Community Survey, American Fact Finder, Selected Population Profile in the United States (Asian Indian Alone)," http://factfinder.census.gov (retrieved January 22, 2010); "The Market: Potential and Opportunity."

146. Jason Richwine, "Indian Americans: The New Model Minority," *Forbes* 02.24.09, http://www.forbes.com/2009/02/24/bobby-jindal-indian-americans-opinions-contributors_immigrants_minority.html (retrieved January 13, 2010). For a critique, see Shiwani Srivastava, "Nobody's Model Minority," *The Root,* March 16, 2009, http://www.theroot.com/views/nobodys-model-minority (retrieved January 13, 2010). The survey data are for GLBT Asian Indians and are reported in Alain Dangerous and Cabrini Vianney, *Living in the Margins* (Washington, DC: National Gay and Lesbian Task Force Policy Institute, 2007), Table 1. See also Arlene Newman, "Festival Reflects Indians' Growth," *The New York Times,* August 18, 1991, sec. 12NJ, p. 1; Joel Kotkin, "Asian Indians in California Spotlight After Years in Shadows," *The Washington Post,* May 6, 1990, p. H2.

147. See Boxall, "Asian Indians Remake Silicon Valley."

148. "Prepared Testimony of Karen Narasaki," Federal News Service, June 26, 1997.

149. Leland Saito, personal communication, Fall 1998.

150. Angela Kim and Christine Yeh, "Stereotypes of Asian American Students," *ERIC Digest,* February 2002, http://searcheric.org/digests/ed462510.html (retrieved December 21, 2006). The quotation is from Press Release, Japanese American Citizens League, August 2008, http://www.jacl.org/public_policy/ response.htm (retrieved January 4, 2010).

151. U.S. Commission on Civil Rights, Civil Rights Issues Facing Asian Americans in the 1990s, pp. 68–99. The San Diego study is in Somini Sengupta, "Not All Asian Americans Prospering, Study Reports; Students' Academic Success Obscuring Needs," *Dallas Morning News,* November 14, 1997, p. 44A; other study reports are in Sonia M. Pérez, Ka Ying Yang, Marian Wright Edelman, and James M. Jones, "Growing Up American," *Children of Immigrant Families* 14 (Summer 2004): 119–138. The 2009 study is in Committee of 100, *Still The "Other?" Public Attitudes toward Chinese and Asian Americans,* pp. 14–21. See also Li-yuan J. Liao and Patrica J. Larke, "The Voices of Thirteen Chinese and Taiwanese Parents Sharing Views about Their Children Attending Chinese

Heritage Schools," *US-China Education Review* 5 (December 2008): 1–2.

152. Kim and Yeh, "Stereotypes of Asian American Students." Quote is from Michelle Ott, "The Incidence of Anti-Asian Violence in High Schools," Bates College, 1994, cited in Peter Nien-Chu Kiang, "We Could Shape It: Organizing for Asian Pacific American Student Empowerment," in *Asian Americans*, ed. Fong and Shinagawa, p. 126; Asian American Legal Defense and Education Fund, "Educational Equity," www.aaldef.org/education.php (retrieved December 13, 2006).

153. "Philippine News: Rising Harassment of Asian American Students," November 21, 2007, http://www.asianam.org/hate.htm (retrieved January 25, 2010).

154. Quote is from Long Le, "The Dark Side of the Asian American 'Model Student,'" August 2, 2006, http://news.newamericamedia.org/news (retrieved January 5, 2007)

155. Donna Leinwand, "Racist Threats Set Penn State on Edge," *USA Today*, May 3, 2001, p. 3A; Press Release, Japanese American Citizens League, http://www.jacl.org/public_policy/response.htm (retrieved January 4, 2010).

156. U.S. Bureau of the Census, *Statistical Abstract of the United States 1994* (Washington, DC: U.S. Government Printing Office, 1994), pp. 49, 157; U.S. Bureau of the Census, "2008 American Community Survey, American Fact Finder: Select Population Profile [for various groups]," http:// factfinder.census.gov/ (retrieved January 25, 2010).

157. Schuppe and Kinkhabwala, "Education a Family Affair"; Melita Marie Garza, "Asians Feel Bias Built on Perceptions," *Chicago Tribune*, August 7, 1994, p. C1.

158. Eloise Salholz et al., "Do Colleges Set Asian Quotas?" *Newsweek*, February 9, 1987, p. 60; Timothy Egan, "Asian-Americans Challenge Ideas of Race in U.S. Universities," *International Herald Tribune*, January 7, 2007, www.nytimes.com/2007/01/07/world/americas/07iht-asians.4125275.html?pagewanted=1&_r=1 (retrieved January 12, 2010).

159. U.S. Commission on Civil Rights, *Civil Rights Issues Facing Asian Americans in the 1990s*, pp. 109–112.

160. Egan, "Asian-Americans Challenge Ideas of Race in U.S. Universities."

161. Madore, "Long-Quiet Asian Group Starts to Mobilize," p. 7.

162. Ronald Takaki, "Is Race Surmountable? Thomas Sowell's Celebration of Japanese-American 'Success,'" in *Ethnicity and the Work Force*, ed. Winston A. Van Horne (Madison: University of Wisconsin Press, 1985), pp. 218–220.

163. Senate Judiciary Committee, "Capitol Hill Hearings," September 20, 1991; "Prepared Testimony of Karen Narasaki," Federal News Service, June 26, 1997; for recent positions, see www.napaba.org.

164. Mogelonsky, "Asian-Indian Americans," pp. 32–38; Takaki, *Strangers from a Different Shore*, p. 473.

165. Mia Tuan, *Forever Foreigners or Honorary Whites?: The Asian American Experience Today* (New Brunswick, NJ: Rutgers University Press, 1998), p. 155; Chou and Feagin, *The Myth of the Model Minority*, pp. 78–135.

166. Kitano and Daniels, *Asian Americans*, pp. 190–192; Takaki, *Strangers from a Different Shore*, p. 473.

167. Saito, *Race and Politics*, p. 61; Chou and Feagin, *The Myth of the Model Minority*, pp. 38, 150.

168. Rubén G. Rumbaut, "The Coming of the Second Generation: Immigration and Ethnic Mobility in Southern California," *AAPSS Annals* 620 (November 2008): 217–219.

169. Scott Gold, "A Generation Removed: Lessons and Legacies 25 Years After Vietnam," *The Los Angeles Times*, April 28, 2000, p. M3; Andrew Vontz, "Hanoi Heart Throbs," *Los Angeles Times*, February 19, 2006, http://www.latimes.com/news/local/orange/la-tm-nuvpop8feb19,1,5473095.story (retrieved January 26, 2010).

170. Daniels, *Coming to America*, p. 367; Reimers, *Still the Golden Door*, p. 111; Hyunsun Choi, "Religious-Based Social Capital in the Los Angeles Korean Community," University of Southern California, paper presented at American Sociological Association annual meeting, August 13–16, 2005.

171. Karen Pyke, "'The Normal American Family' as an Interpretive Structure of Family Life among Adult Children of Korean and Vietnamese Immigrants," unpublished paper, University of Florida, Gainesville, 1997; Lisa Park, *Consuming Citizenship: Children of Asian Immigrant Entrepreneurs* (Palo Alto, CA: Stanford University Press, 2005), passim; Christine Yeh, "Age, Acculturation, Cultural Adjustment, and Mental Health Symptoms of Chinese, Korean, and Japanese Immigrant Youths," *Cultural Diversity and Ethnic Minority Psychology* 9 (2003): 34–48. See also Chou and Feagin, *The Myth of the Model Minority*, pp. 116–151.

172. Durriya Z. Khairullah and Zahid Y. Khairullah, "Behavioural Acculturation and Demographic Characteristics of Asian Indian Immigrants in the United States of America," *International Journal of Sociology* 19 (1999): 57–80; Boxall, "Asian Indians Remake Silicon Valley"; Sharmila Rudrappa, *Becoming American: Indian Immigrants and the Cultures of Citizenship* (New Brunswick, NJ: Rutgers University Press, 2004), passim.

173. John Dillin, "More Blacks Enter Middle Class," *The Christian Science Monitor* (August 9, 1991): 7; Shinagawa and Pang, "Asian American Panethnicity and Intermarriage," in *Asian Americans*, ed. Fong and Shinagawa, p. 341.

174. C. N. Le and J. J. Huang, "Interracial Dating and Marriage," http://www.asian-nation.org/interracial.shtml (retrieved January 10, 2010). See also Shinagawa and Pang, "Asian American Panethnicity and Intermarriage," pp. 334–343.

175. Shinagawa and Pang, "Asian American Panethnicity and Intermarriage," pp. 334–343.

176. Kumiko Nemoto, "Intimacy, Desire, and the Construction of Self in Relationships between Asian American Women and White American Men," *Journal of Asian American Studies* 9 (2006): 51. See also Nadia Kim, "Patriarchy Is So Third World: Korean Immigrant Women and Migrating White Western Masculinity," *Social Problems* 53 (2006): 519–536.

177. Nazli Kibria, "The Construction of 'Asian American': Reflections on Intermarriage and Ethnic Identity among Second-Generation Chinese and Korean Americans," *Ethnic and Racial Studies* 20 (July 1997): 523–544; see also Nazli Kibria, *Becoming Asian American: Second Generation Chinese and Korean American Identities* (Baltimore, MD: Johns Hopkins University Press, 2002), pp. 175–199.

178. Shinagawa and Pang, "Asian American Panethnicity and Intermarriage," p. 343.

179. B. Suzuki, "Education and the Socialization of Asian Americans," in *Asian Americans: Social and Psychological Perspectives*, ed. R. Endo, S. Sue, and N. Wagner (Palo Alto, CA: Science & Behavior Books, 1980), pp. 155–178; Chou and Feagin, *The Myth of the Model Minority*, pp. 42–108.

180. Robert G. Lee, *Orientals: Asian Americans in Popular Culture* (Philadelphia: Temple University Press, 1999), pp. 188, 189.

181. Ishmael Reed, "America's Color Bind: The Modeling of Minorities," *San Francisco Examiner*, November 19, 1987, p. A20; "Success Story of One Minority Group in the U.S.," *U.S. News & World Report*, December 26, 1966, pp. 73–76.

182. We draw here on Feagin, *Racist America*, 2nd ed., Chapter 7.

183. See, for example, Dinesh D'Souza, *The End of Racism: Principles for a Multiracial Society* (New York: The Free Press, 1995).

184. Frank Wu, "Neither Black nor White: Asian Americans and Affirmative Action," *Boston College Third World Law Journal* 15 (1995): 249–250.

185. Gary Y. Okihiro, "Is Yellow Black or White?" in *Asian Americans: Experiences and Perspectives*, ed. Fong and Shinagawa, p. 75.

186. Nadia Y. Kim, "Critical Thoughts on Asian American Assimilation in the Whitening Literature," *Social Forces* 86 (2007): 574.

187. Mimi Ko Cruz, "Study Finds Paradoxes in Orange County's Korean American Community," *Inside*, May 12, 2009, http://calstate.fullerton.edu/news/Inside/2009/oc-korean- american-study.html (retrieved January 26, 2010). (The research study was done by Mikyong Kim-Goh.)

188. Richard L. Zweigenhaft and William Domhoff, *Diversity in the Power Elite: Have Women and Minorities Reached the Top?* (New Haven, CT: Yale University Press, 1998); Min Zhou, "Growing Up American: The Challenge Confronting Immigrant Children and Children of

Immigrants," *Annual Review of Sociology* 23 (1997): 63–95.

189. Gloria Luz R. Martinez and Wayne J. Villemez, "Assimilation in the United States: Occupational Attainment of Asian Americans, 1980," paper presented at the American Sociological Association meetings, Chicago, 1987, pp. 31–32; U.S. Commission on Civil Rights, *Civil Rights Issues Facing Asian Americans in the 1990s*, pp. 103–136.

190. Yen Le Espiritu, "Multiple Identities of Second-Generation Filipinos," in *The Second Generation*, p. 45; the survey is in Committee of 100, *Still The "Other?" Public Attitudes toward Chinese and Asian Americans*, pp. 14–21.

191. Tuan, *Forever Foreigners*, p. 159. Hung Cam Thai, "Formation of Ethnic Identity among Second-Generation Vietnamese Americans," in *The Second Generation*, p. 76; Chou and Feagin, *The Myth of the Model Minority*, pp. 213–216 and passim. See also Vijay Prashad, *The Karma of Brown Folk* (Twin Cities: University of Minnesota Press, 2003), pp. 6–7.

192. Wendy Lin, "Asians, Latinos Rip Voting Plan," *Newsday*, May 29, 1992, p. 4. See also the recent civil rights struggles reported at www.aaldef.org (retrieved January 28, 2010).

193. See Kwang Chung Kim and Won Moo Hurh, "Korean Americans and the 'Success' Image: A Critique," *Amerasia* 10 (Fall/Winter 1983): 15.

194. Daniels, *Coming to America*, pp. 388–389.

Chapter 12

1. "Easy Targets: Arab Americans Fight Bias," tolerance.org, October 7, 2005, www.tolerance.org/news/article_tol .jsp?id=1305.

2. Nadine Naber, "Muslim First, Arab Second: A Strategic Politics of Race and Gender," *The Muslim World* 95 (October 2005): 479–481; we draw here on comments from Karyn Mc-Kinney Marvasti. We are indebted to her and to Gary David, Amir Marvasti, and Pinar Batur for comments on this chapter.

3. See Amir Marvasti and Karyn D. McKinney, *Middle Eastern Lives in America* (Lanham, MD: Rowman & Littlefield, 2004).

4. Joseph R. Haiek, *Arab American Almanac*, 3rd ed. (Glendale, CA: News Circle Publishing, 1984), pp. 20–32.

5. Ibid., p. 33; Gary Orfalea, *The Arab Americans: A History* (Northampton, MA: Olive Branch Press, 2006), pp. 44–46; Haiek, Arab American Almanac, pp. 33–42. See also M. Paul Lewis, ed., *Ethnologue: Languages of the World*, 16th ed. (Dallas, TX: SIL International, 2009).

6. Gary David, *The Mosaic of Middle Eastern Communities in Metropolitan Detroit* (Detroit: United Way Community Services, 1999), pp. 7–9.

7. Nadine Naber, "Ambiguous Insiders: An Investigation of Arab-American Invisibility," *Ethnic and Racial Studies* 23 (January 2000): 41.

8. Table 12.1. See also U.S. Bureau of the Census: "We the People of Arab Ancestry in the United States: Table 1: Population with Arab Ancestry by Detailed Group," published March 2005, www.census.gov/prod/2005pubs/censr-21.pdf.

9. Randa A. Kayyali, *The Arab Americans* (Westport, CT: Greenwood Press, 2006), pp. 58–62; "Arab Americans: Demographics," http://www.aaiusa.org/arab-americans/22/demographics (retrieved February 1, 2010).

10. Naber, "Ambiguous Insiders," pp. 37–61; John Zogby, "Arab America Today," www.arab-aai.org (retrieved January 26, 2001).

11. Alixa Naff, *Becoming American: The Early Arab Immigrant Experience* (Carbondale: Southern Illinois University Press, 1985), pp. 3–4; Zogby, "Arab America Today"; Kayyali, *The Arab Americans*, pp. 24–36.

12. Kayyali, *The Arab Americans*, pp. 24–26.

13. David, *The Mosaic of Middle Eastern Communities in Metropolitan Detroit*, p. 17. See also Marvasti and McKinney, *Middle Eastern Lives in America*.

14. Naff, *Becoming American*, p. 16.

15. David, *The Mosaic of Middle Eastern Communities in Metropolitan Detroit*, pp. 17–19.

16. Michael W. Suleiman, "Introduction: The Arab Immigrant Experience," in *Arabs in America: Building a New Future*, ed. Michael W. Suleiman (Philadelphia: Temple University Press, 1999), p. 7; Haney Lopez, *White by Law: The Legal Construction of Race* (New York: New York University Press, 1996), pp. 204–208.

17. Naber, "Ambiguous Insiders," p. 39.

18. Evelyn Shakir, *Bint Arab: Arab and Arab American Women in the United States* (Westport, CT: Praeger, 1997), p. 81; Kayyali, *The Arab Americans*, p. 53.

19. Erik Love, "'Confronting Islamophobia in the United States: Framing Civil Rights Activism among Middle Eastern Americans," *Patterns of Prejudice* 43 (2009): 402.

20. Edward W. Said, *Orientalism* (New York: Vintage Books, 1979), p. 287; Shelly Shade, "The Image of the Arab in America: Analysis of a Poll on American Attitudes," *Middle East Journal* 35 (Spring 1981): 143–162.

21. Lydia Saad, "Anti-Muslim Feelings Fairly Common in U.S.: Nearly 40% of Americans Admit Feeling Prejudice," Gallup Poll, http://news.aol.com/gallup/story (retrieved January 13, 2007); Love, "Confronting Islamophobia in the United States: Framing Civil Rights Activism among Middle Eastern Americans," pp. 410–411.

22. Terrel Bell, *The Thirteenth Man: A Reagan Cabinet Memoir* (New York: The Free Press, 1988), pp. 103–105.

23. Said, *Orientalism*.

24. Ibid., p. 286; Therese Saliba, "Resisting Invisibility: Arab Americans in Academia and Activism," in *Arabs in America*, p. 310.

25. Matthew W. Hughey and Sahara Muradi, "Laughing Matters: Economies of Hyper-Irony and Manic-Satire in South Park & Family Guy," *Humanity and Society* 33 (2009): 206–237. See also Jamal Amaney and Nadine

Naber, ed., *Race and Arab Americans Before and After 9/11: From Invisible Citizens to Visible Subjects* (Syracuse, NY: Syracuse University Press, 2008).

26. We draw on comments from Karyn McKinney Marvasti (December 2006). The quote is from John Tehranian, "The Last Minstrel Show? Racial Profiling, the War on Terrorism and the Mass Media," *Connecticut Law Review* 41 (February 2009): 811–812.

27. Shakir, *Bint Arab*, p. 1; Karyn McKinney Marvasti, personal communication, December 2006.

28. See "Muslims in the United States: Demography, Beliefs, Institutions," Conference Proceedings, Woodrow Wilson International Center for Scholars, June 18, 2003.

29. Shakir, *Bint Arab*, pp. 2, 5.

30. Kayyali, *The Arab Americans*, p. 80. We draw here on comments from Karyn McKinney Marvasti (December 2006) and "Women in National Parliaments," Interracial-Parliamentary Union, www.ipu.org/wmn-e/classif.htm (retrieved January 13, 2007).

31. Shakir, *Bint Arab*, p. 10.

32. Kristine Ajrouch, "Family and Ethnic Identity in an Arab-American Community," in *Arabs in America*, p. 129; Jen'nan Ghazal Read, "The Sources of Gender Role Attitudes among Christian and Muslim Arab-American Women," *Sociology of Religion* 64 (2003): 207–222.

33. Shakir, *Bint Arab*, p. 112; Susan E. Marshall and Jen'nan Ghazal Read, "Identity Politics among Arab-American Women," *Social Science Quarterly* 84 (December 2003): 875–891.

34. Shakir, *Bint Arab*, p. 81.

35. Joe R. Feagin and Danielle Dirks, "'Who Is White?': College Students' Assessments of Key US Racial and Ethnic Groups," unpublished research manuscript, Texas A&M University, College Station, TX, 2006; Constance A. Flanagan et al., "Ethnic Awareness, Prejudice, and Civic Commitments in Four Ethnic Groups of American Adolescents," *Journal of Youth and Adolescence* 38 (2009): 500–518.

36. Council on American-Islamic Relations, *The Status of Muslim Civil Rights in the United States—2009* (Washington, DC: CAIR, 2009), pp. 1–9; the DRC study is in Alana Semuels, "Workplace Bias against Muslims, Arabs on Rise," *The Los Angeles Times*, October 3, 2006, www.adc.org/index .php?id=2973 (retrieved January 17, 2007). See also Pew Research Center, *Muslim Americans: Middle Class and Mostly Mainstream* (Washington, DC: Pew Research Center, 2007), p. 4.

37. Marvasti and McKinney, *Middle Eastern Lives in America*, pp. 129–132; Fatima Agha Al-Hayani, "Arabs and the American Legal System: Cultural and Political Ramifications," in *Arabs in America*, p. 80. The nurses study is Anahid Kulwicki, "The Effects of September 11 on Arab American Nurses in Metropolitan Detroit," *Journal of Transcultural Nursing* 19 (2008): 134–139. The profiling data are from Tehranian, "The Last Minstrel Show? Racial Profiling, the War on Terrorism and the

Mass Media," pp. 787–789. See also Shakir, *Bint Arab,* p. 116.

38. Said, *Orientalism,* p. 321; on U.S. ethnocentrism with regard to Middle Eastern countries, see Antony J. Blinken, "Winning the War of Ideas," *Washington Quarterly* 25 (Spring 2002): 101–114.

39. Mowahid Shah, "The FBI and the Civil Rights of Arab-Americans," *ADC Issues,* number 5, Washington DC, 1986.

40. Gary David, e-mail communication, March 2001; Naber, "Ambiguous Insiders," p. 49; Leadership Conference on Civil Rights, "Faces of Hate Crimes," www.civil rights.org/programs/hate_crimes/faces/index.htm1#3 (retrieved January 24, 2002).

41. Shakir, *Bint Arab,* p. 86; Kathleen M. Moore, "A Closer Look at Anti-Terrorism Law," in *Arabs in America,* p. 80.

42. American-Arab Anti-Discrimination Committee (ADC), "ADC Fact Sheet: The Condition of Arab Americans Post 9/11," www.adc.org/terror_attack/9-11aftermath .pdf, p. 1 (retrieved January 24, 2002); Peter Finn, "Hijackers Depicted as Elite Group," *The Washington Post,* November 5, 2001, p. Al.

43. American-Arab Anti-Discrimination Committee (ADC), "ADC Fact Sheet: The Condition of Arab Americans Post 9/11," p. 2; we draw here on comments from Karyn McKinney Marvasti (January 2007).

44. Marvasti and McKinney, *Middle Eastern Lives in America,* p. 49; Tehranian, "The Last Minstrel Show? Racial Profiling, the War on Terrorism and the Mass Media," pp. 787–789; Sunita Sohrabji, "FBI Profiling of Muslims on the Rise, Says Asian Law Caucus," *India West,* August 14, 2009, http://news.newamericamedia.org/news/ view_article.html?article_id=11a699af1441226d96c0b7d 4f9d59330 (retrieved January 29, 2010).

45. Meriana Alrabadi, "Did Police Kill Palestinian-American Husien Shehada for Speaking Arabic?" *Washington Report on Middle East Affairs* 28 (7) (September/October 2009): 30–31; Wayne Baker et al., *Citizenship and Crisis: Arab Detroit After 9/11* (New York: Russell Sage, 2009), pp. 1–30.

46. "Islam in the United States, a Tentative Ascent, a Conversation with Yvonne Haddad," http://usinfo.state. gov/usa/islam/hadad.htm (retrieved June 4, 2001); Kathryn A. Ruff, "Scared to Donate," *New York University Journal of Legislation and Public Policy* 9 (2006): 448–449; Council on American-Islamic Relations, *The Status of Muslim Civil Rights in the United States-2009,* pp. 1–9. See also Love, "Confronting Islamophobia in the United States," p. 416.

47. "Hate Crimes against Arab Americans, Muslims, and Sikhs," Leadership Conference on Civil Rights, http:// www .civilrights.org/publications/hatecrimes/arab americans.html (retrieved January 29, 2010); Leadership Conference on Civil Rights Education Fund (LCCREF), *Confronting the New Faces of Hate: Hate Crimes in America, 2009* (Washington, DC: Leadership Conference, 2009), p. 31.

48. "Poll Shows Declining Arab American Support for Bush," Arabic Newspaper Online, www.arabmedia .com/page1.html (retrieved January 17, 2007); "Hamilton College Muslim America Poll," www. hamilton .edu/news/more_news/display.cfm?ID=4607 (retrieved January 17, 2007).

49. Mark Fitzgerald, "Arab Americans Boycott '*Chicago Sun-Times*'" *Jerusalem Post,* November 1, 2000, p. 1; the quotation is from Naber, "Ambiguous Insiders," p. 46. The survey is in David, *The Mosaic of Middle Eastern Communities in Metropolitan Detroit,* p. 39. See also Melani McAlister, *Epic Encounters: Culture, Media, and U.S. Interests in the Middle East, 1945–2000* (Berkeley: University of California Press, 2001).

50. "Muslim-American Activism: Discussion of Legal Issues Facing Muslim Communities in the United States," *Washington Report of Middle Eastern Affairs,* June 2000, pp. 88–89; Love, "Confronting Islamophobia in the United States," p. 417.

51. Nikki Tait, "Immigrants Earn Their Rewards: Arab-American Community," *Financial Times* (February 28, 2000): 6; Gary David, "Intercultural Relationships across the Counter: An Interactional Analysis of In-Situ Service Encounters," unpublished dissertation, Wayne State University, Detroit, MI, 1999; Kayyali, *The Arab Americans,* pp. 142–144.

52. Abdon M. Pallasch, "Arab, Jewish Law Groups Convene; Attorneys Here Seeking Common Ground," *Chicago Sun-Times,* November 10, 2000, p. 12; for more recent efforts, see the Arab-American Bar Association of Illinois website, http://72.14.209.104/ search?q= cache:k3A1of3teO8J:www.arabbar.org/art-govrept .asp+Arab-American+Bar+Association+and+the+ Decalogue+Society+of+Jewish+lawyers&hl=en&gl= us&ct=clnk&cd=7 (retrieved January 16, 2007); Albor Ruiz, "Group Fights Spread of Mideast Hate Here," *New York Daily News,* November 6, 2000, p. 6.

53. Jen'nan Ghazal Read, "More of a Bridge than a Gap: Gender Differences in Arab-American Political Engagement," *Social Science Quarterly* 88 (2007): 1072–1091.

54. Arab American Institute, "2010 Roster of Arab Americans in Public Service & Political Life," www.aaiusa. org/arab-americans/3923 (retrieved February 16, 2010); Teresa Watanabe, "American Muslims Look for Ways to Harness Political Power," *Los Angeles Times,* October 1, 2000, p. B3; Friday Watch-Fire Prayer Alert, Intercessors for America, www.ifapray.org/FridayWatch-FireAlert/FWF-6_23_2006.html (retrieved January 17, 2007).

55. Andrea Stone, "Arab Vote Is Critical in Michigan," *USA Today,* November 1, 2000, p. 12A; Kayyali, *The Arab Americans,* pp. 136–137; Zev Chafets, "Arab Enclave on Pols' Map," *New York Daily News,* November 3, 2000, p. 6; Arab American Institute, "2010 Roster of Arab Americans in Public Service & Political Life"; Casey Kasem, "Famous Arab Americans," Arab American Institute Foundation, www.aaiusa.org/arab-americans/23/

famous-arab-americans (retrieved January 8, 2007); Zogby International, "The 2008 Election: How Arab Americans Will Vote and Why," Conducted for Arab American Institute, September, 2008.

56. Shakir, *Bint Arab,* p. 88; Habib Battah, "Racism Won't Keep Arab Americans From Polls," November 3, 2008, http://www.alternet.org/election08/106010/racism_ isn%27t_keeping_arab_americans_from_the_polls (retrieved January 29, 2010); "AALDEF Releases 2006 Exit Poll Results of Michigan Asian American and Arab American Vote," April 9, 2007, www.aaldef. org/article.php?article_id=261 (retrieved February 15, 2010).

57. Both are quoted in E. R. Shipp, "Anti-Muslim Bigotry Is Bad Political Strategy," *New York Daily News,* November 5, 2000, p. 45.

58. Lydia Saad, "Americans' Support for Israel Unchanged Since Gaza Conflict," Gallup.com, March 3, 2009, www.gallup.com/poll/116308/americans-support-israel-unchanged-gaza-conflict.aspx (retrieved February 16, 2010); Bonnie Squires, "Americans Warming to Arab Cause?" *Philadelphia Daily News,* as reprinted on http:// www.arab-aai.org (retrieved January 26, 2001); Martin Sieff, "Analysis: Poll Adds to Pressure on Israel," UPI Press Release, December 14, 2006.

59. Janine Zacharia, "Arab Americans Send Record Number of Delegates to Democratic Convention," *Jerusalem Post,* August 17, 2000, p. 2; David, *The Mosaic of Middle Eastern Communities in Metropolitan Detroit,* p. 23. See also recent reports at the Arab Community Center for Economic and Social Services (ACCESS), www .accesscommunity.org (retrieved February 16, 2010).

60. The quote is from David, *The Mosaic of Middle Eastern Communities in Metropolitan Detroit,* p. 51; Watanabe, "American Muslims Look for Ways to Harness Political Power," p. B3. See also American Muslim Alliance reports at www.amaweb.org (retrieved February 16, 2010).

61. Naber, "Ambiguous Insiders," pp. 37–61; Zogby, "Arab America Today."

62. U.S. Bureau of the Census, "Population Group: Arab," "2008 American Community Survey," http://factfinder. cen sus.gov (retrieved February 16, 2010).

63. U.S. Bureau of the Census, "Population Group: Arab."

64. Zogby, "Arab America Today"; David, *The Mosaic of Middle Eastern Communities in Metropolitan Detroit,* pp. 9–49; Tait, "Immigrants Earn Their Rewards: Arab-American Community," p. 6; Chafets, "Arab Enclave on Pols' Map," p. 6. See also the list of important Arab American organizations in Detroit area at www.alliedmedia.com/Arab-American/Arab_Organizations.htm (retrieved February 16, 2010).

65. U.S. Bureau of the Census, "Population Group: Arab"; Suleiman, "Introduction," p. 16.

66. David, *The Mosaic of Middle Eastern Communities in Metropolitan Detroit,* p. 40.

67. Jane Adas, "Museum of the City of New York Examines Local Arab Americans," *Washington Report of Middle Eastern Affairs,* April 2000, pp. 51–52, 83. See also Marvin Wingfield, "Arab Americans: Into the Multicultural Mainstream," *Equity & Excellence in Education* 39 (2006): 253–266. One Muslim community school can be seen here: www.mymcs.org/ (retrieved February 16, 2010).

68. Louis Cristillo, "Religiosity, Education and Civic Belonging: Muslim Youth in New York City Public Schools," preliminary report presented at the Muslim Youth in NYC Public Schools Conference, Columbia University, April 30, 2008, pp. 5–9; Diane S. Shammas, "Post-9/11 Arab and Muslim American Community College Students: Ethno-religious Enclaves and Perceived Discrimination," *Community College Journal of Research and Practice* 33 (2009): 283–308.

69. Wendy Schwartz, "Arab American Students in Public Schools," http://eric-web.tc.columbia.edu/digests/ dig142.htm (retrieved June 4, 2001).

70. "Demographics," Arab American Institute, www.aaiusa .org.arab-americans/22/demographics (retrieved February 16, 2010); Kayyali, *The Arab Americans,* p. 100; Pew Research Center, *Muslim Americans: Middle Class and Mostly Mainstream* (Washington, DC: Pew Research Center, 2007).

71. Rosina J. Hassoun, *Arab Americans in Michigan* (Lansing: Michigan State University Press, 2005); Kathleen Benson and Philip M. Kayal (eds.), *A Community of Many Worlds: Arab Americans in New York* (New York: City Museum of City of New York, 2002), pp. 12–16.

72. "Islam in the United States, a Tentative Ascent, a Conversation with Yvonne Haddad"; U.S. Diplomatic Mission to Germany, "Religions of America," http://usa. usembassy.de/society-religion.htm (retrieved January 18, 2007).

73. Shakir, *Bint Arab,* pp. 115–116; Aminah Mohammad-Arif, *Salaam America: South Asian Muslims in New York* (New York: Anthem Press, 2002), pp. 1–75.

74. Pew Research Center, *Muslim Americans,* pp. 1–6. See also Abdul Malik, "Muslims in America: Profile 2001," www.soundvision.com/yearinreview/2001/profile .shtml (retrieved June 4, 2001). On the contemporary diversity in world Islam, see Gary Leupp, "Challenging Ignorance on Islam: A Ten-Point Primer for Americans," http://soundvision.com/info/peace/primer. asp (retrieved February 16, 2010).

75. "Islam in the United States, a Tentative Ascent, a Conversation with Yvonne Haddad"; Cristillo, "Religiosity, Education and Civic Belonging: Muslim Youth in New York City Public Schools," pp. 5–9. See also numerous discussions at www.iiit.org (retrieved February 18, 2010).

76. Suad Joseph, "Against the Grain of the Nation—The Arab," in *Arabs in America: Building a New Future,* ed. Suleiman, p. 261. Italics are added.

77. Suleiman, "Introduction," p. 15; Andrzej Kulczycki and Arun Peter Lobo, "Patterns, Determinants, and Implications of Intermarriage among Arab Americans,

Journal of Marriage and Family 64 (February 2002): 208–210.

78. Naber, "Ambiguous Insiders," p. 40.
79. Naff, *Becoming American,* p. 15.
80. David, *The Mosaic of Middle Eastern Communities in Metropolitan Detroit,* pp. 32–34.
81. Zogby, "Arab America Today"; Kayyali, *The Arab Americans,* pp. 83–84.
82. Denise Al-Johar, "Muslim Marriages in America: Reflecting New Identities," *The Muslim World* 95 (October 2005): 558–572; Kulczycki and Lobo, "Patterns, Determinants, and Implications of Intermarriage among Arab Americans," pp. 208–210; Shakir, *Bint Arab,* p. 116; Pew Research Center, *Muslim Americans: Middle Class and Mostly Mainstream,* pp. 35–55.
83. Zogby, "Arab America Today"; Kayyali, *The Arab Americans,* pp. 109–110.
84. Gary David and Kenneth Kahtan Ayouby, "Being Arab and Becoming Americanized," unpublished research paper, Bentley College, Waltham, MA, 2001, p. 34. See also Mariam Sami, "As Cap Replaces Kaffiyeh, Arab Parents Look for Help," *New York Times,* November 2, 1997, Sec. 14, p. 10.
85. Richard A. Chapman, "Arab-American Teenagers Share Their Culture in Video," *Chicago Sun-Times,* November 28, 1996, p. 22; see also David, *The Mosaic of Middle Eastern Communities in Metropolitan Detroit,* p. 39.
86. Naber, "Muslim First, Arab Second," p. 494.
87. Quoted in David, *The Mosaic of Middle Eastern Communities in Metropolitan Detroit,* p. 37.
88. David and Ayouby, "Being Arab and Becoming Americanized," p. 35. See also pp. 4, 37.
89. Kristine J. Ajrouch and Amaney Jamal, "Assimilating to a White Identity: The Case of Arab Americans," *International Migration Review* 41 (2007): 860–879.
90. "'White' Isn't Enough, Ethnic Groups Say," United Press International, December 17, 2009, www.upi.com/Top_News/US/2009/12/17/White-isnt-enough-ethnic-groups- say/UPI-65431261069734 (retrieved January 29, 2010).
91. David and Ayouby, "Being Arab and Becoming Americanized," p. 15.
92. Shakir, *Bint Arab,* p. 112; Naber, "Ambiguous Insiders," pp. 50–51.

Chapter 13

1. Nat Hentoff, "Free Expression Comes to Boston Latin," *The Washington Post,* February 8, 1992, p. A21.
2. Quoted in Ilan Stavans, *The Hispanic Condition: Reflections on Culture and Identity in America* (New York: HarperCollins, 1995), p. 166.
3. Ibid., p. 167.
4. U.S. Census Bureau, "An Older and More Diverse Nation by Midcentury," August 2008, http://www.census.gov/Press-Release/www/releases/archives/population/ 012496 .html (retrieved June 12, 2009); S. H. Murdock, *An America Challenged: Population Change and the Future of the United States* (Boulder, CO: Westview Press, 1995), pp. 33–47; Joe R. Feagin, *Racist America: Roots, Current Realities and Future Reparations,* 2nd ed. (New York: Routledge, 2010), pp. 261–263.
5. Buchanan is quoted in Clarence Page, "U.S. Media Should Stop Abetting Intolerance," *Toronto Star,* December 27, 1991, p. A27; Pat Buchanan, *State of Emergency, The Third World Invasion and Conquest of America* (New York: Thomas Dunne Books, 2006).
6. Samuel P. Huntington, "The Erosion of American National Interests," *Foreign Affairs* (September/October 1997): 28.
7. Arthur Schlesinger, *The Disuniting of America: Reflections on a Multicultural Society* (New York: W. W. Norton, 1991), pp. 13, 124–125.
8. U.S. Department of Homeland Security, "Yearbook of Immigration Statistics: 2009, Table 2: Persons Obtaining Legal Permanent Resident Status by Region and Selected Country of Last Residence: Fiscal Years 1820 to 2009," May 4, 2010, http://www.dhs.gov/files/statistics/publications/LPR09.shtm (retrieved May 22, 2010); see also Immigration and Naturalization Service, *Fiscal Year 1998 Statistical Yearbook* (Washington, DC: U.S. Government Printing Office, 1999), Table 2, www.ins.gov/graphics/aboutins/statistics/98immtbl.pdf (retrieved August 31, 2001). Note that the data are incomplete for certain time periods and that the definition of some countries has sometimes changed at different times.
9. Andrew Piatt, "The Crux of the Immigration Question," *North American Review* 199 (June 1914): 866, quoted in Rita J. Simon and Susan H. Alexander, *The Ambivalent Welcome: Print Media, Public Opinion, and Immigration* (Westport, CT: Praeger, 1993), p. 59.
10. U.S. Bureau of the Census, "2008 American Community Survey, American Fact Finder: Selected Population Profile in the United States," [Various Asian American groups], http://factfinder.census.gov (retrieved January 3, 2010); U.S. Census Bureau, Table DP-1: Profile of General Demographic Characteristics for the United States: 2000, www.census.gov (retrieved August 29, 2001).
11. Jeffery S. Passel and D'Vera Cohn, *U.S. Population Projections: 2005-2050* (Washington, DC: Pew Research Center, 2008), www.pewhispanic.org/files/reports/85 .pdf (retrieved February 19, 2010); Wendy Lin, "Stakes are High in Lottery for U.S. Green Cards," *Newsday,* October 13, 1991, p. 19. For a list of U.S. immigration acts, see http://en.wikipedia.org/wiki/List_of_United_States_immigration_ legislation (retrieved February 19, 2010).
12. Pew Research Center, "America's Immigration Quandary: No Consensus on Immigration Problem or Proposed Fixes," http://people-press.org/reports/display.php3? PageID=1045 (retrieved January 19,

2007); Scott Keeter, "Where the Public Stands on Immigration Reform," Pew Research Center, November 23, 2009, http://pewresearch.org/pubs/1421/where-the-public-stands-on-immigration-reform (retrieved February 19, 2010). The *New York Times* and *Washington Post* surveys are cited in "Fact Sheet: Public Opinion on Immigration," ImmigrationWorksUSA.org, http://www.immigrationworksusa.org/uploaded/file/IW_polling_round-up.pdf (retrieved December 1, 2009). The poll on the Arizona law is at "Broad Approval for New Arizona Immigration Law: Democrats Divided, But Support Key Provisions," Pew Research Center for the People and the Press, http://people-press.org/report/613/arizona-immigration-law (accessed May 20, 2010).

13. The CEA report is cited in Shawn Foster, "Immigrants: Blessing or Curse for Utah?" *Salt Lake Tribune*, November 10, 1994, p. A1; the National Academy report is quoted in Center for Continuing Study of the California Economy, "The Impact of Immigration on the California Economy," California, September 2005, p. 40. On national and local impact, see Lonnie Stevans, "The Relationship Among African American Male Earnings, Employment, Incarceration and Immigration: A Time Series Approach," http://mpra.ub.uni-muenchen.de/5594/MPRAPaperNo.5594, posted07.November2007 (accessed February 21, 2010); and George J. Borjas, Jeffrey Grogger, and Gordon H. Hanson, "Immigration and African-American Employment Opportunities: The Response of Wages, Employment, and Incarceration to Labor Supply Shocks," National Bureau of Economic Research, www.nber.org/papers/w12518 (retrieved February 21, 2010).

14. Immigration and Naturalization Service, *Fiscal Year 1998 Statistical Yearbook* (Washington, DC: U.S. Government Printing Office, 1999), Tables 1–3, www.ins.gov/graphics/aboutins/statistics/98immtbl.pdf (retrieved August 31, 2001). Offce of Immigration Statistics, *Yearbook of Immigration Statistics: 2008* (Washington, DC: U.S. Department of Homeland Security, 2009), pp. 4–8. See also www.census.gov (accessed February 21, 2010).

15. Offce of Immigration Statistics, *Yearbook of Immigration Statistics: 2008*, p. 48; and www.census.gov (accessed February 21, 2010).

16. Quoted in Keith Henderson, "Immigration as an Economic Engine," *The Christian Science Monitor*, March 27, 1992, p. 9. See also Ben Wattenberg, *The First Universal Nation* (New York: The Free Press, 1990).

17. Hector Tobar and Robin Fields, "21st-Century Cities: What Is Happening in Urban America?" *Milwaukee Journal Sentinel*, May 11, 2001, p. 19A.

18. Kenneth W. Gronbach, *The Age Curve: How to Profit from the Coming Demographic Storm* (New York: Amacom, 2008); Juan Gonzalez, *Harvest of Empire: A History of Latinos in America* (New York: Penguin Books, 2000), pp. xii–xix.

19. Israel Zangwill, *The Melting Pot* (New York: Macmillan, 1925), p. 33.

20. Milton M. Gordon, *Assimilation in American Life* (New York: Oxford University Press, 1964), pp. 72–73.

21. Mitchell Chang, "Measuring the Impact of a Diversity Requirement on Students' Level of Racial Prejudice," University of California, Los Angeles, 1999, http://209.85.165.104/search?q=cache:M0zg0lQn2NUJ:www.diversityweb.org/digest/W00/research2.html+Universities+have+a+diversity+requirement%22&hl=en&gl=us&ct=clnk&cd=1 (retrieved January 19, 2007); Terry Lefton, "Building Bridges in the Big Apple," *Teaching Tolerance* 1(1) (Spring 1992): 8–13; Ralph Blumenthal, "Black Youth Is Killed by Whites; Brooklyn Attack Is Called Racial," *The New York Times*, August 25, 1989, p. A1; for late 2000s data on colleges and universities, see www.diversityweb.org.

22. For many resources and information on *Teaching Tolerance*, see www.tolerance.org (retrieved February 22, 2010).

23. Quoted in Itabari Njeri, "Beyond the Melting Pot: In America, Blending in Was Once the Ideal," *The Los Angeles Times*, January 13, 1991, p. E1. On "strong" multiculturalism, see Ella Shohat and Robert Stam, *Unthinking Eurocentrism: Multiculturalism and the Media* (New York: Routledge, 1994), pp. 46–49.

24. Arthur Schlesinger Jr., "Speaking Up: A Look at Noteworthy Addresses in the Southland," *The Los Angeles Times*, February 7, 1992, p. B2.

25. Andrés Torres, *Between Melting Pot and Mosaic: African Americans and Puerto Ricans in the New York Political Economy* (Philadelphia: Temple University Press, 1995), pp. 2–6.

26. Ibid., p. 4; see also Amitai Etzioni, "Community of Communities," *Washington Quarterly* 19 (Summer 1996): 127–138.

27. Bobbie Harville, "History: Knowledge Is Lacking; Americans' Understanding of the Country's History Is Thin, a New Survey Reveals," *Dayton Daily News*, July 14, 1996, p. 15A; Anne D. Neal, Jerry L. Martin, and Mashad Moses, "Losing America's Memory: Historical Illiteracy in the 21st Century," report of the American Council of Trustees and Alumni, February 21, 2000, pp. 1-6.

28. James W. Loewen, *Teaching What **Really** Happened: How to Avoid the Tyranny of Textbooks and Get Students Excited about Doing History* (New York: Teachers College Press, 2010), pp. 7–8 and note 9; James W. Loewen, *Lies My Teacher Told Me: Everything Your American History Textbook Got Wrong* (New York: The New Press, 1995), p. 163.

29. Quoted in Njeri, "Beyond the Melting Pot," p. E1.

30. Joe R. Feagin, *Racist America: Roots, Current Realities, and Future Reparations*, 2nd ed. (New York: Routledge, 2010), pp. 282–305.

31. Ted Gordon and Wahneema Lubiano, "The Statement of the Black Faculty Caucus," in *Debating P.C.*, ed. Paul Berman (New York: Dell, 1992), p. 251.

32. Ibid., pp. 251–253; Feagin, *Racist America*, pp. 259–311.

33. Feagin, *Racist America*, pp. 265–273.
34. Feagin, Ibid., pp. 197–199.
35. Joe R. Feagin and Melvin P. Sikes, *Living with Racism* (Boston: Beacon, 1994), p. 222.
36. William H. Frey, Alan Berube, Audrey Singer, and Jill H. Wilson, "Getting Current Recent: Demographic Trends in Metropolitan America," Brookings Institution, www.brookings.edu/reports/2009/~/media/Files/rc/reports/2009/03_metro_demographic_trends/03_metro_demographic_trends.pdf (retrieved June 12, 2009).
37. William H. Frey, "Diversity Spreads Out," *Living Cities Census Series,* Brookings Institution, March 2006, pp. 19–21; see also William H. Frey, "Immigration, Domestic Migration, and Demographic Balkanization in America: New Evidence from the 1990s," *Population and Development Review* 22 (December 1996): 741–763; and William H. Frey, "The New White Flight," *American Demographics* (April 1994): 1–6.
38. Frey, "Diversity Spreads Out," pp. 18–19.
39. Joe R. Feagin, "The Future of U.S. Society in an Era of Racism, Group Segregation, and Demographic Revolution," in *Sociology for the Twenty-First Century: Continuities and Cutting Edges,* ed. J. L. Abu-Lughod (Chicago: University of Chicago Press, 1999), pp. 199–212; Joe R. Feagin, *The White Racial Frame: Centuries of Racial Framing and Counter-Framing* (New York: Routledge, 2010), pp. 200–220.

Part III

1. W. E. B. DuBois, *The World and Africa* (New York: International Publishers, 1965 [1946]), p. 23.

Chapter 14

1. Peter Turnley et al., "Graceland," *Newsweek,* May 9, 1994, pp. 30–33.
2. Paul Taylor, "In New South Africa, Pace of Change Has Race Tensions Simmering," *The Washington Post,* July 21, 1994, p. A20.
3. Patrick Bond, "From Racial to Class Apartheid: South Africa's Frustrating Decade of Freedom," *Monthly Review* (March 2004): 49; Simon Wood, "Race Against Time," *The Observer,* January 22, 2006, p. 38.
4. Marion Lloyd, "In Brazil, a New Debate over Color," *The Chronicle of Higher Education,* February 13, 2004, p. 6.
5. F. Scott Fitzgerald, *The Great Gatsby* (New York: Penguin Books, 1983), p. 19.
6. For a fuller discussion of certain issues raised here, see Pinar Batur, "Centering on Global Racism and Anti-Racism: From Everyday Life to Global Complexity," *Sociological Spectrum* 19 (1999): 467–484.
7. Pinar Batur, "Racial and Ethnic Inequality and Struggle from the Colonial Era to the Present: Drawing the Global Color Line," in *The Global Color Line: Racial and Ethnic Inequality and Struggle from a Global Perspective,* ed. Pinar Batur and Joe Feagin (Stamford, CT: JAI Press, 1999), pp. 3–21.
8. Zia Sardar, Ashis Nandy, and Merryl Wyn Davies, *Barbaric Others: A Manifesto on Western Racism* (London: Pluto Press, 1993), pp. 8–9.
9. Oliver C. Cox, *Caste, Class and Race: A Study in Social Dynamics* (Garden City, NY: Doubleday, 1948), pp. 331–332.
10. Ibid., p. 334.
11. Albert Memmi, *The Colonizer and the Colonized* (New York: Orion Press, 1965).
12. Ronald Takaki, *Iron Cages* (New York: Oxford University Press, 1990), p. 12.
13. Joseph Arthur de Gobineau, *Selected Political Writings,* ed. M. D. Biddiss (New York: Harper & Row, 1970), p. 136.
14. Pinar Batur, "Racial and Ethnic Inequality."
15. Frantz Fanon, "The Pitfalls of National Consciousness," and "On National Culture," in *The Wretched of the Earth,* trans. Constance Farrington (New York: Grove Press, 1963); Anthony Brewer, *Marxist Theories of Imperialism* (New York: Routledge, 1986).
16. Albert Memmi, *The Pillar of Salt* (Boston: Beacon Press, 1992), p. 331.
17. Pinar Batur, "Centering on Global Racism."
18. Leonard Thompson, *A History of South Africa* (New Haven, CT: Yale University Press, 1990); Nigel Worden, *The Making of Modern South Africa: Conquest, Segregation and Apartheid* (Oxford: Blackwell, 1994); Basil Davidson, *Africa in History* (New York: Collier Books, 1991); Roland Oliver and Anthony Atmore, *Africa Since 1800,* 3rd ed. (Cambridge: Cambridge University Press, 1989); Joseph Harris, *Africans and Their History* (New York: Mentor, 1987).
19. Leonard Thompson, *Political Mythology of Apartheid* (New Haven, CT: Yale University Press, 1985), p. 71.
20. Ibid., pp. 72–73.
21. Worden, *Making of Modern South Africa,* pp. 11–12.
22. Thompson, *Political Mythology of Apartheid,* p. 75.
23. Ibid., p. 76.
24. Ibid., p. 70.
25. Davidson, *Africa in History,* p. 269.
26. Thompson, *History of South Africa,* pp. 111–112.
27. Allister Sparks, *The Mind of South Africa* (New York: Knopf, 1990), pp. 148–149.
28. The quote is from Thompson, *History of South Africa,* p. 184; see also Sparks, *Mind of South Africa,* p. 153.
29. Merle Lipton, *Capitalism and Apartheid: South Africa, 1910–1984* (Totowa, NJ: Rowman & Allenheld, 1985), pp. 14–15.
30. Thompson, *History of South Africa;* Oliver and Atmore, *Africa Since 1800,* p. 295.
31. Thompson, *History of South Africa,* p. 206; Lipton, *Capitalism and Apartheid.*
32. Francis Meli, *South Africa Belongs to Us: A History of the ANC* (Bloomington: Indiana University Press, 1988).

33. Nozipho Diseko, "The Origins and Development of the South African Student's Movement (SASM): 1968–1976," *Journal of South African Studies* 18 (March 1991): 40–62.

34. Howard Barrell, "The Turn to the Masses: The African National Congress' Strategic Review of 1978–1979," *Journal of South African Studies* 18 (March 1991): 64–92.

35. Bill Keller, "In South Africa, a White 'Third Force' of Violence Is Confirmed," *The New York Times*, March 20, 1994, sec. 4, p. 5.

36. Thompson, *History of South Africa*.

37. Bill Keller, "Rival Visions of a Post-Apartheid Future Divide South Africa's Zulus," *The New York Times*, April 4, 1994, p. A1; Tom Masland and Joseph Conteras, "Ballots or Bullets," *Newsweek*, April 11, 1994, pp. 34–37.

38. Bond, "From Racial to Class Apartheid"; Vivek Aurora and L.A. Ricci, "Unemployment and Labor Market," *IMF: South Africa* (Washington: IMF, 2006).

39. Harry Bearan, "South African Leader Said to Be the Father of Twenty," *New York Times*, February 2, 2010, p. A1; Linda Vergnani, "South African President's Views on AIDS Cloud International Gathering of Scientists," *The Chronicle of Higher Education*, July 7, 2000, p. A43.

40. Clare Kapp, "South African's Hope for a New Era in HIV/AIDS Policies," *Lancet* (November 18, 2006): 1759.

41. Janis van der Westhuizen, "Alarms over AIDS in South Africa," *Alternatives* 30 (2005): 276.

42. "Race About Race: South Africa's Racial Election," *The Economist* (December 9, 2000): 5.

43. Frantz Fanon, *Black Skin, White Masks*, trans. Charles Mark- mann (New York: Grove Weidenfeld, 1967), p. 87.

44. "The Colours of Brazil," *The Economist* (May 10, 1986): 42.

45. Lloyd, "In Brazil, a New Debate over Color," p. 6.

46. Charles Whitaker, "Blacks in Brazil: The Myth and the Reality," *Ebony* (February 1991: 41, 60–64.

47. Lloyd, "In Brazil, a New Debate over Color," p. 6.

48. Daniela Hart, "Racial Bias Entrenched," *Chronicle of Higher Education* (July 20, 1988): A31–A32.

49. E. Bradford Burns, *A History of Brazil*, 3rd ed. (Ithaca, NY: Cornell University Press, 1993), pp. 23–27.

50. Thomas Skidmore and Peter Smith, *Modern Latin America*, 2nd ed. (Oxford: Oxford University Press, 1994), p. 140; Burns, *History of Brazil*, pp. 216–217.

51. Michael Hanchard, *Orpheus and Power: The Movimento Negro of Rio de Janeiro and São Paulo, Brazil, 1945–1988* (Princeton, NJ: Princeton University Press, 1994), pp. 43–45; Jan Rocha, "Brazil's Racial Democracy," BBCNews, April 19, 2000. http://news.bbc.co.uk/2/hi/americas/719134.stm (retrieved February 11, 2010).

52. Thomas Skidmore, *Black into White: Race and Nationality in Brazilian Thought* (Oxford: Oxford University Press, 1974), pp. 48–69; Dain Borges, "Puffy, Ugly, Slothful and Inert: Degeneration in Brazilian Social Thought, 1880–1940," *Journal of Latin American Studies* 25 (1993): 235–256.

53. Thomas Sanders, "Racial Discrimination and Black Consciousness in Brazil," *American Universities Field Staff Reports* 42 (1981); Hanchard, *Orpheus and Power*.

54. Sanders, "Racial Discrimination and Black Consciousness in Brazil," p. 2; Robert Plummer, "Brazil's Admen Face Billboard Ban," BBCNews, September 19, 2006, http://news.bbc.co.uk/2/hi/business/5355692.stm (retrieved February 11, 2010).

55. George Andrews, "Racial Inequality in Brazil and the United States: A Statistical Comparison," *Journal of Social History* 26 (1992): 234; see also Peggy Webster and Jeffrey Dwyer, "The Cost of Being Nonwhite in Brazil," *Sociology and Social Research* 72 (1988): 136–142.

56. Andrews, "Racial Inequality in Brazil and the United States," pp. 256–257.

57. Mala Htun, "Racial Quotas for a Racial Democracy," NACLA Report on the Americas, January–February 2005, pp. 21–22. The Santos quote is from Gary Duffy, "Racial Legacy that Haunts Brazil," BBCNews, November 4, 2009, http://news.bbc.co.uk/2/hi/8338593.stm (retrieved February 11, 2010).

58. Howard Winant, "Rethinking Race in Brazil," *Journal of Latin American Studies* 24 (1992): 173–192.

59. Anthony Faiola, "Yet Another Fresh Start for Brazil," *Washington Post* National Weekly Edition, October 20, 1997, p. 19.

60. David Kennedy, "Who Are Brazil's Indigenas: Contributions of Census Data Analysis to Anthropological Demography on Indigenous Populations," *Human Organization* 59 (2000): 311; "Threat to Brazil's Indians," *Geographical* 73 (June 2001): 12.

61. The quote is from Duffy, "Racial Legacy that Haunts Brazil." See also "Brazil's Unfinished Battle for Racial Democracy," *The Economist* (April 22, 2000): 31.

62. Francisco Oliviera, "A Bible and an Automatic," *Index on Censorship* 28 (January 1999): 115.

63. Quoted in Whitaker, "Racial Bias Entrenched."

64. Nicole Roberge, "Brazil Experiences the Growing Pains of Affirmative Action," *Diverse Education*, June 1, 2006, p. 16.

65. Ibid.

66. Lloyd, "In Brazil, a New Debate over Color." Teles is quoted in Duffy, "Racial Legacy that Haunts Brazil."

67. Fanon, *Wretched of the Earth*, p. 41.

68. Pierre Birnbaum, *Anti-Semitism in France: A Political History from Leon Blum to the Present*, trans. Miriam Kochan (Oxford: Blackwell, 1992), p. 1.

69. Stephen Wilson, *Ideology and Experience: Anti-Semitism in France at the Time of the Dreyfus Affair* (Rutherford, NJ: Fairleigh Dickinson University Press, 1982).

70. Alan Riding, "Mitterand's Mistakes: Vichy Past Is Unveiled," *The New York Times*, September 9, 1994, p. A4.

71. Maxim Silverman, *Deconstructing the Nation: Immigration, Racism and Citizenship in Modern France* (London: Routledge, 1992), p. 10.

72. Douglas Johnson, "The Making of the French Nation," in *The National Question in Europe in Historical Context*,

ed. Mikulas Teich and Roy Porter (Cambridge: Cambridge University Press, 1993), p. 59.

73. Silverman, *Deconstructing the Nation*, pp. 3–4.

74. R. D. Grillo, *Ideologies and Institutions in Urban France* (Cambridge: Cambridge University Press, 1985), p. 65.

75. Silverman, *Deconstructing the Nation*, p. 3.

76. Julia Kristeva, *Nations Without Nationalism* (New York: Columbia University Press, 1993), pp. 97–98; Catherine Wihtol De Wenden, "North African Immigration and the French Political Imaginary," in *Race, Discourse and Power in France*, ed. Maxim Silverman (Brookfield, VT: Gower, 1991), p. 108.

77. "Israelis Say Anti-Semitism Peaked in 2009," *Huffington Post*, January 24, 2010, http://www.huffingtonpost .com/ 2010/01/25/israeli-report-says-anti_n_435245 .html (retrieved February 11, 2010). Daniel Singer, "Liberté, Egalité, Racisme?, *Nation*, October 21, 1996, p. 19.

78. "First French Racism Poll Released," *BBCNews*, January 31, 2007, http://news.bbc.co.uk/2/hi/europe/ 6317799.stm (retrieved February 11, 2010).

79. Bruce Crumley, "Racism Unfiltered in France," *Time*, January 6, 2007, www.time.com/time/world/article/ 0,8599,1574817,00.html (retrieved February 11, 2010).

80. Kristeva, *Nations Without Nationalism*, pp. 13–14.

81. Chris Woodall, "Arabicide in France: An Interview with Fausto Giudice," *Race and Class* 35 (1993): 21–33.

82. Ibid.

83. Youssef Ibrahim, "France Bans Muslim Scarf in Its Schools," *The New York Times*, September 11, 1994, p. 4.

84. The Sarkozy quotes are from "Sarkozy Says Colonial Rule Unjust," *BBCNews*, December 3, 2007, http://news .bbc.co.uk/2/hi/africa/7124548.stm (retrieved February 11, 2010). See also Letitia Creamean, "Membership of Foreigners: Algerians in France," *Arab Studies Quarterly* 16 (1996): 49–67.

85. Alice Chasan, "Border Skirmishes: European Integration vs. Ugly Atavisms," *World Press Review*, January 2000, p. 2.

86. "French TV Executive, Former TV Host Fined for Racist Song Performed on Air About Blacks," *Jet*, April 1, 1996, p. 65.

87. Robert Aldrich, "Colonial Past, Post-Colonial Present," *History Australia* 3 (2006): 14.1–14.10.

88. Frank Johnson, "The Rioters Want 'liberté, egalité, fraternité'; What They Don't Want Is an Islamic State," *The Spectator*, November 19, 2005, p. 32.

89. Stephanie Giry, "France and Its Muslims (Terrorism)," *Foreign Affairs* 85 (September–October 2006): 87.

90. Pinar Batur, "The Discourse of Counterattack: Ethnic Movements and the Formation of Ethnic Identity," Ph.D. dissertation, University of Texas, Austin, 1992.

91. Samuel Totten and W. S. Parson, *The Century of Genocide* (New York: Routledge, 2004), p. xxviii.

92. Ibid., p. xxxix.

93. Scott Straus, "Darfur and the Genocide Debate," *Foreign Affairs* 84 (2004): 123–133.

94. Asafa Jalata, "State Terrorism and Globalization: The Cases of Ethiopia and Sudan," *International Journal of Comparative Sociology* 46 (2005): 79–102.

95. Paul Salopek, "Shattered Sudan," *National Geographic* (February 2003): 2; Karen Lange, "The Nuba: Still Standing," *National Geographic* (February 2003): 4.

96. Straus, "Darfur and the Genocide Debate."

97. Cynthia E. Smith and Tony Pipa, "The Politics of Genocide: U.S. Rhetoric vs. Inaction in Darfur, 7 April–26 September 2004," *Kennedy School Review* 6 (2004): 131–141.

98. Nouraee Andisheh, "Don't Panic!" *Weekly Planet* 18/40 (2006): 16.

99. "80 Percent of Darfur Conflict Deaths Due to Disease," Reuters, January 21, 2010, http://www.reuters.com/ article/idUSTRE60L55Y20100122 (retrieved February 11, 2010); Marlise Simons and Nei MacFarquhar, "Court Issues Arrest Warrant for Sudan's Leader, *The New York Times*, March 5, 2009, www.nytimes.com/ 2009/03/05/world/africa/05court.html (retrieved February 11, 2010).

Index

Photo Credits

Preface and Chapter 1: p. xxi, Arthur Tilley/Taxi/Getty Images; p. 4, Esbin Anderson/The Image Works; p. 9, AP Wide World Photos; p. 12, Jonathan Nourok/PhotoEdit, Inc.; p. 21, Ray Ellis/Photo Researchers, Inc.

Chapter 2: p. 26, Kunio Awaki/Corbis–NY; p. 31, Corbis–NY; p. 37, A. Ramey/PhotoEdit, Inc.; p. 42, Merritt Vincent/ PhotoEdit, Inc.

Chapter 3: p. 65, The Granger Collection; p. 67, Corbis–NY; p. 73, Steven Rubin/The Image Works

Chapter 4: p. 84, Rudi Von Brief/PhotoEdit; p. 87, Library of Congress; p. 92, Corbis–NY; p. 104, Michael Appleton/NY Daily News Archive/Getty Images; p. 106, Getty Images– Hulton Archive Photos

Chapter 5: p. 114, Newscom; p. 119, AP Wide World Photos; p. 123, Tannen Maury/The Image Works; p. 128, Corbis– New York

Chapter 6: p. 137, © Anders Ryman/Alamy; p. 141, Corbis–NY; p. 158, Syracuse Newspapers/David Lassman/The Image Works; p. 160, Ed Lalo/Time Life Pictures/Getty Images; p. 163, Shutterstock.com

Chapter 7: p. 168, © Radius Images/Alamy; p. 179, AP Photo/Al Behrman; p. 193, Corbis–NY; p. 195, © Jeremy Sutton–Hibbert/Alamy; p. 201, © Allstar Picture Library/Alamy

Chapter 8: p. 208, © A. Ramey/ PhotoEdit; p. 214, Joe Raedle/ Getty Images; p. 229, Getty Images, Inc.–Agence France Presse; p. 233, AP Wide World Photos; p. 241, © Richard Levine/Alamy

Chapter 9: p. 248, © Jeff Greenberg/Alamy; p. 263, Chris Hondros/Getty Images; p. 267, © Eric Bechtold/Alamy; p. 270, AP Wide World Photos; p. 277, Sylwia Kapuscinski/Getty Images

Chapter 10: p. 283, © Visions of America, LLC/Alamy; p. 291, AP Wide World Photos; p. 293, Tim Boyle/Getty News; p. 300, Christian Simonpiet/Corbis–NY

Chapter 11: p. 307, Marty Heitner; p. 321, AP Wide World Photos; p. 323, AP Wide World Photos; p. 326, David Longstreath/AP Wide World Photos; p. 333, Redux Pictures; p. 337, Bob Daemmrich/ The Image Works

Chapter 12: p. 346, © Jim West/Alamy; p. 356, Bill Pugliano/Getty Images; p. 357, Justin Sullivan/Getty Images; p. 361, Paul Sancya/AP Wide World Photos; p. 362, AP Wide World Photos

Chapter 13: p. 367; Bettmann/Corbis; p. 370, Paul Sakuma/AP Wide World Photos; p. 374, Lara Jo Regan/Getty News Images; p. 377, AP Wide World Photos

Chapter 14: p. 384, Jean–Jaques Gonzal/The Image Works; p. 390, Obed Zilwa/AP Wide World Photos; p. 392, Eraldo Peres/AP Wide World Photos; p. 397, Laurent Rebours/AP Wide World Photos